INTRODUCTION TO FINANCE

Markets, Investments, and Financial Management

BICENTENNIAL
1807
✦WILEY
2007
BICENTENNIAL

THE WILEY BICENTENNIAL—KNOWLEDGE FOR GENERATIONS

*E*ach generation has its unique needs and aspirations. When Charles Wiley first opened his small printing shop in lower Manhattan in 1807, it was a generation of boundless potential searching for an identity. And we were there, helping to define a new American literary tradition. Over half a century later, in the midst of the Second Industrial Revolution, it was a generation focused on building the future. Once again, we were there, supplying the critical scientific, technical, and engineering knowledge that helped frame the world. Throughout the 20th Century, and into the new millennium, nations began to reach out beyond their own borders and a new international community was born. Wiley was there, expanding its operations around the world to enable a global exchange of ideas, opinions, and know-how.

For 200 years, Wiley has been an integral part of each generation's journey, enabling the flow of information and understanding necessary to meet their needs and fulfill their aspirations. Today, bold new technologies are changing the way we live and learn. Wiley will be there, providing you the must-have knowledge you need to imagine new worlds, new possibilities, and new opportunities.

Generations come and go, but you can always count on Wiley to provide you the knowledge you need, when and where you need it!

WILLIAM J. PESCE
PRESIDENT AND CHIEF EXECUTIVE OFFICER

PETER BOOTH WILEY
CHAIRMAN OF THE BOARD

INTRODUCTION TO FINANCE

Markets, Investments, and Financial Management

THIRTEENTH EDITION

Ronald W. Melicher

Professor of Finance
University of Colorado at Boulder

Edgar A. Norton

Professor of Finance
Illinois State University

John Wiley & Sons, Inc.

Executive Publisher *Don Fowley*
Associate Publisher *Judith Joseph*
Associate Editor *Brian Kamins*
Executive Marketing Manager *Amy Scholz*
Editorial Assistant *Sarah Vernon*
Design Director *Harry Nolan*
Senior Designer *Kevin Murphy*
Senior Production Editor *Patricia McFadden*
Senior Media editor *Allison Morris*

This book was set in by Aptara and printed and bound by Courier/Westford. The cover was printed by Lehigh Press, Inc.

This book is printed on acid free paper. ∞

To order books or for customer service please, call 1-800-CALL WILEY (225-5945).

ISBN-13 978-0470-12892-3
ISBN-10 0470-12892-5

Printed in the United States of America

10 9 8 7 6 5 4 3

• PREFACE •

The thirteenth edition of *Introduction to Finance: Markets, Investments, and Financial Management* builds upon the successes of previous editions while delivering fresh and up-to-date coverage of the field of finance. Our text supports a balanced first course in finance in which students are exposed to multiple perspectives on financial markets, investing, and financial management.

This edition contains several major changes that meet the needs of both professors and students in the first course in finance. First, we have streamlined much of the institutional material. Reviewer and user feedback informed us that students learn much of this material in a money and banking or financial institutions course. Thus, we've kept the institutional content and information about financial markets that is most relevant for a finance overview.

Second, the aspect of *finance* that is most familiar and visible to students is the behavior of the stock market and investing, so we've expanded our coverage of investments. We hope our expanded coverage will continue to whet students' appetites and attract them to finance for further study, if not a career. The characteristics, valuation, and risks for bond and stock investments are now covered in two separate chapters rather than a single chapter. We review the material in a less compressed manner, allowing us to discuss topics more fully within a student-friendly pedagogy. A major innovation is the new Chapter 10, which deals with the practical issues of investing. It wraps up some of the issues raised in Part 2: Investments while setting the stage for Part 3: Financial Management.

Third, we've expanded the financial management (also known as business finance) section of the text. Previously, we tried to cover a lot of material in one capital budgeting chapter; now we have two chapters on this topic. Our improved pedagogy offers one chapter that focuses on methods of evaluating capital projects, and a second offers insights into estimating project cash flows. Many students who select financial management as a career path often obtain a first job working in treasury management. Thus we offer two chapters, one on managing working capital and the other on short-term business financing.

These improvements have been incorporated with an eye on book length. As in previous editions, we present eighteen chapters covering the three major finance topics: basics, investments, and management. For the student who does not plan to take additional courses in finance, this book provides a valuable overview of the major concepts of the discipline; for the student who will take additional courses in finance, the overview provides a solid foundation upon which future courses can build.

Introduction to Finance is meant to be used in a course whose purpose is to survey the foundations of the finance discipline. As such, it is designed to meet the needs of students in a variety of programs. Specifically, this text can be used in the following types of courses:

1. As the first course in finance at a college or university where the department wants to expose students to a broad foundational survey of the discipline

2. As the first and only course in finance for nonfinance business students

3. As an appropriate text to use at a school that seeks to provide liberal arts majors with a business minor or business concentration)

4. As a lower-division service course whose goal is to attract freshmen and sophomores to business and to become finance majors

The philosophy behind this book is threefold. First, we believe that a basic understanding of the complex world of finance should begin with a survey course that covers an introduction to financial markets, investments, and financial management or business finance. With this textbook, students can immediately acquire an integrated perspective on the interrelationships among these three areas. They will appreciate how both businesses and individuals are affected by markets and institutions, as well as how markets and institutions can be used to help meet individual or firm goals.

Second, we wrote the book as an introductory survey to the field of finance with a readable and user-friendly focus in mind. We seek to convey basic knowledge, concepts, and terms that will serve the nonfinance major well into the future and that will form a foundation upon which the finance major can build. Some finer points, discussions of theory, and complicated topics are reserved for "Learning Extensions" in selected chapters. We aim to make students using our text financially literate and cognizant of the richness of the field of finance. It provides a good foundation for students to build upon in later courses in financial management, investments, or financial markets.

Third, we focus on the practice of finance in the settings of markets, investments, and financial management. We focus on the descriptive in each of these fields. We don't want students to be unable to see the forest of finance because the trees of quantitative methods obscure their view or scare them away. When we do introduce equations and mathematical concepts that are applicable to finance, we show step-by-step solutions. We show step-by-step financial calculator keystrokes using both TI and HP calculators. We use Excel spreadsheets to highlight their use in solving fiance problems.

Part 1 of the book contains five chapters on the financial system with primary emphasis on financial markets and the tools and skills necessary to better understand how financial markets work. We begin with an overview of the three main subfields of finance, then we identify the "six principles of finance"—money has a time value; higher returns are expected for taking on more risk; diversification of investments can reduce risk; financial markets are efficient in pricing securities; manager and stockholder objectives may differ; and reputation matters—which is followed by a discussion of career opportunities. We discuss the topic of finance and the roles and functions of the financial system in a nation's economy. The role of banks, other financial intermediaries, and the Federal Reserve are reviewed, as are their functions in the financial system. Part 1 also covers the savings-investment process and identifies and discusses various financial assets.

Next we discuss factors that determine interest rates and we conclude Part 1 with coverage of time value of money concepts. Interest rates are introduced, and the discussion centers on making the student aware of the different influences on the level of interest rates and why they change over time. Because interest rates measure the cost of moving money across time, this section reviews basic time value of money concepts with many worked-out examples, including the keystrokes that students can use with financial calculators.

The five chapters of Part 2 focus on investments. The fundamentals of investment risks and returns are presented, followed by a discussion of the characteristics and valuation of first bonds and then stocks. Students learn to apply time value of money concepts to find the prices of these securities. Since much of investing encompasses recognizing and controlling risk, we review the risks inherent in investing in different fixed income and equity securities. Our attention then turns to a discussion of the basics of investment banking and the operations of securities markets. Advanced classes may want to review the basics of financial derivatives, which are explained in a Learning Extension to Chapter 9's securities markets discussion. Part 2 concludes with a discussion of practical investment implications, such as the need to diversify and the futility of trying to "beat the market" if financial markets are efficient.

In Part 3, the final eight chapters of the text introduce students to financial management. Different ways in which to organize businesses are reviewed, and the financial implications of each organizational form are highlighted. Accounting concepts such as the balance sheet, income statement, and statement of cash flows are introduced with simple examples. Financial ratios, which assist in the process of analyzing a firm's strengths and weaknesses, are also discussed; we review their use in helping managers plan for future asset and financing needs.

We introduce students to how to evaluate business investment and the process for estimating cash flows. We also cover capital structure concepts, as they relate to the choosing of a capital structure mix, and the cost of financial capital. Strategies for managing a firm's current assets and current liabilities are examined, as are the funding sources firms use to tap financial markets for short-term financing. We conclude the text with a discussion of international finance, including exchange rates and the financing of international transactions.

By learning about markets (including institutions), investments, and management as the three major strands of finance, students will finish their course with a greater understanding of how these three fields interrelate. Financial markets will be seen as the arena to which businesses and financial institutions go to raise funds and the mechanism through which individuals can invest their savings to meet their future goals. The investments topic is important in facilitating the savings-investment process. Understanding the trade-off of risk and return, as well as the valuation of bonds and stocks, is essential to both investors and businesses trying to raise financial capital. Understanding how securities markets work is equally important since financial management uses information it obtains from securities and other financial markets to efficiently and profitably manage assets and to raise needed funds in a cost-efficient manner.

A broad exposure to the discipline of finance will meet the needs of non-majors who should know the basics of finance so they can read the *Wall Street Journal* and other business periodicals intelligently. It will also help the non-finance major work effectively as a member of a cross-functional work team—a team that will include finance professionals. This overview of the field of finance will also start the finance major off on the right foot. Rather than receiving a compartmentalized view of finance—through the corporate finance lens that many texts often use—the finance major will receive a practical introduction to the different disciplines of finance and will better appreciate their relationships to one another.

This edition contains several important improvements. First, since we have several new or totally revised chapters we have added additional end-of-chapter questions and problems to expand the scope of problems to be assigned and for students to practice. Second, we highlight applications of the principles of finance with the use of a "Principle" icon in the margin when a specific finance principle is discussed. Although "Reputation matters" is an important principle of finance, we specifically emphasize the role of ethics in finance by placing an "Ethics" icon in the margin when ethical concepts are discussed. Similarly, issues with global applications are highlighted with a "Global" icon in the margin.

Third, spreadsheets are a powerful tool in finance, both as a means to solve problems and as a skill set most business majors should develop. We assist students in developing this skill by showing, in appropriate places, how to set up a spreadsheet and how to use Excel's functions to solve finance problems.

Part 1, the first five chapters of the text, has been heavily rewritten and reorganized to emphasize financial markets and the concepts and tools necessary to understand how interest rates are determined and the importance of time value of money in finance. In addition to these broad improvements, all the chapters have been updated and revised; specific notable changes in this thirteenth edition include the following:

PART 1: FINANCE BASICS

Chapter 1, The Financial Environment: Revised and refocused as the first chapter in Part 1. We define *finance* and identify the "six principles of finance" which we refer to at various points in the text. These principles are that money has a time value, higher returns are expected for taking on more risk, diversification of investments can reduce risk, financial markets are efficient in pricing securities, manager and stockholder objectives may differ, and reputation matters in financial dealings. Developments in the international monetary system are discussed.

Chapter 2, Banks and Other Financial Intermediaries: We describe the major financial intermediaries and their roles in the financial system, then the structure of banks in terms of bank charters, branch banking, bank holding companies, and how commercial banking and investment banking have differed. The chapter briefly discusses the structure of the Federal Reserve System and how the Fed carries out its monetary policy objectives. The characteristics of having a fractional reserve system, along with structural characteristics of selected foreign central banks, are also described.

Chapter 3, Savings-Investment Process and Financial Assets: We begin with a discussion of national economic policy objectives, gross domestic product and capital formation, and the four policy maker groups that establish fiscal and monetary policy. We discuss the process of transferring savings into investments, the creation of savings, and major sources of savings. We present current information on the savings patterns of individuals and corporations. Factors affecting savings, as well as the life stages of individuals and corporations, are discussed.

Chapter 4, Interest Rates: The supply and demand for loanable funds are presented. We then cover the determinants of market interest rates, which include a real rate of interest, an inflation premium and possible premiums for default risk, maturity risk, and liquidity risk. We also discuss the term or maturity structure of interest rates. We review default risk and default risk premiums and their role in affecting the interest rates and issuance of "junk" or high-yield bonds.

Chapter 5, Time Value of Money: The importance of compounding (earning interest on interest) in building wealth over time and discounting future cash flows back to the present for decision making purposes is conveyed. We present examples showing how to make the necessary calculations with formulas, interest factor tables, step-by-step financial calculator keystrokes, and Excel spreadsheets, both with formulas keyed in by the user and with Excel's preprogrammed financial functions.

PART 2: INVESTMENTS

Chapter 6, Return and Risk: We moved this chapter forward in this edition to build upon the time value "return" calculations of Chapter 5. Though mathematical in nature, we also show the sources of risk that arise in a firm's income statement and operating decisions.

Chapter 7, Bonds: Characteristics and Valuation contains a revised discussion of bond characteristics, including the growth over time of the high-yield sector and the fact that highly rated corporate bonds have become scarce. Spreadsheet examples show how to apply time value concepts to calculate bond prices and yields.

Chapter 8, Stocks: Characteristics and Valuation explains the advantages (in addition to higher potential returns) of investing in equities: inflation hedge, growth in value, growth in income, and tax benefits. Dividends and stock repurchases are introduced in this chapter, too, as are rationales for their use. Spreadsheet examples show how to apply time value concepts to calculate stock prices (using constant growth and supernormal growth models).

Chapter 9, Securities Markets: The discussion of the process of going public includes Dutch auction IPOs, of which Google is the most well-known example in recent years. Sections on ethics and changes in stock market trading—which after being static for decades is ever-changing because of technology, global alliances, and changing regulation—have been rewritten and improved. A new feature is a discussion of what makes a "good" market.

Chapter 10, Investment Implications: This is an applications chapter. Having reviewed the background of various securities and how they are traded, this chapter addresses some practical aspects of investing, including efficient markets, active versus passive investing, the process of managing a portfolio, and the measure of risk in a portfolio context. Ways for the small investor to invest are reviewed, too, such as mutual funds and ETFs.

PART 3: FINANCIAL MANAGEMENT

Chapter 11, Business Organization and Financial Data: The finance principle relating to the possibility that manager and stockholder objectives may differ—the principal–agent problem—is discussed. Ethical issues associated with trying to reduce the "agency problem" by using stock options as an incentive mechanism to managers are discussed. We also discuss ethical issues brought on by self-serving managers and the efforts to control managers through regulatory responses from Congress (Sarbanes-Oxley) and the SEC.

Chapter 12, Financial Analysis and Long-Term Financial Planning: Financial ratio analysis is illustrated for a hypothetical firm in a two-year comparative format and over several years against an industry norm for comparative purposes. Long-Term financial planning methods, including percentage of sales technique, cost-volume-profit analysis, and the degree of operating leverage, are discussed.

Chapter 13, Evaluating Business Investments: Concepts such as NPV and IRR are discussed, as is the important practical point of trying to discover potentially attractive projects and sources of positive NPV projects. Spreadsheets are used to compute measures such as NPV, IRR, modified IRR, and profitability index, and to graph the NPV profile.

Chapter 14, Estimating Project Cash Flows: In this new separate chapter, we relate the format of a project's cash flow statement to something that should be familiar to students, namely a firm's statement of cash flows from Chapter 11. We present many examples to show how to estimate cash flows at the beginning and end of a project, as well as during the project's life.

Chapter 15, Capital Structure and Cost of Capital contains updated discussions of trends in the use of debt by corporations and differences in the use of debt by smaller and larger corporations. Some tie-in to earlier chapters is purposefully done to help students see the relationship between the discussion of bonds and stocks from an investor's perspective (Chapters 7 and 8) and the corporate financial structure decision. Data from real firms are used to help students compare capital structure strategies across firms.

Chapter 16, Managing Working Capital: The discussion and examples of collection and disbursement float strategies have been expanded and clarified. Investment policy statements, a growing topic in Treasury management, are discussed as a means of protecting the liquidity and safety of a firm's excess cash while using the funds to earn returns. The chapter-ending section on innovations reviews XML and radio frequency identification tags (RFID) as tools for enhancing cash management and inventory management. Data from real firms are used to help students compare the use and level of current assets across firms.

Chapter 17, Short-Term Business Financing: The section dealing with providers of short-term financing has been revised, reorganized, and rewritten to improve pedagogy and to update the material. Data from real firms are used to help students compare short-term financing strategies across firms.

Chapter 18, International Finance and Trade provides updated information on the evolution of the international monetary system, the European Union, the European Monetary Union, and the euro. Currency exchange markets and rates are discussed. When conducting business internationally, possible differences in ethical behavior across cultures and countries are noted. The process of financing international trade also is discussed.

LEARNING AND TEACHING AIDS

The thirteenth edition of *Introduction to Finance* offers the following aids for students and instructors:

CHAPTER OPENERS: Each chapter begins with these elements:

- *Chapter Learning Objectives* can be used by students to review the chapter's main points and instructors can use as a basis for in-class lecture or discussion.
- *Where We Have Been* reminds students of what was covered in the previous chapters.
- *Where We Are Going* previews future chapters.
- *How This Chapter Applies to Me* explains how the content of the chapter, no matter how technical or business specific, contains applications relevant to the individual student.

APPLYING FINANCE TO. . . : Sidebars show how the topic of each chapter relates to the finance fields of institutions and markets, investments, and financial management.

INTERNET MARGIN NOTES: We direct the student to relevant Web sites at different points in each chapter.

MARGIN DEFINITIONS: Margin definitions of key terms assist students in learning the language of finance.

CONCEPT CHECKS: These assessment features appear in the margins near the end of every section to quiz students on what they have just learned and how well they've learned it. Concept Checks reinforce the topical material and help students determine what they need to review.

MARGIN ICONS: Symbols in the margin indicate discussions of finance principles, financial or business ethical issues, and global or international discussions, and Internet activities.

SPREADSHEET ILLUSTRATIONS: We show how to use spreadsheets to solve problems and to teach students about the power of spreadsheet functions and analysis.

BOXED FEATURES: Throughout the book, sidebar boxes are used to focus on current topics or applications of interest. They are designed to illustrate concepts and practices in the dynamic field of finance.

- *Small Business Practice* boxes highlight aspects of the chapter topics relating directly to small businesses and entrepreneurship.
- *Career Opportunities in Finance* boxes provide information about various careers in finance and appear in most chapters.

CAREER PROFILES: These profiles feature individuals who, in an interview format, discuss their jobs and the skills needed to obtain positions in different areas of finance. Some of the positions reviewed are trust officer, business valuation analyst, money manager, collections manager, treasurer, and venture capitalist. Our hope is that the Career Profiles will stimulate discussion and interest so students will consider pursuing a career in finance.

LEARNING EXTENSIONS: Chapter appendixes, which we refer to as Learning Extensions, are included for many chapters. These extensions provide additional in-depth coverage of topics related to their respective chapters, and many challenge students to use their mathematical skills.

END-OF-CHAPTER MATERIALS: Each chapter provides an extensive range of assessment material:

- End-of-chapter *Discussion Questions* that review chapter material
- *Problems* for students to solve and exercise their mathematical skills
- More difficult *Challenge Problems,* which should be solved by using spreadsheets

COMPANION WEB SITE: The text's Web site at www.wiley.com/college/melicher contains contains a myriad of resources and links to aid both learning and teaching, including Power-Point presentation materials.

SPREADSHEET SOFTWARE: A set of Lotus- and Excel-compatible templates, developed by Robert Ritchey of Texas Tech University, are available on the text Web site. Students can use the templates to help solve some of the end-of-chapter problems and challenge problems.

INSTRUCTOR'S RESOURCE CD: This CD contains an electronic version of all the instructor's supplements, including the Instructor's Manual, Test Bank, Computerized Test Bank, and PowerPoint lecture presentations of text material, including slides of many of the figures from the text.

INSTRUCTOR'S MANUAL AND TEST BANK: The Instructor's Manual is available to adopters of this text. It features detailed chapter outlines, lecture tips, and answers to end-of-chapter questions and problems. The manual also includes an extensive test bank of over 1,500 true-false and multiple-choice examination questions with answers, newly revised and expanded for this edition by Daniel Borgia of Florida Gulf Coast University.

COMPUTERIZED TEST BANK: This program is for use on a PC running Windows. The Computerized Test Bank contains content from the test bank provided within a test generating program that allows instructors to customize their exams.

ACKNOWLEDGMENTS

We would like to thank the Wiley Publishing team of Judith R. Joseph, Associate Publisher; Brian Kamins, Associate Editor, for their role in preparing and publishing the thirteenth edition of *Introduction to Finance*.

In addition, we are especially grateful to the reviewers of this and previous editions for their comments and constructive criticisms:

Jeff Jewell, *Lipscomb University*
Lester Hadsell, *University at Albany*
Amir Tovakkol, *Kansas State University*
Tim Alzheimer, *Montana State University*
Alan Questell, *Richmond Community College*
David Zalewski, *Providence College*
John K. Mullen, *Clarkson University*

Tim Alzheimer, *Montana State University*
Allan Blair, *Palm Beach Atlantic College*
Stewart Bonem, *Cincinnati State Technical and Community College*
Joseph M. Byers, *Community College of Allegheny County, South Campus*
Robert L. Chapman, *Orlando College*
William Chittenden, *Texas State University*
Will Crittendon, *Bronx Community College*
David R. Durst, *University of Akron*
Sharon H. Garrison, *Florida Atlantic University*
Asim Ghosh, *Saint Joseph's University*
Irene M. Hammerbacher, *Iona College*
Kim Hansen, *Mid-State Technical College*
Jeff Hines, *Davenport College*
Ed Krohn, *Miami Dade Community College*
P. John Limberopoulos, *University of Colorado-Boulder*
John K. Mullen, *Clarkson University*
Michael Murray, *Winona State University*
Michael Owen, *Montana State University*
Alan Questell, *Richmond Community College*
Ernest Scarbrough, *Arizona State University*
Amir Tavakkol, *Kansas State University*
Jim Washam, *Arkansas State University*
Howard Whitney, *Franklin University*
David Zalewski, *Providence College*

Comments from students and teachers who have used prior editions of this book also are greatly appreciated, as is the assistance from the dozens of reviewers who have commented about the prior editions of this textbook. Special recognition goes to Carl Dauten, who coauthored the first four editions, and Merle Welshans who was a coauthor on the first nine editions of *Finance*. Finally, and perhaps most important, we wish to thank our families for their understanding and support during the writing of the thirteenth edition.

Ronald W. Melicher, *Boulder, Colorado*
Edgar A. Norton, *Normal, Illinois*

• BRIEF CONTENTS •

• CONTENTS •

INTRODUCTION TO FINANCE

Markets, Investments, and Financial Management

PART I

FINANCIAL MARKETS

INTRODUCTION

Ask someone what he or she thinks "finance" is about. You'll probably get a variety of responses: "It deals with money." "It's what my bank does." "The New York Stock Exchange has something to do with it." "It's how businesses and people get the money they need—you know, borrowing and stuff like that." And they'll all be correct!

Finance is a broad field. It involves national and international systems of banking and financing business. It also deals with the process you go through to get a car loan and what a business does when planning for its future needs.

Within the general field of finance, there are three areas of study—financial institutions and markets, investments, and financial management. These areas are illustrated in the accompanying diagram. Financial institutions collect funds from savers and lend them to or invest them in businesses or people that need cash. Examples of financial institutions are commercial banks, investment banks, insurance companies, and mutual funds. Financial institutions operate as part of the financial system. The financial system is the environment of finance. It includes the laws and regulations that affect financial transactions. The financial system encompasses the Federal Reserve System, which controls the supply of money in the U.S. economy. It also consists of the mechanisms that have been constructed to facilitate the flow of money and financial securities among countries.

Financial markets represent ways for bringing together those that have money to invest with those that need funds. Financial markets, which include markets for mortgages, securities, and currencies, are necessary for a financial system to operate efficiently. Part 1 of this book examines the financial system and the role of financial markets in it. While we provide some discussion of the roles of financial institutions, we focus on topics designed to help better understand how financial markets operate. Included is the need to understand how interest rates are determined and that money has a time value.

Securities markets play important roles in helping businesses and governments raise new funds. Securities markets also facilitate the transfer of securities between investors. A securities market can be a central location for the trading of financial claims, such as the New York Stock Exchange. It may also take the form of a communications network, as with the over-the-counter market, which is another means by which stocks and bonds can be traded. When people invest funds, lend or borrow money, or buy or sell shares of a company's stock, they are participating in the financial markets. Part 2 of this book examines the role of securities markets and the process of investing in bonds and stocks.

The third area of the field of finance is financial management. Financial management studies how a business should manage its assets, liabilities, and equity to produce a good or service. Whether or not a firm offers a new product or expands production, or how it invests excess cash, are examples of decisions that financial managers are involved with. Financial managers are constantly working with financial institutions and watching financial market trends as they make investment and financing decisions. Part 3 discusses how financial concepts can help managers better manage their firms.

It is important to recognize that there are few clear distinctions or separations between the three areas of finance. The diagram intentionally shows institutions and markets, investments, and financial management overlapping one another. Financial institutions operate in the environment of the financial markets and work to meet the financial needs of individuals and businesses. Financial managers do analyses and make decisions based on information they obtain from the financial markets. They also work with financial institutions when they need to raise funds and when they have excess funds to invest. Participants investing in the financial markets use information from financial institutions and firms to evaluate different investments in securities such as stocks, bonds, and certificates of deposit. A person working in one field must be knowledgeable about all three. Thus this book is designed to provide you with a survey of all three areas of finance.

Part 1, "Financial Markets," presents an overview of the financial system and its important components of policy makers, a monetary system, financial institutions, and financial markets. To enhance the understanding of how financial markets operate, we also discuss the determinants of interest rates and time value of money concept.

Financial institutions operate within the financial system to facilitate the work of the financial markets. For example, you can put your savings in a bank and earn interest. But your money just doesn't sit in the bank. The bank takes your deposit and the money from other depositors and lends it to Kathy, who needs a short-term loan for her business; to Ron for a college loan; and to Roger and Maria, who borrow the money to help buy a house. Banks bring together savers and those who need money, such as Kathy, Ron, Roger, and Maria. The interest rate the depositors earn and the interest rate that borrowers pay are determined by national and even international economic forces. Just what the bank does with depositors' money and how it reviews loan applications is determined to some extent by bank regulators and financial market participants, such as the Federal Reserve Board. Decisions by the president and Congress relating to fiscal policies and regulatory laws may also directly influence financial institutions and markets and alter the financial system.

Chapter 1 begins with an overview of the three sub-fields of finance, identifies the six principles of finance, and provides materials on the financial system, the monetary system, and the role and functions of money. Chapter 2 provides descriptive materials on the roles of banks and other financial intermediaries in the economy, as well as reviews the role of the Federal Reserve in establishing monetary policy in a fractional reserve banking system. Chapter 3 covers the savings-investment process and identifies and discusses various financial assets important in a well-functioning financial system. To enhance the understanding of financial markets operations, Chapter 4 discusses the factors that determine the level of interest rates in the financial markets. Chapter 5 describes and discusses the time value of money which also influences how securities are priced in the financial markets.

• CHAPTER 1 •

The Financial Environment

Chapter Learning Objectives

AFTER STUDYING THIS CHAPTER, YOU SHOULD BE ABLE TO:

- Define what is meant by *finance*.
- Describe the six principles of finance.
- Explain why finance should be studied.
- Identify and discuss some career opportunities in finance.
- Describe the financial functions performed in an effective financial system.
- Describe the functions and development of money.
- Briefly explain the M1, M2, and M3 definitions of the money supply.
- Explain possible relationships between money supply and economic activity.
- Comment on developments in the international monetary system.

Where We Have Been...

As we progress through this book, we will start each chapter with a brief review of previously covered materials. This will provide you with a reference base for understanding the transition from topic to topic. After completing the text, you will be at the beginning of what we hope is a successful business career—possibly one in finance.

Where We Are Going...

Part 1 of this text focuses on developing an understanding of financial markets and important basics of finance. In this first chapter we present an overview of the financial environment within which we live and work. Money and money supply are defined, and the importance of controlling the growth of the money supply is discussed. In Chapter 2 we discuss banks and other financial intermediaries that operate within the financial system. The remaining chapters in Part 1 address the supply-investment process and financial assets, interest rate characteristics, and the time value of money.

How This Chapter Applies to Me...

While it is impossible to predict what life has in store for each of us in terms of health, family, and career, everyone can be a productive member of society. Nearly all of us will take part in making social, political, and economic decisions. A basic understanding of the financial environment that encompasses economic and financial systems will help you in making informed economic choices.

Each of us needs money. While you may feel you need more or less money than your friends, money is necessary for each of us to conduct day-to-day activities. You may have to buy gasoline for your car or pay for public transportation to school or work. You may need money for lunch or supplies. You may even want to borrow to purchase a house someday. After reading this chapter you should have a clearer understanding of the functions and types of money available to you.

John Kenneth Galbraith, a U.S. economist, said the following about money:

> *Money is a singular thing. It ranks with love as man's greatest source of joy. And with death as his greatest source of anxiety. Over all history it has oppressed nearly all people in one of two ways: either it has been abundant and very unreliable, or reliable and very scarce.*

Why should any "thing" be so important? Money is what makes the financial system work. Money is a measure of wealth. Money can be used to purchase goods and services. Money is acceptable to repay debts. Creating and transferring money are integral parts of the capital formation process. However, too much money in an economy is associated with unsustainable economic growth and rapidly rising prices. On the other hand, too little money in an economy is associated with poor economic performance and sometimes recession.

WHAT IS FINANCE?

finance
study of how individuals, institutions, governments, and businesses acquire, spend, and manage financial resources

The financial environment encompasses the financial system, institutions or intermediaries (we will use these terms interchangeably throughout this text), financial markets, and individuals that make the economy operate efficiently. *Finance* is the study of how individuals, institutions, governments, and businesses acquire, spend, and manage money and other financial assets. Understanding finance is important to all students regardless of the discipline or area of study because nearly all business and economic decisions have financial implications. The decision to spend or consume now (for new clothes or dinner at a fancy restaurant) rather than save or invest (for spending or consuming more in the future) is an everyday decision that we all face.

financial institutions
intermediaries that help the financial system operate efficiently and transfer funds from savers and investors to individuals, businesses, and governments that seek to spend or invest the funds

Figure 1.1 depicts the three areas of finance—institutions and markets, investments, and financial management—within the financial environment. Note that while we identify three distinct finance areas, these areas do not operate in isolation but rather interact or intersect with each other. Our focus in this book is to provide the reader with exposure to all three areas, as well as to show how they are integrated. Of course, students pursuing a major or area of emphasis in finance will take multiple courses in one or more of these areas.

financial markets
locations or electronic forums that facilitate the flow of funds among investors, businesses, and governments

Financial institutions are organizations or intermediaries that help the financial system operate efficiently and transfer funds from savers and investors to individuals, businesses, and governments that seek to spend or invest the funds in physical assets (inventories, buildings, and equipment). *Financial markets* are physical locations or electronic forums that facilitate the flow of funds among investors, businesses, and governments. The *investments* area involves the sale or marketing of securities, the analysis of securities, and the management of investment risk

investments
involves sale or marketing of securities, the analysis of securities, and the management of investment risk through portfolio diversification

FIGURE 1.1
The Financial Environment

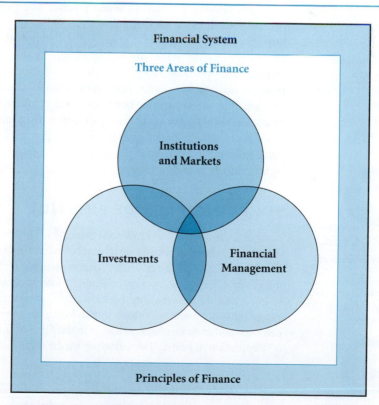

financial management
involves financial planning, asset management, and fund-raising decisions to enhance the value of businesses

through portfolio diversification. **Financial management** involves financial planning, asset management, and fund-raising decisions to enhance the value of businesses.

Finance has its origins in economics and accounting. Economists use a supply-and-demand framework to explain how the prices and quantities of goods and services are determined in a free-market economic system. Accountants provide the record-keeping mechanism for showing ownership of the financial instruments used in the flow of financial funds between savers and borrowers. Accountants also record revenues, expenses, and profitability of organizations that produce and exchange goods and services.

Efficient methods of production and specialization of labor can exist only if there is an effective means of paying for raw materials and final products. Businesses can obtain the money needed to buy capital goods such as machinery and equipment only if a mechanism has been established for making savings available for investment. Similarly, federal and other governmental units, such as state and local governments and tax districts, can carry out their wide range of activities only if efficient means exist for raising money, for making payments, and for borrowing.

Financial institutions, financial markets, and investment and financial management are crucial elements of the financial environment and well-developed financial systems. Financial institutions are intermediaries, such as banks, insurance companies, and investment companies that engage in financial activities to aid the flow of funds from savers to borrowers or investors. Financial markets provide the mechanism for allocating financial resources or funds from savers to borrowers. Individuals make decisions as investors and financial managers. Investors include savers and lenders as well as equity investors. While we focus on financial managers in this book, we recognize that individuals also must be continuously involved in managing their personal finances. Investment management involves making decisions relating to issuing and investing in stocks and bonds. Financial management in business involves making decisions relating to the efficient use of financial resources in the production and sale of goods and services. The goal of the financial manager in a profit-seeking organization is to maximize the owners' wealth. This is accomplished through effective financial planning and analysis, asset management, and the acquisition of financial capital. Financial managers in not-for-profit organizations aim to provide a desired level of services at acceptable costs and perform the same financial management functions as their for-profit counterparts.

As we progress through this book, we offer two themes within the financial institutions and markets, investments, and financial management topic areas. In each chapter we provide boxed materials relating to small business practice and personal financial planning. Successful businesses typically progress through a series of life-cycle stages—from the idea stage to exiting the business. More specifically, the successful business typically moves through five stages: development stage, startup stage, survival stage, rapid growth stage, and maturity stage. **Entrepreneurial finance** is the study of how growth-driven, performance-focused, early-stage (from development through early rapid growth) firms raise financial capital and manage their operations and assets. Our small business practice boxes focus on operational and financial issues faced by early-stage firms. **Personal finance** is the study of how individuals prepare for financial emergencies, protect against premature death and the loss of property, and accumulate wealth over time. Our personal financial planning discussions throughout the text focus on planning decisions made by individuals in regard to saving and investing their financial resources.

entrepreneurial finance
study of how growth-driven, performance-focused, early-stage firms raise financial capital and manage operations and assets

personal finance
study of how individuals prepare for financial emergencies, protect against premature death and property losses, and accumulate wealth

SIX PRINCIPLES OF FINANCE

Finance is founded on six important principles. The first five relate to the economic behavior of individuals, and the sixth focuses on ethical behavior. Knowing about these principles will help us understand how managers, investors, and others incorporate time and risk in their decisions, as well as why the desire to earn excess returns leads to information-efficient financial markets in which prices reflect available information. Unfortunately, sometimes greed associated with the desire to earn excess returns causes individuals to risk losing their reputations by engaging in questionable ethical behavior and even unethical behavior in the form of fraud or other illegal activities. The bottom line is "Reputation matters!" The following are the six principles that serve as the foundation of finance:

- Money has a time value.
- Higher returns are expected for taking on more risk.
- Diversification of investments can reduce risk.

CONCEPT CHECK

What are the three areas of finance?

What two finance themes are carried throughout this book?

FINANCE PRINCIPLE

- Financial markets are efficient in pricing securities.
- Manager and stockholder objectives may differ.
- Reputation matters.

TIME VALUE OF MONEY

Let's look at these principles one by one. Money in hand today is worth more than the promise of receiving the same amount in the future. The *time value* of money exists because a sum of money today could be invested and grow over time. For example, assume that you have $1,000 today and that it could earn $60 (6 percent) interest over the next year. Thus, $1,000 today would be worth $1,060 at the end of one year (i.e., $1,000 plus $60). As a result, a dollar today is worth more than a dollar received a year from now. The time value of money principle helps us understand the economic behavior of individuals and the economic decisions of the institutions and businesses that they run. This finance principle is apparent in many of our day-to-day activities, and knowledge of it will help us better understand the implications of time-varying money decisions. We explore the details of the time value of money in Chapter 5, but this first principle of finance will be apparent throughout this book.

RISK VERSUS RETURN

A trade-off exists between risk and expected return in all types of investments—both assets and securities. Risk is the uncertainty about the outcome or payoff of an investment in the future. For example, you might invest $1,000 in a business venture today. After one year, the firm might be bankrupt, and you would lose your total investment. On the other hand, after one year your investment might be worth $2,400. This variability in possible outcomes is your *risk*. Instead, you might invest your $1,000 in a U.S. government security, where after one year the value may be $950 or $1,100. Rational investors would consider the business venture investment to be riskier and would choose this investment only if they feel the expected return is high enough to justify the greater risk. Investors make these trade-off decisions every day.

Business managers make similar trade-off decisions when they choose between different projects in which they could invest. Understanding the *risk-return trade-off* principle also helps us understand how individuals make economic decisions. While we specifically explore the trade-off between risk and expected return in greater detail in Part 2, this second principle of finance is involved in many financial decisions throughout this text.

DIVERSIFICATION OF RISK

While higher returns are expected for taking on more risk, all investment risk is not the same. In fact, some risk can be removed or *diversified* by investing in several different assets or securities. Let's return to the example involving a $1,000 investment in a business venture where after one year the investment would provide a return of either zero dollars or $2,400. Now, let's assume that there also is an opportunity to invest $1,000 in a second unrelated business venture in which the outcomes would also be zero dollars or $2,400. Let's further assume that we will put one-half of our $1,000 investment funds in each investment opportunity such that the individual outcomes for each $500 investment would be zero dollars or $1,200.

While it is possible that both investments could lose everything (i.e., return zero dollars) or return $1,200 each (a total of $2,400), it is also possible that one investment would go broke and the other would return $1,200. So, four outcomes are now possible:

	COMBINED INVESTMENT	POSSIBLE RETURNS	COMBINED RETURN
Outcome 1	$1,000	$0 + $0 =	$0
Outcome 2	$1,000	$0 + $1,200 =	$1,200
Outcome 3	$1,000	$1,200 + $0 =	$1,200
Outcome 4	$1,000	$1,000 + $1,000 =	$2,400

If each outcome has an equal one-fourth (25 percent) chance of occurring, most of us would prefer this diversified investment. While it is true that our combined investment of $1,000 ($500 in each investment) at the extremes could still return zero dollars or $2,400, it is also true that we have a 50 percent chance of getting $1,200 back for our $1,000 investment. As a result, most of us would prefer investing in the combined or diversified investment rather than in either of the two investments separately. We will explore the benefits of investment diversification in Part 2 of this text.

FINANCIAL MARKETS ARE EFFICIENT

A fourth finance-related aspect of economic behavior is that individuals seek to find undervalued and overvalued investment opportunities involving both real and financial assets. It is human nature, economically speaking, to search for investment opportunities that will provide returns higher than those expected for undertaking a specified level of risk. This attempt by many to earn excess returns, or to "beat the market," leads to financial markets being information efficient. However, at the same time it becomes almost impossible to consistently earn returns higher than those expected in a risk-return trade-off framework. Rather than looking at this fourth principle of finance as a negative consequence of human economic behavior, we prefer to couch it positively in that it leads to information-efficient financial markets.

A financial market is said to be information efficient if at any point the prices of securities reflect all information available to the public. When new information becomes available, prices quickly change to reflect that information. For example, let's assume that a firm's stock is currently trading at $20 per share. If the market is efficient, both potential buyers and sellers of the stock know that $20 per share is a fair price. Trades should be at $20, or near to it, if the demand (potential buyers) and supply (potential sellers) are in reasonable balance. Now, let's assume that the firm announces the production of a new product that is expected to substantially increase sales and profits. Investors might react by bidding up the price to, say, $25 per share to reflect this new information. Assuming this new information is assessed properly, the new fair price becomes $25 per share. This informational efficiency of financial markets exists because a large number of professionals are continually searching for mispriced securities. Of course, as soon as new information is discovered, it becomes immediately reflected in the price of the associated security. Information-efficient financial markets play an important role in the marketing and transferring of financial assets between investors by providing liquidity and fair prices. The importance of information efficient financial markets is examined throughout this text and specifically in Chapters 9 and 10.

MANAGEMENT VERSUS OWNER OBJECTIVES

A fifth principle of finance relates to the fact that management objectives may differ from owner objectives. Owners or equity investors want to maximize the returns on their investments but often hire professional managers to run their firms. However, managers may seek to emphasize the size of firm sales or assets, have company jets or helicopters available for their travel, and be given company-paid country club memberships. Owner returns may suffer as a result of manager objectives. To bring manager objectives in line with owner objectives, it often is necessary to tie manager compensation to measures of performance beneficial to owners. Managers are often given a portion of the ownership positions in privately held firms and are provided stock options and bonuses tied to stock price performance in publicly traded firms.

The possible conflict between managers and owners is sometimes called the *principal-agent problem*. We explore this problem in greater detail and describe how owners provide incentives to managers to manage in the best interests of equity investors or owners in Chapter 11.

REPUTATION MATTERS

ETHICAL ISSUES

ethical behavior
how an individual or organization treats others legally, fairly, and honestly

The sixth principle of finance is "Reputation matters!" An individual's reputation reflects his or her ethical standards or behavior. **Ethical behavior** is how an individual or organization treats others legally, fairly, and honestly. Of course, the ethical behavior of organizations reflects the ethical behaviors of their directors, officers, and managers. For institutions or businesses to be successful, they must have the trust and confidence of their customers, employees, and owners, as well as the community and society within which they operate. All would agree that firms have an ethical responsibility to provide safe products and services, to have safe working conditions for employees, and to not pollute or destroy the environment. Laws and regulations exist to ensure minimum levels of protection and the difference between unethical and ethical behavior. Examples of high ethical behavior include when firms establish product-safety and working-condition standards well above the legal or regulatory standards.

Unfortunately, and possibly due in part to the greed for excess returns (such as higher salaries, bonuses, more valuable stock options, personal perquisites, etc.), directors, officers, managers, and other individuals sometimes are guilty of unethical behavior for engaging in fraudulent or other illegal activities. Reputations are destroyed, criminal activities are prosecuted, and involved individuals may receive jail sentences. The unethical behavior of directors, officers, and managers also may lead to a loss of reputation and even destruction of the institutions and businesses for which they work.

Many examples of fraudulent and illegal unethical behavior have been cited in the financial press over the past few decades, and most seem to be tied to greed for personal gain. In such cases, confidential information was used for personal benefit, illegal payments were made to gain business, accounting fraud was committed, business assets were converted to personal use, and so forth. In the early 1980s, a number of savings and loan association managers were found to have engaged in fraudulent and unethical practices, and some managers were prosecuted and sent to prison while their institutions were dissolved or merged with other institutions.

In the late 1980s and early 1990s, fraudulent activities and unethical behavior by investment banking firms resulted in several high-profile financial wheeler-dealers going to prison. This resulted in the collapse of Drexel, Burnham, Lambert and the near collapse of Salomon Brothers. By the early part of the twenty-first century, such major firms as Enron, its auditor Arthur Andersen, and WorldCom ceased to exist because of fraudulent and unethical behavior on the part of their managers and officers. In addition, key officials of Tyco and Adelphia were charged with illegal actions and fraud. Even more recently, managers and officers of mutual funds have been indicted for fraudulent and unethical business practices.

While the financial press chooses to highlight examples of unethical behavior, most individuals exhibit sound ethical behavior in their personal and business dealings and practices. In fact, the sixth principle of finance depends on most individuals practicing high-quality ethical behavior and believing that reputation matters. To be successful, an organization or business must have the trust and confidence of its various constituencies, including customers, employees, owners, and the community. High-quality ethical behavior involves treating others fairly and honestly and goes beyond just meeting legal and regulatory requirements. High reputation value reflects high-quality ethical behavior, so employing high ethical standards is the right thing to do. Many organizations and businesses have developed and follow their own code of ethics. The importance of practicing sound ethical behavior is discussed throughout this text.

CONCEPT CHECK

What are the six principles of finance?

INTERNET ACTIVITY

Go to the Small Business Administration Web site, http://www.sba.gov, and explore what is involved in deciding whether to start a new business.

WHY STUDY FINANCE?

There are several reasons to study finance. You have just learned about the six principles of finance that are predicated on the economic and ethical behavior of humans. Knowledge of these principles and the content of this text should help you make informed economic decisions, personal and business investment decisions, and career decisions.

1. *To make informed economic decisions.*

As we will see, the operation of the financial system and the performance of the economy are influenced by policy makers. Individuals elect many of these policy makers in the United States, such as the president and members of Congress. Since these elected officials have the power to alter the financial system by creating laws and their decisions can influence economic activity, it is important that individuals be informed when making political and economic choices. Do you want a balanced budget, lower taxes, free international trade, low inflation, and full employment? Whatever your financial and economic goals may be, you need to be an informed participant if you wish to make a difference. Every individual should attain a basic understanding of finance as it applies to the financial system. Part 1 of this book focuses on understanding the basics of finance: the financial environment, financial intermediaries, the savings-investment process and types of financial assets, the structure of interest rates, and the time value of money.

2. *To make informed personal and business investment decisions.*

   An understanding of finance should help you better understand how the institution, government unit, or business that you work for finances its operations. At a personal level, the understanding of investments will enable you to better manage your financial resources and provide the basis for making sound decisions for accumulating wealth over time. Thus, in addition to understanding finance basics relating to the financial system and the economy, you also need to develop an understanding of the factors that influence interest rates and security prices. Part 2 of this book focuses on understanding the characteristics of stocks and bonds and how they are valued, securities markets, and how to make risk-versus-return investment decisions.

3. *To make informed career decisions based on a basic understanding of business finance.*

   Even if your business interest is in a nonfinance career or professional activity, you likely will need to interact with finance professionals both within and outside your firm or organization. Doing so will require a basic knowledge of the concepts, tools, and applications of financial management. Part 3 of this book focuses on providing you with an understanding of how finance is applied within a firm by focusing on decision making by financial managers.

CONCEPT CHECK

Give three reasons for studying finance.

Of course, you may be interested in pursuing a career in finance or at least want to know what people who work in finance actually do. Throughout this text, you will find discussions of career opportunities in finance, as well as a boxed feature entitled Career Opportunities in Finance.

CAREERS IN FINANCE

Career opportunities in finance are available in financial management, depository financial institutions, contractual savings and real property organizations, and securities markets and investment firms. While you may aspire to own your own business or to be a chief executive officer (CEO) or chief financial officer (CFO) in a major corporation, most of us must begin our careers in an entry-level position. Following are some of the ways to get started in a finance career.

1. *Financial management.*

   Larger businesses or corporations divide their finance activities into treasury and control functions, whereas smaller firms often combine these functions. The treasurer is responsible for managing the firm's cash, acquiring and managing the firm's assets, and selling stocks and bonds to raise the financial capital necessary to conduct business. The controller is responsible for cost accounting, financial accounting, and tax record-keeping activities. Entry-level career opportunities include the following:

   • *Cash management analyst:* involves monitoring and managing the firm's day-to-day cash inflows and outflows

- *Capital expenditures analyst:* involves estimating cash flows and evaluating asset investment opportunities
- *Credit analyst:* involves evaluating credit applications and collecting amounts owed by credit customers
- *Financial analyst:* involves evaluating financial performance and preparing financial plans
- *Cost analyst:* involves comparing actual operations against budgeted operations
- *Tax analyst:* involves preparing financial statements for tax purposes

2. **Depository financial institutions.**

Banks and other depository institutions offer the opportunity to start a finance career in consumer or commercial lending. Banks also hold and manage trust funds for individuals and other organizations. Entry-level career opportunities include the following:

- *Loan analyst:* involves evaluating consumer and/or commercial loan applications
- *Bank teller:* involves assisting customers with their day-to-day checking and banking transactions
- *Investments research analyst:* involves conducting research on investment opportunities for a bank trust department

3. **Contractual savings and real property organizations.**

Insurance companies, pension funds, and real estate firms also provide opportunities for starting a career in finance. These institutions need a variety of employees willing to blend marketing or selling efforts with financial expertise. Entry-level career opportunities include the following:

- *Insurance agent (broker):* involves selling insurance to individuals and businesses and participating in the processing of claims
- *Research analyst:* involves analyzing the investment potential of real property and securities for pension fund holdings
- *Real estate agent (broker):* involves marketing and selling or leasing residential or commercial property
- *Mortgage analyst:* involves analyzing real estate loan applications and assisting in the arranging of mortgage financing

4. **Securities markets and investment firms.**

Securities firms and various investment-related businesses provide opportunities to start a finance career in the investments area. Opportunities include buying and selling seasoned securities, analyzing securities for investment potential, marketing new securities issues, and even helping individuals plan and manage their personal financial resources. Entry-level career opportunities include the following:

- *Stockbroker (account executive):* involves assisting clients in purchasing stocks and bonds and building investment wealth
- *Security analyst:* involves analyzing and making recommendations on the investment potential of specific securities
- *Investment banking analyst:* involves conducting financial analysis and valuation of new securities being issued
- *Financial planner assistant:* involves analyzing individual client insurance needs and investment plans to meet retirement goals

While we have focused on entry-level careers in profit-motivated businesses and financial organizations, careers in finance are also available in government or not-for-profit organizations. Finance opportunities at the federal or state government levels include managing cash funds, making asset expenditure decisions, and issuing debt securities to raise funds. Hospitals and other not-for-profit organizations also need expert financial managers to manage assets, control costs, and obtain funds. Financial and other analysts are hired both by government units and not-for-profit organizations to perform these tasks.

All these entry-level finance job opportunities also can be found in the international setting. For example, many businesses engaged in producing and marketing products and services in foreign markets often offer employees opportunities for international job assignments. Large U.S. banks also offer international job experiences through their foreign banking operations. Furthermore, since worldwide securities markets exist, securities analysts and financial planners often must analyze and visit foreign-based firms.

At the end of each chapter, you will find a Career Profile feature about a real person. In addition, several more detailed Career Opportunities in Finance boxes are presented in selected chapters. We hope these materials provide a better understanding of some of the many career opportunities that exist in the finance field. We are also sure that new finance job opportunities will occur in the future as the field continues to develop and change. It is now time to begin learning about finance!

OVERVIEW OF THE FINANCIAL SYSTEM

CHARACTERISTICS AND COMPONENTS

financial system
interaction of intermediaries, markets, instruments, policy makers, and regulations to aid the flow from savings to investments

The ***financial system*** is a complex mix of financial intermediaries, markets, instruments, policy makers, and regulations that interact to expedite the flow of financial capital from savings into investment. Figure 1.2 provides an overview of the U.S. financial system. First, an effective financial system must have several sets of *policy makers* who pass laws and make decisions relating to fiscal and monetary policies. These policy makers include the president, Congress, and the U.S. Treasury, plus the Federal Reserve Board. Since the United States operates within a global economy, political and economic actions of foreign policy makers influence, although indirectly, the U.S. financial system and its operations.

FIGURE 1.2
Graphic View of the U.S. Financial System

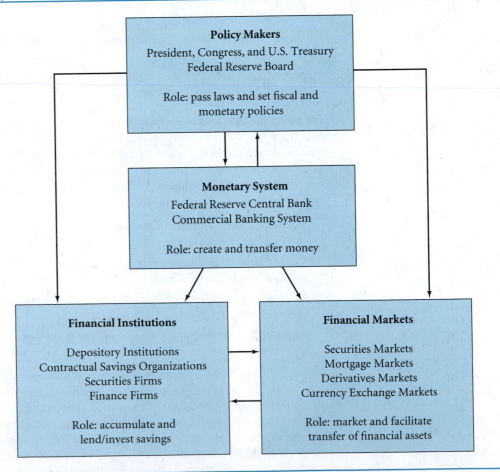

CONCEPT CHECK
What are the major areas for possible careers in finance?

INTERNET ACTIVITY

Go to the Federal Reserve Board Web site, http://www. federalreserve.gov, and find information on the current money supply. Determine the current size of M1 and its four components, as well as the size of M2 and M3.

INTERNET ACTIVITY

Go to the Business Week Web site, http://www.businessweek. com, and identify a major business development relating to the financial environment.

CONCEPT CHECK

What five requirements are necessary for a financial system to be effective?

Second, an effective financial system needs an efficient **monetary system** that is comprised of a central bank and a banking system that is able to create and transfer a stable medium of exchange called *money*. In the United States, the dollar is the medium of exchange, the central bank is the Federal Reserve System, and the banking system is commonly referred to as the commercial banking system.

Third, an effective financial system also must have *financial institutions* or intermediaries that support capital formation either by channeling savings into investment in physical assets or by fostering direct financial investments by individuals in financial institutions and businesses. Four types of financial intermediaries are listed in Figure 1.2. Depository institutions, contractual savings organizations, securities firms, and finance firms are discussed in Chapter 2. The process of accumulating and then lending and investing savings is referred to as the *savings-investment process*.

A fourth requirement of an effective financial system, although not depicted in Figure 1.2, is the need for financial assets or instruments necessary for the savings-investment process to work efficiently. We cover these finance basics in Chapter 3.

Fifth, an effective financial system must also have *financial markets* that facilitate the transfer of financial assets among individuals, institutions, businesses, and governments. Figure 1.2 identifies four types of financial markets—securities markets, mortgage markets, derivatives markets, and currency exchange markets. We briefly discuss these markets in Chapter 3 and then provide more detailed discussions of securities and derivatives markets in Part 2 and currency exchange markets in Part 3 of the text.

A financial system must make possible the creation of productive capital on a scale large enough to meet the demands of the economy. *Productive capital formation* takes place whenever resources are used to produce buildings, machinery, or other equipment for the production of goods for consumers or producers. In a simple economy, such as a self-sufficient, one-person farm, this process takes place directly. For example, the farmer creates capital by building a barn. In a highly developed economy, productive capital formation typically takes place indirectly. If individuals, businesses, or governmental units do not need to spend all their current income, they save some of it. If these savings are placed with a financial institution, they will be made available in the form of loans to others who use them to buy buildings, machinery, or equipment. The indirect process of productive capital formation can work only if the proper legal financial assets or instruments and financial intermediaries exist. Then savers will feel secure transferring their savings to businesses and other institutions that need the savings. The role of depositories and other intermediaries in the financial system is discussed in Chapter 2.

Financial markets are necessary for productive capital formation. They are needed to transfer financial assets, such as stocks and bonds, and to convert such assets into cash. They encourage investment by providing the means for savers to convert their financial assets quickly and easily into cash when needed. For example, millions of people are willing to invest billions of dollars in IBM, General Electric, and other companies because the New York Stock Exchange makes it possible to sell their shares to other investors easily and quickly.

FINANCIAL SYSTEM COMPONENTS AND FINANCIAL FUNCTIONS

We can express the roles of the monetary system, financial institutions, and financial markets as financial functions that are necessary in an effective financial system. Figure 1.3 indicates that the monetary system is responsible for creating and transferring money. Financial institutions efficiently accumulate savings and then lend or invest these savings. Financial institutions play important roles in the savings-investment process both through financial intermediation activities and in facilitating direct investments by individuals. Financial markets, along with certain securities firms, are responsible for marketing and transferring financial assets or claims.

Creating Money

Since money is something that is accepted as payment for goods, services, and debts, its value lies in its purchasing power. Money is the most generalized claim to wealth, since it can be exchanged for almost anything else. Most transactions in today's economy involve money, and most would not take place if money were not available.

One of the most significant functions of the monetary system within the financial system is creating money, which serves as a medium of exchange. In the United States, the Federal Reserve

FIGURE 1.3
Three Financial System Components and Their Financial Functions

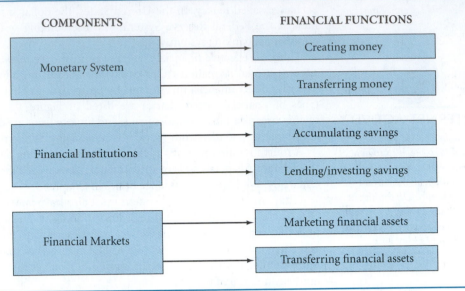

System is primarily responsible for the amount of money that is created, although most of the money is actually created by depository institutions. A sufficient amount of money is essential if economic activity is to take place at an efficient rate. Having too little money constrains economic growth. Having too much money often results in increases in the prices of goods and services.

Transferring Money

Individuals and businesses hold money for purchases or payments they expect to make in the near future. One way to hold money is in checkable deposits at depository institutions. When money is held in this form, payments can be made easily by check. The check is an order to the depository institution to transfer money to the party who received the check. This is a great convenience, since checks can be written for the exact amount of payments, can be safely sent in the mail, and provide a record of payment. Institutions can also transfer funds between accounts electronically, making payments without paper checks. Funds transfers can be made by telephone, at automated teller machines (ATMs) connected to a bank's computer, and via the Internet.

Accumulating Savings

A function performed by financial institutions is the accumulation or gathering of individual savings. Most individuals, businesses, and organizations do not want to take the risks involved in having cash on hand. Even if relatively small, cash amounts are put into a depository institution for safekeeping. When all the deposits are accumulated in one place, they can be used for loans and investments in amounts much larger than any individual depositor could supply. Depository institutions regularly conduct advertising campaigns and other promotional activities to attract deposits.

Lending and Investing Savings

Another basic function of financial institutions is lending and investing. The money that has been put into these intermediaries may be lent to businesses, farmers, consumers, institutions, and governmental units. It may be lent for varying periods and for different purposes, such as to buy equipment or to pay current bills. Some financial institutions make loans of almost all types. Others specialize in only one or two types of lending. Still other financial institutions invest all or part of their accumulated savings in the stock of a business or in debt obligations of businesses or other institutions.

Marketing Financial Assets

New financial instruments and securities are created and sold in the primary securities market. For example, a business may want to sell shares of ownership, called *stock,* to the general public. It can do so directly, but the process of finding individuals interested in investing funds in that business is likely to be difficult, costly, and time-consuming. One particular financial intermediary—an investment banking firm—can handle the sale of shares of ownership. The function of the investment banking firm is essentially one of merchandising. Brokerage firms market existing, or "seasoned," instruments and securities.

Transferring Financial Assets

Several types of financial institutions facilitate or assist the processes of lending and selling securities. Brokerage firms market and facilitate the transferring of existing or seasoned instruments and securities. Also, if shares of stock are to be sold to the general public, it is desirable to have a ready market in which such stocks can be resold when the investor desires. Organized stock exchanges and the over-the-counter market provide active secondary markets for existing securities. The ability to buy and sell securities both quickly and at fair-market values is important in an efficient financial system.

CONCEPT CHECK

What are the financial functions that take place in the financial system?

THE IMPORTANCE AND FUNCTIONS OF MONEY

money
anything that is generally accepted as payment

Money is anything generally accepted as a means of paying for goods and services and for paying off debts. For something to serve successfully as money, it must be easily divisible so that exchanges can take place in small or large quantities, relatively inexpensive to store and transfer, and reasonably stable in value over time. Money must perform three basic functions, serving as a medium of exchange, a store of value, and a standard of value.

medium of exchange
the basic function of money

Money was first developed to serve as a **medium of exchange** to facilitate transactions. Primitive economies consisted largely of self-sufficient units or groups that lived by means of hunting, fishing, and simple agriculture and had little need or occasion to exchange goods or services. As economies developed, however, the process of exchange became important. Some individuals specialized, to a degree at least, in herding sheep, raising grain, or shaping gold as metalsmiths. To aid in the exchanging of goods for goods, called **barter**, tables of relative values were developed from experience. For example, a table might show the number of furs, measures of grain, or amount of cloth agreed to equal one cow. This arrangement eased exchanges, but the process still had many serious drawbacks. For example, if a person had a cow and wanted to trade it for some nuts and furs, he or she would need to find someone who had an excess of both of these items to trade. The need for a simpler means of exchange led to the development of money, with its relatively low storage and transfer costs, to be used as a medium of exchange.

barter
exchange of goods or services without using money

store of value
money held for some period of time before it is spent

Money also may be held as a **store of value**. That is, money may be spent immediately after it is received or after it has been held for some time. While money is held, it is a liquid asset and provides its owner with flexibility, but the owner pays for this flexibility by giving up the potential return that could be earned through investment or the satisfaction that could be gained from spending it for goods and services. Money can perform its function as a store of value only if its "purchasing power" is relatively stable over time. Under this condition, the spending decision is separated from the income decision. Once income is received, the holder of the income can choose to spend it or save it. If the decision is to save, then that money can be made available through the savings-investment process to those who may want to invest now.

liquidity
how easily an asset can be exchanged for money

Any asset other than money can also serve as a store of value as long as that asset can be converted into money quickly and without significant loss of value. We refer to this quality—the ease with which an asset can be exchanged for money or other assets—as **liquidity**. Money is perfectly liquid since it is a generally accepted medium of exchange. Other assets, such as savings deposits held at depository institutions, approach the liquidity of money. The existence of such liquid assets reduces the need for holding money itself as a store of value.

standard of value
function of money that occurs when prices and debts are stated in terms of the monetary unit

Money also serves as a **standard of value**, which means that prices and contracts for deferred payments are expressed in terms of the monetary unit. For example, in the United States, prices

CONCEPT CHECK

What are the three functions performed by money?

and debts are usually expressed in terms of dollars without stating whether the purchase will be cash or credit. Of course, if money is to perform its function as a standard of value, it is essential that the value of the monetary unit be relatively stable over time. For example, if one dollar can be used to purchase two ballpoint pens today but only one tomorrow, such money would not be very effective as either a store of value or a standard of value.

THE DEVELOPMENT OF MONEY IN THE UNITED STATES

The two basic components of money supply in the United States are physical money (coin and currency) and deposit money. The following review of the development of money in the United States will explore the characteristics of money today, as well as how well U.S. money performs the three functions of money.

PHYSICAL MONEY (COIN AND PAPER CURRENCY)

The first function of "successful" money is that it serves as a medium of exchange. Physical money is the coin and paper currency used to purchase goods and services and to settle debts. We will first examine how U.S. coins have changed in terms of their precious metal (gold and silver) content over time. Then, we will examine how U.S. paper currency has changed in terms of both its physical characteristics and "backing" with precious metals.

U.S. Coins

While barter was undoubtedly important in early American history, the government moved swiftly toward a monetary system based on precious metals that would serve as an efficient medium of exchange. During much of the seventeenth and eighteenth centuries, the American colonies relied primarily on the Spanish dollar to conduct business transactions.[1] In 1785 the word *dollar* was adopted by the U.S. Congress as the standard monetary unit or standard of value. The first monetary act in the United States, passed in 1792, provided for a **bimetallic standard** based on both gold and silver. The dollar was defined in both grains of pure silver and grains of pure gold. All gold and silver coins were to be **full-bodied money** because their metal content was worth the same as their face values. For example, one silver dollar was to contain one dollar's worth of silver, a ten-dollar gold coin was to contain ten dollars' worth of gold, and so on.

A law enacted in 1837 modified the weight for the silver dollar to 412.5 grains of silver with .900 fineness. Copper of .100 fineness was used to make the coins last longer. The result was that each dollar contained .77344 ounce of pure silver. Since the value of the silver content was to be $1, silver was valued at $1.29 per ounce ($1/.77344). The peace-type dollar was produced from 1921 to 1935. The Franklin half-dollar, produced from 1948 to 1963, contained .36169 ounce of pure silver. Since silver prices had been gradually rising, the Franklin half-dollar was full-bodied money at a silver price of $1.38 ($.50/.36169). Depending on the prevailing market price of silver, a silver coin such as the half-dollar could be less than, greater than, or exactly full-bodied. For full-bodied money, its store of value was reflected in the then-current value of its precious metal content. As long as the price of precious metals moved in unison with the prices of goods and services, this money's store of value reflected the store of purchasing power.

Rapidly rising silver prices in the 1960s, however, made silver coins worth more as melted-down bullion than their face values. As a result, the U.S. government "debased" its full-bodied money by replacing silver content with copper and nickel. Coins with face values higher than the value of their metal content are called **token coins**. The Eisenhower dollar was minted from 1971 to 1978. Kennedy half-dollars were full-bodied coins in 1964, were changed to silver-clad (reduced silver content) coins from 1965 to 1970, and have been copper-nickel–clad coins since 1971.

The production of gold coins began in 1795 with the $5 and $10 coins. The issuance of full-bodied gold dollars was authorized in 1849, and production continued through 1889. For several decades, the value of a U.S. dollar was expressed both in terms of silver and gold. All gold coin

bimetallic standard
monetary standard based on two metals, usually silver and gold

full-bodied money
coins that contain the same value in metal as their face value

token coins
coins containing metal of less value than their stated value

---

1. The Spanish dollar often was cut into eight pieces or "bits" to make change. If you have heard the U.S. quarter-dollar referred to as "two bits," you now know that this term originated from cutting the Spanish dollar into "pieces of eight."

production was stopped in 1933, and in 1934 U.S. citizens were prohibited from holding monetary gold in the United States. This restriction was extended to gold held abroad by U.S. citizens in 1961. All restrictions on holding gold in money form were removed in 1975.

Paper Currency

The evolution and use of paper currency in the United States have been characterized by a very erratic history. While some paper money was issued by individual colonies, the first effort of a government to issue paper money occurred when the Continental Congress authorized the issuance of notes called Continentals to finance the Revolutionary War. While these notes were denominated in dollars, they had no backing in either silver or gold. Rather, they were backed only by possible future tax revenues to be gathered when the colonies became independent. As you might guess, the Continentals soon became worthless. This led to a long period of distrust of paper money. After a brief experience with two national banks, U.S. banking went through a period of no federal regulation and nonuniformity in operating laws. State-chartered banks issued their own paper currency almost at will and in many cases with no or little backing of their notes with gold or silver deposits.[2]

representative full-bodied money
paper money fully backed by a precious metal

Paper money may be either representative full-bodied money or fiat money. **Representative full-bodied money** is paper money that is backed by an amount of precious metal equal in value to the face amount of the paper money. The U.S. government has issued two types of representative full-bodied money. Gold certificates were issued from 1865 through 1928. Since they could be redeemed for gold with a value equal to the paper currency's face amount, they were "as good as gold." However, since most gold certificates were issued in large denominations, they were not intended to be used in general circulation but rather to settle institutional gold accounts. The issuance of silver certificates was authorized beginning in 1878. A switch to "small-size" silver certificates occurred in 1929, and they continued to be issued and used through 1963. These certificates could be exchanged for silver dollars or silver bullion when presented to the U.S. Treasury. Of course, like full-bodied silver coins, these silver certificates became worth more in terms of the bullion value of silver relative to their face values as silver prices began climbing in the 1960s. As a result, redemption of silver certificates in silver dollars was halted in 1964 by the U.S. government, and in 1968 redemption in silver bullion also was stopped.

fiat money
legal tender proclaimed to be money by law

Today, almost all paper money in circulation is in the form of Federal Reserve Notes, which were authorized under the *Federal Reserve Act of 1913*. These notes, which are not backed by either gold or silver, are called **fiat money** because the government decreed the notes to be "legal tender" for purposes of making payments and discharging public and private debts. Of course, the copper-nickel–clad, or token, coins of today are also fiat money because their metal content values are less than their face values.

The reliance on the use of fiat money can be problematic. First, fiat money generally becomes worthless if the issuing government fails. For example, Confederate currency was issued during the U.S. Civil War, but when the Confederacy lost the war this fiat money became worthless. Second, since there is no required backing in gold or silver, it is relatively easy to issue more and more fiat money. Issuing too much money can, in turn, lead to rising prices and a lack of confidence in the government. An effective monetary system with a strong central bank and prudent policy makers are needed when a financial system relies on fiat money to carry out its transactions.

Several major changes in Federal Reserve Notes have taken place over time. In 1929, the size of the notes was reduced about 30 percent from large notes (7.42 inches by 3.13 inches) to small notes (6.14 inches by 2.61 inches). This change made production less expensive and made it easier to handle and less costly to store and transfer paper money.

ETHICAL ISSUES

When it comes to money, the behavior of individuals ranges from exhibiting high ethical standards down to deceit, fraud, and even counterfeiting activities. How you acquire and deal with money affects your reputation. Individuals who work hard, follow the law, and treat other individuals they are involved with in money transactions fairly and honestly are able to find success, accumulate wealth, and build high-quality reputations. However, probably almost from

---

2. By 1865, it was estimated that about one-third of the circulating paper currency was counterfeit. As a result, the U.S. Treasury established the U.S. Secret Service to control counterfeiting activities.

INTERNET ACTIVITY

Go to the U.S. Treasury Web site, http://www.treas.gov, and find information on the features and characteristics of "large portrait" U.S. paper currency. Write a brief summary of your findings.

CONCEPT CHECK

What is meant by full-bodied money?

What is meant by fiat money?

the origins of money creation, some individuals driven by greed have engaged in counterfeiting activities to illegally get money rather than work for it. It is difficult for most of us to understand such extreme unethical behavior, which typically results in getting caught, serving prison time, and destroying the reputations of those involved.

Unfortunately, attempts to counterfeit or illegally copy U.S. currency constitute big business for some individuals and organizations. Furthermore, the ability to counterfeit currency has been aided in recent years by the introduction of high-quality color copiers. To thwart counterfeiting efforts, the U.S. Treasury Department's Bureau of Engraving and Printing has developed new currency designs in recent years. A new series of notes that made use of microprinting and an embedded security strip was introduced in 1990 to improve security and to make counterfeiting more difficult. A more complete design change began with the $100 "large portrait" bill in 1996. Large-portrait $50 bills were introduced in 1997, and large-portrait $20 bills were placed in circulation in 1998. New $5 and $10 bills were introduced in 2000. Today only the $1 bill continues to use the small-portrait format.

The larger portrait was placed off-center to allow the inclusion of a watermark that is visible from both sides when held up against a light. Such bills contain a vertically embedded security thread, which glows red when exposed to ultraviolet light, at the far left of the portrait. Color-shifting ink, fine line printing, and microprinting were added. Beginning in 2003, peach and light-blue hues were added to the previous green-and-black bills of U.S. currency.

These anti-counterfeiting efforts, while very costly, are essential to maintaining the public's trust and confidence in fiat money. Of course, it is important to remember that even though the appearance of U.S. paper money may be changing, the government honors all previously issued U.S. paper currency at full face value. There is no requirement or time limit for exchanging old notes for new ones. Old notes continue to remain in circulation until depository institutions return them to the Federal Reserve to be retired.

Deposit Money

The use of physical (coin and currency) money to complete transactions can be costly and inefficient if large amounts and/or long distances are involved. As a result of these constraints on the use of physical money, along with confidence in the banking system, a special type of credit money called *deposit money* has grown readily in importance in the U.S. monetary system. **Credit money** is money backed by the creditworthiness of the issuer.[3] **Deposit money** is backed by the creditworthiness of the depository institution that issued the deposit.

Deposit money takes the form of demand deposits held at commercial banks or other checkable deposits held at S&Ls, savings banks, and credit unions. A demand deposit gets its name from the fact that the owner of a deposit account "demands" that all or a portion of the amount in his or her demand deposit account be transferred to another individual or organization. Checks or drafts have traditionally been used to transfer demand deposit or other checkable deposit amounts. Let's illustrate this concept with an example. The ABC business firm deposits $1,000 at First Bank to set up a $1,000 demand deposit account in ABC's name. ABC then writes a $1,000 check against its deposit account and sends the check to an equipment manufacturer as payment for purchase of equipment. The equipment manufacturer deposits the check in its own demand deposit account in a bank (e.g., Last Bank). The check then must be processed and cleared through the banking system. That is, it must be returned to First Bank, which will pay the check amount to Last Bank and deduct $1,000 from the business firm's demand deposit account at First Bank.

The processing of paper checks is time-consuming and costly. An alternative is to electronically transfer funds to and from checkable deposit accounts. Rather than issuing payroll checks, employers can have their employees' wages deposited directly in the employees' checking accounts. Individuals can have regular payments such as mortgage payments or insurance premiums automatically deducted from their accounts. Electronic funds transfers by telephone (*phone banking*) or via the Internet (*online banking*), for payment of utility bills, credit card balances, and so forth, are increasingly common.

credit money
money worth more than what it is made of

deposit money
money backed by the creditworthiness of the depository institution that issued the deposit

---

3. Fiat money is a form of credit money. However, while the government declares fiat money to be "legal tender," other forms of credit money such as deposit money do not have governmental support or backing.

FIGURE 1.4

Definitions of Money Supply Measures and Seasonally Adjusted Totals for December 2005

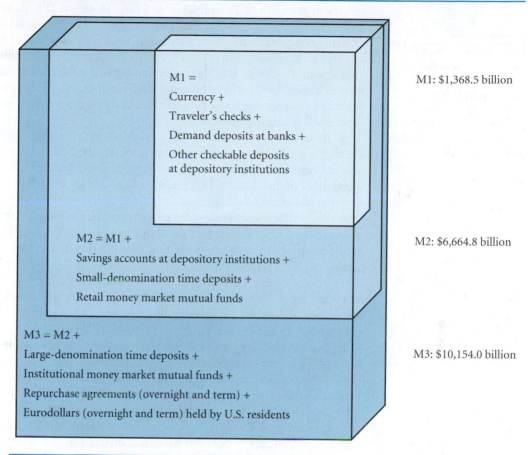

M1 =

Currency +

Traveler's checks +

Demand deposits at banks +

Other checkable deposits
at depository institutions

M1: $1,368.5 billion

M2 = M1 +

Savings accounts at depository institutions +

Small-denomination time deposits +

Retail money market mutual funds

M2: $6,664.8 billion

M3 = M2 +

Large-denomination time deposits +

Institutional money market mutual funds +

Repurchase agreements (overnight and term) +

Eurodollars (overnight and term) held by U.S. residents

M3: $10,154.0 billion

Source: *Statistical Supplement to the Federal Reserve Bulletin* (January 2007), p. 13.

U.S. MONEY SUPPLY TODAY

Now that you have a basic understanding of how money developed in the United States, it is time to examine how the money supply or *money stock* is measured today. Since we are trying to "count" the money supply in the financial system as of a point in time, this can also be viewed as the amount of money stock on a particular date. We start with a narrow definition of the money supply and then consider broader definitions. Figure 1.4 shows several definitions of money supply in use today.

M1 MONEY SUPPLY

M1 money supply
consists of currency, travelers'
checks, demand deposits, and
other checkable deposits

As noted, the basic function of money is that it must be acceptable as a medium of exchange. The M1 definition of the money supply includes only types of money that meet this basic function. More specifically, the **M1 money supply** consists of currency, traveler's checks, demand deposits, and other checkable deposits at depository institutions. The following table shows the components (seasonally adjusted) of M1 and their relative sizes as of December 2005, as reported in the *Statistical Supplement to the Federal Reserve Bulletin*:

M1 COMPONENT	$ (BILLIONS)	PERCENTAGE
Currency	723.4	52.9
Traveler's checks	7.3	.5
Demand deposits	320.5	23.4
Other checkable deposits	317.3	23.2
Total M1	**1,368.5**	**100.0**

INTERNET ACTIVITY

*Go to the St. Louis Federal
Reserve Bank's Web site,
http://www.stls.frb.org, and
access the FRED database.
Find the current size of the M1
money supply and the annual
gross domestic product (GDP)
and calculate the velocity of
money.*

All four components are types of credit money. Currency is U.S. physical money in the form of coins and paper currency. The coins are token money, and the paper currency is fiat money in the form of Federal Reserve Notes. However, U.S. currency (both coins and paper money) is readily accepted for making payments and retiring debts and thus serves as an important medium of exchange. Currency comprises a little over half of the M1 money supply. Traveler's checks, offered by banks and other organizations, promise to pay on demand the face amounts of the checks with their acceptance based on the creditworthiness of the issuer. Since traveler's checks are a widely accepted medium of exchange, they qualify as a component of the M1 money supply. Even so, their relative importance is small, as indicated by the fact that they represent less than 1 percent of the M1 total.

As noted, demand deposits (checking accounts) at commercial banks and other checkable deposits at savings and loan associations (S&Ls), savings banks, and credit unions also are considered to be credit money, since these deposits are backed solely by the creditworthiness of the issuing institutions when checks are presented for collection. Demand deposits at commercial banks account for 24 percent of the money supply. Other checkable deposits, which also represent 24 percent of M1, include automatic transfer service (ATS) accounts and negotiable order of withdrawal (NOW) accounts at depository institutions, credit union share draft accounts, and demand deposits at S&Ls, credit unions, and savings banks.

Taken together, demand deposit and other checkable deposit accounts comprise a little less than half of the M1 money supply. This high percentage shows the importance of the banking system and its money-creating function within the monetary system and in terms of the broader U.S. financial system.

Before moving to a broader definition of the money supply, it is important to consider some of the adjustments or exclusions that take place when estimating the M1 money supply or stock. M1 measures transaction balances. These are sums of money that can be spent without first converting them to some other asset and that are held for anticipated or unanticipated purchases or payments in the immediate future. Essentially, only those amounts that represent the purchasing power of units in the U.S. economy other than the federal government are counted. Specifically excluded from M1 is currency in the vaults of depository institutions or held by the Federal Reserve and the U.S. Treasury. Demand deposits owed to depository institutions, the federal government, and foreign banks and governments also are excluded. Adjustment is also made to avoid double-counting checks being processed. The vault cash and deposits belonging to depository institutions do not represent purchasing power and are, therefore, not money. However, they serve as reserves, an important element of the U.S. financial system that is discussed in Chapter 2.

M2 MONEY SUPPLY

M2 money supply
*consists of M1 plus highly
liquid financial assets
including savings accounts,
small time deposits, and
retail money market mutual
funds*

The Federal Reserve's second definition of the money stock, M2, is a broader measure than M1 because it emphasizes money as a store of value in addition to its function as a medium of exchange. In general terms, the **M2 money supply** includes M1 plus highly liquid financial assets, including savings accounts, small time deposits, and retail money market mutual funds. Most of the financial assets added to M2 provide their owners with a higher rate of return than would M1 components. More specifically, M2 adds to M1 savings deposits, money market deposit accounts (MMDAs), and small-denomination time deposits (under $100,000) at depository institutions, plus balances in retail money market mutual funds (MMMFs) in which initial investments are less than $50,000.

Figure 1.4 shows that M2, at $6,664.8 billion, is nearly five times the size of M1. Some of the owners of the assets included in M2 hold them as long-term savings instruments. Other individuals and firms hold these M2 specific assets even though they plan to spend the funds within a few days because the assets are very liquid. M1 thus understates purchasing power by the amount of these M2 balances held for transaction purposes.

The components of M2 illustrate the difficulties the Federal Reserve has faced in drawing the boundaries of these definitions. For example, MMDAs provide check-writing privileges and can therefore be used for transaction purposes. Some analysts argue on this basis that MMDA balances should be part of M1. The Federal Reserve has included MMDA balances in M2 but not in M1 because MMDAs are different from traditional money components and because MMDAs seem to be used more as savings instruments than as transaction balances. On the other hand, it can be argued that small time deposits should be excluded from M2 because they are not, in practice, very liquid. Holders of small time deposits that they wish to cash in before maturity are penalized by having to forfeit some of the interest they have earned. However, small time deposits are included because they are considered to be close substitutes for some of the other savings instruments included in M2. Savings deposits, including MMDAs, at depository institutions are greater than the M1 total.

money market mutual funds (MMMFs)
issue shares to customers and invest the proceeds in highly liquid, very short maturity, interest-bearing debt instruments

Money market mutual funds (MMMFs) issue shares to customers and invest the proceeds in highly liquid, very-short-maturity, interest-bearing debt instruments called *money market investments*. MMMFs get their name from the type of investments they make. The nature of their investments, coupled with daily payment of interest, keeps MMMF shares valued at $1. Many MMMFs allow shareholders to write checks against their accounts. When checks are cleared and presented to the MMMF for payment, the number of shares owned by the shareholder is reduced accordingly. This process, of course, is very similar to writing checks against checkable deposits held at depository institutions. However, the Federal Reserve does not include retail MMMF balances in M1 because it decided that consumers use the accounts more as a store of purchasing power and less as a medium of exchange. Retail MMMF balances were $810 billion at the end of 2003 and thus are a little less than two-thirds the size of M1.

M3 MONEY SUPPLY

M3 money supply
consists of M2 plus large time deposits and institutional money market mutual funds

M3 takes an even broader view of money as a store of value. In general, the *M3 money supply* includes M2 plus large time deposits and institutional money market mutual funds. Figure 1.4 shows that M3 was $10,154.0 billion or more than seven times M1 at the end of 2005. More specifically, M3 includes large time deposits (over $100,000), balances in institutional MMMFs (minimum initial investments of $50,000), *repurchase agreements* (overnight and term) issued by depository institutions, and Eurodollars (overnight and term) held by U.S. residents in the United Kingdom and Canada and at foreign branches of U.S. banks. (A repurchase agreement is essentially a way of making a loan. The lender buys an asset, usually securities, from the borrower, thus providing funds to the borrower. The borrower repays by buying back the asset at a prearranged time and price. Overnight repurchase agreements, or RPs, and Eurodollars are repaid the next day. Term RPs and Eurodollars are held for a longer time.)

EXCLUSIONS FROM THE MONEY SUPPLY

The Federal Reserve excludes certain stores of value and borrowings from its money supply definitions. For example, stock and bond mutual funds held by individuals represent stores of value, and some even permit limited check writing against these accounts. However, because the value of shares in these funds often fluctuates widely and individuals may hold these security investments for a long time, the Federal Reserve does not consider these part of the money supply.

credit cards
provide predetermined credit limits to consumers when the cards are issued

Credit cards provide predetermined credit limits to consumers at the time the cards are issued. No checkable or other deposits are established at the time of issue. Thus neither credit card limits nor outstanding balances are part of the money supply. Rather, credit cards just allow their holders to borrow up to a predetermined limit. However, the use of credit cards can affect the rate of turnover of the money supply and may contribute to money supply expansion. If credit card borrowing stimulates the demand for goods and services, a given money supply can support a higher level of economic activity. (We explore the relationship between money supply and economic activity in the next section.) Also, when you use your credit card to purchase a product for, say, $50 at a retailer, the bank that issued the credit card lends you $50 and increases the retailer's demand deposit account by $50. As your credit card balance increases as you purchase goods and services on credit, the checkable deposit accounts of those who sold the goods and services also increase. Of course, users of credit cards must eventually pay off their debts.

CONCEPT CHECK

What are the three standard measures of the money supply?

POLICY IMPLICATIONS: MONEY SUPPLY AND ECONOMIC ACTIVITY

Economists generally believe that money supply matters when they try to manage economic activity. They have observed that economic activity, money supply, and the price levels of goods and services generally move together over time. However, economists disagree about how these relationships are to be explained.

The output of goods and services in the economy is referred to as the ***gross domestic product (GDP)***. Since we typically measure output in current dollars, we measure "nominal" GDP. Some economists, called *monetarists*, believe that the amount of money in circulation determines the level of GDP or economic activity. If we divide GDP by the money supply (MS), we get the number of times the money supply turns over to produce GDP. Economists refer to the turnover of money as the *velocity of money*. More specifically, the ***velocity of money*** measures the rate of circulation of the money supply. For example, if the annual GDP is $15 million and the MS is $5 million, the velocity of money (VM) is three times (i.e., $15 million/$5 million). In alternative form, we can say that:

$$MS \times VM = GDP \tag{1.1}$$

For our example, we have:

$$\$5 \text{ million} \times 3 = \$15 \text{ million}$$

Economists also express nominal GDP as being equal to real output (RO) times the price level (PL) of goods and services, or:

$$RO \times PL = GDP \tag{1.2}$$

For example, if the real output in the economy is 150,000 products and the average price is $100, the GDP is $15 million (i.e., 150,000 × $100). Putting these two equations together, we have:

$$MS \times VM = RO \times PL \tag{1.3}$$

An increase in the money supply and/or velocity causes nominal GDP to increase. For nominal GDP to increase, real output and/or price levels must increase. For example, let's assume the money supply increases by 10 percent or $500,000 to $5.5 million while the velocity stays at three times. Nominal GDP will increase to:

$$5.5 \text{ million} \times 3 = 16.5 \text{ million}$$

And, since GDP equals RO × PL, some change in real output or price level (or a combination of the two) needs to take place. One possibility is for real output to increase by 15,000 products or units to 165,000 with no change in prices. GDP then would be:

$$165,000 \text{ units} \times 100 = 16.5 \text{ million}$$

Monetarists also believe that when the money supply exceeds the amount of money demanded, the public will spend more rapidly, causing real economic activity or prices to rise. A too-rapid rate of growth in the money supply will ultimately result in rising prices or inflation because excess money will be used to bid up the prices of existing goods. ***Inflation*** is a rise or increase in the prices of goods and services that is not offset by increases in their quality. Because of the difficulty of measuring changes in quality, a more operational definition of inflation is a continuing rise in prices. For example, instead of the $1.5 million increase in GDP from $15 million to $16.5 million being due to a 10 percent increase in the money supply, the increase might have been due solely to inflation. Let's assume that the quantity of products sold remains at the original 150,000-unit level but that the average price increases by 10 percent to $110. GDP would be calculated as:

$$150,000 \text{ units} \times 110 = 16.5 \text{ million}$$

Of course, almost unlimited combinations of real outputs and price levels, including reducing one of the variables, could produce the same new GDP.

gross domestic product (GDP)
a measure of the output of goods and services in an economy

velocity of money
the rate of circulation of the money supply

inflation
rise in prices not offset by increases in quality

Other economists, called Keynesians in honor of John Maynard Keynes, believe that a change in the money supply has a less direct relationship with GDP. They argue that a change in money supply first causes a change in interest rate levels, which, in turn, alters the demand for goods and services. For example, an increase in the money supply might cause interest rates to fall (at least initially) because more money is being supplied than is being demanded. Lower interest rates, in turn, will lead to an increase in consumption and/or investment spending, causing the GDP to grow.[4] In contrast, a decrease in the money supply will likely cause interest rates to rise. As a result, the GDP will grow more slowly, or even decline, depending on how the higher interest rates affect consumption and spending decisions.

As you might guess, it is not possible to say that one group of economists (monetarists or Keynesians) is right and the other is wrong. The ability to identify relationships among GDP, money supply, and price levels has been complicated by the fact that the velocity of money has increased and the various measures of the money supply have grown at different rates. M1 velocity has increased as credit card usage has replaced the more traditional use of currency and deposit money when purchasing goods and services. The velocity of M1 money also has increased as the public has made more use of money market mutual funds and other liquid accounts that serve as stores of value relative to their usage of traditional deposit money in demand and other checkable accounts.

The M1 measure of the money supply grew at nearly a double-digit rate during the first part of the 1990s. Many economists thought that such growth might lead to higher inflation. However, over the same period, M2 and M3 grew much more slowly. The net result, along with other developments in the economy, was a decline in inflation rates measured in terms of changes in consumer prices. Money supply growth remained moderate and inflation low during the last half of the 1990s and the first few years of the twenty-first century.

However, we must be careful when trying to interpret the near-term impact of changes in the money supply. Decreasing regulation and increasing competition among financial institutions have led to changes in the types of deposit money that individuals use for medium-of-exchange purposes. Likewise, there are ongoing changes in how individuals use liquid financial asset accounts for store-of-value purposes. Thus, recent changes in growth rates for different definitions of the money supply reflect in part changes in how individuals pay bills and store purchasing power. This is one reason why the Federal Reserve simultaneously keeps track of several measures of the money supply.

GLOBAL DISCUSSION

INTERNET ACTIVITY

Go to the Wall Street Journal *Web site at http://www. careerjournal.com, and find information relating to job hunting.*

currency exchange rate
value of one currency relative to another

THE INTERNATIONAL MONETARY SYSTEM

Historically, the international monetary system was tied to the gold standard. An international gold standard was used to conduct most international trade during the latter part of the 1800s and the early part of the 1900s. However, a breakdown in the gold standard occurred during World War I, and less formal exchange systems continued during the worldwide depression of the 1930s and during World War II.

In 1944 many of the world's economic powers met at Bretton Woods, New Hampshire. They agreed to an international monetary system tied to the U.S. dollar or gold via fixed or pegged exchange rates. One ounce of gold was set equal to $35. Each participating country then had its currency pegged to either gold or the U.S. dollar. This system of fixed exchange rates became known as the Bretton Woods System and was maintained through 1971.

By early 1973, major currencies were allowed to float against each other, resulting in a flexible or floating exchange rate system. While free market forces are allowed to operate today, central monetary authorities attempt to intervene in exchange markets when they believe that exchange rates between two currencies are harming world trade and the global economy. This actually makes the current international monetary system a managed floating exchange rate system.

Virtually all international transactions now involve the exchange of currencies or checkable deposits denominated in various currencies. Exchanges occur either for goods and services, for financial claims, or for other currencies. The value of one currency relative to another, called the **currency exchange rate,** depends on the supply of and demand for each currency relative to the

---

4. If the increase in money supply leads to price level increases (inflation), nominal interest rates that include inflation expectations might actually increase. The determinants of market interest rates are presented in Chapter 4.

other. The supply of a currency in international markets depends largely on the imports of the issuing country—that is, how much of its currency a country spends in world markets. Demand for a currency depends on the amount of exports that currency will buy from the issuing country. Demand also depends on the confidence of market participants in the restraint and stability of the monetary authority issuing the currency. If demand for a particular currency falls relative to its supply, the exchange rate falls and the international purchasing power of that nation's money supply drops. Domestic inflation, political instability, or an excess of imports over exports can cause one currency to decline relative to another currency. If a currency is widely accepted, the demand for it may be increased by the desire of people worldwide to hold it as an international medium of exchange. Such is the case of the U.S. dollar, which is widely held internationally because of its general acceptance and ability to hold its value. International finance is discussed in detail in Chapter 18.

A major international development occurred on January 1, 2002, when twelve European countries gave up their individual currencies and adopted a unified currency called the *euro.* For example, the French gave up the franc, the Germans the mark, and the Italians the lira to be part of the European Union (EU). It is interesting to note that all members of the EU do not currently use the euro either because they have chosen to keep their own national currencies or do not qualify for adoption due to fiscal deficit and other constraints. The creation of the euro was accompanied by the formation of the European Central Bank, which replaces the central banks of each of the participating countries.

euro
a single currency that has replaced the individual currencies of twelve member countries of the European Union

Although our focus is on the U.S. monetary system, we operate in a global economy. Thus we must interact with other monetary systems, and a change in either the European Union or Japanese monetary systems will directly affect the U.S. monetary system. For example, when the European Central Bank increases interest rates in the Europe Union, the value of the U.S. dollar weakens relative to the euro. This increases the cost of products imported into the United States unless the Federal Reserve takes countering actions.

THE PLAN OF STUDY

INTERNET ACTIVITY

The Monster.com Web site, http://www.monster.com, provides information on current finance jobs that are available. Click on "Select Category" and then "Finance/Economics" and list some of the entry-level finance positions available.

The subject matter of this book includes the entire scope of the financial environment from the perspective of the financial system and the three areas of finance—institutions and markets, investments, and financial management. You will learn about the markets in which funds are traded and the institutions and intermediaries that participate in and assist these flows of funds. You will learn about the investments area of finance, including the characteristics of debt and equity securities that are issued, the markets where securities are traded, and investment risk-return concepts. You will study the financial management principles and concepts that guide financial managers to make sound financial planning, asset acquisition, and financing decisions. International finance applications also are integrated throughout the text.

Part 1 focuses on the role financial markets play in the financial system and financial basics that underlie how markets operate. This first chapter provided an overview of an effective financial system, including the need for policy makers, a monetary system, financial institutions or

CAREER OPPORTUNITIES IN FINANCE
You Are Likely to Have More than One Business Career

Students are advised today to prepare for several business careers during their working lifetimes. Corporate America continues to restructure and reinvent itself. At the same time, new industries associated with the information age are developing, and old industries are dropping by the wayside. These developments make it even more likely that each of you will have the opportunity for multiple business careers.

Graduates of Harvard University are periodically surveyed concerning their work experiences and careers. Responses to one survey of individuals twenty-five years after graduation found that

over half had worked for four or more employers, while one-fourth had been fired (or in kinder terms "involuntarily terminated"). Over half of the men and women respondents had had at least two substantially different careers, and in many instances significant retraining was required.

Remember as you read this book that even if you don't currently plan on a career in finance, learning about finance might become very important to you later in your working lifetime. And, no matter where your business career takes you, you will always need to know and understand your personal finances.

intermediaries, financial assets or instruments, and financial markets. The functions of money and the importance of understanding the money supply. comprised of a central bank and a banking system for creating and transferring money, were also presented. Chapter 2 provides a more in-depth discussion of banks and other financial intermediaries that perform the financial functions of accumulating savings. Chapter 3 focuses on the savings and investment process and describes the financial assets or instruments that are important to producing effective lending and investing the savings of individuals and others. Chapter 4 discusses the structure and characteristics of interest rates. We conclude Part 1 with a chapter on the time value of money, which is one of the six principles of finance that you must understand clearly if you are to function and operate effectively when making personal finance decisions and in the field of finance.

Part 2 is concerned with the investments area of finance. Chapter 6 discusses return and risk basics. Chapter 7 covers the characteristics and valuation of bonds, while Chapter 8 focuses on the characteristics and valuation of equity or stocks. Chapter 9 discusses the characteristics and workings of the securities markets. Part 2 concludes with Chapter 10, which describes various investment implications that are important when trying to make sound investment decisions.

Part 3 focuses on the financial management of businesses. We begin Chapter 11 with an introduction and overview of the types of business organizations and follow with a review of basic financial statements and financial data important to the financial manager. Chapter 12 discusses the need for, and the way in which to conduct, financial analysis of past performance. Chapter 13 focuses on evaluating business investments. Chapter 14 covers the estimation of projected cash flows and is followed by Chapter 15, which focuses on capital structure and the cost of capital. Chapter 16 provides a discussion of managing working capital. Chapter 17 discusses short-term business financing. We conclude Part 3 with Chapter 18 on international finance and trade.

Of course, as we illustrated in Figure 1.1, the three areas of finance are not independent but rather are continually interacting or overlapping. For example, financial institutions provide an important financial intermediation role by getting individual savings into the hands of businesses so that financial managers can efficiently use and invest those funds. Financial managers also rely heavily on the investments area of finance when carrying out their financial management activities. Corporations often need to raise funds in the primary securities markets, and secondary securities markets, in turn, provide investors with the liquidity of being able to buy and sell previously issued securities. Our approach in this book is to provide survey exposure to all three areas of finance by covering finance basics, investments, and financial management topics.

CONCEPT CHECK

What do the three parts of this book cover?

APPLYING FINANCE TO . . .

INSTITUTIONS AND MARKETS

Financial institutions and financial markets are necessary components of an efficient financial system. Institutions perform an important financial intermediation role by gathering the savings of individuals and then lending the pooled savings to businesses that want to make investments.

The monetary system is composed of a central bank, the Federal Reserve System, and a banking system. For the monetary and financial systems to work, money must be accepted as the medium of exchange by each of us. Commercial banks in the aggregate help create and transfer money and thus help the monetary system operate efficiently. Other financial institutions also help in the savings-investment process when individual savings are pooled and lent or invested in business firms.

INVESTMENTS

Securities markets are also important components of an efficient financial system. The primary securities market facilitates raising funds by issuing new debt and equity securities. The secondary market for securities facilitates the transfer of ownership of existing securities among investors.

Money is the fundamental store of wealth. While we often think of money in terms of coin and currency, the money supply also includes demand and other checkable deposits. Some definitions of the money supply also include savings accounts, time deposits, and money market mutual funds. An individual's net worth consists of real assets such as automobiles and houses, mutual fund shares held, and holdings of the various types of money less any debts.

FINANCIAL MANAGEMENT

Businesses seek to raise additional funds to finance investment in inventories, equipment, and buildings needed to support growth in sales. Bank loans are important financing sources, along with the proceeds from the issuance of new debt and equity securities.

Business firms rely on financial institutions to help them raise funds from the savings of individuals. Businesses need money to conduct their day-to-day operations and need an efficient monetary system for collecting funds from customers and for paying their own bills in a timely fashion. The primary securities markets are where businesses sell or issue their securities and raise financial capital to grow their businesses.

DON PARSONS
Partner, Centennial Funds

BS, Electrical Engineering,
Northwestern
MBA, Finance, University of Michigan

"We'll lose our entire investment in almost half of the companies we fund."

Q: *You work in the venture capital industry. Please explain what that means.*

A: Our firm looks for entrepreneurial companies, especially in the high-tech field, where we can make an equity investment and hopefully produce a high return on our investment over a five-to-nine-year period. We also take an active role with the entrepreneurs to help them succeed.

Q: *What kind of help do entrepreneurs need?*

A: Most entrepreneurs are experts in their specific fields—computers, electronics, whatever—but they're not experts in starting a business and making it profitable. We provide experience that can help a small company avoid common mistakes and improve its chance of survival.

Q: *But success is not guaranteed.*

A: Not at all. According to industry averages, we'll lose our entire investment in almost half of the companies we fund. And only a handful turn into huge successes like Microsoft or Intel, which started very small. In the case of a big success, we might make fifty times our original investment. But these few big successes must make up for the many that don't survive.

Q: *Describe an entry-level position in venture capital.*

A: I started as an investment analyst, which is really an apprentice kind of position. I was assigned to a different partner every six months, and I helped those partners evaluate potential investment in new companies. There's a lot of research involved—in the industry, the technology, the product, the management team of the company—and the investment analyst does a lot of that research. Then we compile our findings into a very comprehensive report that is used to make the investment recommendation.

Q: *How were you qualified to evaluate these start-up companies?*

A: I have an electrical engineering degree and worked with IBM during and after college. At IBM I was involved with the design of several of its early personal computers, so I learned a lot about the development process of new technology products. Not everyone brings a technology background into this business, but many do. It has helped me a lot. After IBM I got my MBA, which enabled me to gain the financial skills necessary to evaluate investment opportunities.

Q: *What skills help you most in your job?*

A: There are many aspects to building a successful company, so the job requires a broad set of skills. You have to understand the technology, the finances, tax considerations, the legal and securities aspects, negotiation, and whatever other issues arise. You must be able to successfully interact with many different people. And parallel thinking is also an absolute requirement. If you can't juggle multiple issues and multiple projects, you would find this a very frustrating business.

Q: *What's the toughest part of this job?*

A: It's difficult to evaluate your results. It may be four, seven, ten years before we can tell if a new company is going to survive, much less succeed. It keeps you humble.

SUMMARY

Finance is the study of how businesses and others acquire, spend, and manage money and other financial resources. More specifically, finance is composed of three areas—financial institutions and markets, investments, and financial management. However, these three areas are not independent of one another but rather intersect or overlap. A survey approach to the study of finance thus covers all three areas.

An effective financial system requires policy makers, a monetary system, and financial institutions and financial markets to facilitate the flow of financial capital from savings into investments. Policy makers pass laws and set fiscal and monetary policies designed to manage the economy. A monetary system creates and transfers money. Financial institutions accumulate and lend/invest individual savings. Financial markets facilitate the transfer of securities and other financial assets. All these activities operate together to create a smoothly running and efficient financial system.

A working knowledge of the U.S. monetary system is essential to understanding the broader U.S. financial system and how businesses and financial institutions operate within the financial system. The monetary system is responsible for creating and transferring money and is intertwined with the savings-investment process. Major participants in the monetary system in the United States include a central bank called the Federal Reserve and a banking system composed of depository institutions. Money must provide several functions for a monetary system to be successful: it must serve as a medium of exchange, as a store of value, and as a standard of value.

Early U.S. coins were full-bodied money in that the value of their precious metal content was equal to their face value. Today, U.S. coins are token coins in that they are no longer backed by precious metals but instead by the creditworthiness of the U.S. government. For some time, the government issued gold certificate notes and silver certificate notes that were considered representative full-bodied money because they could be exchanged for precious metals worth the same as the face value of the notes. Today, U.S. paper currency is fiat money, which gets its name from the government decreeing that the notes are legal tender for paying public and private debts. Deposit money is demand deposit and other checkable deposit balances held at depository institutions and backed by the creditworthiness of the issuing institutions.

As the U.S. monetary system became more complex, definitions of the money supply changed as forms of payment increased to meet the needs of the economy. Today, the money supply is measured in terms of M1, M2, and M3, which add a variety of liquid assets to more traditional measures of the supply of money. M1 focuses on currency and deposit money that serve primarily as mediums of exchange. M2 and M3 add types of money that are viewed more as stores of value, such as money market mutual funds. We also discussed the relationship between money supply and economic activity and briefly covered the international monetary system.

KEY TERMS

barter	financial institutions	medium of exchange
bimetallic standard	financial management	monetary system
credit cards	financial markets	money
credit money	financial system	money market mutual funds (MMMFs)
currency exchange rate	full-bodied money	personal finance
debit cards	gross domestic product (GDP)	representative full-bodied money
deposit money	inflation	standard of value
entrepreneurial finance	investments	store of value
ethical behavior	liquidity	token coins
euro	M1 money supply	velocity of money
fiat money	M2 money supply	
finance	M3 money supply	

DISCUSSION QUESTIONS

1. What is finance?

2. What are the three areas of finance?

3. Briefly describe the terms *entrepreneurial finance* and *personal finance.*

4. What are the six principles of finance?

5. Describe what is meant by *ethical behavior.*

6. Identify and briefly describe several reasons for studying finance.

7. Indicate some of the career opportunities in finance available to business graduates today.

8. What are the basic requirements of an effective financial system?

9. Identify and briefly describe the financial functions in the financial system.

10. What are the basic functions of money?

11. Briefly describe the development of money, from barter to the use of precious metals.

12. What is the difference between full-bodied money and token coins?

13. Describe how representative full-bodied money and fiat money differ.

14. What is deposit money, and how is it "backed"?

15. What are debit cards, and how are they used?

16. Describe the M1 definition of the money supply and indicate the relative significance of the M1 components.

17. How does M2 differ from M1? What are money market mutual funds?

18. Describe the M3 measure of the money supply.

19. Briefly describe the monetarists' view of the relationship between money supply and economic activity.

20. How do Keynesians view the relationship between money supply and economic activity?

21. Briefly describe the development of the international monetary system.

EXERCISES

1. The U.S. financial system is composed of: (1) policy makers, (2) a monetary system, (3) financial institutions, and (4) financial markets. Indicate which of these components is associated with each of the following roles:

   a. accumulate and lend/invest savings

   b. create and transfer money

   c. pass laws and set fiscal and monetary policies

   d. market and facilitate transfer of financial assets

2. In business, ethical dilemmas or situations occur frequently. Laws and regulations exist to define what is unethical behavior. However, the practicing of high-quality ethical behavior often goes beyond just meeting laws and regulations. Indicate how you would respond to the following situations:

   a. Your boss has just told you that tomorrow the Federal Drug Administration will announce its approval of your firm's marketing of a new breakthrough drug. As a result of this information, you are considering purchasing shares of stock in your firm this afternoon. What would you do?

   b. In the past, your firm has been in compliance with regulatory standards relating to product safety. However, you have heard through the company grapevine that recently some of your firm's products have failed, resulting in injuries to customers. You are considering quitting your job due to personal moral concerns. What would you do?

3. Obtain a current issue of *Business Week*. Identify and be prepared to discuss an article that relates to one of the three areas of finance discussed in this chapter. Read and be prepared to discuss an article in the magazine's "Finance" section.

4. Obtain a current issue of *Business Week*. Turn to the "International Business" section and identify a global or international issue that relates to the study of finance from the perspective of the financial environment.

5. Go to the U.S. Small Business Administration (SBA) Web site, http://www.sba.gov, and search for sources of information on start-

ing a new business. Identify and prepare a written summary of the *startup basics* described on the SBA site.

6. Obtain a current issue of the *Statistical Supplement to the Federal Reserve Bulletin*. Compare the present size of M1, M2, and M3 money stock measures with the December 2005 figures presented in Figure 1.4. Also find the current sizes of these M1 components: currency, travelers' checks, demand deposits, and other checkable deposits. Express each component as a percentage of M1 and compare your percentages with those presented in the U.S. Money Supply Today section of this chapter.

7. Find several recent issues of *Business Week*. Review the "Economic Analysis" section for articles relating to developments in the U.S. monetary system. Also examine the "International Business" section for possible developments occurring in foreign monetary systems.

8. All of us are faced with ethical decisions involving money almost every day. For example, we all probably have seen money in the form of coin or currency lying on the ground or floor somewhere. We also may have at some time discovered a lost wallet. Should we keep what we find or not? Sometimes we hear the finders-keepers argument used to rationalize such a decision. Should it matter if the amount of money is small or large? Should it matter if no one else is around or there is no evidence of who lost the money? How would you react to the following scenarios?

   a. You find a dollar bill lying on the ground. No one else is close by. You consider picking it up, acknowledging your good luck, and putting it in your pocket. What would you do?

   b. While you are shopping in a grocery store, you see a wallet lying on the floor. You don't know who dropped it. You consider holding on to it until you get home and then searching for the owner's identification so that you might contact him or her about your finding the wallet. Alternatively, you could just give the wallet to the store manager. What would you do?

PROBLEMS

1. Using the following information determine the size of the M1 money supply.

Currency	$700 billion
Money market mutual funds	$2,000 billion
Demand deposits	$300 billion
Other checkable deposits	$300 billion
Traveler's checks	$10 billion

2. Using the following information determine the size of the demand deposits component of the M1 money supply.

Currency	$350 million
Traveler's checks	$10 million
Other checkable deposits	$200 million
Small time deposits	$100 million
M1 money supply	$800 million

3. The following are the components of the M1 money supply at the end of 2007. What will be the size of the M1 money supply at the end of 2008 if currency grows by 10 percent, demand deposits grow by 5 percent, other checkable deposits grow by 8 percent, and the amount of traveler's checks stays the same?

Currency	$700 billion
Demand deposits	$300 billion
Other checkable deposits	$300 billion
Traveler's checks	$10 billion

4. The following information is available to you: travelers' checks = $1 million; coin and paper currency = $30 million; repurchase agreements and Eurodollars = $15 million; demand deposits = $25 million; retail money market mutual funds = $60 million; savings accounts at depository institutions = $40 million; checkable deposits at depository institutions = $35 million; large-denomination time deposits = $50 million; institutional money market mutual funds = $65 million; and small-denomination time deposits = $45 million. Using Federal Reserve definitions, determine the dollar sizes of the following:

   a. M1 money supply

   b. M2 money supply

   c. M3 money supply

5. A country's gross domestic product (GDP) is $20 billion and its money supply (MS) is $5 billion.

   a. What is the country's velocity of money (VM)?

   b. If the MS stays at the same level next year while the velocity of money "turns over" 4.5 times, what would be the level of GDP?

   c. Assume that the VM will turn over four times next year. If the country wants a GDP of $22 billion at the end of next year, what will the size of the money supply have to be? What percentage increase in the MS will be necessary to achieve the target GDP?

6. Assume that the real output (RO) for a country is expected to be 2.4 million products.

   a. If the price level (PL) is $250 per product, what will be the amount of the gross national product (GDP)?

   b. Now assume that the GDP is projected to be $8 million next year. What will the PL of the products need to be to reach the GDP target?

   c. Now assume that the RO of 2.4 million products is composed of equal amounts of two types of products. The first product sells for $100 each, and the second product sells for $500 each. What will be the size of the GDP?

7. Assume that a country estimates its M1 money supply at $20 million. A broader measure of the money supply, M2, is $50 million. The country's gross domestic product is $100 million. Production or real output for the country is 500,000 units or products.

   a. Determine the velocity of money based on the M1 money supply.

   b. Determine the velocity of money based on the M2 money supply.

   c. Determine the average price for the real output.

8. Using the data in problem 7 along with the monetarists' view of the relationship between money supply and GDP, answer the following:

   a. If the M1 money supply increases by 10 percent and the M1 velocity of money does not change, what is the expected value of the GDP for next year?

   b. Based on the information from (a), if real output does not change next year, what is the expected average price for the products? What percentage change, if any, would take place in the price level?

   c. If the M2 money supply decreases by 10 percent and the M2 velocity of money does not change, what is the expected value of GDP next year?

   d. Based on information from (c), if the price level does not change next year, what is the expected real output in units or products?

9. The following information was gathered for the XYZ economy: velocity of money = 3.8 times; average price level = $85; and real output = 10,000 units.

   a. What is the nominal GDP for the XYZ economy?

   b. What is the size of the money supply for the XYZ economy?

   c. If real output increases by 10 percent next year, but the price level and velocity of money do not change, what money supply amount will be needed to support this real growth in economic activity?

   d. What money supply will be needed to support economic activity next year if real output increases to 12,000 units, the average price increases to $90, and velocity increases to four times?

10. The One Product economy, which produces and sells only personal computers (PCs), expects that next year it can sell 500 more, or 12,500 PCs. Nominal GDP was $20 million this year, and the money supply was $7 million. The central bank for the One Product economy plans to increase the money supply by 10 percent next year.

   a. What was the average selling price for the personal computers this year?

   b. What is the expected average selling price next year for personal computers if the velocity of money remains at this year's turnover rate? What percentage change in price level is expected to occur?

   c. If the objective is to keep the price level the same next year (i.e., no inflation), for what percentage increase in the money supply should the central bank plan?

   d. How would your answer in (c) change if the velocity of money is expected to be three times next year? What is it now?

11. **Challenge Problem** The following problem requires a basic knowledge about probabilities and the calculation of expected values. The problem is more easily solved using Excel spreadsheet software.

Scenario	A	B	C	D	E	Metric
Probability	.10	.20	.40	.20	.10	Percent
Velocity of money	1.75	2.5	3.0	3.5	4.25	Turnover
Real output	375	450	500	550	625	Units in thousands
Price level	75	90	100	110	125	Dollars

   a. Calculate the dollar amount of the money supply under each scenario or outcome.

   b. Calculate the expected value of the money supply, taking into consideration each scenario and its probability of occurrence.

   c. Scenario C is most likely given that its probability of occurrence is 40 percent. Show how the amount of the money supply would change holding real output at 500,000 units and the price level at $100 for each of the velocity of money turnover rates (you have previously calculated the money supply under Scenario C for a turnover of 3.0 times).

   d. Repeat the Scenario C exercise in (c), but now hold the velocity of money at 3.0 times and price level at $100 and allow real output to change.

   e. Repeat the Scenario C exercise in (c), but now hold the velocity of money at 3.0 times and real output at 500,000 units and allow the price level to change.

• CHAPTER 2 •

Banks and Other Financial Intermediaries

Chapter Learning Objectives

AFTER STUDYING THIS CHAPTER, YOU SHOULD BE ABLE TO:

- Describe the major financial intermediaries and their roles in the financial system.
- Describe the differences between commercial banking and investment banking.
- Identify the functions of banks and of the banking system.
- Discuss general regulation of the banking system and how depositors' funds are protected.
- Describe the structure of banks in terms of bank charters, branch banking, and bank holding companies.
- Briefly describe the structure of the Federal Reserve System.
- Discuss how the Federal Reserve uses reserve requirements, the discount rate, and open market operations to carry out monetary policy.
- Explain the meaning of a fractional reserve system.
- Explain the meaning of the monetary base and the money multiplier.
- Discuss structural characteristics of central banks located in selected foreign countries.

Where We Have Been. . .

In Chapter 1, we provided a discussion of the three areas of finance (financial institutions and markets, investments, and financial management) and the six principles of finance. We also presented an overview of the components and financial functions carried out in the financial system, including the need to create and transfer money. Money has three functions, which are a medium of exchange, a store of value, and a standard of value. An understanding of how money developed in the United States over time, as well as knowing current definitions of the U.S. money supply, will be useful as we move through this text. Understanding the relationship between the money supply and the economy helps us understand how the actions of policy makers influence interest rates, economic activity, and the financial system itself.

Where We Are Going. . .

As we move through Part 1, we continue to examine important finance basics that help us understand how financial markets operate. Chapter 3 focuses on the savings-investment process and types of financial assets available to individuals and other investors. Chapter 4 discusses how interest rates, or the "price" of money, are determined in the financial markets. Market interest rates reflect a default risk-free cost of money plus premiums for liquidity, default risk, and maturity. Chapter 5 introduces "time" as a factor when determining rates of return on investments. Recall from Chapter 1 that the time value of money is an important finance principle.

How This Chapter Applies to Me. . .

You probably have a checking account at a depository institution. You may also have a savings account or own some shares in a mutual fund. You may even have a loan on an automobile or a home mortgage. Each of these activities requires an interaction with a financial institution or intermediary. After reading this chapter, you should have a better understanding of what depository and other financial intermediaries do in accumulating and lending or investing savings, the financial assets or instruments available to individuals and businesses, and financial markets that aid in the marketing and transferring of financial assets.

Webster's New English Dictionary defines *bank* as

> an establishment for the deposit, custody, and issue of money, for making loans and discounts, and for making easier the exchange of funds by checks, notes, etc.

Webster also defines *bank* as

> the funds of a gambling establishment; the fund or pool by the banker or dealer in some gambling games.

Most of us associate the first definition with our perception of banks and banking in the United States. However, throughout history and even recently the second definition seems to fit some situations. For example, isolated fraudulent behavior on the part of some commercial bank and S&L officers has resulted in criminal indictments and even in prison sentences. Overall, of course, banks and other financial intermediaries have performed admirably well in getting savings to investors and contributing to an efficient financial system.

TYPES AND ROLES OF FINANCIAL INTERMEDIARIES

The current system of financial institutions or intermediaries in the United States, like the monetary system, evolved to meet the needs of the country's citizens and to facilitate the savings-investment process. Individuals may save and grow their savings with the assistance of financial institutions. While individuals can invest directly in the securities of business firms and government units, most individuals invest indirectly through financial institutions that do the lending and investing for them. ***Financial intermediation*** is the process by which individual savings are accumulated in depository institutions and, in turn, lent or invested.

Figure 2.1 shows the major types of financial intermediaries grouped into four categories: depository institutions, contractual savings organizations, securities firms, and finance companies. ***Depository institutions*** accept deposits or savings from individuals and then lend these pooled savings to businesses, governments, and individuals. Depository institutions include commercial banks, savings and loan associations (S&Ls), savings banks, and credit unions. ***Contractual savings organizations*** collect premiums on insurance policies and employee/employer contributions from pension fund participants and provide retirement benefits and insurance against major financial losses. Insurance companies and pension funds are the two important forms of contractual savings organizations.

Securities firms accept and invest individual savings and also facilitate the sale and transfer of securities between investors. In addition to pooling individual savings and investments,

---

financial intermediation
process by which savings are accumulated in depository institutions and then lent or invested

depository institutions
accept deposits from individuals and then lend pooled deposits to businesses, governments, and individuals

contractual savings organizations
collect premiums and contributions from participants and provide insurance against major financial losses and retirement benefits

securities firms
accept and invest individual savings and also facilitate the sale and transfer of securities between investors

---

FIGURE 2.1

Types of Financial Intermediaries

FINANCIAL INSTITUTIONS CATEGORIES	PRIMARY SOURCES OF FUNDS
DEPOSITORY INSTITUTIONS	
Commercial banks	Individual savings
Savings and loan associations	Individual savings
Savings banks	Individual savings
Credit unions	Individual savings
CONTRACTUAL SAVINGS ORGANIZATIONS	
Insurance companies	Premiums paid on policies
Pension funds	Employee/employer contributions
SECURITIES FIRMS	
Investment companies (mutual funds)	Individual savings (investments)
Investment banking firms	Other financial institutions
Brokerage firms	Other financial institutions
FINANCE FIRMS	
Finance companies	Other financial institutions
Mortgage banking firms	Other financial institutions

finance firms
provide loans directly to consumers and businesses and help borrowers obtain mortgage loans on real property

CONCEPT CHECK

What is meant by financial intermediation?

What are the four major categories of financial institutions?

commercial banks
depository institutions that accept deposits, issue check-writing accounts, and make loans

thrift institutions
noncommercial bank depository institutions that accumulate individual savings and primarily make consumer and mortgage loans

savings bank
accepts the savings of individuals and lends pooled savings to individuals primarily in the form of mortgage loans

savings and loan association
accepts individual savings and lends pooled savings to individuals, primarily in the form of mortgage loans, and businesses

credit union
a cooperative nonprofit organization that exists primarily to provide member depositors with consumer credit

CONCEPT CHECK

What are the four types of depository institutions?

securities firms receive funds from other financial intermediaries. Investment companies (mutual funds), investment banking firms, and brokerage firms are the primary types of securities firms that we will cover. **Finance firms** provide loans directly to consumers and businesses, and they help borrowers obtain mortgage loans on real property. When discussing finance firms in this textbook, the emphasis is on finance companies and mortgage banking firms.

Few of today's financial intermediaries existed during the American colonial period. Only commercial banks and insurance companies (life and property) can be traced back prior to 1800. Savings banks and S&Ls began developing during the early 1800s. Investment banking firms (and organized securities exchanges) also can be traced back to the first half of the 1800s. No new major financial intermediaries evolved during the last half of the nineteenth century. Credit unions, pension funds, mutual funds, and finance companies came into existence during the early part of the 1900s. Thus, throughout much of the 1900s and into the twenty-first century, emphasis has been on redefining and restructuring existing financial intermediaries rather than introducing new ones.

DEPOSITORY INSTITUTIONS

When we refer to banks and the banking system in the United States, we primarily think in terms of commercial banking. **Commercial banks** are depository institutions that accept deposits, issue check-writing accounts, and make loans to businesses and individuals. In addition to commercial banks, depository institutions also include three types of thrift institutions. **Thrift institutions** are noncommercial bank depository institutions referred to as savings and loan associations, savings banks, and credit unions, all of which accumulate individual savings and lend primarily to other individuals. Savings and loan associations engage in some lending to businesses but focus primarily on loans to individuals. Savings banks and credit unions focus on providing consumer and home mortgage loans to individuals seeking to purchase items such as automobiles and houses.

Savings banks made their appearance in 1812, emphasizing individual thrift savings and safety of principal. A **savings bank** accepts the savings of individuals and lends pooled savings to individuals primarily in the form of mortgage loans. Very often the trustees of these banks are prominent local citizens, serving without pay, who regard their service as an important civic duty. Today, savings banks operate almost entirely in New England, New York, and New Jersey, with most of their assets continuing to be invested in mortgage loans.

Savings and loan associations, known also as savings and loans or S&Ls, came on the scene in 1831. First known as building societies, then as building and loan associations, their basic mission was to provide home mortgage financing. In distinguishing between savings banks and savings and loans, it might be said that originally the emphasis of savings banks was on thrift and the safety of savings while the emphasis of S&Ls was on home financing. Today, a **savings and loan association** accepts individual savings and lends pooled savings to individuals, primarily in the form of mortgage loans, and to businesses. In contrast with the limited geographic expansion of savings banking, savings and loan activity spread throughout the United States.

Credit unions came on the scene in the United States much later than the other thrift institutions. A **credit union** is a cooperative nonprofit organization that exists primarily to provide member depositors with consumer credit, including the financing of automobiles and the purchase of homes. Membership in credit unions is composed of individuals who possess common bonds of association, such as occupation, residence, or church affiliation. These institutions derive their funds almost entirely from the savings of their members. The first official credit union was formed in the United States in 1909, but it was not until the 1920s that credit unions became important as a special form of depository institution.

Figure 2.2 illustrates graphically the process of getting funds from individual savers and investors into the hands of *business firms* that want to make investments to maintain and grow their firms. Individuals make deposits in commercial banks that in turn make loans to and purchase debt securities of business firms. Since thrift institutions focus primarily on gathering the savings of individuals and in turn lending those funds to individuals, they are not depicted on Figure 2.2.

FIGURE 2.2
Role of Financial Intermediaries in Directing Savings to Business Firms

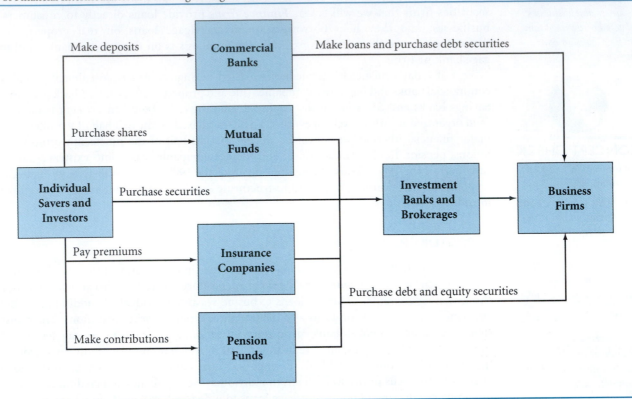

CONTRACTUAL SAVINGS ORGANIZATIONS

Contractual savings organizations in the form of insurance companies and pension funds play important roles by collecting premiums and contributions and using these pooled funds to purchase the debt and equity securities of business firms, as depicted in Figure 2.2. Of course, contractual savings organizations also actively purchase the debt securities issued by governmental units. *Insurance companies* provide financial protection to individuals and businesses for life, property, liability, and health uncertainties. Policyholders pay premiums to insurance companies that invest these funds until the insured claims must be paid. Life insurance provides economic security for dependents in the event of premature death of the insured individual. Health insurance provides protection against possible catastrophic medical expenses in the event that the insured individual becomes ill or is in an accident. Property insurance protects a policyholder against possible financial loss from fire, theft, and other insured perils. Liability insurance protects a policyholder against possible financial loss from a claim of negligence charged by another individual.

Pension funds receive contributions from employees and/or their employers and invest the proceeds on behalf of the employees. The purpose of a pension plan is to provide income during an individual's retirement years. Pension funds are either private pension plans or government-sponsored plans. Many business organizations provide private pension plans for their employees. A private pension plan may be either insured or noninsured. A contractual plan with a life insurance company is an insured plan. An uninsured plan uses a trustee, often a commercial bank or trust company, to manage, invest, and distribute benefits as established in the trust arrangement. Government-sponsored plans may involve either the federal government or state and local governments. Social Security is the largest federal pension plan. The Social Security plan is funded by currently working individuals paying Social Security taxes. Social Security is designed to provide only minimum retirement benefits, so most individuals will need to accumulate additional funds before retirement. The federal government also provides pension plans for its employees, who are known as civil servants, as well as for military employees. State and local government pension plans typically are established to cover teachers, police and fire employees, and their other civil servants.

insurance companies
provide financial protection to individuals and businesses for life, property, liability, and health uncertainties

pension funds
receive contributions from employees and/or their employers and invest the proceeds on behalf of the employees for use during their retirement years

CONCEPT CHECK

What are the two basic types of contractual savings organizations?

SECURITIES FIRMS

Securities firms perform several financial functions. Some securities firms are active in the savings-investment process, while others concentrate primarily on marketing new securities and facilitating the transfer of existing securities between investors. ***Investment companies*** sell shares in their firms to individuals and others and invest the pooled proceeds in corporate and government securities. An investment company may be either a closed-end fund or an open-end fund. A *closed-end fund* issues a fixed number of its shares to investors and invests the pooled funds in securities. Shares in a closed-end fund are bought and sold in secondary securities markets once they have been initially issued.

An *open-end fund,* typically called a ***mutual fund,*** can issue an unlimited number of its shares to its investors and use the pooled proceeds to purchase corporate and government securities. However, unlike a closed-end fund, investors purchase new shares or redeem old shares directly with their mutual fund rather than buying and selling the shares in a secondary securities market. Figure 2.2, which focuses on getting funds to business firms, depicts the important role that mutual funds play by selling shares in their funds to individual investors and then using the proceeds to purchase debt and equity securities issued by business firms. Mutual funds grow by investing the funds of their existing investors in securities that will pay or distribute cash and will appreciate in value. Successful mutual funds attract more investor funds and, in turn, invest in more securities.

Investment banking firms, also referred to as *investment banks,* sell or market new securities issued by businesses to individual and institutional investors. ***Brokerage firms*** assist individuals who want to purchase new or existing securities issues or who want to sell previously purchased securities. Investment banking and brokerage activities are often combined in the same firms. However, in contrast with mutual funds, investment banking firms and brokerage firms do not gather the savings of individuals but rather market or sell securities issued by corporations directly to individuals, as depicted in Figure 2.2. Investment banking and brokerage firms obtain financial capital to carry out their activities from their own resources or from other financial institutions.

FINANCE FIRMS

Although finance firms are an important type of financial institution, they are not included in Figure 2.2 because they focus largely on providing loans to individuals for meeting credit needs and purchasing durable goods and homes. ***Finance companies*** provide loans directly to consumers and businesses or aid individuals in obtaining financing. Sales and consumer finance companies lend to individuals. *Sales finance companies* finance installment loan purchases of automobiles and other durable goods, such as washers, dryers, and refrigerators. *Consumer finance companies* provide small loans to individuals and households. *Commercial finance companies* provide loans to businesses that are unable to obtain financing from commercial banks. However, commercial finance companies are not included in Figure 2.2 because they do not accumulate the savings of individuals but rather get funds for making loans to businesses from other financial institutions.

Mortgage banking firms or mortgage companies help individuals obtain mortgage loans by bringing together borrowers and institutional investors. A *mortgage loan* is a loan on real property, such as a house, whereby the borrower pledges the property as collateral to guarantee that the loan will be repaid. The primary mortgage market, where home and other real property loans are "originated," is very important to the success of the financial system. Traditionally, once a mortgage loan was originated it was held by the lender until maturity or until the loan was prepaid. However, as individual mortgage loans have become more standardized, secondary mortgage markets have arisen, in which existing real property mortgages are bought and sold.

OVERVIEW OF THE BANKING SYSTEM

We now turn our attention to the development of a basic understanding of the current U.S. banking system. First we describe the traditional differences between commercial banking and investment banking and their combination to provide universal banking. Then we cover the functions of banks and the banking system.

---

investment companies sell shares in their firms to individuals and others and invest the pooled proceeds in corporate and government securities

mutual fund open-end investment company that can issue an unlimited number of its shares to its investors and use the pooled proceeds to purchase corporate and government securities

investment banking firms sell or market new securities issued by businesses to individual and institutional investors

brokerage firms assist individuals to purchase new or existing securities issues or to sell previously purchased securities

CONCEPT CHECK

What are some basic types of securities firms?

finance companies provide loans directly to consumers and businesses or aid individuals in obtaining financing of durable goods and homes

mortgage banking firms originate mortgage loans on homes and other real property by bringing together borrowers and institutional investors

CONCEPT CHECK

What are two basic types of finance firms?

COMMERCIAL, INVESTMENT, AND UNIVERSAL BANKING

A *commercial bank* accepts deposits, issues check-writing accounts to facilitate making purchases and paying bills, and makes loans to individuals and businesses. In contrast, an *investment bank* helps businesses sell their new debt and equity securities to raise financial capital. This is typically done by first purchasing the new securities issued by business corporations and then reselling the shares to individual and institutional investors.

Glass-Steagall Act of 1933
provided for separation of commercial banking and investment banking activities in the United States

Notice in Figure 2.2 that commercial banks and investment banks are shown as being separate intermediaries. This reflects the fact that in the midst of the Great Depression Congress passed the *Banking Act of 1933*, commonly known as the **Glass-Steagall Act of 1933** in recognition of the individuals responsible for introducing and supporting the act. This act provided for the separation of commercial banking and investment banking in the United States. Many banks failed during the late 1920s and early 1930s, and efforts were undertaken to assess why that happened. Some politicians, regulators, and others thought that many of the bank failures had been caused, in part, by investment banking activities involving underwriting and the holding of equity securities. The result was passage of the Glass-Steagall Act.

Gramm-Leach-Bliley Act of 1999
repealed the separation of commercial banking and investment banking provided for in the Glass-Steagall Act

universal bank
bank that engages in both commercial banking and investment banking activities

After more than six decades, the Glass-Steagall Act was repealed with the passage of the **Gramm-Leach-Bliley Act of 1999**. When Glass-Stegall was enacted, many officials and individuals believed that government regulation was the answer to avoiding banking excesses and mismanagement. Today the belief is that competition and free markets represent the best way to manage banking risks and create stability in the financial system. Commercial banks are no longer prohibited from engaging in investment banking and insurance underwriting. Likewise, insurance companies and investment banking firms can now engage in commercial banking. Universal banking now is permitted in the United States, as in various other countries. A **universal bank** is a bank that engages in both commercial banking and investment banking. Germany also has universal banking, and the United Kingdom does not legally separate commercial banking from investment banking.

FUNCTIONS OF BANKS AND THE BANKING SYSTEM

banking system
commercial banks, savings and loans, savings banks, and credit unions that operate in the U.S. financial system

Depository institutions accept deposits, make loans, and issue checkable deposit accounts. Like commercial banks, savings and loan associations (also called *savings and loans* or *S&Ls*), savings banks, and credit unions perform these activities. The U.S. **banking system** includes commercial banks, savings and loans, savings banks, and credit unions. It is common practice today to refer to all depository institutions as banks. Banks and the banking system perform five functions: (1) accepting deposits, (2) issuing checkable deposit accounts, (3) granting loans, (4) clearing checks, (5) creating deposit money, and (6) raising financial capital for businesses (investment banking).

SMALL BUSINESS PRACTICE
Where Should You Start Your Small Business?

Today, with modern telecommunication facilities and the Internet, many small businesses can be located wherever their owners want to live and work. At the same time, certain cities and areas in the United States seem to be more conducive to helping small businesses succeed.

Each year the Dun & Bradstreet Company (http://www.dnb.com) "scores" cities to determine which ones provide the best climate and support for small businesses. Five categories are evaluated. First, the "local government attitude toward business" is evaluated in terms of local corporate tax rates and other factors. Second, "local business performance" is assessed in terms of business failure rates and debt payment delinquencies. Third, "local economic growth" is evaluated based on growth in employment and in average wages. The fourth category assesses firms' "risk" reflected in the likelihood that a firm

will fail. This is based on firms' payment record, operating history, and financial health. The fifth category examines "affordability," as indicated by changes in a cost-of-living index, as well as how wages are growing.

Several factors were found to be common across many of the top cities on the Dun & Bradstreet (D&B) list. Many cities housed strong high-technology and telecommunications firms. Venture capital investments were growing in many of these cities, indicating confidence in local entrepreneurs. Also, top cities often offered innovative small-business programs designed to help entrepreneurs and other small businesses to obtain financial capital. If, or when, you decide to start your own business, you might consider locating in one of the cities designated as best for small business by D&B.

Source: "D&B and Entrepreneur's 20 Best Cities for Small Business," *Dun & Bradstreet,* http://www.dnb.com.

CONCEPT CHECK

In the past, how did commercial banks differ from investment banks?

What are the functions performed today by banks and the banking system?

In accepting deposits, banks provide a safe place for the public to keep money for future use. Individuals and businesses seldom wish to spend their money as it becomes available; without depository facilities, such funds may lie idle. The banking system puts the accumulated deposits to use through loans to persons and businesses that have an immediate use for them. This, of course, is the financial intermediation activity of depository institutions in the savings-investment process.

By creating deposit money, banks play an important role in the payments process or mechanism in place in the U.S. financial system. Through check writing against demand and other checkable deposits, it is easier for individuals and businesses to make purchases and to pay bills or debts. Of course, it is not enough just to permit check writing; there must also be an efficient mechanism for processing the checks so they can be presented to the bank that authorized the check for payment.

EARLY DEVELOPMENT OF THE U.S. BANKING SYSTEM

Before we examine the current structure of the banking industry, we will review a little U.S. banking history. We know you are about to ask "Why should I learn anything about the history of banking?" First, a basic understanding of how the banking system evolved should help us better understand how and why the system operates the way it does today. Second, it has been said that "Those who don't study history are doomed to repeat its mistakes."

Until the Civil War, banking in the United States developed under confusing and difficult circumstances. The population lived for the most part on farms. Families were self-sufficient, and transportation and communications were poor. The friction between those who supported a strong central government and those who did not existed in the early years of U.S. history, as it does today. Those living in the new country had little experience in money and financial management, and much controversy raged over the power to charter and regulate banks.

Early Chartered Banks

During the colonial period small, unincorporated banks were established to ease the shortage of financial capital for businesses. Their operations consisted largely of issuing their own paper money. Outside of larger towns, deposit banking was of minor significance. It was not until 1782 that the first incorporated bank, the Bank of North America, was created. It was established in Philadelphia by Robert Morris to assist in financing prior expenditures from the Revolutionary War. This bank set a good example for successful banking: its notes served as a circulating medium of exchange, it lent liberally to the U.S. government, and it redeemed its own notes in metallic coins upon demand. Two years later the Bank of Massachusetts and the Bank of New York were established. These three incorporated banks were the only such banks until 1790.

First Bank of the United States

Alexander Hamilton was the first secretary of the Treasury of the United States. For several years he had harbored the idea of a federally chartered bank that would adequately support the rapidly growing economy and would give financial assistance to the government during its crises. His recommendations were submitted to the House of Representatives of the United States in 1790, and in 1791 a twenty-year charter was issued to the First Bank of the United States. This bank served the nation effectively by issuing notes, transferring funds from region to region, and curbing the excessive note issues of state banks by presenting such notes periodically to the issuing banks for redemption. However, strong opposition existed to the renewal of its charter, and it ceased operations in 1811. The antagonism of state banking interests was an important cause of the demise of the First Bank.

Following the expiration of the charter of the First Bank, the number of state banks increased rapidly, as did the volume of their note issues. Abuses of banking privileges were extensive. The capital of many banks was largely fictitious, and a flood of irredeemable notes was issued to the public.

Second Bank of the United States

The Second Bank of the United States was chartered primarily to restore order to the chaotic banking situation that had developed after the First Bank of the United States ceased operations in 1811. Like the First Bank, the Second Bank received a twenty-year federal charter. It began operations in 1816 and ably served individuals, businesses, and the government. It accepted deposits, made loans, and issued notes. Furthermore, it restrained the note-issuing practices of state banks by periodically presenting their notes for redemption. The Second Bank also served as the fiscal agent for the government. It received all deposits of government funds and reported regularly on all government receipts and expenditures.

In 1833 President Andrew Jackson and many of his associates began such a vigorous campaign against the Second Bank that it became apparent its charter would not be renewed when it expired in 1836. Jackson claimed that the bank was being run to benefit private interests and was operated in such a way as to weaken government policies. Like the First Bank, the Second Bank became a victim of political pressure. Not until 1863 was another bank in the United States to receive a federal charter.

State Banks from 1836 to the Civil War

When the Second Bank's charter expired, the excesses that had plagued the period between 1811 and 1816 began again. This period is characterized as one of "wildcat" banking.[1] Although many state banks operated on a conservative and very sound basis, the majority engaged in risky banking practices through excessive note issues, lack of adequate bank capital, and insufficient reserves against their notes and deposits.

Because the notes of even well-established banks were often of inferior quality, it was easy for skillful counterfeiters to increase the denomination of notes. Also, because of the poor communications that existed between various sections of the country, it was often quite difficult for a banker to be certain whether notes presented for payment were real. Skillfully prepared counterfeit notes frequently circulated with greater freedom than did the legitimate notes of weak and little-known banks.

In spite of the many abuses of state banks during this period, New York, Massachusetts, and Louisiana originated sound banking legislation, much of which provided the basis for the establishment of the National Banking System in 1863.

REGULATION OF THE BANKING SYSTEM

This section provides a brief review of major legislation that has shaped the development of the U.S. banking system. We separate our discussion into general banking legislation, the savings and loan crisis, and legislation enacted to protect depositors' funds.

GENERAL BANKING LEGISLATION

A variety of laws have been passed in the United States to regulate the banking system. Early laws focused on establishing first a system of federally chartered banks and then a system of central banks. More recent legislation has focused on deregulating banking activities and improving the effectiveness of monetary policy.

National Banking Act of 1864

In 1864 the *National Banking Act* made it possible for banks to receive federal charters. This legislation provided the basis for the present national banking laws. As in the cases of the First and Second Banks of the United States, the reasons for federal interest in the banking system were to provide for a sound banking system and to curb the excesses of the state banks. An important additional purpose of the National Banking Act was to provide financing for the Civil War. Secretary of the Treasury Salmon P. Chase and others believed that government bonds could be sold to the nationally chartered banks, which could in turn issue their own notes based in part on the government bonds they had purchased.

Through the National Banking Act, various steps were taken to promote safe banking practices. Among other specifics, minimum capital requirements were established for banks with federal charters, loans were regulated with respect to safety and liquidity, a system of supervision and examination was instituted, and minimum reserve requirements against notes and

CONCEPT CHECK

Why was the First Bank of the United States authorized and what did it do?

INTERNET ACTIVITY

Go to the Citibank Web site, http://www.citibank.com. Find information on the savings alternatives and interest rates currently being paid.

---

1. This nickname was used to refer to banks located in wilderness areas that were more accessible to wildcats than people. This made it difficult for anyone to redeem these banks' notes.

deposits were established. In general, while these reform measures were constructive, they also were viewed by some as being too restrictive. For example, loans against real estate were not allowed. Much of the criticism of the national banking system, in fact, was caused by the inflexibility of its rules.

Federal Reserve Act of 1913

The *Federal Reserve Act of 1913* brought to the U.S. economy a system of central banks. The Federal Reserve System was designed to eliminate many of the weaknesses that had persisted under the National Banking Act and to increase the effectiveness of commercial banking in general. It included not only strong central domination of banking practices but also many services for commercial banks. The structure and functions of the Federal Reserve System, as well as the implementation and management of monetary policy, are discussed later in this chapter.

Depository Institutions Deregulation and Monetary Control Act of 1980

In 1980 President Jimmy Carter signed into law the *Depository Institutions Deregulation and Monetary Control Act,* which for ease of reference is often just called the *Monetary Control Act.* This act represents a major step toward deregulating banking in the United States and improving the effectiveness of monetary policy. The two main provisions of the act are deregulation and monetary control.

Depository Institutions Deregulation

The Depository Institutions Deregulation part of the Monetary Control Act was designed to reduce or eliminate interest rate limitations imposed on the banking system, increase the various sources of funds, and expand the uses of the funds of S&Ls. To enhance competition among depository institutions, Title IV of the Monetary Control Act amended the Home Owners' Loan Act of 1933. Federally chartered S&Ls were permitted to invest up to one-fifth of their assets in corporate debt securities, commercial paper, and consumer loans. Prior residential mortgage loan restrictions relating to geographical areas and first mortgage lending requirements were removed. Greater authority was also permitted for granting real estate development and construction loans by federally chartered S&Ls. In addition, federal savings banks were allowed to make a small number of commercial loans and accept some checkable deposits.

Monetary Control

The Monetary Control Act was designed to extend the Federal Reserve's control to thrift institutions and to commercial banks that are not members of the system. This was accomplished by extending both reserve requirements and general controls to these institutions. Because the Federal Reserve (the Fed) had more stringent regulations than many state regulatory agencies, many commercial banks had given up their membership in the system to become state-chartered nonmember banks. The Monetary Control Act, therefore, has had the effect of halting the declining system membership by transferring much regulatory control from the state to the federal level.

Garn-St. Germain Depository Institutions Act of 1982

There had been high hopes that the Monetary Control Act would have a quick and beneficial effect on the banking system, as well as on the effectiveness of monetary control by the Federal Reserve. However, this was not the case. Of special significance was the dramatic increase in interest rates in late 1980 and 1981. S&Ls and savings banks were faced with heavy increases in their cost of funds as depositors shifted from low-interest passbook savings to the higher-yielding accounts and savings certificates. Rapidly increasing federal deficits and troubles in the automobile and housing industries added to the demand for legislation to address these problems. The *Garn-St. Germain Act of 1982* resulted.

Although the Garn-St. Germain Act had many provisions, its principal focus was to assist the savings and loan industry, which had deteriorated to dangerous levels. Depository institutions in general were authorized, among other things, to issue a new money market deposit account with no regulated interest rate ceiling. S&Ls were authorized to make nonresidential real estate loans, commercial loans, and variable-rate mortgages.

Gramm-Leach-Bliley Act of 1999

As previously noted, the Gramm-Leach-Bliley Act of 1999 repealed the separation of commercial banking and investment banking provided for in the Glass-Steagall Act of 1933. Commercial banks are again allowed to engage in investment banking and insurance underwriting. Likewise, investment banks and insurance companies are allowed to engage in commercial banking.

THE SAVINGS AND LOAN CRISIS

During the last half of the 1980s and the first half of the 1990s, well over 2,000 savings and loan associations were closed or merged into other organizations. The bottom line for why this happened is that S&Ls failed because of mismanagement and greed that led to fraudulent activities on the part of some of the institutions' officers.

The S&L business historically has been a difficult one. S&Ls borrow short-term by accepting the deposits of savers and paying interest on the savings. S&Ls in turn provide long-term mortgage loans to help finance homes. As long as short-term and long-term interest rates remain relatively the same, S&Ls are concerned primarily with illiquidity due to lending long-term but borrowing short-term. When many depositors want their money back, S&Ls may be forced to liquidate their mortgage loans even at unfavorable prices. When short-term interest rates rise as they did in the late 1980s, S&Ls may find themselves paying higher interest rates to depositors than they are earning on their mortgage loans. Unfortunately, S&L managements did not handle the illiquidity and rising short-term interest rate developments very well.

To make matters worse, S&L managements were ill prepared for the consequences of deregulation. Authorization in the early 1980s to invest funds in a wide range of higher-yielding investments permitted many savings and loan associations to run wild by supporting speculative office buildings and other commercial ventures. This resulted not only in overbuilding at inflated costs, but as the promoters were unable to honor the terms of their loan contracts many S&Ls became insolvent. Deregulation also permitted S&Ls to invest in "junk" bonds, which are low-quality, high-risk bonds issued by businesses. Many of these bonds were defaulted on by their issuers, resulting in even greater pressures on S&L operations.

ETHICAL ISSUES

Mismanagement was a major reason for the collapse of much of the S&L industry. This problem was exacerbated by the fact that greed also led to fraudulent behavior on the part of some S&L officers and managers. Depositors' funds were used to pay exorbitant salaries, purchase expensive automobiles and yachts for personal use, and so forth. Top officers borrowed excessively from their own S&Ls and in at least one instance S&L presidents of two associations made loans to each other using depositors' funds.[2]

Evidence suggests that the S&L industry was run by unethical individuals prior to the 1980s. Apparently, deregulation provided the opportunity for unscrupulous individuals from outside the industry to pursue personal greed by becoming officers and managers of S&Ls. Of course, the opportunity for greed associated with deregulation also resulted in some existing S&L officers' behaving unethically and even committing fraud. Individuals who acted illegally were prosecuted, some served prison terms, and reputations were lost. Failure to treat depositors and other constituents honestly and fairly resulted in lost confidence and trust and surely contributed to the demise of many S&Ls.

INTERNET ACTIVITY

Go to the Chase Personal Banking Web site, http://www.chase.com. Find information on types of personal loans and their costs.

The Federal Savings and Loan Insurance Corporation (FSLIC) had insured the deposits of most S&L depositors since the early 1930s. However, because of the number and size of the S&L failures, the FSLIC was bankrupt by early 1988. As a result, the *Financial Institutions Reform, Recovery, and Enforcement Act (FIRREA)* was passed in 1989. FIRREA provided for the termination of the FSLIC and the formation of the Savings Association Insurance Fund (SAIF). Also, the Office of Thrift Supervision (OTS) took over the regulation of S&Ls from the Federal Home Loan Bank Board (FHLBB). The act also required S&Ls to commit more of their assets to home loans, restricted S&Ls from holding junk bonds, and allowed commercial banks to purchase S&Ls.

---

2. The savings and loan crisis has been studied by many. The following three books provide interesting insights into mismanagement practices and unethical behavior by certain S&L officers: Stephen Pizzo, Mary Fricker, and Paul Muolo, *Inside Job: The Looting of America's Savings and Loans* (New York: McGraw-Hill, 1989); Lawrence J. White, *The S&L Debacle* (New York: Oxford University Press, 1991); and Kathleen Day, *S&L Hell* (New York: W.W. Norton & Company, 1993).

Congress created the Resolution Trust Corporation (RTC) in 1988 to take over and dispose of the assets of failed associations by finding acquirers or through liquidations. For some failed S&Ls, deposit transfers were made to sound organizations for a fee without requiring the assumption of any of the defunct S&L's poor-quality assets. Some risky assets of failed S&Ls, such as junk bonds, were purchased at deep discount prices by the RTC and later resold. Assets of failed S&Ls that acquiring firms did not want were disposed of by the RTC. Congress shut down the RTC in 1995.

Commercial banks have suffered some of the same difficulties as the S&Ls. However, losses from international loans, agricultural loans, and from loans to the petroleum industry have been more significant for commercial banks—many banks had to be merged with other banks. Savings banks and credit unions experienced some difficulties as well but to a lesser extent.

PROTECTION OF DEPOSITORS' FUNDS

As a result of bank "runs" during the late 1920s and early 1930s caused by many depositors trying to retrieve their deposited funds at the same time, insurance protection laws for deposits at depository institutions were passed to restore the confidence of depositors. The Federal Deposit Insurance Corporation (FDIC) was created in 1933 to protect deposits in banks. This was followed by federal legislation that created the Federal Savings and Loan Insurance Corporation (FSLIC) and the National Credit Union Share Insurance Fund (NCUSIF) to protect deposits in S&Ls and credit unions, respectively. Of course, as previously noted the S&L crisis of the 1980s led to the insolvency of the FSLIC and its replacement with SAIF, which is now the insuring agency for S&Ls. Over the years the limitation on deposit account insurance was increased, until by 1980 it was set at $100,000 per account, with this amount still in force today.

The pool of funds available to the FDIC for covering insured depositors is called the *Bank Insurance Fund* and consists of annual insurance premiums collected from commercial banks. Prior to 1991 all banks paid the same premium rate on their deposits. Thus, riskier banks were being subsidized by safer banks. *The Federal Deposit Insurance Corporation Improvement Act of 1991 (FDICIA)* was enacted, in part, to address this problem. The FDICIA provided for differences in deposit premiums based on the relative riskiness of banks.

One of the special problems of insuring bank losses has been the practice and assumption that some banks are "too big to fail"—that is, too big in the sense that the problems created by losses may extend far beyond the failed bank. It is on this basis that all depositors have received 100 percent coverage of their funds even though coverage of only the first $100,000 deposited is guaranteed by law. This practice tended to reduce the incentive for large depositors to exercise market discipline and created an incentive for large deposits to be shifted to "too big to fail" banks. Congress addressed this issue with the FDICIA, which generally requires that failed banks be handled in such a way as to provide the lowest cost to the FDIC. Limited exceptions, however, were provided if very serious adverse effects on economic conditions could be expected as a result of any failure of big banks.

STRUCTURE OF BANKS

Bank structure is characterized by how a bank is established, the extent to which branching takes place, and whether a holding company organizational structure is used. This section addresses each of these structural characteristics in terms of commercial banks and includes commentary on how the other three depository institutions are structured.

BANK CHARTERS

dual banking system
allows commercial banks to obtain charters either from the federal government or a state government

To start and operate a bank or other depository institution, a charter must be obtained that spells out the powers of the institution. Commercial banks may obtain charters either from the federal government or from a state government, making the United States a **dual banking system**. While federal and state charters exhibit many similarities, federally chartered banks must include the word *national* in their titles while state chartered banks may not use the word. Federally chartered banks also must be members of the Federal Reserve System and the Federal Deposit Insurance Corporation. State-chartered banks are not required to join either the Federal Reserve or the FDIC, although today almost all banks are covered by federal deposit insurance.

CAREER OPPORTUNITIES IN FINANCE
Financial Institutions

Opportunities

Financial institutions, such as banks, S&Ls, and credit unions, assist businesses and individuals with the flow of funds between borrowers. Financial intermediary jobs provide the chance to work with individuals, small businesses, and large corporations on a variety of financial matters, and therefore provide invaluable business world experience. In addition, individuals interested in finance may find numerous entry-level jobs with strong advancement opportunities.

Jobs

Loan analyst
Loan officer
Financial economist

Responsibilities

A *loan analyst* evaluates loan applicants in terms of their creditworthiness and ability to repay. Since these types of loans are usually for one or more years, the loan analyst must monitor and reevaluate outstanding loans on a periodic basis.

A *loan officer* is responsible for generating new loan business and managing existing loans. As such, a loan officer must have the ability to address the needs of existing clients while simultaneously identifying and actively pursuing new clients.

A *financial economist* analyzes business conditions over time and prepares forecasts of economic activity and employment trends. This information is crucial for lending institutions so that they do not make unwise loans.

Education

The level of education needed varies among different jobs. However, all these jobs require a solid background in economics and finance, as well as experience with computers, statistics, and communication.

According to FDIC statistics, over 8,000 commercial banks are insured by the FDIC. About one-fourth of these banks held national charters, and the remaining three-fourths were state chartered. Less than 20 percent of state banks were members of the Federal Reserve. For some time, concern was expressed that the Federal Reserve might not be able to administer monetary policy effectively if it could not regulate nonmember state banks. This concern disappeared at the beginning of the 1980s when reserve requirements set by the Federal Reserve for member banks were extended to state nonmember banks.

Savings and loan associations and credit unions also can obtain federal or state charters. Savings banks are state chartered. According to FDIC statistics, more than 1,500 savings institutions are FDIC-insured, and about three-fifths of these held federal charters and two-fifths had state charters. Credit unions are not included in FDIC statistics because they are not insured by the FDIC.

FDIC-insured commercial banks hold assets in excess of $6 trillion. The total assets of FDIC-insured savings institutions are more than $1 trillion. Credit unions rank third in terms of the value of assets held. Savings banks are a distant fourth. Thus, while S&Ls, credit unions, and savings banks are important components of the banking system, we will continue to focus on commercial banks because of their dominant role in the banking system.

DEGREE OF BRANCH BANKING

Commercial banks wanting to operate branches away from their home offices are restricted by state laws as to the number of offices they are permitted, as well as where the offices may be located. **Unit banking** means that a bank can have only one full-service office. Back in the 1960s about one-third of the states were unit banking states; today there are no unit-banking states. Colorado was the last unit banking state before it began permitting some form of limited branching in 1991.

In addition to unit banking, there is limited banking and statewide banking. States with **limited branch banking** permit banks under their jurisdiction to locate offices within a geographically defined (e.g., within a county) distance of their main office. **Statewide branch banking** means, as the name implies, that banks can operate offices throughout the state. Back in the 1960s, about one-third of the states permitted limited branching and about one-third permitted statewide branching. Today, statewide branching is permitted in most states.

One of the particular merits of branch banking is that these systems are less likely to fail than independent unit banks. In a branch banking system, a wide diversification of investments can be made. Therefore, the temporary reverses of a single community are not as likely to cause the

INTERNET ACTIVITY

Go to the Web site of the U.S. Small Business Administration, http://www.sba.gov. Find information about small business lending in the United States and write a brief summary.

unit banking
exists when a bank can have only one full-service office

limited branch banking
allows additional banking offices within a geographically defined distance of a bank's main office

statewide branch banking
allows banks to operate offices throughout a state

complete failure of an entire banking chain. This is true primarily of those branch systems that operate over wide geographical areas rather than in a single metropolitan area.

The independent bank cannot rely on other banks to offset local economic problems. It is on this point that branch banking operations appear to have their strongest support. The banking system as a whole cannot be proud of the record of bank failures in the United States. However, opponents of branch banking have pointed out that the failure of a system of banks, although less frequent, is far more serious.

Points of view vary on the pros and cons of branch banking among bank customers. The placement of branches in or near shopping centers, airports, and other centers of activity is convenient for consumers. The ability to make deposits or to withdraw funds at a branch is a special advantage for the elderly. Businesses may satisfy very large borrowing requirements by dealing with a bank that has been able to grow to a substantial size through its branch operations.

BANK HOLDING COMPANIES

one bank holding companies (OBHCs) *permits a firm to own and control only one bank*

multibank holding companies (MBHCs) *permits a firm to own and control two or more banks*

A bank may be independently owned by investors, or it may be owned by a holding company. As the name suggests, a holding company owns and controls other organizations or firms. *One-bank holding companies (OBHCs)* own only one bank. *Multibank holding companies (MBHCs)* own and control two or more banks. Both OBHCs and MBHCs may also own other businesses permitted by law. The policies of banks controlled by a holding company are determined by the parent company and coordinated for the purposes of that organization. The holding company itself may or may not engage in direct banking activities. The banks controlled by the holding company may operate branches.

Little control over bank holding companies was in place until the depression years of the early 1930s. Bank holding companies did not come under the jurisdiction of either state or federal control unless they also engaged directly in banking operations themselves. The Banking Act of 1933 and the Securities Acts of 1933 and 1934 imposed limited control on bank holding companies, but it remained for the *Bank Holding Company Act of 1956* to establish clear authority over these operations.

The Bank Holding Company Act defined a bank holding company as one that directly or indirectly owns, controls, or holds the power to vote 25 percent or more of the voting shares of each of two or more banks. Thus, the act of 1956 regulated MBHCs but not OBHCs. MBHCs were not permitted to engage in nonfinancial activities, and financial activities were restricted primarily to direct banking activities. As a result, while the MBHCs were heavily restricted during the 1960s in terms of their nonbanking activities, the OBHCs diversified widely into nonfinancial areas, including manufacturing, retailing, and transportation.

The Bank Holding Company Amendments of 1970 allowed bank holding companies to acquire companies with activities closely related to banking, such as credit card operations, insurance, and data processing services. The 1970 amendments also brought the OBHCs under the provisions of the 1956 act. Thus, while MBHCs were granted more flexibility in terms of banking-related activities, OBHCs had to divest their nonfinancial holdings. Today, bank holding companies control over three-fourths of the banks in the United States and most of the banking assets.

The liberalization of regulations relating to interstate banking is as significant as the liberalization of branch banking within states. All states currently permit the acquisition of banks by out-of-state bank holding companies. In contrast, only one state permitted interstate banking before 1982. However, while some state laws still limit entry to banking organizations from nearby states in what is called *regional reciprocal*, states are increasingly permitting entry on a nationwide basis, which is known as *national reciprocal* or *open-entry*. Recent congressional actions have paved the way for passage of nationwide banking legislation. In anticipation, large banking mergers have been occurring to establish nationwide banking systems.

CONCEPT CHECK

How are banks chartered in the United States, and what types of branch banking are permitted?

What is the difference between an OBHC and an MBHC?

GLOBAL DISCUSSION

international banking *when banks operate in more than one country*

INTERNATIONAL BANKING AND FOREIGN SYSTEMS

Banks with headquarters in one country may open offices or branches in other countries. When banks operate in more than one country, we call this **international banking**. European banks dominated international banking until the 1960s, when world trade began expanding rapidly and multinational corporations increased in number and size. As a response to these and other developments involving international trade, U.S. banks began opening offices in foreign countries and establishing correspondent banking arrangements with foreign banks. In essence, as U.S. corporations began expanding their operations in other countries, the U.S. banks with which they were working followed them. Likewise, the growing importance of the U.S. dollar in international transactions and the movement by foreign corporations to invest in the United States resulted in foreign banks opening offices in the United States. Today, U.S. banks are actively involved throughout the world with major operations in Europe, Asia, and Latin America, and foreign banks have opened hundreds of offices in the United States.

Traditionally, banking in the United States has been highly regulated to protect depositor funds and to maintain citizen confidence in the U.S. banking system. European and most other countries generally have adopted less restrictive approaches to bank regulation. This led to a competitive disadvantage for U.S. domestic banks relative to foreign-owned banks. The result was the passage of the *International Banking Act (IBA)* of 1978, which was intended to provide a "level playing field" for all banks. Some of the provisions included restricting foreign banks in terms of their U.S. interstate banking activities and giving authority to the Federal Reserve to impose reserve requirements on foreign banks. Rules against nonbanking operations for U.S. banks were extended to foreign banks operating in the United States. Congress strengthened regulations relating to foreign banks by enacting the *Foreign Bank Supervision Enhancement Act* in 1991. This act requires that the Federal Reserve give its approval before foreign banks can open offices in the United States and that the Federal Reserve examine U.S. offices of foreign banks each year.

While most countries have central banking systems that operate much like the U.S. Federal Reserve System, some countries allow their banks to engage in both commercial banking and investment banking. This is called *universal banking,* as we discussed previously in this chapter. Germany's largest banks participate in both types of banking and thus are *universal banks.* The United Kingdom does not restrict its banks from engaging in both commercial banking and investment banking. However, British banks traditionally have been either "clearing banks," which are similar to U.S. commercial banks, or "merchant banks," which are similar to U.S. investment banks. In recent years, some British clearing banks have formed subsidiaries to perform a wide range of investment banking activities. Likewise, merchant banks are expanding beyond investment banking. As a result, banking consolidations are taking place and the United Kingdom is moving more toward universal banking. Commercial banking and investment banking are separated in Japan. As previously noted, the passage of the Gramm-Leach-Bliley Act of 1999 now allows U.S. banks to participate in both commercial and investment banking activities.

German banks are allowed to own shares of stock in German firms and also are permitted to vote those shares. Japanese banks also are allowed to own common stock in their business customer firms as well as to engage in various cross-holdings of stock involving other Japanese firms and banks. United Kingdom banks are not actively involved with the firms with which conduct business. While stock ownership in business firms by banks is not restricted in the United Kingdom, British banks are generally risk averse to ownership of common stock.

CONCEPT CHECK

What is international banking, and why has it grown in importance?

What is universal banking, and which country has important universal banks?

Federal Reserve System (Fed)
U.S. central bank that sets monetary policy and regulates banking system

central bank
a government agency that facilitates the operation of the financial system and regulates money supply growth

THE FEDERAL RESERVE SYSTEM

The **Federal Reserve System (Fed)** is the central bank of the United States and is responsible for setting monetary policy and regulating the banking system. A **central bank** is a government-established organization responsible for supervising and regulating the banking system and for creating and regulating the money supply. While central bank activities may differ somewhat from country to country, central banks typically play an important role in a country's payments system. It is also common for a central bank to lend money to its member banks, hold its own reserves, and be responsible for creating money.

The Federal Reserve System consists of five components:

- Member banks
- Federal Reserve District Banks
- Board of Governors
- Federal Open Market Committee
- Advisory Committees

These five components are depicted in Figure 2.3.

FIGURE 2.3

Organization of the Federal Reserve System

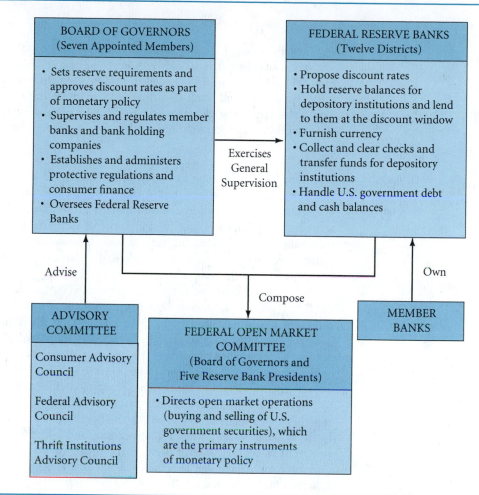

MEMBER BANKS

The Federal Reserve Act provided that all national banks were to become members of the Fed. In addition, state-chartered banks were permitted to join the system if they could show evidence of a satisfactory financial condition. The Federal Reserve Act also required that all member banks purchase capital stock of the Reserve District Bank of their district up to a maximum of 6 percent of their paid-in capital and surplus. In practice, however, member banks have had to pay only 3 percent; the remainder is subject to call at the discretion of the Fed. Member banks are limited to a maximum of 6 percent dividends on the stock of the Reserve District Bank that they hold. The Reserve District Banks, therefore, are private institutions owned by the many member banks of the Federal Reserve.

State-chartered banks are permitted to withdraw from membership with the Federal Reserve six months after written notice has been submitted to the Reserve District Bank of their district. In such cases, the stock originally purchased by the withdrawing member is canceled, and a refund is made for all money paid in.

Approximately 3,500, or about one-third, of the nation's commercial banks are members of the Federal Reserve. This includes all commercial banks with national charters, plus roughly one-fifth of the state-chartered banks. These member banks hold approximately three-fourths of the deposits of all commercial banks. National banks control about three-fifths of the total assets of all FDIC-insured commercial banks, and the state-chartered banks that belong to the Federal Reserve control another one-fourth of total assets. Even these figures understate the importance of the Federal Reserve in the nation's financial system. As previously indicated, the Monetary Control Act of 1980 generally eliminated distinctions between banks that are members of the

INTERNET ACTIVITY

Go to the Federal Reserve Bank of St. Louis Web site, http://www.stls.frb.org, for Federal Reserve Economic Data (referred to as FRED) and find the current discount rate charged by Federal Reserve Banks on loans to depository institutions. Describe any recent changes in discount rates.

Federal Reserve and other depository institutions by applying comparable reserve and reporting requirements to all these institutions.

FEDERAL RESERVE DISTRICT B\ANKS

The Federal Reserve Act of 1913 provided for the establishment of twelve Federal Reserve districts. Each district is served by a Federal Reserve District Bank. Figure 2.3 indicates that district banks have a wide range of responsibilities, including holding reserve balances for depository institutions and lending to them at the prevailing discount (interest) rate. The district banks also issue new currency and withdraw damaged currency from circulation, as well as collect and clear checks and transfer funds for depository institutions.

Directors and Officers

Each Reserve District Bank has corporate officers and a board of directors. The selection of officers and directors is unlike that of other corporations. Each Reserve District Bank has on its board nine directors, who must be residents of the district in which they serve. The directors serve terms of three years, with appointments staggered so that three directors are appointed each year. To ensure that the various economic elements of the Federal Reserve districts are represented, the nine members of the board of directors are divided into three groups: *Class A, Class B,* and *Class C.*

Both Class A and Class B directors are elected by the member banks of the Federal Reserve district. The Class A directors represent member banks of the district, and the Class B directors represent nonbanking interests. These nonbanking interests are commerce, agriculture, and industry. The Class C directors are appointed by the Board of Governors of the Federal Reserve System. These persons may not be stockholders, directors, or employees of existing banks.

The majority of the directors of the Reserve District Banks are elected by the member banks of each district. However, the three nonbanking members of each board appointed by the Board of Governors of the Federal Reserve System are in a more strategic position than the other board members. One member appointed by the Board of Governors is designated chairperson of the board of directors and Federal Reserve agent, and a second member is appointed deputy chairperson. The Federal Reserve agent is the Board of Governors' representative at each Reserve District Bank. He or she is responsible for maintaining the collateral that backs the Federal Reserve notes issued by each Reserve District Bank.

Each Reserve District Bank also has a president and first vice president, who are appointed by its board of directors and approved by the Board of Governors. A Reserve District Bank may have several additional vice presidents. The president is responsible for executing policies established by the board of directors and for the general administration of Reserve District Bank affairs. All other officers and personnel of the Reserve District Bank are subject to the authority of the president.

Federal Reserve Branch Banks

In addition to the twelve Reserve District Banks, twenty-five Branch Banks have been established. These Branch Banks are for the most part in geographical areas not conveniently served by the Reserve District Banks themselves. For this reason, the geographically large western Federal Reserve districts are home to most of the Reserve Branch Banks. The San Francisco district has four, the Dallas district has three, and the Atlanta district has five Branch Banks. The New York Federal Reserve district, on the other hand, has only one Branch Bank, while the Boston district has none.

BOARD OF GOVERNORS

Fed Board of Governors
seven-member board of the
Federal Reserve that sets
monetary policy

The ***Fed Board of Governors***, or formally the Board of Governors (BOG) of the Federal Reserve System, is composed of seven members and is responsible for setting monetary policy. Each member is appointed for a term of fourteen years. The purpose of the fourteen-year term undoubtedly was to reduce political pressure on the board. Board members can be of any political party, and no specific provision concerns the qualifications a member must have. All members are appointed by the president of the United States with the advice and consent of the U.S. Senate. One member is designated as the chairperson and another as the vice-chairperson.

The appointive power of the president and the ability of Congress to alter the board's structure make the Fed Board of Governors a dependent political structure. However, it enjoys much independence in its operations. The Board of Governors of the Federal Reserve System is, in fact, one of the most powerful monetary organizations in the world. The chair of the board plays an especially influential role in policy formulation. Because the board attempts to achieve its goals without political considerations, disagreement between the administration in power and the board is common. From time to time, pressures from Congress or the president have undoubtedly influenced the board's decisions, but the board's semi-independence generally prevails.

Figure 2.3 illustrates how the Board of Governors establishes monetary policy. It sets reserve requirements and reviews and approves the discount rate actions of the twelve Reserve District Banks. It also operates through the Federal Open Market Committee to control the money supply as a means of meetings monetary policy objectives. These monetary policy instruments are explored in more detail later in the chapter.

In addition to setting the nation's monetary policy, the Fed BOG directs and coordinates the activities of the twelve Reserve District Banks under its jurisdiction. It is responsible for approving the applications of state-chartered banks applying for membership in the system and for recommending the removal of officers and directors of member banks when they break rules established by the Fed and other regulatory authorities. In addition, the board implements many of the credit control devices that have come into existence since the mid-1960s, such as the *Truth-in-Lending Act*, the *Equal Credit Opportunity Act*, and the *Home Mortgage Disclosure Act*.

The Fed Board of Governors also publishes the *Federal Reserve Bulletin*, which carries articles of current interest and offers a convenient source of the statistics compiled by the Fed. The BOG and all twelve of the Reserve District Banks engage in intensive research in monetary matters.

FEDERAL OPEN MARKET COMMITTEE

As early as 1922, efforts were made to coordinate the timing of purchases and sales of securities by the Federal Reserve District Banks to achieve desirable national monetary policy objectives. The Federal Open Market Committee (FOMC), with the additional powers granted to it by the *Banking Act of 1935*, has full control over all open-market operations of the Reserve District Banks. As noted in Figure 2.3, this committee consists of the seven members of the Board of Governors of the Federal Reserve, plus five presidents (one of whom must be from New York) of Reserve District Banks. The FMOC conducts open-market operations through the process of buying and selling U.S. government securities. These activities represent the primary method for carrying out monetary policies.

ADVISORY COMMITTEES

The three major advisory committees of the Federal Reserve System are listed in Figure 2.3. The Federal Advisory Council provides advice and general information on banking-related issues to the Fed Board of Governors. Each of the twelve Federal Reserve Districts elects one member to serve on the council. The membership of the Consumer Advisory Council is composed of representatives from depository institutions and their customers and, as the committee title suggests, provides advice relating to consumer issues. The Thrift Institutions Advisory Council consists of members from savings and loans associations, savings banks, and credit unions and provides advice on issues that directly affect thrift institutions.

MONETARY POLICY FUNCTIONS AND INSTRUMENTS

The primary responsibility of the Federal Reserve is to formulate **monetary policy**, which involves regulating the growth of the supply of money, and thereby regulating its cost and availability. By exercising its influence on the monetary system of the United States, the Federal Reserve performs a unique and important function: to promote economic stability. It is notable that the system's broad powers to affect economic stabilization and monetary control were not present when the Fed came into existence in 1913. At that time, the system was meant to help the money supply contract and expand as dictated by economic conditions, serve as bankers' banks in times of economic crisis, provide a more effective check clearance system, and establish a

INTERNET ACTIVITY

Each of the twelve Federal Reserve District Banks has its own Web site and tries to specialize in specific types of information. For example, go to the Federal Reserve Bank of San Francisco's Web site, http://www.frbsf.org, and find information on the history of U.S. paper money. Go to the Federal Reserve Bank of Minneapolis's Web site, http://www.minneapolisfed. org, and find information on the storage and safekeeping of the world's gold supply.

monetary policy
formulated by the Federal Reserve to regulate money supply growth

more effective regulatory system. Much of these responsibilities initially fell to the twelve Reserve District Banks, but as the scope of responsibility for the monetary system was broadened, power was concentrated with the Board of Governors. Today the responsibilities of the Federal Reserve may be described as those relating to monetary policy, to supervision and regulation, and to services provided for depository institutions and the government.

The basic policy instruments of the Fed that allow it to increase or decrease the money supply are the following:

- Changing reserve requirements
- Changing the discount rate
- Conducting open-market operations

The Federal Reserve sets reserve requirements for depository institutions (banks, for short), sets the interest rate at which to lend to banks, and executes open-market operations. By setting reserve requirements, the Federal Reserve establishes the maximum amount of deposits the banking system can support with a given level of reserves. The amount of reserves can be affected directly through open-market operations, thereby causing a contraction or expansion of deposits by the banking system. Discount or interest rate policy on loans to banks also affects the availability of reserves to banks and influences the way they adjust to changes in their reserve positions. Thus the Federal Reserve has a set of tools that together enable it to influence the size of the money supply to attain the Fed's broader economic objectives.

RESERVE REQUIREMENTS

The banking system of the United States is referred to as a "fractional reserve system" because banks are required by the Fed to hold reserves equal to a specified percentage of their deposits. This system is discussed in greater detail in the next section. **Bank reserves** are defined as vault cash and deposits held at the Reserve District Banks. **Required reserves** are the minimum amount of bank reserves that must be held by banks. The **required reserves ratio** is the percentage of deposits that must be held as reserves. If a depository institution has reserves in excess of the required amount, it may lend them out. This is how institutions earn a return, and it is also a way in which the money supply is expanded. In the U.S. system of fractional reserves, control of the volume of checkable deposits depends primarily on reserve management.

The banking system has **excess reserves** when bank reserves are greater than required reserves. The closer to the required minimum the banking system maintains its reserves, the tighter the control the Fed has over the money creation process through its other instruments. If the banking system has close to the minimum of reserves (that is, if excess reserves are near zero), then a reduction of reserves forces the system to tighten credit to reduce deposits. If substantial excess reserves exist, the pressure of reduced reserves is not felt so strongly. When reserves are added to the banking system, depositories may expand their lending but are not forced to do so. However, since depositories earn no interest on reserves, profit maximizing motivates them to lend out excess reserves to the fullest extent consistent with their liquidity requirements. When interest rates are high, this motivation is especially strong.

The ability to change reserve requirements is a powerful tool the Fed uses infrequently. For a number of reasons, the Fed prefers to use open-market operations to change reserves rather than to change reserve requirements. If reserve requirements are changed, the maximum amount of deposits that can be supported by a given level of reserves changes. It is possible to contract total deposits and the money supply by raising reserve requirements while holding the dollar amount of reserves constant. Lowering reserve requirements provides the basis for expanding money and credit.

DISCOUNT RATE POLICY

The Fed serves as a lender to depository institutions. Banks can go to the Fed's "discount window" and borrow funds to meet reserve requirements, depositor withdrawal demands, and even business loan demands. The **Fed discount rate** is the interest rate that a bank must pay to borrow from its regional Federal Reserve District Bank. While each Fed Bank sets its own discount rate, the rates have been similar across all twelve Reserve District Banks in recent years. The Fed sets the interest rate on these loans to banks and thus can influence the money supply by

bank reserves
vault cash and deposits held at Federal Reserve District Banks

required reserves
the minimum amount of total reserves that a depository institution must hold

required reserves ratio
percentage of deposits that must be held as reserves

excess reserves
the amount by which total reserves are greater than required reserves

Fed discount rate
interest rate that a bank must pay to borrow from its regional Federal Reserve District Bank

raising or lowering the cost of borrowing from the Fed. Higher interest rates will discourage banks from borrowing, while lower rates will encourage borrowing. Increased borrowing will allow banks to expand their assets and deposit holdings, and vice versa.

Loans to depository institutions by the Reserve District Banks may take two forms. One option allows the borrowing institution to receive an advance, or loan, secured by its own promissory note together with "eligible paper" it owns. In the second option, the borrower may discount, or sell to the Reserve District Bank, its eligible paper, which includes securities of the U.S. government and federal agencies, promissory notes, mortgages of acceptable quality, and bankers' acceptances. This discounting process underlies the use of the terms *discount window* and *discount rate policy.*

OPEN-MARKET OPERATIONS

open-market operations
buying and selling of securities by the Federal Reserve to alter the supply of money

The most used instrument of monetary policy is **open-market operations**, the buying and selling of securities in the "open market" by the Fed through its Federal Open Market Committee (FOMC) to alter bank reserves. The Fed can purchase securities to put additional reserves at the disposal of the banking system or sell securities to reduce bank reserves. You might ask "Where does the Fed get securities to sell?" A brief look at the Fed's balance sheet will help provide an answer.

The Fed's assets are primarily held in the form of government and government agency securities, which generally represent over 85 percent of total assets. Coins and cash in the process of collection are about 2 percent of total assets. The remainder is assets that include gold certificates and Fed premises. Federal Reserve Notes (recall the discussion of fiat money in Chapter 1) represent nearly 90 percent of the Fed's total liabilities and capital. Deposits in the form of depository institution reserves held at the Reserve District Banks are about 7 percent of the total. Other liabilities, particularly U.S. Treasury deposits, and capital in the form of stock purchased by member banks and surplus earned from operations make up the remaining total liabilities and capital.

FRACTIONAL RESERVE SYSTEM

The banking system of the United States can change the volume of deposits as the need for funds by individuals, businesses, and governments change. This ability to alter the size of the money supply is based on the use of a **fractional reserve system**. In the U.S. fractional reserve system, banks must hold with the Fed reserves equal to a certain percentage of their deposits. To understand the deposit expansion and contraction process, one must study the operations of banks as units in a banking system and the relationship of bank loans to deposits and to bank reserves.

fractional reserve system
reserves held with the Fed that are equal to a certain percentage of bank deposits

In analyzing deposit expansion, it is helpful to distinguish between primary deposits and derivative deposits. For example, the deposit of a check drawn on the Fed is a **primary deposit** because it adds new reserves to the bank where deposited and to the banking system. A **derivative deposit** occurs when reserves created from a primary deposit are made available to borrowers through bank loans. Borrowers then deposit the loans so they can write checks against the funds. When a check is written and deposited in another bank, there is no change in total reserves of the banking system. The increase in reserves at the bank where the check is deposited is offset by a decrease in reserves at the bank on which the check is drawn. Banks must keep reserves against both primary and derivative deposits.

primary deposit
deposit that adds new reserves to a bank

derivative deposit
deposit of funds that were borrowed from the reserves of primary deposits

When reserves were first required by law, the purpose was to assure depositors that banks had the ability to handle withdrawals of cash. This was before the establishment of the Federal Reserve System, which made it possible for a healthy bank to obtain additional funds in time of need. Depositor confidence is now based on deposit insurance and more complete and competent bank examinations by governmental agencies. Today, the basic function of reserve requirements is to provide a means for regulating deposit expansion and contraction.

Deposit creation takes place as a result of the operations of the whole system of banks, but it arises out of the independent transactions of individual banks. To explain the process, therefore, let's consider the loan activities of a single bank. Let's focus first on the bank itself, then on its relationship to a system of banks. This approach is somewhat artificial since a bank practically never acts independently of the actions of other banks, but it has been adopted to clarify the process. Furthermore, it helps explain the belief of some bankers that they cannot create deposits, since they only lend funds placed on deposit in their banks by their depositors. This analysis shows how a system of banks, in which each bank is carrying on its local activities, can do what an individual banker cannot do.

To begin, let us assume that a bank receives a primary deposit of $10,000 and that it must keep reserves of 20 percent against deposits. The $10,000 becomes a cash asset to the bank, as well as a $10,000 liability, since it must stand ready to honor a withdrawal of the money. The bank statement, ignoring all other items, would then show the following:

ASSETS		LIABILITIES	
Reserves	$10,000	Deposits	$10,000

Against this new deposit of $10,000 the bank must keep required reserves of 20 percent, or $2,000. Excess reserves are reserves above the level of required reserves, and the bank now has $8,000 of excess reserves available.

It may appear that the banker could proceed to make loans for $40,000, since all that is needed is a 20 percent reserve ($8,000 in this case) against the resulting checkable deposits. If this were attempted, however, the banker would soon be in difficulty. Since bank loans are usually obtained just before a demand for funds, checks would very likely be written against the deposit accounts almost at once. Many of these checks would be deposited in other banks, and the lending bank would be faced with a demand for cash as checks were presented for collection. This demand could reach the full $40,000. Since the bank has only $8,000 to meet it, it could not follow such a course and remain in business.

The amount that the banker can safely lend is the $8,000 of excess reserves. If more is lent, the banker runs the risk of not being able to make payments on checks. After an $8,000 loan, the books show the following:

ASSETS		LIABILITIES	
Reserves	$10,000	Deposits	$18,000
Loans	$ 8,000		

If a check were written for the full amount of the derivative deposit ($8,000) and sent to a bank in another city for deposit, the lending bank would lose all its excess reserves. This may be seen from its books, which would appear as follows:

ASSETS		LIABILITIES	
Reserves	$2,000	Deposits	$10,000
Loans	$8,000		

In practice a bank may be able to lend somewhat more than the $8,000 in this example because banks frequently require customers to keep an average deposit balance of about 15 to 20 percent of the loan. The whole of the additional $1,500 to $2,000 cannot be lent safely, because an average balance of $1,500 to $2,000 does not prevent the full amount of the loan from being used for a period of time. With an average balance in each derivative deposit account, however, not all accounts will be drawn to zero at the same time. Therefore, some additional funds will be available for loans.

It may be argued that a banker will feel certain that some checks written against the bank will be redeposited in the same bank and that therefore larger sums can be lent. However, because any bank is only one of thousands, the banker cannot usually count on such redepositing of funds. Banks cannot run the risk of being caught short of reserves. Thus, when an individual bank receives a new primary deposit, it cannot lend the full amount of that deposit but only the amount available as excess reserves. From the point of view of an individual bank, therefore, deposit creation appears impossible. Because a part of every new deposit cannot be lent out because of reserve requirements, the volume of additional loans is less than new primary deposits.

It is important to recognize this fact: *What cannot be done by an individual bank can be done by the banking system.* This occurs when many banks are expanding loans and derivative deposits

TABLE 2.1
Multiple Expansion of Deposits—20 Percent Reserve Ratio

	ASSETS				LIABILITIES
	RESERVES				
	TOTAL	REQUIRED	EXCESS	LOANS AND INVESTMENTS	CHECKABLE DEPOSITS
Initial Reserves	$1,000	$ 200	$800	$ 0	$1,000
Stage 1	1,000	360	640	800	1,800
Stage 2	1,000	488	512	1,440	2,440
Stage 3	1,000	590	410	1,952	2,952
Stage 4	1,000	672	328	2,362	3,362
Stage 5	1,000	738	262	2,690	3,690
Stage 6	1,000	790	210	2,952	3,952
Stage 7	1,000	832	168	3,162	4,162
Stage 8	1,000	866	134	3,330	4,330
Stage 9	1,000	893	107	3,464	4,464
Stage 10	1,000	914	86	3,571	4,571
.	.	.	.	.	.
.	.	.	.	.	.
.	.	.	.	.	.
Final Stage	$1,000	$1,000	$ 0	$4,000	$5,000

at the same time. Table 2.1 further illustrates the deposit expansion process for a 20 percent reserve ratio. A primary deposit of $1,000 is injected into the banking system, making excess reserves of $800 available for loans and investments. Eventually, $5,000 in checkable deposits will be created.

The multiple expansion in the money supply created by the banking system through its expansion of checkable deposits also can be expressed in formula form as follows:

$$\text{Change in checkable deposits} = \frac{\text{Increase in excess reserves}}{\text{Required reserves ratio}} \quad (2.1)$$

We define the terms *excess reserves* and *required reserves ratio* in the next section. For our purposes, the maximum increase in the amount of checkable deposits is determined by dividing a new inflow of reserves into the banking system by the percentage of checkable deposits that must be held in reserves.

In the example presented in Table 2.1, the maximum expansion in the checkable deposits component of the money supply would be as follows:

$$\text{Change in checkable deposits} = \$1,000 \div .20 = \$5,000$$

which is the same as the final-stage figure shown for checkable deposit liabilities. The maximum increase in deposits (and money supply) that can result from a specific increase in excess reserves can be referred to as a *money multiplier*. In our very basic example, the money multiplier (m) is equal to 1 divided by the required reserves ratio, or $m = 1 \div .20 = 5$. However, in the complex U.S. economy, several factors or "leakages" reduce the ability to reach the maximum expansion in the money supply depicted in this simplified example. A more realistic money multiplier ratio is discussed in the next section.

THE MONETARY BASE AND THE MONEY MULTIPLIER

Previously in this chapter we examined the deposit multiplying capacity of the banking system. Recall the example in Table 2.1, in which excess reserves of $1,000 were introduced into a banking system having a 20 percent required reserves ratio, resulting in a deposit expansion of $5,000. This can also be viewed as a money multiplier of 5.

In the complex U.S. financial system, the money multiplier is not quite so straightforward. It is useful to focus on the relationship between the monetary base and the money supply to better understand the complexity of the money multiplier. The **monetary base** is defined as banking system reserves plus currency held by the public. More specifically, the monetary base consists of reserve deposits held in Reserve District Banks, vault cash or currency held by depository institutions, and currency held by the nonbank public. The **money multiplier** is the number of times the monetary base can be expanded or magnified to produce a given money supply level. Conceptually, the M1 definition of the money supply is the monetary base (MB) multiplied by the money multiplier (m). In equation form we have:

$$M1 = MB \times m \tag{2.2}$$

The size and stability of the money multiplier are important because the Fed can control the monetary base, but it cannot directly control the size of the money supply. Changes in the money supply are caused by changes in the monetary base, in the money multiplier, or in both. The Fed can change the size of the monetary base through open-market operations or changes in the reserve ratio. The money multiplier is not constant. It can and does fluctuate over time, depending on actions taken by the Fed, the nonbank public, and the U.S. Treasury.

As of December 2005, the money multiplier was approximately 1.73, as determined by dividing the $1,373.2 billion M1 money stock by the $793.4 billion monetary base.[3] Taking into account the actions of the nonbank public and the Treasury, the formula for the money multiplier in today's financial system can be expressed as:[4]

$$m = \frac{(1 + k)}{[r(1 + t + g) + k]} \tag{2.3}$$

where
  r = the ratio of reserves to total deposits (checkable, noncheckable time and savings, and government)
  k = the ratio of currency held by the nonbank public to checkable deposits
  t = the ratio of noncheckable deposits to checkable deposits
  g = the ratio of government deposits to checkable deposits

Let's illustrate how the size of the money multiplier is determined by returning to our previous example of a 20 percent reserve ratio. Recall that in a simpler financial system, the money multiplier would be determined as $1 \div r$ or $1 \div .20$, which equals 5. However, in the complex U.S. system, we also need to consider leakages into currency held by the nonbank public, noncheckable time and savings deposits, and government deposits. Let's further assume that the reserve ratio applies to total deposits, a k of 40 percent, a t of 15 percent, and a g of 10 percent. The money multiplier then would be estimated as:

$$m = \frac{(1 + .40)}{[.20(1 + .15 + .10) + .40]} = \frac{1.40}{.65} = 2.15$$

Of course, if a change occurred in any of the components, the money multiplier would adjust accordingly, as would the size of the money supply.

In Chapter 1 we briefly discussed the link between the money supply and economic activity. Recall that the money supply (M1) is linked to the gross domestic product (GDP) via the velocity or turnover of money. More specifically, the **velocity of money** measures the rate of circulation of the money supply. It is expressed as the average number of times each dollar is spent on purchases of goods and services and is calculated as nominal GDP (GDP in current dollars)

---

monetary base
banking system reserves plus currency held by the public

money multiplier
number of times the monetary base can be expanded or magnified to produce a given money supply level

velocity of money
the rate of circulation of the money supply

---

3. *Statistical Supplement to the Federal Reserve Bulletin* (January 2007), pp. 12–13.
4. The reader interested in understanding how the money multiplier is derived will find a discussion in most financial institutions and markets textbooks.

divided by M1. Changes in the growth rates for money supply (M1g) and money velocity (M1Vg) affect the growth rate in real economic activity (RGDPg) and the rate of inflation (Ig) and can be expressed in equation form as follows:

$$M1_g + M1V_g = RGDP_g + I_g \qquad (2.4)$$

For example, if the velocity of money remains relatively constant, then a link between money supply and the nominal GDP should be observable. Likewise, after nominal GDP is adjusted for inflation, the resulting real GDP growth can be examined relative to M1 growth rates. Changes in money supply have been found to lead to changes in economic activity.

The ability to predict M1 velocity in addition to money supply changes is important in making successful monetary policy. Fed M1 growth targets need to take into consideration expected velocity movements to achieve the desired effects on real GDP and inflation. It would be naive, however, to believe that regulating and controlling the supply of money and credit are all that is needed to manage the complex U.S. economy. We also know that economic activity is affected by government actions concerning government spending, taxation, and the management of our public debt.

GLOBAL DISCUSSION

CENTRAL BANKS IN OTHER COUNTRIES

Central banks in other developed countries, like the U.S. Fed, are responsible for regulating the money supply, safeguarding the currency, and carrying out the monetary policy of each of those countries. Most other countries have a single central bank with branches that differ from the Fed's twelve Reserve District Banks. Of course, the Fed Board of Governors has effectively centralized control of U.S. monetary policy.

Empirical evidence shows a link between central bank independence from government intervention and inflation and economic growth rates. In countries where central banks are relatively independent from their governments, inflation rates have generally been lower and economic growth rates higher than in countries where central banks are closely tied to their governments.

Three economically important foreign central banks are those from the United Kingdom, Japan, and the European Monetary Union. The central bank in the United Kingdom is the *Bank of England (BOE)*. It was created well before the formation of the Federal Reserve System in 1913. The BOE is managed by a governor and five additional officers, all of whom are appointed for five-year terms. The BOE governor reports to the chancellor, who has final responsibility for setting monetary policy. In contrast with the United States, commercial banks in Great Britain are not required to hold reserves at the Bank of England. Great Britain does not legally separate commercial banking and investment banking activities.

The central bank of Japan, called the *Bank of Japan (BOJ),* was created in 1947. The top official of the BOJ is the governor, who heads the Policy Board, which is the central decision-making authority. The governor and some members of the board are appointed by the Japanese equivalent of the U.S. Congress, and other board members are appointed by the finance minister. Japanese commercial banks, like their U.S. counterparts, are required to hold reserves on deposit with the BOJ, and banks can borrow at an official discount rate from the BOJ.

European Central Bank (ECB)
conducts monetary policy for the twelve European countries that adopted the euro as their common currency

The **European Central Bank (ECB)** conducts monetary policy for the twelve European countries that formed the *European Monetary Union* and adopted the euro as their common currency at the beginning of 1999. Euro notes and coins were officially introduced at the beginning of 2002, and all twelve individual national currencies were withdrawn as legal tender by July 1, 2002. The ECB, which is headquartered in Frankfurt, Germany, is responsible for controlling inflation and for managing the value of the euro relative to other currencies. The ECB structure is somewhat similar to that of the U.S. Fed in that the twelve national central banks of the euro countries operate much like the twelve Federal Reserve District Banks. Like the Fed BOG, the governing council of the ECB includes governors from some of the national central banks. Each national central bank is responsible for managing payment systems and furnishing currency and credit in its home country.

MOKEY SHEA
Private Banking Relationship Manager

Key Trust Company of Florida
BA, Political Science
University of Maine

"The whole basis for this service is that I become very familiar with the personal finances of the client."

Q: *What is private banking?*

A: Private banking means providing very personalized and specialized services to high-net-worth individuals and families.

Q: *What kind of services are involved?*

A: We use a team approach to meet the needs of these clients. I supply the checking, savings, and mortgage instruments, the normal retail banking pieces. There is a brokerage officer on the team who provides investment services. Then we have a trust officer who deals with issues such as estate planning. It's not unusual for a bank or other financial services company to provide all these functions. What's new about private banking is that we all work as a team rather than independently.

Q: *How high does a client's net worth need to be to qualify?*

A: There are several criteria we look for, but in general we look for investable assets of $250,000. This would be above and beyond whatever they have invested in real estate. We're located in Naples, Florida, which has an unusual number of wealthy retirees who fit the profile we look for. There are other banks in town that require even higher net worth to qualify for their private banking services.

Q: *You're a "relationship manager." What is that?*

A: The whole basis for this service is that I become very familiar with and involved in the personal finances of the client. The more I know about their financial situation and needs, the better our team can meet those needs. It really is a relationship. I get to know their families, learn about their lifestyles, discuss their futures, including what happens after they die. So the term *relationship manager* is very accurate.

Q: *You were a branch manager for Key Bank before you took your current position. How would you describe that experience?*

A: I ran a branch in Maine with about a dozen employees. In that setting you need to be a true jack-of-all-trades. At nine o'clock I might open a savings account for a twelve-year-old who has a paper route. At ten o'clock I might discuss a $100,000 business loan. At eleven o'clock I might open a checking account for a small business. So I was dealing with every imaginable kind of client. Plus I had the management and operations responsibilities. I was essentially running a small bank. I had profitability targets I needed to meet and other requirements set at our main office.

Q: *Do you miss anything about that job?*

A: It was a tough job because it combined the sales and management roles. Either one of those roles is plenty of work. Doing both demands a lot. The thing I miss the most is working with new businesses and watching them grow from ideas into successes. Most of my private banking clients are past the point of starting a new business. But what I like about my current job is that I get so involved with my clients. I can be much more focused on them and spend more time with them than in the branch environment where it's a continuous stream of different people all day long.

APPLYING FINANCE TO . . .

INSTITUTIONS AND MARKETS

Commercial banks, insurance companies, pension funds, and mutual funds play important roles in getting the savings of individuals into the hands of business firms so that investments can be made to maintain and grow the businesses. Investment banks sell or market new securities issued by businesses to individual and institutional investors. The Fed is the U.S. central bank, which supervises and regulates the banking system. The Fed, along with depository institutions, creates and transfers money. Monetary policy actions of the Fed affect the primary financial markets for debt obligations, influencing the availability of bank loans and the interest rates that must be paid on those loans.

INVESTMENTS

Bank loans to businesses and other debt obligations, such as small certificates of deposit, originate in the primary debt obligations market. However, since they are specific arrangements with business borrowers and depositors, these debt obligations do not trade in a secondary debt obligations market. Investment banking firms and brokerage houses help businesses market their new debt and equity securities issues so that funds can be raised in addition to those provided by banks. Securities markets are also affected by Fed actions. An increase in reserve requirements will restrict the amount of individual savings that would be available to make loans. Other Fed actions may cause banks to raise loan interest rates and cause the economy to slow down and security prices to decline. When the Fed raises the discount rate, banks react to protect their profit margins by raising their lending rates to individuals and businesses.

FINANCIAL MANAGEMENT

Financial managers borrow from commercial banks and depend on the banking system to help support day-to-day operating activities that involve producing and selling their products and services. Business firms depend on the banking system having a highly efficient check clearing system so that cash outflows and inflows can be reasonably balanced. Financial managers also rely on mutual funds, insurance companies, and pension funds to buy their new security issues. Financial management activities are directly affected by Fed monetary policy actions. A tightening of monetary policy makes it more difficult and costly for businesses to borrow funds and for financial managers to sell new stocks and bonds in the primary securities markets. Of course, an easing of monetary policy will make it easier for financial managers to raise financial capital, and they will be able to do so at lower interest rates.

SUMMARY

This chapter began with a review of the financial institutions that currently play major roles in the financial system. We provided an overview of the banking system followed by a comparison of commercial banking, investment banking, and universal banking. We then discussed the six current functions of banks and the banking system: (1) accepting deposits, (2) granting loans, (3) issuing checkable deposit accounts, (4) clearing checks, (5) creating deposit money, and (6) investment banking. We also reviewed banking prior to the Civil War.

We next presented a discussion of regulation of the banking system, including general banking legislation, the savings and loan crisis, and how depositors' funds are protected. Our attention turned to the structure and operation of U.S. banks. Banks may obtain either state or federal charters, which makes the United States a dual banking system. Individual states have the authority to decide whether banks can operate branches in their states. Today, most states permit statewide branching. Banks may be independently owned or owned by either a one-bank holding company (OBHC) or a multibank holding company (MBHC). Next, the development of international banking and some examples of foreign banking systems compared to the U.S. banking system were described.

While the movement to a central banking system in the United States was a slow process, the Federal Reserve Act was finally passed in 1913. Coverage focused on the organization and structure of the Federal Reserve System in terms of membership, Federal Reserve District Banks, the Board of Governors, and the Federal Open Market Committee. National banks must belong to the Federal Reserve System, while state-chartered banks and other depository institutions can elect to join the Federal Reserve.

The basic policy instruments of the Fed include setting reserve requirements, lending to depository institutions at the discount rate, and conducting open-market operations involving the purchase and sale of U.S. government securities. Open-market operations are the primary method used today for carrying out monetary policy objectives.

The last section of the chapter described some of the characteristics of central banks in the United Kingdom, Japan, and the European Monetary Union.

KEY TERMS

bank reserves	credit union	Fed Board of Governors
banking system	depository institutions	Fed discount rate
brokerage firms	derivative deposit	Federal Reserve System (Fed)
central bank	dual banking system	finance firms
commercial banks	excess reserves	finance companies
contractual savings organizations	European Central Bank (ECB)	financial intermediation

fractional reserve system	money multiplier	savings bank
Glass-Steagall Act of 1933	mortgage banking firms	savings and loan association
Gramm-Leach-Bliley Act of 1999	multibank holding companies (MBHCs)	securities firms
insurance companies	mutual fund	statewide branch banking
international banking	one-bank holding companies (OBHCs)	thrift institutions
investment banking firms	open-market operations	unit banking
investment companies	pension funds	universal bank
limited branch banking	primary deposit	velocity of money
monetary base	required reserves	
monetary policy	required reserves ratio	

DISCUSSION QUESTIONS

1. Identify the major financial intermediaries that have roles in directing savings to business firms.

2. Identify what are depository institutions, and briefly describe why and when thrift institutions were founded.

3. Identify and briefly describe types of contractual savings organizations, securities firms, and finance firms.

4. Compare commercial banking with investment banking. What is universal banking?

5. Describe the functions of banks and the banking system.

6. How did the First Bank of the United States serve the nation? Also briefly describe why the Second Bank of the United States was chartered.

7. Why was it considered necessary to create the Federal Reserve System when the United States already had the benefits of the National Banking Act?

8. Comment on the objectives of the Depository Institutions Deregulation and Monetary Control Act of 1980.

9. Why was the Garn-St. Germain Depository Institutions Act thought to be necessary?

10. What was the Gramm-Leach-Bliley Act designed to do?

11. Describe the reasons for the savings and loan crisis that occurred during the 1980s.

12. How are depositors' funds protected today in the United States?

13. Describe the structure of banks in terms of bank charters, branch banking, and bank holding companies.

14. Define what is meant by international banking. Describe how some foreign banking systems differ from the U.S. banking system.

15. Describe the organizational structure of the Federal Reserve System in terms of its five major components.

16. Explain how the banking interests and large, medium, and small businesses are represented on the board of directors of each Reserve District Bank.

17. What is a Reserve Branch Bank? How many such branches exist, and where are most of them located?

18. How are members of the Board of Governors of the Federal Reserve System appointed? To what extent are they subject to political pressures?

19. Identify and briefly describe the three instruments that may be used by the Fed to set monetary policy.

20. Reserve District Banks have at times been described as "bankers' banks" because of their lending powers. What is meant by this statement?

21. Describe the two "targets" that the Fed can use when establishing monetary policy. Which target has the Fed focused on in recent years?

22. What is meant by a fractional reserve system?

23. Explain the potential for deposit expansion when required reserves average 10 percent and $2,000 in excess reserves are deposited in the banking system.

24. What is the difference between the monetary base and total bank reserves?

25. Briefly describe what is meant by the money multiplier, and indicate the factors that affect its magnitude or size.

26. Define the velocity of money, and explain why it is important to anticipate changes in money velocity.

27. Why does it seem to be important to regulate and control the supply of money?

EXERCISES

1. Indicate which of the following financial institutions are considered to be (1) depository institutions and (2) contractual savings organizations.

    a. commercial banks   c. pension funds

    b. insurance companies   d. credit unions

2. Match the following financial institutions with their primary source of funds.

    a. commercial banks   1. premiums paid on policies

    b. insurance companies   2. employee/employer contributions

    c. pension funds   3. other financial institutions

    d. finance companies   4. individual savings

3. Use information presented in this chapter to identify specific examples of financial institutions that operated in the United States prior to 1800. Also, provide specific examples of financial institutions that first began operating during the early part of the twentieth century.

4. Banks provide checking account services, accept savings deposits, and lend to borrowers. In other words, they are in the money business. We all have heard stories of banks or their partner firms "misplacing" or "losing" bags of money. Lending rates are also subject to change periodically. Both of these situations can produce ethical dilemmas or decisions. How would you react to the following scenarios?

    a. You are walking down the street and see a large money bag with "First National Bank" printed on it. The bag is sitting on the sidewalk in front of a local office of First National Bank. You are considering whether to pick up the bag, check its contents, and then try to find the owner. Alternatively, you could pick up the money bag and take it to the local police station or return it directly to the bank itself. What would you do?

b. You are a loan officer of First National Bank. The owner of a small business has come into the bank today and is requesting an immediate $100,000 loan for which she has appropriate collateral. You also know that the bank is going to reduce its lending interest rate to small businesses next week. You could make the loan now or inform the small business owner that she could get a lower rate if the loan request is delayed. What would you do?

5. Obtain a current issue of the *Statistical Supplement to the Federal Reserve Bulletin* and use it to accomplish the following:

a. Find M1 and the monetary base and then estimate the money multiplier.

b. Determine the nominal gross domestic product (GDP in current dollars). Estimate the velocity of money using M1 from (a) and nominal GDP.

c. Indicate how the money multiplier and the velocity of money have changed between two recent years.

PROBLEMS

1. A new bank has vault cash of $1 million and $5 million in deposits held at its Federal Reserve District Bank.

   a. If the required reserves ratio is 8 percent, what dollar amount of deposits can the bank have?

   b. If the bank holds $65 million in deposits and currently holds bank reserves such that excess reserves are zero, what required reserves ratio is implied?

   c. If the new bank holds $1 million in excess reserves and the required reserves ratio is 8 percent, what level of deposits are being held?

2. A bank has $110 million in deposits and holds $10 million in vault cash.

   a. If the required reserves ratio is 10 percent, what dollar amount of reserves must be held at the Federal Reserve District Bank?

   b. How would your answer to (a) change if the required reserves ratio was increased to 12 percent?

   c. Now, if total bank reserves were $15 million with $2 million considered to be excess reserves, what required reserves ratio is implied?

3. Your Friendly National Bank holds $50 million in reserves at its Federal Reserve District Bank. The required reserves ratio is 12 percent.

   a. If the bank has $600 million in deposits, what amount of vault cash would be needed for the bank to be in compliance with the required reserves ratio?

   b. If the bank holds $10 million in vault cash, determine the required reserves ratio that would be needed for the bank to avoid a reserves deficit.

   c. If the Friendly National Bank experiences a required reserves deficit, what actions can it take to be in compliance with the existing required reserves ratio?

4. Assume that Bank A receives a primary deposit of $100,000 and that it must keep reserves of 10 percent against deposits.

   a. Prepare a simple balance sheet of assets and liabilities for the bank immediately after the deposit is received.

   b. Assume Bank A makes a loan in the amount that can be "safely lent." Show what the bank's balance sheet of assets and liabilities would look like immediately after the loan.

   c. Now assume that a check in the amount of the "derivative deposit" created in (b) was written and sent to another bank. Show what Bank A's (the lending bank's) balance sheet of assets and liabilities would look like after the check is written.

5. The SIMPLEX financial system is characterized by a required reserves ratio of 11 percent; initial excess reserves are $1 million, and there are no currency or other leakages.

   a. What would be the maximum amount of checkable deposits after deposit expansion and what would be the money multiplier?

   b. How would your answer to (a) change if the reserve requirement had been 9 percent?

6. Assume a financial system has a monetary base of $25 million. The required reserves ratio is 10 percent and there are no leakages in the system.

   a. What is the size of the money multiplier?

   b. What will be the system's money supply?

   c. How would the money supply change if the reserve ratio is increased to 14 percent?

7. The BASIC financial system has a required reserves ratio of 15 percent; initial excess reserves are $5 million, cash held by the public is $1 million and is expected to stay at that level, and there are no other leakages or adjustments in the system.

   a. What would be the money multiplier and the maximum amount of checkable deposits?

   b. What would be the money supply amount in this system after deposit expansion?

   c. Assume that the cash held by the public drops to $500,000 with an equal amount becoming excess reserves and that the required reserves ratio drops to 12 percent. What would be the new money supply amount?

8. The COMPLEX financial system has these relationships: the ratio of reserves to total deposits is 12 percent and the ratio of noncheckable deposits to checkable deposits is 40 percent. In addition, currency held by the nonbank public amounts to 15 percent of checkable deposits. The ratio of government deposits to checkable deposits is 8 percent, and the monetary base is $300 million.

   a. Determine the size of the M1 money multiplier and the size of the money supply.

   b. If the ratio of currency in circulation to checkable deposits were to drop to 13 percent while the other ratios remained the same, what would be the impact on the money supply?

c. If the ratio of government deposits to checkable deposits increases to 10 percent while the other ratios remain the same, what would be the impact on the money supply?

d. What would happen to the money supply if the reserve requirement increased to 14 percent while noncheckable deposits to checkable deposits fell to 35 percent? Assume the other ratios remain as originally stated.

9. **Challenge Problem** ABBIX has a complex financial system with the following relationships: The ratio of required reserves to total deposits is 15 percent, and the ratio of noncheckable deposits to checkable deposits is 40 percent. In addition, currency held by the nonbank public amounts to 20 percent of checkable deposits. The ratio of government deposits to checkable deposits is 8 percent. Initial excess reserves are $900 million.

a. Determine the M1 multiplier and the maximum dollar amount of checkable deposits.

b. Determine the size of the M1 money supply.

c. What will happen to ABBIX's money multiplier if the reserve requirement decreases to 10 percent while the ratio of noncheckable deposits to checkable deposits falls to 30 percent? Assume the other ratios remain as originally stated.

d. Based on the information in (c), estimate the maximum dollar amount of checkable deposits, as well as the size of the M1 money supply.

e. Assume that ABBIX has a target M1 money supply of $2.8 billion. The only variable that you have direct control over is the required reserves ratio. What would the required reserves ratio have to be to reach the target M1 money supply amount? Assume the other original ratio relationships hold.

f. Now assume that currency held by the nonbank public drops to 15 percent of checkable deposits and that ABBIX's target money supply is changed to $3.0 billion. What would the required reserves ratio have to be to reach the new target M1 money supply amount? Assume that the other original ratio relationships hold.

• CHAPTER 3 •

Savings-Investment Process and Financial Assets

Chapter Learning Objectives

AFTER STUDYING THIS CHAPTER, YOU SHOULD BE ABLE TO:

- Briefly describe the objectives of national economic policy.
- Identify and briefly describe the major components of the gross domestic product.
- Identify the major policy maker groups and describe their primary responsibilities.
- Discuss the three ways money is transferred from savers to businesses.
- Identify the major sources of savings in the United States.
- Identify and describe the factors that affect savings.
- Discuss what is meant by real assets versus financial assets.
- Identify major financial instruments that have maturities of up to one year.
- Identify major financial instruments and securities that have very long or no maturities.
- Describe the four types of financial markets.

Where We Have Been. . .

In Chapter 1 you learned about the role of finance and were able to answer this question: What is finance? Chapter 1 also provided you with information about the development and importance of money in an efficient financial system. Chapter 2 covered the importance of commercial banks and other financial intermediaries in helping the financial system operate smoothly. In Chapter 2 you learned about the Federal Reserve System and its monetary policy functions and instruments. After reading Chapter 3 you should have a better understanding of who the U.S. policy makers are, their roles in the savings-investment process, and what the major types of financial instruments are.

Where We Are Going. . .

In Chapter 4 you will be introduced to the structure of interest rates. You will learn about the supply and demand for loanable funds and the determinants of nominal or market interest rates, as well as the characteristics of U.S. Treasury debt obligations, which are considered to be free of default risk. Our attention then turns to the term or maturity structure of interest rates. Next we cover inflation premiums and price movements. The last section of that chapter examines default risk premiums. Chapter 5 focuses on the time value of money, which is one of the six principles of finance. Investors expect to be compensated for holding investments for a period of time between when they make their investments and when they receive the return of their investments.

How This Chapter Applies to Me. . .

Every day you are faced with deciding whether to "consume more" or to "save." For example, after buying dinner at a restaurant you may still have a few dollars left in the form of extra income, possibly from a part-time job while you are in college. What will you do with the money? You might buy a new CD or take a friend to the movie theater. Alternatively, you might decide to place the money in a savings account at a bank. The process of intermediation then moves your discretionary money from savings into investment. Of course, saving is not without cost. Each time you make a decision to save, you are foregoing current consumption. This action on your part not to immediately consume all your income helps the economy grow.

Our parents and other "experts" have likely provided similar advice to each of us about the importance of saving for a "rainy" day. Of course, they were telling us not to consume all of our current income but, rather, to put some aside for an unexpected financial need—that is, a "rainy day." Such an action of saving not only provides protection against unanticipated future expenditures for the individual but also allows investment. You are probably not a saver at this stage in your life. We say this because most individuals are spenders of their parents' earnings and savings during their formative years from birth through college. At the time of college graduation, most individuals have little or no savings but possess "earning power." As earnings exceed expenditures, individuals have the opportunity to save in a variety of ways ranging from short-term money market investments (considered to be cash) to long-term real estate investments in the form of home ownership.

As you move through your life cycle, you likely will have the opportunity to invest in stocks and bonds. Likewise, having an understanding of the types of financial assets that are used by businesses to finance and grow their businesses will be of value to those of you who pursue business careers.

NATIONAL ECONOMIC POLICY OBJECTIVES

The first panacea for a mismanaged nation is inflation of the currency; the second is war. Both bring a temporary prosperity; both bring a permanent ruin. Both are the refuge of political and economic opportunists.

Ernest Hemingway

Most of us would agree with Hemingway that currency inflation and war are not acceptable economic objectives. While people with differing views debate the proper role of government, there is broad agreement that decisions by government policy makers to levy taxes and make expenditures significantly affect the lives of each of us. In addition to the checks and balances offered by two political parties, the Fed is expected to operate independently of the government but also in the best interests of the country and its people. There is also a strong tradition in the United States that national economic objectives should be pursued with minimum interference to the economic freedom of individuals.

The *Employment Act of 1946* and the *Full Employment and Balanced Growth Act of 1978*, which is typically referred to as the *Humphrey-Hawkins Act*, spell out the role of the U.S. government in carrying out the economic goals of economic growth and stable prices. Most of us also would agree that economic growth is good if it leads to improved living standards for the people. However, for this to occur, economic growth must be accompanied by stable prices and high and stable employment levels. The relationship between the money supply and demand affects the level of prices and economic activity in our market economy. Therefore, the process by which the money supply is increased and decreased is a very important factor to the success of the economy. Since we live in a global environment, our economic well-being also depends on achieving a reasonable balance in international trade and other transactions. To summarize, our country's economic policy actions are directed toward these four general goals:

- Economic growth
- High employment
- Price stability
- Balance in international transactions

Accompanying these economic goals is also a desire for stability in interest rates, financial markets, and foreign exchange markets.

ECONOMIC GROWTH

The standard of living of U.S. citizens has increased dramatically during the history of the United States as a result of the growth of the economy and its productivity. Of course, growth means more than merely increasing total output. It requires that output increase faster than the population so that the average output per person expands. Growth is a function of two components: an increasing stock of productive resources—the labor force and stock of capital—and improved technology and skills.

gross domestic product (GDP)

measures the output of goods and services in an economy

The output of goods and services in an economy is referred to as the **gross domestic product (GDP)**. The United States began the 1980s with a double-dip recession or economic downturn in "real" terms (i.e., after price changes have been factored out). A mild economic decline occurred in 1980, followed by a deeper decline that lasted from mid-1981 through most of 1982. The GDP then grew in real terms throughout the remainder of the 1980s before a mild downturn began in mid-1990 and lasted through the first quarter of 1991. Although some industries underwent substantial downsizing and restructuring, the economy continued to grow in real terms throughout the 1990s. As we moved into the twenty-first century, economic growth slowed both domestically and worldwide, resulting in a U.S. recession in 2001. However, renewed economic growth has continued since then.

HIGH EMPLOYMENT

Unemployment represents a loss of potential output and imposes costs on the entire economy. The economic and psychological costs are especially hard on the unemployed. While there is some disagreement over what we should consider full employment, it is a stated objective of the U.S. government to promote stability of employment and production at levels close to the national potential. This aim seeks to avoid large changes in economic activity, minimizing the hardships that accompany loss of jobs and output.

The U.S. unemployment rate reached double-digit levels during the early 1980s with a peak at about 11 percent near the end of 1982. As the economy began expanding, unemployment levels declined throughout the remainder of the 1980s until the rate fell below 5.5 percent. The recession that began in mid-1990, along with other job dislocations associated with corporate downsizing and restructuring, resulted in an unemployment rate exceeding 7.5 percent in 1992. The remainder of the 1990s was characterized by a steady decline in the unemployment rate to a level below 4.5 percent. As the country entered the twenty-first century, economic activity slowed and the unemployment level began rising. However, with an economic recovery beginning in 2002 employment opportunities have been improving and the unemployment level has shown a modest decline.

PRICE STABILITY

In recent decades the importance of stable prices has become well accepted but difficult to achieve. Consistently stable prices help create an environment in which the other economic goals are more easily reached. **Inflation** occurs when a rise or increase in the prices of goods and services is not offset by increases in the quality of those goods and services. Inflation discourages investment by increasing the uncertainty about future returns. Therefore, high inflation rates are no longer considered acceptable as a price to pay for high levels of employment.

inflation

occurs when an increase in the price of goods or services is not offset by an increase in quality

Inflation was at double-digit levels during the early 1980s, and this was reflected in record-high interest rates. However, as the economy turned down in the 1981–1982 recession, inflation rates also started down and continued down until inflation fell below 3 percent. After a brief rise at the beginning of the 1990s, inflation steadily declined to 2 percent and continued at very low levels in the early years of the twenty-first century. However, the Fed began expressing concern in 2004 about possible rising inflation and reacted by increasing the federal funds rate, with the result being continued low inflation rates to date.

BALANCE IN INTERNATIONAL TRANSACTIONS

The increasing importance of international trade and international capital markets has resulted in a new emphasis on worldwide financial affairs. The U.S. economy is so large that the actions taken with respect to the country's own national affairs also influence the economies of other nations. Economic policy makers, therefore, must always maintain a worldview rather than a narrow nationalistic approach.

Nations that produce and sell (export) more than they buy (import) will have a net capital inflow or surplus, and vice versa. For example, Japan has used its large surplus of exports over imports with the United States to make investments in the United States. Nations that continually operate with international trade deficits will become increasingly weaker economically, while those with consistent surpluses will become economically stronger. Movement toward

international financial equilibrium over time thus is in the best interests of worldwide trade and economic growth.

During the 1980s and 1990s, the United States consistently operated with a large negative trade balance. In other words, its imports of goods and services have consistently exceeded its exports of goods and products. U.S. service exports are generally larger than its service imports. However, the much larger negative merchandise trade or goods balance results in a negative overall trade balance. This negative trade balance remains of great concern to policy makers today. Unfortunately, throughout the first part of the twenty-first century the negative trade balances, particularly with China, have been increasing in size.

GROSS DOMESTIC PRODUCT AND CAPITAL FORMATION

All of a nation's output of goods and services may be consumed, or a portion of them may be saved. Individuals consume by making expenditures on durable and nondurable goods and services. Governments consume by purchasing goods and services. If all output is not consumed, savings can be invested to construct residential and commercial structures, manufacture producers' durable equipment, and increase business inventories. This process is termed **capital formation** and results in economic growth.

Recall that *gross domestic product (GDP)* is a nation's output of goods and services achieved over a specified period, such as one year. Increases in GDP over time measure the extent of economic growth, which is one of the country's national economic policy objectives. In Chapter 1 we focused on the relationship between GDP and monetary policy in terms of the money supply and velocity.

GDP is composed of consumption and investment components, as well as the net export of goods and services. More specifically, GDP consists of four components:

- Personal consumption expenditures
- Government expenditures, including gross investment
- Gross private domestic investment
- Net exports of goods and services

Personal consumption expenditures (PCE) indicate expenditures by individuals for durable goods, nondurable goods, and services. We all like to eat, buy clothes, have roofs over our heads, enjoy the comforts of heating and cooling, benefit from interior lighting, own automobiles and televisions, receive education, travel, and get haircuts and other services. The fact is we consume throughout our lives. Depending on where we are in our life cycles, we typically meet our consumption desires by spending our parents' earnings and savings during our formative years from birth through college graduation, generating our own earnings during our working lives, and spending our own savings during our retirement years.

Government expenditures (GE) include expenditures for goods and services plus gross investments by both the federal and the state and local governments. The federal government spends over one-half of its total expenditures on direct payments to individuals in the form of health, Social Security, and income security support. This should not be a surprise since some would argue that the "elected representatives of the people run the U.S. government for the benefit of the people."

Gross private domestic investment (GPDI) measures fixed investment in residential and nonresidential structures, producers' durable equipment, and changes in business inventories. The final component of GDP is the *net exports (NE)* of goods and services, or exports minus imports.

In equation form, we have:

$$GDP = PCE + GE + GPDI + NE \tag{3.1}$$

Consumption is reflected by the sum of personal consumption expenditures and government purchases of goods and services. Savings used for capital formation produce the gross private domestic investment. In addition, if the exports of goods and services exceed imports, GDP will be higher.

Table 3.1 shows the breakdown in these components for the United States for 2003 and 2006. For 2006 the gross domestic product was $13.3 trillion. Personal consumption expenditures of $9.3 trillion accounted for about 70 percent of GDP and show the importance of the individual in sustaining and improving the standard of living as reflected in GNP growth over time.

capital formation
process of constructing real property, manufacturing producers' durable equipment, and increasing business inventories

personal consumption expenditures (PCE)
expenditures by individuals for durable goods, nondurable goods, and services

government expenditures (GE)
expenditures for goods and services plus gross investments by federal, state, and local governments

gross private domestic investment (GPDI)
investment in residential and nonresidential structures, producers' durable equipment, and business inventories

net exports (NE)
exports of goods and services minus imports

INTERNET ACTIVITY

Go to the Web site of the Federal Reserve Bank of St. Louis, http://www.stls.frb.org. Access the Federal Reserve Economic Database (FRED) and find the current size of the U.S. gross domestic product (GDP) and its major components.

CONCEPT CHECK

What are personal consumption expenditures (PCE)?

What is meant by gross private domestic investment (GPDI)?

TABLE 3.1

Gross Domestic Product Consumption, Investment, and International Components ($ Billions)

	2003	2006
Total gross domestic product	**$10,987.9**	**$13,253.9**
Personal consumption expenditures	**7,757.4**	**9,270.8**
Durable goods	941.6	1,071.3
Nondurable goods	2,209.7	2,716.0
Services	4,606.2	5,483.6
Gross private domestic investment	**1,670.6**	**2,218.4**
Fixed investment	1,673.0	2,165.0
Nonresidential	1,110.6	1,397.9
Structures	259.2	411.6
Equipment and software	851.3	986.2
Residential structures	562.4	767.1
Change in private inventories	−2.4	53.4
Net exports of goods and services	**−495.0**	**−761.8**
Exports	1,048.9	1,466.2
Imports	1,543.8	2,228.0
Government consumption expenditures and gross investment	**2,054.8**	**2,526.4**
Federal	757.2	926.4
State and local	1,297.6	1,600.0

Source: *Survey of Current Business* (June 2004 and February 2006), p. D-3.

Government expenditures, in the form of consumption and gross investment, amounted to $2.5 trillion. Capital formation measured in terms of GPDI was $2.2 trillion. Net exports of goods and services amounted to a negative amount of nearly $.8 trillion in 2006.

FOUR POLICY MAKER GROUPS

Government and private policy makers often are maligned in the press, and sometimes even by themselves. For example, President Ronald Reagan said this in 1986:

> *The government's view of the economy could be summed up in a few short phrases: If it moves, tax it. If it keeps moving, regulate it. And if it stops moving, subsidize it.*

While this statement is somewhat humorous to most of us, it also serves to start us thinking about what should be the United States' broad-based economic objectives and what mechanisms

SMALL BUSINESS PRACTICE
Typical Life Cycle Patterns for the Small Venture Firm

A successful entrepreneurial firm will typically progress through several stages of financing. The first stage is called the *seed* or *development stage*. Here a firm works on an idea, development of a concept, or prototype product and may conduct some preliminary market research. If the firm is successful in producing a product or delivering a service, it moves into the start-up stage. Financing will be needed for "working capital" investments in inventories and to extend trade credit to customers. A manufacturing start-up also will need to invest in plant and equipment.

A third stage can be viewed as the *breakeven* stage, when the firm is now starting to generate enough revenues to cover its operating costs. A fourth stage represents the *recovery of investment* stage. If the firm continues to be successful, the fifth stage results in the *maximum generation of profits*. This occurs because cash flows from operations far exceed new capital expenditure requirements, as well as additional investment in working capital. A sixth stage may be viewed as *maturity* or *stability*.

Timmons and Spinelli report that it takes an average of two and a half years for a firm to break even from an operating standpoint and over six years on average to recover initial equity investments.* Of course, some firms will recover initial investment more rapidly, while others will fail or not progress beyond the start-up stage. Ultimately, a plan is needed for how the successful entrepreneur will "exit" or leave the business. For example, the firm could be sold or merged with another firm.

*Jeffry A. Timmons and Stephen Spinelli, *New Venture Creation,* 7th ed. (New York: McGraw-Hill/Irwin, 2007), pp. 390–391.

FIGURE 3.1

Policy Makers and Economic Policy Objectives

Policy Makers	Types of Policies or Decisions	Economic Objectives
Federal Reserve System The President Congress U.S. Treasury	Monetary Policy Fiscal Policy Debt Management	Economic Growth High Employment Price Stability International Balance

are needed for achieving these objectives. A system of checks and balances is needed to ensure that policy makers will operate in the best interests of the people of the United States. The president and Congress pass laws and set fiscal policy, while the Fed sets monetary policy and attempts to regulate the supply of money and the availability of credit.

Four groups of policy makers are actively involved in achieving the economic policy objectives of the United States:

- Federal Reserve System
- The president
- Congress
- U.S. Treasury

Figure 3.1 illustrates how the four groups use monetary and fiscal policies, supported by debt management practices, to carry out the four economic objectives of economic growth, stable prices, high employment, and balance in international transactions.

As discussed previously, the Fed establishes monetary policy, and we will see later in this chapter how the money supply is actually changed. **Fiscal policy** reflects government influence on economic activity through taxation and expenditure plans. Fiscal policy is carried out by the president and Congress. The U.S. Treasury supports economic policy objectives through its debt management practices.

fiscal policy
government influence on economic activity through taxation and expenditure plans

ETHICAL BEHAVIOR IN GOVERNMENT

ETHICAL ISSUES

Since World War II, eleven individuals have served as president of the United States. One would expect that the leader of the United States should and would exhibit a very high level of moral and ethical behavior. We expect the people of the United States to practice sound ethical behavior by treating others fairly and honestly. Certainly, the president has the opportunity to lead by example.

Two recent presidents, Richard Nixon (who served as president during 1969–1974) and William Clinton (who served as president during 1993–2001), were each accused of unethical behavior while president. Nixon resigned on August 9, 1974, just before he was about to be impeached because of the Watergate offices break-in and scandal. In 1998, Clinton became the second president to be impeached by the House of Representatives. Clinton's handling of personal indiscretions with a White House intern led to his trial in the Senate. He was found not guilty and completed his second term.[1]

Unethical behavior in government has not been limited to presidents. There also have been accounts of unethical behavior on the part of members of Congress. Some have been convicted in criminal court. Since the mid-1970s at least twelve members have received prison sentences for such activities as accepting bribes, taking part in kickback schemes, extortion, illegal sex offenses, and mail fraud. While the activities of these individuals have tainted Congress, by far most members behave ethically both personally and professionally when representing the people who elected them. It is important to remember that the U.S. government and society have overcome the isolated unethical behavior of a few leaders.

---

1. For a further discussion of past U.S. presidents, see Frank Freidel and Hugh S. Sidey, *The Presidents of the United States of America*, Willard, OH: R. R. Donnelley and Sons, 1996.

POLICY MAKERS IN THE EUROPEAN ECONOMIC UNION

As in the United States, European governments use monetary and fiscal policies to try to achieve similar economic goals, such as economic growth and price stability. In December 1991, the members of the *European Union (EU)* signed the *Maastricht Treaty* in Maastricht, Netherlands. The objective was to converge their economies, fix member country exchange rates, and introduce the euro as a common currency at the beginning of 1999. Monetary and fiscal policy actions of each country were to focus on maintaining price stability, keeping government budget deficits below 3 percent of gross domestic product (GDP) and total government debt below 60 percent of GDP, and maintaining stability in relative currency exchange rates. Twelve members of the EU ratified the Maastricht Treaty and adopted the euro as their common currency; they are known as the *European Monetary Union (EMU)*.

It is striking that twelve countries with widely different applications of monetary and fiscal policies in the past could agree on similar economic and financial objectives. While each country continues to formulate its own fiscal policies today, the *European Central Bank (ECB)* focuses on maintaining price stability across the twelve EMU member countries. The sheer size of the EMU also means that European policy makers and U.S. policy makers must work closely together in trying to achieve the worldwide goals of economic growth and price stability.

GOVERNMENT INFLUENCE ON THE ECONOMY

The federal government plays a dual role in the economy. In its traditional role it provides services that cannot be provided as efficiently by the private sector. In this role it acts like a firm, employing resources and producing a product. The magnitude of this role and its influence on economic activity has led to its more modern role: guiding or regulating the economy. The decisions of a number of policy-making entities must be coordinated to achieve the desired economic objectives.

A government raises funds to pay for its activities in three ways:

- Levies taxes
- Borrows
- Prints money for its own use

Because the last option has tempted some governments, with disastrous results, Congress delegated the power to create money to the Fed. The U.S. federal government collects taxes to pay for most of its spending, and it borrows, competing for funds in the financial system, to finance its deficits.

To illustrate the complex nature of the government's influence on the economy, consider the many effects of a federal deficit. To finance it, the government competes with other borrowers in the financial system. This absorbs savings, and it may raise interest rates. Private investment may be reduced if it becomes more difficult for firms to borrow the funds needed. On the other hand, a deficit stimulates economic activity. The government is either spending more or collecting less in taxes, or both, leaving more income for consumers to spend. The larger the deficit, the more total spending, or aggregate demand, there will be. In some circumstances this stimulation of the economy generates enough extra income and savings to finance both the deficit and additional investment by firms.

Furthermore, the Fed may buy government securities, financing some of the deficit and providing additional reserves to the banking system, thus increasing the money supply. This process is known as **monetizing the debt**. The Fed has at times monetized some of the deficit, especially during World Wars I and II. It does not do so now since that would be counter to current monetary policy. It would also have a significant impact on the financial markets. The competition for funds would make it more difficult for some borrowers to meet their financing needs. The characteristics and maturities of debt sold by the Treasury would determine which sectors were most affected.

The decisions of policy makers enter this process at a number of points. The president and the Council of Economic Advisors formulate a *fiscal policy:* the relationship of the Treasury's tax

monetizing the debt
Fed increases the money supply to help offset the demand for increased funds to finance the deficit

plans to its expenditure plans to influence the economy of the nation. Congress must pass legislation authorizing the Treasury's plan or a variation of it. The Treasury is actually responsible for collecting taxes and disbursing funds and for the huge task of debt management, which includes financing current deficits and refinancing the outstanding debt of the government. As discussed in Chapter 2, the Fed contributes to the attainment of the nation's economic goals by formulating monetary policy. It uses its powers to regulate the growth of the money supply and thus influence interest rates and the availability of loans.

The principal responsibilities of these policy makers have not always been the same. When the Fed was established in 1913, most of the power to regulate money and credit was placed in its hands. However, as the public debt grew during World War I, the Great Depression of the 1930s, and World War II, the Treasury became vitally interested in credit conditions. Policies that affect interest rates and the size of the money supply affect the Treasury directly, since it is the largest borrower in the nation. Therefore, the U.S. Treasury took over primary responsibility for managing the federal debt. In managing the large public debt and various trust funds placed under its jurisdiction, the Treasury has the power to influence the money market materially. The Fed came back into its own in the 1950s and is now the chief architect of monetary policy.

When it is felt that the Fed is not being responsive to the needs of the economy, the president will usually exercise pressure. The president also formulates budgetary and fiscal policy, but Congress must pass legislation to implement these policies. Congress regularly exercises its authority to modify presidential proposals before passing legislation. In short, there is much overlap of influence among those who make policy decisions. All three types of policies, however, are directed toward achieving the four objectives: economic growth, high employment, price stability, and a balance in international transactions.

It should not be surprising that the policy instruments of the various policy makers at times put them at cross purposes. A long-standing debate continues over the balance between full employment and price stability. A particular policy that leads toward one may make the other more difficult to achieve, yet each objective has its supporters. As with all governmental policy, economic objectives are necessarily subject to compromise and trade-offs.

CONCEPT CHECK

What is fiscal policy?

What is monetizing the debt?

TRANSFERRING SAVINGS INTO INVESTMENTS

savings-investment process

involves the direct or indirect transfer of individual savings to business firms in exchange for their securities

The ***savings-investment process*** involves the direct or indirect transfer of individual savings to business firms in exchange for their financial instruments or securities. A broader view of the savings-investment process would include the exchange of pooled individual savings for mortgages or other loans to individuals wanting to buy houses or make other purchases. Pooled individual savings to purchase and hold debt securities issued by governmental units also could be included in a broader view of the savings-investment process.

However, our primary focus throughout this book is on the savings-investment process involving businesses. Figure 3.2 shows three ways whereby money is transferred from savers to a business firm. As illustrated in the top part, savers can directly purchase the securities (stocks or debt instruments) of a business firm by exchanging money for the firm's securities. No type of financial intermediary is used in this type of savings-investment transaction since it involves only a saver and the business firm.

The use of indirect transfers is the more common way by which money is transferred from savers to investors. The middle part of Figure 3.2 shows how the transfer process usually takes place when savers purchase new securities issued by a business. You should recall from Chapter 1 that this indirect transfer involves use of the primary securities market. In this process, investment banking firms operate to bring savers and security issuers together. Savers provide money to purchase the business firm's securities. However, rather than a direct transfer taking place, investment banking firms often first purchase the securities from the issuing firm and then resell the securities to the savers. However, no additional securities are created in this type of indirect transfer.

The bottom part of Figure 3.2 illustrates the typical capital formation process involving a financial institution. Savers deposit or invest money with a financial institution such as a bank, insurance company, or mutual fund. The financial intermediary issues its own securities to the saver. For example, a saver may give money in the form of currency to a bank in exchange for the

FIGURE 3.2

Savings-Investment Process: From Individual Savers to a Business Firm

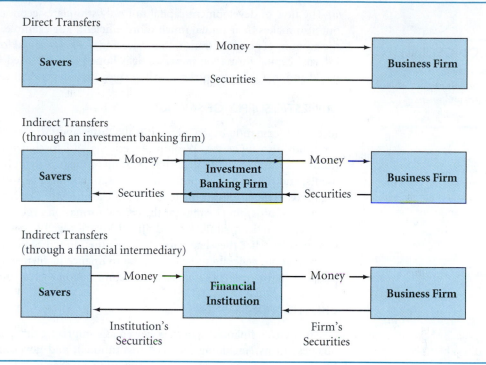

CONCEPT CHECK

What is the savings-investment process?

bank's certificate of deposit (CD). The bank, in turn, may lend money to a business firm in exchange for that firm's "I owe you" (IOU) in the form of a loan. As money passes from savers through a financial institution to a business firm, a debt instrument or security is created by the financial institution and by the business firm. This is the process of financial intermediation that was discussed in Chapter 1.

HISTORICAL ROLE AND CREATION OF SAVINGS

As the size of U.S. businesses expanded, the importance of accumulating and converting large amounts of financial capital to business use increased. The corporate form of organization provided a convenient and flexible legal arrangement for bringing together available financial capital. These advantages of the corporation over sole proprietorship, or private ownership, and partnership are described in Chapter 11.

Developments in public transportation were often too costly and speculative for private promoters to undertake. The magnitude of early canal, turnpike, and railroad construction was such that the government undertook much of the financing of these projects. In fact, until the end of the nineteenth century, governmental units contributed more funding to these efforts than did private interests. Since this government financing was accomplished largely through bond issues rather than current revenues, the ultimate source of funds was the savings of individuals who bought the bonds.

FOREIGN SOURCES OF SAVINGS

Foreign investors purchased large amounts of the securities sold by government and private promoters to develop the United States. In particular, foreign capital played a decisive role in the development of the nation's early transportation system.

The huge role that foreign capital played in the economic development of the United States is found in the developing nations of today. These nations now face many of the financial problems that the United States experienced during its early years. Private savings in many of these countries are negligible because almost all current income must be used for immediate consumption. Individual nations and such international organizations as the World Bank supply large amounts of capital to the developing nations of the world to increase their productive capacity.

The flow of development capital not only stimulates economic expansion in these countries but also makes their capital much more efficient. For example, speedier transportation reduces the amount of goods in transit, thus releasing working capital for other purposes. In due time, as internal capital formation increases, it is hoped that the need for foreign capital will be eliminated and that these countries can then enjoy an independent capital formation process.

DOMESTIC SUPPLY OF SAVINGS

As capital formation began increasing at a faster and faster rate after the Civil War, the demand for funds also increased. Wealthy Americans and foreign investors could no longer provide funds at a rapid enough rate. Britain was investing heavily in India because of political commitments, and the other European countries were not large or wealthy enough to continue supplying funds in quantities adequate to sustain U.S. growth. The American family soon took over the function of providing savings for the capital formation process. Per capita income rose to a level at which American families could afford luxuries well beyond the subsistence level and could save part of what they had earned. Thus, the United States gradually developed to the stage where it could generate sufficient capital to finance its own expansion. Ultimately the result was a change in the country's status from a debtor nation to a creditor nation.

CREATION OF SAVINGS

Today the U.S. financial system is viewed as comprising three basic economic units: individuals, business firms (including financial institutions), and governments (federal, state, and local). *Savings* occur when all of an economic unit's income is not consumed and are represented by the accumulation of cash and other financial assets. *Savings surplus* occurs when an economic unit, such as individuals taken as a group, has current income that exceeds its direct investment in real assets. These surplus savings are made available to savings deficit units. For example, business firms as a group are often unable to meet all their plant and equipment investment needs out of *undistributed profits* or earnings retained in the business, which are profits remaining after taxes and, in the case of corporations, after the cash dividends are paid to stockholders. When expenditures on real assets exceed current income, a *savings deficit* situation exists and it becomes necessary to acquire funds from a savings surplus unit.

MAJOR SOURCES OF SAVINGS

An important savings sector in the economy is the savings of individuals called *personal saving*. In equation form, we have:

$$\text{Personal saving} = \text{personal income} - \text{personal current taxes} - \text{personal outlays} \quad (3.2)$$

Personal income includes compensation of employees, personal income of persons with capital consumption adjustment, personal interest and dividend income, and net government social benefits to persons. Personal income less personal current taxes equals disposable personal income. Then, subtracting personal outlays (personal consumption expenditures, personal nonmortgage interest payments, and personal current transfer payments made primarily to the government) equals personal saving.

Voluntary savings are savings in the form of financial assets held or set aside for use in the future. *Contractual savings* are savings accumulated on a regular schedule for a specified length of time by prior agreement. An example is the accumulation of reserves in insurance and pension funds. Contractual savings are not determined by current decisions. They are disciplined by previous commitments that the saver has some incentive to honor.

It is from individuals that most financial intermediaries accumulate capital. Individuals as a group consistently represent a savings surplus unit. Corporations also represent an important source of savings. However, their large demand for investment funds, as is also the case for unincorporated business firms, generally results in a net need for external funds. While financial intermediaries can also save, their primary role in the U.S. financial system is to aid the savings-investment process. The U.S. government on balance has operated as a savings deficit unit in

CONCEPT CHECK

How were the savings of individuals important in the early development of the United States?

savings
income that is not consumed but is held in the form of cash and other financial assets

savings surplus
occurs when current income exceeds investment in real assets

undistributed profits
proportion of after-tax profits retained by corporations

savings deficit
occurs when investment in real assets exceeds current income

CONCEPT CHECK

What is the difference between savings surplus and savings deficit units?

personal saving
savings of individuals equal to personal income less personal current taxes less personal outlays

voluntary savings
savings held or set aside by choice for future use

contractual savings
savings accumulated on a regular schedule by prior agreement

INTERNET ACTIVITY

Go to the Web site of the Federal Reserve Bank of St. Louis, http://www.stls.frb.org. Access the Federal Reserve Economic Database (FRED) and find current information on the size of disposable personal income and personal savings.

TABLE 3.2
Personal Savings in the United States ($ Billions)

	2003	2006
Personal income	$9,208.0	$10,897.4
Less: personal current taxes	991.5	1,362.6
Disposable personal income	8,216.5	9,534.8
Less: personal outlays	8,043.0	9,626.8
Personal savings	173.5	−92.0
Savings rate (personal savings/disposable personal income)	2.1%	−1.0%

Sources: *Survey of Current Business* (June 2004 and February 2007), p. D-18.

recent years. Thus, the ability to provide adequate funds to meet investment needs primarily depends on the savings of individuals and corporations.

PERSONAL SAVINGS

Table 3.2 shows personal savings in the United States for 2003 and 2006. Personal income rose from $9.2 trillion in 2003 to $10.9 trillion in 2006. Personal current taxes also increased, and individuals increased their personal outlays from $8.0 trillion to $9.6 trillion. As a result, personal savings decreased from $173.5 billion in 2003 to a negative $92 billion in 2006. Thus, in terms of the personal savings rate in the United States, which is personal savings as a percentage of disposable personal income, the change was from 2.1 percent to −1.0 percent from 2003 to 2006. The 2003 U.S. savings rate is considerably below the personal savings rates in Japan and Western Europe, and the negative 2006 savings rate in the United States is very rare.

U.S. personal savings rates were higher in the past. For example, savings rates calculated from *Federal Reserve Bulletin* data for each five-year interval from 1960 through 2000 were as follows:

YEAR	SAVINGS RATES (%)	YEAR	SAVINGS RATES (%)
1960	5.8	1985	4.5
1965	7.0	1990	4.3
1970	8.1	1995	4.8
1975	9.2	2000	1.0
1980	7.1		

Notice that the savings rate increased from below 6 percent in 1960 to more than 9 percent by 1975. Tax reform in the form of lower personal income tax rates in the mid-1960s and in the 1970s may have contributed to this higher personal savings rate. However, the savings rate declined to less than 5 percent by 1985 and remained below 5 percent in 1990 and 1995 before dropping dramatically to the 1 percent level in 2000. Of course, we know from the data in Table 3.2 that the personal savings rate in the United States has declined dramatically—and even turned negative in 2006.

Individuals maintain savings for a number of reasons. They set aside a part of their current income to make mortgage payments on loans used to purchase homes. They also save to acquire costly durable consumer goods, such as cars and appliances. Savings are set aside by individuals to meet unforeseeable financial needs. These savings are not set aside for specific future consumption; instead, they represent emergency or rainy-day funds. Individuals may also save for such long-term foreseeable spending as children's college education or for retirement. For short periods, people may save a portion of current income simply because desirable goods and services are not available for purchase.

A number of media are available in which to maintain savings, ranging in liquidity from cash balances to stocks and bonds. Three factors usually influence a person's choice of medium: liquidity, degree of safety, and return. Various types of financial instruments and securities that individuals may hold are discussed later in this chapter.

CONCEPT CHECK

What are the differences between voluntary savings and contractual savings?

TABLE 3.3

Nonfinancial Corporate Savings in the United States ($ Billions)

	2003	2006 (Q3)
Profits before taxes (with IVA and CCAdj)	$617.0	943.9
Less: tax liabilities	129.4	299.6
Profits after taxes	487.6	644.3
Less: dividends	271.8	407.5
Undistributed profits	215.8	236.8
Retention rate (undistributed profits/profits after taxes)	46.3%	36.8%
Addenda:		
Profits before taxes (with IVA and CCAdj)	$617.0	943.9
Inventory valuation adjustment (IVA)	−12.6	−38.2
Capital consumption adjustment (CCAdj)	207.1	−137.1
Adjusted profits before taxes	422.6	1,119.2

Source: *Survey of Current Business* (June 2004 and February 2007), p. D-17.

Table 3.3 shows nonfinancial corporate savings in the United States for 2003 and the third quarter of 2006. Corporate profits before taxes increased from $617.0 billion in 2003 to $943.9 billion in 2006. At the same time, tax liabilities increased from $129.4 billion to $299.6 billion, which resulted in an increase in profits after taxes from $487.6 billion in 2003 to $644.3 billion in 2006. These developments reflect the continuing economic growth since the 2001 recession.

CORPORATE SAVINGS

Corporations save by producing profits after taxes and then not paying all these profits out to investors in the form of dividends. The proportion of after-tax profits retained in the organization is referred to as *undistributed profits*. Corporate profits that were not distributed to owners amounted to $215.8 billion in 2003 and $236.8 billion in 2006 and resulted in *retention rates* (undistributed profits divided by profits after taxes) of 46.3 percent and 36.8 percent, respectively.

Table 3.3 refers to nonfinancial corporate profits before taxes and includes an inventory valuation adjustment (IVA) and a capital consumption adjustment (CCAdj). Inventory values may increase or decrease in a given year and thus can affect nonfinancial corporate profits before taxes. **Capital consumption adjustment**, also called *depreciation,* is the estimate of the "using up" of plant and equipment assets for business purposes. By subtracting the IVA and CCAdj amounts from the profits before taxes (including IVA and CCAdj), the results were adjusted profits before taxes of $422.6 billion in 2003 and $1,119.2 billion in 2006.

Corporate saving for short-term working capital purposes is by far the most important reason for accumulating financial assets. Seasonal business changes create an uneven demand for corporate operating assets, such as inventories and accounts receivable. Because of these seasonal changes, cash inflow is seldom in just the right amount and at the right time to accommodate the increased levels of operating assets. Quarterly corporate income tax liabilities also impose the necessity of accumulating financial assets. The short-term accumulation of financial assets on the part of business corporations does not add to the level of long-term savings of the economy as a whole. However, these funds do enter the monetary stream and become available to users of short-term borrowed funds. As such, these short-term savings serve to meet a part of the demand for funds of consumers, government, and other businesses. A corporation typically holds this type of savings in the form of checkable deposits with commercial banks, short-term obligations of the federal government, commercial paper, and certificates of deposit issued by commercial banks. These financial assets meet the requirements of safety and liquidity.

Corporations also engage in the savings process to meet planned spending in the future. Reserves are often set up to provide all or part of the cost of construction, purchase of equipment, or major maintenance and repairs to existing facilities. Savings committed to these purposes are often invested in securities that have longer maturities and higher yields than those held for short-term business purposes. These securities include the debt obligations of both corporations and government and, to a limited extent, corporate stock.

capital consumption adjustment

estimates of the "using up," or depreciation, of plant and equipment assets for business purposes

CONCEPT CHECK

What are capital consumption adjustments?

How do corporations save?

FACTORS AFFECTING SAVINGS

Several factors influence the total amount of savings in any given period:

- Levels of income
- Economic expectations
- Cyclical influences
- Life stage of the individual saver or corporation

The precise relationship between savings and consumption is the subject of much debate and continuing study, however, and we limit our observations here to broad generalizations.

LEVELS OF INCOME

For our purposes, savings have been defined as current income minus tax payments and consumption spending. Keeping this definition in mind, let us explore the effect of changes in income on the levels of savings of individuals. As income falls, the individual attempts to maintain his or her present standard of living as long as possible. In so doing, the proportion of his or her consumption spending increases and total savings diminish. As income is further reduced, the individual may be forced to curtail consumption spending, which results in a lower standard of living. Such reduction is reasonably limited, however, since the basic needs of the individual, or family unit, must be met. Not only will personal savings be eliminated when income is drastically reduced, but the individual may also *dissave*—that is, spend accumulated savings rather than further reduce consumption spending.

> *dissave*
> *to liquidate savings for consumption uses*

As income increases, the individual will again be in a position to save. However, the saving will not necessarily begin immediately, as the individual may desire to buy the things that he or she could not afford during the low-income period. The amount of this need, notably for durable consumer goods, largely determines the rate of increase in savings during periods of income recovery.

On the whole, income levels are closely associated with levels of employment. Changes in business activity, in turn, influence employment levels. Downturns in the economy during 1980, 1981–1982, 1990, and 2001 resulted in declines in employment levels and correspondingly lowered levels of income. Post–World War II unemployment highs of the early 1980s exceeded 10 percent. During the decade of the 1990s unemployment averaged less than 5 percent, with deviations resulting in higher levels in the 1990 and 2001 recessions.

ECONOMIC EXPECTATIONS

The anticipation of future events has a significant effect on savings. If individuals believe that their incomes will decrease in the near future, they may curtail their spending to establish a reserve for the expected period of low income. For example, a worker anticipating a protracted labor dispute may increase current savings as partial protection against the financial impact of a strike.

Expectations of a general increase in price levels may also have a strong influence on the liquidity that savers want to maintain. The prospect of price increases in consumer durable goods may cause an increase in their sales as individuals try to buy before prices increase. Savings are thus quickly converted to consumer spending. Corporate savings, too, may be reduced as a result of price increase expectations. In addition to committing funds to plant and office equipment before price increases take place, corporations typically increase their inventory positions. As for the individual, the prospect of an interruption in the supply of inventory because of a labor strike or other cause often results in a rapid stockpiling of raw materials and merchandise. The prospect of price decreases and of large production capacity has the opposite effect: The liquidity and financial assets of a business increase relative to its operating assets.

Unprecedented price increases during the inflationary 1970s led many individuals to develop a "buy it now because it will cost more later" philosophy. This resulted in a classic example of the impact of price increase expectations on the spend–save decisions of individuals. Inflation peaked at double-digit levels at the beginning of the 1980s. However, after some upward pressure in the form of price increases at the end of the 1980s, inflation during the 1990s and the early years of the twenty-first century has been in the 2 percent to 3 percent range.

ECONOMIC CYCLES

Cyclical movements in the economy are the primary cause of changes in levels of income. Cyclical movements affect not only the amounts but also the types of savings. Economic cycles may be viewed in terms of the two- to four-year traditional business cycle or in terms of much longer cycles that correspond with generations of people.

Let's begin with a discussion that concentrates on the traditional business cycle. In general, interest rates on securities with short maturities are lower than interest rates on long-term maturities.[2] However, when economic activity is peaking, short-term interest rates are higher than long-term interest rates, generally because interest rates are high because inflation rates are high and the Fed raises short-term interest rates even further to slow economic activity and reduce inflation. As a recession deepens, short-term interest rates fall faster than long-term interest rates. Finally, when interest rates get low enough, businesses will find it attractive to borrow and grow. The savings rate usually goes down in a recessionary period and savers emphasize liquidity and safety when they do save. When the economy is growing, individuals usually save more and may hold their savings in riskier short-term securities.

Harry Dent, Jr., discusses much longer cycles based on *generation waves,* with the largest generation wave in the history of the United States being the baby boom wave.[3] In his view, a generation wave consists of birth wave, innovation wave, spending wave, and organization wave components or stages. These components correspond with birth, coming of age, adulthood, and maturity. For the baby boom generation, the birth wave peaked in the early 1950s. The innovation wave peaked in the 1980s. This was a period of rapid introduction of new technologies, and the country began the movement from a production economy to an information economy. According to Dent, the spending wave, in turn, which will peak early in this century, has driven the economic successes of the 1990s. The last stage will peak when the baby boomers reach age sixty-five in roughly 2025. While a lot of economists are skeptical about broad-based generalizations made by Harry Dent and others, all will agree that the economic clout of a large number of individuals moving through their life cycles at about the same time can influence the economy and the securities markets.

CONCEPT CHECK

What are general factors that affect savings?

LIFE STAGES OF THE INDIVIDUAL SAVER

The pattern of savings over an individual's life span follows a somewhat predictable pattern when viewed over the total population. A successful individual life cycle would have the following stages:

- Formative/education developing
- Career starting/family creating
- Wealth building
- Retirement enjoying

Individuals save very little during their formative and education developing stage simply because little income is produced. They typically consume a portion of their parents' earnings and savings, which is substantial if they attend college. As they enter their career starting and family creating stage, they possess little savings but have large "earning power" potential. Their income increases. However, expenses also increase during these early family-forming years. Saving and investing typically focus on purchasing a home and accruing life and disability insurance.

By the time an individual reaches his or her wealth building stage, two new factors result in increased savings. First, income is typically much higher than at any previous time; second, the expense of raising and educating children has been reduced or eliminated. Thus it is this group that typically saves the most. At the retirement-enjoying stage, the individual's income is sharply reduced. He or she may now begin the process of *dissaving.* Pension fund payments, along with accumulated savings, are drawn upon for current living expenses.

---

2. We discuss the term or maturity structure of interest rates in detail in Chapter 4.

3. Harry Dent Jr., *The Great Boom Ahead,* New York: Hyperion, 1993. Also see Harry Dent, Jr., *The Roaring 2000s,* New York: Simon & Schuster, 1998.

The level of savings of individuals is therefore a function of the age composition of the population as a whole. A population shift to a large proportion of individuals in the productive middle-age years would result in a greater savings potential. These views of the life stages of the individual saver are consistent with the generation-wave approach described by Harry Dent, Jr. That is, if a large number of individuals are moving through their individual life cycles at approximately the same time, their combined efforts will have a major impact on the overall economy. On a collective basis, they spend at about the same time and are also likely to save at about the same time. Spending has kept the U.S. economy in almost continual growth since the early 1980s, and saving/investing in retirement plans and directly in mutual funds (which in turn buy bonds and stocks) helped the stock market reach historical highs during the 1990s. However, since then a substantial decline in stock prices preceded a downturn in economic activity at the beginning of the twenty-first century.

LIFE STAGES OF THE CORPORATION

Just as the financial savings of an individual are governed in part by age, so the financial savings generated by a business firm are a function of its life stage. The following are the life cycle stages of a successful business firm:

- Start-up stage
- Survival stage
- Rapid growth stage
- Maturity stage

It is true, of course, that not all business firms proceed through a fixed life-stage cycle. To the extent, however, that a firm experiences the typical pattern of starting up, surviving, vigorous growth, and ultimate maturity, its flow of financial savings may experience a predictable pattern.

During the development of the business idea and starting the business stage, the firm is spending cash rather than building cash. The business firm typically continues to burn cash as it tries to find a successful operating niche. During the early part of the expansion years (rapid growth stage) of a successful business, the volume of physical assets typically increases rapidly. So rapid is this growth that the firm is unable to establish a strong position with respect to its financial assets. Indeed, it is during these years of the corporate life cycle that there is a large need for borrowed capital. At this time the corporation is typically a heavy user of financial assets rather than a provider.

As the firm reaches the second part of its rapid growth stage, it begins building surplus or "free" cash flow and increasing the firm's value. Free cash is money available after funds have been reinvested in the firm to sustain its growth. As the enterprise matures and its growth slows down to a long-run sustainable growth rate, it reaches its peak of savings. Earnings and cash flows are high, and commitment of funds to increased operating assets is reduced. The maturity stage can last almost indefinitely as long as the firm remains competitive in its industry. Of course, sometimes a firm's products or services are no longer competitive or needed by consumers and the firm again starts consuming more cash than it brings in. Such firms will eventually cease to exist.

TYPES OF ASSETS

As discussed in Chapter 1, money is the fundamental measure of value or wealth. In addition to money, an individual or a business also measures its wealth in terms of the real and financial assets or claims (in addition to money) that it holds. **Real assets** are physical or tangible assets that provide value or wealth to their owners. Examples are the direct ownership of land, buildings or homes, equipment, furniture, inventories, durable goods, and even precious metals.

Financial assets are intangible contracts, often backed by real assets, which provide value or wealth to their owners. Examples are debt instruments, equity securities, and other financial contracts. Many financial assets provide for a future payment of cash or money, often greater than the initial amount borrowed or paid for the financial asset. A loan to you to purchase an automobile usually provides for the lender to hold the auto title (ownership) until the loan is

CONCEPT CHECK

How does the pattern of savings usually differ over an individual's lifetime?

CONCEPT CHECK

What are some of the stages in a typical corporate life cycle?

real assets
physical assets that provide value or wealth to their owners

financial assets
contractual assets often backed by real assets that provide value or wealth to their owners

repaid. Long-term debt issued by a corporation may represent a claim against specific assets, such as buildings and equipment, or the general assets of the issuer. A mortgage loan to you will be backed by the house against which the loan is made. In addition to the need to repay the amount borrowed, most debt instruments also provide the payment of interest to compensate the lenders for the period of time between when money is lent and when money is repaid.

Although money (currency) is tangible in that you can physically hold it and it is a store of value, it is considered to be a financial asset. For example, when the public holds currency issued today by the U.S. government, the currency is a financial asset and has "value" because the government decreed it to be "legal tender" for making payments and discharging debts. At the same time, currency is a financial liability to the government.

While money is the fundamental measure of wealth, a the net worth of a business firm or an individual usually consists of more than just money. A business firm measures its *net worth* as its assets (both real and financial) less its financial liabilities reflecting money owed. **Individual net worth** is the sum of an individual's money, real assets, and other financial assets or claims against others less the individual's debt obligations. Recall that real assets include the automobile that you own, your house (if you have one) and its contents, clothes, and even jewelry or precious stones. You may also own shares of stock in a mutual fund; while this is a financial asset, it is still part of your net worth. However, you may have borrowed from a bank to purchase your auto, and you probably have a mortgage loan on the house you purchased. These are financial claims held by others against some of your real property. You must subtract debt obligations or financial claims against you or your real property in order to determine your individual net worth. It is estimated that there are about 8 million millionaires in the world with about 2.5 million of them in the United States.[4] If you wish to join this group someday, you will have to accumulate a net worth in excess of $1 million. Good luck!

individual net worth
an individual's money, real assets, and other financial assets less the individual's debt obligations

CONCEPT CHECK

What are real assets?

What are financial assets?

TYPES OF FINANCIAL INSTRUMENTS OR SECURITIES

Figure 3.3 indicates the major types of financial instruments and securities that are issued and traded in financial markets. A **Treasury bill** is a short-term debt obligation issued by the U.S. federal government to meet its short-term borrowing needs when imbalances exist between tax revenues and government expenditures. Treasury bills are generally issued with maturities between three months (technically ninety days) and one year. Investors buy Treasury bills for safety and liquidity reasons. First, it is extremely unlikely that the federal government will default on its debt obligations. Second, there is an active *secondary* money market for Treasury bills, so investors can easily sell them at any time before maturity if cash needs arise.

A **negotiable certificate of deposit (CD)** is a short-term debt instrument issued by depository institutions to individual or institutional depositors. Negotiable certificates of deposit are issued by commercial banks in denominations of $100,000 or more, with typical maturities ranging

Treasury bill
short-term debt obligation issued by the U.S. federal government

negotiable certificate of deposit (CD)
short-term debt instrument issued by depository institutions that can be traded in secondary markets

FIGURE 3.3

Types of Financial Instruments and Securities

INSTRUMENTS OR SECURITIES	ISSUERS	MATURITIES
Treasury bills	U.S. government	Up to 1 year
Negotiable certificates of deposit (CDs)	Commercial banks	Less than 1 year
Commercial paper	Corporations	Less than 1 year
Bankers' acceptances	Commercial banks	Less than 1 year
Eurodollar deposits	Commercial banks	Up to 1 year
Mortgages	Financial Intermediaries	Up to about 30 years
Treasury bonds	U.S. government	Up to about 30 years
Municipal bonds	State/local governments	Up to about 30 years
Corporate bonds	Corporations	Up to about 30 years
Corporate stocks	Corporations	None

4. To learn more about how people become wealthy and some of their characteristics, see Thomas J. Stanley and William D. Danko, *The Millionaire Next Door* (New York: Pocket Books, 1996) and Thomas J. Stanley, *The Millionaire Mind* (Kansas City, MO: Andrews McMeel Publishing, 2001).

from one month to one year. Negotiable CDs are money market securities with an active secondary market that allows short-term investors to easily match their cash or liquidity needs when they arise. It is important to recognize that negotiable CDs differ from smaller-denomination CD time deposits offered by depository institutions to individual depositors. Small-deposit CDs are nonnegotiable and must be redeemed with the issuer, and thus no secondary securities market exists for them. In fact, owners of nonnegotiable CDs redeemed before maturity usually are charged an interest deduction penalty.

Businesses often find it necessary to borrow short-term to meet temporary imbalances between when cash is received from sales and when bills must be paid. *Commercial paper* is a short-term unsecured promissory note issued by a corporation with high-quality credit. Maturities on commercial paper are generally one to three months in length. However, since there is an active secondary money market for commercial paper, purchasers can easily sell their commercial paper holdings at any time to meet their cash needs.

A *bankers' acceptance* is a promise of future payment for goods or services purchased on credit by a firm and guaranteed by a bank. This form of debt instrument is used to finance exports and imports and plays an important role in fostering international trade. For example, an exporter may not know the financial quality of a foreign firm that may wish to purchase the exporter's products on credit. Having a bank "accept" or guarantee the importer's debt obligation removes the exporter's concern about being paid.

A *Eurodollar deposit*, sometimes just referred to as *Eurodollars,* is U.S. dollar funds placed in a foreign bank that remain denominated in U.S. dollars. For example, a demand or time deposit denominated in U.S. dollars held in a U.S. bank that is transferred to a foreign bank, or overseas branch of a U.S. bank, becomes a Eurodollar deposit. This is so because the deposit remains denominated in U.S. dollars and not in the currency of the country where the foreign bank operates.

A *mortgage* is a loan against which a borrower pledges real property as collateral for the loan. In the event the debt is not repaid, the lender can use proceeds from the sale of the real property to extinguish any remaining loan interest or principal balance. Individuals rely heavily on residential mortgages to assist them in owning their own homes. Businesses also often find it worthwhile to borrow against the real property they own.

Bonds are long-term debt instruments issued by government units and business corporations. A *Treasury bond,* sometimes referred to as a *note* for shorter securities, is a debt instrument or security issued by the U.S. federal government with a typical maturity ranging from five to twenty years. Treasury bonds are sold to raise funds needed to reconcile longer-term imbalances between tax receipts and government expenditures. These bonds have very low risks of default, and investors know that they are easily marketable in the secondary securities market. For example, if an investor initially purchases a twenty-year federal government bond and later identifies another investment opportunity, the bond can be easily sold in the secondary capital market. A *municipal bond* is a debt instrument or security issued by a state or local government. Maturities on state and local government bonds, like Treasury bonds, often are in the five-year to twenty-year range. However, municipal bonds issued to build airports or bridges may have their maturities set approximately equal to the expected lives of the assets being financed. Some investors find municipal bonds to be attractive investments because the interest paid on these securities is exempt from federal income taxes and because these bonds also can be sold in a secondary market.

Corporations issue financial instruments or securities, called *debt* and *equity,* to raise funds to acquire real assets to support the operations of their firms. Corporate debt instruments are bonds and equity securities are stocks. A *corporate bond* is a debt instrument issued by a corporation to raise long-term funds. Corporate bonds are typically issued with five- to twenty-year maturities and may be secured by the pledge of real property, plant, or equipment, or they may be issued with only the backing of the general credit strength of the corporation. (Various types of corporate bonds and their characteristics are discussed in later chapters.) A share of *common stock* represents an ownership interest in a corporation. Corporations often issue new shares of their common stocks to raise funds for capital expenditures and investments in inventories. Active secondary markets exist for trading the common stocks of larger corporations after the stocks are initially issued. Corporations also can issue various classes of common stock, another type of stock called *preferred stock,* and even securities that are convertible into shares of common stock, as will be discussed later.

commercial paper
short-term unsecured promissory note issued by a corporation with high-quality credit

bankers' acceptance
promise of future payment for credit purchases by a firm and guaranteed by a bank

Eurodollar deposit
funds placed in a foreign bank that remain denominated in U.S. dollars

mortgage
loan against which a borrower pledges real property as collateral for the loan

Treasury bond
long-term debt instrument issued by the U.S. federal government

municipal bond
long-term debt instrument issued by a state or local government

corporate bond
debt instrument issued by a corporation to raise long-term funds

common stock
ownership interest in a corporation

COMFORT WENDEL
Trust Officer, Fifth Third Bank

BA, Economics,
Smith College

"I really act more as a consultant than as a true salesperson."

Q: *You're a trust officer at Fifth Third Bank. What does your job entail?*

A: I help companies select, set up, and manage retirement plans for their employees.

Q: *If I owned or managed a company, what would you do for me?*

A: First, I would take the time to learn about your firm and help you choose the kind of retirement plan that makes sense for your company's workforce, budget, and growth prospects. I would work directly with your upper management to ensure the plan is set up properly. I would then conduct enrollment seminars to help employees understand and hopefully participate in the plan.

Q: *So you're involved during the sales process and afterward.*

A: Right. I spend approximately 30 percent of my time working with prospects. During the sales process I really act more as a consultant than as a true salesperson. The rest of my time is spent working with the approximately forty existing client plans I am responsible for. I am considered the "relationship officer" so I address not only retirement plan issues but also other customer service needs that the client may have. I also spend a considerable amount of time selling the retirement plan to the employees.

Q: *What does the employee education entail?*

A: Since most of the plans we manage are 401(k) plans that involve employee contributions through payroll deduction, we explain the importance of saving for retirement. We often have to convince people that they can afford to save. We also focus on investment basics. We explain stocks, bonds, and mutual funds and help them select the investment strategy appropriate for their risk tolerance and age.

Q: *How did you end up in this job?*

A: When I got out of college I looked into several bank training programs. I liked Fifth Third's because it included two- to three-month "rotations" in different areas of the bank. That's how I learned about the department I work in now.

Q: *What skills help you most in your job?*

A: It's definitely a people-oriented job. I have continual contact with clients, prospects, and employees and also manage a team of people who do all the day-to-day detail work for our clients. People skills and communication skills are very important. Obviously financial and analytical skills are important, but oddly enough I've found that my ability to write has been a big help, too. I am constantly sending letters to clients and attorneys and preparing proposals and employee presentation materials. Thinking on your feet and public speaking help, too.

Q: *You went to Smith, an all-women's college. Now you work in banking, which historically has been a male-dominated business. Has it been a difficult adjustment?*

A: Smith was a great preparation for the business world. At Smith all the student leadership positions are held by women. Smith gave me the self-confidence to assert myself and move forward. I wasn't afraid to take responsibility and speak my mind when I got to Fifth Third because that was standard procedure at Smith.

CONCEPT CHECK

What financial instruments typically have maturities up to one year?

What financial instruments and securities typically have maturities in excess of one year?

primary markets
markets in which financial instruments and securities are initially offered or sold with the proceeds going to the issuer

secondary markets
markets in which previously issued or "seasoned" instruments or securities are traded.

money markets
markets in which debt instruments of one year or less are traded

capital markets
markets for debt securities with maturities longer than one year and corporate stocks

securities markets
physical locations or electronic forums where debt and equity securities are sold and traded

mortgage markets
where mortgage loans, backed by real property are originated and sometimes traded

derivatives markets
facilitate purchase and sale of derivative securities, which are financial contracts that derive their values from underlying securities

Corporations also can use derivative securities to insure or hedge against various financial risks. A **derivative security** is a financial contract that derives its value from the value of another asset, such as a bond or stock. The use of derivatives is explored in Chapter 9.

TYPES OF FINANCIAL MARKETS

Now that we have identified some of the major financial instruments or securities that are important to an efficiently operating financial system, we can turn to a brief discussion of the markets where such financial assets are initially offered, along with where these instruments and securities are bought and sold or are traded. **Primary markets** are markets in which financial instruments and securities are initially offered or sold with the proceeds going to the issuer. For example, "new" issues of bonds or stocks might be privately placed with a financial intermediary or sold to the general public in the primary market. **Secondary markets** are markets in which previously issued or "seasoned" instruments or securities are traded. In contrast with primary market issues, no proceeds are received by the issuing corporations when financial instruments or securities are sold in secondary markets. Rather, funds are only exchanged between the buyers and sellers of seasoned securities.

Debt and equity securities are the primary types of financial claims that are actively traded in secondary markets. **Money markets** are the markets in which debt securities with maturities of one year or less are traded. **Capital markets** include debt instruments with maturities longer than one year and corporate stocks or equity securities.

There are four types of secondary financial markets: securities markets, mortgage markets, derivatives markets, and currency exchange markets. Most of us have some idea about the markets for securities. **Securities markets** are physical locations or electronic forums where previously issued debt and equity securities are sold and traded. Debt instruments or bonds are obligations to repay borrowed funds. Federal, state, and local governments can issue debt instruments, while business corporations and financial institutions can issue both debt instruments and equity securities, which are ownership rights in businesses and institutions.

Corporations can raise "new" funds either through a *private placement,* which involves issuing new securities directly to specific investors, or through an *initial public offering* (IPO), which involves selling new securities to the general public.

All proceeds, less issuing costs, from the sale of new securities go to the issuing business. The primary market, where new issues are sold, is the only "market" where the security issuer directly benefits (receives funds) from the sale of its securities. Purchasers of "new" securities can either hold the securities or sell them in the secondary securities markets.

Secondary markets for securities facilitate the transfer of previously issued securities from existing investors to new investors. Security transactions or transfers typically take place on organized security exchanges or in the electronic over-the-counter market. Individuals and other investors can actively buy and sell existing securities in the secondary market. While these secondary market investors may make gains or losses on their securities investments, the issuer of the securities does not benefit (or lose) from these activities. Primary and secondary securities markets are discussed in detail in Chapter 11.

Mortgage markets are markets in which mortgage instruments or loans, backed by real property in the form of buildings and houses, are originated and sometimes traded in a secondary market. *Mortgage loans* are usually long-term loans backed by real property, and typically they are repaid in monthly installments of interest and a partial repayment of the loan amount that was borrowed. If a mortgage loan is not repaid by the borrower, the lender can seize and sell the pledged real property under foreclosure laws. While buying and selling individual home mortgages in a secondary market remains a difficult undertaking, in recent years standardized high-quality mortgages have been "pooled" together into mortgage-backed securities that have active secondary markets. Home mortgage loans to individuals are made available primarily through depository institutions and mortgage companies.

Derivatives markets facilitate the purchase and sale of derivative securities, which are financial contracts that derive their values from underlying securities or from other related financial assets. A familiar form of derivative security is the opportunity to buy or sell a corporation's equity securities for a specified price and within a certain amount of time. Derivative securities

currency exchange markets
electronic markets in which financial intermediaries buy and sell various currencies on behalf of businesses and other clients

CONCEPT CHECK

What are the four types of financial markets?

may be used to speculate on the future price direction of the underlying financial assets, or to reduce price risk associated with holding the underlying financial assets. Organized exchanges handle standardized derivative security contracts, while negotiated contracts are handled in electronic markets often involving commercial banks or other financial institutions. Derivative securities are discussed in Chapter 9.

Currency exchange markets (also called *foreign exchange* or *FOREX markets*) are electronic markets in which banks and institutional traders buy and sell various currencies on behalf of businesses and other clients. In the global economy, consumers may want to purchase goods produced, or services provided, in other countries. Likewise, an investor residing in one country may wish to hold securities issued in another country. For example, a U.S. consumer may wish to purchase a product in a foreign country. If the product is priced in the foreign country's currency, to complete the transaction it may be necessary to exchange U.S. dollars for the foreign currency. Businesses that sell their products in foreign countries usually receive payment in the corresponding foreign currencies. However, because the relative values of currencies may change, firms often use the currency exchange markets to reduce the risk of holding too much of certain currencies. Currency exchange rates and currency exchange markets are discussed in Chapter 18.

APPLYING FINANCE TO . . .

INSTITUTIONS AND MARKETS

The savings-investment process provides three ways for individual savers to transfer money to business firms. Direct transfers occur when savers give money to a business firm in exchange for the business firm's debt or equity securities. Savers may also make indirect transfers. Money may be transferred through an investment banking firm from individual savers to a business firm. An indirect transfer also may be made through a financial institution whereby savers first loan money to the financial institution by purchasing its debt instruments. The financial institution, in turn, loans the money it received from savers to the business firm by buying the firm's debt securities.

INVESTMENTS

Governments issue debt securities to finance their needs, and corporations issue both debt and equity securities to maintain and grow their businesses. The savings of individuals are the primary source for raising financial capital by governments and corporations. Financial institutions gather savings and make the savings available to governments and corporations in the primary securities markets. The factors that determine interest rates for borrowing financial capital are discussed in Chapter 4. Factors affecting the valuation of bonds and stocks are covered in Chapters 7 and 8.

FINANCIAL MANAGEMENT

Financial managers often must raise additional amounts of debt and equity funds to finance the plans for their firms. While they may depend somewhat on loans from banks, they may also need to attract financial capital by selling bonds or stocks either privately or publicly. A decision to raise funds must be accompanied with the willingness to pay the required interest rates established in the marketplace or selling stock at a market-determined price. The need by business firms for financial capital will also depend on economic conditions and the business firm's life cycle stage.

SUMMARY

This chapter initially focused on identifying and discussing the U.S. national economic policy objectives of economic growth, high employment, price stability, and the need for a balance in international transactions. We then discussed gross domestic product (GDP) and its four components: personal consumption expenditures (PCE), government expenditures (GE), gross private domestic investment (GPDI), and net exports (NE). This was followed by the identification and discussion of the four policy maker groups, which include the Federal Reserve System, the president, Congress, and the U.S. Treasury. How the government can influence the economy by levying taxes, borrowing, or printing money for its own use also was discussed.

We next turned our attention to understanding the savings-investment process whereby funds are transferred from individual savings to business firms in exchange for the business firms' financial instruments or securities. This was followed by a brief review of the historical role and creation of savings in the U.S. The three basic economic units were identified as individuals, business firms (including financial intermediaries), and governments. Major sources of savings in the United States come from individuals and business firms. Factors that affect the level of savings include levels of income, economic expectations, cyclical influences, and the life stage of the individual saver or corporation.

Real assets and financial assets were identified. Then major types of financial instruments or securities were discussed. Financial instruments with maturities up to one year include Treasury bills, negotiable certificates of deposit, commercial paper, bankers' acceptances, and Eurodollar deposits. Financial instruments and securities with long-term or no maturities include mortgages, Treasury bonds, municipal bonds, corporate bonds, and common stocks. The four major types of financial markets are securities markets, mortgage markets, derivatives markets, and currency exchange markets.

KEY TERMS

bankers' acceptance

capital consumption adjustment

capital formation

capital markets

commercial paper

common stock

contractual savings

corporate bond

currency exchange markets

derivative security

derivatives market

dissave

Eurodollar deposit

financial assets

fiscal policy

government expenditures (GE)

gross domestic product (GDP)

gross private domestic investment (GPDI)

individual net worth

inflation

monetizing the debt

money markets

mortgage

mortgage markets

municipal bond

negotiable certificate of deposit (CD)

net exports (NE)

personal consumption expenditures (PCE)

personal saving

primary markets

real assets

savings

savings deficit

savings-investment process

savings surplus

secondary markets

securities markets

Treasury bill

Treasury bond

voluntary savings

undistributed profits

DISCUSSION QUESTIONS

1. List and briefly describe the economic policy objectives of the United States.

2. What is meant by the term *capital formation?*

3. Describe the major components of gross domestic product.

4. What are the four major policy maker groups? Describe the relationship among policy makers, types of policies, and policy objectives.

5. What is meant by the savings-investment process?

6. Describe the three basic ways whereby money is transferred from savers to a business firm.

7. Briefly describe the historical role of savings in the United States.

8. What are savings surplus and savings deficit units? Indicate which economic units are generally of one type or the other.

9. Define *personal saving.* Also, differentiate between voluntary and contractual savings.

10. Describe the recent levels of savings rates in the United States.

11. How and why do corporations save?

12. Describe the principal factors that influence the level of savings by individuals.

13. How do economic cycle movements affect the media or types of savings by businesses?

14. What are the life cycle stages of individuals? How does each stage relate to the amount and type of individual savings?

15. What are the life cycle stages of corporations and other business firms? Explain how financial savings generated by a business are a function of its life cycle stage.

16. What are real assets, and what are financial assets?

17. Identify and describe major types of financial instruments that have maturities up to one year in length.

18. Identify and describe major types of financial instruments and securities that have long-term or no maturities.

19. How do primary markets compare to secondary markets?

20. How do money markets compare to capital markets?

21. Identify and briefly explain the four types of financial markets.

EXERCISES

1. The U.S. government has four important policy objectives. The achievement of these objectives is the responsibility of monetary policy, fiscal policy, and debt management carried out by the Federal Reserve System, the president, Congress, and the U.S. Treasury. Identify the four economic policy objectives, and describe the responsibilities of the various policy makers in trying to achieve these objectives.

2. The president and members of Congress are elected by the people and are expected to behave ethically. Let's assume that you are a recently elected member of Congress. A special-interest lobbying group is offering to contribute funds to your next election campaign in the hope that you will support legislation being proposed by others that will help the group achieve its stated objectives. What would you do?

3. Obtain a current issue of the *Survey of Current Business* and determine the following:

   a. The current personal savings rate in the United States

   b. The amount of current corporate savings as reflected in the amount of undistributed profits

4. Match the following financial instruments and securities with their issuers.

Instruments/Securities	Issuers
a. corporate stocks	1. commercial banks
b. Treasury bonds	2. corporations
c. municipal bonds	3. U. S. government
d. negotiable certificates of deposit	4. state/local governments

5. Match the following financial instruments and securities with their typical maturities.

Instruments/Securities	Maturities
a. corporate stocks	1. less than one year
b. Treasury bills	2. no maturity
c. mortgages	3. up to about thirty years
d. commercial paper	4. up to one year

6. Obtain a current issue of the *Statistical Supplement to the Federal Reserve Bulletin*. Identify and compare interest rates for the past three years for U.S. federal government Treasury bills and bonds (refer to Figure 3.3).

PROBLEMS

1. A very small country's gross domestic product is $12 million.
   a. If government expenditures amount to $7.5 million and gross private domestic investment is $5.5 million, what would be the amount of net exports of goods and services?
   b. How would your answer change in (a) if the gross domestic product had been $14 million?

2. Personal income amounted to $17 million last year. Personal current taxes amounted to $4 million and personal outlays for consumption expenditures, nonmortgage interest, and so forth were $12 million.
   a. What was the amount of disposable personal income last year?
   b. What was the amount of personal saving last year?
   c. Calculate personal saving as a percentage of disposable personal income.

3. The components that comprise a nation's gross domestic product were identified and discussed in this chapter. Assume the following accounts and amounts were reported by a nation last year: government expenditures (purchases of goods and services) were $5.5 billion; personal consumption expenditures were $40.5 billion; gross private domestic investment amounted to $20 billion; capital consumption allowances were $4 billion; personal savings were estimated at $2 billion; imports of goods and services amounted to $6.5 billion; and exports of goods and services were $5 billion.
   a. Determine the nation's gross domestic product.
   b. How would your answer change if the dollar amounts of imports and exports were reversed?

4. Assume that some of the data provided in problem 1 change next year. Specifically, government expenditures increase by 10 percent; gross private domestic investment declines by 10 percent; and imports of goods and services drop to $6 billion. Assume the other information as given remains the same next year.
   a. Determine the nation's gross domestic product for next year.
   b. How would your answer change in (a) if personal consumption expenditures are only $35 billion next year and capital consumption allowances actually increase by 10 percent?

5. A nation's gross domestic product is $600 million. Its personal consumption expenditures are $350 million, and government expenditures are $100 million. Net exports of goods and services amount to $50 million.
   a. Determine the nation's gross private domestic investment.
   b. If imports exceed exports by $25 million, how would your answer to (a) change?

6. A nation's gross domestic product is stated in U.S. dollars at $40 million. The dollar value of one unit of the nation's currency (FC) is $0.25.
   a. Determine the value of GDP in FCs.
   b. How would your answer change if the dollar value of one FC increases to $0.30?

7. A country in Southeast Asia states its gross domestic product in terms of yen. Assume that last year its GDP was 50 billion yen when one U.S. dollar could be exchanged for 120 yen.
   a. Determine the country's GDP in terms of U.S. dollars for last year.
   b. Assume that the GDP increases to 55 billion yen for this year while the dollar value of one yen is now $0.01. Determine the country's GDP in terms of U.S. dollars for this year.
   c. Show how your answer in (b) would change if one U.S. dollar could be exchanged for 110 yen.

8. **Challenge Problem** (*Note:* This exercise requires knowledge of probabilities and expected values.) Following are data relating to a nation's operations last year:

Capital consumption allowances	$150 million
Undistributed corporate profits	40 million
Personal consumption expenditures	450 million
Personal savings	50 million
Corporate inventory valuation adjustment	25 million
Federal government deficit	230 million
Government expenditures	10 million
State and local governments surplus	1 million
Net exports of goods and services	22 million
Gross private domestic investment	200 million

   a. Determine the nation's gross domestic product (GDP).
   b. How would your answer change in (a) if exports of goods and services were $5 million and imports were 80 percent of exports?
   c. Show how the GDP in (a) would change under the following three scenarios:
   Scenario 1 (probability of .20): the GDP components would be 120 percent of their values in (a).
   Scenario 2 (probability of .50): the GDP component values used in (a) would occur.
   Scenario 3 (probability of .30): the GDP components would be 75 percent of their values in (a).
   d. Determine the nation's gross savings last year.
   e. Show how your answer in (d) would change if each account simultaneously increases by 10 percent.
   f. Show how your answer in (d) would change if each account simultaneously decreases by 10 percent.
   g. Show how your answer in (d) would have changed if capital consumption allowances had been 10 percent less and personal consumption expenditures had been $400 million.

• CHAPTER 4 •

Interest Rates

Chapter Learning Objectives

AFTER STUDYING THIS CHAPTER, YOU SHOULD BE ABLE TO:

- Describe how interest rates change in response to shifts in the supply and demand for loanable funds.
- Identify major historical movements in interest rates in the United States.
- Describe what is meant by the *loanable funds theory* of interest rates.
- Identify the major determinants of market interest rates.
- Describe the types of marketable securities issued by the U.S. Treasury.
- Describe the ownership of Treasury securities and the maturity distribution of the federal debt.
- Explain what is meant by the *term* or *maturity structure* of interest rates.
- Identify and briefly describe the three theories used to explain the term structure of interest rates.
- Identify broad historical price level changes in the United States and other economies and discuss their causes.
- Describe the various types of inflation and their causes.
- Discuss the effect of default risk premiums on the level of long-term interest rates.

Where We Have Been. . .

In Chapter 3 you learned about the savings-investment process as it takes place in the United States. The gross domestic product (GDP) and capital formation were discussed. GDP is composed of personal consumption expenditures, government purchases, gross private domestic investment and the net export of goods and services. You should also understand the major sources of savings and factors that affect savings. You also should be able to identify and briefly describe major financial instruments and securities that facilitate the savings-investment process and sometimes trade in financial markets.

Where We Are Going. . .

Chapter 5 focuses on the time value of money. By saving and investing, money can "grow" over time through the compounding of interest. We first cover simple interest and then turn to compounding of current investments (determining future values) and discounting of future cash receipts (finding present values). You will also be introduced to annuities, which are investments that involve constant periodic payments or receipts of cash. You will then be ready to start Part 2 of this text, which begins with a focus on risk-return considerations when making investment decisions. In Part 2 we also cover the valuation of bonds and stocks and other investment topics.

How This Chapter Applies to Me. . .

It is nearly impossible to get through the day without seeing some reference to interest rates on saving or borrowing money. You may see interest rates being offered on savings accounts by depository institutions, interest rates on new and used automobiles, and even the rate at which you could borrow for a loan to pay your tuition or to purchase a home. Your cost of borrowing will generally be higher when you are just starting your working career and your credit quality has not yet been established. Understanding the factors that determine the level of interest rates hopefully will help you make more informed decisions concerning when to spend, save, and borrow.

We all have been tempted by the advertisements for goods and services that suggest we should buy now and pay later. These advertisements are hoping that we will decide that the value of "more" current consumption to us is worth the added interest that we will have to pay on the funds that we must borrow to finance this consumption.

Sometimes individuals like to consume more now, even though they don't have the money to pay for this consumption. For example, you may see a pair of shoes in a store window that you "have to have right now." Maybe you don't currently have the money to pay for the shoes. Don't despair; if you have a credit card, the credit card issuer may lend you the money to pay for the shoes. In return, you will have to pay back the amount borrowed plus interest on the loan.

You might also be considering making a current investment in your future by borrowing money to go to college. In this case, you hope that your current education will lead to an increase in your future earning power, out of which you will have to repay your student loan. When you purchased your shoes on credit, you decided to consume now and pay later for this current consumption. When you decide to invest in your education, you expect that future earnings will be larger, making it easier to repay the student loan. Businesses also borrow to make investments in inventory, plant, and equipment that will earn profits sufficient to pay interest, repay the amount borrowed, and provide returns to equity investors. In this chapter we focus on the cost or price of borrowing funds. An understanding of interest rates—what causes them to change and how they relate to changes in the economy—is of fundamental importance in the world of finance.

SUPPLY AND DEMAND FOR LOANABLE FUNDS

Lenders are willing to supply funds to borrowers as long as lenders can earn a satisfactory return on their loans (i.e., an amount greater than that which was lent). Borrowers will demand funds from lenders as long as borrowers can invest the funds so as to earn a satisfactory return above the cost of their loans. Actually, the supply and demand for loanable funds will take place as long as both lenders and borrowers have the expectation of satisfactory returns. Of course, returns received may differ from those expected because of inflation, failure to repay loans, and poor investments. Return experiences will, in turn, affect future supply-and-demand relationships for loanable funds.

interest rate

price that equates the demand for and supply of loanable funds

The basic price that equates the demand for and supply of loanable funds in the financial markets is the *interest rate*. Figure 4.1 depicts how interest rates are determined in the financial markets. Graph A shows the interest rate (r) that clears the market by bringing the demand (D_1) by borrowers for funds in equilibrium with the supply (S_1) by lenders of funds. For illustrative

FIGURE 4.1

Interest Rate Determination in the Financial Markets

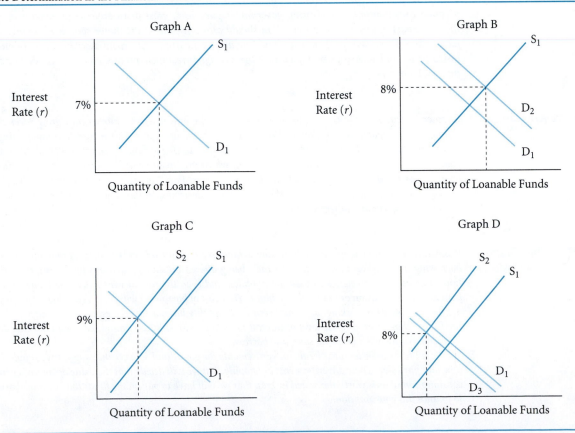

purposes we have arbitrarily chosen a rate of 7 percent as the cost or price that makes savings equal to investment (i.e., where the supply and demand curves intersect).

Interest rates may move from an equilibrium level if an unanticipated change or "shock" causes the demand for, or supply of, loanable funds to change. For example, an increase in the desire to invest in business assets because of an expanding economy might cause the demand for loanable funds to increase or shift upward (i.e., from D_1 to D_2 in Figure 4.1). The result, depicted in Graph B, will be an increase or rise in interest rates to, say, 8 percent, assuming no immediate adjustment in the supply of funds. Of course, as higher interest rates become available to savers, savings may increase, which could cause the supply of loanable funds to increase. A decline in business activity would be expected to have the opposite impact on interest rates.

Graph C in Figure 4.1 depicts an unanticipated increase in inflation, which leads lenders (suppliers) to require a higher rate of interest. This is shown by the shift in supply from S_1 to S_2, which for illustrative purposes shows an increase in the interest rate from 7 percent to 9 percent. At this point, we have not taken into consideration the fact that borrowers also may adjust their demand for loanable funds because of the likelihood of more costly loans. Graph D depicts the situation that borrowers (users) may cut back on their demand for loanable funds from D_1 to D_3 because of the unanticipated increase in inflation. For example, this would occur if borrowers felt that their higher borrowing costs could not be passed on to their customers, and thus the returns on their investments would be adversely affected by the higher inflation rates. Instead of the unanticipated increase in inflation shock causing the interest rate to rise to 9 percent, the new equilibrium rate where supply equals demand (investment) might be only 8 percent.

CONCEPT CHECK

How are interest rates determined in the financial markets?

HISTORICAL CHANGES IN U.S. INTEREST RATE LEVELS

Interest rates for loanable funds have varied throughout the history of the United States as the result of shifting supply and demand. Since just after the Civil War, there have been four periods of rising or relatively high long-term interest rates and four periods of low or falling interest rates on long-term loans and investments. The rapid economic expansion after the Civil War caused the first period of rising interest rates from 1864 to 1873. The second period, from 1905 to 1920, was based on both large-scale prewar expansion and the inflation associated with World War I. The third period, from 1927 to 1933, was due to the economic boom from 1927 to 1929 and the unsettled conditions in the securities markets during the early part of the Depression, from 1929 to 1933. The rapid economic expansion following World War II led to the last period, from 1946 to the early 1980s.

The first period of falling interest rates was from 1873 to 1905. As the public debt was paid off and funds became widely available, the supply of funds grew more rapidly than the demand for them. Prices and interest rates fell, even though the economy was moving forward. The same general factors were at work in the second period, 1920 to 1927. The third period of low interest rates, from 1933 to 1946, resulted from the government's actions in fighting the Great Depression and continued during World War II, when interest rates were pegged, or set.

Beginning in 1966 interest rates entered a period of unusual increases, leading to the highest rates in U.S. history. This increase in rates began as a result of the Vietnam War. It continued in the 1970s because of a policy of on-again, off-again price controls and increased demands for capital arising from ecological concerns and the energy crisis. Furthermore, several periods of poor crops coupled with sharp price increases for crude oil caused worldwide inflation. Interest rates peaked at the beginning of the 1980s, with short-term rates above 20 percent and long-term rates in the high teens. In summary, double-digit inflation, a somewhat tight monetary policy, and heavy borrowing demand by business contributed to these record levels.

The fourth period of declining long-term interest rates began after 1982, when rates peaked, and continued into 2004. Inflation rates dropped dramatically from double-digit levels during the beginning of the 1980s and remained around 2 to 3 percent after the early 1990s. The decline in inflation rates seems to have been the primary reason long-term interest rates have also trended downward.

Short-term interest rates generally move up and down with the business cycle. Therefore, they show many more periods of expansion and contraction. Both long-term and short-term interest rates tend to rise in prosperity periods during which the economy is expanding rapidly. The only major exception was during World War II, when interest rates were pegged. During this period the money supply increased rapidly, laying the base for postwar inflation.

LOANABLE FUNDS THEORY

loanable funds theory
states that interest rates are a function of the supply of and demand for loanable funds

The **loanable funds theory** holds that interest rates are a function of the supply of and demand for loanable funds. This is a flow theory, in that it focuses on the relative supply and demand of loanable funds during a specified period. How the supply of and the demand for loanable funds interact determines both the interest rate and the quantity of funds that flows through the financial markets during any period. If the supply of funds increases, holding demand constant, interest rates will tend to fall. Likewise, an increase in the demand for loans will tend to drive up interest rates. This is depicted in Graph B of Figure 4.1.

Sources of Loanable Funds

There are two basic sources of loanable funds:

- Current savings
- Expansion of deposits by depository institutions

The supply of savings comes from all sectors of the economy, and most of it flows through U.S. financial institutions. Individuals may save part of their incomes, either as voluntary savings or through contractual savings programs, such as purchasing whole life or endowment insurance policies or repaying installment or mortgage loans. Governmental units and nonprofit institutions sometimes have funds in excess of current expenditures. Corporations may have savings available because they are not paying out all their earnings as dividends. Depreciation allowances that are not being used currently to buy new capital equipment to replace older equipment may also be available for lending.

Pension funds, both governmental and private, provide another source of saving. These funds, which are building up large reserves to meet future commitments, are available for investment.

Some savings are invested as ownership equity in businesses either directly in single proprietorships or partnerships or by buying stock in corporations. This is, however, only a small part of total savings. The bulk of the total savings each year is available as loanable funds. Funds may be loaned directly: for example, when someone lends money to a friend to enable the friend to expand business operations. However, most savings are loaned through financial institutions, one of whose basic functions is the accumulation of savings.

The other basic source of loanable funds is that created by the banking system. Banks and other depository institutions not only channel savings to borrowers but also create deposits, which are

---

SMALL BUSINESS PRACTICE
The Family Business or Venture

Family businesses continue to be very popular in the United States. For publicly held firms, corporate goals may differ in part from the goals of managers. For closely held firms that are not family owned, the business goals and the personal goals of owner/managers are closely aligned. For family-owned or family-controlled firms, a third set of goals—family goals—also must be considered. When family goals are closely aligned with the business and manager goals, the business can benefit from family sharing and closeness. However, when family goals differ from business and/or manager goals, conflict and an argumentative environment may prevail. In such instances, family-controlled businesses often fail or the family is forced to sell.

Jeffry Timmons lists several problems unique to family businesses or ventures.* First, problems of control, fairness, and equity often exist. For example, family members may have different ideas

as to how the business should be run. Fairness and equity issues relate to the division of work and relative contributions to running the business. Second is the issue of credibility, whereby founding parents find it difficult to believe that their children can perform in a manner comparable to their own.

Third is a potential problem relating to family dynamics. Since it often is difficult to separate business operations from family life, tensions in one area often spill over into the other area. Fourth is the problem of deciding succession. If succession is to involve a next-generation family member, the founder must disengage his or her ownership rights and delegate an increased level of responsibility to the new person in control. For succession to succeed, the founder must be willing to assume the role of advisor to the family member who was selected to run the firm in the future.

---

*Jeffry A. Timmons, *New Venture Creation*, 4th ed. (Boston: Irwin/McGraw-Hill, 1994). Also see Jeffry A. Timmons and Stephen Spinelli, *New Venture Creation*, 7th ed. (New York: McGraw-Hill/Irwin, 2007), Chapter 17.

CONCEPT CHECK

What are the basic sources of loanable funds?

the most widely used form of money in the U.S. economy. This process was discussed in Chapter 2. Net additions to the money supply are a source of loanable funds; during periods when the money supply contracts, the flow of loanable funds drops below the level of current savings.

Loanable funds can be grouped in several ways. They may be divided into short-term funds and long-term funds. We can also group funds by (1) use, such as business credit, consumer credit, agricultural credit, and government credit, and (2) the institutions supplying each type.

Factors Affecting the Supply of Loanable Funds

Many factors affect the supply of loanable funds. Both sources of funds have some tendency to increase as interest rates rise. However, this effect is often small compared to other factors that limit or otherwise affect the volume of savings or the ability of the banking system to expand deposits.

Volume of Savings

The major factor that determines the volume of savings, corporate as well as individual, is the level of national income. When income is high, savings are high; when it is low, savings are low. The pattern of income taxes—both the level of the tax and the tax rates in various income brackets—also influences savings volume. Furthermore, the tax treatment of savings itself influences the amount of income saved. For example, the tax deferral on (or postponement of) savings placed in individual retirement accounts (IRAs), increases the volume of savings.

The age of the population has an important effect on the volume of savings. As discussed in Chapter 3, little saving is done during the formative and education-building stage or during the family-creating stage. Therefore, an economy with a large share of young couples with children will have less total savings than one with more people in the older wealth-building stage.

The volume of savings also depends on the factors that affect indirect savings. The more effectively the life insurance industry promotes the sale of whole life and endowment insurance policies, the larger the volume of savings. The higher the demand for private pension funds (which accumulate contributions during working years to make payments on retirement), the larger the volume of savings. The effect of interest rates on such savings is often just the opposite of the normal effect of price on supply. As interest rates decrease, more money must be paid for insurance for the same amount of coverage, because a smaller amount of interest will be earned from the reinvestment of premiums and earnings. Inversely, as interest rates rise, less money needs to be put into reserves to get the same objectives. The same is true of the amount of money that must be put into annuities and pension funds.

When savings result from the use of consumer credit, the effect of interest rates is delayed. For example, assume a car is bought with a three-year loan. Savings, in the form of repaying the loan, must go on for three years regardless of changes in interest rates. There may even be an opposite effect in the case of a mortgage because, if interest rates drop substantially, the loan can be refinanced. At the lower interest rate, the same dollar payments provide a larger amount for repayment of principal—that is, for saving.

Expansion of Deposits by Depository Institutions

The amount of short-term credit available depends largely on the lending policies of commercial banks and other depository institutions and on the policies of the Federal Reserve System. Lenders are influenced by such factors as present business conditions and future prospects. However, the Federal Reserve has great control over the ability of the banking system to create new deposits, as discussed in Chapter 2.

How much long-term credit of different types is available depends on the policies of the different suppliers of credit. Since depository institutions do not play a major role in this field, the money supply is not expanded directly to meet long-term credit demands. Indirectly, however, their policies and those of the Federal Reserve are very important: if the banking system expands the money supply to meet short-term needs, a larger proportion of the supply of loanable funds can be used for long-term credit.

Liquidity Attitudes

How lenders see the future has a significant effect on the supply of loanable funds, both long term and short term. Lenders may feel that the economic outlook is so uncertain that they are reluctant to lend their money. This liquidity preference can be so strong that large amounts of funds lie idle, as they did during the depression in the 1930s. Lenders may also prefer liquidity because they expect either interest rates to go up in the near future or opportunities for direct investment to be more favorable. Thus, liquidity attitudes may result in keeping some funds idle that would normally be available for lending.

Effect of Interest Rates on the Demand for Loanable Funds

The demand for loanable funds comes from all sectors of the economy. Business borrows to finance current operations and to buy plant and equipment. Farmers borrow to meet short-term and long-term needs. Institutions such as hospitals and schools borrow primarily to finance new buildings and equipment. Individuals finance the purchase of homes with long-term loans and purchase durable goods or cover emergencies with intermediate- and short-term loans. Governmental units borrow to finance public buildings, bridge the gap between expenditures and tax receipts, and meet budget deficits. The factors affecting the demand for loanable funds are different for each type of borrower. We have considered such factors in detail when analyzing the various types of credit. Therefore, this discussion covers only how interest rates affect the major types of borrowing.

Historically, one of the biggest borrowers has been the federal government, and Congress generally gives little consideration to interest rates in its spending programs. Minor changes in interest rates do not affect short-term business borrowing. However, historical evidence shows that large increases in short-term interest rates do lead to a decrease in the demand for bank loans and other forms of short-term business borrowing.

Changes in long-term interest rates also affect long-term business borrowing. Most corporations put off long-term borrowing when rates are up if they expect rates to go down in the near future.

Likewise, minor changes in interest rates have little effect on consumer borrowing. For short-term installment loans, the monthly repayments of principal are so large compared to the interest cost that the total effect on the repayment schedule is small. However, larger interest rate changes have strongly influenced consumer borrowing in the past. This happened in recent years when home mortgage rates reached historically high levels and new housing starts declined sharply.

CONCEPT CHECK

How do interest rates influence the demand for loanable funds?

Roles of the Banking System and of the Government

While the effect of interest rates on loanable funds varies, both the supply of and the demand for loanable funds are affected by the actions of the banking system and the government. When depository institutions expand credit by increasing the total volume of short-term loans, the supply of loanable funds increases. When credit contracts, the supply of loanable funds decreases. The actions of the Federal Reserve in setting discount rates, buying securities in the open market, and changing reserve requirements also affect the supply of loanable funds. In fact, all actions that affect the level of banking system reserves and creation of checkable deposits affect the supply of loanable funds in the market.

Government borrowing has become a major influence on demand for funds and will remain so for the foreseeable future. Government surpluses or deficits make funds available in the market or take them out of the market in substantial amounts. Treasury debt management policies also affect the supply-and-demand relationships for short-, intermediate-, and long-term funds.

The financial markets are thus under the influence of the Treasury, and the Federal Reserve strongly influences the supply of funds. The Treasury, through tax policies and other government programs, also plays a role on this side of the market. However, the Treasury's major influence is on the demand for funds, as it borrows heavily to finance federal deficits.

International Factors Affecting Interest Rates

Interest rates in the United States are now no longer influenced only by domestic factors. The large trade surpluses with China and Japan, with their accumulation of funds to invest, have had important influences on the rates the federal government pays in issuing new securities. This international influence adds to the critical need to balance the national budget and to avoid the frequency of financing. As production has shifted to many other countries, investment has also shifted. In short, the Treasury and the Federal Reserve must now carefully consider the influence of international movements of funds on domestic interest rates.

CONCEPT CHECK

What are the major factors that affect the supply of loanable funds?

DETERMINANTS OF MARKET INTEREST RATES

nominal interest rate
interest rate that is observed in the marketplace

real rate of interest
interest rate on a risk-free debt instrument when no inflation is expected

inflation premium
average inflation rate expected over the life of the security

default risk premium
compensation for the possibility a borrower will fail to pay interest and/or principal when due

maturity risk premium
compensation expected by investors due to interest rate risk on debt instruments with longer maturities

interest rate risk
possible price fluctuations in fixed-rate debt instruments associated with changes in market interest rates

liquidity premium
compensation for securities that cannot easily be converted to cash without major price discounts

CONCEPT CHECK

What is the nominal interest rate and what is meant by the real rate of interest?

What are the definitions of the following: default risk premium, maturity risk premium, and liquidity premium?

What is interest rate risk?

risk-free rate of interest
interest rate on a debt instrument with no default, maturity, or liquidity risks (Treasury securities are the closest example)

In addition to supply-and-demand relationships, interest rates are determined by a number of specific factors. First, the interest rate (*r*) that we observe in the marketplace is called a **nominal interest rate** because it includes a premium for expected inflation. Second, a nominal interest rate that is not free from the risk of default by the borrower also will have a *default risk premium*. Thus, in its simplest form, the nominal interest rate can be expressed as:

$$r = RR + IP + DRP \qquad (4.1)$$

where RR is the real rate of interest, IP is an inflation premium, and DRP is the default risk premium.

The **real rate of interest** is the interest rate on a risk-free financial debt instrument when no inflation is expected. The **inflation premium** is the average inflation rate expected over the life of the instrument.

The **default risk premium (DRP)** indicates compensation for the possibility that the borrower will not pay interest and/or repay principal according to the financial instrument's contractual arrangements. The DRP reflects the application of the risk-return principle of finance presented in Chapter 1. In essence, "higher returns are expected for taking on more risk." This is a higher "expected" return because the issuer may default on some of the contractual returns. Of course, the actual "realized" return on a default risky debt investment could be substantially less than the expected return. At the extreme, the debt security investor could lose all of his or her investment. The DRP is discussed further in the last section of this chapter. The risk-return finance principle to stock investments and to portfolios of securities is further extended in Chapter 8. Instead of a default risk premium, the concentration is on "stock risk premiums" and "market risk premiums."

To cover both short-term and long-term debt instruments, two additional premiums are frequently added to the equation that explains nominal interest rates. This expanded version can be expressed as:

$$r = RR + IP + DRP + MRP + LP \qquad (4.2)$$

where MRP is the maturity risk premium and LP is the liquidity premium on a financial instrument.

The **maturity risk premium** is the added return expected by lenders or investors because of interest rate risk on instruments with longer maturities. **Interest rate risk** reflects the possibility of changes or fluctuations in market values of fixed-rate debt instruments as market interest rates change over time. There is an inverse relationship in the marketplace between debt instrument values or prices and nominal interest rates. For example, if interest rates rise from, say, 7 percent to 8 percent because of a previously unanticipated inflation rate increase, the values of outstanding debt instruments will decline. Furthermore, the longer the remaining life until maturity, the greater the reductions in a fixed-rate debt instrument's value to a given interest rate increase. These concepts with numerical calculations are explored in Chapter 7.

The **liquidity premium** is the compensation for those financial debt instruments that cannot be easily converted to cash at prices close to their estimated fair market values. For example, a corporation's low-quality bond may be traded very infrequently. As a consequence, a bondholder who wishes to sell tomorrow may find it difficult to sell except at a very large discount in price.

Those factors that influence the nominal interest rate are discussed throughout the remainder of this chapter, beginning with the concept of a risk-free interest rate and a discussion of why U.S. Treasury securities are used as the best estimate of the risk-free rate. Other sections focus on the term or maturity structure of interest rates, inflation expectations and associated premiums, and default risk and liquidity premium considerations.

RISK-FREE SECURITIES: U.S. TREASURY DEBT OBLIGATIONS

By combining the real rate of interest and the inflation premium, we have the **risk-free rate of interest**, which in the United States is represented by U.S. Treasury debt instruments or securities. It is generally believed that even with the large national debt, the U.S. government is not going to renege on its obligations to pay interest and repay principal at maturity on its debt securities. Thus, we view U.S. Treasury securities as being default-risk free. Technically, a truly risk-free financial instrument also has no liquidity risk or maturity risk (as reflected by interest rate risk). Treasury marketable securities are considered to have virtually no liquidity risk, and only longer-term Treasury securities have maturity or interest rate risk associated with changes in market-determined interest rates that occur over time.

Economists have estimated that the annual real rate of interest in the United States and other countries has averaged in the 2 to 4 percent range in recent years. One way of looking at the risk-free rate is to say that this is the minimum rate of interest necessary to get individuals and businesses to save. There must be an incentive to invest or save idle cash holdings. One such incentive is the expectation of some real rate of return above expected inflation levels. For illustrative purposes, let's assume 3 percent is the current expectation for a real rate of return. Let's also assume that the nominal interest rate is currently 7 percent for a one-year Treasury security.

Given these assumptions, we can turn to Equation 4.1 to determine the average inflation expectations of holders or investors as follows:

$$7\% = RR + IP + DRP$$
$$7\% = 3\% + IP + 0\%$$
$$IP = 7\% - 3\% = 4\%$$

Thus, investors expect a 4 percent inflation rate over the next year; if they also want a real rate of return of 3 percent, the nominal interest rate must be 7 percent.

Let's now also use the expanded equation to explain nominal interest rates as expressed in Equation 4.2. However, since this is a Treasury security there is no liquidity premium and no maturity risk premium if we are planning to hold the security until its maturity at the end of one year. Thus, Equation 4.2 would be used as follows to find the average expected inflation rate:

$$7\% = RR + IP + DRP + MRP + LP$$
$$7\% = 3\% + IP + 0\% + 0\% + 0\%$$
$$IP = 7\% - 3\% - 4\%$$

Of course, the answer has not changed and is still 4 percent, since there were no additional risk premiums. The impact of a maturity risk premium is introduced after discussion of the types of marketable securities issued by the Treasury.

CONCEPT CHECK

What is the risk-free rate of interest?

MARKETABLE OBLIGATIONS

marketable government securities
securities that may be bought and sold through the usual market channels

Marketable government securities, as the term implies, are those that can be purchased and sold through customary market channels. Large commercial banks and securities dealers maintain markets for these obligations. In addition, nearly all other securities firms and commercial banks, large or small, will help their customers purchase and sell federal obligations by routing orders to institutions that do maintain markets in them. The investments of institutional investors and large personal investors in federal obligations are centered almost exclusively in the marketable issues. These marketable issues are bills, notes, and bonds, the difference between them being their maturity at time of issue. Although the maturity of an obligation is reduced as it remains in effect, the obligation continues to be called by its original descriptive title. Thus, a twenty-year Treasury bond continues to be described in the quotation sheets as a bond throughout its life.

Treasury Bills

Treasury bills
federal obligations issued with maturities up to one year

Treasury bills are issued with maturities up to one year and thus are the shortest maturities of federal obligations. They are typically issued for 91 days, with some issues carrying maturities of 182 days. Treasury bills with a maturity of one year are also issued at auction every four weeks. Issues of Treasury bills are offered each week by the Treasury to refund the part of the total volume of bills that matures. In effect, the 91-day Treasury bills mature and are rolled over in thirteen weeks. Each week, approximately one-thirteenth of the total volume of such bills is refunded.

When the flow of cash revenues into the Treasury is too small to meet expenditure requirements, additional bills are issued. During those periods of the year when revenues exceed expenditures, Treasury bills are allowed to mature without being refunded. Treasury bills, therefore, provide the Treasury with a convenient financial mechanism to adjust for the lack of a regular revenue flow into the Treasury. The volume of bills may also be increased or decreased in response to general surpluses or deficits in the federal budget from year to year.

Treasury bills are issued on a discount basis and mature at par. Each week the Treasury bills to be sold are awarded to the highest bidders. Dealers and other investors submit sealed binds. Upon being opened, these bids are arrayed from highest to lowest. Those bidders asking the least discount (offering the highest price) are placed high in the array. The bids are then accepted in the order of their position in the array until all bills are awarded. Bidders seeking a higher discount (offering a lower price) may fail to receive any bills that particular week. Investors interested in purchasing small volumes of Treasury bills ($10,000 to $500,000) may submit their orders on an average competitive price basis. The Treasury deducts these small orders from the total volume of bills to be sold. The remaining bills are allotted on the competitive basis described above. Then these small orders are executed at a discount equal to the average of the successful competitive bids for large orders.

Investors are not limited to purchasing Treasury bills on their original issue. Because Treasury bills are issued weekly, a wide range of maturities in the over-the-counter market is available. The Treasury bonds, notes, and bills section of the *Wall Street Journal* shows available maturities from one week to one year. The bid and ask quotations are shown in terms of annual yield equivalents. The prices of the various issues obtained from a dealer would reflect a discount based on these yields. Because of their short maturities and their absence of risk, Treasury bills provide the lowest yield available on taxable domestic obligations. Although some business corporations and individuals invest in Treasury bills, by far the most important holders of these obligations are commercial banks.

Treasury Notes

Treasury notes
federal obligations usually issued for maturities of two to five years

Treasury notes are issued at specified interest rates usually for maturities ranging from two to five years. These intermediate-term federal obligations are also held largely by commercial banks.

Treasury Bonds

Treasury bonds
federal obligations issued with maturities over five years and often for twenty or even thirty years

Treasury bonds typically have original maturities in excess of five years and often are issued for twenty and sometimes even thirty years. These bonds bear interest at stated rates. Many issues of these bonds are *callable,* or paid off, by the government several years before their maturity. For example, a twenty-year bond issued in 1995 may be described as having a maturity of 2005–2010. This issue may be called for redemption at par as early as 2005 but in no event later than 20010. The longest maturity of Treasury bonds is thirty years. Dealers maintain active markets for the purchase and sale of Treasury bonds and the other marketable securities of the government.

All marketable obligations of the federal government, with the exception of Treasury bills, are offered to the public through the Federal Reserve Banks at prices and yields set in advance. Investors place their orders for new issues, and these orders are filled from the available supply of the new issue. If orders are larger than available supply, investors may be allotted only a part of the amount they requested.

Treasury bonds, because of at least initial long-term maturities, are subject to maturity or interest rate risk. Treasury notes with shorter maturities are affected to a lesser extent. For illustrative purposes, let's assume that the nominal interest rate on ten-year Treasury bonds is currently 9 percent. Let's further assume that investors expect the inflation rate will average 4 percent over the next ten years. By applying Equation 4.2 we can find the maturity risk premium to be:

$$9\% = RR + IP + DRP + MRP + LP$$
$$9\% = 3\% + 4\% + 0\% + MRP + 0\%$$
$$MRP = 9\% - 3\% - 4\% = 2\%$$

CONCEPT CHECK

How do Treasury bills, Treasury notes, and Treasury bonds differ?

Our interpretation is that the holders or investors require a 2 percent maturity risk premium to compensate them for the possibility of volatility in the price of their Treasury bonds over the next ten years. If market-determined interest rates rise and investors are forced to sell before maturity, the bonds will be sold at a loss. Furthermore, even if these investors hold their bonds to maturity and redeem them with the government at the original purchase price, the investors would have lost the opportunity of the higher interest rates being paid in the marketplace. This is what is meant by *interest rate risk*. Of course, if market-determined interest rates decline after the bonds are purchased, bond prices will rise above the original purchase price.

DEALER SYSTEM

CONCEPT CHECK

What is the dealer system for marketable U.S. government securities?

dealer system
comprised of a small group of dealers in government securities with an effective marketing network throughout the United States.

The **dealer system** for marketable U.S. government securities occupies a central position in the nation's financial markets. The smooth operation of the money markets depends on a closely linked network of dealers and brokers. Dealers report their daily activity in U.S. government securities to the Federal Reserve Bank of New York. In recent years, there have been on average forty to fifty such dealers, with a little less than half being commercial banks and the remainder being nonbank dealers. New dealers are added only when they can demonstrate a satisfactory responsibility and volume of activity. The dealers buy and sell securities for their own account, arrange transactions with both their customers and other dealers, and also purchase debt directly from the Treasury for resale to investors. Dealers do not typically charge commissions on their trades. Rather, they hope to sell securities at prices above the levels at which they were bought. The dealers' capacity to handle large Treasury financing has expanded enough in recent years to handle the substantial growth in the government securities market. In addition to the dealers' markets, new issues of federal government securities may be purchased directly at the Federal Reserve Banks.

TAX STATUS OF FEDERAL OBLIGATIONS

Until March 1941, interest on all obligations of the federal government was exempt from all taxes. The interest on all federal obligations is now subject to ordinary income taxes and tax rates. The Public Debt Act of 1941 terminated the issuance of tax-free federal obligations. Since that time, all issues previously sold to the public have matured or have been called for redemption. Income from the obligations of the federal government is exempt from all state and local taxes. Federal obligations, however, are subject to federal and state inheritance, estate, or gift taxes.

OWNERSHIP OF PUBLIC DEBT SECURITIES

nonmarketable government securities
issues that cannot be transferred between persons or institutions and must be redeemed with the U.S. government

The U.S. national debt must be financed and refinanced through the issuance of government securities, both marketable and nonmarketable. **Nonmarketable government securities** are those securities that cannot be transferred to other persons or institutions and can be redeemed only by being turned in to the U.S. government. The sheer size of the national debt, over $8.5 trillion in late 2006, makes the financing process a difficult one. In fact, the United States must rely on the willingness of foreign and international investors to hold a substantial portion of the outstanding interest-bearing public debt securities issued to finance the national debt.

The ownership of public debt securities, by group or category, is shown in Table 4.1. Private investors owned approximately 48 percent of the total outstanding federal debt securities in 2003 and in 2006. The percentage of federal debt held by U.S. government accounts (agencies and trust funds) and Federal Reserve Banks also remained relatively constant at 52 percent. Even though overall private ownership of the U.S. federal debt remained roughly constant between 2003 and 2006, foreign and international investors increased their holdings from almost 22 percent to slightly over 25 percent of the total public debt in 2006. This shows the continuing importance of foreign and international investors in financing the U.S. national debt. No other category of private investors held more than about 6 percent of the total federal debt outstanding in 2006.

TABLE 4.1
Ownership of Public Debt of U.S. Treasury Securities (% of Total Debt)

	2003	2006 (SEPT)
Federal Reserve and government accounts	51.7%	52.1%
Private investors		
Foreign and international investors	21.9	25.1
State and local governments	5.2	5.5
U.S. savings bonds	2.9	2.4
Depository institutions	2.2	1.3
Insurance companies	2.0	1.9
Mutual funds	4.0	2.8
Pension funds	4.5	3.8
Other miscellaneous groups of investors*	5.6	5.1
Total private investors	**48.3%**	**47.9%**
Total U.S. agencies and private investors	**100.0%**	**100.0%**
Dollar Amount of Public Debt ($ Trillions)	$7.0	$8.5

Includes individuals, corporate and other businesses, dealers and brokers, government-sponsored agencies, bank personal trusts and estates, and other investors.

Source: *Economic Report of the President* (February 2007), Table B-89.

CONCEPT CHECK

What are nonmarketable government securities?

During the last half of the 1980s, the annual increase in foreign ownership was due primarily to the flow of Japanese capital to this country. Japanese investment in real estate and corporate securities has been well publicized. However, as the dollar declined relative to the Japanese yen and other major foreign currencies, investment in U.S. assets became less attractive after interest and other returns were converted back into the foreign currencies. In recent years interest on the part of Europeans and Chinese has increased. The large trade surpluses China has been having with the United States has resulted in the Chinese holding ever-increasing amounts of U.S. financial assets.

MATURITY DISTRIBUTION OF MARKETABLE DEBT SECURITIES

The various types of marketable obligations of the federal government have already been described in this section. However, the terms of bills, notes, and bonds describe the general maturity ranges only at the time of issue. To determine the maturity distribution of all obligations, therefore, it is necessary to observe the remaining life of each issue regardless of its class. The maturity distribution and average length of marketable interest-bearing federal obligations are shown in Table 4.2. Notice that the average maturity decreased from five years and one month in 2003 to four years and nine months in September 2006.

The heavy concentration of debt in the very short maturity range (within one year) has improved from about 38 percent in 2003 to about 32 percent of the total amount outstanding in 2006. However, this heavy concentration in very short-term maturities poses a special problem for the Treasury. This also is a problem for the securities markets because the government is constantly selling additional securities to replace those that mature. The heavy concentration of short-term

TABLE 4.2
Average Length and Maturity Distribution of Marketable Interest-Bearing Federal Obligations
(% of Total Marketable Debt)

MATURITY CLASS	2003	2006
Within 1 year	37.7%	32.1%
1–5 years	34.1	37.3
5–10 years	12.5	17.8
10–20 years	8.7	8.0
20 years and over	7.0	4.8
Total	100.0%	100.0%
Average maturity of all marketable issues:	5 years, 1 month	4 years, 9 months

Source: *Economic Report of the President* (February 2007), Table B-88.

maturities will not necessarily change by simply issuing a larger number of long-term obligations. Like all institutions that seek funds in the financial markets, the Treasury has to offer securities that will be readily accepted by the investing public. Furthermore, the magnitude of federal financing is such that radical changes in maturity distributions can upset the financial markets and the economy in general. The management of the federal debt has become an especially challenging financial problem, and much time and energy are spent in meeting the challenge.

If the Treasury refunds maturing issues with new short-term obligations, the average maturity of the total debt is reduced. As time passes, longer-term issues are brought into shorter-dated categories. Net cash borrowing that results from budgetary deficits must take the form of maturities that are at least as long as the average of the marketable debt if the average maturity is not to be reduced. The average length of the marketable debt reached a low level of two years and five months in late 1975. Since that time, progress has been made in raising the length of maturities—although the average maturity is again under five years—by selling long-term obligations.

One of the new debt-management techniques used to extend the average maturity of the marketable debt without disturbing the financial markets is *advance refunding*. This occurs when the Treasury offers the owners of a given issue the opportunity to exchange their holdings well in advance of the holdings' regular maturity for new securities of longer maturity.

In summary, the Treasury is the largest and most active borrower in the financial markets. The Treasury is continuously in the process of borrowing and refinancing. Its financial actions are tremendous in contrast with all other forms of financing, including those of the largest business corporations. Yet, the financial system of the nation is well adapted to accommodate its needs smoothly. Indeed, the very existence of a public debt of this magnitude is predicated on the existence of a highly refined monetary and credit system.

CONCEPT CHECK

What is the average maturity of U.S. marketable debt securities?

TERM OR MATURITY STRUCTURE OF INTEREST RATES

The **term structure** of interest rates indicates the relationship between interest rates or yields and the maturity of comparable quality debt instruments. This relationship is typically depicted through the graphic presentation of a **yield curve**. A properly constructed yield curve must first reflect securities of similar default risk. Second, the yield curve must represent a particular point in time, and the interest rates should reflect yields for the remaining time to maturity. That is, the yields should not only include stated interest rates but also consider that instruments and securities could be selling above or below their redemption values. (The process for calculating yields to maturity is shown in Chapter 5.) Third, the yield curve must show yields on a number of securities with differing lengths of time to maturity.

U.S. government securities provide the best basis for constructing yield curves because Treasury securities are considered to be risk free, as previously noted in terms of default risk. Table 4.3 contains interest rates for Treasury securities at selected dates and for various maturities. In early 1980 the annual inflation rate was in double digits. As a result, interest rates were very high even though the economy was in a mild recession. Longer-term interest rates were even higher in March 1982, even though the economy was in a deep recession. Apparently, investors still were expecting the high levels of inflation to continue. However, by the latter part of the 1980s interest rates had dropped dramatically because of reduced inflation. Interest rates on one-year Treasury bills were at 6 percent in March 1991, compared with 14 percent in March 1980. Interest rates declined further as the economy began expanding from a mild recession at the beginning of the

term structure

relationship between interest rates or yields and the time to maturity for debt instruments of comparable quality

yield curve

graphic presentation of the term structure of interest rates at a given point in time

TABLE 4.3

Term Structure of Interest Rates for Treasury Securities at Selected Dates (%)

TERM TO MATURITY	MARCH 1980	MARCH 1982	NOVEMBER 2001	NOVEMBER 2003	OCTOBER 2006
6 months	15.0%	12.8%	1.9%	1.0%	4.9%
1 year	14.0	12.5	2.2	1.3	5.0
5 years	13.5	14.0	4.0	3.3	4.7
10 years	12.8	13.9	4.7	4.3	4.7
20 years	12.5	13.8	5.3	5.2	4.9
30 years	12.3	13.5	5.1	NA	NA

Source: *Federal Reserve Bulletin* and *Statistical Supplement to the Federal Reserve Bulletin*, various issues.

1990s. By November 1998, after the Fed first pushed up short-term interest rates in an effort to head off possible renewed inflation and then lowered rates in an effort to avoid a recession during the mid-1990s, interest rates were relatively flat across different maturities. The Fed lowered its discount rate many times during the first years of the twenty-first century due to concern about an economic downturn, and by November 2001 short-term interest rates had dropped to about 2 percent. Short-term interest rates continued to fall and were at about 1 percent in November 2003. However, in an effort to keep inflation under control, the Fed forced short-term interest rates higher in recent years so that short-term rates reached about 5 percent in October 2006.

Figure 4.2 shows yield curves for March 1980, November 2003, and October 2006 reflecting the plotting of the corresponding data in Table 4.3. Because of high inflation rates and monetary policy trying to constrain economic activity, the March 1980 yield curve was both downward sloping and at very high overall interest rate levels. In contrast, the yield curve for November 2003 was upward sloping and much lower overall due to lower expected inflation rates and efforts by monetary policy to stimulate economic activity. By October 2006, the yield curve was nearly flat across all maturities with a variation only between about 4.7 percent and 5.0 percent. This flattening of the yield curve was attributable primarily to the Fed's effort to raise short-term interest rates as a way of possibly combating the possibility of increases in inflation rates.

RELATIONSHIP BETWEEN YIELD CURVES AND THE ECONOMY

Historical evidence suggests that interest rates generally rise during periods of economic expansion and fall during economic contraction. Therefore, the term structure of interest rates as depicted by yield curves shifts upward or downward with changes in economic activity. Interest rate levels generally are the lowest at the bottom of a recession and the highest at the top of an expansion period. Furthermore, when the economy is moving out of a recession, the yield curve slopes upward. The curve begins to flatten out during the latter stages of an expansion and typically starts sloping downward when economic activity peaks. As the economy turns downward, interest rates begin falling and the yield curve again goes through a flattening-out phase, to become upward sloping when economic activity again reaches a low point.

TERM STRUCTURE THEORIES

Three theories are commonly used to explain the term structure of interest rates. The **expectations theory** contends that the shape of a yield curve reflects investor expectations about future inflation rates. If the yield curve is flat, expectations are that the current short-term inflation rate will remain essentially unchanged over time. When the yield curve is downward sloping, investors expect inflation rates to be lower in the future. Recall from Figure 4.2 that the shape of

CONCEPT CHECK

What is meant by term structure of interest rates?

What is the definition of a yield curve?

expectations theory states that the shape of the yield curve indicates investor expectations about future inflation rates

FIGURE 4.2

Yield Curves for Treasury Securities at Selected Dates

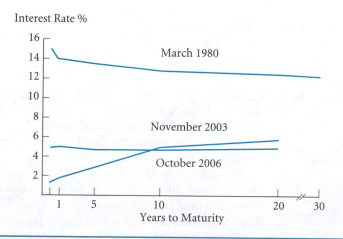

Source: Federal Reserve Bulletin and *Statistical Supplement to the Federal Reserve Bulletin,* various issues.

the yield curve in March 1980 was downward sloping. Thus, investors believed that the double-digit inflation rates prevailing in 1980 were expected to decline in the future. In contrast, the relatively flat yield curve in November 1998 suggested that investors expected the low inflation rates in late 1998 to remain at low levels in the future and that the economy would continue to grow at a moderate rate. The upward-sloping yield curve in November 2001 occurred at the end of the 2001 recession. The yield curve continued to be upward sloping in November 2003 as economic activity continued to increase. The flattening of the yield curve by October 2006 caused some concern about the possibility of a slowdown in economic activity.

To differentiate yield curve shapes in terms of Equations 4.1 and 4.2, first recall that the liquidity and the default risk premiums are zero for Treasury securities. Thus, Equation 4.2 for Treasury securities becomes Equation 4.1 plus a maturity risk premium (MRP). However, the expectations theory in its purest form also assumes the MRP to be zero. Given this assumption, we have reduced Equation 4.2 back to Equation 4.1 such that the yield curve reflects only the real rate (RR) of interest plus the expectation for an inflation premium (IP) over the life of the security.

Let's assume that the current rates of interest or yields are one-year Treasury bills = 7 percent; two-year Treasury notes = 8 percent; and ten-year Treasury bonds = 9 percent. Using a 3 percent real rate of return, we have the following relationships:

MATURITY	R	=	RR	+	IP
1-year	7%	=	3%	+	4%
2-year	8%	=	3%	+	5%
10-year	9%	=	3%	+	6%

Thus, the inflation rate is expected to be 4 percent over the next year. However, the inflation rate is expected to average 5 percent per year over the next two years; or if inflation is 4 percent the first year, then the rate for the second year must be more than 5 percent. Working with simple averages, 5 percent average inflation times two years means that the total inflation will be 10 percent. Thus, 10 percent less 4 percent means that inflation in the second year must be 6 percent.

For years three through ten, inflation must exceed 6 percent annually to average 6 percent over the ten-year period. We can find the simple average by starting with the fact that inflation will be 60 percent (6 percent times 10 years) over the full ten-year period. And, 60 percent less the 10 percent for the first two years means that cumulative inflation for the last eight years will be 50 percent. Then, dividing 50 percent by eight means that inflation will have to average 6.25 percent over years three through ten. In summary, we have:

TIME PERIOD	AVERAGE INFLATION		NUMBER OF YEARS		CUMULATIVE INFLATION
Year 1	4%	×	1	=	4%
Year 2	6%	×	1	=	6%
Years 3–10	6.25%	×	8	=	50%
Total inflation					**60%**
Total years					**10**
Average inflation (60% ÷ 10 years)					6%

These are only simple arithmetic averages. Technically, we have ignored the impact of the compounding of inflation rates over time. The concept of compounding is presented in Chapter 5, which focuses on the time value of money.

The **liquidity preference theory** holds that investors or debt instrument holders prefer to invest short term so that they have greater liquidity and less maturity or interest rate risk. Lenders also prefer to lend short term because of the risk of higher inflation rates and greater uncertainty about default risk in the future. Borrowers prefer to borrow long term so that they have more time to repay loans. The net result is a willingness to accept lower interest rates on short-term loans as a trade-off for greater liquidity and lower interest rate risk.

The **market segmentation theory** holds that securities of different maturities are not perfect substitutes for one another. For example, because of their demand and other deposit liabilities,

---

INTERNET ACTIVITY

Go to the Web site of the Federal Reserve Bank of St. Louis, http://www.stls.frb.org, and access the FRED database. Find current interest rates for different maturities of U.S. Treasury securities and construct the yield curve.

liquidity preference theory

states that investors are willing to accept lower interest rates on short-term debt securities that provide greater liquidity and less interest rate risk

market segmentation theory

states that interest rates may differ because securities of different maturities are not perfect substitutes for each other

commercial banks concentrate their activities on short-term securities. On the other hand, the nature of insurance company and pension fund liabilities allows these firms to concentrate holdings in long-term securities. Thus, supply-and-demand factors in each market segment affect the shape of the yield curve. Thus, in some time periods interest rates on intermediate-term Treasury securities may be higher (or lower) than those for both short-term and long-term treasuries.

INFLATION PREMIUMS AND PRICE MOVEMENTS

Actions or factors that change the value of the money unit or the supply of money and credit affect the whole economy. The change affects first the supply of loanable funds and interest rates and, later, both the demand for and the supply of goods in general. **Inflation**, as previously defined, is an increase in the price of goods or services that is not offset by an increase in quality. Recall that when investors expect higher inflation rates, they will require higher nominal interest rates so that a real rate of return will remain after the inflation. A clearer understanding of investor expectations about inflation premiums can be had by first reviewing past price movements, then exploring possible types of inflation.

HISTORICAL INTERNATIONAL PRICE MOVEMENTS

Changes in the money supply or in the amount of metal in the money unit have influenced prices since the earliest records of civilization. The money standard in ancient Babylon was in terms of silver and barley. The earliest available price records show that one shekel of silver was equal to 240 measures of grain. At the time of Hammurabi, about 1750 B.C., a shekel in silver was worth between 150 and 180 measures of grain, while in the following century it declined to 90 measures. After Persia conquered Babylonia in 539 B.C., the value of the silver shekel was recorded as between 15 and 40 measures of grain.

Alexander the Great probably caused the greatest inflationary period in ancient history when he captured the large gold hoards of Persia and took them to Greece. Inflation was high for some years, but twenty years after Alexander's death, a period of deflation began and lasted over fifty years.

The first recorded cases of deliberate currency debasement (lowering the value) occurred in the Greek city-states. The government would debase currency by calling in all coins and issuing new ones containing less of the precious metals. This must have been a convenient form of inflation, for there are many such cases in the records of Greek city-states.

Ancient Rome

During the Punic Wars, devaluation led to inflation as the heavy bronze coin was reduced in stages from one pound to one ounce. Similar inflation occurred in Roman history. Augustus brought so much precious metal from Egypt that prices rose and interest rates fell. From the time of Nero, debasements were frequent. The weight of gold coins was gradually reduced, and silver coins had baser metals added to them so that they were finally only 2 percent silver. Few attempts were made to arrest or reverse this process of debasement of coins as the populace adjusted to the process. When Aurelian tried to improve the coinage by adding to its precious metal content, he was resisted so strongly that armed rebellion broke out.

The Middle Ages Through Modern Times

During the Middle Ages princes and kings debased the coinage to get more revenue. The rulers of France used this ploy more than others, and records show that profit from debasement was sometimes greater than the total of all other revenues.

An important example of inflation followed the arrival of Europeans in America. Gold and silver poured into Spain from Mexico and Peru. Since the riches were used to buy goods from other countries, they were distributed over the continent and to England. Prices rose in Spain and in most of Europe, but not in proportion to the increase in gold and silver stocks. This was because trade increased and because many people hoarded the precious metals.

Paper money was not used generally until the end of the seventeenth century. The first outstanding example of inflation due to the issuing of an excessive amount of paper money was in France. In 1719 the government gave Scottish banker John Law a charter for a bank that could

CONCEPT CHECK

What is the expectations theory in terms of the term structure of interest rates?

What is the liquidity preference theory?

What is the market segmentation theory?

GLOBAL DISCUSSION

inflation

occurs when an increase in the price of goods or services is not offset by an increase in quality

CONCEPT CHECK

What do we mean by the term inflation?

What was the first example of rapid inflation after paper money began being used?

issue paper money. The note circulation of his bank amounted to almost 2,700 million livres (the monetary unit in use at that time in France), against which he had coin of only 21 million livres and bullion of 27 million livres. Prices went up rapidly, but they fell just as fast when Law's bank failed. Afterward, the money supply was again restricted.

The next outstanding period of inflation was during the time of the American Revolution. For example, France's revolutionary government issued paper currency in huge quantities. This currency, called assignats, declined to 0.5 percent of its face value.

Spectacular inflation also took place in Germany in 1923, when prices soared to astronomical heights. During World War II, runaway inflation took place in China and Hungary, as well as in other countries.

Monetary factors have often affected price levels in the United States, especially during major wars.

INFLATION IN THE UNITED STATES

Revolutionary War

The war that brought the United States into being was financed mainly by inflation. The Second Continental Congress had no real authority to levy taxes and thus found it difficult to raise money. As a result the congress decided to issue notes for $2 million. It issued more and more notes until the total rose to over $240 million. The individual states issued $200 million more. Since the notes were crudely engraved, counterfeiting was common, adding to the total of circulating currency. Continental currency depreciated in value so rapidly that the expression "not worth a continental" became a part of the American language.

War of 1812

During the War of 1812, the government tried to avoid repeating the inflationary measures of the Revolutionary War. However, since the war was not popular in New England, it was impossible to finance it by taxation and borrowing. Paper currency was issued in a somewhat disguised form: bonds of small denomination bearing no interest and having no maturity date. The wholesale price index, based on 100 as the 1910–1914 average prices, rose from 131 in 1812 to 182 in 1814. Prices declined to about the prewar level by 1816 and continued downward as depression hit the economy.

Civil War

The Mexican War (1846–1848) did not involve the total economy to any extent and led to no inflationary price movements. The Civil War (1861–1865), however, was financed partly by issuing paper money. In the war's early stages, the U.S. Congress could not raise enough money by taxes and borrowing to finance all expenditures, and therefore it resorted to inflation by issuing U.S. Notes with no backing, known as *greenbacks*. In all, $450 million was authorized. Even though this was but a fraction of the cost of the war, prices went up substantially. Wholesale prices on a base of 100 increased from 93 in 1860 to 185 in 1865. Attempts to retire the greenbacks at the end of the war led to deflation and depression in 1866. As a result, the law withdrawing greenbacks was repealed.

World War I

Although the U.S. government did not print money to finance World War I, it did practice other inflationary policies. About one-third of the cost of the war was raised by taxes and two-thirds of the cost by borrowing. The banking system provided much of this credit, which added to the money supply. People were even persuaded to use Liberty Bonds as collateral for bank loans to buy other bonds. The wholesale price index rose from 99 in 1914 to 226 in 1920. Then, as credit expansion was finally restricted in 1921, it dropped to 141 in 1922.

World War II and the Postwar Period

The government used fewer inflationary policies to finance World War II. Nevertheless, the banking system still took up large sums of bonds. By the end of the war, the debt of the federal government had increased by $207 billion. Bank holdings of government bonds had increased by almost $60 billion. Prices went up by only about one-third during the war because they were held in check after the first year by price and wage controls. They then rose rapidly when the controls were lifted after the war. In 1948 wholesale prices had risen to 236 from a level of 110 in 1939.

Wholesale prices increased during the Korean War and again during the 1955–1957 expansion in economic activity, as the economy recovered from the 1954 recession. Consumer goods prices continued to move upward during practically the entire postwar period, increasing gradually even in those years in which wholesale prices hardly changed.

Recent Decades

Figure 4.3 shows the consumer price index (CPI) for all items in the index and when food and energy are excluded since the early 1970s. Wholesale consumer goods prices again increased substantially when the Vietnam War escalated after mid-1965. Prices continued upward after American participation in the Vietnam War was reduced in the early 1970s. After American participation in the war ended in 1974, prices rose at the most rapid levels since World War I. Inflation was worldwide in the middle 1970s; its effects were much worse in many other industrial countries than in the United States.

As the 1970s ended, economists realized the full impact of a philosophy based on a high inflation rate. Many economists thought high inflation could keep unemployment down permanently, even though history shows that it does not. The government's efforts to control interest rates by increasing the money supply reinforced people's doubts that such policies would reduce inflation and high interest rates. By October 1979 the Federal Reserve System abandoned this failed approach to interest rate control and adopted a policy of monetary growth control. The result was twofold. First, there was a far greater volatility in interest rates as the Federal Reserve concentrated on monetary factors. Second, during the first three quarters of 1980 some monetary restraint was exercised. This monetary restraint depressed production and employment. The Federal Reserve System quickly backed off from this position of restraint, and by the end of 1980 a far greater level of monetary stimulus had driven interest rates to new peaks.

By this time the prime rate had risen to 21.5 percent and three-month Treasury bills had doubled in yield from their midyear lows. These high interest rates had a profound negative effect on such interest-sensitive industries as housing and automobiles. The Fed reversed the rapid growth of money supply throughout 1981 and until late in 1982. Unemployment climbed as the effects of monetary restraint were imposed on the economy, but the back of inflation was broken. By the end of 1982 economic recovery was in place, along with an easing of monetary restraint.

Figure 4.3 shows that inflation stayed at moderate levels beginning in 1983 and continuing through most of the remainder of the 1980s until near the end of the decade. After peaking in 1990 above a 6 percent annual rate, the CPI stayed at about 3 percent until 1997, when the

INTERNET ACTIVITY

Go to the Web site of the Council of Economic Advisors, http://www.whitehouse.gov/cea/pubs.html, *and access the* Economic Report of the President. *Next access the statistical appendix tables and find current inflation rates based on the consumer price index for all items and when food and energy prices are excluded.*

FIGURE 4.3
Consumer Price Index

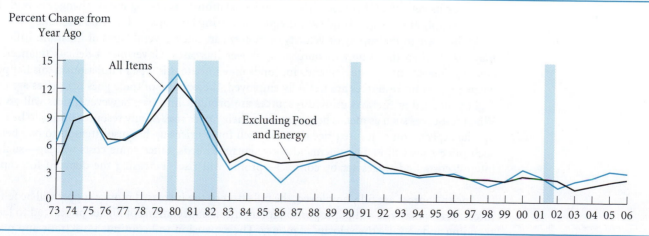

Source: Economic Report of the President and Federal Reserve Bulletin, various issues.

cost-push inflation
occurs when prices are raised to cover rising production costs, such as wages

demand-pull inflation
occurs during economic expansions when demand for goods and services is greater than supply

inflation rate dropped even further. In early 1994 the Fed moved toward a tighter monetary policy in an effort to keep inflation from rising. As the country finished the 1990s and moved into the early twenty-first century, inflation rates remained at relatively low levels. For 2006 the CPI for all items was 3.2 percent; the CPI adjusted to exclude food and energy was 2.5 percent.

TYPES OF INFLATION

Inflation may be associated with a change in costs, a change in the money supply, speculation, and so-called administrative pressures.

Price Changes Initiated by a Change in Costs

The price level can sometimes increase without the original impulse coming from either the money supply or its velocity. If costs rise faster than productivity increases, as when wages go up, businesses with some control over prices will try to raise them to cover the higher costs. Such increases are likely to be effective when the demand for goods is strong compared to the supply. The need for more funds to meet production and distribution at higher prices usually causes the money supply and velocity to increase. This type of inflation is called **cost-push inflation**, as this rise in prices comes from the cost side, not from increases in the money supply. Prices may not go up, however, if the monetary authorities restrict credit expansion. In that case only the most efficient businesses will have enough demand to operate profitably. As a result, some resources will be unemployed.

Cost-push inflation is different from inflation caused by an increase in the money supply, which is called **demand-pull inflation** and may be defined as an excessive demand for goods and services during periods of economic expansion as a result of large increases in the money supply. In practice, both aspects of inflation are likely to occur at the same time, since cost-push inflation can occur only in industries in which labor negotiations are carried out industrywide and in which management has the ability to increase prices.

Demand-pull inflation may also be caused by changes in demand in particular industries. The demand for petroleum, for example, may be greater than demand in general, so that prices rise in this industry before they rise generally. The first raise is likely to be in the basic materials themselves, leading to increased profits in the industries that produce them. Labor will press for wage increases to get its share of the total value of output, and thus labor costs also rise. Price rises in basic industries lead to price increases in the industries that use their products. Wage increases in one major industry are also likely to lead to demands for similar increases in other industries and among the nonorganized workers in such industries. The process set into motion can lead to general changes in prices, provided the monetary authorities do not restrict credit so as to prevent it.

Price Changes Initiated by a Change in the Money Supply

The way in which factors that affect prices relate to one another is quite complex. The following discussion considers the adjustments that take place when the primary change is in the money supply or its velocity. Of course, more complex relationships arising out of changes in both the money supply and the goods side of the equation during business cycles could also take place.

An increase in the supply or velocity of money can cause several types of inflation. Inflation may result when the supply of purchasing power increases. Government deficits financed by creating deposits or private demands for funds may initiate this type of inflation. If this happens when people and resources are not fully employed, the volume of trade goes up; prices are only slightly affected at first. As unused resources are brought into use, however, prices will go up. When resources such as metals become scarce, their prices rise. As any resource begins to be used up, the expectation of future price rises will itself force prices up because attempts to buy before such price rises will increase demand above current needs. Since some costs will lag—such as interest costs and wages set by contract—profits will rise, increasing the demand for capital goods.

Once resources are fully employed, the full effect of the increased money supply will be felt on prices. Prices may rise out of proportion for a time as expectations of higher prices lead to faster spending and so raise the velocity of money. The expansion will continue until trade and prices are in balance at the new levels of the money supply. Velocity will probably drop somewhat from those levels during the period of rising prices, since the desire to buy goods before the price goes up has disappeared.

Even if the supply of money is increased when people and resources are fully employed, prices may not go up proportionately. Higher prices increase profits for a time and so lead to a demand for more capital and labor. Thus, previously unemployed spouses, retired workers, and similar groups begin to enter the labor force. Businesses may use capital more fully by having two or three shifts use the same machines.

Demand-pull inflation traditionally exists during periods of economic expansion when the demand for goods and services exceeds the available supply of such goods and services. A second version of inflation also associated with increases in the money supply occurs because of monetization of the U.S. government debt. Recall from Chapter 5 that the Treasury finances government deficits by selling U.S. government securities to the public, commercial banks, or the Federal Reserve. When the Federal Reserve purchases U.S. government securities, reserves must be created to pay for the purchases. This, in turn, may lead to higher inflation because of an increase in money supply and bank reserves.

Speculation and Administrative Inflation

speculative inflation
caused by the expectation that prices will continue to rise, resulting in increased buying to avoid even higher future prices

When an increased money supply causes inflation, it can lead to the additional price pressure called ***speculative inflation***. Since prices have risen for some time, people believe that they will keep on rising. Inflation becomes self-generating for a time because, instead of higher prices resulting in lower demand, people may buy more to get goods before their prices go still higher, as happened in the late 1970s. This effect may be confined to certain areas, as it was to land prices in the 1920s Florida land boom or to security prices in the 1928–1929 stock market boom. Such a price rise leads to an increase in velocity as speculators try to turn over their funds as rapidly as possible and many others try to buy ahead of needs before there are further price rises.

For three decades, until the early 1980s, price pressures and inflation were continual despite occasional policies of strict credit restraint. During this long period, in fact, prices continued upward in recession periods, although at a slower rate than in prosperity periods. The need to restrain price rises hampered the Fed's ability to promote growth and fight recessions. Prices and other economic developments during this period led many to feel that the economy had developed a long-run *inflationary bias*. However, the continued low inflation rates in the late 1980s and the 1990s may have curtailed these beliefs, at least for a while.

Those economists who believe that long-run inflationary bias will continue do so on the basis of the following factors. First, prices and wages tend to rise during periods of boom in a competitive economy. This tendency is reinforced by wage contracts that provide escalator clauses to keep wages in line with prices and by wage increases that are sometimes greater than increases in productivity. Second, during recessions, prices tend to remain stable rather than decrease. This is because major unions have long-run contracts calling for annual wage increases no matter what economic conditions are at the time. The tendency of large corporations to rely on nonprice competition (advertising, and style and color changes) and to reduce output rather than cut prices also keeps prices stable. Furthermore, if prices do decline drastically in a field, the government is likely to step in with programs to help take excess supplies off the market. There is little doubt that prices would decline in a severe and prolonged depression. Government takes action to counter resulting unemployment, however, before the economy reaches such a level. Thus we no longer experience the downward price pressure of a depression.

administrative inflation
the tendency of prices, aided by union–corporation contracts, to rise during economic expansion and to resist declines during recessions

The inflation resulting from these factors is called ***administrative inflation***. This is to distinguish it from the type of inflation that happens when demand exceeds the available supply of goods, either because demand is increasing faster than supply in the early stages of a recovery period or because demand from monetary expansion by the banking system or the government exceeds available supply.

CONCEPT CHECK

What is the difference between cost-push inflation and demand-pull inflation?

What is meant by the terms speculative inflation *and* administrative inflation?

Traditional monetary policy is not wholly effective against administrative inflation. If money supplies are restricted enough, prices can be kept in line; this will lead to long-term unemployment and slow growth. It is also difficult for new firms and small growing firms to get credit since lending policies are likely to be conservative. The government must develop new tools to deal with administrative inflation effectively.

FINANCE PRINCIPLE

default risk
risk that a borrower will not
pay interest and/or principal
on a loan when due

DEFAULT RISK PREMIUMS

Investors are said to be "risk averse"—that is, they expect to be compensated with higher returns for taking on more risk in the form of greater uncertainty about return variability or outcome. This is the principle of finance known as the *risk-return principle,* or "higher returns are expected for taking on more risk" principle. **Default risk** is the risk that a borrower will not pay interest and/or repay the principal on a loan or other debt instrument according to the agreed contractual terms. The consequence may be a lower-than-expected interest rate or yield or even a complete loss of the amount originally lent. The premium for default risk will increase as the probability of default increases.

To examine default risk premiums for debt securities, it is necessary to hold some of the other risk premiums constant. By referring to Equation 4.2 we can develop a procedure for measuring that portion of a nominal interest rate (r) attributable to default risk. Recall that the nominal interest rate is a function of a real interest rate, an inflation premium, a default risk premium, a maturity risk premium, and a liquidity risk premium.

First, we constrain our analysis to the long-term capital markets by considering only long-term Treasury bonds and long-term corporate bonds. By focusing on long-term securities, the maturity risk will be the same for all the bonds and can be set at zero for analysis purposes. We have also said that the liquidity premium is zero for Treasury securities because they can be readily sold without requiring a substantial price discount. Corporate securities are less liquid than Treasury securities. However, we can minimize any possible liquidity premiums by considering the bonds of large corporations. This also allows us to set the liquidity premium at zero for analysis purposes.

For the following example, assume that the real rate is 3 percent, the nominal interest rate is 8 percent for long-term Treasury bonds, and high-quality corporate bonds have a 9 percent nominal interest rate. Using Equation 4.2, we have:

$$r = RR + IP + DRP + MRP + LP$$
$$9\% = 3\% + 5\% + DRP + 0\% + 0\%$$
$$DRP = 9\% - 3\% - 5\% - 0\% - 0\% = 1\%$$

Since the 8 percent Treasury bond represents the risk-free rate of interest, subtracting the 3 percent real rate results in a long-term average annual inflation premium of 5 percent. Another way of looking at the default risk premium (assuming zero maturity risk and liquidity premiums) is that it is the difference between the interest rates on the risky (corporate) and risk-free (Treasury) securities. In our example, we have:

$$DRP = 9\% - 8\% = 1\%$$

Thus investors require a 1 percent premium to hold or invest in the corporate bond instead of the Treasury bond.

Another corporate bond with a higher default risk may carry an interest rate of, say, 11 percent. If the other assumptions used above are retained, the DRP would be:

$$11\% = 3\% + 5\% + DRP + 0\% + 0\%$$
$$DRP = 11\% - 3\% - 5\% - 0\% - 0\% = 3\%$$

Alternatively, we could find DRP as follows:

$$DRP = 11\% - 8\% = 3\%$$

Thus, to get investors to invest in these riskier corporate bonds, a default risk premium of 3 percentage points must be offered above the interest rate or yield on Treasury bonds.

The examination of actual default risk premiums in Table 4.4 shows long-term interest rates for Treasury bonds and two corporate bonds with different degrees of default risk. The characteristics of corporate bonds are discussed more fully in Chapter 7, but here it can be said that one way potential default risk is measured is through bond ratings. The highest rating, Aaa, indicates the lowest likelihood of default. Investors in Aaa bonds require a small default risk premium over Treasury bonds. Baa-rated bonds have higher default risks but still are considered to be of reasonably high quality. **Investment grade bonds** have ratings of Baa or higher and meet financial institution (banks, pension funds, insurance companies, etc.) investment standards.

investment grade bonds
ratings of Baa or higher that
meet financial institution
investment standards

TABLE 4.4
Default Risk Premiums on Corporate Bonds at Selected Dates (%)

	MARCH 1980	MARCH 1982	NOVEMBER 2001	NOVEMBER 2003	OCTOBER 2006
Aaa-rated corporate bonds	13.0	14.6	7.0	5.7	5.5
Less: 20-year Treasury bonds	12.5	13.8	5.3	5.2	4.9
Equals: default risk premium on Aaa bonds	.5	.8	1.7	.5	.6
Baa-rated corporate bonds	14.5	16.8	7.8	6.7	6.4
Less: 20-year Treasury bonds	12.5	13.8	5.3	5.2	4.9
Equals: default risk premium on Baa bonds	2.0	3.0	2.5	1.5	1.5

Source: Federal Reserve Bulletin and *Statistical Supplement to the Federal Reserve Bulletin,* various issues.

INTERNET ACTIVITY

Go to the Web site of the Federal Reserve Bank of St. Louis, http://www.stls.frb.org, and access the FRED database. Find current interest rates for long-term Treasury bonds, as well as Aaa and Baa corporate bonds, and indicate the size of default risk premiums.

ETHICAL ISSUES

In March 1980 the default risk premium on corporate Aaa bonds over twenty-year Treasuries was 0.5 percentage point (i.e., 13.0% − 12.5%). The default risk premium of the highest-quality corporate bonds over Treasury bonds generally falls in the range of 0.5 to 0.75 percentage points. In fact, the default risk premium was about 0.8 percentage point in March 1982 when the economy was in a deep recession. The default risk premium on Aaa-rated corporate bonds had increased to unusually high 1.7 percentage points in November 2001, reflecting an economic downturn and concerns about terrorism in the United States. However, by November 2003, the premium on Aaa-rated corporate bonds over the interest rate on twenty-year Treasury bonds was only 0.5 percentage point, which is considered to be low, historically speaking. The October 2006 risk premium for Aaa-rated bonds remained low at a 0.6 percentage point differential over twenty-year Treasury bonds.

The default risk premiums on Baa corporate bonds are generally better indicators of investor pessimism or optimism about economic expectations than are those on Aaa bonds. More firms fail or suffer financial distress during periods of recession than during periods of economic expansion. Thus, investors tend to require higher premiums to compensate for default risk when the economy is in a recession or is expected to enter one. Notice in Table 4.4 that the risk premium on Baa-rated bonds was 2 percentage points in March 1980 (14.5% − 12.5%) and then increased to 3 percentage points in March 1982, when a deep recession existed. The default risk premium on Baa-rated bonds was 2.5 percentage points in November 2001 and reflected concerns about the slowing of economic activity in the United States and continued uncertainty after the terrorist attack on September 11, 2001. However, by November 2003 the risk premium on Baa-rated corporate debt had dropped to a relatively low 1.5 percentage points. As of October 2006 the risk premium on Baa-rated corporate debt remained at 1.5 percentage points over the interest rate on twenty-year Treasury bonds.

high-yield or junk bonds
bonds that have a relatively high probability of default

Sometimes corporations issue bonds with ratings lower than Baa. These are called **high-yield or junk bonds** because they have a substantial probability of default. While many institutional investors are restricted to investing in only investment-grade (rated Baa or higher) corporate debt, others are permitted to invest in high-yield, high-risk corporate debt. Recall the discussion in Chapter 2 about the savings and loan associations crisis that was caused in part by corporate defaults on high-yield or junk bonds that were held by S&Ls. Michael Milken, who was at Drexel Burnham Lambert at the time, was instrumental in getting those S&Ls and other institutions allowed to purchase junk bonds to do so. Some individuals would argue that the purchasers of junk bonds were sophisticated enough to make rational risk-return decisions; *caveat emptor*—let the buyer beware. Other individuals charged that unethical and illegal behavior on the part of the marketers of junk bonds contributed to the failure of many of the issuers of the bonds as well as the purchasers (particularly S&Ls) of the bonds. In 1989, Milken was sent to prison and Drexel Burnham Lambert went bankrupt.

CONCEPT CHECK

What is default risk? What is a default risk premium, and how is it calculated?

LESLIE L. ROGERS
President, Telecapital Solutions, Inc.

BA, Psychology,
University of Michigan

"Lending combines the knowledge of credit, industry characteristics, and financial products."

Q: *Why did you become a consultant after twenty years in banking and corporate finance?*

A: My role as a corporate finance consultant gives me the opportunity to use everything that I learned in my banking and corporate finance positions. I enjoy the flexibility of working with different companies and managing my own schedule. I can focus on the larger economic picture and provide unbiased advice about finance as well as the impact of business decisions on operations, marketing, and sales. Other positives include the freedom to be creative and personally impact the success of my clients.

Q: *What were some of the highlights of your career?*

A: I started at Dun and Bradstreet as a credit analyst, where I learned the fundamentals of credit and the importance of paying bills on time to establish a record of responsibility. My job involved the research and preparation of credit reports about companies. Then I began what turned into a twenty-year career in banking, which is a dynamic way to become acquainted with the interrelationship of finance, economics, and credit. I started as an internal bank credit-auditor for a major New York City bank, reviewing the credit of companies that had already received loans and assessing the company's ongoing ability to repay the loan. I was promoted from credit to lending, eventually becoming a vice president and department head. Lending combines the knowledge of credit, industry characteristics, and financial products. I particularly enjoyed becoming an industry specialist. Lending also requires sales skills, to match the right types of loans and other financial products to the customer.

As managing director, treasury, of Lucent Technologies' North America Customer Finance Group, I arranged project financing. My market and credit analysis skills were especially valuable in assessing the customer's ability to pay, particularly when we financed the sale ourselves.

Q: *What skills are important for a career in finance?*

A: Obviously, a firm grounding in accounting is a must. You should know how each journal entry affects the company and its relationship to the balance sheet, income statement, and cash flow statement. You must also understand the firm's business environment—the economics of its industry and the countries in which it operates. Interpersonal skills are extremely important as well.

Q: *Why is it important to understand financial management, even if you work in IT, marketing, or operations?*

A: Cash is the foundation of a viable business model. Personnel in all areas must understand their role in the creation, distribution, and retention of cash. You must be familiar with the cash cycle (the conversion of orders to cash receipts) of your own company, as well as its suppliers and customers. The sales team must be able to evaluate a prospective customer's ability to pay. Operations personnel should understand the effect of each purchasing, maintenance, and inventory decision on the cash cycle of the company. IT must provide the systems to turn the sale into cash. Interdepartmental communication is essential. Each department must prepare budgets based on sound assumptions and be able to analyze the costs and benefits of proposed capital projects.

APPLYING FINANCE TO . . .

INSTITUTIONS AND MARKETS

Depository institutions make profits by achieving a spread between the interest rates they pay individuals on savings accounts and the interest rates they charge businesses and other individuals for loans. Interest rates are also important to financial institutions, such as insurance companies and pension funds, that accumulate premiums and contributions and invest these proceeds in government and corporate securities for the benefit of their policyholders and employees. The government depends on financial institutions holding or owning an important portion of the U.S. Treasury securities issued to finance the national debt.

INVESTMENTS

Interest rates are set in the financial markets based on the supply and demand for loanable funds. The cost or price of home mortgage loans depends on the supply and demand for such loans in mortgage markets. Interest rates offered on Treasury debt securities reflect a real rate of interest and an expected inflation premium. Corporate bond borrowers must pay a default risk premium above the interest rate being offered on government debt securities. Corporate issuers of high-quality investment-grade bonds pay lower default risk premiums relative to issuers of lower-quality bonds. Observed interest rates may also reflect a maturity risk premium and/or a liquidity premium.

FINANCIAL MANAGEMENT

The prevailing level of interest rates is particularly important to financial managers. When interest rates are high, businesses will find it less profitable to borrow from financial institutions or in the securities markets because investment in inventories, plant, and equipment will look less attractive. Likewise, when interest rates are relatively low, loans are generally readily available and stock prices are usually high. Thus, financial managers often find it attractive to grow their businesses during periods when funds to finance the expansion activities can be borrowed at relatively low interest rates or when they can issue new shares of their common stocks at relatively high prices.

SUMMARY

This chapter began by illustrating how interest rates change given shifts in demand and/or supply curves. The loanable funds theory for explaining interest rates was presented. Then the following determinants of market interest rates were discussed: real rate of interest, inflation premium, default risk premium, maturity risk premium, and liquidity premium.

Three types of U.S. Treasury securities (bills, notes, and bonds) were identified and described. Then, the term structure of interest rates was defined and depicted with a yield curve graph. Next, the three theories used to explain the term structure, expectations, liquidity preference, and market segmentation were presented. Major historical price movements were identified, and the types of inflation—cost-push, demand-pull, speculative, and administrative—were described. The final topic focused on how default risk premiums are estimated and what causes them to change over time.

KEY TERMS

administrative inflation
cost-push inflation
dealer system
default risk
default risk premium
demand-pull inflation
expectations theory
high-yield or junk bonds
inflation
inflation premium

interest rate
interest rate risk
investment grade bonds
liquidity preference theory
liquidity premium
loanable funds theory
market segmentation theory
marketable government securities
maturity risk premium
nominal interest rate

nonmarketable government obligations
real rate of interest
risk-free rate of interest
speculative inflation
term structure
Treasury bills
Treasury bonds
Treasury notes
yield curve

DISCUSSION QUESTIONS

1. What is meant by the term *interest rate*, and how is it determined?

2. Describe how interest rates may adjust to an unanticipated increase in inflation.

3. Identify major periods of rising interest rates in U.S. history and describe some of the underlying reasons for these interest rate movements.

4. How does the loanable funds theory explain the level of interest rates?

5. What are the main sources of loanable funds? Indicate and briefly discuss the factors that affect the supply of loanable funds.

6. Indicate the sources of demand for loanable funds and discuss the factors that affect the demand for loanable funds.

7. What are the factors, in addition to supply and demand relationships, that determine market interest rates?

8. What are the types of marketable obligations issued by the Treasury?

9. Explain the mechanics of issuing Treasury bills, indicating how the price of a new issue is determined.

10. Describe the dealer system for marketable U.S. government obligations.

11. What is meant by the tax status of income from federal obligations?

12. Describe any significant changes in the ownership pattern of federal debt securities in recent years.

13. What have been the recent developments in the maturity distribution of marketable interest-bearing federal debt?

14. Describe the process of advance refunding of the federal debt.

15. What is the term *structure of interest rates,* and how is it expressed?

16. Identify and describe the three basic theories used to explain the term *structure of interest rates.*

17. Describe the process by which inflation took place historically before modern times.

18. Discuss the early periods of inflation based on the issue of paper money.

19. What was the basis for inflation during World Wars I and II?

20. Discuss the causes of the major periods of inflation in American history.

21. Explain the process by which price changes may be initiated by a general change in costs.

22. How can a change in the money supply lead to a change in the price level?

23. What is meant by the speculative type of inflation?

24. What is meant by a default risk premium?

25. How can a default risk premium change over time?

EXERCISES

1. Obtain a current issue of the *Statistical Supplement to the Federal Reserve Bulletin* and find interest rates on U.S. Treasury securities and on corporate bonds with different bond ratings.

   a. Prepare a yield curve or term structure of interest rates.

   b. Identify existing default risk premiums between long-term Treasury bonds and corporate bonds.

2. As an economist for a major bank, you are asked to explain the present substantial increase in the price level, notwithstanding the fact that neither the money supply nor the velocity of money has increased. How can this occur?

3. As an advisor to the U.S. Treasury, you have been asked to comment on a proposal for easing the burden of interest on the national debt. This proposal calls for the elimination of federal taxes on interest received from Treasury debt obligations. Comment on the proposal.

4. As one of several advisors to the secretary of the U.S. Treasury, you have been asked to submit a memo in connection with the average maturity of the obligations of the federal government. The basic premise is that the average maturity is far too short. As a result, issues of debt are coming due with great frequency and need

constant reissue. On the other hand, the economy shows signs of weakness. It is considered unwise to issue long-term obligations and absorb investment funds that might otherwise be invested in employment-producing construction and other private-sector support. Based on these conditions, what course of action do you recommend to the secretary of the U.S. Treasury?

5. Assume a condition in which the economy is strong, with relatively high employment. For one reason or another, the money supply is increasing at a high rate, with little evidence of money creation slowing down. Assuming the money supply continues to increase, describe the evolving effect on price levels.

6. Assume you are employed as an investment advisor. You are working with a retired individual who depends on her income from her investments to meet her day-to-day expenditures. She would like to find a way of increasing the current income from her investments. A new high-yield or junk bond issue has come to your attention. If you sell these high-yield bonds to a client, you will earn a higher-than-average fee. You wonder whether this would be a win-win investment for your retired client, who is seeking higher current income, and for you, who would benefit in terms of increased fees. What would you do?

PROBLEMS

1. You are considering an investment in a one-year government debt security with a yield of 5 percent or a highly liquid corporate debt security with a yield of 6.5 percent. The expected inflation rate for the next year is expected to be 2.5 percent.

   a. What would be your real rate earned on either of the two investments?

   b. What would be the default risk premium on the corporate debt security?

2. Inflation is expected to be 3 percent over the next year. You desire an annual real rate of return of 2.5 percent on your investments.

   a. What nominal rate of interest would have to be offered on a one-year Treasury security for you to consider making an investment?

   b. A one-year corporate debt security is being offered at 2 percentage points over the one-year Treasury security rate that meets your requirement in (a). What would be the nominal interest rate on the corporate security?

3. Find the nominal interest rate for a debt security given the following information: real rate = 2 percent, liquidity premium = 2 percent, default risk premium = 4 percent, maturity risk premium = 3 percent, and inflation premium = 3 percent.

4. Find the default risk premium for a debt security given the following information: inflation premium = 3 percent, maturity risk premium = 2.5 percent, real rate = 3 percent, liquidity premium = 0 percent, and nominal interest rate = 10 percent.

5. Find the default risk premium for a debt security given the following information: inflation premium = 2.5 percent, maturity risk premium = 2.5 percent, real rate = 3 percent, liquidity premium = 1.5 percent, and nominal interest rate = 14 percent.

6. Assume that the interest rate on a one-year Treasury bill is 6 percent and the rate on a two-year Treasury note is 7 percent.

   a. If the expected real rate of interest is 3 percent, determine the inflation premium on the Treasury bill.

   b. If the maturity risk premium is expected to be zero, determine the inflation premium on the Treasury note.

   c. What is the expected inflation premium for the second year?

7. A Treasury note with a maturity of four years carries a nominal rate of interest of 10 percent. In contrast, an eight-year Treasury bond has a yield of 8 percent.

   a. If inflation is expected to average 7 percent over the first four years, what is the expected real rate of interest?

   b. If the inflation rate is expected to be 5 percent for the first year, calculate the average annual rate of inflation for years 2 through 4.

   c. If the maturity risk premium is expected to be zero between the two Treasury securities, what will be the average annual inflation rate expected over years 5 through 8?

8. The interest rate on a ten-year Treasury bond is 9.25 percent. A comparable-maturity Aaa-rated corporate bond is yielding 10 percent. Another comparable-maturity but lower-quality corporate bond has a yield of 14 percent, which includes a liquidity premium of 1.5 percent.

   a. Determine the default risk premium on the Aaa-rated bond.

   b. Determine the default risk premium on the lower-quality corporate bond.

9. A corporate bond has a nominal interest rate of 12 percent. This bond is not very liquid and consequently requires a 2 percent liquidity premium. The bond is of low quality and thus has a default risk premium of 2.5 percent. The bond has a remaining life of twenty-five years, resulting in a maturity risk premium of 1.5 percent.

   a. Estimate the nominal interest rate on a Treasury bond.

   b. What would be the inflation premium on the Treasury bond if investors required a real rate of interest of 2.5 percent?

10. **Challenge Problem** Following are some selected interest rates.

MATURITY OR TERM	RATE	TYPE OF SECURITY
1 year	4.0%	Corporate loan (high quality)
1 year	5.0%	Corporate loan (low quality)
1 year	3.5%	Treasury bill
5 years	5.0%	Treasury note
5 years	6.5%	Corporate bond (high quality)
5 years	8.0%	Corporate bond (low quality)
10 years	10.5%	Corporate bond (low quality)
10 years	8.5%	Corporate bond (high quality)
10 years	7.0%	Treasury bond
20 years	7.5%	Treasury bond
20 years	9.5%	Corporate bond (high quality)
20 years	12.0%	Corporate bond (low quality)

   a. Plot a yield curve using interest rates for government default risk-free securities.

   b. Plot a yield curve using corporate debt securities with low default risk (high quality) and a separate yield curve for low-quality corporate debt securities.

   c. Measure the amount of default risk premiums, assuming constant inflation rate expectations and no maturity or liquidity risk premiums on any of the debt securities for both high-quality and low-quality corporate securities based on information from (a) and (b). Describe and discuss why differences might exist between high-quality and low-quality corporate debt securities.

   d. Identify the average expected inflation rate at each maturity level in (a) if the real rate is expected to average 2 percent per year and if there are no maturity risk premiums expected on Treasury securities.

   e. Using information from (d), calculate the average annual expected inflation rate over years 2 through 5. Also calculate the average annual expected inflation rates for years 6 through 10 and for years 11 through 20.

   f. Based on the information from (e), reestimate the maturity risk premiums for high-quality and low-quality corporate debt securities. Describe what seems to be occurring over time and between differences in default risks.

• CHAPTER 5 •

Time Value of Money

Chapter Learning Objectives

AFTER STUDYING THIS CHAPTER, YOU SHOULD BE ABLE TO:

- Explain what is meant by the time value of money.
- Describe the concept of simple interest.
- Describe the process of compounding.
- Describe discounting to determine present values.
- Find interest rates and time requirements for problems involving compounding or discounting.
- Describe the meaning of an ordinary annuity.
- Find interest rates and time requirements for problems involving annuities.
- Calculate annual annuity payments.
- Make compounding and discounting calculations using time intervals that are less than one year.
- Describe the difference between the annual percentage rate and the effective annual rate.
- Describe the meaning of an annuity due (in the *Learning Extension*).

Where We Have Been...

In Chapter 4 you learned how interest rates are determined in the financial markets. The supply of and demand for loanable funds were discussed along with the determinants of market or "nominal" interest rates. You should recall that the determinants are the real rate of interest, an inflation premium, and a default risk premium for risky debt. A maturity risk premium adjusts for differences in lives or maturities, and there also may be a liquidity premium. You also learned about the characteristics of U.S. government debt securities and the term or maturity structure of interest rates. You now should know how inflation premiums and price movements affect interest rates, as well as why default risk premiums exist and how they are measured.

Where We Are Going...

Chapter 6 focuses on financial return and risk concepts. Chapters 7 and 8 then discuss the characteristics and valuations of bonds and stocks. You will learn about the long-term external financing sources available to and used by businesses. You will then explore the characteristics and features of both debt and equity capital. Next, the general principles of valuation, which build on the time value of money (covered in this chapter), and how bonds and stocks are valued will be covered. Calculating rates of return is the last topic in Chapter 8. In Chapter 9 you will focus on the characteristics and operation of primary and secondary securities markets. Chapter 10, the last chapter in Part 2, will focus on investment implications.

How This Chapter Applies to Me...

You probably have experienced the need to save money to buy an automobile or to pay for your tuition. Your savings grow more rapidly when you can earn interest on previously earned interest in addition to interest on the starting amount of your savings. This is known as compounding and means that the longer you save the faster your savings will grow and the larger will be your down payment on your automobile purchase or the more money you will have for your tuition. An understanding of compounding also will be useful to you when investing in stocks and bonds and planning for eventual retirement.

Most of us would agree that if other things are equal:

> *More money is better than less money.*

Most of us also would agree:

> *Money today is worth more than the same amount of money received in the future.*

Of course, the value of an additional dollar is not necessarily the same for all individuals. For example, a person subsisting at the poverty level would likely find an added dollar to be worth more in "economic terms" than would an extra dollar to a millionaire or billionaire. It is probably safe to say that having an added dollar today has more "economic worth" to you or us than it would to Bill Gates, the founder and CEO of the Microsoft Corporation. At the same time, his personal desire or drive for accumulating more dollars is likely to be greater than your desires.

This chapter makes no attempt to consider the economic or psychic values of more money to a specific individual. Rather, it concentrates on the pillar of finance, initially presented in Chapter 1, stating that "Money has a time value." The focus here is on how money can grow or increase over time, as well as how money has a lower worth today if one has to wait to receive the money sometime in the future. This occurs because one loses the opportunity of earning interest on the money by not being able to save or invest the money today.

Financial calculators or spreadsheet software programs will perform the calculations and procedures discussed in this chapter. However, the calculation procedures are first described in detail to enhance the understanding of the logic involved in the concepts of the time value of money. By learning to work the problems the "long way," using step-by-step calculations, following the steps given for financial calculators, spreadsheet programs, and tables-based calculations should make more sense. Students are encouraged to explore using multiple problem-solving methods.

FINANCE PRINCIPLE

BASIC CONCEPTS

time value of money
math of finance whereby interest is earned over time by saving or investing money

To understand the pricing and valuation of bonds, stocks, and real asset investments, we must first understand some basic finance math concepts. The ***time value of money*** is the math of finance whereby interest is earned over time by saving or investing money. Money can increase or grow over time if we can save (invest) it and earn a return on our savings (investment). Let's begin with a savings account illustration. Assume you have $1,000 to save or invest; this is your *principal*. The ***present value (PV)*** of a savings or an investment is its amount or value today. For our example, this is your $1,000.

present value
amount or value today of savings or an investment

A bank offers to accept your savings for one year and agrees to pay to you an 8 percent interest rate for use of your $1,000. This amounts to $80 in interest (0.08 × $1,000). The total payment by the bank at the end of one year is $1,080 ($1,000 principal plus $80 in interest). This $1,080 is referred to as the future value or value after one year. The ***future value (FV)*** of a savings amount or investment is its value at a specified time or date in the future. In general word terms, we have:

future value
value at a specified time or date in the future of a savings amount or investment

$$\text{Future value} = \text{Present value} + (\text{Present value} \times \text{Interest rate})$$

or

$$\text{Future value} = \text{Present value} \times (1 + \text{Interest rate})$$

In our example, we have:

$$\text{Future value} = \$1,000 + (\$1,000 \times 0.08)$$
$$= \$1,080$$

or

$$\text{Future value} = \$1,000 \times 1.08$$
$$= \$1,080$$

Let's now assume that your $1,000 investment remains on deposit for two years but that the bank pays only ***simple interest***, which is interest earned only on the investment's principal. In word terms, we have:

simple interest
interest earned only on the investment's principal

$$\text{Future value} = \text{Present value} \times [1 + (\text{Interest rate}) \times (\text{number of periods})]$$

For our example, this becomes:

$$\text{Future value} = \$1,000 \times [1 + (0.08 \times 2)]$$
$$= \$1,000 \times 1.16$$
$$= \$1,160$$

What is the time value of money?

What do we mean by present value and future value?

What is simple interest?

Another bank will pay you a 10 percent interest rate on your money. Thus, you would receive $100 in interest ($1,000 × 0.10) or a return at the end of one year of $1,100 ($1,000 × 1.10) from this second bank. While the $20 difference in return between the two banks ($1,100 versus $1,080) is not great, it has some importance to most people. For a two-year deposit for which simple interest is paid annually, the difference increases to $40. The second bank would return $1,200 ($1,000 × 1.20) to you versus $1,160 from the first bank. If the funds were invested for ten years, we would accumulate $1,000 × [1 + (0.08 × 10)] or $1,800 at the first bank. At the second bank we would have $1,000 × [1 + (0.10 × 10)] or $2,000, a $200 difference. This interest rate differential between the two banks will become even more important when we introduce the concept of *compounding*.

COMPOUNDING TO DETERMINE FUTURE VALUES

compounding
arithmetic process whereby an initial value increases or grows at a compound interest rate over time to reach a value in the future

compound interest
earning interest on interest in addition to interest on the principal or initial investment

Compounding is an arithmetic process whereby an initial value increases or grows at a *compound interest* rate over time to reach a value in the future. **Compound interest** involves earning interest on interest in addition to interest on the principal or initial investment. To understand compounding, let's assume that you leave the investment with a bank for more than one year. For example, the first bank accepts your $1,000 deposit now, adds $80 at the end of one year, retains the $1,080 for the second year, and pays you interest at an 8 percent rate. The bank returns your initial deposit plus accumulated interest at the end of the second year. How much will you receive as a future value? In word terms, we have:

$$\text{Future value} = \text{Present value} \times [(1 + \text{Interest rate}) \times (1 + \text{Interest rate})]$$

For our two-year investment example, we have:

$$\begin{aligned}
\text{Future value} &= \$1,000 \times (1.08) \times (1.08) \\
&= \$1,000 \times 1.1664 \\
&= \$1,166.40 \\
&= \$1,166 \text{ (rounded)}
\end{aligned}$$

A timeline also can be used to illustrate this two-year example as follows:

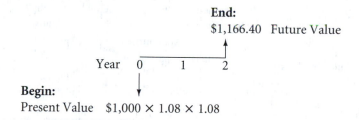

Thus, for a one-year investment, the return would be $1,080 ($1,000 × 1.08), which is the same as the return on a simple-interest investment, as was previously shown. However, a two-year investment at an 8 percent compound interest rate will return $1,166.40, compared to $1,160 using an 8 percent simple interest rate.

The compounding concept also can be expressed in equation form as:

$$FV_n = PV(1 + r)^n \qquad (5.1)$$

where FV is the future value, PV is the present value, r is the interest rate, and n is the number of periods in years.

For our $1,000 deposit, 8 percent, two-year example, we have:

$$\begin{aligned}
FV_2 &= \$1,000 (1 + 0.08)^2 \\
&= \$1,000(1.1164) \\
&= \$1,166.40 \\
&= \$1,166 \text{ (rounded)}
\end{aligned}$$

If we extend the time period to ten years, the $1,000 deposit would grow to:

$$FV_{10} = \$1,000(1 + 0.08)^{10}$$
$$= \$1,000(2.1589)$$
$$= \$2,158.90$$
$$= \$2,159 \text{ (rounded)}$$

Texas Instruments (TI) and Hewlett Packard (HP) make two popular types of financial calculators. However, they are programmed differently.[1] Reference is made to the use of TI and HP calculators when discussing calculator solutions throughout the remainder of this chapter. Other available financial calculators are usually programmed like either the TI or HP calculators. What is important is that if you are going to use a financial calculator to solve time value of money problems, you must understand how your particular calculator works.

Most financial calculators are programmed to readily find future values. Typically, financial calculators will have a present value key (PV), a future value key (FV), a number of time periods key (N), an interest rate key (usually designated %i), and a compute key (usually designated as CPT). If you have a financial calculator, you can verify the future value result for the ten-year example.

First, clear any values stored in the calculator's memory. Next, enter 1000 and press the PV key (some financial calculators require that you enter the present value amount as a minus value because it is an investment or outflow). Then, enter 8 and press the %i key (most financial calculators are programmed so that you enter whole numbers rather than decimals for the interest rate). Next, enter 10 for the number of time periods (usually years) and press the N key. Finally, press the CPT key followed by the FV key to calculate the future value of 2,158.93, which rounds to $2,159. Actually, financial calculators are programmed to calculate answers to twelve significant digits.

Financial Calculator Solution:

Inputs:	10	8	1000
	N	%i	PV
Press:	CPT	FV	
Solution:	2158.93		

Computer spreadsheet programs also are available for finding future values. Following is the same problem solved using Microsoft's Excel spreadsheet program. For presentation purposes, the solution only for the two-year version of the problem is shown graphically. That is, how much would you accumulate after two years if you invested $1,000 at an 8 percent interest rate with annual compounding?

Spreadsheet Solution:

	A	B	C	D
1	Interest Rate	0.08		
2	Time Period	0	1	2
3	Cash Flow	-1000	0	0
4	Future Value (FV)		1080.00	1166.40
5				
6	Financial Function			
7	FV Solution:			$1,166.40

We set up our spreadsheet with descriptive labels in cells A1 through A4. We then solve the compound interest problem by placing the interest rate in decimal form (0.08) in Cell B1. The

---

1. For problems involving PVs and FVs, HP calculators require one of the values to be entered as a negative. In contrast, both PVs and FVs are entered as positive values in TI calculators, and the internal program makes one of the values negative for calculation purposes. Other TI and HP differences when entering data also are noted later in this chapter.

Venture capitalists represent an important source of financing for small businesses. Venture capitalists, of course, are in the business of providing financial capital to small businesses with the expectation of earning a return on their investments commensurate with the risks associated with those investments. A typical "exit strategy" of venture capitalists is to maintain an investment in a firm for approximately five years and, if the investment is successful, then sell the firm to another company or take the firm public in an initial public offering (IPO).

A venture capitalist usually will invest in a small business by either taking a direct ownership position in the form of common stock or by accepting the firm's bond plus an "equity kicker" or the right to purchase a certain portion of the firm (e.g., 50 percent). For example, let's assume that a venture capitalist invests $5 million in a firm. In return, the venture capitalist receives shares of stock representing 50

percent ownership in the firm. Let's assume that the firm can be sold for $40 million at the end of five years. What will be the rate of return that the venture capitalist will earn on the $10 million investment? The present value is $5 million and the future value is $20 million (i.e., $40 million times .5, or 50 percent). Since, we know the time period is five years, we solve for the interest rate r. Using a financial calculator results in a compound interest rate (%i) of 32.0 percent.

What would have been the venture capitalist's rate of return if the firm had been sold for $40 million at the end of six years instead of at the end of five years? Again, the present value is $5 million, the future value is $20 million, and the time period is six years. Solving for the interest rate yields 26.0 percent. Thus, if the sale of the firm is delayed by one year, the compound rate of return on the venture capitalist's investment drops 6 percentage points from 32 percent down to 26 percent.

time periods are placed on Row 2, beginning with period 0 (the current period) in Cell B2 and so forth. The cash flow of -1000 (an outflow) is listed in cell B3. Since this is a simple problem, we first replicate the basic "by hand" calculations in spreadsheet format and the future value calculations beginning in C4 and continuing to D4.

In Cell C4 we place the formula $= -\text{B3}*(1+\text{B1})$, which reflects compounding the $1,000 $1,000 investment at 8 percent interest for one year. Cell D4 shows compounding of the investment at 8 percent for a second year and can be calculated as $\text{C4}*(1+\text{B1})$. So, compounding at a 8 percent interest rate results in a future value of $1,166.40 after two years. Of course, we could have made the FV calculation in one step as $= -\text{B3}*(1+\text{B1})^\wedge 2$, which also produces $1,166.40.

Excel and other spreadsheet programs have built-in "financial functions" so that spreadsheet solutions do not have to be calculated the "long way." The bottom portion of the spreadsheet solution example illustrates the use of the financial function for future value. Click on the Excel financial wizard (*fx*) icon, then Financial, then FV, then OK to bring up the dialogue box where the FV components for the problem at hand are requested. The equation is FV(Rate, Nper, Pmt, PV, Type). The Rate is 0.08; Nper is the number of time periods, or 2 in the preceding example; Pmt is 0, since there are no periodic payments; PV is -1000; and Type is 0, reflecting that payments occur at the end of the period. Thus we would have FV(0.08,2,0,-1000,0). Clicking OK results in an FV of $1,166.40, or $1,166 rounded. Of course, rather than inserting numbers, one could insert specific cell references in the FV function.

If the investment had been compounded for ten years, the FV function inputs would have been FV(0.08,10,0,-1000,0). Clicking OK would result in an answer of $2,158.92, or $2,159 rounded.

In addition, tables have been prepared to simplify the calculation effort if financial calculators or spreadsheet programs are not available. Equation 5.1 can be rewritten as:

$$FV_n = PV(FVIF_{r,n}) \qquad (5.2)$$

where the $(1 + r)^n$ part of Equation 5.1 is replaced by a future value interest factor (FVIF) corresponding to a specific interest rate and a specified time period.

Table 5.1 shows FVIF values carried to three decimal places for a partial range of interest rates and time periods. (Table 1 in the Appendix is a more comprehensive FVIF table.) Let's use Table 5.1 to find the future value of $1,000 invested at an 8 percent compound interest rate for a ten-year period, notice that at the intersection of the 8 percent column and ten years, we find an FVIF of 2.159. Putting this information into Equation 5.2 gives the following solution:

Table-Based Solution:

$$FV_{10} = \$1,000(2.159)$$
$$= \$2,159$$

TABLE 5.1
Future Value Interest Factor (FVIF) of $1

YEAR	5%	6%	7%	8%	9%	10%
1	1.050	1.060	1.070	1.080	1.090	1.100
2	1.102	1.124	1.145	1.166	1.188	1.210
3	1.158	1.191	1.225	1.260	1.295	1.331
4	1.216	1.262	1.311	1.360	1.412	1.464
5	1.276	1.338	1.403	1.469	1.539	1.611
6	1.340	1.419	1.501	1.587	1.677	1.772
7	1.407	1.504	1.606	1.714	1.828	1.949
8	1.477	1.594	1.718	1.851	1.993	2.144
9	1.551	1.689	1.838	1.999	2.172	2.358
10	1.629	1.791	1.967	2.159	2.367	2.594

INTERNET ACTIVITY

Go to the Chase Bank Web site, www.chase.com. Access "Personal Finance" and then "Banking" and identify the interest rates being paid on certificates of deposit (CDs) of various maturities and amounts.

Further examination of Table 5.1 shows how a $1 investment grows or increases with various combinations of interest rates and time periods. For example, if another bank offers to pay you a 10 percent interest rate compounded annually, notice that the FVIF at the intersection of 10 percent and ten years would be 2.594, making your $1,000 investment worth $2,594 ($1,000 × 2.594). Now the difference between the 8 percent and 10 percent rates is much more significant at $435 ($2,594 − $2,159) than the $200 difference that occurred with simple compounding over ten years. Thus, we see the advantage of being able to compound at even slightly higher interest rates over a period of years.

The compounding or growth process also can be depicted in graphic form. Figure 5.1 shows graphic relationships among future values, interest rates, and time periods. For example, notice how $1 will grow differently over a ten-year period at 5 percent versus 10 percent interest rates. Of course, if no interest is being earned, then the initial $1 investment will remain at $1 no matter how long the investment is held. At a 10 percent interest rate, the initial $1 grows to $2.59 (rounded) after ten years. This compares with $1.63 (rounded) after ten years if the interest rate is only 5 percent. Notice that the future value increases at an increasing rate as the interest rate is increased and as the time period is lengthened.

FIGURE 5.1
Future Value, Interest Rate, and Time Period Relationships

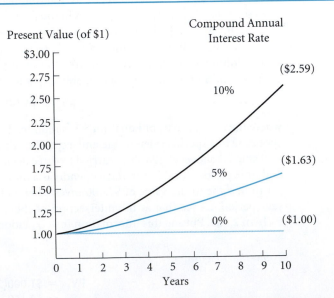

INFLATION OR PURCHASING POWER IMPLICATIONS

The compounding process described in the preceding section does not say anything about the purchasing power of the initial $1 investment at some point in the future. As seen, $1 growing at a 10 percent interest rate would be worth $2.59 (rounded) at the end of ten years. With zero inflation, you could purchase $2.59 of the same quality of goods after ten years relative to what you could purchase now. However, if the stated or *nominal* interest rate is 10 percent and the inflation rate is 5 percent, then in terms of increased purchasing power the "net" or differential compounding rate would be 5 percent (10 percent − 5 percent) and $1 would have an inflation-adjusted value of $1.63 after ten years. This translates into an increased purchasing power of $0.63 ($1.63 − $1.00).

Also note that if the compound inflation rate is equal to the compound interest rate, the purchasing power would not change. For example, if in Figure 5.1 both the inflation and interest rates were 5 percent, the purchasing power of $1 would remain the same over time. Thus, to make this concept operational, subtract the expected inflation rate from the stated interest rate and compound the remaining (differential) interest rate to determine the change in purchasing power over a stated time period. For example, if the interest rate is 10 percent and the inflation rate is 3 percent, the savings or investment should be compounded at a differential 7 percent rate. Turning to Table 5.1, we see that $1 invested at a 7 percent interest rate for ten years would grow to $1.967 ($1.97 rounded) in terms of purchasing power. Of course, the actual dollar value would be $2.594 ($2.59 rounded).

Financial contracts (e.g., savings deposits and bank loans) in countries that have experienced high and volatile inflation rates sometimes have been linked to a consumer price or similar inflation index. Such actions are designed to reduce the exposure to inflation risk for both savers and lenders. Since the interest rate they receive on their savings deposits will vary with the rate of inflation, savers receive purchasing power protection. As inflation rises, so will the rate of interest individuals receive on their savings deposits such that purchasing power will be maintained.

Bank lenders are similarly protected against changing inflation rates, since the rates they charge on their loans will also vary with changes in inflation rates. At least in theory, banks will be able to maintain a profit spread between the interest rates they pay to savers and the higher interest rates they lend at to borrowers because inflation affects both financial contracts. Of course, if the borrowers are business firms, they need to be able to pass on higher prices for their products and services to consumers to be able to maintain profit margins when interest rates are rising along with increases in inflation.

GLOBAL DISCUSSION

CONCEPT CHECK

What do we mean by the term compounding?

What is compound interest?

DISCOUNTING TO DETERMINE PRESENT VALUES

Most financial management decisions involve present values rather than future values. For example, a financial manager who is considering purchasing an asset wants to know what the asset is worth now rather than at the end of some future time period. The reason that an asset has value is because it will produce a stream of future cash benefits. To determine its value now in time period zero, we have to discount or reduce the future cash benefits to their present value. **Discounting** is an arithmetic process whereby a future value decreases at a compound interest rate over time to reach a present value.

Let's illustrate discounting with a simple example involving an investment. Assume that a bank or other borrower offers to pay you $1,000 at the end of one year in return for using $1,000 of your money now. If you are willing to accept a zero rate of return, you might make the investment. Most of us would not jump at an offer like this! Rather, we would require some return on our investment. To receive a return of, say, 8 percent, you would invest less than $1,000 now. The amount to be invested would be determined by dividing the $1,000 that is due at the end of one year by one plus the interest rate of 8 percent. This results in an investment amount of $925.93 ($1,000 ÷ 1.08), or $926 rounded. Alternatively, the $1,000 could have been multiplied by 1 ÷ 1.08, or 0.9259 (when carried to four decimal places) to get $925.90, or $926 rounded.

Let's now assume that you will not receive the $1,000 for two years and the compound interest rate is 8 percent. What dollar amount (present value) would you be willing to invest? In word terms, we have:

discounting
arithmetic process whereby a future value decreases at a compound interest rate over time to reach a present value

$$\text{Present value} = \text{Future value} \times \{[1 \div (1 + \text{Interest rate})] \times [1 \div (1 + \text{Interest rate})]\}$$

For our two-year investment example, we get:

$$\begin{aligned}
\text{Present value} &= \$1{,}000 \times (1 \div 1.08) \times (1 \div 1.08) \\
&= \$1{,}000 \times (0.9259) \times (0.9259) \\
&= \$1{,}000 \times 0.8573 \\
&= \$857.30
\end{aligned}$$

A timeline also can be used to illustrate this two-year example as follows:

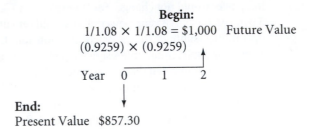

Begin:

$1/1.08 \times 1/1.08 = \$1{,}000$ Future Value

$(0.9259) \times (0.9259)$

Year 0 1 2

End:

Present Value $857.30

Thus, for a one-year investment, the present value would be $925.90 ($1,000 × 1 ÷ 1.08, or 0.9259). A two-year investment would have a present value of only $857.30 ($1,000 × 0.9259 × 0.9259).

The discounting concept can be expressed in equation form as:

$$PV = FV_n \div (1 + r)^n$$

or

$$PV = FV_n[1 \div (1 + r)^n] \tag{5.3}$$

where the individual terms are the same as those defined for the future value equation. Notice that the future value equation has simply been rewritten to solve for the present value. For the $1,000, 8 percent, two-year example, we have:

$$\begin{aligned}
PV &= \$1{,}000[1 \div (1 + 0.08)^2] \\
&= \$1{,}000(1 \div 1.1164) \\
&= \$1{,}000(0.8573) \\
&= \$857.30 \\
&= \$857 \text{ (rounded)}
\end{aligned}$$

If we extend the time period to ten years, the $1,000 future value would decrease to:

$$\begin{aligned}
PV &= \$1{,}000[1 \div (1 + 0.08)^{10}] \\
&= \$1{,}000(1 \div 2.1589) \\
&= \$1{,}000(0.4632) \\
&= \$463.20 \\
&= \$463 \text{ (rounded)}
\end{aligned}$$

Most financial calculators are programmed to readily find present values. As noted, financial calculators typically have a present value (PV) key, a future value (FV) key, a number of time periods (N) key, an interest rate (%i) key, and a compute (CPT) key. If you have a financial calculator, you can verify the present value result for the ten-year example. First, clear the calculator. Then, enter 1000 (or −1000 for some calculators to find a positive PV) and press the FV key, enter 8 and press the %i key, and enter 10 and press the N key. Finally, press the CPT key followed by the PV key to calculate the present value of 463.19, which rounds to $463.

Financial Calculator Solution:

Inputs: 10   8   1000

[N]   [%i]   [FV]

Press: [CPT]   [PV]

Solution: 463.19

Excel or another spreadsheet program also can be used to find present values. For a simple present value problem, we show the calculation by hand in spreadsheet format, as well as using the preprogrammed PV financial function. What would be the present value of receiving $1,000 two years from now if the annual discount rate is 8 percent?

Spreadsheet Solution:

	A	B	C	D
1	Interest Rate	0.08		
2	Time Period	0	1	2
3	Cash Flow	0	0	1000
4	Present Value	857.34	925.93	
5				
6	Financial Function			
7	PV Solution:	($857.34)		

When making the calculation by hand, we enter 0.08 as the interest rate in Cell B1, then the time periods beginning with 0 in Cell B2 and so forth, and a cash flow of 1000 in Cell D3. In Cell C4 we insert the equation =D3/(1+B1)^1 and get 925.93. Then, in Cell B4 we enter the equation =C4/(1+B1)^1, with the result being 857.34. Of course, we could have solved for the present value in one step by entering in Cell B4 the equation D3/(1+B1)^2 and found 857.34 directly.

The bottom portion of the spreadsheet solution example illustrates the use of Excel's Financial Function, called present value (PV). Click on the Excel financial wizard (*fx*) icon, then Financial, then PV, then OK to bring up the dialogue box where the PV components for the problem at hand are requested. The equation is PV(Rate, Nper, Pmt, FV, Type). The Rate is 0.08; Nper is the number of time periods, or 2 in this example; Pmt is zero since there are no periodic payments; FV is 1000; and Type is 0, reflecting that payments occur at the end of the period. This equates to PV(0.08,2,0,1000,0). Clicking OK results in a PV of −$857.34, or −$857 rounded. Note that the PV function in Excel is programmed to give a negative number much like the PV solutions on most calculators. Of course, rather than inserting numbers, one could insert specific cell references in the PV function.

If the investment had been discounted for ten years, the PV function inputs would have been PV(0.08,10,0,1000,0). Clicking OK would result in an answer of −$463.19, or −$463 rounded.

In addition, tables have been prepared to simplify the calculation effort if financial calculators or computer programs are not available. Equation 5.3 can be rewritten as:

$$PV = FV_n(PVIF_{r,n}) \tag{5.4}$$

where the $1 \div (1 + r)^n$ part of Equation 5.3 is replaced by a present value interest factor (PVIF) corresponding to a specific interest rate and a specified time period.

Table-Based Solution:

Table 5.2 shows PVIF values for a range of interest rates and time periods. (Table 2 in the Appendix is a more comprehensive PVIF table.) Let's use Table 5.2 to find the present value of $1,000 invested at an 8 percent compound interest rate for a ten-year period. Notice that at the intersection of the 8 percent column and ten years, we find a PVIF of 0.463. Putting this information in Equation 5.4 gives the following:

$$PV = \$1,000(0.463)$$
$$= \$463$$

TABLE 5.2
Present Value Interest Factor (PVIF) of $1

YEAR	5%	6%	7%	8%	9%	10%
1	.952	.943	.935	.926	.917	.909
2	.907	.890	.873	.857	.842	.826
3	.864	.840	.816	.794	.772	.751
4	.823	.792	.763	.735	.708	.683
5	.784	.747	.713	.681	.650	.621
6	.746	.705	.666	.630	.596	.564
7	.711	.665	.623	.583	.547	.513
8	.677	.627	.582	.540	.502	.467
9	.645	.592	.544	.500	.460	.424
10	.614	.558	.508	.463	.422	.386

Further examination of Table 5.2 shows how a $1 investment decreases with various combinations of interest rates and time periods. For example, if another bank offers to pay interest at a 10 percent compound rate, the PVIF at the intersection of 10 percent and ten years would be 0.386, resulting in your $1,000 future value being worth an investment of $386 ($1,000 × 0.386). The difference in required investments needed to accumulate $1,000 at the end of ten years between 8 percent and 10 percent interest rates is $77 ($463 − $386). In essence, the present value of a future value decreases as the interest rate increases for a specified time period.

The discounting process also can be depicted in graphic form. Figure 5.2 shows graphic relationships among present values, interest rates, and time periods. For example, notice how a $1 future value will decrease differently over a ten-year period at 5 percent versus 10 percent interest rates. Of course, at a zero interest rate, the present value remains at $1 and is not affected by time. If no interest is being earned, the $1 future value will have a present value of $1 no matter how long the investment is held. At a 5 percent interest rate, the present value of $1 declines to $0.61 (rounded) if an investor has to wait ten years to receive the $1. This compares with a present value of $1 of only $0.39 (rounded) if the interest rate is 10 percent and the investor must wait ten years to receive $1. Notice that the present value decreases at an increasing rate as the interest rate is increased and as the time period is lengthened.

CONCEPT CHECK

What do we mean by discounting?

FIGURE 5.2
Present Value, Interest Rate, and Time Period Relationships

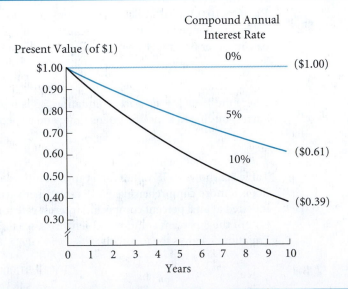

EQUATING PRESENT VALUES AND FUTURE VALUES

Notice that Equations 5.1 and 5.3 are two ways of looking at the same process involving compound interest rates. That is, if we know the future value of an investment, we can find its present value and vice versa. For example, an initial investment of $1,000 will grow to $1,116.40 at the end of two years if the interest rate is 8 percent. Note that to reduce the impact of rounding errors, we are carrying our calculations here to four decimal places:

$$\text{FV}_2 = \$1,000(1 + 0.08)^2$$
$$= \$1,000(1.1664)$$
$$= \$1,166.40$$

Now, what is the present value of a $1,166.40 future value is if we must wait two years to receive the future value amount and if the interest rate is 8 percent? The solution would be:

$$\text{PV} = \$1,166.40[1 \div (1 + 0.08)^2]$$
$$= \$1,166.40(1 \div 1.1664)$$
$$= \$1,166.40(0.8573)$$
$$= \$1,000$$

Thus, an investor should be indifferent about receiving a $1,000 present value now or a $1,166 future value two years from now if the compound interest rate is 8 percent.

CONCEPT CHECK

How do present values and future values relate or equate to each other?

FINDING INTEREST RATES AND TIME REQUIREMENTS

Recall the four variables from the future value (5.1 and 5.2) and present value (5.3 and 5.4) equations: PV = present value, FV = future value, r = interest rate, and n = number of periods. As long as we know the values for any three of these variables, we can solve for the fourth or unknown variable. This is accomplished by using a financial calculator, a financial function in a spreadsheet program, or tables.

INTERNET ACTIVITY

Go to the Citibank Web site, www.citibank.com, and identify the types of credit cards available to individuals and the prevailing interest rates on the credit cards.

SOLVING FOR INTEREST RATES

Assume that the present value of an investment is $1,000, the future value is $1,403, and the time period is five years. What compound interest rate would be earned on this investment?

This problem can be solved using a financial calculator. If a financial calculator is used, enter PV = 1000, FV = 1403, N = 5, and press CPT followed by the %i key to find an r of 7.01, or 7 percent rounded (some calculators may require either the PV entry or FV entry to be negative).

Financial Calculator Solution:

Inputs:	5	1000	1403
	N	PV	FV
Press:	CPT	%i	
Solution:	7.01		

A second way of solving for the interest rate is with a spreadsheet program using a financial function. Excel has a financial function called RATE that makes it possible to solve quickly for the interest rate. Click on the financial wizard (*fx*), then on Financial, then RATE. Entering the requested data and clicking OK gives the following solution:

Spreadsheet Solution:

$$= \text{RATE(Nper, Pmt, PV, FV, Type)}$$
$$= \text{RATE}(5,0,-1000,1403,0)$$
$$= 7.01\%$$

The number of periods (Nper) is 5, there are zero periodic payments (Pmt), the present value is (PV) entered as -1000, the future value (FV) is 1403, and the Type is zero, since cash flows occur at the end of a time period.

Table-Based Solution:

The interest rate answer also can be found by setting up the problem using Equation 5.2 and Table 5.1 as follows:

$$FV_5 = PV(FVIF_{r,5})$$
$$\$1,403 = \$1,000(FVIF_{r,5})$$
$$FVIF_{r,5} = 1.403$$

Since we know that the number of time periods is five, we can turn to Table 5.1 and read across the year-five row until we find FVIF of 1.403. Notice that this occurs under the 7 percent column, indicating that the interest rate r is 7 percent.

We also can work the problem using Equation 5.4 and Table 5.2 as follows:

$$PV = FV_5(PVIF_{r,5})$$
$$\$1,000 = \$1,403(PVIF_{r,5})$$
$$PVIF_{r,5} = 0.713$$

Turning to Table 5.2, we read across the year-five row until we find the PVIF of 0.713. This occurs under the 7 percent column, indicating that the interest rate r is 7 percent.

SOLVING FOR TIME PERIODS

Now let's assume an investment has a present value of $1,000, a future value of $1,403, and an interest rate of 7 percent. What length of time does this investment involve?

This problem can be solved using a financial calculator and entering PV = 1000 (or -1000), FV = 1403, and %i = 7 and then pressing the CPT key followed by the N key to find an n of 5.01, or 5 years rounded.

Financial Calculator Solution:

Inputs:	7		1000	1403
	%i		PV	FV
Press:	CPT		N	
Solution:	5.01			

Spreadsheet Solution:

The number of time periods can also be determined by using the Excel financial function called NPER. Following the sequence described and clicking on the NPER financial function, we have:

$$= NPER(Rate,Pmt,PV,FV,Type)$$
$$= NPER(.07,0,-1000,1403,0)$$
$$= 5.00$$

The interest rate is 7 percent, there are no payments, the present value is -1000, the future value is 1403, and type is zero.

Table-Based Solution:

The answer can also be found by using Equation 5.2 and Table 5.1 as follows:

$$FV_n = PV(FVIF_{7\%,n})$$
$$\$1,403 = \$1,000(FVIF_{7\%,n})$$
$$FVIF_{7\%,n} = 1.403$$

Since we know the interest rate is 7 percent, we can turn to Table 5.1 and read down the 7 percent column until we find the FVIF of 1.403. Notice that this occurs in the year-five row, indicating that the time period n is five years.

We also can work the problem using Equation 5.4 and Table 5.2 as follows:

$$PV = FV_n(PVIF_{7\%,n})$$
$$\$1,000 = \$1,403(PVIF_{7\%,n})$$
$$PVIF_{7\%,n} = .713$$

Turn to Table 5.2, we read down the 7 percent column until we find the PVIF of .713. This occurs at the year-five row, indicating that the time period n is five years.

RULE OF 72

Investors often ask, "How long will it take for my money to double in value at a particular interest rate?" Table 5.1 illustrates the process for answering this question. We pick a particular interest rate and read down the table until we find an FVIF of 2.000. For example, at an 8 percent interest rate, it will take almost exactly nine years (note the FVIF of 1.999) for an investment to double in value. At a 9 percent interest rate, the investment will double in about eight years (FVIF of 1.993). An investment will double in a little over seven years (FVIF of 1.949) if the interest rate is 10 percent.

A shortcut method referred to as the **Rule of 72** can be used to approximate the time required for an investment to double in value. This method is applied by dividing the interest rate into the number 72 to determine the number of years it will take for an investment to double in value. For example, if the interest rate is 8 percent, 72 divided by 8 indicates that the investment will double in value in nine years. Notice that this is the same conclusion drawn from Table 5.1. Likewise, at an interest rate of 10 percent it will take approximately 7.2 years (72 ÷ 10) for an investment to double in value. It is important to be aware that at very low or very high interest rates, the Rule of 72 does not approximate the compounding process as well, and thus a larger estimation error occurs in the time required for an investment to double in value.

Rule of 72
used to approximate the time required for an investment to double in value

CONCEPT CHECK
How is the Rule of 72 used?

FUTURE VALUE OF AN ANNUITY

The previous discussion focuses on cash payments or receipts that occurred only as lump sum present and future values. However, many finance problems involve equal payments or receipts over time, referred to as *annuities*. More specifically, an **annuity** is a series of equal payments (receipts) that occur over a number of time periods.

An **ordinary annuity** exists when the equal payments (receipts) occur at the end of each time period.[2] For example, suppose you want to invest $1,000 per year for three years at an 8 percent interest rate. However, since you will not make your first payment until the end of the first year, this will be an ordinary annuity.

This problem also can be illustrated using a timeline, as follows:

annuity
a series of equal payments (receipts) that occur over a number of time periods

ordinary annuity
equal payments (receipts) occur at the end of each time period

annuity due
exists when equal periodic payments occur at the beginning of each time period

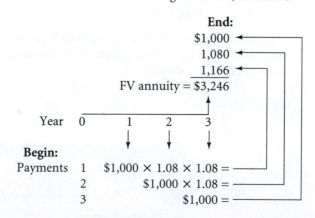

---

2. An **annuity due** exists when equal periodic payments start at the end of time period zero or, in other words, at the beginning of each time period. Annuity due problems are discussed in Learning Extension 5.

Notice that to calculate the future value of this ordinary annuity we must add the future values of the first payment ($1,166), the second payment ($1,080), and the third payment ($1,000). This results in a future value of $3,246. To summarize, since the first payment is made at the end of the first year, it is compounded for two years. The second payment is compounded for one year, and the third payment earns zero interest since the payment is made at the end of the third year.

The future value of this annuity can also be determined by making the following computations:

$$\text{FV ordinary annuity} = \$1,000(1.08)^2 + \$1,000(1.08)^1 + \$1,000(1.08)^0$$
$$= \$1,000(1.166) + \$1,000(1.080) + \$1,000(1.000)$$
$$= \$1,000(3.246)$$
$$= \$3,246$$

While the computational process was relatively easy for the three-year ordinary annuity example, the required calculations become much more cumbersome as the time period is lengthened. As a result, the following equation was derived for finding the future value of an ordinary annuity (FVA):

$$\text{FVA}_n = \text{PMT}\{[(1 + r)^n - 1] \div r\} \tag{5.5}$$

where PMT is the periodic equal payment, r is the compound interest rate, and n is the total number of periods.

Inserting the data from the preceding three-year annuity example results in:

$$\text{FVA}_3 = \$1,000\{[(1 + 0.08)^3 - 1] \div 0.08\}$$
$$= \$1,000[(1.2597 - 1) \div 0.08]$$
$$= \$1,000(3.246)$$
$$= \$3,246$$

Most financial calculators are programmed to readily find future values of annuities. In addition to the previously identified keys, financial calculators also will have a payments (PMT) key for purposes of working problems involving ordinary annuities. The result for the three-year ordinary annuity can be verified using a financial calculator.

First, clear the calculator. Next, enter -1000 (for both TI and HP calculators) and press the PMT key. Then, enter 8 and press the %i key, and enter 3 and press the N key. Finally, press the CPT key and then the FV key to calculate the FVA of 3246.40, which rounds to $3,246. Note that because this problem involves a periodic outflow of $1,000, most financial calculators require that the payment be entered as a negative number to solve for a positive FVA.

Financial Calculator Solution:

Inputs: 3   8 -1000

               | N | | %i | | PMT |

Press: | CPT | | FV |

Solution: 3246.40

Spreadsheet programs also are available for finding future values of annuities. Following is a solution using an Excel spreadsheet and future value (FV). The difference here is that we have a constant periodic payment.

Spreadsheet Solution:

	A	B	C	D	E
1	Interest Rate	0.08			
2	Time Period	0	1	2	3
3	Cash Flow	0	-1000	-1000	-1000
4					
5	Financial Function				
6	FV Solution:				$3,246.40

TABLE 5.3
Future Value Interest Factor (FVIFA) for a $1 Ordinary Annuity

YEAR	5%	6%	7%	8%	9%	10%
1	1.000	1.000	1.000	1.000	1.000	1.000
2	2.050	2.060	2.070	2.080	2.090	2.100
3	3.152	3.184	3.215	3.246	3.278	3.310
4	4.310	4.375	4.440	4.506	4.573	4.641
5	5.526	5.637	5.751	5.867	5.985	6.105
6	6.802	6.975	7.153	7.336	7.523	7.716
7	8.142	8.394	8.654	8.923	9.200	9.487
8	9.549	9.897	10.260	10.637	11.028	11.436
9	11.027	11.491	11.978	12.488	13.021	13.579
10	12.578	13.181	13.816	14.487	15.193	15.937

We solve for the future value of the annuity as follows:

$$= FV(Rate,Nper,Pmt,PV,Type)$$
$$= FV(.08,3,-1000,0,0)$$
$$= \$3,246.40$$

In addition, tables have been prepared to simplify the calculation effort if financial calculators or computer programs are not available. Equation 5.5 can be rewritten as:

$$FVA_n = PMT(FVIFA_{r,n}) \qquad (5.6)$$

where the $[(1 + r)^n - 1] \div r$ part of Equation 5.5 is replaced by a future value interest factor of an annuity (FVIFA) corresponding to a specific interest rate and a specified time period.

Table-Based Solution:

Table 5.3 shows FVIFA values for a partial range of interest rates and time periods. (Table 3 in the Appendix is a more comprehensive FVIFA table.) Let's use Table 5.3 to find the future value of an ordinary annuity involving annual payments of $1,000, an 8 percent interest rate, and a three-year time period. Notice that at the intersection of the 8 percent column and three years, we find a FVIFA of 3.246. Putting this information into Equation 5.6 gives:

$$FVA_3 = \$1,000(3.246)$$
$$= \$3,246$$

CONCEPT CHECK

What is an annuity?

What is an ordinary annuity?

Further examination of Table 5.3 shows how a $1 annuity grows or increases with various combinations of interest rates and time periods. For example, if $1,000 is invested at the end of each year (beginning with year one) for ten years at an 8 percent interest rate, the future value of the annuity would be $14,487 ($1,000 × 14.487). If the interest rate is 10 percent for ten years, the future value of the annuity would be $15,937 ($1,000 × 15.937). These results demonstrate the benefits of higher interest rates on the future values of annuities.

PRESENT VALUE OF AN ANNUITY

Many present value problems also involve cash flow annuities. Usually these are ordinary annuities. Let's assume that we will receive $1,000 per year beginning one year from now for a period of three years at an 8 percent compound interest rate. How much would you be willing to pay now for this stream of future cash flows? Since we are concerned with the value now, this becomes a present value problem.

We can illustrate this problem using a timeline as follows:

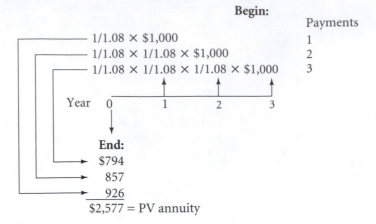

Notice that to calculate the present value of this ordinary annuity we must sum the present values of the first payment ($794), the second payment ($857), and the third payment ($926). This results in a present value of $2,577.

We also can find the present value of this annuity by making the following computations:

$$
\begin{aligned}
\text{PV ordinary annuity} &= \{\$1,000[1 \div (1.08)^1]\} + \{\$1,000[1 \div (1.08)^2]\} \\
&\quad + [\$1,000[1 \div (1.08)^3]\} \\
&= [\$1,000(0.926)] + [\$1,000(0.857)] \\
&\quad + [\$1,000(0.794)] \\
&= \$1,000(2.577) \\
&= \$2,577
\end{aligned}
$$

While the computational process was relatively easy for the preceding three-year ordinary annuity example, the required calculations become much more cumbersome as the time period is lengthened. As a result, the following equation was derived for finding the present value of an ordinary annuity (PVA):

$$
PVA_n = PMT\{[1 - (1 \div (1 + r)^n)] \div r\}
\tag{5.7}
$$

where the various inputs are the same as previously defined.

Inserting the data from the preceding three-year annuity example results in:

$$
\begin{aligned}
PVA_3 &= \$1,000\{[1 - (1 \div (1 + 0.08)^3)] \div 0.08\} \\
&= \$1,000[(1 - 0.7938) \div 0.08] \\
&= \$1,000(0.2062 \div 0.08) \\
&= \$1,000(2.577) \\
&= \$2,577
\end{aligned}
$$

Most financial calculators are programmed to readily find present values of annuities. The result for the three-year present value of an ordinary annuity problem can be verified with a financial calculator. First, clear the calculator. Next, enter 1000 for a TI calculator (or −1000 for an HP calculator) and press the payments (PMT) key. Then, enter 8 and press the %i key, and enter 3 and press the N key. Finally, press the CPT key followed by the PV key to calculate the PVA of 2577.10, which rounds to $2,577.

Financial Calculator Solution:

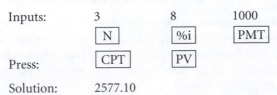

Inputs:	3	8	1000
	N	%i	PMT
Press:	CPT	PV	
Solution:	2577.10		

Spreadsheet programs also are available for finding present values of annuities. Following is an Excel spreadsheet solution:

Spreadsheet Solution:

	A	B	C	D	E
1	Interest Rate	0.08			
2	Time Period	0	1	2	3
3	Cash Flow	0	-1000	-1000	-1000
4					
5	Financial Function				
6	FV Solution:				$3,246.40

Use the previously described present value (PV) financial function provided by Excel, as follows:

$$= \text{PV(Rate,Nper,Pmt,FV,Type)}$$
$$= \text{PV}(.08, 3, -1000, 0, 0)$$
$$= \$2,577.10$$

In addition, tables have been prepared to simplify the calculation effort if financial calculators or computer programs are not available. Equation 5.7 can be rewritten as:

$$\text{PVA}_n = \text{PMT}(\text{PVIFA}_{r,n}) \tag{5.8}$$

where the $\{1 - [1 \div (1 + r)^n]\} \div r$ part of Equation 5.7 is replaced by a present value interest factor of an annuity (PVIFA) corresponding to a specific interest rate and a specified time period.

Table-Based Solution:

Table 5.4 shows PVIFA values for a partial range of interest rates and time periods. (Table 4 in the Appendix is a more comprehensive PVIFA table.) Let's use Table 5.4 to find the present value of an ordinary annuity involving annual payments of $1,000, an 8 percent interest rate, and a three-year time period. Notice that at the intersection of the 8 percent interest rate column and three years, we find a PVIFA of 2.577. Putting this information into Equation 5.8 gives:

$$\text{PVA}_3 = \$1,000(2.577)$$
$$= \$2,577$$

Further examination of Table 5.4 shows how the present value of a $1 annuity decreases with various combinations of interest rates and time periods. For example, if $1,000 is paid at the end of each year (beginning with year one) for ten years at an 8 percent interest rate, the present value of the annuity would be $6,710 ($1,000 × 6.710). If the interest rate is 10 percent for ten years, the present value of the annuity would be $6,145 ($1,000 × 6.145). These results demonstrate the costs of higher interest rates on the present values of annuities.

CONCEPT CHECK

How do we find the present value of an annuity?

TABLE 5.4
Present Value Interest Factor (PVIFA) for a $1 Ordinary Annuity

YEAR	5%	6%	7%	8%	9%	10%
1	0.952	0.943	0.935	0.926	0.917	0.909
2	1.859	1.833	1.808	1.783	1.759	1.736
3	2.273	2.673	2.624	2.577	2.531	2.487
4	3.546	3.465	3.387	3.312	3.240	3.170
5	4.329	4.212	4.100	3.993	3.890	3.791
6	5.076	4.917	4.767	4.623	4.486	4.355
7	5.786	5.582	5.389	5.206	5.033	4.868
8	6.463	6.210	5.971	5.747	5.535	5.335
9	7.108	6.802	6.515	6.247	5.995	5.759
10	7.722	7.360	7.024	6.710	6.418	6.145

INTEREST RATES AND TIME REQUIREMENTS FOR ANNUITIES

How to find or solve for interest rates or time periods for problems involving a lump sum present value or future value was discussed previously in this chapter. That originally involved working with four variables: PV = present value, FV = future value, r = interest rate, and n = number of periods. A fifth variable is now added to reflect payments (PMT) involving annuities.

SOLVING FOR INTEREST RATES

Assume that the future value of an ordinary annuity is $5,751, the annual payment is $1,000, and the time period is five years. What is the interest rate for this problem?

A financial calculator also could be used to solve this problem if either the FV or PV of the ordinary annuity is known. If you have a financial calculator and you know the future value, enter FV = 5751, PMT = −1000 (for both TI and HP calculators), and N = 5. Press the CPT key followed by the %i key to find an r of 7 percent. (*Note:* Some financial calculators will give an error message if the 1000 PMT is entered as a positive number. If the present value of the ordinary annuity is known instead of the future value, the preceding procedure would be followed except that PV = 4100 would be entered instead of the future value amount.)

Financial Calculator Solution:

Inputs:	5		−1000	5751
	$\boxed{\text{N}}$		$\boxed{\text{PMT}}$	$\boxed{\text{FV}}$
Press:	$\boxed{\text{CPT}}$		$\boxed{\text{\%i}}$	
Solution:	7.00			

Spreadsheet Solution:

Excel's RATE financial function also can be used to solve this interest rate of an annuity problem, much as the function was used elsewhere in this chapter for problems without periodic payments. The financial function solution would be:

$$= \text{RATE(Nper,Pmt,PV,FV,Type)}$$
$$= \text{RATE}(5,-1000,0,5751,0)$$
$$= 7.00\%$$

Table-Based Solution:

The answer can be found by setting up the problem using Equation 5.6 and Table 5.3, as follows:

$$FVA_5 = PMT(FVIFA_{r,5})$$
$$\$5,75 = \$1,000(FVIFA_{r,5})$$
$$FVIFA_{r,5} = 5.751$$

Since we know that the number of time periods is five, we can turn to Table 5.3 and read across the year-five row until we find the FVIFA of 5.751. Notice that this occurs under the 7 percent column, indicating that the interest rate r is 7 percent.

Let's now assume that we know that the present value of the preceding ordinary annuity is $4,100. We could then find the interest rate for the problem using present value annuity tables, as follows:

$$PVA_5 = PMT(PVIFA_{r,5})$$
$$\$4,100 = \$1,000(PVIFA_{r,5})$$
$$PVIFA_{r,5} = 4.100$$

Turning to Table 5.4, we read across the year-five row until we find the PVIFA of 4.100. This occurs under the 7 percent column, indicating that the interest rate r is 7 percent.

SOLVING FOR TIME PERIODS

Let's assume that the future value of an ordinary annuity is $5,751, the annual payment is $1,000, and the interest rate is 7 percent. How long would it take for your $1,000 annual investments to grow to $5,751?

We can solve this problem using a financial calculator. We know that the future value of the ordinary annuity is $5,751, so enter FV = 5751, PMT = −1000, %i = 7, and press the CPT key followed by the N key to find an n of five years. If we knew the present value of the annuity instead of the future value, we could work the problem by substituting the PV for the FV.

Financial Calculator Solution:

Inputs:	7		−1000	5751
	%i		PMT	FV
Press:	CPT		N	
Solution:	5.00			

Spreadsheet Solution:

Excel's NPER financial function also can be used to solve for the number of periods in an annuity problem, much as we used the function earlier for problems without periodic payments. The financial function solution would be:

$$= \text{NPER}(\text{Rate,Pmt,PV,FV,Type})$$
$$= \text{NPER}(5, -1000, 0, 5751, 0)$$
$$= 5.00$$

Table-Based Solution:

The problem also can be set up by using Equation 5.6 and Table 5.3 as follows:

$$\text{FVA}_n = \text{PMT}(\text{FVIFA}_{7\%,n})$$
$$\$5,751 = \$1,000(\text{FVIFA}_{7\%,n})$$
$$\text{FVIFA}_{7\%,n} = 5.751$$

Since we know the interest rate is 7 percent, we can turn to Table 5.3 and read down the 7 percent column until we find FVIFA of 5.751. Notice that this occurs in the year-five row, indicating that the n time period is five years.

If we knew the present value of the above ordinary annuity was $4,100, we could also work the problem using Equation 5.8 and Table 5.4, as follows:

$$\text{PVA}_n = \text{PMT}(\text{PVIFA}_{7\%,n})$$
$$\$4,100 = \$1,000(\text{PVIFA}_{7\%,n})$$
$$\text{PVIFA}_{7\%,n} = 4.100$$

Turning to Table 5.4, we read down the 7 percent column, until we find PVIFA of 4.100. This occurs at the year-five row, indicating that the n time period is five years.

SO YOU WANT TO BE A MILLIONAIRE?

A million dollars can be acquired in a number of ways. Probably the easiest legal way is to inherit it. Those of us who won't benefit that way must save a portion of our disposable personal income and then live long enough to take advantage of compounding interest. For example, if you could invest $10,000 now (at the end of time period zero), the following combinations of annual compound interest rates and time periods would make you a millionaire.

INTEREST RATE (%)	TIME (YEARS)
5	94.4
10	48.3
15	33.0
20	25.3

Notice that at a 5 percent compound rate it would take more than ninety-four years to accumulate $1 million. This is probably not acceptable (or possible) for most of us. Even if we could compound our interest at a 20 percent annual rate, it would take a little more than twenty-five years to become a millionaire.

An alternative approach would be to create an investment annuity of $10,000 per year. Now let's show the time required to become a millionaire under the assumption of an ordinary annuity where the first investment will be made one year from now:

INTEREST RATE (%)	TIME (YEARS)
5	36.7
10	25.2
15	19.8
20	16.7

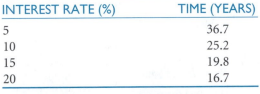

CONCEPT CHECK

What is the process for solving for either interest rates or time period requirements for annuities?

With this approach the time required, particularly at higher interest rates, is more feasible. Compounding at 5 percent would still require making annual investments for nearly thirty-seven years to accumulate $1 million. At 10 percent, it would take a little more than twenty-five years to attain that goal. Of course the most critical factor, which might be easier said than done, is the ability to come up with $10,000 per year out of disposable personal income. Good luck!

DETERMINING ANNUAL ANNUITY PAYMENTS

It is necessary in many instances to determine the periodic equal payment required for an annuity. For example, you may wish to accumulate $10,000 at the end of five years from now by making equal annual payments beginning one year from now. If you can invest at a compound 6 percent interest rate, what will be the amount of each of your annual payments?

This is a future value of an ordinary annuity problem. Using a financial calculator, the annual payment (PMT) would be found as follows:

Financial Calculator Solution:

Inputs: 7   5   10,000
             %i   N   FV

Press: CPT   PMT

Solution: 1773.96

Spreadsheet Solution:

Excel's PMT financial function also can be used to solve for the annual payment amount. The financial function solution would be:

$$= PMT(Rate, PV, FV, Type)$$
$$= PMT(5, 0, 10000, 0)$$
$$= -\$1,773.96$$

Notice that the financial function solution gives a negative value for the payment solution, as was the case when solving for the present value amount in a previous example.

TABLE 5.5

Sample Loan Amortization Schedule

YEAR	ANNUAL PAYMENT	INTEREST PAYMENT	PRINCIPAL REPAYMENT	LOAN BALANCE
0	—	—	—	$20,000
1	$8,042	$2,000	$6,042	13,958
2	8,042	1,396	6,646	7,312
3	8,042	731	7,311*	0

Because of rounding, the final principal repayment is off by $1.

Table-Based Solution:

a. Equation 5.6 and Table 5.3 also can be used, as follows:

$$FVA_n = PMT(FVIFA_{r,n})$$
$$\$10{,}000 = PMT(FVIFA_{6\%,5})$$
$$\$10{,}000 = PMT(5.637)$$
$$PMT = \$1{,}773.99$$
$$= \$1{,}774 \text{ (rounded)}$$

The FVIFA factor of 5.637 is taken from Table 5.3 at the intersection of the 6 percent column and the year-five row.

For another example, we might want to find the equal payment necessary to pay off, or *amortize,* a loan or real estate mortgage. An ***amortized loan*** is repaid in equal payments over a specified time period. Let's assume that a lender offers you a $20,000, 10-percent interest rate, three-year loan that is to be fully amortized with three annual payments. The first payment will be due one year from the loan date, making the loan an ordinary annuity. How much will you have to pay each year?

This is a present value problem because the $20,000 is the value or amount of the loan now. The annual payment can be found with a financial calculator, a financial function in a spreadsheet program, or via a table-based approach using Equation 5.8 and Table 5.4, as follows:

$$PVA_n = PMT(PVIFA_{10\%,3})$$
$$\$20{,}000 = PMT(2.487)$$
$$PMT = \$8{,}041.82$$
$$= \$8{,}042 \text{ (rounded)}$$

The PVIFA factor of 2.487 is taken from Table 5.4 at the intersection of the 10 percent column and the year-three row.

Table 5.5 illustrates the repayment process with a ***loan amortization schedule***, which shows the breakdown of each payment between interest and principal, as well as the remaining balance after each payment. Since the interest rate is 10 percent, the first year interest will total $2,000 ($20,000 × 0.10). Subsequent interest payments are based on the remaining loan balances, which are smaller each year (also referred to as the *declining balance*). Since $6,042 ($8,042 − $2,000) of the first year's $8,042 payment is used to repay part of the principal, the second year's interest payment will only be $1,396 ($13,958 × 0.10). The third and last payment covers the final year's interest of $731 plus the remaining principal balance.

This loan amortization process is the same as that used to determine monthly payments on home mortgages. However, because the discounting interval is very short, it would be unwieldy to calculate the monthly payment the long way for a typical thirty-year loan. Therefore, a financial calculator or spreadsheet program is used.

amortized loan
a loan repaid in equal payments over a specified time period

loan amortization schedule
a schedule of the breakdown of each payment between interest and principal, as well as the remaining balance after each payment

CONCEPT CHECK

What do we mean by an amortized loan?

What is a loan amortization schedule?

MORE FREQUENT COMPOUNDING OR DISCOUNTING INTERVALS

In many situations, compounding or discounting may occur more often than annually. For example, recall from the beginning of this chapter the $1,000 that could be invested at one bank at an 8 percent annual interest rate for two years. Remember that the future value at the end of two years was:

$$FV_2 = \$1,000(1.08)^2$$
$$= \$1,000(1.166)$$
$$= \$1,166.40$$

Now let's assume that another bank offers the same 8 percent interest rate but with semiannual (twice a year) compounding. We can find the future value of this investment by modifying Equation 5.1 as follows:

$$FV_n = PV(1 + r \div m)^{n \times m} \qquad (5.9)$$

where m is the number of compounding periods per year.

For this problem:

$$FV_2 = \$1,000(1 + 0.08 \div 2)^{2 \times 2}$$
$$= \$1,000(1.04)^4$$
$$= \$1,000(1.1699)$$
$$= \$1,169.90$$

Thus, by compounding semiannually the future value would increase by $3.50.

The more-frequent-than-annual compounding process can be described operationally as follows. First, divide the annual interest rate of 8 percent by the number of times compounding is to take place during the year ($0.08 \div 2 = 0.04$). We also need to increase the total number of periods to reflect semiannual compounding. To do this, multiply the number of years for the loan times the frequency of compounding within a year (2 years × 2 = 4 periods).

Previously in this chapter, it was shown that a $1,000 investment at an 8 percent interest rate would grow to $2,158.92 or $2,159 (rounded) at the end of ten years. However, if semiannual compounding had been available, the future value of the $1,000 investment would have been:

$$FV_{20} = \$1,000(1.04)^{20}$$
$$= \$1,000(2.1911)$$
$$= \$2,191.10$$

The following subsection shows how the financial calculator solution would be found.

Financial Calculator Solution:

Inputs:	20		4		1000	
	N		%i		PV	
Press:	CPT		FV			
Solution:	2191.12					

Spreadsheet Solution:

The Excel FV function inputs would be:

$$= FV(0.04, 20, 0, -1000, 0)$$
$$= \$2,191.12$$

CONCEPT CHECK

What is the process for compounding or discounting quarterly rather than annually?

Table-Based Solution:

The future value interest factor (FVIF) can also be found in Table 1 in the Appendix. When a three decimal place table is used, the factor is 2.191 with a future value of $2,191 (rounded). Notice that semiannual compounding will result in $32 more than the $2,159 earned with annual compounding. It follows that more frequent compounding, such as quarterly or monthly, produces even higher earnings.

The process described also applies to discounting problems when discounting occurs more frequently than annually. The use of financial calculators and spreadsheet programs are more expedient as the frequency of compounding or discounting within a year increases.

COST OF CONSUMER CREDIT

UNETHICAL LENDERS

ETHICAL ISSUES

usury
the act of lending money at
an excessively high interest
rate

Throughout history there have been many examples of individuals being charged exorbitant interest rates on loans. There is a word, *usury*, for this type of action. *Usury* is the act of lending money at an excessively high interest rate. Lenders who exhibited such unethical behavior were sometimes referred to as "loan sharks." Lenders, of course, are in the business of making a rate of return on the money that they have to lend. Without question, lenders deserve to earn a fair rate of return to compensate them for their time and the risk that the borrower will not repay the interest and/or principal on time or in full.

In Chapter 4, we defined this added compensation as a risk premium above the prevailing risk-free rate. Good ethical behavior is consistent with treating borrowers honestly and fairly. However, because of the existence of unethical lenders, various laws have made usury illegal. While it is illegal to charge usurious rates of interest, some unscrupulous lenders still try to behave unethically when making loans to consumers. Congress passed the *Consumer Credit Protection Act of 1968*, which prohibits excessively high-priced credit transactions; Regulation Z enacts the Truth in Lending section of the act, whereby the Federal Reserve has the responsibility of making consumers aware of the costs of alternative forms of credit. Lenders must disclose all loan costs (interest amounts, service charges, loan and finder fees, etc.) as well as the *annual percentage rate* of charge or interest. It is unfortunate, but a fact of life, that because of the unethical behavior of some lenders, laws must be enacted to protect consumers.

APR VERSUS EAR

annual percentage rate
(APR)

determined by multiplying
the interest rate charged per
period by the number of
periods in a year

Banks, finance companies, and other lenders are required by the Truth in Lending law to disclose their lending interest rates on credit extended to consumers. Such a rate is called a contract or stated rate, or more frequently, an *annual percentage rate (APR)*. The method of calculating the APR on a loan is set by law. The APR is the interest rate r charged per period multiplied by the number of periods in a year m:

$$\text{APR} = r \times m \tag{5.10}$$

Thus, a car loan that charges interest of 1 percent per month has an APR of 12 percent (i.e., 1 percent times 12 months). An unpaid credit card balance that incurs interest charges of 1.5 percent per month has an APR of 18 percent (1.5 times 12 months).

effective annual rate
(EAR)

measures the true interest
rate when compounding
occurs more frequently than
once a year

However, the APR misstates the true interest rate. The *effective annual rate (EAR)*, sometimes called the *annual effective yield*, is the true opportunity cost measure of the interest rate, as it considers the effects of periodic compounding. For example, say an unpaid January balance of $100 on a credit card accumulates interest at the rate of 1.5 percent per month. The interest charge is added to the unpaid balance; if left unpaid, February's balance will be $101.50. If the bill remains unpaid through February, the 1.5 percent monthly charge is levied based on the total unpaid balance of $101.50. In other words, interest is assessed on previous months' unpaid interest charges. Thus, since interest compounds, the APR formula will *understate* the true or effective interest cost. This will always be true except in the special case where the number of periods is one per year—that is, in annual compounding situations.

If the periodic interest charge r is known, the EAR is found by using Equation 5.11:

$$\text{EAR} = (1 + r)^m - 1 \tag{5.11}$$

INTERNET ACTIVITY

Go to the Board of Governors
of the Federal Reserve Web site,
www.federalreserve.gov, and
access consumer information
and consumer credit and find
information on the cost of
credit, including the APR.

where m is the number of periods per year.

If the APR is known instead, divide the APR by m and use the resulting number for r in Equation 5.11.[3]

As an example of the effective annual rate concept, let's find the true annual interest cost of a credit card that advertises an 18 percent APR. Since credit card charges are typically assessed monthly, m, the number of periods per year is 12. Thus, the monthly interest rate is:

$$r = \text{APR} \div m = 18\% \div 12 = 1.5\%$$

---

3. Some financial calculators are preprogrammed with an "interest rate conversion" function, with which one can easily switch between an EAR (sometimes called EFF% for the "effective" rate) and the APR.

"We take a resource, the money of our clients, and produce a product, which is the return on their investment."

Q: *Before you took your current position, you worked in the business valuation field. What is that?*

A: There are a number of circumstances when the owner of a business may need to determine the value of his or her firm. For instance, if I was going to sell part of the ownership of my company to someone else, I'd need to know how to price it. Or if I was going to use it as collateral for a loan, I'd need to demonstrate the value to the lender.

Q: *How did you determine a company's value?*

A: There are several methods. Sometimes we would look for similar firms that had been sold recently and use those as comparisons. Or we'd look for similar firms that are publicly traded and look at the value of their stock. In other cases we would look at their present value from a cash flow perspective.

Q: *Describe that process.*

A: It's not unlike the process you would use to determine the value of a stock or bond. We'd look at the discounted value of the projected cash flow for the next five years and then the terminal value, which is the amount you would expect to sell the business for in five years, again discounted to present value.

Q: *Now you're a portfolio manager.*

A: Right. I basically invest other people's money. In a way it's like a manufacturing business. We take a resource, the money of our clients, and produce a product, which is the return on their investment. We manage about $180 million currently.

Q: *How do you decide what to invest in?*

A: Our investment strategy could be described as fairly complex. We look for firms with quite specific capital conditions. We look at their existing debt (bonds) and their existing equity (stock) values. When we see a certain relationship between those values, we see an opportunity to make a positive return. Applying our strategy, we will often end up buying a company's bonds and selling its stock short.

Q: *Why would this strategy work?*

A: In very simple terms, when we see certain stock and bond values, we conclude that there is a misvaluation, that the stock is overpriced relative to the bond, for instance. So if we're right, we're able to take advantage of that misvaluation by buying the underpriced security and shorting the overpriced one. As I said, it's a fairly complex strategy.

Q: *What do you do on a daily basis?*

A: I spend essentially the entire day on the telephone, discussing the value of securities, mostly with brokers. Since the bonds we buy are not traded on an exchange like stocks, I may need to call four or five sources for those bonds to determine the going price. The other piece of my job is to manage the existing portfolio, making day-to-day adjustments based on the changing values of securities. Using the metaphor of a manufacturing business, I adjust the settings on the production line so the products are manufactured correctly.

APPLYING FINANCE TO . . .

INSTITUTIONS AND MARKETS

Depository institutions offer savings accounts and certificates of deposit (CDs) to individual savers. To entice individuals to save with them, these financial institutions often state annual percentage rates but compound the interest more frequently than once a year. The result is that the effective annual rate (EAR) is higher than the stated annual percentage rate (APR). Of course, since most financial institutions depend on the spread between their cost of obtaining funds and their lending rates, they must balance the effective annual rates at which they borrow and lend. Credit card loans typically provide for monthly compounding so that the EAR is higher than the APR.

INVESTMENTS

Most financial decisions are based on the rate at which an investment is compounded or a future value is discounted. Savers are interested in growing or compounding their savings over time and know the longer an investment can compound the more rapidly it will grow in value at a specified interest rate. Investors make plans, based on the compound rates of return they expect to earn on their investments, about when they can buy a home, when they can send their children to college, and when they can retire. The ability to compound interest more frequently than once a year means that investors can reach their goals sooner or at lower interest rates.

FINANCIAL MANAGEMENT

Financial managers borrow from banks and issue debt to raise funds to maintain and grow their firms. While some business loans are simple interest loans, others take the form of fully amortized loans, whereby annuity payments are composed of a declining interest portion and a rising principal repayment portion over the life of the loan. Investors, of course, expect to earn compound rates of return on their debt and equity investments held for more than a year. Financial managers accordingly must invest funds in capital projects that will generate excess cash flows sufficient in amount to provide investors with their expected rates of return.

From Equation 5.11, the EAR is:

$$(1 + 0.015)^{12} - 1 = 1.1956 - 1 = 0.1956, \text{ or } 19.56\%$$

The true interest charge on a credit card with an 18 percent APR is really 19.56 percent! When the annual stated rate stays the same, more frequent interest compounding helps savers earn more interest over the course of a year. For example, is it better to put your money in an account offering option (1) 8 percent interest per year, compounded quarterly or option (2) 8 percent interest per year, compounded monthly?

Compounding interest quarterly means that the bank is paying interest four times a year to its depositors. Option (1) involved four periods per year and a periodic interest rate r of 8 percent divided by 4, or 2 percent. Every dollar invested under option (1) will grow to $1.0824 [$1(1 + 0.02)^4] after one year's time. Another way of expressing this is that the effective annual rate of 8 percent compounded quarterly is 8.24 percent.

Under option (2), the relevant time period is one month and the periodic interest rate is 8 percent ÷ 12 or 0.67 percent. Every dollar invested under option (2) will grow to $1.0830 [$1(1 + 0.0067)^{12}]. Thus, the effective annual rate of 8 percent compounded monthly is 8.30 percent.

As option (2) gives the depositor more interest over the course of a year, depositors should choose it over option (1). This example illustrates that, for the same APR or stated rate, more frequent compounding increases the future value of an investor's funds more quickly.

CONCEPT CHECK

What do we mean by the annual percentage rate (APR) on a loan?

What is the effective annual rate (EAR) on a loan?

SUMMARY

This chapter has introduced the reader to the concept of the time value of money, which is the basis of many financial applications. It began with an explanation and illustration of simple interest whereby on starts with a present value amount as it grows to a future value in one time period. Then, compounding interest over several time periods to determine future values was discussed. This was followed with a discussion and illustrations of the concept of discounting to determine present values, then how to find interest rates and time requirements were covered in problems involving future and present values.

Future value problems involving ordinary annuities were described, and the calculation process illustrated. This was followed

with a section on how to calculate the present value of an ordinary annuity. Solving for either interest rates or time periods was then discussed in problems involving annuities. The next section focused on how to determine annual annuity payments. This is particularly useful for finding periodic payments for loans that are amortized (repaid in equal payments) over their lives.

The last two sections of the chapter addressed how to handle more frequent compounding or discounting intervals and a comparison of two interest rate concepts, the annual percentage rate versus the effective annual rate.

The Learning Extension that follows covers the meaning of an annuity due and will illustrate some annuity due problems.

KEY TERMS

amortized loan	discounting	Rule of 72
annual percentage rate (APR)	effective annual rate (EAR)	simple interest
annuity	future value	time value of money
annuity due	loan amortization schedule	usury
compounding	ordinary annuity	
compound interest	present value	

DISCUSSION QUESTIONS

1. Briefly describe what is meant by the time value of money.

2. Explain the meaning of simple interest.

3. Describe the process of compounding and the meaning of compound interest.

4. Briefly describe how inflation or purchasing power impacts stated or nominal interest rates.

5. What is the meaning of discounting? Give an illustration.

6. Briefly explain how present values and future values are related.

7. Describe the process for solving for the interest rate in present and future value problems.

8. Describe the process for solving for the time period in present and future value problems.

9. How can the Rule of 72 be used to determine how long it will take for an investment to double in value?

10. What is an ordinary annuity?

11. Briefly describe how to solve for the interest rate or the time period in annuity problems.

12. Describe the process for determining the size of a constant periodic payment that is necessary to fully amortize a loan.

13. Describe what is meant by compounding or discounting more often than annually.

14. What is *usury*, and how does it relate to the cost of consumer credit?

15. Explain the difference between the annual percentage rate and the effective annual rate.

EXERCISES

1. Obtain a current issue of the Statistical Supplement to the *Federal Reserve Bulletin* and find interest rates on *consumer credit*. Find average interest rates charged by commercial banks on new automobile loans, personal loans, and credit card plans.

   a. For the most recent year, compare the average level of interest rates among the three types of loans.

   b. Compare trends in the cost of consumer credit provided by commercial banks over the past three years.

2. Obtain a current issue of the Statistical Supplement to the *Federal Reserve Bulletin* and go to the "Consumer Credit" information section. For the most recent year, compare the interest rates charged by auto finance companies on loans for new and used cars. Also compare the trend in the cost of loans from auto finance companies over the past three years.

3. Assume that your partner and you are in the consumer lending business. A customer, talking with your partner, is discussing the possibility of obtaining a $10,000 loan for three months. The potential borrower seems distressed and says he needs the loan by tomorrow or several of his relatively new appliances will be repossessed by the manufacturers. You overhear your partner saying that that in order to process the loan within one day there will be a $1,000 processing fee so that $11,000 in principal will have to be repaid in order to have $10,000 to spend now. Furthermore, because the money is needed now and is for only three months the interest charge will be 6 percent per month. What would you do?

PROBLEMS

1. You are asked to find the future value of $10,000 invested now after five years if the annual interest rate is 8 percent.

   a. What would be the future value if the interest rate is a simple interest rate?

   b. What would be the future value if the interest rate is a compound interest rate?

2. Determine the future values if $5,000 is invested in each of the following situations:

   a. 5 percent for ten years

   b. 7 percent for seven years

   c. 9 percent for four years

3. You are planning to invest $2,500 today for three years at a nominal interest rate of 9 percent with annual compounding.

   a. What would be the future value of your investment?

   b. Now assume that inflation is expected to be 3 percent per year over the same three-year period. What would be the investment's future value in terms of purchasing power?

   c. What would be the investment's future value in terms of purchasing power if inflation occurs at a 9 percent annual rate?

4. Determine the present values if $5,000 is received in the future (i.e., at the end of each indicated time period) in each of the following situations:

   a. 5 percent for ten years

   b. 7 percent for seven years

   c. 9 percent for four years

5. Determine the present value if $15,000 is to be received at the end of eight years and the discount rate is 9 percent. How would your answer change if you had to wait six years to receive the $15,000?

6. Assume you are planning to invest $5,000 each year for six years and will earn 10 percent per year. Determine the future value of this annuity if your first $5,000 is invested at the end of the first year.

7. What is the present value of a loan that calls for the payment of $500 per year for six years if the discount rate is 10 percent and the first payment will be made one year from now? How would your answer change if the $500 per year occurred for ten years?

8. Determine the annual payment on a $500,000, 12 percent business loan from a commercial bank that is to be amortized over a five-year period.

9. Determine the annual payment on a $15,000 loan that is to be amortized over a four-year period and carries a 10 percent interest rate. Also prepare a loan amortization schedule for this loan.

10. Assume a bank loan requires an interest payment of $85 per year and a principal payment of $1,000 at the end of the loan's eight-year life.

    a. How much could this loan be sold for to another bank if loans of similar quality carried an 8.5 percent interest rate? That is, what would be the present value of this loan?

    b. Now, if interest rates on other similar quality loans are 10 percent, what would be the present value of this loan?

    c. What would be the present value of the loan if the interest rate is 8 percent on similar-quality loans?

11. Use a financial calculator or computer software program to answer the following questions:

    a. What would be the future value of $15,555 invested now if it earns interest at 14.5 percent for seven years?

    b. What would be the future value of $19,378 invested now if the money remains deposited for eight years and the annual interest rate is 18 percent?

12. Use a financial calculator or computer software program to answer the following questions:

    a. What is the present value of $359,000 that is to be received at the end of twenty-three years if the discount rate is 11 percent?

    b. How would your answer change in (a) if the $359,000 is to be received at the end of twenty years?

13. Use a financial calculator or computer software program to answer the following questions:

    a. What would be the future value of $7,455 invested annually for nine years beginning one year from now if the annual interest rate is 19 percent?

    b. What would be the present value of a $9,532 annuity for which the first payment will be made beginning one year from now, payments will last for twenty-seven years, and the annual interest rate is 13 percent?

14. Use a financial calculator or computer software program to answer the following questions.

    a. What would be the future value of $19,378 invested now if the money remains deposited for eight years, the annual interest rate is 18 percent, and interest on the investment is compounded semiannually?

    b. How would your answer for (a) change if quarterly compounding were used?

    c. What is the present value of $359,000 that is to be received at the end of twenty-three years, the discount rate is 11 percent, and semiannual discounting occurs?

    d. How would your answer for (a) change if monthly discounting were used?

15. What would be the present value of a $9,532 annuity for which the first payment will be made beginning one year from now, payments will last for twenty-seven years, the annual interest rate is 13 percent, quarterly discounting occurs, and $2,383 is invested at the end of each quarter?

16. Answer the following questions:

    a. What is the annual percentage rate (APR) on a loan that charges interest of .75 percent per month?

    b. What is the effective annual rate (EAR) on the loan described in (a)?

17. You have recently seen a credit card advertisement stating that the annual percentage rate is 12 percent. If the credit card requires monthly payments, what is the effective annual rate of interest on the loan?

18. A credit card advertisement states that the annual percentage rate is 21 percent. If the credit card requires quarterly payments, what is the effective annual rate of interest on the loan?

19. **Challenge Problem** (*Note:* A computer spreadsheet software program or a financial calculator that can handle uneven cash flow streams will be needed to solve the following problems.) The following cash flow streams are expected to result from three investment opportunities.

YEAR	INVESTMENT STABLE	INVESTMENT DECLINING	INVESTMENT GROWING
1	$20,000	$35,000	$10,000
2	20,000	30,000	15,000
3	20,000	20,000	20,000
4	20,000	5,000	30,000
5	20,000	0	50,000

    a. Find the present values at the end of time period zero for each of these three investments if the discount rate is 15 percent. Also find the present values for each investment using 10 percent and 20 percent discount rates.

    b. Find the future values of these three investments at the end of year five if the compound interest rate is 12.5 percent. Also find the future values for each investment using 2.5 percent and 22.5 percent compound rates.

    c. Find the present values of the three investments using a 15 percent annual discount rate but with quarterly discounting. Also find the present values for both semiannual and monthly discounting for a 15 percent stated annual rate.

    d. Find the future values of the three investments using a 12.5 percent annual compound rate but with quarterly compounding. Also find the future values for both semiannual and monthly compounding for a 12.5 percent stated annual rate.

    e. Assume that the present value for each of the three investments is $75,000. What is the annual interest rate (%i) for each investment?

    f. Show how your answers would change in (e) if quarterly discounting takes place.

    g. Assume that the future value for each of the three investments is $150,000. What is the annual interest rate (%i) for each investment? (*Note:* (e) and (g) are independent of each other.)

    h. Show how your answers would change in (g) if quarterly compounding takes place.

LEARNING EXTENSION 5

Annuity Due Problems

FUTURE VALUE OF AN ANNUITY DUE

In contrast with an ordinary annuity, an *annuity due* exists when the equal periodic payments occur at the beginning of each period. Let's return to the example used in the "Future Value of an Annuity" section in this chapter. Recall that the problem involved a three-year annuity, $1,000 annual payments, and an 8 percent interest rate. However, let's assume that the first payment now is made at the beginning of the first year, namely at time zero. This will allow the first $1,000 payment to earn interest for three years, the second payment to earn interest for two years, and the third payment to earn interest for one year.

The calculation process to find the future value of this annuity due problem can be demonstrated as follows:

$$
\begin{aligned}
\text{FV annuity due} &= \$1,000(1.08)^3 + \$1,000(1.08)^2 + \$1,000(1.08)^1 \\
&= \$1,000(1.260) + \$1,000(1.166) + \$1,000(1.080) \\
&= \$1,000(1.260 + 1.166 + 1.080) \\
&= \$1,000(3.506) \\
&= \$3,506
\end{aligned}
$$

Notice that by making the first payment now, the future value of this annuity at the end of three years will be $3,506. This contrasts with a future value of $3,246 if payments are delayed by one year, as would be the case with an ordinary annuity.

Table-Based Solution:

Equation 5.6 can be easily modified to handle annuity due problems as follows:

$$
\text{FVAD}_n = \text{PMT}(\text{FVIFA}_{r,n})(1 + r) \tag{LE5.1}
$$

where FVAD is the future value of an annuity due and the $(1 + r)$ factor effectively compounds each payment by one more year to reflect the fact that payments start at the beginning of each period.

In this problem, the annual payment is $1,000, the time period is three years, and the interest rate is 8 percent. Using Equation LE5.1, the future value of this annuity due would be:

$$
\begin{aligned}
\text{FVAD}_3 &= \$1,000(\text{FVIFA}_{8\%,3})(1 + 0.08) \\
&= \$1,000(3.246)(1.08) \\
&= \$1,000(3.506) \\
&= \$3,506
\end{aligned}
$$

The FVIFA of 3.246 comes from Table 5.3 at the intersection of the 8 percent interest rate column and the year-three row.

Annuity due problems also can be solved with financial calculators. In fact, most financial calculators have a DUE key (or a switch) for shifting payments from the end of time periods to the beginning of time periods. If you have a financial calculator, you can verify the future value of an annuity due result for the three-year annuity problem. First, clear the calculator. Next, enter -1000 (for both TI and HP calculators) and press the PMT key. Then enter 8 and press the %i key, and enter 3 and press the N key. Finally, instead of pressing the CPT key, press the DUE key followed by the FV key to find the future value of an annuity due of 3506.11, which rounds to $3,506.

Financial Calculator Solution:

Inputs: 3   8 -1000
           | N | | %i | | PMT |

Press: | DUE | | FV |

Solution: 3506.11

Spreadsheet Solution:

The future value of an annuity due is solved with a problem by again using Excel's future value (FV) financial function, but adjusting for when the cash flows occur, as follows:

$$= FV(Rate, Nper, Pmt, PV, Type)$$
$$= FV(.08, 3, -1000, 0, 1)$$
$$= \$3,506.11$$

Note that the "Type" value was given a "1" to indicate the beginning of period cash flows. Recall that previously we used a "0" value in "Type" to reflect cash flows occurring at the end of each time period.

PRESENT VALUE OF AN ANNUITY DUE

Occasionally, you will have to do present value annuity due problems. For example, leasing arrangements often require the person leasing equipment to make the first payment at the time the equipment is delivered. Let's illustrate by assuming that lease payments of $1,000 will be made at the beginning of each year for three years. If the appropriate interest rate is 8 percent, what is the present value of this annuity due leasing problem?

The calculation process to find the present value of this annuity due problem can be demonstrated, as follows:

$$PV \text{ annuity due} = \$1,000[1 \div (1.08)^0] + \$1,000[1 \div (1.08)^1] + \$1,000[1 \div (1.08)^2]$$
$$= \$1,000(1.000) + \$1,000(0.926) + \$1,000(0.857)$$
$$= \$1,000(2.783)$$
$$= \$2,783$$

Notice that by making the first payment now, the present value of this annuity is $2,783. This contrasts with a present value of $2,577 if payments are delayed by one year, as would be the case with an ordinary annuity.

Table-Based Solution:

Equation 5.8 can be easily modified to handle annuity due problems, as follows:

$$PVAD_n = PMT(PVIFA_{r,n})(1 + r) \tag{LE5.2}$$

where PVAD is the present value of an annuity due and the $(1 + r)$ factor effectively compounds each payment by one more year to reflect the fact that payments start at the beginning of each period.

In the preceding problem, the annual payment is $1,000, the time period is three years, and the interest rate is 8 percent. Using Equation LE5.2, the present value of this annuity due would be:

$$PVAD_3 = \$1{,}000[(PVIFA_{8\%,3})(1 + 0.08)]$$
$$= \$1{,}000[(2.577)(1.08)]$$
$$= \$1{,}000(2.783)$$
$$= \$2{,}783$$

The PVIFA of 2.577 comes from Table 5.4 at the intersection of the 8 percent interest rate column and the year-three row. Present value annuity due problems also can be solved with computer software programs and financial calculators.

If you have a financial calculator, you can verify the present value of an annuity due result for the preceding three-year annuity problem. First, clear the calculator. Next, enter 1000 for TI calculators (or −1000 for HP calculators) and press the PMT key. Then enter 8 and press the %i key, and enter 3 and press the N key. Finally, instead of pressing the CPT key, press the DUE key followed by the PV key to find the present value of an annuity due of 2783.26, which rounds to $2,783.

Financial Calculator Solution:

Inputs:	3	8	1000
	N	%i	PMT
Press:	DUE	PV	
Solution:	2783.26		

Spreadsheet Solution:

The present value of an annuity due problem is solved by again using Excel's present value (PV) financial function, but adjusting for when the cash flows occur, as follows:

$$= PV(Rate,Nper,Pmt,FV,Type)$$
$$= PV(.08,3, - 1000,0,1)$$
$$= \$2{,}783.26$$

Note that the "Type" value was given a "1" to indicate beginning of period cash flows. Recall that previously we used a "0" value in "Type" to reflect cash flows occurring at the end of each time period.

INTEREST RATES AND TIME REQUIREMENTS FOR ANNUITY DUE PROBLEMS

Tables containing FVIFA and PVIFA factors are not readily available for annuity due problems. Thus, it is better to use a spreadsheet program or a financial calculator when trying to find the interest rate for an annuity due problem. Let's assume that the future value of an annuity due problem is $6,153, each payment is $1,000, and the time period is five years. What is the interest rate on this problem? If you have a financial calculator, enter FV = 6153, PMT = −1000, and N = 5. Press the DUE key and the %i key to find an r of 7 percent.

Financial Calculator Solution:

Inputs:	5	−1000	6153
	N	PMT	FV
Press:	DUE	%i	
Solution:	7.00		

Spreadsheet Solution:

Excel's RATE financial function also can be used to solve for the interest rate involving an annuity due problem. The process is very similar to the one used for an ordinary annuity problem except that a "1" value in "Type" is entered to indicate that cash flows occur at the beginning of each time period. The financial function solution would be:

$$= RATE(Nper,Pmt,PV,FV,Type)$$
$$= RATE(5,-1000,0,6153,1)$$
$$= 7.00\%$$

The n time periods involved in an annuity due problem also can be determined using either a computer software program or a financial calculator. For example, in the preceding problem let's assume we know the interest rate is 7 percent, the future value is $6,153, and the payment is $1,000 (entered as −1000). What we don't know is the number of time periods required. We can solve for N as follows:

Financial Calculator Solution:

Inputs:	7		−1000	6153
	%i		PMT	FV
Press:	DUE		N	
Solution:	5.00			

Spreadsheet Solution:

Excel's NPER financial function also can be used to solve for the number of periods in an annuity due problem. However, in contrast with an ordinary annuity, a value of "1" for "Type" must be entered to indicate that the cash flows occur at the beginning of the time periods. The financial function solution would be:

$$= NPER(Rate,Pmt,PV,FV,Type)$$
$$= NPER(7,-1000,0,6153,1)$$
$$= 5.00$$

Of course the same process could be used for finding either interest rates or the number of time periods if the present value of the annuity due instead of the future value were known. This would be done by substituting the PV value for the FV value in financial calculator or spreadsheet calculations.

QUESTIONS AND PROBLEMS

1. Assume you are planning to invest $100 each year for four years and will earn 10 percent per year. Determine the future value of this annuity due problem if your first $100 is invested now.

2. Assume you are planning to invest $5,000 each year for six years and will earn 10 percent per year. Determine the future value of this annuity due problem if your first $5,000 is invested now.

3. What is the present value of a five-year lease arrangement with an interest rate of 9 percent that requires annual payments of $10,000 per year with the first payment being due now?

4. Use a financial calculator to solve for the interest rate involved in the following future value of an annuity due problem. The future value is $57,000, the annual payment is $7,500, and the time period is six years.

5. **Challenge Problem** (*Note:* This problem requires access to a spreadsheet software package or a financial calculator that can handle uneven cash flows.) Following are the cash flows for three investments (originally presented in end-of-chapter problem 17) that actually occur at the beginning of each year rather than at the end of each year.

YEAR	INVESTMENT STABLE	INVESTMENT DECLINING	INVESTMENT GROWING
1	$20,000	$35,000	$10,000
2	20,000	30,000	15,000
3	20,000	20,000	20,000
4	20,000	5,000	30,000
5	20,000	0	50,000

a. Find the present values at the end of time period zero for each of these three investments if the discount rate is 15 percent.

b. Find the future values of these three investments at the end of year five if the compound interest rate is 12.5 percent.

c. Assume that the present value for each of the three investments is $75,000. What is the annual interest rate (%i) for each investment?

d. Assume that the future value for each of the three investments is $150,000. What is the annual interest rate (%i) for each investment? (*Note:* (c) and (d) are independent of each other.)

P A R T 2

INVESTMENTS

INTRODUCTION

The field of finance is composed of three areas—institutions and markets, investments, and financial management. These areas are illustrated in the accompanying diagram. Part 2 focuses on the investments area of finance. Investments involve the sale or marketing of securities, the analysis and valuation of securities and other financial claims, and the management of investment risk through holding diversified portfolios. Money flows into the financial markets from households' and firms' retained earnings. Funds flow into financial institutions such as banks and life insurance companies, which, in turn, invest the funds in various securities such as stocks and bonds, as well as other financial claims. Financial claims are anything that has a debt or equity claim on income or property, such as a car loan, a mortgage, or an equity investment in a small partnership. Financial institutions facilitate the work of the financial markets by directing funds from savers to those individuals, firms, or governments who need funds to finance current operations or growth. Part 1 dealt with the operations of the financial markets in general within the context of the financial system.

Part 2 introduces many of the important concepts and tools that financial institutions and investors use in the financial markets. For example, no one would want to invest (except perhaps altruistically) $100 now and expect to receive only their $100 back after one year. How much can we expect to receive for our $100 investment? The answer is determined in the financial markets. As with any other market, the financial markets consider demand and supply forces to determine the "price" of money, namely the interest rate or the expected return on an investment. The amount of interest received on a certificate of deposit or a bond, or the expected return on a common stock investment, all depends on the workings of the financial markets and the marketplace's evaluation of the investment opportunity.

It is through the investing process that institutions, firms, and individual investors come together. Firms and governments go to the financial markets, seeking investors and institutions to whom they can sell financial securities. Investors and institutions participate in the financial markets, seeking profitable investments to help meet their goals. For an investor, the goal may be a comfortable retirement or accumulating funds to purchase a car or house. For financial institutions, the higher the returns they earn on prudent investments, the greater will be their profits and the stronger their competitive position. A financial institution that prudently earns higher returns in the financial markets will be able to offer current and potential customers higher interest rates on their deposits than a competitor whose financial market returns are lower.

Part 2 introduces us to the concepts, securities, and mechanisms of investing. Chapter 6 takes the concept of "return" from chapter 5's time value of money discussion and examines where "return" comes from and what comprises an investment return. Chapters 7 and 8 introduce us to bonds and stocks. We review their characteristics and we use the time value concepts from Chapter 5 in a pragmatic manner to see how we can estimate their value and what affects the riskiness of each type of investment. We also learn how to read and interpret information about bonds and stocks from information presented in financial newspaper and the internet.

Chapter 9 delves deeper into the workings of the securities markets. It focuses on the processes that institutions and firms use to issue securities and the process that investors use when buying or selling securities. Chapter 10 completes our overview of investing by examining some of the practical issues facing investors, such as the efficiency of markets, diversification, managing a portfolio, developing appropriate portfolio goals and objectives, and the tools that investors and securities market participants use to evaluate and to control investment risk.

• CHAPTER 6 •

Return and Risk

Chapter Learning Objectives

AFTER STUDYING THIS CHAPTER, YOU SHOULD BE ABLE TO:

- Describe the difference between historical and expected rates of return.
- Know how to compute arithmetic averages, variances, and standard deviations using return data for a single financial asset.
- Know the historical rates of return and risk for different securities.
- Explain how to calculate the expected return on a portfolio of securities.
- Understand how and why the combining of securities into portfolios reduces the overall or portfolio risk.
- Explain the difference between systematic and unsystematic risk.

Where We Have Been...

We know investors take their savings and direct it in various ways: some to bank accounts, some to stocks, bonds, or other investment vehicles. Investors direct their savings to various instruments by considering a number of factors: How safe is my money? Am I willing to risk a loss in hopes of achieving a large gain? What happens to my investment if security market prices rise or fall?

Where We Are Going...

The concepts of risk and return presented in this chapter are important not only to investors; they are important to the businesses that issue the bonds and stocks that investors purchase. Businesses use a variety of short-term and long-term financing tools; the level of interest rates, expected return, and risk will guide firms as they make financing choices (Chapters 7, 8, and 15) and their investment decisions (Chapter 13).

How This Chapter Applies to Me...

Perhaps no other chapter can affect your investing future more than this discussion of financial risk and return. When coupled the discussion of stock and bond valuation in Chapter 7 and Chapter 8, along with Chapter 10's perspective on investment implications, you will have a good working knowledge of investment fundamentals.

Peter Bernstein, a well-known financial consultant and researcher, gives us some insights into the word "risk":

> *The word "risk" derives from the early Italian risicare, which means "to dare." In this sense, risk is a choice rather than a fate. The actions we dare to take, which depend on how free we are to make choices, are what the story of risk is all about.*

A closer look at financial risk is the main topic of this chapter.

Investors place their funds in stocks, bonds, and other investments to try to attain their financial goals, but stock and bond market values rise and fall over time, based on what happens to interest rates, economic expectations, and other factors. Since no one can predict the future, the returns earned on investments are, for the most part, not known. Some may look backward and see how different investments performed in the past and predict that future returns will be similar. Others do sophisticated economic and financial analyses in order to estimate future returns.

In this chapter we will first learn how risk is measured relative to the average return for a single investment. We also review historical data showing the risk-return relationship. We will see that higher risk investments must compensate investors over time with higher expected returns. Our emphasis then shifts to a discussion of risk sources and the effect of combining assets in a portfolio. This leads to a discussion of the use and advantages of portfolio diversification. We conclude the chapter with a discussion of systematic versus unsystematic risk.

RETURNS

Chapter 5 showed how to do several types of "future value" time value of money problems. In the first type, the unknown quantity to be calculated was the future value. In this type of problem we knew how much we were investing, for how long, and what rate of return (or interest rate) we would earn:

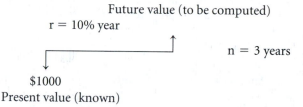

Future value (to be computed)

r = 10% year

n = 3 years

$1000
Present value (known)

How to compute the future value was shown as $FV_3 = PV(1 + r)^n = \$1000 (1 + .10)^3 = \$1,331$.

A second type of problem changed what was known and what was unknown. In this second type of problem we knew the future value of our investment and we needed to compute what rate of return would allow us to reach our goal.

Future value = $1331

r to be computed

n = 3 years

$1000
Present value (known)

For example, if you had $1,000 to invest today and wanted to have $1,331 at the end of three years, what rate of return would you need to earn? Solving the future value equation for r:

$$FV_3 = PV(1 + r)^n = \$1000(1 + r)^3 = \$1331$$

We find a 10 percent annual return is needed to reach that goal.

If we place our funds in a three-year bank certificate of deposit (CD), we will earn the same interest rate each year. However, the return from an investment will not necessarily be a constant interest rate over time. In fact, except for special situations such as a CD with a constant interest rate, the return earned on an investment will likely be neither an "interest rate" nor constant over time.

Rather than being comprised of an "interest rate" only, returns on an investment have two basic sources: *income* and *changes in price*. The return on a bank CD arises only from income, which is accrued solely from the interest rate it earns. The return on an investment in, say, gold, arises only from the change in gold's price over time. Other investments, such as an investment in a company's stock, a bond, or an apartment building may have some return coming from income (dividends on a stock, interest on a bond, or rent from apartment leases) and from changes in the value of the stock, bond, or piece of real estate.

The change in price, or value, of an investment is called a **capital gain** if the value of the asset rises. It is called a **capital loss** if the investment's value falls. So the return on an investment can be defined as:

Return = income + changes in price

or

Return = income + capital gain or loss

capital gain
source of return arising from an increase (gain) of an asset's value or price

capital loss
source of return arising from a decrease (loss) of an asset's value or price

In the real world, returns are not constant over time. As illustrated in Chapter 4, interest rates vary over time based upon economic conditions, including the supply and demand for funds and the level of inflation. Although a CD rate may be "locked in" until the CD matures, interest rates, dividends, rent, and asset prices on other investments will rise—or fall—over time. Very few investment opportunities offer a definite return that is constant over time.

Let's take another look at the second type of future value problem—where the future value or goal is known and we need to calculate the return needed to meet the goal. In the preceding problem, we wanted to invest $1,000 today and have $1,331 in three years. Solving the problem, we learned we needed to earn 10 percent per year, but that return is an average compounded return. In other words, we don't need to earn exactly 10.0 percent each year. In some years the return may be higher, in others it may be lower; we just need to average 10 percent per year on a compounded basis. For example, from our problem solution we know $1,000 (1 + .10) (1 + .10)(1 + .10) equals $1,331.

However, the following set of returns will allow us to meet our third-year target as well: a first year gain of 30 percent, a second year loss of 20 percent, and a third year return of 28 percent:

$$\$1000(1 + .30)(1 - .20)(1 + .28) = \$1331.$$

Another possible set of returns is 5 percent, 12 percent, and 13.2 percent:

$$\$1000(1 + .05)(1 + .12)(1 + .132) = \$1331$$

Still another set of returns is −10 percent, 6 percent, and 39.5 percent:

$$\$1000(1 - .10)(1 + .06)(1 + .395) = \$1331$$

Each of these three combinations of annual returns averages to a compounded annual return of 10 percent. An infinite number of potential sets of returns allow $1,000 to grow to $1,331 over time. Each possible combination allows us to meet our goal of having $1,331 after three years; each possible combination will have an average annual compounded return of 10 percent, but they will differ on their risk level. A safe alternative would be to earn 10 percent each year for three years, but earning 30 percent in year 1, losing 20 percent in year 2, and earning 28 percent in year 3 is a much riskier means of averaging 10 percent a year.

In the real world, we can rarely choose the sequence of investment returns we will earn. Some investments are safer than others in that they offer more consistent or constant returns over time; others are riskier, offering more variable returns. As we learned from the second principle of finance, higher returns typically are associated with higher levels of risk. In the next section, we'll take a look at how to measure return and risk over time so we can better compare investment alternatives.

HISTORICAL RETURN AND RISK FOR A SINGLE FINANCIAL ASSET

Figure 6.1 shows monthly prices for the stocks of two firms: Walgreens and Microsoft. We can compute monthly returns on both of these stocks, taking their price changes and dividends into consideration. The monthly return is computed as:

Dollar return = Stock price at end of month − stock price at beginning of month + dividends

To put things in terms of a percentage return, the month's percentage return is:

Percentage return = Dollar return/stock price at the beginning of the month

For example, in one month Walgreens' stock went from $33.63 per share at the beginning of the month to $34.31 at the end of the month. No dividends were paid that month. The dollar return is simply:

Dollar return = $34.31 − $33.63 = $0.68

FIGURE 6.1
Walgreens and Microsoft Stock Prices, 2001–2006

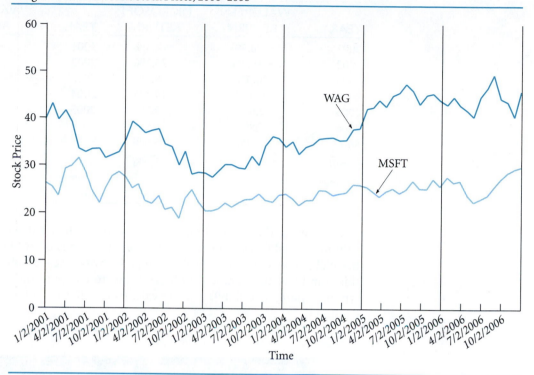

The monthly percentage return is $0.68/33.63 = 0.02022 or 2.022 percent.

If a dividend were received, that amount would be added to the dollar return. For example, if a dividend of four cents had been received during the month, the dollar return would have been:

$$\text{Dollar return} = \$34.31 - \$33.63 + \$0.04 = \$0.72$$

The monthly percentage return is $0.72/33.63 = 0.02141 or 2.141 percent.

One way to measure the risk of an asset is to examine the variability of its returns. For comparison, an analyst may want to determine the level of return and the variability in returns for these two stocks to see whether investors in the higher-risk stock earned a higher return over time to compensate or adequately reward them for the higher risk.[1]

ARITHMETIC AVERAGE ANNUAL RATES OF RETURN

If historical, or ex-post, data on a stock's returns are known, the analyst can easily compute historical average return and risk measures. If R_t represents the stock's return for period t, the *arithmetic average return*, $\overline{R}$, over n periods is given by:

$$\overline{R} = \sum_{t=1}^{n} [R_t]/n \tag{6.1}$$

The "Σ" symbol means to add or to sum the returns. We compute the arithmetic average return by adding the periodic returns and dividing the sum by n, the number of observations.

Let's assume that Padric held shares of Walgreens stock over a recent six-year period and that Serinca owned shares of Microsoft over the same six-year period. Following is a list of annual rates of returns over the six years for Walgreens and Microsoft stock:

---

1. For simplicity, we use stocks in our discussion here. The concepts are applicable to any asset.

	PERCENTAGE FORM			DECIMAL FORM	
YEAR	WALGREENS RETURN	MICROSOFT RETURN	YEAR	WALGREENS RETURN	MICROSOFT RETURN
2001	−10.7%	4.4%	2001	−0.107	0.044
2002	−19.3%	−25.5%	2002	−0.193	−0.255
2003	20.3%	18.7%	2003	0.203	0.187
2004	24.6%	19.3%	2004	0.246	0.193
2005	2.6%	9.7%	2005	0.026	0.097
2006	7.8%	8.9%	2006	0.078	0.089
Sum	25.3%	35.6%	Sum	0253	0.356
Sum/6 = Average Return	4.2%	5.9%	Sum/6 = Average Return	0.042	0.059

Performing this calculation in Excel is straightforward. Placing the annual returns in columns B and C, as shown in the following screen shot, we use the SUM function to add the Walgreens returns in cells B2 through B7 by typing =SUM(B2:B7) in cell B8. We divide this sum by 6, the number of observations, to compute the average Walgreens return by typing =B8/6 in cell B9. Similar calculations for the Microsoft data are entered into column C.

We can also compute the average return by using a special Excel function. If we entered =AVERAGE(B2:B7) in cell B8, we would obtain the same result of 4.2 percent.

Walgreens stock has an arithmetic average annual rate of return over these six years of 4.2 percent, whereas the average annual return for Microsoft stock over the same six-year period was 5.9 percent. If we are willing to ignore risk as reflected in the variability of returns, an investment in Microsoft stock might be the preferred among the two. However, all investors do not have the same tolerance for uncertainty or risk associated with possibly wide swings in Microsoft's returns. Let's now see how we might quantify this variability in past returns.

VARIANCE AS A MEASURE OF RISK

The historical risk of a stock can be measured by the variability of its returns in relation to this average. Some quantitative measures of this variability are the variance, standard

deviations
computed as a periodic return minus the average return

variance
derived by summing the squared deviations and dividing by n−1

deviation, and coefficient of variation. All these measures use **deviations** of periodic returns from the average return, that is, $R_t - \bar{R}$, where $\bar{R}$ denotes the average arithmetic return over some time frame.

Note that the sum of the deviations, $\Sigma(R_t - \bar{R})$, is always zero.

The **variance**, σ^2, from a sample of data, is computed by summing the squared deviations and dividing by n − 1. (You may recall from a prior course in statistics that when a sample is drawn from a population, dividing by n − 1 observations instead of n observations provides a more accurate estimate of the variance and standard deviation characteristics of the population.)

$$\sigma^2 = \sum_{t=1}^{n} (R_t - \bar{R})^2/(n - 1) \tag{6.2}$$

Stated in words, we first find the average annual return, $\bar{R}$ over the time period being analyzed. Second, subtract the average return from the individual annual returns. Third, square each individual difference. Fourth, sum the squared differences and then divide this sum by the number of observations minus 1 to get the variance.

We now can find the historical variance in returns for Walgreens and Microsoft stocks over the past six years, as shown in Table 6.1. The results indicate an estimated variance of 292.8%^{2} for Walgreens and 271.7%^{2} for Microsoft. The units, percent squared (%^{2}) may seem odd, but they are the result of the variance calculation in which the deviations are squared before they are added together and divided by (n − 1).

Use of the SUM function and other Excel operators make these calculations less tedious. Of special note is the Excel function VAR. For example, if Walgreens' returns are in cells B2 through B7, typing =VAR(B2:B7) into another cell computes and displays the variance of Walgreens' returns.

STANDARD DEVIATION AS A MEASURE OF RISK

standard deviation
the square root of the variance

Squaring the deviations can make variance difficult to interpret. What do units such as percent squared or dollars squared tell an investor about a stock's risk? Because of this difficulty, analysts often prefer to use the **standard deviation**, σ, which is simply the square root of the variance:

$$\sigma = \sqrt{\sigma^2} \tag{6.3}$$

The standard deviation formula gives units of measurement that match those of the return data. Taking the square root of the variance of 292.8 for Walgreens stock gives a standard deviation of 17.1 percent. This compares to a standard deviation of 16.5 percent (i.e., the square root of 271.7) for Microsoft. Thus, Microsoft has both a relatively higher average return (5.9 percent versus 4.2 percent) and a lower standard deviation (16.5 percent versus 17.1 percent) when compared to Walgreens for the time period we studied.

TABLE 6.1
Finding the Variances for the Returns on Walgreens and Microsoft

		WALGREENS						MICROSOFT			
YEAR	RETURN		AVERAGE		DEVIATION	DEVIATION SQUARED	YEAR	RETURN		AVERAGE		DEVIATION	DEVIATION SQUARED
2006	7.8%	−	4.2%	=	3.6%	12.99%	2006	8.9%	−	5.9%	=	3.0%	9.22%
2005	2.6%	−	4.2%	=	−1.6%	2.40%	2005	9.7%	−	5.9%	=	3.8%	14.37%
2004	24.6%	−	4.2%	=	20.4%	414.41%	2004	19.3%	−	5.9%	=	13.4%	180.74%
2003	20.3%	−	4.2%	=	16.1%	259.54%	2003	18.7%	−	5.9%	=	12.8%	164.89%
2002	−19.3%	−	4.2%	=	−23.5%	552.70%	2002	−25.5%	−	5.9%	=	−31.4%	987.09%
2001	−10.7%	−	4.2%	=	−14.9%	221.85%	2001	4.4%	−	5.9%	=	−1.5%	2.36%
Sum						1463.89%^{2}	Sum						1358.68%^{2}
Variance = Sum/(6 − 1) =						292.8%^{2}	Variance = Sum/(6 − 1) =						271.7%^{2}

The square root also can be found using a financial calculator with a square root key as follows:

Financial Calculator Solution:

Walgreens stock		Microsoft stock	
Inputs	292.8	271.7	
Press	√	√	
Solution	17.1	16.5	

Spreadsheets can be used, too. Since we know the standard deviation is the square root of the variance, Excel's SQRT function can be used by keying in =SQRT(cell containing the variance). To make the calculation simpler, we can use the STDEV function. If Walgreens' returns are in cells B2 through B7, using =STDEV(B2:B7) in another cell computes the standard deviation.

Our results that Microsoft had a higher return than Walgreens and a lower standard deviation indicate only what has happened in the recent past and are based on only six years of data. This small sample is by no means a violation of the second principle of finance that higher returns are expected for taking on more risk. Figure 6.2 shows the behavior of stock prices for Walgreens (WAG) and Microsoft (MSFT) for a number of years. It is clear that over time Microsoft's stock has offered more price variability than Walgreens while offering larger percentage gains.

Looking at historical annual returns on these stocks will tell us what their price range has been—namely, how low and how high each stock price has been. If we have reason to believe the near future will be similar to the time period studied, we can use the standard deviation to help give an investor an intuitive feel for the possible range of returns that can occur. As shown in Figure 6.3, if the underlying distribution of returns is continuous and approximately normal (that is, bell-shaped), then we expect 68 percent of actual periodic returns to fall within one standard deviation of the mean, that is $\bar{R} \pm 1\sigma$. About 95 percent of observed returns will fall within two standard deviations of the average: $\bar{R} \pm 2\sigma$. Actual returns should

FIGURE 6.2

Behavior of Stock Prices for Walgreens (WAG) and Microsoft (MSFT) for a Number of Years

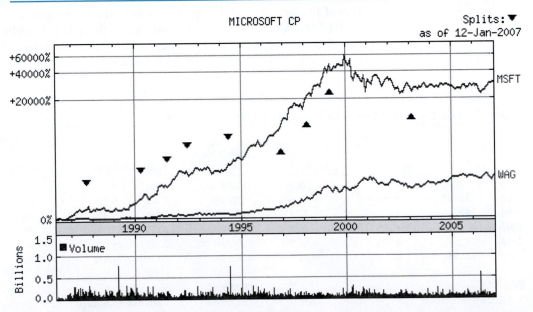

Source: http://finance.yahoo.com Accessed January 15, 2007.

FIGURE 6.3
Normal Distributions

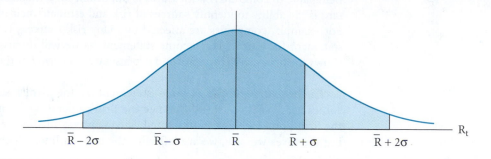

fall within three standard deviations of the mean, $\bar{R} \pm 3\sigma$, about 99 percent of the time. Thus, if the mean and standard deviation are known, a rough range for expected returns over time can be estimated.

Applying this to our data for Walgreens and Microsoft, and assuming that returns over a long period of time were approximately normally distributed and our six years of observations were a reasonable representation of returns over the long run, then Table 6.2 shows the range of possible outcomes along with approximate probabilities of occurrence. In other words, we can say that 95 percent of the time the annual return on Walgreens' stock will fall between −30.0 percent and +38.4 percent, with an expected average annual return of 4.2 percent. For Microsoft, 95 percent of the time the annual return will fall within the range of −27.0 percent and +38.9 percent and the expected average annual return will be 5.9 percent. However with the overall stock market averaging about 10 percent annual return, it is likely that future return distributions for Walgreens and Microsoft will offer investors better returns.

One problem with using the standard deviation as a measure of risk is that we cannot tell which stock is riskier by looking at the standard deviation alone. For example, suppose stock A has an average annual return of 8 percent and an annual standard deviation of 16 percent while stock B has an average annual return of 12 percent annual standard deviation of 20 percent per year. Stock B clearly has a higher standard deviation, but it also had a higher average annual return of 12 percent versus 8 percent for stock A. Which stock is the riskier?

The *coefficient of variation (CV)* is a measure of risk per unit of return. It allows us to make comparisons because it controls for the size of the average. The coefficient of variation is computed as:

$$CV = \sigma/\bar{R} \tag{6.4}$$

A higher coefficient of variation indicates more risk per unit of return. A lower coefficient of variation indicates less risk per unit of return. Stock A has a coefficient of variation of 16/8 or 2.0, meaning it offers 2.0 units of risk for every unit of return. Stock B has a coefficient of variation of 20/12 or 1.67 units of risk per unit of return. Based upon the coefficient of variation, stock A is the riskier security based upon its units of risk for every one percentage point of return.

INTERNET ACTIVITY

Stock price data are available at finance.yahoo.com. Daily, weekly, and monthly stock prices, adjusted for stock splits, can be downloaded into a spreadsheet. You can use the data to compute returns, average returns over a time period, and risk measures.

coefficient of variation
measures the risk per unit of return

CONCEPT CHECK

How is average return computed?

Describe three ways to measure risk.

TABLE 6.2
Distribution of Returns for Walgreens and Microsoft

STOCK	PERCENT OF RETURNS	ANNUAL RETURN ESTIMATES		
		DOWNSIDE (%)	AVERAGE (%)	UPSIDE (%)
Walgreens	68	−12.9%	4.2%	21.3%
	95	−30.0%	4.2%	38.4%
	99	−47.1%	4.2%	55.6%
Microsoft	68	−10.6%	5.9%	22.4%
	95	−27.0%	5.9%	38.9%
	99	−43.5%	5.9%	55.4%

WHERE DOES RISK COME FROM?

Being able to compute risk measures is important for a financial analyst. Perhaps more important is the ability to identify sources of risk and estimate their impact on different investments. For example, companies are affected by many risk sources. Table 6.3 shows a simple income statement for a firm. The income statement, as we will discuss in more detail in Chapter 11, shows the firm's sales revenues and expenses over a period of time, such as a month, quarter, or year.

The top line of the income statement is the firm's sales. From this, expenses are subtracted. We'll call this difference the firm's operating income. Next, interest expenses on the firm's borrowings are subtracted, leaving pretax income or income before taxes. Subtracting the taxes we owe, we are left with the bottom line, which is our net income or income after taxes.

Table 6.3 lists sources of risk that affect these components of the income statement.

Business Risk:

Business risk is caused by changes in quantity sold, changes in the firm's markup on its sales (the price−cost margin), and its level of fixed costs. It leads to variation in a firm's operating income over time.

For example, when the cost of an input increases—such as rising labor costs, oil prices, or raw material costs—competitive pressures may not allow a firm to increase its selling prices to offset the increase expenses. This lowers the price−cost margin and, if all else is constant, will reduce the firm's operating profit. On the other hand, fixed costs can lead to variations in operating profit over time, too. Fixed costs are fixed in that they don't change in the face of higher or lower selling prices or quantity sold. When much of a firm's costs are fixed by contract (as in the case of a labor union agreement, supply contracts, and lease agreements), a decline in sales revenues is not matched by a decline in expenses. Falling sales combined with stable expenses result in declining operating profits.

> **business risk**
> *variations in operating income over time because of variations in unit sales, price−cost margin, and/or fixed expenses*

TABLE 6.3

A Firm's Income Statement Reflects Sources of Risk

COMPONENTS OF A FIRM'S INCOME STATEMENT	POTENTIAL SOURCES OF RISK
Revenue	*Business Risk:* changes in quantity sold; varying price−cost margin
	Exchange Rate Risk: changes in U.S. dollars received from overseas sales
	Purchasing Power Risk: inability to raise prices at the same pace as expenses
Less: *Expenses*	*Business Risk:* amount of fixed costs
	Exchange Rate Risk: changes in U.S. dollars paid to overseas suppliers
	Purchasing Power Risk: inflation increases costs
Equals: Operating Income	
Less: *Interest Expense*	*Financial Risk:* amount of fixed financial expenses
	Interest Rate Risk: effect of changing interest rates on variable rate debt
Equals: Income Before Taxes	
Less: *Taxes*	*Tax Risk:* changes in tax rates, laws, surcharges either at home or overseas
Equals: *Net Income*	

Other sources of profit variability include the following:

Exchange Rate Risk:

exchange rate risk
effect on revenues and expenses from variations in the value of the U.S. dollar in terms of other currencies

An **exchange rate risk** arises when a U.S. firm makes an overseas transaction in which it makes or receives payment in a foreign currency. If it receives payment in a foreign currency, U.S. dollar sales revenues will fall and rise over time, depending upon whether the dollar is getting stronger (it takes more units of foreign currency to purchase one U.S. dollar) or weaker (fewer units of foreign currency are needed to purchase one U.S. dollar).

Conversely, if the firm needs to pay overseas suppliers in nondollar currency, the firm's dollar-based expenses will fall and rise depending upon whether the dollar strengthens or weakens. To summarize, the following are true if all else is held constant:

	U.S. DOLLAR REVENUES INCREASE FROM OVERSEAS SALES IF:	U.S. DOLLAR REVENUES DECREASE FROM OVERSEAS SALES IF:	U.S. DOLLAR EXPENSES INCREASE TO PAY OVERSEAS SUPPLIERS IF:	U.S. DOLLAR EXPENSES DECREASE TO PAY OVERSEAS SUPPLIERS IF:
U.S. dollar strengthens		X		X
U.S. dollar weakens	X		X	

Purchasing Power Risk:

purchasing power risk
changes in inflation affect revenues, expenses, and profitability

When inflation increases costs and can hurt the firm's profitability if it cannot raise prices to compensate for the increased expenses, **purchasing power risk** occurs.

Financial Risk:

financial risk
variations in income before taxes over time because fixed interest expenses do not change when operating income rises or falls

Financial risk is experienced when a firm with debt outstanding that requires fixed interest payments faces a situation similar to a firm with fixed operating expenses (see the preceding section on "Business Risk"). If sales decline and operating income falls, the fixed interest costs still must be paid if the firm is to remain in operation, leading to declines in interest before taxes. On the other hand, rising levels of operating profit do not cause the fixed financial cost to change, so more of the increased operating profit passes through to become an increase in income before taxes.

Interest Rate Risk:

interest rate risk
variations in interest expense unrelated to sales or operating income arising from changes in the level of interest rates in the economy

Interest rate risk occurs when some of a firm's debt has interest rates that vary according to the level of interest rates in the economy. Such changes in the cost of borrowing are usually not related to changes in the firm's sales or operating profits. Thus, variability in interest rates can increase or reduce income before taxes irrespective of sales trends.

Tax Risk:

tax risk
variations in a firm's tax rate and tax-related charges over time due to changing tax laws and regulations

Changes in tax rates, laws, and surcharges, either at home or overseas, add another layer of **tax risk** and potential variability to a firm's income.

EXPECTED MEASURES OF RETURN AND RISK

ex-ante
expected or forecasted

The use of historical data to look backward is valuable for examining returns and performance over time, but today's investment and business decisions must be made by looking forward, not backward. Future returns will depend upon decisions made today and upon future events. We need to develop a way to estimate expected, or **ex-ante**, measures of return and risk.

A popular method of forecasting future returns is to develop scenarios of future states of nature. A state of nature includes a set of economic trends and business conditions. The investor cannot control or predict what future states of nature will occur. One set of scenarios could be the following:

1. *Boom economy:* The domestic economy will grow at an above-average pace; inflation will increase slowly; interest rate trends will be slightly upward. Company sales will be assisted by a healthy export environment.

2. *Normal conditions:* The domestic economy will grow at a pace close to its long-run average. Inflation rates and interest rates will be relatively stable. No major disruptions in export markets are expected.
3. *Recession:* The domestic economy will grow slowly or may contract. Inflation will peak and start to decline; short-term interest rates will fall. Slow export markets will lead to lower levels of foreign sales.

Each of the three preceding scenarios is a state of nature. The states of nature can be complicated or simple, few or many, but as a whole they should include all reasonable (and maybe a few unreasonable) possible future environments. These three scenarios assumed that inflation, interest rate, and a firm's exports will follow the trends in the overall domestic economy. This, of course, does not have to be the case. A more complex set of states of nature may include separate scenarios for the domestic economy, inflation, interest rates, exports, and any other variables deemed important by the investment analyst.

Once the possible states of nature are projected, the analyst must assign a probability, or a chance of occurrence, to each one. For the three preceding scenarios, suppose the first scenario of a growing economy has a probability (p_1) of 0.30; the second scenario of normal conditions has a probability (p_2) of 0.40; the third recession scenario has a probability (p_3) of 0.30. In reality, these probabilities are developed from a combination of the analyst's experience or gut feeling, surveying other analysts on their beliefs, economic and industry forecasts, monetary policy, and a review of what has happened in the past under similar conditions. There is no pat formula that can be used to determine probabilities for each state of nature. The only rules are that each state of nature needs a nonnegative probability assigned to it and that the probabilities of all the states of nature must sum to 1.00.

The analyst must also forecast the stock's return for the year under each state of nature. If the three preceding states of nature are being used, analysts may forecast a 20 percent return under good economic conditions, 10 percent in normal times, and −5 percent in a recession.

The expected return can be found using Equation 6.5:

$$\text{Expected return } E(R) = \sum_{i=1}^{n} p_i R_i \qquad (6.5)$$

where p_i = probability of the ith scenario and R_i = the forecasted return in the ith scenario.

The expected return $E(R)$ is a weighted average of the different state of nature returns, where the weights are the probabilities of each occurring state of nature. Using the probabilities and forecasted returns cited, the expected return using Equation 6.5 is:

$$E(R) = (0.3)(20) + (0.4)(10) + (0.3)(-5) = 8.5\%$$

This number, or any other so calculated, represents the average return if the state of nature scenarios could be replicated many times under identical conditions. In any one year, if the state of nature estimates are correct, the outcome will be either *boom* (and a return of 20 percent), *normal* (10 percent return), or *recession* (return of −5 percent). If the cycle could be repeated many times, the average return over the cycles would be 8.5 percent. Thus, the expected return does not refer to the expected outcome of a particular situation. It refers only to the long-run average outcome that would occur if the situation could be replicated many, many times. However, this concept does provide analysts with an intuitive measure of central tendency. It also allows us to develop measures of possible return variability, or risk.[2]

As for historical data, measures of dispersion or variance can be computed once the average or expected value is found. The variance, σ^2, is found by using Equation 6.6:

$$\sigma^2 = \sum_{i=1}^{n} p_i [R_i - E(R)]^2 \qquad (6.6)$$

---

2. The process of computing expected returns from scenarios is not easy to apply practically. Thus, some analysts prefer to estimate expected returns from historical return data and forecasts of future conditions by adding various asset risk premiums, such as a default risk or a liquidity risk premium, to the expected nominal interest rate. For example, an investor may believe a stock investment in AT&T deserves a risk premium of 5 percent over the nominal interest rate. If Treasury bills are currently offering a return of 4 percent, the expected return on an investment in AT&T stock would be 4 percent plus 5 percent, or 9 percent. When using this method, however, it becomes difficult to estimate measures of future risk.

SMALL BUSINESS PRACTICE
Should You Start Your Own Business?

Most of us would agree that it is not possible for someone else to answer the question "Should you start your own business?" However, an article by Joshua Hyatt titled "Should You Start a Business?" in *Small Business Success,* a supplement to *Inc.* magazine, provides a list of questions that you should ask yourself. First, "Is my idea good enough?" While it is not necessary for your idea to be a revolutionary breakthrough, you must believe in it yourself and be willing to commit the time and effort necessary to make it both useful and exciting to others.

You also should ask "Do I have the management skills I'll need?" "How important is money to me?" "Can I live with the risk?" People who start companies don't necessarily do so because they thrive on

risk. Rather, some entrepreneurs actually see the starting of a new business as being less risky than the alternative risk of working for a large company. Hyatt attributes the following quote to Paul Hawken of the firm Smith & Hawken: "The best entrepreneurs are risk avoiders. They identify the risk, and then they take actions to minimize the effects of it."

The final question that Hyatt suggests that you ask is "What do I tell my family?" It is important to talk with family members about the time, money, and energy commitment that you will have to make if you decide to start your own business. Hyatt also suggests the following: "Have a fallback plan. You can't make the boldest moves with your business if you feel you can't afford to be wrong."

As with historical or ex-post measures, the standard deviation is simply the square root of the variance. The coefficient of variation is the standard deviation divided by the expected return. As with ex-post or historical data, the coefficient of variation is easily interpreted: it represents the risk per unit of expected return.

Let's compute the variance, standard deviation, and coefficient of variation for the stock return using the same three scenarios we have developed. The stock return forecast was 20 percent in an economic boom (30 percent probability), 10 percent in a normal economy (40 percent probability), and −5 percent in a recession (30 percent probability). The expected return was computed to be 8.5 percent. Using Equation 6.6, the variance of the forecast is:

$$\sigma^2 = (0.3)(20 - 8.5)^2 + (0.4)(10 - 8.5)^2 + (0.3)(-5 - 8.5)^2$$
$$= 39.675 + 0.90 + 54.675$$
$$= 95.25\%^2$$

The standard deviation will be the square root of this number, or 9.76 percent. The coefficient of variation is the standard deviation divided by the expected return, or 9.76/8.5 = 1.15.

Is it practical to develop states of nature, determine their expected probabilities, and estimate expected return and risk? In other words, do investors really do these calculations? There is evidence that scenario analysis does have practical implications. First, when the Federal Reserve Board is expected to decide to act to change short-term interest rates, market watchers and investors anticipate what the Fed may do. Periodicals such as the *Wall Street Journal* and *USA Today* survey practitioners on their expectations of Fed action. One news article presented this analysis prior to an expected interest rate cut by the Fed:[3]

INTERNET ACTIVITY

Perform an Internet search for "scenario analysis" to see what examples you can find of this method. To learn more about simulation analysis, visit www.decisioneering.com, the Web site of a firm that markets simulation software.

SCENARIO	PROBABILITY	LIKELY MARKET RESPONSE
No rate cut	Very unlikely	Stocks and bonds plunge
Quarter-point cut	Possible	Stocks and bonds fall
Half-point cut	Likely	Stocks and bonds could rise, at least initially
Three-quarter point cut, or more	Unlikely	Stocks and bonds surge

The market evidently anticipated the Fed's actions; that day the Fed announced it would attempt to reduce short-term rates by one-half point, which was the "likely" scenario. The stock market closed virtually unchanged; that day the Dow Jones Industrial Average closed down just 4.36 points (or 0.04 percent of the index's value), while the NASDAQ Composite Index closed up 3.66 points (0.18 percent).[4] As another example, several months later, the market anticipated a quarter-point reduction, from 2.00 percent to 1.75 percent, in the federal funds rate; when the

---

3. E. S. Browning, "Investors Hold Breath, Awaiting Rate Cut," *Wall Street Journal* (May 15, 2001), p. C1.
4. E. S. Browning, "Fed Delivers Expected Rate Cut, but Investors' Reaction Is Muted," *Wall Street Journal* (May 16, 2001), p. C1.

Fed did announce the rate cut to 1.75 percent, both the Dow Jones Average and S&P 500 indexes moved less than 0.33 percent, reflecting that the market anticipated the move.[5]

The second insight is related to the first: namely, that although each individual investor may not compute a scenario analysis, the markets as a whole behave as if they do. Expected changes, news, or announcements will generally have little effect on security prices. So if an investor follows the consensus set of beliefs, the investor will find it difficult to earn above-average returns, after adjusting for risk differences. To make above-average returns without undue risk, an investor must do analysis, show where the consensus belief is incorrect, and invest accordingly. If the analysis is correct, the investor's investments should benefit.

The third insight, a more complex form of decision analysis than scenario analysis, is called *simulation*. Rather than using a limited number of states of nature with specific values for, say, inflation, economic growth, and so on, simulation allows many different combinations of the important variables that may determine stock returns. After running the analysis several thousand times, the computer can compute the average return from the simulation runs and the standard deviation of the returns. This technique is used by businesses for a variety of decisions involving uncertain revenues or expenses.

HISTORICAL RETURNS AND RISK OF DIFFERENT ASSETS

In Chapter 5 we learned that the value of an asset is the present value of the expected cash flows that arise from owning the asset. To compute a present value, we need to know the size and timing of expected future cash flows from an asset. We also must know the appropriate discount rate, or the required rate of return, at which to discount expected cash flows back to the present. Chapter 4 identified three components of the required rate of return: the real risk-free rate of return, inflation expectations, and a risk premium.

The first two components are the same for all investments. Their combined effect is approximated by the yield on a short-term Treasury bill. Expected returns differ as a result of different risk premiums. Thus, finance professionals say that *risk drives expected return*, as does the second principle of finance: *a low-risk investment will have a lower expected return than a high-risk investment*. High-risk investments will have to offer investors higher expected returns to convince (typically) risk-averse people to place their savings at risk. Thus, longer-term Treasury bonds will have to offer investors higher expected returns than Treasury bills. Common stock, by virtue of its equity claim and low priority on company cash flows and assets, will have to offer investors a still larger expected return to compensate for its risk.

Evidence that high returns go hand in hand with high risk is seen in Table 6.4, which reports the average annual returns and standard deviations for different types of investments. The return distributions for common stocks have a large standard deviation, indicating much more risk than for bond investments. Clearly, however, investors who undertake such risk earn high rewards over the long haul, since stock returns reward investors more than conservative bond investments.

The return and risk measures for long-term government bonds show that less risk does result in less return. The average annual return of Treasury bills is the lowest in the table, as is the standard deviation of their returns over time.

Although future returns and risk cannot be predicted precisely from past measures, the data in Table 6.4 do present information that investors find useful when considering the relative risks and rewards of different investment strategies. It is important to note that risk is a real factor for investors to consider. Just because large company stocks have an arithmetic average return of 11.8 percent does not mean we necessarily should expect the stock market to rise by that amount each year. As the standard deviation of the annual returns indicates, 11.8 percent is the average return over a long time frame, during which there were substantial deviations—both positive and negative—from the average. The behavior of the stock market in 2000–2002, particularly the technology sector, should remind us that market returns are not always positive. The S&P 500

5. E. S. Browning, "Stocks Fall Back Before Meeting of Fed on Rates," *Wall Street Journal* (December 11, 2001), pp. C1, C17; E. S. Browning, "Fed Pessimism and Merck News Abet Late-Day Selloff," *Wall Street Journal* (December 12, 2001), pp. C1, C19.

TABLE 6.4

Historical Returns and Standard Deviations of Returns from Different Assets, 1928–2006

ASSET	TREASURY BILLS	TREASURY BONDS	COMMON STOCKS	INFLATION RATE
Average Annual Return	3.9%	5.2%	11.8%	3.2%
Standard Deviation	3.1%	7.5%	19.9%	4.1%

Source: Damodaran Online (home page for Professor Aswath Damodaran), http://www.stern. nyu.edu/ ~adamodar (accessed January 2007).

CONCEPT CHECK

Explain what is meant by "Risk drives expected return."

How does Table 6.4 illustrate the concept that risk drives expected return?

stock market index lost over 9 percent in value during calendar year 2000, over 12 percent during 2001, and over 22 percent in 2002. The technology sector was very hard hit during this time, as bankruptcies and oversupply resulted in some sectors losing 60 percent or more in value in 2000, with losses continuing through 2002.

PORTFOLIO RETURNS AND RISK

Let's return to our previous discussion of the stocks of Walgreens and Microsoft. Recall that Padric received an historical arithmetic average annual rate of return of 4.2 percent on Walgreens stock with a standard deviation of 17.1 percent over six years. Serinca's historical average return and risk achieved by investing in Microsoft over the same six-year period were 5.9 percent and 16.5 percent, respectively.

Mary also is considering investing in common stocks but is considering purchasing both Microsoft and Walgreens shares. This latter choice would be an example of building or forming a portfolio. A **portfolio** is any combination of financial assets or investments.

portfolio
any combination of financial assets or investments

Mary realizes that future returns and risks for these two stocks may differ from the recent past. She estimates the following for Walgreens and Microsoft:

	WALGREENS	MICROSOFT
Expected Return	7%	12%
Standard Deviation Forecast	11%	20%

CAREER OPPORTUNITIES IN FINANCE
Personal Financial Planning

Opportunities

Personal financial planning involves preparing for emergencies and protecting against catastrophes such as premature death and the loss of real assets. Personal financial planning also involves planning for the accumulation of wealth during an individual's working career to provide an adequate standard of living after retirement. Job opportunities include the fields of insurance (life, health, and property) and investments (money management, individual bonds and stocks, and mutual funds).

Jobs

Financial planner
Financial advisor

Responsibilities

A financial planner helps individuals develop personal financial plans that include establishing current and future financial goals and assists individuals in setting up steps for carrying out the goals. Financial goals are set for cash reserves, insurance protection, and investing or saving to accumulate wealth over an individual's working lifetime.

A financial advisor focuses on maintaining and increasing the investment wealth of individuals. Investment advice is given in reference to the existing stage in the individual's life cycle, as well as in terms of the individual's attitude toward investment risk. Advice is given on the target mix among cash reserves, bonds, and stocks. Specific investment recommendations also may be provided.

Education

A bachelor's degree usually is a prerequisite. Additional education and training often are needed in the insurance and securities areas. Certification programs must be completed to sell securities. A Certified Financial Planner designation also is available.

EXPECTED RETURN ON A PORTFOLIO

The expected rate of return on a portfolio, $E(R_p)$, is simply the weighted average of the expected returns, $E(R_i)$, of the individual assets in the portfolio:

$$E(R_p) = \sum_{i=1}^{n} w_i E(R_i) \qquad (6.7)$$

where w_i is the weight of the ith asset, or the proportion of the portfolio invested in that asset. The sum of these weights must equal 1.0.

Let's assume that Mary is willing to invest 50 percent of her investment funds in Walgreens and 50 percent in Microsoft. We can use Equation 6.7 to compute her expected portfolio return, assuming expected annual returns of 7.0 percent for Walgreens and 12.0 percent for Microsoft. Again, assuming these are average expected returns, we have:

$$E(R_p) = 0.50(7.0\%) + 0.50(12.0\%) = 3.5\% + 6.0\% = 9.5\%$$

Now, let's assume that Ramon is willing to accept a little more variability in his portfolio returns relative to Mary as a trade-off for a higher expected return. Consequently, Ramon has decided to invest 25 percent of his investment funds in Walgreens and 75 percent in Microsoft. Using the expected annual returns for each stock, the expected average annual return on his portfolio would be:

$$E(R_p) = 0.25(7.0\%) + 0.75(12.0\%) = 1.75\% + 9.0\% = 10.5\%$$

VARIANCE AND STANDARD DEVIATION OF RETURN ON A PORTFOLIO

The total risk of a portfolio can be measured by its variance or the standard deviation of its returns. Extending the concept of portfolio return, one might think that the variance of a portfolio is simply a weighted average of asset variances. Unfortunately, this first guess is not correct and we cannot use an equation like Equation 6.7. To see why, look at the time series of returns illustrated in Figure 6.4.

Consider the relationship between stocks and Treasury bonds. Stock prices are affected primarily by expectations of future economic growth, while Treasury bond prices are mainly affected by changes in the level of interest rates. At times stock and bond returns will move together; at other times they will move in opposite directions.

Figure 6.4a indicates this general condition. It shows the returns of a stock index and a bond index. Bond returns were generally less volatile than stock returns over the 1990–2006 time period.

Suppose, however, that by investors placing funds in each, stocks and bonds are combined in a portfolio. The portfolio's combined return in Figure 6.4b shows less risk. Why do the portfolio returns vary so much less?

Lower portfolio variability arises from the benefits of diversification. **Diversification** occurs when we invest in several different assets rather than just a single one. The benefits of diversification are greatest, as we see in Figure 6.4, when an asset return has a **negative correlation**—that is, it tends to move in opposite directions, such as from 2000 through 2003 in Figure 6.4a. Two sets of data are said to have a **positive correlation** if their returns move together over time, as did the bonds and stock returns during the 1992–1998 time frame.

Although the calculation of this measure is beyond the scope of this text,[6] **correlation** is a statistical concept that relates movements in one set of returns to movements in another set over time. Part of many investors' strategy is to have investments in their portfolio that are not highly positively correlated with each other. The less positive or the more negative the correlation, the greater the risk reduction benefits from diversifying into different assets. This means that although the individual assets may be risky, combining them in a portfolio may result in levels of portfolio risk below that of any of the constituent assets.

diversification
occurs when we invest in several different assets rather than just a single one

negative correlation
occurs when two time series tend to move in opposite directions

positive correlation
occurs when two time series tend to move in conjunction with each other

correlation
statistical concept that relates movements in one set of returns to movements in another set over time

TO DIVERSIFY OR NOT TO DIVERSIFY?

The idea behind diversification is that at times some investments will do well while some are performing poorly, and vice versa. Since it is difficult to forecast efficient markets, we should

FIGURE 6.4A
Stock and Treasury Bond Returns

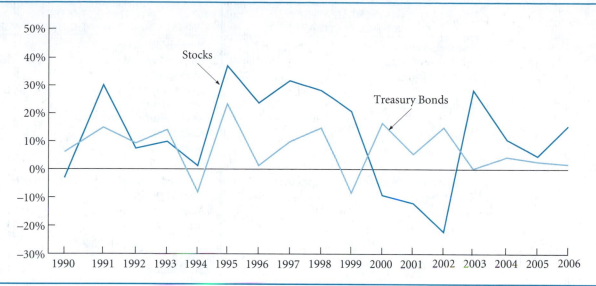

FIGURE 6.4B
Portfolio of 50 Percent Stocks and 50 Percent Bonds

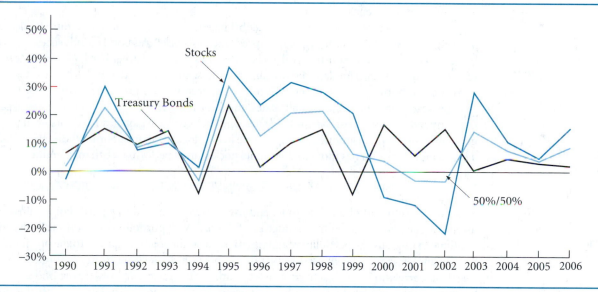

FINANCE PRINCIPLE

spread our funds across several different investments to prevent a large exposure to any one investment. An example of the benefits of diversification is found in Table 6.5.

Our time frame is twenty-five years; $10,000 invested over this time frame at an average annual rate of 7 percent gives us $54,274.33 in our account. However, what might happen if we divide our $10,000 initial investment into five subaccounts, investing $2,000 in each one? Suppose one of the investments turns out to be a total failure and we lose the entire $2,000 invested. The second investment earns no return at all; twenty-five years later, we still have $2,000 in that account. The third subaccount earns a meager 5 percent annual average return over the twenty-five years. The fourth and fifth subaccounts perform better, one earning 10 percent and the other 12 percent on an average annual basis. Even though some accounts perform poorly, investing $2,000 in each of these five subaccounts will grow to become

6. The development and calculation of correlations for portfolios can be found in most investments textbooks. See, for example, Frank K. Reilly and Edgar A. Norton, *Investments,* 7th edition (Mason, OH: South-Western College Publishing, 2006), Chapter 8.

TABLE 6.5

An Illustration of Diversification for a $10,000 Investment over Twenty-Five Years

INVESTMENT STRATEGY 1: ALL FUNDS IN ONE ASSET		INVESTMENT STRATEGY 2: INVEST EQUALLY IN FIVE DIFFERENT ASSETS	
Number of assets	1	Number of assets	5
Initial investment	$10,000	Amount invested per asset	$2,000
Number of years	25	Number of years	25
		5 asset returns (annual)	
Annual asset return	7%	Asset 1 return	−100%
		Asset 2 return	0%
		Asset 3 return	5%
		Asset 4 return	10%
		Asset 5 return	12%
Total accumulation at end of time frame:		Total accumulation at end of time frame:	
Total funds =	$54,274.33	Asset 1	$0.00
		Asset 2	$2,000.00
		Asset 3	$6,772.71
		Asset 4	$21,669.41
		Asset 5	$34,000.13
		Total funds	$64,442.25

$64,442.25 over twenty-five years, a gain of more than $10,000 over our single-basket strategy, which earned 7 percent.

To benefit from the opportunities in a global investment marketplace, investors should consider investing in a way that cuts across asset classes (such as stocks and bonds), industries, and country borders. The U.S. auto industry used to be known as the Big Three: Ford, General Motors, and Chrysler, but Toyota, Honda, and Korean imports such as Hyundai and Kia have taken much market share from U.S.-headquartered firms. Also, even though firms such as Ford or Coca-Cola may be headquartered in the United States, much of their product sales and revenue streams are from beyond the borders of the United States, and they compete globally. Investors need to look for good investments no matter where they may be in the global economy. Some studies have found that a firm's industry sector has more to do with its stock market performance than a "country" effect.[7]

PORTFOLIO RISK AND THE NUMBER OF INVESTMENTS IN THE PORTFOLIO

What happens to portfolio risk as more and more assets are added to a portfolio? Adding a second asset to a one-asset portfolio may reduce portfolio risk. Will portfolio risk continue to decline if we continue to diversify the portfolio by adding a third, a tenth, or a fiftieth asset to the portfolio?

The answer is no. The greatest reductions in portfolio risk come from combining assets with negative correlations. As each new asset reduces the variability of a portfolio's returns, it becomes more difficult to find still more assets that have low correlations with the portfolio because all assets share a common environment. In U.S. markets, most assets' returns react in some way to the ups and downs of the business cycle. Once a portfolio includes a certain number of assets, the pervasive effects of national economic and financial market trends reduce the likelihood that further diversification can offer significant benefits.

We may look beyond national borders and include non-U.S. assets in the portfolio to gain some additional reduction in portfolio risk, since the world's economies and financial markets do not move in lockstep. Even though the global product and financial markets are becoming more and more integrated, remaining differences suggest that a well-diversified global asset portfolio will have a lower total risk than a well-diversified portfolio of U.S. assets. Even with a choice of global assets, however, diversification benefits are limited. The world's economies do not move in lockstep, but neither do they have large negative correlations. Eventually the benefits of further diversification will disappear.

---

7. Craig Karmin, "Investing Overseas Reduces the Riskiness of a Portfolio," *Wall Street Journal* (January 29, 2001), p. R15; Phyllis Feinberg, "Importance of Sectors Grows for International Investors," *Pensions and Investments* (November 27, 2000), p. 56.

FIGURE 6.5

Risk and Portfolio Diversification

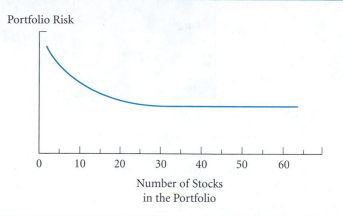

U.S. stock market data confirm this expected pattern.[8] By constructing a number of sample portfolios, with one stock, two stocks, three stocks, and so on, researchers have found that average portfolio risk declines as additional securities are added to the portfolio, as shown in Figure 6.5. After a portfolio includes twenty to thirty stocks, the risk reduction effect of adding more stocks is almost nil. The total risk of a well-diversified portfolio of U.S. stocks appears to be about one-half the risk of the average one-stock portfolio. In other words, constructing a well-diversified portfolio of about twenty stocks can reduce overall portfolio risk by one-half!

Further reductions in portfolio risk are documented when international securities are included in the analysis. It appears that only about fifteen international stocks are needed to exhaust the risk-reducing benefits of diversification. The total risk of a well-diversified international portfolio of stocks is about one-third of the risk of an average one-stock portfolio—that is, up to two-thirds of portfolio risk can be eliminated in a well-diversified international portfolio!

SYSTEMATIC AND UNSYSTEMATIC RISK

Figure 6.6 can be used to show that two types of risk affect both individual assets and portfolios of assets: risk that can be diversified away, and risk that cannot be diversified away.

Figure 6.6 resembles Figure 6.5 but with labels for these types of risks. The risk that is diversified away as assets are added to a portfolio is the firm- and industry-specific risk, or the microeconomic risk. This is known as **unsystematic risk**. Table 6.6 lists several sources of risk.

unsystematic risk
risk that can be diversified away

Information that has negative implications for one firm may contain good news for another firm. For example, news of rising oil prices may be bad news for airlines but good news for oil companies. The announcement of the resignation of a well-respected CEO may

FIGURE 6.6

Risk and Portfolio Diversification

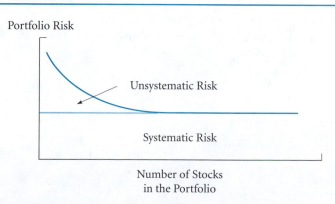

---

8. J. Evans and S. H. Archer, "Diversification and the Reduction of Dispersion: An Empirical Analysis," *Journal of Finance* (December 1968), pp. 761–67.

MIKE HACKMAN
Insurance and Investment Broker
Hackman Financial Group

BS, Business
Miami University

"Finding new clients is by far the most difficult part of my job."

Q: *What does an insurance and investment Broker do?*

A: We provide several services. We help small companies set up their employee benefit packages. Depending on the company, this could include medical insurance, 401(k) savings plans, disability plans, or other special benefit programs. We also work with individual investors.

Q: *What do you do for individuals?*

A: We help them identify and meet their financial goals. I know that sounds sort of obvious, but everything we do revolves around the client's goals. Investments that are perfect for financing a child's college education may be terrible for funding a comfortable retirement. So we spend a lot of time discussing with the client exactly what they wish to accomplish.

Q: *And once you understand their goals. . . .*

A: Then we look for the appropriate investment vehicles to meet those goals. We have access to the entire investment spectrum—life insurance, mutual funds, annuities, and everything else. There are so many options that most individuals do not have the time or information necessary to evaluate even a small percentage of them. There are over 8,000 mutual funds alone.

Q: *So, you simplify their choices.*

A: Yes. We spend lots of time and energy looking at the performance of various investment options. Then we make suggestions that match the client's goals. In most cases, we'll suggest a diversified portfolio. Diversification helps reduce downward risk in bad years and provide good performance in up years.

Q: *Do you execute the trades for your clients?*

A: We work with a broker/dealer in Florida that executes trades for our customers based on our instructions. For that service, the broker/dealer keeps a portion of the commission.

Q: *Occasionally we see the term* churning *in reports about unscrupulous brokers. What does it mean?*

A: Churning is when a broker suggests an investment strategy where there is an unnecessary amount of buying and selling of securities. And the purpose of the frequent trades is not to benefit the client but to generate high commissions for the broker. Anyone serious about making a living in this business learns quickly that it is a relationship business. If you lose the trust of your clients by churning an account or making some other bad move, they won't be clients for very long. And if you can't keep your existing clients, that means you need to keep finding new ones.

Q: *Is that difficult?*

A: Finding new clients is by far the most difficult part of my job. I work strictly on the referrals and introductions of my clients and other people I meet. That's why it's so important for me to provide sound and ethical advice.

TABLE 6.6
Examples of Risk

DIVERSIFIABLE RISK (ALSO KNOWN AS UNSYSTEMATIC RISK OR FIRM-SPECIFIC RISK OR MICRO RISK)	UNDIVERSIFIABLE RISK (ALSO KNOWN AS SYSTEMATIC RISK, MARKET RISK, OR MACRO RISK)
Business Risk	Market Risk
Financial Risk	Interest Rate Risk
Event Risk	Purchasing Power Risk
Tax Risk	Exchange Rate Risk
Liquidity Risk	

systematic risk (market risk)
risk that cannot be eliminated through diversification

CONCEPT CHECK

Why is a measure of portfolio risk not a simple average of component asset variances?

How does correlation between assets affect portfolio variance?

What is diversification?

What is the difference between systematic and unsystematic risk?

be bad for the company but good for competing firms. One firm's announcement of its intentions to build a technologically advanced plant may mean bad news for its competitors. In a well-diversified portfolio of firms from different industries, the effects of good news for one firm may effectively cancel out bad news for another firm. The overall impact of such news on the portfolio's returns should approach zero. In this way, diversification can effectively eliminate unsystematic risk. A well-diversified portfolio can reduce the effects on portfolio returns of firm- or industry-specific events, such as strikes, technological advances, and entry and exit of competitors, to zero.

Diversification cannot eliminate risk that is inherent in the macro economy. This undiversifiable risk is called **systematic risk**, or **market risk**. General financial market trends affect most companies in similar ways. Macroeconomic events such as changes in GDP, war, major political events, rising optimism or pessimism among investors, tax increases or cuts, or a stronger or weaker dollar have broad effects on product and financial markets. Even a well-diversified portfolio cannot escape these effects. Table 6.6 lists several sources of unsystematic risk.

Thus, the total risk of an asset has two components: unsystematic or firm-specific risk and systematic or market risk:

$$\text{Total risk (portfolio variance)} = \text{systematic risk} + \text{unsystematic risk}$$

PERSONAL FINANCIAL PLANNING
Diversification for the Small Investor

Most people do not have the time and expertise needed to manage an asset portfolio. For many, acquiring the investment capital is difficult, too. Fortunately, such "small" investors, as they are called, have a way to obtain professional investment management and portfolio diversification. They can use investment companies.

An investment company is a corporation that invests the pooled funds of savers. Many investment companies purchase the stocks and bonds of corporations. Others specialize in holding short-term commercial paper, bank CDs, and U.S. Treasury bills and are known as money market mutual funds. The funds of many investors are pooled for the primary purpose of obtaining expert management and wide diversity in security investments. Both the number and the size of investment companies have increased rapidly in the past decade.

Classification of Investment Companies

Investment companies are of two types: closed-end funds and mutual, or open-ended, funds, which are much more popular. Both types have the common objective of achieving intelligent diversification, or variety of investments, for the pooled funds of individuals.

Closed-End Funds

Ordinarily, money is initially raised to invest by selling stock or ownership shares in a closed-end fund. Owners of closed-end fund shares may sell their shares just as they would with any corporate security—that is, by selling them to other investors. The shares of closed-end funds are traded either on an organized securities exchange or in the over-the-counter market.

Mutual (Open-Ended) Funds

A mutual fund can invest in equity and debt securities, and it uses dividends and interest from these securities to pay dividends to shareholders. In contrast with closed-end funds, mutual funds continually sell shares to willing investors. Shareholders may sell their shares back to the mutual fund at any time. The purchase and selling prices of mutual fund shares are related to the fund's net asset value. A fund's net asset value is the per-share market value of the securities that the fund owns. Some large and well-known mutual fund companies are Fidelity, Vanguard, T. Rowe Price, and Scudder.

Securities and Exchange Commission data indicate that more than 8,000 mutual funds hold assets in the form of corporate and government securities in excess of $10 trillion—a popular method of investing indeed!

In practice and in theory, few investors have only one asset; rather, they own a portfolio of assets.[9] The unsystematic, microeconomic component of an asset's total risk disappears in a well-diversified portfolio. That means the risk that remains the systematic risk (that is, the sensitivity of the asset's returns to macroeconomic events) is the only risk that should matter to financial markets. When financial markets evaluate the trade-off between risk and expected return, they really focus on the trade-off between systematic risk and expected return. We'll examine this more closely in Chapter 10, "Investment Implications".

APPLYING FINANCE TO . . .

INSTITUTIONS AND MARKETS	INVESTMENTS	FINANCIAL MANAGEMENT
Banks, brokerages, pension funds, insurance companies—and financial institutions of all types—evaluate expected return, risk, and portfolios for their own investments and those of their clients. Markets transmit perceived changes in asset risk and expected return through changes in security prices.	The trade-off between risk and expected return is a foundational concept in finance, cutting across markets, investments, and financial management. Knowing how to compute and evaluate return and risk and knowing the important role that correlations play can help investors put together well-diversified portfolios.	Actions by investors affect a firm's stock price and the market interest rates on its bonds. Price changes relative to competing firms and the overall market inform management how investors view their actions.

SUMMARY

Financial risk and return concepts are among the most mathematical and confusing to the first-time finance student, but they are vital to understanding financial markets, institutions, and management. Much of modern investment analysis, portfolio management, and corporate finance is based upon the topics introduced in this chapter.

Historical returns are computed from past income cash flows and price changes. From annualized returns we can determine the average return on an asset over time, as well as measures of risk

(variance, standard deviation, and the coefficient of variation). Scenario analysis is a widely used tool for estimating expected return and risk.

When assets are combined into portfolios, diversification effects may mitigate the effects of each individual asset's risk. When some assets' returns are poor, others may perform well. Adding assets to a portfolio may help reduce portfolio risk, but after a certain point, all unsystematic risk has been diversified away and only systematic risk remains.

KEY TERMS

business risk

capital gain

capital loss

coefficient of variation (CV)

correlation

deviations

diversification

ex-ante

exchange rate risk

financial risk

interest rate risk

negative correlation

portfolio

positive correlation

purchasing power risk

standard deviation

systematic risk (market risk)

tax risk

unsystematic risk

variance

DISCUSSION QUESTIONS

1. Explain how a percentage return is calculated, and describe the calculation of an arithmetic average return.

2. Describe how the variance and standard deviation are calculated and indicate how they are used as measures of risk.

3. What is meant by the coefficient of variation? How is it used as a measure of risk?

4. Business risk has three possible sources. What are they?

---

9. Ownership by individual investors of shares of diversified mutual funds helps to achieve overall diversification for an investor.

5. What are sources of risk facing a firm that are reflected on its income statement?

6. Suppose in the preceding year that the U.S. dollar strengthens against other currencies. Explain its effect on U.S. dollar revenues and expenses for a global firm headquartered in the United States.

7. Describe the meaning of a *state of nature,* and explain how this concept is used to provide expected measures of return and risk.

8. Explain the historical relationships between return and risk for common stocks versus corporate bonds.

9. Define what is meant by a *portfolio,* and describe how the expected return on a portfolio is computed.

10. Explain the terms *diversification* and *correlation* in the context of forming portfolios.

11. Explain the fallacy of this statement: "I'd rather put my money into a single high-earning asset than into a portfolio of diversified investments. I'll earn more money with the single asset."

12. Describe what happens to portfolio risk as more and more assets are added to a portfolio. Are there advantages to international diversification?

13. How does systematic risk differ from unsystematic risk?

14. Classify each of the following as an example of systematic or unsystematic risk:

   a. The labor unions at Caterpillar, Inc. declared a strike yesterday.

   b. Contrary to what polls predicted, the president was reelected.

   c. Disagreement about inflation policy leads to a fall in the euro relative to the dollar.

   d. The computer industry suffers lower profits because of aggressive pricing strategies on new desktop computers.

   e. Every Christmas selling season, there is a "hot" toy that many parents try to purchase for their child.

PROBLEMS

1. From the following information, compute the average annual return, the variance, standard deviation, and coefficient of variation for each asset.

ASSET	ANNUAL RETURNS
A	5%, 10%, 15%, 4%
B	−6%, 20%, 2%, −5%, 10%
C	12%, 15%, 17%
D	10%, −10%, 20%, −15%, 8%, −7%

2. Based upon your answers to question 1, which asset appears riskiest based on standard deviation? Based on coefficient of variation?

3. Recalling the definitions of risk premiums from Chapter 4 and using the Treasury bill return in Table 6.4 as an approximation to the nominal risk-free rate, what is the risk premium from investing in each of the other asset classes listed in Table 6.4?

4. What is the real, or after-inflation, return from each of the asset classes listed in Table 6.4?

5. The countries of Stabilato and Variato have the following average returns and standard deviations for their stocks, bond, and short-term government securities. What range of returns should you expect to earn 95 percent of the time for each asset class if you invested in Stabilato's securities? From investing in Variato's securities?

STABILATO ASSET	AVERAGE RETURN	STANDARD DEVIATION
Stocks	8%	3%
Bonds	5%	2%
Short-term government debt	3%	1%

VARIATO ASSET	AVERAGE RETURN	STANDARD DEVIATION
Stocks	15%	13%
Bonds	10%	8%
Short-term government debt	6%	3%

6. Using the following information, compute the percentage returns for the following securities:

SECURITY	PRICE TODAY	PRICE ONE YEAR AGO	DIVIDENDS RECEIVED	INTEREST RECEIVED
RoadRunner stock	$20.05	$18.67	$0.50	
Wiley Coyote stock	$33.42	$45.79	$1.10	
Acme long-term bonds	$1,015.38	$991.78		$100.00
Acme short-term bonds	$996.63	$989.84		$45.75
Xlingshot stock	$5.43	$3.45	$0.02	

7. Given her evaluation of current economic conditions, Ima Nutt believes there is a 20 percent probability of recession, a 50 percent chance of continued steady growth, and a 30 percent probability of inflationary growth. For each possibility, Ima has developed an interest rate forecast for long-term Treasury bond interest rates:

ECONOMIC FORECAST	INTEREST RATE FORECAST
Recession	6 percent
Constant growth	9 percent
Inflation	14 percent

   a. What is the expected interest rate under Ima's forecast?
   b. What is the variance and standard deviation of Ima's interest rate forecast?
   c. What is the coefficient of variation of Ima's interest rate forecast?
   d. If the current long-term Treasury bond interest rate is 8 percent, should Ima consider purchasing a Treasury bond? Why or why not?

8. Ima is considering a purchase of Wallnut Company stock. Using the same scenarios and probabilities as in problem 7, she estimates Wallnut's return is −5 percent in a recession, 20 percent in constant growth, and 10 percent in inflation.

   a. What is Ima's expected return forecast for Wallnut stock?
   b. What is the standard deviation of the forecast?

c. If Wallnut's current price is $20 per share and is expected to pay a dividend of $0.80 per share next year, what price does Ima expect Wallnut to sell for in one year?

9. Ima's sister, Uma, has completed her own analysis of the economy and Wallnut's stock. Uma used recession, constant growth, and inflation scenarios, but she used different probabilities and expected stock returns. Uma believes the probability of recession is quite high, at 60 percent, and that in a recession Wallnut's stock return will be −20 percent. Uma believes the scenarios of constant growth and inflation are equally likely and that Wallnut's returns will be 15 percent in the constant growth scenario and 10 percent under the inflation scenario.

a. What is Uma's expected return forecast for Wallnut stock?
b. What is the standard deviation of the forecast?
c. If Wallnut's current price is $20.00 per share and is expected to pay a dividend of $0.80 per share next year, what price does Uma expect Wallnut to sell for in one year?

10. In addition to being used to forecast security returns, scenario analysis has many practical applications. In this problem, scenario analysis is used to forecast an exchange rate. Jim Danday's forecast for the euro/dollar exchange rate depends upon what the U.S. Federal Reserve and European central bankers do to their countries' money supply (MS). Jim is considering the following scenarios and exchange rate forecasts:

CENTRAL BANK BEHAVIOR	PROBABILITY OF BEHAVIOR FORECAST	JIM'S FORECAST EXCHANGE RATE
European banks increase MS growth; U.S. banks do not	.20	1.15 €/$
European and U.S. banks maintain constant MS growth	.30	1.0 5 €/$
U.S. banks increase MS growth; European banks do not	.35	0.95 €/$
U.S. and European banks increase MS growth	.15	0.85 €/$

a. What is Jim's expected exchange rate forecast?
b. What is the variance of Jim's exchange rate forecast?
c. What is the coefficient of variation of Jim's exchange rate forecast?

11. Using the data in Table 6.4, calculate and interpret the coefficient of variation for each asset class.

12. The following are annual stock return data on Krahamco and Avery Edit, Inc.:

YEAR	KRAHAMCO	AVERY EDIT
2004	10%	−3%
2005	15%	0%
2006	−10%	15%
2007	5%	10%

a. What is the average return, variance, and standard deviation for each stock?
b. What is the expected portfolio return on a portfolio comprised of the following:
25 percent Krahamco and 75 percent Avery Edit?
50 percent Krahamco and 50 percent Avery Edit?
75 percent Krahamco and 25 percent Avery Edit?

c. Without doing any calculations, would you expect the correlation between the returns on Krahamco and Avery Edit's stock to be positive, negative, or zero? Why?

13. The following are annual stock return data on AAB Company and YYZ, Inc.:

YEAR	AAB	YYZ
2003	0%	5%
2004	5%	10%
2005	10%	15%
2006	15%	20%
2007	−10%	−20%

a. What is the average return, variance, and standard deviation for each stock?
b. If the conditions in the future are expected to be like those in the past few years, what comprises the expected portfolio return on a portfolio comprised of the following?
25 percent AAB and 75 percent YYZ?
50 percent AAB and 50 percent YYZ?
75 percent AAB and 25 percent YYZ?
c. Without doing any calculations, would you expect the correlation between the returns on AAB and YYZ's stock to be positive, negative, or zero? Why?

14. Estimate the weights (w_i) for assets in the following three portfolios, given the following information about the portfolio holdings:

	PRICE	NUMBER OF SECURITIES
A. Stock A	$25	200
Stock B	$53	100
Stock C	$119	100
B. Bond A	$975	10
Bond B	$1,020	20
Bond C	$888	10
Bond D	$1,150	10
C. Stock A	$25	1,000
Stock C	$119	500
Bond D	$1,150	20
D. Stock B	$53	1,000
Stock C	$119	100
Bond A	$975	20
Bond B	$1,020	10

15. Tim's portfolio contains two stocks, Lightco and Shineco. Last year his portfolio returned 14 percent. Lightco's return was 5 percent and Shineco returned 20 percent. What are the weights of each in Tim's portfolio?

The following year Tim adds a third stock, Brightco, and reallocates his funds among the three stocks. Lightco and Shineco have the same weight in the portfolio and Brightco's weight is one-half of Lightco's weight. During the year Lightco returns 10 percent, Shineco returns 12 percent, and Brightco loses 5 percent. What was the return on Tim's portfolio?

16. **EXCEL** Spreadsheets are useful for computing statistics: averages, standard deviation, variance, and correlation are included as built-in functions. The following are the recent monthly stock return data for ExxonMobil (XOM) and Microsoft (MSFT). Using a spreadsheet and its functions, compute the average, variance, standard deviation, and correlation between the returns for these stocks. What does the correlation between the returns imply for a portfolio containing both stocks?

MONTH	XOM RETURN	MSFT RETURN
November	−4.6%	10.4%
October	0.1%	13.6%
September	−1.9%	−10.3%
August	−3.3%	−13.8%
July	−4.4%	−9.3%
June	−1.6%	5.5%
May	0.7%	2.1%
April	9.4%	23.9%
March	−0.1%	−7.3%
February	−3.2%	−3.4%

17. **EXCEL** If the conditions in the future are expected to be like those in the past, what are the expected portfolio return and the standard deviation of a portfolio comprised of the following?

   a. 25 percent XOM and 75 percent MSFT?
   b. 50 percent XOM and 50 percent MSFT?
   c. 75 percent XOM and 25 percent MSFT?

18. **EXCEL** Construct a spreadsheet to replicate the analysis of Table 6.5. That is, assume $10,000 is invested in a single asset that returns 7 percent annually for twenty-five years and $2,000 is placed in five different investments, earning returns of −100 percent, 0 percent, 5 percent, 10 percent, and 12 percent, respectively, over the twenty-five-year time frame. For each of the following questions, begin with the original scenario presented in Table 6.5:

   a. Experiment with the return on the fifth asset. How low can the return go and still have the diversified portfolio earn a higher return than the single-asset portfolio?

   b. What happens to the value of the diversified portfolio if the first two investments are both a total loss?

   c. Suppose the single-asset portfolio earns a return of 8 percent annually. How does the return of the single-asset portfolio compare to that of the five-asset portfolio? How does it compare if the single-asset portfolio earns a 6 percent annual return?

   d. Assume that Asset 1 of the diversified portfolio remains a total loss (−100 percent return) and Asset 2 earns no return. Make a table showing how sensitive the portfolio returns are to a one percentage point change in the return of each of the other three assets. In other words, how is the diversified portfolio's value affected if the return on Asset 3 is 4 percent or 6 percent? If the return on Asset 4 is 9 percent or 11 percent? If the return on Asset 5 is 11 percent? 13 percent? How does the total portfolio value change if each of the three assets' returns are one percentage point lower than in Table 6.5? If they are one percentage point higher?

   e. Using the sensitivity analysis of (c) and (d), explain how the two portfolios differ in their sensitivity to different returns on their assets. What are the implications of this for choosing between a single asset portfolio and a diversified portfolio?

LEARNING EXTENSION 6

Arithmetic Average Return and Geometric (Compounded) Average Return

At the beginning of this chapter, we wanted to invest $1,000 today and have $1,331 in three years. Solving the problem using time value of money techniques, we saw that an annual return of 10 percent will allow our $1,000 investment to grow to $1,331. However, then we noted that we don't need to earn exactly 10.0 percent each year. In some years the return may be higher, in others it may be lower; we just need to average 10 percent per year on a compounded basis. We computed that the following sets of annual returns will allow our investment to grow to $1,331:

$$\$1000(1 + .10)(1 + .10)(1 + .10) = \$1331$$
$$\$1000(1 + .30)(1 - .20)(1 + .28) = \$1331$$
$$\$1000(1 + .05)(1 + .12)(1 + .132) = \$1331$$
$$\$1000(1 - .10)(1 + .06)(1 + .395) = \$1331$$

Table LE6.1 shows a number of other returns in years 1, 2, and 3 that result in a future value of $1,331 for our investment. It leads us to a discussion of the difference between an arithmetic average and the geometric (or compounded) average return. These are two different concepts, and each is important in finance.

Table LE6.1 shows ten different variations in annual returns that create a future value of $1,331 with a compound return of 10 percent—but the arithmetic average return of these ten possibilities varies greatly.

TABLE LE6.1

Ways to Earn 10 Percent Compounded Average Over Three Years So $1000 Will Grow To $1,331

YEAR 1	YEAR 2	YEAR 3	FUTURE VALUE IN YEAR 3	ARITHMETIC AVERAGE	VARIANCE	STANDARD DEVIATION	COMPOUNDED AVERAGE ANNUAL RETURN
10.0%	10.0%	10.0%	$1,331.00	10.00%	0.00%	0.00%	10.00%
5.0%	12.0%	13.2%	$1,331.23	10.07%	19.61%	4.43%	10.01%
15.0%	5.0%	10.2%	$1,331.00	10.08%	25.02%	5.00%	10.00%
10.0%	18.0%	2.5%	$1,331.00	10.18%	59.76%	7.73%	10.00%
20.0%	20.0%	−7.6%	$1,331.00	10.81%	253.36%	15.92%	10.00%
12.0%	30.0%	−8.6%	$1,331.00	11.14%	372.76%	19.31%	10.00%
−10.0%	6.0%	39.5%	$1,330.83	11.83%	638.08%	25.26%	10.00%
30.0%	−20.0%	28.0%	$1,331.20	12.67%	801.33%	28.31%	10.01%
−10.0%	−5.0%	55.7%	$1,331.00	13.56%	1336.51%	36.56%	10.00%
10.0%	−20.0%	51.3%	$1,331.00	13.75%	1279.69%	35.77%	10.00%

The *arithmetic average* was the focus of much of Chapter 6 and was introduced in Equation 6.1 (copied below as Equation LE6.1)—namely, it is the sum of the periodic returns divided by the number of periods:

$$\overline{R} = \sum_{t=1}^{n} [R_t]/n \qquad (LE6.1)$$

The *compound return,* also known as the *geometric average,* was the quantity used in our Chapter 5 time value of money examples. Whenever we used present value or future value concepts, we were compounding the discount rate over the requisite number of years involved in the problem.

We can estimate the compound return using historical returns. For simplicity, we'll assume we are using annual returns. First, each of the annual returns has to be expressed as a decimal rather than a percent; that is, 10 percent is expressed as 0.10.

Second, we add one to each return; this is called the *return relative.* The return relative of 0.10 is $1 + 0.10$ or 1.10; if the return is -10 percent, the decimal form is -0.10 and the return relative is $1 - 0.10$ or 0.90.

Third, the return relatives are multiplied together. Whatever gains occur in the first year are compounded by the gains (or losses) of the second year, and so forth.

Fourth, if we have *n* years of return data, we take the nth root of the product of the return relatives and subtract one. The resulting answer is the geometric average, or compounded average return, over the *n* years of time. In terms of a formula, we have:

$$R_G = [\Pi \, (\text{return relative})]^{1/n} - 1$$

where the Π symbol means "multiply."

We've already computed the arithmetic average annual returns for Walgreens (4.2%) and Microsoft (5.9%). Let's use the data to compute their geometric average returns.

	WAG RETURN (%)	MSFT RETURN (%)	WAG RETURN (DECIMAL)	MSFT RETURN (DECIMAL)	RETURN RELATIVE WAG	RETURN RELATIVE MSFT
2001	−10.7%	4.4%	−0.107	0.044	0.893	1.044
2002	−19.3%	−25.5%	−0.193	−0.255	0.807	0.745
2003	20.3%	18.7%	0.203	0.187	1.203	1.187
2004	24.6%	19.3%	0.246	0.193	1.246	1.193
2005	2.6%	9.7%	0.026	0.097	1.026	1.097
2006	7.8%	8.9%	0.078	0.089	1.078	1.089

Multiplying the return relatives for Walgreens:

$$(0.893)(0.807)(1.203)(1.246)(1.026)(1.078) = 1.1947$$

As we have six years of annual returns, we take the sixth root of this number, and subtract one from it:

$$(1.1947)^{1/6} - 1 = 1.0301 - 1 = 0.0301, \text{ or } 3.01\% \text{ is the geometric average return.}$$

For Microsoft, the geometric average return is:

$$[(1.044)(0.745)(1.187)(1.193)(1.097)(1.089)^{1/6} - 1 = [1.3158]^{1/6} - 1 = 1.0468 - 1 = 0.0468, \text{ or } 4.68\%$$

When the annual rates of return are all equal for the period under review, the geometric average return will equal the arithmetic average. For example, look at the top row of Table LE6.1; the return is 10 percent in each of the three years, and that results in the arithmetic average and geometric average both equaling 10 percent.

If the rates of return vary over the years, the geometric mean will always be lower than the arithmetic mean. The difference between the two mean values will depend on the variability in the rates of return. The larger the standard deviation—that is, the greater the risk or variability in the annual returns—the greater will be the difference between the arithmetic and geometric means. This is indeed the case in Table LE6.1; the larger the standard deviation, the greater the difference between the arithmetic return and the geometric return.

TWO MEASURES: WHICH TO USE?

Does it matter which measure—arithmetic mean or geometric mean—we use? The answer is it depends.

We must compute the arithmetic mean whenever we want to compute the variance or standard deviation of returns. These risk measures require us to first compute the arithmetic mean and to use that value to compute deviations from the arithmetic mean.

Besides this mathematical requirement, the arithmetic mean provides the best estimate of the asset's return in any one year. If the arithmetic mean is 10 percent, our best estimate for next year's return, unless economic or market changes material change, is 10 percent.

Investors are typically concerned with long-term performance when comparing alternative investments. The geometric average return is considered a superior measure of the long-term mean rate of return because it indicates the compound annual rate of return based on the ending value of the investment versus its beginning value. In the context of the Walgreens data, this means that $1 invested in Walgreens stock in January 2001 would have grown to a little over $1.19 in value (with dividends reinvested) by December 2006. The product of the return relatives, 1.1947, represents how a $1 investment would have grown over the time period under study.[10]

Although the arithmetic average provides a good indication of the expected rate of return for an investment during an individual year, it is biased upward if you are attempting to measure an asset's long-term performance. This is obvious for a volatile security. Consider, for example, a security that increases in price from $10 to $20 (a 100 percent increase) during year 1 and drops back to $10 during year 2 (a 50 percent decrease), so the security's end-of-year 2 value is the same as at the beginning of year 1. The annual returns are:

YEAR	BEGINNING VALUE	ENDING VALUE	RETURN (%)	RETURN (DECIMAL)	RETURN RELATIVE (=1 + RETURN DECIMAL)
1	10	20	100%	1.00	2.00
2	20	10	−50%	−0.50	0.50

This would give an arithmetic mean rate of return of:

$$[(100\%) + (-50\%)]/2 = 50/2 = 25\%$$

Intuitively, this investment brought no change in wealth and therefore no return, yet the arithmetic mean rate of return is computed to be 25 percent.

The geometric mean rate of return would be:

$$[(2.00)(0.50)]^{1/2} - 1 = (1.00)^{1/2} - 1 = 0.00 \text{ or } 0\%$$

This answer of a 0 percent rate of return accurately measures the fact that there was no change in wealth from this investment.

Another actual example of this is the performance of a mutual fund during the stock market decline that started in 2000. The ProFund Ultra OTC mutual fund lost 94.7 percent of its value during the March 2000–April 2001 time period; it subsequently rose in value by 95.6 percent in May 2001. A simple arithmetic average will lead the unknowing investor to believe his investment has broken even during this time period: [(−94.7 + 95.6)/2 = 0.45% arithmetic average return]. However, investors looking at their account statements (and readers of this book) will know that March 2000 investors still face a substantial loss: a $1,000 investment in March 2000 was worth about $103.67 in May 2001.[11]

An awareness of both methods of computing mean rates of return is important because published accounts of investment performance or descriptions of financial research will use both

---

10. The product of the return relatives is known as the *cumulative wealth index*. It indicates the wealth generated by each dollar invested at the beginning of the time frame.

11. The story of a large percentage loss followed by a large percentage gain can be seen in Karen Damato, "Doing the Math: Tech Investors' Road to Recovery Is Long," *Wall Street Journal*, May 18, 2001, p. C1.

TABLE LE6.2

Historical Arithmetic and Geometric Returns and Standard Deviations of Returns from Different Assets, 1928–2006

ASSET	TREASURY BILLS	TREASURY BONDS	COMMON STOCKS	INFLATION RATE
Average Arithmetic Annual Return	3.9%	5.2%	11.8%	3.2%
Geometric or compounded average return	3.85%	4.95%	9.86%	3.15%
Standard Deviation	3.1%	7.5%	19.9%	4.1%

Source: Damodaran Online (home page for Professor Aswath Damodaran), http://www.stern.nyu.edu/ ~adamodar (accessed January 2007).

measures of average historical returns. We will also use both throughout this book. Currently, most studies dealing with long-run historical rates of return include both arithmetic and geometric mean rates of return. For example, Table LE 6.2 shows the arithmetic and geometric average returns for the assets shown in Table 6.4.

QUESTIONS AND PROBLEMS

1. How does the geometric or compounded average return relate to the computed discount rate in a time value of money problem?

2. Explain how to compute the geometric average return.

3. "The larger the standard deviation, the greater the difference between the arithmetic average return and the geometric average return." Do Table LE6.1 and Table LE6.2 illustrate this point? Explain.

4. Using the following data, find the arithmetic mean and the geometric mean for ExxonMobil, AMR, and the S&P 500 returns.

	EXXONMOBIL RETURN	AMR RETURN	S&P 500 RETURN
2001	−2.6%	−36.2%	−17.3%
2002	−7.7%	−88.4%	−24.3%
2003	25.9%	465.5%	32.2%
2004	32.4%	−47.6%	4.4%
2005	26.3%	164.0%	8.4%
2006	22.5%	44.8%	10.7%

5. How much would $100 invested in ExxonMobil at the beginning of 2001 be worth at the end of 2006? If it were invested in AMR stock? In the S&P 500?

6. What is the relationship between the arithmetic mean and geometric mean you computed in problem 4 and the variation in returns for each of the return series?

• CHAPTER 7 •

Bonds: Characteristics and Valuation

Chapter Learning Objectives

AFTER STUDYING THIS CHAPTER, YOU SHOULD BE ABLE TO:

- Identify the major sources of external long-term financing for corporations.
- Describe major characteristics of corporate bonds.
- Explain how financial securities are valued in general and specifically for bonds.

Where We Have Been. . .

The financial system is comprised of a number of participants—banks, insurance companies, credit unions, and individuals, among others. Some borrow or lend funds; others seek to sell or purchase ownership rights, or common stock, in firms. We've seen how investors are willing to give up their money today in the expectation of receiving a return in the future that will exceed the inflation rate and reward them for the risk of their investment. Time value of money principles (present value, future value) help both borrowers and lenders determine items such as how much to borrow, repayment schedules, and the return on an investment. This chapter looks at this process from the perspective of the bond market.

Where We Are Going. . .

We will learn about stocks, their characteristics, and their valuation in Chapter 8. Bonds and stocks are traded in securities markets, which will be the topic of Chapter 9. The investment implications of these securities is the topic of Chapter 10, and we'll learn more about how firms make the decision to issue debt or equity in Chapter 15, "Capital Structure and the Cost of Capital." Additional sources of funds for business financing are discussed in Chapter 17, "Short-Term Business Financing."

How This Chapter Applies to Me. . .

Time value of money is one of the most important concepts in finance. In this chapter we will consider applications of time value concepts to the bond investor. As a financial manager, this chapter will introduce you to various types of capital market securities and their features so you will know more about the financing choices facing firms.

Ralph Waldo Emerson wrote,

Wilt thou seal up the avenues of ill? Pay every debt, as if God wrote the bill!

Borrowing money brings with it the obligation to repay the debt. Individuals and firms who do not repay their borrowing may find themselves unable to borrow again in the future and, worse yet, filing for bankruptcy. However, prudent use of debt by issuers can help finance the purchase of capital, equipment, houses, and so forth. We'll learn more about the corporate decision to borrow in a future chapter. In this chapter we'll begin to learn about the characteristics of bonds from an investor's perspective.

In Chapter 2, we described **financial assets** as claims against the income or assets of individuals, businesses, and governments. Businesses obtain long-term external financial capital either by borrowing or by obtaining equity funds. Long-term borrowing can be privately negotiated or can be obtained by issuing debt obligations called bonds. Equity

financial assets
claims against the income or assets of individuals, businesses, and governments

capital may be obtained either by finding new partners with financial capital to invest or by issuing shares through the public markets. This chapter describes the characteristics of bonds and applies the time value of money techniques from Chapter 5 to see how to value bonds. In Chapter 8, we'll discuss the characteristics of stocks and tools used to value them.

LONG-TERM EXTERNAL FINANCING SOURCES FOR BUSINESSES

Businesses obtain long-term financing from internal funds, which are generated from profits, and external funds, which are obtained from capital markets. Some firms will have little need for external funds. They may be able to generate sufficient internal funds to satisfy their need for capital, or they may require little investment in fixed assets (for example, firms operating in service industries). Other businesses, such as high-technology firms that experience rapid growth, cannot generate enough internal funds for their capital needs and may be forced to seek financing, often from the capital markets.

The proportion of internal to external financing varies over the business cycle. During periods of economic expansion, firms usually rely more on external funds because the funds needed for investment opportunities outstrip the firms' ability to finance them internally. During periods of economic contraction, the reverse is true. As profitable investment opportunities become fewer, the rate of investment is reduced and reliance on external capital markets decreases.

Long-term funds are obtained by issuing corporate bonds and stocks. Table 7.1 shows that the total of new security issues amounted to more than $2,070 billion in 2004 and $2,400 billion in 2005. Most of the annual funds raised from security issues come from corporate bond sales. In fact, corporate bonds accounted for approximately 88 percent of total new security issues from 1995 to 2005. Firms issue more bonds than equities for two basic reasons. First, as we will see in Chapter 15, it is cheaper to borrow than to raise equity financing. Second, bonds and other loans have a maturity date, when they expire or come due; at times, new bonds are sold to repay maturing ones. Equity, on the other hand, never matures. Firms can repurchase their outstanding stock, or the shares of one firm may be merged or acquired by another firm. That is the reason the "net issues" line for common stocks shows negative numbers. Over the time period covered in Table 7.1, corporations have been net repurchasers, rather than net issuers, of new equity.

INTERNET ACTIVITY

Examine recent financing activity and data at the Federal Reserve Board and U.S. Securities and Exchange Commission Web sites, www.federalreserve.gov and www.sec.gov.

Table 7.1 further shows that annually corporations have been raising approximately 90 percent of their publicly held long-term debt funds by selling their bonds through public issues in the United States. The second important method of raising long-term debt funds is through private sales or placements in the United States. Public security issues are offered for sale to all investors, must be approved by the U.S. Securities and Exchange Commission (SEC), and are accompanied by public disclosure of the firm's financial statements and other information. Private placements are sold to specific qualified investors and do not go through SEC scrutiny, nor do they require public disclosure of company information. Since private sales are "private" we do not have good data on these sales over time.

GLOBAL DISCUSSION

U.S. firms may also borrow funds overseas. This percentage varies over this time frame, from 4.5 percent in 2001 to over 15 percent in 2000. There are four reasons why U.S. firms raise funds outside of the United States. First, if they have overseas plants or factories, it may make financial sense to raise funds in the country in which the plant is built. Second, financing costs such as interest rates are sometimes lower overseas, although the recent downtrend in overseas financing may be due to lower interest rates in the United States. Third, if securities are issued outside of the United States, the issuer avoids the costly and time-consuming SEC approval process. Fourth, the growing number of large bond offerings (issues of $1 billion or more at one time) causes issuers to seek access to the global capital markets to find buyers.[1]

The bottom of Table 7.1 and Figure 7.1 show the mix between external (bonds and stocks) and internal (retained profits) financing for U.S. corporations. Because of merger, acquisition, and stock buyback activity, external public equity has fallen by an average of 9 percent annually in recent years (this trend began in the 1980s). To make up for the shortfall, publicly issued bonds have increased relative to retained earnings as a funding source. Since the late 1990s, about 85 percent of net financing have come from bonds.

---

1. Gregory Zuckerman, "Cautious Bond Investors Have Issuers Thinking Big," *Wall Street Journal* (July 27, 1998), pp. C1, C23.

TABLE 7.1

Public Offerings of Bonds and Stocks ($ billions)

	2000		2001		2002		2003		2004		2005		AVERAGE
	AMOUNT	PERCENT	AMOUNT	PERCENT	AMOUNT	PERCENT	AMOUNT	PERCENT	AMOUNT	PERCENT	AMOUNT	PERCENT	PERCENT
New Security Issues													
Corporate Bonds	807.3	85.7%	1253.4	90.7%	1152.2	91.3%	1692.3	93.2%	1923.1	92.9%	2323.7	95.3%	87.8%
Public offerings, Corporate Stocks	134.9	14.3%	128.6	9.3%	110.4	8.7%	123.3	6.8%	147.6	7.1%	115.3	4.7%	12.2%
Total	**942.2**	**100.0%**	**1382.0**	**100.0%**	**1262.6**	**100.0%**	**1815.6**	**100.0%**	**2070.7**	**100.0%**	**2439.0**	**100.0%**	**100.0%**
Bonds by Type of Offering													
Public, domestic	684.5	84.8%	1197.1	95.5%	1065.9	92.5%	1579.3	93.3%	1737.3	90.3%	2141.5	92.2%	88.5%
Sold Abroad	122.8	15.2%	56.4	4.5%	86.2	7.5%	112.9	6.7%	185.8	9.7%	182.2	7.8%	11.5%
Total	**807.3**	**100.0%**	**1253.5**	**100.0%**	**1152.1**	**100.0%**	**1692.2**	**100.0%**	**1923.1**	**100.0%**	**2323.7**	**100.0%**	**100.0%**
Stocks by Type of Offering													
Common shares issued	134.9		128.6		110.4		123.3		147.6		115.3		
Common shares repurchased	238.5		134.1		74.9		102.6		165.9		434.1		
Net issues	−103.6		−5.5		35.5		20.7		−18.3		−318.8		
Retained earnings (internal financing) by corporations	174.8		196.0		310.8		376.5		397.3		440.0		
Net long term financing raised	878.5		1,443.9		1,498.5		2,089.5		2,302.1		2,444.9		
Net percent from bonds		91.9%		86.8%		76.9%		81.0%		83.5%		95.0%	84.7%
Net percent from common stock		−11.8%		−0.4%		2.4%		1.0%		−0.8%		−13.0%	−9.4%
Net percent from internal financing		19.9%		13.6%		20.7%		18.0%		17.3%		18.0%	24.7%
		100.0%		**100.0%**		**100.0%**		**100.0%**		**100.0%**		**100.0%**	**100.0%**

Source: *Federal Reverse Bulletin* (tables 1.46, 1.57), *Economic Report of the President* (Table B-90), various issues.

CONCEPT CHECK

Which security is more frequently issued: stocks or bonds?

Why would a U.S. firm issue bonds overseas?

How important are internal equity and external equity as a financing source for U.S. corporations?

FIGURE 7.1

Net Percent of Financing from Bonds, New Stock Issues, and Retained Earnings, 1995–2005

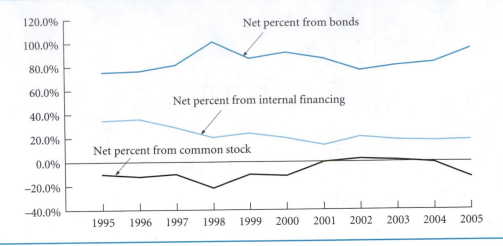

DEBT CAPITAL

par value (face value)
principal amount that the issuer is obligated to repay at maturity

GLOBAL DISCUSSION

coupon payments
interest payments paid to the bondholders; typically equals coupon rate multiplied by par value

A debt agreement is really a contract between lenders and the firm. As such, holders of debt capital have certain rights and privileges not enjoyed by the firm's owners (those holding shares of common stock) in a corporation. A debt holder may force the firm to abide by the terms of the debt contract even if the result is reorganization or bankruptcy of the firm. The periodic interest payments due the holders of debt securities must be paid or else the creditors can force the firm into bankruptcy. Table 7.2 summarizes important characteristics of bonds, which are reviewed in this section.

Except for rarely issued perpetuities,[2] all debt issues have maturity dates when issuers are obligated to pay the bonds' principal (*par value* or *face value*) to bondholders. In the United States par value is usually $1,000 for corporate bonds. All but zero-coupon issues pay interest, called *coupon payments*. If a bond has an 8 percent coupon and a par value of $1,000, it pays annual interest of 8 percent of $1,000 or $0.08 \times \$1,000 = \$80$. A bond with a 10 percent coupon would pay interest of $100 per year. Eurobonds, which are bonds issued in Europe, pay a single annual coupon interest payment. In the United States, bonds pay interest semiannually; an 8 percent coupon will pay interest of $40 every six months during the life of the bond.

Bondholders have legal status as creditors, not owners, of the firm. As such, they have priority claims on the firm's cash flows and assets. This means that bondholders must receive their interest payments before the firm's owners receive their dividends. In case of bankruptcy, the debt holders

TABLE 7.2

Common Elements of Bonds

Represent borrowed funds
Contractual agreement between a borrower and lender (indenture)
Senior claim on assets and cash flow
No voting rights
Par value
Having a bond rating improves the issue's marketability to investors
Covenants

Interest:	Tax-deductible to the issuing firm. Usually fixed over the issue's life but can be variable as the indenture allows coupon rate on new issues affected by market interest rates and bond rating
Maturity:	Usually fixed, can be affected by convertibility, call and put provisions, sinking fund, extendibility features in the indenture
Security:	Can have senior claim on specific assets pledged in case of default or can be unsecured (debenture or subordinated [junior claim] debenture)

2. A *perpetuity* is a bond without a maturity date. Its owners and heirs receive interest payments in perpetuity as long as the firm exists.

must receive the funds owed to them before funds are distributed to the firm's owners. Because of this first claim on a firm's cash flow and assets, debt is a less risky investment than equity.

Offsetting the advantages of owning debt is its lower return. The interest payments creditors receive usually are considerably less over a period of years than the returns received by equity holders. Also, as long as the corporation meets its contractual obligations, the creditors have little choice in its management and control, except for those formal agreements and restrictions that are stated in the loan contract.

Long-term corporate debt securities fall into two categories: secured obligations and unsecured obligations. A single firm can have many types of debt contracts outstanding. Although ownership of many shares of stock may be evidenced by a single stock certificate, the bondholder has a separate security for each bond owned. Bonds can be either registered or bearer bonds. Bonds currently issued in the United States are **registered bonds**, in that the issuer knows the bondholders' names and interest payments are sent directly to the bondholder. **Bearer bonds** have coupons that are literally clipped from the side of the bond certificate and presented, like a check, to a bank for payment. Thus, the bond issuer does not know who is receiving the interest payments. Bearer bonds are more prevalent outside of the United States. Regulations prevent their issuance in the United States, primarily because unscrupulous investors may evade income taxes on the clipped coupons.

Bonds can be sold in the public market, following registration with the SEC, and traded by investors. There is a private market, too; bonds can be sold in a private placement to qualified investors, typically institutional investors such as insurance companies and wealthy individuals. It is important to note that other forms of debt capital exist in addition to bonds. Businesses can borrow from banks; commercial finance companies are a popular source of debt financing, a topic that will be further discussed in Chapter 17.

WHO BUYS BONDS?

The U.S. Treasury has a Treasury Direct program to sell Treasury securities directly to individual investors. However, the main buyers of Treasury bonds are large institutions, such as pension funds or insurance companies, who hold them for investment purposes; other buyers, such as investment banks, may purchase them and then resell them to smaller investors.

Similarly, corporate debt markets are oriented toward the large institutional investor who can purchase millions of dollars of bonds at a time. Several innovative firms, such as IBM, UPS, Caterpillar, and GE Capital, initiated programs in recent years to sell $1,000 par value bonds directly to the retail, or individual, investor. Called SmartNotes, medium-term notes, or direct access notes (depending on the issuer and the investment banker selling them), the programs target small investors who have only a few thousand rather than millions to invest in bonds.

ETHICAL ISSUES

registered bonds
the issuer knows the names of the bondholders, and the interest payments are sent directly to the bondholder

bearer bonds
have coupons that are literally clipped and presented, like a check, to the bank for payment; the bond issuer does not know who is receiving the interest payments

INTERNET ACTIVITY

Learn more about these financing options by visiting www.treasurydirect.gov, www.directnotes.com, www.smartnotes.com, and www.internotes.com.

SMALL BUSINESS PRACTICE
Financing Sources for the Start-Up Firm

So you want to start your own business? All businesses require some initial financial capital to carry out the firm's operations. A service business requires less financial capital than would a manufacturing business. Both need working capital in the form of inventories and possibly accounts receivable if sales are made on credit terms. In addition, a manufacturing business requires fixed assets to manufacture the products that are to be sold.

Now that you have decided to start a new business, where are you going to get the necessary financial capital? First, you use your own assets. You may have some accumulated savings to use and/or have some financial assets in the form of stocks and bonds that can be sold. Second, you can turn to family and friends for financial support. You can either borrow from family members and friends or offer them a partial ownership (equity) position in the firm.

A small business can sometimes get outside financing from business angels or venture capitalists. Angels are wealthy individuals who provide financial capital to small businesses, usually during their early development. Venture capitalists organize partnerships that specialize in providing debt and equity capital to small businesses in their development and early expansion stages. The partners in a venture capital pool typically include insurance companies, endowment funds, and other institutional investors.

After a firm begins operations, some financing may be obtained from customers and/or suppliers. Large customers may be willing to lend to you in the form of advance partial payments on products that have not yet been completed. Suppliers often will give small businesses credit, in some cases for several months, on purchases of materials and supplies. Bank financing is another source of possible outside financing for the small business once operations have begun. The federal government through the Small Business Administration provides an additional source of financing for small businesses. Many states and local communities also provide financing assistance to small businesses.

ETHICAL ISSUES

CONCEPT CHECK

Why are bond returns expected to be lower than stock returns?

Are covenants important to bond investors? Why or why not?

ETHICAL ISSUES

BOND COVENANTS

The **trust indenture** is an extensive document and includes in great detail the various provisions and covenants of the loan arrangement. A **trustee** represents the bondholders to ensure the bond issuer respects the indenture's provisions. In essence, the indenture is a contract between the bondholders and the issuing firm. The indenture details the par value of the issue, its maturity date, and coupon rate. A bond indenture may also include **bond covenants**, which can impose restrictions or extra duties on the firm.

Examples of covenants include stipulations that the firm must maintain a minimum level of net working capital,[3] keep pledged assets in good working order, and send audited financial statements to bondholders. Others include restrictions on the amount of the firm's debt, its dividend payments, the amount and type of additional covenants it may undertake, and asset sales.

These examples illustrate the purpose of covenants: to protect the bondholders' stake in the firm. Bonds have value, first, because of the firm's ability to pay coupon interest and, second, because of the value of the assets or collateral backing the bonds in case of default. Without proper covenant protection, the value of a bond can decline sharply if a firm's liquidity and assets depreciate or if its debt grows disproportionately to its equity. These provisions affect the bond rating (see the following section) of the issue and the firm's financing costs, since bonds giving greater protection to the investor can be sold with lower coupon rates. The firm must decide if the restrictions and duties in the covenants are worth the access to lower-cost funds. Covenants are important to bondholders. Holders of RJR-Nabisco bonds owned high-quality, A-rated bonds prior to the firm's takeover in 1988 by a leveraged buyout. After the buyout, large quantities of new debt were issued; RJR-Nabisco's original bonds were given a lower rating and fell by 17 percent in value. Lawsuits by disgruntled bondholders against the takeover were unfruitful. The courts decided that the bondholders should have sought protection against such increases in the firm's debt load by seeking appropriate covenant language before investing, rather than running to the courts after the fact to correct their mistake. Covenants are the best way for bondholders to protect themselves against dubious management actions or decisions.

For example, some bonds allow the investor to force the firm to redeem them if the credit rating falls below a certain level; others, such as Deutsche Telekom's $14.5 billion issue in 2000, increase the coupon rate (in this case by fifty basis points or 0.50 percentage points) if the bond rating falls below an A rating. Bond ratings are discussed in the next section.

BOND RATINGS

Most bond issuers purchase **bond ratings** from one or more agencies such as Standard & Poor's (S&P), Moody's, or Fitch. For a one-time fee of about $25,000, the rater examines the credit quality of the firm (e.g., its ability to pay the promised coupon interest), the indenture provisions, covenants, and the expected trends of firm and industry operations. From its analysis and discussions with management, the agency assigns a bond rating, as shown in Table 7.3, that indicates the likelihood of default (nonpayment of coupon or par value, or violation of the bond indenture) on the bond issue.[4] In addition, the rating agency commits to continually reexamine the issue's risk. For example, should the financial position of the firm weaken or improve, S&P may place the issue on its *Credit Watch* list with negative or positive implications. Shortly thereafter, S&P will either downgrade, upgrade, or reaffirm the original rating.

Despite the initial cost and the issuer's concern of a lower-than-expected rating, a bond rating makes it much easier to sell the bonds to the public. The rating acts as a signal to the market that an independent agency has examined the qualities of the issuer and the bond issue and has determined that the credit risk of the bond issue justifies the published rating. An unrated bond issue will likely obtain a cool reception from investors. Investors may have good reason to wonder, "What is the firm trying to hide? If this really was an attractive bond issue, the firm would have had it rated." In addition, certain types of investors, such as pension funds and insurance companies, may face restrictions against purchasing unrated public debt.

A bond's security or collateral provisions affect its credit rating. Bonds with junior or unsecured claims receive lower bond ratings, leading investors to demand higher yields to compensate

---

3. This is a measure of a firm's ability to repay short-term bills as they come due. Net working capital is discussed further in Chapter 12, Financial Analysis and Long-Term Planning and Chapter 16, Managing Working Capital.

4. For a review of S&P's rating process, see G. Hessol, "Financial Management and Credit Ratings," *Midland Corporate Finance Journal* (Fall 1985), pp. 49–52.

TABLE 7.3

Examples of Bond Rating Categories

MOODY'S	STANDARD & POOR'S	FITCH	
Aaa	AAA	AAA	Best quality, least credit risk
Aa1	AA+	AA+	High quality, slightly more risk than a top-rated bond
Aa2	AA	AA	
Aa3	AA−	AA−	
A1	A+	A+	Upper-medium grade, possible future credit quality difficulties
A2	A	A	
A3	A−	A−	
Baa1	BBB+	BBB+	Medium-quality bonds
Baa2	BBB	BBB	
Baa3	BBB−		
Ba1	BB+	BB+	Speculative issues, greater credit risk
Ba2	BB	BB	
Ba3	BB−	BB−	
B1	B+	B+	Very speculative, likelihood of future default
B2	B	B	
B3	B−	B−	
Caa	CCC	CCC	Highly speculative, either in default or high likelihood of going into default
Ca	CC	CC	
C	C	C	
	D	DDD	
		DD	
		D	

for the higher risk. Thus bond issues of a single firm can have different bond ratings if their security provisions differ.

Table 7.3 shows that investment grade bonds are those with ratings of Baa3, BBB−, or better. They are called "investment grade" as historically investors (both individuals and managed funds, such as bank trust department portfolios and pension funds) were allowed to invest in such bonds. Bonds below "investment grade" were deemed too risky for such conservative portfolios and were not allowed to be held.

Times and regulations change, however, and bonds that are below investment grade—that is, that have ratings of Ba1, BB+, or lower—have gained a spot in many investment portfolios. Known as **junk bonds** or (euphemistically) **high-yield bonds**, they are higher risk, but offer higher expected returns, and do have benefits in lowering unsystematic risk in diversified portfolios. Formerly, issuing companies would seek the highest bond rating possible for new issues for two reasons. First, having high-rated debt added prestige to the company; a AAA-rated firm was viewed as being well-managed, financially stable, and strong. In addition, such bonds gave the appearance of a safe investment and, as they were investment-grade, would find demand by investors such as trust departments and pension funds. The second main reason for seeking a high bond rating is that the higher rating saves the firm interest expense as coupon rates on highly rated bonds are lower (because of the risk-expected return trade-off) than on lower-rated bonds.

However, the growth of the high-yield sector of the bond market has attracted both investors and issuers. Some firms prefer to issue debt rather than dividend-paying common stock as interest payments are tax deductible to the issuer. Others, as part of the firm's financial strategy, have issued bonds and used the funds to repurchase shares of common stock. Investors have noted that having junk bonds in a portfolio offers potential return enhancements and may help to diversify risk.

Over time, the stigma attached to "junk" bonds has diminished. Both issuers and investors are more amenable to these securities. For example, in 1980 less than a third of S&P-rated bonds were not investment quality—and many of those were "fallen angels,"—that is, bonds that were originally issued as investment grade but whose rates fell into the junk category because the issuing firm ran into financial difficulty.

junk bonds or high-yield bonds
bonds with ratings that are below investment grade— that is, bonds that are Ba1, BB+, or lower

By the late 1980s more than half of rated debt was in the high-yield category, and by 2007 over 70 percent of S&P-rated firms had junk bonds outstanding. The number of AAA- and AA-rated companies fell from 17 percent of issuers in 1980 to only 2 percent in 2007; B-rated bonds, on the other hands, have grown from 7 percent of issues in 1980 to over 40 percent of issues in 2007. Only six nonfinancial firms had a AAA rating in 2007: General Electric, ExxonMobil, Pfizer, United Parcel Service, Automatic Data Processing, and Johnson & Johnson.[5]

BONDHOLDER SECURITY

An important attribute of a bond issue that affects its rating is the security, collateral, or assets that are pledged to back the bond issue. In case the bond issuer defaults and misses a payment of coupon interest or principal, the collateral can be sold and distributed to the bond investors. It helps make their investment in the issue more secure. There are a number of different types of bonds, each offering different levels of security to their investors.

Mortgage bonds, despite their name, are not secured by home mortgages. Rather, they are backed or secured by specifically pledged property of a firm. As a rule, the mortgage applies only to real estate, buildings, and other assets classified as real property. For a corporation that issues bonds to expand its plant facilities, the mortgage usually includes only a lien, or legal claim, on the facilities to be constructed.

When a parcel of real estate has more than one mortgage lien against it, the *first* mortgage filed for recording at the appropriate government office, generally the county recorder's office, has priority. The bonds outstanding against the mortgage are known as *first mortgage bonds;* if a second lien is filed, the bonds issued are *second mortgage bonds.*

The bonds outstanding against all mortgages subsequently recorded are known by the order in which they are filed, such as second or third mortgage bonds. Because first mortgage bonds have priority with respect to asset distribution if the business fails, they generally provide a lower yield to investors than the later liens. An *equipment trust certificate* is a type of mortgage bond that gives the bondholder a claim to specific "rolling stock" (movable assets), such as railroad cars or airplanes. The serial numbers of the specific items of rolling stock are listed in the bond indenture, and the collateral is periodically examined by the trustee to ensure its proper maintenance and repair.

There are two basic types of mortgage bonds. A *closed-end mortgage bond* does not permit future bond issues to be secured by any of the assets pledged as security under the closed-end issue. Alternatively, an *open-end mortgage bond* is one that allows the same assets to be used as security in future issues. As a rule, open-end mortgages usually stipulate that any additional real property acquired by the company automatically becomes a part of the property secured under the mortgage. This provides added protection to the lender.

Debenture bonds are unsecured obligations and depend on the general credit strength of the corporation for their security. They represent no specific pledge of property; their holders are classed as general creditors of the corporation equal with the holders of promissory notes and trade creditors. Debenture bonds are used by governmental bodies and by many industrial and utility corporations. The riskiest type of bond is a *subordinated debenture*. As the name implies, the claims of these bondholders are subordinate, or junior, to the claims of debenture holders. Most junk bonds or high-yield bonds are subordinated debentures.

Another bond market innovation is *asset securitization*. Securitization involves issuing bonds whose coupon and principal payments arise from another existing cash flow stream. Suppose a mortgage lender by virtue of previously issued mortgages has a steady cash flow stream coming into the firm. By selling bonds that use that cash flow stream as collateral, the mortgage banker can receive funds today rather than waiting for the mortgages to be paid off over time.[6] Principal and interest on the newly issued bonds will be paid by homeowners'

INTERNET ACTIVITY

Learn about the rating agencies and their processes at the following Web sites: www.standardandpoors.com, www.moodys.com, and www.fitchratings.com.

mortgage bonds
backed or secured by specifically pledged property of a firm (real estate, buildings, and other assets classified as real property)

equipment trust certificate
gives the bondholder a claim to specific "rolling stock" (movable assets), such as railroad cars or airplanes

closed-end mortgage bond
does not permit future bond issues to be secured by any of the assets pledged as security to it

open-end mortgage bond
allows the same assets to be used as security in future issues

debenture bonds
unsecured obligations that depend on the general credit strength of the corporation for their security

subordinated debenture
claims of these bonds are subordinate or junior to the claims of the debenture holders

---

5. Sereno Ng, "Junk Turns Golden, but May Be Laced with Tinsel", *Wall Street Journal,* January 4, 2007, page C1, C2; Nicholas Riccio, "The Rise of "B" Rated Companies and Their Staying Power as an Asset Class," S&P's *CreditWeek,* January 3, 2007.

6. Collateralized bonds pledge securities to protect bondholders against loss in case of default. An example of collateralized bonds is collateralized mortgage obligations (CMOs) sold by firms and agencies involved in the housing market. The CMO is backed by a pool of mortgages. Frank J. Fabozzi, *Fixed Income Analysis* (New Hope, PA: Frank J. Fabozzi Associates, 2000), and Frank J. Fabozzi with Steven V. Mann, ed., *The Handbook of Fixed-Income Securities,* 7th ed. (Chicago: McGraw-Hill, 2005).

mortgage payments; in essence, the mortgage payments will "pass through" the original mortgage lender to the investor who purchased the mortgage-backed securities. Not all the interest payments are passed on, however; the mortgage lender will be paid a servicing fee from these cash flows as compensation for collecting the mortgage payments and distributing them to the bondholders.

Securitization allows the original lender to reduce its risk exposure, as any homeowner defaults are now a risk borne by the investor. In addition, the lender receives new funds which can, in turn, form the basis for new loans and new issues of mortgage-backed securities.

Many other cash flow streams are amenable to securitization. Payment streams based on credit card receivables and auto loans have been packaged as bonds and sold to investors. And the cash flow streams that pay the bond's interest and principal don't necessarily have to be debt-related. Music artists who collect royalties from past recordings have taken advantage of securitization. In 1997 British rock star David Bowie initiated this trend by his involvement in a $55 million bond deal in which royalty rights from his past recordings were pooled and sold to investors. Interest on the bonds will be paid by the royalty cash flow generated by compact disk, radio playtime, and music and ringtone downloads.[7] Other innovations include offering bonds backed by pools of insurance contracts. Interest on such bonds is paid from the policy premiums of the contract holders. Many times, however, these bonds have provisions for future payoffs that are affected by the existence of catastrophes such as hurricanes or earthquakes.[8]

TIME TO MATURITY

GLOBAL DISCUSSION

A straight bond will have a set time to maturity. That is, it will pay coupon interest every six months until the bond matures, at which time the final interest payment is made and the bond's par value is paid to investors. But a variety of features can affect the bond's final maturity.

Geography can play a role. U.S. firms routinely issue bonds with ten- to thirty-year maturities, and even longer in some instances. Bonds in the European market rarely extend their maturity past the seven-to-ten-year range, but this may change over time as European firms are starting to access the capital markets more and rely on bank debt less for their longer-term financing needs.[9]

convertible bond
can be changed or converted, at the investor's option, into a specific number of shares of the issuer's common stock

conversion ratio
number of shares into which a convertible bond can be converted

conversion value
stock price times the conversion ratio

callable bonds
can be redeemed prior to maturity by the issuing firm

A **convertible bond** can be changed or converted, at the investor's option, into a specified number of shares of the issuer's common stock (defined as the bond's **conversion ratio**). The conversion ratio is set initially to make conversion unattractive. If the firm meets with success, however, its stock price will rise and the bond's price will be affected by its **conversion value** (the stock price times the conversion ratio) rather than just its value as a straight bond. For example, suppose a firm has just issued a $1,000 par value convertible bond. Its conversion ratio is 30 and the stock currently sells for $25 a share. The conversion value of the bond is 30 × $25/share or $750. It makes sense to hold onto the bond rather than convert a bond with a purchase price of about $1,000 into stock that is worth only $750. Should the stock's price rise to $40, the bond's conversion value will be 30 × $40/share or $1,200. Now it may be appropriate for an investor to convert his or her bond into the more valuable shares. Why would a firm issue convertible bonds? Some may do so as a way to raise equity at a time when either the firm's stock or the overall stock market is out of favor. By selling convertible bonds a firm can raise capital now and erase the debt from their books when the bonds are converted after the stock price rises.

Callable bonds can be redeemed prior to maturity by the firm. Such bonds will be called and redeemed if, for example, a decline in interest rates makes it attractive for the firm to issue lower coupon debt to replace high-coupon debt. A firm with cash from successful marketing efforts or a recent stock issue also may decide to retire its callable debt.

7. Karen Richardson, "Bankers Hope for a Reprise of 'Bowie Bonds,'" *Wall Street Journal*, August 23, 2005, page C1, C3; anonymous, "Iron Maiden Bank Finishes $30 Million Sale of Bonds," *Wall Street Journal*, February 9, 1999, p. C23.I.S; "Bowie Ch-Ch-Changes the Market," *CFO* (April 1997); see also Patrick McGeehan, "Rock 'n' Roll Bonds Tap Investors' Faith in Future Royalties," *Wall Street Journal*, February 10, 1998, p. C21.

8. Patrick McGeehan, "Investment Banks Are Moving Fast to Offer Securities Backed by Pools of Insurance Policies," *Wall Street Journal*, June 15, 1998, p. C4.

9. Aline van Duyn, "Euro Corporate Bonds Give the Dollar a Run for its Money," *Financial Times* (June 29, 2001), p. 16.

call price

price paid to the investor for redemption prior to maturity, typically par value plus a call premium of one year's interest

Most indentures state that, if called, callable bonds must be redeemed at their **call price**, typically par value plus a call premium of one year's interest. Thus, to call a 12 percent coupon, $1,000 par value bond, an issuer must pay the bondholder $1,120.

Investors in callable bonds are said to be subject to **call risk**. Despite receiving the call price, investors are usually not pleased when their bonds are called away. As bonds are typically called after a substantial decline in interest rates, the call eliminates their high coupon payments; investors will have to reinvest the proceeds in bonds that offer lower yields.

call risk

risk of having a bond called away and reinvesting the proceeds at a lower interest rate

To attract investors, callable bonds must offer higher coupons or yields than noncallable bonds of similar credit quality and maturity. Many indentures specify a **call deferment period** immediately after the bond issue during which the bonds cannot be called.

Putable bonds (sometimes called **retractable bonds**) allow investors to force the issuer to redeem them prior to maturity. Indenture terms differ as to the circumstances when an investor can "put" the bond to the issuer prior to the maturity date and receive its par value. Some bond issues can be put only on certain dates. Some can be put to the issuer in case of a bond rating downgrade.[10] The put option allows the investor to receive the full face value of the bond, plus accrued interest. Since this protection is valuable, investors "pay" for it in the form of a lower coupon rate.

call deferment period

specified period of time after the issue during which the bonds cannot be called

Extendable notes have their coupons reset every two or three years to reflect the current interest rate environment and any changes in the firm's credit quality. At each reset, the investor may accept the new coupon rate (and thus effectively extend the maturity of the investment) or put the bonds back to the firm.

putable bonds (retractable bonds)

allow the investor to force the issuer to redeem the bonds prior to maturity

An indenture may require the firm to retire the bond issue over time through payments to a sinking fund. A **sinking fund** requires the issuer to retire specified portions of the bond issue over time. This provides for an orderly and steady retirement of debt over time. Sinking funds are more common in bonds issued by firms with lower credit ratings. A higher-quality issuer may have only a small annual sinking fund obligation due to a perceived ability to repay investors' principal at maturity.

extendable notes

have their coupons reset every two or three years to reflect the current interest rate environment and any changes in the firm's creditworthiness; the investor can accept the new coupon rate or put the bonds back to the firm

INCOME FROM BONDS

A typical bond will pay a fixed amount of interest each year over the bond's life. As previously noted, U.S. bonds pay interest semiannually while Eurobonds pay interest annually.

sinking fund

requirement that the firm retire specific portions of the bond issue over time

Although most bonds pay a fixed coupon rate, some bonds have coupon payments that vary over time. The bond's indenture may tie coupon payments to an underlying market interest rate so that the interest payment will always be a certain level above or will be a specified percentage of a market interest rate, such as the ten-year Treasury note rate. Others, such as the Deutsche Telekom bond issue previously mentioned, will have a coupon rate that will increase if the bond's rating falls.

Zero coupon bonds pay no interest over the life of the bond. The investor buys the bond at a steep discount from its par value; the return to the investor over time is the difference between the purchase price and the bond's par value when it matures. A drawback to taxable investors is that the IRS assumes interest is paid over the life of the bond so the investor must pay tax on interest he or she doesn't receive. Because of these tax implications, zero coupon bonds are best suited for tax-exempt investment accounts such as IRAs or tax-exempt investment organizations such as pension funds.

Why would an investor purchase a zero-coupon bond? Many bond investors have long-term time horizons before the invested funds are needed (to pay for a child's college education, personal retirement, or other financial goals). Such investors will not spend the bond's coupon interest when it is received; they will reinvest it in other securities. When regular bonds are purchased by these investors, they face the risk of not knowing what the return will be on the reinvested coupons over the life of the bond. Interest rates may rise, fall, or cycle up and down over the life of the investment. Zero coupon bonds eliminate this uncertainty by, in essence, locking in the return (the difference between the price paid and the par value) when the bond is purchased.

---

10. Another way to offer protection in the face of a ratings downgrade is for the issue's coupon rate to rise to compensate for the higher credit risk.

A large risk faced by bond investors is an unexpected change in inflation. An unexpected increase in inflation can cause lower real returns to an investor as the bond's fixed interest rate does not adjust to varying inflation. In 1997 the U.S. Treasury offered an innovation to investors in U.S. debt: inflation-protected Treasury notes.[11] Issued in $1,000 minimum denominations, the principal value of the notes change in accordance with changes in the consumer price index (CPI).[12]

Here's how *Treasury Inflation Protected Securities (TIPS)* work: Interest payments are computed based upon the inflation-adjusted principal value. In times of rising consumer prices, both the principal value and interest payments rise in line with inflation. Should the CPI fall, the principal amount is reduced accordingly. For example, suppose an inflation-indexed note with a $1,000 par value is sold at a 3 percent interest rate. If inflation over the next year is 4 percent, the principal value rises to $1,000 plus 4 percent or $1,040. The annual interest payment will be 3 percent of $1,040, 0.03 × $1,040, or $31.20. With 4 percent inflation, the principal rises by 4 percent ($1,000 to $1,040) as does the interest ($30 to $31.20).

Although the principal is not paid until the note matures, the IRS considers the year-by-year change in principal as taxable income in the year in which the change in value is made. In the preceding example, the investor will pay taxes on $71.20—the $31.20 in interest received and the $40 increase in principal value. Because of this, these bonds will be most attractive for tax-exempt or tax-deferred investments, such as pension funds and individual IRA accounts.[13] To make the inflation protection more affordable to smaller investors, in 1998 the U.S. Treasury announced plans to offer inflation-protected U.S. savings bonds.

In addition, several corporations, such as Merrill Lynch, Morgan Stanley, Household International, Fannie Mae, and Sallie May, have issued inflation-protected bonds. Several banks, for example LaSalle Bank and Standard Federal Bank, have inflation-protected certificates of deposit.[14]

There are so many variations in bondholder security, maturity, and income payouts among bond issues for the same reason there are different computers, carbonated beverages, and pizza: namely, to meet different needs in the market, or in the case of bonds, to meet the needs of different types of borrowers and lenders. Some borrowers reduce borrowing costs by offering lenders better collateral; others want to maintain flexibility (or they have no collateral to offer) so they issue debentures and pay higher interest rates. From the lenders' perspective, zero-coupon bonds may be attractive as they eliminate reinvestment risk (the risk of reinvesting coupon income at lower interest rates). Similarly, sinking funds, call, put, or convertability provisions are attractive to different investors in ever-changing market environments.

CONCEPT CHECK

What information does a bond rating give to investors?

How does a collateralized bond differ from a mortgage bond?

Which offers investors greater protection: a mortgage bond, a debenture, or a subordinated debenture? Why?

Explain what a conversion feature does on a bond. What does it mean when a bond is callable?

GLOBAL DISCUSSION

Eurodollar bonds
dollar-denominated bonds
sold outside the United States

GLOBAL BOND MARKET

Many U.S. corporations have issued *Eurodollar bonds*, which are dollar-denominated bonds that are sold outside the United States. Because of this, they escape review by the SEC, somewhat reducing the expense of issuing the bonds. Eurodollar bonds usually have fixed coupons with annual coupon payments. Most mature in five to ten years, so they are not attractive for firms that want to issue long-term debt. Most Eurodollar bonds are debentures. This is not a major concern to investors, as only the largest, financially strongest firms have access to the Eurobond market. Investors *do* care that the bonds are sold in bearer form, because investors can remain anonymous and evade taxes on coupon income. Some

---

11. Inflation-adjusted bonds have been offered by other countries for some time. For example, Israel first offered these securities in 1955, the United Kingdom in 1981, Australia in 1985, Canada in 1991, and Sweden in 1994.

12. Because of the initial popularity of the inflation-adjusted T-notes, some federal agencies (Federal Home Loan Bank Board, Tennessee Valley Authority) have issued inflation-indexed notes as well.

13. Gregory Zuckerman, "Inflation-Indexed Bonds Attract Fans," *Wall Street Journal*, May 20, 1999, p. C1; Pu Shen, "Features and Risks of Treasury Inflation Protection Securities," *Federal Reserve Bank of Kansas City Economic Review* (First Quarter, 1998), pp. 23–38.

14. Aaron Lucchetti, "Inflation Rears its Head . . . If Only on New Bond Issues," *Wall Street Journal*, January 28, 2004, pp. C1, C4; Christine Richard, "Corporations, Banks Issue Debt with an Inflation-Wary Hook," *Wall Street Journal*, September 24, 2003, p. C5.

PERSONAL FINANCIAL PLANNING
Investing in Ladders and Barbells

As a first introduction to stocks and bonds, this chapter is filled with applications to personal finance. From knowledge about the different types of stocks and bonds to how to read the stock and bond listings in the newspaper, to basic valuation principles, all these tools and concepts can be used by individual investors as well as professionals.

Let's look at one application for a bond investor. Because of the "seesaw effect," lower interest rates cause bond prices to rise and higher interest rates cause lower bond prices. However, the yield curve doesn't just shift up and down over time. Sometimes it twists: this means that short-term rates rise while long-term rates are stable or falling, or long-term rates rise while short-term rates are stable or falling. To avoid having their holdings hit by sudden moves in short-term or long-term rates, some investors employ a "ladder" strategy.

This strategy invests an equal amount of money in bonds over a range of maturities, so interest rate cycles will average out over the business cycle to reduce the bond investor's risk. Others chose a "barbell" approach, with approximately equal amounts of short-term bonds and long-term bonds purchased. By clumping holdings at either end of the maturity spectrum, the investor hopes to smooth out the effect of interest rate fluctuations on his bond portfolio.

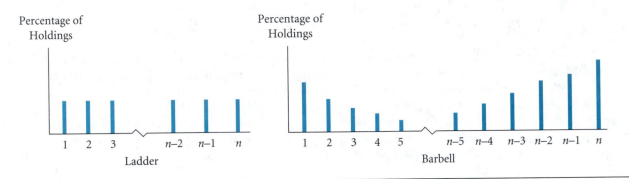

researchers believe that this is the main reason that Eurodollar bond interest rates are low relative to U.S. rates.[15]

U.S. firms aren't the only issuers of securities outside their national borders. For example, foreign firms can issue securities in the United States if they follow U.S. security registration procedures. **Yankee bonds** are U.S. dollar-denominated bonds that are issued in the United States by a foreign issuer. Some issuers find the longer maturities of Yankees attractive to meet long-term financing needs. Japanese firms often find it necessary to issue bonds outside their national borders. Regulations and a requirement for mandatory bank guarantees on publicly traded debt in Japan limit the market for Japanese domestic debt issues to only the largest, blue-chip firms. While Eurodollar bonds typically mature in five to ten years, Yankees may have maturities as long as thirty years. Nonetheless, the euro (€) is becoming a strong competitor to the U.S. dollar for firms that want to raise funds in a currency that has broad appeal to many investors.[16]

Increasingly, the international bond market is ignoring national boundaries. A growing number of debt issues are being sold globally. In 1989, the World Bank was the first issuer of **global bonds**. Global bonds usually are denominated in U.S. dollars. As they are marketed globally, their offering sizes typically exceed $1 billion. In addition to the World Bank, issuers include the governments of Finland and Italy and corporations such as Deutsche Telekom ($14.5 billion raised), Ford Motor Credit ($8.6 billion), Tecnost International Finance (Netherlands) ($8.3 billion), AT&T ($8 billion), Glitnir Bank (Iceland) ($1.25 billion), and Wal-Mart ($5.8 billion).

Yankee bonds
dollar-denominated bonds issued in the United States by a foreign issuer

global bonds
generally denominated in U.S. dollars and marketed globally

READING BOND QUOTES

Figure 7.2 shows some of the bond quotation information that is available in the financial press or Web sites such as http://finance.yahoo.com and http://wsjmarkets.com. The exhibit highlights a bond

15. W. Marr and J. Trimble, "The Persistent Borrowing Advantage of Eurodollar Bonds: A Plausible Explanation," *Journal of Applied Corporate Finance* (Summer 1988), pp. 65–70.

16. Aline van Duyn, "Euro Corporate Bonds Give the Dollar a Run for its Money," *Financial Times* (June 29, 2001), p. 16.

FIGURE 7.2

Sample Bond Quotation

COMPANY (TICKER)	COUPON	MATURITY	LAST PRICE	LAST YIELD	EST SPREAD	UST	EST. $ VOL (000s)
Ford Motor Credit (F) 7.000		2013	105.296	6.25	236	5	230,068

quote for a hypothetical bond issued by Ford Motor Credit, the subsidiary of Ford Motor that raises funds to finance car loans and leases.

The ticker symbol (F) refers to Ford's common stock; in stock trading ticker symbols are used as a shorthand notation rather than full company names. The Ford Credit bond has a coupon rate of 7.000 percent. If its par value is $1,000, as are most corporate bonds, then Ford Credit pays interest of 7 percent of $1,000, or 0.0700 × 1,000 = $70.00 per year or $35.00 every six months. The bond matures (that is, the principal repayment comes due) in 2013. The "Last Price" reports the closing price of the bond, expressed as a percentage of par value. Since its par value is $1,000, a closing price of 105.296 percent of par gives a value for the bond of $1,052.96.

A commonly used term that is simple to compute is the *current yield* of a bond. We calculate current yield by dividing the annual coupon interest by the current price. The Ford Credit bond's current yield is $70.00/$1,052.96 = 6.65 percent. The current yield does not adequately represent the return on a bond investment as it considers income return only and ignores price changes.

The yield to maturity is a better measure of investor return on a bond and is shown by the "Last Yield" in Figure 7.2. **Yield to maturity** represents an estimate of the investor's return on the bond if it were purchased today and held to maturity. The yield to maturity is calculated using the bond's coupon, par value, last price, and time to maturity. Here the yield is presented to us as 6.252 percent. (On page 187 you will learn to compute a bond's yield to maturity.) The "Estimated Spread" is the difference between the yield to maturity on the Ford Credit bond and a similar-maturity U.S. Treasury bond. Here, the spread is 236 basis points or 2.36 percent (one basis point represents 0.01 percentage points). The spread is computed from the yield to maturity on a Treasury security that matures in five years, as seen by the number under the "UST" column. Since any corporate bond is riskier than Treasury securities because of default or credit risk, the spread will always be positive. Since the Ford Credit bond has a yield to maturity of 6.252 percent, the five-year Treasury security must have a yield to maturity of about 6.252 percent − 2.36 percent = 3.89 percent.

The "Vol" column represents actual bond trading volume in thousands of dollars for this Ford Credit bond. The market value (quantity traded times last price) of the trading volume is $230,068,000. With a last price of $1,052.96, the approximate number of this type of Ford Credit bond that traded is $230,068,000/$1,052.96 = 218,496.

The following is a typical price quote in the financial pages for Treasury bonds:

RATE	MATURITY MO/YR	BID	ASKED	CHG.	ASKED YLD
4.000	Feb 14	100:27	100:28	−1	3.89

The coupon rate for the bond is 4.000 percent of par value, meaning that a $1,000 par value bond will pay $40 of interest annually, in two semiannual payments of $20. The bond matures in February of 2014. Treasury bond prices are expressed as percentages of par value and in 32nds of a point. The bid price, which is the price received by investors selling bonds, is 100 27/32 percent of par, or $1,008.4375. The ask price, which is paid by investors purchasing the bonds, is 100 28/32 of par or $1,008.75. The bid-ask spread represents dealer profit, or $0.3125 per $1,000 par value bond. Spreads are often an indicator of how liquid a security is; the narrower the bid-ask spread, the greater the liquidity (and, usually, the greater the trading volume). The change in price from the previous day was −1/32 of a percentage point. The yield to maturity, based on the asked price, is 3.89 percent. Note that this is the

yield to maturity
represents an estimate of the investor's return on the bond if it was purchased today and held to maturity

INTERNET ACTIVITY

Learn more about the bond market and prices at www.bonds-online.com and http://www.investinginbonds.com.

same bond as the "UST" bond used in the Ford Credit quote in Figure 7.2. The five-year Treasury security yield to maturity we estimated agrees with the data in the Treasury security quote.

A fine point: The asked yield in the Treasury security quote will slightly understate the true yield to maturity. It is determined by computing the semiannual yield given the coupon payments, ask price, and par value and then doubling it. To be exact, we would compound the semiannual yield over two half-year periods. That is, if the reported asked yield is 3.89 percent, the computed semiannual yield is 3.89/2, or 1.945 percent. Compounding this over two semiannual periods gives a truer estimate of the yield to maturity, $(1 + 0.01945)^2 - 1$, which equals 3.93 percent.

VALUATION PRINCIPLES

In Chapter 5 we learned how to find the present value of a series of future cash flows. The present value represents the current worth of the future cash flows. In other words, it represents the price someone would be willing to pay today in order to receive the expected future cash flows. For example, from page 122, an investor would be willing to pay $2,577 to receive a three-year annuity of $1,000 at an 8 percent discount rate.

All securities are valued on the basis of the cash inflows they are expected to provide to their owners or investors. Thus, mathematically we have:

$$\text{price} = [CF_1/(1 + r)^1] + [CF_2/(1 + r)^2] + \cdots + [CF_n/(1 + r)^n] \qquad (7.1)$$

or

$$\text{price} = \sum_{t=1}^{n} [CF_t/(1 + r)^t] \qquad (7.1a)$$

that is, value or current price should equal the present value of expected future cash flows.

Recall from Chapters 4 and 5 that the r represents the appropriate discount rate or the rate of return required by investors. For securities with no default risk, such as Treasury bonds, r reflects the combination of the real risk-free rate and expected inflation as measured by the nominal risk-free rate. For securities with default risk, such as the bonds and stocks issued by corporations, the r represents a nominal risk-free rate plus a premium to reflect default risk. For illustration purposes, let's assume that a security is expected to pay its owner $100 per year for five years. Let's also assume that investors expect a 10 percent annual compound rate of return on this investment. The 10 percent rate is based on a risk-free rate of 6 percent plus a 4 percent default risk premium. Now, what should be the security's current or present value?

The answer can be determined by using present value tables, a financial calculator, or a computer software program. For example, using Table 2 (Present Value of $1) in this book's appendix, we can identify the appropriate present value interest factors (PVIF) at 10 percent as follows:

YEAR	CASH FLOW	×	PVIF @ 10%	=	PRESENT VALUE
1	$100		0.909		$90.90
2	100		0.826		82.60
3	100		0.751		75.10
4	100		0.683		68.30
5	100		0.621		62.10
					price = $379.00

Thus, the current or present value of the security at a 10 percent discount rate should be $379. Notice how the preceding table resembles a spreadsheet. Indeed, spreadsheets are powerful tools for developing models to evaluate bonds and stocks. Using Excel we can create a table to do this calculation:

	A	B	C	D
1				
2	Interest rate:	10%		
3	Number of years:	5		
4				
5	Year	Cash Flow	PVIF	Present Value
6	1	$100	0.909	$90.91
7	2	$100	0.826	$82.64
8	3	$100	0.751	$75.13
9	4	$100	0.683	$68.30
10	5	$100	0.621	$62.09
11				$379.08

where the present value interest factor formula in cell C6 is = 1/(1+B2)^A6. In cell C6, the present value interest factor is computed as $1/(1 + 0.10)^1$ or 0.909 (to three decimal places). In cell C7, the interest rate remains the same, but the exponent changes to reflect that the cash flow is discounted back two years: = 1/(1+B2)^A7. The spreadsheet calculates this as $1/(1 + 0.10)^2$-or 0.826. We use the SUM function to add the numbers in cell D11: =SUM(D6:D10). Of course, since the security's cash flow reflects a $100 five-year annuity, we could have used Table 4 (Present Value of a $1 Ordinary Annuity) in this book's appendix to determine the security's present value as follows:

$$\text{price} = \text{cash flow annuity} \times \text{PVIFA @ 10\%}$$
$$= \$100 \times 3.791$$
$$= \$379.10$$

where PVIFA refers to the present value interest factor of an annuity. Notice that there is a slight rounding error due to the use of three-digit tables.

The security's present value also can be determined by using a financial calculator as follows. First, clear the calculator's memory. Next, enter 100 (or −100, depending on the calculator) using the annuity or payments (PMT) key. Then, enter 10 and press the %i key and enter 5 and press the N key. Finally, press the compute (CPT) key followed by the present value (PV) key to calculate the security's current value of $379.08.

Financial Calculator Solution:

Inputs: 5   10   −100
         [N]   [%i]   [PMT]

Press: [CPT]   [PV]

Solution: 379.08

Excel's PV function can compute the present value of an annuity, too. Recall that the PV function has the form PV (periodic interest rate, number of periods, payment, future value, type). To solve for this five-year annuity, we can use the Excel spreadsheet:

	A	B
1	Interest rate:	10%
2	Number of years:	5
3	Cash flow	$100
4		
5	Present value of the annuity:	-$379.08
6		
7		
8		
9		
10		

where the Excel function in cell B5 will be =PV(B1,B2,B3,0,0). Cell B1 contains the interest rate; the number of years in the annuity, 5, is found in cell B2; and the periodic annuity payment, $100, is in cell B3.

The desired future savings (future value) is zero for the current problem. Since we are computing a regular annuity, we can either omit the final item or enter "0" in the final position. The Excel PV function returns a negative number. Recalling the cash flow diagrams from Chapter 5, if the $100 annuity represents cash inflows to an investor, the present value must represent an outflow—namely, the price an investor is willing to pay to receive a five-year annuity of $100. By convention, cash outflows are negative numbers and inflows are positive. Should you prefer not to have a negative present value number, simply insert a negative sign before the PV command: =−PV(B1,B2,B3,0,0) so the spreadsheet returns a positive present value:

	A	B
1	Interest rate:	10%
2	Number of years:	5
3	Cash flow	$100
4		
5	Present value of the annuity:	$379.08
6		

Now we are ready to determine the values of bonds. Conceptually, bond valuation is very similar to many of the present value examples covered in Chapter 5.

CONCEPT CHECK

What is the relationship between the present value of future cash flows and the price an investor should be willing to pay for a security?

What does r represent in Equation 7.1?

VALUATION OF BONDS

Corporate and government bonds usually provide for periodic payments of interest plus the return of the amount borrowed or par value when the bond matures. Equation 7.1 can be modified to incorporate these bond cash flows.

DETERMINING A BOND'S PRESENT VALUE

The value of a bond with annual coupon payments can be expressed as follows:

$$\text{price} = \text{PV (expected future cash flows)}$$
$$= [C_1/(1 + r_b)^1] + [C_2/(1 + r_b)^2] + \cdots$$
$$+ [C_n/(1 + r_b)^n] + [\text{Par}_n/(1 + r_b)^n] \tag{7.2}$$

$$= \sum_{t=1}^{n} [C_t/(1 + r_b)^t] + [\text{Par}_n/(1 + r_b)^n] \tag{7.2a}$$

$$= \text{PV (coupon annuity)} + \text{PV (principal)}$$

where
Price = the bond's value now or in period zero,
C　　= the coupon payment,
Par　= the bond's principal amount,
r_b　　= the rate of return required by investors on this quality or risk class of bonds, given its bond rating; if coupons are paid semiannually, this is the semiannual required rate of return.

In other words, we use both Equation 5.7 (present value of an annuity) and Equation 5.3 (present value of a single amount) to compute a bond's price. We first find the present value of the bond's expected coupon payments. Second, we compute the present value of the bond's principal payment. Third, we add together these two present values to find the bond's price. A point to watch for is the type of bond we are dealing with; Eurobonds pay coupon interest once a year, whereas U.S. bonds pay interest twice a year, delivering one-half of the annual coupon to bondholders every six months.

Thus, for U.S. bonds, we need to adjust the calculation of Equation 7.2a for semiannual cash flows. In this circumstance, n, the number of periods, equals:

$$n = 2 \times \text{the number of years until maturity}$$

and the required rate of return, r_b, is the rate that compounds to equal the market interest rate:

$$(1 + \text{market rate}) = (1 + r_b)^2$$

That is, the market rate is the effective interest rate (EAR) in Equation 5.11; the bond's required periodic rate is found by:

$$r_b = (1 + \text{market rate})^{1/2} - 1$$

Most corporate bonds are issued in $1,000 denominations. To illustrate how a corporate bond's value is calculated, let's assume that a bond with $1,000 face value has a coupon rate of 8 percent and a ten-year life before maturity. Thus an investor will receive $80 ($1,000 × 0.08) annually; for U.S. corporate bonds, half of this annual amount, $40, will be paid every six months, with the $1,000 paid at the end of ten years. We determine the bond's present value based on the interest rate required by investors on similar quality bonds. Let's assume investors require an 8.16 percent rate of return on bonds of similar quality.

With semiannual coupons, the number of periods is twenty (2 × 10 years) and the periodic interest is $r_b = (1 + \text{market rate})^{1/2} - 1 = (1 + 0.0816)^{1/2} - 1 = 0.04$ or 4.0 percent.

We need to discount the $40 coupon annuity portion of the bond at the PVIFA at 4 percent for twenty periods, which is 13.590 (see Table 4 in this book's appendix). Since the $1,000 principal will be received only at the end of twenty periods, we use 0.456, the PVIF at 4 percent for twenty years from Table 2 in this book's appendix.[17]

Taking these together, we have:

$$\begin{aligned}
\$40 \times 13.590 &= \$543.60 \\
\$1,000 \times 0.456 &= \underline{456.00} \\
\text{Bond value} &= \$999.60
\end{aligned}$$

which rounds to $1,000. Thus the bond is worth $1,000 and will remain so as long as investors require the 8.16 percent market rate of return on bonds of this maturity and risk.

Rather than use tables, we can compute bond prices using a financial calculator's functions or with spreadsheets. The following spreadsheet format shows that the price of the preceding bond is $1,000.00:

	A	B	C
1			
2	Computing Bond Price using EAR (effective annual rate)		
3	Coupon Rate	8.00%	
4	Number of years until maturity	10.00	
5	Number of coupon payments per year	2.00	
6	Par Value	$1,000.00	
7	Market rate	8.16%	(EAR)
8			
9	Compute periodic interest rate:	4.00%	equals [(1 + B7)^(1/B5)] minus 1
10	Compute number of periods:	20.00	equals B4 * B5
11	Compute coupon cash flow:	$40.00	equals (B3 *B6)/B5
12			
13	Bond price	$1,000.00	equals -PV(B9, B10, B11, B6, 0)
14			

---

17. For bonds paying semiannual coupons, we must not think in terms of the number of years, but rather the number of periods. Because the 4 percent periodic rate of return is a semiannual rate, we use twenty semiannual periods of time in both the coupon and par value present value calculations.

As an alternative, we can use ten years as the time frame for the par value calculation, but only if we use the annualized market interest rate of 8.16 percent as the discount rate. Doing so, the present value of the $1,000 par value is $1,000 × (1/1.0816)^{10} = $1,000 × 0.456 = $456.00, the same value as we received using the semiannual rate of 4 percent over twenty semiannual periods.

However, what if investors required a 10.25 percent return, or yield, on bonds of similar qual-ity? The bond must then fall in price to compensate for the fact that only $80 in annual interest is received by the investor. A market return of 10.25 percent corresponds to a semiannual return of $(1 + 0.1025)^{1/2} - 1 = 0.05$ or 5.0 percent. The appropriate discount factors at 5 percent for twenty years from Tables 2 and 4 in the appendix would be:

$$
\begin{aligned}
\$40 \times 12.462 &= \$498.48 \\
\$1{,}000 \times 0.377 &= \underline{377.00} \\
\text{Bond value} &= \$875.48
\end{aligned}
$$

Using the preceding spreadsheet and changing the value of cell B7 from 8.16 percent to 10.25 percent, we easily find the new price of the bond, $875.38. The spreadsheet's price is more accurate as interest factors from the financial tables are rounded to only three decimal places. The benefit of this calculation with spreadsheets is clear: once we appropriately design the spreadsheet, we can change our inputs or assumptions and see the effect on the bond's price.

Microsoft Excel

File Edit View Insert Format Tools Data Window Help

100% Arial

Reply with Changes... End Review

A15

	A	B	C	D	E
1					
2	Computing Bond Price using EAR (effective annual rate)				
3	Coupon Rate	8.00%			
4	Number of years until maturity	10.00			
5	Number of coupon payments per year	2.00			
6	Par Value	$1,000.00			
7	Market rate	10.25%	(EAR)		
8					
9	Compute periodic interest rate:	5.00%	equals [(1 + B7)^(1/B5)] minus 1		
10	Compute number of periods:	20.00	equals B4 * B5		
11	Compute coupon cash flow:	$40.00	equals (B3 *B6)/B5		
12					
13	Bond price	$875.38	equals -PV(B9, B10, B11, B6, 0)		
14					
15					

Thus an investor would be willing to pay about $875 (rounded) for the bond. Although annual coupon payment remains at $80, a new investor would earn a 10.25 percent return because she or he would pay only $875 now and get back $1,000 at the end of ten years. A bond that sells below par value, such as this one, is said to be selling at a *discount* and is called a ***discount bond***. Someone who purchases this discount bond today and holds it to maturity will receive, in addition to the stream of coupon interest payments, a gain of $125, which is the difference between the bond's price ($875) and its principal repayment ($1,000). A bond's price will reflect changes in market conditions while it remains outstanding. With its fixed 8 percent coupon rate, this bond will no longer be attractive to investors when alternative investments are yielding 10.25 percent. The bond's market price will have to fall in order to offer buyers a combined return of 10.25 percent from the coupon payments and the par value. Thus, bond prices fall as interest rates rise.

discount bond
bond that is selling below par value

If investors required less than an 8 percent (e.g., 6.09 percent) return for bonds of this quality, then the previously described bond would have a value greater than $1,000; investors would find the bond's 8 percent coupon attractive when other bonds are offering closer to 6 percent. If it was selling to yield a return of 6.09 percent to investors, the bond's price will rise to $1,149.08 (check this on your own). When a bond's price exceeds its par value, it is selling at a *premium,* and it is called a ***premium bond***. The investor who holds the bond until maturity will receive the above-market coupon payments of 8 percent per year, offset by a loss of $149 (the difference between its purchase price and par value). In most cases where the bond sells at a premium, interest rates have fallen after the bond's issue. This bond's 8 percent coupon rate makes it very attractive to investors; buying pressure increases its price until its overall yield matches the market rate of 6.09 percent.

premium bond
bond that is selling in excess of its par value

CALCULATING THE YIELD TO MATURITY

Many times, rather than compute price, investors want to estimate the return on a bond investment if they hold it until it matures (this is the yield to maturity or YTM).[18] Financial calculators and computer spreadsheet packages such as Excel can be used to find the exact return. An approximate answer for the yield to maturity can be obtained by using the following formula:

$$\text{Approximate yield to maturity} = \frac{\text{Annual interest} + \dfrac{\text{par} - \text{price}}{\text{No. of years until maturity}}}{\dfrac{\text{par} + \text{price}}{2}} \qquad (7.3)$$

The numerator of Equation 7.3 equals the annual coupon interest plus a straight-line amortization of the difference between the current price and par value. It represents an approximation of the annual dollar return the bondholder expects to receive, as over time the bond's value will rise or fall so it equals its par value at maturity. This estimated annual return is divided by the average of the bond's par value and its current price to give us an approximate yield or percentage return if the bond is held until maturity.

From the preceding example, we know that if the bond can be purchased for $875, it offers investors a 10.25 percent return. Let's use Equation 7.3 to estimate the approximate yield to maturity if we know the price is $875, annual coupons are $80, and the bond matures in ten years with a par value of $1,000:

$$\text{Approximate yield to maturity} = \frac{\$80 + \dfrac{\$1000 - \$875}{10}}{\dfrac{\$1000 + \$875}{2}}$$

$$= 0.0987 \text{ or } 9.87 \text{ percent}$$

The approximate answer of 9.87 percent is somewhat close to the exact yield to maturity of 10.25 percent but certainly shows the approximate nature of the formula. Of course, the use of a financial calculator will give us a precise answer for the yield to maturity. We illustrate the calculation process for a ten-year (or, rather, twenty-period) bond paying interest of $40 per period and a $1,000 principal repayment at maturity. First, we assume the bond is currently trading at $1,000. Second, we assume the price to be $875.48.

Financial Calculator Solution: $1,000 Current Price:

Inputs:	20	1,000	40	1,000
	N	PV	PMT	FV
Press:	CPT	%i		
Solution:	4.00			

A periodic return of 4 percent is the same as an annual yield to maturity of 8.16 percent.[19] Now let's see the yield to maturity when the bond is trading at $875.48:

---

18. The yield to maturity (YTM) calculation assumes that all coupon cash flows are reinvested at the YTM throughout the bond's life. The realized compound yield (RCY) calculation allows the investor to compute the expected return on a bond using another, perhaps more realistic, return for how the bond's coupons are reinvested. The RCY calculation is done in two steps. First, the future value of all the bond's cash flows is computed using the assumed reinvestment rate. Second, the rate that equates the bond's current price and the future value of cash flows is calculated; this rate is the RCY.

For example, a bond investor may expect interest rates to fall to the point where the reinvestment rate on ten-year bonds becomes 6.09 percent. That means the $40 semiannual coupons are likely to be reinvested at a semiannual rate of only 3 percent. After ten years (or twenty periods), the future value of the $40 coupons will be $40 × 26.870 (FVIFA factor for 3 percent and twenty years from Table 3 in this book's appendix) or $1,074.80. Adding the par value to be received at that time, the future value of all the bond's cash inflows is $2,074.80. If the current price of the bond is $1,000, the annual RCY is found by solving the future value equation for r: $FV = PV(1 + r)^n = \$2,074.80 = 1,000(1 + r)^{10}$. Solving for r, the realized compound yield is 7.57 percent.

19. Annualized yield to maturity = $(1 + 0.04)^2 - 1 = 0.0816$ or 8.16 percent.

Financial Calculator Solution: $875.48 Current Price:

Inputs:	20	875.48	40	1,000
	N	PV	PMT	FV
Press:	CPT	%i		
Solution:	5.00			

which corresponds to an annual yield to maturity of 10.25 percent.[20]

Given what we know about bonds and our time value of money techniques, the following will be true, if all other influences are kept constant:

CONCEPT CHECK

How do you go about computing a bond's price?

What is a discount bond? A premium bond?

Given two bonds identical in all respects except one pays coupons annually and the other pays coupons semiannually, which one will have the higher price? Why?

- The larger the coupon interest, the higher the bond's price. We've already seen that with a yield to maturity of 8.16 percent, a ten-year bond that pays annual interest of $80 will have a present value or price of $1,000. A bond that is identical except it has a 10 percent coupon rate will have a price of $50 × 13.590 + $1,000 × 0.456 = $1,135.50.

- The more frequent the coupon payments (e.g., semiannually instead of annually), the higher the bond's price, as some cash flows occur sooner in time than they would otherwise. For example, with semiannual coupon payments, the 8 percent coupon bond is worth $1,000 when the market interest rate is 8.16 percent. If this bond were a Eurobond, with annual coupon payments, its price would be slightly lower, at $989.34 (check this answer using Equations 5.3 and 5.7).

- The higher the yield to maturity, the lower the price of the bond; the lower the yield to maturity, the higher the bond's price. We have already seen this; when a ten-year bond with an 8 percent coupon sells at an 8.16 percent yield to maturity, its price is $1,000; when it sells at a 10.25 percent yield to maturity, its price is $875; its price is $1,149 when the yield to maturity falls to 6.09 percent. More risky bonds (those with lower bond ratings) will have higher required yields and will sell at lower prices or with higher coupon rates.

RISK IN BOND VALUATION

Investors in domestic bonds face three types of risk: credit risk, interest rate risk, and reinvestment rate risk. Investors in foreign bonds are subject to two additional risks: political risk and exchange rate risk.

Credit Risk

credit risk (default risk)
the chance of nonpayment or delayed payment of interest or principal

The cash flows to be received by bond market investors are not certain; like individuals, corporate debtors may pay interest payments late or not at all. They may fail to repay principal at maturity. To compensate investors for this **credit risk** or **default risk**, rates of return on corporate bonds are higher than those on government securities with the same terms to maturity.

Government securities are presumed to be free of credit risk. In general, as investors perceive a higher likelihood of default, they demand higher default-risk premiums. Since perceptions of a bond's default risk may change over its term, the bond's yield to maturity may also change, even if all else remains constant. Firms such as Moody's, Standard & Poor's, and Fitch provide information on the riskiness of individual bond issues through their bond ratings. The bond rating is a measure of a bond's default risk.

The default risk premium is measured by the difference in the yield to maturity, or spread, of two bonds of equal time to maturity. If a ten-year Treasury note has a yield of 5.4 percent and a ten-year Baa-rated corporate bond has a yield of 7.4 percent, the Baa–Treasury spread of 2.0 percentage points represents the default risk premium earned by investors who are willing to carry the extra risk of a Baa-rated bond.

Credit risk spreads are not constant; they fluctuate based upon credit conditions and investors' willingness to take on risk. In good economic times when investors are optimistic, spreads generally narrow; in uncertain times or in a recession, there is a *flight to quality* as

---

20. We can design a spreadsheet to incorporate the inputs and calculation of Equation 7.3. We can also use several Excel functions (IRR, YIELD, YIELDMAT) to compute the exact yield to maturity, but their application is too advanced for the current discussion.

FIGURE 7.3

Credit Risk Spreads, 1975–2006

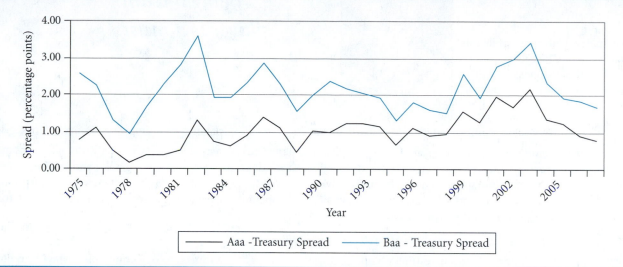

ETHICAL ISSUES

investors prefer safer securities and credit spreads widen. Figure 7.3 shows the behavior of spreads between Baa-rated bonds and Treasuries and Aaa-rated bonds and Treasuries over time.

Ethics plays a role in determining a bond's rating. If management, through fraud or accounting gimmickry, make a firm appear more profitable or financially stable, the firm's bonds may have higher bond ratings than they should. After accounting irregularities were discovered at Enron, which at the time was one of the largest energy firms in the United States, its bond rating dropped to junk levels and its bank loans came due as a result of failing to meet its loan covenants.

Interest Rate Risk

interest rate risk
fluctuating interest rates lead to varying asset prices. In the context of bonds, rising (falling) interest rates result in falling (rising) bond prices

As we introduced in the discussion of premium and discount bonds, bond prices change in response to changes in interest rates. We know the general level of interest rates in an economy does not remain fixed; rather, it fluctuates. For example, interest rates will change in response to changes in investors' expectations about future inflation rates. In Figure 7.4 we can see that the "seesaw effect" means that a rise in interest rates renders the fixed coupon interest payments on a bond less attractive, lowering its price. Therefore, bondholders are subject to the risk of capital loss from such interest rate changes should the bonds have to be sold prior to maturity.

horizon risk premium (horizon spread)
the difference in return earned by investing in a longer-term bond that has the same credit risk as a shorter-term bond

All else being equal, a longer term to maturity increases the sensitivity of a bond's price to a given change in interest rates, as the discount rate change compounds over a longer time period. Similarly, a lower coupon rate also increases the sensitivity of the bond's price to market interest rate changes. This occurs because lower coupon bonds have most of their cash flow occurring further into the future, when the par value is paid.

FIGURE 7.4

Relationship Between Current Interest Rates and Bond Prices: The Seesaw Effect

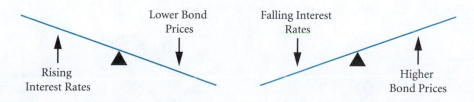

TINA LONGFIELD
Associate, Investment Banking Division
Credit Suisse First Boston

BA, Accountancy, University of Illinois
MBA, University of Chicago
Graduate School of Business

"Being a team player is a must."

Q: *How does an investment bank like Credit Suisse First Boston help clients set and implement financial strategy?*

A: Credit Suisse First Boston (CSFB) is a leading global investment bank serving institutional, corporate, government, and individual clients. Its businesses include securities underwriting, sales and trading, investment banking, private equity, financial advisory services, investment research, venture capital, correspondent brokerage services, and asset management. We operate in over eighty-nine locations across more than thirty-seven countries on six continents.

Q: *What are your responsibilities as an associate at CSFB?*

A: I work in the firm's investment banking division and specialize in technology companies. The technology group serves a wide range of clients, from large established companies to start-ups. As an associate in the corporate finance area, I work with our clients to help in such areas as determining alternative capital structures, choosing a financing strategy in ever-changing market environments, and introducing ideas for mergers and acquisitions. Of course, once a client chooses to implement a financing strategy, I work with a team to execute the transaction, such as an initial public offering (IPO) or a convertible financing transaction. Business development—marketing ideas to potential clients—is also an important part of my job.

Q: *Is there a typical career path at investment banking firms?*

A: Yes. BAs enter an analyst program. After an intensive training program covering accounting, corporate finance, and financial modeling, you're often assigned to an industry, product, or geographical group where you learn to apply these basics and become an integral member of the group. At the end of two to three years, many analysts go to business school to earn their MBA. An investment bank also hires MBAs, who often have three or more years of work experience as associates. After several years of investment banking experience with a variety of clients and transactions, associates are considered for promotion to the next level, which is vice president.

Q: *Sounds like a challenging job. What skills do you need to be successful?*

A: Good analytical skills are, of course, helpful to provide both analysis and the interpretation of numbers. Being a team payer is a must; we often work in small groups that can change from transaction to transaction. Creativity and overall communication skills are very important, as is the ability to work in a fast-paced environment. As an analyst, it's an advantage to have introductory classes in finance, accounting, and economics, but it's not a necessity, because of the intensive training program everybody is put through. As you become more experienced, product and industry-specific knowledge, as well as the ability to see the big picture, is important, so you can provide the best advice on the range of financing and strategic alternatives available to the client.

Q: *What do you like best about your work?*

A: This job is always changing—no two days are the same. One day I could be working with a young private company looking to raise equity, and the next I could be focused on helping a client sell a distressed unit of his or her company. One of the most rewarding experiences I probably have is the strategic dialogue I have with a lot of influential decision makers, who are looking to raise significant amounts of money and deciding how to put it to work. I also enjoy working with the people at CSFB. This job requires long hours, so liking your colleagues is a key factor in job satisfaction.

FIGURE 7.5

Horizon (Time) Spreads on Treasury Securities

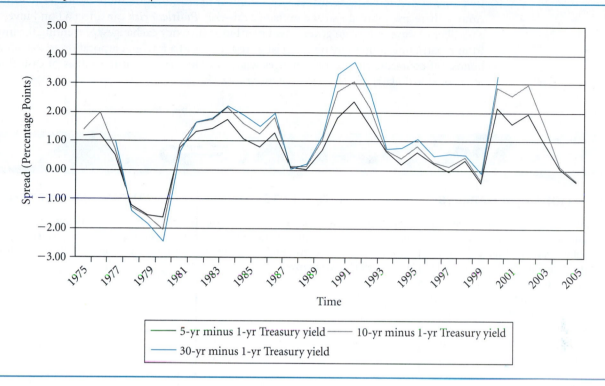

——— 5-yr minus 1-yr Treasury yield ——— 10-yr minus 1-yr Treasury yield
——— 30-yr minus 1-yr Treasury yield

CONCEPT CHECK

What risks are faced by domestic bond investors?

What is the seesaw effect?

What special risks are faced by investors in foreign bonds?

political risk

actions by a sovereign nation to interrupt or change the value of cash flows accruing to foreign investments

reinvestment rate risk (rollover risk)

fluctuating interest rates cause coupon or interest payments to be reinvested at different interest rates over time

GLOBAL DISCUSSION

Because of *interest rate risk*, investors will demand a larger risk premium for bonds whose price is especially sensitive to market interest rate changes. Hence, we would expect higher yields to maturity for long-term bonds with low coupon rates than for short-term bonds with high coupon rates. The *horizon risk premium* or *horizon spread* is the difference in return earned by investing in a longer-term bond that has the same credit risk as a shorter-term bond. For example, suppose a five-year Treasury note has a yield of 4.7 percent and a ten-year Treasury note has a yield of 5.4 percent. The difference of 0.7 percentage point is the horizon spread, representing the extra return expected to be earned by investors in the longer-term notes for their exposure to higher levels of interest rate risk. Figure 7.5 shows horizon spreads for five-, ten-, and thirty-year Treasury securities, compared with one-year Treasury bills.[21]

The negative spreads around 1979, 2001, and 2006 occurred when the yield curve was inverted, when short-term rates exceeded long-term rates. This typically happens before a recession begins, when short-term rates are rising because of inflationary pressures at the time. Some experts feel, however, that the inverted yield curve in 2006 does not predict a soon-coming recession. They argue that easy monetary policy, both in the United States and worldwide, created a great deal of liquidity in financial markets. Indeed, in 2006 and early 2007 there was no sign of a restrictive monetary policy by the Fed and credit spreads (see Figure 7.5) remained low. If investors feared a soon-coming recession, credit spreads would widen due to a flight to quality.

Reinvestment Rate Risk

The return an investor receives from a bond investment equals the bond's yield to maturity only if the coupon payments can be reinvested at a rate equal to the bond's yield to maturity. Recall the form of the interest factor in bond price (Equation 7.2): $(1 + r_b)^n$. This assumes that all the cash flows are reinvested at the periodic rate r_b. If the coupons are reinvested at a lower rate, the investor's actual yield over time will be less than the bond's yield to maturity. Thus, *reinvestment rate risk (rollover risk)* occurs when fluctuating interest rates cause coupon payments to be reinvested at different interest rates. Another illustration of reinvestment rate risk occurs when maturing bank CDs are rolled over into new CDs. The risk benefits the investor when the new CD rate is higher than the maturing CD rate; it works against the investor when the new CD rate is lower. It is this risk that zero coupon securities eliminate, as they have no intermediate cash flows requiring reinvestment.

21. The U.S. Treasury did not issue thirty-year securities in 2002–2005.

Risks of Nondomestic Bonds

Investors in nondomestic securities face a number of risks beyond those of domestic securities. Among these are political risk and exchange rate risk. *Political risk* can affect a bond investor in a number of ways. A foreign government may block currency exchanges, preventing the investor from repatriating coupon income. Social unrest may lead a foreign corporation to default on its bonds. Of course, exchange rate changes will cause fluctuations in the values of cash flows in terms of U.S. dollars; this is called *exchange rate risk*.

APPLYING FINANCE TO . . .

INSTITUTIONS AND MARKETS

Bond trading occurs in capital markets. Some institutions, such as investment banks, facilitate trading of these securities and develop different variations (callable, putable) to meet the needs of different kinds of issuers and investors. For other institutions, bonds are another means in addition to bank loans, private placements, mortgages, and so forth of supplying capital to those needing access to funds.

INVESTMENTS

Bonds are tools used by investors; they are purchased in an attempt to meet an investor's goals and risk preferences over the investor's time horizon.

FINANCIAL MANAGEMENT

Bonds are a source of long-term financing for asset acquisition, implementing long-term strategies, and acquiring other firms.

SUMMARY

One purpose of this chapter has been to examine the characteristics of bonds. Whereas corporations are net purchasers of stock, in recent years they have issued large quantities of debt to finance their activities. A second major purpose of this chapter has been to determine security values by applying time value of money techniques to the cash flows that investors receive from bond investments. The current price of the securities should equal the present value of future expected cash flows. If security prices are already known, these techniques can also be used to estimate the yield to maturity from a bond investment.

Stock and debt offerings are major sources of long-term funds for businesses. Bonds offer investors a fixed income flow and priority in terms of liquidation. Bond covenants, which are found in the indenture, list some of the obligations of the issuer toward the bondholders. Bonds can be secured by corporate assets or can be unsecured; unsecured bonds are called debentures. Bond ratings assess both the collateral underlying the bonds, as well as the ability of the issuers to make timely payments of interest and principal. Bonds can be sold overseas by U.S. issuers; non-U.S. firms can issue bonds in the United States, as long as SEC requirements are fulfilled.

Though considered to be safer investments than common stock, bond investments are not without risks. Credit risk, the possibility of a firm missing an interest or principal payment, is indicated by the bond rating of the issue. Interest rate risk causes bond prices to rise (fall) as interest rates fall (rise). Related to the risk of changing interest rates on bond prices is the risk of uncertain reinvestment rates on the bond's cash flows over time. Finally, investors who purchase bonds from issuers outside their domestic borders face political and exchange risk in their investment.

KEY TERMS

bearer bonds

bond rating

call deferment period

call price

call risk

callable bond

closed-end mortgage bond

collateralized bonds

conversion ratio

conversion value

convertible bond

coupon payments

covenants

credit risk (default risk)

debenture bonds

discount bond

equipment trust certificate

Eurodollar bonds

exchange rate risk

extendable notes

financial assets

global bonds

horizon risk premium (horizon spread)

interest rate risk

junk bonds or high-yield bonds

mortgage bonds

open-end mortgage bond

par value (face value)

political risk

premium bond

putable bonds	sinking fund	Yankee bonds
registered bonds	subordinated debenture	yield to maturity (YTM)
reinvestment rate risk (rollover risk)	trustee	
retractable bonds	trust indenture	

DISCUSSION QUESTIONS

1. Describe the relationship between internal and external financing in meeting the long-term financial needs of a firm.

2. What are the major sources of long-term funds available to business corporations? Indicate their relative importance.

3. Why would firms raise capital in markets other than their domestic or home market?

4. Can bonds be purchased only by large institutional investors? Explain.

5. How does a TIPS bond differ from the typical U.S. Treasury security?

6. Describe what is meant by *bond covenants*.

7. What are bond ratings?

8. Briefly describe the types of bonds that can be issued to provide bondholder security.

9. What is meant by the following terms: *convertible bonds, callable bonds, putable bonds,* and *Eurodollar bonds?*

10. Why are investment-grade bonds given that name? Why are *junk bonds* also known as *high-yield bonds?*

11. Why might a firm want to maintain a high bond rating? What has been happening to bond ratings in recent years?

12. Why might an investor find a zero-coupon bond to be an attractive investment?

13. Briefly describe how securities are valued.

14. Describe the process for valuing a bond.

15. What is meant by the *yield to maturity* on a bond?

16. Briefly describe the types of risk faced by investors in domestic bonds. Also indicate the additional risks associated with nondomestic bonds.

17. What risk does a zero-coupon bond address?

18. According to the behavior of interest rates in Figure 7.3, were investors more concerned or less concerned about risk over the 2002–2006 time period? Explain.

19. What does it signify when the horizon spreads in Figure 7.5 dip below the X-axis? Why do some feel that this was not to be the case in 2006?

20. How do you think credit spreads behave over the course of the economic cycle?

21. What is a *"flight to quality?"* Under what economic conditions might we see this?

PROBLEMS

1. Compute the annual interest payments and principal amount for a Treasury Inflation-Protected Security with a par value of $1,000 and a 3 percent interest rate if inflation is 4 percent in year 1, 5 percent in year 2, and 6 percent in year 3.

2. Judy Johnson is choosing between investing in two Treasury securities that mature in five years and have par values of $1,000. One is a Treasury note paying an annual coupon of 5.06 percent. The other is a TIPS that pays 3 percent interest annually.

   a. If inflation remains constant at 2 percent annually over the next five years, what will be Judy's annual interest income from the TIPS bond? From the Treasury note?

   b. How much interest will Judy receive over the five years from the Treasury note? From the TIPS?

   c. When each bond matures, what par value will Judy receive from the Treasury note? From the TIPS?

   d. After five years, what is Judy's total income (interest + par) from each bond? Should she use this total as a way of deciding which bond to purchase?

3. Using the regular Treasury note from the previous problem:

   a. What is its price if investors' required rate of return is 6.09 percent on similar bonds? Treasury notes pay interest semi-annually.

   b. Erron Corporation wants to issue five-year notes, but investors require a credit risk spread of 3 percentage points. What is the anticipated coupon rate on the Erron notes?

4. Assume a $1,000 face value bond has a coupon rate of 8.5 percent, pays interest semiannually, and has an eight-year life. If investors are willing to accept a 10.25 percent rate of return on bonds of similar quality, what is the present value or worth of this bond?

5. Referring to the previous problem:

   a. By how much would the value of the bond in Problem 4 change if investors wanted an 8 percent rate of return?

   b. A bond with the same par value and coupon rate as the bond in Problem 4 has fourteen years until maturity. If investors will use a 10.25 percent discount rate to value this bond, by how much should its price differ from the bond in Problem 4?

6. The Garcia Company's bonds have a face value of $1,000, will mature in ten years, and carry a coupon rate of 16 percent. Assume interest payments are made semiannually:

   a. Determine the present value of the bond's cash flows if the required rate of return is 16.64 percent.

   b. How would your answer change if the required rate of return is 12.36 percent?

7. Judith, Inc. bonds mature in eight years and pay a semiannual coupon of $55. The bond's par value is $1,000:

   a. What is their current price if the market interest rate for bonds of similar quality is 9.2 percent?

   b. A change in Fed policy increases market interest rates 0.50 percentage point from their level in (a). What is the percentage change in the value of Judith, Inc. bonds from their value in (a)?

c. Better profits for Judith, Inc. reduce the market interest rate for the company's bonds to 9.0 percent. What is the percentage change in the value of Judith, Inc. bonds from the answer in (b)?

8. Kamins Corporation has two bond issues outstanding, each with a par value of $1,000. Information about each follows. Suppose market interest rates rise 1 percentage point across the yield curve. What will be the change in price for each of the bonds? Does this tell us anything about the relationship between time to maturity and interest rate risk?

Bond A: 5 years to maturity, 8 percent coupon, 9 percent market interest rate

Bond B: 12 years to maturity, 8 percent coupon, 9 percent market interest rate

9. Billon Corporation has two bond issues outstanding, each with a par value of $1,000. Information about each follows. Suppose market interest rates rise 1 percentage point across the yield curve. What will be the change in price for each of the bonds? Does this tell us anything about the relationship between coupon rate and interest rate risk?

Bond A: 10 years to maturity, 0 percent coupon, 9.62 percent market interest rate

Bond B: 10 years to maturity, 10 percent coupon, 9.62 percent market interest rate

10. Koppen Corporation has two bond issues outstanding, each with a par value of $1,000. Information about each follows. Suppose market interest rates rise 1 percentage point across the yield curve. What will be the change in price for each of the bonds? Does this tell us anything about the relationship between frequency of cash flows and interest rate risk?

Bond A: This bond is a Eurobond. It has 10 years to maturity, pays a 7 percent coupon, and has an 11.3 percent market interest rate.

Bond B: This bond is issued in the United States. It has 10 years to maturity, pays a 7 percent coupon, and has an 11.3 percent market interest rate.

11. BVA Inc. has two bond issues outstanding, each with a par value of $1,000. Information about each follows. Suppose market interest rates rise 1 percentage point across the yield curve. What will be the change in price for each of the bonds? Does this tell us anything about the relationship between initial yield to maturity and interest rate risk?

Bond A: 12 years to maturity, 7 percent coupon, and 12.36 percent market interest rate on this BB-rated bond

Bond B: 12 years to maturity, 7 percent coupon, and 10.25 percent market interest rate on this A-rated bond

12. What is the approximate yield to maturity (use Equation 7.3) and the exact yield to maturity (use a calculator) for the following bonds? Assume these are bonds issued in the United States:

a. 10 years to maturity, 6 percent coupon rate, current price $950

b. 16 years to maturity, 0 percent coupon rate, current price $339

c. 25 years to maturity, 8.5 percent coupon rate, current price $1,030

13. On Thursday the following bond quotation appears in the newspaper. Interpret each item that appears in the quote and compute its current yield:

COMPANY (TICKER) COUPON		MAT.	LAST PRICE	LAST YIELD	EST SPREAD	EST UST	$VOL (000s)
Wal-Mart Stores							
WMT	4.550	May 1, 2013	99.270	4.649	47	10	66,830

14. Perusing the corporate bond quotations, you write down some summary information:

COMPANY (TICKER) COUPON		MAT.	LAST PRICE	LAST YIELD	EST SPREAD	EST UST	$VOL (000s)
Wal-Mart Stores							
WMT	4.550	10 years	99.270	4.649	47	10	66,830
Wal-Mart Stores							
WMT	4.125	8 years	99.554	4.200	2	10	50,320
Liberty Media							
L	5.700	10 years	102.750	5.314	112	10	26,045
Ford Motor Credit							
F	7.250	8 years	107.407	6.012	183	10	22,863

a. Which company is the riskiest? Why?

b. Which bond has the highest default risk? Why?

c. Why would Wal-Mart have two bonds trading at different yields?

d. Compute the current yield for each of the four bonds.

e. Compute yield to maturity for each of the four bonds.

15. You run across the following bond quotation on a Friday.

RATE	MATURITY MO/YR	BID	ASKED	CHG.	ASKED YLD
7.500	Nov 24	131:06	131:07	−9	5.04

a. What kind of security is it?

b. Interpret the meaning of the information contained in the quote.

c. Suppose a corporate bond with the same time to maturity has a credit risk spread of 250 basis points. What should be the yield to maturity for the corporate bond?

16. **Challenge Problem** A $1,000 face value bond issued by the Dysane Company currently pays total annual interest of $79 per year and has a thirteen-year life.

a. What is the present value, or worth, of this bond if investors are currently willing to accept a 10 percent annual rate of return on bonds of similar quality if the bond is a Eurobond?

b. How would your answer in (a) change if the bond is a U.S. bond?

c. How would your answer in (b) change if, one year from now, investors only required a 6.5 percent annual rate of return on bond investments similar in quality to the Dysane bond?

d. Suppose the original bond can be purchased for $925. What is the bond's yield to maturity?

17. **Challenge Problem**

a. You own a two-bond portfolio. Each has a par value of $1,000. Bond A matures in five years, has a coupon rate of 8 percent, and has an annual yield to maturity of 9.20 percent. Bond B matures in fifteen years, has a coupon rate of 8 percent and has an annual yield to maturity of 9.20 percent.

Both bonds pay interest semiannually. What is the value of your portfolio? What happens to the value of your portfolio if each yield to maturity rises by one percentage point?

b. Rather than own a five-year bond and a fifteen-year bond, suppose you sell both of them and invest in two ten-year bonds. Each has a coupon rate of 8 percent (semiannual coupons) and has a yield to maturity of 9.20 percent. What is the value of your portfolio? What happens to the value of your portfolio if the yield to maturity on the bonds rises by one percentage point?

c. Based upon your answers to (a) and (b), evaluate the price changes between the two portfolios. Were the price changes the same? Why or why not?

18. **EXCEL** A bond with a par value of $1,000 has a coupon rate of 7 percent and matures in fifteen years. Using a spreadsheet program, graph its price versus different yields to maturity, ranging from 1 percent to 20 percent. Is the relationship between price and yield linear? Why or why not?

• CHAPTER 8 •

Stocks: Characteristics and Valuation

Chapter Learning Objectives

AFTER STUDYING THIS CHAPTER, YOU SHOULD BE ABLE TO:

* Identify the reasons why investors seek stocks for an investment vehicle.
* Describe major characteristics of preferred stock.
* Describe the major characteristics of common stock.
* Describe the process for issuing dividends by a firm.
* Explain how financial securities are valued in general and specifically for stocks.

Where We Have Been. . .

The financial system is comprised of a number of participants—banks, insurance companies, mutual funds, pension funds, among others. Some borrow or lend funds; others seek to sell or purchase ownership rights, or common stock, in firms. Prior chapters have looked at the concepts of risk and return on investments. Chapter 7 examined bonds in some detail. This chapter will help you learn about the characteristics of common stock and the problems we face in trying to place a value on a share of stock.

Where We Are Going. . .

The operations of the securities markets and the implications of investing and creating portfolios of bonds and stocks are the topics of Chapters 9 and 10. Of course, before we can invest in a security it has to be issued. We'll learn more about how firms make the decision to issue debt or equity in Chapter 15, "Capital Structure and the Cost of Capital."

How This Chapter Applies to Me. . .

Time value of money is one of the most important concepts in finance. In this chapter we will see applications of time value concepts to the stock investor. Unlike bond coupons, which are determined contractually, income from stock investments, in the form of dividends, is not a legal obligation of the issuing firm. This chapter examines the process a firm goes through to issue dividends.

A famous Mark Twain quote refers to investing in stocks:

> *October. That month is especially dangerous for investing in stocks. Other dangerous months include August, January, June, March, November, July, February, April, December, May and September.*

That pretty much covers them all! In this chapter we'll learn about the characteristics of stock and some of the issues that arise when trying to place a value of stock.

Table 7.1 in Chapter 7 shows that, except for the year 2000, stock issues have been less than 10 percent of new security issues. The table shows, in many years, that the net amount of stock issued has been negative—indicating that, because of mergers, acquisition, and stock buybacks, the quantity of common stock has shrunk. Corporate America has, on average, been raising capital through bonds and its own profits (internal financing)—as well as through some vehicles not shown on Table 7.1, such as bank loans.

However, we are in no danger of the stock market disappearing. Stock issues by new and growing firms are a vital source of external financing. Banks, the bond market, and other lenders are hesitant to give funds to smaller firms with an uncertain future or to give vast sums to firms with high-growth potential. The market for private and public equity (stock) helps to meet the needs of growing firms. The equity markets also help firms with heavy debt loads issue shares of stock to help pay down some of the interest-bearing debt.

From the investors' perspective, investing in the stock market is, for many, the best means available for enjoying the benefits of corporate wealth creation. As firms grow in size, profitability, market share, and market value, the value of the shares of stock often grows, too. This helps investors to meet their financial goals, such as preparing to meet the needs of paying for the eventual college education of a small child or their own retirement.

ADVANTAGES TO INVESTORS FROM INVESTING IN COMMON STOCKS

Unlike most other securities available to investors, equity—common stock, specifically—offers investors four major advantages. It provides protection over time against inflation, it offers opportunity for growth in value, it offers opportunity for growth in income, and it has tax advantages, too. We'll examine each of these in turn.

INFLATION HEDGE

First, common stock is an *inflation hedge*—that is, we expect it to provide protection over time against inflation, namely against a decline in the purchasing power of our investment portfolio. To see why, we've replicated Table 6.4 as Table 8.1.

The returns shown in Table 8.1 are **nominal returns**—that is, they represent the actual dollars-and-cents returns that investors would receive if the effects of inflation are ignored. They also assume no taxes are paid on the returns.

Table 8.2 displays the nominal return information from Table 8.1 and also shows the effects of taxation and inflation on the nominal returns. The second column of Table 8.2 repeats the nominal returns from Table 8.1. The third column shows the real return. **Real returns** show the change in purchasing power—in other words, they control for the effects of inflation over time. A 10 percent nominal return in an environment with 10 percent inflation does not represent a gain in purchasing power; indeed, a 10 percent return is needed just to maintain one's current purchasing power in the face of such an inflation rate. The investor's real return in such a case is zero percent: 10 percent nominal return less 10 percent inflation equals a real return of zero.

Subtracting the average inflation rate of 3.20 percent from the nominal returns of Treasury bills, Treasury bonds, and common stocks, we compute the real average annual returns shown in column 3 of Table 8.2. The returns on the Treasury securities do not look as attractive as before.

Yet to see the correct effects of inflation, we need to examine the returns on an after-tax basis. Investing in securities means paying taxes on the income we receive and the change in price between when we purchased the security and when we sell it. Column 4 of Table 8.2 assumes a 25 percent tax rate on overall returns; thus, the nominal after-tax returns in column 4 are 75 percent of the nominal pre-tax returns in column 2. This is our broad estimate of the nominal return an investor would keep from investing in these securities. The final column shows the after-tax return on a real basis; that is, we subtract the average inflation rate of 3.20 percent from the column 4 nominal after-tax returns to estimate real after-tax returns.

This clearly shows the value of stock investing. Considering the combined effects of taxes and inflation, common stocks are the financial assets that provide the best opportunity to gain value on an after-tax, after-inflation basis. An inflation hedge is expected to provide protection against inflation over time; historically, the real returns on common stocks have done so, even after considering taxes. The effect on investor wealth is negative for Treasury bills with an average real

nominal returns
the actual value received; does not include the effect of inflation

real returns
the value received in terms of purchasing power; subtracts the effect of inflation from the current nominal value

FINANCE PRINCIPLE

TABLE 8.1

Historical Returns and Standard Deviations of Returns from Different Assets, 1928–2006

ASSET	TREASURY BILLS	TREASURY BONDS	COMMON STOCKS	INFLATION RATE
Average Annual Return	3.9%	5.2%	11.8%	3.2%
Standard Deviation	3.1%	7.5%	19.9%	4.1%

Source: Home Page for Aswath Damodaran, http://www.stern.nyu.edu/~adamodar (accessed January 2007).

TABLE 8.2

Historical Returns from Different Assests, 1928–2006

Asset	NOMINAL AVERAGE ANNUAL RETURN	REAL AVERAGE ANNUAL RETURN = nominal return minus inflation rate	NOMINAL AFTER-TAX RETURN; TAX RATE IS 25% = nominal return × (1 − tax rate)	REAL AFTER-TAX RETURN = nominal return × (1 − tax rate) minus inflation rate
Inflation Rate	3.20%			
Treasury Bills	3.90%	0.70%	2.93%	−0.28%
Treasury Bonds	5.20%	2.00%	3.90%	0.70%
Common Stocks	11.80%	8.60%	8.85%	5.65%

Source: Home Page for Aswath Damodaran, http://www.stern.nyu.edu/~adamodar (accessed January 2007) and author calculations.

after-tax return of −0.28 percent. Treasury bonds do offer a positive but rather small return of 0.70 percent. Common stocks have earned average real after-tax returns that surpass those of Treasury securities.[1]

OPPORTUNITY FOR GROWTH IN VALUE

The second advantage to investors for purchasing common stock is the opportunity for growth in value over time. Table 8.2 illustrates this point as well. Common stocks offer superior real after-tax returns compared to Treasury bills and Treasury bonds. That is, they not only act as an inflation hedge, but the average long-term return on stocks sufficiently exceeded the inflation rate so as to provide real inflation-adjusted growth to an investor's stock portfolio. Table 8.3 shows the growth, in real, inflation-adjusted terms, of $1,000 invested in each of the three assets over the 1928–2006 time frame. Treasury bills lost wealth in real terms—a fact we already knew because the estimated real after-tax return is negative. Treasury bonds offered a modest growth in real wealth, but common stocks offered a substantial increase in real wealth over the time frame.

As we see in Table 8.4, we don't have to wait the seventy-nine years between 1928 and 2006 to gain stock's growth opportunities. When looking at each of the seventy-nine one-year periods between 1928 and 2006, stocks earned a superior return in fifty-two of them. When using a five-year time horizon, stocks earned better returns than Treasury bonds in fifty-eight out of seventy-five such five-year time periods from 1928 to 2006. Over each ten-year time frame, stocks earned higher returns in sixty out of seventy time periods. With a time horizon of twenty years or longer, stocks earned higher returns in all such time periods.

Of course, we are studying historical data while we will be investing in the future. We cannot tell for certain what future returns will be, on a real or nominal basis, for stocks or bonds, but we know the second principle of finance states that higher expected returns and

TABLE 8.3

Real (Inflation-Adjusted) Value in 2006 of $1,000 Invested in 1928

ASSET	REAL AFTER-TAX RETURN	REAL DOLLAR VALUE AT END OF 2006 (after taxes)
Treasury Bills	−0.28%	$804.49
Treasury Bonds	0.70%	$1,735.11
Common Stocks	5.65%	$76,858.27

---

1. Other assets, notably real estate, exist that are considered to be inflation hedges, but they are not financial assets. TIPS bonds (discussed in Chapter 7) provide inflation protection but are not expected to offer the level of real after-tax returns of stocks. Municipal bonds that are exempt from federal taxes may offer positive real after-tax returns, but data are not available on their performance over long periods of time. The long-term nature of municipal bonds will, as with most bonds, make them susceptible to interest rate risk if inflation rates rise during their time to maturity.

TABLE 8.4
Comparison of Returns for Stocks and Treasury Bonds, 1928–2006

	NUMBER OF TIME PERIODS STOCK RETURN > TREASURY BOND RETURNS	
Any 1-year period	52	Out of 79 such periods
Any consecutive 5-year period	58	Out of 75 such periods
Any consecutive 10-year period	60	Out of 70 such periods
Any consecutive 20-year period	60	Out of 60 such periods

Source: Author calculations.

higher risk go together. Thus, we expect over time that higher-risk stocks will earn higher returns than Treasury bonds.

OPPORTUNITY FOR GROWTH IN INCOME

Part of the growth in value from stock arises from dividend income. Rising dividend income is a significant component of stock investment returns. From 1949–2006, the nominal growth in dividend income was over 2,450 percent. That is, $1 in dividend income in the stock market in 1949 would have, on average, grown to over $25 in 2006. Interest rates on Treasury bills, Treasury bonds, or any other fixed income security did not increase that rapidly over this time frame. Between these years, the consumer price index rose 735 percent, implying a substantial real growth in dividend income.[2] For investors on "fixed" incomes, such as retirees, stock dividends offer the possibility of income growth from dividends. Most bond investments do not offer such income growth opportunities.[3]

TAX ADVANTAGES

The fourth and final advantage to investing in stocks is the tax advantage from doing so. Under U.S. tax law, bond coupon income (as well as income from T-bills, CDs, and savings accounts) is taxed as ordinary income. So a person in the 25 percent tax bracket (meaning the next dollar of income is taxed at 25 percent) keeps only 75 percent of interest earned; the remaining 25 percent is taxes paid or payable to the government. Certain qualifying dividends, however, are taxed at either a 5 percent or 15 percent rate. The specific dividend tax rate depends on the investor's taxable income. The main point is that the tax rate on qualifying dividends is less than the investor's tax rate that applies for the next dollar received from other income sources.

In addition to the lower tax on dividend income, taxes due on increases in the value of your investment may be lower, too. Increases in the value of the investment are called **capital gains** (decreases are *capital losses*). Taxes are lowered in two ways. First, taxes on any increase in value of your investment are deferred until the stock is sold. So if you purchased stock five years ago for $500 and it has a current value of $1,100, the $600 capital gain is not taxable unless you sell the stock today. As long as you hold the stock, the taxes on any gains are deferred. Taxes on any change in the stock's value come due only after the stock is sold.

Second, even after selling the stock for a profit the investor can pay lower taxes than on other income sources. If the investor owned the stock for more than one year, the capital gain is considered a long-term capital gain and is taxed at a rate lower than the investor's **marginal tax rate**, which is the tax rate the investor would pay on the next dollar of income. The long-term capital gains tax rate will be either 5 percent or 15 percent, depending on the investor's taxable income. If the stock is sold before owning it for a year, any gains are taxed at the investor's marginal income tax rate.

What happens if the stock declines in value so the investor is facing a capital loss? A full discussion of the U.S. tax code is not possible here, but basically if an investor sells an asset at a capital loss, the loss can be deducted from any capital gain before taxes are calculated. This has the potential effect of reducing or eliminating any tax on the investor's capital gains. Suppose

capital gains
increases in the value of an asset (decreases are called capital losses)

marginal tax rate
tax rate on the next dollar of income received

2. Calculations based on data found in the *Economic Report of the President*. Data in the report goes back only to 1949.

3. *Two caveats:* First, TIPS bonds will have increasing coupon income over time as the coupon rate rises with inflation. Second, the level of bond income is higher at the initial starting point than dividend income from the average stock. For example, in 2006 the dividend yield on the S&P 500 stock index was 1.8 percent, far below the level of coupon income possible from bank CDs or Treasury notes/bonds (which was about 5 percent to 6 percent, depending upon time to maturity).

stock A is sold with a long-term capital gain of $1,000 and stock B is sold with a long-term capital loss of $600. The net long-term capital gain for the investor will be $1,000 − $600 = $400. The investor will pay tax, at either the 5 percent or 15 percent marginal rate, on the $400 net long-term capital gain. If the investor had total long-term capital losses of $1,000, the net long-term capital gain would be zero, and no capital gains taxes would be owed.

The deferral of taxes until an asset is sold and the lower long-term capital gains tax rates apply to most assets. Thus, gains in the price of a bond can be deferred until the bond is sold, or the lower capital gains tax rates can apply if a bond is held for longer than a year before being sold. However, the price change that occurs over the life of a discount bond (the discount price, say $900, will naturally rise toward the $1,000 par value as the bond nears maturity) is considered to be income, not capital gain, by the Internal Revenue Service. Thus, all else being constant, an investment in common stock is likely to have tax advantages over investments in bonds and other income-producing securities such as CDs.

This section reviewed the advantages of investing in stock. The next section discusses some of the details relating to common stock, preferred stock—including ownership claims, voting rights, and dividends.

CORPORATE EQUITY CAPITAL

Corporate equity capital is the financial capital supplied by the owners of a corporation. This ownership claim is represented by the **stock certificate**, as shown in Figure 8.1. The stock certificate shows the type of stock held by the owner, the name of the company, the name of the stock's owner, and the signatures of certain company officers. Stock certificates generally are issued for 100 shares (called a *round lot*) or multiples thereof. The stock certificate also has a space on the reverse for its assignment in the event that it is transferred to another person. As a protection against forgery, all signatures on transferred stock certificates usually are certified by a commercial bank's representative or a stock broker.

When a stockholder sells his or her shares, the assigned stock certificate is forwarded to the company by the broker, and it is destroyed by the secretary of the corporation. A new certificate

CONCEPT CHECK

Why is the net amount of common stock issued negative in some years?

Why might investors want to invest in common stock?

How does a real return differ from a nominal return?

corporate equity capital
financial capital supplied by the owners of a corporation

stock certificate
certificate showing an ownership claim of a specific company

FIGURE 8.1
Common Stock Certificates

is issued to the new owner, whose name will then be carried on the stock record. For larger corporations an official transfer agent, generally a trust company or a bank, is appointed for this task. The larger corporations may also have an independent stock registrar to supervise the transfer of securities. When an investor sells stock, the stock certificate must be delivered to the stockbroker within three business days (called T + 3). When stock is purchased, adequate funds must be brought to the broker within three business days. As technology advances, so do regulations. In past years the requirement was T + 5; it is now T + 3. In the planning stages the requirement is T + 1 for settling trades. Instantaneous settlement, called STP or *straight through processing*, occurs when all systems are tied together electronically.

Stock certificates can be kept in the owner's name and in his or her possession. Many investors find it convenient, however, to keep their stock holdings in **street name**. Stock held in street name is kept in the name of the brokerage house, but the broker's accounting system keeps track of dividends, proxy voting, and so on. Some investors find it convenient to keep shares in street name; there is no need for the investor to safeguard the certificates, and delivery of the certificates within the T + 3 time frame is automatic.

Equity securities of the corporation may be grouped broadly into two classes: common stock and preferred stock. We discuss each in the following section.

COMMON STOCK

Common stock (see Table 8.5) represents ownership shares in a corporation. Ownership gives common stockholders certain rights and privileges that bondholders do not have. Common shareholders can vote to select the corporation's board of directors. The board of directors, in turn, exercises general control over the firm. In addition to voting for the board, common shareholders may also vote on major issues facing the firm, such as corporate charter changes and mergers.

The common shareholders have a claim on all business profits that remain after the holders of all other classes of debt and equity securities have received their coupon payments or returns. However, the firm may wish to retain some of those profits to reinvest in the firm to finance modernization, expansion, and growth. When so declared by the board of directors, owners of a firm's common stock receive dividend payments. The dividend is typically a cash payment that allows shareholders to receive some income from their investment. To many investors, an attractive characteristic of common stock dividends is their potential to increase over time. As a firm achieves success, its profits should grow and the shareholders can expect to see the dollar amount of their dividends rise. Of course, success and growth are not guaranteed. A firm may experience poor earnings or losses, in which case shareholders bear the risk of smaller dividends or even the elimination of dividend payments until the firm's financial situation improves.

The common stockholders have the lowest standing when a business venture is liquidated or fails. All creditors, bondholders, and preferred stockholders must, as a rule, be paid in full before common stockholders receive proceeds from liquidation. As with dividends, all bankruptcy or liquidation proceeds remaining after prior obligations are settled accrue to the common stockholders. Yet it is rare when the proceeds of an asset sale from a bankrupt corporation fulfill the

street name
allows stock to be held in the name of the brokerage house

common stock
represents ownership shares in a corporation

TABLE 8.5
Elements of Common Stock

- Represents an ownership claim
- Board of directors oversees firm on behalf of shareholders; enforces corporate charter
- Voting rights for board members and other important issues allowed by corporate charter
- Lowest claim on assets and cash flow
- Par value is meaningless; many firms have very low or no-par stock
- *Dividends:* Received only if declared by the firm's board
  Paid out from after-tax earnings and cash flow; not tax deductible
  Taxable when received by shareholder
  Can vary over time
- *Maturity:* Never; stock remains in existence until firm goes bankrupt, merges with another firm, or is acquired by another firm

claims of creditors and preferred stockholders. Common stockholders generally receive little, if anything, from liquidation proceedings. The common stockholders, therefore, are affected hardest by business failure, just as they enjoy the primary benefits of business success.

The common stock of a corporation may be assigned a ***par value***, or stated value, in the certificate of incorporation. The par value usually bears little relationship to the current price or book value of the stock. It is used mainly for accounting purposes and some legal needs.[4]

Common stock may be divided into special groups, generally Class A and Class B, to permit the acquisition of additional capital without diluting the control of the business. When a corporation issues two classes of common stock, it will often give voting rights to only one class, generally Class B. Except for voting, owners of Class A stock will usually have most, if not all, of the other rights and privileges of common stockholders. Issuing nonvoting equity securities is opposed by some government agencies, including the Securities and Exchange Commission, because it permits the concentration of ownership control. The New York Stock Exchange refuses to list the common stock of corporations that issue nonvoting classes of common stock.

At times, different stock classes are created following an acquisition of one corporation by another. For example, Class E and Class H shares of General Motors (GM) stock were issued in the past to help finance GM's acquisition of EDS and Hughes Aircraft, respectively. The dividends on GM's Class E and H shares were related to the earnings of their respective subsidiary.

American Depository Receipts (ADRs) represent shares of common stock that trade on a foreign stock exchange. The receipts can be traded on U.S. exchanges. We'll learn more about ADRs in Chapter 9, "Securities Markets."

PREFERRED STOCK

Preferred stock (see Table 8.6) is an equity security that has a preference, or senior claim, to the firm's earnings and assets over common stock. Preferred shareholders must receive their fixed dividends before common shareholders can receive a dividend. In liquidation, the claims of the preferred shareholders are to be satisfied before common shareholders receive any proceeds. In contrast with common stock, preferred stock generally carries a stated fixed dividend. The dividend is specified as either a percentage of par value or a fixed number of dollars per year.

For example, a preferred stock may be a "9 percent preferred," meaning that its annual dividend is 9 percent of its par or stated value. In such cases, unlike common stock, a preferred stock's par value does have important meaning, much like par value for a bond. The dividend for no-par preferred stock is stated in terms of a dollar amount—for example, preferred as to dividends in the amount of $9 annually. The holder of preferred stock accepts the limitation on the amount of dividends as a fair exchange for the priority held in the earnings and assets of the company.

Thus, unlike with common stock, the par value of a preferred stock is important: dividends often are expressed as a percentage of par, and the par value represents the holder's claim on corporate assets in case of liquidation. Additionally, when shares of preferred stock are first issued, the initial selling price is frequently close to the share's par value.[5]

Because preferred stocks are frequently nonvoting, many corporations issue them as a means of obtaining equity capital without diluting the control of current stockholders. Unlike coupon interest on bonds, the fixed preferred stock dividend is not a tax-deductible expense. A major source of preferred stock issues are regulated public utilities, such as gas and electric companies. For regulated firms, the nondeductibility of dividends is not as much of a concern as for other firms, because the utilities' tax payments affect the rates they are allowed to charge.

For foreign firms to issue preferred stock, they must do so in the United States. The U.S. security markets are the only public financial markets in which preferred stock is sold.

---

par value
stated value of a stock; accounting and legal concept bearing no relationship to a firm's stock price or book value

CONCEPT CHECK

What rights and privileges do common shareholders have that bondholders do not?

What extra risks do shareholders face that bondholders do not?

preferred stock
equity security that has preference, or a senior claim, to the firm's earnings and assets over common stock

---

4. To show further that par value has little significance, consider that most states permit corporations to issue no-par stock.

5. A recent innovation is *hybrid capital,* a security that is concerned with equity for accounting purposes but whose payments to security holders are tax-deductible to the firm—thus it appears to be a perfect combination of advantages of both equity and debt. The details of issuing such capital can be difficult and involve aspects of accounting treatment, securities law, and bank regulation, and so are beyond the scope of our discussion.

TABLE 8.6
Elements of Preferred Stock

- Does not represent an ownership claim
- No voting rights unless dividends are missed
- Claim on assets and cash flow lies between those of bondholders (specifically, subordinated debenture holders) and common shareholders
- Par value is meaningful as it can determine the fixed annual dividend
- *Dividends:* Annual dividends stated either as a dollar amount or as a percentage of par value
  - Received only if declared by the firm's board
  - Paid out from after-tax earnings and cash flow; not tax deductible
  - Taxable when received by shareholder
  - May be cumulative
- *Maturity:* Unless it has a callable or convertible feature, the stock never matures; remains in existence until firm goes bankrupt, merges with another firm, or is acquired by another firm.

cumulative preferred stock

requires that before dividends on common stock are paid, preferred dividends must be paid not only for the current period, but also for all previous periods in which preferred dividends were missed

noncumulative preferred stock

makes no provision for the accumulation of past missed dividends

callable preferred stock

gives the corporation the right to retire the preferred stock at its option

convertible preferred stock

has a special provision that makes it possible to convert it to common stock of the corporation, generally at the stockholder's option

participating preferred stock

allows preferred shareholders to receive a larger dividend under certain conditions when common shareholder dividends increase

Preferred stock may have special features. For example, it may be cumulative or noncumulative. **Cumulative preferred stock** requires that before dividends on common stock are paid, preferred dividends must be paid not only for the current period but also for all previous periods in which preferred dividends were missed. It is important to remember that, unlike debt holders, the preferred stockholders cannot force the payment of their dividends. They may have to wait until earnings are adequate to pay dividends. Cumulative preferred stock offers some protection for periods during which dividends are not declared.

Noncumulative preferred stock, on the other hand, makes no provision for the accumulation of unpaid dividends. The result may be that management may be tempted to declare preferred dividends only when it appears that sufficient earnings are available to pay common stock dividends as well. Practically all modern preferred stock is cumulative.

Callable preferred stock gives the corporation the right to retire the preferred stock at its option. **Convertible preferred stock** has a special provision that makes it possible to convert it to common stock of the corporation, generally at the stockholder's option. This, like many of the special features that preferred stock may have, exists primarily to attract investors to buy securities at times when distribution would otherwise be difficult. Preferred stock that is both cumulative and convertible is a popular financing choice for investors purchasing shares of stock in small firms with high growth potential.

Participating preferred stock allows preferred shareholders to participate with common shareholders when larger dividend payouts are available. Holders get a larger dividend, if sufficient earnings exist and if common shareholders will be getting a dividend larger than the preferred shareholders. It is a rarely used feature except in some private equity and venture capital investments.

The one tax advantage of preferred stock goes to corporate investors who purchase another firm's preferred. When one corporation buys stock of another firm, 70 percent of the dividend income received by the corporation is exempt from taxes. Thus, for every $100 of dividend income, only $30 is taxable to an investing corporation.

READING STOCK QUOTES

Information on stock prices is available from a number of print resources (such as the *Wall Street Journal* and other newspapers with financial sections) and the Internet. Figure 8.2 shows stock quotation information that is available on these print and online resources.

The information from print sources reflects trading that occurred on the previous business day; online information many times reflects current trading information but with a fifteen- to twenty-minute delay in reporting. Information, such as that presented in Figure 8.2, is available on stock prices, recent trends or volatility in prices, the dividend paid by the company, and its earnings per share.

For example, Figure 8.2 shows Microsoft's ticker symbol, MSFT. Tickers are shorthand notation for a stock. Rather than keying in a firm's full name many times, only the ticker needs to be entered to obtain information. Microsoft's stock is traded on the NASDAQ, an over-the-counter exchange we'll discuss in Chapter 9. At the time this information was accessed, the most recent

CONCEPT CHECK

How is preferred stock similar to a bond? To common stock?

What is meant by the term cumulative preferred stock?

FIGURE 8.2

Stock Quotation Information

Firm name: Microsoft	Ticker: MSFT
Market: NASDAQ	YTD range: $29.40–$31.48
Last Trade: $30.43	52-week range: $21.46–$31.48
Change: −0.17	Volume (1000s): 14831
	P/E: 24.3
	Dividend: $0.40
	Dividend Yield: 1.31%

Source: http://finance.yahoo.com; www.marketwatch.com; http://moneycentral.msn.com (accessed January 29, 2007).

trade for Microsoft stock was for $30.43 a share. If a round lot (100 shares) was purchased at this price, the cost of purchasing the shares would be $30.43 × 100 shares = $3,043 plus any commissions. The price of Microsoft stock fell 17 cents from the end of the previous trading day; that means the closing or final price of the previous trading day was 17 cents higher, namely $30.43 + 0.17 = $30.60. Stocks are now traded in decimals (they used to be traded in units of $\frac{1}{8}$ so prices such as $30\frac{1}{8}$, $30\frac{1}{2}$, $32\frac{7}{8}$ and so forth would appear in the newspapers). If only the price of the final trade of the day is reported (as may be the case for newspaper listings), it appears under the label of *close* to represent the day's closing price for the stock.

Looking at the information in the second column of Figure 8.2, we see that Microsoft's stock price has varied from a low of $29.40 to a high of $31.48 over the course of the year (YTD means year to date). Over the past fifty-two weeks, however, Microsoft's stock has varied from a low price of $21.46 to a high of $31.48. This wide range (the high price is about 50 percent higher than the low price) is not uncommon. Review for yourself the fifty-two-week ranges of different stocks from a current issue of the *Wall Street Journal*.

The volume of trading in Microsoft stock from the previous trading day was approximately 14,831,000 shares. Many times the volume is printed in terms of 1000s (14831) or 100s (148310) to save space.

The column labeled PE gives the price/earnings ratio of the stock. This value is computed by dividing the firm's latest annual earnings per share into its current stock price. Newspaper stock listings report only integer values of P/E ratios, so they would list Microsoft's P/E ratio as 24. Using the stock's price and the P/E ratio, we can estimate Microsoft's earnings per share:

$$\text{Price/EPS} = 24.3 = (\$30.44)/\text{EPS}$$

INTERNET ACTIVITY

Get stock price quotes online and learn more about stock investing at http://www.fool.com and http://finance.yahoo.com. Try the investment calculators at these sites and at http://www.financenter.com.

so our approximation for EPS is $1.25.

Next, the table lists the twelve-month dividend paid by the firm; Microsoft paid $0.40 per share in dividends to its owners over the past twelve months. The final piece of information in the table is the dividend yield of the stock. The dividend yield is calculated as the stock's annual dividend divided by its current price. Since the current price is $30.43, the dividend yield is $0.40/$30.43, or 1.31 percent. In newspaper listings this may be rounded to 1.3 percent as the stock listings allow for only one decimal place.

Dots (. . .) or "NA" will appear as the dividend or dividend yield for some stocks. This indicates that the firm did not pay dividends in the previous twelve months. Similarly, lack of a number for the firm's P/E indicates a firm with a negative net income.

INNOVATION IN COMMON STOCKS

Although started in the mid-1980s with acquisitions by General Motors of Electronic Data Systems (EDS) and Hughes Aircraft, tracking stocks gained popularity in the late 1990s and early 2000s. When it acquired these firms, GM offered stock for the firm's shareholders that would be driven by the fortunes of each new subsidiary rather than GM as a whole. Investment bankers and corporate executives rediscovered this idea a few years ago as a way to separate, on paper, the fortunes of a "hot" subsidiary from its sluggish parent company.

A tracking stock is issued by the parent company to track a subsidiary rather than the entire firm. Shares can be sold and capital raised to help the subsidiary fund growth. Unlike common stock, though, the tracking shares have no ownership claim on the subsidiary; the parent company (and the parent's shareholders) retain all ownership in it. Tracking stock is thus very much different from the case of a spinoff where the parent sells the subsidiary to another firm or in a public offering and the new owners truly do own the firm. Since the parent retains ownership, the tracking stock merely cuts the pieces of the firm's cash flow pie differently; it does not increase the size of the pie. In other words, the value of the tracking stock plus the parent firm's stock after the tracking stock has been issued should closely approximate the pre-tracking stock value of the entire firm.

Although tracking stocks may have some claim on the division's cash flow, the parent company still has control over where the cash goes. Some have claimed tracking stocks are a way to give incentives to managers in the subsidiaries as they can get paid in tracking shares or can receive options on the tracking stock of a successful subsidiary rather than in the stodgy parent. Firms that have issued tracking stock include AT&T, Cendant, Disney, DuPont, and Dow Jones, although many of them have since cancelled the tracking stocks by pulling them back into the parent firm. Studies have shown that the performance of tracking stocks has lagged that of the parent firms. One reason for this is that the subsidiary is still very much a part of the firm; there is no reason why "2 + 2 = 5" synergies would be created to create more value out of the same company merely by offering tracking shares in a subsidiary.[6]

As we saw in Chapter 7, bonds have many different characteristics with respect to time to maturity, coupon income payouts, callable, put options, and so forth. With only a few exceptions, equity has fewer variations. Except for some variations across preferred equity issues (callable, participating, convertible) or different voting rights and dividend rights for common stock, there are not many variations of publicly traded equity issues.

CONCEPT CHECK

What does the "volume" notation mean in Figure 8.2?

What dividend does Microsoft pay its common shareholders?

What does the P/E ratio indicate?

What do tracking stocks track?

DIVIDENDS AND STOCK REPURCHASES

The process of paying coupon interest on bonds is rather straightforward; it is a payment that is legally required under the terms of the bond's indenture. Only when a firm contacts the trustee and states that it will not be able to pay the required interest because of financial difficulty does the process become complex and legalistic.

Dividends, as we've learned, are not a legal obligation of the firm and as such may be skipped, decreased, increased, stopped, and started according to the collective wisdom of the corporation's board of directors. When they are paid, they are typically paid on a quarterly basis, four times over the course of a year. In this section we'll review the process a firm follows to declare and issue a cash dividend. We'll also review why firms pay dividends and about other means that firms use to increase shareholder value via stock dividends, stock splits, and share repurchases.

PROCESS OF ISSUING CASH DIVIDENDS

As dividend payments are not automatic in the sense that bond interest is, there is a process to be followed. First, the firm's board of directors—who oversee the firm's managers and who are to

6. Matt Krantz, "Remember Tracking Stocks? Most Are History," *USA Today*, September 21, 2004, http://www.usatoday.com/money/markets/us/2004-09-20-notrack_x.htm(accessed January 29, 2007); Robert McGough, "Tracking Stocks Fail to Justify Their Buzz, A Study Finds," *Wall Street Journal*, April 25, 2000, pp. C1, C2; Burton G. Malkiel, "Tracking Stocks Are Likely to Derail," *Wall Street Journal*, February 14, 2000, p. A42.

FIGURE 8.3

Time Line for Declaring and Issuing a Cash Dividend

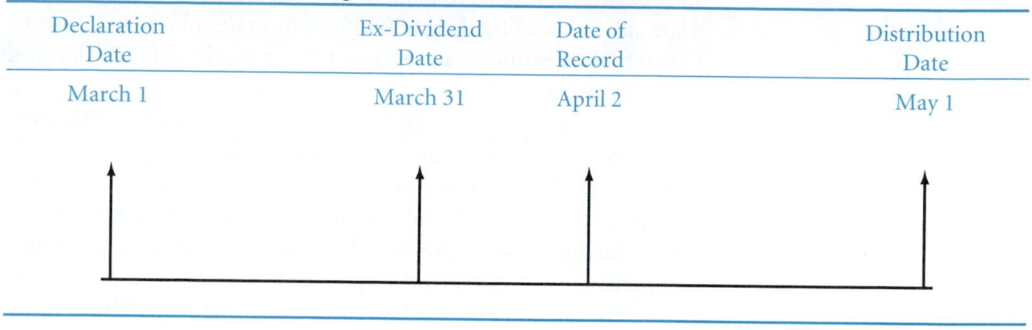

Declaration Date	Ex-Dividend Date	Date of Record	Distribution Date
March 1	March 31	April 2	May 1

declaration date

the date the board of directors announces that a dividend is declared or is forthcoming

distribution date

date on which the dividend is to be paid to shareholders

date of record

those owning the stock on this date will receive the declared dividend on the distribution date

ex-dividend date

two working days before the date of record; trades on and after this trade do not include the right to receive the declared dividend

dividend reinvestment plans (DRIPs)

allow shareholders to easily purchase additional shares with their dividends

make decisions for the benefit for the firm's common shareholders[7]—must declare that a cash dividend will be paid. On this *declaration date* they will announce the amount of the dividend per share that will be paid on the *distribution date* to those who own stock as of the *date of record*. The time line of this process is shown in Figure 8.3.

The board declares that a dividend will be paid on the *declaration date*, for example March 1. The announcement will include information on the amount of the dividend and when the dividend will be paid (the *distribution date*, which is May 1 in Figure 8.3). The board will also announce the *date of record*; dividends will only be paid to those who own shares of the firm's stock on this date. Figure 8.3 shows the date of record as April 2.

We learned earlier that stock trades are processed in "T + 3", that is, it takes up to three days before a stock purchase or sale is recorded. Thus, our time line needs one more date: the *ex-dividend date*. The ex-dividend date is two working days before the date of record. Stock trades on or after the ex-dividend date will not include the expectation of the dividend. In our time line, assuming that April 2 falls on a Wednesday, the ex-dividend date will be two working days before—that is, Monday, March 31. Anyone wanting to purchase shares in order to receive the dividend needs to purchase them before March 31.

What should happen to the stock price on the ex-dividend date? If there were no other influences, we would expect the price of the stock to fall by an amount equal to the dividend. If stock is trading for $27.50 with a declared quarterly dividend of $0.30, we expect the price to fall to $27.20 on the ex-dividend date.

Many firms offer shareholders the choice to receive a check for the amount of their dividends or to reinvest the dividends in the firm's stock. *Dividend reinvestment plans (DRIPs)* allow shareholders to purchase additional shares automatically with all or part of the investor's dividends. Fractional shares can be purchased, and DRIP purchases have no or very low commissions.

Suppose an investor owns sufficient shares to receive $10 in dividends on a stock from its quarterly declared dividend. If the stock price is $25, the DRIP program allows the investor to purchase $10/$25 or 0.40 share of the firm's stock. If the stock price is $8, the investor's reinvested dividends will purchase $10/$8 or 1.25 shares of the stock.

If the investor favors the stock and wants to continue holding it, participating in a DRIP is an easy way of purchasing additional shares over time without any direct cash outlay. It also allows income returns to be reinvested to facilitate compounding returns over time. However, as with all dividends, the declared dividend is taxable as income. Whether the dividends are received as cash or reinvested, the investor must pay taxes on them.

HOW DO FIRMS DECIDE ON THE DOLLAR AMOUNT OF DIVIDENDS?

dividend payout ratio

dividends per share divided by earnings per share

Most firms that issue dividends try to maintain a consistent *dividend payout ratio*, which is dividends per share divided by earnings per share. Microsoft's dividend payout ratio, using the information from Figure 8.2 and our calculations, is its dividend of $0.40 per share divided by our calculation of earnings per share, $1.25:

Dividend payout ratio = $0.40/$1.25 = 0.32 or 32 percent

---

7. The board of directors is discussed more fully in Chapter 11: Business Organization and Financial Data.

How about the case of a firm that wants to start paying dividends? Microsoft's decision to start paying dividends in 2003 was prompted by its cash balance of $48 billion; its decision to pay a special dividend totaling $30 billion to shareholders in 2004 arose as its cash balance had risen to $60 billion. Suffice it to say, most firms that initiate dividends do not generate as much cash as does Microsoft.

A key component of the "How much?" decision is the level of dividends sustainable over time. A firm does not want to announce it will begin paying dividends only at a later time to have to reduce or eliminate the dividend due to the need to conserve cash. Dividends are thought to send a signal to investors about management's view of the future cash-generating ability of the firm. Managers—and the board of directors—have private information about the strategies, competitive responses, and opportunities facing the firm that the investing public does not know. Thus, if the firm decides to increase dividends, that is a positive signal or indicator to the financial markets that management believes the future for the firm looks either stable or to be improving. A reduction in dividends is taken to be a pessimistic indicator of the firm's future, so firms try to set dividends so future reductions are unlikely given their current perspective on the firm's future.

Thus, most firms that start paying dividends will do so at a rather low level—perhaps just a penny a share. The fact that management and the board are sufficiently confident to issue a dividend is a positive signal to the financial markets. Over time, as the firm generates more cash, the firm will increase its dollar amount of dividends per share, as well as its dividend payout ratio. After a while, the firm will determine a *target dividend payout ratio* that it seeks to maintain over time. However, dividends will not automatically rise along with earnings. If future earnings rise, dividends will not increase until the board feels the higher level of earnings is sustainable over time (remember, firms do not want to ever cut the dollar amount of the dividends per share if they can possibly avoid it). If the higher earnings appear to be sustainable over time, the firm will adjust the dividends per share accordingly toward the target dividend payout ratio.[8] Some call this the **target dividend payout policy**.

Some firms follow a different dividend strategy of consistently paying a low regular dividend but declaring a **special dividend** when times are particularly good. For a firm in a cyclical industry, with sales and earnings that are highly variable, this may be a strategy to conserve cash during industry recessions while maintaining the low but stable regular dividend. Shareholders are rewarded when rising earnings allow the company to declare an extra or special dividend. While such a dividend policy may help management control its cash balance, such a strategy is not favored by investors, who generally prefer certainty to uncertainty.

Other dividend payment strategies suffer from the same drawback of creating investor uncertainly due to variable dividend levels. The **residual dividend policy** states that dividends will vary based upon how much excess funds the firm has from year to year. Under a **constant payout ratio** strategy, the firm pays a constant percentage of earnings as dividends, so as earnings rise and fall so does the dollar amount of dividends. Please note that this is not the same as the target payout policy. The firm adjusts dividends around the target over time, depending on earnings sustainability; some years the actual payout ratio will exceed the target and others will be under it in order to have stable, predictable changes in dividends. The constant payout ratio maintains the payout ratio at the expense of a varying dollar amount of dividends per share.

Several factors will be considered by the board of directors and management as they consider the level of dividend payout. The following are some of these factors:

- *Ability of the firm to generate cash to sustain the level of dividends.* Recall that investors do not react well to reductions in dividends. If a dividend level is thought to be unsustainable, the firm's stock price will fall as investors sell the stock.

- *Legal and contractual considerations.* Dividends, when they are paid, reduce a firm's equity. A firm cannot pay dividends if doing so will reduce the firm's equity below the par value of the common stock. In addition, a bond's indenture (or loan agreement with a bank) may

target dividend payout policy
the dividend payout ratio adjusts over time to a target level set by management

special dividend
an extra dividend declared by the firm over and above its regular dividend payout

residual dividend policy
dividends vary over time based on the firm's excess funds

constant payout ratio
the declared dividends are a constant percentage of the firm's earnings

---

8. Discussions of dividend policy theories and practice are available in Julio Brandon and David L. Ikenberry, "Reappearing Dividends," *Journal of Applied Corporate Finance*, Fall 2004, 16(4), 89–100; Alon Brav, John R. Graham, Campbell R. Harvey, and Roni Michaely, "Payout Policy in the 21st Century" (April 2003), NBER Working Paper No. W9657, available at Web site of the Social Science Research Network (SSRN): http://ssrn.com/abstract-5398560 (accessed July 11, 2007).

restrict the dollar amount of dividends to ensure adequate cash is available to pay loan interest and principal.

• *Growth opportunities.* Growing firms require capital—they will likely want to reinvest all profits into the company to help finance expansion and movement into new products or markets. Growing firms may seek additional funds from loans, bond issues, and new issues of stock. It is unlikely that firms facing growth opportunities will want to initiate or significantly increase their dividends.

• *Cost of other financing sources.* Dividends are paid, for the most part, from internally generated funds—that is, cash that remains after the firm's bills, interest, and taxes are paid. If a firm has the ability to easily raise cash from low-cost external financing sources, it will be better able to maintain a higher level of dividends. Firms that can raise outside financing only by paying high interest rates or by issuing new shares of stock will likely have lower levels of dividends.

• *Tax rates.* Prior to 2003, dividend income was viewed as unattractive by some investors because dividend income was taxed as income, at the investors' marginal income tax rate, which exceeded 30 percent (combined federal and state tax rates) for many. Then the Jobs and Growth Tax Relief Reconciliation Act of 2003 reduced the top federal tax rate on dividends from 38 percent to 15 percent, the same as the top rate on long-term capital gains. Although surveys of financial officers indicate that tax rates are not a first-order concern when setting dividends, many firms markedly increased dividends after the law was passed.

In addition to cash dividends, the firm's board of directors can announce other decisions, such as a stock dividend or stock split, which at first glance appear to benefit shareholders; as we shall soon see, their affect on the value of a firm's stock and the wealth of shareholders is zero. However, there is one other decision the board can make that positively affects shareholders—a stock buyback, or share repurchase, program. We'll examine these in turn.

STOCK DIVIDENDS AND STOCK SPLITS

A **stock dividend** is what it sounds like: a dividend paid with shares of stock rather than cash. Rather than mention a dollar figure, the announcement will state that the firm is distributing a 5 percent (or "X" percent) stock dividend, but a stock dividend has no net effect on the wealth of the shareholders. To see why, consider the following.

CUL8R Incorporated stock is currently priced at $10 a share, and 100,000 shares are outstanding; the total market value of the firm is $10 × 100,000 or $1 million. Suppose you own 1,000 shares, so you own 1 percent of the shares outstanding and the value of your holdings is $10 × 1,000 shares or $10,000. CUL8R's board has declared a 10 percent stock dividend, so now you own 1,100 shares.

Are you any richer? The answer is no: you still own 1 percent of the shares outstanding, and the value of your CUL8R holdings is still $10,000. You own 1,100 shares but the number of shares outstanding is now 10 percent larger, too. There are now 110,000 total shares, and you still own 1 percent of this total. Nothing has happened to the value or the earnings ability of the firm with this paper transaction, so the firm's stock price will fall and will equal $1 million/110,000 shares or approximately $9.09. Some account entries will affect the firm's equity account, but the total amount of equity in the accounting statements will remain the same.[9] The bottom line is that a stock dividend distributes nothing to shareholders and removes nothing from the firm. No value is transferred.

A **stock split** has a similar effect. The firm distributes extra shares for every share owned in a stock split. For example, a firm may announce a *two-for-one* stock split; this has the effect of doubling the number of shares outstanding and doubling the holdings of each investor. However, as in the case of a stock dividend, the net effect on investor wealth is zero. You may own twice as many shares, but the stock price will be cut in half, leaving your ownership stake (both in terms of value and percentage owned) the same as it was before the stock split. Occasionally a firm will

CONCEPT CHECK

Why is the decision to reduce dividends not well received by investors?

What policies might a board follow in setting a firm's dividend?

What five influences affect a board's dividend decision?

stock dividend
a dividend in which investors receive shares of stock rather than cash

stock split
the firms distribute additional shares for every share owned

---

9. The firm's combined value of its par value and additional paid-in capital accounts will rise by the market value of the stock dividend, but the firm's retained earnings account will decline by this amount so the firm's equity account remains constant.

announce a *reverse split*, in which multiple shares are combined to form one new share. For example, a *one-for-four* reverse split means four old shares are now equal to one new share. When this happens, the stock price will change, so once again there is no change in the investor's wealth.

You may have noted that there is not much of a difference between a stock split and a stock dividend. They both involve paper transactions in which the number of shares is increased but prices adjust downward to maintain investor wealth at a constant level. By way of accounting convention, a distribution of five shares for four (a 25 percent stock dividend) is considered to be a stock split; a distribution of less than five for four (less than a 25 percent stock dividend) is considered to be a stock dividend.[10]

Why do some firms offer stock dividends or do stock splits? Since they have no value effects, the impact is mainly psychological. Stock dividends are a way to make investors think they are receiving something of value when in reality they are not. Some practitioners believe there is an optimal range for a stock price. Prices that are "too high" will scare away investors because of the large capital investment needed to purchase shares. Prices that are "too low" make the stock appear speculative. Stock dividends and splits can reduce or increase market prices to keep them within an optimal range of $20 to $80. But many successful firms have stock prices far exceeding this range; in 2007 Google stock was selling for over $500 a share and Berkshire Hathaway A shares have traded at over $100,000 a share. Stocks with low prices (say, less than $5 a share) bear a stigma of being lower-quality speculative issues, and some have done reverse splits to raise their stock price. Yet research studies show what we intuitively know: there is no shareholder value created in splits, reverse splits, or stock dividends.

SHARE REPURCHASES

Rather than distribute funds to shareholders in the form of earnings, a firm can repurchase its shares. For example, in January 2007 Walgreens announced the following:

> The board of directors of Walgreen Co. (NYSE, NASDAQ:WAG) today announced a new stock repurchase program of up to $1 billion, which the company plans to execute over the next four years. . . . Walgreens President and CEO Jeffrey A. Rein said, "The repurchase program is a continued vote of confidence in our company and our future, and reflects our commitment to increase shareholder value."[11]

At the same time Walgreens also announced a dividend, so stock repurchases can occur along with dividend payouts. Why would a firm repurchase its own shares of stock? Small purchases (relative to the total amount of shares outstanding) acquire shares used in management stock-option incentive programs, in which managers can purchase shares of stock at prespecified prices (more will be said about this in Chapter 11, "Business Organization and Financial Data"). Other firms purchase shares of their own stock to use in stock-based acquisitions of other firms—that is, they repurchase shares from current shareholders and then distribute them to owners of a newly acquired firm.

A major reason for doing this is to reward longer-term shareholders by enhancing the value of the firm's shares. Under current U.S. tax law, dividends are taxed when issued, regardless if the shareholder receives cash or reinvests them in a DRIP program. marginal income tax rate—that is, the same tax rate they would pay in the next dollar earned, whether that dollar comes from salary, commission, dividends, or interest. This rate may be as high as 35 percent, depending on the person's income level.

However, increases in stock prices are not taxed until the shares are sold, and if the shares have been held longer than one year the maximum tax on capital gain (the increase in value) is 15 percent. This tax savings is thought by some researchers to be a major reason for the increase in stock repurchases in recent years.

Another reason for stock repurchases is that the firm has the cash and sees its own stock as one of its most attractive investment alternatives. Rather than investing in expanding the business

---

10. There is a distinction in what happens to the equity account in the case of a stock split. For a stock split, the only change is to the number of shares outstanding and to the stock's par value (if any). None of the dollar amounts in the equity accounts change. So if a firm has 100,000 shares outstanding of $1 par value stock and it announces a two-for-one stock split, the number of share outstanding becomes 200,000 and the par value becomes $0.50.

11. "Walgreens Co. Authorizes $1 Billion Stock Repurchase Program," accessed at http://news.walgreens.com/article_display.cfm?article_id-52406 (accessed February 2, 2007).

to new markets, the firm's board of directors and top managers believe the firm's stock is under-valued and offers potential returns. The stock can be purchased now at what is perceived to be a low price and reissued later, after the stock price increases. This is, metaphorically, a firm "putting its money where its mouth is." This was a popular reason given for stock repurchases during the 2000–2002 stock market decline. On the other hand, it is an indicator that management is doing a poor job in identifying new corporate strategies for increasing the stock's value.

This section discussed the process of declaring and issuing dividends on equity securities. The following section applies the time value of money principles presented in Chapter 5 to expected cash flows from equity investments. The process of valuation is important to business managers considering ways to issue securities, as well as to investors who must make security buy and sell decisions.

VALUATION OF STOCKS

In Chapter 5 we learned how to find the present value of a series of future cash flows. The present value represents the current worth of the future cash flows; in other words, it represents the price someone would be willing to pay today to receive the expected future cash flows. For example, from page 122, an investor would be willing to pay $2,577 in order to receive a three-year annuity of $1,000 at an 8 percent discount rate.

All securities are valued on the basis of the cash inflows that they are expected to provide to their owners or investors. As we saw in Chapter 7, Equation 7.1:

$$\text{price} = [CF_1/(1 + r)^1] + [CF_2/(1 + r)^2] + \cdots + [CF_n/(1 + r)^n] \tag{8.1}$$

or

$$\text{price} = \sum_{t=1}^{n} [CF_t/(1 + r)^t] \tag{8.1a}$$

that is, value or current price should equal the present value of expected future cash flows.

In Chapter 7 we applied this general formula to the case of bond pricing. The cash flows from a typical bond are straightforward: the bond has a known and definite life, has fixed coupon payments paid on a regular basis, pays a known par value or principal when the bond matures, and should have a discount rate (yield to maturity) close to that of bonds with similar credit ratings.

Although the principle for determining an appropriate stock price is the same as that for determining a bond price, equity does not offer the certainty of bond cash flows. Common and preferred stocks are generally assumed to have infinite lives. For common stock, relevant cash flows (dividend payments) will likely be variable over time. Finally, determining an appropriate rate at which to discount future dividends is difficult. Despite these difficulties, in this section we will see that the present value of all future dividends should equal a stock's current price and that some simplifying assumptions can make the task of determining stock value much easier. Our discussion in this section focuses on common stock. As we will see, the method for valuing preferred stock is a special case of common stock valuation.

It may seem rather strange to treat the stock price as nothing more than the present value of all future dividends. Who buys stock with no intention of ever selling it, even after retirement? Investors generally buy stock with the intention of selling it at some future time ranging from a few hours to thirty years or longer. Despite the length of any one investor's time horizon, the current price of any dividend-paying common stock should equal the present value of all future dividends:[12]

$$\text{price} = \sum_{t=1}^{n} [D_t/(1 + r_s)^t] \tag{8.2}$$

12. Here is the intuition behind this statement. A stock is purchased today, in year T, with the plan of selling it in year T + 1. What should its current price be? The current price should equal the present value of dividends over year T and the selling price in year T + 1.

But what will be the price of the stock in year T + 1? Suppose another investor plans on buying the stock at the beginning of year T + 1 and selling it a year later in year T + 2. As before, the price of the stock at the beginning of year T + 1 should be the present value of the dividends paid in year T + 1 plus the selling price in year T + 2.

Through substitution, today's price will be the present value of the dividends in year T and T + 1 plus the expected selling price in year T + 2. We can continue extending this exercise through many years: year T + 3, T + 4, and so on. The result is that today's stock price will be the sum of the present value of future dividends.

What if a corporation currently pays no dividends and has no plans to pay dividends in the foreseeable future? The value of this company's stock will not be zero. First, just because the firm has no plans to pay dividends does not mean that it never will. To finance rapid growth, young firms often retain all their earnings; when they mature, they often begin paying out a portion of earnings as dividends. Second, although the firm may not pay dividends to shareholders it may be generating cash (or have the potential to do so). The cash or profits can be claimed by the firm's new owner if the firm is acquired or merged, and so its current price should reflect this value. Third, at the very least, the firm's stock should be worth the per-share liquidation value of its assets; for a going concern, the firm is worth the discounted cash flow value that can be captured by an acquirer.

Estimating all future dividend payments is impractical. Matters can be simplified considerably if we assume that the firm's dividends will remain constant or will grow at a constant rate over time.

VALUING STOCKS WITH CONSTANT DIVIDENDS

If the firm's dividends are expected to remain constant, so that $D_0 = D_1 = D_2 \ldots$, we can treat its stock as a perpetuity. We know that preferred stock dividends are constant over time, so this situation is most applicable for valuing shares of preferred stock. The present value of a perpetuity is the cash flow divided by the discount rate. For stocks with constant dividends, this means that Equation 8.2 becomes:

$$P_0 = D_0/r_s \tag{8.3}$$

Many preferred stocks are valued using Equation 8.3 since preferred stocks typically pay a constant dollar dividend and do not usually have finite lives or maturities. For example, if the FY Corporation's preferred stock currently pays a $2 dividend and investors require a 10 percent rate of return on preferred stocks of similar risk, the preferred stock's present value is:

$$P_0 = \$2/0.10 = \$20.00$$

For a preferred stock with no stated maturity and a constant dividend, changes in price will occur only if the rate of return expected by investors changes.

VALUING STOCKS WITH CONSTANT DIVIDEND GROWTH RATES

Many firms have sales and earnings that increase over time; their dividends may rise, as well. If we assume that a firm's dividends grow at an annual rate of g percent, next year's dividend, D_1, will be $D_0(1 + g)$; the dividend in two years will be $D_0(1 + g)^2$. Generalizing, we have:

$$D_t = D_0(1 + g)^t$$

Equation 8.2 now can be shown in expanded form as:

$$P_0 = [D_0(1 + g)]/(1 + r_s) + [D_0(1 + g)^2]/(1 + r_s)^2 + [D_0(1 + g)^3]/(1 + r_s)^3 + \cdots$$

As long as the dividend growth rate g is less than the discount rate r_s, each future term will be smaller than the preceding term. Although technically the number of terms is infinite, the present value of dividends received further and further into the future become closer and closer to zero. By accepting the fact that the sum of all these terms is finite, Equation 8.2 becomes:

$$P_0 = D_1/(r_s - g) \tag{8.4}$$

Gordon model (constant dividend growth model)
a means of estimating common stock prices by assuming constant dividend growth over time

This result is known as the ***Gordon model*** or the ***constant dividend growth model.*** The model assumes that a dividend is currently being paid and that this dividend will grow or increase at a constant rate over time. Of course, the assumption of constant growth in dividends may not be realistic for a firm that is experiencing a period of high growth (or negative growth—that is, declining revenues). Neither will constant dividend growth be a workable assumption for a firm whose dividends rise and fall over the business cycle.

Let's assume that the cash dividend per share for XYZ Company for last year was $1.89 and is expected to be $2.05 at the end of this year. This represents a percentage increase of 8.5 percent [($2.05 − $1.89)/$1.89]. If investors expect a 12 percent rate of return, then the estimated current stock value (P_0) would be:

$$P_0 = \$1.89(1.085)/(0.12 - 0.085) = (\$2.05/0.035) = \$58.59$$

Thus, if investors believed that the cash dividends would grow at an 8.5 percent rate indefinitely into the future and expected a 12 percent rate of return, they would pay $58.59 for the stock.

A simple spreadsheet can compute stock price using the constant growth assumption:

From this discussion, we can see that there are four major influences on a stock's price. First is the firm's earnings per share and second is the firm's dividend payout ratio; together, they determine a firm's dollar amount of dividends. The third influence is the firm's expected growth rate in dividends, which will itself be affected by a number of firm, industry, and economic influences. Fourth is the shareholders' required return; from Chapter 4, we know this return is itself affected by the real interest rate in the economy, the expected inflation rate, and a risk premium to compensate investors for purchasing risky equities.

We can use the constant dividend growth model to solve for any of the four unknown variables (price, dividends, required return, and growth) as long as the other three are known. For example, rearranging Equation 8.4, we can use the market price of the stock to calculate the market's required return for the stock:

$$r_s = D_1/P_0 + g$$

that is, the dividend yield plus the expected growth rate.

Similarly, using an estimate for the required return, we can estimate the market's consensus estimate for future dividend growth:

$$g = (P_0 \cdot r - D_0)/(P_0 + D_0)$$

This is especially valuable as a check against overoptimism on the part of investors when valuing a growth stock—that is, one whose earnings are expected to continue growing at a fast rate over time. At the height of the Internet stock bubble in 1999–2000, stocks of technology firms were priced assuming that 20 percent to 30 percent growth or higher was expected indefinitely. Such growth is not possible for long periods of time, so it was only a matter of time before their stock prices tumbled after slower sales resulted in slower earnings and cash flow growth for these firms.

TWO-STAGE GROWTH MODELS

The assumption of a smooth and constant growth rate over time may not be true for some firms. The firm and industry life cycle is such that a period of fast and variable growth is followed by a period of slower, more consistent growth, and cyclical firms will have growth rates that fluctuate with the business cycle. One way to address this reality is to use a two-stage growth model. The model assumes that supernormal growth will occur for the firm over a short period of time, after which "normal" and relatively constant growth will occur.[13] To value these stocks, we use:

$$P_0 = [D_0(1 + g)]/(1 + r_s) + [D_0(1 + g)^2]/(1 + r_s)^2 + \_\cdots\_ + \tag{8.5}$$
$$[D_0(1 + g)^n]/(1 + r_s)^n + Price_n/(1 + r_s)^n$$

That is, we estimate the dividends for each year of the n-year supernormal growth period and compute their present value; we add to this the present value of the stock price in year n. The year n price is estimated by the constant dividend growth model; since dividends are expected to grow at a consistent rate after year n, we find their value as of year n and discount it back to the present. Without the notation of Equation 8.5, the process is:

1. Estimate the dividends for each year of the supernormal growth period.
2. Since constant growth begins in year n + 1, find the price of the stock in year n using the Gordon model.
3. Sum the present value of the dividends in each of the supernormal growth years and the present value of the stock price in year n.

For example, let's assume Kraham Corporation's stock is in a growth period; dividends are expected to grow 20 percent annually for the next three years, at which time the firm will grow at a "normal" rate of 7 percent. If investors require a 10 percent return on their investment in a stock with Kraham's risk and the firm just paid a dividend of 50 cents a share, what is a fair price for the stock?

The first step is to estimate the dividends in the supernormal growth period. With a current dividend of $0.50 and 20 percent growth, these are the dividends:

YEAR	DIVIDEND
1	$(0.50)(1 + 0.20) = \$0.60$
2	$(0.60)(1 + 0.20) = \$0.72$
3	$(0.72)(1 + 0.20) = \$0.86$

The second step is to estimate the stock price in year 3. After year 3 the dividends are expected to grow at a normal growth rate of 7 percent. Using the constant dividend growth model, we find:

$$P_n = D_{n+1}/(r_s - g) = P_3 = D_4/(r_s - g) = \$0.86(1 + 0.07)/(0.10 - 0.07)$$
$$= 0.92/0.03 = \$30.67$$

INTERNET ACTIVITY

Examine estimates on the future earnings of firms at http://www.zacks.com and http://www.whispernumber. com. Another great resource of stock analysis is www.fool.com.

The third and final step of the process is to sum the present values of the supernormal growth dividends and the year-3 price at the 10 percent required rate of return for Kraham stock. We have:

$$P_0 = \$0.60/(1.10) + \$0.72/(1.10)^2 + \$0.86/(1.10)^3 + \$30.67/(1.10)^3 = \$24.83$$

According to the two-stage model, investors should be willing to pay $24.83 a share for Kraham Corporation stock.

---

13. Some use a three-stage growth model in which a period of supernormal growth is followed by a period of above-normal but declining growth rates until a sustainable constant growth rate is achieved.

A simple spreadsheet design can incorporate the inputs and calculations for this three-year supernormal growth stock:

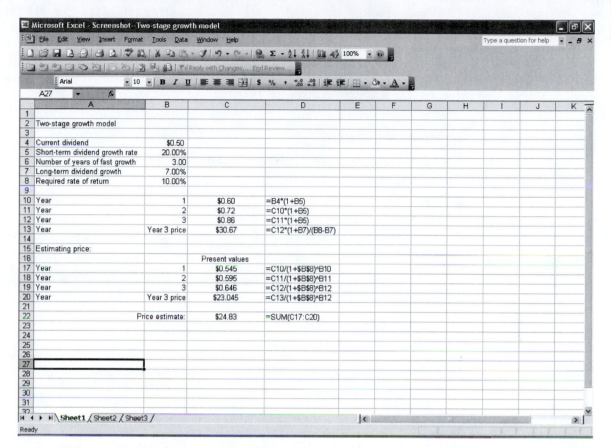

Using this spreadsheet, if we change the supernormal growth assumption (cell B5) to 30 percent, the stock should trade at $31.55 a share. Leaving the growth rate assumption at 20 percent, if we change the long-term dividend growth to only 5 percent (cell B7), the stock should sell for $15.42.

RISK IN STOCK VALUATION

ETHICAL ISSUES

CONCEPT CHECK

What challenges must be faced when determining a value for a firm's common shares?

What risks do shareholders face that can lead to fluctuations in share values?

Investors in common stocks face a number of risks that bondholders do not. This additional risk leads them to require a higher rate of return on a firm's stock than on its debt securities. For example, in the event of corporate failure, the claims of stockholders have lower priority than those of bondholders, so stockholders face a greater risk of loss than bondholders. Dividends can be variable and omitted, whereas bond cash flows have a legal obligation to be met.

Poor ethical decisions and poor management are another source of risk for stock investors in that such decisions can lower future cash flows and raise the required rate of return demanded by future investors. Accounting gimmickry and decisions by self-serving managers (more will be said about this in Chapter 11) can hurt stock prices, as happened with Enron, WorldCom, and Tyco. Poor customer–supplier relations, allegations of poor-quality products, and poor communications, as occurred between Ford Motor Company and one of its tire suppliers, Firestone, hurt both companies and their shareholders.

If the general level of interest rates rises, investors will demand a higher required rate of return on stocks to maintain their risk premium differential over debt securities. This will force stock prices downward. Therefore, stockholders risk losses from any general upward movement of market interest rates.

Also, future dividends, or dividend growth rates, are not known with certainty at the time stock is purchased. If poor corporate performance or adverse general economic conditions lead

JAMIE BREEN
Marketing
Disciplined Investment Advisors

BS Radio, TV, and Film
Northwestern University
MBA Marketing/Finance
Northwestern University

"For lack of a more specific title, I'm the marketing guy."

Q: *Describe the firm you work for.*

A: I work for Disciplined Investment Advisors, which is a small money management firm. We manage (invest) money for corporate pension funds.

Q: *You say it's a small firm. How small?*

A: We manage over a billion dollars for our clients. That's a lot of money, but compared to a Fidelity with several hundred billion, we're definitely at the lower end. In the industry we'd be called a "boutique" firm.

Q: *And what do you do there?*

A: For lack of a more specific title, I'm the marketing guy. It's my job to spread the word about what we do, generate new clients, and keep existing ones.

Q: *So you call on pension fund managers?*

A: Yes, that's part of it. Our clients all have a person or team in charge of managing the pension fund, trying to invest it profitably and safely. So I call on those people. But there's another group of people that I spend even more time with. They are the outside consultants that help the pension managers decide whom to hire.

Q: *What do you do with these consultants?*

A: Basically I try to demonstrate to them that we are a good firm to recommend to their clients. I present them with information about our investment strategy and our performance during previous periods. But more important than the numbers is demonstrating to the consultants that we can help them look good, that we can make a professional presentation to their clients, explain our strategy coherently, and so on.

Q: *So if you impress the consultant, the consultant may recommend you to take over the investing of a company's pension fund?*

A: Part of a company's pension fund. To diversify, most funds divide the investment job between a number of companies like ours. Four or five for a smaller fund, up to a hundred or more for a very large corporation.

Q: *Is this a competitive business?*

A: It's very competitive because there's so much money involved. There are probably a thousand money managers that we could conceivably compete against. So even if our results are excellent, say in the top quartile, there are another 250 companies that can say the same thing.

Q: *So how do you differentiate yourself from the crowd?*

A: One of the unique aspects of our company is that it was founded by university professors, true experts in the field of finance. So part of our message is based on the amount and quality of research that backs up our investment strategy. We provide both the pension fund managers and the consultants with a great deal of research data and information that helps them do their jobs. In return we hope to be selected to manage their money. And the other piece of the puzzle is simply to establish trust and credibility. Like any other sales job.

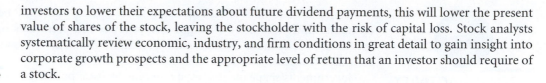

investors to lower their expectations about future dividend payments, this will lower the present value of shares of the stock, leaving the stockholder with the risk of capital loss. Stock analysts systematically review economic, industry, and firm conditions in great detail to gain insight into corporate growth prospects and the appropriate level of return that an investor should require of a stock.

INTERNET ACTIVITY

Read analysis and expectations of overseas economic activity from sites such as www. morganstanley.com (search for "Global Economic Forum") and download exchange rate data from sites such as https:// www. federalreserve.gov/Releases.

VALUATION AND THE FINANCIAL ENVIRONMENT

The price of an asset is the present value of future cash flows; the discount rate used in the present value calculation is the required rate of return on the investment. Future cash flows of firms and the required returns of investors are affected by the global and domestic economic environments and the competition faced by firms. Slower sales or higher expenses can harm a firm's ability to pay its bond interest or dividends or to reinvest in its future growth. Besides affecting cash flows, these can affect investors' required rates of return by increasing risk premiums or credit spreads. Inflation pressures and capital market changes influence the level of interest rates and required returns.

GLOBAL ECONOMIC INFLUENCES

GLOBAL DISCUSSION

Two main overseas influences will affect firms.[14] First is the condition of overseas economies.

Growth in foreign economies will increase the demand for U.S. exports. Similarly, sluggish foreign demand will harm overseas sales and hurt the financial position of firms doing business overseas. The rate of economic growth overseas can affect the conditions faced by domestic firms, too, as growing demand globally may make it easier to raise prices and sluggish demand overseas may lead to intense competition in the U.S. market.

The second influence is the behavior of exchange rates: the price of a currency in terms of another currency. A change in exchange rates over time has two effects on the firm. Changing exchange rates lead to higher or lower U.S. dollar cash flows from overseas sales, more competitively priced import goods, or changing input costs. Thus, changing exchange rates affect profitability by influencing sales, price competition, and expenses. Second, changing exchange rates affect the level of domestic interest rates. Expectations of a weaker U.S. dollar can lead to higher U.S. interest rates; to attract capital, U.S. rates will have to rise to compensate foreign investors for expected currency losses because of the weaker dollar.[15] Conversely, a stronger dollar can result in lower U.S. interest rates.

DOMESTIC ECONOMIC INFLUENCES

INTERNET ACTIVITY

The Economic Report of the President *is available on the Internet, as are its data tables; see also the Economics Statistics Briefing Room of the White House, http://www.whitehouse. gov/fsbr/esbr.html. Other good sources of domestic economic analysis and data include the Federal Reserve's Web site, http://www.federalreserve.gov; see especially the* Beige Book *analysis of economic conditions across the regions of the country. The Federal Reserve Bank of St. Louis Web site, http://www. stls.frb.org, has links to the FRED database and to education and analysis sites.*

Individuals can spend only what they have (income and savings) or what their future earning capacity will allow them to borrow. Consumption spending (spending by individuals for items such as food, cars, clothes, computers, and so forth) comprises about two-thirds of gross domestic product, GDP, in the United States. Generally, higher disposable incomes (that is, income after taxes) lead to higher levels of consumption spending. Higher levels of spending mean inventories are reduced and companies need to produce more and hire additional workers to meet sales demand. Corporations will spend to obtain supplies and workers based upon expectations of future demand. Similarly, they will invest in additional plant and equipment based upon expected future sales and income. Economic growth results in higher levels of consumer spending and corporate investment, which in turn stimulate job growth and additional demand. Slow or negative growth can lead to layoffs, pessimistic expectations, and reduced consumer and corporate spending. These effects will directly influence company profits and cash flows.

14. By "overseas," we refer to events outside of the U.S. domestic economy, whether water separates the countries or not. Thus, although the United States shares a land border with two countries, to a U.S. firm the economies of Canada and Mexico are overseas economies.

15. To understand this effect, suppose initially the exchange rate between the U.S. dollar and euro is $1 = €1. Analysts anticipate the dollar will weaken over the year to $1 = €0.95. The European investor who invests €1 for every $1 of investment now expects to receive dollars worth only €0.95 next year. The investor will require a higher expected return on his U.S. investment to compensate for the effects of the weakening dollar. This is similar to a U.S. investor seeking protection from anticipated inflation by increasing the required rate of return to reflect inflationary expectations.

CONCEPT CHECK

How can the growth of overseas economies affect the value of a U.S. firm's stock?

Why do stock and bond investors need to be aware of expectations in the exchange rate market?

How do fiscal policy, monetary policy, and consumer spending affect the outlook for securities markets?

How does competition affect a firm's profits over time?

Economic conditions affect required returns, too. Investors will be more optimistic in good economic times and more willing to accept lower-risk premiums on bond and stock investments. In poor economic times, credit spreads will rise as investors want to place their funds in safer investments.

Governments shape the domestic economy by fiscal policy (government spending and taxation decisions) and monetary policy. These decisions may affect consumer disposable income (fiscal policy) and the level of interest rates and inflation expectations (monetary policy) and, therefore, affect the valuation of the bond and stock markets.

Some industry sectors are sensitive to changes in consumer spending. Sales by auto manufacturers, computer firms, and other manufacturers of high-priced items will rise and fall by greater amounts over the business cycle than will food or pharmaceutical firms. Changes in interest rates affect some industries more than others, too: banks and the housing industry (and sellers of large household appliances) are sensitive to changes in interest rates more than, say, book and music publishers or restaurants.

INDUSTRY AND COMPETITION

A firm's profits are determined by its sales revenues, expenses, and taxes. We've already mentioned taxes and some influences on sales and expenses in our discussion of global and domestic economies. In addition, industry competition and the firm's position within the industry will have a large impact on its ability to generate profits over time. Tight competition means it will be difficult to raise prices to increase sales revenue or profitability. Nonprice forms of competition, such as customer service, product innovation, and using technology to the fullest extent in the manufacturing and sales process, may hurt profits by increasing expenses if the features do not generate sufficient sales. Competition may not come only from similar firms; for example, a variety of "entertainment" firms, from music to theater to movies to sports teams, vie for consumers' dollars. Both trucking firms and railroads compete for freight transportation; cable and satellite firms compete in the home television markets (and for Internet service, along with telephone service providers). Changes in the cost and availability of raw materials, labor, and energy can adversely affect a firm's competitive place in the market.

The influences of competition and supply ultimately affect a firm's profitability and investors' perceptions of the firm's risk. This, in turn, will affect its bond and stock prices. The most attractive firms for investing will be firms with a competitive advantage over their rivals. They may offer a high-quality product, or be the low-cost producer, or be innovators in the use of technology, or offer the best customer support. Whatever the source of the advantage, if they can build and maintain their advantage over time, they will reap above-normal profits and be attractive investments.

SUMMARY

One purpose of this chapter has been to review the characteristics of preferred and common stock. A second major purpose has been to determine security values by applying time value of money techniques to the cash flows that investors receive from these investments. The current price of a share of stock should equal the present value of future expected cash flows. If security prices are already known, these techniques can also be used to estimate investment returns. In the case of the constant dividend growth model, we can use known stock prices and estimates of returns to compute the market's consensus about the dividend growth rate.

Most equity offerings are sales of common stock. Preferred stock gives holders preference over common shareholders with respect to dividends and liquidation. Unlike the common shareholders, though, the (usually) fixed dividend received by preferred share-

holders does not allow them to enjoy the benefits of future profit growth. Many investors buy common shares and expect dividends to rise over time.

The financial system and the economic environment are inseparable inputs to analyzing stocks. Firms' cash flows—and the outlook for their shares—are affected by the global economy and domestic economy as growth overseas and at home will affect demand for the firm's products and will affect its costs, too. Industry competition and technological change can make last year's "sure thing" become this year's bankruptcy filing. Changing demand and supply for funds, fluctuating exchange rates, and monetary policy will influence inflationary expectations and required returns on securities. Much of what was learned in economics and in Part I of this book has implications for the behavior of the financial markets over time.

KEY TERMS

callable preferred stock

capital gains

common stock

constant payout policy

convertible preferred stock

corporate equity capital

cumulative preferred stock

date of record

declaration date

distribution date

dividend payout ratio

dividend reinvestment plans (DRIPs)

ex-dividend date

Gordon model (constant dividend growth model)

marginal tax rate

nominal returns

noncumulative preferred stock

participating preferred stock

par value

preferred stock

real returns

residual dividend policy

special dividend

stock certificate

stock dividend

stock split

street name

target dividend payout policy

DISCUSSION QUESTIONS

1. Why study stocks if the net amount of stock issues is negative?

2. What are four main advantages of investing in common stock?

3. Why should investors consider common stock as an investment vehicle if they have a long-term time horizon?

4. Why does dividend income growth exceed that of bond income growth over a period of time?

5. Explain the difference in taxation between stock dividend income and bond interest income.

6. What is a capital gain? Is it taxed the same way as dividends?

7. "Taxes on capital gains can be deferred." Explain what is meant by this statement.

8. Explain how a capital loss on the sale of a firm's stock can affect an investor's taxes.

9. What is a round lot of common stock?

10. List the principal features of a stock certificate. How are stock certificates transferred from person to person?

11. Describe some of the characteristics of common stock.

12. List and briefly explain the special features usually associated with preferred stock.

13. Explain the process for issuing dividends on shares of common stock.

14. How do firms decide how much of their earnings to distribute as dividends?

15. Explain how an investor may view a stock dividend, a stock split, and a stock repurchase plan with regard to the value of his stock holdings.

16. Briefly describe how securities are valued.

17. Describe the process for valuing a preferred stock.

18. Describe the process for valuing a common stock when the cash dividend is expected to grow at a constant rate.

19. Describe the process for valuing common stock using the two-stage growth model.

20. Discuss the risks faced by common shareholders that are not related to the general level of interest rates.

21. Under what economic forecast would you believe an auto manufacturer would be a good investment? A computer manufacturer?

22. Discuss how changes in exchange rates can affect the outlook for both global and domestic firms.

23. What can looking at data on inventories tell us about the condition of the economy? Data on business expansion or investment plans?

24. Is industry competition good or bad if you are looking for attractive stock investments?

25. Give examples of firms you believe have been successful over time because of each of the following traits:

   a. They are industry leaders in quality.

   b. They are the low-cost producer.

   c. They are innovative.

   d. They offer superior customer service.

26. Energy prices are forecast to go higher. How would this affect your decision to purchase the stocks of (a) ExxonMobil? (b) American Airlines? (c) Ford? (d) Archer Daniels Midland, a food processor?

PROBLEMS

1. RCMP, Inc. shares rose 10 percent in value last year while the inflation rate was 3.5 percent. What was the real return on the stock? If an investor sold the stock after one year and paid taxes on the investment at a 15 percent tax rate, what is the real after-tax return on the investment?

2. Find the real return on the following investments:

STOCK	NOMINAL RETURN	INFLATION
A	10%	3%
B	15%	8%
C	−5%	2%

3. Find the real return, nominal after-tax return, and real after-tax return on the following:

STOCK	NOMINAL RETURN	INFLATION	TAX RATE
X	13.5%	5%	15%
Y	8.7%	4.7%	25%
Z	5.2%	2.5%	28%

4. Global Cycles (GC) offers investors a DRIP program. An investor purchases 100 shares of GC at a price of $20 per share on January 2. How many shares will the investor own on December 31 if the

following dividends are paid and the investor participates in the DRIP program (assume the firm allows fractional shares and accounts for them up to three decimal places)? If the stock's price is $27.50 on December 31, what is the value of her investment in GC?

March 1: dividend paid of $0.50 per share; stock price $21

June 1: dividend paid of $0.50 per share; stock price $22.50

September 1: dividend paid of $0.55 per share; stock price $19

December 1: dividend paid of $0.55 per share; stock price $25

5. If a stock's earnings per share are $2, what will be the dividend per share if the payout ratio is 40 percent? If the following year's earnings per share are $2.10, what will be the payout ratio if the firm wants to maintain dividend growth of 8 percent?

6. You purchased 200 shares of H2O Corporation stock at a price of $20 per share. Consider each of the following announcements separately. What will be the price of the stock after each change? How many shares will you own? What will be the total value of your holdings (value of stock plus any income)?

   a. The firm announces a 10 percent stock dividend.

   b. The firm announces a two-for-one stock split

   c. The firm announces a $0.50 per share dividend (in your answer use the price of the stock on the ex-dividend date).

   d. The firm announces it will repurchase 10 percent of its shares; you do not offer to sell any of your shares.

7. The Fridge-Air Company's preferred stock pays a dividend of $4.50 per share annually. If the required rate of return on comparable quality preferred stocks is 14 percent, calculate the value of Fridge-Air's preferred stock.

8. The Joseph Company has a stock issue that pays a fixed dividend of $3 per share annually. Investors believe the nominal risk-free rate is 4 percent and that this stock should have a risk premium of 6 percent. What should be the value of this stock?

9. The Lo Company earned $2.60 per share and paid a dividend of $1.30 per share in the year just ended. Earnings and dividends per share are expected to grow at a rate of 5 percent per year in the future. Determine the value of the stock:

   a. if the required rate of return is 12 percent.

   b. if the required rate of return is 15 percent.

   c. Given your answers to (a) and (b), how are stock prices affected by changes in investor's required rates of return?

10. The French Thaler and Company's stock has paid dividends of $1.60 over the past 12 months. Its historical growth rate of dividends has been 8 percent, but analysts expect the growth to slow to 5 percent annually for the foreseeable future.

    a. Determine the value of the stock if the required rate of return on stocks of similar risk is 15 percent.

    b. If analysts believe the risk premium on the stock should be reduced by 2 percentage points, what is the new required rate of return on French Thaler and Company stock? By how much should its price change from the answer you computed in (a)?

11. Mercier Corporation's stock is selling for $95. It has just paid a dividend of $5 a share. The expected growth rate in dividends is 8 percent.

    a. What is the required rate of return on this stock?

    b. Using your answer to (a), suppose Mercier announces developments that should lead to dividend increases of 10 percent annually. What will be the new value of Mercier's stock?

    c. Again using your answer to (a), suppose developments occur that leave investors expecting that dividends will not change from their current levels in the foreseeable future. Now what will be the value of Mercier stock?

    d. From your answers to (b) and (c), how important are investors' expectations of future dividend growth to the current stock price?

12. The common stock of RMW Inc. is selling at $88 a share. It just paid a dividend of $4. Investors expect a return of 15 percent on their investment in RMW Inc. From this information, what is the expected growth rate of future dividends?

13. Lerman Company has preferred stock outstanding. It pays an annual dividend of $10. If its current price is $70, what is the discount rate investors are using to value the stock?

14. Interpret the following stock price quote. In addition, what is Sizzler's approximate earnings per share? What was the stock's closing price the previous day?

YTD % CHG	52 WEEKS HI	52 WEEKS LO	STOCK	SYM	DIV	YLD %	PE	VOL 100s	LAST	NET CHG
+17.3	7.13	5.00	Sizzlr	SZ	0.16	2.7	25	844	6	−0.25

15. **Challenge Problem** Ritter Incorporated just paid a dividend of $2 per share. Its management team has just announced a technological breakthrough that is expected to result in a temporary increase in sales, profits, and common stock dividends. Analysts expect the firm's per-share dividends to be $2.50 next year, $3 in two years, and $3.50 in three years. After that, normal dividend growth of 5 percent is expected to resume. If shareholders expect a 15 percent return on their investment in Ritter, what should the firm's stock price be?

16. **Challenge Problem** Tough times have hit the retail store chain of Brador, Inc. Analysts expect its dividend of $1 a share to fall by 50 percent next year and another 50 percent the following year before it returns to its normal growth pattern of 3 percent a year. If investors expect a return of 18 percent on their investment in Brador stock, what should its current stock price be?

17. **EXCEL** JW Corp has a dividend of $0.50. The dividend is growing at a 6 percent rate over time. Based on the stock's risk, investors require an 11 percent rate of return.

    a. Using the constant dividend growth model, what should be the stock's price?

    b. Estimate the firm's dividends for the next ten years and find their present value. What proportion of the stock's price is based upon dividends that are expected to occur more than ten years into the future?

    c. What proportion of the firm's price is based upon dividends that are expected to occur more than five years into the future?

18. **EXCEL** A firm's dividends are expected to grow 20 percent a year for the next five years and then trend downward by 3 percentage points per year until they stabilize at a constant growth rate of 5 percent. The current dividend is $0.80 a share, and the stock's required rate of return is 13 percent. What should be its current price? If these growth expectations come to pass, what will be its price four years from now? Eight years from now?

LEARNING EXTENSION 8
Annualizing Rates of Return

An investment provides two sources of returns: income and price changes. Bonds pay coupon interest (income) and, as we saw in Chapter 7, fluctuating market interest rates can lead to changing bond prices and capital gains or losses. Stocks may pay dividends (a source of investor income) and rise or fall in value over time, leading to capital gains or losses. Such is the case with other investment vehicles, such as real estate or mutual funds.

HOLDING PERIOD RETURNS

The dollar return on a single financial asset held for a specific time, or holding period, is given by:

$$\text{Dollar return} = \text{Income received} + \text{Price change} \qquad \text{(LE8.1)}$$

Suppose that during the time Amy held a share of stock, she received dividends of $2 while the stock price rose from a purchase price of $25 to its current level of $30. Should Amy sell the stock today, her dollar return would be:

$$\text{Dollar return} = \text{Income received} + \text{Price change}$$
$$= \$2 + (\$30 - \$25)$$
$$\$7 = \$2 + \$5$$

She received $2 in dividends, and the value of her investment rose by $5 for a total dollar return of $7. To compare this investment return with others, it is best to measure the dollar return relative to the initial price paid for the stock. This percentage return is simply the dollar return divided by the initial price of the stock:

$$\text{Percentage return} = (\text{Dollar return}/\text{Initial price}) \qquad \text{(LE8.2)}$$

Amy's percentage return was:

$$\text{Percentage return} = (\text{Dollar return}/\text{Initial price}) = (\$7/\$25) = 0.28 \text{ or } 28 \text{ percent}$$

ANNUALIZED RATES OF RETURN

To compare accurately the returns on one investment with another, they should be measured over equal time periods, such as a year, a month, or a day. By convention, most investors use annual returns as a means by which to compare investments. To *annualize a return* means to state it as the annual return that would result in the observed percentage return. Equation LE8.3 gives us a formula for determining annualized returns:

$$\text{Annualized return} = (1 + \text{percentage return})^{1/n} - 1 \qquad \text{(LE8.3)}$$

where n is the number of years an investment was held.

For a one-year example, Amy's annualized return is the same as her percentage return. This can be shown as follows:

$$\text{Annualized return} = (1 + 0.28)^{1/1} - 1$$
$$= (1.28)^1 - 1 = 1.28 - 1 = 0.28 \text{ or } 28 \text{ percent}$$

Notice that the superscript fraction 1/1 indicates that Amy's investment was for one year. When investments are held for longer than one year, the fraction becomes less than one, indicating that the percentage return must be spread over a longer time period. For example, if Amy's investment was purchased two years ago, her annualized return would be:

$$\text{Annualized return} = (1 + 0.28)^{1/2} - 1$$
$$= (1.28)^{0.5} - 1 = 1.131 - 1 = 0.131 \text{ or } 13.1 \text{ percent}$$

Also notice that the annualized return is not just the 28 percent total return divided by two years, or 14 percent, which would be a simple average annual return. Rather, the annualized return measured by Equation LE8.3 also captures the compounding or discounting effects of holding investments longer than one year.

It should now be apparent that as the investment holding period lengthens, the annualized return gets progressively smaller. For example, let's now assume that Amy earned her 28 percent total return over a period of four years. Her annualized return would be calculated as:

$$\text{Annualized return} = (1 + 0.28)^{1/4} - 1$$
$$= (1.28)^{0.25} - 1 = 1.064 - 1 = 0.064 \text{ or } 6.4 \text{ percent}$$

A financial calculator can be used to simplify the calculation effort, as follows.

Financial Calculator Solution—1-Year Investment

Exponent	$1/n = 1/1 = 1$							
Input	1.28	Y^x	then	1	$=$	-1	$=$	
Solution	0.28							

Financial Calculator Solution—2-Year Investment

Exponent	$1/n = 1/2 = 0.5$							
Input	1.28	Y^x	then	0.5	$=$	-1	$=$	
Solution	0.131							

Financial Calculator Solution—4-Year Investment

Exponent	$1/n = 1/4 = 0.25$							
Input	1.28	Y^x	then	0.25	$=$	-1	$=$	
Solution	0.064							

Annualized returns also can be calculated for investments that are held for less than one year. Let's assume that Amy held her investment for only nine months while earning a percentage return of 28 percent. What would be Amy's annualized return under this scenario?

$$\text{Annualized return} = (1 + 0.28)^{1/(9/12)} - 1$$
$$= (1.28)^{1/0.75} - 1 = (1.28)^{1.33} - 1 = 1.389 - 1 = 0.389 \text{ or } 38.9 \text{ percent}$$

Because most individual and institutional investors are interested in comparing annualized returns, it is important that you know how to compute percentage returns and how to annualize them.

PROBLEMS

1. Given the following information, compute annualized returns:

ASSET	INCOME	PRICE CHANGE	INITIAL PRICE	TIME PERIOD
A	$2	$6	$29	15 months
B	0	10	40	11 months
C	50	70	30	7 years
D	3	−8	20	24 months

2. Given the following information, compute annualized returns:

ASSET	PURCHASE PRICE	CURRENT PRICE	INCOME RECEIVED	TIME PERIOD
A	$20	$26	$2	75 weeks
B	15	18	0.40	3 months
C	150	130	0	2 years
D	3.50	3.00	0.20	8 months

• CHAPTER 9 •

Securities Markets

Chapter Learning Objectives

AFTER STUDYING THIS CHAPTER, YOU SHOULD BE ABLE TO:

- Describe the processes and institutions used by businesses to distribute new securities to the investing public.
- Outline the recent difficulties and changes in structure of the investment banking industry.
- Describe how securities are traded among investors.
- Identify the regulatory mechanisms by which the securities exchanges and the over-the-counter markets are controlled.
- Explain influences that affect broker commissions.

Where We Have Been...

For the savings process to work, funds must be routed from savings to the users of funds. Banks and other financial institutions assist with this process; so do securities markets. Chapters 7 and 8 introduced us to the characteristics of stocks and bonds, how they can be priced using time value concepts, and the risks that investors face when holding them.

Supply and demand forces in financial markets set market prices for securities. Interest rates and asset prices rise and fall based upon investors' and issuers' desires to buy and sell securities.

Where We Are Going...

The process of raising funds in securities markets is important for business firms. A firm's ability to raise funds will be the topic of future chapters: long-term fund-raising is the focus of Chapter 15's capital structure discussion, and short-term financing is discussed in Chapter 17.

How This Chapter Applies to Me...

Securities markets—typically the secondary markets such as the New York Stock Exchange—are in the news every day. Stock and bond indexes reflect the changing values of securities over time. Investors' decisions and reactions to news events lead to changes in interest rates, bond prices, and stock prices. Movements in market prices affect personal wealth. Many people make decisions, either through direct investment or through their decisions regarding where to place their 401(k) or Individual Retirement Account (IRA) investments that involve the securities markets. As a financial manager, the trend in your firm's stock price over time, relative to competitors and the overall market, is a reflection of how investors view your firm's prospects.

The goal of every investor is to *buy low and sell high.* Will Rogers, the famous American humorist, gave his own thoughts on how to succeed in investing:

> Buy a stock that will go up in value. If it doesn't go up, don't buy it!

Of course, the ability to buy securities at a low price and to sell them at a higher price is the goal of every investor, but it isn't easy to do. In this chapter we'll learn how securities are issued, about the different markets in which they are traded, and how investors can buy and sell securities.

ISSUING SECURITIES: PRIMARY SECURITIES MARKETS

primary market
original issue market in which securities are initially sold

secondary market
market in which securities are traded among investors

flotation
initial sale of newly issued debt or equity securities

initial public offering (IPO)
initial sale of equity to the public

investment bankers (underwriters)
assist corporations by raising money through the marketing of corporate securities to the securities markets

public offering
sale of securities to the investing public

private placement
sale of securities to a small group of private investors

due diligence
detailed study of a corporation

prospectus
highly regulated document that details the issuer's operations and finances and must be provided to each buyer of a newly issued security

underwriting agreement
contract in which the investment banker agrees to buy securities at a predetermined price and then resell them to investors

offer price
price at which the security is sold to the investors

Recall from Chapter 1 that newly created securities are sold in the **primary market** while existing securities are traded in the **secondary market**. The initial sale of newly issued debt or equity securities is called a **flotation**; the initial sale of equity to the public is called an **initial public offering (IPO)**. To raise money, corporations usually use the services of firms, called **investment bankers (underwriters)**, whose main activity is marketing securities and dealing with the securities markets. Investment bankers act as intermediaries between corporations and the general public when corporations want to raise capital.

PRIMARY MARKET FUNCTIONS OF INVESTMENT BANKERS

Although the specific activities of investment bankers differ depending upon their size and financial resources, the functions of investment bankers include originating, underwriting, and selling newly issued securities.

Originating

Most of the larger investment banking firms engage in originating securities. As an originator, the investment bank seeks to identify firms that may benefit from a **public offering**, which is a sale of securities to the investing public, or a **private placement**, which is a sale of securities to a small group of private investors. The Securities and Exchange Commission (SEC) regulates the public offering process. The private placement process has fewer regulations, but the securities can only be sold to investors who meet certain SEC-regulated guidelines for wealth and investment knowledge. Most of this section will focus on the role of an investment bank in a public offering.

Once the investment bank identifies a firm that may want to sell securities, the investment bank attempts to sell itself to the issuer as the best investment bank to handle the offering.[1] Once an agreement is reached, the investment bank makes a detailed study (called **due diligence**) of the corporation. The investment bank uses this information to determine the best means of raising the needed funds. The investment banker will recommend the types, terms, and offering price of securities that should be sold.[2] He or she also aids the corporation in preparing the registration and informational materials required by the Securities and Exchange Commission.

One important and carefully regulated piece of information is the **prospectus**, which details the issuer's finances and must be provided to each buyer of the security. Some of the questions one chief financial officer used to quiz prospective investment banking partners for his firm's IPOs are listed in Table 9.1. These questions cover several of the underwriting, selling, and after-market aspects of the going-public process, which we will discuss below.

Another piece of advice the investment bank gives firms that want to have an initial public offering is when to go public. At times, the investing public is particularly interested in firms operating in certain industries or that develop certain technologies. Firms that go public in "hot" IPO markets—when investors are anxious to buy new issues and prices are bid up, sometimes to twice or three times their initial offering price—are likely to receive better prices for their shares than if they go public in a "cold" market when investors are less receptive to new stock issues.

Underwriting

Investment bankers not only help to sell securities to the investing public; they also sometimes assume the risk arising from the possibility that such securities may not be purchased by investors. This occurs when the investment banker enters into an **underwriting agreement** with the issuing corporation. As shown in Figure 9.1, with an underwriting agreement securities are purchased at a predetermined or "firm commitment" price by the underwriters, who then sell them to investors at the **offer price**. The difference between the offer price and the price paid by

---

1. For one firm's process of selecting an investment banker, see Alix Nyberg, "The Tough Go Shopping," *CFO* (January 2001), pp. 89–93; Orin C. Smith, "Wanted: The Right Investment Banker," *Financial Executive* (November/December 1994): pp. 14–18. Mr. Smith describes his firm's experience of "going public" when he was chief financial officer of Starbucks Coffee Company.

2. Chapter 15, "Capital Structure and the Cost of Capital," details some of the items a firm and its investment bank will consider before deciding the type of securities to be sold.

TABLE 9.1

Selections from One Firm's Quiz for Potential Investment Banking Firms Interested in Doing Its IPO

1. How would you position our company in relation to the market and its competition?
2. What companies would you choose as comparable companies from a valuation standpoint? How do you value our company and why?
3. Explain your pricing strategy for our firm's public offering and contrast it with at least four other recent IPOs that you have managed or co-managed.
4. How frequently will research reports be published during the two years following the offering? Present examples of frequency of your research for other IPOs in the last two years.
5. Under what circumstances would you stop research coverage of the company? Have you dropped coverage of any companies you have taken public in the last three years?
6. Please prepare a table that demonstrates your trading performance post-IPO for five or six high-profile IPOs that you have managed in the last twelve to eighteen months.

Source: Based upon Alix Nyberg, "The Tough Go Shopping," *CFO* (January 2001), p. 90.

spread
difference between the offer price and the price paid by the investment bank

the investment bank is called a **spread**. The spread is revenue to the investment bank, which is used to cover the bank's expenses and to provide a profit from its underwriting activities.

The issuer has virtually no price risk in a firm commitment offering once the offer price is set. The issuer receives the proceeds from the sale immediately, which it can then spend on the purposes outlined in the prospectus. The investment bank carries, or underwrites, the risk of fluctuating stock prices. The investment bank carries the risk of loss, or at least the possibility of a smaller spread than expected, should the market's perception of the issuer change or an economic event (such as an unexpected attempt by the Fed to increase interest rates) result in a stock market decline before the investment bank can sell all the securities. As we shall see in a later section, though, the phenomenon of *underpricing* or first-day price increases for IPOs is prevalent and reduces the possibility of an investment banker losing money on a firm commitment underwriting.

best-effort agreement
agreement by the investment banker to sell securities of the issuing corporation; assumes no risk for the possible failure of the flotation

Another means of offering securities is called best-effort selling. Under a **best-effort agreement**, investment bankers try to sell the securities of the issuing corporation, but they assume no risk for a possible failure of the flotation. The investment bankers are paid a fee or commission for those securities they sell. The best-effort agreement is typically used when the investment bankers anticipate that there may be some difficulty in selling the securities and they are unwilling to assume the underwriting risk. From the perspective of investors, an investment bank putting its money at risk with a firm commitment underwriting agreement would be preferable. Investors should view a best-effort offering with some concern. If the investment banker is not willing to support the firm's security sale, why should other investors?

Firms that are already public and wish to raise additional funds have several choices. They can sell additional securities by using the underwriting process, as previously discussed. They also can choose to use shelf registration, sell securities to a private party, have a rights offering, or seek competitive bids. We discuss each of these in the following paragraphs.

Shelf Registration

The Securities and Exchange Commission's (SEC) Rule 415 allows firms to register security issues (both debt and equity) and then "put them on the shelf" for sale any time over the

FIGURE 9.1

Diagram of a Firm Commitment Underwriting

succeeding two years. Once registered, the securities can be offered for sale by submitting a short statement to the SEC whenever the firm needs the funds or market conditions are attractive. The *shelf registration* process saves issuers both time and money. There is no cost or penalty for registering shelf securities and then not issuing them. Filing fees are relatively low, and the firm can take some securities from the shelf and sell them immediately through one underwriter and then sell more later with another underwriter. Not every firm can use shelf registration. Firms must meet several size, credit quality, and ethics requirements:

1. The market value of the firm's common stock must be at least $150 million.
2. It must have made no defaults on its debt in the previous three years.
3. The firm's debt must be investment grade (rated BBB or better).
4. The firm must not have been found guilty of violating the Securities Exchange Act of 1934 in the previous three years.

shelf registration
allows firms to register security issues (both debt and equity) with the SEC and have them available to sell for two years

ETHICAL ISSUES

Sell Securities to a Private Party

A publicly held firm can choose to sell securities in a private placement. To keep current shareholders from suspecting any "sweetheart deals," privately placed equity is typically sold at a slight premium to the stock's current market price.

Private equity sales may occur if the firm is the rumored or actual target of a hostile takeover. Management may try to stall the takeover or stop it by selling a large block of voting stock to an investor or syndicate that seems more friendly. Occasionally news stories contain articles of rumored deals involving firms in financial difficulty that are seeking equity infusions to keep them afloat.

Private placements of equity may also fulfill a need for an emergency infusion of equity. Since the shares are not being sold in a public offering, the private placement avoids SEC registration and subsequent publicity. The private sale must follow other SEC regulations, however. The firm must disclose the sale after it occurs, and the private investors must meet SEC requirements as "accredited investors." Basically, accredited investors are those who are considered knowledgeable enough or sufficiently strong enough financially to invest without the protection provided by the SEC's registration process. Accredited investors can include wealthy individuals with investment experience as well as financial institutions, such as insurance companies and pension funds.

Rights Offerings

Under the charters of some corporations, if additional shares of common stock, or any security that may be converted to common stock, are to be issued, the securities must be offered for sale first to the existing common stockholders. That is, the existing shareholders have **preemptive rights** to purchase newly issued securities. The purpose of this regulation is to permit existing stockholders to maintain their proportional share of ownership. Once popular in the United States, rights offerings among public corporations became infrequent during the 1980s and 1990s, although they are still used among privately held firms. On the other hand, rights offerings remain popular among public firms in Europe.

preemptive rights
securities for sale must be offered first to existing common shareholders

Competitive Bidding

State, local, and federal government bond issues, as well as those of governmental agencies, usually require competitive bidding by investment bankers before awarding underwriting agreements. This is also the case for debt and equity securities issued by some public utilities. Large, financially strong firms occasionally will announce that they are seeking competitive bids on a new security offering. Under these circumstances, there may be little initial negotiation between the investment houses and the issuer. In these cases, the issuer decides upon the size of the issue and the type of security that it wishes to sell. Then it invites the investment banking houses to offer bids for handling the securities. The investment banking group offering the highest price for the securities, while also providing information showing it will be able to carry through a successful flotation, will usually be awarded the contract.

A great deal of disagreement has existed about the relative advantages and disadvantages of competitive bidding by investment banking houses. Investment bankers strongly contend that the continuing advice they give is essential to an economical and efficient distribution of an issuer's primary market securities. Others contend that competitive bidding enables corporations to sell their securities at higher prices than would otherwise be the case.

Dutch auction
an offering process in which investors bid on prices and number of securities they wish to purchase; the securities are sold at the highest price that allows all the offered securities to be sold

INTERNET ACTIVITY

Go to http://www.openipo.com to visit the Web site of an investment bank (WR Hambrecht & Co.) that uses Dutch auctions in initial public offerings it underwrites.

A variation of competitive bidding—which usually occurs when issuers seek bids solely from investment banking firms—is the **Dutch auction** bidding process, which allows smaller firms and individual investors to purchase securities. The U.S. Treasury uses a Dutch auction; some IPOs use the Dutch auction mechanism, too. Most notable was the Google stock public offering in 2004. The process begins when the issuer and its investment banks determine a price range for the stock. After setting up an account with one of the underwriters, investors place bid prices for the number of shares they want to purchase via Internet, fax, or telephone. Bidders can place bids outside the price range if they believe demand will be higher (higher bid price) or weaker (lower bid price) than expected by underwriters. At the close of the bidding period, the underwriters determine the highest bid, or clearing price, at which all the offered shares are sold.

For example, suppose a firm, Yoogle, wants to issue 100 million shares in a Dutch auction IPO. For a simple example, assume only five bids are made:

BIDDER	PRICE	NUMBER OF SHARES
A	$20.50	25 million
B	$20.47	25 million
C	$20.45	25 million
D	$20.43	25 million
E	$20.40	25 million

The clearing price is $20.43; the number of shares to be purchased at that price or higher allows all the offered shares to be sold. Investors A, B, C, and D will be able to purchase their desired number of shares, and investor E will receive no shares in the IPO.

If two or more investors place bids at the clearing price, the offering firm can make one of three choices. First, it can increase the offering size to absorb the extra demand; second, it can sell shares on a pro-rata basis to the lowest bidders; and third, it can sell shares on a pro-rata basis to all successful bidders. To illustrate, here is what would happen if investors D and E had each placed a bid of $20.43 for 25 million shares: At the clearing price of $20.43, there are orders for 125 million shares, but only 100 million shares are offered. Under the first option, Yoogle can decide (if the prospectus gives Yoogle permission to do so) to increase the offering size to 125 million shares and sell the desired amount to each investor. With the second option, Yoogle allocates 75 million shares to bidders A, B, and C, and splits the remaining 25 million shares between bidders D and E in proportion to the size of their bids. Since they both wanted the same number of shares, the remaining shares are divided evenly, with bidders D and E each receiving 12.5 million shares. Under the third option, with 100 million shares to sell and clearing price demand for 125 million, each investor receives 100/125 or 80 percent of their desired number of shares. That is, bidders A, B, C, D, and E will receive 25 million × 0.80 shares or 20 million shares each.

Selling

The amount of securities sold in public offerings is quite large. In 2003 over $5.3 trillion of equity and debt were raised; in 2006 over $7.6 trillion worth of debt and equity securities were sold in the primary market. A list of leading investment banking firms will include Citigroup, J.P. Morgan, Deutsche Bank, Morgan Stanley, Merrill Lynch, Goldman Sachs, and UBS.[3] To assist the underwriting and best-effort process, the majority of large investment banking houses maintain "retail" outlets throughout the nation. Retail selling is selling to individual investors. There are also many independent retail brokerage outlets not large enough or financially strong enough to engage in major originating and underwriting functions. These independents may be able to assist the major investment banks in selling new issues. Like the underwriters, they depend upon the resale of securities at a price above their cost to cover expenses and provide profit from operations. A few of the large investment banking houses do not sell to individuals. Rather, they confine their activities entirely to originating, underwriting, and selling securities to institutional investors. Institutional investors are large investors such as insurance companies, pension funds, investment companies, and other large financial institutions.

---

3. The first issue of the *Wall Street Journal* each year contains a summary of the prior year's largest IPOs and leading underwriting firms.

FIGURE 9.2

A Security Offering Announcement, or Tombstone

This announcement is under no circumstances to be construed as an offer to sell or as a solicitation of an offer to buy any of these securities. The offering is made only by the Prospectus.

New Issue   December 5, 1995

10,350,000 Shares

Boston Chicken, Inc.

Common Stock

Price $34.50 Per Share

Copies of the Prospectus may be obtained from any State or jurisdiction in which this announcement is circulated from only such of the undersigned or other dealers or brokers as may lawfully offer these securities in such State or jurisdiction.

Merrill Lynch & Co.		Alex. Brown & Sons Incorporated
Dean Witter Reynolds Inc.	A.G. Edwards & Sons, Inc.	Goldman, Sachs & Co.
Montgomery Securities	Morgan Stanley & Co. Incorporated	Oppenheimer & Co., Inc.
Piper Jaffray Inc.	Prudential Securities Incorporated	Schroder Wertheim & Co.
Smith Barney Inc.		Nesbitt Burns Securities Inc.
Arnhold and S. Bleichroeder, Inc.	J. C. Bradford & Co.	Equitable Securities Corporation
EVEREN Securities, Inc.	Hanifen, Imhoff Inc.	Interstate/Johnson Lane Corporation
Janney Montgomery Scott Inc.	Edward D. Jones & Co.	Ladenburg, Thalmann & Co. Inc.
Legg Mason Wood Walker Incorporated	Principal Financial Securities, Inc.	Pryor, McClendon, Counts & Co., Inc.
Rauscher Pierce Refsnes, Inc.	Wessels, Arnold & Henderson, L.L.C.	Wheat First Butcher Singer

Regulatory authorities permit announcements of security offerings to be placed in newspapers and other publications. These announcements, called **tombstones**, are very restricted in wording and must not seem to be soliciting sales. An announcement is shown in Figure 9.2. Note that this tombstone is careful to point out that "This is neither an offer to sell nor a solicitation of an offer to buy any of these securities." The word *tombstone* apparently derives from the small amount of information it provides and the large amount of white space it features. Boston Chicken was seeking to sell 10.35 million shares of common stock at an offer price of $34.50 a share. The underwriters are shown on the bottom of the announcement in Figure 9.2.

The investment bank or banks chosen to originate and handle a flotation are called the lead bankers. In the issue shown in Figure 9.2, the two firms listed at the top, Merrill Lynch and Alex. Brown, are the lead bankers. These lead bankers formed a **syndicate** of several investment banking firms to participate in the underwriting and distribution of the issue. Syndicate members are listed under the lead bankers, in alphabetical order, in the tombstone ad. For very large issues, many firms may be part of the syndicate. For an $8 billion Kraft Foods IPO in 2001, about seventy-five firms, including the lead bankers, were part of the syndicate.

The period after a new issue is initially sold to the public is called the *aftermarket*. This period may vary from a few hours to several weeks. During this period the members of the syndicate may not sell the securities for less than the offering price. Investors who decide to sell their newly purchased securities may depress the market price temporarily, so the syndicate steps in to buy back the securities in order to prevent a larger price drop. This is called *market stabilization*. Although the Securities Exchange Act of 1934 prohibits manipulation of this sort by all others, underwriters are permitted to buy shares if the market price falls below the offering price. If market stabilization is allowed for a particular issue, it must be stipulated in the prospectus. If part of an issue remains unsold after a period of time, for example thirty days, members may leave the syndicate and sell their securities at whatever price the market will allow. The lead underwriter decides when the syndicate is to break up, freeing members to sell at the prevailing market price.

As an example of underwriting risk, at times the lead banker is left holding many more shares of an offering than it would like. Even such well-known and respected investment banks as Merrill Lynch, Goldman Sachs, and Morgan Stanley are sometimes left with substantial amounts of stock.[4] Merrill Lynch and its investment funds once owned over one-half of the outstanding shares of First USA Inc., a credit card company, more than three months after its initial public offering. Bond offerings can turn sour because of unexpected interest rate increases in the economy or credit deterioration by the firm. Convertible bonds—bonds that can be converted to shares of common stock at predetermined prices—are sometimes shunned by investors if the conversion and other features are not to their liking. Rumors were that J.P. Morgan was left owning 80 percent of a convertible bond offering in 2000 for LSI Logic, a semiconductor firm; this was at the peak of the technology bull market. As the bear market continued into 2001, other firms, including CSFB, Salomon Smith Barney, and Merrill Lynch, were still holding large stakes of convertible bond issues.[5] However, underwriting is a lucrative business; in 2006 investment bankers earned $42 billion in underwriting fees.

COST OF GOING PUBLIC

One of the drawbacks of going public is its cost. The issuing firm faces direct out-of-pocket costs for accountants' and lawyers' fees, printing expenses, and filing fees.

In addition, the firm faces two additional costs, which together represent the difference between the market value of the firm's shares in the aftermarket and the actual proceeds the firm receives from the underwriters. The first of these costs is the spread, as discussed previously. The second cost, *underpricing*, represents the difference between the aftermarket stock price and the offering price. Underpricing represents money left on the table, or money the firm could have received had the offer price better approximated the aftermarket value of the stock. For example, suppose a firm raises $15 million by selling one million shares at an offer price of $15. By the close of trading on the first day, the firm's stock price is $20. The firm's market value rose (20 − 15) × 1 million shares or $5 million. Had the securities originally been offered at $20, the firm might have received an additional $5 million for the stock. Some would argue that the firm left $5 million "on the table," financing it could have received had the stock been priced better. To view this another way, if the offer price had been $20, the firm could have raised $15 million by selling only 750,000 shares.

Studies of IPOs in the United States indicate that firms' IPOs are, on average, underpriced more if it is a smaller issue, if it is issued by a technology firm, if the firm has benefited from venture capital financing, and if the issue's underwriters are more prestigious.[6] Underpricing is

aftermarket
period of time during which members of the syndicate may not sell the securities for less than the initial offering price

market stabilization
intervention of the syndicate to repurchase securities in order to maintain their price at the offer price

INTERNET ACTIVITY

Review recent offerings and position openings at investment banking firms such as Merrill Lynch (http://www.ml.com) and Morgan Stanley (http://www.morganstanley.com).

CONCEPT CHECK

What are the three primary market functions of investment banks?

How does an underwriting agreement differ from a best-effort offering?

What is a tombstone ad?

underpricing
represents the difference between the aftermarket stock price and the offering price

4. Alexandra Peers and Craig Torres, "Underwriters Hold Huge Stakes in IPOs," *Wall Street Journal* (August 12, 1992), p. C1.

5. Suzanne McGee, "First Boston's 'Son of Tyco' Deal Goes Sour," *Wall Street Journal* (February 15, 2001), page C1, C16; Gregory Zuckerman, "Stalled Convertible: J.P. Morgan Is Left Holding $400 Million of LSI Bond Issue," *Wall Street Journal* (March 2, 2000), pp. C1, C19.

6. For reviews of these studies, see Jay R. Ritter, "Investment Bank and Securities Issuance," in George Constantinides, Milton Harris, and Rene Stulz, eds., *Handbook of the Economics of Finance* (Amsterdam: North-Holland Pub Co., 2002).

GLOBAL DISCUSSION

TABLE 9.2
Average Initial Returns for Thirty-Nine Countries

COUNTRY	SAMPLE SIZE	TIME PERIOD	AVERAGE INITIAL RETURN
Australia	920	1976–2005	20.0%
Austria	83	1984–2002	6.3%
Belgium	93	1984–2004	14.2%
Brazil	62	1979–1990	78.5%
Canada	540	1971–2002	7.0%
Chile	55	1982–1997	8.8%
China	1,124	1992–2000	267.0%
Denmark	117	1984–1998	5.4%
Finland	99	1984–1997	10.1%
France	571	1983–2000	11.6%
Germany	545	1978–2001	31.1%
Greece	363	1976–2005	25.1%
Hong Kong	857	1980–2001	17.3%
India	2,713	1990–2004	95.4%
Indonesia	265	1989–2003	20.2%
Iran	279	1991–2004	22.4%
Israel	285	1990–1994	12.1%
Italy	181	1985–2001	21.7%
Japan	1,689	1970–2001	28.4%
Korea	477	1980–1996	74.3%
Malaysia	401	1980–1998	104.1%
Mexico	37	1987–1990	33.0%
Netherlands	143	1982–1999	10.2%
New Zealand	201	1979–1999	23.0%
Nigeria	63	1989–1993	19.1%
Norway	68	1984–1996	12.5%
Philippines	104	1987–1997	22.7%
Poland	140	1991–1998	27.4%
Portugal	21	1992–1998	10.6%
Singapore	441	1973–2001	29.6%
South Africa	118	1980–1991	32.7%
Spain	99	1986–1998	10.7%
Sweden	332	1980–1998	30.5%
Switzerland	120	1983–2000	34.9%
Taiwan	293	1986–1998	31.1%
Thailand	292	1987–1997	46.7%
Turkey	282	1990–2004	10.8%
United Kingdom	3,122	1959–2001	17.4%
United States	**15,333**	**1960–2005**	**18.1%**

Source: From Tim Loughran, Jay R. Ritter, and Kristian Rydquist, "Initial Public Offerings: International Insights," *Pacific-Basin Finance Journal* (June 1994), vol. 2, pp. 165–199, updated October 24, 2006, available on http://bear.cba.ufl.edu/ritter/index.html.

not only a U.S. occurrence; Table 9.2 shows that studies in many countries find large first-day returns to IPOs, indicating underpricing. Why underpricing occurs is a matter of debate among researchers; it evidently isn't dependent upon a country's security markets, regulations, or trading mechanisms since it occurs in so many different countries. Some theories that have been proposed include cases where some investors have better information (presumably via their own research) than others regarding the attractiveness of an IPO; in order to give incentive for the uninformed investors to continue to purchase primary market equity offerings, they on average must earn profits, via underpricing. Other theories deal with irrational investor behavior: investors wanting to purchase shares but are unable to in the public offering frantically bid up the prices of shares to purchase them from those who did purchase IPO shares.

Together, these three costs—direct costs, the spread, and underpricing—are the **flotation costs** of an IPO. The flotation costs of an issue depend upon a number of factors, including the size of the offering, the issuing firm's earnings, its industry, and the condition of the stock

flotation costs
comprised of direct costs, the spread, and underpricing

TABLE 9.3

Number of Offerings and Average First-Day Returns (Underpricing) of Initial Public Offerings in 1975–2006

YEAR	NUMBER OF OFFERINGS	AVERAGE FIRST-DAY RETURN
1975	12	−1.5
1976	26	1.9
1977	15	3.6
1978	20	11.2
1979	39	8.5
1980	75	13.9
1981	197	6.2
1982	81	10.7
1983	521	9.0
1984	222	2.5
1985	216	6.2
1986	480	5.9
1987	341	5.6
1988	128	5.4
1989	119	7.9
1990	112	10.5
1991	287	11.7
1992	395	10.1
1993	505	12.7
1994	412	9.8
1995	461	21.1
1996	687	17.0
1997	483	13.9
1998	317	20.1
1999	487	69.6
2000	385	55.4
2001	81	13.7
2002	70	8.6
2003	68	12.4
2004	186	12.2
2005	169	9.8
2006	155	12.2

INTERNET ACTIVITY

Web sites of a firm involved in the Internet IPO market include WR Hambrecht & Co. (http://www.wrhambrecht.com). An information source on public offerings is http://www.ipo.com.

First-day returns are computed as the percentage return from the offering price to the first closing market price.
Source: Jay R. Ritter, "Some Factoids About the 2006 IPO Market," unpublished, (accessed December 29, 2006 at http://bear.cba.ufl.edu/ritter).

INTERNET ACTIVITY

Jay Ritter of the University of Florida's Warrington College of Business is a leading academic researcher on IPOs. His Web site, http://bear.cba.ufl.edu/ritter, offers data and recent research findings on IPOs.

market. The flotation costs, relative to the amount raised, are usually lower for a firm commitment offering than a best-efforts offering. Best-efforts offerings have higher costs for two reasons. First, typically it is higher-risk firms that utilize best-efforts offerings, so the banker charges higher fees to compensate for his extra efforts. Second, on average, best-efforts offerings raise smaller amounts of money (so the fixed costs of preparing the offering are spread over fewer shares sold). One study found that for U.S. corporations the average costs for *initial public offerings* (IPOs) of equity, not including underpricing, averaged 11.0 percent of the proceeds. For *seasoned equity offerings* (SEOs)—that is, follow-on equity offerings of firms that already have public equity outstanding—these costs averaged 7.1 percent. For convertible bonds, the costs averaged 3.8 percent. For straight debt issues, issuing costs averaged 2.2 percent, although they were sensitive to the credit rating of the issue.[7]

Studies have shown that underpricing varies over time and with IPO volume. In addition, IPO volume is cyclical: periods of frantic IPO activity alternate with periods when few firms go public. There is a close relationship between IPO volume and underpricing. Periods of "hot IPO markets" have heavy IPO volume with large underpricing; periods of low IPO volume or "cold IPO markets" show less underpricing. The data in Table 9.3 show these patterns since 1975. Note

---

7. Inmoo Lee, Scott Lochhead, Jay Ritter, and Quanshui Zhao, "The Costs of Raising Capital," *Journal of Financial Research*, vol. 19, no. 1 (Spring 1996).

the hot IPO markets in the late 1990s and the cooler markets in the early 1980s, late 1980s, and after the turn of the millennium.

Innovations Among Investment Banking Firms

As we saw in Chapters 7 and 8, investment banking firms have tried to meet the needs of both issuers and investors by developing many variations of *debt* and *equity*. As far as the process of underwriting is concerned, the Internet has had an impact, albeit relatively minor, on public offerings. Some firms have tried using the Internet as a means to sell securities to small investors and to reduce the amount of underpricing of securities. Most investment banks are large, well-capitalized firms. Investors who receive IPO shares in an offering are typically large institutional clients of the investment banks and their favored retail customers (those with large brokerage accounts who do a lot of trading). The Internet has the potential to make investors more equal by allowing them to bid for shares in Dutch auctions. By selling shares to the highest bidders, all investors are treated equally; if a small investor bids a higher price than an investment bank, she will receive her requested number of shares first. Second, by seeking bids, the hope is that the average price received by the issuing firm will exceed the price it would receive in a firm commitment underwriting. Bond offerings have been made available on the Internet, too. Internotes, Direct Access Notes, and Direct Access Bonds are examples of firms and names given to bonds sold via the Internet. Corporations, government agencies, and municipalities have issued bonds using the Internet.[8]

INTERNET ACTIVITY

Visit the sites of firms that facilitate Internet bond offerings: http://www. internotes.com, http://www. directnotes.com, and http:// www.directaccessbonds .com.

Another means of going public for a private firm is to merge with or acquire a public firm. This is how the New York Stock Exchange "went public"; it purchased the electronic communications network (ECN) firm Archipelago Holdings. The new firm combines trading technology the "old way"—on the New York Stock Exchange floor—and with modern technology.

In an example of market excess in recent years, *special purpose acquisition companies* (SPACs) have grown more popular. A SPAC is a firm that goes public but has no operations. The funds raised in the IPO are held in reserve as the SPAC's management seeks firms (private or public) to acquire. Thus, such an IPO is really buying an expectation that the SPAC's managers are competent and can soon find an attractive firm with which to merge. Ordinarily the SPAC prospectus states that if a merger or acquisition is not forthcoming within eighteen to twenty-four months the IPO funds will be returned to investors, less commissions and other fees.[9]

OTHER FUNCTIONS OF INVESTMENT BANKING FIRMS

Investment banking firms engage in many activities beyond their primary function of distributing long-term security instruments. For example, they have traditionally dominated the commercial paper market. Commercial paper is an important source of short-term financing for business that we will discuss in Chapter 17. Through buying and selling commercial paper, investment bankers assist with the short-term cash flow needs of many businesses. Four investment banking firms dominate commercial paper activities. They are Goldman, Sachs & Co.; Merrill Lynch & Co.; Credit Suisse First Boston Corporation; and Lehman Brothers.

In recent years merger and acquisition activities (M & A) have increased in importance for many investment banking firms. Firms with strong M & A departments compete intensely for the highly profitable activity of corporate mergers or acquisitions. Investment banking firms act on behalf of corporate clients in identifying firms that may be suitable for merger. Very large fees are charged for this service.

Other activities of investment bankers include the management of pension and endowment funds for businesses, colleges, churches, hospitals, and other institutions. In many cases, officers of investment banking firms are on the boards of directors of major corporations. In this capacity they are able to offer financial advice and participate in the financial planning of the firm. Investment bankers also provide financial counseling on a fee basis.

---

8. Rachel Koning, "Chicago Bonds Go Straight to Buyers," *Wall Street Journal* (September 15, 2005), p. D2; Emily S. Plishner, "E-bonds: Will They Fly?," *CFO* (March 2001), pp. 87–92; Terzah Ewing, "Too Hot an IPO? Andover.net's 252% Pop Raises Questions About Underwriter's 'Dutch Auction,'" *Wall Street Journal* (December 9, 1999), pp. C1, C23; John Thackray, "A Kinder, Gentler IPO?," *CFO* (October 1999), pp. 41–42; Silvia Ascarelli, "Investment Bank Niche Thrives for Online IPOs," *Wall Street Journal* (October 18, 1999), p. A431.

9. Karen Richardson and Peter Lattman, "Financiers Now Say 'Trust Us'," *Wall Street Journal* (February 1, 2007), p. C1.

Not all investment bankers engage in every one of these activities. The size of the firm largely dictates the various services it provides. Some firms, known as *boutiques,* specialize in only a few activities, such as mergers or underwriting IPOs for high-technology firms.

ETHICAL ISSUES

INTERNET ACTIVITY

An overview of various regulations and the EDGAR (Electronic Data Gathering and Retrieval) system for required SEC filings can be found at http://www.sec.gov.

broker

one who assists in the trading process by buying or selling securities in the market for an investor

dealer

satisfies the investor's trades by buying and selling securities from its own inventory

blue-sky laws

protect the investor from fraudulent security offerings

INVESTMENT BANKING REGULATION

Federal regulation of investment banking is administered primarily under the provisions of the Securities Act of 1933. The chief purposes of the act are (1) to provide full, fair, and accurate disclosure of the character of newly issued securities offered for sale and (2) to prevent fraud in the sale of such securities. The first purpose is achieved by requiring that the issuer file a registration statement with the Securities and Exchange Commission and deliver a prospectus to potential investors. The SEC, however, does not pass judgment on the investment merit of any securities. It is illegal for a seller of securities to represent the SEC's approval of a registration statement as a recommendation of investment quality. The philosophy behind the Securities Act of 1933 is that the most effective regulatory device is the requirement that complete and accurate information be disclosed for securities on which investment decisions may be made. Although the SEC does not guarantee the accuracy of any statement made by an issuer of securities in a registration statement or prospectus, legal action may be taken against officers and other representatives of the issuing company for any false or incorrect statements. Full disclosure is, therefore, instrumental in accomplishing the second purpose: fraud prevention.

The Securities Exchange Act of 1934 established the Securities and Exchange Commission (SEC) and gave it authority over the securities markets. All brokers and dealers doing business in the organized markets must register with the SEC. A **broker** assists the trading process by buying or selling securities in the market for an investor. A **dealer** satisfies investors' trades by buying and selling securities from his own inventory. In addition, attempts to manipulate securities prices were declared illegal.

In addition to federal regulation of investment banking, most states have **blue-sky laws** to protect investors from fraudulent security offerings. Blue-sky laws apparently get their name from the efforts of some unscrupulous operators who, if not restricted, would promise to sell investors pieces of the blue sky. Because state laws differ in their specific regulations, the federal government is the primary regulator of investment banking. The most common violation of state blue-sky laws is that of misrepresenting the financial condition and asset position of companies.

The Glass-Steagall Act of 1933 ended the ability of commercial banks to act as underwriters of newly issued securities. There were many commercial bank failures during the Great Depression, and at the time there was thought to be evidence that some of the failures resulted from the underwriting activities and poor equity investments of banks. With the passage of the Gramm-Leach-Bliley Act, the walls between commercial banking and investment banking are falling and the traditional boundaries among insurance, commercial banks, investment banks, and other financial institutions are becoming blurrier.

SMALL BUSINESS PRACTICE
Business Angels: Who Are They?

Business angels are private investors who provide start-up capital for small businesses. Angels, although wealthy individuals, seldom invest more that $100,000 in a firm. The annual investment in the angel market is estimated to be $20 billion. In addition to providing financing, angels provide valuable advice and sometimes help with the preparation of business plans. Robert Gaston completed a survey of over 400 angel investors for the U.S. Small Business Administration and found the following:

Angels typically are entrepreneurs, and over 80 percent are business owners or managers. Angels will consider small investments, are usually older than the individuals they are trying to help, and are the largest source of small business financial capital. Iris Lorenz-Fife

in *Financing Your Business* (Prentice Hall, 1997) provides valuable advice on how to attract angels and react when they respond, along with a checklist for the small business person to examine in terms of deciding whether angels are right for you.

Angels usually identify small business investment opportunities through word of mouth referrals from bankers, accountants, lawyers, and business consultants. Angels are attracted to individuals who have the drive to succeed.

When an angel responds to your business plan, make sure that you spell out the amount, timing, and length of the investment. Also spell out in advance the degree of involvement of the angel in your firm's operations.

TRADING SECURITIES: SECONDARY SECURITIES MARKETS

The primary market, we've learned, is where securities are first issued; the issuer sells the securities in an offering to investors. Any trading of the securities thereafter occurs in the secondary market. The secondary markets provide liquidity to investors who wish to sell securities. It is safe to say that, were it not for secondary securities markets for trading between investors, there would be no primary market for the initial sale of securities. Selling securities to investors would be difficult if investors had no easy way to profit from their holdings or no way to sell them for cash. They allow investors to shift their assets into different securities and different markets. Secondary markets provide pricing information, thus providing a means to evaluate a firm's management and for management to determine how investors are interpreting its actions. The secondary market for securities has two components: organized security exchanges, which have physical trading floors, and the over-the-counter market, a network of independent dealers and agents who communicate and trade electronically rather than on a trading floor. The New York Stock Exchange is the prime example of an organized exchange while NASDAQ is an over-the-counter market.

A firm that fares poorly is penalized by pressure placed on the firm's management by its stockholders as market prices of its securities fall in the secondary market. In addition, when such a firm seeks new capital, it will have to provide a higher expected return to investors. The position of a firm's management becomes increasingly vulnerable as business deteriorates. Ultimately the firm's directors may replace management, or the firm may be a target of a takeover attempt.

ORGANIZED SECURITY EXCHANGES

An organized securities exchange is a location with a trading floor where all trading takes place under rules created by the exchange. Organized exchanges in the United States include the New York Stock Exchange (NYSE) and the American Stock Exchange (AMEX), as well as several regional exchanges, such as the Boston, Chicago, Cincinnati, Philadelphia, and Pacific Stock Exchanges. Only the New York Stock Exchange and American Stock Exchange, both located in New York City, may be considered truly national in scope, although the regionals trade both local and national issues, including *dual-listed* stocks, those traded on more than one exchange.

arbitrage
purchasing a security on one exchange at one price while selling it on another

The organized stock exchanges use the latest in electronic communications. This helps to ensure an internally efficient trading mechanism whereby orders are tracked and processed quickly. It ensures that prices on the different exchanges are identical, so a trader cannot **arbitrage**, or purchase a security on one exchange at one price while selling it on another, at a different price, to lock in a riskless profit. The present methods of transmitting information within cities and between cities are in sharp contrast to the devices used before the introduction of the telegraph in 1844, when quotations were conveyed between New York and Philadelphia through signal flags in the daytime and light signals at night from high point to high point across New Jersey. Although cumbersome compared with modern methods, quotations were often transmitted in this manner in as little as ten minutes.

Because of its relative importance and because in most respects its operations are typical of those of the other exchanges, the New York Stock Exchange, sometimes called the "Big Board," will provide the basis for the following description of exchange organization and activities.

STRUCTURE OF THE NEW YORK STOCK EXCHANGE

Like all the stock exchanges in the nation, the objective of the New York Stock Exchange (NYSE) is to provide a convenient meeting place where buyers and sellers of securities or their representatives may conduct business. In addition, the NYSE provides facilities for the settlement of transactions, establishes rules for the trading processes and the activities of its members, provides publicity for the transactions, and establishes standards for the corporations whose securities are traded on the exchange.

Before it became a public firm and changed its parent firm's name to NYSE Group in March 2006, trading on the NYSE was facilitated by its 1,366 members who held "seats" on the exchange. After its merger with Archipelago Holdings and public offering, the NYSE began offering about 1,500 trading licenses for sale. The licenses—called SEATS (Stock Exchange

floor brokers
two types: house brokers and independent brokers

commission (house) brokers
act as agents to execute customers' orders for securities purchases and sales

independent brokers
independent brokers who handle the commission brokers' overflow

registered traders
buy and sell stocks for their own account

specialists
assigned dealers who have the responsibility of making a market in an assigned security

market maker
specialist who maintains an inventory of relevant securities and stands ready to buy or sell to maintain a fair and orderly market

ETHICAL ISSUES

INTERNET ACTIVITY

LaBranche and Company is a NYSE specialist firm; its Web site is http://www.labranche. com. Names of other specialist firms, and NYSE seat holders, are available on the NYSE Web site, http://www. nyse.com.

Auction Trading System) for the sake of tradition—allow members to access to the trading floor, as well as electronic trading access. Former seat holders were able to purchase trading licenses, and they also received cash and shares of the new publicly held firm valued between $4–$5 million.[10]

The NYSE has three basic types of members: specialists, floor brokers, and registered traders. In turn, there are two variations of floor brokers: commission (house) brokers and independent brokers.

The largest group of members on the NYSE is the house brokers. The key function of **house (commission) brokers** is to act as agents to execute customers' orders for securities purchases and sales. In return the broker receives a commission for the service. Merrill Lynch owns several seats used by its house brokers. **Independent brokers** handle the house brokers' overflow. When trading volume is particularly heavy, house brokers will ask an independent broker to help them in handling their orders. **Registered traders** are individuals who purchase a seat on the exchange to buy and sell stocks for their own account. Since they do their own trading, they do not pay any commissions. They may also be on retainer from a brokerage house, often a regional firm that does not want its own seat on the exchange.

Specialists, or assigned dealers, have the responsibility of making a market in an assigned security. Each stock is assigned to a specialist, who has a trading post on the exchange floor.[11] All trades in a specialist's assigned stock need to take place at the specialist's post. As a **market maker**, the specialist maintains an inventory of the security in question and stands ready to buy or sell to maintain a fair and orderly market. That means the specialist must be ready to purchase shares of the assigned stock when there are many sellers and must be willing to sell shares when traders want to buy. Exchange regulations require the specialist to maintain an orderly market, meaning that trading prices should not change by more than a few cents (stocks are traded in decimals, so the smallest difference in price can be one cent). The specialist maintains bid-and-asked prices for the security, and the margin between the two prices represents the specialist's gross profit. The bid price is that price the buyer is willing to pay for the securities (thus, it represents the investor's selling price). The ask price is the price at which the owner is willing to sell securities (thus, it represents the investors' purchase price). If the current bid price from brokers is 50.00 and the current ask price is 50.05, the specialist may enter a bid of 50.02 or 50.03 or a lower ask price in order to lower the spread and maintain market order.

A penny may not seem like much, but an extra penny per share profit on the billion shares traded each day on the NYSE can add to a sizable sum. Specialist firms have been accused of placing their own interests above those of their customers. Front-running occurs when a specialist trades to take advantage of information it has (but others do not) about large buy or sell orders that will soon be placed. An example would be buying a stock for $23.27 while knowing that in a few minutes a customer will place a large buy order that will likely push the price higher to $23.30 or $23.32.

Another example of profiting from trades is *negative obligation*, which occurs when a specialist intervenes in a trade when that assistance is unnecessary. It occurs when a specialist buys shares from a seller then immediately sells them to a buyer at a higher price. The specialist should have allowed the two traders to trade between themselves without the specialist making a profit. In 2004, the NYSE and SEC fined five specialist firms $240 million for such tactics. The NYSE received sanctions, too, from the Securities and Exchange Commission and was forced to add staff and funds to increase its oversight of regulations and trading.

Other exchanges face ethics issues, too. We discuss the NASDAQ over-the-counter market in the section entitled "Over-the-Counter Market" on page 242; in the late 1990s, two dozen firms involved in NASDAQ trading were accused of setting unfairly high trading commissions and were fined a total of $900 million.

---

10. Associated Press, "NYSE Approves Merger with Electronic Trading Company http://www.iht.com/Articles/2005/12/07/News/Web.1207.Nyse.php (accessed February 11, 2007); Liz Moyer, "A Piece of the Action," http://www.forbes.com/management/2005/11/14/nyse-merger-lawsuit-cx_lm_1115nyse.html (accessed February 11, 2007).

11. More correctly, the listed firm chooses which specialist firm to use. The seven specialist firms are Banc of America Specialists; Bear Wagner Specialists; Kellogg Specialists; LaBranche & Co.; SIG Specialists; Spear, Leeds and Kellogg Specialists; and Van Der Moolen Specialists.

bid
price offered by a potential buyer

ask
price requested by the seller

spread
difference between the bid and ask prices

Listing Securities

All securities must be listed before they may be traded on the New York Stock Exchange. To qualify for listing its security, a corporation must meet certain requirements regarding profitability, total value of outstanding stock, or stockholder's equity. Over time the NYSE revamped its listing standards in an attempt to attract more high-growth firms (which had been favoring the NASDAQ over-the-counter market for listings) and more foreign companies. The new standards are summarized in Table 9.4. The corporation also pays a fee for the privilege of being listed. The original listing fee ranges from $150,000 to $250,000. Continuing annual fees range from $35,000 to $500,000, depending on the number of outstanding shares. The acceptance of the security by the exchange for listing on the Big Board does not constitute endorsement of its quality.

The American Stock Exchange and all the regional exchanges permit unlisted trading privileges, as well as listed trading privileges. The distinction between these two lies primarily in the method by which the security is placed on the exchange for trading. For unlisted securities, the exchange itself (instead of the issuing corporation) recommends the securities for trading privileges. The SEC must approve unlisted trading privileges. The securities of approximately 1,000 corporations carry unlisted trading privileges on the nation's stock exchanges.

Security Transactions

Buying and selling securities is similar to buying and selling other items in a negotiated market. Whether you want to sell a house or a car, you have a price you are asking potential buyers to pay. Buyers of your house or car will likely not want to pay your price but will offer their own price, a bid, to see if you will agree to sell your item for a lower price. In security transactions, potential buyers place **bid** prices, as in an auction, and sellers have their **ask** prices. The difference between the lower bid and higher ask is the **spread**. The narrower the spread, the more liquid the market and the quicker a transaction can be made.

TABLE 9.4
New York Stock Exchange Listing Requirements

NYSE, U.S. FIRMS	NYSE, NON-U.S. FIRMS
Number of Shareholders, Trading Volume, and Market Value	
I. (a) 2,000 owners of 100 shares; *or* (b) 2,200 total shareholders and average monthly trading volume in the past 6 months of 100,000 shares; *or* (c) 500 shareholders with average monthly trading volume over the past year of 1,000,000 shares II. 1.1 million shares outstanding III. Market Value: $100 million ($60 million for IPOs)	I. (a) 5,000 owners of 100 shares worldwide; (b) 2.5 million shares outstanding worldwide; *and* (c) market value of $100 million worldwide
Earnings, Cash Flow, and Revenues	
I. Pretax earnings of $10.0 million in past three years, with $2.0 million in each of the two preceding years; *or* II. Positive operating cash flow in each of last three years with a cumulative total of $25 million for these years; *or* III. Revenues of $75 million for the past year and an average market capitalization (number of shares × stock price) of $750 million	I. Pretax earnings of $100 million in past three years, with $25 million in each of the two most recent years; *and* II. Cumulative operating cash flow of $100 million over the past three years with at least $25 million in each of the two most recent years with an average market capitalization of $500 million; *or* III. Revenues of $75 million for the past year and an average market capitalization of $750 million

CONCEPT CHECK

How do secondary securities markets assist the function of primary markets?

Describe the four types of members of the New York Stock Exchange.

Internet sites inform us (with a time delay, unless you purchase access to real-time data) what the bid and ask prices for a security are throughout the day. For example, a quote from such a site for Microsoft stock may show:

Bid: 30.42 × 50900
Ask: 30.43 × 50800

This means that there is demand for 50,900 shares by potential buyers at that point during the day and that the highest bid price for Microsoft shares is $30.42. There are 50,800 shares offered for sale at that time, and the lowest asking price is $30.43. With trading in pennies, this is the tightest spread possible since only one cent separates the bid and ask prices. This shows that Microsoft stock, at least in this snapshot of time, is quite liquid.

Investors can place a number of different types of orders to buy or sell securities. In order to trade, they need to contact a stock brokerage firm where they can set up an account. The investor can then specify the type of order to be placed, as well as the number of shares to be traded in specific firms. Securities orders to buy and sell can be market, limit, or stop-loss orders.

Market Order

market order
open order of an immediate purchase or sale at the best possible price

An order for immediate purchase or sale at the best possible price is a **market order**. The brokerage firm that receives an order to trade shares of stock listed on the New York Stock Exchange at the best price possible transmits the order to its New York office, where the order is transmitted to its commission broker on the floor of the exchange.

Limit Order

limit order
maximum buying price (limit buy) or the minimum selling price (limit sell) specified by the investor

In a **limit order**, the maximum buying price (limit buy) or the minimum selling price (limit sell) is specified by the investor. For example, if a commission broker has a limit buy order at 50 from an investor and other brokers have ask prices higher than 50, the order could not be filled at that moment. The broker will wait until a price of 50 or less becomes available. Usually any limit order that is not quite close to the current market price is turned over to the specialist, who places it in his or her **central limit order book**. The specialist will make the trade for the commission broker when the price comes within the limit. Of course, if the price of the stock progresses upward rather than downward, the order will not be completed. Limit orders may be placed to expire at the end of one day, one week, one month, or on a good-until-canceled basis.

central limit order book
limit "book" in which the specialist keeps unexecuted limit orders

Stop-Loss Order

stop-loss order
order to sell stock at the market price when the price of the stock falls to a specified level

A **stop-loss order** is an order to sell stock at the market price when the price of the stock falls to a specified level. The stockholder may protect gains or limit losses due to a fall in the price of the stock by placing a stop-loss order at a price a few points below the current market price. For example, an investor paying $50 for shares of stock may place a stop-loss order at a price of $45. If the price does fall to $45, the commission broker sells the shares for as high a price as possible. This order does not guarantee a price of $45 to the seller, since by the time the stock is actually sold, a rapidly declining stock price may have fallen to well below $45. On the other hand, if the stock price does not reach the specified price, the order will not be executed.

These orders can be used to protect profits. If the stock increases in price after its purchase, the investor can cancel the old stop-loss order and issue a new one at a higher price.

Short Sale

short sale
sale of securities that the seller does not own

A **short sale** is sale of securities that the seller does not own. An investor will want to short a stock if she feels the price will decline in the future. Shares of the stock are borrowed by the broker and sold in the stock market. In the event that a price decline does occur, the short seller covers the resulting short position by buying enough stock to repay the lender. If any dividends are paid during the time the stock is shorted, the short seller must pay the dividends owed on the borrowed shares.

street name
an investor's securities are kept in the name of the brokerage house to facilitate record keeping, settlement, safety against loss or theft, and so on

For example, suppose Amy thinks AT&T's stock price will fall in the future because of intense competition in the telecommunications industry. She contacts her broker, for example Merrill Lynch, and gives instructions to sell 100 shares of AT&T short. The broker in turn arranges to borrow the necessary stock, probably from another Merrill Lynch investor who has the stock in **street name**, meaning that the investor keeps the stock certificates at the brokerage firm rather than having personal possession of them. Having sold the borrowed stock, the brokerage house keeps the proceeds of the sale as collateral. In this example, if the securities were sold at $40, Merrill Lynch would keep the proceeds from the 100 shares, $4,000, in Amy's account. Let's say the stock drops to a price of $36 and Amy wants to cover her short position. She tells her broker to buy 100 shares, which costs her $3,600. Merrill Lynch returns the newly purchased shares to the account from which they were borrowed. Amy sold $4,000 worth of stock and purchased $3,600 worth of stock after it fell in price; the difference, $400, is Amy's profit, ignoring broker- age commissions. The person from whose account the shares were borrowed will never know that they were borrowed; Merrill Lynch's internal record keeping will keep track of all such transactions.

If the price of AT&T stock rises, the short seller must still cover her short position at some future time. If the price rises to $45 a share and the position is closed, Amy will pay $4,500 to purchase 100 shares to cover her position. Amy will suffer a loss of $4,000–$4,500, or $500, from her short sale.

Because short sales have an important effect on the market for securities, the SEC regulates them closely. Heavy short sale trades can place undue pressure on a firm's stock price. Among the restrictions on short sales is one relating to selling only on an up-tick. This means that a short sale can take place only when the last change in the market price of the stock from transaction to transaction was an increase. For example, if the most recent transaction prices were 39.95, 39.95, 40.00, 40.00, 40.00, the short sale would be allowed as the last price change was an increase. A short sale would not be allowed if the most recent transactions prices were, for example, 40.07, 40.01, 40.00 or 40.10, 40.00, 40.00, since the most recent price change was a decrease.

In addition, both Federal Reserve System and New York Stock Exchange regulations require the short seller to maintain a margin or deposit of at least 50 percent of the price of the stock with the broker. Loans of stock are callable on twenty-four hours notice.

Buying on Margin

buying on margin
investor borrows money and invests it along with his or her own funds in securities

Buying on margin means that the investor borrows money and invests it along with his own funds in securities. The securities so purchased become collateral for the loan. The *margin* is the minimum percentage of the purchase price that the investor must pay in cash. In other words, margin is the ratio of the investor's equity (own money) to the market value of the security. To buy on margin, the investor must have a margin account with the brokerage firm, which in turn arranges the necessary financing with banks.

margin
minimum percentage of the purchase price that must represent the investor's equity or unborrowed funds

Margin trading is risky; it magnifies the profits as well as the losses from investment positions. For example, suppose an investor borrows $20,000 and combines it with $30,000 of his own money to purchase $50,000 worth of stocks. His initial margin is 60 percent ($30,000 of his own money divided by the $50,000 value of the securities). Should the market value of his stock rise 10 percent to $55,000, the value of his equity rises to $35,000:

Market value of securities	$55,000
Less: borrowed funds	$20,000
Value of investor's position	$35,000

This increase in value to $35,000 represents a gain of 16.7 percent ($5,000/$30,000). A 10 percent rise in the stock's value increased the value of the investor's position by 16.7 percent because of the use of margin.

Margin also magnifies losses. If the value of the securities falls by 10 percent to $45,000, the value of the investor's equity would fall to $25,000:

Market value of securities	$45,000
Less: borrowed funds	$20,000
Value of investor's position	$25,000

margin call
investor faces the option of either closing the position or investing additional cash to increase the position's equity or margin

This loss in value to $25,000 represents a loss of 16.7 percent. A 10 percent fall in the stock's value decreased the value of the investor's position by 16.7 percent because of the use of margin.

Should the value of the securities used as collateral in a margin trade begin to decline, the investor may receive a **margin call** from the brokerage firm. The investor will face a choice of either closing out the position or investing additional cash to increase the position's equity or margin. If the market price of the pledged securities continues to decline and the investor fails to provide the new margin amount, the brokerage house will sell the securities. Under current Federal Reserve regulations, investors must have an ***initial margin*** of at least 50 percent when entering into a margined trade. The minimum ***maintenance margin*** to which the position can fall is 25 percent before the broker will have to close out the position. Depending upon the individual investor's creditworthiness, a brokerage firm can impose more stringent margin requirements.

The combination of falling prices, margin calls, and sales of securities can develop into a downward spiral for securities prices. This kind of spiral played an important role in the stock market crash of 1929. At that time there was no regulatory restraint on margin sales and, in fact, margins of only 10 percent were common.

Record Keeping

When a trade takes place, the information is sent to a central computer system that, in turn, sends the information to display screens across the nation. This consolidated report includes all transactions on the New York Stock Exchange, as well as those on the regional exchanges and other markets trading NYSE-listed stocks. Trades can be for a ***round lot*** of 100 shares or an ***odd lot***, a trade of less than 100 shares.[12] The details of the purchase transaction are also sent to the central office of the exchange and then to the brokerage office where the order was originally placed. Trade information is also sent to the registrar of the company whose shares were traded. The company needs this information so new certificates can be issued in either the name of the investor or the brokerage firm (if the shares are to be kept in street name). Likewise, records will be updated so dividends, annual reports, and shareholder voting material can be sent to the proper person.

A security is bought in *street name* when the brokerage house buys the security in its own name on behalf of the investor. The advantage of this is that the investor may sell securities by simply phoning the broker without the necessity of signing and delivering the certificates. New regulations imposed in 1995 require stock trades to be settled in three days. Before this regulation, settlement did not have to take place until five days after the trade. This "T+3" requirement means funds to purchase shares or stock certificates of shares that were sold must be presented to the stockbroker within three days of the stock trade. This shorter settlement time should make street name accounts more appealing to investors. Plans are underway for a "T+1" one-day settlement requirement, and hopes exist for an all-electronic process that would make settlement immediate.

Program Trading

Around 1975 stocks began to be traded not only individually but also in packages or programs. ***Program trading*** is a technique for trading stocks as a group rather than individually; it is defined as the trading for a group of at least fifteen different stocks with a value of at least $1 million. At first program trades were simply trades of any portfolio of stocks held by an equity manager who wanted to change the portfolio's composition for any number of reasons. Today the portfolios traded in package form are often made up of the stocks included in a stock index, such as the Standard & Poor's 500. In 2006, nearly 50 percent of all NYSE trading volume was program trades, but it was not unusual for that percentage to rise to 70 percent or more during times of volatile market prices. The most active program traders include Morgan Stanley, Merrill Lynch, UBS, Credit Suisse First Boston, and Goldman Sachs.

A wide range of portfolio trading strategies is now described as program trading. The best known form of program trading is known as *index arbitrage,* when traders buy and sell stocks with offsetting trades in futures and options in order to lock in profits from price differences between these different markets.[13] In much of the 1990s, about 20–30 percent of program trading was because of index arbitrage. Program traders use computers to keep track of prices in the different markets and to give an execution signal when appropriate. At the moment the signal is given, the orders for the stocks are sent directly to the NYSE trading floor for execution by the

---

initial margin
initial equity percentage

maintenance margin
minimum margin to which an investment may fall before a margin call will be placed

round lot
sale or purchase of 100 shares

odd lot
sale or purchase of less than 100 shares

INTERNET ACTIVITY

Examples of how trades are placed can be found on the Web sites of several exchanges, including http://www.nyse.com and http://www.nasdaq.com.

program trading
technique for trading stocks as a group rather than individually; defined as a minimum of at least fifteen different stocks with a minimum value of $1 million

---

12. For a few high-priced stocks listed on the New York Stock Exchange, a round lot is ten shares.

13. Futures and options are discussed in this chapter's Learning Extension.

CONCEPT CHECK

How does a limit order differ from a stop order?

How does a short sale work?

What does "buying on margin" mean?

proper specialist. The use of computers allows trades to be accomplished more quickly. This can cause problems if price movements trigger simultaneous sales orders by a number of large program traders. A serious plunge in market prices may occur. As a result, efforts have been made to control some aspects of program trading by limiting its use on days when the Dow Jones Industrial Average rises or falls more than 180 points (in spring 2007; this limit is reset quarterly based on the level of the Industrial Average. Current values are available at http://www.nyse.com/press/circuit_breakers.html).

Over-the-Counter Market

In addition to the organized exchanges, the other major secondary market for securities trading is the *over-the-counter market* or OTC. The largest OTC market is the NASDAQ system; "NASDAQ" stands for National Association of Securities Dealers Automated Quotation system. Although the NASDAQ trades more than twice as many issues as the NYSE, the OTC is comprised mainly of stocks of smaller firms, although companies such as Intel, Microsoft, Novell, and Apple Computer are listed on it.

There are several differences between the organized exchanges and the OTC market. Organized exchanges have a central trading location or floor, such as the NYSE trading floor on Wall Street in New York City. The OTC is a telecommunications network linking brokers and dealers that trade OTC stocks. The organized exchanges have specialists that make markets and control trading in listed stocks; the OTC has no specialists. Instead, OTC dealers buy from and sell for their own account to the public, other dealers, and commission brokers. In a sense, they operate in the manner of any merchant. They have an inventory, comprised of the securities in which they specialize, that they hope to sell at a price enough above their purchase price to make a profit. The OTC markets argue that theirs is a competitive system, with multiple dealers making a market in a company's stock.

INTERNET ACTIVITY

The NASDAQ Web site is http://www.nasdaq.com.

To trade in an OTC stock, an investor contacts his broker, who then checks a computer listing of dealers for that particular stock. After determining which dealer has the highest bid price or lowest ask price, the broker contacts the dealer to confirm the price and to execute the transaction.

The OTC market is regulated by the Maloney Act of 1938. This act amended the Securities Exchange Act of 1934 to extend SEC control to the OTC market. The law created the legal basis for OTC brokers and dealers to form national self-regulating trade associations. This was one instance where business itself requested government regulation. It stemmed from the fact that honest dealers in the investment field had little protection against bad publicity resulting from the unscrupulous practices of a few OTC dealers. Under this provision one association, the National Association of Security Dealers (NASD), was formed. All rules adopted by the NASD must be reported to the SEC. The SEC has the authority to take away any powers of the NASD.

ETHICAL ISSUES

The NASD has established a lengthy set of rules and regulations intended to ensure fair practices and responsibility on the part of the association's members. Any broker or dealer engaged in OTC activities is eligible to become a member of the NASD as long as it can prove a record of responsible operation and the broker or dealer is willing to accept the NASD code of ethics.

Third and Fourth Security Markets

It should not be surprising that an activity as broad as the security market would give rise to special arrangements. Despite their names, the third and fourth markets are two additional types of secondary markets that have evolved over time.

The **third market** is a market for large blocks of listed shares that operates outside the confines of the organized exchanges. In the third market, blocks of stock (units of 10,000 shares) are traded OTC. The participants in the third market are large institutions (such as mutual funds, insurance companies, and pension funds) that often need to trade large blocks of shares. Brokers assist the institutions in the third market by bringing buyers and sellers together and, in return, receive a fee.

The **fourth market** is even further removed from the world of organized securities trading. Electronic communications networks, or ECNs, are computerized trading systems that automatically match buy and sell orders at specified prices. Certain large institutional investors arrange purchases and sales of securities among themselves without the benefit of a broker or dealer. They subscribe to an electronic network in which offers to buy or sell are made known to other

third market
market for large blocks of listed stocks that operates outside the confines of the organized exchanges

fourth market
large institutional investors arrange the purchase and sale of securities among themselves without the benefit of broker or dealer

subscribers. The offers are made in code, and institutions wishing to accept a buy or sell offer know the identity of the other party only upon acceptance of the offer. A fee is paid to the network provider when the trade is completed. Those who support fourth-market trading argue that transfers are often quicker and more economical, but the confidentiality is also an important feature to many firms.

WHAT MAKES A GOOD MARKET?

NYSE, AMEX, NASDAQ, third market, fourth market—what are the requirements for a good market? What makes one market better for trading than another for a certain type of transaction?

Competition exists in our product markets. For example, the local Wal-Mart store is a marketplace for buying and selling goods—except that Wal-Mart is the lone seller and we, the consumers, are the buyers. Other large stores nearby compete for the consumer dollar, wanting you to enter their store and to "trade" with them.

Competition exists among exchanges, too. The NYSE, NASDAQ, and others are encouraging firms to list their shares with them so the exchange benefits from the trading volume. For example, the NYSE has been perceived as listing only quality firms that have many shareholders and a history of financial success, as seen in the listing requirements in Table 9.4. The NASDAQ has allowed smaller firms and those without a financial track record to list with it. The NASDAQ's emphasis over time on technology (as trading occurs via market makers and computers rather than in a physical location) has attracted many "high tech" firms, such as Microsoft, Intel, Cisco Systems and Dell Computer, to list their shares on the NASDAQ.

One exchange will boast of quicker execution of trades to encourage investors to trade securities on that exchange rather than a competitor's. For example, the NASDAQ has argued that its technology will allow faster trade execution than the NYSE's specialist system. Over time, the NYSE has responded by automating some trades that did not require interaction with a specialist.

A good market will have four characteristics: liquidity, quick and accurate execution of trades, reasonable listing requirements, and low costs. Let's discuss each of these in turn.

A market is *liquid* if trades are executed quickly at a price close to fair market value. Generally, a market needs to have breadth and depth to be liquid. If a market is liquid, it will have tighter (or smaller) bid–ask spreads.

A market has depth if it can absorb large buy and sell orders without disrupting prices. This may mean there are investors with deep pockets willing to take the opposite side of a large trade or there are many traders each of whom is willing to help execute the trade. A broad market, or one with breadth, attracts many traders. In general, having many traders make a market more competitive; a few large traders may be able to set prices in their own favor rather than allowing competitive forces to determine price levels. Generally, trading is more liquid if the difference between the bidder's buy and the seller's ask price is small. Otherwise, large price jumps can occur, depending on how anxious a trader is to execute his buy or sell order.

The second characteristic, *quick and accurate execution of trades,* is reasonably self-explanatory. The quicker the sale or purchase is executed, the quicker the investor can receive confirmation and know the transaction price. Studies have indicated that small stock transactions done electronically average one-tenth of a second to execute, whereas larger transactions can take up to ten seconds.[14] Size of the trade, the liquidity of the stock, and the venue affect the transaction time. Computer trading is quickest, NYSE specialist trading is the slowest, with NASDAQ dealers lying in-between, but a quick transaction does not meet the investor's need without good record keeping to verify the price of the transactions. Portfolio managers (to measure the performance of their stock selections) and individual traders (for tax records) need accurate transaction records.

Reasonable listing requirements allow investors to know the quality of the firms that are listed. The NYSE has the highest standards, in terms of stock ownership, earnings, and cash flow, but many firms that could meet the NYSE standards decide to list their shares elsewhere, believing costs may be cheaper and investor trade execution faster on another exchange. Nonetheless,

14. Gregory Crawford, "Inconsistency Haunts Investor Equity Trades, Report Says," *Pensions and Investments* (January 9, 2006), p. 28.

INTERNET ACTIVITY

Examples of ECNs are Instinet, http://www.instinet.com, and Arcavision (now part of the NYSE) http://www.arcavision.com.

CONCEPT CHECK

How does trading OTC differ from trading at the New York Stock Exchange?

How do the third and fourth markets differ from the New York Stock Exchange?

PERSONAL FINANCIAL PLANNING
Stock Market Indexes

"What did the market do today?" is an often-heard question in financial circles. Although the question sounds ambiguous (Which market?), the speakers and their intended listener know which market: the stock market, specifically the performance of the Dow Jones Industrial Average (DJIA). As we mention in this chapter, the DJIA is comprised of only thirty firms, but they are thirty very large firms whose market capitalization (that is, the number of shares multiplied by the stock price) is quite large compared to those of other firms. There are literally dozens of stock market indexes, and even more examples of indexes abound for the bond markets.

Indexes are very popular for several reasons. First, they are a means of representing the movement and returns to the overall market or a segment of the market. The DJIA 30, S&P 500, and Wilshire 5000 are measures of stock market performance. The NYSE, AMEX, and NASDAQ indexes measure performance of the New York, American, and OTC stock markets.

Second, indexes are a useful comparison when you want to benchmark the performance of a portfolio. If your investment advisor recommends a portfolio of stocks that rose 10 percent in value while the S&P 500 rose 20 percent, you may feel his recommendations weren't too good. On the other hand, if his selections were all OTC stocks and the NASDAQ index rose only 5 percent, you may judge his performance more favorably.

Third, indexes themselves are gaining popularity as investments. Rather than try to invest to "beat the market"—which is difficult to do, as we'll see in Chapter 10 with the discussion of efficient capital markets—more and more investors are believing the saying "If you can't beat them, join them." They are choosing to invest in the stocks and bonds that comprise an index in the hope of matching the index's performance over time. Many mutual funds exist so the small investor can do this quickly and easily just by purchasing shares of the mutual fund.

CONCEPT CHECK

What are four characteristics of a good market?

How do market breadth and market depth differ?

the average size and profitability are lower for NASDAQ firms than for NYSE firms. The *pink sheet* (an OTC market, now computerized, that started trading speculative issues listed on pink sheets of paper) has no listing fees and has quotes provided only by dealers making a market in the stock; the firm has little role to play.[15] Its securities will be fairly speculative.

Finally, a good market will offer reasonable listing fees to issuers (lest it price itself out of the market for listings) and *low costs* to traders. Costs to investors include the commissions paid for stock or bond purchases but also "hidden" costs. Hidden costs include the lack of breadth (i.e., many traders) so a buyer must pay the higher ask price for the security (or the seller must accept the lower bid price). Another hidden cost includes price pressure, which is another indicator of a market that lacks good liquidity. Price pressure occurs with a large trade moving the market before it can be fully executed. Professional traders learn to parcel out large trades into smaller trades and to work with several dealers or market makers to minimize price changes that occur because of the large transaction, but a market that can absorb such trades is a benefit to investors.

A WORD ON COMMISSIONS

It costs money to trade securities. About the only market participants who don't pay commissions are the exchange specialists and registered traders on the NYSE and dealers in OTC stocks.

Stock commissions vary from brokerage firm to brokerage firm. Some brokerage firms, those called "full-service" brokerages, not only assist your trades but also have research staffs that analyze firms and make recommendations on which stocks to buy or sell. Their analysts write research reports that are available to the firm's brokerage customers. Examples of full-service brokerages include Merrill Lynch, A.G. Edwards, and Morgan Stanley.

INTERNET ACTIVITY

Merrill Lynch (http://www. ml.com) is a full-service broker; Charles Schwab (http://www.schwab.com) is a premier discount broker that offers stock trading, some research, mutual funds, annuities, and life insurance. An example of an online broker is http://www.etrade.com.

"Discount" brokerages are for investors who just want someone to do their stock transactions. Investors who do not desire or need the extra services of a full-service broker use discounters. The stereotypical discount investor makes his or her own investment decisions and wishes to trade at the lowest possible costs. Examples of discount brokerages include Brown and Company, Charles Schwab, Muriel Siebert, and Olde Discount.

A new innovation that is shaking up the traditional stock brokerage industry is the deep discount broker and the ability to trade stocks over the Internet. With low overhead costs and offers of basic services, stock trading on some Internet-based brokerages are quite inexpensive, even compared to discount brokers. Falling commissions and ease of access make online trading

---

15. "Yellow sheets" refer to over-the-counter bond market quotations for smaller and lower-quality bond issues.

attractive to those who make their own investment decisions. Trading commissions for some online brokerages are under $7 a trade.

Commissions on security trades depend upon several additional factors. Commissions generally are lower on more liquid securities (more actively traded securities or securities with a popular secondary market). Commissions generally are higher, as a proportion of the market value of the securities purchased, for smaller trades that involve fewer shares or lower-priced shares. Many brokerages charge a minimum commission that may make small trades relatively costly. They also charge a transaction fee to cover their costs of processing the trade. Others assess fees if your account is inactive for a year; in other words, even if you don't trade, you still pay the broker some fees. As with so many other things in life, a wise investor will shop around for the brokerage firm and broker that best meets his or her particular needs.

It is possible to buy shares of some companies without going through a stockbroker. Some firms sell their shares directly to the public; this is called *direct investing*. Other firms allow shareholders to add to their stock holdings through dividend reinvestment plans; as the name implies, the shareholder's dividends are used to purchase shares (including partial or fractional shares) of the firm.

CONCEPT CHECK

What factors affect the size of a commission on a trade?

Why has stock trading on the Internet increased so rapidly in recent years?

SECURITY MARKET INDEXES

If one listens to the radio, watches television, or reads the newspaper, the words "Dow Jones Industrial Average" or "Standard & Poor's 500 Stock Index" will be encountered daily. The thirty stocks that are part of the Dow Jones Industrial Average are listed in Table 9.5. You are probably familiar with most of their names.

Market indexes are useful for keeping track of trends in an overall market (such as the NYSE index, which tracks all stocks listed in the NYSE) or a sector (the S&P 400 industrials summarizes the movements in 400 stocks of industrial firms) or specific industries (Dow Jones's various industry indexes, such as banks, autos, chemicals, retail, and many others). Market indexes exist for many countries' securities markets, including a variety of both stock and bond market indexes.

There are many ways in which an index can be constructed; the previous paragraph shows that indexes can cover different security market segments. Indexes also can be computed in different ways. For example, the Dow Jones Industrial Average of thirty large "blue-chip" stocks is based upon a sum of their prices; it is an example of a price-weighted index. The S&P 500 stock index is computed in part by summing the market values—the stock price times the number of shares outstanding—of the 500 component stocks; it is an example of a value-weighted index. Still other indexes are based upon other computational schemes.

The 500 stocks comprising the S&P 500 are not the largest 500 firms or the 500 stocks with the largest market values. A nineteen-member committee of Standard & Poor's Corporation selects the stocks in the index. The committee tries to have each industry represented in the S&P 500 index in proportion to its presence among all publicly traded stocks. Most of the changes that occur in the S&P 500 index occur because of firms' mergers, acquisitions, or bankruptcies. Because it is an index based upon market values, large market-value firms, or "large capitalization" stocks as they are called, are the main influences on the index's movements over time.

TABLE 9.5

Stocks in the Dow Jones Industrial Average (as of July 2007)

Alcoa	Altria	American Express
American International Group	AT&T	Boeing
Caterpillar	Citigroup	Coca-Cola
DuPont	ExxonMobil	General Electric
General Motors	Hewlett Packard	Home Depot
Honeywell	IBM	Intel
Johnson & Johnson	J P Morgan Chase	McDonald's
Merck	Microsoft	3M
Pfizer	Procter and Gamble	United Technologies
Verizon	Wal-Mart	Walt Disney

Bond indexes exist, too; Lehman Brothers (Treasury bonds) and Merrill Lynch (corporate bonds) publish bond indexes that show trends in their respective markets. Indexes will favor intermediate-term Treasury securities, longer-term agencies, and corporate bonds.

FOREIGN SECURITIES

The growth in the market value of foreign securities has occurred because of general economic expansion, deregulation of exchange rates, and liberalization of the regulation of equity markets. The integration of the world's markets is emphasized by the fact that many securities are listed on several markets. The London Stock Exchange, for example, has over 500 foreign listings, of which about 200 are U.S. firms. The major U.S. stock markets—the NYSE, AMEX, and NASDAQ—trade about 600 foreign stocks. Foreign stocks can be traded in the United States if they are registered with the Securities and Exchange Commission.

Foreign companies raise funds in the United States for reasons similar to why U.S. firms will tap overseas markets: to gain access to new funding sources and to finance overseas assets with overseas financing. Foreign companies also want a presence in the United States because of the breadth and depth of U.S. capital markets. Companies can find an audience there for their shares and raise huge amounts of capital. Some leading world economies have stock markets that are all but ignored by their citizens. Germans prefer the safety of savings accounts and bonds; only 13 percent own stocks. Only 7 percent of Japanese own shares.[16] One reason for this is the Japanese government's pension systems, which diminish the need to invest long-term for one's retirement; another is a culture that favors conservative investment strategies.

INTERNET ACTIVITY

The ADR index was developed by the Bank of New York. See it on the Internet at http://www.adrbny.com.

Investors and professional money managers have found it increasingly important to diversify their investments among the world's markets. Such diversification makes possible a broader search for investment values and can reduce the risk in investment portfolios.[17]

Investment in foreign shares by U.S. investors may be facilitated through the use of ***American depository receipts (ADRs)***. These ADRs are traded on U.S. exchanges and are as negotiable as other securities. They are created when a broker purchases shares of a foreign company's stock in its local stock market. The shares are then delivered to a U.S. bank's local custodian bank in the foreign country. The bank then issues depository receipts. There is not necessarily a one-to-one relationship between shares and depository receipts; one depository receipt may represent five, ten, or more shares of the foreign company's stock. ADRs allow U.S. investors to invest in foreign firms without the problems of settling overseas trades or having to personally exchange currencies. ADRs are traded in dollars, and dividends are paid in dollars as well. ***Global depository receipts (GDRs)*** are similar to ADRs, but they are listed on the London Stock Exchange. U.S. investors can buy GDRs through a broker in the United States.

American depository receipts (ADRs) receipts that represent foreign shares to U.S. investors

global depository receipts (GDRs) listed on the London Stock Exchange; facilitate trading in foreign shares

As securities markets become more global, more and more foreign firms will seek to have their shares or ADRs listed on a U.S. exchange. There are nearly 2,200 ADRs from ninety countries, although significant trading occurs in only a small portion of them.[18] Leading ADRs include telecom firms Nokia (Finland), Ericsson (Sweden), Vodafone (U.K.) and oil firms BP (U.K.) and Royal Dutch Petroleum (Netherlands). Listing an ADR allows U.S. investors more easily to trade a foreign firm's shares. It also gives the foreign firm easier access to a large pool of U.S. investment capital. There is an ADR Index to track price trends.

CONCEPT CHECK

What does an index measure? What are ADRs?

ETHICAL ISSUES

INSIDE INFORMATION AND OTHER ETHICAL ISSUES

The capital markets are successful in allocating capital because of their integrity. Should investors lose confidence in the fairness of the capital markets, all will lose; investors lose an attractive means for investing funds, and issuers will lose access to low-cost public capital.

16. Sara Calian and Silvia Ascorelli, "Europeans Lose Love for Stocks," *Wall Street Journal* (May 12, 2004), p. C1; and Craig Karmin, "The Global Shareholder," *Wall Street Journal* (May 8, 2000), p. R4.

17. The topic of diversification and its effect on the risk of an investment portfolio is discussed in Chapter 6; we'll expand on it in Chapter 10.

18. Craig Karmin, "ADR Issuance Surges as Firms Abroad Tap Market for Capital," *Wall Street Journal* (December 8, 2000), p. C12.

CAREER OPPORTUNITIES IN FINANCE
Field: Securities Markets

Opportunities

Individuals and institutions invest in stocks and bonds to finance assets and to create wealth. Many times, as with large corporations, these investments for any given day may be in the millions of dollars. Most investors, however, have neither the time nor the resources to properly plan these investments. Instead, investors turn to securities specialists to plan and execute investment decisions.

Jobs like these require that individuals have the ability to make sound decisions quickly under heavy pressure. For those who excel, though, the opportunities are limitless. Brokerage firms, bank trust departments, and insurance companies typically hire professionals in this field.

Jobs

Account executive

Securities analyst

Responsibilities

An *account executive,* or securities broker, sells stocks and bonds to individual and institutional customers and manages client funds consistent with client risk-taking objectives. In addition, an account executive must actively pursue new clients and learn about new investment possibilities. Securities firms typically hire account executives to fill entry-level positions. A *securities analyst* includes being a securities analyst or a securities trader for brokerage firms. A securities analyst must evaluate the value of stocks and bonds and present this information to, or act on this information for, investors.

Education

A strong background in finance, economics, and marketing is necessary for these jobs. In addition, these jobs require the ability to communicate and negotiate effectively.

Some persons who deal in securities and have access to nonpublic or private information about mergers, new security offerings, or earnings announcements may be tempted to trade to take advantage of this information. Taking advantage of one's privileged access to information can lead to large profits from timely purchases or sales (or short sales) of securities. In the United States taking advantage of private "inside" information is thought to be unfair to other investors. These factors, combined with the ease with which inside information can be used, explain why insider trading is not allowed under provisions of the Securities Exchange Act of 1934.

The most obvious opportunity for insider trading is that for personnel of a corporation who, by virtue of their duties, have knowledge of developments that are destined to have an impact on the price of the corporation's stock. However, "insiders" are not limited to corporate personnel. Investment bankers, by virtue of their relationship with such corporations, may be aware of corporate difficulties, major officer changes, or merger possibilities. They, too, must take great care to avoid using such information illegally. Even blue-collar workers at printing firms that print prospectuses or merger offers have been found guilty of trading on private information based upon what they have read from their presses.

Because the insider-trading law is not very clear, it is often difficult to tell when it is illegal to turn a tip into a profit. For example, a stock analyst may discover, through routine interviews with corporate officers, information destined to have an impact on the price of the company's stock. Such information conveyed to the analyst's clients may be, and has been considered to be, insider trading. The almost frantic efforts of large firms to control insider trading is understandable in light of the damage that can occur to their reputations. It is understandable, too, that the SEC has resorted to very strong efforts to resolve the question that continues to exist with respect to a meaningful and fair definition of insider information. After all, it is the investing public without access to this information who pays the price for insider information abuses. Regulation FD mandates full disclosure of material nonpublic information that was sometimes disclosed to a select few, such as security analysts or large institutional investors. Insight into higher or lower earnings, for example, could result in those receiving the information—and their clients—trading securities to make a profit (or avoid a loss) at the expense of others not privileged to have access to the information. Regulation FD mandates that if a company official discloses material nonpublic information to certain individuals, it must announce the information to all via public disclosure.

Another breach of investor confidence can occur via *churning,* which is what happens when a broker constantly buys and sells securities from a client's portfolio in an effort to generate commissions. Rather than making decisions that are in the client's best interest, frequent

JOHN MURPHY
Independent Floor Broker,
New York Stock Exchange

BA, History/Business
St. Bonaventure University

> "I pay $130,000
> a year for the privilege
> of making trades."

Q: *What does an independent floor broker do?*

A: I buy and sell stocks on the floor of the New York Stock Exchange. "Independent" means I'm not an employee of any of the big brokerage houses. I'm self-employed.

Q: *For whom are you making trades?*

A: I have a few of my own clients and I make trades for them, but the vast majority of my business is overflow for larger brokers. When Merrill Lynch, for instance, has so many customer orders that its own floor traders can't get them all executed in a timely fashion, I am given a portion of the orders to execute for them. Then Merrill pays me a commission for the work I've done.

Q: *Describe what happens on a trade.*

A: Let's say Merrill has a customer that wants to buy 2,000 shares of company X stock at $20 per share or less. Merrill would give me a piece of paper with those instructions. I would then go to the specific area of the floor where company X is traded. I would ask the specialist in company X stock what price people are willing to sell that stock for. If he has a seller at $20 per share or less, he executes the trade.

Q: *What actually happens when it is executed?*

A: The specialist records Merrill as the buyer and whoever the seller is, the number of shares, and the price. And that's pretty much it. I would then go on to the next order. Now if my order is for a larger volume of shares, say 200,000 shares, I may need to stay there for a while executing a bunch of smaller trades. It might take fifty separate trades to come up with 200,000 shares. And I want to make these buys at the lowest possible cost. If I can save an eighth of a point on each share, that's a savings of $25,000.

Q: *Do you only trade certain stocks?*

A: No, I move all over the floor during the course of the day. I might trade twenty-five to thirty different issues on a given day. And that may involve several hundred individual orders.

Q: *Sometimes we see the Chicago Board of Trade on television, with traders yelling out bids and making hand signals to each other. Is the New York Stock Exchange like that?*

A: Not really. On the New York Stock Exchange, all trades take place through the specialist. In fact, many trades, especially smaller ones, are completed via computer instead of by a trader on the floor. The specialist matches up buy and sell orders from brokerages on his computer screen. It's not as wild as the Board of Trade, but it still can get pretty hectic. Recently the trading volume on the exchange has been quite high, which means everyone on the floor has lots of trades to execute as quickly as possible. If prices are moving up or down quickly, the urgency is even greater.

Q: *Do you own a seat on the exchange?*

A: No. There is a finite number of seats, or memberships, on the exchange. To make trades there you need to either buy a seat, which costs more than a million dollars now, or lease one, which is what I do. I pay $130,000 a year for the privilege of making trades.

commission-generating trades may be made by brokers with selfish motives. There are some times when frequent trading may be appropriate, but it should occur only within the client's investing guidelines and with the client's interests at heart.

Unfortunately, the millions of dollars paid in investment banking fees result in occasional scandal by some who make poor choices. In 2003 several investment banking firms were fined $1.4 billion for ethical lapses. Evidence showed stock analysts, whose stock recommendations should be unbiased, were sometimes rewarded for writing favorable reports to attract investment banking clients. Recall the first-day returns from IPOs in Table 9.3; in another ethical lapse, some banks allocated IPO shares to top officers of their client firms—or to firms they wanted to attract as clients. Allocating shares that may enjoy a quick "pop" in price is a means of bribing clients. In addition to paying large fines, firms must separate stock research from investment banking practices and offer clients independent investment research written by analysts from other firms.

Because ethics and integrity are at the center of fair and well-functioning securities markets, major professional certifications, such as the Chartered Financial Analyst (CFA®) and Certified Financial Planner (CFP™), have ethics as a central part of their certification programs.

CHANGES IN THE STRUCTURE OF THE STOCK MARKET

In an effort to increase the technological and informational efficiency of the stock market, the SEC has actively promoted major changes in the structure of stock market activities and institutions. Many of the changes proposed have long met with resistance from existing interests, especially the NYSE. However, many of the SEC's recommendations have been adopted, and many more will be instituted in due time. The NYSE, which many times resisted change that would deemphasize its specialist trading structure, gained new leadership in 2003 and since then has been embracing technology and globalization. As NASDAQ founder Gordon Macklin said in 1987, "How long do you think people are going to stand in a marble hall and trade?"[19]

Indeed, an important change relates to electronic technology. Technology exists to link organized exchanges and OTC markets electronically. The SEC would like to see the stock market take the form of one giant trading floor, all at the command of the broker. The broker would be able to tell which market has the best quote on each stock by punching buttons on the quotation machine. Bid and asked prices on covered stocks would be available in all markets. In a step toward this, the NASDAQ offers *dual-listing* to NYSE firms, meaning that NYSE-listed stocks can choose to have their shares listed on the NASDAQ. Instituted in 2004, the first firms to take advantage of dual listing were Apache Corp. (stock symbol: APA), Cadence Design Systems (CDN), Charles Schwab Corp. (SCH), Countrywide Financial (CFC), Hewlett-Packard (HPQ), and Walgreens (WAG).

Technology can link national markets to one another, worldwide. Long the purview of national market regulators, stock exchanges are now reaching across national boundaries to link up and in some cases merge with other exchanges. The New York Stock Exchange and Euronext, a major European exchange, agreed in 2006 to a merger. In 2007 the NASDAQ owned over 25 percent of the London Stock Exchange and was seeking its own merger with it. In addition to Euronext, alliances or cross-ownership agreements exist between the NYSE and the National Stock Exchange of India; the NYSE and the Tokyo Stock exchange; and the Tokyo Stock Exchange also has made alliance agreements with the Singapore Exchange and the Korea Exchange.[20] Look for this trend to continue!

The goal of global alliances and mergers is to make international investing and capital raising easier. One goal of the NYSE–Euronext merger is to cross-list shares on the two exchanges; this will make it easier for U.S. investors to trade securities listed on Euronext, and for European investors to trade U.S. stocks. Higher commissions, currency translation, and difficulties in settling trades are large hindrances to investing overseas; efficiencies in having global alliances will make investing in overseas firms easier, quicker, and less expensive.

19. Stephen Miller, "Gordon Macklin, 1928–2007: Ushering in Age of the Electronic Stock Market," *Wall Street Journal* (February 3, 2007), p. A8.
20. Gaston F. Ceron, "NYSE and Tokyo Tie a Knot," *Wall Street Journal* (February 1, 2007), p. C2.

The European Community is moving toward greater integration of its financial services, too. Markets in Financial Instruments Directive (MiFID) has the goals of creating a single market for investment services across the European Union and creating a single set of regulations for financial services firms. MiFID has three main objectives: (a) to create a single EU market for investment services; (b) to coordinate responses to innovations in the securities markets, and (c) increased protection for investors in a cross-country market.

Technological change has and will continue to drive much of the innovation in securities markets. Regulators in the United States, Europe, and Asia will have to try to keep up with change without hurting the potential for increased efficiencies. Electronic trading has been occurring for some time; the NASDAQ has an electronic European exchange that it hopes will be the forerunner of an all-European exchange. Another European electronic exchange, Virt-X, is a joint effort of the Swiss exchange and London's Trade-point trading platform.

Which model—NYSE's specialists or the electronic trading—is better? For the most part, both systems work to give investors swift trade execution and the best price available. For quicker trades, some will give the advantage to an electronic market. For the best price (lowest price for buyers, highest price for sellers) some argue that the NYSE's specialists can intervene to offer better prices to traders. For clearing large trades, the advantage goes to the NYSE; it has more trading volume and offers greater liquidity for handling large transactions.

Highly automated securities exchanges now exist in the major money-center cities of the world, permitting trading on a global basis. Because of varying time zones, trading is now possible twenty-four hours a day. Trading and settlement (issuing securities and collecting funds) go hand in hand; currently the United States has a T+3 settlement standard, meaning that all stock trades have to be settled in cash within three business days. With advancing technology, a standard of T+1, next-day settlement, may become regulatory reality by the middle of the decade.

APPLYING FINANCE TO . . .

INSTITUTIONS AND MARKETS

One can easily argue that securities markets exist because of the development of financial institutions and intermediaries over time to collect and allocate capital. In particular, investment banks and brokerage houses help firms and governments raise funds in the public and private markets. They assist investors who want to trade securities and help to provide liquidity to the financial system.

INVESTMENTS

Investors and analysts need to know the different ways to trade (long, short, margin) in securities markets and the risks of each. It is their desire to trade that creates a need for the securities markets and the institutions that facilitate their trading. New information is quickly evaluated by investors as a whole and reflected in changing market prices.

FINANCIAL MANAGEMENT

Firms raise capital in the primary markets. Initial public offerings and secondary offerings are an important undertaking for financial managers who take their firms public; others in private firms will arrange private placements or loans from banks, insurance companies, and other institutions. Securities markets set the interest rates and security prices for the firm; these are a reflection of the quality of the firm, risk, and investors' expectations of future cash flows.

SUMMARY

The accumulation of funds by business establishments to finance plant, equipment, and working capital is a necessary process of an industrial society. In this chapter we described the role of the investment banking industry in facilitating this process. The accumulation of funds is supported by the existence of a secondary market for securities. The constant buying and selling of securities not only provides the investor with the confidence that his or her investment is liquid and can be converted easily to cash but also provides information to the firm's managers. Businesses that prosper are rewarded by securities

that enjoy price increases. The secondary market is made up principally of the organized securities exchanges and the over-the-counter markets. Investing in foreign securities can take place by using ADRs.

Trading on the basis of inside or private information is illegal in U.S. markets, although such trading is accepted as the norm in some overseas securities markets. In the United States, ethical norms are such that society frowns upon those who, by virtue of their position or access to information, take advantage of their shareholders for personal gain.

KEY TERMS

aftermarket	house (commission) brokers	prospectus
American depository receipts (ADRs)	independent brokers	public offering
ask	initial margin	registered traders
best-effort agreement	initial public offering (IPO)	round lot
bid	investment bankers (underwriters)	secondary market
blue-sky laws	limit order	shelf registration
broker	maintenance margin	short sale
buying on margin	margin	specialists
central limit order book	margin call	spread
commission (house) brokers	market maker	stop-loss order
dealer	market order	street name
due diligence	market stabilization	syndicate
Dutch auction	odd lot	third market
floor brokers	offer price	tombstones
flotation	pre-emptive rights	underpricing
flotation costs	primary market	underwriters
fourth market	private placement	underwriting agreement
global depository receipts (GDRs)	program trading	

DISCUSSION QUESTIONS

1. Why do corporations employ investment bankers?

2. Identify the primary market functions of investment bankers.

3. Discuss how investment bankers assume risk in the process of marketing securities of corporations. How do investment bankers try to minimize these risks?

4. Briefly describe the process of competitive bidding and discuss its relative advantages and disadvantages.

5. Explain what is meant by *market stabilization*.

6. Identify the costs associated with going public.

7. Briefly describe how investment banking is regulated.

8. Describe the inroads into investment banking being made by commercial banks.

9. In 2003, several investment banking firms were fined $1.4 billion for ethics abuses related to the underwriting process. Will this be a deterrent for ethical lapses?

10. What are some of the characteristics of an organized securities exchange?

11. Describe the four basic types of members of the New York Stock Exchange.

12. Why is there a difference at some point in time between bid and ask prices for a specific security?

13. Describe the differences among the following three types of orders: market, limit, and stop loss.

14. What is meant by a *short sale?*

15. Describe the meaning of *buying on margin.*

16. What is meant by *program trading?*

17. Describe several differences between the organized exchanges and the over-the-counter (OTC) market.

18. What factors differentiate a *good market* from a *poor market?*

19. What influences affect a security's liquidity?

20. Why may a stock trade that takes one second to execute be preferable to a trade that takes nine seconds to execute?

21. How do the third and fourth markets differ from other secondary markets?

22. What are some factors that influence the commission on a stock trade with a broker?

23. Give some examples of market indexes. Why are there so many different indexes?

24. What are American depository receipts (ADRs)?

25. Why is it illegal to trade on insider information?

26. What is Regulation FD, and how does it affect security trading?

27. Visit the Web site of the CFA Institute, http://cfainstitute.org. Type the word *ethics* into the site's search field. Discuss, in your own words, the ethics issues that the CFA Institute is analyzing or discussing.

28. Visit the Web site of the CFP Board, http://www.cfp.net. Type the word *ethics* into the site's search field. Describe a few of the pages that appear from the search.

29. What are the advantages of having a specialist-based trading system? An electronic trading system?

30. Discuss this statement: "Technology and globalization are two current forces impacting stock exchanges."

PROBLEMS

1. You are the president and chief executive officer of a family-owned manufacturing firm with assets of $45 million. The company articles of incorporation and state laws place no restrictions on the sale of stock to outsiders. An unexpected opportunity to expand arises that will require an additional investment of $14 million. A commitment must be made quickly if this opportunity is to be taken. Existing stockholders are not in a position to provide the additional investment. You wish to maintain family control of the firm regardless of which form of financing you might undertake. As a first step, you decide to contact an investment banking firm.

   a. What considerations might be important in the selection of an investment banking firm?

   b. A member of your board has asked if you have considered competitive bids for the distribution of your securities compared with a negotiated contract with a particular firm. What factors are involved in this decision?

   c. Assuming that you have decided upon a negotiated contract, what are the first questions that you would ask of the firm chosen to represent you?

   d. As the investment banker, what would be your first actions before offering advice?

   e. Assuming the investment banking firm is willing to distribute your securities, describe the alternative plans that might be included in a contract with the banking firm.

   f. How does the investment banking firm establish a selling strategy?

   g. How might the investment banking firm protect itself against a drop in the price of the security during the selling process?

   h. What follow-up services will be provided by the banking firm following a successful distribution of the securities?

   i. Three years later as an individual investor you decide to add to your own holding of the security, but only at a price that you consider appropriate. What form of order might you place with your broker?

2. In late 2007 you purchased the common stock of a company that has reported significant earnings increases in nearly every quarter since your purchase. The price of the stock increased from $12 a share at the time of the purchase to a current level of $45. Notwithstanding the success of the company, competitors are gaining much strength. Further, your analysis indicates that the stock may be overpriced based on your projection of future earnings growth. Your analysis, however, was the same one year ago, and the earnings have continued to increase. Actions that you might take range from an outright sale of the stock (and the payment of capital gains tax) to doing nothing and continuing to hold the shares. You reflect on these choices as well as other actions that could be taken. Describe the various actions that you might take and their implications.

3. Which of the following securities is likely to be the most liquid according to this data? Explain.

STOCK	BID	ASK
R	$39.43	$39.55
S	13.67	13.77
T	116.02	116.25

4. You purchased shares of Broussard Company using 50 percent margin; you invested a total of $20,000 (buying 1,000 shares at a price of $20 per share) by using $10,000 of your own funds and borrowing $10,000. Determine your percentage profit or loss under the following situations (ignore borrowing costs, dividends, and taxes). In addition, what would the percentage profit and loss be in these scenarios if margin were not used?

   a. The stock price rises to $23 a share.

   b. The stock price rises to $30 a share.

   c. The stock price falls to $16 a share.

   d. The stock price falls to $10 a share.

5. Currently the price of Mattco stock is $30 a share. You have $30,000 of your own funds to invest. Using the maximum margin allowed, what is your percentage profit or loss under the following situations (ignore dividends and taxes)? What would the percentage profit or loss be in each situation if margin were not used?

   a. You purchase the stock and it rises to $33 a share.

   b. You purchase the stock and it rises to $35 a share.

   c. You purchase the stock and it falls to $25 a share.

   d. You purchase the stock and it falls to $20 a share.

6. The Trio Index is comprised of three stocks, Eins, Zwei, and Tri. Following are their current prices:

STOCK	PRICE AT TIME (t)
Eins	$10
Zwei	$20
Tri	$40

   a. Between now and the next time period, the stock prices of Eins and Zwei increase 10 percent while Tri increases 20 percent. What is the percentage change in the price-weighted Trio Index?

   b. Suppose instead that the price of Eins increases 20 percent while Zwei and Tri rise 10 percent. What is the percentage change in the price-weighted Trio Index? Why does it differ from the answer to (a)?

7. The following four stocks are part of an index:

STOCK	# OF SHARES OUTSTANDING	PRICE AT TIME (t)	PRICE AT TIME t+1
Eeny	100	10	15
Meeny	50	20	22
Miney	50	30	28
Moe	20	40	42

   a. Compute a price-weighted index by adding the prices of the shares at time t and time t+1. What is the percentage change in the index?

   b. Compute a value-weighted index by adding the market values at time t and time t+1. What is the percentage change in the index?

   c. Why is there a difference between your answers to (a) and (b)?

car accident. We pay an up-front price or premium to buy a certain level of protection for a limited amount of time. This is comparable to the concept of hedging with derivatives; hedging with derivatives can protect the investor from large adverse price fluctuations in the value of an asset.

The volume of outstanding derivatives has increased dramatically. In 1986, one estimate was that $2 trillion in value was traded; this rose to nearly $10 trillion in 1991, over $40 trillion on a worldwide basis by the end of 1995, and $370 trillion in 2006.[21]

Speculation, or investing in derivatives in anticipation of a favorable change in the cash market price, is a very risky investment strategy. Speculators are not hedging an underlying investment. They hope for a price move that will bring them profits. The complexity of some derivatives has resulted in some investors undertaking risks that they were not (so they say!) aware of. In recent years, firms such as Barings PLC, Gibson Greetings, Metallgesellschaft, Procter & Gamble, and several municipalities and colleges have suffered large losses and even bankruptcy because of inappropriate speculation in the derivatives markets. In the following pages, we describe several basic derivative securities.

FUTURES CONTRACTS

futures contract
a contract obligating the owner to purchase (or sell) the underlying asset at a specified price on a specified day

A **futures contract** obligates the owner to purchase the underlying asset at a specified price: **exercise price (strike price)** on a specified day. Exchange-traded futures contracts are traded on major futures exchanges. Exchange-traded futures contracts are standardized as to terms and conditions, such as quality and quantity of the underlying asset and expiration dates (for example, corn delivered under a futures contract must meet certain moisture content standards, among others). This standardization allows futures to be bought and sold, just as common stocks are bought and sold in secondary markets. Someone purchasing (selling) a futures contract can negate the obligation by selling (purchasing) the identical type of contract. This is called a *reversing trade*.

exercise price (strike price)
price at which the asset can be traded under a futures or option contract

Today, futures contracts are traded not only on agricultural goods and precious metals but also on oil, stock indexes, interest rates, and currencies. Some exchanges on which futures contracts are traded are listed in Table LE9.1.

initial margin
deposited funds necessary to purchase a derivatives contract

When entering a contract, such as a futures contract, one takes a risk on the creditworthiness of the entity on the other side of the transaction. Fortunately, exchange-traded futures carry little credit or default risk. Purchasers and sellers of futures are required to deposit funds, or **initial margin**, in a margin account with the exchange's clearing corporation or clearinghouse. The

TABLE LE9.1
Selected U.S. Futures Exchanges

Chicago Board of Trade (CBOT). The Board of Trade handles futures contracts for agricultural commodities such as corn, wheat, and soybeans. It is also a leading marketplace for trading in financial futures contracts, especially those involving Treasury securities. Web site: http://www.cbot.com.

Chicago Mercantile Exchange (CME). "The Merc" handles trading in stock index, interest rate, and foreign currency futures. Web site: http://www.cme.com.

New York Mercantile Exchange (NYMEX). Metals and energy-related futures contracts, including crude oil, gasoline, heating oil, natural gas, electricity, gold, silver, copper, aluminum, and platinum, are traded on the NYMEX. Web site: http://www.nymex.com.

New York Board of Trade (NYBOT). Formerly known as the Coffee, Sugar, and Cocoa Exchange, the NYBOT offers contracts for these items, as well as for cotton, orange juice, ethanol, and several currency and equity indexes. Web site: http://www.nybot.com.

Note: In fall 2006 the CBOT and CME announced a merger; if approved by government regulators and their members, the new entity (tentatively) will be known as CME Group Inc., a CME/Chicago Board of Trade Company. (As of this writing, the merger had not been finalized.)

21. Fabio Fornari and Serge Jeanneau, "Derivatives Markets," *BIS Quarterly Review* (March 2004), published by the Bank for International Settlements, Basle, Switzerland. Updated data are available at http://www.bis.org. The value mentioned in this statistic is "notational" value, not the actual value of securities traded. Notational value is used to compute the size of the cash flow that is actually exchanged among market participants. Most futures contracts, for example, require a margin requirement of only 3 to 6 percent of the contract's notional value.

FIGURE LE9.1
Listing of the S&P 500 Futures Contract

MTH/STRIKE	OPEN	SESSION HIGH	SESSION LOW	LAST	SETT	PT CHGE	EST VOL	— SETT	PRIOR DAY VOL	— INT
MAR 07	1443.00	1433.60	1438.30	1440.30	—	−260	4796	1442.90	40378	591922

http://www.cme.com/trading/dta/del/delayed_quote.html?ProductSymbol=SP&ProductFoiType=FUT&ProductVenue=R&ProductType=idx accessed February 12, 2007.

settlement price
approximate daily closing price of a futures contract

initial margin requirement is usually 3 to 6 percent of the price of the contract. Funds are added to or subtracted from the margin account daily, reflecting that day's price changes in the futures contract. At the end of each trading day, a special exchange committee determines an approximate closing price, called the **settlement price**. Thus, futures are cash-settled every day through this process, known as "marking to the market." As is the case with common stocks, should an investor's margin account become too low, the maintenance margin limit will be reached. The investor must place additional funds in the margin account or have his position closed.

Thus, rather than buying or selling futures from a specific investor, the futures exchange becomes the counterparty to all transactions. Should an investor default, the exchange covers any losses rather than a specific investor. However, the daily settling of accounts through marking to the market and maintenance margin requirements help to prevent an investor's losses from growing indefinitely until contract maturity.

Figure LE9.1 presents an example of the futures quotation page from the Chicago Mercantile Exchange (Merc) Web site, http://www.cme.com. Suppose you were considering buying a futures contract on the S&P 500 stock market index. Each contract has a value equal to $250 times the value of the S&P 500 stock index. The value of the contract traded on the Merc will, over time, closely follow the variations in the actual value of the S&P 500 index in the cash or spot market. The March contract opened the day at $1,443.00 per contract (thus having a total contract value of $1,443.00 × $250 or $360,750), and it had so far during the day's trading had a high of $1,443.60 and a low of $1,438.30. The price of the last recorded transaction was $1,440.30, which is down 260 points (read this as $2.60 in terms of contract price) from the previous day's close.

The settlement price, which is roughly the closing price, is the price at which contracts are marked to market; trading is still ongoing for the day when the data were downloaded, so no settlement price is given. Trading volume thus far for the day was 4,796 contracts. Data from the previous trading day shows a settlement price of $1,442.90 (notice, that this is indeed $2.60 higher than the current last price). The previous day's trading volume was 40,378 contracts. The open interest, which is the number of contracts currently outstanding, is 591,922.

OPTIONS

option
financial contract giving the owner the choice of buying or selling an item at a specified price on or before a specified date

An **option** is a financial contract that gives the owner the option or choice of buying or selling a particular good at a specified price (called the *strike price* or *exercise price*) on or before a specified time or expiration date. Most of us are familiar with option arrangements of one sort or another.

In some ways a sports or theater ticket is an option. We can exercise it by attending the event at the appropriate time and place, or we can choose not to attend and let the ticket expire worthless. As another example of an option, the owner of real estate may be paid a certain amount of money in return for a contract to purchase property within a certain time period at a specified price. If the option holder does not exercise the purchase privilege according to the terms of the contract, the option expires.

call option
an option to buy assets at a specified price on or before a specified date

A contract for the purchase of securities is a **call option**. A **put option** is a contract for the sale of securities within a specific time period and at a specified price. Similar to futures trading, exchange-traded options are standardized in terms of expiration dates, exercise prices, and the quantity and quality of the underlying asset upon which the contract is based. Thus, exchange-traded options are liquid. A secondary market exists for trading in them. While the Chicago Board Options Exchange remains the main market, the New York, American, Pacific, and

put option
an option to sell assets at a specified price on or before a specified date

FIGURE LE9.2
Stock Option Quotations

Microsoft
Current Stock Price: $25.62

	CALL			PUT		
	LAST	VOL	OPEN INT.	LAST	VOL	OPEN INT.
09 January 20	6.90	336	7451	1.20	100	39387
09 January 30	2.00	17	136164	5.60	10	87389

option writer
seller of an option contract

option premium
the price paid for the option contract

INTERNET ACTIVITY

The Web sites of futures and options exchanges offer visitors the chance to see time-delayed quotes. See, for example, the Chicago Mercantile Exchange, http://www.cme.com; Chicago Board of Trade, http://www.cbot.com; and Chicago Board Options Exchange, http://www.cboe.com.

Philadelphia exchanges also deal in option contracts. Today, options are traded on individual stocks, bonds, currencies, metal, and a wide variety of financial indexes. While most exchange-traded options contracts expire in less than a year, the Chicago Board Options Exchange offers long-lived options on select stocks. Long-term Equity Anticipation Securities (LEAPs) have expiration dates up to three years in the future.

Through the organized exchanges, the individual investor can now sell or create the options. The seller of option contracts is the **option writer**. The price paid for the option itself is the **option premium**. It is what a call buyer must pay for the right to acquire the asset at a given price at some time in the future and what a put buyer must pay for the right to sell the asset at a given price at some time in the future. The seller or writer of the option receives the premium upon sale of the option contract.

Figure LE9.2 presents an example of an option quotation from the Chicago Board Options Exchange. Suppose you were considering buying a call on Microsoft, and the current price of Microsoft's stock is $25.62. The Web site contains information on a variety of call and put options for Microsoft. We focus here on a LEAPS contract. The notation "09January20" refers to the contract's expiration date (January 2009) and strike price ($20). If you had done the last trade on the Microsoft 09 January 20 call, the price would have been $6.90 per option. Because each contract is for 100 calls, the total cost of buying the call option would have been $690.00. During the day, 336 contracts were traded. The number of outstanding 09 January 20 call option contracts is 7,451. The information on the 09 January 20 put option and the 09 January 30 contracts is interpreted similarly.

OPTION PAYOFF DIAGRAMS

Futures carry an obligation to execute the contract (unless offset by another contract so the investor's net position is zero). An option contract is just that—it gives the owner the option to purchase (call option) or sell (put option) an asset. Thus, if exercising the option will cause the owner to lose wealth, the option can expire unexercised and have a value of zero. Whereas losses on futures can grow as a result of adverse moves in the value of the underlying asset, the owner of an option contract may be able to limit losses by merely choosing not to exercise the contract.

How valuable is a call option? Suppose Microsoft's January 20 option is about to expire and the price of Microsoft's stock is $25.62. If the call option's price were $3.00, investors could buy the option for $3.00 and immediately choose to exercise it, since they could buy the stock by paying only $20 a share. They will then sell these shares at Microsoft's market price of $25.62 and receive a profit of $2.62 (they paid a total of $3.00 [option] plus $20 [exercise price] or $23.00; selling the stock for $25.62 results in a $2.62 profit). This is an example of an *arbitrage* operation in which mispricing between two different markets leads to risk-free opportunities to profit.

Other investors would also want to take advantage of this opportunity. The buying pressure in the options market and selling pressure in the stock market by arbitragers would cause the option and/or stock prices to change and eliminate the risk-free profit opportunity. Thus, if the Microsoft January 20 call option were about to expire, its price would have to be $5.62 to eliminate arbitrage opportunities. With a price of $5.62, investors would be indifferent between buying the stock for $25.62 or buying the call for $5.62 and exercising it (total cost, $5.62 + $20 = $25.62).

FIGURE LE9.3
Payoff Diagram for Call and Put Options

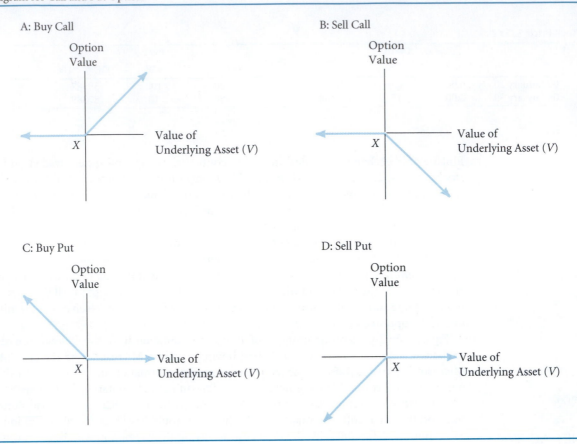

On the other hand, suppose the January 30 call option for Microsoft was also about to expire. With the price of Microsoft stock at $25.62, an investor that pays any price for the option is making a mistake; why pay for an option to purchase the stock at $30 per share when the stock can be purchased now for only $25.62 per share? The value of the about-to-expire January 30 call option would be zero.

To summarize: just before it expires, the intrinsic value of a call option will either be the asset's value minus the exercise price (if the asset's value exceeds the exercise price) or zero (if the asset's value is less than the strike price). If we let V equal the market value of the underlying asset (say, the Microsoft stock price) and X denote the option's exercise price, the value of an option just prior to expiration will be the maximum of $V - X$ or 0. This can be written Max[0, $V - X$]. Panel A in Figure LE9.3 illustrates a payoff diagram for a call option.

The payoff diagram for the seller or writer of the call option is shown in panel B of Figure LE9.3; it is the opposite of the payoff to the option buyer. For the option writer, increases in the asset's price above the exercise price are harmful, since the call option allows the buyer to purchase the higher-priced asset at the lower exercise price. In the case of the January 20 call option, the writer may be forced to sell Microsoft stock for only $20 a share when its market value is $25.62 per share. As the stock's value climbs, the call writer faces a larger loss.

Payoff diagrams for put option buyers and writers are shown in panels C and D in Figure LE9.3. The put option allows the owner to sell the underlying asset at the exercise price, so the put option becomes more valuable to the buyer as the value of the asset falls below the exercise price.

Let's look at the Microsoft January 30 put option. Arbitrage will ensure that this put option's price will be at least $4.38. For example, should the put's price be $0.50, arbitragers will buy the put for $0.50 and will buy the stock for $25.62; they will then immediately exercise the put, forcing the put writer to purchase their stock at the exercise price of $30. The arbitragers will gain a risk-free profit of $3.88 on every share (they paid $0.50 [put option] + $25.62 [stock's market value] or

$26.12; selling the stock by exercising the put gives them $30, for a profit of $30 − $26.12 = $3.88). Thus, if the put option is about to expire, its price should be $30, $30 − $25.62 or $4.38 to prevent arbitrage.

If the January 30 put option was about to expire and the stock's price is $35, the value of the put option would be worthless. No one would want to buy a put option that gives them the right to sell Microsoft at $30 a share when they can sell the stock on the NASDAQ, where Microsoft is traded, for the current market price of $35.

This example shows the intrinsic value of the put option at expiration is the maximum of $X − V$ or zero, or Max[0, $X − V$]. As the asset's value falls below the exercise price X, the value of the put option rises in correspondence with the fall of the asset's value, as seen in panel C of Figure LE9.3.

The situation is reversed for the writer or seller of the put option. The payoff diagram for the writer of the put is shown in panel D of Figure LE9.3. As the asset's value falls below the exercise price, the put writer will be forced to purchase the asset for more than its current market value and will suffer a loss. For example, with the January 30 put option, the put writer may have to purchase the stock at the $30 exercise price, thereby paying $4.38 more than the stock's current market price of $25.62.

at-the-money
an option's exercise price is close to the market price of the underlying asset

Here's some more option terminology: an option is ***at-the-money*** if its exercise price just happens to equal the current market price of the underlying asset. An ***in-the-money*** option has a positive intrinsic value; that is, for a call (put) option, the underlying asset price exceeds (is below) the strike price, X. An ***out-of-the-money*** option has a zero intrinsic value; that is, for a call (put) option, the underlying asset price is below (exceeds) the strike price, X.

in-the-money
the option has an intrinsic value

Thus far, to keep the analysis at a basic level, we have only reviewed the intrinsic value of options. In reality, the option's value will equal its intrinsic value only at expiration. At all other times, the option's premium or price will exceed its intrinsic value. A major reason for this is time. The longer the time to expiration, the greater the chance of the option becoming in-the-money (if it was originally at- or out-of-the-money) or to become even more in-the-money than it originally was. Another important influence on the option premium is the variability in the price of the underlying asset. The greater the asset's variability over time, the greater the chance of the option going in-the-money and increasing in value. Therefore, high volatility in the price of the underlying asset *increases* the option premium for both puts and calls.

out-of-the-money
the option has no intrinsic value

SUMMARY

From recent headlines to investment seminars, derivatives are an investment vehicle that will become more and more prevalent. This Learning Extension has reviewed two types of derivatives: futures and options.

A futures contract represents an obligation to buy or sell the underlying asset at a specified price by a certain date. An options contract is similar, except the owner has the option not to exercise the contract.

Futures contracts can be used to "lock in" prices now for a transaction that will not occur until sometime later. They can be used to

reduce the risk of price fluctuations. For example, the risk of changing prices in a long (you own it) asset position can be countered by a short (sell) position in an appropriate futures contract. The increases in the value of one position will offset the decreases in the value of the other.

Options are useful for hedging positions as well. Some options positions, such as buying a call option, have the added benefit of maintaining profit potential should the value of the underlying asset rise while limiting the dollar losses should the underlying asset's value fall.

KEY TERMS

arbitrage

at-the-money

call option

derivative security

exercise price (strike price)

futures contract

hedge

initial margin

in-the-money

option

option premium

option writer

out-of-the-money

put option

settlement price

spot market

DISCUSSION QUESTIONS

1. Briefly describe what is meant by a derivative security.

2. What is a futures contract?

3. What is an option contract?

4. Indicate the difference between a call option and a put option.

PROBLEMS

1. Determine the intrinsic values of the following call options when the stock is selling at $32 just prior to expiration of the options:

    a. $25 call price

    b. $30 call price

    c. $35 call price

2. Determine the intrinsic values of the following put options when the stock is selling at $63 just prior to expiration of the options:

    a. $55 put price

    b. $65 put price

    c. $75 put price

• CHAPTER 10 •

Investment Implications

Chapter Learning Objectives

AFTER STUDYING THIS CHAPTER, YOU SHOULD BE ABLE TO:

- Define investment and describe reasons for investing.
- Understand the concept of market efficiency and explain the three types of efficient markets.
- Describe the role of systematic risk, beta, and market portfolio in the Capital Asset Pricing Model.
- Know the stages of the investor life cycle.
- Understand the four-step portfolio management process.
- Explain the two investment objectives and five constraints that can appear in an investor policy statement.
- Describe the implications of active and passive investing for asset allocation and security selection strategies.
- Explain investment vehicles available for the small investor that provide diversification and professional management.
- Understand the importance of ethics in investment-related positions.

Where We Have Been. . . . *We've covered the basics of risk and return (Chapter 6); the characteristics of bonds and stocks (Chapters 7 and 8); and how these securities are traded (Chapter 9). Now we will pull together this and other information to introduce some of the practical implications of investing.*

Where We Are Going . . . *Although this chapter concludes the investment section, we are not finished with the concepts discussed here. The financial markets provide important information to financial managers. The next section of this book explains tools and concepts of corporate financial management. Monitoring security prices and their reactions to news events are important inputs to corporate decisions.*

How This Chapter Applies to Me . . . *The last few chapters have covered much ground with respect to investment topics. This chapter ties together some of what we've learned. We focus on information—both theory and practice—that is used by investment professionals and financial planners. Obviously one chapter can't cover all the insights and information related to personal investing, but this chapter will give you a good foundation to build upon in future coursework, reading, or Web browsing.*

Peter Lynch, a well-known mutual fund manager, shared how he invested in stocks:

"The key to making money in stocks is not to get scared out of them."

Some investors like to invest in the "hot fad" or the "next sure thing." In investing, there are few sure things and this month's fad can be next month's flop. A good investing philosophy is like the fable of the tortoise and the hare: slow and steady wins the (investing) race.

WHY INVEST?

The answer to the question "Why invest?" is similar to the answer to "Why go to college?" You hope to enjoy life more because of the learning you'll gain at college. You will likely face more opportunities for advancement because of a college degree, and studies have shown that, on average, those with a college degree earn more in salary and benefits over their working career. You are investing in yourself now and hope to benefit in the future.

So it is with the use of money. We can do two activities with your funds: spend them now or save them with plans to spend the money some time in the future. This trade-off of *present* spending for a higher level of *future* spending is the reason for saving. What you do with the savings to make them increase over time is *investment*.

INVESTMENT DEFINED

investment
setting aside funds for a period of time in order to receive expected future benefits

FINANCE PRINCIPLE

When we make an ***investment***, we set aside current funds in the expectation of receiving future funds that will compensate us for (1) the time the funds are committed, (2) the expected rate of inflation, and (3) the risk of the investment.[1] A key word here is *expectation*. Many investments contain risks so that the actual future payments may be higher or lower than expected. Someone may buy shares of common stock, expecting to earn a positive return, but the value of the shares could fall because of an overall stock market decline or because investors are not willing to pay such a high price for the stock.

The three sources of compensation are similar to concepts we learned in Chapter 4, "Interest Rates." One source of return is the real risk-free rate, or the "pure" time value of money. If we found a risk-free investment in an economic environment with no expected inflation, we would still need some incentive to invest (rather than spend) our funds. This is the real risk-free rate of interest. In the U.S. economy, the closest investments to such a security are the Treasury Inflation-Indexed Notes (they are also called Treasury Inflation-Protected Notes, or TIPS for short). The U.S. Treasury is the lowest-risk issuer of securities in our economy. Such securities have coupon payments and principal values that rise with the inflation rate so they protect investors from future inflation. Figure 10.1 shows recent market yield on a five-year TIPS note that

FIGURE 10.1
Yields on a Treasury Inflation-Indexed Note Due 2010

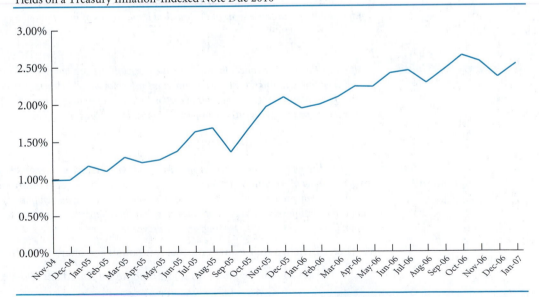

Source: "Economic Data–Fred," Federal Reserve Board of St. Louis, http://research.stlouisfed.org/fred2 (accessed February 13, 2007).

---

1. Some items that do not qualify as investments include gambling (the expected future return is less than the amount paid); property insurance (it is protection against loss; it is a good risk management tool but does not offer a greater expected return than the premiums paid, otherwise the insurance company would go bankrupt); consumer durables, such as a car or computer, which are wasting assets (they may last several years, but they decrease in value over time).

FIGURE 10.2

Six-Month Treasury Bill Rates

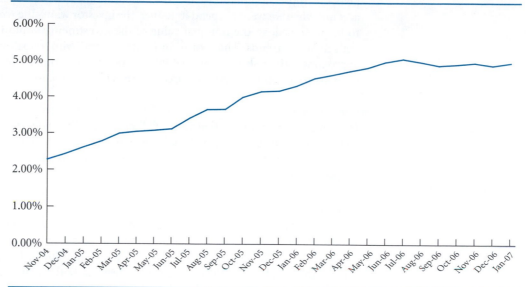

matures in 2010. Because of their low-risk, inflation-protected features, the yield on such notes is the closest measure we have to the real interest rate in the U.S. economy.

The second source of return is the expected inflation rate. Unless we are buying a TIPS bond, we will want to protect the purchasing power of the dollars we expect to receive in the future. If next year's inflation rate is anticipated to be 5 percent, we would not want to invest in a security that pays only 2 percent interest because if we invested $100 today our money will grow to only $102 in a year—and the purchasing power of those funds will be less than the $100 we have today! If inflation over the year is indeed 5 percent, in one year our funds will have the purchasing power of $102/1.05, or the equivalent of $97.14 today.

FINANCE PRINCIPLE

The nominal risk-free interest rate is the interest rate that combines the real risk-free rate with the market's expectations for future inflation. Our best estimate of the nominal risk-free rate is the return offered by U.S. Treasury securities. Figure 10.2 shows a graph of T-bill rates. The difference between the TIPS rates and the T-bill rates is an estimate of the market's expectations for inflation.

The third source of return is the risk premium. In all but the safest investments, the expectation of future income, dividends, or security prices may be incorrect. Riskier securities need to offer higher-risk premiums to give investors incentive to purchase them. As we learned in Chapter 4, "Interest Rates," sources of risk include maturity risk, credit or default risk, interest rate risk, and liquidity risk. In Chapter 6 we learned about other risk sources: business risk, financial risk, and systematic risk. We will learn more about systematic risk later in this chapter.

REASONS FOR INVESTING

People invest for many different reasons. Following is a review of some of the main reasons.

Income

Investments can be made in the hope of providing future income. Usually investors want income to begin in the immediate future (such as when a bond or an annuity is purchased). You first learned of the term *annuity* in Chapter 5 as a series of equal cash flows. Similarly, in the language of investing, an **annuity** is an investment vehicle that promises to pay income over a stated number of years. It may be for a fixed period of time, say ten years, or it may be a promise to pay income over the investor's lifetime. The promised payment may be fixed (say $1000 a month), or it may be variable, dependent upon the investment returns of the company selling the annuity contract.

annuity

an investment vehicle, many times sold by financial services firms, that promises to pay a stated amount of money over a stated number of years

Capital Preservation

Generally a conservative, low-risk, investment strategy, in capital preservation the investor wants to be sure the funds will be available, with little or no risk of loss in purchasing power, at a future point in time. As such, the term *capital preservation,* though used by many, is misleading, as it gives the impression that if we invest $1,000 we want to be reasonably sure $1,000 will be in our account when we want to spend it. Rather, the investor wants the *real* value of the invested capital to be preserved, so the nominal value of the investment should increase at a pace consistent with inflation trends. The return on funds invested with a goal of capital preservation should approximate the risk-free nominal interest rate in an economy for a nontaxable investment. If taxes are to be paid, a higher required return is needed to compensate for the tax payment.

Capital Appreciation

Investments are made so that funds will grow in value, primarily through price appreciation, to help fund a future need such as retirement savings or a child's college education. Typically, investments made with capital appreciation in mind have some risk exposure to get the desired returns.

Total Return

This strategy is similar to that of capital appreciation as the goal is to have the portfolio grow over time to meet a future need. Capital appreciation seeks to do this primarily through capital gains, but the total return strategy seeks to increase portfolio value by both capital gains and reinvesting current income. Because the total return strategy has both income and capital gains components, its risk exposure lies between that of the current income and capital appreciation strategies.

Minimize Taxes

Taxes are a fact of financial life. Some investments are made with the goal of legally deferring or eliminating taxes on investments. For example, the U.S. tax code allows some investments to earn returns on a deferred basis—meaning no taxes will be paid on investment returns until they are withdrawn from the account. Examples of such tax-deferred investments include employer-sponsored 401(k) plans and IRA accounts. Money set aside in a college savings plan (529 plan) can grow tax-deferred and the funds can be used, tax-free, to help pay college expenses. Municipal bonds are bonds issued by state, city, and local governments. The coupon interest on such bonds is exempt from federal taxes, and they can be attractive investments for someone in a high marginal tax bracket.

A person's reason for investing may involve just one of these motivations or several. For example, a retired person may want to invest a portion of their wealth to generate income while the remainder is invested for capital appreciation purposes. A university endowment fund may also invest funds to generate income while seeking a capital preservation or appreciation strategy, too.

CONCEPT CHECK

What is an investment?

What are the three sources of investment returns?

Explain the five reasons for investing.

EFFICIENT CAPITAL MARKETS

The secret to successful investing is simple: buy low and sell high. That is, purchase the security (stock, bond, or other asset) at a low price and sell it when its price is higher. Yet this simple rule is difficult to implement in practice. It is difficult to tell when a security's price is "low"—sufficiently low that it is safe to assume it will rise in value over time. Much analysis of security price behavior indicates that it is very difficult to "outsmart" the financial markets—that is, even professionals cannot consistently buy low and sell high and earn better returns (after adjusting for risk) than those returns earned by an investor who buys securities and holds onto them for a long period of time. This is the result if markets are "efficient." This section discusses this important and practical aspect of investing.

Prices on securities change over the course of time. As we learned in Chapters 7 and 8, security prices are determined by the pattern of expected cash flows and a discount rate. Therefore, any change in price must reflect a change in expected cash flows, the discount rate, or both. Sometimes identifiable news can cause assets' prices to change. Unexpected good news may cause investors to view an asset as less risky or to expect increases in future cash flows. Either reaction leads to an increase in an asset's price. Unexpected bad news can cause an opposite reaction: the asset may be viewed as more risky, or its future cash flows may be expected to fall. Either reaction results in a falling asset price.

FIGURE 10.3

Price Reaction in Efficient and Inefficient Markets

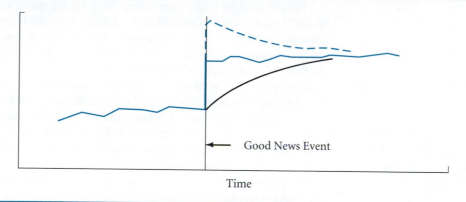

*Examples of price reaction in an efficient market (—) and inefficient markets following good news about a company. An inefficient market with an overreaction is indicated by (- - -); an inefficient market with an underreaction is indicated by (—).

efficient market

market in which prices adjust quickly after the arrival of new information and the price change reflects the economic value of the information, on average

A market with systems that allow for quick execution of customers' trades is said to be operationally efficient. If a market adjusts prices quickly after the arrival of important news surprises, it is said to be an *informationally efficient market,* or an **efficient market**. If the market for Microsoft stock is efficient, we should see a quick price change shortly after any announcement of an unexpected event that affects sales, earnings, or new products or after an unexpected announcement by a major competitor. A quick movement in the price of a stock such as Microsoft should take no longer than several minutes. After this price adjustment, future price changes should appear to be random—that is, the initial price reaction to the news should, on average, fully reflect the effects of the news.

In an efficient market, only unexpected news or surprises should cause prices to move markedly up or down. Expected events should have no impact on asset prices, since investors' expectations would already be reflected in their trading patterns and the asset's price. For example, if investors expected Microsoft to announce that earnings for the past year rose 10 percent, Microsoft's current stock price should reflect that expectation. If Microsoft does indeed announce a 10 percent earnings increase, no significant price change should occur since Microsoft's stock price already reflected that information. If, however, Microsoft announced an earnings increase of 20 percent (a good-news surprise) or an earnings decline of 5 percent (a bad-news surprise), the market would quickly adjust Microsoft's price in reaction to the unexpected news.

Every time Microsoft's stock price changes in reaction to new information, it should show no continuing tendency to rise or fall after the price adjustment. Figure 10.3 illustrates this. After new information hits the market and the price adjusts, no steady trend in either direction should persist.

This is similar to our Chapter 6 discussion about scenario analysis and the market's analysis of expected actions by the Fed. The market will anticipate moves by the Fed; when the expected change occurs, prices do not move appreciably. Thus, any expected news, about a company or the economy, should have little effect on the markets. Unexpected news will lead to price changes.

Any consistent trend in the same direction as the price change would be evidence of an *inefficient market* that does not quickly and correctly process new information to properly determine asset prices. Likewise, evidence of price corrections or reversals after the immediate reaction to news implies an inefficient market that overreacts to news.

In an efficient market, it is difficult to consistently find stocks whose prices do not fairly reflect the present values of future expected cash flows. Prices will quickly change when the arrival of new information indicates that an upward or downward revision in this present value is appropriate.

This means that investors in an efficient market cannot consistently earn above-average profits (after controlling for risk differences among assets) from trades made after new information arrives at the market. The price adjustment occurs so rapidly that buy or sell orders placed after the announcement cannot, in the long run, result in risk-adjusted returns above the market's average return. An order to buy after the arrival of good news may result in large profits, but such a gain will occur only by chance, as will comparable losses. Stock price trends always return to their random ways after initially adjusting to the new information.

Efficient markets result from interactions among many market participants, each analyzing available information in pursuit of advantage. Also, the information flows they analyze will be random, both in timing and content (since, in an efficient market, no one can consistently predict tomorrow's news). The profit motive leads investors to try to buy low and sell high on the basis of new information and their interpretation of it. Hordes of investors analyzing all available information about the economy and individual firms quickly identify incorrectly priced stocks. Resulting trading pushes those stocks to their correct levels. This causes prices in an efficient market to move in a ***random walk***, meaning that they appear to fluctuate randomly over time, driven by the random arrival of new information.[2]

Different assumptions about how much information is reflected in prices give rise to different types of market efficiency. A market in which prices reflect all knowledge, including past and current publicly known and private information, is a ***strong-form efficient market***. In such an efficient market, even corporate officers and other insiders cannot earn above-average, risk-adjusted profits from buying and selling stock. Even their detailed, exclusive information is already reflected in current stock prices. Few markets can ever pass the test of strong-form efficiency, and insiders can profit from information not known by others. As discussed in Chapter 9, that is one reason why U.S. laws prohibit insider trading, or trading based on important, nonpublic information.

In a ***semi-strong-form efficient market***, all public information, both past and current, is reflected in asset prices. The U.S. stock market appears to be a fairly good example of a semi-strong-form efficient market. News about the economy or individual companies appears to produce quick stock price changes without subsequent trends or price reversals.

A ***weak-form efficient market*** is a market in which prices reflect all past information, such as information in last year's annual report, previous earnings announcements, and other past news. Some investors, called ***chartists (technicians)***, examine graphs of past price movements, number of shares bought and sold, and other figures to try to predict future price movements. A weak-form efficient market implies that such investors are wasting their time; they cannot earn above-average, risk-adjusted profits by projecting past trends in market variables.

Market efficiency has several important practical implications. First, efficient markets make it difficult for investors to invest to consistently "beat the market" by earning above-average returns after taking risk differences into account. Thus, over time, more and more individual and institutional investors have chosen to *index,* that is, to invest in securities that comprise the market indexes (such as the Standard & Poor's 500 or Merrill Lynch's corporate bond index) rather than to try to choose specific stocks or bonds. Indexers try to match the market's performance by placing funds in securities in the same proportion as their weight in the chosen index.[3] Over virtually any ten- to fifteen-year period, anywhere from two-thirds to three-quarters of professionally managed U.S. diversified stock mutual funds earned lower returns than did a broad stock market index. Figure 10.4 shows that, except for one year (2000), professional mutual fund managers generally earned lower returns than the broad Wilshire 5000 stock market index in recent years. This is evidence in favor of the efficient market hypothesis.

Second, for corporate financial managers, stock price reactions to a firm's announcements of dividend changes, mergers, and strategies will present a fair view of how the marketplace feels about management's actions. Announcements followed by stock price declines indicate that the market believes the decision will hurt future cash flows or will increase the riskiness of the firm. Announcements followed by stock price increases indicate that investors feel future cash flows will rise or risk will fall. By watching the market, managers can see how investors perceive their actions.

Now that we have discussed how difficult it is to earn rates of return higher than risk-adjusted "market" returns, what is an investor to do? In the next section, we take a closer look at the

---

random walk

prices appear to fluctuate randomly over time, driven by the random arrival of new information

strong-form efficient market

market in which prices reflect all public and private knowledge, including past and current information

semi-strong-form efficient market

market in which all public information, both current and past, is reflected in asset prices

weak-form efficient market

market in which prices reflect all past information

chartists (technicians)

study graphs of past price movements, volume, etc., to try to predict future prices

INTERNET ACTIVITY

Go to http://finance.yahoo.com and see who are the day's biggest price gainers and losers in the stock market. What news may have caused these price changes?

---

2. The insightful reader may be wondering how prices can demonstrate a random walk when evidence presented earlier in Chapter 8 shows common stocks increasing in value by almost 12 percent per year on average. Such a return seems to imply an upward trend, not random deviations. Market efficiency does not eliminate long-run upward and downward trends in the economy; it simply means investors cannot consistently predict which stocks will outperform or underperform the market averages on a risk-adjusted basis.

3. In practice, it is difficult for index funds to exactly match the performance of the chosen index because of the index fund managers' need to reinvest dividend or coupon income over time, as well as their need to handle cash coming in from new investors and to sell shares from investors who want to take their money out of the index fund.

FIGURE 10.4

Percentage of General Equity Mutual Funds with Returns Less than the Wilshire 5000 Stock Market Index

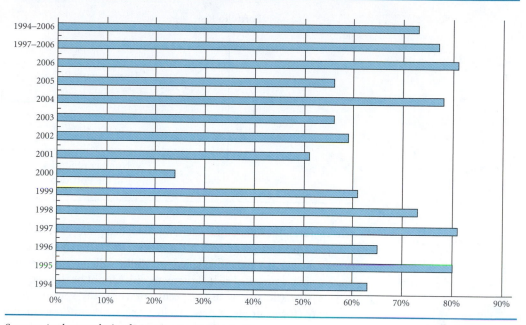

Source: Author analysis of Morningstar *Principia Pro.*

CONCEPT CHECK

What is an efficient market?

If price trends are predictable, would that be an indication of an efficient or inefficient market? Explain your answer.

How does a semi-strong efficient market differ from a weakly efficient market?

trade-off between expected return and risk and the role of systematic and unsystematic risk—concepts we first reviewed in Chapter 6.

CAPITAL ASSET PRICING MODEL

If markets are efficient, is there still a trade-off between risk and expected return? If so, what should this trade-off look like?

To answer this question, let's review a bit of what we learned in Chapter 6. Figure 6.5 is reproduced here as Figure 10.5. It shows how portfolio risk changes as the number of stocks added to it increases. Generally portfolio risk declines up to a point; after that, portfolio risk is fairly constant as additional stocks are added to the portfolio. We can split the risk of a portfolio (and for that matter, the risk of a security) into two broad types of risk: systematic risk and unsystematic risk, as shown in Figure 10.6.

As we learned in Chapter 6, the reason for this is that all stocks (and more generally, all securities) are affected by systematic or market risk. The U.S. economy's economic trends, changes in

FIGURE 10.5

Risk and Portfolio Diversification

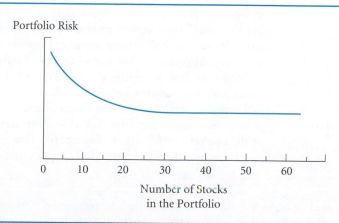

FIGURE 10.6
Risk and Portfolio Diversification

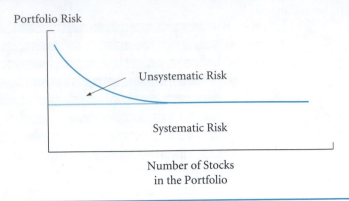

interest rates, the U.S. dollar exchange rate, Fed policy, and so on are pervasive and affect returns and risk on most securities. All securities are affected by macroeconomic and other national events, so even a well-diversified portfolio will have some exposure to these systematic, or marketwide, sources of risk. Systematic risk cannot be diversified away.

Unsystematic risk is asset-specific or company-specific risk. What is good news for one company (for example, a new product or patent announcement) may be considered bad news for another competitor. What is considered good news for one sector of the economy (rising oil prices for oil-producers) is bad news for another (sectors dependent upon oil and gasoline, such as transportation industries). As more securities are added to a portfolio, the effects of unsystematic risk are diversified away as the positive effects and negative effects on different companies and sectors cancel each other out, leaving only the broad systematic risk exposure.

This has an important implication for the trade-off between expected return and risk. What is "risk"? As we have reviewed, only systematic risk should matter because prudent investors can and should diversify their portfolios to eliminate unsystematic risk. Only systematic risk should remain, so only systematic risk will affect an asset's returns over time.

Regardless of their total risk (or standard deviation of returns), assets with higher levels of systematic risk should have higher expected returns; assets with lower levels of systematic risk should have lower levels of expected returns. From this perspective, we see that it is not an asset's total risk that is important. What is important is how the asset affects the risk of the overall portfolio.

For example, what is the systematic risk of short-term Treasury bills? Purchasing a T-bill "locks in" a short-term return that is considered risk free since it is backed by the full faith and credit of the U.S. government. While an investor owns that security, the return is not affected by economic events. In other words, the systematic risk of a T-bill investment is zero—or as close to zero as we can have in this world! If an investor adds T-bills to a portfolio, the effect on the overall portfolio will be a lowering of its systematic risk. Combining risky assets with a zero-risk asset will lower the overall systematic risk of the portfolio.

For another example, from historical data researchers have found that gold, by itself, is a risky investment. It offers no income stream and its price fluctuates, sometimes with high volatility, but in combination with common stocks an investment in gold can reduce a portfolio's total risk. The reason is that common stocks usually perform poorly when investors fear inflation, whereas gold prices tend to rise when higher inflation is expected. So, including gold in a stock portfolio can have a negative effect on risk—that is, it can make the portfolio less risky. Gold, at times, may have *negative* systematic risk.

From the perspective of the financial markets, the **market portfolio**—one that contains all risky assets—is the portfolio that truly eliminates all unsystematic risk. The only risk contained in the market portfolio is systematic risk. That means that as the value of the market portfolio fluctuates over time, the pure effect of systematic risk is seen.[4]

systematic risk (market risk)
risk that cannot be eliminated through diversification

unsystematic risk
unsystematic risk: risk that can be diversified away

market portfolio
portfolio that contains all risky assets

---

4. It is only in the case of the market portfolio that the standard deviation (or variance) of returns shows the effect of systematic risk; for all other less than perfectly diversified portfolios, the portfolio's variance measures a combination of systematic and unsystematic risk influences.

FIGURE 10.7

Comparing Asset Returns and Market Portfolio Returns Over Time with Those of the Market Portfolio

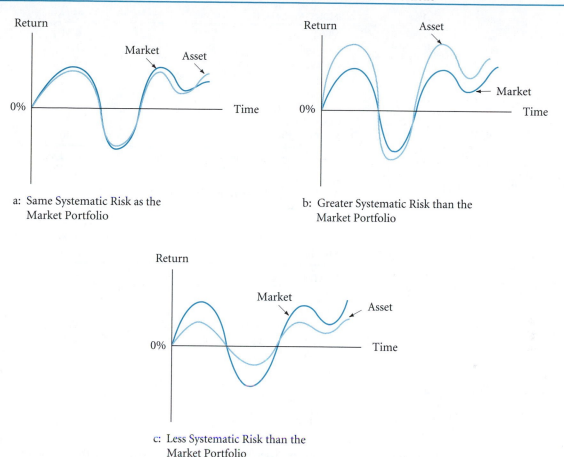

a: Same Systematic Risk as the
   Market Portfolio

b: Greater Systematic Risk than the
   Market Portfolio

c: Less Systematic Risk than the
   Market Portfolio

Since the market portfolio contains all risky assets, some assets that are especially sensitive to changes in macroeconomic variables, such as interest rates or GDP, will have higher exposures to systematic risk than the overall market portfolio. Some assets' returns will be less sensitive to these influences and will have less systematic risk. One way we can measure an asset's systematic risk is by comparing its returns over time to those of the market portfolio. Those assets whose returns rise and fall in line with the overall market will have the same systematic risk exposure as the market portfolio (see Figure 10.7a). Assets whose returns are more volatile (they typically rise higher and fall lower) than those of the market portfolio have systematic risk exposures that exceed those of the market portfolio (Figure 10.7b). Assets whose returns are less volatile (their returns don't rise as high or fall as low as the market portfolio) have less systematic risk exposure than the market portfolio (Figure 10.7c).

From this "portfolio perspective," an asset's risk is measured not by standard deviation but by its systematic risk, namely how it affects the risk of the overall portfolio. Assets with higher systematic risk will tend to increase the systematic risk (and the expected return) of the portfolios in which they appear. Assets with low levels of systematic risk will tend to lower the systematic risk (and the expected return) of the portfolios in which they appear.

Capital Asset Pricing Model (CAPM)
states that expected return on an asset depends on its level of systematic risk

These insights are the basis for the **Capital Asset Pricing Model (CAPM)**, which states that the expected return on an asset depends upon its level of systematic risk. The asset's systematic risk is measured relative to that of the market portfolio. In other words, the relative risk of an asset is that asset's contribution to the risk of a well-diversified portfolio.

beta
measure of an asset's systematic risk

Under the CAPM, **beta** (β) is the measure of an asset's systematic risk. Beta is a measure of relative risk. Beta measures the volatility or variability of an asset's returns relative to the market portfolio. For example, if an asset's returns are half as volatile as those of the market portfolio, its beta will be 0.5. That means that if the market portfolio changes in value by 10 percent, on average the asset's

TABLE 10.1
Examples of Stock Betas

INDUSTRIAL FIRMS	BETA
AT&T	0.41
Caterpillar	1.94
Coca-Cola	0.60
Disney	1.09
DuPont	1.25
General Electric	0.44
General Motors	1.34
McDonald's	1.40

TRANSPORTATION FIRMS	BETA
Alaska Air	2.30
AMR (parent of American Airlines)	3.70
Burlington Northern Santa Fe	1.31
CSX	1.41
FDX (parent of Federal Express)	1.06
J.B. Hunt	1.37

UTILITIES	BETA
Allegheny Energy	0.25
Ameren	0.32
American Electric Power	0.57
Consolidated Edison	0.27
DTE Energy	0.41
Florida Public Utilities	0.94

Source: http://finance.yahoo.com (accessed February 18, 2007).

value changes by 0.5 as much, or 5 percent. If an asset's beta equals 1.4, then the asset's returns are 40 percent more volatile than the market. When the market changes in value by 10 percent, the asset's value changes, on average, by 1.4 times 10 percent, or 14 percent. With this definition of beta, the beta of the market portfolio, β_{MKT}, is 1.0. By definition, the market is exactly as volatile as itself!

Assets that are more volatile than the market, or equivalently those that have greater systematic risk than the market, have betas greater than 1.0. Whatever the market return is, these assets' average returns are larger in absolute value. Assets that are less volatile than the market—that is, those that have less systematic risk—have betas less than 1.0. These assets' returns, on average, are less in absolute value than those of the market. Table 10.1 lists the historic betas for some stocks.

In practice, there is no true identifiable "market" portfolio; there are just too many assets, including the value of natural resources and human capital (investments in training, educating, and developing) to attempt to measure returns on such a portfolio. Investment professionals use a proxy, or substitute, for the true market portfolio. A popular measure of the market portfolio is a broad stock market index, such as the S&P 500 index or the NYSE index. Typically, when an asset's beta is estimated, it is measured relative to that of the S&P 500 stock market index. How to estimate a stock's beta is the topic of this chapter's Learning Extension.

CONCEPT CHECK

What is the market portfolio?

What is the relationship between systematic risk and a portfolio's variability relative to the market portfolio?

What is beta?

INDIVIDUAL INVESTOR LIFE CYCLE

Financial plans and investment needs are as different as each individual. Investment needs change over a person's life cycle. How individuals structure their financial plan should be related to their age, financial status, future plans, needs and risk preferences.

LIFE CYCLE INVESTMENT STRATEGIES

net worth

a person's assets (what they own) minus their liabilities (what they owe)

The investment needs and strategies—the "how to" of investing—will change over a person's lifetime. The needs of a typical college graduate, working in her or his first full-time job, will differ from the middle-aged person with two children in college. College graduates may have a negative **net worth**—that is, what they own (their assets) may be less than what they owe (their liabilities or bills).

TABLE 10.2
Benefits of Investing Early

		VALUE OF AN INITIAL $10,000 INVESTMENT	VALUE OF INVESTING $2,000 ANNUALLY	VALUE OF THE INITIAL INVESTMENT PLUS THE ANNUAL INVESTMENT
INTEREST RATE	7.0%			
Number of years	20	$ 38,696.84	$ 81,990.98	$120,687.83
Number of years	30	$ 76,122.55	$188,921.57	$265,044.12
Number of years	40	$149,744.58	$399,270.22	$549,014.80
INTEREST RATE	8.0%			
Number of years	20	$ 46,609.57	$ 91,523.93	$138,133.50
Number of years	30	$100,626.57	$226,566.42	$327,192.99
Number of years	40	$217,245.21	$518,113.04	$735,358.25

They may face student and car loans to repay, and they may be making plans to get married or trying to save for an "emergency" fund. The older individual may have a positive net worth due to past savings and home equity but will still face debts, such as credit cards, car loans, and mortgages—in addition to needing to pay their college tuition bills while also trying to save for retirement.

Although each individual's needs are different, some general traits affect most investors over the life cycle. Let's look at four life-cycle phases: accumulation, consolidation, spending, and gifting.

In the **accumulation phase** individuals are saving and investing money to satisfy shorter-term and longer-term goals. Shorter-term goals may include a down payment on a house; longer-term goals may include paying for a child's college education and saving for retirement. People in the accumulation phase tend to be in the early-to-middle years of their working careers, say around twenty-two to thirty-five years of age. Their net worth is small, and debt obligations from car loans or from college loans may be heavy.

From what we know about the time value of value, enough cannot be said about the wisdom of investing early and regularly in one's life. Compound interest, as we saw in future value problems in Chapter 5, works to our advantage if we can budget our income so money can be set aside for investment purposes. Table 10.2 shows growth from an initial $10,000 investment over twenty, thirty, and forty years at an assumed annual return of 7 percent. The middle-aged person who invests $10,000 "when they can afford it" will only reap the benefits of compounding for twenty years or so before retirement. The younger person who saves will reap much higher benefits if the funds remain invested for thirty or forty years.

Table 10.2 indicates that regularly investing $2,000 a year reaps large benefits from compounding interest, too. Someone who can invest $2,000 every year over forty years will have nearly $400,000 over forty years at an average return of 7 percent. The person who waits to invest "when they can afford it" will earn compound returns over a shorter period of time and will have a smaller amount of savings, about $82,000 over ten years and $189,000 over twenty years.

If a person is fortunate enough to invest $10,000 *and* then invest $2,000 each year thereafter for forty years, she will have accumulated over half a million dollars after forty years. If the funds are invested more aggressively (probably a larger percentage in common stock investments) and earn an average of 8 percent annually, the nest egg will total nearly three-quarters of a million dollars.

In the **consolidation phase** of the investment life cycle, a person's earnings exceed expenses. Most early-career debts have been paid (except for the home mortgage) and an emergency cash fund established. The ability to save is greater because of salary raises and/or promotions. Savings may be directed to some shorter-term goals, such as vacations or children's college savings, but the focus is also on longer-term goals such as retirement. The long-term benefits of compounding will be of some help, but the advantage is to start saving early in life.

The **spending phase** typically begins when individuals retire. One's focus shifts from saving money to wisely spending it. Income is provided from the investments made during the working lifetime—employer pension plans, IRAs, and other investing—and from government sources such as Social Security. The average sixty-five-year-old person in the United States has a life expectancy of

accumulation phase
phase of the investing life cycle when the emphasis is on building a foundation for attaining future investment goals

FINANCE PRINCIPLE

consolidation phase
stage of the investment life cycle when earnings exceed expenses, providing funds for longer-term financial goals

spending phase
stage of the investment life cycle during the retirement years

about twenty more years. Thus, although the primary investment focus may be on income generation or capital preservation, some funds should still be invested with the goal of capital appreciation.

The *gifting phase* may occur at the same time as the spending phase. In this stage, income and net worth are sufficient to cover expected personal expenses while maintaining a reserve for uncertainties. The excess income or wealth can be used to gift relatives or friends or to make sizable charitable donations to favored causes.

A well-developed policy statement considers these needs over an investor's lifetime. The following sections detail the process for managing a portfolio, constructing an investment policy, and monitoring its applicability to the investor over time.

THE PORTFOLIO MANAGEMENT PROCESS

The process of planning for one's financial goals should not be left to accident or an attitude of "I'll save what I can and hope for the best." The process of managing an investment portfolio should begin early, as funds are budgeted to go into a savings plan, and never stops. The process of managing a portfolio has four steps:

1. Evaluate personal needs, risk tolerance, and long-term asset returns.
2. Examine current financial market conditions and expectations. Create a plan for investing in the current environment based on Step 1's longer-term plan.
3. Implement the plan by investing in various securities to create the portfolio.
4. Monitor the performance of the portfolio and the needs of the investor. Update and revise Steps 1 and 2 and implement changes as needed.

We'll review each of these steps in turn.

The first step in the portfolio management process is for the investor, either alone or with the assistance of an investment adviser, to construct a *policy statement*. In the policy statement investors specify their financial goals, risk preferences, and investing constraints. The policy statement lists the type of assets the investor wishes to invest in (which will include general asset classes such as stocks and bonds rather than specific firm names), as well as the long-term target allocation to each asset class (such as "Over time my investments will be 60 percent in stocks and 40 percent in bonds"). All investment decisions are based on the policy statement to ensure that they are appropriate for the investor. We will examine the process of constructing a policy statement later in this chapter. Because investor needs change over time, the policy statement must be periodically reviewed and updated. That is part of the fourth step of the portfolio management process.

In the second step of the portfolio management process, the investor or advisor should study current financial and economic conditions and forecast future trends. Using the policy statement percentage as a guideline, decisions are made for how the individual should invest in the current market. So, if the policy statement mentions a long-term target investment mix of 60 percent stocks and 40 percent bonds and the investor believes the stock market will offer above-average returns in the next year or so, the investor may want to invest, say, 65 percent or 70 percent of the funds in stocks as of today. If the stock market outlook was more pessimistic, they may decide to invest only 55 percent or 50 percent of the portfolio in stocks at the current time. Because the economy, interest rates, and company outlooks are dynamic, the portfolio will require constant monitoring, rebalancing, and updating to reflect changes in financial market expectations, which occurs in the fourth step of the portfolio management process.

The third step of the portfolio management process is to construct the portfolio. With the investor's policy statement and financial market forecasts, the investor and any advisers determine how to allocate available funds across different countries, asset classes, and specific investment vehicles, such as stocks, bonds, mutual funds, and so on. This involves constructing a portfolio that will minimize the investor's risks while meeting the needs specified in the policy statement.

The fourth step in the portfolio management process is to monitor the investor's needs and financial market conditions. When necessary, the advisor and client will update the policy statement and modify the longer-term investment strategy accordingly. Periodic rebalancing of the portfolio should occur if the asset allocation strays too much from its target level.[5]

---

gifting phase
stage of the investment life cycle that occurs if personal wealth is sufficient so that planning for distributing funds to others, while alive or in a will, happens

CONCEPT CHECK

What are the four stages of the investor life cycle?

How would you expect a person's net worth to change over the life cycle?

policy statement
investor specifies financial goals, constraints, and types of assets in which to invest

---

5. This can happen, for example, if high returns in the stock market result in faster growth in the equity portion of the portfolio relative to bonds. If stocks represent a higher percentage allocation in the overall portfolio than originally desired, some stocks should be sold and the proceeds reinvested in other assets.

CREATING THE POLICY STATEMENT

The first step of the portfolio management process is to construct a policy statement. To do so, the investor—alone or with the help of an investment advisor—needs to thoughtfully consider the financial implications of his or her fears and goals. The policy statement will include the investor's investment objectives and constraints.

There are two investment objectives: risk and return. As we learned in Chapter 6, risk and return go hand in hand, so a discussion of one implicitly includes the other. The investing constraints that should be discussed in the policy statement include these five areas:

1. *Liquidity Needs*—Does the investor need to access funds quickly to pay expenses or purchase items?
2. *Time Horizon*—What is the investor's time frame for achieving his/her goals?
3. *Taxes*—What is the investor's tax situation, and what steps should be taken to minimize the tax implication of his or her investment decisions?
4. *Legal/Regulatory Factors*—Many regulations affect the investment process and transferring funds from one account to another; restrictions on any strategy must be identified.
5. *Unique Needs and Preferences*—Each investor is different; specific needs and preferences should be considered when constructing the investment strategy.

We'll consider these objectives and constraints one by one and illustrate them in the context of a "typical" twenty-five-year-old investor.

Investment Objectives

The **investment objectives** are the investor's investment goals expressed in terms of both risk and return. Focusing only on a return goal ignores the risk inherent in trying to achieve the return goal. This causes problems for two reasons: first, an aggressive return goal may be inappropriate if the investor is not able and/or willing to take on high amounts of risk that go along with the expected return; second, expressing goals only in terms of returns can lead to inappropriate and even unethical investment practices by a portfolio manager, such as the use of high-risk investment strategies or account churning, which involves moving quickly in and out of commission-generating investments in an attempt to buy low and sell high.

A careful analysis of the client's risk tolerance should precede any discussion of return objectives. Investment firms usually give their clients a survey to gauge their risk tolerance. Sometimes investment periodicals and Web sites contain tests that individuals can take to help them determine their risk tolerance.

Risk tolerance is more than a function of an individual's psychological makeup; it is affected by other factors, such as an individual's family situation (for example, marital status and the number and ages of children), age, current net worth, and future income expectations. All else being equal, individuals with higher incomes have a greater propensity to take risk because their incomes can help cover any shortfall. Likewise, a person with a larger net worth can afford to place some assets in risky investments while the remaining assets provide a cushion against losses. A younger person is likely to be able to invest in riskier assets as they have a longer investment time horizon to recover any shorter-term losses.

A person's return objective may be stated in terms of an absolute return (e.g., seek an annual average return of 8 percent) or relative percentage return (such as exceed the inflation rate by an average of 3 percent annually). It may also be stated in terms of a general goal, such as capital preservation, current income, capital appreciation, or total return.

What is an appropriate investment objective for our typical twenty-five-year-old investor? First we'll make some assumptions: he has a job with managerial potential, is a valued employee, has adequate insurance coverage, and has enough money in the bank to provide for an emergency fund. Let's also assume that his current long-term goal is to build a retirement fund. Depending on his risk tolerance, he will likely select an investment strategy that has moderate to high amounts of risk because the income stream from his job will grow over time. For his retirement fund goal, a total return or capital appreciation objective would be most appropriate. Here's a possible objective statement:

Invest funds in a variety of moderate to higher risk investments. The average risk of the equity portfolio should exceed that of a broad stock market index such as the NYSE stock index. Equity exposure should range from 80 percent to 95 percent of the total portfolio with at least 10 percent of the funds invested overseas. Remaining funds should be invested in intermediate- and long-term notes and bonds.

Investment Constraints

investment constraints
liquidity needs, time horizon, taxes, legal/regulatory factors, unique needs and preferences

In addition to twin investment objectives of risk and expected return, investors may face some or all of the five *investment constraints* listed previously.

Liquidity Needs

liquid
an asset can be quickly exchanged for cash at a price close to its fair market value

An asset is **liquid** if it can be quickly converted to cash at a price close to fair market value. Generally, assets are more liquid if many traders are interested in a fairly standardized product or if the investment has sufficient demand to attract many investors. Treasury bills are a highly liquid security; shares of Microsoft and ExxonMobil are likely to be liquid as well. Typically, real estate and some corporate bonds are not very liquid.

Investors may have liquidity needs that the investment plan must take into consideration. For example, those saving for retirement may need funds for shorter-term purposes such as buying a car, a house, or making college tuition payments. A wealthy individual (called a "high net worth" investor) with sizable tax obligations needs adequate liquidity to raise cash to pay taxes without upsetting their investment plan.

Our typical twenty-five-year-old investor probably has little need for liquidity as he focuses on his long-term retirement fund goal. This constraint may change, however, should he face a period of unemployment or should near-term goals, such as honeymoon expenses or a house down payment, enter the picture.

Time Horizon

We've mentioned the possibility of short-term and long-term financial goals, so time horizon as an investment constraint is somewhat familiar to us. Investors with longer investment horizons generally can tolerate greater portfolio risk and invest more aggressively ("aggressive" investing means placing a higher proportion of investment dollars in risky assets such as stocks or real estate). Such investors can invest more aggressively because any shortfalls or losses can be overcome by returns earned in subsequent years. On the other hand, investors with shorter time horizons generally favor less risky investments because losses are harder to overcome during a short time frame.

Because of life expectancy, the twenty-five-year-old investor has a long investment time horizon. He will work for another thirty to forty years and will enjoy, on average, a twenty-year retirement. The twenty-five-year-old will probably have a greater proportion of his portfolio in equities including stocks in small firms and international firms than someone with a shorter investing time horizon.

Tax Concerns

marginal tax rate
tax rate paid on the next dollar's worth of income

Taxable income from interest, dividends, or rents is taxable at the investor's marginal tax rate. The marginal tax rate is the proportion of the next one dollar in income paid as taxes. Table 10.3 shows the marginal tax rates for different levels of taxable income. As of 2007, the top federal marginal tax rate was 35 percent.[6]

The **marginal tax rate** is the part of each additional dollar in income that is paid as tax. Thus, a married person, filing jointly, with an income of $50,000 will have a marginal tax rate of 15 percent. The 15 percent marginal tax rate should be used to determine after-tax returns on investments. The

---

6. Some students may be curious about the tax implications of selling assets. Capital gains or losses arise from asset price changes. They are taxed differently than income. Income is taxed when it is received; capital gains or losses are taxed only when an asset is sold and the gain or loss, relative to its initial cost, is realized. Unrealized capital gains or losses reflect the price change in currently held assets that have *not* been sold; the tax liability on unrealized capital gains can be deferred indefinitely. Realized capital gains occur when an appreciated asset has been sold; taxes are due on the realized capital gains only. A short-term capital gain occurs if the asset was owned for one year or less; a long-term capital gain occurs if the asset was owned longer than one year. The tax rate on short-term capital gains is the same as the taxpayer's regular income tax rate in Table 10.3. Tax rates are lower for long-term capital gains; as of 2007 the maximum tax rate on long-term capital gains is 15 percent. A popular strategy for minimizing taxes is to try to own an asset for at least a year before selling so it qualifies for the lower long-term capital gains tax rate. A second popular tax-minimizing strategy is to sell securities with losses to balance out any securities you sold with capital gains. The tax code allows investors to subtract the dollar amount of long-term losses from any long-term gains and to subtract the dollar amount of short-term losses from any short-term gains. Reducing the amount of taxable gains lowers the investor's tax bill.

TABLE 10.3
Individual Marginal Tax Rates, 2006

SINGLE		
IF TAXABLE INCOME IS OVER—	**BUT NOT OVER—**	**THE TAX IS:**
$0	$7,550	10% of the amount over $0
$7,550	$30,650	$755 plus 15% of the amount over $7,550
$30,650	$74,200	$4,220.00 plus 25% of the amount over $30,650
$74,200	$154,800	$15,107.50 plus 28% of the amount over $74,200
$154,800	$336,550	$37,675.50 plus 33% of the amount over $154,800
$336,550	No limit	$97,653.00 plus 35% of the amount over $336,550

MARRIED FILING JOINTLY		
IF TAXABLE INCOME IS OVER—	**BUT NOT OVER—**	**THE TAX IS:**
$0	$15,100	10% of the amount over $0
$15,100	$61,300	$1,510.00 plus 15% of the amount over $15,100
$61,300	$123,700	$8,440.00 plus 25% of the amount over $61,300
$123,700	$188,450	$24,040.00 plus 28% of the amount over $123,700
$188,450	$336,550	$42,170.00 plus 33% of the amount over $188,450
$336,550	No limit	$91,043.00 plus 35% of the amount over $336,550

For updates, go to the IRS Web site, http://www.irs.gov.

average tax rate
total taxes divided by income

average tax rate is simply a person's total tax payment divided by income. It represents the average tax paid on each dollar the person earned. From Table 10.3, it can be seen that a married person, filing jointly, will pay $6,745 in tax on a $50,000 income [$1,510 plus .15($50,000 − $15,100)]. His or her average tax rate is $6,745/$50,000 or 13.5 percent.

Another tax factor is that some sources of income are exempt from taxes. Coupon interest on municipal bonds (bonds issued by a state, city, or other local governing body) is exempt from federal taxes. Further, if the investor purchases municipal bonds issued by a locality in the state in which they live, the interest is usually exempt from both state and federal income tax. Thus, high-income individuals have an incentive to purchase municipal bonds, rather than taxable corporate bonds, to reduce their tax liabilities.

To decide which is better to purchase—taxable or municipal bonds—the investor needs to do a short calculation. Municipals will always offer lower interest rates than corporate bonds of similar risk and maturity since the municipal bond (muni) interest is tax free. If an investor incorrectly compares the municipal interest with the corporate bond, he is comparing an after-tax return on the muni with the before-tax return on the corporate. To make the right decision the investor needs to consider the before-tax return on both types of bonds—or the after-tax return.

Suppose you are in the 25 percent marginal tax bracket (meaning you pay 25 cents on each additional dollar of income). You have a choice between a municipal bond paying 4 percent coupon interest and a corporate bond with a 5.0 percent coupon. If their risks and time to maturity are similar, which bond should you buy? You'll want to purchase the bond that will give you the greater income after taxes are paid. The municipal bond's after-tax coupon rate is the same as the before-tax rate: 4 percent. The corporate bond pays a 5.0 percent coupon, but after you pay 25 percent of it in taxes you'll have left only 3.75 percent—that is, 5.0 percent × (1 − .25) = 3.75 percent. In this case, to lower your tax bill, you'll prefer the municipal bond.[7]

The bonds can be compared in one other way by calculating the equivalent taxable yield on the muni. The equivalent taxable yield:

$$\text{Equivalent Taxable Yield} = \text{municipal yield}/(1 - \text{marginal tax rate})$$

is the taxable interest rate that results in the same after-tax interest rate (4 percent in this case) as the municipal bond.

In our example, the equivalent taxable yield is 4 percent/(1 − .25) = 5.33 percent. That is, the muni offers the same after-tax return as a taxable corporate bond paying a 5.33 percent coupon.

---

7. By the way this example is constructed we are ignoring any tax implications from a capital gain or loss situation. We are also ignoring the implications of the Alternative Minimum Tax (AMT). Such topics are beyond the scope of this book.

Comparing these numbers, the muni's equivalent taxable yield of 5.33 percent exceeds that of the 5 percent corporate bond. Whether you look at these bonds using after-tax or equivalent taxable yields, the analysis brings us to the same conclusion: buy the municipal security.

Another important means of reducing tax liabilities is to defer the tax payment. Based upon time value of money principles, you know that the present value of a dollar amount declines as the time period until payment increases. The tax code allows several ways for investors to invest money and not pay taxes on interest, dividends, and capital appreciation until a future time.

Contributions to a traditional IRA (individual retirement account) can be beneficial on two counts. First, the money invested in the traditional IRA may qualify as a tax deduction and reduce taxable income if certain income limits are met. Second, taxes are deferred on the IRA investment returns—meaning taxes are not paid until the funds are withdrawn from the account.

The benefits of deferring taxes can dramatically compound over time. For example, if we invest $1000 in a traditional IRA and the funds earn 8 percent, after 30 years the account will be worth $10,062.66 as the account grows on a tax-deferred basis. Suppose the funds were invested at 8 percent but were placed in taxable investments. If we assume a 28 percent marginal (combined federal and state) tax rate, the funds will grow to only $5,365.91—about one-half as much. What happens if we withdraw the funds from the traditional IRA account and pay taxes at a 28 percent marginal tax rate? We'll have an after-tax amount of $10,062.66 × (1 − 0.28) = $7,245.12—still greater than the funds in the taxable account.

The Tax Reform Act of 1997 created another individual retirement account: the Roth IRA. Unlike the traditional IRA, Roth IRA contributions are not tax deductible, so they do not reduce taxable income. However, funds invested in a Roth IRA can grow on a tax-deferred basis, but unlike the traditional IRA the funds in the Roth can be withdrawn, tax free, if the funds are invested for at least five years and they are withdrawn after the investor reaches age $59\frac{1}{2}$. Tax-free withdrawals are possible at younger ages if the funds are to be used for college education expenses or first-time home purchases. This is an attractive option for investors, especially those in lower marginal tax brackets.[8] Investors can have both traditional IRA and Roth IRA accounts, but they cannot invest money in them in the same year.

In addition to traditional and Roth IRA accounts, investors have other tax-deferred investment choices. For example, many companies offer employees 401(k) plans. Like a traditional IRA, a 401(k) plan allows the employee to reduce taxable income by making tax-deferred investments. In some plans the employer will match the employee's contributions up to a specified limit. For example, if the employer has a "3 percent match," any contributions by employees up to 3 percent of their salary will be matched dollar for dollar by the employer. This allows employees to double their investment with little risk!

Another investment option—although it should not be consider a primary vehicle for investing—is a whole life insurance contract. A full discussion of whole life (as well as universal life and variable life insurance) contracts is beyond the scope of this discussion. Life insurance should be used, primarily, as a means of providing for loved ones in the event of premature death. But the way that whole life insurance is structured, part of the premiums paid for the insurance are invested. These invested funds, called the *cash value of the life insurance contract,* will accumulate and grow tax free until the funds are withdrawn. Should the contract holder live long enough, the funds can be used to supplement retirement income or for other financial needs.

How do taxes affect our typical twenty-five-year-old investor? He is probably in a fairly low tax bracket, so detailed tax planning will not be a major concern. Tax-exempt income, such as that available from municipals, also will not be a concern. Nonetheless, tax-deferred investing should be an important part of his investment strategy. He should invest as much as possible into tax-deferred plans such as a traditional IRA or Roth IRA and should take advantage of a 401(k) plan if his employer offers it.

Legal and Regulatory Factors

The investment process and the financial markets are highly regulated and subject to numerous laws. At times, these legal and regulatory factors constrain the investment strategies of individuals and institutions.

---

8. For such investors the opportunity cost of the lost tax deduction will be less but the benefits of future tax-free withdrawals—even if income and their marginal tax bracket are higher—are great.

TABLE 10.4

Where U.S. Households Invest Their Financial Assets: Percentage of Financial Assets Held in Various Forms

TYPE OF FINANCIAL ASSET	1989	1992	1995	1998	2001	2004
Transaction accounts	19.1%	17.5%	14.0%	11.4%	11.5%	13.2
Certificates of deposit	10.2	8.1	5.7	4.3	3.1	3.7
Savings bonds	1.5	1.1	1.3	0.7	0.7	0.5
Bonds	10.2	8.4	6.3	4.3	4.6	5.3
Stocks	15.0	16.5	15.7	22.7	21.6	17.6
Mutual funds (excluding money market funds)	5.3	7.7	12.7	12.5	12.2	14.7
Retirement accounts	21.5	25.5	27.9	27.5	28.4	32.0
Cash value of life insurance	6.0	6.0	7.2	6.4	5.3	3.0
Other financial assets	11.4	9.2	9.3	10.3	12.6	10.1
Total	100.0	100.0	100.0	100.0	100.0	100.0
Financial assets as a percentage of total household assets	30.4	31.5	36.6	40.6	42.0	35.7

Source: A. M. Aizcorbe, A. B. Kennickell, and K. B. Moore, *Recent Changes in U.S. Family Finances: Results from the 1998 and 2001 Survey of Consumer Finances* (Washington, DC: Federal Reserve Board of Governors, 2003); and Brian K. Bucks, Arthur B. Kennickell, and Kevin B. Moore, *Recent Changes in U.S. Family Finances: Results from the 2001 and 2004 Survey of Consumer Finances* (Washington, DC: Federal Reserve Board of Governors, 2007).

For example, except for a few exceptions, funds removed from a regular IRA, Roth IRA, or 401(k) plan before age $59\frac{1}{2}$ are taxable and subject to an additional 10 percent withdrawal penalty. You may also be familiar with the tagline in many bank CD advertisements: "Substantial interest penalty upon early withdrawal." Regulations and rules such as these may make such investments unattractive for investors with substantial liquidity needs in their portfolios.

All investors must respect securities laws, such as insider trading prohibitions against the purchase and sale of securities on the basis of important information that is not publicly known. Typically, the people possessing such private or inside information are the firm's managers, who have a duty to act in their shareholders' best interests. Trading securities based on inside information violates the trust the shareholders have placed with management. Such managers are seeking personal financial gain from their privileged access to information rather than doing what is best for shareholders.

For our typical twenty-five-year-old investor, legal and regulatory matters will be of little concern, with the possible exception of insider trading laws and the penalties associated with early withdrawal of funds from tax-deferred retirement accounts.

Unique Needs and Preferences

This category covers the individual and peculiar concerns of each investor. Some investors may want to exclude certain companies from their portfolio on the basis of personal preference or for social consciousness reasons. For example, an investor may request that no firms that manufacture or sell tobacco, alcohol, pornography, or environmentally harmful products be included in their portfolio.

Another example of a personal constraint is a person's available time and expertise for managing their portfolio. Busy people may prefer to hire a trusted adviser to manage their investments. Retirees, on the other hand, may have available time but believe they lack the expertise to choose and monitor investments, so they may seek professional advice.

Because each investor is unique, the implications of this final constraint differ for each person. There is no "typical" twenty-five-year-old investor in this regard. Each individual will have to decide—and then communicate specific goals in a well-constructed policy statement.

How do U.S. households invest or save their funds? Table 10.4 shows the data from the Survey of Consumer Finances, a Federal Reserve Board-sponsored survey that is conducted every three years. Checking accounts (transactions accounts), CDs, U.S. savings bonds, and bonds have declined as a percentage of owned financial assets over time. However, stocks, mutual funds, and retirement accounts have increased in relative ownership, possibly in part due to the baby boom generation getting older and saving more for retirement. Financial assets average about 35 percent

CONCEPT CHECK

What are the four steps in the portfolio management process?

What objectives and constraints should appear in the investment policy statement?

of overall household assets. This percentage will rise and fall due to stock market fluctuations and the value of real estate (the major asset owned by most families is their house).

INVESTMENT STRATEGIES

There are many financial assets in which to invest and many security analysis and portfolio management strategies from which to choose. Each investment analyst must determine his or her own strengths and use them to the best of his or her ability to try to optimally manage a portfolio or to discover value in the securities markets. Creating a portfolio involves two sets of decisions. The first set involves what asset allocation to use and what securities to purchase in each asset class. The second set of decisions deals with whether to use active investing or passive investing. We'll examine both sets of decisions in this section.

The overall collection of assets owned by an individual or institution is called a *portfolio*. A portfolio contains securities from one or more asset classes, such as stocks, bonds, mortgages, and so on. Using the investor's objectives and constraints, the investor must decide on an appropriate **asset allocation**—that is, what percentage of the portfolio should be in each of the different asset classes. The asset allocation decision has a large bearing on the expected return and risk of the portfolio since some assets (e.g., stocks) are riskier than others (e.g., bonds).

Once the asset allocation is determined, the security selection process begins, which involves deciding which specific securities to purchase for the portfolio. Once made, the asset allocation and security selection decisions are not permanent; markets change, expectations change, the circumstances surrounding the portfolio and the client change. The asset allocation and the securities comprising the portfolio will have to be monitored and revised on a periodic basis. How one determines an asset allocation decision and security selection strategy depends upon one's investing philosophy—that is, should an investor pursue an active investment management role or a passive one? Table 10.5 lists various possibilities under each philosophy.

An **active investment philosophy** has the investor, or the person managing the investor's funds, making continual decisions about what assets and securities to buy, sell, or hold. An active investor scans the economic climate and determines its implications for various industries, sectors, and firms. The motto of the active investor is to "buy low and sell high." Active investors try to time the market by purchasing securities and increasing the percentage invested in an asset class when their values are anticipated to rise. Conversely, securities are sold and the percentage of a portfolio invested in an asset class is reduced when prices are thought to have reached a peak and/or are in danger of falling.

A **passive investment philosophy** involves making an initial decision about investments and then holding onto them until one of two situations happen. The first situation is that the investor's or the financial market outlook materially changes. The second is that an asset class allocation reaches an upper or lower limit and that the portfolio needs to be "rebalanced" back to its initial asset allocation. An example of the first event is as a person ages his or her ability and willingness to tolerate risk (usually) declines; over time, the allocation in a passive portfolio would be readjusted to lower the allocation to stocks and increase the allocation to bonds even if the outlook for stocks is positive. With respect to the second event, usually a portfolio will be created with an initial asset allocation—for example, 60 percent stocks and 40 percent bonds—and limits will be set for each allocation, say plus or minus 10 percent. This means the stock portion of the portfolio can vary from 50 percent to 70 percent and the bond allocation can vary

---

asset allocation
the percentage of the portfolio invested in each asset class

active investment philosophy
financial markets are continually evaluated to determine what securities or assets to buy, sell, or hold in an effort to time the market's highs and lows.

passive investment philosophy
a buy-and-hold investment strategy in which securities or assets are not traded unless the investor's or financial market outlook materially changes or rebalancing is needed.

TABLE 10.5
Investment Philosophies

	ASSET ALLOCATION DECISION	SECURITY SELECTION DECISION
Active	Market timing	Stock picking by top-down or bottom-up approach
Passive	Maintain predetermined allocation with periodic rebalancing	Try to track a well-known market index

from 30 percent to 50 percent. If an allocation goes above or below its bounds, the portfolio will be rebalanced, meaning assets will be sold and others purchased to restore the portfolio to its initial allocation of 60/40. The motto of the passive investor is "buy and hold" until something causes the need to change the portfolio's composition.

A manager with an active security selection philosophy will try to identify which securities will likely do well over the coming period of time; these will be purchased, and securities from the portfolio that are expected to underperform, or do poorly compared to the market, in the coming months will be sold. Such managers typically have a "top-down" or "bottom-up" approach to security analysis. Top-down adherents will examine the economic picture to get overviews of which sectors are expected to perform well and which are expected to perform poorly over the next year. After these sectors are identified, stocks are purchased from companies that are expected to do well in industries that are expected to perform well given the economic forecast. Bottom-up stock pickers focus on firms with good management, a good strategy, and a good product that will likely gain market share and increase the firm's earnings in the future.

A passive investor has a simpler security selection task; once an asset allocation has been determined, she will invest the funds to track, as closely as possible, a selected market index, such as the S&P 500 stock index or the Lehman Brothers bond index. Such investors believe the securities markets are 100 percent efficient, so as the saying goes, "If you can't beat 'em, join 'em." They follow the indexes rather than try to earn above-average returns for a given risk level by security selection.

A manager can be "active" in one decision and "passive" in another. For example, a manager who believes she can forecast when the stock market will outperform the bond market (and vice versa) but does not have skill in selecting specific securities to purchase may be active in the asset allocation decision but will implement the strategy by investing in indexes. For another example, a manager with perceived strengths in stock picking will abide by a consistent asset allocation but will manage the portfolio by actively analyzing and selecting the securities to include in it.

From the discussion in this chapter, we can list the following four "truths" of investing that should guide your investing decisions:

FINANCE PRINCIPLE

1. *There is a trade-off between risk and expected return:* higher-risk securities and higher-risk portfolios should be expected to earn higher returns. The risk is this: they may not actually earn the higher returns!
2. *U.S. financial markets are nearly efficient:* new information (what is truly "new" in the news) will be reflected in current stock prices and interest rates.
3. *Investors should focus on what they can keep:* that is, be aware of the tax consequences of your investing decisions. Similarly, investments with higher expenses (commissions or fees) will lower the returns you get. Seek low-expense investments.
4. *Diversify:* regardless of how "sure" you may be of an investment, whether it is a stock or money managed by a wise portfolio manager, it is best to spread your funds across different assets in different industries—even consider placing some funds in investments outside the United States to further reduce systematic risk from U.S. financial markets.

CONCEPT CHECK

What are the two sets of decisions that are made when creating a portfolio?

How does an active investing strategy differ from a passive investment strategy?

WAYS TO INVEST FOR THE SMALL INVESTOR

It may be difficult for the individual investor to invest alone; it takes a lot of money to buy sufficient securities to form a well-diversified portfolio, and the time and expertise involved in researching the economy, industries, and companies are more than the typical working person has. Fortunately, several investing tools are available to give the small investor access to a diversified portfolio and professional management. In this section we review mutual funds, closed-end investment companies, exchange-traded funds (ETFs), and variable annuities.

MUTUAL FUNDS

mutual fund (open-end investment company) *pools funds from investors and purchases securities; fund shares are bought and sold from the investment company*

A **mutual fund (open-end investment company)** invests a pool of funds belonging to many individuals in a portfolio of individual investments, such as stocks and bonds. As an example, an investment company might initially sell 10 million shares to the public at $10 a share for a total of $100 million. If this common stock fund emphasized blue-chip stocks, the manager would invest

closed-end investment company

sells shares in an IPO and uses them to purchase securities; fund shares are traded on stock exchanges

the proceeds of the sale ($100 million less any commissions) in the stock of such companies as ExxonMobil, Microsoft, Wal-Mart, General Motors, and General Electric. Therefore, each individual who bought shares of the investment company would own a percentage of the investment company's total portfolio. Mutual funds are called open-end investment companies as shares in the fund are bought and sold directly from the investment company. Thus, the number of shares is "open-ended"—it can grow indefinitely if investors wish to invest in the fund.

The value of the mutual fund shares depends on the value of the portfolio of stocks. Suppose the number of shares remains at 10 million and the market value of the stocks in the portfolio increases to $115 million (net of any liabilities).[9] Then each original share of the investment company is worth $11.50 ($115 million/10 million shares). This per share value is the net asset value (NAV) of the investment company. It equals the total market value of all its assets, net of liabilities, divided by the number of fund shares outstanding:

$$\text{Net Asset Value} = \frac{\text{Market value of assets minus liabilities}}{\text{Number of shares outstanding}} \tag{10.1}$$

If investors wish to purchase fund shares, the price per share they pay is the NAV (plus any commissions). If an investor wishes to sell their shares, they contact the investment company and receive an amount equal to the NAV for each share they sell.

Well-known mutual fund firms such as Vanguard, Fidelity, T. Rowe Price, and others offer dozens of different funds under the name of the firm. As with the many products you see in a supermarket, the wide variety of funds—focusing on different aspects of stock and bond markets—offered by the same firm will appeal to the risk–return preferences of different investors. Most fund companies allow investors to transfer money or switch investments among funds within the company at low or no cost as economic or personal conditions change. This "family of funds" concept promotes flexibility and also increases the total capital the investment firm manages. Fidelity Investments, the nation's largest investment company, offers more than two hundred mutual funds.

A lesser-known type of investment company is known as a **closed-end investment company**. It is "closed-end" as after the company sells an initial offering of shares it does not issue additional shares, nor does it redeem the shares. Investors who want to buy or sell closed-end investment company shares after the initial offering must trade through a broker, much like trading shares of stock in any publicly listed company. A disadvantage of investing in closed-end funds is that their market price rarely equals their NAV. Many times the funds sell at a discount, meaning the market price is less than the fund's NAV. Sometimes closed-end funds sell at a premium, meaning their market price exceeds NAV. The reason for this is a much-studied part of finance. Some believe the difference between a closed-end fund's price and NAV can represent a lack of liquidity in the fund's shares. Others believe it measures the sentiment of small investors—as they are the typical purchasers of closed-end fund shares.

There are similarities between mutual funds, closed-end funds, and exchange-traded funds (ETFs, discussed in the next section), but as seen in Table 10.6, mutual funds are by far the more popular investment option.

TABLE 10.6
Popularity of Mutual Funds, Closed-End Funds, ETFs, and Variable Annuities in 2006

	MUTUAL FUNDS	CLOSED-END INVESTMENT COMPANY	EXCHANGE-TRADED FUNDS	VARIABLE ANNUITIES
Net Total Assets ($ billions)	$10,413.7	$285.8	$422.5	$1,291.2
Total Number of Funds	8,117	640	357	N/A
Net Assets for Stock Funds ($ billions)	$5,909.6	$110.4	$401.9	$761.8
Number of Stock Funds	4,765	196	351	N/A

Source: Investment Company Institute Web site (http://www.ici.org).

---

9. Liabilities may include money borrowed in order to purchase additional securities (this is known as trading on *margin*) or payables for management fees and for securities purchased but not yet paid for. The amount of liabilities is usually quite small, less than 1 percent, compared to the total assets of a mutual fund.

The popularity of mutual funds is due to the attractive features they offer individual investors. Some advantages of using mutual funds include:

1. *Liquidity:* Investors buy and sell shares directly from the mutual fund. Such trades are priced at the NAV at the close of trading on the day (or sometimes the day after) the order arrives at the fund.
2. *Diversification:* Money invested in the fund is automatically diversified across all the fund's investments. Mutual funds allow a small investor to get ownership in a diversified portfolio for as little as $100 or less, depending on the fund's minimum investment requirements.
3. *Professional management and record keeping:* The mutual fund's professional managers research economic and company trends to judge what securities to purchase and when to trade them. The fund managers keep track of all fund share purchases, as well as income and capital gains (or losses) from the fund's investments, and allocates them to each shareholder.
4. *Choice and flexibility:* Fund "families" offer a wide variety of funds to meet the investment goals of individuals. Fund families allow fund investors no-cost or very low-cost switching from one fund to another.
5. *Indexing:* If an investor believes that markets are reasonably efficient, they can select mutual fund investments in "index" funds, which are especially designed and managed to track a broad market index, such as the S&P 500 for stocks or the Lehman Brothers Aggregate Bond Index for bonds.

Although closed-end funds, exchange-traded funds (ETFs), and variable annuities offer some of these features, only mutual funds offer all of them.

EXCHANGE-TRADED FUNDS

exchange-traded funds (ETFs)
shares represent ownership of a basket of securities, and investors can trade the ETF shares on a stock exchange or convert them into the underlying securities it represents

Although many more assets are held in mutual funds, ETFs are rapidly gaining in popularity. They have surpassed their much-older cousin, the closed-end investment company, in assets. First issued in 1993, **exchange-traded funds (ETFs)** attracted nearly $7 billion in 1997, $80 billion in early 2002, over $160 billion of investor's funds in 2004, and over $420 by 2006.

An ETF is similar to a closed-end fund in that ETF shares trade on an exchange and the shares represent ownership in a basket of securities. Unlike an actively managed closed-end fund, though, the ETF is passively managed by a sponsor to mirror an index.

Unlike closed-end funds for which the market price of the fund can deviate substantially from NAV, exchange-traded funds offer a unique method for keeping market price close to NAV: large institutional investors can assemble baskets of the underlying stocks and exchange them for ETF shares if the ETF is selling at a price above its NAV. Similarly, if the ETF is selling at a price below NAV, the institutional investors can buy ETF shares and convert them to the underlying securities. This ability to convert ETF shares into shares of the underlying securities (or vice versa) keeps the ETF price very close to its NAV.

Whereas index mutual fund shares can be purchased or redeemed by investors only once a day (using the day's closing price to determine NAV), an ETF trades throughout the day, much like any other publicly traded security.

ETFs can focus on broad indexes such as the S&P 500 (SPDRs), investment styles such as value and growth (iShares S&P 500 Growth Index Fund), sectors such as energy (SPDR Energy), countries (iShares MSCI-Taiwan), and regions (iShares MSCI-EAFE). Expenses are usually low on ETFs; the SPDR 500, which replicates the S&P 500 index, has an expense ratio of 0.17 percent compared to the low-cost Vanguard Index 500 fund's expense ratio of 0.18 percent and the average stock mutual funds' ratio of about 1.52 percent.

Although expenses are low, a drawback to ETF shares is that they can only be purchased and sold on exchanges. Since brokerage commissions will increase the cost of trading ETFs, they are not a good vehicle if frequent purchases or regular monthly purchases from savings are planned. Lastly, some ETFs do not frequently trade, so it may be difficult at times to quickly purchase or exit an investment—that is, they may have some liquidity risk.

INTERNET ACTIVITY

Learn more about ETFs from some sponsoring firms:
http://www.ishares.com,
http://www.powershares.com,
and http://www.vanguard.com.

JOEL RASSMAN
Senior Vice President, Chief Financial
Officer, Toll Brothers, Inc.

BA, University of New York—
City College
Certified Public Accountant

*"Interest rate changes affect
our business in several ways."*

CAREER PROFILES

Q: *What type of company is Toll Brothers?*

A: Toll Brothers, Inc., the nation's leading builder of luxury homes, operates in twenty-one states. The publicly traded company builds customized single-family and attached homes and develops country club and/or golf course communities and active-adult communities. We operate our own architectural, engineering, mortgage, title, land development and land sale, home security, landscape, lumber distribution, house component assembly, and manufacturing units.

Q: *What are your general responsibilities as CFO at Toll Brothers?*

A: I oversee Wall Street relationships, investor relations, finance, borrowing and bank relationships, treasury functions, taxes, accounting, audit, and risk management. I also serve as an internal consultant for many other aspects of the business.

Q: *How do changing levels of interest rates affect the home-building industry?*

A: Interest rate changes affect our business several ways. Most homebuyers use mortgages to finance their acquisition. If long-term interest rates rise, so do a buyer's monthly payments, and fewer families can afford a home. Changing rates also affect the costs of owning a home versus renting an apartment. Because first-time homebuyers tend to have less disposable income, they are much more sensitive to changing interest rates. Luxury homebuyers buying their third or fourth homes are generally less sensitive. Also, the spread between long-term and short-term rates affects homebuyers' choice of fixed-rate or variable-rate mortgages. Because we borrow to finance our business, our interest costs on floating-rate debt change as rates fluctuate.

Q: *What external funding does Toll Brothers use to finance its activities, and how do interest rates change your financing strategy?*

A: We use many funding sources to finance our business. We have issued new stock in the public markets and used most types of debt instruments: convertible subordinated debentures, bonds, notes, bank term loans and revolving credit, and mortgages for our commercial operations and fixed asset financing. We determine which vehicle to use by analyzing the market and comparing costs of each alternative, choosing the vehicle that minimizes costs while best matching risk and related life of the asset. As a business, you should not finance long-term risk with short-term money.

Q: *What skills make you good at your job?*

A: I understand how business, taxes, finance, and accounting interrelate. Arranging financing that meet the needs of the borrower and lender/investor requires knowledge of capital markets, bank markets, and investors' needs. Patience and understanding other people's needs is a must, as is willingness to listen to others. Most better ideas come from new ideas with successful existing practices. It's also important to think out of the box and look for innovative ways of solving problems. Equally important is the fact that I enjoy what I do.

Q: *How should someone prepare for a career in real estate finance?*

A: Real estate finance is a broad field with such varied opportunities that multiple paths can lead to success. Find an environment that lets you experience different types of transactions and develop multiple skills and a mentor who will explain the reasons behind each transaction. In the right environment you learn something new every day—I still do after thirty-four years in real estate, often from questions people ask.

282

VARIABLE ANNUITY

Another mutual fund look-alike is a variable annuity, a security offered by insurance companies and subsidiaries of a few mutual fund companies. A ***variable annuity*** offers investors the choice of several funds in which to invest. Unlike mutual funds, closed-end funds, and ETFs, the funds invested in variable annuity units grow tax deferred over time. Taxes are paid only when annuity units are redeemed and converted to cash.

A variable annuity is an insurance product since in the case of death the investor's beneficiaries will receive funds that are no less than the initial investment less any subsequent withdrawals. This insurance benefit is of most practical importance if the market declines after the investment is made and the investor passes away before the market recovers. If the investor lives long enough, upon the investor's retirement the annuity will pay an income stream as long as the policyholder lives, so a long-lived annuitant can end up earning a nice return on his invested funds.

CONCEPT CHECK

What is a mutual fund?

What is an exchange-traded fund?

How does a variable annuity differ from a mutual fund?

A disadvantage of an annuity is its higher costs. In addition to expenses for managing the fund, investors pay a *mortality fee* for the insurance protection and promise of a lifelong annuity. Because of this, total annual expenses on a variable annuity usually exceed 2 percent on stock and bond funds, which far exceeds the average expense ratios of most mutual funds.

Since the annuity pays an income stream, another disadvantage is that all investment gains, even those arising from capital gains, are taxed at (higher) income tax rates rather than (lower) capital gains tax rates. Additionally, variable annuity families offer fewer investment options than do mutual fund families. Although some switching of accounts is allowed, the variety of choices is limited.

ETHICS AND JOB OPPORTUNITIES IN INVESTMENTS

ETHICAL ISSUES

Important components of the financial markets are the laws and regulations governing them. Without regulatory bodies and laws, the financial markets and securities trading would be hampered. Regulations dealing with deposit insurance in banks, the required discussion of risks in a new security prospectus, laws forbidding corporate "insiders" to use their privileged information for private gain, and requirements for fair dealings by brokers and dealers when trading for clients work to increase the public's sense of trust and confidence in the financial markets. Individuals who deal with clients must be registered in the state in which they work and must register with the Securities and Exchange Commission.

Regulations often arise from past abuses or problems. Many of the long-standing regulations in U.S. markets (the Securities Act of 1933 and the Securities Exchange Act of 1934) resulted from the situation surrounding the stock market crash of 1929. More recently, the Sarbanes-Oxley Act of 2002 arose from corporate accounting scandals. The oversight provided by corporate boards and external auditors failed in some companies, and as a result false financial statements hid the true condition of a company. Once uncovered, corporate failure, bankruptcy, job losses, pension losses, and criminal charges involved companies such as Enron, WorldCom, Tyco, Arthur Andersen, and HealthSouth.

Unfortunately, others entrusted with people's savings sometimes have been found less than worthy. Several mutual fund firms and investment banks have been accused of wrongdoing in recent years. Stock analysts who worked at investment banking firms wrote false and optimistic research reports, hoping to attract or to keep clients using their firm's lucrative, high-fee investment banking business. Others allocated shares of "hot" or popular IPOs to top executives of firms that used the firm's investment banking business. Persons and firms involved in such unethical dealings include Jack Grubman of Salomon Smith Barney and Henry Blodgett of Merrill Lynch.[10]

To help maintain the professionalism and ethics of the investments field, professional designations have been developed. Very few persons with the CFA® or CFP™ designations were involved in these scandals because of the ethics training that is part of these programs. Persons who receive the designations, by passing exams and having a requisite amount of work experience, show they have a certain level of expertise in their field and agree to abide by

---

10. See the list of corporate scandals at http://www.marketwatch.com/news/features/scandal_sheet.asp (accessed July 7, 2007).

TABLE 10.7
Ethical Standards in Investment Professional Certifications

CHARTERED FINANCIAL ANALYST (CFA®) STANDARDS OF PROFESSIONAL CONDUCT	CERTIFIED FINANCIAL PLANNER (CFP™) CODE OF ETHICS AND PROFESSIONAL RESPONSIBILITY
Standard I: Fundamental Responsibilities	These Principles of the Code express the professional recognition of its responsibilities to the public, to clients, to colleagues, and to employers. They apply to all CFP designees and provide guidance to them in the performance of their professional services.
Standard II: Relationships with and Responsibilities to the Profession	
Standard III: Relationships with and Responsibilities to the Employer	
Standard IV: Relationships with and Responsibilities to Clients and Prospects	Principle 1: Integrity
Standard V: Relationships with and Responsibilities to the Investing Public	Principle 2: Objectivity
For additional details, see http://www.cfainstitute.org.	Principle 3: Competence
	Principle 4: Fairness
	Principle 5: Confidentiality
	Principle 6: Professionalism
	Principle 7: Diligence
	For additional details, see http://www.cfp.net.

CONCEPT CHECK

What major laws have been created due to ethical lapses in the market?

How do professional designations incorporate ethics awareness?

a code of ethics and professional standards in their dealings with clients and their employer. An overview of expected behaviors for holders of two investment professional certifications is given in Table 10.7.

Ethics is an important concern in investments-related professions since practitioners advise clients and invest or handle large sums of money. Virtually any career path within the investments field has federal or state regulations on behavior in addition to those required from an earned professional designation. Additional information about investments-related careers can be found on the Web pages of financial firms, such as http://www.ml.com, http://www.smithbarney.com, http://www.schwab.com, and http://www.agedwards.com.

KEY TERMS

accumulation phase

active investment philosophy

annuity

asset allocation

average tax rate

beta

Capital Asset Pricing Model (CAPM)

chartists (technicians)

closed-end investment company

consolidation phase

efficient market

exchange-traded funds (ETFs)

gifting phase

investment

investment constraints

investment objectives

liquid

marginal tax rate

market portfolio

mutual fund (open-end investment company)

net worth

objectives

passive investment philosophy

policy statement

random walk

semi-strong-form efficient market

spending phase

strong-form efficient market

systematic risk (market risk)

variable annuity

unsystematic risk

weak-form efficient market

DISCUSSION QUESTIONS

1. What is an investment? How does it differ from gambling or buying insurance?

2. How does a strategy of "capital preservation" differ from minimizing the chance of loss to maintain the nominal value of the invested dollars?

3. What are the three sources of return we should expect to receive prior to investing? How can each be measured?

4. What are the five reasons or strategies for investing?

5. How does the capital appreciation strategy differ from total return strategy?

6. Explain what is meant by *market efficiency*. What are the characteristics of an efficient market?

7. What are the differences among the weak, semi-strong, and strong forms of the efficient market hypothesis?

8. What type of market efficiency—none, weak, semi-strong, or strong—is reflected in each of the following statements?

   a. I know which stocks are going to rise in value by looking at their price changes over the past two weeks.

   b. Returns earned by company officers trading their own firm's stock are no higher than those of other investors.

c. If a firm announces lower-than-expected earnings, you know the price will fall over a few days.

d. By the time I heard the news about the dividend increase, the stock had already risen by a substantial amount.

e. Whatever the stock market does in January, it will continue to move in that direction for the rest of the year.

f. As soon as the chairman of the Federal Reserve gave his testimony to Congress about future monetary policy, interest rates rose and stock prices dropped.

9. Explain if you agree or disagree with this statement: "After the merger announcement the stock price increased greatly. Then it fell for the next one or two days before becoming relatively stable. This is proof against the efficient market hypothesis."

10. How do mutual fund return data present evidence for or against efficient markets? Explain.

11. What is meant by the Capital Asset Pricing Model? Describe how it relates to expected return and risk.

12. Define the concept of *beta*, and describe what it measures.

13. What is the market portfolio? Can we invest in such a portfolio?

14. Describe how a person's saving and investing behaviors differ across the investor life cycle stages.

15. What is the portfolio management process?

16. Discuss the role of the policy statement to the portfolio management process.

17. How might the two investment objectives and the five constraints differ for a soon-to-be-retired sixty-five-year-old when compared to the twenty-five-year-old discussed in this chapter?

18. How does an active investment strategy differ from a passive investment strategy?

19. Is the rebalancing of a portfolio when one asset allocation becomes too high or too low consistent with being a "passive" investor? Why or why not?

20. For what reasons are mutual funds such a popular investment vehicle?

21. How are a mutual fund, closed-end fund, ETF, and variable annuity similar?

22. What are the differences between the following?

a. mutual fund and closed-end fund

b. closed-end fund and ETF

c. mutual fund and variable annuity

23. What are some ethical issues that have plagued the investments and securities industry?

24. How do professional designations raise ethical awareness among practitioners?

PROBLEMS

1. Go to the Federal Reserve of St. Louis Web site (http://research. stlouisfed.org/fred2) and download data for T-bills, T-notes, and TIPS securities. What do their differences tell you about changing inflationary expectations over time in the financial markets? About changing horizon (time) premiums?

2. Construct a spreadsheet similar to the one in Table 10.2 to show the effect of investing $2,000 annually at an average return of 6 percent over ten, twenty, thirty, and forty years.

3. Suppose you wish to retire in thirty years. Which investment option is better, assuming a 7 percent average return:

a. Invest $2,000 a year for the first ten years and nothing for the following twenty years.

b. Wait ten years and invest $2,000 a year for the next twenty years until you retire.

4. Using the tax information in Table 10.3, how much in federal tax should each of the following people pay?

a. Married couple earning $60,000

b. Single person earning $60,000

5. For the persons in Problem 4, what is the marginal tax rate for each? What is their average tax rate?

6. Which of the following is a better investment for someone in the 25 percent tax bracket? Assume the time to maturity and risk is similar for each. Also, how do the answers to (a) and (b) change if the investor's marginal tax rate is 33 percent?

a. Municipal bond sold at par with a coupon of 4.5 percent versus a corporate bond with a coupon of 5.7 percent

b. Municipal bond sold at par with a coupon of 5 percent versus a corporate bond with a coupon of 7 percent

7. Compute the NAV of each of the following funds:

FUND	ASSETS	LIABILITIES	NUMBER OF SHARES	AVERAGE RETURN
JimJ Fund	$1,000	$0	975	8.8%
Mackey Fund	$1,458	$98	579	10.3%
Aimz Fund	$777	$165	759	7.7%
MSN Fund	$3,316	$33	957	4.0%

LEARNING EXTENSION 10

Estimating Beta

We can estimate beta for a stock or portfolio of stocks relative to the overall stock market using simple linear regression analysis. The reader might recall the following equation from a prior course in statistics. However, prior work in statistics is not necessary to grasp the following concepts. In simple equation form we have:

$$R_i = \alpha + \beta R_{MKT} + e_i \qquad \text{(LE10.1)}$$

where α = the alpha or intercept term, β = the beta or slope coefficient that shows the size of the impact that market returns (R_{MKT}) have on stock returns (R_i), and e_i = an error term reflecting the fact that changes in market returns are not likely to fully explain changes in stock returns. This straight line is shown in Figure LE10.1.

Some computer software programs and sophisticated financial calculators can perform the necessary calculations and find the beta coefficient with little effort. Spreadsheet software can perform this analysis, too. In addition, we can estimate beta the "long way" by using relatively simple calculations that can be done by hand or by using a simple calculator. We will demonstrate the long way of estimating beta so that the reader can develop a better understanding of the underlying process.

Let's begin by using the monthly returns over a recent six-month period between the market, as measured by the S&P 500 and Microsoft (in practice, beta is often computed using sixty months' worth of data, but we will use only six months for the purposes of this illustration):

MONTH	MSFT RETURN	S&P 500 RETURN
1	−2.0%	−1.7%
2	4.8%	−1.7%
3	−6.0%	−1.6%
4	−4.1%	1.2%
5	1.0%	1.7%
6	6.5%	5.1%

We now want to measure the systematic risk of Microsoft relative to the market. Let's first plot these returns on the graph in Figure LE10.2. The market's returns are plotted along the x (horizontal) axis since we are interested in examining how Microsoft's returns move with or respond to the market's returns. Microsoft's monthly returns are plotted along the y (vertical) axis. Notice that there is a positive (upward-sloping) relationship between the returns on the market and Microsoft's returns. We also have inserted a line across the scatter plot of annual returns. In addition to having a positive relationship, the steepness of the slope of the line reflects how much Microsoft's returns respond to a change in the market's returns. Thus, the beta coefficient is the slope of this line and indicates the sensitivity of Microsoft's returns to the market's returns.

Now let's calculate the slope or beta of the relationship between the returns on the market and returns on Microsoft. The calculations used to estimate beta are shown in Table LE10.1. A beta of 0.93 indicates that Microsoft was less risky than the market over this time frame. More specifically, based on six months of past data, we can say that on average a 1 percent increase (decrease) in the monthly return on the market was accompanied by a 0.93 percentage increase

FIGURE LE10.1

Graph of $R_i = \alpha + \beta R_{MKT} + e_i$

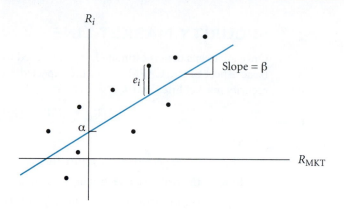

FIGURE LE10.2

Plot of Returns for Microsoft and the S&P 500

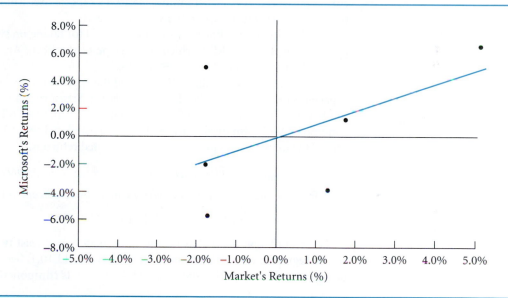

TABLE LE10.1

How to Calculate a Beta Coefficient or Measure of Systematic Risk

MONTH	RATES OF RETURN S&P 500 X-AXIS	MICROSOFT Y-AXIS	MARKET'S RETURNS SQUARED X^2	PRODUCT OF THE RETURNS $X \times Y$
1	−1.70%	−2.00%	2.89%	3.40%
2	−1.70	4.80	2.89	−8.16
3	−1.60	−6.00	2.56	9.60
4	1.20	−4.10	1.44	−4.92
5	1.70	1.00	2.89	1.70
6	5.10	6.50	26.01	33.15
	Sum X = 3.00%	Sum Y = 0.20%	Sum X^2 = 38.68%	Sum XY = 34.77%

Estimating beta where n = 6 is the number of observations:

$$\beta = \frac{n \sum xy - (\sum x)(\sum y)}{n \sum x^2 - (\sum x)^2} = \frac{6(34.77) - (3.00)(0.20)}{6(38.68) - (3.0)(3.0)} = \frac{208.02}{223.08} = 0.93$$

(decrease) in Microsoft's monthly returns. It is important to note that our estimate was based on only six observations. Normally, betas are estimated using many more data points.

SECURITY MARKET LINE

Once an asset's beta is estimated, it can be used to form the basis of return predictions. Another basic aspect of the CAPM is that the expected return/risk trade-off for an asset is given by the security market line (SML):

$$E(R_i) = RFR + [E(R_{MKT}) - RFR]\beta_i \qquad (LE10.2)$$

where:

$E(R_i)$ = the expected rate of return for asset i

RFR = the risk-free rate, usually measured by the rate of return on Treasury bills

β_i = the measure of systematic risk (beta) for asset i

$E(R_{MKT})$ = the expected return on the market portfolio

The security market line is shown in Figure LE10.3. Note that the dependent variable in this relationship is the expected return on the asset and the independent variable is β_i. The asset's risk, as measured by beta, determines the asset's expected return. It is an asset's or portfolio's risk that determines return expectations, not vice versa.

The security market line shows that the reward for taking on systematic risk is the market risk premium, $E(R_{MKT}) - RFR$, which is the slope of the SML. An asset's risk premium, or extra expected return, equals $[E(R_{MKT}) - RFR]\beta_i$.

To illustrate the use of the SML, let's find the expected return on AT&T stock if the market is expected to rise 9 percent. We'll assume that the Treasury bill rate is 4.0 percent. We'll need to use Equation LE10.2, the security market line, to estimate AT&T's expected return under these conditions. We'll also need to use AT&T's beta listed in Table 10.1. Using its recent beta of 0.41, should the market rise 8 percent, AT&T's expected return is:

$$E(R_{AT\&T}) = 4 + [9 - 4] \times 0.41 = 6.05 \text{ percent}$$

If, for example, the market portfolio were to fall by 15 percent, AT&T's expected return would be:

$$E(R_{AT\&T}) = 4 + [-15 - 4] \times 0.41 = -3.79 \text{ percent}$$

The beta of a *portfolio* of assets can be estimated in at least two ways. First, portfolio returns can be regressed on market returns using Equation LE10.1. Second, the beta of a portfolio can be estimated by computing the weighted average of its component's betas:

$$Beta_p = \sum_{t=1}^{n} w_i \, beta_i \qquad (LE10.3)$$

FIGURE LE10.3
Security Market Line

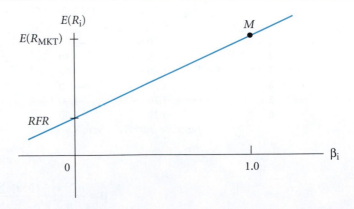

where w_i is the weight of the ith asset in the portfolio. Unlike the portfolio variance risk measure, the systematic risk of a portfolio does equal the weighted average of its component's systematic risk.

Beta has several practical uses in finance. It is used to determine investors' required rate of return on an investment. It also is used to develop estimates of shareholders' required returns on their investments. Also, as we have seen here, beta is a valuable measure of the systematic risk of an asset.

QUESTIONS AND PROBLEMS

1. Stock market forecasters are predicting that the stock market will rise a modest 5 percent next year. Given the beta of each of the following stocks, what is the expected change in each stock's value?

FIRM	BETA
BCD	1.25
NOP	0.70
WXY	1.10
ZYX	1.00

2. Suppose the estimated security market line is $E(R_i) = 4.0 + 7(\beta_i)$.

   a. What is the current Treasury bill rate?

   b. What is the current market risk premium?

   c. What is the current expected market return?

   d. Explain what beta (β_i) measures.

3. Financial researchers at Smith Sharon, an investment bank, estimate the current security market line as $E(R_i) = 4.5 + 6.8(\beta_i)$.

   a. Explain what happens to expected return as beta increases from 1.0 to 2.0.

   b. Suppose an asset has a beta of -1.0. What is the expected return on this asset? Would anyone want to invest in it? Why or why not?

4. Answer the following:

   a. What was the risk-free rate in the economy for the year if Stevens Incorporated's stock has a 14 percent return, a beta of 0.85, and a 15 percent market return?

   b. The stock market of another company had a return of 20 percent. What would you estimate its beta to be?

5. You've collected data on the betas of various mutual funds. Each fund and its beta are listed in the following table:

MUTUAL FUND	BETA
Weak Fund	0.23
Fido Fund	0.77
Vanwatch	1.05
Temper	1.33

   a. Estimate the beta of your fund holdings if you held equal proportions of each of the listed funds.

   b. Estimate the beta of your fund holdings if you had 20 percent of your investments in the Weak fund, 40 percent in Fido, 15 percent in Vanwatch, and the remainder in Temper.

6. Using your answers to (a) and (b) in Problem 5, estimate your portfolio's expected return if the security market line is estimated as $E(R_i) = 5.2 + 8.4(\beta_i)$.

7. **EXCEL** Spreadsheets can do the work for us of computing beta. Use Excel's slope function to estimate the beta of Microsoft using the data in Table LE10.1. Use the intercept function to estimate the alpha or intercept term of the regression line.

8. **EXCEL** Following are return data for Walgreens and the S&P 500 for nine months:

MONTH	WALGREENS RETURN	S&P 500 RETURN
1	2.0%	7.5%
2	-5.9%	1.8%
3	0.2%	-8.2%
4	2.0%	-6.4%
5	-2.2%	-1.1%
6	-14.3%	-2.5%
7	-6.0%	0.5%
8	4.9%	7.7%
9	-7.9%	-6.4%

   a. Estimate the intercept (alpha) and beta for Walgreens stock using spreadsheet functions.

   b. Interpret what the slope estimate means to a stock analyst.

   c. Compute the R-squared of the regression using Excel's RSQ function. What does the R-squared tell us about the relationship between the returns of Walgreen and those of the market?

P A R T 3

FINANCIAL MANAGEMENT

INTRODUCTION

The field of finance is comprised of three areas—institutions and markets, investments, and financial management. These areas are illustrated in the accompanying diagram. Part 3 deals with the applications of finance within a business firm. The practice of financial management requires businesspeople to work with financial institutions in the context of the financial markets. If Allgreens needs a short-term loan to help finance inventory for the Christmas selling season, it can go to a bank for the loan. But the interest rate that Allgreens pays will be affected by the current level of interest rates in the economy, which is determined by a variety of economic conditions. If Allgreens needs to raise many millions of dollars to finance new expansion and construction, it can work with another type of financial institution, an investment bank, which will help Allgreens sell bonds or shares of common stock to raise the needed funds. The interest rate on the bonds and the price of the stock are determined by the conditions of the financial markets.

Institutions and investors pay close attention to a firm's financial management policies. Market participants glean information from a firm's financial statements, namely its balance sheet, income statement, and statement of cash flows. Changes in a firm's financial condition inform investors of a firm's strengthening or weakening position against its competitors. Investors and lending institutions may express concern if a firm's financing policy changes so that it begins to use much more debt financing than it has in the past.

A firm's managers use information that they obtain from the financial markets and institutions. They will keep their eyes on the firm's stock price. Changes in the stock price may reflect investor happiness or dissatisfaction with the company and its management's decisions. Managers will use interest rate and stock price information from the financial markets to evaluate the firm's own investments in its lines of business. The level of short-term interest rates, the level of long-term interest rates, and stock prices will influence management's decisions about how to raise funds to finance the firm's activities.

Chapter 11 introduces the various ways a business can be organized and the financial implications of each organizational form. We discuss the financial goal of maximizing shareholder wealth as well as the three basic accounting statements: the balance sheet, income statement, and statement of cash flows. Chapter 12 continues the discussion of financial statements by showing how the information contained in them can be used to evaluate a firm's strengths and weaknesses. We review how managers use financial statement relationships to estimate the firm's future asset and financing needs.

In Chapter 13 the focus changes to managing a firm's long-term assets. We introduce capital budgeting, which is a financial technique for deciding in which assets a firm should invest. Chapter 14 shows, through many examples, the process of estimating cash flows for a possible capital budgeting project.

Chapter 15 discusses factors that influence firms' long-term financing choices. We bring the financial markets front and center in our discussion of how a firm uses financial information to determine its financing costs and how the financing costs affect its capital budgeting choices.

Any firm will have both short-term and long-term investment and financing needs. Chapter 16 discusses strategies and methods for managing a firm's short-term assets, such as cash, accounts receivable, and inventory. We show how a cash budget can be used to estimate a firm's future short-term financing needs. Chapter 17 reviews various sources of short-term financing for businesses, including bank loans, trade credit, and many other non-bank financing sources.

Finance is a global phenomenon. Investors in any country can invest in virtually any other country; similarly, firms can raise capital in global markets. A recession in Europe can affect interest rates in the U.S. The final chapter reviews the role of financial markets, institutions, investors, and business firms in the setting of international trade and finance.

• CHAPTER 11 •

Business Organization and Financial Data

Chapter Learning Objectives

AFTER STUDYING THIS CHAPTER, YOU SHOULD BE ABLE TO:

• Describe the three major forms of business organization.
• Provide a brief description of the income statement.
• Provide a brief description of the balance sheet.
• Provide a brief description of the statement of cash flows.
• Identify the goal and functions of financial management.
• Describe the agency relationships in a business organization and their implications for financial management.
• Discuss tax law implications (in Learning Extension 11)

Where We Have Been. . .

We've seen how the financial system supports the flow of funds from saving units to those who need to borrow funds or raise equity by selling shares. Financial markets, interest rates, securities prices, and risk and return considerations help direct funds efficiently to their best purpose to help the global economy run as smoothly as possible. One of the biggest users of capital in the financial markets are businesses, from the entrepreneur seeking start-up financing, to the firm issuing shares for the first time in an IPO, to an exporter arranging overseas financing for a purchase. No discussion of finance is complete without a look at financial management—how businesses use the financial system and markets to raise funds and direct capital to keep their firms running and to meet customers' needs.

Where We Are Going. . .

How a business is organized has implications for a manager's incentives. Financial statement information is valuable to investors and managers to help them make appropriate decisions. We'll see applications of these concepts in the next few chapters, including financial analysis (Chapter 12), capital project analysis (Chapters 13 and 14), and managing working capital (Chapter 16).

How This Chapter Applies to Me. . .

Rather than accept the first job offered to you, try to work for a company with a mission and vision that relate to your personal values. Statistics show, on average, people have five to seven different "careers" during their working lives as their employers and career paths change. You will probably not stay with the firm that hires you after graduation, but you want that first job and all successive positions to be a "fit" for your values and lifestyle. Annual reports are important sources of information to you, both as an investor and employee, about the firm.

Successful businesses prepare financial plans. To make this point more clearly, we provide the following quotation from an unknown author:

> *Failure to plan is planning to fail.*

An important part of planning is to do financial planning for a firm. All businesses require financing. Money is needed to finance plant and equipment and to support current opera-

292

tions. Some firms require very little capital, and the industries in which these firms operate have a vast number of competitors. Any field of activity that requires little financial capital is open to a host of people who want to establish their own business, such as Internet Web site designers or financial counselors. At the other extreme are businesses that require huge amounts of financial capital to operate even on a minimum scale. In the auto and steel industries, for example, because of capital requirements, only a few large firms dominate in national or regional markets.

We begin this chapter with a brief preview of some of the factors to consider when deciding to start a business. One of the decisions to be made is how the business will be organized. We discuss issues relating to a firm's goals and problems that can arise if a firm's owners are not the same people as the firm's managers.

The remainder of the chapter focuses on the financial data provided by business firms. Those firms organized as corporations must provide a summary of their financial performance in an annual report to their shareholders. Included in annual reports are three basic financial statements—the income statement, the balance sheet, and the statement of cash flows—that businesses need to prepare. Even individually owned or closely held firms need to prepare financial statements for tax purposes. Just as important, these financial statements contain much of the language of business, such as revenues, expenses, assets, liabilities, and equity. The financial statements are analyzed by the firm's managers, the firm's competitors, banks, and other financial market participants who are considering buying or selling the firm's securities. In this chapter's Learning Extension, we discuss taxation and depreciation concepts that business managers must understand if they are to be successful in managing their businesses.

STARTING A BUSINESS

In our market economy, individuals have the freedom to establish any legal business they choose. However, they must have adequate financial capital of their own or be able to arrange the necessary financing. The success of a business in raising funds for operations depends on its profit potential.

STRATEGIC PLAN WITH A VISION OR MISSION

mission statement
statement of a firm's reason for being; sometimes called a vision statement

A business should begin with a vision or **mission statement** that is consistent with the planned overall strategy. The vision or mission should indicate what the firm wants to produce, distribute, and sell or indicate what services it wants to provide. The statement helps declare the company's main reason for being; in times when new opportunities look attractive, the firm's managers should go back and read the mission statement to ensure their actions are consistent with it. Comments on quality objectives and customer and owner focus also are typically found in vision and mission statements. Some statements are idealistic in their views.

Both small and large companies formulate strategic plans with visions and missions. Let's take a look at some of these statements.[1] For example, Ben & Jerry's Ice Cream Company has the following detailed statement of mission:

> *Ben & Jerry's is founded on and dedicated to a sustainable corporate concept of linked prosperity. Our mission consists of three interrelated parts:*
>
> ***Product Mission:*** *To make, distribute and sell the finest quality all natural ice cream and euphoric concoctions with a continued commitment to incorporating wholesome, natural ingredients and promoting business practices that respect the Earth and the environment.*
>
> ***Economic Mission:*** *To operate the Company on a sustainable financial basis of profitable growth, increasing value for our stakeholders and expanding opportunities for development and career growth for our employees.*
>
> ***Social Mission:*** *To operate the company in a way that actively recognizes the central role that business plays in society by initiating innovative ways to improve the quality of life locally, nationally and internationally.*

---

1. The mission statements we use in this chapter were found on each company's Web site.

Central to the mission of Ben & Jerry's is the belief that all three parts must thrive equally in a manner that commands deep respect for individuals in and outside the company and supports the communities of which they are a part.

Wendy's, the company that sells Wendy's Old Fashioned Hamburgers and other products, wants to:

Deliver superior quality products and services for our customers and communities through leadership, innovation, and partnerships.

Wells Fargo, a nationwide diversified financial services company providing banking, insurance, investments, and other financial services, has the following vision:

We want to satisfy all of our customers' financial needs, help them succeed financially, be the premier provider of financial services in every one of our markets, and be known as one of America's great companies.

Merck & Company, Inc., one of the world's largest pharmaceutical companies, states that:

The mission of Merck is to provide society with superior products and services—innovations and solutions that improve the quality of life and satisfy customer needs and to provide employees with meaningful work and advancement opportunities and investors with a superior rate of return.

Dell is a well-known computer and peripheral manufacturer. Its mission statement is short and to the point:

Dell's mission is to be the most successful computer company in the world at delivering the best customer experience in markets we serve.

BUSINESS AND FINANCIAL GOALS

A guiding force behind top management's decisions should be the mission statement. At the same time, the mission statement should not be carved in stone; it should be periodically reviewed to ensure it is up-to-date and reflects market needs in a dynamic, global economy. On the other hand, a business cannot chase every idea developed by its managers. Businesses need to stick to what they do best, or in the parlance of management, strategic goals should be related to the firm's core competencies.[2] Businesses must support their visions and missions with business and financial goals or plans—sometimes referred to as operating plans. Such plans may include specific numeric goals for customer satisfaction ratings, market share, and return to shareholders. Such plans allow managers to track their progress toward achieving the plan and mission of the firm.

Attracting and acquiring financing are necessary to obtain the factors of production required to conduct business operations. Allocation of these factors is largely automatic under the market system. Resources flow smoothly to those businesses that through their past operations and the promise of profitable future operations are able to pay for them. Investors, as providers of debt and equity capital, expect a return on their investment. As we saw in Chapter 6, actual returns usually differ from expected returns. This is the risk faced by investors, but the investor or the financial intermediary who assumes an unusually large risk does so with the full expectation that, if things go well with the firm, the rewards for the investment will be very great. Where the possible risk is very small, the potential reward is small. As explained in Chapter 6, there is a trade-off between expected return and risk. Investment funds flow both to risky firms and very safe firms, invested according to the intermediary's or the investors' risk preferences.

FORMS OF BUSINESS ORGANIZATION IN THE UNITED STATES

Three major forms of business ownership are used in the United States: proprietorship, partnership, and corporation. Proprietorships are the most widely used form, although they are generally the smallest organizations in terms of assets. About 72 percent of U.S. firms are proprietorships,

INTERNET ACTIVITY

Most corporations' Web sites will have links to their mission or vision statements. Visit the home pages of firms you are familiar with and find their missions. The Web sites of the firms mentioned in this section are http://www.benjerry.com, http://www.wendys.com, http://www.wellsfargo.com, http://www.merck.com, and http://www.dell.com.

CONCEPT CHECK

What is a mission or vision statement?

Why is a mission statement important to a firm?

Why won't investors' money only be invested in large, safe firms?

2. C. K. Prahalad and G. Hamel, "The Core Competence of the Corporation," *Harvard Business Review* (May–June 1990), 79–91.

SMALL BUSINESS PRACTICE
Habits of Successful Small Companies

As we know, hundreds of thousands of firms start up each year. Many will fail or go out of business for various reasons. Some will struggle while a few will thrive. You probably are ready to ask: What are some of the characteristics or "habits" of firms that become successful? Well an article by Leslie Brokaw titled "The Truth about Start-Ups" in *Small Business Success,* a supplement to *Inc.* magazine, has identified some of these habits. Each year *Inc.* identifies the fifty fastest-growing companies in the United States. These firms often are examined in an effort to identify common characteristics or habits. Following are some findings.

Successful small rapidly growing firms "often rely on team efforts." We often credit the success of a start-up to a single founder or CEO. Rather, many successful firms are started by team efforts in

the form of founding partners. Successful firms generally are "headed by people who know their line of work." Past professional experience in their fields is a common characteristic of successful entrepreneurs. Brokaw also suggests that successful companies are founded and built by "people who have started other businesses." For example, many of the *Inc.* 500 CEOs had started at least one other business prior to their current business.

Brokaw also suggests that highly successful, rapidly growing firms are "disproportionately manufacturers, and they're high tech." For example, nearly one-half of the *Inc.* 500 companies view themselves as being high-tech ventures. These rapidly growing firms also "are not owned by the founders alone." Many of the CEOs of *Inc.* 500 companies own less than 50 percent of the equity in their businesses.

about 8 percent are partnerships, and the remaining 20 percent are corporations. In terms of revenues, 85 percent of sales are generated by corporations, about 10 percent by partnerships, and about 5 percent by proprietorships.[3]

The choice of a legal form of organization for a business is a strategic matter from many points of view. Managerial lines of authority and control, legal responsibility, and the allocation of income and risk are all directly related to the form the organization takes. In this chapter we look at the relationship between the legal form of organization and its sources and methods of financing and its allocation of risk. Table 11.1 summarizes some of the points of this discussion.

PROPRIETORSHIP

proprietorship
business venture that is owned by a single individual who personally receives all profits and assumes all responsibility for the debts and losses of the business

The **proprietorship**, sometimes called a sole proprietorship, is a business venture that is owned by a single individual who personally receives all profits and assumes all responsibility for the debts and losses of the business. Typically the owner is the manager; he or she is in total control of the firm. It is hard to separate the owner from the firm. Proprietorships far outnumber all other forms of business organization in the United States. However, the economic power of these firms, as measured by number of employees and size of payrolls, is far less than that of the nation's corporations.

The financial capital of proprietorships is many times limited to the savings of the owner and funds that may be borrowed from friends, relatives, and banks. The investment made by the owner is called **equity capital** or owner's equity. As the business grows and larger investments in capital are required, the owner may reach the point where additional funds cannot be borrowed without an increase in owner's equity. Lenders will generally insist on an increase in the owner's equity because that equity provides a margin of safety for the lender.

equity capital
investment made by the owner into the company

This point is where the proprietorship form of organization displays its basic weakness. In many cases, the owner's original investment exhausts his or her personal resources and often those of friends and relatives. Unless profits from the venture are great enough to meet the increased equity needs, the firm is prevented from achieving its maximum growth. At this stage it may be necessary to adopt a form of organization more appropriate for capital-raising purposes.

In addition, the life of the proprietorship is limited to that of the proprietor. When the proprietor dies, the business ends. Another weakness is the difficulty in transferring ownership (sometimes called ownership "liquidity") of the proprietorship. It can be difficult to sell a proprietorship. Among the complicating factors is that the firm is likely to sell at a discount, or for a percentage, of its value because of the difficulty in determining the business's past profitability, cash flows, risks, and future market potential. Much of what has made the proprietorship successful may be the proprietor herself or at least the information that is in the proprietor's mind.

---

3. Data are taken from the *Statistical Abstract of the United States,* 2007 edition.

TABLE 11.1
Organizational Forms and Financial Characteristics

ORGANIZATIONAL FORM	NUMBER OF OWNERS	OWNER'S LIABILITY	EQUITY CAPITAL SOURCES	EASE OF START-UP	TAXATION	LIQUIDITY OF OWNERSHIP	LIFE SPAN
Proprietorship	1	Unlimited	Self, friends, relatives	Simple	Personal taxation	Difficult to sell	Linked to owner
Partnership (general)	>1	Unlimited, jointly and severally	Partners, friends, relatives	Not difficult	Personal taxation	Difficult to sell	Linked to owners
Limited partnership	At least 1 general, any number of limited partners	Limited partners' liability is limited to partners' investment	General and limited partners	More difficult	Personal taxation	Usually poor	Linked to general partner
Corporation	Unlimited	Limited to shareholders' investment	Common stock offerings	Difficult	Corporate taxation, but dividends are taxed twice, both as corporate earnings and personal income	Can be very liquid	Unlimited
Subchapter S corporation	<35	Limited to shareholders' investment	Sub S equity investors	Difficult	Income flows to shareholders for taxation at personal rates	Usually poor	Unlimited
Limited liability company (LLC)	Unlimited	Limited to owners' investment	Common stock offerings	Difficult	Income flows to shareholders for taxation at personal rates	Poor	Linked to current shareholders

Another weakness of proprietorships is that the owner's liability for debts of the firm is unlimited. Creditors may take not only the assets of the business to settle claims but also the personal assets of the proprietor. Thus the proprietor may find his or her home and personal property under claim if the assets of the business are not sufficient to meet the demands of creditors. The unlimited liability of the owner is, therefore, a serious disadvantage of the proprietorship.

On the positive side, a proprietorship business is easily started with minimal expense and generally has fewer government regulations to comply with than does a corporation. Profits from a proprietorship are taxed at personal or individual rates rather than at corporate income tax rates. Furthermore, it is relatively easy to convert a business that was established as a proprietorship into a corporation when the need to finance growth warrants such a move.

partnership
form of business organization in which two or more people own a business operated for profit

PARTNERSHIP

A ***partnership*** form of business organization exists when two or more persons own a business operated for profit. Although the partnership resembles the proprietorship to some degree, there are important differences. See Table 11.1 for a summary.

Undoubtedly, one of the major reasons for the popularity of the partnership arrangement is that it allows individuals to pool their resources of money, property, equipment, knowledge, and business skills without the complications that often accompany incorporation. A partnership form may exist from the beginning of a business operation. In other cases a firm that began as a proprietorship may reach the point where additional growth is impossible without increased equity capital. Bringing in new equity investors by converting to a partnership arrangement is one method of increasing the equity capital of a firm.

The number of partners that may be taken into a business venture is theoretically unlimited. However, the managerial difficulties and conflicts arising with many partners limit their number to a practical size. Thus the partnership, like the proprietorship, eventually suffers from a lack of large amounts of equity capital. It is unusual to find more than a few partners in an industrial or commercial firm.

Similar to the proprietorship, the life of a partnership is linked to that of its partners. Should a partner leave or die, the partnership officially dissolves unless a new partnership agreement is drafted. For purposes of taxation, the partnership's profits (and losses) are distributed to the partners and are taxable to the individual partner. Like proprietorships, partnerships have typically illiquid ownership stakes. Partners' shares of most small to medium businesses are often sold at a discount that reflects their lack of liquidity, their lack of majority control over the firm, and the need for the new partner to "fit" with the existing partners.

Like the proprietor, the members of a partnership team risk their personal assets as well as their investments in the business venture. In addition, if one of the partners negotiates a contract that results in substantial loss, each partner suffers a portion of the loss, based on a previously determined agreement on distribution of profits and losses. The other partners may, however, sue the offending partner if there is any violation of the articles of co-partnership.

More serious, perhaps, is a partner's liability for the actions of the business. In legal terms each partner is both jointly and severally liable for the partnership's debts. Under partnership law, each partner has unlimited liability for all the debts of the firm. This permits creditors to claim assets from one or more of the partners if the remaining partners are unable to cover their share of the loss.

limited partnership
has at least one general partner who has unlimited liability; the liability of the limited partners is limited to their investment

limited partners
face limited liability; their personal assets cannot be touched to settle the firm's debt

These liability risks describe a general partnership. A **limited partnership** addresses the liability concern by identifying at least one general partner who has unlimited liability. The remaining **limited partners** face liability limited to their investments in the firm—their personal assets cannot be attached to settle the firm's debts. They are also limited in that they cannot participate in the operations of the firm. Operating decisions may be made only by the general partners. Some sports teams (such as the New York Yankees) are owned by limited partnerships. Broadway theater productions and real estate management and construction firms are other popular limited partnership vehicles.

SMALL BUSINESS PRACTICE
The Family Business or Venture

Family businesses continue to be very popular in the United States. For publicly held firms, corporate goals and the goals of managers may differ. For closely held firms that are nonfamily owned, the business goals and the personal goals of owner/managers are closely aligned. For family-owned or family-controlled firms, a third set of goals—family goals—also must be considered. When family goals are closely aligned with the business and manager goals, the business can benefit from family sharing and closeness. However, when family goals differ from business and/or manager goals, conflict and an argumentative environment may prevail. In such instances, such family-controlled businesses often fail or the family is forced to sell.

Jeffry Timmons in his book titled *New Venture Creation* lists several problems that are unique to family businesses or ventures. First, problems of "control, fairness, and equity" often exist. For example, family members may have different ideas on how the business should be run. Fairness and equity issues relate to the division of work and relative contributions to running the business. Second is the issue of "credibility," whereby founding parents find it difficult to believe that their children can perform in a manner comparable to their own.

Third is a potential problem relating to "family dynamics." Since it often is difficult to separate business operations from family life, tensions in one area often spill over into the other area. Fourth is the problem of deciding succession. If succession is to involve a next-generation family member, the founder must disengage his or her ownership "rights" and delegate an increased level of responsibility to the new person in control. For successful succession to take place, the founder must be willing to assume the role of an advisor to the next-generation family member who was selected to run the firm in the future.

CORPORATION

corporation

legal entity created under state law with unending life that offers limited financial liability to its owners

A *corporation* is a legal entity created under state law in the United States with an unending life and limited financial liability to its owners. (See Table 11.1 for a comparison of organizational forms.) In the case of Dartmouth College versus Woodward in 1819, Chief Justice of the Supreme Court John Marshall described the status of the corporation as follows:

> A corporation is an artificial being, invisible, intangible, and existing only in contemplation of law. Being the mere creature of law, it possesses only those properties which the charter of its creation confers upon it, either expressly, or as incidental to its very existence. . . . Among the most important are immortality and individuality—properties by which a perpetual succession of persons are considered as the same and may act as a single individual.

In essence, the law has created an artificial being that has the rights, duties, and powers of a person. The definition includes the concept of many people united into one body that does not change its identity with changes in ownership. Advantages of being organized as a corporation include unlimited corporate life that is not tied to that of the owners, the ability to attract outside capital, limited financial liability for the owners, and the ease with which ownership can be transferred from investor to investor.

A corporation that has existed only a short time, like most new ventures, usually finds it difficult to attract investment funds from outsiders. The corporate form of organization does not by itself ensure a flow of investment funds into the business. Rather, it removes several of the barriers to the flow of capital that exist in other forms of business organization. But it is only after a corporation appears to offer attractive returns for investors that these special features of the corporate form become significant. One of the important reasons corporations can accumulate large sums of capital is that they are allowed to sell capital stock. The stock may be offered to existing stockholders or to new investors in amounts suited to their purposes. As we discussed in Chapter 9, a firm can go public by registering its shares with the Securities and Exchange Commission (SEC) and then selling them to the investing public. A corporation that has not gone through this process is a privately held corporation.

One of the advantages for corporate stockholders is the limitation on liability. Ordinarily, creditors and other claimants may look only to the assets of the corporation for satisfaction of their claims. They cannot take the personal assets of the owners (stockholders). This advantage is particularly appealing to the owner of a business who has built up considerable personal wealth and has other business interests. The limitation on liability may also make it possible for promoters of new ventures to attract wealthy investors who would otherwise be unwilling to risk claims against their personal property.

On the other hand, the corporate form of organization may not always protect stockholders from personal risk beyond their investment when a business is relatively new or in a weak financial condition. Creditors may simply require that one or more of the stockholders add their signatures to the obligation of the corporation, making them personally liable for the obligation. After a corporation has established a good credit reputation, however, creditors and suppliers seldom insist on personal guarantees on the part of the stockholders.

Another important advantage of the corporation is the ease with which ownership may be transferred. Corporate stock may be transferred freely from one person to another. The purchaser of the stock then has all the rights and privileges formerly held by the seller. The corporation is not a party to the transfer of ownership and has no power to interfere with the sale or purchase of its stock. In contrast, there must be unanimous approval of the members of a partnership before a new partner can be brought into the business.

charter

provides the corporate name, indicates the intended business activities, provides names and addresses of directors, and indicates how a firm will be capitalized with stock

bylaws

rules established to govern the corporation; they deal with how the firm will be managed and the rights of the stockholder

However, just like proprietorships and partnerships, the corporate form of organization has its drawbacks. First, setting up a corporation is more time-consuming and costly because of legal requirements. Individuals who wish to incorporate must hire a lawyer to prepare both a charter and a set of bylaws. The **charter** provides a corporate name, indicates the intended business activities, provides the names and addresses of directors, and indicates how the firm will be capitalized with stock. A corporation is chartered in a specific state by filing the charter with the secretary of that state. The **bylaws** are the rules established to govern the corporation and include how the firm will be managed, how directors will be elected, and the rights of stockholders. After beginning operation, the corporation must file financial and tax statements with state and federal government agencies.

subchapter S corporation
has fewer than 35 shareholders, none of which is another corporation. Its income is taxed only once, as personal income of the shareholders

limited liability company (LLC)
organizational form whose owners have limited liability; the firm can have an unlimited number of shareholders; income is taxed only once as personal income of the shareholders

CONCEPT CHECK

In what ways does a proprietorship differ from a partnership?

In what ways does a proprietorship differ from a corporation?

How do the subchapter S and LLC organizational forms address some of the problems of the corporation organizational form?

INTERNET ACTIVITY

The Web site of the Securities and Exchange Commission, http://www.sec.gov, gives users access to public corporations' financial filings through its EDGAR (electronic data gathering and retrieval) system.

annual report
contains descriptive information and numerical records on the operating and financial performance of a firm during the past year

A second drawback of the corporate form of organization relates to the fact that corporate earnings distributed as shareholder dividends are subject to double taxation. That is, corporate earnings are taxed once at the appropriate corporate income tax rate. Then, if the corporation pays out a portion of its after-tax earnings in the form of dividends, the stockholders must pay personal income taxes on this income.

Two special forms of corporate organization in the United States summarized in Table 11.1 allow dividends to escape double taxation. A **subchapter S corporation** (named for the section of the tax code that discusses this organization) must have fewer than thirty-five shareholders, none of whom is another corporation. Income from a subchapter S corporation flows untaxed to the shareholders. Thus, it is taxed only once, as personal income of the shareholders.

A **limited liability company (LLC)** organizational form is similar to a subchapter S corporation: It offers owners limited liability, and its income is taxed only once as personal income of the shareholder.[4] Unlike a subchapter S corporation, however, an LLC can have an unlimited number of shareholders, including other corporations. The LLC can sell shares without completing the costly and time-consuming process of registering them with the SEC, which is a requirement for standard corporations that sell their securities to the public. The LLC structure has drawbacks in that, should an owner leave, all others must formally agree to continue the firm. Also, all of the LLC's owners must take active roles in managing the company. To protect partners from unlimited liability, some large accounting firms formerly set up as partnerships, such as PricewaterhouseCoopers, have become LLCs. Other partnerships have decided to go the corporate route to limit the partners' liability and to gain access to the capital market; Goldman Sachs, an investment banking firm, has converted from partnership to corporate status.

Many countries' laws recognize the corporate form of organization. American corporations may use the suffixes Inc. or Corp. to designate themselves. British corporations use the suffix PLC, which stands for public limited company; limited refers to shareholders' liability in the firm. The suffix AG following the names of firms in Germany, Austria, Switzerland, and Liechtenstein is an abbreviation for Aktiengesellschaft, which means corporation.

It is up to the firm's owners to weigh the pros and cons and determine which organizational form suits the needs of their firm best. Each has its own implications for taxation, control by the owners, ability to trade ownership positions, limitations on liability, firm life, and raising capital.

THE ANNUAL REPORT

An important component of manager-owner communication is the firm's financial statements. Firms organized as proprietorships or partnerships are not required to prepare financial reports or statements except for tax purposes. Of course, it is important for proprietors and partners to gather financial data so as to be able to evaluate their financial performance over time. Requests for bank loans will need to be accompanied by recent financial statements, too.

In contrast, companies organized as corporations are required to prepare financial reports annually for the benefit of their shareholders. Public corporations also are required to file annual reports with the SEC.

An **annual report** contains descriptive information on operating and financial performance during the past year, a discussion of current and future business opportunities, and financial statements that provide a numerical record of financial performance. Usually financial highlights are provided on the first page or two followed by a letter to the stockholders by the firm's Chairman of the Board and Chief Executive Officer (CEO). The CEO summarizes the financial results for the year and identifies the firm's strengths, such as employee talents and the size of its customer base. After the CEO's letter, most companies describe their current business areas, future opportunities, and financial goals, such as a target return on equity or earnings growth rate.

Three important financial statements are provided in the annual report. These are the statement of income (sometimes called the statement of operations), the balance sheet (sometimes called the statement of financial position), and the statement of cash flows. Detailed notes to

---

4. LLCs are available in every state; state offices can provide details on how to establish an LLC (or any other organizational form). Some states allow LLPs, limited liability partnerships. An LLC can be established by a single person; LLPs require two or more persons. LLPs are similar in some states to limited partnerships except that the LLP structure gives limited liability to the general partner.

these financial statements also are provided by management. Annual reports also typically provide a five- or ten-year summary of selected financial data for the firm.

CONCEPT CHECK

What is the purpose of the annual report?

What three important financial statements are found in the annual report?

generally accepted accounting principles (GAAP)

set of guidelines as to the form and manner in which accounting information should be presented

ACCOUNTING PRINCIPLES

Among the inputs used to construct the financial statements are *generally accepted accounting principles (GAAP)*, which are formulated by the Financial Accounting Standards Board (FASB). The FASB recognizes it would be improper for all companies to use identical and restrictive accounting principles. Some flexibility and choice are needed as industries and firms within industries differ in their operating environments. On the negative side, this flexibility can result in firms that, at first glance, appear healthier than they really are, and we'll see some examples of deceptive accounting in a future section. It is the task of the financial analyst to dig deep into the available financial information to separate those firms that appear attractive from those that really are in good financial shape.[5] Fortunately, FASB requires that financial statements include footnotes. These footnotes inform analysts of which accounting principles were used by the firm.

Accounting information is vitally important for financial managers, investors, and financial institutions. But there are some important differences in how accounting information is constructed and what interests finance personnel. Table 11.2 lists some important differences.

Much of accounting practice is based on the accrual concept. Under accrual accounting, revenues and their associated expenses are recognized when a sale occurs, regardless of when cash revenues or expenses really occur. Let's use the example of a set of living room furniture that is sold in June. The sofa was constructed the previous November; the coffee table was manufactured in March; other pieces were also finished in the spring. Although the manufacturer's raw materials suppliers and the workers that made the furniture were paid a long time ago—last year in the case of the sofa—the expenses will not appear on the firm's accounting books until the set is sold in June. At that time, the selling price of the living room set and its associated expenses are recorded using accrual accounting principles. It is interesting to note that the sales figure may be misleading, too. Although sales revenue may be "booked" in June when the furniture sells, the actual cash receipts from the sale may not come in until later if the store is financing the purchase for the buyer.

From the financial manager's perspective, cash is what matters most. He had to pay the firm's suppliers last year and the workers over the last several months. He also knows, because the customer will pay for her purchase under the monthly installment plan, that although revenue is recognized in June, the actual cash from the sale will come in over several months; the customer will not be finished paying for the furniture until the following year. The cash flows, or the cash expenses and cash revenues, occur over the space of many months and three calendar years. Yet, under accrual accounting, the accounting revenues and expenses all appear to have occurred this year, in the month of June, and although the firm may appear profitable, it may be very cash

TABLE 11.2

Comparison of Accounting and Financial Perspectives

ACCOUNTING FOCUS	FINANCE FOCUS
Matching revenue and expenses (accrual concept)	Identifying cash inflows and outflows
Use of different accounting principles can lead to manipulation of financial statements	Track the cash flows to assess the "quality" of reported assets and earnings
Seek to measure firm profitability	Measure cash usage
Emphasis is historical	Looks forward
Attempts to track assets and depreciate them	Market value of assets

---

5. It is interesting to note that, although U.S. firms must conform their financial statements to GAAP, the U.S. government does not. In fact, a review of federal government accounting records found them to be woefully deficient. Fourteen of twenty-four departments and agencies flunked a corporate-style review of their books. Departments with accounting problems included the Treasury Department, Commerce Department, and the Departments of Agriculture, Health and Human Services, Transportation, and Defense. See Jacob M. Schlesinger, "U.S. Fails to Meet Standard Accounting Methods," *Wall Street Journal* (March 31, 1998), pp. A2, A6.

poor because of the lag between cash outflows and cash inflows. Whereas from an historical perspective the furniture store may be making a profit, what matters to the firm's treasurer (and the firm's lenders) is what cash inflows are expected in the near future so the firm can continue to stay in business and pay its bills in a timely manner.

Another difference is in how accountants and financial managers view assets. In the manufacturing economy, fixed assets are depreciated according to set schedules so their accounting value declines over time. However, for many firms today, the most important assets are people, brand identity, technological innovation, and organizational knowledge rather than "hard" assets. Accountants are grappling with ways to value such "intangible" assets.[6]

As this example illustrates, an analyst may have to "dig deeper" to obtain a true picture of the items featured in the firm's financial statements. In the following sections, we review the firm's major financial statements and their components.

An issue that managers and investors have had to grapple with is international accounting standards. Every nation has its own set of standards, some of which are very different from U.S. GAAP. Table 11.3 presents several examples of the differences in profit that can arise depending on which country's accounting standards are followed. The International Accounting Standards Board (IASB) has been working for over twenty years on a set of international accounting standards so it will be easier to compare firms' financials across borders. It is hoped by many analysts that these standards will soon be acceptable alternatives in many countries, making inter-country firm comparisons and analyses easier than they are now.[7]

GLOBAL DISCUSSION

CONCEPT CHECK

What are GAAP?

How does the accrual concept affect financial statement data?

INCOME STATEMENT

income statement
reports the revenues generated and expenses incurred by the firm over an accounting period

The *income statement* reports the revenues generated and expenses incurred by a firm over an accounting period such as a quarter or year. The accrual concept is used to construct the income statement. Table 11.4 presents income statements for the Allgreens Corporation for 2005 and 2006. In 2006, Allgreens had net revenues of $32.5 billion compared with $28.7 billion for 2005, which reflects an increase of over 13 percent. After deducting production costs and other expenses incurred in running the business, Allgreens' net income was $1,176 million in 2006, more than a 15 percent increase over 2005's net income of $1,019 million.

Let's now look at some of the major income statement accounts in greater detail. The starting point of the income statement reflects the revenues or sales generated from the operations of the business. Quite often gross revenues are larger than net revenues. This is due to sales returns and allowances that may occur over the time period reflected in the income statement. Sometimes

TABLE 11.3

Comparing Profits: Home Country Accounting Standards Versus U.S. GAAP

FIRM	YEAR	HOME COUNTRY PROFIT (STATED IN TERMS OF THE U.S. DOLLAR)	U.S. GAAP PROFIT (STATED IN TERMS OF THE U.S. DOLLAR)
DaimlerBenz (Germany)	1992	$97 million	$–548 million
SmithKline Beecham (U.K.)	1993	$1.5 billion	$1.2 billion
British Airways (U.K.)	1993	$535 million	$353 million
Hoechst AG (Germany)	1995	$1.2 billion	$–40 million
Hoechst AG (Germany)	1996	$1.4 billion	$708 million

Sources: Elizabeth MacDonald, "The Outlook: Fixing Tower of Babel in Global Accounting," *Wall Street Journal* (May 11, 1998), p. A1; Ian Springsteel, "All for One, or None for All?" *CFO* (April 1998), pp. 103–105; Anita Raghaven and Michael R. Sesit, "Foreign Firms Raise More and More Money in the U.S. Markets," *Wall Street Journal* (October 5, 1993), p. A1.

---

6. Thomas E. Weber, "Intangibles Are Tough to Value, but the Payoff Matters in Dot-Com Era," *Wall Street Journal* (May 14, 2001), p. B1.

7. Eric L. Reiner, "Fusing Together Financial Standards," *Treasury and Risk Management* (March 2001), pp. 53–54; Elizabeth MacDonald, "The Outlook: Fixing Tower of Babel in Global Accounting," *Wall Street Journal* (May 11, 1998), p. A1; Ian Springsteel, "All for One, or None for All?" *CFO* (April 1998), pp. 103–105.

TABLE 11.4

Income Statements for Allgreens ($ in millions)

	2006	2005
Revenue	$32,505.40	$28,681.10
Cost of Goods Sold	$23,360.10	$20,768.80
GROSS PROFIT	**$9,145.30**	**$7,912.30**
Selling, General & Administrative Expense	$6,950.90	$5,980.80
Depreciation	$346.10	$307.30
OPERATING INCOME	**$1,848.30**	**$1,624.20**
Interest Expense	$0.00	$0.00
Other Expenses (Income)	($40.40)	($13.10)
INCOME BEFORE TAXES	**$1,888.70**	**$1,637.30**
Income Taxes	$713.00	$618.10
NET INCOME	**$1,175.70**	**$1,019.20**
EPS (as reported)	$1.14	$0.99
Weighted Avg. Shares Outstanding (000)	1,031,580	1,032,271

when customers make early payment on their bills, cash discounts are given by the firm. Also, if customers buy in very large quantities, trade discounts may be given. Thus discounts will reduce gross revenues.

The costs of producing or manufacturing the products sold to earn revenues are grouped under cost of goods sold. These expenses reflect costs directly involved in production, such as raw materials, labor, and overhead, and thus vary with the level of production output.

Selling, general, and marketing expenses tend to be stable or fixed in nature and cover requirements such as record keeping and preparing financial and accounting statements. These expenses also reflect the costs associated with selling the firm's products. This includes salaries and/or commissions generated by the sales force as well as promotional and advertising expenditures.

Depreciation is an estimate of the reduction in the economic value of the firm's plant and equipment during the time period covered by the income statement. This one-time-period depreciation is accumulated over time, and the accumulated depreciation appears in the balance sheet. No cash outflow is associated with depreciation, so depreciation is considered to be a noncash expense.

Operating income is a firm's income before interest and income taxes and is sometimes referred to as earnings before interest and taxes (EBIT).

Interest expense is subtracted from operating income. When a portion of a firm's assets are financed with liabilities, interest charges usually result. This is true for bank loans and long-term corporate bonds. Operating income less interest expense gives the firm's pretax earnings, or earnings before taxes.

Businesses are required to pay federal income taxes on any profits. Most states also tax business profits. Taxable earnings or profit are defined as income remaining after all other expenses except income taxes have been deducted from revenues. Effective income tax rates can vary substantially, depending on whether the firm is organized as a proprietorship, partnership, or corporation. More information on taxes appears in this chapter's Learning Extension.

The net income or profits remaining after income taxes are paid reflects the earnings available to the owners of the business. This income may be retained in the business to reduce existing liabilities, increase current assets, and/or acquire additional fixed assets. On the other hand, some or all of the income may be distributed to the owners of the business.

Because of accrual accounting, it is important to note that a firm's net income over some period is not necessarily the same as its cash flow. The amount of cash flowing into the firm can be higher or lower than the net income figure.

For a corporation, it is also common to show a firm's net income on a per-share basis. This is referred to as the earnings per share (EPS) and is calculated by dividing the net income by the number of shares of common stock that are outstanding. For Allgreens, EPS increased from $0.99 in 2005 to $1.14 in 2006. This is a 15 percent increase, very similar to the percentage increase in net income, as the number of shares outstanding changed less than 1 percent during the year.

In some instances, corporations have both preferred and common stockholders. Dividends are paid to these "preferred" stockholders out of net income; the remaining earnings are called income available to common stockholders. For example, if Allgreens had paid $200 million in preferred stock dividends in 2006, the remaining earnings available for common stockholders would have been $975.7 million and the EPS to common stockholders would have been $0.95 ($975.7 million/1,031,580,000 shares).

Corporations frequently pay cash dividends to their common stockholders. The percentage of net income or earnings paid out as dividends is referred to as the dividend payout ratio. For example, in 2006 Allgreens paid common stock dividends of $152.4 million (this figure is given in Table 11.6); this represents a dividend payout ratio of 13.0 percent ($152.4 million/ $1,175.7 million). The remaining earnings are retained in the business. On a per-share basis, the dividends per share (DPS) in 2006 were about $0.15 ($152.4 million/1,031,580,000 shares).

THE BALANCE SHEET

The **balance sheet** is a statement of a company's financial position as of a particular date, usually at the end of a quarter or year. Whereas the income statement reflects the firm's operations over time, the balance sheet is a snapshot at a point in time. It reveals two broad categories of information: (1) the **assets**, financial and physical items, owned by a business; and (2) the claims of creditors and owners in the business assets. The creditors' claims, which are the financial obligations of the business, are referred to as **liabilities**. The company's **equity** is the funds supplied by the owners and represents their residual claim on the firm.

In addition to providing a snapshot of a firm's financial condition, the balance sheet also reveals much of the inner workings of the company's financial structure. The various types of assets indicate at once the results of recent business operations and the capacity for future operations. The creditors' claims and the owners' equity in the assets reveal the sources from which these assets have been derived. The term *balance sheet* itself indicates a relationship of equality between the assets of the business and the sources of funds used to obtain them that may be expressed as follows:

$$\text{Assets} = \text{Liabilities} + \text{Owners' Equity}$$

This "balance sheet equation" or "accounting identity" shows that every dollar of a firm's assets must be financed by a dollar of liabilities (typically some type of credit or borrowing), a dollar of owners' equity, or some combination of the two. The firm's asset total shows what the firm owns; the total of liabilities and equity shows what the firm owes to its creditors and owners.

The balance sheet for the Allgreens Corporation shown in Table 11.5 reveals this equality of assets and the financial interests in the assets. Total assets were $11,405.9 million in 2006, a 15.5 percent increase over 2005's asset level of $9,878.8 million.

Total liabilities increased from $3,648.6 million to $4,210.2 million, which is a 15.4 percent increase. Owners' equity, which for Allgreens is stockholders' equity, provided the balancing figure with $7,195.7 in 2006 and $6,230.2 in 2005. This was an increase of 15.5 percent.

ASSETS

Assets that are most liquid are typically listed first. By *liquidity* we are referring to the time it usually takes to convert the assets into cash. Two broad groups—current assets and fixed assets—are identified on the balance sheet.

The **current assets** of a business include cash and other assets that are expected to be converted into cash within one year. Current assets thus represent the **working capital** needed to carry out the normal operations of the business. The principal current assets of a business are typically its cash and marketable securities, accounts receivable, and inventories.

Cash and marketable securities include cash on hand and cash on deposit with banks; marketable securities, such as commercial paper issued by other firms; and U.S. government securities in the form of Treasury bills, notes, and bonds.

Accounts receivable generally arise from the sale of products, merchandise, or services on credit. The buyer's debts to the business are generally paid according to the credit terms of the

---

CONCEPT CHECK

What does the income statement measure for a firm?

Describe the items found in a typical firm's income statement.

balance sheet
statement of a company's financial position as of a particular date

assets
financial and physical items owned by a business

liabilities
creditors' claims on a firm

equity
funds supplied by the owners that represent their residual claim on the firm

current assets
cash and all other assets that are expected to be converted into cash within one year

working capital
assets needed to carry out the normal operations of the business

TABLE 11.5
Balance Sheets for Allgreens ($ in millions)

	2006	2005
Cash & Marketable Securities	$1,017.1	$449.9
Accounts Receivable	$1,017.8	$954.8
Inventories	$4,202.7	$3,645.2
Other Current Assets	$120.5	$116.6
Total Current Assets	$6,358.1	$5,166.5
Net Fixed Assets	$4,940.0	$4,591.4
Other Long-Term Assets	$107.8	$120.9
TOTAL ASSETS	**$11,405.9**	**$9,878.8**
Accounts Payable	$2,077.0	$1,836.4
Notes Payable	$0.0	$0.0
Other Current Liabilities	$1,343.5	$1,118.8
Total Current Liabilities	$3,420.5	$2,955.2
Long-Term Debt	$0.0	$0.0
Other Liabilities	$789.7	$693.4
TOTAL LIABILITIES	**$4,210.2**	**$3,648.6**
Preferred Equity	$0.0	$0.0
Common Equity	$777.9	$828.5
Retained Earnings	$6,417.8	$5,401.7
Stockholders' Equity	$7,195.7	$6,230.2
TOTAL LIABILITIES & EQUITY	**$11,405.9**	**$9,878.8**

sale. Some firms also have notes receivable. A note receivable is a written promise by a debtor of the business to pay a specified sum of money on or before a stated date. Notes receivable may come into existence in several ways. For example, overdue accounts receivable may be converted to notes receivable at the insistence of the seller or upon special request by the buyer. Notes receivable may also occur as a result of short-term loans made by the business to its employees or to other persons or businesses.

The materials and products on hand that will be sold or transformed into a product are shown as inventories on the balance sheet. Generally, a manufacturing firm categorizes its inventories in terms of raw materials, goods in the process of manufacture, and finished goods. Sometimes the balance sheet will reveal the amount of inventory in each of these categories.

Fixed assets are the physical facilities used in the production, storage, display, and distribution of the products of a firm. These assets normally provide many years of service. The principal fixed assets are plant and equipment and land.

In a manufacturing firm, a large investment in plant and equipment is usually required. As products are manufactured, some of the economic value of this plant and equipment lessens. This is called **depreciation**, and accountants reflect this use of real assets by charging off depreciation against the original cost of plant and equipment. Thus the net fixed assets information at any point in time is supposed to reflect their remaining useful lives. The net is calculated by subtracting the amount of depreciation that has accumulated over time from the gross plant and equipment. The topic of depreciation is discussed further in this chapter's Learning Extension.

Some firms own the land or real property on which their buildings or manufacturing plants are constructed. Other firms may own other land for expansion or investment purposes. The original cost of land owned is reflected on the firm's balance sheet. Under the tax code land cannot be depreciated.

depreciation
devaluing a physical asset over the period of its expected life

LIABILITIES

Liabilities are the debts of a business. They come into existence through direct borrowing, purchases of goods and services on credit, and the accrual of obligations such as wages and income taxes. Liabilities are classified as current and long-term.

The current liabilities of a business may be defined as those obligations that must be paid within one year. They include accounts payable, notes payable, and accrued liabilities that are to be met out of current funds and operations. Although the cash on hand plus marketable securities of the Allgreens Company is $1,017.1 million compared with current liabilities of $3,420.5, it is expected that normal business operations will convert receivables and inventory into cash in time to meet current liabilities as they become due.

Accounts payable are debts that arise primarily from the purchase of goods and supplies on credit terms. Accounts payable arising from the purchase of inventory on credit terms represent trade credit financing as opposed to direct short-term borrowing from banks and other lenders. An account payable shown on one firm's balance sheet appears as an account receivable on the balance sheet of the firm from which goods were purchased.

A note payable is a written promise to pay a specified amount of money to a creditor on or before a certain date. The most common occurrence of a note payable takes place when a business borrows money from a bank on a short-term basis to purchase materials or for other current operating requirements.

Current liabilities that reflect amounts owed but not yet due as of the date of the balance sheet are called accrued liabilities or accruals. The most common form of accruals are wages payable and taxes payable. These accounts exist because wages are typically paid weekly, biweekly, or monthly and income taxes are paid quarterly.

Business debts with maturities greater than one year are long-term liabilities. As we reviewed in Chapter 9, one of the common methods used by businesses for obtaining a long-term loan is to offer a mortgage to a lender as collateral for a corporate bond. In the event that the borrowing business fails to meet the obligations of the loan contract, the mortgage may be foreclosed. That is, the property may be seized through appropriate legal channels and sold to satisfy the indebtedness.

OWNERS' EQUITY

All businesses have owners' equity in one form or another. Owners' equity is the investment of the owners or owner in the business. It initially results from a cash outlay to purchase assets to operate the business. In some cases, the owners of a business may place their own assets, such as machinery, real estate, or equipment, with the firm for its operation. In addition to contributing cash or property, owners' equity may also be increased by allowing profits to remain with the business. On the balance sheet, the amount of owners' equity is always represented by the difference between total assets and total liabilities of the business. It reflects the owners' claims on the assets of the business as opposed to the creditors' claims.

In the case of a corporation, the owners' equity is usually broken down into three different accounts, as we show for Allgreens in Table 11.6. Allgreens has no preferred stock outstanding, so that account balance is zero. The common stock account reflects the number of outstanding shares of common stock carried at a stated or par value and the capital paid in excess of par. It is worth noting that the par value is an arbitrary value and thus is not related to a firm's stock price or market value. If we divide the common stock account amount by number of shares outstanding, $777.9 million/1,031,580,000 shares, the average selling price over time is about $0.75 per share. The actual selling price of stock in Allgreens' equity offerings was undoubtedly higher than this, but the effects of stock splits and repurchases over time have changed the effective per-share price.[8]

The third account is called the retained earnings account, and it shows the accumulated undistributed earnings (i.e., earnings not paid out as dividends) within the corporation over time. These retained earnings do not represent cash. They have been invested in the firm's current and/or fixed assets. Together these three accounts comprise the corporation's equity.

CONCEPT CHECK

What is the accounting identity? What does it show?

Describe the items that appear on a typical balance sheet.

---

8. Let's say a firm issues 1 million shares of stock at a price of $20 per share so its common stock account shows $20 million. Some time later, the firm has a two-for-one stock split, so that each shareholder now owns twice as many shares, but the market price of the stock is halved. The common stock account still shows the original paid balance of $20 million, but with twice as many shares outstanding it appears the average offering price per share is $20 million/ 2 million shares or $10 per share.

STATEMENT OF CASH FLOWS

In addition to the income statement and balance sheet, corporate annual reports also try to measure changes in cash flows. The previously described financial statements are prepared using an accrual accounting system whereby items are recorded as incurred but not necessarily when cash is received or disbursed. For example, a sale of $100 is recorded as a sale this year even though the cash is not expected to be collected until next year.

statement of cash flows
provides a summary of the
cash inflows (sources) and
cash outflows (uses) during a
specified accounting period

A **statement of cash flows** provides a summary of the cash inflows (sources) and cash outflows (uses) during a specified accounting period.[9] The statement consists of three sections: operating activities, investing activities, and financing activities. The primary approach to construct a statement of cash flows begins with the net income from the income statement as a cash inflow. We then add back any noncash deductions such as depreciation, which was deducted by accounting principles although no cash outflow occurred. The other "cash flow" adjustments are made by examining the differences in the accounts from two consecutive balance sheets. More specifically, cash flows are determined as follows:

SOURCES

1. Amount of net income plus amount of depreciation
2. Decrease in an asset account
3. Increase in a liability account
4. Increase in an equity account

USES

1. Increase in an asset account
2. Decrease in a liability account
3. Decrease in an equity account
4. Amount of cash dividends

Let's examine these more closely:

- **Assets.** The purchase of raw materials or fixed assets requires spending or investing cash. Thus, increases in assets are a use and are therefore subtracted in the statement of cash flows. In contrast, collection of accounts receivable or sale of an asset brings cash into the firm; reductions in asset accounts are a source and are added in the statement of cash flows.

- **Liabilities and equity.** Borrowing money from a bank (increase in liability) or receiving an added investment from a partner or stockholder (increase in equity) represents a source of cash to the firm. In contrast, paying off a bank loan (decrease in liability) or repurchasing shares of stock (decrease in equity) is a use of cash.

Changes in the cash account are not included. Rather, in the statement of cash flows, all of the firm's sources and uses of cash are added together. Their sum equals the change in the firm's cash account. If the statement of cash flows is constructed correctly, the sum of the items should equal the difference in the cash account between the two balance sheets used to generate it.

Table 11.6 shows the statement of cash flows for the Allgreens Company based on the 2006 income statement and the balance sheets as of fiscal year-end 2005 and 2006. Notice that cash flows are grouped on the basis of operating activities, investing activities, and financing activities. Sources of funds from operations begin with net income of $1,175.7 million plus depreciation of $346.1 million to reflect the fact that depreciation is a noncash charge against the firm's revenues. Allgreens also generated additional sources of cash from operations by increasing its accounts payable by $240.6 million and other current liabilities by $224.7 million. Uses of cash from operations were in the form of a $63.0 million increase in accounts receivable and a $557.5 million increase in inventories. Along with other operating activities, the overall result was a net cash inflow from operations during 2006 of $1,009.4 million. The cash from

---

9. For an overview of how to analyze a statement of cash flows, see Anne Tergesen, "The Ins and Outs of Cash Flow," *BusinessWeek* (January 22, 2001), pp. 102–104.

TABLE 11.6
Statement of Cash Flows, Allgreens ($ in millions)

	2006
OPERATING ACTIVITIES	
Net Income (Loss)	$1,175.7
Depreciation	$346.1
Increase in Accounts Receivable	($63.0)
Increase in Inventories	($557.5)
(Increase) Decrease in Other Current Assets	($3.9)
Increase in Accounts Payable	$240.6
Increase in Other Current Liabilities	$224.7
Other Adjustments, Net	(353.3)
CASH FROM OPERATIONS	**$1,009.4**
INVESTING ACTIVITIES	
Purchase of Property, Plant, and Equipment	($348.6)
Sale of Property, Plant & Equipment	$13.1
Cash In (Out) Flow	$96.3
CASH FROM INVESTMENTS	**($239.2)**
FINANCING ACTIVITIES	
Issuance of Capital Stock	
Repurchase of Capital Stock	($50.6)
Debt Increase (Decrease)	$0.0
Dividends	(152.4)
Other Cash In (Out) Flow	
CASH FROM FINANCING	**(203.0)**
Effect of Exchange Rates	
NET CHANGE IN CASH	**$567.2**

CONCEPT CHECK

How does the statement of cash flows relate income statement information to balance sheet information?

What kind of transactions lead to a source of funds? A use of funds?

operations is an important figure for businesses. It may be negative for growing firms, but generally a firm cannot exist long if it continually creates net cash outflows from its operations.

Table 11.6 shows that Allgreens invested funds in plant and equipment in 2006. The net cash outflow from financing activities amounted to $203.0 million during 2006. This net figure includes the payment of cash dividends amounting to $152.4 million and a buyback of stock.

The overall result of operating, investing, and financing activities during 2006 was a $567.2 million increase in the cash and marketable securities account. This is further verified by the fact that Table 11.5 shows the year-end 2006 cash and marketable securities balance of $1,017.1 million is $567.2 million higher than 2005's figure of $449.9 million.

FINANCIAL STATEMENTS OF DIFFERENT COMPANIES

Financial statements tell investors of differences in how companies operate. Across industries, the composition of firms' assets and liabilities will differ. Similarly, how firms generate earnings will depend upon the characteristics of the industry in which they compete and the products or service they offer to consumers. It is difficult directly to compare the financial statements of different firms. Because of size differences among firms the dollar level of assets, liabilities, and expenses will be hard to compare.

A means of addressing the size problem to aid firm comparisons is to use ***common-size financial statements.*** Common-size financial statements express balance sheet numbers as a percent of total assets and income statement numbers as a percentage of revenue. This way comparison between firms is based on relative numbers rather than absolute dollar figures.

Table 11.7 shows how common-size financial statements can aid the comparison of three different firms. Allgreens is a leading firm in the retail drug store industry; Tinysoft is a major software and operating system provider; BigOil is a leading firm in the oil industry. The differences

common-size financial statements
expresses balance sheet dollar figures as a percent of total assets and income statement numbers as a percent of total revenue to facilitate comparisons between different-size firms

TABLE 11.7
Common Size Financial Statements

BALANCE SHEET $ MILLIONS	ALLGREENS 2006	PERCENT OF ASSETS	TINYSOFT 2006	PERCENT OF ASSETS	BIGOIL 2006	PERCENT OF ASSETS
Cash & Marketable Securities	1,017.1	8.9%	49,048.0	61.6%	10,626.0	6.1%
Accounts Receivable	1,017.8	8.9%	5,196.0	6.5%	24,309.0	13.9%
Inventories	4,202.7	36.8%	640.0	0.8%	8,957.0	5.1%
Other Current Assets	120.5	1.1%	4,089.0	5.1%	2,068.0	1.2%
Total Current Assets	6,358.1	55.7%	58,973.0	74.1%	45,960.0	26.4%
Net Fixed Assets	4,940.0	43.3%	2,223.0	2.8%	104,965.0	60.2%
Other Long Term Assets	107.8	0.9%	18,375.0	23.1%	23,353.0	13.4%
TOTAL ASSETS	**11,405.9**	**100.0%**	**79,571.0**	**100.0%**	**174,278.0**	**100.0%**
Accounts Payable	2,077.0	18.2%	1,573.0	2.0%	15,334.0	8.8%
Short-Term Debt	0.0	0.0%	0.0	0.0%	4,789.0	2.7%
Other Current Liabilities	1,343.5	11.8%	12,401.0	15.6%	18,263.0	10.5%
Total Current Liabilities	3,420.5	30.0%	13,974.0	17.6%	38,386.0	22.0%
Long-Term Debt	0.0	0.0%	0.0	0.0%	4,756.0	2.7%
Other Liabilities	789.7	6.9%	4,577.0	5.8%	41,221.0	23.7%
TOTAL LIABILITIES	**4,210.2**	**36.9%**	**18,551.0**	**23.3%**	**84,363.0**	**48.4%**
Preferred Equity	0.0	0.0%	0.0	0.0%	0.0	0.0%
Common Stockholders' Equity	7,195.7	63.1%	61,020.0	76.7%	89,915.0	51.6%
TOTAL LIABILITIES & EQUITY	11,405.9	100.0%	79,571.0	100.0%	174,278.0	100.0%

INCOME STATEMENT $ MILLIONS	ALLGREENS 2006	PERCENT REVENUE	TINYSOFT 2006	PERCENT OF REVENUE	BIGOIL 2006	PERCENT OF REVENUE
Revenue	32,505.4	100.0%	32,187	100.0%	213,199	100.0%
Cost of Goods Sold	23,360.1	71.9%	4,247	13.2%	129,928	60.9%
GROSS PROFIT	**9,145.3**	**28.1%**	**27,940**	**86.8%**	**83,271**	**39.1%**
Selling, General & Admin.	6,950.9	21.4%	8,625	26.8%	51,041	23.9%
Depreciation	346.1	1.1%	1,439	4.5%	9,047	4.2%
Research & Development	0.0	0.0%	4,659	14.5%	0	0.0%
OPERATING INCOME	**1,848.3**	**5.7%**	**13,217**	**41.1%**	**23,183**	**10.9%**
Interest Expense	0.0	0.0%	0	0.0%	207	0.1%
Other Expenses (Income)	(40.4)	(0.1%)	(1,509)	(4.7%)	(8,990)	(4.2%)
INCOME BEFORE TAXES	**1,888.7**	**5.8%**	**14,726**	**45.8%**	**31,966**	**15.0%**
Income Taxes	713.0	2.2%	4,733	14.7%	11,006	5.2%
NET INCOME	**1,175.7**	**3.6%**	**9,993**	**31.0%**	**20,960**	**9.8%**

among the industries in which these firms operate is apparent when looking at their common-size financial statements.

Looking briefly at the balance sheets, we note the capital-intensive nature of oil exploration and refining as BigOil only has 26 percent of its assets in current assets while the reminder are long-term assets; Allgreens and Tinysoft have over half of their assets in the form of current assets. Noting differences in the composition of current assets, Allgreens has most of its current assets in inventory, which is expected for a retail establishment. BigOil has more current assets in accounts receivable from its oil sales. Tinysoft is cash-rich with over 60 percent of its total assets in the form of cash; this comprises over 80 percent of its current assets.

As a retail establishment, Allgreens has the largest percentage of accounts payable (18.2 percent) and the largest proportion of financing in the form of current liabilities (30.0 percent). Because of its large relative use of fixed assets, BigOil has a large percentage of liability financing (its total liabilities are 48.4 percent of its assets). Tinysoft has relatively few fixed assets; most of its capital is in the form of software code and organizational and human capital, which lenders can't take possession of in case of financial difficulty. Thus, Tinysoft's equity financing, almost 80 percent, is much larger than that of Allgreens and BigOil.

The balance sheets provide insight into how a firm generates a product or service and how it finances itself. The income statement shows the effects of the firm's production operations, financing, competition, and industry characteristics. Tinysoft by far had the most profitable year, with income after taxes equal to 31.0 percent of revenue. Tinysoft's income statement shows that the actual production of software (placing code on CDs or other media and packaging it) is rather low; its cost of goods sold is only 13.2 percent of sales, and its gross profit is a huge 86.8 percent. Allgreens, operating in a markup retail environment, has a much higher cost of goods sold (71.9 percent of revenue) and lower gross profit (28.1 percent). Overhead in the form of selling, general, and administrative expenses is relatively higher for Tinysoft. We see the need to invest in product and manufacturing to stay ahead of competitors in the size of Tinysoft's R&D expense (14.5 percent of sales). All three firms use little long-term debt financing; this is clear from the common-size balance sheet. It is also reflected in the common-size income statement with the low percentage of interest expense for each firm.

Common-size statements are easily computed using spreadsheet software. Below we place the 2006 income statement data for Allgreens in an Excel spreadsheet. Revenue is in cell B3, costs of goods sold in B4, and so on. To compute the common-size income statement we merely divide these numbers by the revenue, cell B3. The formulas in column C show this. Using spreadsheets it is easy to convert balance sheet and income statement data into common-size format.

	A	B	C
1	INCOME STATEMENT	ALLGREENS	PERCENT OF
2	$ MILLIONS	2003	REVENUE
3	Revenue	32,505.4	=B3/B3
4	Cost of Goods Sold	23,360.1	=B4/B3
5	**GROSS PROFIT**	9,145.3	=B5/B3
6	Selling, General and Admin.	6,950.9	=B6/B3
7	Depreciation	346.1	=B7/B3
8	Research and Development	0.0	=B8/B3
9	**OPERATING INCOME**	1,848.3	=B9/B3
10	Interest Expense	0.0	=B10/B3
11	Other Expenses (Income)	-40.4	=B11/B3
12	**INCOME BEFORE TAXES**	1,888.7	=B12/B3
13	Income Taxes	713.0	=B13/B3
14	**NET INCOME**	1,175.7	=B14/B3

CONCEPT CHECK

How do common-size financial statements assist with comparing different firms?

Explain how manufacturing and competitive strategies can be seen in common-size financial statements.

In this section we've seen how the tool of common-size statements can be used to compare firms of different sizes in different industries. Examining the percentages gives us insight into the competition in these three industries and the firms' methods of serving their markets.

GOAL OF A FIRM

Although a firm may have a mission statement espousing goals of quality, customer service, offering quality products at fair prices, and so on, such qualitative statements are really only a means to an end. The firm's managers need a definite measurable benchmark against which to evaluate alternatives. The goal of any firm should be financial, namely the maximization of the owners' (or the common shareholders') wealth.

Creditors have a fixed claim that usually doesn't change with variations in the value of the firm's assets over time. As we learned in Chapter 8, shareholders have a residual or junior claim on the firm's assets. Therefore variations in a firm's value will be mainly reflected in the fluctuating value of the owners' or shareholders' wealth in the firm. Managers will want to select strategies that are expected to increase shareholders' wealth. Alternatives that harm shareholders' wealth should be rejected.[10]

This view is consistent with the process of attracting and acquiring capital and investing it to earn rates of return in excess of the investors' expected returns. If a firm is able to do this, the excess return will accrue to the firm's owners, the shareholders.

---

10. Some mandatory projects such as the need to retrofit factories due to regulation changes may be costly and harm shareholder wealth. In this case, if several alternatives exist, the project that hurts shareholder wealth the least should be chosen. This may include the option of going out of business, if the new regulations are too costly to obey.

MEASURING SHAREHOLDER WEALTH

Shareholder wealth is measurable and observable daily in the financial sections of newspapers (at least for firms whose common stock is publicly traded). Shareholder wealth is nothing more than the market value of a firm's common stock. This market value of the shareholders' claim on a firm is equal to:

$$\text{Shareholder wealth} = \text{Common stock price} \times \text{Number of common shares outstanding}$$

This relationship allows analysts to keep track of changes in shareholder wealth on a regular basis to see which firms are most successful at returning value to shareholders. *As long as the number of common stock shares outstanding does not change appreciably, the market's perception of the firm and of its management's actions appears in the firm's stock price.*

For shareholder wealth maximization to be a realistic goal, the financial markets need to provide reasonably accurate information about the value of a firm. The stock market is sometimes criticized in the popular press as being shortsighted and unpredictable. Can it really determine a fair value for the firm? The evidence on efficient markets from Chapter 10 suggests that it can. Many studies show that the market is oriented toward the long-run health and well-being of firms.[11] The weight of evidence favors the idea that the market generally does price stocks fairly. Recall Figure 10.4; it shows the market's quick reaction, as seen in changing stock prices, to firms' announcing earnings that were higher (or lower) than expected. Stock price changes in this example directly show the effect on firm value from the market's evaluation of the news.

ETHICAL ISSUES

Focusing on shareholder value does not mean other aspects of good management are ignored. Smart managers make decisions to service customers in a cost-efficient manner. Many studies have showed the value-enhancement that occurs from maintaining the current customer base rather than having to continually find new customers to take the place of dissatisfied ones. Similarly, smart managers treat and pay employees fairly. Table 11.8 shows the effect of unsatisfying jobs, employee turnover, and the cost impact of needing to hire and train replacement workers. Unmotivated and unhappy employees become unproductive employees who increase costs and prevent the firm from satisfying its goals. By focusing on firm value, managers work to maintain satisfactory relationships with financing sources so funds will be available to finance future

TABLE 11.8
Happy and Productive Employees Help Increase Shareholder Wealth

A. SELECTED INDUSTRYWIDE COSTS OF REPLACING EMPLOYEES	ANNUAL TURNOVER RATE	INDUSTRYWIDE COSTS (DIRECT REPLACEMENT COSTS ONLY) ($ BILLIONS)	COSTS AS A PERCENTAGE OF INDUSTRY EARNINGS
Specialty Retail	97%	23.2	50%
Call Centers	31	5.4	43
High-Tech	25	44.3	43
Fast Food	123	3.4	16

Source: Sibson & Co.

B. TURNOVER RATES AND HIRING COSTS	ANNUAL TURNOVER RATE	COST PER NEW HIRE
Banking	16.0%	$6,110
Consumer Products	23.0	$17,450
Insurance	13.1	$9,902
Manufacturing	17.8	$11,408
Pharmaceuticals	12.6	$13,632
Telecommunications	21.0	$7,176

Source: Saratoga[SM] Institute.

11. See the tables in David Stires, "America's Best and Worst Wealth Creators," *Fortune* (December 10, 2001), pp. 137–142, and in and Alfred Rappaport, "CFOs and Strategists: Forging a Common Framework," *Harvard Business Review* (May–June 1992), p. 87. Both of these articles have tables with estimates of the value of firms' future growth as reflected in current stock prices.

growth needs. Focusing on shareholder wealth is the best means of helping the long-term survival of the firm in a dynamic, global economy.

Shareholder wealth as a measure of firm performance is objective, forward-looking, and incorporates all influences on the firm and its stakeholders. No other measure of firm performance is so inclusive and practical for evaluating a firm's strategies.

A measure to identify successful firms that is growing in popularity is **market value added (MVA).** The MVA measures the value created by the firm's managers. It equals the market value of the firm's liabilities and equity minus the amount of money investors paid to the firm (this is the "book value" of liabilities and equity found in the firm's financial statements) when these securities were first issued. That is, market value added (MVA) equals:

MVA = Market value of stock + Market value of debt − Book value of stock − Book value of debt

Usually, a firm's market value of debt closely approximates its book value, so a close estimate of MVA is the market value of equity less the book value of equity. Stern Stewart & Company, a financial consulting firm, regularly reports firms' MVAs.

LINKING STRATEGY AND FINANCIAL PLANS

A firm's managers will want to pay close attention to movements in a company's stock price over time. These movements inform managers of how financial market participants view the risk and potential return from investing in the firm. If investors perceive the risk is too great relative to expected returns, they will sell the firm's stock and reinvest their money elsewhere.

To provide a link between a firm's strategy and its financial plans, managers can first review the firm's performance in the financial markets and determine why the firm's stock price performed better or worse than its competitors in the eyes of investors. Managers can then take this information and examine the firm's internal operations. They need to examine financial measures to see how the firm has been generating cash, where this cash is being invested in the firm (new products, subsidiaries, etc.), and the return earned on these investments. Managers can then determine where poor returns are being earned and they can take corrective steps. Managers will want to evaluate the firm's operations and new project proposals with an eye toward the firm's stock price. Projects that will add to shareholder wealth should be chosen for implementation. Projects that are expected to reduce shareholder wealth should be cast aside.

Executing a firm's financial strategy entails more than just looking at numbers on a computer spreadsheet. It includes making necessary adjustments to the firm's use of debt, equity, and its dividend policy to create more value to shareholders. It includes seeking new markets or customers for the firm's products; controlling costs or prudently raising prices; and efficiently using the firm's assets. In addition, to publicize its plans for creating value, management will want to communicate key components of its plan to shareholders and the financial markets. Other activities include ethically using accounting principles and the tax code to minimize the firm's taxes; increasing the efficiency of the firm's cash management; and managing the firm's risk exposures. Many of these topics are discussed in upcoming chapters.

CRITERION FOR NONPUBLIC FIRMS

An obvious question to ask is which criterion to employ for organizations that have no observable market prices: for example, a small closely held company or a nonprofit organization. The answer lies in the factors that cause any productive asset to have value. From our discussion in Chapter 5 on the time value of money, we know assets have value because of the size, timing, and risk of their cash flows. Management needs to balance the risks, timing, and sizes of the cash flows of the organization to maximize what the decision maker believes would be the market value of owner's equity if it were traded in the financial markets.

Owner-managers of small firms face a different situation, however. Since they own their firms, they seek to maximize their own wealth, but this wealth may defy clear expression in dollar terms. Nonmonetary benefits may be personally important to the owner-manager, such as maintaining control of the firm, keeping the business in the family, or having adequate leisure time. From a purely monetary perspective, owner-managers may not be maximizing the

market value added (MVA)

market value added measures the value created by the firm's managers

ETHICAL ISSUES

ETHICAL ISSUES

CONCEPT CHECK

What should be the goal of a firm?

What information might a changing stock price give to managers?

What should be the goal of a firm that does not have publicly traded stock?

Does focusing on stock price necessarily lead to unethical behavior by managers?

financial wealth of the firm, but as the owners they have to answer only to themselves as long as they make timely payments to their creditors and employees. Their decisions will attempt to maximize their total personal wealth, which includes both monetary and nonmonetary components.

WHAT ABOUT ETHICS?

Critics frequently argue that emphasizing shareholder wealth may lead managers to focus on quick fixes to problems, even resorting to unethical behavior to maintain firm value. Some managers, unfortunately, do make decisions to ignore product quality or safety, worker safety, or the well-being of communities, or they use deceitful selling practices. As long as these practices are not discovered or publicized, they may help keep shareholder value higher than it should be. But let's take a closer look at this type of behavior.

Unethical managers will make improper decisions regardless of the performance measure, so using shareholder value as a performance measure probably will not affect such abusive practices. By inflating firm revenues, keeping costs artificially low, or diverting scarce resources from important to less productive uses, unethical practices would improve virtually any performance measure, be it sales, costs, or market share. Thus to blame ethical lapses on financial measures of firm performance is inappropriate.

In fact, focusing on firm value may help to keep management's eyes on the longer-term consequences of its actions. Firms engaged in unethical or careless behavior run the risk of having this behavior exposed. Such revelations can harm the firm's reputation and shareholder value for extended periods as customers and employees feel their trust has been violated. Some evidence from a recent study suggests that firms with a social conscience may gain more financially in the marketplace.[12] An important aspect of corporate ethics is the control systems that a firm has in place to discourage such activity and to catch it if it occurs. As shareholders are many and dispersed, it falls to the board and corporate governance to ensure managers are working for the shareholders' best interests rather than for a "quick fix" or their own selfish interests.

CORPORATE GOVERNANCE

ETHICAL ISSUES

principals
owners of the firm

agents
hired by the principals to run the firm

In most proprietorships and partnerships the owners are the managers and they play an active role in managing the business, but in many firms someone other than the owners makes business decisions; there is a separation of ownership and control. For example, professional managers run public corporations in the place of the shareholders. This arrangement may result in ethics problems; for example, dishonest managers can make decisions that increase expenses to benefit themselves (such as company-owned vacation villas, corporate jets, high salaries) over shareholders. Or they can send stock prices higher by manipulating transactions and accounting rules so the firm appears more profitable than it really is.

Unfortunately, the early 2000s brought a number of corporate scandals to light. Some stock analysts and their investment banking firms were accused of "hyping" stocks to attract lucrative investment banking fees. Firms such as Enron, Global Crossing, Parmalat, Rite-Aid, Tyco, WorldCom, and Xerox were accused of incorrect accounting practices and had to restate past year's financials; some executives were fined and sent to jail. Arthur Andersen, a venerable accounting firm, is restricted from doing further auditing work after employees shredded documents relating to Enron's accounting irregularities. Most of the scandals were caused by poor ethical decisions dealing with accounting practices that inflated earnings—and stock prices.

PRINCIPAL–AGENT PROBLEM

In legal parlance, the **principals**, or owners of the firm, hire managers (the **agents**) to run the firm. The agents should run the firm with the best interests of the principals in mind. However,

---

12. Justin Martin, "Good Citizenship Is Good Business," *Fortune* (March 21, 1994), pp. 15–16. In addition, having your firm named in an unfavorable light in the financial and public press is costly over time. An example is Daniel Fisher, "Shell Game: How Enron Concealed Losses, Inflated Earnings and Hid Secret Deals From the Authorities," *Forbes* (January 7, 2002).

principal–agent problem
conflict of interest between the principals and agents

ethical lapses, self-interest, or the principals' lack of trust in the agent can lead to conflicts of interest and suspicions between the two parties. This problem in corporate governance is called the ***principal–agent problem***. The possible conflict between manager and owner objectives is one of the basic finance principles set out in Chapter 1.

In a corporation, the common shareholders of a firm elect a board of directors. In theory, the board is to oversee managers and to ensure that they are working in the best interests of the shareholders. Often, however, in practice the board has a closer relationship with management than with the shareholders. For example, it is not unusual for top management to sit on the firm's board of directors, and the firm's top managers often nominate candidates for board seats. For example, as recently as 1995 the board of Archer-Daniels-Midland, a grain processor, included the firm's CEO and three of his relatives. Other firms have had relatives of management as members of the board's audit committees, the important group that oversees the firm's financial controls.[13] These relationships can obscure loyalties and make the board a toothless watchdog for shareholders' interests.

Managers, acting as agents, may seek their own self-interest by increasing their salaries, the size of their staffs, or their perquisites. Better known as "perks," the latter include club memberships, use of company planes or luxurious company cars, gardening expenses, low- or no-interest loans and lifetime benefits, such as paid long-term care insurance, use of company cars and drivers, and access to company planes. Firms may also do business with other businesses in which the CEO has an ownership stake, blurring the distinction between doing what is best for shareholders and doing favors for the top officer.[14]

Many managers like their jobs, their salaries, their perks, and their positions of power. Acting in their own self-interest, they would like to keep their jobs. This is never better seen than when one firm tries to take over or merge with another firm. Often these takeovers include an offer to buy a firm's shares from its shareholders at a price above its current market price. There have been a number of situations when the target firm's management, in conjunction with its board, seek to fight a takeover attempt, or they may try to preempt such merger or acquisition attempts by changing the corporate charter so that takeovers are difficult to pursue. Examples of such delaying tactics, or ***poison pills***, include provisions that require super-majorities (for example, two-thirds) of existing shareholders to approve any takeover, provisions to allow the board to authorize and issue large quantities of stock in the event of a takeover attempt, or provisions to make expensive payouts to existing managers in the face of any successful buyout. Although managers may state that such actions are being taken with shareholders' best interests at heart, a possible consequence of their actions is to preserve their own jobs and income in the face of a takeover. However, in the face of investor unrest related to corporate scandals, fewer firms are adopting poison pills and some are taking steps to eliminate them or are allowing their provisions to expire. In recent years Circuit City, Goodyear, FirstEnergy, PG&E, and Raytheon have eliminated poison pills.[15]

Because of these behaviors, the principal–agent problem imposes ***agency costs*** on shareholders. Agency costs are the tangible and intangible expenses borne by shareholders because of the actual or potential self-serving actions of managers. Agency costs include explicit, out-of-pocket expenses. Examples of these costs include the costs of auditing financial statements to verify their accuracy; purchasing liability insurance for board members and top managers; monitoring managers' actions by the board or by independent consultants; and paying inflated managerial salaries and perks.

Implicit agency costs do not have a direct expense associated with them, but they harm shareholders anyway. Implicit agency costs include restrictions placed against managerial actions (e.g., requiring shareholder votes for some major decisions) and covenants or restrictions placed on the firm by a lender.[16]

The end result of the principal–agent problem is a reduction in firm value. Investors will not pay as much for the firm's stock because they realize that the principal–agent problem and its

poison pills
provisions in a corporate charter that make a corporate takeover more unattractive

agency costs
tangible and intangible expenses borne by shareholders because of the actual or potential self-serving actions of managers

13. Joann S. Lublin and Elizabeth MacDonald, "More Independent Audit Committees Are Sought," *Wall Street Journal* (February 8, 1999), p. A2.

14. Timothy D. Schellhardt and Joann S. Lublin, "All the Rage Among CEOs: Lifetime Perks," *Wall Street Journal* (July 6, 1999), pp. A17, A24; Anonymous, "In a Cost-Cutting Era, Many CEOs Enjoy Imperial Perks," *Wall Street Journal* (March 7, 1995), pp. B1, B10.

15. Robin Sidel, "Where Are All the Poison Pills?" *Wall Street Journal* (March 2, 2004), pp. C1, C5.

16. Such covenants are placed on the firm to protect the lender's position and to ensure that available cash flow will be directed to repay the loan.

attendant costs lower the firm's value. Agency costs will decline, and firm value will rise, as principals' trust and confidence in their agents rises. We will discuss some ways of reducing agency costs in the next section.

REDUCING AGENCY PROBLEMS

Two basic approaches can be used to reduce the consequences of managers making self-serving decisions. First, managers' incentives can be aligned to more closely match those of shareholders. A frequently used method for doing this in the past was to offer ***stock options*** to managers. The options allow managers to purchase, at a future time, a stated number of the firm's shares at a specific price. If the firm's stock price rises, the value of the shares, and therefore the managers' wealth, also rises. Decisions that detract from the best interest of shareholders will affect management by making the stock options less valuable.[17] But stock option plans are subject to several criticisms. One is the past practice (since corrected by a revised accounting standard) of not reflecting the difference between market price and the (low) stock option price in the company's income statement; now it must be shown on the income statement as an expense. Another problem with stock options is that managers are able to receive huge bonuses because economic conditions create a rising stock market, regardless of their managerial skill. When the stock market falls, not all managers are financially harmed as some firms chose to revalue their stock options at lower prices.[18] Finally, stock options were blamed for some of the ethical lapses of managers in the late 1990s; accounting decisions to push up a firm's earnings can result in sharp stock price changes and a windfall for managers who cash in their options.

Restricted stock is gaining popularity as a way to align managers' interests with those of shareholders without the bad consequences of stock options. Restricted stock is given to employees, but they cannot sell it until it vests, which typically occurs after three to five years. Employees who leave the firm before the stock vests lose their restricted shares. Under some company plans, top managers forfeit restricted shares if the firm has poor financial performance or they miss financial targets. Restricted stock's time to vest is typically longer than that of shorter-term stock options, and it has less upside (large return) potential. But whereas stock options can become worthless if the stock price does not rise sufficiently, restricted shares will retain some value as long as the firm doesn't go bankrupt. In addition, holders receive dividends of restricted shares, even before they vest.

A second tool for controlling self-serving managers is to have closer oversight to make them more accountable. In the wake of corporate and accounting scandals, legislative mandate of controls is supplementing oversight by corporate boards. Some firms are increasing the number of independent directors (i.e., individuals who are not part of the firm's management) on their boards. The Sarbanes-Oxley Act of 2002 was passed by the U.S. Congress in response to some of the previously cited corporate accounting and ethical scandals. Nicknamed "SOX" or "Sarbox," the act established the following standards:

- Creation of the Public Company Accounting Oversight Board (PCAOB) with five members, which reports to the SEC. PCOAB registers firms that conduct corporate accounting audits; establishes auditing, quality control, ethical and independence standards for such firms; and literally audits the auditors in that the board can inspect their work and initiate disciplinary proceedings against firms that violate their standards and provisions of SOX.

- To try to eliminate conflicts of interest, accounting firms cannot perform other functions (bookkeeping, financial system consulting, etc.) in firms for which they perform audits. To try to maintain independence, the lead auditor must be changed at least every five years. The auditors must present their report to the board of directors' audit committee. The audit committee must contain at least one "financial expert" as defined by the act. Only independent (that is, directors who, except for their board service, do not work or do paid consulting for the firm) directors can sit on the audit committee.

stock options
allow managers to purchase a stated number of the firm's shares at a specified price

ETHICAL ISSUES

restricted stock
shares of stock awarded to managers that vest, or become saleable, after a stated number of years

ETHICAL ISSUES

---

17. Business periodicals and the press usually publicize the largest CEO salaries for the previous year. Such salaries can reach $50 million or more. The news reports fail to recognize much of this CEO income comes from exercising stock options. A CEO can make a lot of money on stock options if he or she performs the job well and raises the stock price.

18. Ruth Simon and Ianthe Jeanne Dugan, "Options Overdose," *Wall Street Journal* (June 4, 2001), pp. C1, C17; Ken Brown, "Now, Some Hope for Their Stock to Tank," *Wall Street Journal* (June 4, 2001), pp. C1, C2.

- To enhance corporate responsibilities, the CEO and CFO of the firm must certify that the firm's financial reports conform to SOX requirements and good accounting practice. Jail (up to ten years) and/or fines (up to $1 million) await the officer who signs an incorrect statement. Corporations can no longer make loans to its officers and directors. In addition, firms must draft a code of ethics for its senior officers and have policies in place to protect "whistleblowers," that is, persons who report alleged wrong doing by the firm.

- Security analysts study corporations and write research reports regarding the prospects of a firm's stock, bonds, and other securities. Many times an analyst works for an investment banking firm that can earn large fees by assisting corporations in its primary market offerings. SOX contains several provisions to ensure there are no conflicts of interest between the analysts' firm and possible investment banking clients. First, the research function must be separate from the investment banking function; research reports cannot be reviewed or approved by the investment banking arm of a Wall Street firm prior to the report's publication. Second, security analysts cannot be paid based upon the investment banking fees generated by favorable research reports written about the firm's clients. Third, reports must disclose if the security analyst owns any of the securities issued by the firm about which he or she is making a recommendation.

CONCEPT CHECK

What is the principal–agent problem?

What are agency costs? Give some examples.

What steps can be taken to reduce agency costs?

Both Sarbanes-Oxley and actions by the stock exchanges require more independent directors on corporate boards. Independent directors should be more inclined to carefully analyze management's strategies and proposals and their effects on shareholder value. In addition, major institutional investors, such as pension funds and mutual funds, are becoming more vocal. Some are taking active roles in overseeing the performance of companies in which they hold stock by requesting meetings with management, criticizing management actions, and suggesting shareholder votes on issues of importance to the firm.

Increased trust in the financial system and greater accounting transparency help shareholder wealth. Several studies have shown that firms in countries with better corporate governance regulations have experienced higher stock returns.[19] Attempts to tighten corporate governance and reduce agency costs by regulation are gaining popularity overseas. A recent study by the Organization for Economic Cooperation and Development (OECD) recommends a number of so-called "U.S. management style" initiatives for its member countries. The report recommends that companies around the world adopt practices such as shareholder wealth maximization, stronger shareholder rights to remove directors and to nominate and elect directors; independent boards of directors to oversee managers; avoiding security analyst conflicts of interest; independent auditors and whistleblower protection.[20]

FINANCE IN THE ORGANIZATION CHART

chief financial officer (CFO)

responsible for the controller and the treasury functions of a firm

treasurer

oversees the traditional functions of financial analysis

controller

manages accounting, cost analysis, and tax planning

In all but the smallest of firms, a top manager with the title *chief financial officer (CFO)* or vice president of finance usually reports to the president. Managers of two areas usually report to the CFO: the firm's *treasurer* and its *controller* (Figure 11.1). The firm's treasurer oversees the traditional functions of financial analysis: capital budgeting, short-term and long-term financing decisions, and current asset management. The controller traditionally manages accounting, cost analysis, and tax planning.

Compensation for financial officers at large public corporations is quite attractive, but of course hard work, long hours, and excellent skills in analytics, communication, and working with people are expected. The typical pay packages of CFOs, treasurers, and controllers at large firms include salary, annual incentive pay, long-term incentive pay (which includes both cash and restricted stock, that is, stock that cannot be sold for a specified number of years), and stock options. In 2003, the average CFO's pay package at these large corporations totaled over $3.2

19. Phillip Day, "Corporate Governance Can Be Strong Indicator of Stock Performance Within Emerging Markets," *Wall Street Journal* (May 1, 2001), p. C14; Craig Karmin, "Corporate-Governance Issues Hamper Emerging Markets," *Wall Street Journal* (November 8, 2000), pp. C1, C14; Robert L. Simison, "Firms World-Wide Should Adopt Ideas of U.S. Management, Panel Tells OECD," *Wall Street Journal* (April 2, 1998), p. A6.

20. Christopher Rhoads, "OECD Proposes Global Guidelines to Govern Firms," *Wall Street Journal* (January 12, 2004), and "OECD Countries Agree to New Corporate Governance Principles" (April 22, 2004), accessed at http://www.oecd.org/document/22/0,2340,en_2649_201185_31558102_1_1_1_1,00.html during May 2004.

WENDY WILSON
Audit Senior Manager
Ernst & Young, LLP

BS, Accounting
University of Richmond
Certified Public Accountant

"A bean-counter personality wouldn't last long here."

Q: *What's the difference between public accounting and private accounting?*

A: We are public accountants, meaning we provide accounting services to other companies. Private accounting refers to the internal accounting departments you would find in large companies.

Q: *What services do you provide for your clients?*

A: Our company provides three main categories of service: audit, tax, and consulting. I'm in the audit division. We review the financial statements that our clients compile and certify that they are based on generally accepted accounting principles and that they are free of what we call material misstatements.

Q: *So you evaluate the financial statements and the methods used to develop them. If you find they are in order, then what?*

A: We would then put in writing what we found, that the financial statements were audited and appear to fairly represent the financial standing of the company. The clients can then use our opinion to demonstrate the validity of their financial statements to their stockholders or to a bank when seeking a loan.

Q: *Do you physically review all of the financial records of your clients?*

A: The smaller the client the more likely we are to look at its individual transactions to see if they were reported correctly. With large clients we look more for the proper systems and controls. But we could never look at all of the records of any client. That would be extremely time-consuming and expensive.

Q: *What's the toughest part of the job?*

A: Because almost every company's fiscal year ends on December 31, we have an extremely busy season from January to March. We work very long hours in that stretch, sixty hours a week, at least. On the other hand, once the busy season ends we have a liberal vacation policy and excellent benefits. So you pay your dues during the winter, and the rest of the year isn't so bad.

Q: *What do you enjoy most about your job?*

A: I work with a lot of excellent people, both clients and coworkers. I manage several projects at a time and work with different people and issues on each, so there's lots of variety.

Q: *There are some stereotypes about accountants. Any comments?*

A: The image of accountants as bean counters hunched over their adding machines is not accurate at all. We work with such a broad range of clients that we have to have good people skills. A bean-counter personality wouldn't last long here.

FIGURE 11.1
Position of Finance in a Typical Organization Chart

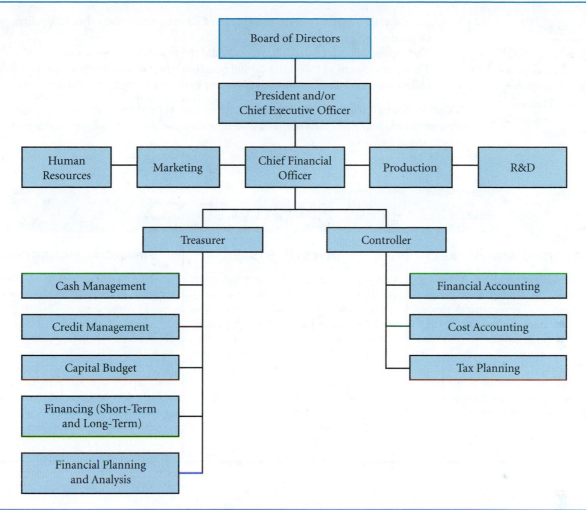

million while the average treasurer package was $918,000 and the average controller's was $1,078,000. Fortune 500 company chief executive officers (CEOs) received an average compensation package of $13.5 million in 2005.[21]

A firm's strategy for business success is plotted by its top officers and, in the case of a corporation, its board of directors. Often, this strategy will be reflected in the composition of the firm's balance sheet, as seen in Figure 11.2. Those involved in planning the firm's

FIGURE 11.2
Balance Sheet

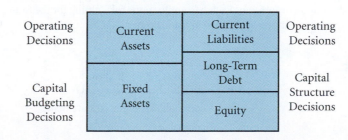

21. John Labate, "Losing Altitude in a Stiff Wind." *Treasury and Risk Management* (May 2004), p. 24. Also see "Morgan's Mack Sees Hefty Pay Raise," CNNMoney.com, http://money.cnn.com/2007/02/23/news/companies/morgan_compensation/index.htm (accessed July 11, 2007).

CONCEPT CHECK

What are typical titles for a firm's top financial officers?

How does a firm's balance sheet relate a firm's strategies?

strategy follow the structure provided by the balance sheet in answering several basic questions:

1. The capital budgeting question. What fixed or long-term assets should the firm purchase to produce its product?
2. The capital structure question. How should the firm finance these purchases?
3. The operations or net working capital question. How should the firm manage inventory, collect payments from customers, pay suppliers, and manage its cash account?

The following chapters will delve into these topics to show you the data that financial managers need, how they analyze them, and how they use the shareholder wealth maximization goals to make decisions.

APPLYING FINANCE TO . . .

INSTITUTIONS AND MARKETS

Lending decisions are made on the basis of who is responsible for repaying; in small firms, the proprietor or owner may have to personally guarantee any loans to the firm.

Creditworthiness (ability to repay) and collateral are paramount to the lending decision. The markets and lending institutions will pay close attention to the firm's financial statements when making a loan and while the loan is outstanding.

INVESTMENTS

Corporate governance and principal–agent problems are well known to the financial markets and professional investors who work for mutual funds and pension funds. Firm values can rise or fall depending on whether the market perceives management's actions as serving its shareholders or entrenching managers. All investors, including bond- and stockholders, will be interested in the information contained in a firm's financial statements.

FINANCIAL MANAGEMENT

A firm's organizational form affects how its earnings are taxed and how easy it is to transfer ownership.

A growing firm has to make decisions about how it may want to increase its equity base; choices include going public and becoming a public corporation or growing more slowly if it wants to stay private as a nonpublic corporation, partnership, or proprietorship. Financial statements tell investors and competitors much about the performance of a public company.

SUMMARY

Finance provides the basic tools managers can use when seeking to maximize the wealth of the owners. By maintaining the firm's vision or mission when setting operating goals, managers should evaluate strategies and seek to increase shareholder wealth. Separation of firm ownership and control leads to the principal–agent problem. Agents (managers) may act in their own self-interest rather than in the owners' interest. There are several means of reducing the effects of the agency problem, including linking the compensation of managers to the firm's stock price performance and increasing information about managers' decisions to the firm's owners.

A firm can be organized in one of three basic ways: as a proprietorship, a partnership, or a corporation. Each has implications for capital-raising ability, ease of transferring ownership, and taxation.

A basic introduction to finance should also review the firm's accounting statements. The balance sheet indicates the firm's assets and how they were financed by various liabilities and equity as of a point in time. The income statement shows the level of the firm's revenues and expenses over a specific period. The statement of cash flows indicates the influences affecting the firm's cash account over time.

In the following chapter we will use the various accounts listed on the balance sheet and income statement to illustrate some of the duties of a financial analyst. We'll see how to study a firm's financial position and how the financial statements can be used when planning for the future.

KEY TERMS

agency costs

agents

annual report

assets

balance sheet

bylaws

charter

chief financial officer (CFO)

common-size financial statements

controller

corporation

current assets

depreciation

equity

equity capital

generally accepted accounting principles (GAAP)

income statement

liabilities

limited liability company (LLC)

limited partners

limited partnership	principal–agent problem	stock options
market value added (MVA)	principals	subchapter S corporation
mission statement	proprietorship	treasurer
partnership	restricted stock	working capital
poison pills	statement of cash flows	

DISCUSSION QUESTIONS

1. It has often been said that a business should begin with a vision or mission statement. Explain what this means.

2. How do the financial markets accommodate the needs of both risky firms and very safe firms?

3. Identify and briefly describe the three major forms of business ownership used in the United States.

4. What are the differences in owner liability in proprietorships and partnerships versus corporations?

5. Briefly describe the differences between a subchapter S corporation and a limited liability company.

6. What types of information are included in an annual report?

7. General accounting practice is based on the accrual concept. Explain what this means and briefly describe how this compares with the financial manager's focus on cash.

8. What is the purpose of the income statement? Also briefly identify and describe the major types of expenses that are shown on the typical income statement.

9. What is the purpose of the balance sheet? Briefly identify and describe the major types of assets and the claims of creditors and owners shown on the typical balance sheet.

10. Describe the three different accounts that comprise the owners' equity section on a typical corporate balance sheet.

11. What is a statement of cash flows? What are the three standard sections contained in a statement of cash flows?

12. How can common-size financial statements be used?

13. How are industry operating differences reflected in firms' financial statements?

14. Describe the financial goal espoused by business firms.

15. Briefly explain how shareholder wealth is measured.

16. What does it mean when a firm's MVA is negative?

17. How are financial strategy and financial plans linked together?

18. What is meant by the principal–agent problem in the context of corporate governance?

19. Discuss some ways agents can make self-serving decisions.

20. What are the two main solutions for reducing the adverse effects of agency problems?

21. What is restricted stock? How does it improve managerial incentives compared to the use of stock options?

22. Describe four provisions of the Sarbanes-Oxley Act.

23. What are the responsibilities of a firm's controller?

24. Briefly describe the financial responsibilities undertaken by a firm's treasurer.

PROBLEMS

1. Use the "balance sheet equation" to determine owners' equity if liabilities are $5 million and assets are $10 million.

2. Use your knowledge of balance sheets to fill in the missing amounts:

ASSETS	
Cash	$10,000
Accounts receivable	100,000
Inventory	_____
Total current assets	220,000
Gross plant and equipment	500,000
Less: accumulated depreciation	_____
Net plant and equipment	375,000
Total assets	_____

LIABILITIES	
Accounts payable	$12,000
Notes payable	50,000
Total current liabilities	_____
Long-term debt	_____
Total liabilities	190,000
Common stock ($1 par, 100,000 shares)	_____
Paid-in capital	_____
Retained earnings	150,000
Total stockholders' equity	_____
Total liabilities and equity	_____

3. Use your knowledge of balance sheets to fill in the missing amounts:

ASSETS	
Cash	$ 50,000
Accounts receivable	80,000
Inventory	100,000
Total current assets	_____
Gross plant and equipment	_____
Less: accumulated depreciation	130,000
Net plant and equipment	600,000
Total assets	_____

LIABILITIES

Accounts payable	$12,000
Notes payable	50,000
Total current liabilities	_____
Long-term debt	_____
Total liabilities	_____
Common stock ($1 par, 100,000 shares)	_____
Paid-in capital	250,000
Retained earnings	200,000
Total stockholders' equity	_____
Total liabilities and equity	$830,000

4. Use your knowledge of balance sheets and common-size statements to fill in the missing dollar amounts:

ASSETS

Cash	$25,000	3.4%
Accounts receivable	$125,000	
Inventory	_____	27.1%
Total current assets	$350,000	_____
Gross plant and equipment	_____	95.0%
Less: accumulated depreciation	$313,000	42.5%
Net plant and equipment	_____	_____
Total assets	$737,000	100.0%

LIABILITIES

Accounts payable	_____	15.7%
Notes payable	$29,000	3.9%
Total current liabilities	_____	_____
Long-term debt	$248,000	33.6%
Total liabilities	$393,000	_____
Common stock ($.01 par, 450,000 shares)	$4,500	0.6%
Paid-in capital	$220,500	29.9%
Retained earnings	_____	_____
Total stockholders' equity	$344,000	46.7%
Total liabilities and equity	_____	100.0%

5. Use your knowledge of income statements to fill in the missing items:

Sales	
Cost of goods sold	$575,000
Gross profit	1,600,000
General and administrative expense	200,000
Selling and marketing expense	_____
Depreciation	50,000
Operating income	_____
Interest	100,000
Income before taxes	_____
Income taxes (30%)	_____
Net income	$700,000

6. Use the following information to construct an income statement:

Interest	$25,000
Sales	$950,000
Income tax rate	25%
Selling and marketing expenses	$160,000

General and administrative expenses	$200,000
Gross profit	$550,000
Depreciation	$30,000
Cost of goods sold	$400,000

7. Use the following information to construct an income statement:

Cost of goods sold	$684,000
Gross profit	$546,000
General and administrative expense	$159,000
Selling and marketing expense	$134,000
Operating income	$228,000
Income before taxes	$87,000
Income tax rate	27%

8. Use your knowledge of income statements and common-size statements to fill in the missing dollar amounts:

Sales	$2,876,200	100.0%
Cost of goods sold	_____	74.7%
Gross profit	_____	25.3%
General and administrative expense	$250,000	8.7%
Selling and marketing expense	$140,000	4.9%
Depreciation	_____	3.8%
Operating income	$229,000	8.0%
Interest	_____	4.6%
Income before taxes	$97,000	3.4%
Income taxes (25%)	$24,250	0.8%
Net income	_____	2.5%

9. **Challenge Problem** Use a spreadsheet to construct a common-size balance sheet from the data in problem 2 and a common-size income statement from the data in problem 5.

10. Use the following income statement and balance sheet information to put together a statement of cash flows.

	2006
Sales	$1,230,000
Cost of goods sold	$684,000
Gross profit	$546,000
General and administrative expense	$159,000
Selling and marketing expense	$134,000
Depreciation	$25,000
Operating income	$228,000
Interest	$141,000
Income before taxes	$87,000
Income taxes (27%)	$23,490
Net income	$63,510
Dividends paid	$25,000

ASSETS	2006	2005
Cash	$25,000	$21,990
Accounts receivable	$125,000	$115,000
Inventory	$200,000	$215,000
Total current assets	$350,000	$351,990
Gross plant and equipment	$700,000	$475,000
Less: accumulated depreciation	$313,000	$288,000
Net plant and equipment	$387,000	$187,000
Total assets	$737,000	$538,990

LIABILITIES	2006	2005
Accounts payable	$116,000	$103,000
Notes payable	$29,000	$29,000
Total current liabilities	$145,000	$132,000
Long-term debt	$248,000	$152,000
Total liabilities	$393,000	$284,000
Common stock ($.01 par)	$4,500	$4,000
Paid-in capital	$220,500	$170,500
Retained earnings	$119,000	$80,490
Total stockholders' equity	$344,000	$254,990
Total liabilities and equity	$737,000	$538,990

11. **Challenge Problem** Using the financial statements below,

   a. Compute common-size financial statements.

   b. Put together a statement of cash flows of the firm. Where did the firm invest funds during the year? How did it finance these purchases?

Income Statements for Global Manufacturing, Inc.

YEARS ENDED DECEMBER 31	2006	2005
Net revenues or sales	$700,000	$600,000
Cost of goods sold	450,000	375,000
Gross profit	250,000	225,000
Operating expenses:		
General and administrative	95,000	95,000
Selling and marketing	56,000	50,000
Depreciation	25,000	20,000
Operating income	74,000	60,000
Interest	14,000	10,000
Income before taxes	60,000	50,000
Income taxes (40%)	24,000	20,000
Net income	$36,000	$30,000
Number of shares outstanding	50,000	50,000
Earnings per share	$0.72	$0.60

Balance Sheets for Global Manufacturing, Inc.

YEARS ENDED DECEMBER 31	2006	2005
ASSETS		
Cash and marketable securities	$25,000	$20,000
Accounts receivable	100,000	80,000
Inventories	125,000	100,000
Total current assets	250,000	200,000
Gross plant and equipment	300,000	225,000
Less: accumulated depreciation	−100,000	−75,000
Net plant and equipment	200,000	150,000
Land	50,000	50,000
Total fixed assets	250,000	200,000
Total assets	$500,000	$400,000
LIABILITIES AND EQUITY		
Accounts payable	$78,000	$65,000
Notes payable	34,000	10,000
Accrued liabilities	30,000	25,000
Total current liabilities	142,000	100,000
Long-term debt	140,000	100,000
Total liabilities	$282,000	$200,000
Common stock ($1 par, 50,000 shares)	$50,000	$50,000
Paid-in capital	100,000	100,000
Retained earnings	68,000	50,000
Total stockholders' equity	218,000	200,000
Total liabilities and equity	$500,000	$400,000

12. Compare and contrast the two common-size balance sheets below. Which one do you think may belong to an auto manufacturer? To a computer manufacturer?

Common-Size Balance Sheets

ASSETS	FIRM A	FIRM B
Cash	26.7%	10.6%
Accounts receivable	18.8%	0.9%
Inventory	1.7%	2.9%
Other current assets	7.9%	5.0%
Total current assets	55.1%	19.4%
Net plant and equipment	7.9%	13.3%
Other long-term assets	37.1%	67.3%
Total assets	100.0%	100.0%

LIABILITIES	FIRM A	FIRM B
Accounts payable	37.9%	6.5%
Notes payable	0.0%	0.6%
Other current liabilities	18.5%	19.0%
Total current liabilities	56.4%	26.0%
Long-term debt	2.6%	56.3%
Other liabilities	8.4%	13.9%
Total liabilities	67.5%	96.3%
Common equity	0.8%	1.0%
Retained earnings	31.7%	2.7%
Total stockholders' equity	32.5%	3.7%
Total liabilities and equity	100.0%	100.0%

13. Compare and contrast the two common-size balance sheets below. Which one do you think may belong to a supermarket? To a jeweler?

Common-Size Balance Sheets

ASSETS	FIRM A	FIRM B
Cash	5.3%	2.7%
Accounts receivable	4.1%	0.0%
Inventory	37.5%	61.7%
Other current assets	5.9%	4.1%
Total current assets	52.8%	68.5%
Net plant and equipment	35.1%	20.6%
Other long-term assets	12.4%	11.0%
Total assets	100.0%	100.0%

LIABILITIES	FIRM A	FIRM B
Accounts payable	19.6%	23.8%
Notes payable	0.1%	0.0%
Other current liabilities	16.8%	3.6%
Total current liabilities	36.5%	27.4%
Long-term debt	11.9%	14.2%
Other liabilities	14.7%	8.0%
Total liabilities	63.1%	49.6%
Common equity	4.9%	4.9%
Retained earnings	32.0%	45.5%
Total stockholders' equity	36.9%	50.4%
Total liabilities and equity	100.0%	100.0%

14. **Challenge Problem** Using the following financial statements:

   a. compute common-size financial statements.

   b. compute year-to-year percentage changes in the various accounts.

   c. What insights about the firm can you obtain from this analysis?

Balance Sheet—Yearly Data ($ in millions)

	2006	2005	2004	2003	2002
Cash & Cash Equivalents	16.9	12.8	141.8	144.0	73.0
Accounts Receivable	798.3	614.5	486.5	373.0	376.0
Inventories	3,482.4	2,830.8	2,462.6	2,027.0	1,733.0
Other Current Assets	96.3	92.0	130.8	79.0	144.0
Net Fixed Assets	4,345.3	3,428.2	2,593.9	2,144.0	1,754.0
Other Long-Term Assets	94.6	125.4	91.1	135.0	127.0
TOTAL ASSETS	8,833.8	7,103.7	5,906.7	4,902.0	4,207.0
Accounts Payable	1,546.8	1,364.0	1,130.3	907.0	813.0
Short-Term Debt	440.7	0.0	0.0	0.0	0.0
Other Current Liabilities	1,024.1	939.7	793.5	673.0	626.0
Long-Term Debt	0.0	0.0	0.0	0.0	0.0
Other Liabilities	615.0	566.0	498.6	473.0	395.0
TOTAL LIABILITIES	3,626.6	2,869.7	2,422.4	2,053.0	1,834.0
Preferred Equity	0.0	0.0	0.0	0.0	0.0
Common Equity	676.3	446.2	337.3	196.0	107.0
Retained Earnings	4,530.9	3,787.8	3,147.0	2,653.0	2,266.0
STOCKHOLDERS' EQUITY	5,207.2	4,234.0	3,484.3	2,849.0	2,373.0
TOTAL LIAB. & EQUITY	8,833.8	7,103.7	5,906.7	4,902.0	4,207.0

Income Statement—Yearly Data ($ in millions)

	2006	2005	2004	2003	2002
Revenue	24,623.0	21,206.9	17,838.8	15,307.0	13,363.0
Cost of Goods Sold	17,779.7	15,235.8	12,768.5	10,951.0	9,518.0
Selling, General and Admin.	5,175.8	4,516.9	3,844.8	3,332.0	2,973.0
Depreciation and Amort.	269.2	230.1	210.1	189.0	164.0
Research and Development	0.0	0.0	0.0	0.0	0.0
OPERATING INCOME	1,398.3	1,224.1	1,015.4	835.0	708.0
Interest Expense	3.1	0.4	0.4	1.0	2.0
Other Expenses (Income)	(27.5)	(39.6)	(12.3)	(43.0)	(6.0)
INCOME BEFORE TAXES	1,422.27	1,263.3	1,027.3	877.0	712.0
Income Taxes	537.1	486.4	403.2	340.0	276.0
INCOME AFTER TAXES	885.6	776.9	624.1	537.0	436.0
EPS (as reported)	0.86	0.76	0.62	0.54	0.44

LEARNING EXTENSION 11

Federal Income Taxation

In addition to financing and risk factors, income tax liabilities also may differ for each form of business organization selected. Income from partnerships and proprietorships is combined with other personal income for tax purposes. We show the 2006 rate schedules for (1) a married couple filing jointly and (2) a single person.

FILING STATUS	TAXABLE INCOME	MARGINAL TAX RATE
Married Filing Jointly	$1–15,100	10%
	15,101–61,300	15
	61,301–123,700	25
	123,701–188,450	28
	188,451–336,550	33
	over $336,550	35
Single	$1–7,550	10%
	7,551–30,650	15
	30,651–74,200	25
	74,201–154,800	28
	154,801–336,550	33
	over $336,550	35

A cursory observation shows that personal income tax rates are progressive tax rates because the higher the income, the larger the percentage of income that must be paid in taxes. For example, let's assume that the taxable income from a proprietorship is $50,000 and that the owner does not have any additional income. If the owner is married and filing a joint return and the spouse has no reportable income, the income will be taxed as follows:

$$
\begin{array}{rll}
0.10 \times \$15,100 = & \$1,510 \\
\underline{0.15 \times \quad 34,900 = } & \underline{5,235} \\
\$50,000 & \$6,745
\end{array}
$$

The marginal tax rate is the rate paid on the last dollar of income. In our example it is 15 percent and applies to that portion of the taxable income above $14,000. The average tax rate is determined by dividing the tax amount of $6,745 by the $50,000 in taxable income; it equals 13.5 percent. The marginal tax rate is the rate that is most important when making business decisions. It shows the percentage of new income that will be paid to the government or, alternatively, that will be lost to the firm because of tax obligations.

A proprietor with $50,000 in taxable income who is single would pay the following taxes:

$$
\begin{array}{rll}
0.10 \times \$7,550 = & \$755 \\
0.15 \times 23,100 = & 3,465 \\
\underline{0.25 \times 19,350 = } & \underline{4,837.50} \\
\$50,000 & \$9,057.50
\end{array}
$$

The single proprietor earning $50,000 faces a higher marginal tax rate, 25 percent, and an average tax rate of $9,057.50/$50,000 or 18.1 percent.

Personal taxable income as examined is considered to be *ordinary taxable income* and is taxed when it is received. Capital gains or losses arise from asset price changes on capital assets such as real estate, bonds, and stocks. Capital gains or losses are taxed only when the asset is sold and the gain or loss is realized. *Unrealized capital gains* reflect the price appreciation of currently held assets that have not been sold; the tax liability on unrealized capital gains can be deferred indefinitely. Capital gains become taxable only after the asset has been sold for a price higher than its cost or basis. If appreciated assets are passed on to an heir upon the investor's death, the basis of the assets is considered to be their value on the date of the holder's death. The heirs can then sell the assets and not pay capital gains tax. *Realized capital gains* occur when an appreciated asset has been sold; taxes are due on the realized capital gains only.

Capital gains taxes are paid on realized capital gains. The top capital gain tax rate is 15 percent for assets held longer than twelve months. For taxpayers in the 15 percent tax bracket the capital gains tax rate is only 5 percent. Two things are for certain; the ever-changing tax laws will increase record-keeping requirements and they will keep tax advisors busy.

Corporations, in contrast with proprietorships and partnerships, are taxed as separate entities. In 2006 the corporate tax rates on their taxable income was:

TAXABLE INCOME	TAX RATE
$1–50,000	15%
50,001–75,000	25
75,001–100,000	34
100,001–335,000	39
335,001–10,000,000	34
10,000,001–15,000,000	35
15,000,001–18,333,333	38
Over 18,333,333	35

The 39 percent tax rate for income between $100,000 and $335,000 is designed to recapture the benefits of the 15.0 percent and 25 percent rates. A similar recapture occurs for taxable income between $15 million and $18.3 million. Because of this, the average and marginal tax rates are both 35 percent for corporate incomes over $18,333,333.

A corporation with taxable income of $50,000 pays $7,500 (a 15 percent marginal and average rate), compared with $6,745 for a proprietor who is married and filing a joint return or $9,057.50 for a proprietor who is single. However, income distributed from after-tax corporate profits to owners is taxed again in the form of personal ordinary income. Thus, deciding whether there would be an income tax advantage associated with being taxed as a corporation rather than a proprietorship or partnership is a complex undertaking.

A corporation with taxable income of $200,000 would have the following tax obligation:

$$
\begin{array}{rcl}
0.15 \times \$50,000 &=& \$7,500.00 \\
0.25 \times 25,000 &=& 6,250.00 \\
0.34 \times 25,000 &=& 8,500.00 \\
0.39 \times 100,000 &=& 39,000.00 \\
\hline
\$200,000 && \$61,250.00
\end{array}
$$

The marginal tax rate would be 39 percent, and the average tax rate would be 30.6 percent ($61,250/$200,000).

A corporation pays taxes on its taxable income. Then, if cash from profits is distributed as dividends to stockholders, the stockholders must pay personal income taxes. This means that money paid out to the owners is taxed twice—once at the corporate level and once as personal income. Small businesses can sometimes qualify as S corporations under the Internal Revenue Code. These organizations receive the limited liability of a corporation but are taxed as proprietorships or partnerships. Thus, the S corporation avoids double taxation because the business is taxed as a proprietorship or partnership. Whether or not this taxation option is selected depends on the level of the owner's personal tax bracket.

Businesses also have the opportunity to carry operating losses backward for two years and forward for twenty years to offset taxable income. A new business corporation that loses, for example, $50,000 the first year can offset only taxable income earned in future years. However, initial losses by a new proprietorship or partnership can be first carried back against personal income taxes paid by owners, entitling them to tax refunds. This can be helpful for a new business that has limited funds.

DEPRECIATION BASICS

Depreciation write-offs are particularly important to businesses because depreciation is deductible from income before taxes and thus reduces the firm's income-tax liability. The following example illustrates the impact of deducting versus not deducting $20,000 in depreciation before computing income-tax liabilities.

	WITH DEPRECIATION	WITHOUT DEPRECIATION
Income before depreciation and income taxes	$100,000	$100,000
Less: Depreciation	20,000	0
Income before taxes	80,000	100,000
Less: Income taxes (@ 30%)	24,000	30,000
Net income	**$56,000**	**$70,000**

The depreciation deduction shields income from taxes. Notice that income before taxes is lower when depreciation is deducted, so the amount of income taxes paid is lower as well. This is an example of the *depreciation tax shield*. With depreciation, taxes are reduced by $6,000. The depreciation tax shield is equal to the tax rate multiplied by the depreciation expense. In this case, it is $0.30 \times \$20,000$, or $6,000.

The effects of the depreciation tax shield is seen in the operating cash flow calculation as well. Ignoring any changes in the current asset and current liability accounts, operating cash flow is net income plus depreciation. With the depreciation deduction, the operating cash flow is $56,000 + $20,000 = $76,000. This is $6,000 higher than the operating cash flow without depreciation, $70,000 + $0 = $70,000.

A FEW WORDS ON DEPRECIATION METHODS

IRS tax regulations allow two basic depreciation methods: straight-line depreciation and the modified accelerated cost recovery system (MACRS).

Annual straight-line depreciation expense is computed by dividing the asset's cost by an estimate of its useful life. The annual straight-line depreciation expense for an asset that costs $100,000 and is expected to be used for eight years is $100,000/8 = $12,500.

MACRS depreciates assets by an accelerated method. In essence, MACRS depreciates assets using the double-declining balance method until it becomes advantageous to use straight-line depreciation over the asset's remaining life.

To ensure some uniformity, it assigns assets to depreciation classes:

3-year class	Designated tools and equipment used in research
5-year class	Cars, trucks, and some office equipment such as computers and copiers
7-year class	Other office equipment and industrial machinery
10-year class	Other long-lived equipment
27.5-year class	Residential real estate
31.5-year class	Commercial and industrial real estate

Assets in the 27.5- or 31.5-year classes must be depreciated with the straight-line method over the appropriate number of years. In addition, with some exceptions, MACRS follows a half-year convention. The asset receives a half-year's worth of depreciation in the year it is acquired, regardless of when it is actually purchased. Thus, assets in the three-year class are actually depreciated over four years. The owner writes off a half year of depreciation in year 1, a full year of depreciation in each of years 2 and 3, and the remaining half year of depreciation in year 4.

Annual depreciation percentages are given in the chart that follows. To determine an asset's annual depreciation expense, the cost of the asset is multiplied by the percentage for the appropriate asset class in the appropriate year.

ASSET CLASS YEAR OF OWNERSHIP	3-YEAR	5-YEAR	7-YEAR	10-YEAR
1	33.33%	20.00%	14.29%	10.00%
2	44.45	32.00	24.49	18.00
3	14.81	19.20	17.49	14.40
4	7.41	11.52	12.49	11.52
5		11.52	8.93	9.22
6		5.76	8.92	7.37
7			8.93	6.55
8			4.46	6.55
9				6.56
10				6.55
11				3.28

For example, let's assume that a business purchases a computer system for $10,000. The amount that could be written off or depreciated each year would be as follows:

YEAR	PURCHASE PRICE		DEPRECIATION PERCENTAGE		DEPRECIATION AMOUNT
1	$10,000	×	0.2000	=	2,000
2	10,000	×	0.3200	=	3,200
3	10,000	×	0.1920	=	1,920
4	10,000	×	0.1152	=	1,152
5	10,000	×	0.1152	=	1,152
6	10,000	×	0.0576	=	576
			Total		$10,000

Thus, the computer system would be fully depreciated by the end of six years. Of course, the computer system may have an economic or useful life that is either less than or more than its depreciable life.

QUESTIONS AND PROBLEMS

1. Why is it said that the personal income tax rate in the United States is progressive?

2. Corporate tax rates vary with the amount of taxable income. What currently is the range (lowest and highest) of corporate tax rates in the United States?

3. What is meant by the statement "Depreciation provides a tax shield?" Explain how this works.

4. Determine the marginal and average tax rates under the tax law for corporations with the following amounts of taxable income:

   a. $60,000
   b. $150,000
   c. $500,000

5. Calculate the tax obligation for a corporation with pretax earnings of:

   a. $60,000
   b. $150,000
   c. $500,000

d. What would be the personal tax obligation of a person filing her taxes under the "single" filing status if she had the preceding pretax income levels?

e. How would your answers change in (d) if the filing status was "married filing jointly?"

6. Find the annual depreciation expenses for the following items:

   a. Original cost is $35,000 for an asset in the three-year class.
   b. Original cost is $70,000 for an asset in the five-year class.

7. Assume a corporation earns $75,000 in pretax income.

   a. Determine the firm's income tax liability.
   b. Calculate the firm's average income tax rate.

8. Assume that a corporation purchases a new piece of equipment for $90,000. The equipment qualifies for a three-year class life for depreciation purposes.

   a. What is the dollar amount of depreciation that can be taken in the first year?
   b. Determine the depreciation for the remaining years.

• CHAPTER 12 •

Financial Analysis and Long-Term Planning

Chapter Learning Objectives

AFTER STUDYING THIS CHAPTER, YOU SHOULD BE ABLE TO:

- Describe what is meant by financial statement analysis.
- Describe the five basic types of financial ratios.
- Indicate what is meant by Du Pont analysis and indicate its major components.
- Explain the importance of the quality of financial statements.
- Describe the link between asset investment requirements and sales growth.
- Describe how internally generated financing occurs.
- Describe how additional external financing requirements are determined.
- Describe the cost-volume-profit analysis concept.

Where We Have Been. . .

The previous chapter introduced the three basic financial statements and some basics of accounting—the language of business. Not only do financial market participants such as bondholders, shareholders, and bankers analyze the financial statements, so do the firm's managers to help them assess their own firm and their firm's competition, and to plan for future strategies and financing needs.

Where We Are Going. . .

A myriad of financial market participants will use and analyze financial statement information, particularly bankers, other lenders, suppliers, investors, and even some of the firm's customers. We will see how and why they need this information in future chapters, especially Chapter 15, "Capital Structure and the Cost of Capital," and Chapter 17, "Short-Term Business Financing."

How This Chapter Applies to Me. . .

Publicly available data can be analyzed to show workers and investors how well the firm is doing. For private firms, statement analysis and industry comparisons contain similar information for internal use. A few simple ratio calculations can tell you as an employee or investor how well a firm is doing and how it is making profits.

This chapter gives insight into how lenders make decisions about lending money to you. They will review your personal "balance sheet" (assets and debts) and income statement (monthly income and checking account information) when you apply for a car loan or mortgage.

Warren Buffett, CEO of Berkshire Hathaway, Inc., is well regarded as a financial genius and for his insightful letters to his shareholders that appear in his firm's annual report. In 1987 he wrote:

> *Oftentimes in his shareholders' letter, a CEO will go on for pages detailing corporate performance that is woefully inadequate. He will nonetheless end with a warm paragraph describing his managerial comrades as "our most precious asset." Such comments sometimes make you wonder what the other assets can possibly be.*

INTERNET ACTIVITY

Copies of Buffet's past chairman's letters are available at Berkshire Hathaway's Web site, http://www.berkshirehathaway.com.

Part of being a good manager is managing both people and assets well. Successful financial analysis and planning require an understanding of both a firm's external and internal environments. Prior chapters have discussed important external influences affecting firms such as fluctuations in inflation, interest rates, exchange rates, and government policy. The firm's internal environment includes items that can be affected by management, such as organizational structure, worker motivation and productivity, cost control, and the firm's plant and operations.

There are, of course, a number of interrelationships between a firm's external and internal environment. Firm sales will be affected by the state of the economy, management's ability to handle growth, and the quality and marketing of the firm's product. Pricing decisions are influenced by the state of the economy, actions by competitors, and the firm's production costs. The joint impact of the external and internal environment on a firm is best reflected in the firm's financial statements. These statements provide measures of the success or failure of the firm's strategies and policies, quantified in financial terms. Such information is valuable to the firm's managers as well as to stock and bond analysts, bank loan officers, and competitors. The information found on the financial statements is invaluable for analyzing a firm's past as well as for planning for its future.

For investors, how we view the results from analyzing financial statements will depend upon the economic environment, too. For example, a firm with high debt ratios may be an attractive investment at the end of a recession as economic growth begins. Rapidly expanding sales will generate cash to pay interest, leaving high levels of profits. Of course, the same debt ratios at the end of a period of economic growth, with a recession growing near, may make the firm appear very unattractive for investment purposes.

This chapter addresses how to analyze a firm's financial statements to identify a firm's strengths and weaknesses. We also discuss using financial statement information for financial planning and forecasting purposes, including estimating future asset needs and capital requirements.

FINANCIAL STATEMENT ANALYSIS

The financial statements discussed in Chapter 11 were designed to report a firm's financial position at a point in time, as well as the results of its operations over a period of time. The real usefulness of these statements comes from the help they provide in predicting the firm's future earnings and dividends along with the risks associated with these variables.

Financial statement analysis can affect nonfinance operations of a firm. For example, a salesperson could lose a new customer and a sales commission should a check of the customer's financial statements lead to the conclusion that the customer is a bad credit risk. An analysis that indicates excessive levels of inventories could lead to a change in the firm's pricing and marketing strategies, and it could affect the firm's production plan, even leading to worker layoffs.

A firm's management reviews its financial statements to determine if progress is being made toward company goals. Internal documents based on this analysis inform division managers of the status of their divisions and product lines and how these results compare to the year's plan.

Many individuals and organizations analyze firms' financial statements. A firm that seeks credit, either from a supplier firm or a bank, typically must submit financial statements for examination. Potential purchasers of a firm's bonds will analyze financial statements in order to gauge the firm's ability to make timely payments of interest and principal. Potential shareholders should examine financial statements as they are an excellent source of firm information. Present shareholders will want to examine financial statements to monitor firm performance.

CONCEPT CHECK

Describe how financial statements are used by a variety of different groups to discover information about a firm.

RATIO ANALYSIS OF BALANCE SHEET AND INCOME STATEMENT

ratio analysis
financial technique that involves dividing various financial statement numbers into one another

In this section we discuss **ratio analysis** as a means by which to gain insight regarding a firm's strengths and weaknesses. Ratios are constructed by dividing various financial statement numbers into one another. The ratios can then be examined to determine more easily trends and reasons for changes in the financial statement quantities. Ratios are valuable tools, as they standardize balance sheet and income statement numbers. Thus differences in firm size will not affect the analysis. A firm with $10 billion in sales can be easily compared to a firm with $1 billion or $200 million in sales.

Three basic categories of ratio analysis are used. First, financial ratios can be used in **trend** or **time series analysis** to evaluate a firm's performance over time. Second, ratios are used in **cross-sectional analysis**, in which different firms are compared at the same point in time. Third, **industry comparative analysis** is used to compare a firm's ratios against average ratios for other companies in the firm's industry. This allows the analyst to evaluate the firm's financial performance relative to industry norms.

Comparing a firm's ratios to average industry ratios requires extreme caution. Some sources of industry data report the average for each ratio; others report the median; others report the interquartile range for each ratio (that is, the range for the middle 50 percent of ratio values reported by firms in the industry).

Other difficulties can arise as well. First, by their nature, industry ratios are narrowly focused on a specific industry, but the operations of large firms such as GE, ExxonMobil, and IBM often cross many industry boundaries.

Second, accounting standards often differ among firms in an industry. This can create confusion, particularly when some firms in the industry adopt new accounting standards (set forth by FASB, the Financial Accounting Standards Board) before others. Adopting standards early can affect a firm's ratios by making them appear unusually high or low compared to the industry average.

Third, care must be taken when comparing different types of firms in the same industry. In one industry there may be both very large and small firms; both multinational and domestic firms; firms that operate nationally; and those that focus only on limited geographic markets.

Fourth, analysts and sources of public information on ratios may compute ratios differently. Some may use after-tax earnings, some pre-tax earnings; others may assume "debt" refers only to long-term debt while others include all liabilities as debt. Make sure you are aware of how a resource defines its ratios before using it for analysis.

A firm's financial statements are the best information source for time series or cross-sectional analysis. These materials appear in annual reports as well as 10-Q and 10-K filings with the Securities and Exchange Commission.

Data for industry average financial ratios are published by a number of organizations, such as Dun & Bradstreet, Risk Management Association (formerly known as Robert Morris Associates), Financial Dynamics, Standard & Poor's, and the Federal Trade Commission. These information sources are readily available at most libraries. In addition, analysts can create their own industry financial ratios by obtaining financial statement information on a firm and its competitors. The financial statement items can be added across the firms to give an "industry" balance sheet or income statement. This data can be used to compute ratios for comparison against the firm in question.

How an analyst interprets a ratio depends on for whom the analyst works. Whether a ratio appears favorable or unfavorable depends on the perspective of the user. For example, a short-term creditor such as a bank loan officer wants most to see a high degree of liquidity. This analyst is somewhat less concerned with a firm's profitability. An equity holder would rather see less liquidity and more profitability. Therefore the analyst must keep in mind the perspective of the user in evaluating and interpreting the information contained in financial ratios.

CONCEPT CHECK

Why is financial statement analysis important?

Describe the three types of financial statement analysis.

What can industry average data tell analysts about a firm?

TYPES OF FINANCIAL RATIOS

Many types of ratios can be calculated from financial statement data or stock market information. However, it is common practice to group ratios into five basic categories:

1. Liquidity ratios
2. Asset management ratios
3. Financial leverage ratios
4. Profitability ratios
5. Market value ratios

The first four categories are based on information taken from a firm's income statements and balance sheets. The fifth category relates stock market information to financial statement items. We will use the financial statements for Allgreens that were introduced in Chapter 11 to illustrate how financial statement analysis is conducted. Tables 12.1 and 12.2 contain the balance sheets

TABLE 12.1

Balance Sheet for Allgreens ($ in millions)

	2006	2005	2004	2003
ASSETS				
Cash & Marketable Securities	$1,017.10	$449.90	$16.90	$12.80
Accounts Receivable	$1,017.80	$954.80	$798.30	$614.50
Inventories	$4,202.70	$3,645.20	$3,482.40	$2,830.80
Other Current Assets	$120.50	$116.60	$96.30	$92.00
Total Current Assets	$6,358.10	$5,166.50	$4,393.90	$3,550.10
Net Fixed Assets	$4,940.00	$4,591.40	$4,345.30	$3,428.20
Other Long-Term Assets	$107.80	$120.90	$94.60	$125.40
Total Fixed Assets	$5,047.80	$4,712.30	$4,439.90	$3,553.60
Total Assets	$11,405.90	$9,878.80	$8,833.80	$7,103.70
LIABILITIES AND EQUITY				
Accounts Payable	$2,077.00	$1,836.40	$1,546.80	$1,364.00
Notes Payable	$0.00	$0.00	$440.70	$0.00
Other Current Liabilities	$1,343.50	$1,118.80	$1,024.10	$939.70
Total Current Liabilities	$3,420.50	$2,955.20	$3,011.60	$2,303.70
Long-Term Debt	$0.00	$0.00	$0.00	$0.00
Other Liabilities	$789.70	$693.40	$615.00	$566.00
Total Liabilities	$4,210.20	$3,648.60	$3,626.60	$2,869.70
Common Equity	$777.90	$828.50	$676.30	$446.20
Retained Earnings	$6,417.80	$5,401.70	$4,530.90	$3,787.80
Total Stockholders' Equity	$7,195.70	$6,230.20	$5,207.20	$4,234.00
Total Liabilities and Equity	$11,405.90	$9,878.80	$8,833.80	$7,103.70

and income statements for several years for Allgreens. For comparative purposes, for each ratio group we present graphs of Allgreens' ratios, as well as hypothetical average ratios for the retail drug store industry over the 2000–2006 time period.[1]

LIQUIDITY RATIOS AND ANALYSIS

The less liquid the firm, the greater the risk of insolvency or default. Because debt obligations are paid with cash, the firm's cash flows ultimately determine solvency.

INTERNET ACTIVITY

Various industry ratios and industry analyses are available for different firms on Web sites such as http://finance.yahoo. com (enter a stock ticker symbol to get a price quote; then click on "profile"; once on the profile page, click on "ratio comparison") and http:// www.hoovers.com. Other Web sites containing financial information will be a corporation's home page, http://www.sec.gov/edgar. shtml for the SEC's EDGAR database of public firm filings, and http://www.multex.com.

TABLE 12.2

Income Statements for Allgreens ($ in millions)

	2006	2005	2004	2003
Revenue	$32,505.40	$28,681.10	$24,623.00	$21,206.90
Cost of Goods Sold	$23,360.10	$20,768.80	$17,779.70	$15,235.80
Gross Profit	$9,145.30	$7,912.30	$6,843.30	$5,971.10
Selling, General & Administrative	$6,950.90	$5,980.80	$5,175.80	$4,516.90
Depreciation	$346.10	$307.30	$269.20	$230.10
Operating Income	$1,848.30	$1,624.20	$1,398.30	$1,224.10
Interest Expense	$0.00	$0.00	$3.10	$0.40
Other Expenses (Income)	($40.40)	($13.10)	($27.50)	($39.60)
Income Before Taxes	$1,888.70	$1,637.30	$1,422.70	$1,263.30
Income Taxes	$713.00	$618.10	$537.10	$486.40
Net Income	$1,175.70	$1,019.20	$885.60	$776.90
Number of Shares Outstanding (000s)	1,031,580	1,032,271	1,028,947	1,019,889
Earnings Per Share	$1.14	$0.99	$0.86	$0.76

---

1. Average industry ratios were prepared solely for comparison purposes in this chapter and are not intended to be actual ratios.

We can estimate the firm's liquidity position by examining specific balance sheet items. *Liquidity ratios* indicate the ability to meet short-term obligations to creditors as they mature or come due. This form of liquidity analysis focuses on the relationship between current assets and current liabilities, and the rapidity with which receivables and inventory turn into cash during normal business operations. This means that the immediate source of cash funds for paying bills must be cash on hand, proceeds from the sale of marketable securities, or the collection of accounts receivable. Additional liquidity also comes from inventory that can be sold and thus converted into cash either directly through cash sales or indirectly through credit sales (accounts receivable).

The dollar amount of a firm's **net working capital**, or its current assets minus current liabilities, is sometimes used as a measure of liquidity. Two popular ratios are also used to gauge a firm's liquidity position. The *current ratio* is a measure of a company's ability to pay off its short-term debt as it comes due. The current ratio is computed by dividing the current assets by the current liabilities. Both assets and liabilities with maturities of one year or less are considered to be current for financial statement purposes.

A low current ratio (low relative to, say, industry norms) may indicate a company faces difficulty in paying its bills. A high value for the current ratio, however, does not necessarily imply greater liquidity. It may suggest that funds are not being efficiently employed within the firm. Excessive amounts of inventory, accounts receivable, or idle cash balances could contribute to a high current ratio.

We can now calculate the current ratio for 2006 and 2005 as follows:

CURRENT RATIO:

2006: (Current Assets/Current Liabilities) = $6,358.1/$3,420.5 = 1.86 times
2005: $5,166.5/$2,955.2 = 1.75 times

Table 12.1 shows a large increase in Allgreens' cash account in 2006 and that both accounts receivables and inventory rose. At first glance, analysts may need to be wary of slow-paying accounts or sales slowdowns (because of the inventory rise), but Table 12.2 shows that Allgreens had a healthy sales increase of over 13 percent in 2006.

The *quick ratio*, or *acid test ratio*, is computed by dividing the sum of cash, marketable securities, and accounts receivable by the current liabilities. This comparison eliminates inventories from consideration since inventories are among the least liquid of the major current asset categories because they must first be converted to sales.

In general, a ratio of 1.0 indicates a reasonably liquid position in that an immediate liquidation of marketable securities at their current values and the collection of all accounts receivable, plus cash on hand, would be adequate to cover the firm's current liabilities. However, as this ratio declines, the firm must rely increasingly on converting inventories to sales in order to meet current liabilities as they come due. Allgreens' quick ratios for 2006 and 2005 are:

QUICK RATIO:

2006: [(Cash + Accounts Receivable)/Current Liabilities] = ($1,017.1 + $1,017.8)/$3,420.5 = 0.59 times
2005: ($449.9 + $954.8)/$2,955.2 = 0.48 times

According to the financial statement data, Allgreens' quick ratio is well below 1.0. As we will soon see, this is not a major cause for concern in the retail drugstore industry. In this industry, we expect lower quick ratios as much of their current assets are inventory awaiting sale on their store shelves and warehouses.

When assessing the firm's liquidity position, financial managers also are interested in how trade credit from suppliers, which we call accounts payable, is being used and paid for. This analysis requires taking data from a firm's income statement in addition to the balance sheet. The *average payment period* is computed by dividing the year-end accounts payable amount by the firm's average cost of goods sold per day. We calculate the average daily cost of goods sold by dividing the income statement's cost of goods sold amount by 365 days in a year.

AVERAGE PAYMENT PERIOD

$$\frac{\text{Accounts Payable}}{\text{Cost of Goods Sold}/365} = \text{Accounts Payable/Cost of Goods Sold per Day:}$$

$$2006: \frac{\$2,077.0}{\$23,360.1/365} = \$2,077.0/\$64.00 = 32.5 \text{ days}$$

$$2005: \frac{\$1,836.4}{\$20,768.8/365} = \$1,836.4/\$56.90 = 32.3 \text{ days}$$

CONCEPT CHECK

What do liquidity ratios measure?

Name three liquidity ratios and describe what they tell about a firm.

On average, it takes Allgreens a little over one month to pay its suppliers.

Figure 12.1 illustrates the trend of Allgreens' liquidity ratios in comparison to their industry averages. The industry's current and quick ratios rose slightly while the average payment period fell over the 2000–2006 period. Allgreens' current and quick ratios are above those of the industry in 2000 and 2001, but their relative positions reversed in 2003. Since 2003, Allgreens' liquidity ratios have recovered and have moved closer to those of the industry.

Allgreens' average payment period has remained constant, about thirty-two days, during this period. This is about ten days quicker than the industry until 2003 when the industry average decreased so that both the industry and Allgreens paid their bills, on average, in thirty-two days.

FIGURE 12.1
Liquidity Ratios

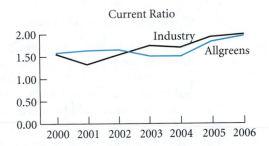

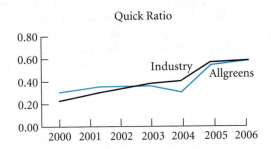

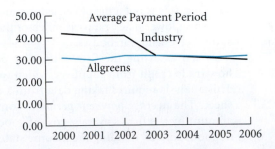

ASSET MANAGEMENT RATIOS AND ANALYSIS

asset management ratios
indicate extent to which
assets are used to support
sales

Asset management ratios indicate the extent to which assets are turned over, or used to support sales. These are also sometimes referred to as activity or utilization ratios, and each ratio in this category relates financial performance on the income statement with items on the balance sheet. Thus, we will be using information for Allgreens from Tables 12.1 and 12.2.

The *total assets turnover ratio* is computed by dividing net sales by the firm's total assets. It indicates how efficiently the firm is utilizing its total assets to produce revenues or sales. It is a measure of the dollars of sales generated by one dollar of the firm's assets. Generally, the more efficiently assets are used, the higher a firm's profits. The size of the ratio is significantly influenced by characteristics of the industry within which the firm operates. Capital-intensive electric utilities might have asset turnover ratios as low as 0.33, indicating that they require $3 of investment in assets in order to produce $1 in revenues. In contrast, retail food chains with asset turnovers as high as 10 would require a $0.10 investment in assets to produce $1 in sales. A typical manufacturing firm has an asset turnover of about 1.5. Allgreens' 2005 and 2006 total assets turnover ratios are calculated as follows:

TOTAL ASSETS TURNOVER:

2006: (Net Sales/Total Assets) = $32,505.4/$11,405.9 = 2.85 times

2005: $28,681.1/$9,878.8 = 2.90 times

Asset utilization was consistent between 2005 and 2006, with each $1 in assets supporting slightly less than $3 in sales.

The *fixed assets turnover ratio* is computed by dividing net sales by the firm's fixed assets and indicates the extent to which long-term assets are being used to produce sales. Similar to the interpretation given to the total asset turnover, the fixed assets turnover represents the dollars of sales generated by each dollar of fixed assets. Investment in plant and equipment is usually quite expensive. Consequently unused or idle capacity is very costly and often represents a major factor in a firm's poor operating performance. On the other hand, a high (compared to competitors or the industry average) fixed assets turnover ratio is not necessarily a favorable sign; it may come about because of efficient use of assets (good) or because of the firm's use of technologically obsolete equipment that has small book values because of the effects of accumulated depreciation (poor). An astute analyst will do research to determine which is the case for the firm under analysis.

FIXED ASSETS TURNOVER:

2006: (Net Sales/Fixed Assets) = $32,505.4/$4,940.0 = 6.58 times

2005: $28,681.1/$4,591.4 = 6.25 times

Allgreens' fixed assets turnover increased from 6.25 to 6.58, indicating that sales increased more rapidly than fixed assets. In percentage terms, net fixed assets increased 7.6 percent [i.e., ($4,940.0 − $4,591.4)/$4,591.4] compared to 13.3 percent for sales [i.e., ($32,505.4 − $28,681.1)/$28,681.1]. In light of an increase in the fixed asset turnover, it may be surprising that total asset turnover fell slightly from 2005 to 2006. For this to happen, it means Allgreens used its working capital less efficiently. This is what occurred, as current assets grew 23 percent, compared to the 13.3 percent and 7.6 percent increases in sales and fixed assets.

The *average collection period* is calculated as the year-end accounts receivable divided by the average net sales per day and thus indicates the average number of days that sales are outstanding. In other words, it reports the number of days it takes, on average, to collect credit sales made to the firm's customers. The average collection period measures the days of financing that a firm extends to its customers.[2] Because of this, a shorter average collection period is usually preferred to a longer one. Another measure that can be used to provide this same information is the receivables turnover. The receivables turnover is computed by dividing annual sales, preferably credit sales, by the year-end accounts receivable. If the receivables turnover is six, this means that, on the average, the average collection period is about two months (12 months divided by

---

2. In some ways the average collection period is the "mirror image" of the average payment period, which is the average number of days the firm's suppliers extend credit to the firm.

the turnover ratio of 6). If the turnover is four times, the firm has an average collection period of about three months (twelve months divided by the turnover ratio of four). Allgreens' average collection periods for 2006 and 2005 were:

AVERAGE COLLECTION PERIOD:

$$\frac{\text{Accounts Receivable}}{\text{Net Sales}/365} = (\text{Accounts Receivable/Net Sales per Day}):$$

$$2006: \frac{\$1,017.8}{\$32,505.4/365} = \$1,017.8/\$89.06 = 11.4 \text{ days}$$

$$2005: \frac{\$954.8}{\$28,681.1/365} = \$954.8/\$78.58 = 12.2 \text{ days}$$

Allgreens' average collection period fell slightly. In essence, Allgreens obtained funds from its customers three-quarters of a day more quickly, on average, from 2005 to 2006. Comparing the average collection and payment periods, Allgreens is in a positive situation, as it collects from its customers about twenty days faster than it pays its suppliers. This has positive implications for Allgreens' asset efficiency and for its liquidity.

In general, compared to an industry average, an unusually low number of days required to collect sales for a particular line of business may indicate an unnecessarily tight internal credit policy that could result in lost sales. The firm may be selecting only the best customers, or may be insisting on unusually strict payment terms. On the other hand, a very high average collection period may indicate that the firm has too lax a policy concerning customer quality and/or credit payment terms. Thus, in trying to decide on a proper credit policy, it is important to monitor trends over time, as well as to compare the firm's average collection period relative to industry norms. We will explore credit policies in greater detail in Chapter 16.

The *inventory turnover ratio* is computed by dividing the cost of goods sold by the year-end inventory.[3] Here we are seeking to determine how efficiently the amount of inventory is being managed so that on the one hand the firm does not have to finance excess inventory and on the other hand adequate inventory supplies exist in order to avoid costly stock-outs. Stated differently, the inventory turnover ratio indicates whether the inventory is out of line in relation to the volume of sales when compared against industry norms or when tracked over time for a specific firm.[4]

INVENTORY TURNOVER:

2006: (Cost of Goods Sold/Inventory) = $\$23,360.1/\$4,202.7 = 5.56$ times

2005: $\$20,768.8/3,645.2 = 5.70$ times

Allgreens' annual inventory turnover decreased slightly from 5.70 in 2005 to 5.56 in 2006.

Inventory management requires a delicate balance between having too low an inventory turnover, which increases the likelihood of holding obsolete inventory, and too high an inventory turnover, which could lead to stock-outs and lost sales. These concepts will be discussed in greater detail in Chapter 16.

When a firm is growing rapidly (or even shrinking rapidly), the use of year-end data might distort the comparison of ratios over time. To avoid such possible distortions, we can use the average inventory (beginning plus ending balances divided by two) to calculate inventory turnovers for comparison purposes.[5] Likewise, average data for other balance sheet accounts should be used when rapid growth or contraction is taking place for a specific firm.

---

3. Cost of goods sold often is used to compute this ratio instead of sales in order to remove the impact of profit margins on inventory turnover. Profit margins can vary over time, thus making it more difficult to interpret the relationship between volume and inventory.

4. The decline in fortunes for telecom firms during 2000–2001 was clearly evident in the behavior of their inventory turnover ratios. Rising inventories and falling sales led to plummeting profits, cash positions, and stock prices for many firms. See Ken Brown, "Some Tech Investors Shift Hopes to 2002," *Wall Street Journal* (February 21, 2001), pp. C1, C2.

5. For firms with highly seasonal sales, the average of the inventory balance from the firm's quarterly balance sheets (which are distributed to shareholders of public firms) also can be used.

CONCEPT CHECK

Figure 12.2 illustrates Allgreens' asset management ratios in comparison to the industry average between 2000 and 2006. With the exception of the fixed assets turnover ratio, Allgreens had more favorable asset management ratios than the industry, but as we saw with the liquidity ratios, there has been a narrowing of the advantage Allgreens has had over its industry competitors.

FINANCIAL LEVERAGE RATIOS AND ANALYSIS

Financial leverage ratios indicate the extent to which borrowed or debt funds are used to finance assets, as well as the ability of the firm to meet its debt payment obligations.

The total debt to total assets ratio is computed by dividing the total debt or total liabilities of the business by the total assets. This ratio shows the portion of the total assets financed by all creditors and debtors. We obtain the relevant balance sheet information for Allgreens from Table 12.1.

FIGURE 12.2

Asset Management Ratios

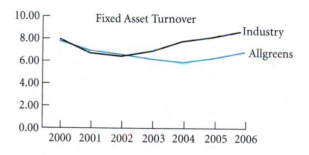

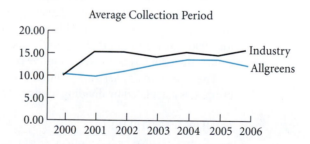

CAREER OPPORTUNITIES IN FINANCE
Business Financial Planning

Opportunities
A business may be small, with a relatively small budget and a straightforward market, or large, with a budget well over $1 billion and a multinational market. In either case, analysts and planners play an important and necessary role in preserving the financial well-being of their firm. These jobs, therefore, are challenging, often unpredictable, and exciting. The risks are often high, but so are the rewards.

Jobs
Financial Analyst
Treasury Analyst
Credit Analyst

Responsibilities
A financial analyst calculates a firm's past and ongoing financial performance relative to other firms in the same industry and/or a firm's own performance over time. Once this information is gathered, a financial analyst evaluates the results and presents these findings to other departments of the firm.

A treasury analyst prepares short-term and longer-term financial plans. A short-term financial plan generally involves estimating monthly cash needs for one year into the future. Business firms also typically prepare five-year plans based on sales forecasts and estimates of capital expenditures needed to support the sales forecasts. A treasury analyst would make annual estimates of the external financing needed to support these sales targets over each five-year plan.

A credit analyst evaluates the creditworthiness of both a firm's potential customers and existing credit customers. Decisions whether to extend credit in the form of short-term financing are based on an assessment of the applicant's liquidity and ability to pay. In cases where credit has been extended, the credit analyst monitors credit customers for possible changes in the liquidity or the ability to pay in the short run.

Education
These positions require at least a bachelor's degree along with a solid background in finance, economics, accounting, and computers.

TOTAL DEBT TO TOTAL ASSETS:

2006: (Total Debt/Total Assets) = $4,210.2/$11,405.9 = 0.369 = 36.9%

2005: 3,648.6/9,878.8 = 0.369 = 36.9%

Allgreens' total debt ratio has not changed, meaning that the firm's debt load grew at approximately the same rate as its asset base.

Compared to industry averages, a total debt to asset ratio that is relatively high tells the financial manager that the opportunities for securing additional borrowed funds are limited. Additional debt funds may be more costly in terms of the rate of interest that will have to be paid. Lenders will want higher expected returns to compensate for their risk of lending to a firm that has a high proportion of debt to assets. It is also possible to have too low a ratio of total debt to total assets. This can be quite costly to the firm.[6] Since interest expenses are deductible for income tax purposes, the government in effect pays a portion of the debt financing costs. Furthermore, as we will see in Chapter 15, a firm's debt costs are lower than the effective costs of equity.

Sometimes a debt ratio is calculated that shows the total debt in relation to the dollars the owners have put in the firm. This is referred to as the total debt to equity ratio. Allgreens' ratio for 2006 was 0.59 ($4,210.2/$7,195.7) and 0.59 ($3,648.6/$6,230.2) in 2005. For every dollar of equity, the firm has borrowed about 59 cents.

The *equity multiplier ratio*, which provides still another way of looking at the firm's debt burden, is calculated by dividing total assets by the firm's total equity.

EQUITY MULTIPLIER:

2006: (Total Assets/Total Equity) = $11,405.9/$7,195.7 = 1.59

2005: $9,878.8/$6,230.2 = 1.59

Similar to the total debt to total assets ratio, the equity multiplier was unchanged between 2005 and 2006. Since Allgreens does not have long-term debt outstanding, these modest changes in the debt ratios occur because of changes in short-term debt or Allgreens' other liabilities, such as pension fund or health care benefits for workers.

---

6. A low debt ratio can arise from the continued profitability of a firm and its additions to retained earnings. These additions to retained earnings will increase the level of equity relative to debt unless the firm issues additional debt or repurchases outstanding shares of stock.

At first glance, this last ratio appears to have little to do with leverage; it is simply total assets divided by stockholders' equity. But recall the accounting identity: Assets = Liabilities + Equity; more assets relative to equity suggests greater use of debt. Thus, larger values of the equity multiplier imply a greater use of leverage by the firm. This can also be seen by rewriting the equity multiplier using the accounting identity:

$$(\text{Total Assets/Equity}) = [(\text{Liabilities} + \text{Equity})/\text{Equity}] = (\text{Liabilities/Equity}) + 1$$

This is simply one plus the debt to equity ratio. Clearly, more reliance on debt results in a larger equity multiplier. While the equity multiplier does not add to the information derived from the other debt ratios, it is useful when financial analysis is conducted using certain financial models, as we will explain later in this chapter.

In addition to calculating debt ratios, the financial manager should be interested in the firm's ability to meet or service its interest and principal repayment obligations on the borrowed funds. This is accomplished through the calculation of interest coverage and fixed charge coverage ratios. These ratios make use of information directly from the income statement or from footnotes to a firm's financial statements.

The *interest coverage,* or *times-interest-earned ratio,* is calculated by dividing the firm's operating income or earnings before interest and taxes (EBIT) by the annual interest expense. Using data from Allgreens' 2003 and 2004 financial statements, since no interest was paid in 2005 and 2006, we have:

INTEREST COVERAGE:

2004: (Earnings Before Interest & Taxes/Interest Expense) = $1,398.3/$3.10 = 451.1 times

2003: $1,224.10/$0.40 = 3,060.3 times

Allgreens' interest coverage ratios are not defined for 2005 and 2006 since interest-paying notes payable and long-term debt are both zero on the firm's balance sheet in 2005 and 2006.

The interest coverage figure indicates the extent to which the operating income or EBIT level could decline before the ability to pay interest obligations would be impeded. Suppose a firm's interest coverage ratio is 5.0. This would mean that Allgreens' operating income could drop to 20 percent, or one-fifth (in general, to one divided by the interest coverage), of its current level and interest payments still could be met.

sinking fund payments
*periodic bond principal
repayments to a trustee*

In addition to interest payments, there may be other fixed charges, such as rental or lease payments and periodic bond principal repayments, that are typically referred to as **sinking fund payments**. The fixed charge coverage ratio indicates the ability of a firm to meet its contractual obligations for interest, leases, and debt principal repayments out of its operating income.

Rental or lease payments are deductible on the income statement prior to the payment of income taxes just as is the case with interest expenses. In contrast, a sinking fund payment is a repayment of debt and thus is not a deductible expense for income tax purposes. However, to be consistent with the other data, we must adjust the sinking fund payment to a before-tax basis. We do this by dividing the after-tax amount by one minus the effective tax rate.

While footnotes to Allgreens' balance sheets are not provided in Table 12.1, examination of the footnotes in Allgreens' annual reports shows property lease payments of $1,187.0 million in 2006 and $897.9 million in 2005. Allgreens has no interest-bearing liabilities, and it has no sinking fund obligations. We compute the fixed charge coverage ratio as follows. First, the numerator in the ratio must reflect earnings before interest, lease payments, and taxes, which we determine by adding the lease payment amount to the operating income or EBIT amount. Second, the denominator needs to show all relevant expenses on a before-tax basis.

FIXED CHARGE COVERAGE:

$$\frac{\text{Earnings Before Interest, Lease Payments, and Taxes}}{\text{Interest} + \text{Lease Payments} + [(\text{Sinking Fund Payment})/(1-\text{Tax Rate})]}$$

$$2006: \frac{\$1,848.3 + \$1,187.0}{\$0 + \$1,187.0 + \$0} = \$3,035.3/\$1,187.0 = 2.56$$

$$2005: \frac{\$1,624.2 + \$897.9}{\$0 + \$897.9 + \$0} = \$2,522.1/\$897.9 = 2.81$$

CONCEPT CHECK

What do financial leverage ratios tell analysts about a firm?

Does a debt to assets ratio that is too high signal potential bad news about a firm? How about one that is well below the industry average?

This is a marked difference from the interest coverage ratio. Information in Allgreens' annual report to shareholders tells us that the firm usually leases its store space rather than purchasing it. These long-term leases are a substitute for debt financing for Allgreens.

The graphs of Allgreens' financial leverage ratios in Figure 12.3 shows industry debt ratios declining slightly during the 2000–2006 time period. The deterioration in the industry's interest coverage, from about 9 in 2000 to about 3 in 2006, was a concern. Since the industry debt load rose only slightly until 2002, the decline in interest coverage was due to falling earnings. Since then, however, the industry's interest coverage ratio has recovered.

In contrast to the retail drugstore industry, Allgreens' debt ratio declined slightly while its interest coverage ratio was either at extremely high levels or was undefined because of the absence of interest-bearing debt (thus, we do not show Allgreens' interest coverage ratio in Figure 12.3). From looking at Allgreens, we can make three important conclusions. First, not all liabilities are contractual debt. Allgreens has a debt to assets ratio of about 40 percent but has no interest-bearing short-term (notes payable) or long-term (long-term debt) on its balance sheet. Second, not all liabilities require interest to be paid. Again, Allgreens has a debt ratio of 40 percent but virtually no interest payments. Third, to get a truer perspective of a firm's financial situation all contractual fixed charges, including interest, lease payments, and sinking fund payments, should be examined. This requires some reading of the footnotes and other information in the firm's financial statements. Allgreens' sky-high interest coverage ratio is brought back to earth when fixed charges are considered and a fixed charge coverage ratio is computed.

FIGURE 12.3
Financial Leverage Ratios

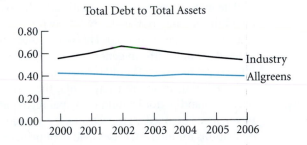

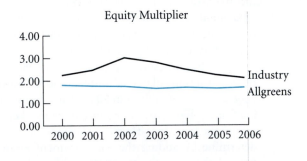

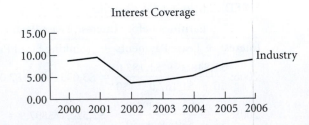

PROFITABILITY RATIOS AND ANALYSIS

Profitability ratios indicate the firm's ability to generate returns on its sales, assets, and equity. Two basic profit margin ratios are important to the financial manager: the operating profit margin and the net profit margin. The *operating profit margin* is calculated as the firm's earnings before interest and taxes divided by net sales. This ratio indicates the firm's ability to control operating expenses relative to sales. Table 12.2 contains income statement information for the Allgreens Corporation and provides the necessary information for determining the operating profit margin.

OPERATING PROFIT MARGIN:

2006: (Earnings Before Interest & Taxes/Net Sales) = $1,848.3/$32,505.4 = 0.0569 = 5.69%

2005: 1,624.2/28,681.1 = 0.0566 = 5.66%

These results indicate that Allgreens was able to slightly improve its operating profitability from 2005 to 2006. Whether it was because of higher selling prices or lower costs, operating profit (EBIT) rose about 13.8 percent on a sales increase of about 13.3 percent.

The *net profit margin,* a widely used measure of firm profitability, is calculated as the firm's net income after taxes divided by net sales. In addition to considering operating expenses, this ratio also indicates the ability to earn a return after meeting interest and tax obligations. Allgreens' net profit margin shows a slight improvement in 2006 over 2005:

NET PROFIT MARGIN:

2006: (Net Income/Net Sales) = $1,175.7/$32,505.4 = 0.0362 = 3.62%

2005: $1,019.2/$28,681.1 = 0.0355 = 3.55%

Three basic rate of return measures on assets and equity are important to the financial manager. The *operating return on assets* is computed as the earnings before interest and taxes divided by total assets. Notice that this ratio focuses on the firm's operating performance and ignores how the firm is financed and taxed. Relevant data for Allgreens must be taken from both Tables 12.1 and 12.2.

OPERATING RETURN ON ASSETS:

2006: (Earnings Before Interest & Taxes/Total Assets) = $1,848.3/$11,405.9 = 0.162 = 16.2%

2005: $1,624.2/$9,878.8 = 0.164 = 16.4%

Allgreens' operating return on assets was consistent in these two years.

The net return on total assets, commonly referred to as the *return on total assets,* is measured as the firm's net income divided by total assets. Here we measure the return on investment in assets after a firm has covered its operating expenses, interest costs, and tax obligations. Allgreens' return on total assets remained constant in 2005 and 2006:

RETURN ON TOTAL ASSETS:

2006: (Net Income/Total Assets) = $1,175.7/$11,405.9 = 0.103 = 10.3%

2005: $1,019.2/$9,878.8 = 0.103 = 10.3%

Recall how Allgreens leases many of its stores. This not only reduces its financing needs but reduces its level of fixed and total assets. In turn, this can help to increase asset-based profitability ratios, such as the return on total assets, if indeed the firm is profitable.

A final profitability ratio is the *return on equity.* It measures the return that shareholders earned on their equity invested in the firm. The return on equity is measured as the firm's net income divided by stockholders' equity. This ratio reflects the fact that a portion of a firm's total assets are financed with borrowed funds. As with the return on assets, Allgreens' return on equity remained virtually the same from 2005 to 2006:

RETURN ON EQUITY:

2006: (Net Income/Common Equity) = $1,175.7/$7,195.7 = 0.163 = 16.3%

2005: $1,019.2/$6,230.2 = 0.164 = 16.4%

CONCEPT CHECK

What do profitability ratios measure?

Figure 12.4 indicates that industry profitability ratios were below those of Allgreens during 2000–2006. Industry profitability fell sharply in 2002 and 2003 while Allgreens was able to maintain its profitability. As of 2006, Allgreens is more cost efficient (as seen in its higher operating and net profit margins) and generates more profit from its asset and equity base (as seen in the operating return on assets, return on total assets, and return on equity) than the retail drugstore industry as a whole.

FIGURE 12.4
Profitability Ratios

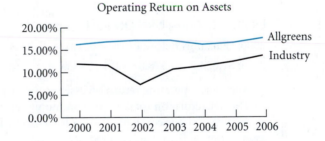

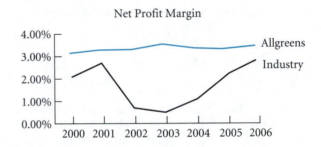

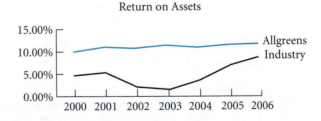

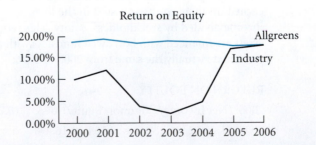

MARKET VALUE RATIOS AND ANALYSIS

market value ratios
indicate the value of a firm in the marketplace relative to financial statement values

The **market value ratios** indicate the willingness of investors to value a firm in the marketplace relative to financial statement values. A firm's profitability, risk, quality of management, and many other factors are reflected in its stock and security prices by the efficient financial markets. Financial statements are historical in nature; the financial markets are forward looking.[7] We know that stock prices seem to reflect much of the known information about a company and are fairly good indicators of a company's true value. Hence, market value ratios indicate the market's assessment of the value of the firm's securities.

The *price/earnings,* or *P/E, ratio,* is simply the market price of the firm's common stock divided by its annual earnings per share. Sometimes called the *earnings multiple,* the P/E ratio shows how much investors are willing to pay for each dollar of the firm's earnings per share. Earnings per share comes from the income statement, so it is sensitive to the many factors that affect net income. Though earnings per share cannot reflect the value of the firm's patents or assets, human resources, culture, quality of management, or its risk, stock prices can and do reflect all these factors. Comparing a firm's P/E relative to that of the stock market as a whole, or the firm's competitors, indicates the market's perceptions of the true value of the company.

The *price-to-book-value ratio* measures the market's value of the firm relative to balance sheet equity. The book value of equity is simply the difference between the book values of assets and liabilities appearing on the balance sheet.[8] The price-to-book-value ratio is the market price per share divided by the book value of equity per share. A higher ratio suggests that investors are more optimistic about the market value of a firm's assets, its intangible assets, and its managers' abilities.

Figure 12.5 shows levels and trends in the P/E ratio and price/book ratio for Allgreens and the retail drugstore industry. Just as our analysis of financial statement ratios pointed out, Allgreens' higher profitability and consistency in its ratios over time has translated into higher relative market valuations. The market is optimistic in its valuation of Allgreens' future prospects. Both the earnings multiple and price/book ratios have fallen for Allgreens and the industry, but Allgreens' ratios continue to exceed those of the industry.

ETHICAL ISSUES

CONCEPT CHECK

What do market value ratios tell managers about the financial market's view of a firm?

What is meant by a "quality" balance sheet or a "quality" income statement?

Financial managers and analysts often talk about the quality of a firm's earnings or the quality of its balance sheet. This has nothing to do with the size of a firm's earnings or assets or who audited the financial statements. Quality financial statements are those that accurately reflect the firm's true economic condition. In other words, various accounting rules were not used to inflate its earnings or assets to make the firm look stronger than it really is. Thus, for a quality income statement, the firm's sales revenues are likely to be repeated in the future. Earnings are not affected by one-time charges. A quality balance sheet will represent inventory that is marketable, not out of fashion or technologically obsolete. It will represent limited debt, indicating the firm could easily borrow money should the need arise. The firm's assets will have market values that exceed their accounting book values; in other words, the firm's assets will not be inflated by intangible assets such as "goodwill" or "patents." All else constant, a firm with higher-quality financial statements will have higher market value ratios. This occurs as the market will recognize and reward the economic reality of a firm's earnings and assets that are not temporarily bloated by accounting gimmicks.

Note how attempts to play accounting tricks will affect the firm's ratios. Overstating existing inventory can have the affect of making current cost of goods sold appear lower, thus inflating profits. Booking revenue in advance of true sales to customers will inflate both sales and profits. The effect of such actions will be to increase profitability and asset management ratios. Unfortunately, watching for accounting tricks or outright fraud is necessary for investors, as episodes with companies in different industries such as telecommunications equipment (Lucent), dot-com firms (many), and energy trading (Enron) have shown in recent years.[9]

7. Recall from Chapter 8 that stock prices are in part based upon investors' *expectations* of *future* dividend growth.

8. Typically it is equal to stockholders' equity.

9. Jonathan Weil, John Emshwiller, and Scot J. Paltrow, "Arthur Andersen Says It Disposed of Documents That Related to Enron," *Wall Street Journal* (January 11, 2002), pp. A1, A4; Dennis K. Berman and Rebecca Blumenstein, "Behind Lucent's Woes: All-Out Revenue Goal and Pressure to Meet It," *Wall Street Journal* (March 29, 2001), pp. A1, A8; Jonathan Weil, "Going Concerns: Did Accountants Fail to Flag Problems at Dot-Com Casualties?" *Wall Street Journal* (February 9, 2001), pp. C1, C2.

FIGURE 12.5
Market Value Ratios

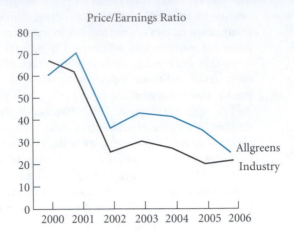

Price/Earnings Ratio

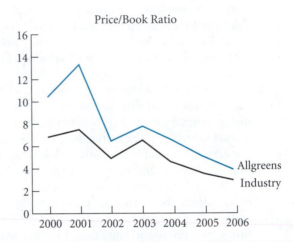

Price/Book Ratio

SUMMARY OF RATIO ANALYSIS FOR ALLGREENS

Let's review and summarize what we've learned about Allgreens by computing its ratios and comparing them to the industry averages. The liquidity ratios show consistency over time, but the favorable gap between Allgreens and its industry average ratios has narrowed or been

SMALL BUSINESS PRACTICE
Why Do Businesses Fail?

The Dun and Bradstreet Corporation reports that on average over 60,000 businesses fail each year. The U.S. Department of Labor estimates that business terminations generally exceed 800,000 per year. Thus, many firms cease to exist for reasons other than bankruptcy. Businesses are merged with other firms or sold to others, or they just shut down operations.

The U.S. Small Business Administration (SBA), in its annual report titled "The Facts About Small Business," finds that nearly one-fourth of all firms are dissolved less than two years after starting operation. Over one-half of new businesses cease operating within four years of operation. Approximately 70 percent of all new businesses don't exist after eight years of operation.

A study by the SBA of business failures found that nearly one-half of the failures were associated with economic factors such as inadequate sales or a lack of profits. Of the failures that don't cite economic factors, nearly 40 percent (or about 20 percent of total failures) are attributed to inadequate financial capital or too much debt. Other reasons include inadequate business or management experience, business or family conflicts, disasters, and even fraud. From these findings, it is apparent that having adequate business, management, and financial education are important factors in determining whether a business venture will be successful.

reversed. This is true of the asset management ratios, too; Allgreens' historical advantages have disappeared.

Should Allgreens need to raise money quickly, it should be able to issue debt, as Allgreens' debt ratios are lower than the industry averages (debt to assets, equity multiplier) and its interest coverage. A truer picture would include fixed charges such as lease payments in the analysis. Allgreens' fixed charge coverage ratio shows that the firm does have an income cushion before it would have trouble meeting its stated lease payments.

Part of Allgreens' successes can be traced to good control (higher than average operating profit margin and operating return on assets) and, until recently, superior asset management. The receivables collection period is shorter than average as well. The combination of good cost control and efficient asset management has resulted in good profitability compared to industry average trends (net profit margin, return on total assets, return on equity). The stock market has recognized Allgreens' abilities and Allgreens' market value ratios (price/earnings, market/book) are above those of the industry.

DU PONT METHOD OF RATIO ANALYSIS

How does a supermarket generate profits? In general, supermarkets have very low profit margins. Many of its goods are sold for pennies above cost. Profits are generated by rapid turnover. The shelves are restocked daily with new items to take the place of items that were purchased. Thus, supermarkets generally have high asset turnover ratios. Jewelry stores generate their profits differently. They typically have very high profit margins but low turnover. Jewelry items may sit on the shelf for months at a time until they are sold.

This indicates that there are two basic methods by which a firm can generate a return on its assets. It can offer low prices and low profit margins while seeking high sales volumes on commodity products, like a supermarket, or it can sell its quality or differentiated goods at high prices and rely mainly on high profit margins to generate returns on low sales, like a jewelry store.

The return on total assets ratio can be used to examine this relationship and to determine how a given firm generates profits. The return on assets can be broken into two components. It equals the product of the profit margin and total asset turnover ratio:

$$\text{Return on total assets} = \text{Profit margin} \times \text{Total asset turnover}$$

$$(\text{Net income/Assets}) = (\text{Net income/Sales}) \times (\text{Sales/Total assets})$$

A supermarket's profit margin may be 1 percent, but its total asset turnover may be 10. This would give it a return on total assets of 1 percent × 10 or 10 percent. A jewelry store may have a 25 percent profit margin and have a very low asset turnover of 0.40, also giving it a return on total assets of 10 percent (25 percent × 0.40). Year-to-year variations in a firm's return on total assets can be explained by changes in its profit margin, total asset turnover, or both.

Like the return on total assets, return on equity can be broken down into component parts to tell us why the level of return changes from year to year or why two firms' returns on equity differ. The return on equity is identical to return on total assets multiplied by the equity multiplier:

$$(\text{Net income/Equity}) = (\text{Net income/Total assets}) \times (\text{Total assets/Equity})$$

We just saw how the return on total assets is itself comprised of two other ratios, so return on equity can be expanded to:

$$\text{Return on equity} = \text{Profit margin} \times \text{Asset turnover} \times \text{Equity multiplier}$$

$$(\text{Net income/Equity}) = (\text{Net income/Sales}) \times (\text{Sales/Total assets}) \times (\text{Total assets/Equity})$$

Thus, a firm's return on equity may differ from one year to the next, or from a competitor's, as a result of differences in profit margin, asset turnover, or leverage. Unlike the other measures of profitability, return on equity directly reflects a firm's use of leverage, or debt. If a firm uses relatively more liabilities to finance assets, the equity multiplier will rise, and, holding other factors constant, the firm's return on equity will increase. This leveraging of a firm's return on equity does not imply greater operating efficiency, only a greater use of debt financing.

Du Pont analysis
technique of breaking down return on total assets and return on equity into their component parts

CONCEPT CHECK

What is Du Pont analysis?

Describe the reasons why a firm's ROE might increase from one year to the next.

This technique of breaking return on total assets and return on equity into their component parts is called **Du Pont analysis**, named after the company that popularized it. Figure 12.6 illustrates how Du Pont analysis can break return on equity and return on total assets into different components (profit margin, total asset turnover, and equity multiplier) and how these components can, in turn, be broken into their constituent parts for analysis. Thus an indication that a firm's return on equity has increased as a result of higher turnover can lead to study of the turnover ratio, using data from several years, to determine if the increase has resulted from higher sales volume, better management of assets, or some combination of the two.

Table 12.3 illustrates the use of Du Pont analysis to explain the changes in Allgreens' return on equity during 2003–2006. Between 2003 and 2004, the main reason for the decrease in Allgreens' return on equity was a decrease in the net profit margin and asset efficiency. Between 2004–2006, Allgreens' profit margin and asset efficiency ratios recovered, but return on equity fell as its use of leverage declined. Managers and analysts generally prefer to see increases in the return on equity arising from increased profitability or increased asset efficiency and decreases in ROE occurring because of reductions in leverage.

FIGURE 12.6
The Du Pont System of Financial Analysis

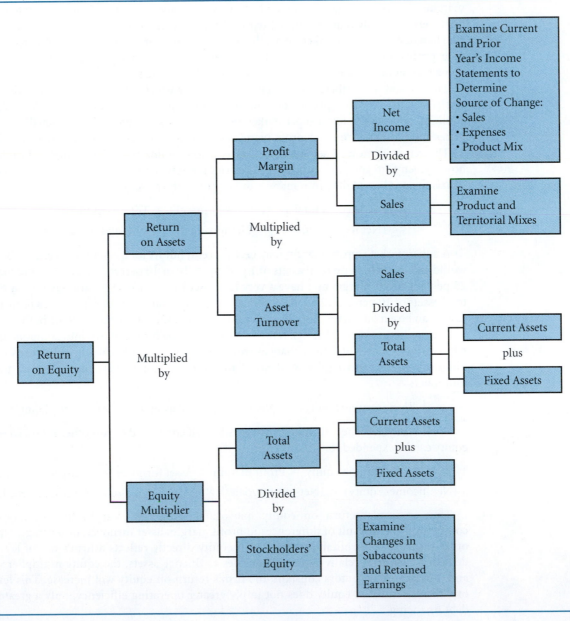

TABLE 12.3
Du Pont Analysis of Allgreens, Inc.

YEAR	NET INCOME / SALES	×	SALES / TOTAL ASSETS	×	TOTAL ASSETS / EQUITY	=	NET INCOME* / EQUITY
2003	3.66%		2.99		1.68		18.35
2004	3.60		2.79		1.70		17.01
2005	3.55		2.90		1.59		16.36
2006	3.62		2.85		1.59		16.34

*Return on equity is as reported in the text. The product of the three components may not equal this number exactly because of rounding.

LONG-TERM FINANCIAL PLANNING

Financial ratios and financial statement relationships can be used to analyze firms and their competitors, as we have just seen. But they have a second important practical use: managers can use them to assist in the firm's financial planning process.

To plan, it is necessary to look forward. We all have perfect hindsight, but foresight is what determines the success of a business. Long-range plans covering several years must be prepared to project growth in sales, assets, and employees. First, a sales forecast needs to be made that includes expected developments in the economy and reflects possible competitive pressures from other businesses. The sales forecast then must be supported by plans for an adequate investment in assets. For example, a manufacturing firm may need to invest in plant and equipment to produce an inventory that will fill forecasted sales orders. After determining the size of the necessary investment, plans must be made for estimating the amount of financing needed and how to acquire it. Adequate investment in human resources must be planned for as well.

In addition to long-range financial plans or budgets, the financial manager is concerned with near-term cash inflows and outflows associated with the business. Cash flows are often monitored on a daily basis for large firms while small firms may make only monthly cash budgets.

Financial analysis using ratios goes hand in hand with successful financial planning. An established firm should conduct a financial ratio analysis of past performance to aid in developing realistic future plans. The new firm should analyze the performance characteristics of other firms in the same industry before making plans.

In the remainder of this chapter, we focus on long-term financial planning techniques. The first, the percentage of sales technique, will illustrate how a sales forecast and knowledge of the firm's balance sheet and income statement can be used to estimate the firm's long-term asset and financing needs. The second, cost-volume-profit analysis, reviews a method a firm can use to determine the profitability of different sales levels and how many product units it needs to sell in order to turn a profit.

PERCENTAGE OF SALES TECHNIQUE

budgets
financial plans indicating expected revenues, spending, and investment needs

Financial planning begins with a sales forecast for one or more years. These sales forecasts are the basis for written financial plans referred to as **budgets**. For established firms, sales forecasts are usually based on historical sales data that are used in statistical analyses to project into the future. Adjustments may be made to reflect possible changes in sales growth due to expected economic conditions, new products, and so forth. For example, a firm's sales may have been growing at a 10 percent average annual rate in the past. However, if a recession is anticipated, management might forecast only a zero percent growth rate for the next year. In contrast, a booming economic climate might be associated with a 15 percent annual growth rate. New firms without sales histories have to rely on information from the experiences of other firms in their industry. Accurate sales forecasting is an essential element of successful financial management.

Asset Investment Requirements

After determining a sales forecast, plans must be made to acquire the assets necessary to support the new sales level. The relationship of assets and sales is shown in the total assets turnover ratio, which, as we learned, equals sales divided by total assets.

Recall from previously in this chapter that Allgreens had an assets turnover ratio of 2.85 based on 2006 sales of $32,505.4 and total assets of $11,405.9. By taking the inverse of this ratio, total assets divided by net sales, we can express assets as a percent of sales, which would be about 35 percent ($11,405.9/$32,505.4). This number can be used to help forecast future asset needs. For example, suppose we forecast sales to rise 15 percent. This means we estimate $4,876 increase in net sales ($32,505.4 × 15%). This, in turn, results in an anticipated increase in new asset investment of about $1,707 ($4,876 × 35%). Remember, the financial statements are in terms of millions of dollars, so $1,707 represents $1.707 billion.

Table 12.4 shows each major balance sheet item expressed as a percent of sales over the time period 2003–2006, as well as the average percentage during this time frame for Allgreens.[10] After forecasting sales, we can use the average percentages in Table 12.4 to determine changes in various balance sheet accounts. This is the percent-of-sales method for forecasting asset investment requirements. Actual asset investment required to support a specific sales increase may be altered if either of two developments occur: if the asset turnover ratio changes or if certain fixed assets do not have to be increased.

First, if Allgreens could slightly improve its asset turnover ratio from about 3.0 to 4.0, then assets would be only 25.0 (that is, 1/4.0) percent of sales. This would mean that a $4,876 increase in sales would require an asset investment of about $4,876 × 0.25 or $1,219, or roughly $488 ($1,707 − $1,219) less than the earlier calculation.

Second, fixed assets such as land or buildings might not have to be increased each year along with an increase in sales. The deciding factor usually is whether the firm currently has excess production capacity. For example, according to Table 12.4, if only current assets are expected to increase with sales next year, then the asset investment requirements would be about $878 ($4,876 × 18%).

Internally Generated Financing

Internally generated funds for financing new asset investments come from profits. Let's assume that for Allgreens the $1,707 asset investment scenario will be what is needed next year. We are now ready to plan how to finance these assets from anticipated profits or external sources. The average profit margin during 2003–2006 for Allgreens was 3.6 percent. If net sales are expected to rise by 15 percent next year to $37,381.21 and the profit margin is expected to hold, then profits would be projected at about $1,345.72 ($37,381.21 × 3.6 percent). Examining the dividend record in Allgreens' annual report, we learn that the firm pays about 20 percent of earnings to shareholders as dividends. After paying dividends, we expect Allgreens to have $1,076.58 (80 percent of $1,345.72) in internally generated funds to finance the expected $1,707 expansion in assets. The remaining $630.42 in additional assets will have to be financed with external funds. These can be either short-term debt, long-term debt, or equity funds. Let's consider how the financial manager might plan the mix of short-term and long-term funds from external sources.

External Financing Requirements

Allgreens can expect that a portion of its asset financing requirements will be met by almost automatic increases in certain current liability accounts such as accounts payable and accrued liabilities. To meet planned sales increases, more credit purchases of inventory items will be necessary to support the higher sales level. Increases also are expected in accrued wages and taxes. These almost-automatic increases in liability accounts reduce the need for other external financing. As they usually rise and fall along with sales, these current liability accounts provide a spontaneous or automatic source of financing.

Table 12.4 shows that accounts payable plus other current liabilities have averaged 11 percent of sales for Allgreens. Based on the expected increase in sales, accounts payable and other current liabilities would be expected to rise and provide about $536.36 ($4,876 × 11 percent) in spontaneous short-term funds. This leaves an external financing need for Allgreens of about $94.06 ($630.42 minus $536.36) to cover the asset investment requirements. Management might choose to borrow the amount from a commercial bank, issue long-term debt, or request more equity funds from the owners.

---

10. Note that this is not the same as the common-size balance sheet from Chapter 11. The common-size balance sheet divides each item by total assets; the percentage-of-sales balance sheet divides each item by sales.

TABLE 12.4
Percent-of-Sales Balance Sheets for Allgreens, 2003–2006

	2006	2005	2004	2003	AVERAGE
ASSETS					
Cash & Marketable Securities	3.1%	1.6%	0.1%	0.1%	1.2%
Accounts Receivable	3.1%	3.3%	3.2%	2.9%	3.1%
Inventories	12.9%	12.7%	14.1%	13.3%	13.3%
Other Current Assets	0.4%	0.4%	0.4%	0.4%	0.4%
Total Current Assets	19.6%	18.0%	17.8%	16.7%	18.0%
Net Fixed Assets	15.2%	16.0%	17.6%	16.2%	16.3%
Other Long-Term Assets	0.3%	0.4%	0.4%	0.6%	0.4%
Total Fixed Assets	15.5%	16.4%	18.0%	16.8%	16.7%
Total Assets	35.1%	34.4%	35.9%	33.5%	34.7%
LIABILITIES AND EQUITY					
Accounts Payable	6.4%	6.4%	6.3%	6.4%	6.4%
Notes Payable	0.0%	0.0%	1.8%	0.0%	0.4%
Other Current Liabilities	4.1%	3.9%	4.2%	4.4%	4.2%
Total Current Liabilities	10.5%	10.3%	12.2%	10.9%	11.0%
Long-Term Debt	0.0%	0.0%	0.0%	0.0%	0.0%
Other Liabilities	2.4%	2.4%	2.5%	2.7%	2.5%
Total Liabilities	13.0%	12.7%	14.7%	13.5%	13.5%
Common Equity	2.4%	2.9%	2.7%	2.1%	2.5%
Retained Earnings	19.7%	18.8%	18.4%	17.9%	18.7%
Total Stockholders' Equity	22.1%	21.7%	21.1%	20.0%	21.2%
Total Liabilities and Equity	35.1%	34.4%	35.9%	33.5%	34.7%

CONCEPT CHECK

How can ratios be used to help managers do financial planning?

Describe the percentage of sales technique for forecasting a firm's external financing needs.

To summarize briefly, the amount of new external funds needed to finance asset additions can be calculated as follows:

1. Forecast the dollar amount of the expected sales increase:
   Sales expected to grow 15%: new sales = 1.15 × $32,505.4 = $37,381.21
   Dollar amount of sales increase = 15% × $32,505.4 = $4,876 (or $37,381.21 − $32,505.40)
2. Determine the dollar amount of new asset investment necessary to support the sales increase.
   Additional assets = 35% × $4,876 = $1,707
3. Subtract the expected amount of retained profits from the planned asset investment.
   Expected profit = 3.6% × $37,381.21 = $1,345.72
   Expected addition to retained earnings = 0.80 × $1,345.72 = $1,076.58
4. Subtract the amount of spontaneous increases expected in accounts payable and accrued liabilities from the planned asset investment.
   Expected spontaneous financing = 11% × $4,876 = $536.36
5. The remaining dollar amount of asset investments determines the external financing needs (EFN).
   EFN
   = Change in assets − addition to retained earnings − spontaneous financing
   = $1,707.00 − $1,076.58 − $536.36
   = $94.06

COST-VOLUME-PROFIT ANALYSIS

cost-volume-profit analysis
used by managers for financial planning to estimate the firm's operating profits at different levels of unit sales

breakeven analysis
used to estimate how many units of product must be sold in order for the firm to break even or have a zero profit

Cost-volume-profit analysis represents another tool used by managers for financial planning purposes. It can be used to estimate the firm's operating profits at different levels of unit sales. A variation, called **breakeven analysis**, can be used to estimate how many units of product must be sold in order for the firm to "break even" or have a zero profit.

As an example of cost-volume-profit analysis, let's assume that a Allgreens store is considering adding a new product to its stores. It will be sold for $10 per item. The variable costs—in this case, the cost of purchasing the item from its manufacturer—will be $6. Fixed costs—mostly various administrative overhead expenses of tracking inventory and dealing with the supplier—are expected to be $1,000 annually. Management is interested in knowing what level of operating profit will occur if unit sales are 2,000 per year.

From the format of an income statement (for example, Table 12.2), we know that sales revenues minus various costs gives us operating profit or earnings before interest and taxes (EBIT). Sales can be expressed as unit price multiplied by quantity sold, or (P)(Q). The costs can be expressed by variable costs and fixed costs. The variable cost per unit (VC) times the quantity sold (Q) gives us total variable cost: (VC)(Q). Total fixed costs, FC, are constant; they are called "fixed" because they do not change with increases or decreases in output. Thus, we can find operating income as follows:

$$\text{EBIT} = \text{Sales} - \text{Variable costs} - \text{Fixed costs}$$

In terms of our symbols, this becomes:

$$\text{EBIT} = (P)(Q) - (VC)(Q) - FC \tag{12.1}$$

For our new product example, we have:

$$\begin{aligned}
\text{EBIT} &= \$10(2,000) - \$6(2,000) - \$1,000 \\
&= \$20,000 - \$12,000 - \$1,000 \\
&= \$20,000 - \$13,000 \\
&= \$7,000
\end{aligned}$$

If sales reach 2,000 units per year, the firm expects an increase in operating profit of $7,000.

Management also may want to know how many units will have to be sold in order to break even. That is, what volume needs to be reached so that the amount of total revenues equals total costs (variable costs plus fixed costs)? At this point, operating income or EBIT is zero. The breakeven point in units can be calculated by setting equation 12.1 equal to zero:

$$\text{EBIT} = (P)(Q) - (VC)(Q) - FC = 0$$

The quantity of unit sales that solves this equation is the breakeven quantity; we'll call this Q_{BE}. Solving this equation for the breakeven quantity, we have:

$$Q_{BE} = \frac{FC}{P - VC} \tag{12.2}$$

Using data from the new product example, we have:

$$Q_{BE} = \frac{\$1,000}{\$10 - \$6} = (\$1,000/\$4) = 250 \text{ units}$$

The firm must sell 250 units of the new product to break even. This can be confirmed by substituting the relevant information in equation 12.1 as follows:

$$\begin{aligned}
\text{EBIT} &= \$10(250) - \$6(250) - \$1,000 \\
&= \$2,500 - \$1,500 - \$1,000 \\
&= \$2,500 - \$2,500 \\
&= 0
\end{aligned}$$

contribution margin
contribution of each unit sold that goes toward paying fixed costs

The breakeven point in units, depicted graphically in Figure 12.7, occurs when total revenues equal total costs. The breakeven point in sales dollars is equal to the selling price per unit times the breakeven point in units. In our example, we have $10 times 250 units or $2,500.

The denominator of equation 12.2, (P − VC), is called the **contribution margin**. It represents the contribution of each unit sold toward paying the annual fixed costs. In our example, for every unit sold at a price of $10, $6 of the revenue covers the variable costs; the remainder, ($10 − $6) or $4, is the contribution toward paying the fixed costs. Since fixed costs are $1,000, the firm must sell $1,000/$4 units or 250 units before the fixed costs are covered.

CONCEPT CHECK

What is breakeven analysis?

What does the contribution margin measure?

DEGREE OF OPERATING LEVERAGE

A firm's sales revenues are rarely constant. The variability of sales or revenues over time indicates a basic operating business risk that must be considered when developing financial plans. In addition, changes in the amount of income shown on the income statement are affected by both

FIGURE 12.7

Cost-Volume-Profit Relationships

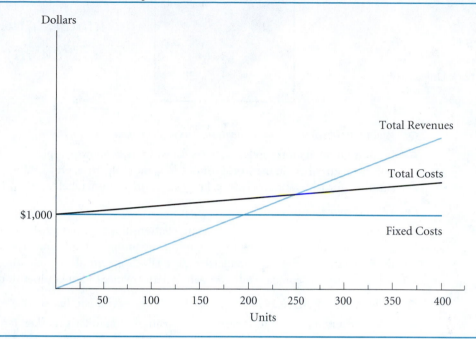

changes in sales and the use of fixed versus variable costs. As we'll see in this section, the greater the amount of fixed costs, the more variable will be operating profit.

The following portion of an income statement based on Allgreens' data illustrates this point. Based on historical averages, we estimate variable costs, mainly Allgreens' cost of goods sold, to be 72 percent of sales. Similarly, we assume Allgreens' selling, general, and administrative expenses are fixed as are depreciation expenses.

		CURRENT SITUATION ($ MILLIONS)
Net sales	$32,500.00	
Less variable costs	$23,400.00	(Cost of goods sold has averaged about 72% of sales)
Less fixed costs	$7,300.00	(Assume SG&A expenses and depreciation remain fixed)
Earnings before interest and taxes (Operating income)	$ 1,800.00	

Let's examine the impact of both a 10 percent decrease and a 10 percent increase in next year's sales on the firm's operating income or earnings before interest and taxes (EBIT). The revised partial income statement would appear as follows:

	PERCENT CHANGE IN SALES		
	−10%	BASE	10%
Net sales	$29,250	$32,500	$35,750
Less: variable costs (72% of sales)	$21,060	$23,400	$25,740
Less fixed costs	$7,300	$7,300	$7,300
Earnings before interest and taxes	$890	$1,800	$2,710
Percent change in operating income from the current level	−50.6%		50.6%

A 10 percent change in sales becomes magnified or leveraged into a 50.6 percent change in operating income. Operating income changes by such a large amount relative to the change in sales because some costs are fixed and do not change as revenues rise and fall.

SUSAN COLROSS
Director, Corporate Finance
Leap

BS, Finance
New York University

It is important for me to understand how investors view my company."

Q: *What type of wireless communications services does Leap provide?*

A: Leap's unlimited local wireless service, called Cricket, allows people to make all their local calls and receive calls from anywhere in the world for one low, monthly price. Our goal is to make wireless communications simple, affordable, and worry free. Leap was spun off from Qualcomm in 1998.

Q: *What is your role at Leap?*

A: My primary role with Leap is managing relationships with our existing lenders, as well as negotiating new agreements. In that role, it is important for me to understand how investors view my company and make their investment choices. Financial ratio analysis is critical in evaluating our business performance and helping investors compare our company's performance to our competition.

Q: *What ratios are especially important in the telecommunications industry?*

A: Leverage and liquidity ratios carry great significance in today's market, largely because of the recent decline in the telecommunications sector. Many of the failed telecom companies had trouble repaying debt or were unable to raise the capital needed to survive a downturn in market conditions.

Some of our loan agreements test ratios on a regular basis to assure our lenders that the business is operating as they expected, to indicate how much of the company's total funding comes from debt, and to demonstrate whether we will have cash available for debt service payments. We must send our lenders a report showing compliance with these ratios each quarter.

Q: *How does Leap approach financial planning?*

A: Our major financial models integrate capital budgeting and operational planning. To project revenues, we look at market size, anticipated market share, the revenue our expected customers will generate, and how long we expect them to remain customers. We then identify our costs: building and running a wireless network in a specific location and customer acquisition. Projecting revenues and expenses involves many variables, and the finance group must work closely with the network planners. Once revenues and expenses are understood, we can take both a short-term and long-term view of capital we need to raise to sustain or grow our business.

Q: *What do you like best about your job?*

A: I really enjoy the fact that when I come into the office, I'm never quite sure what transaction or market condition I will face. I have enough balance between the routine and surprises to keep me challenged and interested throughout the day. The two skills I find most helpful to me on a day-to-day basis—in addition, of course, to such givens as financial analysis and computer skills—may surprise you. One is to always read footnotes and column headings! Footnotes point out very important facts and, together with column headings, may change the information you derive from numbers or keep you from using them in the wrong manner. The other is communication. It's not just an ability to be heard, but more often it's an ability to really understand what others are saying to you. Being able to understand a situation, not just some of the facts, gives one a greater ability to be a problem solver and a leader in the career of your choice.

The **degree of operating leverage (DOL)** measures the sensitivity of operating income to changes in the level of output:

$$DOL = \frac{\% \text{ change in EBIT}}{\% \text{ change in sales}}$$

For Allgreens, the degree of operating leverage is:

$$DOL = \frac{\% \text{ change in EBIT}}{\% \text{ change in sales}} = \frac{50.6\%}{10\%} = 5.06$$

That is, if net sales increase by 10 percent next year, from $32,500 to $35,750, operating income is expected to rise from $1,800 to $2,710, a $910 or 50.6 percent increase ($910/$1,800.00 = 50.6 percent). Thus, a 50.6 percent change in operating income divided by a 10 percent change in net sales produces a 5.06 magnification or leverage effect. DOL also works in reverse and provides negative leverage when net sales decline. A 10 percent decline in sales volume becomes a 50.6 percent decline in operating income.

DOL can be represented by the following formula as well:

$$DOL = \frac{Q(P - VC)}{Q(P - VC) - FC} = \frac{\text{Sales} - \text{total variable costs}}{\text{Sales} - \text{total variable costs} - \text{fixed costs}}$$

This relationship allows us to determine the degree of operating leverage with only one observation of sales, variable costs, and fixed costs. In the preceding example, the sales were $32,500, variable costs were $23,400, and fixed costs were $7,300. That means DOL equals:

$$DOL = \frac{\$32,500 - \$23,400}{\$32,500 - \$23,400 - \$7,300} = \frac{\$9,100}{\$1,800} = 5.06$$

which is the same result as when we used percentage changes in operating income and sales to estimate DOL. A DOL of 5.06 means that a 10 percent change in sales is expected to result in a (5.06)(10 percent) = 50.6 percent change in EBIT.

If we know a firm's degree of operating leverage, we can estimate the effect of a change in sales on operating income. If the degree of operating leverage is 5.06, a forecasted increase in sales of 5 percent is expected to increase operating income by (5 percent)(5.06) = 25.30 percent.

The operating leverage effect is solely due to the level of fixed costs. Suppose that Allgreens' fixed costs were higher, for example $8,000 instead of $7,300. With sales of $32,500, variable costs of $23,400, and fixed costs of $8,000, EBIT will be $1,100:

	CURRENT SITUATION
Net sales	$32,500
Less variable costs	$23,400
Less fixed costs	$8,000
Earnings before interest and taxes (Operating income)	$ 1,100

The effect of this higher level of fixed costs and operating leverage on EBIT is:

	PERCENT CHANGE IN SALES		
	−10%	BASE	10%
Net sales	$29,250	$32,500	$35,750
Less: variable costs (72% of sales)	$21,060	$23,400	$25,740
Less fixed costs	$8,000	$8,000	$8,000
Earnings before interest and taxes	$190	$1,100	$2,010
Percent change in operating income from the current level	−82.7%		82.7%

CONCEPT CHECK

What does the degree of operating leverage measure?

What is the source of a firm's operating leverage?

A 10 percent change in sales becomes magnified or leveraged into an 82.7 percent change in operating income! With the increase to $8,000 in fixed costs, the degree of operating leverage is now 82.7 percent/10 percent or 8.27.

The magnification or leverage effect is solely due to the level of fixed costs. A higher level of fixed costs results in a higher level of operating leverage. This makes operating income more sensitive to changes in sales volume. Sophisticated financial planning models take into consideration the impact of operating leverage when projecting the next year's income.

APPLYING FINANCE TO . . .

INSTITUTIONS AND MARKETS

If a firm has strong financials, it is easier for it to sell securities through an investment bank or to obtain loans from banks, insurance companies, and other lenders. Financial statement analysis is an important part of the capital allocation process to determine the likelihood of repayment of borrowed funds.

Several different types of ratios discussed in this chapter may appear in bond or loan covenants (particularly those dealing with liquidity and debt).

INVESTMENTS

The economy, characteristics of the firm's industry, and competitive influences on the firm are reflected in financial statements and how analysts examine them. A firm's strategy and its success or failure, as well as the firm's strengths and weaknesses, will become evident, too, in financial statement analysis. This information will help you determine if you should invest, not invest, or sell your investment in a firm's securities. Shareholders (owners) and bondholders (lenders) each have different concerns and focuses when examining financial ratios.

FINANCIAL MANAGEMENT

Financial statements show managers how the firm is progressing toward its goals. Some managers may try to "manage earnings" to reduce earnings variability and to hit earnings targets to satisfy investor expectations. Managers know investors and other market participants will closely examine and analyze the firm's financials.

Managers' decisions about new strategies and initiatives should be reflected in improving financial ratios compared to the firm's competitors. Microdata, not available to the public, on specific product and market performance will assist managerial decision making.

SUMMARY

Financial statements, introduced in Chapter 11, are useful only if managers and financial analysts know how to use them. The focus of this chapter has been on the practical application of financial statements for analysis and financial forecasting. The information in financial statements can be examined by using various financial ratios. The ratios control for size differences between firms or for firm growth over time. By examining one firm's ratios over time or in conjunction with an industry average, managers and analysts can pinpoint areas of strength and weakness in both their firm and in their competitors.

Liquidity ratios are useful in determining the ability of a firm to pay its short-term obligations. Asset management ratios measure how efficiently the firm's assets are used. Financial leverage ratios provide information on the firm's use of debt to finance its assets. Profitability ratios measure the ability of a firm to earn a return on its sales, assets, and equity. Analysts and managers also use market-based ratios to see how the financial marketplace evaluates the firm and its peers.

Changes in a ratio over time are caused by relative changes in the ratio's numerator and denominator and their components. Financial analysis does not stop with the calculation of a ratio. Changes in ratios over time or differences in ratios between firms should be explained. Du Pont analysis is one such tool for examining return on equity. Changes in the return on equity occur because of changes in the profit margin, total asset turnover, financial leverage, or some combination of these.

Financial planning uses the financial statement relationships to estimate future asset and financing needs. The percentage-of-sales method uses the relationship between balance sheet accounts and sales to estimate future asset needs. Combining a sales forecast, profit margin, and dividend policy, managers can estimate the increase in retained earnings that will provide internally generated financing. The difference between the forecasted increase in assets and the internally generated financing (such as additions to retained earnings and spontaneous current liability growth) equals the external financing the firm needs to plan to raise. Other tools, such as cost-volume-profit analysis, breakeven analysis, and operating leverage, can also be used to forecast future profits and to analyze the financial structure of a firm.

KEY TERMS

asset management ratios	degree of operating leverage	net working capital
breakeven analysis	Du Pont analysis	profitability ratios
budgets	financial leverage ratios	ratio analysis
contribution margin	industry comparative analysis	sinking fund payments
cost-volume-profit analysis	liquidity ratios	trend or time series analysis
cross-sectional analysis	market value ratios	

DISCUSSION QUESTIONS

1. List some reasons why financial statement analysis is conducted. Identify some of the participants that analyze firms' financial statements.

2. What is ratio analysis? Also briefly describe the three basic categories or ways that ratio analysis is used.

3. Identify the types of ratios that are used to analyze a firm's financial performance based on its income statements and balance sheets.

4. Which type or category of ratios relates stock market information to financial statement items?

5. What do liquidity ratios indicate? Identify some basic liquidity ratios.

6. What do asset management ratios indicate? Identify some basic asset management ratios.

7. What do financial leverage ratios indicate? Identify some measures of financial leverage.

8. What do profitability ratios indicate? Identify some measures of profitability.

9. What do market value ratios indicate? Identify some market value ratios.

10. Describe the Du Pont method or system of ratio analysis. What are the two major components of the system?

11. How is the Du Pont system related to both the balance sheet and the income statement?

12. How is the process of financial planning used to estimate asset investment requirements?

13. Explain how internally generated funds are used to reduce the need for external financing to fund asset investments.

14. Explain how financial planning is used to determine a firm's external financing requirements.

15. What is cost-volume-profit analysis? How can it be used by a firm?

16. What is the purpose of knowing the breakeven point?

17. What will happen to the breakeven point if the contribution margin rises (falls)?

18. What does a firm's degree of operating leverage (DOL) indicate?

19. Describe what would happen to the DOL if all costs are fixed? Variable?

PROBLEMS

1. The Robinson Company has the following current assets and current liabilities for these two years:

	2005	2006
Cash and marketable securities	$50,000	$50,000
Accounts receivable	300,000	350,000
Inventories	350,000	500,000
Total current assets	$700,000	$900,000
Accounts payable	$200,000	$250,000
Bank loan	0	150,000
Accruals	150,000	200,000
Total current liabilities	$350,000	$600,000

   a. Compare the current ratios between the two years.

   b. Compare the acid-test ratios between 2005 and 2006. Comment on your findings.

2. The Robinson Company had a cost of goods sold of $1,000,000 in 2005 and $1,200,000 in 2006.

   a. Calculate the inventory turnover for each year. Comment on your findings.

   b. What would have been the amount of inventories in 2006 if the 2005 turnover ratio had been maintained?

3. The Dayco Manufacturing Company had the following financial statement results for last year. Net sales were $1.2 million with net income of $90,000. Total assets at year-end amounted to $900,000.

   a. Calculate Dayco's total asset turnover ratio and its profit margin.

   b. Show how the two ratios in (a) can be used to determine Dayco's rate of return on assets.

   c. Dayco operates in the same industry as Allgreens, whose industry ratios are these: Return on assets: 11%; Total asset turnover: 2.5 times; Net profit margin: 3.6%. Compare Dayco's performance against the industry averages.

4. Next year Allgreens expects its sales to reach $35,000 with an investment in total assets of $12,750. Net income of $1,725 is anticipated.

   a. Use the Du Pont system to compare Allgreens' anticipated performance against its 2005 and 2006 results. Comment on your findings.

   b. How would Allgreens compare with the industry if the industry ratios (see Problem 3) remain the same?

5. Following are selected financial data in thousands of dollars for the Hunter Corporation.

	2006	2005
Current assets	$500	$400
Fixed assets, net	700	600
Total assets	1,200	1,000
Current liabilities	300	200
Long-term debt	200	200
Common equity	700	600
Total liabilities and equity	$1,200	$1,000
Net sales	$1,500	$1,200
Total expenses	−1,390	−1,100
Net income	110	100

   a. Calculate Hunter's rate of return on total assets in 2006 and in 2005. Did the ratio improve or worsen?

   b. Diagram the expanded Du Pont system for Hunter for 2006. Insert the appropriate dollar amounts wherever possible.

   c. Use the Du Pont system to calculate the return on assets for the two years, and determine why they changed.

6. Following are financial statements for the Genatron Manufacturing Corporation for 2006 and 2005.

   a. Apply Du Pont analysis to both the 2006 and 2005 financial statements' data.

   b. Explain how financial performance differed between 2006 and 2005.

GENATRON MANUFACTURING CORPORATION

BALANCE SHEET	2006	2005
ASSETS		
Cash	$40,000	$50,000
Accounts receivable	260,000	200,000
Inventory	500,000	450,000
Total current assets	800,000	700,000
Fixed assets, net	400,000	300,000
Total assets	$1,200,000	$1,000,000
LIABILITIES AND EQUITY		
Accounts Payable	$170,000	$130,000
Bank loan	90,000	90,000
Accruals	70,000	50,000
Total current liabilities	330,000	270,000
Long-term debt, 12%	400,000	300,000
Common stock, $10 par	300,000	300,000
Capital surplus	50,000	50,000
Retained earnings	120,000	80,000
Total liabilities & equity	$1,200,000	$1,000,000

INCOME STATEMENT	2006	2005
Net sales	$1,500,000	$1,300,000
Cost of goods sold	900,000	780,000
Gross profit	600,000	520,000
Expenses: general		
& administrative	150,000	150,000
Marketing	150,000	130,000
Depreciation	53,000	40,000
Interest	57,000	45,000
Earnings before taxes	190,000	155,000
Income taxes	76,000	62,000
Net income	$114,000	$93,000

7. This problem uses the financial statements for the Genatron Manufacturing Corporation for the years 2006 and 2005 from Problem 6.

   a. Calculate Genatron's dollar amount of net working capital in each year.

   b. Calculate the current ratio and the acid-test ratio in each year.

   c. Calculate the average collection period and the inventory turnover ratio in each year.

   d. What changes in the management of Genatron's current assets seem to have occurred between the two years?

8. Genatron Manufacturing expects its sales to increase by 10 percent in 2007. Estimate the firm's external financing needs by using the percent-of-sales method for the 2006 data. Assume that no excess capacity exists and that one-half of the 2006 net income will be retained in the business.

9. Rework Problem 8 assuming that Genatron Manufacturing expects its sales to increase by 20 percent in 2007. What is the amount of external financing needed?

10. Genatron wants to estimate what will happen to its income before interest and taxes if its net sales change from the 2006 level of $1,500,000. Refer to Genatron's 2006 income statement, shown in Problem 6, where the income before interest and taxes is $247,000. Assume that the cost of goods sold are variable expenses and that the other operating expenses are fixed.

a. Calculate the expected amount of income before interest and taxes for both a 10 percent decrease and a 10 percent increase in net sales for next year.

b. Determine the percentage change in income before interest and taxes given your calculations in (a), and determine the degree of operating leverage.

11. **Challenge Problem** Using the information in Tables 12.1 and 12.2, compute the financial ratios we discussed in this chapter for Allgreens using the 2004 and 2003 data.

12. **Challenge Problem** Below are financial statements for Global Manufacturing. After computing the ratios we discussed in this chapter, discuss strong and weak points of Global's performance.

DECEMBER 31	2006	2005	2004
ASSETS			
Cash and marketable securities	$25,000	$20,000	$16,000
Accounts receivable	100,000	80,000	56,000
Inventories	125,000	100,000	80,000
Total current assets	250,000	200,000	152,000
Gross plant and equipment	300,000	225,000	200,000
Less: accumulated depreciation	−100,000	−75,000	−50,000
Net plant and equipment	200,000	150,000	150,000
Land	50,000	50,000	50,000
Total fixed assets	250,000	200,000	200,000
Total assets	$500,000	$400,000	$352,000
LIABILITIES AND EQUITY			
Accounts payable	$78,000	$65,000	$58,000
Notes payable	34,000	10,000	10,000
Accrued liabilities	30,000	25,000	25,000
Total current liabilities	142,000	100,000	93,000
Long-term debt	140,000	100,000	71,000
Total liabilities	$282,000	$200,000	$164,000
Common stock			
($1 par, 50,000 shares)	$50,000	$50,000	$50,000
Paid-in capital	100,000	100,000	100,000
Retained earnings	68,000	50,000	38,000
Total stockholders' equity	218,000	200,000	188,000
Total liabilities and equity	$500,000	$400,000	$352,000

YEARS ENDED DECEMBER 31	2006	2005	2004
Net revenues or sales	$700,000	$600,000	$540,000
Cost of goods sold	450,000	375,000	338,000
Gross profit	250,000	225,000	202,000
Operating expenses:			
General and administrative	95,000	95,000	95,000
Selling and marketing	56,000	50,000	45,000
Depreciation	25,000	20,000	15,000
Operating income	74,000	60,000	47,000
Interest	14,000	10,000	7,000
Income before taxes	60,000	50,000	40,000
Income taxes (40%)	24,000	20,000	16,000
Net income	$36,000	$30,000	$24,000
Number of shares outstanding	50,000	50,000	50,000
Earnings per share	$0.72	$0.60	$0.48

13. Following are the consolidated financial statements for Global Manufacturing's industry. Use Du Pont analysis on the industry financial statements to determine why industry return on equity changed from year to year.

Balance Sheets for INDUSTRY

DECEMBER 31	2006	2005	2004
ASSETS			
Cash and marketable securities	$30,000	$25,000	$20,000
Accounts receivable	110,000	90,000	60,000
Inventories	100,000	80,000	80,000
Total current assets	240,000	195,000	160,000
Gross plant and equipment	250,000	220,000	200,000
Less: accumulated depreciation	−100,000	−65,000	−50,000
Net plant and equipment	150,000	155,000	150,000
Land	50,000	50,000	50,000
Total fixed assets	200,000	205,000	200,000
Total assets	$440,000	$400,000	$360,000
LIABILITIES AND EQUITY			
Accounts payable	$58,000	$50,000	$45,000
Notes payable	50,000	50,000	50,000
Accrued liabilities	0	0	0
Total current liabilities	108,000	100,000	95,000
Long-term debt	32,000	20,000	15,000
Total liabilities	$140,000	$120,000	$110,000
Total stockholders' equity	300,000	280,000	250,000
Total liabilities and equity	$440,000	$400,000	$360,000

INCOME STATEMENTS FOR INDUSTRY: YEARS ENDED

DECEMBER 31	2006	2005	2004
Net revenues or sales	$1,100,000	$1,000,000	$900,000
Cost of goods sold	700,000	650,000	600,000
Gross profit	$400,000	$350,000	$300,000
Operating expenses:			
General and administrative	143,000	135,000	130,000
Selling and marketing	88,000	80,000	70,000
Depreciation	44,000	40,000	36,000
Operating income	125,000	95,000	64,000
Interest	15,000	15,000	14,000
Income before taxes	110,000	80,000	50,000
Income taxes (40%)	44,000	32,000	20,000
Net income	$66,000	$48,000	$30,000

14. Compare the reasons for the changes in return on equity for Global Manufacturing and its industry.

15. Challenge Problem Compute the financial ratios for Global Manufacturing's industry. Using Global's ratios from Problem 12, graph the firm's and industry ratios as we've done in this chapter. Analyze Global's performance in comparison to its industry.

16. Challenge Problem Evaluate the performance of Johnson & Johnson in comparison to its industry.

	JOHNSON & JOHNSON		INDUSTRY	
RATIO	YEAR 1	YEAR 2	YEAR 1	YEAR 2
Current Ratio	1.62	1.57	1.54	1.68
Quick Ratio	0.80	0.78	1.01	1.01
Total Asset Turnover	1.15	1.00	0.86	0.90
Fixed Asset Turnover	2.01	1.75	2.59	3.27
Average Collection Period	53.65	60.33	67.13	75.62
Inventory Turnover	2.79	2.45	2.16	2.05

Total Debt to Total Assets	0.55	0.55	0.53	0.51
Equity Multiplier	2.20	2.20	2.13	2.02
Interest Coverage	19.51	14.86	16.90	14.40
Net Profit Margin	12.6%	12.7%	14.2%	14.2%
Return on Assets	14.6%	12.8%	12.2%	11.7%
Return on Equity	32.1%	28.2%	26.1%	25.8%
Price/Earnings	16.38	17.55	21.45	22.03
Price/Book	5.18	4.94	3.93	3.78

17. Associated Containers Company is planning to manufacture and sell plastic pencil holders. Direct labor and raw materials will be $2.28 per unit. Fixed costs are $15,300 and the expected selling price is $3.49 per unit. Use spreadsheet calculations to answer the following questions:

a. Determine the breakeven point (where operating profit is zero) in units and dollars.

b. How much profit or loss before interest and taxes will there be if 10,825 units are sold?

c. What will the selling price per unit have to be if 13,650 units are sold in order to break even?

d. How much will variable costs per unit have to be to break even if only 9,500 units are expected to be sold and the selling price is $3.49?

18. Challenge Problem Graph the revenue and cost lines to estimate the breakeven point for the following data. Compute the breakeven point mathematically.

a. price = $12.95; variable cost/unit = $6.89; fixed costs = $10,000

b. price = $23,995; variable cost/unit = $16,545; fixed costs = $40 million

c. price = $249; variable cost/unit = $50; fixed costs = $800,000

19. This problem uses the two years of financial statements data provided in Problem 6 for the Genatron Manufacturing Corporation.

a. Calculate and compare each current assets account as a percentage of total assets for that year.

b. Calculate and compare each current liabilities account as a percentage of total liabilities and equities for that year.

c. Calculate the current ratio and the acid-test ratio for each year. Describe the changes in liquidity, if any, that occurred between the two years.

20. The Jackman Company had sales of $1,000,000 and net income of $50,000 last year. Sales are expected to increase by 20 percent next year. Selected year-end balance sheet items were:

Current assets	$400,000
Fixed assets	500,000
Total assets	$900,000
Current liabilities	$200,000
Long-term debt	200,000
Owners' equity	500,000
Total liabilities and equity	$900,000

a. Express each balance sheet item as a percent of this year's sales.

b. Estimate the new asset investment requirement for next year, assuming no excess production capacity.

c. Estimate the amount of internally generated funds for next year, assuming all profits will be retained in the firm.

d. If all current liabilities are expected to change spontaneously with sales, what will be their dollar increase next year?

e. Estimate Jackman's external financing requirements for next year.

21. Using the data in the chapter, estimate Allgreens' external financing needs if a 20 percent growth rate is expected.

22. Using Global Manufacturing's financial statements in Problem 12, estimate their external financing needs if 10 percent growth in sales is expected and the firm pays out half of its earnings as dividends.

23. Using the financial statements presented in Problem 12, determine Global Manufacturing's degree of operating leverage in each of the years presented. Assume the cost of goods sold are variable costs and all other costs are fixed.

24. Using your estimate for the degree of operating leverage for Global in 2006 from Problem 23, estimate the level of operating income if the following year's sales (a) rise by 5 percent; (b) fall by 12 percent.

25. Using the financial statements presented in Problem 6, determine Genatron's degree of operating leverage in each of the years presented. Assume the cost of goods sold and marketing expenses are variable costs and all other costs are fixed.

26. Using your estimate for the degree of operating leverage for Genatron in 2006 from Problem 25, estimate the level of operating income if the following year's sales (a) rise by 5 percent; (b) fall by 12 percent.

• CHAPTER 13 •

Evaluating Business Investments

Chapter Learning Objectives

AFTER STUDYING THIS CHAPTER, YOU SHOULD BE ABLE TO:

- Explain how the capital budgeting process should be related to a firm's mission and strategies.
- Identify and describe the five steps in the capital budgeting process.
- Identify and describe the methods or techniques used to make proper capital budgeting decisions.
- Discuss how a project's risk can be incorporated into capital budgeting analysis.

Where We Have Been. . .

In Chapter 11, at the beginning of the financial management section of this book, we considered how firms will have a mission or vision statement—a reason for being. This current chapter will examine how firms can "put feet to their words" and make decisions to purchase fixed assets and pursue strategies to help them fulfill their mission.

Where We Are Going. . .

As a part of capital budgeting, a firm analyzes the expected cash flows from projects under consideration. The process of estimated a project's cash flows is the subject of Chapter 14, "Estimating Project Cash Flows."

How This Chapter Applies to Me. . .

Capital budgeting analysis is a framework for evaluating all business decisions; it is not only a tool for the "financial" types. It causes managers to consider more than a "feel good" or "sounds right" criterion for investing in projects. Whether the investment is one in a business strategy, building a new warehouse, upgrading information technology systems, or investing in human resources, we should try to quantify the benefits and costs of these choices in order to evaluate them properly.

To achieve success over time, a firm's managers must identify and invest in projects that provide positive net present values to maximize shareholder wealth. Good ideas become good strategies when the numbers—cash flow forecasts—show the likelihood of shareholder wealth increasing because of the project. The value of the firm will rise when a capital investment provides the firm with positive cash flows after the amount of the investment has been recovered, the cost of obtaining the necessary financing has been paid, and the timing of the project's cash flows has been taken into consideration.

As first discussed in Chapter 11, every firm should have a vision or mission—a reason for being. To successfully implement its mission, a firm needs to have a competitive advantage. A competitive advantage is the reason why a firm's customers are willing to purchase its products or services rather than another firm's. Large corporations spend millions on researching their customers and competitors to gather information they can use to maintain or expand their competitive advantage. Integral to the process of trying to maintain or expand a firm's competitive advantage are its decisions of what products to offer and what markets or market segments to serve.

CONCEPT CHECK

What is capital budgeting?

Why is it important to a firm?

mutually exclusive projects
selecting one project precludes others from being undertaken

independent projects
projects not in direct competition with one another

CONCEPT CHECK

What kinds of asset decisions can be made with capital budgeting analysis?

A firm is considering two capital budgeting projects. How will the decision to do or not do each project be affected by whether the projects are independent or mutually exclusive?

net present value
present value of a project's cash flows minus its cost

Capital budgeting is the process of identifying, evaluating, and implementing a firm's investment opportunities. Capital budgeting seeks to identify projects that will enhance a firm's competitive advantage and thereby to increase shareholders' wealth. By its nature, capital budgeting involves long-term projects, although capital budgeting techniques also can be applied to working capital decisions.[1] Capital budgeting projects usually require large initial investments and may involve acquiring or constructing plant and equipment. A project's expected time frame may be as short as a year or as long as twenty or thirty years. Projects may include implementing new production technologies, new products, new markets, or mergers. Given their size and duration, the projects undertaken by the firm should reflect its overall strategy for meeting future goals. Given the length of most projects, time value of money concepts should be used to evaluate them.

The typical capital budgeting project involves a large upfront cash outlay, followed by a series of smaller cash inflows and outflows, but the project's cash flows, including the total upfront cost of the project, are not known with certainty before the project starts. The firm must evaluate the size, timing, and risk of the project's cash flows to determine if they enhance shareholder wealth.

The profitability of a firm is affected to the greatest extent by the success of its management in making capital budget investment decisions. A fixed-asset decision will be sound only if it produces a stream of future cash inflows that earns the firm an acceptable rate of return on its invested capital.

MANAGEMENT OF FIXED ASSETS

Fixed-asset management requires financial managers to compare capital expenditures for plant and equipment against the cash flow benefits that will be received from these investments over several years. When properly adjusted benefits exceed expenditures, these projects will help increase the firm's value.

Investment in assets provides the basis for a firm's earning power or profitability. Plant, equipment, training, and infrastructure are employed to manufacture inventories or provide services that will be sold for profit, produce cash inflows, and enhance the firm's value. Proper capital budgeting decisions must be made by the financial manager for this to occur. Some types of decisions include whether to replace existing equipment with new equipment; whether to expand existing product lines by adding more plant and equipment similar to what is in use; or whether to expand into new product areas requiring new types of assets.

Capital budgeting decisions can involve mutually exclusive or independent projects. As an example of *mutually exclusive projects*, two or more machines that perform the same function may be available from competing suppliers, possibly at different costs and with different expected cash benefits. The financial manager is responsible for choosing the best of these alternatives since only one can be chosen. Selecting one project precludes the other from being undertaken. *Independent projects* are not in direct competition with one another. They are to be evaluated based on their expected effect on shareholder wealth. All such projects that enhance shareholder wealth should be included in the firm's capital budget.

In this chapter we focus on only a small part of what is a very complex topic. We present an overview of the capital budgeting process and some techniques that are used to evaluate potential investments. Then we briefly discuss the process of estimating the cash flows that are expected to occur from a capital budgeting project. We then cover how a project's risk can affect the evaluation process.

IDENTIFYING POTENTIAL CAPITAL BUDGET PROJECTS

From Chapters 7 and 8, we know that the market value of an investment is the present value of future cash flows to be received from the investment. The net benefit, or the *net present value*, of an investment is the present value of a project's cash flows minus its cost:

$$\text{Net present value} = \text{Present value of cash flows} - \text{Cost of the project} \qquad (13.1)$$

1. See Terry S. Maness and John T. Zietlow, *Short-Term Financial Management* (Mason, OH: South-Western, 2003); Ned C. Hill and William Sartoris, *Short-Term Financial Management,* 3rd ed. (Englewood Cliffs, NJ: Prentice Hall, 1995).

Should the net present value be positive (the investor pays less than the market value of the investment), the owner's wealth increases by the amount of the net present value. If, for example, the present value of an asset's cash flows is $100 and we can purchase it now for only $80, our wealth rises by $20. If instead we were foolish enough to pay $130 for the investment, our wealth will fall by $30. To maximize shareholder wealth, we need to find assets or capital budgeting projects that have positive net present values.

For businesses to find attractive capital budgeting projects, business managers must search for projects that are related to the firm's present lines of business or future plans. It would be foolish, for example, for a computer manufacturer to consider investing in land and mining equipment to prospect for gold. Despite management beliefs about future trends in gold prices and despite confidence in the ability to find gold, such a project is far afield from the firm's current markets, products, and expertise.

MOGS
Mission, Objectives, Goals, and Strategies

Businesses should seek guidance to focus their search for capital budgeting projects. One popular corporate planning tool, **MOGS** (for Mission, Objectives, Goals, and Strategies), develops project plans that fit well with firm plans. A firm should have in place a MOGS plan, or something similar to it, to give direction to company planning and to help the firm's officers identify potential capital budgeting projects.

Over time managers define and redefine the firm's mission, objectives, goals, and strategies. This long-term plan provides a foundation for the next five to ten years of operating plans for the firm. The long-term plan is operationalized, or implemented, in the annual capital budget. To develop the capital budget, managers must find investment opportunities that fit within the overall strategic objectives of the firm; its position within the various markets it serves; government fiscal, monetary, and tax policies; and the leadership of the firm's management. Attractive capital budgeting projects take the firm from its present position to a desired future market position and, as a consequence, maintain or increase its shareholders' wealth.[2]

SWOT analysis
review of a firm's internal strengths and weaknesses and its external opportunities and threats

SWOT analysis examines a firm's *strengths, weaknesses, opportunities,* and *threats.* It can help managers identify capital budgeting projects that allow the firm to exploit its competitive advantages or prevent others from exploiting its weaknesses. Strengths and weaknesses come from the firm's internal abilities, or lack thereof. Opportunities and threats represent external conditions that affect the firm, such as competitive forces, new technologies, government regulations, and domestic and international economic trends.

Strengths give the firm a comparative advantage in the marketplace. Perceived strengths can include good customer service, high-quality products, strong brand image and customer loyalty, innovative R&D efforts, market leadership, or strong financial resources. Managers must continue to develop, maintain, and defend these strengths through prudent capital investment policies; otherwise they will diminish and shareholder wealth will fall as new and existing competitors take advantage of the weakening firm.

Once identified, strengths can also be used to correct or mitigate a firm's weaknesses. Weaknesses give competitors opportunities to gain advantages over the firm. Once weaknesses are identified, the firm can select capital investments to mitigate or correct them. For example, a domestic producer in a global market can undertake investments that will allow it to export or produce its product overseas. Such a move may also make it easier for the firm to raise money in the future, as it may be able to raise funds in several different financial markets instead of just in its home country.

How can one find positive NPV projects? From economics we learn that economic profits in a competitive market are zero (recall that zero economic profits implies that the firm is earning a fair accounting return on its invested capital). In a competitive marketplace, we should be suspicious of any capital budgeting project that appears to have a positive net present value. Any positive economic profit or positive net present value must arise from one or two sources. One source is a market imperfection or inefficiency (such as an entry barrier or monopoly situation) that prevents competition from driving the net present value to zero. The second source involves cost-saving projects that allow the firm to reduce costs below their current level. Following are some possible projects.

---

2. For a seminal piece on the role of value maximization in a firm versus stakeholder theory or the *balanced scorecard*, see Michael C. Jensen, "Value Maximization, Stakeholder Theory, and the Corporate Objective Function," *Journal of Applied Corporate Finance* (Fall 2001), vol. 14, no. 5, pp. 8–21.

Economies of scale and high capital requirements typically go together. High sales volumes are sometimes needed to cover large fixed costs of plant and equipment. Economies of scale occur as average production cost declines with rising output per period. Any new entrant must (1) have available financing to construct a large-scale factory and (2) be able to sell in sufficient quantity to be cost competitive. These requirements can permit or prevent entry and promote or inhibit positive net present values.

Product differentiation can also generate positive net present values. Differentiation comes from consumers' belief in a difference between firms' products, whether there is a real difference or not. Differentiation leads to an imperfect market where a firm can set higher prices. Potential sources of differentiation include advertising and promotion expenditures to create branding, R&D, and quality differences.

Absolute cost advantages can place competitors at a cost disadvantage. A firm that is a first-mover into a market can learn about the production and distribution process. By being further down the learning curve, the first-mover may have the opportunity to use assets, technology, raw inputs, and personnel more efficiently than its follow-on competitors. Similar advantages can result from possessing proprietary technology that is protected by patents. Early entry into foreign markets can allow the firm to gain experience over its competitors as it can more effectively make inroads into new markets and start to build customer loyalty.

Differences in access to distribution channels can also produce unique advantages by reducing competitors' access to consumers. Shelf space is limited at retail outlets, and store owners are understandably hesitant to take space from a current supplier and give it to a new entrant. A motivated and well-trained sales force may keep competitors from chipping away at a firm's market share. Next time you are at the grocery store, take a look at the varieties of breakfast cereal produced by the large firms in the industry!

Government policy can hinder new and potential entrants and give existing competitors unique advantages. An increasing regulatory burden on an industry can discourage entry by increasing both the complexity and the costs of entry. Domestic industries can seek import quotas to limit the extent of foreign entry and competition. Of course, similar quotas by other countries, perhaps raised in retaliation to the domestic quotas, can hurt the firm that initially sought protection. The policy of a foreign government toward nondomestic producers, as well as the stability of the government, can contribute to the political risk of investing or doing business overseas.

CONCEPT CHECK

What does net present value *mean?*

Should a firm invest in any line of business that looks attractive? Why or why not?

How can SWOT analysis be used to identify capital budgeting projects?

List five sources of positive net present value projects.

PERSONAL FINANCIAL PLANNING
Favorable Attributes of Firms for Investment Purposes

Peter Lynch was the legendary manager of Fidelity Magellan Fund, a mutual fund that invests in stocks. During Lynch's tenure at Magellan, his stock-picking ability rewarded his mutual fund investors with high returns. His investment success and easygoing style make him a popular figure with the media. Although retired from managing mutual funds, Peter is still featured in Fidelity's advertising and company publications.

Lynch identified several attributes of firms that may result in favorable stock market performance. Many of these attributes relate to the capital budgeting process in that they suggest capital budgeting and marketing strategies in which firms may need to invest. Lynch's favorable attributes of firms include the following:

1. A firm's product is not faddish; it is one that consumers will have to purchase time and time again. Repeat sales build profits, market share, and shareholder value.
2. The company should have some comparative advantage over its rivals. Other competitors will try to successfully copy the firm's

product. Capital budgeting investments in technology, innovation, customer research, and building brand loyalty can help build and maintain a comparative advantage over time and enhance shareholder wealth.

3. The firm can benefit from cost reductions. Capital budget projects to create or enhance production, marketing, and distribution efficiencies can increase profitability and stock price.
4. Firms that repurchase their shares or have managers (company insiders) buying shares show that the firm and its insiders are putting their money into the firm. When managers use available funds to reinvest in the firm by purchasing the firm's stock, they are telling investors that, with their inside knowledge, they believe the firm's shares are underpriced. Given all the capital budget projects they face, they've chosen repurchasing stock as one of the more attractive projects to return value to shareholders.

CAPITAL BUDGETING PROCESS

The capital budgeting process involves the preparation and analysis of a business case request for funding, and usually consists of the following five stages:

1. Identification
2. Development
3. Selection
4. Implementation
5. Follow-up

The ***identification stage*** involves finding potential capital investment opportunities and identifying whether a project involves a replacement decision and/or revenue expansion. The ***development stage*** requires estimating relevant cash inflows and outflows. It also involves discussing the pros and cons of each project. Development sometimes requires asking what the strategic impact will be of not doing the project.

The third ***selection stage*** involves applying the appropriate capital budgeting techniques to help make a final accept or reject decision. In the ***implementation stage***, projects that are accepted must be executed in a timely fashion. In the ***follow-up stage***, decisions are periodically tracked, reviewed, analyzed, or audited to determine whether they are meeting expectations. If disappointing results occur, it is sometimes necessary to terminate or abandon previous decisions.

The multinational corporation (MNC) must be taken through the same capital budgeting process just described. In addition, however, managers of MNCs must consider possible added political and economic risks when making their decisions. Risk adjustments may be necessary because of the possibility of seizure of assets, unstable currencies, and weak foreign economies. The impact of foreign exchange controls and foreign tax regulations on a project's cash flows in relation to the final amounts that may be paid to the parent firm must also be taken into account.

In Chapter 11 we stated how a company's mission should guide management in making investment decisions while striving to meet goals and maximize shareholder wealth. We looked at several firms' mission statements in Chapter 11. Let's now briefly review some of the capital projects in which the firms are investing.

Ben & Jerry's: This company's mission, in part, is to produce high-quality all-natural ice cream in innovative flavors, to have profitable growth, and to be socially conscious. It has marketed and introduced several new flavors each year, with names such as Pfish Food and Chunky Monkey, and organic ice cream, such as Strawberry. International expansion has occurred in numerous countries, including Peru, United Kingdom, France, Canada, and South Korea. The firm uses part of its profits to assist nonprofit organizations and social causes that its founders favor.

Wendy's: Growth in sales and earnings in the restaurant industry comes mainly via selling new and innovative products, opening new outlets, and acquisitions. Wendy's invests in new store locations, offers late-night hours to increase sales per location, has built a bakery plant to supply its stores with fresh bread, and has acquired growing niche restaurants. An example is the company's investment in Café Express, a player in the "fast-casual" restaurant segment.

Wells Fargo: This financial institution is implementing a number of strategies to cross-sell products with a special emphasis on home equity loans. Technology investments improve its online financial services capabilities and also improve customer service. Wells Fargo's strategy is to increase customer loyalty and to increase customer satisfaction with bank visits.

Merck: As a pharmaceutical company, Merck's future relies on investing in research and developing a portfolio of products to meet the health needs of consumers. It initiates, curtails, expands, and shepherds a variety of formulations through the FDA drug approval process in order to maintain and grow its future cash flows.

Dell: Growth in sales, both in the United States and abroad, show that Dell is making progress on its mission, which deals with customer experience and product development. Dell invests funds with customer service and satisfaction in mind. It has been successful, as witnessed by the many awards the company has won for the quality and reliability of its products and services. It has diversified, and its offerings now include printers, digital music players, and monitors.

---

identification stage
finding potential capital investment opportunities and identifying whether a project involves a replacement decision and/or revenue expansion

development stage
requires estimating relevant cash inflows and outflows

GLOBAL DISCUSSION

selection stage
applying appropriate capital budgeting techniques to help make a final accept or reject decision

implementation stage
executing accepted projects

follow-up stage
tracking, reviewing, analyzing, or auditing a project's results

INTERNET ACTIVITY

Details of investments can be seen in annual reports and news releases, both of which can be accessed via the firms' Web sites: http://www.benjerry.com, http://www.wendys.com, http://www.wellsfargo.com, http://www.merck.com, and http://www.dell.com.

CONCEPT CHECK

What are the five stages of the capital budgeting process?

CAPITAL BUDGETING TECHNIQUES

FINANCE PRINCIPLE

Appropriate methods or techniques are required to evaluate capital budgeting projects so that proper wealth-maximizing decisions can be made. The techniques used should reflect the time value of money since cash outlays for plant and equipment occur now, while the benefits occur in the future. Five methods—net present value, internal rate of return, modified internal rate of return, profitability index, and payback period—are utilized widely. Of these five methods, the payback period is the *least* preferable because it does not take the time value of money into account.

NET PRESENT VALUE

The net present value (NPV) method is arguably the best method to use to evaluate capital budgeting projects. A project's net present value is calculated as the present value of all cash flows for the life of the project less the initial investment or outlay, as we saw in Equation 13.1. It considers the time value of money and includes all of the project's cash flows in the analysis. In addition, its value measures the project's dollar impact on shareholder wealth. The NPV measures the expected dollar change in shareholder wealth from doing the project. That is, a project with an NPV of $1 million is expected to increase shareholder wealth by $1 million. Thus, projects with positive NPVs are expected to add to shareholder wealth, while projects with negative NPVs should be shunned.

To apply the net present value method, we need to know the project's estimated cash flows and the required rate of return to discount the cash flow. We discuss methods of estimating cash flows in Chapter 14. The required rate of return should reflect the cost of long-term debt and equity capital funds for projects with the same risk as the one under consideration. In the following example, we'll assume that the required rate of return, or **cost of capital**, is 10 percent. In Chapter 15 we review in detail the process of determining the cost of capital.

cost of capital
project's required rate of return

We apply the net present value technique to Projects A and B, whose cash flows are shown in Table 13.1. Assuming a 10 percent cost of capital, the cash flows are multiplied by the 10 percent PVIF from Table 2 in the Appendix to get the present values shown in Table 13.2. Notice that there is no discount factor for the initial outlays because they occur before any time has passed (i.e., in year zero). Positive net present values are shown for both projects. This means that an investment in either project will add to shareholder wealth. However, Project A, with the higher net present value of $1,982, is preferable to Project B, which has a net present value of $988.

A positive NPV means the project's cash inflows are sufficient to repay the initial upfront (time zero) costs as well as the financing cost of 10 percent over the project's life. Since their NPVs are greater than zero, each project's return is greater than the 10 percent cost of capital.

TABLE 13.1

Cash Flow Data for Projects A and B

YEAR	PROJECT A	PROJECT B
1	$5,800	$4,000
2	5,800	4,000
3	5,800	8,000
4	5,800	10,000
5	5,800	10,000

TABLE 13.2

Net Present Value Calculations for Projects A and B

			PROJECT A					PROJECT B		
YEAR	CASH FLOW	×	10% PVIF	=	PRESENT VALUE	CASH FLOW	×	10% PVIF	=	PRESENT VALUE
0 –	$20,000		1.000		−$20,000	−$25,000		1.000		−$25,000
1	$5,800		0.909		$5,272	$4,000		0.909		$3,636
2	$5,800		0.826		$4,791	$4,000		0.826		$3,304
3	$5,800		0.751		$4,356	$8,000		0.751		$6,008
4	$5,800		0.683		$3,961	$10,000		0.683		$6,830
5	$5,800		0.621		$3,602	$10,000		0.621		$6,210
			Net present value = $1,982					Net present value = $ 988		

Financial calculators can compute NPV. For example, for Project A we can enter the following:

For HP 10 B II Financial Calculator:

$-20,000$ CF$_j$
5800 CF$_j$
5800 CF$_j$
5800 CF$_j$
5800 CF$_j$
5800 CF$_j$

10 I/YR (interest rate key)

Pushing the NPV key (some may require pushing a shift on "2nd" key first) next, we have a more exact answer for the NPV: $1,986.56.

For the TI BA II Plus Financial Calculator:

TO	PRESS	DISPLAY
Select Cash Flow worksheet	CF	CFo = 0.00
Enter initial cash flow	20000 +/− **ENTER**	CFo = −20,000
Enter cash flow for first year	↓5800 ENTER	C01 = 5,800
	↓	F01 = 1.00
Enter cash flows for the second year	↓5800 ENTER	C02 = 5,800
	↓	F01 = 1.00
Enter cash flows for the third year	↓5800 ENTER	C03 = 5,800
	↓	F01 = 1.00
Enter cash flows for the fourth year	↓5800 ENTER	C04 = 5,800
	↓	F01 = 1.00
Enter cash flows for the fifth year	↓ 5800 ENTER	C05 = 5,800
	↓	F01 = 1.00

Computing NPV:

TO	PRESS	DISPLAY
Prepare to compute NPV	NPV	I = 0.00
Enter interest rate per period	10 ENTER	I = 10.00
Compute NPV	↓ CPT	NPV = 1,986.56

Doing this calculation for Project B, we find its NPV is $992.01.

A shortcut method can be used to calculate the net present value for Project A. Since the cash inflows form an annuity, we could have used the PVIFA at 10 percent for five years from Table 4 in the Appendix, which is 3.791. The net present value then can be calculated:

$$\$5,800 \times 3.791 = \begin{array}{r} \$21,988 \text{ PV cash inflows} \\ \underline{-20,000 \text{ Initial outlay}} \\ \$1,988 \text{ Net present value} \end{array}$$

The $1,988 net present value figure using PVIFA differs slightly from the $1,982 using PVIF because of rounding the present value interest factors in the Appendix tables. When cash inflows are not in the form of an annuity, as in the case of Project B, the longer calculation process shown in Table 13.2 must be used to find the net present value.

Projects with negative net present values are not acceptable to a firm. They provide returns lower than the cost of capital and would cause the value of the firm to fall. In our example, both Projects A and B have positive NPVs that are acceptable. If they are mutually exclusive projects, managers should chose Project A as its NPV—$1,986.56—is higher than Project B's NPV of $992.01. Clearly, it is important for the financial manager to make capital budgeting decisions on the basis of the expected impact on the firm's value.

Using Spreadsheet Functions

In addition to multiplying with factors found in a present value table or using a financial calculator, electronic spreadsheet packages such as Excel make the task of computing a net present value rather simple, too. Suppose we have the cash flows for Project A in column B, rows 2 through 7 of an Excel spreadsheet:

	Microsoft Excel				
File	Edit View Insert Format Tools Data Window				
				100%	
			Reply with Changes...		
A13		f_x			
	A	B	C	D	E
1	Time	Cash Flow			
2	0	-$20,000			
3	1	$5,800			
4	2	$5,800			
5	3	$5,800			
6	4	$5,800			
7	5	$5,800			
8	NPV =	$1,986.56	=NPV(10%,B3:B7) + B2		
9					
10					

Sheet1 / Sheet2 / Sheet3

Ready

To compute the net present value, we can use Excel's NPV function, with modification. We need to modify its use because Excel's NPV does not calculate net present value as we do in this chapter. Excel's NPV function computes the sum of present values assuming the value in the first cell listed is to be discounted back one period, the value in the second cell is to be discounted back two periods, and so on. Yet most capital budgeting problems have a "time zero" or "current" investment that is not discounted; in our example, the investment of $20,000 at time zero is already expressed in present value terms.

To get around this problem, we use Excel's NPV function to find the sum of the present values in periods one through the end of the project (cells B3 through B7 in our example) and then add the initial negative investment cash outflow of $20,000 in cell B2. In the preceding example, in cell B8 we typed =NPV(10%, B3:B7) + B2, and the spreadsheet computes an exact value of the net present value, $1,986.56.

The NPV function has the form:

$$= \text{NPV(discount rate, cell of time one cash flow: cell of last cash flow)}$$

The discount rate can be typed as a percentage (10%) or as a decimal equivalent (0.1). If you type in the "%" symbol, Excel assumes the number is a percentage, otherwise the decimal equivalent is assumed. Be careful: if you key in "10" rather than "10%," the spreadsheet will use a discount rate of 1,000 percent!

INTERNAL RATE OF RETURN

We know from our discussion of bonds in Chapter 7 that there is an inverse relationship, or "seesaw effect," between bond prices and interest rates. As investors' required rates of return rise, bond prices fall; as investors' required rates of return fall, bond prices rise. A similar relationship exists between NPV and a firm's required rate of return or cost of capital on a project. For a given set of cash flows, a higher cost of capital will lead to a lower NPV; a lower cost of capital, however, will increase a project's NPV. Figure 13.1 shows this relationship, called the **NPV profile**, between NPV and the cost of capital. As the cost of capital on a project rises, the NPV changes from positive, to zero, to negative. The cost of capital at which the NPV is zero deserves special attention.

While the net present value method tells us that both Projects A and B provide expected returns that are greater than 10 percent, we do not know the actual rates of return. The **internal rate of return (IRR) method** finds the return that causes the net present value to be zero, namely the point where the NPV profile crosses the x axis in Figure 13.1. Net present value will equal

CONCEPT CHECK

How is NPV computed?

What does the cost of capital represent?

NPV profile
the graphical relationship between a project's NPV and cost of capital

internal rate of return (IRR) method
return that causes the net present value to be zero

FIGURE 13.1
Relationship Between NPV and Discount Rates

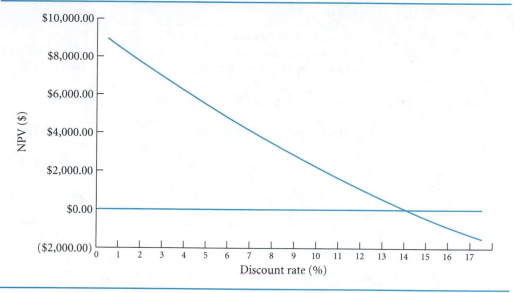

zero when the present value of the cash flows equals the project's initial investment, as seen in Equation 13.2:[3]

$$NPV = \sum_{t=1}^{n} [CF_t/(1 + IRR)^t - \text{Initial Investment}] = 0 \qquad (13.2)$$

A trial-and-error process can be used to find the internal rate of return (IRR), but financial calculators and computer spreadsheets (such as Excel's IRR function) provide much quicker means of estimating internal rates of return.

Let's illustrate the IRR process first for Project A. Because the cash inflows form an annuity, the IRR is easy to find. From Chapter 5 we know:

Present value of an annuity = PVIFA × Annuity cash flow

Rearranging, we divide the initial capital budgeting outlay (PV annuity) by the cash inflow annuity amount to find the present value interest factor for an ordinary annuity:

PVIFA = PV annuity/Annual cash inflow

For Project A the PVIFA is 3.448 ($20,000/5,800). We know this PVIFA of 3.448 is for five years. By turning to Table 4 in the Appendix, "Present Value of a $1 Ordinary Annuity," we can read across the five-year row until we find a PVIFA close to 3.448. It falls between 3.605 (12 percent) and 3.433 (14 percent) but is much closer to the PVIFA at 14 percent. Thus the internal rate of return for Project A is a little less than 14 percent.

Of course, other, more precise, ways to find internal rate of return can be done with financial calculators and computer spreadsheets. Using a financial calculator and Project A's cash flows:

For HP 10 B II Financial Calculator:

$$-20,000 \text{ CF}_j$$
$$5800 \text{ CF}_j$$
$$5800 \text{ CF}_j$$
$$5800 \text{ CF}_j$$
$$5800 \text{ CF}_j$$
$$5800 \text{ CF}_j$$

Pushing the IRR key (for some calculators, you may need to push a shift or "2nd" key before pushing the IRR key). Doing so, we find the IRR is 13.82 percent.

---

3. This method also is used to find the yield to maturity on bonds in Chapter 7.

For the TI BA II Plus Financial Calculator:

TO	PRESS	DISPLAY
Select Cash Flow worksheet	CF	CFo = 0.00
Enter initial cash flow	20000 +/− **ENTER**	CFo = −20,000
Enter cash flow for first year	↓ 5800 ENTER	C01 = 5,800
	↓	F01 = 1.00
Enter cash flows for the second year	↓ 5800 ENTER	C02 = 5,800
	↓	F01 = 1.00
Enter cash flows for the third year	↓ 5800 ENTER	C03 = 5,800
	↓	F01 = 1.00
Enter cash flows for the fourth year	↓ 5800 ENTER	C04 = 5,800
	↓	F01 = 1.00
Enter cash flows for the fifth year	↓ 5800 ENTER	C05 = 5,800
	↓	F01 = 1.00

Computing NPV:

TO	PRESS	DISPLAY
Prepare to compute IRR	IRR	IRR = 0.00
Compute internal rate of return	↓ CPT	IRR=13.82

We can illustrate how to determine the IRR two ways using spreadsheets. We will use Project A, with its annuity cash flows, in these examples. First, we can successively compute values of NPV using different discount rates:

DISCOUNT RATE (%)	PROJECT A'S NPV	
0	$9,000.00	
1	$8,149.90	
2	$7,338.07	
3	$6,562.30	
4	$5,820.57	
5	$5,110.96	
6	$4,431.71	
7	$3,781.15	
8	$3,157.72	
9	$2,559.98	
10	$1,986.56	
11	$1,436.20	
12	$907.70	
13	$399.94	The NPV goes from
14	−$88.13	positive to negative
15	−$557.50	here, so the IRR must
16	−$1,009.10	lie between 13 and 14
17	−$1,443.79	percent.

This shows that the IRR is between 13 and 14 percent. This information can then be used as input into Excel's graphing capabilities, and the NPV profile can be graphed. In fact, that is how we constructed Figure 13.1. The NPV profile gives us a visual perspective of how sensitive the net present value is to a change in the project's cost of capital or discount rate.

The second way to use the spreadsheet is to compute the internal rate of return directly by using Excel's IRR function. Let's assume the time 0 through time 5 cash flows for Project A are in cells B2 through B7, as shown in the following spreadsheet. By keying = IRR(B2:B7) into a cell (B9, in this case) the spreadsheet will compute an exact value of the internal rate of return for Project A:

	Microsoft Excel

```
File  Edit  View  Insert  Format  Tools  Data  Window
```

	A	B	C	D	E
	A12		fx		
1	Time	Cash Flow			
2	0	-$20,000			
3	1	$5,800			
4	2	$5,800			
5	3	$5,800			
6	4	$5,800			
7	5	$5,800			
8	NPV =	$1,986.56	=NPV(10%,B3:B7) + B2		
9	IRR =	13.82%	=IRR(B2:B7)		
10					

Sheet1 / Sheet2 / Sheet3 /

Ready

In our example, the initial (time zero) cash flow is found in cell B2. Cell B7 contains the final cash inflow for time period five. Using the IRR function, we obtain an exact value for Project A's internal rate of return—13.82 percent—the same as we found using a financial calculator.

The IRR function has the form =IRR(cell of time zero cash flow : cell of last cash flow, initial estimate for the IRR). The last item, the initial estimate for the IRR, is optional and we did not use it in the preceding example for Project A. To input an initial guess, we can use percentages (10%) or decimal equivalents (0.10). Many times, we can omit this initial guess and the IRR function will compute the internal rate of return without difficulty.

For Project B, with its unequal cash flows, a financial calculator or spreadsheet program is the best to use. A trial-and-error process can also be used to find the IRR for Project B. Discounting the cash flows at a 10 percent rate results in a positive net present value of $988, as calculated in Table 13.2. A positive net present value indicates that we need to try a higher discount rate, such as 12 percent, to find the discount rate that results in a zero NPV.[4] The 12 percent present value interest factors are taken from Table 2 in the Appendix, "Present Value of $1." In Table 13.3, we calculate that when the cash flows are discounted at a 12 percent rate, the net present value becomes minus $514.

This indicates that the IRR actually falls between 10 and 12 percent. Since minus $514 is closer to zero than $988, you might guess that the IRR is a little above 11 percent. To obtain an exact answer, though, we need to use a financial calculator or electronic spreadsheet. Doing so, we learn that Project B's IRR is 11.3 percent.

Both Projects A and B are acceptable because they provide returns higher than the 10 percent cost of capital. However, if the projects are mutually exclusive, we would select Project A over Project B because A's net present value is higher.[5]

TABLE 13.3

Net Present Value Calculation for Project B Using a 12 Percent Discount Rate

YEAR	CASH FLOW	×	12% PVIF	=	PRESENT VALUE
0	−$25,000		1.000		−$25,000
1	$4,000		0.893		$3,572
2	$4,000		0.797		$3,188
3	$8,000		0.712		$5,696
4	$10,000		0.636		$6,360
5	$10,000		0.567		$5,670
				Net present value =	−$514

---

4. Similar to the "seesaw effect" we learned in bond pricing, a higher discount rate results in a lower NPV, as seen in Figure 13.1.

5. For several reasons, a project with an NPV below that of another project may have a higher IRR than the competing project. That is why it is best to calculate each project's NPV in addition to the IRR. The project with the highest NPV is the one that is expected to add the most to shareholder wealth.

NET PRESENT VALUE AND INTERNAL RATE OF RETURN

The NPV and IRR methods will always agree on whether a project enhances or harms shareholder wealth. If a project returns more than its cost of capital, the NPV is positive. If a project returns less than its cost of capital, the NPV is negative. An issue with the use of IRR is that at times it will rank projects differently than the NPV will. If that occurs, what decision should be made?

If the projects are independent, there is no real issue: the firm should do all projects with positive NPVs—in other words, the firm should do all projects with internal rates of return greater than their required returns.

If the projects are mutually exclusive, however, the decision should be made to follow the rankings created by the NPV method. The NPV measures the change in shareholder wealth that is expected to be generated by the project. As managers should try to maximize shareholder wealth, the project with the higher NPV—*not* the higher IRR—should be preferred.

A second issue with IRR arises when the cash flows of a project alternate in sign: some positive, some negative. In such a case it is mathematically possible to have two—or more—IRRs! For example, consider the case of a project with an initial outlay of $100, a positive cash flow of $300 in year 1, and a cash outflow of −$200 in year 2 because of shutdown costs. Such a project has two IRRs: 0 percent and 100 percent.

$$\text{NPV at} \quad 0\%: -100 + 300/(1 + 0)^1 + -200/(1 + 0)^2 = -100 + 300 - 200 = 0$$
$$\text{NPV at} \ 100\%: -100 + 300/(1 + 1.00)^1 + -200/(1 + 100.0)^2 = -100 + 150 - 50 \ = 0$$

It is easy to think of a real-world project that may require substantial renovations or maintenance over time or that may have large end-of-life decommissioning or shutdown costs. Thus, for this reason NPV, rather than IRR, is the preferred approach.

A common misconception is that the IRR represents the compounded return on the funds originally invested in the project. What IRR really measures is the return earned on the funds that remain internally invested in the project (hence the name, *internal* rate of return). Some cash flows from a project are a return of the principal (original investment), while some pay a return on the remaining balance of funds invested in the project.

To show that the IRR measures the return earned on the funds that remain internally invested in a project, we present the following example. Martin and Barbara have decided to upgrade their business computer system to improve the quality and efficiency of their work. The initial investment is $5,000, and the project will save them $2,010.57 per year. The internal rate of return on the project has been determined to be 10 percent. We show how the IRR represents the return on the year-by-year unrecovered costs of the project.

Following is the cash flow schedule constructed for Martin and Barbara's computer upgrade project.

(1) YEAR	(2) BEGINNING INVESTMENT VALUE	(3) CASH INFLOW (SAVINGS)	(4) 10% RETURN ON THE INVESTED FUNDS (2) × 0.10	(5) REDUCTION IN THE INVESTED FUNDS (3) − (4)	(6) ENDING VALUE OF INVESTED FUNDS (2) − (5)
1	$5,000.00	$2,010.57	$500.00	$1,510.57	$3,489.43
2	3,489.43	2,010.57	348.94	1,661.63	1,827.80
3	1,827.80	2,010.57	182.78	1,827.79	0.01*

CONCEPT CHECK

What is the relationship between the cost of capital and net present value?

What is the relationship between IRR and NPV?

What does the IRR measure?

*Value is not 0.00 due to rounding.

This table shows that the yearly cash saving of $2,010.57 from the computer upgrade project represents both a return on the funds that remain invested (column 4) and a reduction in the funds that remain invested in the project (column 5). The project does not earn a 10 percent return, or $500 annually, on the initial $5,000 investment for all three years. The 10 percent IRR represents the return on the funds that remain invested in the project over its lifetime rather than each year's return on the original investment.

MODIFIED INTERNAL RATE OF RETURN

modified internal rate of
return (MIRR) method
a technique that finds the
return that equates the
present value of a project's
outflows to the future value
of its inflows

The *modified internal rate of return (MIRR) method* solves some of the problems presented by IRR. MIRR rankings of mutually exclusive projects with comparably sized initial investments will agree with the NPV rankings of those projects. Additionally, the MIRR calculation always gives a single answer—it will not give us multiple answers as the IRR approach sometimes does.

MIRR is calculated in a three-step process:

1. Using the required rate of return as the discount rate, find the present value of all cash outflows (for a conventional project, this will be just the initial cost of the project). This step converts all the cash outflows into a lump-sum present value at Time 0.
2. Using the required return as the reinvestment or compounding rate, compute the *future* value of each cash inflow as of the end of the project's life, time *N*, and add them together. This sum is sometimes called the *terminal value*. This step converts all inflows into a lump-sum future value at time *N*.
3. Find the discount rate that equates the present value of the outflows and the future value of the terminal value; this discount rate is the *modified internal rate of return*.

Figure 13.2 illustrates this process using the cash flow data from Project A using a required return of 10 percent.

FIGURE 13.2
MIRR for Project A

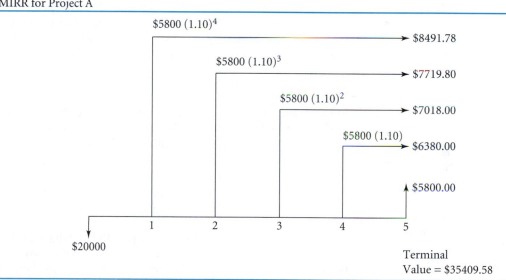

In the first step, the present value of the project's outflows is simply its initial investment: $20,000.

Second, we find the future value of each of the project's inflows as of the end of the fifth and final year of the project. The year 1 cash inflow of $5,800 is compounded over four years to the end of year 5; its future value at the end of year 5 is $8,491.78. The year 2 cash flow is compounded for three years to the end of year 5; its future value at the end of year 5 is $7,719.80. Similarly, we compute the future values for the years 3, 4, and 5 cash inflows. The year 5 cash inflow needs no compounding as it occurs at the end of year 5. Adding the future values together, their sum is $35,409.58; this is the project's terminal value.

Third, we find the discount rate that sets the present value of the outflows equal to the terminal value:

$$FV = PV(1 + r)^n = \$35{,}409.58 = \$20{,}000(1 + r)^5$$

Solving, we find the MIRR is 12.10 percent

Using a spreadsheet, Excel has a function, MIRR, to do this calculation:

	A	B	C	D	E	F
1	Time	Cash Flow				
2	0	-$20,000				
3	1	$5,800				
4	2	$5,800				
5	3	$5,800				
6	4	$5,800				
7	5	$5,800				
8	NPV =	$1,986.56	=NPV(10%,B3:B7) + B2			
9	IRR =	13.82%	=IRR(B2:B7)			
10	MIRR =	12.10%	=MIRR(B2:B7,10%,10%)			

IRR / Multiple IRRs \ **MIRR** /

The MIRR function has the form =MIRR(cell of time zero cash flow : cell of last cash flow, finance rate, reinvestment rate). The finance rate is the interest rate paid on borrowing to finance the cash outflows. The reinvestment rate is the rate used to compound, or to find the future value, of the cash inflows. We used the firm's required rate of return of 10 percent for both of these in this example.

Similar calculations show the MIRR for Project B is 10.86 percent. MIRR ranks Project A (12.10 percent) higher than Project B (10.86 percent); this is the same ranking as NPV gave the projects.

The decision rule for MIRR is similar to that for IRR: a project is acceptable if its MIRR exceeds the project's minimum required return. A drawback to the MIRR is that it is a relative measure of attractiveness; it does not indicate the dollar amount by which projects change shareholder wealth.[6]

CONCEPT CHECK

What is MIRR?

How does the MIRR method improve upon the IRR method?

profitability index (PI)
ratio between the present values of the cash flows and the project's cost

benefit/cost ratio
the profitability index

PROFITABILITY INDEX

Another discounted cash flow (DCF) technique for evaluating capital budgeting projects is the **profitability index (PI)**, also called the **benefit/cost ratio**. The PI method computes the ratio between the present values of the inflows and outflows:

$$PI = \frac{\text{Present value of the cash flows}}{\text{Initial cost}} = \frac{\sum_{t=1}^{N} \frac{CF_t}{(1+r)^t}}{CF_o} \tag{13.3}$$

The PI measures the relative benefits of undertaking a project, namely the present value of benefits received for each dollar invested. A PI of 2, for example, means that the project returns a present value of $2 for every $1 invested. Since it would be foolish to invest in a project that returns less than a dollar for every dollar invested, the profitability index has a natural decision rule: accept a project that has a profitability index greater than 1.0, reject a project that has a PI less than 1.0.

Using the data in Table 13.3, we calculate the present value of Project A's inflows to be $21,982. Since its initial cost is $20,000, Project A has a profitability index of $21,982/$20,000, or 1.099. Project B's cash inflows have a present value of $25,988, so its profitability index is $25,988/$25,000, or 1.040.

The relationship between PI and NPV should be clear. Whenever NPV is positive, PI exceeds 1.0. Likewise, whenever NPV is negative, PI is less than 1.0. Thus, the NPV, IRR, and PI always agree on which projects would enhance shareholder wealth and which would diminish it.

CONCEPT CHECK

What is the profitability index?

What is the relationship between the profitability index and the net present value?

---

6. The reason the MIRR ranks projects in the same order as the NPV method is because the MIRR is a transformation of the NPV calculation. The terminal value calculation in the MIRR method is equal to the future value of the present value of the inflows. For example, for Project A, the present value of the inflows is $21,986.56. At the 10 percent required return, the future value of this amount in year 5 is $21,986.56(1.10)^5 = $35,409.57, which, with some rounding error, is the terminal value we computed.

Conflicts Among Discounted Cash Flow Techniques

NPV, IRR, MIRR, and PI will *always* agree on whether a project should be accepted or rejected. So if the firm is considering only independent projects, it makes little practical difference which method is used. All these methods always give consistent decisions as to whether a given project would increase or decrease shareholder wealth.

However, when mutually exclusive projects are ranked from most attractive to least attractive, NPV may rate them different than the other techniques. The main reason for this is that NPV measures one aspect of the project, whereas IRR and PI measure another.

NPV measures the dollar change in shareholder wealth that arises from undertaking the project. As relative measures of project attractiveness, IRR and PI indicate the rate of profitability a project adds to shareholder wealth—but not the actual dollar amount. A project with a lower IRR or PI may still add more to shareholder value than another mutually exclusive project if the projects have different cash flow patterns, time horizons, or sizes.

Different Cash Flow Patterns

Projects that provide larger cash flows in their early stages can seem to provide more funds than a project with more even cash flows. If the IRR exceeds the firm's required rate of return, the effects of compounding larger cash flows at a rate exceeding the required return may result in the IRR method ranking the project higher than the NPV method. Thus, projects with larger earlier cash flows may have higher IRR rankings than those with larger later cash flows.

Different Time Horizons

A shorter project may free up invested funds sooner and consequently offer a higher IRR. A long-term project's cash flows will remain internally invested in the project for a longer period. Unless those future cash flows are quite large, the discounting process may reduce their perceived present value, eroding the IRR of the longer-term project. The IRR of a desirable project must exceed the project's required return; the NPV formula uses a lower discount rate, so it values later cash flows more favorably than does the IRR calculation.

A quick example will show this point. Suppose Project Short and Project Long both require an initial investment of $100. In two years, Project Short returns a lump sum of $200. Project Long lasts ten times longer and returns ten times more than Project Short; that is, Project Long will return a lump sum of $2,000 in twenty years. A quick calculation will confirm that Project Short has an IRR of 41.42 percent; Project Long has an IRR of 16.16 percent, but at a 10 percent cost of capital, Project Long's NPV ($197.29) exceeds that of Project Short ($65.29).

Different Sizes

Projects with smaller initial investments may have higher PIs and IRRs, but their small size may appear to make them less attractive from an NPV perspective. For example, consider Projects Small and Large:

PROJECT	INITIAL OUTLAY	PV OF CASH FLOWS	NPV	PI
Small	$100.00	$150.00	$50	1.5
Large	$1,000.00	$1,100.00	$100	1.1

The NPV method ranks Project Large first because of its larger NPV, but PI ranks Project Small first.

Thus, rankings among capital budgeting projects may differ for any of the three reasons given. The discounted cash flow methods each provide a different perspective on project attractiveness, but since the goal of the decision process is to maximize shareholder wealth, the NPV approach remains preferred among the others.

PAYBACK PERIOD

The payback period method does not consider the time value of money. We discuss it because it is simple to compute and is still used by some firms. You need to know about this technique and to be able to explain why it should not be used to make investment decisions.

CONCEPT CHECK

Why will projects with larger earlier cash flows tend to have higher IRRs?

Why will shorter projects tend to have higher IRRs?

Why might projects with smaller initial investments have higher IRRs and PIs than projects with larger initial investments?

SMALL BUSINESS PRACTICE
A Small Business Resource Center

Business Week has established the Small Business Resource Center. Access to this center is available to current *Business Week* subscribers at the company's Web site at http://www.businessweek.com/smallbiz/index.html. The center provides a variety of different types of information and also is interactive. A variety of resource information is available on such topics as market research, managing a workforce, finance, and technology.

In addition to information about resources available to small businesses, the center provides services in the form of access to *Business Week* travel and career centers. Daily reports and breaking business stories are provided, along with an Ask Enterprise feature that helps provide answers to questions posed by managers of small businesses.

Information relating to operating and financing a business at various life cycle stages is provided. For example, if you wish to start a new business, you can examine the forms that are necessary to begin operation. Information on financing and growing a business also is provided. In addition, information is provided for owner/managers who are either seeking to sell their firms or trying to find other ways to exit their businesses.

---

payback period method *determines the time in years it will take to recover, or pay back, the initial investment in fixed assets*

The **payback period method** determines the time in years needed to recover, or "pay back," the initial investment in fixed assets. Management will choose the projects whose paybacks are less than a management-specified period.

In cases where the cash benefits form an annuity, the payback period is easily calculated:

$$\text{Payback period} = \text{Initial outlay/Annual cash inflow}$$

For Project A we have:

$$\text{Payback period} = \$20,000/\$5,800 = 3.4 \text{ years}$$

The initial investment outflow for Project B is $25,000. Cash inflows for Project B will total $16,000 ($4,000 + $4,000 + $8,000) for the first three years. This leaves $9,000 ($25,000 − $16,000) still unrecovered. With a $10,000 cash flow expected in year 4, it will take an additional 0.9 of a year ($9,000/$10,000) before the investment is fully recovered. Thus the payback period for Project B is 3.9 years. Based solely on the payback period technique, Project A would be chosen over Project B because it recoups its investment more quickly.

However, the payback period evaluation method suffers from two basic drawbacks. First, the technique does not consider the time value of money. The second limitation is that all cash flows beyond the payback period are ignored. Notice that Project B will return $10,000 in cash inflow in year five, which is substantially more than Project A's fifth-year cash inflow. The possible significance of this difference is overlooked by the payback period method.

A large accounting firm conducted a study of store remodelings and renovations. Their findings are disturbing for some retailers: these investments may never pay for themselves. The study found that large discounters, such as Kmart have payback periods that average twenty years for renovation projects. The IRR on such projects range from 1 percent to 6 percent. For family-apparel specialty stores (such as Eddie Bauer), it was a different story. Their remodeling IRRs were as high as 67 percent with payback periods that averaged nineteen months. (The participants in the study were not revealed; the store names used here are only examples of stores in the different retail categories.)

The study concludes that having a good market position is more important than a renovation project. Poor returns on some stores' renovations apparently occurred because stores were trying to modernize in the face of new competition rather than realigning company strategy to respond to a successful competitor.[7]

CONCEPT CHECK

What is the payback period?

Why is the payback period inferior to NPV as a method for selecting capital budgeting projects?

DIFFERENCE BETWEEN THEORY AND PRACTICE

Thus far, this chapter has presented the basic concepts and techniques of capital budgeting. The capital budgeting process tries to identify projects that will maximize shareholder value. Using the firm's mission and objectives as a guide, managers seek to identify market or product segments where the firm can build, maintain, or expand a competitive advantage.

---

7. Christina Duff, "Discount Retailers Get No Quick Fix from Remodeling Stores, Study Says," *Wall Street Journal* (March 27, 1995), p. A15C.

We have reviewed five capital budgeting techniques: net present value, internal rate of return, modified internal rate of return, profitability index, and payback method. The first four use discounted cash flows to incorporate the time value of money into the analysis. The final method ignores time value considerations. Financial managers favor the use of discounted cash flow techniques.

Theory strongly suggests that analysts should evaluate capital budgeting projects using DCF techniques that incorporate all relevant cash flows, that base decisions on clear and objective criteria, and that indicate the impacts of projects on shareholder wealth. The net present value method clearly satisfies these conditions better than other methods. Surveys of practitioners find, however, that NPV is not all that widely used; even more surprising is the continued popularity of non-DCF techniques as either primary or secondary evaluation methods.

Over time, studies have found that the use of DCF techniques has become more prevalent among practitioners. Surveys indicate that IRR is the most favored capital budgeting analysis technique. The payback is especially popular as a secondary or supplementary method of analysis. One survey found that about 75 percent of CFOs use NPV, IRR, or both to evaluate capital budgeting projects. Surprisingly, over half of the firms computed the payback period, too, to help evaluate projects.[8] A survey of techniques used by multinational firms confirms these results.[9]

Why might real-world decision makers favor IRR and payback over net present value? One reason could be ignorance. Over time, surveys have shown that the use of DCF techniques has become more prevalent, perhaps because business schools have taught students the virtues of the time value of money and NPV. The apparent sustaining power of IRR and payback techniques, however, suggest the possibility of other reasons. Let's examine several of them.

SAFETY MARGIN

Suppose an analyst tells you that the NPV of Project Big is $100,000 while a competing project, Project Small, has an NPV of $60,000. From our previous discussion, you should select Project Big because of its larger NPV. But what if Project Big requires a $5 million investment while Project Small requires only a $600,000 investment? If the present value estimates of Project Big cash flows are off by only 2 percent, the forecasted positive NPV becomes negative. The present value of Project Small's cash flows can deviate from plan by 10 percent before the project turns into a loser.

Suppose instead that the analyst tells you that Project Big's IRR is 10.5 percent, Small's IRR is 15 percent, and the required return is 10.0 percent. Would you feel confident that Project Big is the more attractive project, despite its higher NPV? Perhaps not, as a small change in cash flows could push Project Big's actual IRR below 10 percent.

This rather contrived example illustrates why managers in the real world may prefer to use relative DCF measures such as the IRR or the PI. IRR and PI give the decision maker an intuitive feel for a project's "safety margin." The decision maker will sleep better at night after deciding to undertake a smaller project with a larger safety margin and reject a large project with a small safety margin. Most managers have seen reality defy forecasts and they know that an inadequate safety margin can make taking big investment risks unwise. Post-project audits can give the firm a better perspective on the accuracy or inaccuracy of its cash flow forecasting techniques. This information can help improve management's perspective on the safety cushion needed for a typical project.

SIZE

The effect of different project sizes may also help explain the lack of popularity of the NPV approach. Suppose Project Tiny costs $100 and Project Huge costs $1,000, while Project Huge has only double the NPV of Project Tiny. Managers need to consider what they can do with the extra $900 (the cost of Project Huge minus the cost of Project Tiny). Project Tiny may enhance shareholder wealth more if these funds can be invested elsewhere in positive NPV projects, so that Project Tiny and other projects, when combined together, produce an NPV that exceeds the NPV of Project Huge.

---

8. John R. Graham and Campbell R. Harvey, "The Theory and Practice of Corporate Finance: Evidence from the Field," *Journal of Financial Economics* (2001), vol. 60, no. 1, 187–243.

9. M. Stanley and S. Block, "A Survey of Multinational Capital Budgeting," *Financial Review*, March 1984, pp. 36–54.

MANAGERIAL FLEXIBILITY AND OPTIONS

The popularity of NPV and DCF techniques also suffers because both are difficult to apply in practice to projects that entail future investment opportunities or options. These techniques do not suit some situations in which managerial flexibility can be valuable. For example, if a project involves a joint venture, an R&D effort, or a move into new markets, management may face several choices once the project is underway. After seeing the initial results, management may decide to continue the project as planned, to expand its scope in the face of success, to decrease the scope of the project, to defer further investment, or to abandon the project completely. These kinds of decisions can help improve a project's potential for upside return while limiting its loss potential. Such flexibility is hard to model in terms of cash flows and discount rates. Payback periods, for example, may be useful as a means of giving managers a general feel for how much time a project needs to at least break even and recover its costs. The technique of real options has been developed to use time value of money techniques in situations where managerial flexibility can add value to a project. An example of real options appears in Chapter 14's Learning Extension.

Conflicts may arise when a firm tries to coordinate strategy analysis and shareholder value analysis. The numbers on the analyst's spreadsheet may fail to justify the actions that the corporate planner strongly feels will lead to competitive advantage and future investment opportunities. However, strategic analysis and financial analysis, if properly applied, are compatible. More often than not, conflicts between these two sets of tools result from inadequate estimates of the cash flows from implementing a strategy. Unless the cash flows that result from a strategic plan are estimated correctly, good projects can be rejected on the basis of inaccurate NPVs or IRRs. The process of correctly estimating a project's cash flows is the subject of Chapter 14.

CONCEPT CHECK

What capital budgeting analysis techniques are the most popular primary and secondary evaluation methods among practitioners?

Why might managers prefer methods such as the IRR, PI, or payback method instead of NPV?

RISK-RELATED CONSIDERATIONS

The degree of risk associated with expected cash inflows may vary substantially among different investments. For example, a decision about whether to replace an existing machine with a new, more efficient machine would not involve substantial cash inflow uncertainty because the firm already has some operating experience with the existing machine. Likewise, expansion in existing product lines allows the firm to base cash flow expectations on past operating results and marketing data. These capital budgeting decisions can be made by discounting cash flows at the firm's cost of capital, or required rate of return, because they are comparable in risk to the firm's other assets.

Expansion projects involving new areas, new product lines, and overseas expansion are usually associated with greater cash inflow uncertainty. To compensate for this greater risk, financial managers often apply risk-adjusted discount rates to these cash flows because of the trade-off between risk and expected return. A higher-risk project needs to be evaluated using a higher required rate of return. To use a financial markets analogy, given the current return offered on safe short-term Treasury bills, investors will not want to invest in risky common stocks unless the expected returns are commensurate with the higher risk of stocks. Similarly, managers should not choose higher-risk capital budgeting projects unless the project's expected returns are in line with the risks.

FINANCE PRINCIPLE

risk-adjusted discount rate (RADR)
adjusts the required rate of return at which the analyst discounts a project's cash flows based on the project's risk

The **risk-adjusted discount rate (RADR)** approach adjusts the required rate of return at which the analyst discounts a project's cash flows. Projects with higher (or lower) risk levels demand higher (or lower) discount rates. A project is expected to enhance shareholder wealth only if its NPV based on a risk-adjusted discount rate is positive.

One way to determine project risk-adjusted discount rates is for the firm's managers to use past experience to create risk classes or categories for different types of capital budgeting projects. Each risk category can be given a generic description to indicate the types of projects it should include and a required rate of return or "hurdle rate" to assign those projects.[10]

An example is shown in Table 13.4, which assigns projects of average risk (or those whose risk is about the same as the firm's overall risk) a discount rate equal to the firm's cost of capital. That is, projects of average risk must earn an average return, as defined by the firm's cost of financing. Projects with below-average risk levels are discounted at a rate below the cost of capital. To be

---

10. Another, more complicated technique, is to use the Capital Asset Pricing Model. A beta is calculated for each project based on analysis of firms in lines of business similar to that of the proposed project. The security market line is used with the beta estimate to approximate the project's required return.

TABLE 13.4
Risk Categories, RMEN Corporation

Below-average risk:

Replacement decisions that require no change, or only a minor change, in technology. No change in plant layout required

Discount rate = Cost of capital − 2%

Average risk:

Replacement decisions involving significant changes in technology or plant layout; all cost-saving decisions; expansions and improvements in the firm's main product lines

Discount rate = Cost of capital

Above-average risk:

Applied research and development; introduction of new products not related to major product lines; expansion of production or marketing efforts into developed economies in Europe and Asia

Discount rate = Cost of capital + 2 percent

High risk:

Expansion of production or marketing efforts into less-developed and emerging economies; introduction of products not related to any of the firm's current product lines

Discount rate = Cost of capital + 5 percent

acceptable, projects of above-average risk must earn premiums over the firm's cost of capital. Subjectivity enters this process as management must decide the number of categories, the description of each risk category, and the required rate of return to assign to each category. Differences of opinion or internal firm politics may lead to controversy in classifying a project. Clearly defined category descriptions can minimize such problems.

For example, let's use the data previously presented for Projects A and B to illustrate the use of risk-adjusted discount rates. Let's assume that Projects A and B are independent projects. Project A involves expansion in an existing product line, whereas Project B is for a new product. The firm's 10 percent cost of capital would be the appropriate discount rate for Project A. Recall that this would result in a net present value of $1,982.

In contrast, a higher discount rate for Project B's cash flows of possibly 12 percent—the 10 percent cost of capital plus a 2 percentage points risk premium—might be judged appropriate by the financial manager. This would result in a net present value of minus $514. Thus, on a risk-adjusted basis, Project A would still be acceptable to the firm, but Project B would be rejected. Making adjustments for risk differences is a difficult but necessary task if the financial manager is to make capital budgeting decisions that will increase the value of the firm.

APPLYING FINANCE TO . . .

INSTITUTIONS AND MARKETS

Financial institutions and markets play an indirect role in the capital budgeting process. The participants comprising the markets use the flow of information from the firm and its competitors, as well as economic and industry conditions, to evaluate firms. Their analysis and reactions are seen in the firm's stock price changes and bond rating changes. In turn, market return expectations are used to determine the discount rate in the net present value calculation. This process will be covered in detail in Chapter 15.

INVESTMENTS

Investors, security analysts, and portfolio managers are continually evaluating a firm's performance. Investment in projects likely to return a positive net present value is a sign of forward-thinking managers who have shareholder interests at heart. Stock price and bond ratings respond favorably to a firm's wealth-maximizing capital budgeting and resource allocation decisions.

FINANCIAL MANAGEMENT

A way to operationalize shareholder wealth maximization is to identify and select projects that are expected to have positive net present values. Managers must properly use capital budgeting evaluation techniques, adjust project evaluation for risk, and seek to invest in projects that enhance shareholder value.

TIM KISH
Vice President and
Chief Financial Officer
Illumina Corp.

BBA, Accounting, Michigan State
University
MBA, University of Minnesota

"My role as Illumina's CFO is to maximize the shareholder value of the firm."

Q: *Please describe Illumina and its products.*

A: Illumina is a biotechnology company that develops next-generation tools for the large-scale analysis of genetic variation and function. The information provided by these tools will enable the development of personalized medicine by correlating genetic variation and function with particular disease states, allowing diseases to be detected earlier and more specifically and permitting better choices of drugs for individual patients.

Q: *What are your responsibilities as chief financial officer?*

A: My role as Illumina's CFO is similar to what it would be in most other publicly held companies: to maximize the shareholder value of the firm. I have three broad job responsibilities: raising capital at reasonable rates to fund growth, spending the right amount of money on corporate activities that contribute to growth, and communicating the company's business strategies and results to the financial markets, so that the company's intrinsic value is reflected in its stock price.

Q: *What skills do you need to accomplish these responsibilities?*

A: Successful financial managers must have strong analytical skills. They must understand trends at strategic, commercial, and operational levels, and they must identify and help resolve financial and operating issues. Excellent interpersonal, communication, and persuasion skills are extremely important, too. CFOs do not control operating departments but must convey their business and financial expertise to motivate the behavior of the managers of those departments. They also need managerial and leadership skills so that they are seen as "influencers" in the organization and can develop a highly capable staff.

Q: *How do you make capital investment decisions at Illumina?*

A: Illumina first establishes an annual target amount for its anticipated capital expenditures based on the company's cash flow and the types of assets required to accomplish our corporate objectives. We then carefully review each new investment proposal to ensure that it is consistent with our strategic or operating plans at that time and that the value provided by the asset will exceed its cost by an acceptable margin. We use discounted cash flow analysis to determine if a project's future benefits exceed its total costs, making adjustments to incorporate risk. We also monitor the project once it is underway to make sure that actual costs and benefits are consistent with the original expectations.

Q: *What are the challenges of capital budgeting?*

A: Understanding how to deal with risk and uncertainty. To properly analyze the future value of a project, we have to make assumptions about alternative uses and project cash flows. In many cases we can estimate the economic assumptions and alternatives within reasonable ranges. In those situations we use special techniques to measure the risk that the project will have unfavorable economics.

SUMMARY

A firm's long-term success depends on its strategy and its competitors' actions. The capital budget allocates funds to different projects, usually long-term, that are primarily used to purchase fixed assets to help a firm build or maintain a competitive advantage.

The capital budgeting process is comprised of five stages: identification, development, selection, implementation, and follow-up.

Since the capital budgeting process involves the analysis of cash flows over time, it is best to examine projects using a selection technique that considers the time value of money. The net present value, internal rate of return, modified rate of return, and profitability index are four such methods. A fifth method, the payback period, measures how quickly a project will pay for itself, but it ignores time value concerns. Of these selection methods, the net present value is

the best, as it measures the dollar amount by which a project will change shareholder wealth.

By focusing solely on numbers, financial analysts of capital budgeting projects can lose sight of the strategic importance behind the analysis. On the other hand, strategists need to be made aware of the need for shareholder value-enhancing projects. As with financial market investments, corporate investments should include risk–expected return considerations. Higher-risk projects should be evaluated using higher discount rates.

Chapter 14 examines how firms can estimate cash flows from a proposed project. This is important, as GIGO—"garbage in, garbage out"—will lead to inaccurate estimates of a project's value and may lead to incorrect decisions.

KEY TERMS

benefit/cost ratio

capital budgeting

cost of capital

development stage

follow-up stage

identification stage

implementation stage

independent projects

internal rate of return (IRR) method

modified internal rate of return (MIRR) method

MOGS

mutually exclusive projects

net present value

NPV profile

payback period method

profitability index (PI)

risk-adjusted discount rate (RADR)

selection stage

SWOT analysis

DISCUSSION QUESTIONS

1. What is meant by capital budgeting? Briefly describe some characteristics of capital budgeting.
2. Why is proper management of fixed assets crucial to the success of a firm?
3. How do "mutually exclusive" and "independent" projects differ?
4. Where do businesses find attractive capital budgeting projects?
5. Briefly describe the five stages in the capital budgeting process.
6. Identify some capital budgeting considerations that are unique to multinational corporations.
7. What is meant by a project's net present value? How is it used for choosing among projects?
8. Identify the internal rate of return method and describe how it is used in making capital budgeting decisions.

9. How does the modified internal rate of return measure improve upon the IRR measure?
10. Describe the term *profitability index,* and explain how it is used to compare projects.
11. Why do the NPV, IRR, and profitability index technique sometimes rank projects differently?
12. Describe the payback period method for making capital budgeting decisions.
13. Why might managers want to use other techniques besides NPV to make capital budgeting decisions?
14. What is a risk-adjusted discount rate? How are risk-adjusted discount rates determined for individual projects?

PROBLEMS

1. Find the NPV and PI of a project that costs $1,500 and returns $800 in year 1 and $850 in year 2. Assume the project's cost of capital is 8 percent.

2. Find the NPV and PI of an annuity that pays $500 per year for eight years and costs $2,500. Assume a discount rate of 6 percent.

3. Find the IRR of a project that returns $17,000 three years from now if it costs $12,000.

4. Find the IRR and MIRR of a project if it has estimated cash flows of $5,500 annually for seven years if its year 0 investment is $25,000.

5. For the following projects, compute NPV, IRR, MIRR, profitability index, and payback. If these projects are mutually exclusive,

which one(s) should be done? If they are independent, which one(s) should be undertaken?

	A	B	C	D
Year 0	−1,000	−1,500	−500	−2,000
Year 1	400	500	100	600
Year 2	400	500	300	800
Year 3	400	700	250	200
Year 4	400	200	200	300
Discount rate	10%	12%	15%	8%

6. The Sanders Electric Company is evaluating two projects for possible inclusion in the firm's capital budget. Project M will require

a $37,000 investment while Project O's investment will be $46,000. After-tax cash inflows are estimated as follows for the two projects:

YEAR	PROJECT M	PROJECT O
1	$12,000	$10,000
2	$12,000	$10,000
3	$12,000	$15,000
4	$12,000	$15,000
5	$ 0	$15,000

   a. Determine the payback period for each project.

   b. Calculate the net present value and profitability index for each project based on a 10 percent cost of capital. Which, if either, of the projects is acceptable?

   c. Determine the internal rate of return and modified internal rate of return for Projects M and O.

7. Project R requires an investment of $45,000 and is expected to produce after-tax cash inflows of $15,000 per year for five years. The cost of capital is 10 percent.

   a. Determine the payback period, the net present value, and the profitability index for Project R. Is the project acceptable?

   b. Now assume that the appropriate risk-adjusted discount rate is 14 percent. Calculate the risk-adjusted net present value. Is the project acceptable after adjusting for its greater risk?

   c. Calculate the internal rate of return.

8. Assume that the financial manager of the Sanders Electric Company in Problem 6 believes that Project M is comparable in risk to the firm's other assets. In contrast, there is greater uncertainty concerning Project O's after-tax cash inflows. Sanders Electric uses a 4 percentage point risk premium for riskier projects. The firm's cost of capital is 10 percent.

   a. Determine the risk-adjusted net present values for Project M and Project O, using risk-adjusted discount rates where appropriate.

   b. Are both projects acceptable investments? Which one would you choose?

9. The BioTek Corporation has a basic cost of capital of 15 percent and is considering investing in either or both of the following projects. Project HiTek will require an investment of $453,000, while Project LoTek's investment will be $276,000. The following after-tax cash flows (including the investment outflows in year zero) are estimated for each project:

YEAR	PROJECT HITEK	PROJECT LOTEK
0	$−453,000	$−276,000
1	$132,000	$74,000
2	$169,500	$83,400
3	$193,000	$121,000
4	$150,700	$54,900
5	$102,000	$101,000
6	0	$29,500
7	0	$18,000

   a. Determine the present value of the cash inflows for each project and then calculate their net present values by subtracting the appropriate dollar amount of capital investment. Which, if either, of the projects is acceptable?

   b. Calculate the internal rates of return for Project HiTek and Project LoTek. Which project would be preferred?

   c. Now assume that BioTek uses risk-adjusted discount rates to adjust for differences in risk among different investment opportunities. BioTek projects are discounted at the firm's cost of capital of 15 percent. A risk premium of 3 percentage points is assigned to LoTek-type projects, while a 6 percentage point risk premium is used for projects similar to HiTek. Determine the risk-adjusted present value of the cash inflows for LoTek and HiTek and calculate their risk-adjusted net present values. Should BioTek invest in either, both, or neither project?

• CHAPTER 14 •

Estimating Project
Cash Flows

Chapter Learning
Objectives

AFTER STUDYING THIS CHAPTER, YOU SHOULD BE ABLE TO:

- Identify which cash flows are relevant and which are not relevant for capital budgeting decision purposes.
- Describe the importance of determining the correct base case from which to estimate project cash flows.
- Explain how a project's statement of cash flows differs from that of the overall firm.
- Calculate a project's periodic cash flows given information on a project's revenue and expense implications for a firm.

Where We Have Been...

In Chapter 13 we learned techniques for using cash flow information to make shareholder wealth-maximizing decisions. In this chapter we'll learn how to estimate the cash flows that are vital to this decision-making process.

Where We Are Going...

Once a firm decides which fixed assets and corporate strategies to pursue, it must finance them. This will be the focus of Chapter 15, "Capital Structure and the Cost of Capital."

How This Chapter
Applies to Me...

Proper analysis is needed to identify relevant cash flows to form the basis for a business decision; otherwise dominant personalities and pet projects are the deciding influence rather than objective analysis. Whether the investment is for a business strategy, building a new warehouse, upgrading information technology systems, or developing human resources, or something else, to evaluate them properly we should quantify the benefits and costs of these choices in terms of cash flows.

A mantra or saying of bankers and other lenders is

Watch cash flow.

Many an investor has said

Happiness is a positive cash flow.

Cash is king—not just for paying the bills but for determining the viability of different business strategies. Cash flow, not accounting profits, pays the bills. An investment analyst will study a firm's financial statements to determine a firm's profitability and ability to generate cash. So must the firm's financial analyst focus on cash flows when studying strategies, competitive responses, and reactions to market events.

As we learned in Chapter 13, a firm's managers must identify and invest in projects that provide positive net present values to maximize shareholder wealth. Good ideas become good strategies when the numbers—cash flow forecasts—show the likelihood of shareholder wealth increasing because of the project. The value of the firm will rise when a capital investment provides the firm with positive cash flows after the amount of the investment has been recovered, the cost of obtaining the necessary financing has been paid, and the timing of the project's cash flows has been taken into consideration.

INFORMATION NEEDS

We reviewed the five-step capital budgeting process in Chapter 13. The second stage of the process is the development stage. In this stage we do analysis and research, and we collect the data necessary to estimate a project's cash flows.

Capital budget decisions require a great deal of analysis. Information generation develops three types of data: internal financial data, external economic and political data, and nonfinancial data. These data are used to forecast financial data that are used to estimate a project's cash flows.

Table 14.1 lists data items that may need to be gathered in the information generation stage, depending on the size and scope of the project. Many economic influences can directly impact the success of a project by affecting sales revenues, costs, exchange rates, and overall project cash flows. Regulatory trends and political environment factors, both in the domestic and foreign economies, may help or hinder the success of proposed projects.

Financial data relevant to the project are developed from sources such as marketing research, production analysis, and economic analysis. Using the firm's research and internal data, analysts estimate the cost of the investment, working capital needs, projected cash flows, and financing costs. If public information is available on competitors' lines of business, this also should be incorporated into the analysis, to help estimate potential cash flows and to determine the effects of the project on the competition.

Nonfinancial information relevant to the cash flow estimation process includes data on the means used to distribute products to consumers, quality and quantity of the labor force, dynamics of technological change in the targeted market, and information from a strategic analysis of competitors. Analysts should assess the strengths and weaknesses of competitors and how they will react if the firm undertakes its own project.

To illustrate, in mid-1998 a strike against General Motors (GM) caused GM management to reexamine its capital budgeting plan. GM had been planning to invest $21 billion in its U.S. plants between 1998 and 2002. The prospect of poor labor relations and inefficient union work rules was giving GM leaders second thoughts about its planned U.S. capital investment.[1]

TABLE 14.1

Examples of Data Needed in Project Analysis

EXTERNAL ECONOMIC AND POLITICAL DATA

Business cycle stages
Inflation trends
Interest rate trends
Exchange rate trends
Freedom of cross-border currency flows
Political stability and environment
Regulations
Taxes

INTERNAL FINANCIAL DATA	NONFINANCIAL DATA
Investment costs (fixed assets and working capital)	Distribution channels
Market studies and estimates of revenues, costs, cash flows	Quantity, quality of labor force in different global areas
Financing costs (cost of capital)	Labor-management relations
Transportation costs	Status of technological change in the industry
Publicly available information on competitor's plans, operating results	Competitive analysis of the industry, potential reaction of competitors

---

1. Micheline Maynard, "GM May Rethink Plant Investments," *USA Today* (June 18, 1998), p. 1B.

GLOBAL DISCUSSION

Political risks affect overseas projects; delays have occurred in developing oil fields in Kazakhstan and Turkmenistan because the projects involve building an oil pipeline across politically unstable or unfriendly countries to get the oil to waterways and to oil tankers.[2] A surprise by competitors who introduced a seven-seat model in the European compact minivan market caused Ford to abandon its plans to introduce a five-seat model, after several years and many millions had been spent on design efforts.[3]

Table 14.1 lists some of the information that firms may use to evaluate capital spending projects. For a specific industry example, oil and gas companies ranked the following items from most important to least important on their effect on capital spending decisions:

1. Forecasts of natural gas prices
2. Forecasts of crude oil prices
3. Forecasted demand for natural gas
4. Forecasted demand for crude oil
5. Availability and cost of outside funds to finance projects
6. Regulatory requirements or constraints on projects
7. Tax considerations

Natural gas prices and demand and crude oil prices and demand determine company revenues. Higher prices (demand) will result in higher sales revenues and, all else being constant, higher profits. Since oil and gas are substitute products, oil producers will be interested in natural gas price and demand trends and vice versa. With large oil companies spending billions of dollars a year on capital spending, the ability to raise external funds is a consideration should additions to retained earnings be insufficient to finance all the attractive projects. Because of environmental concerns, production of oil and gas is heavily regulated. The intricacies of the tax code also affect oil and gas investment decisions. Not only do U.S. income taxes affect these companies, but so do depreciation and oil and gas depletion allowances, tax codes of the different countries in which drilling takes place, tax credits for taxes paid to different jurisdictions, and so on. Firms sometimes plan for growing capital budgets when oil and gas prices are low, in order to take advantage of future price upswings and to trim spending when prices are high, since they don't want to overextend themselves before oversupply occurs and prices fall.[4]

A practical problem when analyzing capital budgeting projects is how properly to estimate project cash flows. We consider how to do this in the following section.

ESTIMATING PROJECT CASH FLOWS

This section reviews methods of developing such cash flow forecasts based on input from engineering, economic, and market analyses, as well as from examination of the firm's competitive advantages.

ISOLATING PROJECT CASH FLOWS

stand-alone principle
analysis focuses on the project's own cash flows, uncontaminated by cash flows from the firm's other activities

To estimate properly the cash flows of a proposed capital budgeting project, the project must be viewed separately from the rest of the firm. This ***stand-alone principle*** ensures that analysts focus on the project's own cash flows, uncontaminated by cash flows from the firm's other activities. We should treat the project as its own mini-firm and create financial statements that are specific to the project.

Relevant Project Cash Flows

The relevant cash flows of a project include its incremental after-tax cash flows, any cannibalization or enhancement effects, and opportunity costs.

2. Hugh Pope, "Scramble for Oil in Central Asia Hits Roadblocks," *Wall Street Journal* (March 13, 1998), p. A12.

3. Scott Miller, "Ford Scraps Plans for Compact Minivan, Years in Planning, in Cost-Cutting Effort," *Wall Street Journal* (February 14, 2000), p. A18.

4. Thaddeus Herrick, "Big Oil Firms Trim Exploration Spending," *Wall Street Journal* (September 26, 2000), p. A2; Anne Reifenberg, "Big Oil Opens Capital-Spending Spigot for Overseas Projects Amid Price Slump," *Wall Street Journal* (January 3, 1996), p. A2.

Incremental After-Tax Cash Flows

incremental cash flows
represent the difference between the firm's after-tax cash flows with the project and the firm's after-tax cash flows without the project

base case
firm's after-tax cash flows without the project

ETHICAL ISSUES

The stand-alone principle requires the analyst to examine the future after-tax cash flows that occur only as a result of the project. These are the project's **incremental cash flows**. The cash flows are incremental as they represent the difference between the firm's after-tax cash flows with the project and its **base case**, or the after-tax cash flows without the project. To identify this difference, analysts must try to identify all cash flows that will rise or fall as a consequence of pursuing the future project. This includes any expected changes in revenues, expenses, and depreciation, as well as investments in fixed assets and net working capital.

Managerial estimates need to be checked and verified as part of the capital budget review process; ethical lapses, such as inflating revenues and decreasing expenses to make a project look more attractive, may result in harm to the firm and reductions in shareholder wealth.

Estimating incremental after-tax cash flows for a project requires a more thorough analysis than determining the expected change in cash flows from the firm's current condition. If future strategic moves by competitors are expected to damage or eliminate a firm's competitive advantage, the firm's base case cash flow should reflect this situation. A project's incremental cash flows would then reflect expected changes from this declining trend.

For example, a firm such as Intel must consider competitors' responses when it invests in R&D to develop new computer chips. Intel's base case must include the impact on its sales if it does not develop the next generation of computer chips first. In the fast-moving technology market, being second to market could mean billions of lost sales.

Intel has poured billions into factory improvement and expansion projects to increase its production capacity in order to maintain and increase its competitive advantage over other chip manufacturers and to sustain cash flow growth. Greater capacity means greater economies of scale, lower costs, and better competitive position in the computer chip market. With forecasted chip demand experiencing double-digit growth rates each year, Intel needs additional capacity just to maintain its current market share of the chip market.

Cannibalization or Enhancement

cannibalization
a project robs cash flow from the firm's existing lines of business

Cannibalization occurs when a project robs cash flow from the firm's existing lines of business. When a soft-drink firm is thinking about introducing a new flavor or a new diet product, the firm should consider how the new offering's incremental cash flows will erode the sales and cash flows of the firm's other products. Corporate strategists reportedly considered how the introduction of Pepsi One, a new low-calorie cola soft drink product, would affect sales of Diet Pepsi and Pepsi-Cola.[5] Similarly, Intel engineers and strategists agonized for months before deciding they needed to design a new computer chip to advance the technology of its highly successful ×86 chip (the one that powers Pentium-class computers).[6]

enhancement
increase in the cash flows of the firm's other products that occur because of a new project

Enhancement is less common than cannibalization; it reflects an increase in the cash flows of the firm's other products that occur because of a new project. For example, adding a delicatessen to a grocery store may increase cash flows more than the deli sales alone if new deli customers also purchase grocery items.

Opportunity Costs

opportunity cost
cost of passing up the next best alternative

From economics, we know that an **opportunity cost** is the cost of passing up the next best alternative. For example, the opportunity cost of a building is its market value. By deciding to continue to own it, the firm is forgoing the cash it could receive from selling it. Economics teaches the TINSTAAFL principle: "There is no such thing as a free lunch." Capital budgeting analysis frequently applies this principle to existing assets.

If a firm is thinking about placing a new manufacturing plant in a building it already owns, the firm cannot assume that the building is free and assign it to the project at zero cost. The project's cash flow estimates should include the market value of the building as a cost of investing since this represents cash flows the firm cannot receive from selling the building.

Irrelevant Cash Flows

Now that we've examined some factors that influence cash flow estimates, let's look at some factors that should be excluded.

5. Nikhil Deogun, "Pepsi Takes Aim at Coke with New One-Calorie Drink," *Wall Street Journal* (October 5, 1998), p. B4.
6. David P. Hamilton, "Circuit Break: Gambling It Can Move Beyond PC, Intel Offers a New Microprocessor," *Wall Street Journal* (May 29, 2001), pp. A1, A8.

Sunk Costs

A **sunk cost** is a project-related expense that does not depend on whether or not the project is undertaken. For example, assume that a firm commissioned and paid for a feasibility study for a project last year. The funds for the study are already committed and spent. The study's cost is not an incremental cash flow as it is not affected by the firm's future decision to either pursue or abandon the project. Therefore, the cost must be excluded from the project's cash flow estimates.

Financing Costs

It may seem important to account for financing cash flows such as interest and loan repayments, but there is a very good reason for excluding them from cash flow estimates. Capital budgeting analysis techniques explicitly consider the costs of financing a project when the analysis discounts project cash flows. As we shall discuss more fully in Chapter 15, a project's minimum required rate of return, or cost of capital, incorporates a project's financing costs.

CONCEPT CHECK

What is the stand-alone principle?

What three categories of cash flows are relevant to measure for capital budgeting purposes?

What categories of cash flows are irrelevant for capital budgeting analysis?

APPROACHES TO ESTIMATING PROJECT CASH FLOWS

As an initial step of the financial analysis of a capital budgeting proposal, we should first construct year-by-year projected balance sheets and income statements for the project. Analysis of these forecasted statements tells us what the expected cash flows from the project will be. Changes over time in the project's working capital requirements or investment needs will represent cash inflows or outflows from the project. Similarly, the net income and noncash expenses from the project are part of the project's periodic cash flows, too.

As discussed in Chapter 11, one of the financial statements that must be issued by public firms is the statement of cash flows. In this section we use the format of the statement of cash flows to identify the periodic cash flows of a capital budgeting project.

Recall that a firm's statement of cash flows has three sections. The first, cash flows from operations, reports on cash generated by the firm's day-to-day manufacturing and marketing activities. The second section, cash flows from investments, usually involves data for investments in subsidiaries or the firm's plant and equipment. The third section lists the firm's financing cash flows, including sales and purchases of debt, as well as dividend payments.

Using this format for a capital budgeting project, cash flows from operations summarize the sources of a project's operating cash flows. Cash flows from investing activities report a firm's fixed asset investments in the capital budgeting project. As explained previously, cash flows from financing activities are excluded from a project's cash flow analysis since their impact is measured in the discount rate or cost of capital used to discount a project's cash flow.

Table 14.2 summarizes the similarities between company and project cash flow statements. The following sections explore these relationships in more detail.

TABLE 14.2
Firm Versus Project Statement of Cash Flows

FIRM VERSUS PROJECT STATEMENT OF CASH FLOWS	
THE FIRM'S CASH FLOW STATEMENT	**A PROJECT'S CASH FLOW STATEMENT**
Cash Flow from Operations	**Cash Flow from Operations**
Net Income	Net Income
+ Depreciation	+ Depreciation
+ Current sources	+ Current sources
− Current uses	− Current uses
Cash Flow from Investment Activities	**Cash Flow from Investment Activities**
− Change in gross fixed assets	− Funds invested in the project's fixed assets
− Change in investments	
Cash Flow from Financing Activities	**Cash Flow from Financing Activities**
− Dividends paid	Not applicable
+ Net new bond issues	
+ Net new stock issues	

TABLE 14.3

A Project Income Statement

Project sales	(generally a cash inflow)
− Project costs	(generally a cash outflow)
− Depreciation	(a noncash expense)
EBIT = EBT	(earnings before interest and taxes, which also equals earnings before taxes as financing costs are ignored in cash flow analysis)
− Taxes	(a cash outflow)
= Net income	

CASH FLOW FROM OPERATIONS

Cash flow from operations is, quite simply, a measure of the cash entering and leaving the firm as a result of the firm's business. Cash flow from operations equals net income plus depreciation plus funds from sources arising from changes in current asset and liability accounts minus uses from changes in current asset and liability accounts for a given period of time. A period-by-period project income statement can estimate the net income from a project, as in Table 14.3.

All sales revenues may not be cash inflows. For example, if customers buy the firm's products with credit, some of the increase in sales revenue may increase accounts receivable rather than cash. Similarly, not all costs reflect cash outflows. Such is the case if the firm buys supplies or raw materials on credit. Some expenses may be paid in cash, and others may create changes in accounts payable. For reasons such as these, to compute cash flow we need to include an adjustment—the change in net working capital—to reflect such situations.

Depreciation is a noncash expense. Accounting rules allow us to compute taxable income by deducting depreciation expense from revenues, although no cash leaves the firm. Since it is a noncash expense we add it back—after we compute net income—when we compute operating cash flows.

Thus, a project's operating cash flows are computed as:

Cash flow from operations = Net income + Depreciation − Change in net working capital (14.1)

which, using the project income statement in Table 14.3, is the same as:

$$\text{Operating cash flow} = (\text{Sales} - \text{Costs} - \text{Depreciation}) - \text{Taxes} + \text{Depreciation} \atop - \text{Change in net working capital} \quad (14.2)$$

If the firm's tax rate is denoted by t, the firm's taxes are:

$$\text{Taxes} = t\,(\text{pretax income}) = t\,(\text{Sales} - \text{Costs} - \text{Depreciation}) \quad (14.3)$$

Combining Equations 14.2 and 14.3, we have:

$$\text{Operating cash flow} = (\text{Sales} - \text{Costs} - \text{Depreciation}) - t\,(\text{Sales} - \text{Costs} - \text{Depreciation}) \atop + \text{Depreciation} - \text{Change in net working capital}$$

By simplifying, we have Equation 14.3:

$$(\text{Sales} - \text{Costs} - \text{Depreciation})\,(1 - t) + \text{Depreciation} - \text{Change in net working capital} \quad (14.4)$$

As we demonstrate in some examples toward the end of this chapter, virtually any problem that requires estimating operating cash flows can be solved using Equation 14.4.[7]

---

7. We advocate knowing how to use this one equation in estimating operating cash flows. Other texts propose a variety of formulas, each based on the known information from a specific type of capital budgeting project (revenue-enhancing, cost-saving, etc.) It is easy to show how the following equations are identical to Equation 14.4. We believe that knowing one all-encompassing method is better than keeping track of the different variations. Variations of Equation 14.4. include:

OCF = Net Income + Depreciation − Change in NWC

OCF = Earnings Before Taxes − Taxes + Depreciation − Changes in NWC

OCF = (Sales − Costs) − (tax rate) • (Sales − Costs − Depreciation) − Changes in NWC

OCF = Sales − Costs − Taxes − Change in NWC

OCF = (Sales − Costs)(1 − tax rate) + (tax rate) • Depreciation − Change in NWC

In most cases of capital budgeting analysis, operating cash flow is calculated in part by using the traditional net working capital measure of current assets minus current liabilities. This occurs since typically a project's cash flows are immediately returned to the firm. The project's balance sheet cash account always will be zero. Thus, current sources and current uses can be summarized in the period-by-period change in a project's net working capital.[8]

A confusing point to some is the matter of why we subtract the change in net working capital when computing operating cash flow. To illustrate the reasoning for this, suppose current assets are $700 and current liabilities are $400; this means net working capital is $300. Cash comes into the firm if customers pay $200 of their accounts receivable. This reduces accounts receivable and current assets to $500 ($700 − $200 payment) and net working capital to $100 ($500 current assets − $400 current liabilities). Thus, net working capital decreases when there is a source or inflow of operating cash to the firm. When we *subtract* this *negative* change in net working capital it becomes a *positive* addition to operating cash flow:

$$-(-\$200 \text{ change in net working capital}) = +\$200 \text{ change in operating cash flow}$$

Conversely, suppose with $700 in current assets and $400 in current liabilities (and a net working capital of $700 − $400 = $300) we pay $150 in bills that we owe to suppliers. Cash flows out of the firm and accounts payable fall by $150 as do current liabilities. The new value of current liabilities is $250 ($400 − $150), and the new value for net working capital is $700 − $250 = $450. Net working capital has risen +$150 from $300 to $450. Thus, net working capital increases when there is a use or outflow of operating cash from the firm. When we subtract this increase in net working capital, it becomes a *reduction* to operating cash flow:

$$-(+\$150 \text{ change in net working capital}) = -\$150 \text{ change in operating cash flow}$$

CONCEPT CHECK

How does the format of a firm's statement of cash flows correspond to that of a project's cash flow estimates?

Does an increase in net working capital increase or decrease operating cash flow? Explain.

When developing a project income statement, why does EBIT equal EBT?

CASH FLOW FROM INVESTMENT ACTIVITIES

Cash flow from investment activities will record the firm's period-by-period fixed asset investments in the capital project, namely the plant and equipment necessary to pursue the project. Cash flow from investments is usually negative at the beginning of a project as the firm spends cash to acquire, build, modify, or replace assets. The cash flow from investments may be positive at the end of a project if it sells assets for salvage value.

CASH FLOW FROM FINANCING ACTIVITIES

Capital budgeting analysis excludes cash flows from financing activities. As discussed previously, relevant after-tax financing costs are incorporated into the discount rate used to discount estimated cash flows to the present.

AN EXAMPLE

Now let's look at an example. Suppose you are considering opening a campus ice cream shop. Your initial investment in depreciating assets will be $10,000, and your initial investment in net working capital (NWC)—which will include such inventory items as cones, ice cream, and toppings—will be $3,500. You forecast no future changes in net working capital. You will depreciate fixed assets on a straight-line basis over four years.[9]

The shop's forecasted net income is $0, $1,500, $2,500, and $4,000 over each of the next four years. At the end of four years, you expect to graduate with a bachelor's degree and some entrepreneurial work experience and will sell your enterprise to another student. You hope to be able to sell your business for $12,000. For simplicity, ignore any tax implications from the sale. What are the cash flows from this project?

It is sometimes easier to estimate cash flows if you construct a table, or use a spreadsheet, such as the following one. It summarizes, by year and by cash flow category, the project's incremental after-tax cash flows. For example, at the current time (year 0), the only expected cash

---

8. An exception to this rule is overseas projects. For internal financing purposes or because of currency restraints, some cash may remain with the overseas subsidiary. In this case, an overseas project's cash flows should include only the cash that is returned to the parent firm.

9. Current income tax laws specify allowable methods for depreciating business assets. Accelerated depreciation methods are popular, but they add an unnecessary layer of complexity to the discussion. Straight-line depreciation is a permitted method so we assume it in most of our discussions.

flows are a $10,000 investment in fixed assets and a $3,500 outflow for net working capital. Depreciating the $10,000 in fixed assets on a straight-line basis over four years gives a yearly depreciation expense of $10,000/4 or $2,500.

Year 1 net income is expected to be $0; along with the $2,500 depreciation expense and no change in net working capital, Year 1's operating cash flow is estimated at $2,500. Since you anticipate no investing cash flows, Year 1's total cash flow is estimated to be $2,500.

The cash flows for Years 2, 3, and 4 are computed similarly. In Year 4, the operating cash flows are supplemented by an investing cash flow of $12,000 from the sale of the business. Thus Year 4's total cash flows sum to $18,500: $4,000 from net income, $2,500 from depreciation, and $12,000 from the sale of the business.

| | OPERATING CASH FLOWS | | | INVESTING CASH FLOWS | |
YEAR	NET INCOME +	DEPRECIATION −	CHANGE IN NWC	CHANGE IN FIXED ASSETS =	TOTAL CASH FLOW
0	$0	$0	$−3,500	$−10,000	$−13,500
1	0	2,500	0	0	2,500
2	1,500	2,500	0	0	4,000
3	2,500	2,500	0	0	5,000
4	4,000	2,500	0	12,000	18,500

If 12 percent is your required rate of return, the net present value of this endeavor is $7,236.90, so your personal wealth should rise from opening the ice cream shop.

Depreciation plays an important role in determining operating cash flow. As discussed about, it is a noncash expense. By deducting depreciation expense, a firm lowers its pretax income (earnings before taxes or EBT), its tax bill, and its net income—and it increases its operating cash flow! A short example will show how this deduction *lowers* net income but *raises* operating cash flow.

DEPRECIATION AS A TAX SHIELD

Suppose JohnnyJim Products has $1,000 in sales and expenses for wages and supplies of $300. Let's see how a depreciation expense of $100 affects its profitability and its net income. Table 14.4 shows two income statements: one without depreciation expense and one with depreciation expense. To simplify the example, we'll assume the change in net working capital is zero and that JohnnyJim's tax rate is 40 percent.

Using Equation 14.1, JohnnyJim's operating cash flow with depreciation is:

Cash flow from operations = Net income + Depreciation − Change in net working capital

= $360   + $100   − $0 = $460

and its operating cash flow without depreciation is:

Cash flow from operations = Net income + Depreciation − Change in net working capital

= $420   + $0   − $0 = $420

Although depreciation lowers its net income, JohnnyJim's operating cash flow is $40 higher with depreciation expense than without it. The reason the operating cash flow with depreciation is $40 higher is because JohnnyJim's tax bill is $40 lower. By lowering earnings before taxes,

TABLE 14.4

JohnnyJim Products Income Statements (With and Without Depreciation Expense)

	WITH DEPRECIATION EXPENSE	WITHOUT DEPRECIATION EXPENSE
Sales	$1000	$1000
− Costs	−300	−300
− Depreciation	−100	0
EBT	$600	$700
− Taxes (40%)	240	280
Net Income	$360	$420

depreciation tax shield
tax reduction due to
depreciation of fixed assets;
equals the amount of the
depreciation expense
multiplied by the firm's
tax rate

CONCEPT CHECK

How does depreciation affect a project's cash flows?

What is meant by the term depreciation tax shield?

noncash depreciation expense lowers a cash expense—taxes—by $40. This $40 reduction leads to an operating cash flow that is $40 higher than the case of no depreciation.

The $40 savings in taxes arises from a combination of the tax rate and the depreciation expense. With a 40 percent tax rate, a depreciation expense of $100 increases expenses—and lowers taxes—by (0.40)($100) or $40.

The tax rate multiplied by the depreciation expense—(t)(Depreciation)—is called the **depreciation tax shield**. It represents the tax savings the firm receives from its noncash depreciation expense. With a 40 percent tax rate, a depreciation expense of $100 reduces a firm's tax bill by $40.

Despite political claims that tax incentives are needed to boost capital spending and investment, a healthy economy can do more for capital investment than the most generous politicians. The United States enjoyed a capital spending boom in the 1990s despite not having favorable tax law changes, investment tax credits, or changes in depreciation rules. A good economy with sustained growth and low inflation is the best combination for corporate investment. As one corporate executive said, "We're not sitting on our hands waiting for government tax policy to change. If you want to protect and extend your market position, you invest the money. We would do that no matter what."

Economists do favor incentives, such as a capital gains tax cut, that would increase savings in the economy. Greater savings, all else being constant, would mean lower interest rates, higher stock prices, and lower financing costs for firms buying plant and equipment.[10]

PROJECT STAGES AND CASH FLOW ESTIMATION

How are cash flow estimates developed? In this section we develop a practical overview of how an analyst develops the data to estimate cash flows.

INITIAL OUTLAY

The first cash flow estimate is the initial investment in the project. Engineering estimates may be available for projects that require designing or modifying equipment and buildings. Engineers will examine preliminary designs or architectural sketches and estimate the quantities of various materials needed. Estimates of purchases, transportation costs, and construction expenses can be developed based on current market prices.

Another means of estimating the acquisition or construction cost of a project is to solicit bids from various construction or equipment manufacturers based upon a preliminary set of design specifications. An approximate cost can be determined through discussions with bidding firms. If the firm is large enough that it has an in-house engineering or real estate acquisition staff, this expertise can also be tapped to estimate relevant costs.

The expense of developing cost estimates is a sunk cost. That money is spent and gone whether or not the proposed project is accepted; it should not be included in the project's cash flow estimates. However, the initial outlay estimate must consider opportunity costs if the project will use property or equipment presently owned by the firm.

CONCEPT CHECK

How can a firm estimate the initial investing cash flows for a project?

When might a project's initial outlays include changes in net working capital?

The investment cost estimate may have to be adjusted if the project involves replacing an asset with another, presumably newer and more cost-efficient, model. If the old asset is going to be sold, the investment outlay must be reduced by the after-tax proceeds from the sale of the old asset. (Some of the specifics of adjusting for salvage value are discussed further into this section.)

Finally, even though a project's initial outlay may directly involve property and equipment (investing cash flows), it may also have implications for net working capital (operating cash flows). For example, if a project affects the firm's production process, inventory levels may change. New raw materials needs may affect accounts payable. These kinds of expected changes in net working capital must be included as part of the initial outlay.

CASH FLOWS DURING THE PROJECT'S OPERATING LIFE

Operating cash flows can be estimated using Equation 14.4. The practical difficulty, of course, is determining the amounts for sales, costs, depreciation, taxes, and net working capital changes to enter into the calculations.

10. Joseph Spiers, "The Most Important Economic Event of the Decade," *Fortune* (April 3, 1995), pp. 33–40.

A project with the main purpose of reducing costs should have a presumed impact on sales of zero. Expected cost savings can be derived from engineering estimates or production management techniques. Suppliers can often estimate the potential cost savings from new machines or processes, but these sales claims may not be wholly trustworthy; to verify any claims, the careful manager runs independent tests and trial runs, preferably at the plant that will house the new project.

One asset often replaces another in a cost-saving project. This can involve a difference in depreciation schedules between the old and new asset (not to mention salvage value differences), which the analyst must incorporate into the analysis. More will be said in this chapter about this point when we review an example.

Revenue-enhancing or revenue-sustaining projects build or protect a firm's competitive advantage or extend its market penetration. Market researchers can provide detailed data about new products or features and the costs to develop them to help the financial analyst construct cash flow estimates. Such research may include sales forecasts or information on price, quantity, and quality trends in the market segment. If the project concerns one of the firm's current products, the production staff can often provide data to estimate the cost implications of greater sales. If the project involves a new product offering, engineers or the production staff should be able to provide production cost estimates. Depreciation expense can be estimated from the estimated initial investment outlay for the property or equipment needed for the project.

Net working capital may be expected to change over the course of the project's life. Operating cash flow estimates must reflect these changes in net working capital.

CONCEPT CHECK

How can operating cash flow estimates be developed for cost-saving projects?

How can operating cash flow estimates be developed for revenue-expanding projects?

SALVAGE VALUE AND NWC RECOVERY AT PROJECT TERMINATION

If the project is expected to have a definite life span, the analysis must consider the salvage value of the project's assets. Any increases in net working capital in the course of a project are generally assumed to be recovered by the firm and converted to cash at the project's end.

Any property or equipment that is expected to be sold, either for use by someone else or for scrap, will generate inflows. The cash flow for the sale will have to be adjusted to account for tax implications if the asset's selling price differs from its book value.

Book value (BV) represents an asset's original cost less accumulated depreciation. If at the end of a project the selling price of an asset equals its book value, there is no need for tax adjustments: the after-tax cash flow equals the selling price.

INTERNET ACTIVITY

Some firms sell old equipment on auction sites, such as http://www.ebay.com, in order to recover final or "salvage" cash flows at the end of a project's term. A more business-oriented site is http://www.salvagesale.com.

If the asset's selling price exceeds its book value, then in effect the asset was depreciated too quickly on the firm's books. The amount of the recovered depreciation (Price − BV) is taxed at the firm's marginal tax rate for ordinary income. Thus, the tax owed the government is t(Price − BV). The total after-tax proceeds will be Price − t(Price − BV)—that is, the selling price less the tax obligation.

If the selling price is less than the asset's book value, the firm suffers a loss. This loss reflects failure to depreciate the asset's book value quickly enough. The firm's taxable income is reduced by the amount of the loss, and taxes will be reduced by t(Price − BV).

Note that if t(Price − BV) is positive, the firm owes taxes, reducing the after-tax proceeds of the asset sale; if t(Price − BV) is negative, the firm reduces its tax bill, in essence increasing the after-tax proceeds of the sale. When t(Price − BV) is zero, the transaction causes no tax adjustment to be made. Thus, a general relationship for the after-tax salvage value is:

$$\text{After-tax salvage value} = \text{Price} - t(\text{Price} - \text{BV}) \tag{14.5}$$

Let's look at an example. Assume that an asset originally cost $100, had an expected life of ten years, and was depreciated on a straight-line basis. Seven years later, the firm must determine the after-tax cash flow from selling the asset if the selling price is (a) $50, (b) $30, or (c) $15. Assume the marginal tax rate for ordinary income is 34 percent.

The first thing we need to do is determine the asset's book value; then Equation 14.5 can be used to compute cash flows for three situations. With an original cost of $100 and straight-line depreciation over ten years, its yearly depreciation expense is $100/10 = $10. As seven years have passed, accumulated depreciation is now $70 (7 × $10/year), so the asset's book value is $100 minus $70 or $30.

If the asset's sale price is $50, the firm has recovered some past depreciation and it must reduce the salvage value cash flow by the resulting tax liability. The after-tax salvage value is Price − t(Price − BV) = $50 − 0.34($50 − $30) = $43.20.

If the asset's sale price is $30, this price equals the book value. According to Equation 14.5, the after-tax salvage value is $30: Price − t(Price − BV) = $30 − 0.34($30 − $30) = $30.

If the asset's sale price is $15, the firm suffers a loss as the price is below book value. This means the salvage value cash flow will rise above $15 by the amount of the subsequent tax savings. The after-tax cash flow equals Price − t(Price − BV) = $15 − 0.34($15 − $30) = $20.10,

By their nature, after-tax salvage values are difficult to estimate as both the salvage value and expected future tax rate are uncertain. As a practical matter, if the project termination is many years in the future, the present value of the salvage proceeds will be small and inconsequential to the analysis. If necessary, however, the analyst can try to develop a salvage value forecast in two ways. First, one could try to tap the expertise of those involved in secondary market uses of the asset. Second, one could try to forecast future scrap material prices for the asset. Typically, the after-tax salvage cash flow is calculated using the firm's current tax rate as an estimate for the future tax rate.

The problems of estimating values in the distant future become worse when the project involves a major strategic investment that the firm expects to maintain over a long period of time. In such a situation, the firm may estimate annual cash flows for a number of years (say, ten years) and then attempt to estimate the project's value as a going concern at the end of this time horizon. One method the firm can use to estimate the project's going-concern value is the constant dividend growth model discussed in Chapter 8:

$$\text{Price}_{\text{horizon}} = \frac{\text{Dividend}_{\text{horizon}+1}}{r - g} \qquad (14.6)$$

The salvage value of the project is its going-concern value at the end of the time horizon; the dividend is its expected operating cash flow one year past the horizon. The required rate of return, *r*, is the project's required return. The expected growth rate, *g*, is the analyst's estimate of the constant growth rate for operating cash flows after the horizon.

KEEPING MANAGERS HONEST

The fifth stage of the capital budgeting process we reviewed in Chapter 13—the follow-up—is sometimes called the *audit* or *control phase*. In this stage a firm's financial analyst tracks the spending and results of the firm's current capital budgeting projects.

Many firms review spending during the implementation stage of approved projects. Quarterly reports are often required in which the manager overseeing the project summarizes spending to date, compares it to budgeted amounts, and explains differences between the two. Such oversight during the implementation stage allows top managers to foresee cost overruns. Some firms require projects that are expected to exceed their budgets by a certain dollar amount or percentage to file new appropriation requests to secure the additional funds. Implementation audits allow managers to learn about potential trouble areas so future proposals can account for them in their initial analysis; implementation audits also give top management information on which managers generally provide the best estimates of project costs.

In addition to implementation control, firms should compare forecasted cash flows to actual performance after the project has been completed. This provides data regarding the accuracy over time of cash flow forecasts; this will permit the firm to discover what went right with the project, what went wrong, and why. Audits force management to discover and justify any major deviations of actual performance from forecasted performance. Specific reasons for deviations from budget are needed for the experience to be helpful to all involved.

An effective control system will record the names of the persons who make the estimates so top management can evaluate business units and managers on the accuracy of their estimates. Such a system pinpoints personal responsibility. If, for example, a department head estimates that a proposed expenditure would allow the department to reduce personnel by 10 percent, the department head can be questioned if the proposed cuts do not come to pass. Such a system will control intrafirm agency problems by helping to help reduce "padding,"—that is, overestimating the benefits of favorite or convenient project proposals. This increases the incentives for department heads to manage in ways that help the firm achieve its goals.

The control or postaudit phase sometimes requires the firm to consider terminating or abandoning an approved project. The possibility of abandoning an investment prior to the end of its

CONCEPT CHECK

Why are audits important to project implementation?

What useful information can be discovered by comparing forecasted and actual cash flows?

Which type of cash flow—initial investments, operating flows, or salvage values—are the hardest to estimate?

estimated useful or economic life expands the options available to management and reduces the risk associated with a decision that turns out to be a poor one. This form of contingency planning gives decision makers a second chance when dealing with the economic and political uncertainties of the future.

In a survey, researchers found that three-fourths of responding Fortune 500 firms audited their cash flow estimates.[11] Nearly all the firms that performed audits compared initial investment outlay estimates with actual costs; all evaluated operating cash flow estimates; two-thirds audited salvage value estimates.

About two-thirds of firms that performed audits claimed that actual initial investment outlay estimates usually were within 10 percent of forecasts. Only 43 percent of firms that performed audits could make the same claim with respect to operating cash flows. Over 30 percent of the firms confessed that operating cash flow estimates differed from actual performance by 16 percent or more.[12]

To be successful, the cash flow estimation process requires a commitment by the corporation and its top policy-setting managers; this commitment includes the type of management information system the firm uses to support the estimation process. Past experience in estimating cash flows, requiring cash flow estimates for all projects, and maintaining systematic approaches to cash flow estimation appear to help firms achieve success in accurately forecasting cash flows.

APPLICATIONS

In this section we review practical applications of cash flow estimation for a revenue expanding project, for a cost saving project, and in setting a bid price.

CASH FLOW ESTIMATION FOR A REVENUE EXPANDING PROJECT

Let's examine a firm's decision to build an addition to a present plant in response to a forecast showing rising sales. For simplicity, we'll assume construction for the addition occurs in Year 0. The plant has an expected useful life of five years and can be sold for $1 million at the end of the project. We need to determine the initial outlay, the incremental after-tax operating cash flow, and the salvage value for the project. We will assume the project's minimum required return is 10 percent and its tax rate is 40 percent.

Initial Outlay

The upfront expenses include those that are depreciable for tax purposes and those that are not depreciable. Depreciable outlays include construction labor, materials, preparation and transportation of materials, and equipment in the plant addition. For this example, we'll assume depreciable outlays are $4.5 million in Year 0. Other expenses include costs for additional workers to operate the new plant and expenses associated with hiring, relocating, and training the workers. As with other expenses, this cost is deducted from the project's Year 0 taxable income. The plant managers estimate that these costs will total $0.4 million after tax.

As seen in Table 14.5, the initial after-tax outlays are $4.9 million in Year 0. Of this cost, $4.5 million is depreciable, while the remaining $0.4 million is expensed in Year 0.

TABLE 14.5
Initial Outlays for Plant Addition Project ($ Millions)

	t = 0
Depreciable Outlays	− $4.5
Expensed Cash Outlays, after tax	− 0.4
	− $4.9

11. R. Pohlman, E. Santiago, and F. Markel, "Cash Flow Estimation Practices at Large Firms," *Financial Management*, Summer 1988, pp. 71–78.

12. In Chapter 13, we argued that safety margin concerns may lead managers to prefer selection methods such as IRR and PI over NPV. With error rates such as these, it is easy to see why safety margins would concern analysts and decision makers.

TABLE 14.6

Project Income Statement, for Years 1 through 5 ($ Millions)

Sales	$3.000
− Costs	− 0.635
− Depreciation	− 0.900
EBT	$1.465
− Taxes (40%)	− 0.586
Net income	$0.879

Operating Cash Flow Estimates Using Equation 14.4, spreadsheet format:

TAX RATE: 40%	YEAR 1	YEARS 2-4	YEAR 5
Sales	$3.000	$3.000	$3.000
− Cost	−$0.635	−$0.635	−$0.635
− Depreciation	−$0.900	−$0.900	−$0.900
EBT	$1.465	$1.465	$1.465
× (1 − t)	$0.879	$0.879	$0.879
+ Depreciation	$0.900	$0.900	$0.900
− Change NWC	−$0.100	$0.000	$0.100
Operating CF	$1.679	$1.779	$1.879

Calculating the project's operating cash flow through direct application of Equation 14.4:

(Sales − Costs − Depreciation) (1 − t) + Depreciation − Change in net working capital

= ($3.000 − 0.635 − $0.900)(1 − 0.40) + $0.900 − $0.100 = $1.679 for Year 1

With no further changes in net working capital, the operating cash flow for Years 2 through 4 is

OCF = ($3.000 − 0.635 − $0.900)(1 − 0.40) + $0.900 − $0 = $1.779.

And with the net working capital recovery, operating cash flow in year 5 is:

OCF = ($3.000 − 0.635 − $0.900)(1 − 0.40) + $0.900 − (−$0.1) = $1.879

Incremental After-Tax Operating Cash Flows

For simplicity, assume that the incremental sales and costs arising from the plant addition project will be constant over the five-year life of the addition. Sales are expected to rise by $3.0 million and costs will increase by $0.635 million. Using straight-line depreciation, the depreciable outlays of $4.5 million will increase the firm's depreciation expense by $4.5 million/5 years or $0.90 million per year.

The expected increase in sales volume and production will require more working capital. Net working capital is expected to rise by $0.1 million in Year 1 as the plant goes online. In Year 5, the plant addition will cease operations and the firm will recover the $.1 million.[13]

Table 14.6 presents this data in income statement format and calculates the operating cash flows using Equation 14.4.

Salvage Value

In Year 5, the project will generate a cash inflow as the firm receives the after-tax salvage value of the plant addition and the resale value of equipment from the addition. These items will be fully depreciated by the end of Year 5—that is, their book values will be zero. Their collective market value was given as $1.0 million, so the after-tax salvage value cash flow is:

Price − t(Price − BV) = $1.0 million − 0.4($1.0 million − 0) = $0.600 million

Is the Project Beneficial to Shareholders?

Table 14.7 summarizes the expansion project's incremental cash flows: the net initial outlay, after-tax operating cash flows, an d salvage value determine if the project will increase shareholder wealth. Table 14.7 uses this information to compute the present values of the cash flows, using a 10 percent required return, for the NPV calculation. Since the project's NPV is positive, the plant expansion project should be undertaken; shareholders will benefit from it.

---

13. The funds will be recovered as inventory is sold, accounts receivable are collected, and raw material accounts payable are paid in full.

TABLE 14.7

Cash Flow Summary and NPV Calculation (Millions of Dollars)

YEAR	INITIAL OUTLAY	OPERATING CASH FLOWS	SALVAGE VALUE	TOTAL INCREMENTAL CASH FLOWS	PVIF (10%)	PV OF CASH FLOWS
0	$-4.9	$ 0.000	$ 0.0	$-4.90	1.0000	$-4.90
1	0.0	1.679	0.0	1.679	0.9091	1.53
2	0.0	1.779	0.0	1.779	0.8264	1.47
3	0.0	1.779	0.0	1.779	0.7513	1.34
4	0.0	1.779	0.0	1.779	0.6830	1.22
5	0.0	1.879	0.6	2.479	0.6209	1.54
						NPV = $ 2.20

CASH FLOW ESTIMATION FOR A COST-SAVING PROJECT

For a cost-saving project, the incremental cash flows are usually the difference between the cash flows of two mutually exclusive investments: (1) keeping the existing capital equipment and (2) purchasing new equipment. Suppose that a firm is considering a project to replace an older computer system with a more cost-efficient model. The decision depends on the difference between the cash flows that arise from the initial investment in the new equipment, the operating cash flows, and the salvage values.

Initial Investment Outlay

The total cost of the investment consists of the total outlay required to purchase and prepare the new computer for operation less the after-tax salvage value of the older model. For simplicity, let's assume that the expected useful life of the new computer, three years, equals the expected remaining useful life of the old system.

Table 14.8 lists the depreciable cash outlays. Added to the purchase price of $7,700 are transportation, hookup, and modification costs, which result in a total depreciable cost of $12,000. Table 14.8 also shows the after-tax salvage cash flow of the old system of $3,600. This brings the initial total cash outlay for this project to $12,000 minus $3,600, or $8,400.

Incremental After-Tax Operating Cash Flows

For a cost-saving project, it is safe to assume the incremental sale revenues are zero, so if the firm's revenues are $500,000 they will not change after the project is done. Suppose the estimated costs of operating the old system and the new system are as follows:

	t = 1	t = 2	t = 3
Old computer system	$3,000	$3,500	$4,000
New computer system	$500	$2,000	$3,000

TABLE 14.8

Total Outlays

CASH OUTFLOWS ON THE NEW COMPUTER	
Purchase price	$7,700
Transportation	1,800
Hookup cost	200
Office modification	2,300
Total depreciable outlays	$12,000

CASH INFLOWS FROM DISPOSAL OF OLD COMPUTER	
After-tax salvage value	$3,600

INITIAL INVESTMENT OUTLAY	
Cash outflows for new computer	$12,000
Cash inflow from disposal of old computer	− 3,600
Initial investment outlay	$ 8,400

The incremental depreciation charge is the difference between depreciation charges on the new computer and those on the old one. Using straight-line depreciation, the new computer's depreciation will be its cost of $12,000 divided by three years or $4,000 per year. The future depreciation of the old computer depends on the depreciation method the firm selected at the time of purchase. Assuming that the firm acquired the old computer two years earlier at a cost of $10,000 expecting a life of five years, its straight-line annual depreciation charges are $2,000 per year.

We will assume that replacing one computer system with another will have no impact on the firm's current assets and current liabilities. Thus, changes in net working capital will be zero.

Using a 40 percent tax rate and the preceding information on sales, costs, depreciation, and net working capital, Table 14.9 applies Equation 14.4 to estimate operating cash flows.

In Table 14.9 we apply Equation 14.4 to each year. For example, for the first year we list the operating cash flow components for the old system: costs of $3,000, depreciation of $2,000, and no change in net working capital. We do the same for the new system: costs of $500 and depreciation of $4,000 and no change in net working capital. The incremental operating cash flow of replacing computer systems in the first year is $2,300. Similarly, we find the incremental operating cash flows for year 2 are $1,700 and year 3 are $1,400.

TABLE 14.9
Incremental After-Tax Operating Cash Flows

YEAR 1 TAX RATE: 40%	OLD SYSTEM	NEW SYSTEM	INCREMENTAL CASH FLOWS (NEW − OLD)
Sales	$500,000	$500,000	$0
− Cost	−$3,000	−$500	$2,500
− Depreciation	−$2,000	−$4,000	−$2,000
EBT	$495,000	$495,500	$500
× (1 − t)	$297,000	$297,300	$300
+ Depreciation	$2,000	$4,000	$2,000
− Change NWC	$0	$0	$0
Operating CF	$299,000	$301,300	$2,300

YEAR 2 TAX RATE: 40%	OLD SYSTEM	NEW SYSTEM	INCREMENTAL CASH FLOWS (NEW − OLD)
Sales	$500,000	$500,000	$0
Cost	−$3,500	−$2,000	$1,500
Depreciation	−$2,000	−$4,000	−$2,000
EBT	$494,500	$494,000	−$500
× (1 − t)	$296,700	$296,400	−$300
+ Depreciation	$2,000	$4,000	$2,000
− Change NWC	$0	$0	$0
Operating CF	$298,700	$300,400	$1,700

YEAR 3 TAX RATE: 40%	OLD SYSTEM	NEW SYSTEM	INCREMENTAL CASH FLOWS (NEW − OLD)
Sales	$500,000	$500,000	$0
Cost	−$4,000	−$3,000	$1,000
Depreciation	−$2,000	−$4,000	−$2,000
EBT	$494,000	$493,000	−$1,000
× (1 − t)	$296,400	$295,800	−$600
+ Depreciation	$2,000	$4,000	$2,000
− Change NWC	$0	$0	$0
Operating CF	$298,400	$299,800	$1,400
Summary:	t = 1	t = 2	t = 3
Incremental after-tax OCF	$2,300	$1,700	$1,400

TABLE 14.10
Cash Flow Summary and NPV Calculation

YEAR	INITIAL OUTLAY	OPERATING CASH FLOWS	SALVAGE VALUE	TOTAL INCREMENTAL CASH FLOWS	PVIF (10%)	PV OF CASH FLOWS
0	−$8,400	$0	$0	$8,400	1.0000	−$8,400
1	0	2,300	0	2,300	0.9091	2,091
2	0	1,700	0	1,700	0.8264	1,405
3	0	1,400	600	2,000	0.7513	1,503
					NPV =	−$3,401

Terminal Cash Flows

At the end of the third year, we will assume that the new computer will have a market value of $1,000, whereas the old computer, if kept, will be worthless. Since the old computer system will have a book value and a market value of $0, its after-tax salvage value is $0.

The new computer's book value will be zero after three years. Its after-tax salvage value will be the selling price of $1,000 less the tax obligation of $400 [0.4($1,000 − $0)] or $600. The incremental salvage value cash flow will be $600 (new computer) − $0 (old computer) or $600.

Is the Project Beneficial to Shareholders?

Table 14.10 summarizes the incremental cash flows: the net initial outlay, the after-tax operating cash flows, and the salvage value. Assuming a 10 percent minimum required rate of return, the net present value is −$3,401. The computer replacement project is unacceptable because the negative NPV indicates that the project would decrease shareholder wealth by $3,401.

SETTING A BID PRICE

Often a corporation or government that needs a fixed asset or service will solicit bids for its manufacture. The firm's request for proposals (RFP) will list the desired attributes and specifications of the item. Firms will respond to the RFP with the hope of winning the solicitor's approval by verifying that it can produce the item at the lowest cost. The firm that makes the lowest bid will most likely win the contract.

Before placing a bid in response to an RFP, a firm's financial analysts must first determine the price that will allow the firm to cover its costs and earn a sufficient return so its shareholders aren't harmed. Putting it another way, the bidding firm must determine the minimum price at which the project will have a zero NPV. Any bid below this price would result in a negative NPV and hurt the firm's shareholders. To determine the minimum bid price, the analyst must work backward to develop cash flow estimates consistent with a zero NPV and then convert the cash flow estimates into a unit price.

Suppose you are the chief financial officer for You-go, Inc., a manufacturer of high-quality, motorized bicycles. An RFP from a large city is seeking bids for motorized bicycles for use by police officers on patrol. Your firm's motorized bicycles will require special modifications to make them suitable for police work. Among other requirements, the RFP notes that 100 bicycles will have to be delivered each year for the next three years. Assume You-go's required return on such projects is 20 percent and that the firm's tax rate is 40 percent.

Initial Investment Outlay

To increase production to meet the city's request and to properly modify the cycles for police use, the firm's plant and equipment will need to be expanded at a cost of $120,000 this year. The cost is about $10,000, after tax, to hire and train new workers. Net working capital needs are expected to increase $40,000 this year, as well. The firm will recover this increase in net working capital in the third year as it fills the production requirement.

This brings the total investment to $170,000, including $120,000 in depreciable assets. These assets will be straight-line depreciated over the three years of the project's life; thus, depreciation expense is expected to be $120,000/3 or $40,000 per year.

If the firm wins the bid, labor costs are expected to rise by $50,000 per year. Raw materials expenses will rise by $20,000 per year. Thus, expenses will increase by $70,000 annually as a result of this project.

TABLE 14.11
Cash Flow Summary

YEAR	INITIAL OUTLAY	OPERATING CASH FLOWS	SALVAGE VALUE	TOTAL INCREMENTAL CASH FLOWS
0	−$170,000	$0	$0	−$170,000
1	0	X	0	X
2	0	X	0	X
3	0	X + $40,000	$12,000	X + $52,000

Salvage Value

The salvage value of the specialized equipment needed for this project is expected to be only $20,000 after three years. Since the assets will be fully depreciated to a book value of $0 at the end of three years, the after-tax proceeds from their sale will be $20,000 − 0.4($20,000 − $0) = $12,000.

Estimating Yearly Operating Cash Flows

Table 14.11 summarizes the information that is known so far. The initial outlay totals $170,000 in Year 0 and salvage value is $12,000 in Year 3. The operating cash flows are unknown now, but they will increase by $40,000 in Year 3 due to the recovery of net working capital.

To make this information easier to work with, let's simplify the information presented in the table. Let's add the *present value* of the Year 3 cash inflow of $52,000 to the initial cash outflow of $170,000. This gives a present value of the known cash flows of:

$$-\$170{,}000 + \$52{,}000(1/1.20)^3 = -\$139{,}907.41$$

This removes the effects of the salvage value and the recovery of net working capital from the project's annual cash flows. The cash flows in Years 1 through 3 are now a three-year annuity, with a net Year 0 investment of $139,907.41 in present value terms:

YEAR	CASH FLOW
0	−$139,907.41
1	X
2	X
3	X

The net present value of this series of cash flows is the present value of the three year $X annuity less $139,907.41. To determine the minimum operating cash flow that will leave shareholder wealth unharmed, we set NPV to zero and solve for X:

$$\text{NPV} = 0 = (\$X)(\text{PVIFA for 3 years, 20\%}) - \$139{,}907.41$$

Using interest factor table or a financial calculator, the PVIFA for three years and 20 percent is 2.1065; solving for $X, we find the operating cash flow annuity is $66,417.58.

Using this minimum operating cash flow, we can work backward to determine the minimum sales revenue consistent with a zero-NPV bid. Recall the project's annual costs are $70,000, its annual depreciation expense is $40,000, and the firm's tax rate is 40 percent. We can ignore the change in net working capital as we've already incorporated that in the analysis in Table 14.11 and the cash flow estimate of $66,417.58. Using Equation 14.4 and simplifying we have:

$$\text{Operating cash flow} = (\text{Sales} - \text{Costs} - \text{Depreciation})(1 - t) + \text{Depreciation}$$
$$- \text{Change in net working capital}$$

$$\$66{,}417.58 = (\text{Sales} - \$70{,}000 - \$40{,}000)(1 - 0.40) + \$40{,}000 - 0$$
$$\$66{,}417.58 = (\text{Sales} - \$110{,}000)(0.60) + \$40{,}000$$
$$\$66{,}417.58 = (\text{Sales})(0.60) - \$66{,}000 + \$40{,}000$$
$$\$66{,}417.58 = (\text{Sales})(0.60) - \$26{,}000$$
$$\$92{,}417.58 = (\text{Sales})(0.60)$$

CODY PRESS
Managing Director of Public Finance—
West Coast

Citigroup Global Market, Inc.
BS, Dartmouth College
MBA (Finance),
University of Pennsylvania

*"Common sense and judgement
are very important."*

Q: *What is the purpose of public finance?*

A: The short answer is that we help municipalities and other nonprofit entities solve their financing problems.

Q: *Who are these entities?*

A: Basically you can use the rule that anyone who is tax-exempt and needs to raise money could be a client. Municipalities, museums, counties, states, nonprofit hospitals, and so on. In many cases we will be hired to secure financing for a specific project, such as a bridge or a toll road.

Q: *Let's take a simple example. How would a city finance a bridge?*

A: There could be several options, but in many cases we will help the city issue bonds to generate the money necessary to build the bridge. The city borrows the money by selling bonds and repays it over time, quite possibly through a toll or fee for using the bridge. This is generally a better option than raising taxes because it means that the people who use the bridge pay for it throughout its useful life.

Q: *What role do you play in this transaction?*

A: We work with the municipality on two levels. We work with the elected officials on the higher-level decisions, helping them understand what their options are for raising the funds they need to implement their plans. Then we work with their staff people on the more technical aspects of the bond issue, how it will be structured and so forth. When the bonds are sold, we keep a percentage of the proceeds as our compensation.

Q: *Would you describe your function as sales or management?*

A: It's a combination of both. Several years ago there were twenty people in my group, so I spent more time on management then. Now I have eleven people, so I spend more time on sales. I spend at least two days a week out of the office, meeting mostly with our existing clients.

Q: *Is this a competitive field?*

A: It's very competitive. The size of the market is much smaller now than it was just a few years ago, so we all compete for the available deals.

Q: *What skills do you rely on most?*

A: Common sense and judgment are very important. There are always decisions about where to focus your time and resources, and good judgment is essential in making the right choices. Honesty is an important quality, too.

Q: *What are the career options in this field?*

A: That's an interesting issue. Because public finance is so specialized, it's not easy to move to another field. You really have to be very interested in working with government clients for the long haul, because you may not have a lot of other options.

Solving for Sales to find the minimum total sales revenue, we see it equals $154,029.30 per year. Dividing total annual sales by 100 cycles gives us the minimum bid per cycle, $1,540.29. This unit price represents the lowest price the firm can bid without adversely affecting shareholder wealth.

We see from these applications that to approach a cash flow estimation problem we should first estimate initial cash outlay, including property and equipment expenditures, necessary changes in net working capital, and other start-up expenses, such as hiring new workers. Second, we estimate the periodic operating cash flows using Equation 14.4, making sure to include any changes in net working capital over the lifetime of the project. Third, we estimate after-tax salvage value cash flows. Once we have these three estimates, we can use the Chapter 14 techniques to estimate NPV, IRR, MIRR, profitability index, or payback period.

APPLYING FINANCE TO . . .

INSTITUTIONS AND MARKETS

Cash flow estimates are important to lenders and investors. If a firm needs to raise capital to undertake a capital budgeting project, it may need to share project data and estimated cash flows with lenders or investment bankers. The minimum required rate of return on the project is determined, as we will learn in Chapter 15, by financial institutions and other participants in the capital markets.

INVESTMENTS

Investors, security analysts, and portfolio managers are continually evaluating a firm's performance. If they see a firm investing in questionable projects, they may take action to intervene with the firm's board or to sell their investments. Indicators of questionable projects are those that are not related to the firm's current lines of business or for which the market estimates poor cash flow returns.

FINANCIAL MANAGEMENT

Financial analysts and managers must work with a variety of nonfinancial people—marketers, salespeople, engineers, and such—to try to develop sound estimates of a project's cash flows. It does not help the firm if poor analysis, poor teamwork, or poor communication lead to incorrect decisions.

SUMMARY

Estimating cash flows is a difficult part of evaluating capital budgeting projects. Projected earnings, expenses, and fixed asset investments must be converted into cash flows by using the methods discussed in this chapter.

By focusing solely on numbers, financial analysts of capital budgeting projects can lose sight of the strategic importance behind the analysis. On the other hand, strategists need to be made aware of the need for shareholder value–enhancing projects. Analysts must be sure the financial analysis includes the correct base case, includes cannibalization and competitor retaliation effects, and includes proper risk adjustments. Depreciation expense acts as a tax shield, because it reduces a project's tax bill and works to increase a project's after-tax cash flows.

The process of estimating cash flows for a capital budgeting project must be based upon sound economic principles and thorough competitive analysis. Once managers identify a project that may enhance the firm's future competitive position, various sources—engineers, sales staffs, marketing analyses, competitive analyses, among others—are used to develop estimates of incremental cash flows. The actual calculation of periodic cash flows borrows the format of the statement of cash flows, as discussed in Chapter 11. The main difference is that capital budgeting cash flow analysis ignores specific financing costs. Such costs are taken into account when the cash flows are discounted at the project's required return.

Cash flows must be estimated for three project stages. The first stage covers the initial investment outlay, which may include upfront depreciable and nondepreciable expenses. The second stage covers the remaining time horizon of the project; typically the relevant cash flows are the components of the project's operating expense and income streams. The third stage is the termination of the project; cash flows relevant to this stage include the after-tax salvage value of assets and the recovery of net working capital.

Chapter 15 examines how firms can estimate their cost of capital. This is important, as the cost of financing the firm will be used as the discount rate for evaluating average-risk capital budgeting projects.

KEY TERMS

base case

cannibalization

depreciation tax shield

enhancement

incremental cash flow

opportunity cost

stand-alone principle

sunk cost

DISCUSSION QUESTIONS

1. What kinds of financial data are needed to conduct project analysis?

2. What kinds of nonfinancial information are needed to conduct project analysis?

3. How is the *stand-alone principle* applied when evaluating whether to invest in projects?

4. What are the three types of relevant cash flows to be considered in analyzing a project?

5. What types of cash flows are considered irrelevant when analyzing a project?

6. "Our firm owns property around Chicago that would be an ideal location for the new warehouse. Since we already own the land there isn't any cash flow needed to purchase it." Do you agree or disagree with this statement? Explain

7. "Our bank will finance the product expansion project with a loan interest rate of 10 percent. Make sure the project's cash flow estimates include this interest expense." Do you agree or disagree? Explain.

8. Label each of the following as a cannibalization effect, enhancement effect, or neither. Explain your answers.

   a. A computer manufacturer seeks to produce a high-quality engineering work station, thinking that consumers will believe the firm's standard PC products will also be of higher quality.

   b. An airline offers taxicab service to and from the airport.

   c. A gas station adds service bays and a small convenience store.

   d. A mainframe computer manufacturer begins to sell personal computers.

   e. A snack food manufacturer starts marketing a new line of fat-free snacks.

   f. A firm seeks to export its products to foreign countries.

9. Classify each of the following as a sunk cost, an opportunity cost, or neither.

   a. The firm has spent $1 million thus far to develop the next-generation robotic arm; it is now examining whether the project should continue.

   b. A piece of ground owned by the firm can be used as the site for a new facility.

   c. It is anticipated that another $200,000 of R&D spending will be needed to work out the bugs of a new software package.

10. How is a project's cash flow statement similar to that of a firm? How is it different?

11. Why is depreciation considered to be a *tax shield?*

12. Why is the change in net working capital included in operating cash flow estimates?

13. What information sources are used to develop estimates for the following components of a project?

   a. Initial outlays

   b. Operating life

   c. Salvage value

14. Why might there be tax implications when an asset is sold at the termination of a capital budgeting project?

15. What is a way to keep managers accountable for their capital budgeting forecasts and estimates?

16. Explain the process for estimating cash flows for a revenue-enhancing project.

17. Explain the process for estimating cash flows for a cost-saving project.

18. Explain the process for estimating a bid price by estimating zero-NPV cash flow needs.

PROBLEMS

1. AA Auto Parts Company has a corporate tax rate of 34 percent and depreciation of $19,180. Compute its depreciation tax shield.

2. Suppose the Quick Towing Company purchases a new tow truck. The old truck had a book value of $1,000 and was sold for $1,420. If Quick Towing is in the 34 percent marginal tax bracket, what is the tax liability on the sale of the truck? What is the after-tax cash flow on the sale?

3. A project is estimated to generate sales revenue of $10 million with expenses of $5 million. No change in net working capital is expected. Marginal profits will be taxed at a 35 percent rate. If the project's operating cash flow is $1 million, what is the project's depreciation expense? Its net income?

4. Hammond's Fish Market just purchased a $30,000 forklift truck. It has a five-year useful life. The firm's tax rate is 25 percent.

   a. If the forklift is straight-line depreciated, what is the firm's tax savings from depreciation?

   b. What will be its book value at the end of year 3?

   c. Suppose the forklift can be sold for $10,000 at the end of three years. What is its after-tax salvage value?

5. Compute operating cash flows for the following:

   a. A project that is expected to have sales of $10,000, expenses of $5,000, depreciation of $200, an investment of $50 in net working capital and a 20 percent tax rate.

   b. A project has the simplified project income statement below. In addition, assume that the project requires a $75 investment in net working capital.

Sales	$925.00
− Costs	−315.00
− Depreciation	−100.00
EBIT = EBT	510.00
− Taxes (at 34%)	−174.40
Net Income	336.60

   c. For a capital budgeting proposal, assume this year's cash sales are forecast to be $220, cash expenses $130, and depreciation $80. Assume the firm is in the 30 percent tax bracket.

6. A machine can be purchased for $10,500, including transportation charges, but installation costs will require $1,500 more. The machine

is expected to last four years and produce annual cash revenues of $6,000. Annual cash operating expenses are expected to be $2,000, with depreciation of $3,000 per year. The firm has a 30 percent tax rate. Determine the relevant after-tax cash flows and prepare a cash flow schedule.

7. Use the information in Problem 6 to do the following:

   a. Calculate the payback period for the machine.

   b. If the project's cost of capital is 10 percent, would you recommend buying the machine?

   c. Estimate the internal rate of return for the machine.

8. The Brassy Fin Pet Shop is considering an expansion. Construction will cost $90,000 and will be depreciated to zero, using straight-line depreciation, over five years. Earnings before depreciation are expected to be $20,000 in each of the next five years. The firm's tax rate is 34 percent.

   a. What are the project's cash flows?

   b. Should the project be undertaken if the firm's cost of capital is 11 percent?

9. The following is a simplified project annual income statement for Ma & Pa Incorporated for each year of an eight-year project. Its upfront cost is $2,000. Its cost of capital is 12 percent.

Sales	$925.00
Less cash expenses	310.00
Less depreciation	250.00
Earnings before taxes	$365.00
Less taxes (at 35%)	127.75
Net income	$237.25

   a. Compute the project's after-tax cash flow.

   b. Compute and interpret the project's NPV, IRR, profitability index, and payback period.

10. Lisowski Laptops is examining the possibility of manufacturing and selling a notebook computer that is compatible with both PCs and Macintosh systems and that can receive television signals. Its estimated selling price is $2,500. Variable costs (supplies and labor) will equal $1,500 per unit, and fixed costs per year would approximate $200,000. Up-front investments in plant and equipment will total $270,000, which will be straight-line depreciated over three years. The initial working capital investment will be $100,000 and will rise proportionately with sales. Bill, the CEO, forecasts sales of the laptop will be 50,000 units the first year, 60,000 units the second, and 45,000 units the third year, at which time product life cycles would require closing down production of the model. At that time, the market value of the project's assets will be about $70,000. LL's tax rate is 40 percent and its required return on projects such as this one is 17 percent. Should they offer the new computer?

11. Preston Industries' current sales volume is $100 million a year. Preston is examining the advantages of EDI (electronic data interchange). The technology will allow Preston to electronically communicate with suppliers and customers and to send and receive purchase orders, invoices, and cash. It will save Preston money by lowering costs in the purchasing, customer service, accounts payable, and accounting departments. Initial estimates are that savings will equal $100,000 a year. Investment in EDI technology will include $500,000 in depreciable expenses and $100,000 in nondepreciable expenses. Assets will be depreciated on a straight-line basis for four years. Implementation of EDI is expected to reduce Preston's net working capital by $200,000. Because of changing technology, Preston's president,

Carol, wants to estimate the effect of switching to EDI on shareholder wealth over a four-year time horizon, assuming that advances in technology will make the equipment worthless at the end of four years. At a 30 percent tax rate and 13 percent required rate of return, should Preston Industries switch to EDI?

12. Bart and Morticia, owners of the prestigious Gomez-Addams Office Towers, are concerned about high heating and cooling costs and client complaints of temperature variation within the building. They commissioned an engineering study by Frasco-Prew Associates to identify the cause of the problems and suggest corrective action. Frasco-Prew's basic recommendation is that a new HVAC (heating, ventilation, and air conditioning) system, featuring electronic climate control, be installed in the office towers. Over the next four years, the engineers estimate a new system will reduce heating and cooling costs by $125,000 a year. Cost of the new system will be $500,000 and can be depreciated over four years. Using a 25 percent tax rate and a 14 percent required return, should Bart and Morticia change the HVAC system? Use a four-year time horizon.

13. Casey's Baseball Bats is planning to begin exporting its product to the Asian market. The company estimates up-front expenses of $1 million this year (Year 0) and $3 million next year (Year 1). Operating cash flows in Years 2, 3, and 4 will be (in dollars) $100,000, $200,000, and $400,000, respectively. After Year 4, Casey's expects operating cash flows to grow at 10 percent a year indefinitely. If 15 percent is the required return on the project, what is its NPV?

14. The No-Shoplift Security Company is interested in bidding on a contract to provide a new security system for a large department store chain. The new security system would be phased into ten stores per year for five years. No-Shoplift can purchase the hardware for $50,000 per installation. The labor and material cost per installation is approximately $15,000. In addition, No-Shoplift will need to purchase $100,000 in new equipment for the installation, which will be depreciated to zero using the straight-line method over five years. This equipment will be sold in five years for $25,000. Finally, an investment of $50,000 in net working capital will be needed. Assume that the relevant tax rate is 34 percent. If the No-Shoplift Security Company requires a 10 percent return on its investments, what price should it bid?

15. **Challenge Problem** Annual savings from Project X include a reduction of ten clerical employees with annual salaries of $15,000 each, $8,000 from reduced production delays, $12,000 from lost sales due to inventory stock-outs, and $3,000 in reduced utility costs.

    Project X costs $250,000 and will be depreciated over a five-year period using straight-line depreciation. Incremental expenses of the system include two new operators with annual salaries of $40,000 each and operating expenses of $12,000 per year. The firm's tax rate is 34 percent.

    a. Find Project X's initial cash outlay.

    b. Find the project's operating cash flows over the five-year period.

    c. If the project's required return is 12 percent, should it be implemented?

16. **Challenge Problem** You are considering becoming a franchisee with the Kopy-Kopy Copy and Pizza Delivery Service. For $50,000 they give you training and exclusive territorial rights.

    Equipment can be purchased through the home office for an additional $50,000, all of which will be straight-line depreciated. The home office estimates your territory can generate $100,000 in sales volume in the first year and that sales will grow 10 percent in each of the following four years, at which time you plan on selling the business for $50,000, after tax. From reading the company's brochures and talking to several other franchisees, you believe that costs, excluding depreciation, are about 60 percent of sales. You also know that the home office requires you to pay a 15 percent royalty on your gross sales revenue.

Using a 30 percent tax rate and a 10 percent return requirement, how will this opportunity affect your personal wealth?

17. **Challenge Problem** The ice cream shop described in this chapter's "Approaches to Estimating Project Cash Flows" section has been a smash success. Customers from the next college town are pleading with you to open one closer to them. Based on your operating experience and knowledge of local real estate, you believe that opening a new ice cream shop will require an investment of $20,000 in fixed assets and $3,000 in working capital. Fixed assets will be straight-line depreciated over five years. Preliminary market research indicates that sales revenue in the first year should be about $50,000 and that variable costs, excluding depreciation, will be about 80 percent of sales. To be on the safe side, you assume sales revenue will not change over the next five years. At the end of five years, you estimate you can sell your business, after tax, for $25,000. Using a 28 percent tax rate and a 12 percent required return, should you expand?

18. **Challenge Problem** Sensitivity analysis involves changing one variable at a time in a capital budgeting situation and seeing how NPV changes. Perform sensitivity analysis on each of the following variables from Problem 17 to determine its effect on NPV:

a. Sales can be 10 percent higher or lower than expected each year.

b. Expenses may be 10 percent higher or lower than expected each year.

c. Your initial investment in fixed assets and working capital may be 50 percent higher than originally estimated.

LEARNING EXTENSION 14

Strategic Analysis and Cash Flow Estimation

Proper analysis of a capital spending project must tie together the details of the firm's competitive and strategic analyses and the cash flow estimates of the proposed project. In the end, strategic analysis, marketing analysis, and financial analysis should agree. If they seem to conflict, which may happen when corporate planners strongly favor a project with a negative NPV for "strategic" reasons, everyone involved in the decision must work together to discover the cause of the conflict. Some common problem areas follow.[14]

DETERMINING THE CORRECT BASE CASE

Incremental cash flows were defined as the anticipated changes in cash flow from a base case. The firm's base case projection must assess what the firm's market share and cash flows would be if no new projects are implemented. The firm's planners must recognize that if nothing is done, customers may start buying competitors' products in response to the marketing, new-product development, and/or quality efforts of the competitors. The base case estimate should reflect these potential declines in cash flow.

OVERVALUING STRATEGY

Projects may look more attractive than they really are if the analyst ignores cannibalization effects. The project analysis must also consider the effects of competitor retaliation; should you introduce a new product or innovation, your competition will take action to try to blunt the effectiveness of your strategy.

In addition, analysts need to be careful not to lose sight of the assumptions behind the estimates. Too many analysts start changing a few numbers and playing "What if?" games with their computer spreadsheets to get a positive project NPV. The spreadsheet output may soon lose any relationship with valid economic assumptions.

DEFINE PROJECT BOUNDARIES AT THE CORPORATE LEVEL

Estimates of revenues and costs should take the corporate view, rather than the business unit view. A project may look attractive to business unit managers because, as either an intended or unintended consequence, it shifts revenues or costs from one part of the company to another. Such projects will most likely fail to enhance shareholder value when total corporate incremental cash flows are properly estimated.

---

14. This discussion is based upon P. Barwise, P. Marsh, and R. Wensley, "Must Finance and Strategy Clash?" *Harvard Business Review* (September/October 1989), pp. 85–90.

REAL OPTIONS

Real option analysis is a new type of financial analysis that incorporates strategic thinking better than traditional discounted cash flow analysis does. Real option analysis evaluates investments by recognizing the sources of flexibility that can enhance a project's value.

Traditional discounted cash flow analysis develops a single set of cash flow estimates, applies a market-determined discount rate, and computes a net present value. To be sure, different sets of cash flow estimates can be used via scenario or simulation analysis to give managers a "feel" for potential variability of cash flows and NPVs, but the project's risk, if evaluated correctly, should be reflected in the project's discount rate.

Real options analysis incorporates managerial flexibility into static NPV analysis and can incorporate five different considerations. The first option is waiting to invest; rather than beginning a project this year, there may be value in waiting until next year in order to better evaluate changing technology, input prices, or conditions in their own product market.

The second is a *learning option*. Successful introduction of a product may lead managers to expand a product or innovation more quickly than initially proposed to take advantage of consumer interest and to gain production experience, lock up distribution channels, and shut competitors out of the market.

If success doesn't occur as hoped, there is a third option: the *exit* or *abandonment* option. If initial results from a multistage project are poor, managers can save the firm's value by reducing the size of the initial project or by pulling the plug and stopping the project completely to stop further value-diminishing investments.

A fourth option is *growth opportunities*. Investing may create as-yet-unforeseen opportunities that would not be available if the firm does not do the project. Investing now in a new technology may create options for future growth, market expansion, technology development, and other activities to enhance shareholder value.

A fifth option is *flexibility*. Flexibility adds value; a work disruption in a plant in one country can allow the firm to shift production to another plant elsewhere. Furnaces that can operate with different fuel sources allow the owner to switch to whatever fuel source is less expensive.

Sophisticated real options analysis attempts to evaluate future opportunities represented by these five options. An example illustrates the value of the exit or abandonment option in a simple binomial, or two-choice, framework. In the binomial model, a decision is made to invest and two possible outcomes will occur, usually "success" and "failure." Each outcome occurs with a known probability; for example, we may expect a 45 percent chance of success and a 55 percent chance of failure. We can find the expected cash flow by computing $probability_{success} \times CF_{success} + probability_{failure} \times CF_{failure}$. Let's look at an example and see how real options analysis considers managerial flexibility.[15]

Suppose a mining firm is considering operating a copper mine for an additional year but to do so will need to make additional investments of $1 million in equipment. The mine is almost depleted, and the price of copper is subject to large market fluctuations. Analysts estimate, based upon past movements in copper prices, a 45 percent chance that copper prices will be high and that the cash inflow from operating the mine for an additional year will be $20 million. There is a 55 percent chance of low copper prices, in which case the cash flow is a negative $27 million. The situation is shown in Figure LE14.1.

The expected cash inflow is:

$$E \text{ (inflow)} = .45 \text{ ($20 million)} + .55 \text{ (}-\text{$27 million)} = -\text{$5.85 million}$$

If the risk-adjusted discount rate for the mining project is 15 percent, the NPV of operating the mine for an additional year is:

$$NPV = -\text{$1 million} + (-\text{$5.85 million})/(1 + .15) = -\text{$6.1 million}$$

With a negative NPV, the decision is to not invest in another year's operations and to shut down the mine immediately. However, consider the role of management if it invested in the

---

15. This example is taken from Kathleen T. Hevert, "Real Options Primer: A Practical Synthesis of Concepts and Valuation Approaches," *Journal of Applied Corporate Finance* (Summer 2001), 14(2), pp. 25–40. The entire issue of this journal is comprised of articles illustrating the use of real options analysis. See also Edward Teach, "Will Real Options Take Root?" *CFO* (July 2003), pp. 73–76.

FIGURE LE14.1
Payoff Diagram for Copper Mining Example

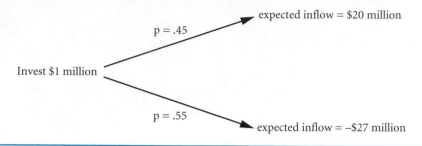

operation but then walked away from it if copper prices remained low. In other words, management would invest the $1 million in new equipment and invest in fixed extraction costs, but if the variable costs of processing the ore do not exceed the market price of copper, the company will abandon the project. In this case, the losses would be restricted to the cost of extraction, not the combined loss of extracting and processing the ore. If the fixed cost of mining the ore is $10 million, we have the situation in Figure LE14.2. There is a 45 percent chance of high copper prices with a subsequent cash inflow of $20 million and a 55 percent chance of low copper prices, in which case the mine would be abandoned, no refining of the mined ore would occur, and the cash flow would be −$10 million, the fixed cost of mining the ore.

With the abandonment option, the expected cash inflow is:

$$E\,(\text{inflow}) = .45\,(\$20\text{ million}) + .55\,(-\$10\text{ million}) = \$3.5\text{ million}$$

Using the risk-adjusted discount rate of 15 percent, the NPV of operating the mine for an additional year is:

$$\text{NPV} = -\$1\text{ million} + (\$3.5\text{ million})/(1 + .15) = \$2.0\text{ million}.$$

Thus we see the value of the real option to abandon the project; having this option raised the NPV from −$6.1 million to $2 million. Real options have value, and real option analysis is a new method to incorporate managerial flexibility into financial analysis.

FIGURE LE14.2
Payoff Diagram for Copper Mining Example with Abandonment

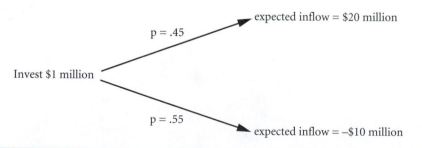

• CHAPTER 15 •

Capital Structure and the Cost of Capital

Chapter Learning Objectives

AFTER STUDYING THIS CHAPTER, YOU SHOULD BE ABLE TO:

- Explain how capital structure affects a firm's capital budgeting discount rate.
- Explain how a firm can determine its cost of debt financing and cost of equity financing.
- Explain how a firm can estimate its cost of capital.
- Explain how a firm's growth potential, dividend policy, and capital structure are related.
- Explain how EBIT/eps analysis can assist management in choosing a capital structure.
- Describe how a firm's business risk and operating leverage may affect its capital structure.
- Describe how a firm's degree of financial leverage and degree of combined leverage can be computed, and explain how to interpret their values.
- Describe the factors that affect a firm's capital structure.

Where We Have Been . . .

We have seen how a firm can familiarize itself with the workings of the financial markets, security pricing, and IPOs (Chapters 7 through 9). Part of the financing decision depends on the firm's asset needs. New asset purchases, restructurings, or corporate strategies may lead to the need for new financing or a new financing strategy for the firm. Likewise, changes in financial market conditions (due to fluctuations in interest rates, stock price, or exchange rates) may make new financial strategies look appealing.

Where We Are Going . . .

Our focus in this chapter is on capital structure or "long-term" financing for a firm, but it also presents another financing-related choice: whether to choose a financing strategy emphasizing short-term sources or long-term sources of funds. We'll explore this option in Chapter 17.

How This Chapter Applies to Me . . .

High levels of consumer debt are used as a harbinger of tough economic times ahead. Similar to a firm, individuals have a capital structure, too. Add up your assets; subtract any debts; the balance is your net worth or "equity." Your own personal capital structure is your mixture of debt and equity that is used to finance what you own and your lifestyle. Like a firm, use of debt without the ability to make interest payments and to reduce the principal can lead to financial distress. The best use of debt for individuals is similar to that of firms: use in moderation and only to help purchase assets with the potential to grow in value, such as a house. Right now, you may be using student loans to finance an investment in yourself: your education. Because of your education, your future earnings potential is expected to be greater than it otherwise would be and gives you the ability to repay the loan.

In Shakespeare's play *Hamlet,* the elder Polonius counsels his son Laertes:

> *Neither a borrower nor a lender be.*

We can tell Polonius did not study modern-day finance! Lending money, in the form of buying bonds, can be an attractive investment strategy for some, and businesses often find themselves needing to borrow or raise funds for short periods or longer periods of time. This chapter looks at the analysis a firm should conduct when funds are needed for longer periods of time.

FIGURE 15.1
The Balance Sheet

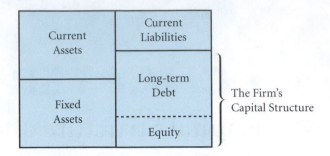

The previous chapters described the capital budgeting process. We learned how to estimate a project's cash flows and how to use techniques, such as NPV and IRR, for evaluating projects. In Chapter 13, we assumed that the project's discount rate, or its cost of capital, was given. In this chapter we'll explain how managers can estimate their firm's cost of capital for an "average risk" project. This discount rate is adjusted up or down, as we learned in Chapter 13, depending on the project's risk.

Before managers can estimate the cost of capital, two inputs are needed. First, they must determine the cost of each financing source. Second, they must determine the appropriate financing mix to use to fund the firm. Once these are known, they can estimate the firm's weighted average cost of capital.

capital structure
firm's mix of debt and equity

A firm's mix of debt and equity used to finance its assets defines the firm's **capital structure**, as seen in Figure 15.1. In this chapter we first review the importance of a firm's capital structure and how the capital structure and the costs of each financing source can be combined to provide an estimate of the weighted average cost of capital (WACC). We'll examine the interrelationship among a firm's growth rate, its dividend policy, and its capital structure decisions. Then we'll review the influences that affect a firm's choice of a capital structure over time.

WHY CHOOSE A CAPITAL STRUCTURE?

optimum debt/equity mix
proportionate use of debt and equity that minimizes the firm's cost of capital

Obviously, a target capital structure is important as it determines the proportion of debt and equity used to estimate a firm's cost of capital. There is, however, a second, even more important reason. The firm's **optimum debt/equity mix** minimizes the firm's **cost of capital**, which in turn helps the firm to maximize shareholder wealth.

cost of capital
minimum acceptable rate of return to a firm on a project

For example, suppose a firm expects cash flows of $20 million annually in perpetuity. Each of the three capital structures shown in Table 15.1 has a different weighted average cost of capital. Following the perpetuity valuation rule from Chapter 5, firm value is computed by dividing the expected cash flow by the firm's cost of capital under each capital structure. Capital Structure 2 in Table 15.1 minimizes the cost of capital at 8 percent, which in turn maximizes the value of the firm at $250 million.

TABLE 15.1
Capital Structure Options

	CAPITAL STRUCTURE 1	CAPITAL STRUCTURE 2	CAPITAL STRUCTURE 3
Debt	25.0%	40.0%	70.0%
Equity	75.0%	60.0%	30.0%
Weighted Average Cost of Capital	10.0%	8.0%	12.5%
Firm value under:			
Capital Structure 1: $20 million/0.10 = $200 million			
Capital Structure 2: $20 million/0.08 = $250 million			
Capital Structure 3: $20 million/0.125 = $160 million			

A nonoptimal capital structure with either too much or too little debt leads to higher financing costs, and the firm will likely reject some capital budgeting projects that could have increased shareholder wealth with an optimal financing mix. For example, suppose a firm has a minimum cost of capital of 8 percent, but poor analysis leads management to choose a capital structure that results in a 10 percent cost of capital. It would then reject an average risk project that costs $100,000 and returns cash flows of $26,000 in Years 1 through 5 at a 10 percent cost of capital (NPV = −$1,434). This project would be acceptable at the minimum possible cost of capital of 8 percent (NPV = $3,818).

There is another, more intuitive way to see the importance of finding the optimal capital structure. A project's NPV represents the increase in shareholders' wealth from undertaking a project. From Chapter 7, we know there is an inverse relationship between value and discount rates (the "seesaw effect"). Thus, a lower weighted average cost of capital gives higher project net present values and results in higher levels of shareholder wealth.

TRENDS IN CORPORATE USE OF DEBT

The ratio of long-term debt to GDP for U.S corporations grew during the 1960s until, as seen in Figure 15.2, the mid-1970s, exceeding 35 percent only for limited occasions. But the relative use of debt then rose until 1989, peaking at a nearly 45 percent of GDP. Many firms restructured themselves financially during the 1980s. Some did so in attempts to lower their cost of capital by taking advantage of the tax deductibility of interest by issuing debt to repurchase common stock, thereby increasing their debt-to-equity ratio (D/E). Other firms went private in the 1980s, fought off takeovers, or acquired other firms, financing the transactions with large amounts of debt. The surge in bankruptcies at the beginning of the 1990s shows the folly of such excessive use of debt.

Into the early 1990s, the ratio of debt to economic activity fell as firms issued equity to strengthen their balance sheets and to reduce the probability of financial distress due to over-borrowing. But as the economy grew in the 1990s, so did the relative use of debt, until the economic slowdown in the early part of the new millennium started to reduce debt levels.

Figure 15.3 shows the relative use of debt-to-equity for different-size firms in the latter part of the 1990s. The figure shows a fairly consistent pattern that smaller firms use relatively more debt

FIGURE 15.2

Corporate Debt as a Percentage of GDP

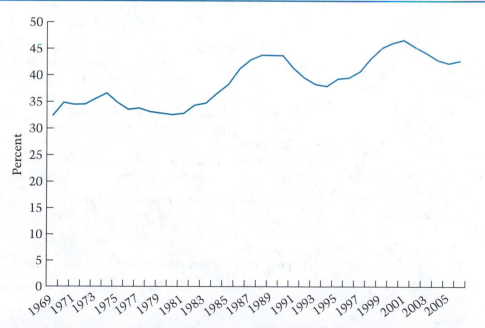

Source: GPO Access, *Economic Report of the President, 2006*, Table B-1, http://www.gpoaccess.gov/eop/download.html (accessed July 15, 2007); and Federal Reserve Board, *Flow of Funds Accounts*, Table of Debt Growth, Borrowings, and Debt Outstanding, http://www.federalreserve.gov/releases/Z1/Current (accessed July 18, 2007).

FIGURE 15.3
Ratios of Debt to Stock Market Equity for Different-Size Firms

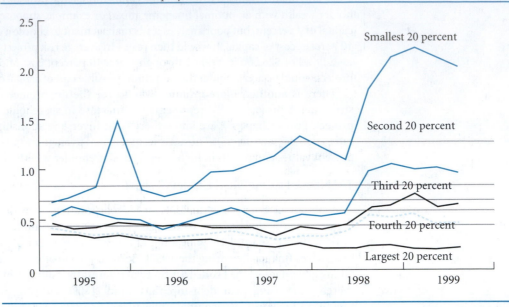

Source: Carol Osler and Gijoon Hong, "Rapidly Rising Corporate Debt: Are Firms Now Vulnerable to an Economic Slowdown?" *Current Issues in Economics and Finance*, vol. 6, no. 7 (June 2000), Federal Reserve District Bank of New York.

than larger firms. This occurs because of the higher relative costs of equity for smaller firms, as well as the better access to capital markets of the larger ones.

CONCEPT CHECK

What are the components of a firm's capital structure?

What is the relationship between a firm's cost of capital and firm value?

Have corporations been using a steady ratio of debt-to-equity over time?

REQUIRED RATE OF RETURN AND THE COST OF CAPITAL

Investors in a project expect to earn a return on their investment. This expected return depends on current capital market conditions (for example, levels of stock prices and interest rates) and the risk of the project. The minimum acceptable rate of return of a project is the return that generates sufficient cash flow to pay investors their expected return.

To illustrate, suppose a firm wants to spend $1,000 on an average-risk capital budgeting project, financing the investment by borrowing $600 and selling $400 worth of common stock. The firm must pay interest on the debt at a rate of 9 percent, while shareholders expect a 15 percent return on their investment. To compensate the firm's investors adequately, the project should generate an annual pretax expected cash flow equal to:

$$\text{Lender's interest} + \text{Shareholders' return} = \text{Annual expected cash flow}$$
$$= (0.09)(\$600) + (0.15)(\$400)$$
$$= \$54 + \$60 = \$114$$

The project's minimum rate of return must then equal:

$$\text{Minimum cash flow/Investment} = \text{Minimum rate of return}$$
$$= \$114/\$1,000 = 11.4 \text{ percent}$$

As another means to determine this, the expected return of each financing source could be weighted by its relative use. The firm is raising 60 percent of the project's funds from debt and 40 percent from equity. This results in a minimum pretax required return of:

$$(0.60)(9 \text{ percent}) + (0.40)(15 \text{ percent}) = 11.4 \text{ percent}$$

CONCEPT CHECK

What is the relationship between a project's cost of capital and its minimum required rate of return?

Why is a weighted average cost used instead of a project's specific cost of financing to determine whether it should be accepted or rejected?

Thus, the required rate of return on a project represents a weighted average of lenders' and owners' return expectations. Since a cash flow or return to an investor represents a cash outflow or a cost to the firm, *the minimum required rate of return is a weighted average of the firm's costs of various sources of capital.* Thus, the required rate of return on a project is equivalent to the project's cost of capital. It is this number that should be used as a discount rate when evaluating a project's NPV. *Required rate of return, cost of capital,* and *discount rate* are different terms for the same concept.

It is fair to ask why the minimum required return is equal to a *weighted* average of financing costs. If a firm can finance a project using all debt at an interest cost of 8 percent, shouldn't the project be accepted if it has a positive NPV using an 8 percent discount rate or if its IRR exceeds 8 percent? The answer is no, not necessarily. Suppose this week a project of average risk is financed by borrowing at 8 percent and has an IRR of 9 percent, so the firm's board votes to accept the project. Next quarter, because the firm's debt ratios are high, the board decides to finance all new projects with equity. If the cost of equity is 15 percent and a potential project with average risk has an IRR of 12 percent, the project will be turned down. It is hard to envision a board that is maximizing the value of the firm accepting projects with 9 percent expected returns while rejecting projects with the same risk that have expected returns of 12 percent! That is why the weighted average cost of capital is used: so project acceptance is not subject specifically to how it is to be financed.

COST OF CAPITAL

Relevant cash flows are incremental after-tax cash flows. To be consistent, these cash flows must be discounted using an incremental after-tax cost of capital. The firm's relevant cost of capital is computed from after-tax financing costs. Firms pay preferred and common stock dividends out of net income, so these expenses already represent after-tax costs to the firm. Because debt interest is paid from pretax income, however, the cost of debt requires adjustment to an after-tax basis before computing the cost of capital.

A project's incremental cash flows must also be discounted at a cost of capital that represents the incremental or marginal cost to the firm of financing the project—that is, the cost of raising one additional dollar of capital. Thus, the cost of debt and equity that determines the cost of capital must come not from historical averages or past costs but, rather, from forward-looking projections of future costs. The firm's analysts need to evaluate investors' expected returns under likely market conditions and then must use these expected returns to compute the firm's marginal future cost of raising funds by each method.

Conceptually, investors' required returns equal the firm's financing costs. The following sections use the valuation concepts for bonds and stocks from Chapters 7 and 8 to find investors' required returns on bonds, preferred stock, and common stock. We then adjust these required returns to reflect the firm's after-tax cost of financing.

COST OF DEBT

The firm's unadjusted cost of debt financing equals the yield to maturity on new debt issues, either a long-term bank loan or a bond issue. The yield to maturity represents the cost to the firm of borrowing funds in the current market environment. The firm's current financing costs determine its current cost of capital.

A firm can determine its cost of debt by several methods. If the firm targets an "A" rating (or any other bond rating), a review of the yields to maturity on A-rated bonds in *Standard & Poor's Bond Guide* can provide an estimate of the firm's current borrowing costs. Several additional factors will affect the firm's specific borrowing costs, including covenants and features of the proposed bond issue, as well as the number of years until the bond or loan matures or comes due. It is important to examine bonds whose ratings and characteristics resemble those the firm wants to match.

In addition, the firm can solicit the advice of investment bankers on the cost of issuing new debt. Or, if the firm has debt currently trading, it can use public market prices and yields to estimate its current cost of debt. The publicly traded bond's yield to maturity can be found using the techniques for determining the internal rate of return on an investment discussed in Chapters 5 and 7. Finally, a firm can seek long-term debt financing from a bank or a consortium of banks. Preliminary discussions with the bankers will indicate a ballpark interest rate that the firm can expect to pay on its borrowing.

The yield estimate, however derived, is an estimate of the coupon rate on newly issued bonds (as bonds are usually issued with prices close to their par value) or the interest rate on a loan. Interest is a pretax expense, so the interest estimate should be adjusted to reflect the tax shield provided by debt financing. If YTM is the pretax interest cost estimate, the after-tax estimate is YTM times $(1 - t)$, where t is the firm's marginal tax rate.[1] Thus the after-tax cost of debt, k_d, is:

$$k_d = YTM(1 - t) \qquad (15.1)$$

Suppose Global Manufacturing has a 40 percent marginal tax rate and it can issue debt with a 10 percent yield to maturity. Its after-tax cost of debt is 10 percent $(1 - 0.40) = 6$ percent.

COST OF PREFERRED STOCK

Chapter 8 explained how to model preferred stock as a perpetuity. The investor pays a price, P, for a share of preferred stock and in return expects to receive D_p of dividends every year, forever. Valuing the stock as perpetuity, the maximum price an investor will pay for a share is D_p/r_p, where r_p represents the rate of return required by investors in the firm's preferred stock. Rearranging the valuation equation to solve for r_p yields:

$$r_p = D_p/P$$

CONCEPT CHECK

How is a firm's after-tax cost of debt determined?

How is a firm's cost of preferred stock calculated?

When issuing preferred stock, the firm will not receive the full price P per share; there will be a flotation cost of F_p per share.[2] Thus, the cost to the firm of preferred stock financing, k_p, is:

$$k_p = D_p/(P - F_p) \qquad (15.2)$$

A firm wants to issue preferred stock that pays an annual dividend of $5 a share. The price of the stock is $55, and the cost of floating a new issue will be $3 a share. The cost of preferred stock to this firm is: $k_p = D_p/(P - F_p) = \$5/(\$55 - \$3) = 0.0962$ or 9.62 percent.

COST OF COMMON EQUITY

Unlike debt and preferred stock, cash flows from common equity are not fixed or known beforehand and their risk is harder to evaluate. In addition, firms have two sources of common equity, retained earnings and new stock issues, and thus two costs of common equity. It may be clear

---

1. In reality, this is an approximation. We know from Chapter 7 that the yield to maturity reflects both interest paid and the difference between market price and par value. Only the interest is tax-deductible to the firm. For coupon-paying bond issues, the coupon rate many times is set so that the market or offering price of the bonds is close to par. In these cases, Equation 15.1 is a close approximation to the cost of debt.

2. Flotation costs were discussed in Chapter 9.

that there is an explicit cost (dividends) associated with issuing new common equity, but even though the firm pays no extra dividends to use retained earnings, they are not a free source of financing. We must consider the opportunity cost of using funds that could have been given to shareholders as dividends.

Retained earnings are the portion of net income that the firm does not distribute as dividends. As owners of the firm, common shareholders have a claim on all its net income, but they receive only the amount that the firm's board of directors declares as dividends.

From the shareholders' perspective, the opportunity cost of retained earnings is the return the shareholders could earn by investing the funds in assets whose risk is similar to that of the firm. Suppose, for example, that shareholders expect a 15 percent return on their investment in a firm's common stock. If the firm could not invest its retained earnings to achieve a risk-adjusted 15 percent expected return, shareholders would be better off receiving 100 percent of its net income as dividends; that way they can reinvest the funds themselves in similar-risk assets that can provide a 15 percent expected return.

To maximize shareholder wealth, management must recognize that retained earnings have a cost. That cost, k_{re}, is the return that shareholders expect from their investment in the firm. We will review two methods of estimating the cost of retained earnings. One method uses the security market line, and the other uses the assumption of constant dividend growth.

Cost of Retained Earnings: Security Market Line Approach

Chapter 10's Learning Extension developed the security market line, or SML, which can provide an estimate of shareholder required return based on a stock's systematic risk.

$$E(R_i) = RFR + \beta_i(R_{MKT} - RFR)$$

The preceding security market line equation gives the required return as a combination of the risk-free return, RFR, and a risk premium that is the product of a stock's systematic risk, measured by β, and the market risk premium ($R_{MKT} - RFR$). The required shareholder return is the opportunity cost the firm must earn on its retained earnings. Thus, an estimate for the cost of retained earnings is:

$$k_{re} = E(R_i) = RFR + \beta_i(R_{MKT} - RFR) \tag{15.3}$$

For example, assume that the current T-bill rate is 4.5 percent and that analysts estimate that the current market risk premium is slightly above its historical average at 9.0 percent. Suppose also that analysts estimate Global Manufacturing's β to be 1.30. What is Global Manufacturing's cost of retained earnings using the SML approach?

All the information we need to apply Equation 15.3 has been presented:

$$k_{re} = E(R_i) = RFR + \beta_i(R_{MKT} - RFR) = 4.5 \text{ percent} + [(1.3)(9 \text{ percent})] = 16.2 \text{ percent}$$

Using the security market line, Global Manufacturing's cost of retained earnings is 16.2 percent.

Cost of Retained Earnings: Constant Dividend Growth Model

Chapter 8 presented the constant dividend growth model to estimate a firm's stock price:

$$P = \frac{D_1}{r_{cs} - g} \tag{15.4}$$

where

P = stock price
g = expected (constant) dividend growth rate
D_1 = next year's expected dividend (equal to the current dividend increased by g percent)
r_{cs} = shareholders' required return on the stock

Rather than use the model to determine a price, however, we can substitute today's actual stock price for P and solve for the shareholders' required rate of return, r_{cs}:

$$k_{re} = r_{cs} = \frac{D_1}{P} + g \tag{15.5}$$

The shareholders' required return represents the firm's cost of retained earnings, k_{re}. The ratio D_1/P represents the current income yield to shareholders from their investment of P.

From the firm's perspective, this ratio represents the ratio of dividends it pays to its current market value. The growth rate, g, represents shareholders' expected capital gain arising from dividend growth. From the firm's perspective, g can be viewed as an opportunity cost of raising equity today. The firm expects to be able to sell equity next year at a price g percent higher.

COST OF NEW COMMON STOCK

flotation costs

costs of issuing stock; includes accounting, legal, and printing costs of offering shares to the public, as well as the commission earned by the investment bankers who market the new securities to investors

To estimate the cost of new equity, we must modify Equation 15.5 to reflect extra cost to the firm of issuing securities in the primary market. The costs of issuing stock, or **flotation costs**, include the accounting, legal, and printing costs of offering shares to the public, as well as the commission or fees earned by the investment bankers who market the new securities to investors. If the flotation cost is F per share, the cost of issuing new common stock, or k_n, is given by Equation 15.6:

$$k_n = \frac{D_1}{P - F} + g \qquad (15.6)$$

Suppose a firm has just paid a dividend of $2.50 a share, its stock price is $50 a share, and the expected growth rate of dividends is 6 percent. The current dividend of $2.50 must be multiplied by a factor to reflect the expected 6 percent growth for D_1, next year's dividend. Using Equation 15.5, the cost of using retained earnings as a financing source is:

$$k_{cs} = \frac{2.50(1 + 0.06)}{\$50} + 0.06 = \frac{\$2.65}{\$50} + 0.06$$

$$= 0.053 + 0.06 = 0.113, \text{ or } 11.3 \text{ percent}$$

If new common stock is to be issued to finance the project and flotation costs are expected to be $4 per share, we need to use Equation 15.6 to estimate the cost of new common equity:

$$k_{cs} = \frac{2.50(1 + 0.06)}{\$50 - \$4} + 0.06 = \frac{\$2.65}{\$46} + 0.06$$

$$= 0.058 + 0.06 = 0.118, \text{ or } 11.8 \text{ percent}$$

CONCEPT CHECK

Should retained earnings be considered a source of free financing to the firm?

How can the cost of retained earnings be determined for a firm? The cost of new common equity?

The cost of using new common stock is 11.8 percent.

We learned about the concept of efficient markets in Chapter 10, namely that current market prices and interest rates reflect all known information, as well as the market's expectations about the future. Financial managers can do little to "fight the market." If managers feel their financing costs are too high, it is usually the case that the market perceives risk that the managers are ignoring. The efficient market ensures that financing costs are in line with the market's perception of firms' risks and expected returns.

WEIGHTED AVERAGE COST OF CAPITAL

We have seen how to compute the costs of the firm's basic capital structure components. Now we will combine the components to find the weighted average of the firm's financing costs.

weighted average cost of capital (WACC)

represents the minimum required rate of return on a capital-budgeting project. It is found by multiplying the marginal cost of each capital structure component by its appropriate weight, and then summing the terms

The firm's **weighted average cost of capital (WACC)** represents the minimum required rate of return on its capital budgeting projects. It is found by multiplying the marginal cost of each capital structure component by its appropriate weight and summing the terms:

$$WACC = w_d k_d + w_p k_p + w_e k_e \qquad (15.7)$$

The weights of debt, preferred equity, and common equity in the firm's capital structure are given by w_d, w_p, and w_e, respectively. As the weighted average cost of capital covers all the firm's capital financing sources, the weights must sum to 1.0.

The firm's cost of common equity, k_e, can reflect the cost of retained earnings, k_{re}, or the cost of new common stock, k_n, whichever is appropriate. Most firms rely on retained earnings to raise the common equity portion of their financial needs. If retained earnings are insufficient, they can issue common stock to meet the shortfall. In this case, k_n is substituted for the cost of common equity.

CAPITAL STRUCTURE WEIGHTS

The weights in Equation 15.7 represent a specific intended financing mix. These target weights represent a mix of debt and equity that the firm will try to achieve or maintain over the planning horizon. As much as possible, the target weights should reflect the combination of debt and equity that management believes will minimize the firm's weighted average cost of capital. The firm should make an effort over time to move toward and maintain its target capital structure mix of debt and equity.

MEASURING THE TARGET WEIGHTS

As the firm moves toward a target capital structure, how will it know when it arrives? There are two ways to measure the mix of debt and equity in the firm's capital structure.

One method uses target weights based on the firm's book values, or balance sheet amounts, of debt and equity. The actual weight of debt in the firm's capital structure equals the book value of its debt divided by the book value of its assets. Similarly, the actual equity weight is the book value of its stockholders' equity divided by total assets. Once the target weights are determined, the firm can issue or repurchase appropriate quantities of debt and equity over time to move the balance sheet numbers toward the target weights.

A second method uses the market values of the firm's debt and equity to compare target and actual weights. The actual weight of debt in the firm's capital structure equals the market value of its debt divided by the market value of its assets. Similarly, the actual equity weight is the market value of the firm's stockholders' equity divided by the market value of its assets. Calculated in this way, bond and stock market price fluctuations, as well as new issues and security repurchases, can move the firm toward—or away from—its target.

Financial theory favors the second method as most appropriate. Current *market* values are used to compute the various costs of financing, so it is intuitive that *market*-based costs should be weighted by *market*-based weights.

The basic capital structure of a firm may include debt, preferred equity, and common equity. In practice, calculating the cost of these components is sometimes complicated by the existence of hybrid financing structures (e.g., convertible debt) and other variations on straight debt, preferred equity, or common equity.[3] (A discussion of this advanced topic is beyond the scope of this book.)

For example, let's compute the weighted average cost of capital for Global Manufacturing. Assume that Global Manufacturing has determined that its target capital structure should include one-third debt and two-thirds common equity. Global Manufacturing's current cost of debt is 6.0 percent, and its current cost of retained earnings is 15.0 percent. What is Global Manufacturing's weighted average cost of capital, assuming that last year's operations generated sufficient retained earnings to finance this year's capital budget?

Since sufficient new retained earnings exist, Global Manufacturing will not need to issue shares to implement its capital budget. Thus, the cost of retained earnings will be used to estimate its weighted average cost of capital. The target capital structure is one-third debt and two-thirds common equity. Using Equation 15.7, Global Manufacturing's weighted average cost of capital is:

$$\text{WACC} = (1/3)(6.0 \text{ percent}) + (2/3)(15.0 \text{ percent})$$

$$= 12.0 \text{ percent}$$

Given current market conditions and Global Manufacturing's target capital structure weights, the firm should use a discount rate of 12.0 percent when computing the NPV for average risk projects.[4]

---

3. For insights into how to handle these more complex financing structures, see Michael C. Ehrhardt, *The Search for Capital* (Boston: Harvard Business School Press, 1994), and Tom Copeland, Tim Koller, and Jack Murrin, *Valuation: Measuring and Managing the Value of Companies*, 3rd ed. (Hoboken, NJ: Wiley, 2000) or most intermediate-level corporate finance textbooks.

4. For a good case study of estimating the cost of capital for firms in the food processing fieftury, see Samuel C. Weaver, "Using Value Line to Estimate the Cost of Capital and Industry Capital Structure," *Journal of Financial Education* (Fall 2003), vol. 29, pp. 55–71.

To compare Global Manufacturing's current capital structure with its target capital structure, let's assume that Global Manufacturing has two bond issues outstanding. One is rated AA and has a yield to maturity of 8.8 percent; the other is rated A and yields 9.5 percent. The firm also has preferred stock and common stock outstanding. The following table shows the current market prices and the number of shares or bonds outstanding. How does Global Manufacturing's current capital structure compare to its target?

SECURITY	CURRENT PRICE	NUMBER OUTSTANDING
AA bonds	$1,050	10,000 bonds
A bonds	1,025	20,000 bonds
Preferred stock	40	250,000 shares
Common stock	50	700,000 shares

To begin, Global Manufacturing's target capital structure of one-third debt and two-thirds common equity does not leave any room for preferred stock. Evidently Global Manufacturing's management has decided not to raise funds in the future with new preferred stock issues. Using the given information, let's compute the market values of Global Manufacturing's securities and their current market value weights and then compare these figures to Global Manufacturing's target capital structure. A security's market value is found by multiplying its market price by the number of bonds or shares currently outstanding. The figures in the preceding table give these market values and weights:

SECURITY	MARKET VALUE ($ MILLIONS)	MARKET WEIGHT
AA bonds	$10.50	0.138
A bonds	20.50	0.270
Preferred stock	10.00	0.132
Common stock	35.00	0.460
Total	$76.00	1.000

Presently, Global Manufacturing's capital structure is comprised of 41 percent debt, about 46 percent common equity, and about 13 percent preferred equity. To move toward its target capital structure, Global Manufacturing may want to issue common stock and use the proceeds to purchase outstanding preferred stock and bonds. There is no need for Global Manufacturing to restructure its finances immediately. The flotation costs and administrative fees of such a program would be prohibitive. Some movement toward the target capital structure would occur if Global Manufacturing could identify several positive-NPV projects. Barring a market downtrend, these projects would increase its market value of equity. Also, it could use future additions to retained earnings to repurchase some outstanding debt or preferred equity.

WHAT DO BUSINESSES USE AS THEIR COST OF CAPITAL?

Surveys of U.S. firms find that most firms use after-tax weighted average costs of capital as their required rates of return for projects. Other methods include management-determined target returns or the cost of some specific source of funds. A survey of U.S.-based multinationals found, surprisingly, that half of them use a single firmwide discount rate to evaluate projects, regardless of risk differences. The most popular method for estimating the cost of equity is the security market line approach; nearly 75 percent of firms use this method. Because of its assumption regarding growth, the constant dividend growth model is not used by many firms; only about 15 percent of firms in a 1999 survey used that method, about half the level found in a 1982 survey.[5]

5. John R. Graham and Campbell R. Harvey, "The Theory and Practice of Corporate Finance: Evidence from the Field," *Journal of Financial Economics,* vol. 60, no. 1 (2001), pp. 187–243; Lawrence J. Gitman and Vincent Mercurio, "Cost of Capital Techniques Used by Major U.S. Firms: Survey and Analysis of Fortune's 1000," *Financial Management,* vol. 14 (1982), pp. 21–29.

DIFFICULTY OF MAKING CAPITAL STRUCTURE DECISIONS

INTERNET ACTIVITY

Cost of capital is included in the calculation of economic value added (the concept of EVA was discussed in Chapter 11). Stern Stewart's Web site, http://www.sternstewart.com contains information on the importance of the cost of capital, as well as practitioner-oriented research reports.

Examining the various influences that affect a firm's capital structure is not an easy task. Unlike NPV or operating cash flow, there is no formula we can use to determine the proportions of debt and equity a firm should use to finance its assets.

However, that does not mean we are totally lost. Financial theory and research on firm behavior have given us a set of guidelines or principles by which to evaluate a firm's proper mix of debt and equity. We also simplify the discussion by referring only to debt and equity, with little distinction between the various types of debt and equity. We discuss some of the variations in debt and equity later in this chapter.

In the following sections, we'll examine a number of interrelationships affecting a firm's capital structure decisions. First is the firm's growth rate. All else being equal, a firm with higher growth levels will need to tap the capital markets more frequently than a slow or no-growth firm. Second, given a firm's growth rate, the need for outside capital depends upon its return on assets and dividend policy. Again, all else being equal, a firm with a larger return on assets can rely more on retained earnings as a source of financing and will favor equity over debt financing. A firm with a large dividend payout will need more outside capital to finance growth. Next we will examine some analytical tools and theories that have been advanced and tested to explain firms' capital structures.

Figure 15.3 showed how debt ratios—one indication of capital structure—can differ among different-size firms. Figure 15.4 shows the ratio of long-term debt to total assets for several firms. The graph shows a wide variation in capital structures. Google, which went public in 2004 and then had a secondary equity offering in 2005, has little debt. Other technology firms—whose true assets are software, ideas, and knowledge rather than brick and mortar—have low debt ratios (Apple, Dell, and Microsoft). Walgreens also has a low ratio of long-term debt to assets, but that is because they lease, rather than own, many of their stores to conserve capital. The firm with the highest level of debt relative to assets is Consolidated Edison. This is no surprise, since as a utility most of its asset base is comprised of fixed assets, which are more amenable to borrowing than are ideas or software. In addition, since its industry is regulated, it will likely be able to charge electric rates sufficient to service the debt interest.

FIGURE 15.4
Long-Term Debt Divided by Total Assets

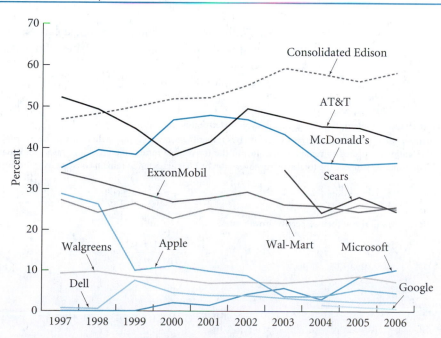

PLANNING GROWTH RATES

A firm's growth is in part determined by management's strategy to acquire or maintain market share in a growing or stable market. But management's plans for future sales, assets, and financing growth may not happen because of the competitive struggle in the marketplace. Growth that is faster or slower than expected may occur.

A simple financial planning tool, the internal growth rate model, is available to determine just how quickly a firm can grow without running short of cash.

INTERNAL GROWTH RATE

internal growth rate
a measure of how quickly a firm can grow without needing additional outside financing

The *internal growth rate* measures how quickly a firm can increase its asset base over the next year without raising outside funds. It does not measure divisional growth, or break down total growth into domestic or international components. The internal growth rate gives a general, companywide value.

It is equal to the ratio of the expected increase in retained earnings over the next year to the current asset base:

$$\frac{\text{Expected change in retained earnings}}{\text{Total assets}}$$

This can also be calculated as:

$$\text{Internal growth rate (g)} = \frac{(\text{RR})(\text{ROA})}{1 - (\text{RR})(\text{ROA})} \qquad (15.8)$$

retention rate
the proportion of each dollar of earnings that is kept by the firm

RR is the firm's retention rate, and ROA is its return on assets. The internal growth rate divides the product of these values by one minus this product.[6] The *retention rate* represents the proportion of every $1 of earnings per share that is retained by the firm; in other words, it is equal to one minus the *dividend payout ratio*.

dividend payout ratio
the proportion of each dollar of earnings that is paid to shareholders as a dividend; equals one minus the retention rate

Suppose a firm pays out 40 percent of its earnings as dividends and has averaged a 15 percent return on assets over the past several years; how quickly can the firm grow without needing to tap outside financing sources? A 40 percent dividend payout ratio means that the firm's retention rate is $1.00 - 0.40 = 0.60$. Of every dollar of net income, the firm distributes $0.40 as dividends and retains $0.60. With a 15 percent return on assets, Equation 15.8 tells us that the internal growth rate for the firm is:

$$\text{Internal growth rate} = \frac{(0.60)(0.15)}{1 - (0.60)(0.15)} = 0.099 \text{ or } 9.9 \text{ percent}$$

If it relies only on new additions to retained earnings to finance asset acquisition and maintains its past profitability and dividend payout, the firm can increase its asset base by a little under 10 percent next year.[7]

---

6. An end-of-chapter problem (number 13) invites you to derive this relationship.

7. Most managers plan and think in terms of sales dollars rather than size, so it may help to relate the internal growth rate to sales growth. If the firm's total asset turnover ratio is expected to remain constant into the foreseeable future, the growth in sales will equal the internal growth rate we have previously computed. For example, suppose the total asset turnover ratio of 2.0 is expected to remain constant over the next few years:

$$\frac{\text{Sales}}{\text{TA}} = 2.0$$

Both sales and assets will rise at their respective growth rates:

$$\frac{\text{Sales}(1 + g_s)}{\text{TA}(1 + g_a)} = 2.0$$

Then

$$2.0 = \frac{(\text{Sales})(1 + g_s)}{(\text{TA})(1 + g_a)} = (2.0)\frac{(1 + g_s)}{(1 + g_a)}$$

This implies that $1 + g_s = 1 + g_a$, or that sales growth will equal asset growth.

The internal growth rate makes the restrictive assumption that the firm will pursue no outside sources of financing. Should the firm grow at its internal growth rate, its retained earnings account will continually rise (assuming profitable sales) while its dollar amount of debt outstanding will remain constant. *Thus, the relative amount of debt in its capital structure declines over time, and the debt level will likely fall below its proportion in management's ideal financing mix.*

SUSTAINABLE GROWTH RATE

Perhaps a more realistic assumption would be to allow management to borrow funds over time to maintain steady capital structure ratios. As the stockholders' equity account rises from new additions to retained earnings, the firm issues new debt to keep its debt-to-equity ratio constant over time.

This rate of growth is the **sustainable growth rate**. It measures how quickly the firm can grow when it uses both internal equity and debt financing to keep its capital structure constant over time. It is computed as follows:

$$\text{Sustainable growth rate} = \frac{(\text{RR})(\text{ROE})}{1 - (\text{RR})(\text{ROE})}$$

As before, RR is the firm's retention rate, which is multiplied by ROE, its return on equity, divided by one minus this product.[8]

Suppose that the firm in the previous example maintains a debt-to-equity ratio of 1.0 (which is equivalent to an equity multiplier of 2.0) to minimize its financing costs. What would be the firm's sustainable growth rate? From the discussion in Chapter 12 of Du Pont analysis, we know that ROE = ROA × equity multiplier.

Since the firm has a return on assets of 15 percent, its ROE equals 15 percent × 2 = 30 percent; with a retention rate of 0.60, the sustainable growth rate equals:

$$\text{Sustainable growth rate} = \frac{(0.60)(0.30)}{1 - (0.60)(0.30)} = 0.2195 \text{ or } 21.95 \text{ percent}$$

Thus, without outside financing, the firm can increase sales and assets by slightly under 10 percent; by maintaining a constant capital structure, the firm can grow by nearly 22 percent if it can maintain its levels of profitability and earnings retention.

EFFECTS OF UNEXPECTEDLY HIGHER (OR LOWER) GROWTH

The internal and sustainable growth rates are planning tools. These formulas cannot make a firm grow by a certain prescribed amount. Changing global competition, political, and credit market conditions can cause actual growth to deviate from planned growth.

The internal and sustainable growth rate relationships suggest that there are three measurable influences on growth: dividend policy (as reflected in the retention rate), profitability (as measured by ROA), and the firm's capital structure (as measured by the equity multiplier). A fourth influence that is much harder to measure is management's preferences and beliefs about the use of external financing rather than relying solely on changes in retained earnings. Should actual growth differ from planned growth, one or more of these factors will have to be adjusted either to prevent financial difficulty or to absorb excess funds.

Dividend Policy

A reduction in the dividend payout ratio implies a higher retention rate and the ability for the firm to grow more quickly, if all else remains constant. Thus, a fast-growing firm may decide to maintain a low dividend payout in an effort to finance its rapid growth. More mature, slower-growing firms usually increase their dividend payout as growth opportunities diminish.

---

sustainable growth rate
the estimate of how quickly a firm may grow by maintaining a constant mix of debt and equity

CONCEPT CHECK

What does the internal growth rate measure?

What does the sustainable growth rate measure?

What causes the difference between them?

---

8. You have a chance to derive this relationship in one of the end-of-chapter problems (number 14).

Profitability

Higher returns on assets generate more net income, larger additions to retained earnings, and faster growth, when all else is held constant. As we learned in the Du Pont analysis discussion in Chapter 12:

$$ROA = \text{profit margin} \times \text{total asset turnover}$$

Management can attempt to change return on assets by influencing these factors should growth outpace or fall short of the planned rate.

Capital Structure

The equity multiplier is determined by the firm's financing policy. A firm that uses a larger amount of debt can support a higher sustainable growth rate, when all else remains constant. If actual growth exceeds the sustainable growth rate, a firm can finance the difference by taking on additional debt.

One or more of these variables must deviate from planned levels to accommodate a difference between planned and actual growth. If a firm's actual growth exceeds the planned rate, management will have to reduce its dividend payout, increase profitability, use more debt, or use a combination of these options. If growth slows, the firm will need to increase its dividend payout, reduce profitability, reduce its use of debt, or choose some combination of these alternatives. If outside financing is needed, the external financing needs calculation from Chapter 12 can help estimate the amount of funds needed.

We examined, via Du Pont analysis, factors affecting profitability in Chapter 12. Next we will examine the role of dividends and retained earnings on firm financing needs.

THE ROLE OF DIVIDENDS AND RETAINED EARNINGS

For a given growth strategy, a firm's dividend decision directly affects its capital structure decision. A firm's profits can be used in one of two ways: distributed as dividends or added to retained earnings. Findings from research shed some light on the role of dividends in corporate finance and how—and how not—to use retained earnings.

But first: do dividends matter to investors? In a world without taxes, brokerage fees, and no net additional financing costs, the answer is no. If a firm's dividends are too low from the perspective of investors, they can sell some shares to generate extra cash. If investors feel that the dividend amount is too high, they can reinvest the excess back into the firm's shares. Whether the firm issues a large or small dividend, the overall cash flows and earning power of the firm will not be changed. In a world without taxes and commissions, it will not matter whether dividends are paid or not.[9]

However, we live in a world with taxes, and many economies tax dividends more heavily than capital gains.[10] So why do firms pay dividends? Why shouldn't the funds be reinvested in the firm or, if no attractive investments are available, why aren't the available funds used to repurchase stock? Here are some reasons.

Dividends Versus Stock Repurchases

Although dividends are taxed more heavily than capital gains, investors like dividends. Many firms have a stable or constant dividend strategy or a dividend growth strategy. Dividends represent income that investors come to rely upon; unlike bond coupons, dividends may become a growing stream of income. Even though stock prices may fall in difficult economic times, dividends are a source of positive return to shareholders. During the past seventy-five years, stock dividends have risen more than 2,250 percent, inflation has risen more than 870 percent, and Treasury bill income has risen about 80 percent. Thus, dividends are commonly thought by investors to be a "safe" and growing source of return.

---

9. In finance, this is the well-known *dividend irrelevance* theorem. Further details can be found in many advanced finance textbooks, as well as in the original research article, M. Miller and F. Modigliani, "Dividend Policy, Growth, and the Valuation of Shares," *Journal of Business*, vol. 43 (October 1961), pp. 411–432.

10. Indeed, taxes on capital gains can be deferred indefinitely. A capital gain must be *realized* (that is, the asset sold for more than the purchase price) before tax becomes due. Thus, investors can hold on to appreciated stock for many years and even pass it on to heirs, without paying tax on the accumulated capital gains. Dividends, on the other hand, are taxable income in the year they are received.

Dividends Versus Retained Earnings

FINANCE PRINCIPLE

In Chapter 11 we discussed agency costs and how managerial incentives may differ from those that are best for shareholders. The temptation to spend what cash we have is strong, for both the corporate executive and the shopper at the mall. Studies find that cash-rich firms destroy value—about seven cents for every dollar of cash reserves held—because they seek acquisitions and projects that typically result in lower firm values. Managers overdiversify and bid too high for their acquisitions.[11] Rather than having to raise capital in financial markets, such firms escape market discipline by relying on internal finance and, on average, make poor investment decisions. Once diversified, the problem continues as firms don't always direct capital to the highest-returning divisions and instead invest in lower-returning subsidiaries. This finding is supported by research in both the U.S. markets and several overseas markets.[12] In fact, some evidence exists that dividends have evolved in some countries because of investor protection laws. In a study of dividend policies of firms in thirty-three countries, those countries with "common law" traditions with excellent investor protection (such as the United States and United Kingdom) have dividend rates higher than countries with "civil law" traditions and weaker investor protection (such as Latin America, Scandinavia, and southern Europe).[13]

Dividends as Signals

GLOBAL DISCUSSION

Dividends can be used by managers to signal or convey information to the markets about the firm's future prospects. Firms do not usually decrease dividends unless absolutely necessary. Dividend changes, particularly increases, are usually permanent in nature, as firms don't want to add to investor risk by varying the dollar amount of dividends every year. This also means that managers won't commit to a dividend increase unless they feel it can be maintained on the basis of the firm's future cash inflows. Thus, a dividend increase is a way of informing the market of management's confidence in the firm's future prospects. Some research has shown a relationship between dividend changes and future firm profitability.[14]

To summarize, to investors dividends are important as they have potential to be a growing source of income. A firm's need to access the capital markets helps the financial marketplace exert market discipline on the firm. Dividends are a credible means for managers to signal the market about their belief in the firm's future cash flows.

But is the tide beginning to shift toward stock repurchases? A massive shift is unlikely to occur for the reasons presented, but some research of the thinking of corporate executives is finding a shift toward favoring stock repurchases. Some executives say they are more flexible than dividends (since, as we saw, a reduction in dividends is interpreted as an indicator of poor future prospects). Stock repurchases can be increased or decreased easily, depending upon the firm's capital budgeting opportunities. Stock repurchases can be used in an attempt to "time" the market—repurchase shares when they are cheap—although adherents of the efficient markets hypothesis would argue that timing is difficult to do on a consistent basis.[15]

The ability of the firm to grow is affected not only by management's strategy and by competitive conditions but also by the firm's access to capital and levels of additions to retained earnings. Jointly, these influences of growth, dividend payout, and the amount of retained earnings determine the firm's need for outside capital. We first learned this in Chapter 12, when estimating a firm's external financing requirements.

---

11. Jarred Harford, "Corporate Cash Reserves and Acquisitions," *Journal of Finance*, vol. 54, no. 6 (December 1999), pp. 1969–1997.

12. Studies of this phenomenon include Karl Lins and Henri Servaes, "International Evidence on the Value of Corporate Diversification," *Journal of Finance*, vol. 54, no. 6 (December 1999), pp. 2215–2239; Raghuram Rajan, Henri Servaes, and Luigi Zingales, "The Cost of Diversity: The Diversification Discount and Inefficient Investment," *Journal of Finance*, vol. 55, no. 1 (February 2000), pp. 35–80; Toni Whited, "Is It Inefficient Investment That Causes the Diversification Discount?," *Journal of Finance*, vol. 56, no. 5 (October 2001), pp. 1667–1691; Owen A. Lamont and Christopher Polk, "The Diversification Discount: Cash Flows Versus Return," *Journal of Finance*, vol. 56, no. 5 (October 2001), pp. 1693–1721.

13. Rafael La Porta, Florencio Lopez-De-Silanes, Andrei Schleifer, and Robert W. Vishny, "Agency Problems and Dividend Policies Around the World," *Journal of Finance*, vol. 55, no. 1 (February 2000), pp. 1–33.

14. Doron Nissim and Amir Ziv, "Dividend Changes and Future Profitability," *Journal of Finance*, vol. 56, no. 6 (December 2001), pp. 2111–2133.

15. Alon Brov, John R. Graham, Campbell R. Harvey, and Roni Michaely, "Payout Policy in the 21st Century," *Journal of Financial Economics*, vol. 77, no. 3 (September 2005), pp. 483–527.

As we saw then, a firm's external financing needs can come from short-term financing sources, such as notes payable and drawing down lines of credit, as well as from spontaneous financing sources such as accounts payable. Starting in the next section, we'll examine influences on a firm's long-term financing strategy. In Chapter 17, we'll review influences on a firm's short-term/long-term financing mix.

EBIT/EPS ANALYSIS

EBIT/eps analysis
allows managers to see how different capital structures affect the earnings and risk levels of their firms

As a first step in capital structure analysis, let's examine how different capital structures affect the earnings and risk of a firm in a simple world with no corporate income taxes. We use a tool of financial analysis called EBIT/eps analysis. **EBIT/eps analysis** allows managers to see how different capital structures affect the earnings and risk levels of their firms. Specifically, it shows the graphical relationship between a firm's operating earnings, or earnings before interest and taxes (EBIT), and earnings per share (eps). If we ignore taxes, these two quantities differ only by the firm's interest expense and by the fact that eps is, of course, net income stated on a per-share basis. Examining scenarios with different EBIT levels can help managers to see the effects of different capital structures on the firm's earnings per share.

Let's assume the Bennett Corporation is considering whether it should restructure its financing. As seen in Table 15.2, Bennett currently finances its $100 million in assets entirely with equity. Under the proposed change, Bennett will issue $50 million in bonds and use this money to repurchase $50 million of its stock (if the stock's price is $25 a share, Bennett will repurchase 2 million shares of stock). Bennett expects to pay 10 percent interest on the new bonds, for an annual interest expense of $5 million.

Assuming that Bennett's expected EBIT for next year is $12 million, let's see how the proposed restructuring may affect earnings per share. For simplicity, we ignore taxes in this example, so earnings per share (eps) will be computed as (EBIT − interest expense) divided by the number of shares. As shown in Table 15.3, the scenario analysis assumes that Bennett's EBIT will be either $12 million, 50 percent lower ($6 million), or 50 percent higher ($18 million). Figure 15.5 graphs the EBIT/eps combinations that result from the scenario analysis of the current and proposed capital structures. For lower EBIT levels, the current all-equity capital structure leads to higher earnings per share. At higher levels of EBIT, the proposed 50 percent equity, 50 percent debt capital structure results in higher levels of eps.

INDIFFERENCE LEVEL

Figure 15.5 clearly shows that the EBIT/eps lines cross. This means that, at some EBIT level, Bennett will be indifferent between the two capital structures, inasmuch as they result in the same earnings per share.

Under Bennett's current capital structure, earnings per share is computed as (EBIT − $0 interest)/4 million shares. Under the proposed structure, earnings per share is calculated as (EBIT − $5 million interest)/2 million shares. To find the level of EBIT where the lines cross—that is, where the combination of earnings per share and EBIT are the same under each capital structure—we set these two earnings per share values equal to each other and solve for EBIT:

$$\frac{EBIT - 0}{4} = \frac{EBIT - 5}{2}$$

TABLE 15.2

Current and Proposed Capital Structures for the Bennett Corporation

	CURRENT	PROPOSED
Total assets	$100 million	$100 million
Debt	$0 million	$50 million
Equity	$100 million	$50 million
Common stock price	$25	$25
Number of shares	4,000,000	2,000,000
Interest rate	10%	10%

TABLE 15.3

Scenario Analysis with Current and Proposed Capital Structures

	CURRENT—NO DEBT, 4 MILLION SHARES (MILLIONS OMITTED)		
	EBIT 50% BELOW EXPECTATIONS	EXPECTED	EBIT 50% ABOVE EXPECTATIONS
EBIT	$6.00	$12.00	$18.00
− I	0.00	0.00	0.00
NI	$6.00	$12.00	$18.00
eps	$1.50	$ 3.00	$ 4.50

	PROPOSED—50% DEBT (10% COUPON), 2 MILLION SHARES (MILLIONS OMITTED)		
	EBIT 50% BELOW EXPECTATIONS	EXPECTED	EBIT 50% ABOVE EXPECTATIONS
EBIT	$6.00	$12.00	$18.00
− I	5.00	5.00	5.00
NI	$1.00	$ 7.00	$13.00
eps	$0.50	$ 3.50	$ 6.50

Doing so, we learn that the earnings per share under the two plans are the same when EBIT equals $10 million.[16] When EBIT exceeds $10 million; the proposed, more highly leveraged capital structure will have the higher earnings per share. When EBIT is less than $10 million, the current, less leveraged capital structure will have the higher earnings per share.

The indifference level of $10 million in EBIT did not occur by chance. It equals the firm's interest cost of 10 percent multiplied by its total assets ($100 million). In other words, if the firm can earn an operating return on assets (EBIT/TA) greater than its interest cost, leverage is beneficial in that it results in higher earnings per share. If the firm's operating return on assets is less than its 10 percent interest cost, leverage is expensive relative to the firm's earning ability and results in a lower earnings per share. If Bennett strongly believes that EBIT will meet expectations at $12 million, the proposed capital structure change is attractive.

EBIT/eps analysis has several practical implications. First, as seen, it shows the ranges of EBIT where a firm may prefer one capital structure over another. The firm may decide to increase or decrease its financial leverage depending on whether its expected EBIT is above or below the indifference EBIT level.

FIGURE 15.5

EBIT/eps Analysis, Bennett Corporation

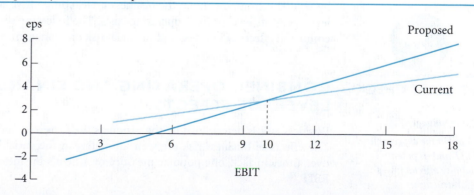

16. By cross-multiplying, 2 EBIT = 4 EBIT − 20. Solving for EBIT, we obtain EBIT = 10.

FIGURE 15.6

Firm Value, Earnings per Share, and Debt Ratios

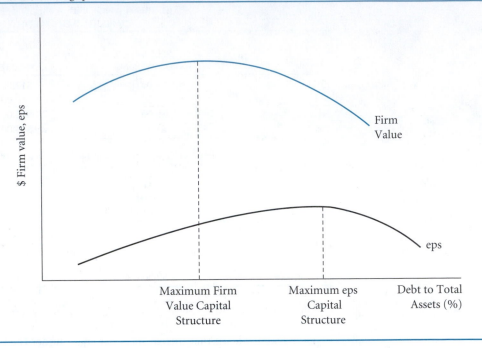

Second, EBIT is not constant over time; it will change, depending on sales growth, industry competitive conditions, and the firm's operating leverage. Variations in EBIT will produce variations in earnings per share. Should the expected EBIT of the firm lie above the indifference EBIT level, the firm's managers need to consider potential variation of earnings in their EBIT forecast. Depending on its uncertainty, management may decide to use a more conservative financing strategy with less debt.

This shows the drawback of using EBIT/eps analysis. It does not adequately capture the risk facing investors and how it affects shareholder wealth. We seek a capital structure that maximizes the value of the firm, not earnings per share. Although earnings per share may rise with financial leverage under certain values of EBIT, the value of earnings per share that maximizes firm value will likely be less than the maximum earnings per value. The firm's investors, both lenders and shareholders, consider the risk of cash flows when valuing investments. A relationship among debt, earnings per share, and firm value appears in Figure 15.6. Because of the risk of excessive debt, the maximum firm value occurs at a lower debt ratio than that of maximum earnings per share.

A firm's **business risk** is measured by its variability in EBIT over time. Business risk is affected by several factors, including the business cycle, competitive pressures, and the firm's operating leverage or its level of fixed operating costs. The following section reviews business risk and the combined effects of business and financial risk on management's choice of a capital structure.

business risk
measured by variability in EBIT over time

CONCEPT CHECK

How is EBIT/eps analysis useful to managers?

How might the expected level of EBIT and its potential variability affect a firm's capital structure?

COMBINED OPERATING AND FINANCIAL LEVERAGE EFFECTS

Business risk is determined by the products the firm sells and the production processes it uses. The effects of business risk are seen ultimately in the variability of operating income or EBIT over time. In fact, one popular measure of a firm's business risk is the standard deviation of EBIT.[17]

---

17. To control for the effects of firm size when comparing different firms, some use the standard deviation of operating return on assets, that is, the standard deviation of EBIT/Total assets.

TABLE 15.4

Effects of Business Risk and Financial Risk on a Simplified Income Statement

IMPACT OF BUSINESS RISK (TOP HALF OF INCOME STATEMENT)	Sales revenue (equals price × quantity sold) Less variable costs (such as labor and materials; equals variable cost per unit × quantity) Less fixed costs (such as rent and depreciation expenses) Earnings before interest and taxes (operating income)
IMPACT OF FINANCIAL RISK (BOTTOM HALF OF INCOME STATEMENT)	Less interest expense (bank loans, bonds, other debt; a fixed expense as it is not dependent on sales) EBT (earnings before taxes) Less taxes (a variable expense, dependent on EBT) Net Income

eps = Net Income/Number of Shares

Table 15.4 shows a simplified income statement. Because business risk is measured by variability in EBIT, line items that affect business risk appear on the top half of the income statement, between sales revenue and EBIT. This suggests that a firm's business risk is affected by three major influences: unit volume or quantity sold; the relationship between selling price and variable costs; and the firm's fixed costs.

UNIT VOLUME VARIABILITY

Variability in the quantity sold of the firm's products or services will cause variation in sales revenue, variable costs, and EBIT. Fluctuating sales volumes can arise from a variety of factors, including pricing strategy from competitive products, new technologies or new products, customer impressions of product or service quality, and other factors affecting customer brand loyalty.

PRICE-VARIABLE COST MARGIN

A second factor affecting business risk is the firm's ability to maintain a constant, positive difference between price and per-unit variable costs. If the margin between price and cost fluctuates, the firm's operating income will fluctuate, too. Competitive pricing pressures, input supply shocks, labor union contracts, and other cost influences can cause the price-variable cost margin to vary over time, thus contributing to business risk.

FIXED COSTS

The variability of sales or revenues over time is a basic operating risk. Furthermore, when fixed operating costs, such as rental payments, lease payments, contractual employee salaries, and general and administrative overhead expenses exist, they create operating leverage and increase business risk. Since fixed costs do not rise and fall along with sales revenues, fluctuating revenues lead to variability in operating income or EBIT. As we learned in Chapter 12, the effect of operating leverage is that a given percentage change in net sales will result in a greater percentage change in operating income or earnings before interest and taxes (EBIT).

Operating leverage affects the top portion of a firm's income statement, as shown in Table 15.4. It relates changes in sales to changes in EBIT or operating income. We saw in Chapter 12 that the effect of fixed operating costs on a firm's business risk can be measured by the degree of operating leverage (DOL). Equation 15.9 repeats these relationships from Chapter 12:

$$\text{DOL} = \frac{\text{Percentage change in EBIT}}{\text{Percentage change in Sales}} = \frac{\text{Sales} - \text{variable cost}}{\text{Sales} - \text{variable cost} - \text{fixed cost}} \quad (15.9)$$

In a similar fashion, when money is borrowed, financial leverage will be created as the firm will have a fixed financial obligation or interest to pay. Financial leverage affects the bottom half of a firm's income statement. A given percentage change in the firm's EBIT will produce a larger percentage change in the firm's net income or earnings per share. A small percentage change in EBIT may be leveraged or magnified into a larger percentage change in net income.

DEGREE OF FINANCIAL LEVERAGE

degree of financial leverage (DFL)
measures the sensitivity of eps to changes in EBIT

A firm's financial risk reflects its interest expense or, in financial jargon, its financial leverage. A quick way to determine a firm's exposure to financial risk is to compute its degree of financial leverage. The *degree of financial leverage (DFL)* measures the sensitivity of earnings per share to changes in EBIT:

$$\text{DFL} = \frac{\text{Percentage change in eps}}{\text{Percentage change in EBIT}} \tag{15.10}$$

This definition clearly suggests that DFL represents the percentage change in eps arising from a 1 percent change in earnings before interest and taxes. For example, a DFL of 1.25 means that the firm's eps will rise (or fall) by 1.25 percent for every 1 percent increase (or decrease) in EBIT; a 1 percent change in EBIT becomes magnified to a 1.25 percent change in eps.

There is a more straightforward way to compute a firm's degree of financial leverage that avoids handling percentage changes in variables. This formula is given in Equation 15.11:

$$\text{DFL} = \frac{\text{EBIT}}{\text{EBIT} - I} = \frac{\text{EBIT}}{\text{EBT}} \tag{15.11}$$

DFL equals the firm's earnings before interest and taxes (EBIT) divided by EBIT minus interest expense, or earnings before taxes (EBT).

Let's use Equation 15.11 to find the degree of financial leverage when EBIT equals $50 and interest expense equals $10, $20, and $0. When EBIT equals $50 and interest expense equals $10, DFL equals $50/($50 − $10) = 1.25.

When interest expense is $20, DFL equals $50/($50 − $20) = 1.67. Higher interest expense leads to greater financial risk and greater eps sensitivity to changes in EBIT.

When the interest expense is zero, the DFL is $50/($50 − $0) = 1.00. That is, the percentage change in eps will be the same as the percentage change in EBIT. Without any fixed financial cost, there is no financial leverage and there is no magnification effect.

TOTAL RISK

Total earnings risk, or total variability in eps, is the result of combining the effects of business risk and financial risk. As shown in Table 15.4, operating leverage and financial leverage combine to magnify a given percentage change in sales to a potentially much greater percentage change in earnings.

combined leverage
effect on earnings produced by the operating and financial leverage

Together, operating and financial leverage produce an effect called *combined leverage*. A firm's *degree of combined leverage (DCL)* is the percentage change in eps share that results from a 1 percent change in sales volume:

$$\text{DCL} = \frac{\text{Percentage change in eps}}{\text{Percentage change in sales}} \tag{15.12}$$

degree of combined leverage (DCL)
percentage change in earnings per share that results from a 1 percent change in sales volume

There is a straightforward relationship between the degrees of operating and financial leverage and the degree of combined leverage. A firm's degree of combined leverage is simply the product of its degree of operating leverage and its degree of financial leverage:[18]

$$\text{DCL} = \text{DOL} \times \text{DFL} \tag{15.13}$$

The DCL represents the impact on eps of the effects of operating leverage and financial leverage on a given change in sales revenue.

---

18. Recall that the degree of operating leverage is the percentage change in EBIT divided by the percentage change in sales; the degree of financial leverage is the percentage change in eps divided by the percentage change in EBIT. Multiplying these two formulas gives the definition of DCL in Equation 15.12:

$$\frac{\text{Percentage change in EBIT}}{\text{Percentage change in sales}} \times \frac{\text{Percentage change in eps}}{\text{Percentage change in EBIT}} =$$

$$\text{DOL} \times \text{DFL} = \frac{\text{Percentage change in eps}}{\text{Percentage change in sales}} = \text{DCL}$$

TABLE 15.5
Effects of Leverage on the Income Statement

		NEXT YEAR	
	THIS YEAR	10% SALES DECREASE	10% SALES INCREASE
Net sales	$700,000	$630,000	$770,000
Less: variable costs (60% of sales)	420,000	378,000	462,000
Less: fixed costs	200,000	200,000	200,000
Earnings before interest and taxes	80,000	52,000	108,000
Less: interest expenses	20,000	20,000	20,000
Income before taxes	60,000	32,000	88,000
Less: income taxes (30%)	18,000	9,600	26,400
Net income	$42,000	$22,400	$61,600
PERCENTAGE CHANGE IN SALES			
Percent change in operating income (EBIT)		−35.0%	+35.0%
Percent change in net income		−46.7%	+46.7%

Let's illustrate this concept with a full income statement for this year and both a 10 percent decrease and a 10 percent increase in net sales for next year, as seen in Table 15.5.

We can estimate directly the individual effects of operating and financial leverage and their combined effects. First, from Chapter 12, the degree of operating leverage (DOL) is estimated as:

$$DOL = \frac{Sales - variable\ cost}{Sales - variable\ cost - fixed\ cost}$$

$$= \frac{\$700,000 - \$420,000}{\$700,000 - \$420,000 - \$200,00} = \frac{\$280,000}{80,000} = 3.50$$

It should be noted that this is the same as the percentage change in EBIT (35 percent) divided by the percentage change in sales (10 percent) in Table 15.5:

$$DOL = \frac{35\%}{10\%} = 3.50$$

The degree of financial leverage (DFL) measures the impact of fixed financial expenses and is estimated as:

$$DFL = \frac{EBIT}{EBIT - I}$$

Thus, DFL is equal to:

$$DFL = \frac{\$80,000}{\$80,000 - \$20,000} = \frac{\$80,000}{\$60,000} = 1.33$$

It should be noted that this is the same as the percentage change in eps (46.7 percent) divided by the percentage change in EBIT (35 percent) in Table 15.5:

$$DFL = \frac{46.7\%}{35.0\%} = 1.33$$

Finally, the degree of combined leverage (DCL) can be estimated by finding the product of the DOL and the DFL as follows:

$$DCL = DOL \times DFL$$

$$= 3.5 \times 1.33$$

$$= 4.66$$

Except for rounding, this is the same as the percentage change in eps (46.7 percent) divided by the percentage change in sales (10 percent): 46.7 percent/10 percent = 4.67.

By knowing the DCL factor, we can now estimate next year's change in net income, assuming no major change occurs in the income tax rate. This is done by multiplying the expected percentage change in net sales by the DCL of 4.67. For example, a 10 percent increase in net sales will increase net income by 46.7 percent (10 percent times the combined leverage factor of 4.67). Of course, combined leverage works in both directions, and a decline in net sales might place the firm in a difficult financial position. A 10 percent decline in sales will be expected to reduce net income and eps by 46.7 percent.

The use of both operating and financial leverage produces a compound impact when a change in net sales occurs. Thus, from an overall risk perspective, it is important for the financial manager to use operating and financial leverage to form an acceptable combined leverage effect.

For example, if a firm's stockholders do not like large amounts of risk, a firm with a high degree of operating leverage may attempt to keep financial leverage low. In other words, it will use relatively less debt and more equity to finance its assets. Likewise, a firm with low business risk (that is, steady sales and low fixed operating expenses), such as an electric utility, can support a higher degree of financial leverage and use relatively more debt financing. There is no evidence that firms adjust their DOLs and DFLs to match some standard degree of combined leverage, but their relationship does imply a potential trade-off between a firm's business and financial risk.

CONCEPT CHECK

What are the effects of financial leverage on earnings per share?

What is the degree of combined leverage? How is it related to DOL and DFL?

INSIGHTS FROM THEORY AND PRACTICE

An insight gained from our discussion of combined leverage is that a firm with greater business risk may be inclined to use less debt in its capital structure, while a firm with less business risk may use more debt in its capital structure. Theories of financial researchers have shed light on additional influences on the capital structure decision.

TAXES AND NONDEBT TAX SHIELDS

Interest on debt is a tax-deductible expense whereas stock dividends are not; dividends are paid from after-tax dollars. This gives firms a tax incentive to use debt financing, but in reality there are limits to the benefits of tax-deductible debt. Business risk leads to variations in EBIT over time, which can lead to uncertainty about the firm's ability to fully use future interest deductions. For example, if a firm has a negative or zero operating income, an interest deduction provides little help; it just makes the pretax losses larger. Firms in lower tax brackets have less tax incentive to borrow than do those in higher tax brackets.

In addition, firms have other tax-deductible expenses besides interest. Various cash and noncash expenses such as depreciation, R&D, and advertising expenses can reduce operating income. Thus, the tax deductibility of debt becomes less important to firms with large nondebt tax shields. Foreign tax credits, granted by the U.S. government to firms that pay taxes to foreign governments, also diminish the impact of the interest deduction.

BANKRUPTCY COSTS

bankruptcy costs
explicit and implicit costs associated with financial distress

static trade-off hypothesis
a theory that states firms attempt to balance the benefits of debt versus its disadvantages to determine an optimal capital structure

The major drawback to debt in the capital structure is its legal requirement for timely payment of interest and principal. As the debt/total asset ratio rises, or as earnings become more volatile, the firm will face higher borrowing costs, driven upward by bond investors requiring higher yields to compensate for additional risk.

A rational marketplace will evaluate the probability and associated costs of bankruptcy for a levered firm. **Bankruptcy costs** include explicit expenses, such as legal and accounting fees and court costs, along with implicit costs, such as the use of management time and skills, in trying to prevent and escape bankruptcy. It is also difficult to market the firm's products and keep good people on staff when the firm is teetering on the brink of bankruptcy.[19] An efficient market will evaluate the present value of the expected bankruptcy costs and reduce its estimate of the value of the firm accordingly.

The **static trade-off hypothesis** states that firms will balance the advantages of debt (its lower cost and tax-deductibility of interest) with its disadvantages (greater possibility of bankruptcy and the value of explicit and implicit bankruptcy costs). This is illustrated in Figure 15.7. At low

---

19. Potential customers shy away from a financially troubled firm in fear that it may not survive to provide warranty service or spare parts for their products. Customers may also fear that financial distress may lead management to reduce customer service or product maintenance (witness the decline in ridership for an airline when it declares bankruptcy). Good employees with marketable skills may decide to change jobs rather than risk unemployment due to business failure.

FIGURE 15.7

The Static Trade-Off Hypothesis: Weighted Average Cost of Capital Versus Debt Ratio

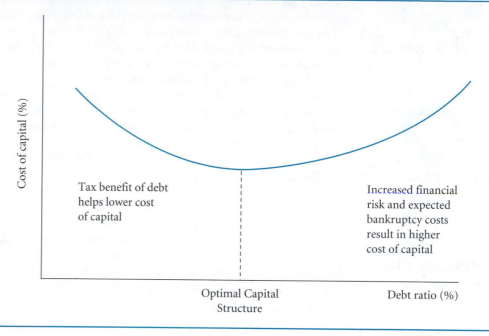

Tax benefit of debt
helps lower cost
of capital

Increased financial
risk and expected
bankruptcy costs
result in higher
cost of capital

Cost of capital (%)

Optimal Capital
Structure

Debt ratio (%)

INTERNET ACTIVITY

Professor Edward Altman's Web site contains links to research on bond default rates and financial distress: http://www.stern.nyu.edu/~ealtman.

levels of debt, increasing the use of debt is beneficial as debt's lower cost helps to lower the weighted average cost of capital and to increase firm value, but further increases in debt beyond the optimal capital structure level actually reduce firm value, as investors' perceptions of the increased cost of bankruptcy outweigh the tax benefits of additional debt.

Bond ratings, discussed in Chapter 7, help guide both investors and managers in evaluating the risk of increasing debt to the capital structure. Studies have shown that the probability of financial distress and bankruptcy rises as a firm's bond ratings decline. Some firms use their bond rating as a guide for their capital structure decision—for example, maintaining debt at a level consistent with an "A" bond rating. To preserve some financing flexibility, firms may try to keep their debt ratios lower than that necessary to maintain their target debt rating. This way, should they need to raise additional debt, they can do so and still be able to maintain their desired rating.

Table 15.6 shows the decline in senior debt ratings over time among U.S. firms. In 1980, 50 percent of firms with rated senior debt had a rating of "A" or higher. In 1999, in good economic times, only 18 percent of firms had an "A" rating or better; by 2006 the proportion had sunk lower, to 11 percent. Of course, this has the opposite effect on low-rated issues; the percentage of junk bonds (rated "BB" or lower) has swelled from 32 percent in 1980 to 71 percent in 2006. Several factors may account for this decline in credit quality, including more risk-tolerant investors, more risk-taking corporate managers, and perceptions of lower bankruptcy costs.

TABLE 15.6

Distribution of U.S. Industrial Senior Debt Ratings, Various Years

RATING	PERCENTAGE OF FIRMS WITH RATING IN 1980	PERCENTAGE OF FIRMS WITH RATING IN 1999	PERCENTAGE OF FIRMS WITH RATING IN 2006
AAA/AA	17	5	2
A	33	13	9
BBB	18	20	18
BB	22	24	25
B	7	32	42
CCC/D	3	6	4

Sources: Serena Ng, "Junk Turns Golden, but May Be Laced with Tinsel," *Wall Street Journal,* January 4, 2007, pp. C1, C2; David Lindorff, "Who Needs a Triple A?" *Treasury and Risk Management* (May/June 2000), pp. 47–48.

FINANCE PRINCIPLE

GLOBAL DISCUSSION

CONCEPT CHECK

As a firm's use of nondebt tax shields rises, how might its use of debt change?

How do bankruptcy costs affect a firm's optimal capital structure?

How do agency costs affect a firm's capital structure?

Why might a firm with many fixed assets use more debt financing relative to a dot-com firm?

AGENCY COSTS

From Chapter 11 we know agency costs are restrictions placed on corporate managers to limit their discretion. They basically measure the cost of distrust between investors and management. To protect bondholders, covenants may require the firm to maintain a minimum level of liquidity or may restrict future debt issues, future dividend payments, or certain forms of financial restructuring. Agency costs may also take the form of explicit expenses, such as a requirement that the firm's finances be audited periodically.

The cost to the firm's shareholders of excessive covenants and interference with management discretion will likely cause firms to shy away from excessive debt in the United States. In other words, the relationship between the level of agency costs and firm debt will look similar to that of bankruptcy costs and firm debt in Figure 15.7. The joint effect of bankruptcy and agency costs will reduce the optimal level of debt financing for a firm below the level that would be appropriate if agency costs were zero.

The situation may be different for non-U.S. companies. Agency costs may differ across national borders as a result of different accounting principles, banking structures, and securities laws and regulations. Firms in the United States and United Kingdom use relatively more equity financing than do firms in France, Germany, and Japan, which use relatively more debt financing. Some argue that these apparent differences can be explained by differences in equity and debt agency costs across the countries.[20] For example, agency costs of equity seem to be lower in the United States and United Kingdom. These countries have more accurate systems of accounting and higher auditing standards than the other countries. Dividends and financial statements are distributed to shareholders more frequently, as well, which allows shareholders to monitor management more easily.

Germany, France, and Japan, on the other hand, all have systems of debt finance that may reduce the agency costs of lending. In these countries, a bank can hold an equity stake in a corporation, meet the bulk of the corporation's borrowing needs, and have representation on the corporate board of directors. Corporations can own stock in other companies and also have representatives on other companies' boards. Companies frequently get financial advice from groups of banks and other large corporations with which they have interlocking directorates. These institutional arrangements greatly reduce the monitoring and agency costs of debt; thus, debt ratios are substantially higher in France, Germany, and Japan.[21]

A FIRM'S ASSETS AND ITS FINANCING POLICY

Firms' asset structures and capital structures are related because of agency costs and bankruptcy costs. Evidence shows that firms with fungible, tangible assets (i.e., assets in place that can be easily sold and used by another firm, such as railroad cars or automobiles) use more debt financing than firms with many intangible assets. Examples of intangible assets include growth opportunities, the value of the firm's R&D efforts, and customer loyalty that is built and maintained through large advertising expenditures.

Agency costs and bankruptcy costs impose lighter burdens on financing for investments in tangible assets. It is much easier for a lender to monitor the use of tangible assets such as physical plant and equipment. Well-developed accounting rules govern methods for tracking the values of such assets. Also, tangible assets can be sold and reused, and they will not lose all their value following a period of financial distress. Such is not necessarily the case for intangible assets whose value mainly resides within the firm.

THE PECKING ORDER HYPOTHESIS

One perspective on firms' capital structure decisions is based on repeated observations of how corporations seem to raise funds over time. The theory behind this perspective is based on the

---

20. See J. Rutherford, "An International Perspective on the Capital Structure Puzzle," *Midland Corporate Finance Journal* (Fall 1985), pp. 60–72. For a perspective on several countries in the Asia Pacific region, see Rataporn Deesomsak, Krishna Paudyal, and Gioia Pescetto, "The Determinants of Capital Structure: Evidence from the Asia Pacific Region," *Journal of Multinational Financial Management*, vol. 14, no. 4–5 (2004), pp. 387–405.

21. Substantially higher debt ratios still exist in these countries after allowing for differences in accounting principles.

belief that management knows more about the firm and its opportunities than does the financial marketplace and that management does not want to be forced to issue equity when stock prices are depressed.

Evidence shows that corporations rely mainly on additions to retained earnings to finance growth and capital budgeting projects. If they need outside financing, firms typically issue debt first, as it imposes lower risk on the investor than equity, and it has a lower cost to the corporation. Should a firm approach its debt capacity, it may well favor hybrid securities, such as convertible bonds, over common stock. As a last resort, the firm will issue common equity. Thus, the firm has a financing "pecking order," rather than a goal to maintain a specific target debt/equity ratio over time.

pecking order hypothesis
a theory that states managers prefer to use additions to retained earnings to finance the firm, then debt, and, as a final resort, new equity

Under this ***pecking order hypothesis***, financial theory implies that firms have no optimal debt/equity ratios.[22] Instead, they follow the pecking order, exhausting internal equity (retained earnings) first and resorting to external equity (new issues of common stock) as a last resort. Observed debt ratios represent nothing more than the cumulative result of a firm's need to use external financing over time and reflect the joint effects of growth, attractive investment opportunities, and dividend policy.

Under the pecking order hypothesis, firms with higher profitability should have lower debt ratios, as these firms' additions to retained earnings reduce their need to borrow. Under the static trade-off hypothesis, a firm with higher profitability should have a lower probability of bankruptcy and a higher tax rate, thus leading to *higher* debt ratios. Most empirical evidence resolves this conflict in favor of the pecking order hypothesis; studies find that more profitable firms tend to have lower debt ratios.

MARKET TIMING

market timing hypothesis
firms try to time the market by selling common stock when their stock price is high and repurchasing shares when their stock price is low

Like the pecking order hypothesis, this perspective is based upon observations of how firms raise funds in practice. The ***market timing hypothesis*** states that firms try to time the equity market by issuing stock when their stock prices are high and repurchasing shares when stock values are low.[23] Research studies have found that firms prefer to issue stock when earnings expectations by the market are overoptimistic. Managers have admitted that over- and undervaluation of their stock is an important consideration in issuing equity.[24] Researchers argue that firms, after issuing or repurchasing equity in apparent attempts to time the equity market, do not move the firm back to its former capital structure over time. Rather, low-leverage firms are those that were, on balance, successful in raising funds when their equity market values were high; high-leverage firms, on average, are those that raised funds when their equity market values were low.

INTERNET ACTIVITY

Cutting-edge research on capital structure issues and many other finance topics can be found via the links on http://www.cob.ohio-state.edu/fin, the home page of the Finance Department at Ohio State University. Another site, http://www.cfo.com, contains items of interest on financing and other corporate finance topics.

An apparent implication of both the pecking order and market timing hypotheses is that the firm has no optimal capital structure. What implication does this have for computing a cost of capital and using it to evaluate capital budgeting projects? The answer: hardly any. Recall that the weighted average cost of capital represents the minimum required return on a firm's average-risk capital budgeting projects. The target capital structure weights reflect management's impression of a capital structure that is sustainable in the long run and that allows financing flexibility over time. Using the target structure and current financing costs, management can compute the weighted average cost of capital. The cost of capital calculation is paramount; should a firm fail to earn an appropriate return on its capital budgeting projects, shareholder wealth and firm value will decline.

Part of the uncertainty over which theoretical perspective may be correct arises from capital structure choices that depart from "plain vanilla" debt and equity. Firms have devised a myriad of financing flavors, as we discuss next.

22. Stewart C. Myers and Nicholas S. Majluf, "Corporate Financing and Investment Decisions when Firms Have Information that Investors Do Not Have," *Journal of Financial Economics*, vol. 13 (1984), pp. 187–221; Stewart C. Myers, "The Capital Structure Puzzle," *Journal of Finance*, vol. 39 (1984), pp. 575–592.
23. Malcolm Baker and Jeffrey Wurgler, "Market Timing and Capital Structure," *Journal of Finance*, vol. 57, no. 1 (February 2002), pp. 1–32.
24. John R. Graham and Campbell R. Harvey, "The Theory and Practice of Corporate Finance: Evidence from the Field," *Journal of Financial Economics*, vol. 60 (2001), pp. 187–243.

PERSONAL FINANCIAL PLANNING
The Effect of Investors on the Firm

In this chapter, the discussions of Part 2, "Investments," and Part 3, "Financial Management," are drawn together. Financial market participants, by deciding where and how to save and invest, affect the level of interest rates in the financial markets. This, in term, determines a firm's cost of debt. A firm cannot determine its borrowing costs; it must accept the interest rates given it by the financial markets. Stock prices are determined by investors' expectations of future firm performance. Optimism (buying) and pessimism (selling) determine

a firm's share price in an efficient market. A firm's cost of capital is affected directly by the investment decisions of many investors.

By changing the firm's capital structure, a firm can affect investors' perceptions of its risk. As seen, the firm's cost of capital affects the firm's value. Decisions to increase or decrease a firm's use of debt are made to determine the capital structure that minimizes the weighted average cost of capital and maximizes the value of investors' holdings in the firm.

BEYOND DEBT AND EQUITY

Bright Wall Street investment bankers have introduced many variations on these two themes in attempts to market new and different instruments to meet the needs of many kinds of issuers and investors.[25] Today firms can choose among various types of security issues, as we saw in Chapters 7 and 8. Consequently, many firms have several layers of debt and several layers of equity on their balance sheets.

Debt can be made convertible to equity. Its maturity can be extended, or shortened, at the firm's option. Debt issues can be made senior or subordinate to other debt issues. Coupon interest rates can be fixed, float up or down along with other interest rates, or be indexed to a commodity price.[26] Some bond issues do not even pay interest. Corporations can issue bonds in the United States or overseas. Bonds can be sold alone, or with warrants attached that allow the bond investor to purchase shares of common stock at predetermined prices over time.

Likewise, equity variations exist. Preferred stock has a claim on the firm that is junior to the bondholder claim but senior to the common shareholder claim. Preferred stock can pay dividends at a fixed or a variable rate.

CONCEPT CHECK

What is the pecking order hypothesis?

What is the marketing timing hypothesis?

Describe some differences that can exist among security issues.

Even types of common stock can differ. Firms can have different classes of common equity. Some classes can provide holders with higher levels of dividend income. Some classes may have superior voting rights. Firms have issued separate classes of equity to finance acquisitions, distributing part of the acquired firm's earnings as dividends to holders of that particular class of stock. Such was the case with General Motors. It issued its Class E stock to finance its acquisition of EDS; dividends on the Class E shares were determined by the earnings of the EDS subsidiary.

All these variations of debt and equity give the firm valuable flexibility. Corporate financial managers' decisions about the structure of a security issue may be more difficult now, but these choices also can allow them to lower the cost of capital and increase firm value.[27]

GUIDELINES FOR FINANCING STRATEGY

We have covered a lot of ground and a lot of controversy in this chapter. Let's now summarize the practical implications of these discussions and list the influences of both theory and real-world evidence on a firm's capital structure decisions.

Business Risk

Firms in the same industry will generally face the same business risks. Many financial managers confess that they examine their competitors' capital structures to help determine if their own

---

25. Finance is not just finance; it sometimes involves marketing research and analysis. Wall Street firms serve two basic sets of customers: issuers and investors. By designing innovative securities to better meet their customers' needs, investment bankers can exploit market niches by being the first mover in a new product area. Such innovation will attract business, enhance income, and increase the firm's reputation among market players.

26. For example, a silver-mining firm whose profits and cash flow are quite sensitive to the market price of silver can reduce its financial leverage by issuing bonds that pay interest at a rate that is related to silver price fluctuations.

27. An accessible review of issues related to capital structure and cost of capital is available in Zander's 8-part series "WACC: Practical Guide for Strategic Decision-Making" found at http://www.gtnews.com/feature/122.cfm (accessible with free registration). Zanders, Treasury and Finance Solutions, is a European-Based consulting firm. Their series on WACC was featured on the gtnews.com Web site from March 2006 to March 2007.

financial strategies are appropriate. A firm's degree of operating leverage affects the amount of debt it can issue. Firms with highly variable EBIT can ill afford to issue large amounts of debt, as the combined effects of high business and financial risk may imperil the future of the firm. In general, greater EBIT variability reduces the firm's reliance on debt.[28]

Taxes and Nondebt Tax Shields

Under current tax regulations, the debt interest deduction is a strong influence in favor of debt. The tax incentive for debt financing can diminish as a firm accumulates nondebt tax shields, such as depreciation expense, R&D, and large advertising outlays.

Mix of Tangible and Intangible Assets

Agency costs and bankruptcy costs can make debt less attractive as a financing alternative for firms with relatively large amounts of intangible assets, such as goodwill, customer loyalty, R&D, and growth opportunities.

Financial Flexibility

Frequently the greatest concern among financial managers is maintaining access to capital. Without the ability to raise financing, a firm may have to pass up attractive investment opportunities, or a temporary cash crunch may push it to the edge of default. Loss of financial flexibility can disrupt the firm more than the strictest bond covenants. Some firms seek financial flexibility by maintaining financial slack or unused debt capacity. One way to do this is to try to maintain an investment-grade bond rating over time or to maintain large lines of credit.

It may be good to have financing that can be eliminated if it is no longer needed. The firm can arrange for debt financing with a maturity matching the expected period of need. For maturity matching, debt holds an important advantage over preferred stock or common stock financing because equity securities do not have a stated maturity that makes it possible to retire them conveniently. We should also note that a lease arrangement for fixed assets is advantageous because the lease term may be set to coincide with the duration of the need for the assets.

Control of the Firm

Common shareholders receive dividends and have voting control of the firm. Additional equity issues will likely reduce per-share dividends and dilute control. If shareholders worry about control, they may force a firm to use more debt financing and less external equity financing.

Profitability

Firms with above-average profitability can reduce flotation costs and restrictive debt covenants by relying on internal equity to finance capital budgeting projects. More profitable firms tend to use less debt financing.

Financial Market Conditions

A firm can minimize its financing costs by issuing debt when interest rates are near cyclical lows, especially if economists forecast rising rates in the future. Likewise, it is advantageous to issue stock when stock prices are high rather than depressed.

Management's Attitude Toward Debt and Risk

When push comes to shove, it is people—the management team—who ultimately make decisions about financing policy. Some management teams may be more conservative and hesitant to issue debt, while others may be more aggressive and willing to increase the firm's financial leverage. Their judgment and expectations for the firm's financial future will affect the firm's capital structure.

CONCEPT CHECK

What influences affect a firm's choice of a capital structure?

---

28. Securities can reduce the adverse effects of price swings that might otherwise contribute to business risk. Bonds with coupons that rise and fall with changes in commodity prices, market interest rates, or foreign currencies can help mitigate the effects of EBIT variations on net income. Firms can reduce political risk exposure from their foreign operations by financing foreign assets with host country bank loans or debt issues.

JEFF YINGLING
Managing Director, Corporate
Finance
Morgan Stanley Dean Witter

BBA, Finance
University of Notre Dame
MBA, Finance
University of Chicago

*"We definitely have ups and
downs with the markets."*

Q: *What is your primary responsibility?*

A: My job is to initiate and maintain investment banking relationships with clients in the utility and telecommunications industries.

Q: *What do you do for these clients?*

A: Our primary role is to help them raise capital through the issuance of equity or debt. We also advise on mergers, acquisitions, and divestitures.

Q: *Explain what happens when the client decides to publicly offer common stock.*

A: We work with the client to assemble the necessary information to register the offering with the Securities and Exchange Commission, analyze the value of the company to determine the price at which to offer the security, and coordinate a series of "road shows" where we and the client present information to potential investors. These road shows help generate awareness and demand for the upcoming stock issue. We also underwrite the issue, which means that we buy the stock for an agreed-upon price up front. The client gets that money minus our commission. Then it's up to our sales force to sell the stock at the higher public offering price.

Q: *What are the major differences between issuing equity as you've just described and selling debt?*

A: There are lots of similarities, but one major difference is the time line. A stock issue generally takes a number of weeks. A bond issue can be concluded in a very short time if necessary. That's because it's much less complicated to determine the value of a bond. Its cash flows, which are a function of the prevailing market interest rates and the credit rating of the company, are known at the time of sale. The value of a common stock issue, on the other hand, is much more subjective because it relates to the value of the company's future earnings and cash flow, which obviously cannot be known in advance. There are many more variables to consider, so it takes longer to analyze.

Q: *What is the normal entry-level point in investment banking?*

A: Someone with an undergraduate degree would normally start as an analyst. An MBA would normally start as an associate. These positions involve the detail-level responsibilities in a transaction such as document preparation, number crunching, and the specifics of the road shows. Each deal is handled by a team of several people, depending on its size and complexity. The work of the analysts and associates is overseen by a more senior person.

Q: *Do the fluctuations of the markets affect your success?*

A: Very much so. When interest rates are low and equity values are high, it is much easier for a company to raise money or complete a merger or acquisition, which means there is more business for us. When the markets are weak, our job is more difficult and the competition is more spirited. We definitely have ups and downs with the markets.

APPLYING FINANCE TO . . .

INSTITUTIONS AND MARKETS	INVESTMENTS	FINANCIAL MANAGEMENT
A firm's capital structure is affected by the costs it faces from raising capital. Depository institutions and investment banks funnel savings to those wanting to raise funds. They do so in a way that helps to lower flotation and other transactions costs associated with raising funds, thereby making it easier for firms to raise capital. Security analysts and bond rating agencies convey opinions to investors regarding the attractiveness of a firm's securities.	Dividends and the price appreciation potential in equity are attractive to many investors. Investors examine a firm's prospects and then "vote with their dollars" by deciding which investments look most attractive from a risk–expected return trade-off. The market prices of a firm's securities and the ratings given the firm's bonds are used as inputs into the firm's decision-making process because they determine the cost of financing the firm's assets and therefore are a cost the firm must consider in its capital budgeting decisions.	Financial managers need to listen to the market. Trends in interest rates will affect the choice of short-term and long-term borrowing by the firm. Changes in stock price that differ from those of the overall market or the firm's industry group send positive or negative messages to managers about how investors evaluate the firm's future prospects. Financial capital is not cheap; the cost of financing assets, whether in the form of higher inventory or equipment, must be part of the firm's investment decisions.

SUMMARY

The capital structure decision is a very difficult but very important one for managers to make. An inappropriate mix of debt and equity can lead to higher financing costs for a firm, which in turn will hurt shareholders' wealth. Once a target capital structure is selected, the cost of each financing source must be estimated before the weighted average cost of capital can be computed. We review how to estimate the cost of debt, cost of preferred stock, the cost of retained earnings, and the cost of new common equity.

This chapter reviewed several tools that can be used to examine a firm's capital structure, including EBIT/eps analysis, business risk, financial risk, and combined leverage. We reviewed findings of several studies, both theoretical and empirical, relating to influences on the capital structure decision, including management's desire to balance the benefits and drawbacks of debt, financing pecking orders, market timing, and agency cost issues, among others.

KEY TERMS

bankruptcy costs	degree of financial leverage (DFL)	optimum debt/equity mix
business risk	dividend payout ratio	pecking order hypothesis
capital structure	EBIT/eps analysis	retention rate
combined leverage	flotation costs	static trade-off hypothesis
cost of capital	internal growth rate	sustainable growth rate
degree of combined leverage (DCL)	market timing hypothesis	weighted average cost of capital (WACC)

DISCUSSION QUESTIONS

1. What is a firm's capital structure?

2. Explain why determining a firm's optimum debt-to-equity mix is important.

3. Briefly describe the trends that have occurred in the corporate use of debt.

4. What is EBIT/eps analysis? What information does it provide managers?

5. Describe the term *indifference level* in conjunction with EBIT/eps analysis.

6. Describe how a firm's business risk can be measured, and indicate how operating leverage impacts business risk.

7. How is financial leverage created? Describe how the degree of financial leverage is calculated.

8. Briefly explain the concepts of *business risk, operating leverage,* and *financial leverage* in terms of an income statement.

9. How might the following influences affect a firm's business risk (consider each separately)?

   a. Imports increase the level of competition.

   b. Labor costs decline.

   c. Health care costs (provided for all employees) increase.

   d. The firm's proportion of Social Security and unemployment insurance taxes rises.

   e. Adoption of new technology allows the firm to produce the same output with fewer employees.

10. How might the following influences affect a firm's financial risk (consider each separately)?

   a. Interest rates on the firm's short-term bank loans are reduced.

   b. The firm refinances a mortgage on one of its buildings at a lower interest rate.

   c. Tax rates decline.

   d. The firm's stock price rises.

   e. The firm suffers a sales and operating income decline.

11. What is meant by the *degree of combined leverage*?

12. Describe how the degree of combined leverage can be determined by the degrees of operating and financial leverage.

13. Briefly explain how the factors of flexibility and timing affect the mix between debt and equity capital.

14. How do corporate control concerns affect a firm's capital structure?

15. The management of Albar Incorporated has decided to increase the firm's use of debt from 30 percent to 45 percent of assets. How will this affect its internal growth rate in the future? Its sustainable growth rate?

16. A booming economy creates an unexpectedly high sales growth rate for a firm with a low internal growth rate. How can the firm respond to this unplanned sales increase?

17. What is the relationship between a firm's cost of capital and investor-required rates of return?

18. How can a firm estimate its cost of debt financing?

19. Describe how the cost of preferred stock is determined.

20. Describe two methods for estimating the cost of retained earnings.

21. How does the cost of new common stock differ from the cost of retained earnings?

22. What is the weighted average cost of capital? Describe how it is calculated.

23. Should book value weights or market value weights be used to evaluate a firm's current capital structure weights? Why?

24. How does management's strategy toward corporate growth and dividends affect its capital structure policy?

25. If a firm is eligible to receive tax credits, how might that affect its use of debt?

26. Describe the reasoning behind the static trade-off hypothesis.

27. How do agency costs affect a firm's optimal capital structure? How can differences in agency costs explain capital structure differences across countries?

28. How do you expect the capital structures of two firms to differ if one is involved in steel production and the other designs software to solve business problems?

29. What implications might the pecking order and market timing hypotheses have for an optimal capital structure? Is the weighted average cost of capital still an important concept under these hypotheses?

PROBLEMS

1. AQ&Q has EBIT of $2 million, total assets of $10 million, stockholders' equity of $4 million, and pretax interest expense of 10 percent.

   a. What is AQ&Q's indifference level of EBIT?

   b. Given its current situation, might it benefit from increasing or decreasing its use of debt? Explain.

   c. Suppose we are told AQ&Q's average tax rate is 40 percent. How does this affect your answers to (a) and (b)?

2. URA, Incorporated, has operating income of $5 million, total assets of $45 million, outstanding debt of $20 million, and annual interest expense of $3 million.

   a. What is URA's indifference level of EBIT?

   b. Given its current situation, might URA benefit from increasing or decreasing its use of debt? Explain.

   c. Suppose forecasted net income is $4 million next year. If it has a 40 percent average tax rate, what will be its expected level of EBIT? Will this forecast change your answer to (b)? Why or why not?

3. Stern's Stews, Inc., is considering a new capital structure. Its current and proposed capital structure are:

	CURRENT	PROPOSED
Total assets	$150 million	$150 million
Debt	$25 million	$100 million
Equity	$125 million	$50 million
Common stock price	$50	$50
Number of shares	2,500,000	1,000,000
Interest rate	12%	12%

Stern's Stews' president expects next year's EBIT to be $20 million, but it may be 25 percent higher or lower. Ignoring taxes, perform an EBIT/eps analysis. What is the indifference level of EBIT? Should Stern's Stews change its capital structure? Why or why not?

4. Faulkner's Fine Fries, Inc. (FFF) is thinking about reducing its debt burden. Given the following capital structure information and an expected EBIT of $50 million (plus or minus 10 percent) next year, should FFF change their capital structure?

	CURRENT	PROPOSED
Total assets	$750 million	$750 million
Debt	$450 million	$300 million
Equity	$300 million	$450 million
Common stock price	$30	$30
Number of shares	10,000,000	15,000,000
Interest rate	12%	12%

5. Redo Problem 4, assuming that the less leveraged capital structure will result in a borrowing cost of 10 percent and a common stock price of $40.

6. A firm has sales of $10 million, variable costs of $4 million, fixed expenses of $1.5 million, interest costs of $2 million, and a 30 percent average tax rate.

a. Compute its DOL, DFL, and DCL.

b. What will be the expected level of EBIT and net income if next year's sales rise 10 percent?

c. What will be the expected level of EBIT and net income if next year's sales fall 20 percent?

7. Following are the income statements for Genatron Manufacturing for 2007 and 2008:

INCOME STATEMENT	2007	2008
Net sales	$1,300,000	$1,500,000
Cost of goods sold	$780,000	$900,000
Gross profit	$520,000	$600,000
General and administrative	$150,000	$150,000
Marketing expenses	$130,000	$150,000
Depreciation	$40,000	$53,000
Interest	$45,000	$57,000
Earnings before taxes	$155,000	$190,000
Income taxes	$62,000	$76,000
Net income	$93,000	$114,000

Assuming one-half of the general and administrative expenses are fixed costs, estimate Genatron's degree of operating leverage, degree of financial leverage, and degree of combined leverage in 2007 and 2008.

8. The Nutrex Corporation wants to calculate its weighted average cost of capital. Its target capital structure weights are 40 percent long-term debt and 60 percent common equity. The before-tax cost of debt is estimated to be 10 percent, and the company is in the 40 percent tax bracket. The current risk-free interest rate is 8 percent on Treasury bills. The expected return on the market is 13 percent and the firm's stock beta is 1.8.

a. What is Nutrex's cost of debt?

b. Estimate Nutrex's expected return on common equity using the security market line.

c. Calculate the after-tax weighted average cost of capital.

9. Following are the balance sheets for the Genatron Manufacturing Corporation for the years 2007 and 2008:

BALANCE SHEET	2007	2008
Cash	$50,000	$40,000
Accounts receivable	$200,000	$260,000
Inventory	$450,000	$500,000
Total current assets	$700,000	$800,000
Fixed assets (net)	$300,000	$400,000
Total assets	$1,000,000	$1,200,000
Bank loan, 10%	$90,000	$90,000
Accounts payable	$130,000	$170,000
Accruals	$50,000	$70,000
Total current liabilities	$270,000	$330,000
Long-term debt, 12%	$300,000	$400,000
Common stock, $10 par	$300,000	$300,000
Capital surplus	$50,000	$50,000
Retained earnings	$80,000	$120,000
Total liabilities and equity	$1,000,000	$1,200,000

a. Calculate the weighted average cost of capital based on book value weights. Assume an after-tax cost of new debt of 8.63 percent and a cost of common equity of 16.5 percent.

b. The current market value of Genatron's long-term debt is $350,000. The common stock price is $20 per share, and 30,000 shares are outstanding. Calculate the WACC using market value weights and the component capital costs in (a).

c. Recalculate the WACC based on both book value and market value weights, assuming that the before-tax cost of debt will be 18 percent, the company is in the 40 percent income tax bracket, and the after-tax cost of common equity capital is 21 percent.

10. The Basic Biotech Corporation wants to determine its weighted average cost of capital. Its target capital structure weights are 50 percent long-term debt and 50 percent common equity. The before-tax cost of debt is estimated to be 10 percent, and the company is in the 30 percent tax bracket. The current risk-free interest rate is 8 percent on Treasury bills. The after-tax cost of common equity capital is 14.5 percent. Calculate the after-tax weighted average cost of capital.

11. **Challenge Problem** Use various Internet resources and information contained in this text to estimate the cost of debt, cost of retained earnings, the cost of new equity, and the weighted average cost of capital for the following firms: Walgreens, Microsoft, and ExxonMobil. As an approximation, use current book value ratios as estimates of their target capital structure weights.

12. **Challenge Problem** Through library or Internet resources, find information regarding the sources of long-term financing for AT&T. What are the current market prices for their outstanding bonds and stock? Estimate their current market value weights. Estimate the cost of each financing source and, assuming the current market value weights equal AT&T's target capital structure, estimate its weighted average cost of capital.

13. Let S = last year's sales revenue; A = last year's total assets; D = last year's total liabilities; E = last year's stockholders' equity; NI/S = the firm's (presumably constant) profit margin, the ratio of net income to sales; g = the firm's expected sales growth rate; RR = the firm's (presumably constant) retention ratio. Using these symbols and relationships you are familiar with, find the following:

a. What will this year's net income equal?

b. How much will be added to stockholders' equity this year?

c. What is this year's level of assets?

d. What is the change in assets between last year and this year?

e. The change in assets computed in (d) has to be financed. Assuming only internal financing is available, compute the firm's internal growth rate. [*Hint:* Set your answers to (b) and (d) equal to each other, and solve for g.]

14. Using the same notation used in the previous problem, now assume that the firm will raise some funds externally to keep the firm's debt-to-equity (D/E) ratio constant.

a. What will this year's net income equal?

b. How much will be added to stockholders' equity this year?

c. If the D/E ratio remains constant, how much external debt can the firm raise this year?

d. What is this year's level of assets?

e. What is the change in assets between this year and the last?

f. The change in assets computed in (e) has to be financed. Assuming a constant debt-to-equity ratio, compute the firm's sustainable growth rate. [*Hint:* Add together your answers to (b) and (c) and set them equal to the solution to (e), then solve for g.]

15. The following are items from recent financial statements from Moss and Mole Manufacturing:

2008 BALANCE SHEET (ALL NUMBERS ARE IN THOUSANDS)

Total assets	$192,000
Stockholders' equity	$44,000
Total liabilities	$148,000

2008 INCOME STATEMENT

Sales	$260,000
Net income	$37,500
Dividends paid	$18,750

a. Find M&MM's internal growth rate.

b. Find its sustainable growth rate.

16. The following information is from the financial statements of Bagle's Biscuits:

2008 BALANCE SHEET (ALL NUMBERS ARE IN MILLIONS)

Total assets	$134.9
Stockholders' equity	$51.7
Total liabilities	$83.2

2008 INCOME STATEMENT

Sales	$137.5
Net income	$8.0
Dividends paid	$3.2

a. Find Bagle's internal growth rate.

b. Compute Bagle's sustainable growth rate.

17. Following are the income statements for Mount Lewis Copy Centers for 2007 and 2008. Data are in thousands of dollars.

	2007	2008
Sales	$20,000	$21,000
Cost of goods sold	$10,000	$10,500
Leases	$2,500	$3,000
Depreciation	$2,000	$2,100
EBIT	$5,500	$5,400
Interest	$3,000	$3,200
EBT	$2,500	$2,200
Taxes (30%)	$750	$660
Net income	$1,750	$1,540

a. Compute and interpret the degree of operating leverage, degree of financial leverage, and degree of combined leverage in 2007. Assume the components of the costs of goods sold are all variable costs.

b. Compute and interpret the degree of operating leverage, degree of financial leverage, and degree of combined leverage in 2008. Assume the components of the costs of goods sold are all variable costs.

c. Why did these numbers change between 2007 and 2008?

18. Using the income statements from the Mount Lewis Copy Centers for 2007 and 2008 in Problem 17, find the percentage change in sales, EBIT, and net income. Use them to compute the degree of operating leverage, financial leverage, and combined leverage.

19. Here's a recent income statement from TC1 Telecommunications Services, Inc. (numbers are in millions):

Sales	$53.7
Costs of goods sold	$20.2
Depreciation	$13.9
EBIT	$19.6
Interest expense	12.4
EBT	$ 7.2
Taxes (25%)	$1.8
Net Income	$5.4

a. Compute TC1's degree of financial, operating, and combined leverage if one-half of the costs of goods sold are variable costs and one-half are fixed costs.

b. Assume during the current year that TC1's sales rise to $59.5 million. What is your estimate of TC1's net income this year?

c. Assume during the current year that TC1's sales fall to $49.3 million. What is your revised estimate for TC1's net income?

20. **Challenge Problem** Company A1 intends to raise $3 million by either of two financing plans:

Plan A: Sell 100,000 shares of stock at $30 net to firm

Plan B: Issue $3 million in long-term bonds with a 10 percent coupon

The firm expects an EBIT of $1 million. Currently A1 has 50,000 shares outstanding and no debt in its capital structure. Its tax rate is 34 percent.

a. What EBIT indifference level is associated with these two proposals?

b. Draw an EBIT/eps graph showing the various levels of eps and EBIT, including the expected EBIT. What should A1 do in this case?

21. **Challenge Problem** Big 10+1 Corp. intends to raise $5 million by one of two financing plans:

Plan A: Sell 1,250,000 shares at $4 per share net to the firm

Plan B: Issue $5 million in ten-year debentures with a 9 percent coupon rate

The firm expects an EBIT level of $800,000. Currently Big 10+1 has 100,000 shares outstanding and $2 million of debt with a 5 percent coupon in its capital structure. The tax rate is 34 percent.

a. Draw an EBIT/eps graph showing the various levels of eps and EBIT.

b. What is the EBIT indifference point?

c. When will eps be zero under either alternative?

d. What type of financing should the firm choose?

e. Suppose under the equity financing option at an EBIT level of $800,000, the firm's P/E ratio is 10; for the debt financing option, the P/E ratio is 7. What should the firm do?

22. **Challenge Problem** Champion Telecommunications is restructuring. Currently Champion has no debt outstanding. After it restructures, debt will be $5 million. The rate offered to bondholders is 10 percent. Champion currently has 700,000 shares outstanding at a market price of $40/share. Earnings per share are expected to rise.

a. What is the minimum level of EBIT that Champion is expecting? Ignore the consequences of taxes.

b. Calculate the minimum level of EBIT that Champion Telecommunications' managers are expecting, if the interest rate on debt is 5 percent.

c. Assume that Champion Telecommunications had EBIT of $2 million; was the leverage beneficial in (a)? In (b)?

• CHAPTER 16 •

Managing Working Capital

Chapter Learning Objectives

AFTER STUDYING THIS CHAPTER, YOU SHOULD BE ABLE TO:

- Explain what is meant by a firm's operating cycle and its cash conversion cycle.
- Describe the impact of the operating cycle on the size of investment in accounts receivable and inventories.
- Explain how seasonal and cyclical trends affect the operating cycle, cash conversion cycle, and investments in current assets.
- Explain how a cash budget is developed and how a treasurer will use it.
- Describe the motives underlying the management of cash and marketable securities.
- Briefly explain what is involved in accounts receivable management and indicate how it is carried out.
- Describe inventory management from the standpoint of the financial manager.

Where We Have Been. . .

The previous chapters have introduced us to financial statements and some ways they can help managers and investors. Financial statements contain data that are used to do ratio analysis and long-term financial planning. In addition to helping users identify trends, ratio analysis can help users analyze a firm's operating condition and can help with short-term financial planning. In previous chapters we examined how to make capital budget decisions, which typically include fixed assets. This chapter focuses on managing current assets.

Where We Are Going. . .

A firm's short-term financing needs will be affected by near-term sales growth and how efficiently the firm manages its working capital accounts. The next chapter, Chapter 17, "Short-Term Business Financing," reviews fund sources to help a firm finance its short-term needs. Ongoing short-term financing needs may reflect a need for permanent long-term financing; factors affecting long-term financing decisions were discussed in Chapters 7 and 8's discussion of bonds and stocks. A related discussion, including the appropriate mix and use of debt and equity, was Chapter 15, "Capital Structure and the Cost of Capital."

How This Chapter Applies to Me. . .

Business practices of managing short-term assets—such as cash—apply directly to personal issues. First, cash flow is important. We can create a personal cash budget, showing when cash inflows are expected to occur (paychecks, stock dividends, cash birthday gifts) and when expected outflows will occur (bills to be paid). Second, just as a business faces expected return/risk choices when wanting to invest extra cash, so do we. How soon will we need to use our extra cash? How much do we want to hold for transaction, precautionary, and speculative purposes? Do we want a safe place to put our excess funds with high liquidity but low return (such as a bank checking account), or should we invest in T-bills (via the Treasury-Direct program) or buy a longer-term CD that offers higher expected returns but lower liquidity?

We begin this chapter with a frequently cited quote from an unknown author:

> *Happiness is a positive cash flow.*

Inventory (representing future hoped-for sales) and accounts receivable (representing past sales and a future promise to pay cash) are important items for a firm. Investments

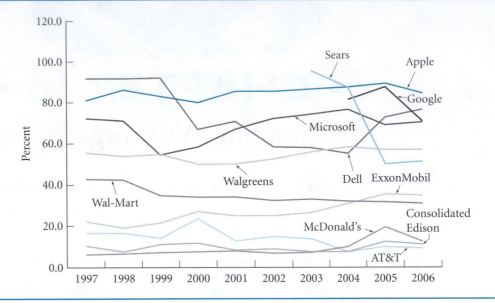

FIGURE 16.1
Ratio of Current Assets to Total Assets, Selected Firms

such as these in working capital must be converted to cash at some future time. A positive cash flow occurs when the cash coming into the firm exceeds the cash leaving the firm.

A firm can invest in both working capital and fixed capital. Working capital is a firm's current assets and consists of cash, marketable securities, accounts receivable, and inventories. Fixed capital is a firm's fixed assets, which include plant, equipment, and property. In this chapter we focus on managing a firm's working capital. The financial manager must decide how much to invest in working capital or current assets and how to finance these current assets.

How important are working capital issues? In a word, *very*. Firms that cannot obtain needed short-term financing are candidates for bankruptcy. Supplies and raw materials are converted to inventory. When sold, inventory may become an account receivable and ultimately cash. Unexpected increases in inventory or receivables can harm a firm's best-laid long-term plans. As with any other asset, increases in current assets must be financed with either liabilities or equity. If poor planning causes a mismatch between assets and financing sources or between cash inflows and cash outflows, bankruptcy is a real possibility.

Current assets typically comprise from one-third to one-half of a firm's total assets. They are affected by the firm's day-to-day marketing, production, and human resource issues. A survey of financial managers found they spend nearly 70 percent of their time dealing with financial planning, budgeting, and working capital issues.[1] Figure 16.1 shows the level and variability over time of the ratio of current assets to total assets for several firms. McDonald's, Consolidated Edison (an electric utility), and AT&T have lower proportions of current assets to total assets, whereas technology firms such as Apple, Dell, Microsoft, and Google have relatively higher levels of current assets to total assets.

The first part of this chapter describes how a firm's operating cycle affects the amount of working capital it carries. Next we review how to prepare and use a cash budget. Our final emphasis is on methods used to manage cash and marketable securities, accounts receivable, and inventories.

OPERATING AND CASH CONVERSION CYCLES

Two important concepts in managing short-term finances are the operating cycle and cash conversion cycle.

FIGURE 16.2
The Operating Cycle

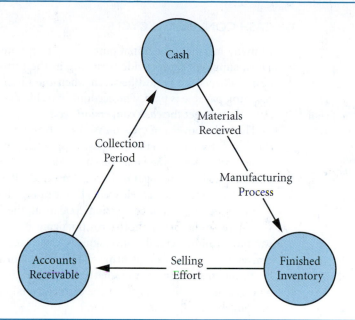

OPERATING CYCLE

The ***operating cycle*** measures the time between receiving raw materials and collecting cash from receivables. Figure 16.2 graphically depicts the operating cycle for a manufacturing firm. Raw materials are purchased and products are manufactured from them to become finished goods. Effort then is made to sell the finished goods. If the goods are sold on credit, then the receivables must be collected. A service firm would have a similar cycle except for the manufacturing stage. That is, finished goods would be purchased, then consumed in the process of providing a service, and receivables collected. Of course, the operating cycles of both service and manufacturing firms would be shortened if sales are made for cash and not on credit.

Figure 16.3 depicts a time line reflecting the operating cycle for a manufacturing firm. The cycle begins with the receipt of raw materials. The inventory period involves producing or processing the materials into final products or finished goods and ends when the finished goods are sold. If the finished goods are sold on credit, the second major period of interest is the accounts receivable period. It covers the time from when the goods are sold until the receivables

FIGURE 16.3
Time Lines for the Operating and Cash Conversion Cycles

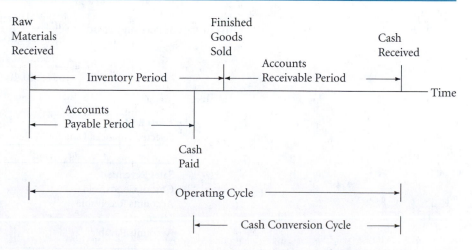

are collected in the form of cash. The inventory period and the accounts receivable period together constitute the firm's operating cycle.

CASH CONVERSION CYCLE

In many instances the initial purchase of raw materials or finished goods for resale is on credit. Thus, suppliers can provide financing in the form of accounts payable. The accounts payable period covers the period between when the order for raw materials is invoiced and when the resulting payable is paid. The accounts payable period is subtracted from the length of the operating cycle to get the ***cash conversion cycle***.

The cash conversion cycle measures a firm's financing gap in terms of time. In other words, it is the time between when the firm pays its suppliers and when it collects money from its customers. It is the time between when materials are ordered and receivables are collected less the time over which payables are outstanding. Of course, if no credit is extended by suppliers, then the operating cycle and the cash conversion cycle would be the same. The cash conversion cycle is shown in Figure 16.3.

Increases in the cash conversion cycle mean the firm must finance itself for a longer time. This will increase the firm's short-term financing needs and financing costs. Financial managers will want to monitor the cash conversion cycle and take action should it begin to lengthen. Shorter cash conversion cycles mean the firm will reduce its short-term financing needs and financing costs.

Two items determine the length of the operating cycle: inventory period and accounts receivable period. Three items affect the cash conversion cycle: inventory period, accounts receivable period, and accounts payable period.

cash conversion cycle
time between a firm's paying its suppliers for inventory and collecting cash from customers on a sale of the finished product

DETERMINING THE LENGTH OF THE OPERATING CYCLE AND CASH CONVERSION CYCLE

We can estimate the length of a firm's operating and cash conversion cycles using information from a firm's income statement and balance sheet. All that needs to be done is to calculate three ratios that will tell us the firm's inventory, accounts receivable, and accounts payable periods. Table 16.1 contains selected balance sheets and income statement items for Walgreens.

Inventory Period

First, we would like to know how many days items were in inventory during 2006—that is, the time between when an order for raw materials was received and when the finished goods were sold. To determine the length of this period, we can use the inventory turnover ratio (cost of goods sold divided by inventories) from Chapter 12. Using the numbers in Table 16.1, the inventory turnover for Walgreens is 5.66 times ($34,240.40/$6,050.40)—that is, Walgreens turns over or transforms its inventory into finished products and sells them 5.66 times a year. To determine the inventory conversion period, we divide the 365 days in a year by this inventory turnover ratio (365/5.66) to get 64.5 days.

As an alternative calculation, we can divide the 2006 year-end inventories amount by the 2006 cost of goods sold (COGS) per day. In ratio form, we have:

$$\text{Inventory conversion period} = \frac{\text{Inventory}}{\text{Cost of goods sold}/365} = \frac{\text{Inventory}}{\text{COGS per day}}$$

$$= \frac{\$6,050.40}{\$34,240.40/365} = \frac{\$6,050.40}{\$93.81} = 64.5 \text{ days}$$

TABLE 16.1
Selected Financial Data for Walgreens ($ Millions)

	2006
Sales Revenue	$47,409.00
Cost of Goods Sold	$34,240.40
Accounts Receivable	$2,062.70
Inventories	$6,050.40
Accounts Payable	$4,039.20

By either method, it took about 64.5 days in 2006 for Walgreens to complete the inventory conversion period.

Accounts Receivable Period

The second step is to determine the average collection period in 2006 for Walgreens. We saw this ratio in Chapter 12. It measures the average time between when a product is sold on credit and cash is received from the buyer. It is calculated as follows:

$$\text{Average collection period} = \frac{\text{Accounts Receivable}}{\text{Net Sales}/365}$$

$$= \frac{\$2,062.70}{\$47,409.00/365} = \frac{\$2,062.70}{\$129.89} = 15.9 \text{ days}$$

It took Walgreens 15.9 days, on average, during 2006 from the time finished goods were sold on credit to when the resulting receivables were actually collected.

The operating cycle is determined as follows:

$$\text{Operating cycle} = \text{Inventory conversion period} + \text{Average collection period}$$

Walgreens' average 2006 operating cycle was 64.5 days to process and sell its inventory, plus 15.9 days to collect its receivables for a total of 80.4 days.

Average Payment Period

The average payment period represents the time it takes Walgreens to pay its suppliers. We were first introduced to this ratio in Chapter 12. The average payment period is calculated by dividing a firm's accounts payable by its cost of goods sold per day. Using the information from Table 16.1, the average payment period is calculated as follows:

$$\text{Average payment period} = \frac{\text{Accounts Payable}}{\text{Cost of goods sold}/365}$$

$$= \frac{\$4,039.20}{\$34,240.40/365} = \frac{\$4,039.20}{\$93.81} = 43.1 \text{ days}$$

Thus, Walgreens was able to get on average about 43.1 days of credit from its suppliers in 2006. The cash conversion cycle is the operating cycle less the average payment period:

$$\text{Cash conversion cycle} = \text{Operating cycle} - \text{Average payment period}$$

CONCEPT CHECK

What is the operating cycle?

What is the cash conversion cycle?

Why would a lengthening cash conversion cycle be a concern to a firm's treasurer?

For Walgreens, we start with an operating cycle of 80.4 days and subtract the average payment period of 43.1 days to arrive at a cash conversion cycle of 37.3 days for 2006. The average time between when Walgreens paid for materials and when it received payment from its customers after a final sale was about thirty-seven days. Managing the cash conversion cycle is a major task of a firm's financial manager. The shorter the cash conversion cycle, the smaller will be the firm's investment in inventory and receivables, and consequently the less will be its financing needs.

WORKING CAPITAL REQUIREMENTS

Let's take a closer look at how the length of the operating cycle affects the amount of funds invested in accounts receivable and inventories. Using Walgreens' 2006 sales of $47,409.00, average sales per day were $129.89 ($47,409.00/365). We also know that in 2006 it took Walgreens an average of 15.9 days to collect its accounts receivable. We can use this information to find Walgreens' average investment in accounts receivable. We multiply the net sales per day of $129.89 times the average collection period:

Receivables investment amount = Net sales per day × Average collection period

Receivables investment amount = $129.89 × 15.9 days = $2,065.3

This should be no surprise to us since we previously used Walgreens' $2,062.70 accounts receivable balance to determine the average collection period. Our calculation shows $2,065.3 instead of $2,062.70 because of rounding involved when we computed the net sales per day and average collection period. However, let's now ask this question: What will the investment be next year in accounts receivable if sales increase by 10 percent to $52,149.90 and the average collection period remains at 15.9 days? Intuitively, if there is a constant relationship between sales and receivables, a 10 percent increase in sales should lead to a 10 percent increase in receivables. An estimate of the new receivables balance would be $2,062.70 (2006 level) plus 10 percent, for a total of $2,268.97.

We can also find the new accounts receivable balance by finding the new sales per day and then multiplying it by the collection period. Dividing $52,149.90 by 365, we get $142.88 sales per day; multiplying it by 15.9 days gives us:

$$\text{Receivables investment amount} = \$142.88 \times 15.9 \text{ days} = \$2,271.79$$

In this case, our initial estimate of $2,268.97 was correct (within rounding of the inputs), because the collection period remained the same. Walgreens' investment in accounts receivable will have to increase by $206.27 (i.e., $2,268.97 − $2,062.70) to support a sales increase of $4,740.9 (i.e., $52,149.90 − $47,409.00) as long as the average collection period remains at 15.9 days.

What will happen if the relationship between sales and accounts receivable does not remain constant? For example, as sales rise or fall over time the accounts receivable period may change. If the economy goes into a recession, the accounts receivable period may rise as customers take longer to pay their bills. Or, focusing the firm's marketing efforts on customers with better-quality credit may allow the firm to increase sales and reduce its receivables balance if more customers pay early. Now we should ask this: What will be the necessary investment in accounts receivable if sales increase to $52,149.90 but Walgreens is able to decrease its average collection period to an even fifteen days? We find the answer to be:

$$\text{Receivables investment amount} = \$142.88 \times 15 \text{ days} = \$2,143.20$$

Thus, a reduction of nearly a full day in the average collection period would mean that the amount of increased investment required in accounts receivable to support a 10 percent increase in sales would be only $80.50 ($2,143.20 − $2,062.70).

A similar analysis can be conducted in terms of inventories. The 2006 cost of goods sold was $34,240.40 for the year, or $93.81 on a per-day basis ($34,240.40/365). We know that in 2006 it took Walgreens on average 64.5 days between when raw materials were received and when the finished goods were sold. By multiplying the average cost of goods per day times the inventory conversion period, we can determine the investment required in inventories:

Inventories investment amount = Average cost of goods sold per day × Inventory conversion period

For Walgreens in 2006 we have:

$$\text{Inventories investment amount} = \$93.81 \times 64.5 \text{ days} = \$6,050.75$$

This, of course, is the same amount, within rounding error, shown for the inventories account in Table 16.1 for Walgreens.

It should be clear that this required investment will change if the cost of goods sold, the inventory conversion period, or both change. For example, let's assume that the firm's cost of goods sold increases by 10 percent to $37,664.44 because of an increase in sales. This would be a new cost of goods sold per day of $103.19 ($37,664.44/365). If the inventory conversion period remains at 64.5 days, the new investment in inventories should be about 10 percent higher, too:

$$\text{Inventories investment amount} = \$103.19 \times 64.5 \text{ days} = \$6,655.76$$

which is an increase of $605.36 ($6,655.76 − $6,050.40) or 10 percent.

Of course, if Walgreens could find a way to lower its inventory conversion period to, say, sixty days, the net impact on the investment in inventories of a 10 percent sales rise would be:

$$\text{Inventories investment amount} = \$103.19 \times 60 \text{ days} = \$6,191.40$$

Thus, even though sales and cost of goods sold increase next year, a decline in the inventory conversion period to sixty days results in a modest increase in the investment in inventories by $141 ($6,191.40 − $6,050.40). Walgreens may be able to achieve a reduction in its inventory conversion period by managing inventories more efficiently. Some strategies for doing this are discussed in the last section of this chapter.

The size of the accounts payable account is also affected by two basic factors: the level of the firm's cost of goods sold and the average payment period. Table 16.1 indicates that the cost of goods sold for Walgreens was $34,240.40 in 2006. On a per-day basis the cost of goods sold was $93.81 ($34,240.40/365). We also previously calculated the 2006 average payment period at 43.1 days. Given this information, we can determine the required amount of accounts payable as follows:

$$\text{Accounts payable} = \text{Cost of goods sold per day} \times \text{Average payment period}$$

For Walgreens in 2006 we have:

$$\text{Accounts payable} = \$93.81 \times 43.1 \text{ days} = \$4,043.21$$

This amount, of course, is the same, within rounding error, as the accounts payable amount shown in Table 16.1 for Walgreens at the end of 2006.

Of course, as a firm's cost of goods sold increases, its credit purchases and thus its accounts payable also should increase. For example, if Walgreens' cost of goods sold increases by 10 percent to $37,664.44 next year, we expect accounts payable, currently $4,039.20, to rise by 10 percent as well, if the payment period does not change. A cost of goods sold of $37,664.44 gives a daily average cost of goods sold of $37,664.44/365 days or $103.19. If the average payment period remains at 43.1 days, the projected amount in the accounts payable account is:

$$\text{Accounts payable} = \$103.19 \times 43.1 \text{ days} = \$4,447.49$$

which represents approximately a 10 percent increase in payables.

It now should be recognized that while an increase in sales and cost of goods sold should result in an increase in the investment in accounts receivable and inventories, these increases will be partially offset by an increase in accounts payable, other things being equal. If the accounts payable period rises to forty-five days, the new accounts payable balance will be:

$$\text{Accounts payable} = \$103.19 \times 45 \text{ days} = \$4,643.55$$

Our estimates of the effects on receivables, inventory, and payables are shown in summary form in Table 16.2 under the assumption that no changes occur in the operating and cash conversion cycles.

Thus, while investment in accounts receivable and inventories would be expected to increase by $811.63 from $8,113.10 to $8,924.73, the expected increase in accounts payable of $408.29 from $4,039.20 to $4,447.49 causes the net impact to be only a $403.34 increase in needed financing. The financial manager will have to plan ahead to obtain the necessary funds to support this expected increase in net working capital. She can obtain funds from short-term financing sources, as discussed in Chapter 17, or she may decide it is appropriate to tap long-term sources, such as stocks and bonds.

Table 16.3 summarizes our estimates of receivables, inventory, and payables if sales and cost of goods sold rise by 10 percent and changes occur in the operating and cash conversion cycles.

TABLE 16.2

Effect of 10 Percent Increase in Sales and Cost of Goods Sold on Receivables, Inventory, and Payables: Base Case

ACCOUNT	2006 RESULTS FOR WALGREENS	10% INCREASE IN SALES AND COST OF GOODS SOLD
Investment		
Accounts Receivable	$2,062.70	$2,268.97
Inventories	$6,050.40	$6,655.76
Total	$8,113.10	$8,924.73
Financing		
Accounts Payable	$4,039.20	$4,447.49
Net Investment		
Investment—Financing	$4,073.90	$4,477.24

Assumptions: Average collection period = 15.9 days; inventory period = 64.0 days; average payment period = 43.1 days.

TABLE 16.3

Effect of 10 Percent Increase in Sales and Cost of Goods Sold on Receivables, Inventory, and Payables: New Assumptions

ACCOUNT	2006 RESULTS FOR WALGREENS	10% INCREASE IN SALES AND COST OF GOODS SOLD
Investment		
Accounts Receivable	$2,062.70	$2,143.20
Inventories	$6,050.40	$6,191.40
Total	$8,113.10	$8,334.60
Financing		
Accounts Payable	$4,039.20	$4,643.55
Net Investment		
Investment—Financing	$4,073.90	$3,691.05

Assumptions: Average collection period = 15 days; inventory period = 60 days; average payment period = 45 days.

CONCEPT CHECK

How are a firm's levels of accounts receivable, inventory, and accounts payable expected to be affected by an increase in sales?

What happens to accounts receivable if both sales and the collection period rise?

Specifically, Table 16.3 shows the effects of an average collection period of fifteen days, an inventory period of sixty days, and a payables period of forty-five days.

The effect of these minor changes in cash conversion cycle components is remarkable. The firm's net investment in these working capital accounts will fall to $3,691.05, nearly $383 less than the current (2006) situation and nearly $790 less than the scenario in Table 16.2.

In a later section, we discuss another important topic: the management of working capital assets. From our discussion, it should be clear that more efficient management of working capital assets and faster cash collection will lessen the firm's needs for financing. Small working capital account balances mean that less debt and external equity financing are needed, saving the firm extra financing expenses. Activities that decrease the cash conversion cycle will reduce the firm's need to obtain financing.

CASH BUDGETS

We have seen how financial ratios can be used to estimate the firm's total financing needs over the course of a year. As we learned in Chapter 12, expected sales growth may require the firm to acquire additional assets, both current and fixed, to support higher sales levels. By combining the sales forecast and the firm's total asset turnover ratio, we can estimate the amount of assets needed to support the sales forecast. The projected increase in assets less the estimated increase in current liabilities and retained earnings will give the financial analyst an estimate of the firm's needs for external financing.

The previous section illustrates a quick means of estimating working capital financing needs by comparing expected changes in current assets and current liabilities. The estimated change in current assets minus the expected change in current liabilities measures the change in working capital. This growth (or decline) in working capital must be financed, via either short-term or long-term financing.

Such methods are appropriate as a first approximation toward estimating a firm's yearly financing needs, but a firm needs more precise information than this. Over the course of a year, large bills may need to be paid before subsequent cash inflows occur. Dividend checks will be mailed to shareholders; workers and suppliers will need to be paid; interest on debt and perhaps even the principal that was borrowed will have to be repaid. During any one week or month the firm's need for cash may far exceed the annual estimates. A firm's treasurer will need to closely track and forecast daily and weekly cash inflows and outflows to ensure that cash is available to pay necessary expenses. Should the firm's cash balance become dangerously low, the treasurer will need to make plans to acquire the needed funds by either borrowing money or selling marketable securities. A *cash budget* is a tool the treasurer uses to forecast future cash flows and to estimate future short-term borrowing needs.

cash budget
tool the treasurer uses to forecast future cash flows and estimate future short-term borrowing needs

CONCEPT CHECK

What is a cash budget? Why is it important?

What three pieces of information do we need to construct a cash budget?

A budget is simply a financial forecast of spending, income, or both. A cash budget details the periodic cash inflows and cash outflows of a firm over some time frame. Small- and medium-size firms may prepare monthly cash budgets, whereas larger firms will forecast cash flows weekly or daily. If cash surpluses are forecast, the treasurer can plan how the firm's excess cash can be invested to earn interest.[2] If a cash deficit is forecast, the treasurer can plan how to best raise the necessary funds. We'll construct a cash budget for a manufacturing firm, Global Manufacturing, in this section. Global Manufacturing's sales pattern is seasonal, with sales typically rising at the end of the calendar year followed by a sharp sales decline at the beginning of the calendar year. We'll see how the decision for the firm to have level production during the year rather than seasonal production will affect its cash needs throughout the year.

To construct a cash budget, three sets of information are needed: the firm's minimum desired cash balance, estimated cash inflows, and estimated cash outflows. We discuss each of these in the following subsections.

MINIMUM DESIRED CASH BALANCE

Most firms have a minimum desired cash balance. Some cash will be needed to pay the month's bills, but extra cash also may be desired because the forecasts of cash inflows and outflows will not be perfect. To protect against lower-than-expected cash inflows (or higher-than-expected cash outflows), a *cash buffer* is needed. The size of the cash buffer depends on several influences, including the firm's ability to acquire financing easily on short notice, the predictability of cash inflows and outflows, and management's preferences.

CASH INFLOWS

The estimates of cash inflows are driven by two main factors: the sales forecast and customer payment patterns. Over any period, the main sources of cash inflows for the firm will be cash sales and collections of receivables. If we know the proportion of cash sales and the percentage of customers who pay their bills every month, we can use sales forecasts to estimate future cash inflows.

Sales forecasts will be affected by seasonal patterns. Obviously, monthly sales figures will differ for swimsuit makers and snow blower manufacturers. Managers can determine seasonal patterns by merely plotting monthly or quarterly sales figures, as in Figure 16.4.

For example, Table 16.4 presents Global Manufacturing's actual November and December 2007 sales and forecasted sales for January, February, March, and April 2008. From Figure 16.4, Global knows that its sales volume is highly seasonal, with a large proportion of sales occurring in the last few months of the year. All of Global's sales are credit sales and become accounts

FIGURE 16.4
Sales Data for Global Manufacturing, Inc., 2005–2007

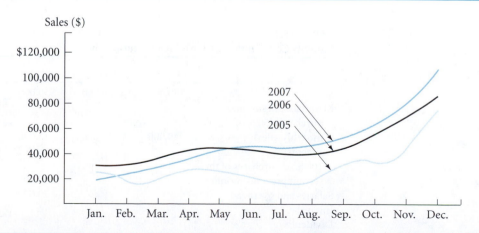

---

2. Unlike personal checking accounts, business checking accounts earn no interest. Thus, the treasurer will want to invest any cash over and above the firm's immediate needs to earn a return on the excess funds.

TABLE 16.4
Monthly Cash Inflows, Global Manufacturing, Inc.

	NOV.	DEC.	JAN.	FEB.	MAR.	APR.
Sales	$80,000	$100,000	$30,000	$40,000	$50,000	$60,000
Collections:						
50% of sales of the previous month		40,000	50,000	15,000	20,000	25,000
50% of sales of the second previous month			40,000	50,000	15,000	20,000
Total cash receipts			$90,000	$65,000	$35,000	$45,000

receivable. From reviewing past payment patterns, Global knows that receivables representing 50 percent of a month's sales are paid one month after purchase, while the remaining 50 percent are paid two months later. Thus, for January to April, each month's cash inflows have two sources: cash comes into the firm equal to 50 percent of the sales volume from the previous month, and cash comes into the firm equal to 50 percent of the sales volume from two months prior. Thus, for January, cash inflows reflect 50 percent of December's sales (50 percent of December's sales equals $50,000) plus 50 percent of November's sales (50 percent of November's sales equals $40,000), for a total expected inflow of $90,000.

CASH OUTFLOWS

Every month Global will have bills to pay, and these cash outflows need to appear in the cash budget. Suppliers of raw materials must be paid, as well as the firm's payroll. Rental or lease payments, utility bills, and so forth are other examples of regular outflows that should be listed in the budget. Interest on borrowing may be due at specific times, as will dividends and tax payments. Any anticipated purchases of plant and equipment also must be listed in the budget. Production, over the course of the year, can be seasonal, rising and falling along with the sales forecast, or level, producing a constant amount of product every month. Here we assume Global uses seasonal production. Later, we will see the effect of a level production schedule on Global's cash budget.

Table 16.5 shows Global's expected cash disbursements. Raw materials and supplies equal to 50 percent of each month's sales are purchased each month. Global pays its suppliers two months after the goods are purchased. Each month's estimated salary and overhead expenses are $20,000. Interest payments of $7,000 are due in February, and a quarterly dividend, expected to be $6,000, is to be paid in March. Quarterly taxes of $3,000 also need to be paid in March. In anticipation of growing sales, Global is planning to purchase $50,000 worth of capital equipment in February.

CONCEPT CHECK

What influences affect the size of a firm's minimum desired cash buffer?

What factors influence the size of a firm's periodic cash inflows?

What affects the size of a firm's periodic cash outflows?

TABLE 16.5
Monthly Cash Outflows, Global Manufacturing, Inc.

	NOV.	DEC.	JAN.	FEB.	MAR.	APR.
Sales	$80,000	$100,000	$30,000	$ 40,000	$50,000	$60,000
Materials and supplies purchases (50% of monthly sales)	40,000	50,000	15,000	20,000	25,000	30,000
Payments 100% of purchases of the second previous month			40,000	50,000	15,000	20,000
Salaries and overhead			20,000	20,000	20,000	20,000
Interest				7,000		
Dividends					6,000	
Taxes					3,000	
Capital expenditures				50,000		
Total cash payments			$60,000	$127,000	$44,000	$40,000

TABLE 16.6

Net Monthly Cash Flows, Seasonal Production, Global Manufacturing, Inc.

	JAN.	FEB.	MAR.	APR.
Total cash receipts	$90,000	$65,000	$35,000	$45,000
less: Total cash payments	$60,000	127,000	$44,000	$40,000
Net cash flow	$30,000	($62,000)	($ 9,000)	$ 5,000

CONSTRUCTING THE CASH BUDGET

After listing all the expected cash inflows and cash outflows for each month, we can estimate the monthly net cash flow. As shown in Table 16.6, this is simply the difference between Global's cash receipts and cash payments from Tables 16.4 and 16.6.

From Table 16.6 we see that January will be a month with a large positive net cash flow, but that February and March are expected to have larger cash outflows than cash inflows. April is expected to have more cash coming into the firm than going from it. To help Global determine its short-term financing needs, we need to put together a fully developed cash budget that indicates Global's minimum desired cash balance, as well as its monthly loan (or loan repayment) needs. We'll assume Global's minimum desired cash balance is $25,000. Should the cash position in any month fall below $25,000, Global's treasurer will need to borrow sufficient funds so that the cash balance is restored to the $25,000 level. Table 16.7 illustrates Global's monthly cash budget.

From Table 16.6, we see that January's net cash flow is $30,000; adding this to Global's beginning-of-January cash balance of $25,000 gives Global a cumulative cash balance of $55,000. Global's treasurer may want to make plans to invest some of this excess cash in marketable securities to earn extra interest income.

The end-of-January cash balance becomes the beginning-of-February cash balance. Adding the $55,000 cash balance to February's net cash flow of −$62,000 means that Global is forecasted to spend $7,000 more in cash than it is expected to have available. To meet the expected payments and to raise the cash balance to its minimum desired level of $25,000, Global's treasurer will need to borrow $7,000 + $25,000, or $32,000, during the month of February. After doing so, the ending cash balance of February will be $25,000.

When March's net cash flow of −$9,000 is added to March's beginning cash balance of $25,000, Global's available cash will be $16,000. To maintain the minimum desired cash balance of $25,000, Global should plan to borrow $9,000. When this is added to the already outstanding loans from February, Global's total loan balance at the end of March will be $32,000 + $9,000, or $41,000. The ending cash balance in March will be $25,000.

April's positive net cash flow, when added to the beginning cash balance, will give Global a positive cash balance of $30,000. This exceeds Global's minimum desired cash balance of $25,000, so in all likelihood the excess cash of $5,000 will be used to repay some of Global's recently acquired debt. By so doing, Global's cumulative loan balance will fall to $36,000.

This example illustrates the usefulness of cash budgeting. Forecasted sales are used to estimate future cash inflows and outflows based on expected payment patterns. The treasurer can plan ahead to invest excess cash or to borrow needed funds. In addition to its value as a planning tool, the cash budget will be a necessary component of any short-term loan request from a bank. The bank will not only want to see when and how much the firm may need to borrow but also when the firm will be able to repay the loan.

TABLE 16.7

Monthly Cash Budget, Seasonal Production, Global Manufacturing, Inc.

	JAN.	FEB.	MAR.	APR.
Net cash flow	$30,000	($62,000)	($ 9,000)	$ 5,000
Beginning cash balance	25,000	55,000	25,000	25,000
Cumulative cash balance	55,000	(7,000)	16,000	30,000
Monthly loan (or repayment)	0	32,000	9,000	(5,000)
Cumulative loan balance	0	32,000	41,000	36,000
Ending cash balance	$55,000	$25,000	$25,000	$25,000

FIGURE 16.5

Changing Composition of Current Assets with Seasonal Sales and Level Production

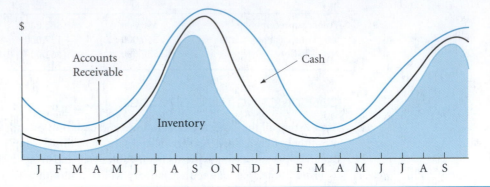

SEASONAL VERSUS LEVEL PRODUCTION

The example assumes that Global uses seasonal production to meet its seasonal sales forecast. Raw materials purchases will rise or fall in anticipation of higher or lower sales. Such a strategy can help minimize the effect of seasonal sales on inventory. Goods are manufactured shortly before they are sold, but seasonal production can lead to other problems, such as idle plant and laid-off workers during slow sales months and production bottlenecks during busy times. Consequently, for better production efficiency, some firms with seasonal sales use a level production plan. Under a level production plan, the same amount of raw material is purchased and the same amount of finished product is manufactured every month. Inventory builds up in anticipation of the higher seasonal sales while cash and accounts receivable are quite low. When the selling season begins, inventories fall and receivables rise. After a time, inventories are nearly exhausted and the firm is collecting cash from its customers. The changing composition of current assets for a firm with a seasonal sales pattern is illustrated in Figure 16.5.

Now let's see how Global's cash budget will be affected if it switches to a level production plan. Table 16.4, the schedule of cash inflows, will not be affected, but Table 16.5 will be changed to reflect a level pattern of materials purchases. We will assume that the amount of materials and supplies over the course of a year is one-half of estimated sales. If forecasted sales are $700,000, this means Global purchases $350,000 of materials over the course of a year, or approximately $29,200 each month. Table 16.8 shows the revised cash outflow schedule assuming purchases, and subsequent payments, of a constant $29,200 each month.

With these new cash payments, Table 16.9 shows the monthly net cash flows and Table 16.10 shows the new cash budget. In January, the level production plan leads to a higher cash balance than under the seasonal plan, but sustained production levels during Global's slow sales months lead to monthly cash deficits in February, March, and April. Under seasonal production, net

TABLE 16.8

Monthly Cash Outflows, Level Production

	NOV.	DEC.	JAN.	FEB.	MAR.	APR.
Sales	$80,000	$100,000	$30,000	$ 40,000	$50,000	$60,000
Materials and supplies purchases (50% of average monthly sales)	29,200	29,200	29,200	29,200	29,200	29,200
Payments (100% of purchases of the second previous month)			29,200	29,200	29,200	29,200
Salaries and overhead			20,000	20,000	20,000	20,000
Interest				7,000		
Dividends					6,000	
Taxes					3,000	
Capital expenditures				50,000		
Total cash payments			$49,200	$106,200	$58,200	$49,200

TABLE 16.9

Net Monthly Cash Flows, Level Production

	JAN.	FEB.	MAR.	APR.
Total cash receipts	$90,000	$65,000	$35,000	$45,000
less: Total cash payments	49,200	106,200	58,200	49,200
Net cash flow	$40,800	($41,200)	($23,200)	($4,200)

TABLE 16.10

Monthly Cash Budget, Level Production

	JAN.	FEB.	MAR.	APR.
Net cash flow	$40,800	($41,200)	($23,200)	($4,200)
Beginning cash balance	25,000	65,800	25,000	25,000
Cumulative cash balance	65,800	24,600	1,800	20,800
Monthly loan (or repayment)	0	400	23,200	4,200
Cumulative loan balance	0	400	23,600	27,800
Ending cash balance	$65,800	$25,000	$25,000	$25,000

CONCEPT CHECK

How is a cash budget constructed?

How will the choice of seasonal or level production affect a firm's monthly cash flows over the course of a year?

cash flow returned to positive in April and some loans could be repaid. With level production, the cumulative loan balance continues to grow through April.

The projections on the cash budget will reflect the firm's marketing efforts, as well as its credit policies, how it manages its receivables, and how it decides to manage its production and inventories. In general, firms with larger receivables balances and easier credit terms will have slower cash receipt inflows, but this must be balanced against the competitive impact of tightening up its receivables management policies. Firms with larger inventories will face large accounts payable balances and larger cash payments than firms operating on leaner inventories and tighter production schedules. Thus, how a firm manages its working capital accounts will be a concern to the company's treasurer. We examine these topics in the next section.

MANAGEMENT OF CURRENT ASSETS

Management of current assets involves the administration of cash and marketable securities, accounts receivable, and inventories. On the one hand, the financial manager should strive to minimize the investment in current assets because of the cost of financing them. On the other hand, adequate cash and marketable securities are necessary for liquidity purposes, acceptable credit terms are necessary to maintain sales, and appropriate inventory levels must be kept to avoid running out of stock and losing sales. Successful management thus requires a continual balancing of the costs and benefits associated with investment in current assets.

CASH AND MARKETABLE SECURITIES MANAGEMENT

Business firms should strive to minimize their cash holdings since, under current law, businesses cannot earn interest on funds in their checking accounts. Some large firms exist with virtually no cash balances, although others hold billions of dollars in cash and marketable securities.[3] For firms that operate with little or no cash, whatever funds they need they obtain from short-term bank loans or overdrafts that are repaid the next day from cash inflows or from selling marketable securities. The greater the ability of a firm to tap short-term sources of financing (discussed in Chapter 17), the less the need to hold cash and marketable securities balances. Firms that do hold cash generally do so for three motives, which we discuss.[4]

3. In the late 1990s Ford's balance sheet showed over $25 billion in cash and marketable securities; the company argued that the cash was needed to help the firm invest for the future and weather economic downturns. This was evidently true, as its cash balance fell to under $5 billion in 2001 before rising to nearly $34 billion at the end of 2006. By 2006 Microsoft had over $34 billion in cash and marketable securities on its balance sheet because of its highly profitable products. Microsoft's cash and marketable securities balance has declined from $48 billion in 2003 due to the firm's dividend and share repurchase program.

4. For a detailed discussion of an empirical study of some of these motives, see T. Opler, L. Pinkowitz, R. Stulz, and R. Williamson, "Corporate Cash Holdings," *Journal of Applied Corporate Finance*, vol. 14, no. 1 (Spring 2001), pp. 55–66, and T. Opler, L. Pinkowitz, R. Stulz, and R. Williamson, "Determinants and Implications of Corporate Cash Holdings," *Journal of Financial Economics*, vol. 52 (1999), pp. 3–46.

INTERNET ACTIVITY

Some cash is necessary to carry on day-to-day operations. This is the **transactions motive** or demand for holding cash. If cash inflows and outflows could be projected with virtual certainty, the transactions demand for cash could theoretically be reduced to zero. Most businesses prepare cash flow forecasts or budgets, trying to predict the amount of cash holdings they will need. However, most firms are forced to hold some cash because of cash flow uncertainties and because minimum cash balances often are required on loans from commercial banks.

Marketable securities are held primarily for **precautionary motives**. These are demands for funds that may be caused by unpredictable events, such as delays in production or in the collection of receivables. Marketable securities can be sold to satisfy such liquidity problems. In the event of strong seasonal sales patterns, marketable securities also can be used to reduce wide fluctuations in short-term financing requirements. Funds may be held for precautionary purposes so the firm can continue to invest in assets—either plant, equipment, and technology—even if future sales and cash flows fall.

Marketable securities may also be held for **speculative motives**. In certain instances a firm might be able to take advantage of unusual cash discounts or price bargains on materials if it can pay quickly with cash. Marketable securities are easily converted into cash for such purposes.

To qualify as a marketable security, an investment must be highly liquid—that is, it must be readily convertible to cash without a large loss of value. Generally this requires that it have a short maturity and that an active secondary market exist so that it can be sold prior to maturity if necessary. The security must also be of high quality, with little chance that the borrower will default. U.S. Treasury bills offer the highest quality, liquidity, and marketability. Other investments that serve well as marketable securities include negotiable certificates of deposit (CDs) and commercial paper, both of which offer higher rates but are more risky and less liquid than Treasury bills. Business firms also can hold excess funds in money market accounts, or they can purchase banker's acceptances or short-term notes of U.S. government agencies. We discuss the characteristics of several financial instruments used as marketable securities below.

U.S. Treasury Bills

Treasury bills are sold at a discount through competitive bidding in a weekly auction. These bills are offered in all parts of the country but sell mostly in New York City. Treasury bills also are actively traded in secondary money markets, again mostly in New York.

Figure 16.6 shows the levels and volatility, or tendency to change rapidly, of three-month Treasury bill yields between 1990 and early 2007. Notice that they were over 8 percent in 1990 and dropped steadily to about 3 percent during 1992–1994. Yields rose to about 6 percent in early 1995 before dropping again and fluctuating about 4 to 6 percent through 1996–2000 and

---

SMALL BUSINESS PRACTICE
Importance of Working Capital Management for Small Businesses

For U.S. manufacturing firms, current assets represent about 40 percent of total assets and current liabilities are about 25 percent of total financing. A financial manager may spend over one-half of his or her time on the management of working capital, and the first job after graduation for many finance students will be in the area of working capital.

The management of working capital is particularly important to the entrepreneurial or venture firm. The need for all types of financial capital is important as the firm moves from a start-up situation to rapid growth in revenues. To reduce financing needs it is important for the small firm to keep only a necessary level of inventories on hand. Too much inventory causes unnecessary financing costs and increases the likelihood of having obsolete, unsalable products. Of course, too little inventory could result in stock-outs and the loss of potential sales.

To be competitive, businesses often must offer credit to their customers, which results in the need to finance accounts receivable.

However, the entrepreneurial or venture firm should not overlook the possibility that customers in some cases can actually provide financing help in the form of advance payments to you. For example, if you produce and sell an important component that is essential to a customer's own product that it markets and sells, your customer may actually be willing to provide partial payments in advance to you to help ensure that you will continue to manufacture the products on time and to maintain adequate quality.

A venture or entrepreneurial firm also may find it advantageous to seek longer repayment terms from suppliers to help finance growth in sales. In fact, sometimes suppliers will negotiate converting accounts payables to notes payable. Such a conversion is usually not without cost to the small business. Rather, to convert an accounts payable with thirty-day terms to a notes payable due in ninety days usually requires the payment of interest on the amount of the notes payable in addition to the amount owed when the accounts payable comes due.

FIGURE 16.6

Short-Term Interest Rates (Shaded Bars Represent Economic Recessions)

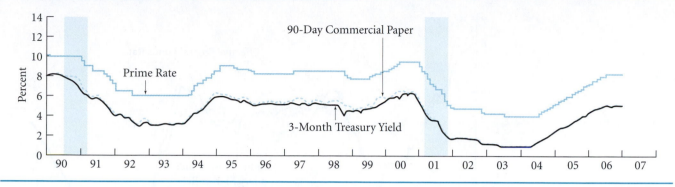

Source: "U.S. Currency at Home and Abroad," *Monetary Trends,* St. Louis Federal Reserve District Bank, March 2007, http://research.stlouisfed.org/publications/mt/20070301/mtpub.pdf (accessed July 16, 2007).

then sharply declined following the Fed's attempts to stimulate the economy in 2001. Rates rose again in 2004–2006 as the Fed increased its discount rate and federal funds rate as economic growth increased demand for loanable funds before easing in late 2006. U.S. Treasury bills are considered to be essentially risk free in that there is virtually no risk of default. Consequently, interest rates are, as expected, higher for other money market instruments of similar maturity at the same point in time.

Figure 16.7 shows recent examples of the yield curve. Some corporate financial managers attempt to "ride the yield curve" when the yield curve is upward sloping by buying longer-term securities rather than short-term with their excess cash. To understand why they do this, recall what happens as we purchase longer-term securities (by "longer-term" in this context, we mean securities that mature in, say, one year, rather than one month). First, longer maturities mean (if the yield curve is upward sloping) higher interest income. Second, as the security nears maturity and if the yield curve is upward sloping, its market yield will fall; we know from Chapter 7 that a falling interest rate results in higher prices for fixed-income securities. Thus, aggressive financial managers ride the curve to try to get higher returns on their investments of excess cash.

Federal Funds

Federal funds are not an investment alternative for excess cash except for financial institutions. At times, a commercial bank or other depository institution may find its reserves are temporarily greater than its required reserves. These temporary excess reserves, *federal funds* as they are called

FIGURE 16.7

Examples of the Yield Curve

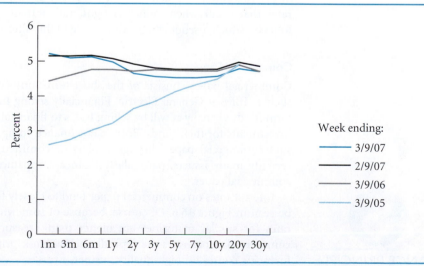

FIGURE 16.8
Federal Funds and 3-Month T-Bill Rates

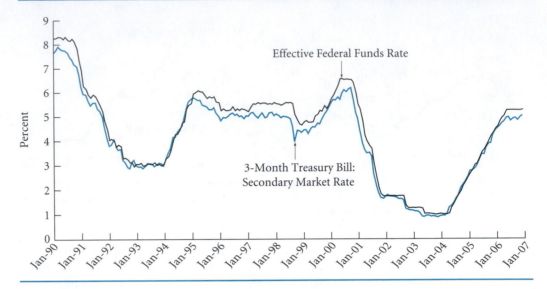

when loaned, are lent on a day-to-day basis to other depository institutions that are temporarily short of reserves.

The lending for a one-day period is generally done by an electronic funds transfer and can be illustrated with an example involving two commercial banks. The deal may be made by one or more telephone calls from the bank wanting to borrow funds, or it may be arranged through a federal funds broker. Funds are electronically transferred from the lending bank's reserve account to the borrowing bank's reserve account at the Federal Reserve Bank. Repayment of the loan plus interest occurs the next day. Many of these transactions are between New York City banks, but banks in other cities also enter the New York money market, usually as lenders. The most common trading unit for federal funds is $1 million, but this is often exceeded.

Federal funds rates usually parallel U.S. Treasury bill rates, as is shown in Figure 16.8. Notice that the federal funds rate has mainly remained above the three-month Treasury bill rate since 1995. Normally the spread, or difference, between the two rates is narrow. During periods of tight money and credit, however, federal funds can be bid up to very high levels. Banks and other depository institutions choose, within limits, between borrowing at the discount rate from the Federal Reserve and borrowing federal funds to meet reserve requirements. If they could be freely substituted for each other, the discount rate set in accordance with monetary policy objectives would set an upper limit for the federal funds rate, since banks would borrow at the lower of the two rates. In practice, however, banks prefer to borrow federal funds, even at the high rates that occur when money is tight, rather than borrow too frequently from the Federal Reserve, which discourages continued use of this alternative.

Commercial Paper

Commercial paper consists of the short-term, unsecured notes of well-known business firms such as IBM or General Electric. Financially strong firms such as these are able to raise short-term funds virtually at will by selling IOUs to financial market participants who seek short-term investments for their funds. Both major finance companies and nonfinancial corporations have sold commercial paper through dealers or commercial paper houses for many years. More recently many issuers, particularly finance companies, have begun to issue or sell their own commercial paper.

Interest rates on commercial paper tend to closely follow Treasury bill rates over time, as can be seen in Figure 16.6. Of course, because of somewhat greater default risk, commercial paper rates for similar maturities are higher than Treasury bill rates at any point in time. Since commercial paper rates are typically below bank prime rates, they are a valuable short-term financing source for high-quality business firms.

FINANCE PRINCIPLE

Negotiable Certificates of Deposit

A certificate of deposit is in essence a receipt issued by a bank in exchange for a deposit of funds. The bank agrees to pay the amount deposited plus interest to the bearer of the receipt on the date specified on the certificate. Many banks had issued such certificates as early as the turn of the last century, but before 1960 they were rarely issued in negotiable form. Negotiable CDs can be traded in the secondary market before maturity.

The volume of negotiable CDs (usually issued in denominations of $100,000 or more) has increased dramatically. Interest rates on these CDs usually parallel rates on other money market instruments such as commercial paper and banker's acceptances and are higher than the less risky Treasury bill rates.

GLOBAL DISCUSSION

Banker's Acceptances

This form of business paper primarily finances exports and imports and, since it is the unconditional obligation of the accepting bank—rather than a firm—generally has a high quality rating. Yields on banker's acceptances closely follow yields on commercial paper.

GLOBAL DISCUSSION

Eurodollars

Eurodollars are deposits placed in foreign banks that remain denominated in U.S. dollars. A demand deposit in a U.S. bank becomes a Eurodollar when the holder of such a deposit transfers it to a foreign bank or an overseas branch of a U.S. bank. After the transfer, the foreign bank holds a claim against the U.S. bank, while the original deposit holder (usually a business firm) now holds a Eurodollar deposit. It is called a Eurodollar deposit because it is still denominated in U.S. dollars rather than in the currency of the country in which the foreign bank operates.

Large commercial banks have raised money by borrowing from the Eurodollar market through their overseas branches. Overseas branches of U.S. banks and banks outside the United States get funds in the Eurodollar market by accepting dollars in interest-bearing time deposit accounts. These dollar deposits are lent anywhere in the world, usually on a short-term basis. Banks generally transfer funds by telephone or electronically, lending large sums without collateral between banks. Banks that handle Eurodollars are located in Europe, with London as the center, and in other financial centers throughout the world, including such places as Singapore and the Bahamas.

Eurodollar deposit liabilities have arisen because the dollar is widely used as an international currency and because foreigners are holding more dollars as a result of the ongoing U.S. balance of payment problems. Eurodollars are supplied by national and international corporations, banks, insurance companies, wealthy individuals, and some foreign governments and agencies. Eurodollar loan recipients also are a diverse group, but commercial banks, multinational corporations, and national corporations are heavy users.

U.S. banks have entered the Eurodollar market through their overseas branches for several major reasons: to finance business activity abroad, to switch Eurodollars into other currencies, and to lend to other Eurodollar banks. The most important reason, and the one that has received the most publicity in the United States, is for banking offices in the United States to borrow Eurodollars from their overseas branches. In this way they get funds at lower costs and during periods of tight money.

Municipal Securities

Securities issued by municipalities—cities, towns, states, school districts, and so forth—pay interest that, under law, is exempt from federal income taxes. For this reason, some companies like to invest some of their excess cash in short-term municipal securities. For a corporation with a 30 percent marginal tax rate, earning an annual rate of 4 percent on municipal securities is equivalent to earning $4/(1-.30)$ or 5.71 percent on taxable securities.

Where do firms invest their short-term cash holdings? U.S. government securities (mainly Treasury bills) are the most popular place to "park" cash, followed by CDs (time deposits), commercial paper, and other short-term investments such as banker's acceptances and Eurodollars.

TABLE 16.11
Sample Short-term Investment Policy Guidelines

INVESTMENT	MAXIMUM INVESTMENT	RATING	MAXIMUM MATURITY
Commercial paper	$15 million/issuer	A1/P1	180 days
Certificates of deposit	$25 million/institution	A1/P1 Bank Rating	270 days
U.S. Treasuries	None	Not applicable	18 months
Municipal securities	$10 million/issuer	A1/MIG1	15 months
Banker's acceptances	$15 million/issuer	A1/P1	120 days

Short-Term Investment Policy Statement

When the firm invests excess cash, it does not want to take undue risks. The funds will be needed in the future to pay bills and dividends, to invest in capital budget projects, or to repurchase outstanding bonds or shares of stock. A firm will seek safety of principal (the amount invested) as the first priority when investing excess cash. A second important consideration is liquidity—the ability to sell the security and raise cash quickly, easily, and at a price close to fair market value. A third consideration—that is ranked last among these three—is return. The risk/return trade-off for investing excess cash is traditionally decided in terms of safe, low-risk securities such as those we've reviewed in this section.

A firm's treasurer will develop guidelines to use when investing the firm's excess cash. These guidelines, called a ***short-term investment policy statement***, will detail the type of securities that the treasurer can invest in, their safety or default rating, maximum amounts that can be invested in each, and the maximum maturity of the securities purchased. Except possibly for U.S. Treasury securities, most short-term investment policy statements will require some degree of diversification. Diversification will keep the firm's cash from being invested in only one or a few issuers to protect against undue risk and potential loss in case an issuer gets in financial trouble. Table 16.11 shows a summary of one firm's short-term investment policy statement. It allows investment in five different short-term securities and limits exposure to any one issuer (except in the case of U.S. Treasuries) by specifying the maximum amount of securities from any one issuer that can be held by the portfolio at any point in time.

Unlike bond ratings, the credit ratings on short-term obligations can be rated A-1, A-2, and A-3 or P-1, P-2, and P-3. Short-term municipal obligations can have "MIG" ratings to designate that they are issued by a municipality. Typically only top-rated securities are allowed to be used when investing excess cash.

Some firms, rather than invest in individual securities, invest in money market mutual funds that are designed especially for use by corporate investors. Such funds will invest in a diversified pool of short-term securities and will face their own self-imposed limits on diversification, ratings, and maximum maturity.

The firm's financial managers will review the investment policy on a periodic basis to determine if limits should be raised or lowered and if the list of permissible securities should be expanded or reduced, but they will always keep the focus on safety and liquidity, with return being a third consideration.

GETTING—AND KEEPING—THE CASH

In addition to prudent investment of excess cash, there is another aspect of cash management: managing the cash conversion cycle by speeding up cash collections to receive cash as quickly as possible from customers (reducing the accounts receivable period) and keeping cash as long as possible (lengthening the accounts payable period). Ethically, there are concerns with lengthening the payables period by paying bills late; it is also bad business, but there are several tools firms use to speed up collections and slow down disbursements. Most of them use the concept of *float*. **Float** is the delay between when funds are sent by a payer to a payee. *Collection float* is the time between when a payer sends payment and the funds are credited to the payee's bank account. *Disbursement float* is the time between when a payer sends payment and when the funds are deducted from the payer's bank account. Individuals can appreciate the concept of float just by comparing their checkbook balance to the bank's record of their checking account balance. The difference between the two amounts arises because of float.

---

short-term investment policy statement
guidelines for the types of securities and diversification requirements to use when investing funds

ETHICAL ISSUES

float
the delay in the payment system between when the funds are sent by a payer and credited to the payee's bank account and deducted from the payer's bank account

By taking steps to reduce collection float or to increase disbursement float the firm's treasurer can reduce the cash conversion cycle. Reducing the cash conversion cycle benefits the firm in two ways. First, as we've seen in this chapter, it reduces the need for external financing. All else being equal, a firm with a cash conversion cycle of thirty days uses less outside financing than one with a cycle of thirty-two days. The second benefit is increased profitability. Extra cash can be invested in securities, used to reduce interest-bearing loans, invested productively in the firm, or distributed to shareholders.

Float, whether we are dealing with collections or disbursements, has three components. First is *delivery* or *transmission* float. This is the delay in transferring the means of payment from the payer (customer) to the payee (the provider of the goods or services). A payment placed in the mail may take several days before it reaches its destination; payments via couriers such as FedEx or DHL may be presented overnight, and electronic transmissions of payments occur with virtually no delivery float.

The second component is *processing float.* Once the payment reaches its destination, an envelope must be opened and its contents processed and entered into the firm's financial processing system. Electronic payments do not come in an envelope, but they must be routed correctly and any differences corrected between invoices and payments.

The third component is *clearing float.* This is the delay in transferring funds between payer and payee because of the banking system. You have probably seen this in your bank statements or in your bank's check availability policy; funds from a check deposited in your account may not be available to you for one to three days. This time is needed for the check to be routed back to the payer's bank and for the payer's bank to transfer funds to your bank.

Seeking ways to reduce the components of collection float is one of the practical issues facing a firm's treasurer. To speed up cash collections from customers, firms can use a **lockbox system**. If you pay your phone bill, utility bill, or credit card bill to a "P.O. Box" address, the firm receiving your payment is probably using a lockbox. Most lockboxes are managed by banks.[5] Several times a day bank personnel will empty the postal box and immediately begin processing and depositing payments from customers. A firm will consider mail delivery times, average number of pieces of mail received, and the average size of the receipts from customers before deciding where the lockboxes should be located geographically.

Preauthorized checks are a means of reducing both delivery and processing delays. If you have monthly expenses automatically deducted from your checking account, that is an example of a preauthorized check; this tool allows firms to regularly deduct payments from customers' bank accounts and is a means to pay utility, cable, and insurance bills. Preauthorized checks are initiated by the company to deduct funds from customers' accounts. Much of the process is automated, thereby reducing delivery and processing delays.

Processing delays (as well as some delivery delays) are reduced by the use of technology. Large incoming payments (say, over $1 million) can be automatically flagged by the lockbox bank and alerts sent to the firm's treasurer. Electronic check images and electronic payments (rather than the use of paper checks) reduce mail and processing delays. Forms recognition technology allows for incoming payments and data to be read electronically and for data to be stored in a form usable to the vendor. Use of the Internet and other electronic means for making payments eliminates delivery float and speeds processing. Lockboxes and preauthorized checks reduce processing delays, as processing is handled by banks, speeding deposit of incoming receipts.

Clearing float is reduced by the Fed and the banking system. Under Check 21, a new law that went into effect in late 2004, payee banks can present electronic or digital images of checks to payer banks for payment, rather than having to physically deliver paper checks. As this technology is adopted, clearing delays will be greatly reduced as this law eliminates the need to physically transport, record, and reconcile billions of paper checks per year.

Fewer options are available for slowing disbursements because of fears of being considered a poor customer at best or unethical at worst. When credit gets tight, the slow-paying customers are the first to be terminated. Most disbursement systems involve selected banks where funds to be disbursed are deposited to maximize float. Many firms use a ***zero-balance account*** in which just enough funds are transferred into an account to cover that day's checks presented for payment.

---

lockbox system
payments are sent to a P.O. box and processed by a bank to reduce collection float

preauthorized checks
regular (typically monthly) deductions by a vendor from a customer's checking account

zero-balance account
an arrangement between a bank and firm to transfer sufficient funds to a disbursement account to cover the day's checks presented to the bank for payment

INTERNET ACTIVITY

Visit http://www.afponline.org, the Web site of the Association for Financial Professionals. The site is specifically oriented toward those working in cash collection, disbursement, management, and investment. Learn about the CTP (Certified Treasury Professional) professional designation while visiting this site.

ETHICAL ISSUES

---

5. Lockbox systems are quite complex for large firms. General Electric uses over 150 lockboxes managed by three banks for collecting receipts from its various global divisions. Richard Gamble, "More than Just a Pretty Image," *Treasury and Risk Management* (May 2004), pp. 41–44.

electronic data interchange
the use of communications and computer systems to convey ordering, invoice, and payment information between suppliers and customers

remote capture
scanning of paper checks to electronically gather and transmit the payment information.

ETHICAL ISSUES

INTERNET ACTIVITY

Visit http://www.nacha.org, the Web site of the National Automated Clearinghouse Association—The Electronic Payments Association to learn more about electronic payment processing.

CONCEPT CHECK

Why do firms hold cash and marketable securities?

List at least four types of marketable securities a firm may use to invest excess cash to earn a short-term return.

What is float? List the components of float.

It may be only a matter of time before float virtually disappears on most business-to-business and person-to-business transactions. The growth of communications systems has resulted in firms using **electronic data interchange** as a means to send invoices and electronic payment for goods and services. Internet trading exchanges and Web-based funds transfer are the next steps in eliminating float.[6]

Another method that is growing in popularity is **remote capture**, which allows the company receiving a check to scan it through a device that records the relevant bank, account, and other payment information. Once scanned, the information can be sent digitally to the firm's bank. Such electronic processing eliminates paper handling and the need to complete a deposit slip listing each of the day's checks. It reduces potential keying errors and greatly reduces float as electronic images are transmitted from the recipient, the recipient's bank, the payer's bank, and the payer's bank account. After scanning, the paper check can then be destroyed or returned to the customer. Some stores have the scanners located by cash registers; the check is returned to the customer after it is run through the scanner, thus helping the customer to keep track of his or her spending and use of checks.

Many persons today use *online bill pay* as a way to pay bills and manage their accounts without having to write a paper check. Similarly, it is costly to businesses to use paper checks. It is less expensive, and less time-consuming, to do business electronically. That is why many businesses pay regular bills, such as payroll, electronically through direct deposit. One study found that a small business paying 100 employees twice a month can save almost $5,800 a year by using direct deposit rather than paper checks. For large businesses the savings adds up to over $1 million per year.[7]

In addition to lower costs, use of an electronic payment mechanism reduces the possibility of fraud and identity theft. Anywhere from three to ten people will handle a paper check before it is returned in a monthly bank statement. Paper checks can be "washed" of the original payee's information and another name inserted for payment. Using a desktop scanner, a person can scan in a check, make changes, and print out a new version of the check to be paid to a different person or with a different amount. Unlike paper checks, electronic payments are made and processed under the very tight computer and network security that exists in banks and in transmissions between banks.

Table 16.12 summarizes various ways to address float so the firm can hold onto its cash for as long as is ethically possible.

TABLE 16.12

Methods to Reduce the Components of Collection and Disbursement Float

COMPONENTS OF FLOAT	TYPES OF FLOAT	
	COLLECTION FLOAT	DISBURSEMENT FLOAT
Delivery	Lockboxes Pre-authorized checks Electronic payments	Selection of disbursement banks to maximize delivery float, clearing float, and to maximize prudent returns on corporate cash (such as using zero-balance accounts)
Processing	Lockboxes Pre-authorized checks Electronic payments Use of technology Digital imaging	
Clearing	Banking system improvements to allow electronic images rather than paper checks	

6. Kenneth N. Kuttner and James J. McAndrews, "Personal On-Line Payments," *Economic Policy Review,* Federal Reserve Bank of New York (December 2001), pp. 35–50; Edward Teach, "Going Virtual," *CFO* (May 2000), pp. 81–88.

7. NACHA—The Electronic Payments Association, *Direct Deposit/Direct Payment General Information,* 2nd edition, June 2003, Herndon, Virginia. Original calculations for the 1st edition made by Joseph D. Tinucci, Tinucci and Associates, Inc., March 2001.

PERSONAL FINANCIAL PLANNING
Efficiency and the Banking System

The average firm has one-third or more of its assets in the form of current assets (cash, accounts receivable, and inventory). Surveys show that almost two-thirds of a financial manager's time and effort is spent on short-term finance issues. Thus, managing working capital and maintaining short-term financing sources (the topic of Chapter 17 are main concerns to a financial manager and to the well-being of the firm. Efforts to cut operating expenses and to increase the firm's efficient use of its working capital can help increase a firm's profits, making it a potentially attractive investment. As mentioned later in this chapter, General Electric's efforts to manage its inventory more efficiently will free up an extra $1 billion in cash, an amount of cash that can be redirected to more productive investments to increase shareholder return.

This chapter points out an important difference between individuals and business firms with respect to cash management. You and I can earn interest on our checking account balance at a bank. Current regulations, however, prevent banks from paying interest on a firm's checking account. Whereas you probably do not mind seeing your checking account balance rise, the fact that such balances do not earn interest for a firm gives firms an incentive to minimize their checking account balances. However, banks who realize the profit potential of developing relationships with businesses have developed ways to get around this. One method is a *zero-balance account (ZBA)*—a checking account whose balance is kept at zero. When one of the firm's checks clears the banking system, the bank moves enough funds into the account to match the amount on the presented check. After payment the ZBA goes back to a zero balance. Another service that banks have developed is the *sweep account*. At the end of the business day, any funds left in a firm's checking account are "swept" out and invested overnight in repurchase agreements and other short-term investments. All this ingenuity, effort, and resources are expended simply because banks cannot pay interest on a firm's checking account as they do on our personal checking accounts!

ACCOUNTS RECEIVABLE MANAGEMENT

The management of receivables involves conducting credit analysis, setting credit terms, and carrying out collection efforts. Taken together, these decision areas determine the level of investment in accounts receivable. The selling of goods on credit is generally driven by industry norms and competitive pressures. The time it takes to collect accounts receivable depends on industry norms for credit terms, as well as the firm's policies for setting credit standards and carrying out collection efforts.

CREDIT ANALYSIS

ETHICAL ISSUES

character
ethical quality upon which one can base a judgment about a customer's willingness to pay bills

capacity
ability to pay bills

capital
adequacy of owners' equity relative to existing liabilities

collateral
whether assets are available to provide security for the potential credit

conditions
current economic climate and state of the business cycle

Credit analysis involves appraising the creditworthiness or quality of a potential customer. It answers the question "Should credit be granted?" The decision is made on the basis of the applicant's character, capacity, capital, collateral, and conditions—the five C's of credit analysis.

Some of these involve an analysis of a potential buyer's financial statements using the ratios we saw in Chapter 12. **Character** is the ethical quality of the applicant on which one can base a judgment about his or her willingness to pay bills and is best judged by reviewing the applicant's past credit history for long overdue or unpaid obligations. **Capacity** is the ability to pay bills and often involves an examination of liquidity ratios. **Capital** indicates the adequacy of owners' equity relative to existing liabilities as the underlying support for creditworthiness. **Collateral** reflects whether assets are available to provide security for the potential credit. **Conditions** refer to the current economic climate and state of the business cycle. All are important considerations in assessing whether the applicant can meet credit obligations.

Once a firm has established its credit quality standards, credit analysis is used to determine whether an applicant is granted credit, rejected, or put into a marginal category. Whether or not credit should be extended to marginal applicants depends on such factors as the prevailing economic conditions and the extent to which the selling firm has excess production capacity. During periods of economic downturn and excess capacity, a firm may need to sell to lower-quality applicants who may be slow paying but are not likely to default.

Your local car dealership provides an example of this. To entice buyers when sales are sluggish, auto manufacturers may offer below-market financing rates, attractive refunds, and/or low (or no) down payment requirements. Sales can rise sharply as a result of aggressive marketing via credit terms. However, large losses can accrue to firms when buyers find themselves unable to repay the loans. This happened to Mitsubishi in 2003 and 2004, and when Mitsubishi tightened its credit standards, sales fell sharply. More than attractive credit terms, the success of a firm requires a product offering good value to customers.

CREDIT-REPORTING AGENCIES

Several sources of credit information are available to help a firm decide whether or not to extend credit. **Credit bureaus** exist to obtain credit information about business firms and individuals. They are nonprofit institutions, established and supported by the businesses they serve.

The local mercantile, or business, credit bureau provides a central record for credit information on firms in the community. Bureau members submit lists of their customers to the bureau. The bureau determines the credit standing of these customers by contacting other bureau members who have extended credit to them. Thus, a member firm need only contact its credit bureau for information on prospective customers rather than deal with many individual firms.

The exchange of mercantile credit information from bureau to bureau is accomplished through the National Credit Interchange System. Credit bureau reports are factual rather than analytical, and it is up to each credit analyst to interpret the facts.

Local retail credit bureaus have been established to consolidate and distribute credit information on individuals in the community. These organizations are generally owned and operated by participating members on a nonprofit basis. A central organization known as the Associated Credit Bureaus of America enables local retail credit bureaus in the United States to transmit credit information from bureau to bureau.

GLOBAL DISCUSSION

American businesses selling to foreign customers encounter all the problems involved in a domestic sale, such as credit checking, plus several others. Among these are increased distance, language differences, complicated shipping and government regulations, differences in legal systems, and political instability. To help exporters with these problems, the National Association of Credit Management established the Foreign Credit Interchange Bureau. Just as local credit bureaus increase their information on business credit risks by pooling credit and collection experience, so the members of the Foreign Credit Interchange Bureau have established a central file of information covering several decades of credit experience. The bureau is located in New York to serve the numerous export and financial organizations there that do business overseas.

INTERNET ACTIVITY

A source of credit information for business customers is Dun & Bradstreet, http://www.dnb.com. Your own personal credit information can be obtained from credit bureau firms such as Equifax (http://www.equifax.com), Experian (http://www.experian.com), and TransUnion Corporation (http://www.tuc.com).

Some private firms also operate as credit-reporting agencies. The best known is Dun & Bradstreet, which has been in operation for well over a century and provides credit information on businesses of all kinds. The information that is assembled and evaluated is brought into the company through many channels. The company employs full- and part-time employees for direct investigation, communicates directly with business establishments by mail to supplement information files, and obtains the financial statements of companies being evaluated. All information filed with public authorities and financial and trade papers is carefully gathered and analyzed to produce a credit analysis. The basic service supplied to the manufacturers, wholesalers, banks, and insurance companies who subscribe to Dun & Bradstreet is rendered in two ways: through written reports on individual businesses and through a reference book.

A Dun & Bradstreet report is typically divided into five sections: (1) rating and summary, (2) trade payments, (3) financial information, (4) operation and location, and (5) history. In addition, six times per year Dun & Bradstreet publishes a composite reference book of ratings on thousands of manufacturers, wholesalers, retailers, and other businesses.

When many customers want to apply for credit, in-depth credit analysis focusing on the five C's is not practical. Companies that offer credit cards use a sophisticated statistical tool called *credit scoring,* which takes information about thousands of customers and, through computer number crunching, develops a formula that tries to predict who is a good credit risk (someone who will likely pay their bill in a timely manner) and who is a poor credit risk. Credit scoring models use quantitative items such as a person's income, past mortgage or credit card payment history, marital status, homeowner/renter status, and current debts to make this determination.

INTERNET ACTIVITY

For more information on credit scoring, see http://www.fairisaac.com, http://www.myfico.com, and http://www.ecredit.com.

Such models will make errors. One person applied for a credit card and was rejected despite having a clean credit record. He earns $123,100 in salary at age forty-one in a job with excellent security. The person was Lawrence B. Lindsey, who at the time was on the Board of Governors of the Federal Reserve System. A man who helps set interest rate and bank policy was rejected because the computer models could not handle the qualitative data that explained why his credit report appeared as it did. Ironically, in an earlier speech, Mr. Lindsey predicted the following about credit scoring: "We will obtain the fairness of the machine, but lose the judgment, talents, and sense of justice that only humans can bring to decision making."[8]

---

8. David Wessel, "A Man Who Governs Credit Is Denied a Toys 'R' Us Card," *Wall Street Journal* (December 14, 1995), p. B1.

CREDIT TERMS AND COLLECTION EFFORTS

trade credit

credit extended on purchases to a firm's customers

Credit extended on purchases to a firm's customers is called **trade credit** and is discussed more fully in Chapter 17. This credit appears as accounts payable on the balance sheet of the customer and as receivables to the seller. The seller sets the terms of the credit. For example, the firm might require full payment in sixty days, expressed as net sixty. If all customers pay promptly in sixty days, this would result in a receivables turnover of 365/60 or about six times a year.[9] Thus, annual net sales of $720,000 would require an average receivables investment of about $120,000. A change in credit terms or in the enforcement of the terms through the collection effort will alter the average investment in receivables. The imposition of net fifty-day terms would lead to an increase in the receivables turnover to 7.3 (365/50) times, and the average investment in receivables would decline to about $100,000 ($720,000/7.3). If it costs, say, 15 percent to finance assets, then the $20,000 reduction in receivables would result in a savings of $3,000 ($20,000 × 15 percent).[10]

We are assuming that a reduction in the credit period and in the receivables portion of the short-term operating cycle will not cause lost sales. The financial manager must be very careful not to impose credit terms that will lower sales and cause lost profits that would more than offset any financing cost savings.

GLOBAL DISCUSSION

In global business, a concern with managing accounts from overseas is the effect of changing exchange rates on the funds received by the firm. For example, suppose a firm sells an item for $50 to customers in the U.S. and for €57 to customers in France based upon an exchange rate of about $1 = €1.14. Over the next sixty days when payment is due, should the dollar strengthen (to, say, $1 = €1.20), the firm will receive only a €57/€1.20 per dollar or $47.5, which will hurt its profitability.

A firm has two ways to handle this issue. First, it can invoice customers in the firm's home currency. That is, a U.S. firm can request payment from a customer in France in terms of the U.S. dollar instead of the euro. This shifts the risk of changing exchange rates to the payer. Second, if a U.S. firm allows customers to pay in their own currencies rather than in U.S. dollars, the firm can hedge, or reduce the risk, of changing exchange rates by using currency futures or options contracts. General information about futures and options contracts is in the Learning Extension to Chapter 9.

The collection effort involves administering past due accounts. Techniques include sending letters, making telephone calls, and even making personal visits for very large customers with past due bills. One credit card company sent Hallmark greeting cards to delinquent customers to encourage them to contact the firm to arrange payment schedules. If the customer continues to fail to pay a bill, then the account may be turned over to a commercial collection firm. If this fails, the last resort is to take legal action.[11] The use of e-mail payment requests is gaining popularity as a means to quickly and cheaply contact customers who are behind in their payments.

A lax collection policy may result in the average collection period for receivables being substantially longer than the credit period stated in the terms. As seen, the average collection period is the ratio of accounts receivable to the average sales per day. For example, a firm might sell on credit terms of net sixty days and have net sales of $720,000 and an accounts receivable balance of $150,000. For this firm, the average collection period is:

$$\frac{\text{Accounts receivable}}{\text{Net sales}/365} = \frac{\$150,000}{\$720,000/365} = \frac{\$150,000}{\$1,973} = 76 \text{ days}$$

This shows that the accounts receivable are outstanding an average of seventy-six days instead of the sixty-day credit period. Increasing credit standards or improving the collection effort might reduce the average collection period to sixty days and the accounts receivable balance to $120,000. Lowering a firm's credit standards or customer credit quality will cause the average

9. The turnover of current asset accounts such as receivables and inventories, like total assets turnover, is an asset utilization ratio. A higher ratio implies better usage of assets.

10. The 15 percent figure represents the cost of financing assets through the firm's liabilities and equity—the right-hand side of the balance sheet. Any change in assets must be financed by a change in liabilities and equity. The 15 percent figure does not represent the cost of managing accounts receivable from a human or technology perspective.

11. See Brenda L. Moore, "Dunning Debtors," *Wall Street Journal* (May 4, 2001), pp. R9, R11, for insights into the process of collecting past-due accounts.

TABLE 16.13
Analysis of a Change in Credit Policy

Marginal or Additional Benefits:

Increased sales (estimate): $100,000
    Additional bad debt expense from change in sales: 5 percent
    0.05 × $100,000 = $5,000 in losses
Net estimated increase in sales: $95,000
    Expected profit margin: 10 percent
Net increase in profits = 0.10 × $95,000 = $9,500
Marginal or Additional Costs:

Increases in asset accounts:
    Accounts receivables average increase: $14,000
    Inventory average increase: $18,000
    Total: $32,000 increase in current assets to be financed
Cost of financing: 15 percent
Net increase in financing costs = 0.15 × $32,000 = $4,800

INTERNET ACTIVITY

Learn more about current issues in short-term finance at http://www.cfo.com and http:// www.treasuryandrisk.com.

FINANCE PRINCIPLE

collection period to lengthen, as poorer-quality customers are generally slower payers. Thus, the financial manager must balance the advantages of increased sales from more customers against the cost of financing higher receivable investments and increased collection costs.

For example, suppose a firm is considering lowering its credit standards to increase sales. Table 16.13 summarizes the analysis to determine if the credit change makes financial sense. The estimated sales will rise by $100,000. Additional bad debt expense from poor credit risks is expected to be 5 percent, leaving a net revenue increase of $95,000. With a profit margin of 10 percent, the incremental benefit of lowering standards is $9,500.

The costs of lowering credit standards will be the cost of financing higher receivables and inventory balances. If sales rise $100,000, the firm expects its average receivables balance will rise by $14,000 and its average inventory balance will rise by $18,000, for an increase of $32,000 in current assets. If the cost of financing these assets is 15 percent, the cost of the looser credit policy is $32,000 × 0.15, or $4,800. The incremental benefit of $9,500 is larger than the incremental cost, $4,800, so the firm should go ahead with its plan. This analysis requires that the additional risks of the looser credit policy are reflected in the cost of financing of 15 percent. This may not be the same as the firm's cost of financing its other assets. Recall from Chapter 6 that expected return and risk are linked; should the added accounts be more risky than the firm's assets as a whole because of their greater risk of nonpayment, the cost of financing the risky assets may need to be adjusted appropriately.

INVENTORY MANAGEMENT

Inventory administration is primarily a production management function. The length of the production process and the production manager's willingness to accept delays will influence the amount invested in raw materials and work in process. The amount of finished goods on hand may vary depending on the firm's willingness to accept stock-outs and lost sales.

Costs of owning raw materials, such as financing, storage, and insurance, need to be balanced against the costs of ordering the materials. Production managers attempt to balance these costs by determining the optimal number of units to order that will minimize inventory costs of total raw materials.

Let's assume that a firm's cost of goods sold is $600,000 and it has inventories on hand of $100,000. Recall that the inventory turnover is computed as follows:

$$\frac{\text{Cost of goods sold}}{\text{Inventories}} = \frac{\$600,000}{\$100,000} = 6 \text{ times}$$

If the firm is able to increase its inventory turnover to, say, eight times, then the investment in inventories could be reduced to $75,000 ($600,000/8) and some financing costs would be saved. However, if a tight inventory policy is imposed, lost sales due to stock-outs could result in lost profits that more than offset financing cost savings. Thus the financial manager must balance possible savings against potential added costs when managing investments in inventories.

The *just-in-time (JIT) inventory control system* is gaining increased acceptance by firms trying to reduce the amount of inventory they must carry. Under this system, substantial coordination is required between the manufacturer and its suppliers so that materials needed in the manufacturing process are delivered just in time to avoid halts in production. For example, automobile manufacturers who used to keep a two-week supply of certain parts now place orders on a daily basis and expect daily shipment and delivery.

Corporate fads may come and go, but one that is sure to stay is the attempt by corporations to reduce their net working capital by reducing their current asset account balances. Some firms have a goal of operating with zero working capital. Although they may not attain it, merely striving for this goal creates opportunities to discover efficiencies, improve production processes and customer relations, and free up cash. At a time when firms need cash to invest in overseas facilities and markets, invest in new technology, and service debt, the uncovering of cash by reducing working capital is similar to finding a treasure chest.

The average Fortune 500 firm has $.20 of working capital for every $1 of sales—a grand total of over $500 billion for all the firms on the list. A small increase in working capital efficiency can have a significant impact on cash flow. Savings from the efforts of individual firms are impressive: Campbell's Soup reduced working capital by $80 million; American Standard has reduced it by $200 million; Quaker Oats also reduced working capital by $200 million. General Electric estimates that increasing inventory turnover by one turn a year will generate $1 billion in freed-up cash. It is no accident that Amazon.com's first year of profitability, 2001, was accompanied by an increase in inventory turnover from 9 to 13; the extra asset efficiency helped to deliver savings and profits to its bottom line.[12]

Cutting working capital generates cash and can increase company earnings. Financing costs should decline as less financing is needed to support large receivables and inventory balances. Costs of warehousing and handling inventory will fall as inventory levels are pared. Slimmed-down current asset balances will lead to reductions in firms' total assets. The result of cost savings and smaller asset bases will mean higher returns on assets and, in all likelihood, increases in shareholder wealth.

A new innovation in inventory management is JIT II. *JIT II* moves the JIT relationship between vendor and purchaser a step closer. The position of the buyer's purchasers or materials planner is eliminated and replaced by a representative of the supplier. This person works closely with the buyer to, at times, manage inventories and issue purchase orders to supply additional materials. The advantages of this system are increased efficiency by reducing inventory, eliminating duplicate positions, and assistance in planning. For JIT II to work effectively, the buyer must have a high degree of trust in the supplier along several dimensions: first, that the supplier's products will continue to meet the buyer's needs, and second, that the proprietary information to which the vendor's representative has access will remain private and will not be shared outside this specific buyer–vendor relationship.

TECHNOLOGY AND WORKING CAPITAL MANAGEMENT

Technology is fast improving the ability of firms to manage cash and receivables, to control inventory, and to communicate with customers and suppliers more efficiently. Firms in industries such as auto manufacturing, oil and gas, and retailing are initiating Internet-based systems, or portals, for ordering items from suppliers. *Portals* are specialized and secure Web sites through which clients can access order and account information. B2B (business-to-business) portals have the promise of lowering procurement and supply-chain costs. They also provide a way for firms to sell excess inventory or assets.

CONCEPT CHECK

Is there a benefit to reducing corporate America's levels of working capital?

What influences the level of a firm's inventory?

What information does inventory turnover provide to managers?

How might improved inventory management techniques help the economy?

What is JIT? JIT II?

INTERNET ACTIVITY

Examples of B2B Web sites include those listed at http://www.internetb2blist.com (food and beverage industry), http://www.agentrics.com (retailing), and http://www.covisint.com (auto).

12. Ronald Fink, "Forget the Float?" *CFO* (July 2001), pp. 54–62; Randy Myers, "Cash Crop", *CFO* (August 2000), pp. 59–82; S. L. Mintz, "Lean Green Machines," *CFO* (July 2000), pp. 76–94; Shawn Tully, "Raiding a Company's Hidden Cash," *Fortune* (August 22, 1994), pp. 82–87.

JEAN DONNELLY
Controller
Fath Management

Certified Public Accountant
BS, Accounting
Purdue University

"Managing people is probably the hardest and most rewarding part of the job."

Q: *Is it correct to describe your work as private accounting?*

A: Yes. I am the controller at Fath Management, which is a real estate management company. I manage the in-house accounting department there.

Q: *What does your job entail?*

A: Our department basically handles all the money that passes in and out of the company, which includes the thousands of rent checks we receive each month from our tenants and all the expenditures necessary to operate our properties. We also produce a variety of monthly reports that show how each property is performing relative to its budget and to the previous year. These reports help us make decisions about upgrading properties and adjusting rents, among other things. I'm also involved in the creation of next year's budget for each property, which we put together in the last quarter of the year.

Q: *Where does the title "Controller" come from?*

A: Part of it relates to financial controls. I design and implement the appropriate financial controls and approvals throughout the company so that cash coming in and going out is handled correctly. These are basically checks and balances to protect Fath's interests.

Q: *Do you have the same kind of busy season at the end of the year that public accountants do?*

A: It is a busy time of year for us. During the winter we assemble our year-end financial statements and the figures needed for our tax returns. We spend a lot of time on taxes. Each of our forty properties has its own tax return, so we have a lot of data to pull together and organize. We have to file returns in the four different states where we own properties, so we have one of the public accounting firms handle the actual return preparation, but we still have to assemble all the required information.

Q: *You previously worked for one of the large, public accounting firms. How would you compare that to your current experience at Fath?*

A: It was an excellent preparation for what I do now. You receive so much training and experience; it's almost like getting another degree. The biggest difference I've found since joining Fath is the size of the organization. Our company has a small management team, and we're expected to do a lot. I interact with the owner of the firm all the time. There's more latitude to make decisions and take the initiative, but there's also the accountability that goes along with that.

Q: *Do you manage a staff?*

A: Yes. The accounting manager, systems administrator, and seven accounting clerks are in my department. I spend a lot of my time doing the traditional managerial tasks—reviewing, training, motivating, disciplining. Managing people is probably the hardest and most rewarding part of the job. I have a great group, and that makes my life a lot easier.

CASH MANAGEMENT

The Internet (and corporate intranets) allows treasurers and other finance personnel to more closely track their firm's cash flows and needs. Information on bank balances, incoming checks, and the status of disbursements are available online through bank portals. The use of the Web allows the transfer of funds between corporate accounts and the initiation of electronic payments and preauthorized check transactions. Traveling executives can access Treasury information online, not just from the firm's main bank but from all of its banking relationships. Access to such information allows the treasurer to forecast and estimate the firm's needs for cash on a day-to-day basis and thus reduce the level of excess cash and keep short-term borrowing at the minimum level needed.

PROCESSING INVOICES AND FLOAT

Technology has revolutionized order processing. Imagine collecting orders by hand, keying them into a computer (sometimes twice as a check against keying errors), printing bills, stuffing envelopes, mailing bills, waiting for customers to pay their bills, processing incoming payments, and reconciling differences, handling the collection process, and writing off bad debts—all very labor and time intensive.

EDI (electronic data interchange) systems helped to computerize some of the payment and collection process. EDI allows a limited amount of invoice information to accompany an electronic bill payment. However, the expanding use of XML in business applications is automating much of this process. Many of you are aware of HTML (hypertext markup language), the language that Web browsers are programmed to read, interpret, and display Web pages. XML, extensible markup language, goes a step beyond HTML. XML tells computer systems what kind of information is being transmitted: financial, invoice, ordering, pictures, and so on, so different computer systems can recognize data and communicate with each other. XML systems will help firms process orders more efficiently and reduce, if not virtually eliminate, processing float.

A variation to XML is *electronic invoice presentment and payments systems (EIPP)*. Working through an Internet portal, vendors and customers can more efficiently process and pay for orders. Consider this example: a client orders ten computers online from a vendor. The automated system collects the order, approves it, and prepares the computers for shipping. When they are delivered, the client realizes one of the computers does not work properly. The client goes online, pulls up the invoice, and marks the disputed item. This starts an automated process that adjusts the invoice to bill the client for the working computers for online payment (perhaps via XML). Others are notified electronically, too, and by way of e-mail the dispute is resolved; either a shipping label is sent so the bad machine can be returned to the vendor, a technician is sent to fix it, or a replacement computer is sent to the client and the invoice adjusted accordingly. EIPP speeds ordering, dispute resolution, and payment collection.

TRACKING INVENTORY

The movement toward JIT, better supplier–buyer communications, and information technology has helped improve sales forecasting and production processes. You are familiar with product scanners at store checkout lines; many times the scanned information is sent directly to suppliers to communicate the necessary size of the next morning's product shipment.

Tracking inventory allows firms to reduce the inventory conversion period (and thus the cash conversion cycle), reduce costs, and track shipments more effectively. Bar codes on boxes are scanned to track inventory in transit between vendor, warehouse, retail store, and checkout counter. RFID (radio frequency identification) tags take inventory tracking one step further. The RFID tag sends out a radio signal to electronic readers that allow companies to know the location of inventory literally on a minute-by-minute basis. RFID tags for cargo containers can send alarms when a break-in has occurred, when a container has been sitting in one location for too long, or in response to violations of preset conditions relating to temperature, air pressure, motion, and so on inside the container. Tracking with such detail can reduce theft and spoilage, as well as inventory levels and the costs of carrying inventory.

CONCEPT CHECK

How is technology improving cash management? Reducing float?

How is technology helping to improve inventory management?

APPLYING FINANCE TO . . .

INSTITUTIONS AND MARKETS

The market determines short-term interest rates, based in part on Fed policy, expectations of future Fed policy and inflation, and the supply/demand of short-term funds. Banks and other financial services firms are eager to attract firms' excess short-term funds so they, in turn, can lend them to entities that desire short-term financing.

INVESTMENTS

Although we usually think that investing involves long-lived assets (bonds, stocks, buildings, corporate strategies), it involves short-term assets, too. Investing excess cash can be a means of increasing profits. The expected risk/return trade-off holds true for both short-term and long-term investments.

FINANCIAL MANAGEMENT

A firm's long-term goal is to maximize shareholder wealth, but it needs to survive the short term first! To do so, the firm needs to maintain its liquidity and manage its cash, receivables, and inventory to satisfy its creditors, suppliers, and customers. A firm with poor cash, credit, and inventory management will have unhappy customers, lenders, and suppliers and may not be in business much longer.

SUMMARY

It is cash, not earnings, that keeps a firm in business. Company treasurers are, therefore, mainly interested in watching a firm's cash flows and forecasting future cash flows to ensure adequate cash is available to pay the firm's obligations when they are due. This chapter discussed several aspects of working capital management that will be of practical concern to those watching the firm's cash flow. A firm's operating cycle measures the time it takes from when raw materials are received, processed into finished goods, and sold to when cash is collected from the sale of the finished products. The cash conversion cycle is similar to the operating cycle except that it measures the time between when the firm pays for its materials purchases and when cash is collected from their sale. Firms with faster inventory turnovers, faster receivables turnovers, and slower average payment periods will have shorter cash conversion cycles. The longer this cycle is, the greater the firm's financing needs and accompanying financing costs. The cycle and its components will be affected by seasonal sales patterns and business cycles.

A cash budget provides a treasurer with some detail on expected cash inflows and outflows. Specifically, it shows the amounts and the source of expected cash inflows and outflows. By using the cash budget, the treasurer can plan how best to invest cash surpluses and borrow to cover cash deficits. Investing excess cash in marketable securities is a process in which the treasurer tries to balance the need for safety and liquidity of the invested funds with the desire to earn returns on the investment. Popular marketable securities investments include Treasury bills, negotiable CDs, commercial paper, and Eurodollar deposits.

Marketing concerns are a major determinant of accounts receivable policies. Production and purchasing issues may dominate the inventory decision. Nonetheless, financial managers need to be part of these strategic discussions and aware of the factors that affect these decisions. More and more firms have realized that significant amounts of cash are tied up in working capital. Attempts to speed up cash collections, slow disbursements, and reduce receivables and inventories can free up cash, lead to more efficient operations, and increase firm profitability and shareholder wealth.

KEY TERMS

capacity
capital
cash budget
cash conversion cycle
character
collateral
conditions

credit bureau
electronic data interchange
float
lockbox system
operating cycle
preauthorized checks
precautionary motives

remote capture
short-term investment policy statement
speculative motives
trade credit
transactions motive
zero-balance account

DISCUSSION QUESTIONS

1. What is meant by *working capital?*

2. Briefly describe a manufacturing firm's operating cycle.

3. Explain how the cash conversion cycle differs from the operating cycle.

4. Describe how the length of the cash conversion cycle is determined.

5. Explain how the length of the operating cycle affects the amount of funds invested in accounts receivable and inventories.

6. What affects the amount of financing provided by accounts payable as viewed in terms of the cash conversion cycle?

7. What is a cash budget? How does the treasurer use forecasts of cash surpluses and cash deficits?

8. Three sets of information are needed to construct a cash budget. Explain what they are.

9. Why might firms want to maintain minimum desired cash balances?

10. What are the sources of cash inflows to a firm over any time frame?

11. What are the sources of cash outflows from a firm over any time frame?

12. How does the choice of level or seasonal production affect a firm's cash over the course of a year?

13. Describe what happens to a firm's current asset accounts if the firm has seasonal sales and it uses (a) level production and if it uses (b) seasonal production.

14. Describe the three motives or reasons for holding cash.

15. What characteristics should an investment have to qualify as an acceptable marketable security?

16. Identify and briefly describe several financial instruments used as marketable securities.

17. Why would a corporation want to invest excess cash in securities issued by a municipality?

18. What are the three main concerns of a treasurer when investing a firm's excess cash?

19. Why is a short-term investment policy statement necessary?

20. What is float? Why is it important to cash management?

21. What are the three components of float? Which float components are under the control of the firm seeking to reduce collection float?

22. What are some strategies a firm can use to speed up its collections by reducing float?

23. How can processing float be reduced?

24. How can a firm use float to slow down its disbursements?

25. Why can't a firm that wants to increase disbursement float simply make payments after the stated due date?

26. How does remote capture reduce float?

27. Besides lower expenses, explain another advantage of using electronic payments rather than paper checks.

28. What is credit analysis? Identify the five C's of credit analysis.

29. Describe various credit-reporting agencies that provide information on business credit applicants.

30. How can a firm control the risk of changing exchange rates when billing an overseas customer?

31. What risks arise when a firm lowers its credit standards to try to increase sales volume?

32. How do credit terms and collection efforts affect the investment in accounts receivable?

33. How is the financial manager involved in the management of inventories?

34. What are the benefits to a firm of reducing its working capital?

35. What is JIT II?

36. How is technology affecting cash management? Order processing?

37. How is technology changing inventory management?

PROBLEMS

1. Pretty Lady Cosmetic Products has an average production process time of forty days. Finished goods are kept on hand for an average of fifteen days before they are sold. Accounts receivable are outstanding an average of thirty-five days, and the firm receives forty days of credit on its purchases from suppliers.

   a. Estimate the average length of the firm's short-term operating cycle. How often would the cycle turn over in a year?

   b. Assume net sales of $1,200,000 and cost of goods sold of $900,000. Determine the average investment in accounts receivable, inventories, and accounts payable. What would be the net financing needs considering only these three accounts?

2. The Robinson Company has the following current assets and current liabilities for these two years:

	2007	2008
Cash and marketable securities	$50,000	$50,000
Accounts receivable	300,000	350,000
Inventories	350,000	500,000
Total current assets	$700,000	$900,000
Accounts payable	$200,000	$250,000
Bank loan	0	150,000
Accruals	150,000	200,000
Total current liabilities	$350,000	$600,000

   a. If sales in 2007 were $1.2 million and sales in 2008 were $1.3 million, and cost of goods sold was 70 percent of sales, how long were Robinson's operating cycles and cash conversion cycles in each of these years?

   b. What caused them to change during this time?

3. The Robinson Company from Problem 2 had net sales of $1,200,000 in 2007 and $1,300,000 in 2008.

   a. Determine the receivables turnover in each year.

   b. Calculate the average collection period for each year.

   c. Based on the receivables turnover for 2007, estimate the investment in receivables if net sales were $1,300,000 in 2008.

   d. How much of a change in the 2008 receivables occurred?

4. Suppose the Robinson Company had a cost of goods sold of $1,000,000 in 2007 and $1,200,000 in 2008.

   a. Calculate the inventory turnover for each year. Comment on your findings.

   b. What would have been the amount of inventories in 2008 if the 2007 turnover ratio had been maintained?

5. Given Robinson's 2007 and 2008 financial information presented in Problems 2 and 4, address the following:

   a. Compute Robinson's operating and cash conversion cycle in each year.

   b. What was Robinson's net investment in working capital each year?

6. Robinson expects its 2009 sales and cost of goods sold to grow by 5 percent over their 2008 levels.

   a. What will be the effect on its levels of receivables, inventories, and payments if the components of its cash conversion cycle remain at their 2008 levels? What will be its net investment in working capital?

   b. What will be the impact on its net investment in working capital in 2009 if Robinson is able to reduce its collection period by five days and its inventory period by six days, as well as increase its payment period by two days?

7. Robinson expects its 2009 sales and cost of goods sold to grow by 20 percent over their 2008 levels.

   a. What will be the effect on its levels of receivables, inventories, and payments if the components of its cash conversion cycle remain at their 2008 levels? What will be its net investment in working capital?

   b. What will be the impact on its net investment in working capital in 2009 if Robinson is able to reduce its inventory period by ten days?

8. Following are financial statements for the Genatron Manufacturing Corporation for the years 2007 and 2008:

Selected Balance Sheet Information

	2007	2008
Cash	$ 50,000	$40,000
Accounts receivable	200,000	260,000
Inventory	450,000	500,000
Total current assets	$700,000	$800,000
Bank loan, 10%	$90,000	$90,000
Accounts payable	130,000	170,000
Accruals	50,000	70,000
Total current liabilities	$270,000	$330,000
Long-term debt, 12%	300,000	400,000

Selected Income Statement Information

	2007	2008
Net sales	$1,300,000	$1,500,000
Cost of goods sold	780,000	900,000
Gross profit	$520,000	$600,000
Net income	$93,000	$114,000

Calculate Genatron's operating cycle and cash conversion cycle for 2007 and 2008. Why did they change between these years?

9. Genatron Manufacturing expects its sales to increase by 10 percent in 2009. Estimate the firm's investment in accounts receivable, inventory, and accounts payable in 2009.

10. With concerns of increased competition, Genatron is planning in case its 2009 sales fall by 5 percent from their 2008 levels. If cost of goods sold and the current asset and liability accounts decrease proportionately:

   a. Calculate the 2009 cash conversion cycle.

   b. Calculate the 2009 net investment in working capital.

11. In Problem 10 we assumed the current asset and liability accounts decrease proportionately with Genatron's sales. This is probably unrealistic following a decline in sales. What will be the impact on the working capital accounts if Genatron's collection period lengthens by five days, its inventory period lengthens by seven days, and its payment period lengthens by three days if the company's sales and COGS fall 5 percent from their 2008 levels?

12. Suppose Global Manufacturing is planning to change its credit policies next year. It anticipates that 10 percent of each month's sales will be for cash, two-thirds of each month's receivables will be collected in the following month, and one-third will be collected two months after their sale. Assuming the Global's sales forecast in Table 16.4 remains the same and the expected cash outflows in Table 16.5 remain the same, determine Global's revised cash budget.

13. Global's suppliers are upset that Global takes two months to pay its accounts payable; they demand that in the following year Global pay its bills within thirty days, or one month after purchase.

   a. Using this new information, update Global's cash outflow forecast shown in Table 16.5.

   b. Using the cash inflows given in Table 16.4, construct a revised cash budget for Global.

14. Of its monthly sales, The Kingsman Company historically has had 25 percent cash sales with the remainder paid within one month. Each month's purchases are equal to 75 percent of the next month's sales forecast; suppliers are paid one month after the purchase. Salary expenses are $50,000 a month, except in January, when bonuses equal to 1 percent of the previous year's sales are paid out. Interest on a bond issue of $10,000 is due in March. Overhead and utilities are expected to be $25,000 monthly. Dividends of $45,000 are to be paid in March. Kingsman's 2008 sales totaled $2 million; December sales were $200,000. Kingsman's estimated sales for January are $100,000; February, $200,000; March, $250,000, and April, $300,000.

   a. What are Kingsman's expected monthly cash inflows during January through April?

   b. What are Kingsman's expected monthly cash outflows during January through April?

   c. Determine Kingsman's monthly cash budget for January through April. Assume a minimum desired cash balance of $40,000 and an ending December cash balance of $50,000.

15. Redo Problem 14, using the following monthly sales estimates:

January	$300,000
February	$250,000
March	$200,000
April	$100,000

16. **Challenge Problem** Using the information provided in Problem 14, construct cash budgets from each of the following scenarios. Use the data from Problem 14 as the base case. What insights do we obtain from a cash budget scenario analysis?

   a. *Best case:* sales are 10 percent higher than the base; purchases are 5 percent lower than the base; cash sales are 30 percent of sales.

   b. *Worst case:* sales are 10 percent lower than the base; purchases are 5 percent higher than the base; cash sales are 15 percent of sales.

17. **Challenge Problem** CDLater's projected sales for the first four months of 200X are:

January	$60,000
February	$55,000
March	$65,000
April	$70,000

The firm expects to collect 10 percent of sales in cash, 60 percent in one month and 25 percent in two months with 5 percent in uncollectible bad debts. Sales for the previous November and December were $55,000 and $80,000, respectively.

   The firm buys raw materials thirty days prior to expected sales—that is, the materials for January are bought by the beginning of December with payment made by the end of December. Materials costs are 58 percent of sales.

Wages for the months of January, February, and March are expected to be $6,000 per month. Other monthly expenses amount, to $5,000 a month and are paid in cash each month. Taxes due for an earlier quarter are paid in the second month of the succeeding quarter. The taxes due for the prior quarter were $9,000.

The firm plans to buy a new car in January for $18,000. An old vehicle will be sold for a net amount of $2,000. A note of $10,000 will be due for payment in February. A quarterly loan installment payment of $7,500 is due in March.

The beginning cash balance in January is $8,000. The company policy is to maintain a minimum cash balance of $5,000. It has an outstanding loan balance of $10,000 in December. Should the firm need to borrow to meet expected monthly shortfalls, the interest cost is 1.5 percent per month and is paid each month on the total amount of borrowed funds outstanding at the end of the previous month.

Prepare a monthly cash budget for January, February, and March.

18. Mattam Corporation's yearly sales are $5 million and its average collection period is thirty-two days. Only 10 percent of sales are for cash and the remainder is credit sales.

a. What is Mattam's investment in accounts receivable?

b. If Mattam extends its credit period, it estimates the average collection period will rise to forty days and that credit sales will increase by 20 percent from current levels. What is the expected increase in Mattam's accounts receivable balance if it extends its credit period?

c. If Mattam's net profit margin is 12 percent, the expected increase in bad debt expense is 10 percent of the new sales, and the cost of financing the increase in receivables is 18 percent, should Mattam extend the credit period?

19. Pa Bell, Inc., wants to increase its credit standards. The company expects sales will fall by $50,000 and bad debt expense will fall by 10 percent of this amount. It has a 15 percent profit margin on its sales. The tougher credit standards will lower the firm's average receivables balance by $10,000 and the average inventory balance by $8,000.

The cost of financing current assets is estimated to be 12 percent. Should Pa Bell adopt the tighter credit standards? Why or why not?

20. Robinson Company (refer to the data in Problems 2, 3, and 4) has a 2008 profit margin of 5 percent. It is examining the possibility of loosening its credit policy. Analysis shows that sales may rise 10 percent, while bad debts on the change in sales will be 2 percent. The cost of financing the increase in current assets is 10 percent.

a. Should Robinson change its credit policy?

b. Using the information stated in the problem, at what profit margin is Robinson indifferent between changing the policy or maintaining its current standard?

c. Using the information stated in the problem, at what financing cost is Robinson indifferent between changing or maintaining the credit policy?

d. Using the information stated in the problem, by what amount can the current assets change so that Robinson is indifferent between changing or maintaining its credit policy?

21. Genatron Manufacturing (refer to Problem 8) is considering changing its credit standards. Analysis shows that sales may fall 5 percent from 2008 levels with no bad debts from the change in sales. The cost of financing the increase in current assets is 8 percent.

a. Should Genatron change its credit policy?

b. Using the information stated in the problem, at what profit margin is Genatron indifferent between changing its policy or maintaining its current standard?

c. Using the information stated in the problem, at what financing cost is Genatron indifferent between changing or maintaining the credit policy?

d. Using the information stated in the problem, by what amount can the current assets change so that Genatron is indifferent between changing or maintaining its credit policy?

• CHAPTER 17 •

Short-Term Business Financing

Chapter Learning Objectives

AFTER STUDYING THIS CHAPTER, YOU SHOULD BE ABLE TO:

- Identify and describe strategies for financing working capital.
- Identify and briefly explain the factors that affect short-term financing requirements.
- Identify the types of unsecured loans made by commercial banks to business borrowers.
- Describe the use of accounts receivable, inventory, and other sources of security for bank loans.
- Explain the characteristics, terms, and costs of trade credit.
- Explain the role of commercial finance companies in providing short-term business financing.
- Briefly describe how factors function as a source of short-term business financing.
- Describe how the Small Business Administration aids businesses in meeting short-term borrowing needs.
- Describe how and why commercial paper is used as a source of short-term financing by large corporations.

Where We Have Been...

The balance sheet identity is total assets equals liabilities plus stockholders' equity. In other words, a firm's assets must be financed from one or a combination of two basic sources: debt and owners' equity. Among the assets that need to be financed are short-term or current assets: cash, marketable securities, accounts receivable, and inventory. Chapter 16 examined some issues relating to managing current assets, including forecasting their level and forecasting short-term borrowing needs (the cash budget). This chapter will discuss basic financing strategies for the firm and will review popular short-term financing sources.

Where We Are Going...

Access to short-term financing and sources of liquidity are the lubricant that keeps a firm's business engine running well. If sources of liquidity and access to credit disappear, chances are the firm will not survive long. Issues faced by a firm that is trying to expand overseas include the need to obtain credit to finance overseas shipments, to deal with changing exchange rates, and to handle the uncertain credit rating of possible customers. Chapter 18 presents the exciting world of international finance.

How This Chapter Applies to Me...

A firm facing liquidity problems may not be a prudent choice as a future employer—its lack of cash and difficulty in attracting financing may make it a candidate for merger or bankruptcy, both of which can be disruptive to one's business career. However, just as businesses need a liquidity buffer and access to liquidity, so do individuals. Personal financial planning experts suggest keeping three to six months of living expenses in a liquid savings account for emergencies or personal crises such as a short-term disability situation or job loss/layoff. For most people, access to short-term credit occurs via credit cards and overreliance on short-term credit can lead—just as it can for a business—to future financial crises unless the high-interest credit card debt is promptly paid.

Willie Sutton, a famous bank robber from years gone by, was once asked in a jail interview why he robbed so many banks. Willie replied,

Because that's where the money is.

That's not a very good life philosophy! Fortunately, there are better ways of obtaining needed financing, and businesses today are not limited only to bank financing.

Many times companies use long-term financing sources, such as the stocks and bonds we discussed in Chapters 7 and 8, to acquire fixed assets. The firm's current assets need to be financed as well, though. Sometimes firms use mainly short-term financing sources to finance current assets, sometimes they rely mainly on long-term sources, and at times they use both.

In this chapter we review several strategies for financing current assets. As we shall see, management must make an important strategic decision when deciding on the relative amounts of short-term and long-term financing that the firm uses to finance its assets. The choices a firm makes affect its financing costs, its liquidity, and even the chance of eventual bankruptcy. The chapter closes with a review of various short-term financing sources that firms can access. The tremendous resources of the nation's banking system make commercial banks the largest provider of short-term loan funds for businesses. Short-term funds also come in the form of trade credit extended between businesses. Other important sources of short-term funds are commercial finance companies, factors, and commercial paper.

STRATEGIES FOR FINANCING WORKING CAPITAL

working capital
a firm's current assets

net working capital
the dollar amount of current assets minus the dollar amount of current liabilities

Working capital includes a firm's current assets, which consist of cash and marketable securities in addition to accounts receivable and inventories. Current liabilities generally consist of accounts payable (trade credit), notes payable (short-term loans), and accrued liabilities. **Net working capital** is defined as current assets less current liabilities. Figure 17.1 shows the basic structure of a balance sheet with general account categories. Assets are either current or fixed; financing sources are either current liabilities, long-term debt, or equity.

From the accounting identity, we know that the sum of the asset accounts must equal the sum of the liability and equity accounts. In Figure 17.1 we see that part of the dollar amount of current assets is financed by current liabilities but that the dollars invested in current assets are also partially financed by the firm's long-term financing mix of long-term debt and equity. When net working capital is positive, it represents the amount of current assets that is financed through long-term financing, as seen in Figure 17.1. If net working capital is negative (current liabilities are greater than current assets), it represents the amount of fixed assets that are financed by current liabilities, as seen in Figure 17.2.

Figure 17.3 shows how assets may fluctuate over time for a growing firm.[1] We have depicted a pattern of rising and falling asset values within each time interval or year because of seasonal sales patterns. As we saw in Chapter 16, seasonal sales variations will have important implications for a firm's current assets. Inventories must be increased to meet seasonal demand, and receivables will rise (and inventories fall) as sales increase. The need for funds will fall as accounts receivable are collected. Thus seasonal variation in sales requires only temporary additional investments in such current assets as inventory and accounts receivable.

FIGURE 17.1
Balance Sheet with Positive Net Working Capital

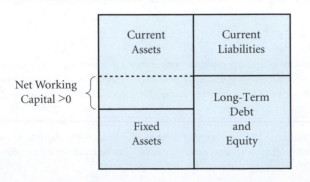

---

1. Whether the sales or asset trend is rising, falling, or stable over time does not affect our conclusions. We merely use a rising asset trend since many firms do enjoy growth over time.

FIGURE 17.2
Balance Sheet with Negative Net Working Capital

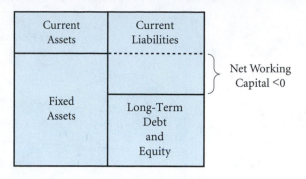

The level of current assets actually has two components: permanent current assets and temporary or fluctuating current assets. Temporary current assets rise and fall because of the seasonal sales fluctuations mentioned. Permanent current assets reflect the minimum investment level in cash, accounts receivable, and inventories needed to support sales.[2] While individual accounts are collected and inventory items sold, they are replaced by others, so the dollar values of the accounts will maintain some minimum level or possibly grow over time as sales rise.

A firm can use several strategies to finance its fixed assets, permanent current assets, and temporary current assets. They are illustrated in Figure 17.4.

MATURITY-MATCHING APPROACH

Panel A of Figure 17.4 shows a balanced approach for financing a firm's assets. Notice that all the fixed assets and the permanent current assets are financed with long-term debt and equity provided by the firm's owners. The temporary current assets are financed by short-term liabilities. The balanced approach also is referred to as the ***maturity-matching approach*** because the financial manager attempts to match the maturities of the assets by financing with comparable

maturity-matching approach
financing strategy that attempts to match the maturities of assets with the maturities of the liabilities with which they are financed

FIGURE 17.3
Asset Trends for a Growing Firm

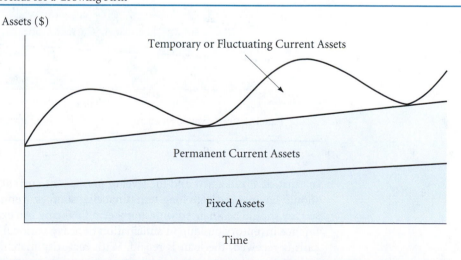

2. For example, recall our Chapter 16 cash budget discussion concerning the firm's minimum desired cash balance; this can be considered a component of the permanent current assets.

FIGURE 17.4
Financing Strategies

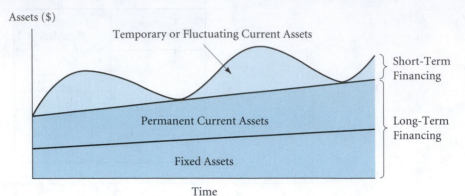

Panel A: Maturity Matching

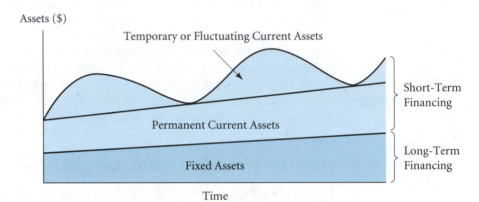

Panel B: Aggressive Financing

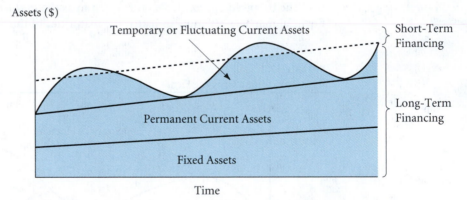

Panel C: Conservative Financing

maturities. Fixed assets and the level of permanent current assets have long maturities, so they should be financed with long-term financing sources. Temporary current assets are short-lived, so they should be financed with short-term financing. An example would be using a bank loan to finance inventory buildup in anticipation of heavy seasonal sales. After the inventory is sold and cash is received, the loan is repaid. With maturity matching, the amount of current assets is greater than that of current liabilities, so net working capital will be positive, as in Figure 17.1. Consequently, firms using maturity matching will have current ratios greater than 1.0.

Panels B and C of Figure 17.4 show two other possible financing strategies. They are deviations from maturity matching. One uses relatively more short-term financing, the other uses relatively more long-term financing than the maturity-matching strategy.

AGGRESSIVE APPROACH

Panel B in Figure 17.4 depicts an aggressive approach to the financing of a firm's current assets in that all current assets, both temporary and permanent, are financed with short-term financing. Only fixed assets are financed with long-term debt and equity funds. Such an approach could result in liquidity problems should sales decline in the future. Since all current assets are financed with current liabilities, the current ratio would be equal to 1.0 under this aggressive scenario. An even more aggressive approach would be for the firm to rely on short-term funds to finance all the current assets, as well as some of the fixed assets. In such a case, the structure of the firm's balance sheet would resemble Figure 17.2, its net working capital would be negative, and its current ratio would be less than 1.0.

CONSERVATIVE APPROACH

Panel C in Figure 17.4 depicts a very conservative approach to the financing of a firm's assets. In this case, except for automatic or "spontaneous" financing provided by accounts payable and accrued liabilities, all the financing is done through long-term debt and equity funds. At times the firm will have excess liquidity, when available funds exceed necessary current asset levels. During these periods the firm will have large cash balances and will probably seek to invest the excess cash in marketable securities. As the amount of current assets is much greater than that of current liabilities, net working capital will be positive and the current ratio will comfortably exceed 1.0.

FINANCE PRINCIPLE

Like many other aspects of finance, deciding how much short-term financing the firm should use relative to long-term financing has risk/return trade-off implications. Recalling our discussion about the yield curve in Chapter 4, we remember that short-term securities generally have lower yields than long-term securities. From the borrower's perspective, that means the cost of paying short-term financing charges (short-term interest rates) will be less than the cost of paying long-term financing charges (long-term interest rates and equity holders' required rates of return).[3]

Compared to a conservative plan that relies more on long-term financing, an aggressive financing plan using relatively more short-term financing will generally have lower financing costs and will, all else being equal, be more profitable. As it comes due, short-term debt is replaced by new short-term debt. This replacement is called "rolling over the debt," but with the expectation of higher return comes higher risk. Short-term interest rates are more volatile than long-term rates, and in periods of tight money or when inflation is a concern short-term rates can rise quickly, sharply increasing the cost of using short-term money. Sources of short-term credit also may disappear. In such a credit crunch, banks may not have enough funds to lend to satisfy demand, and investors may not be willing to purchase the firm's short-term debt. A conservative financing plan has a higher financing cost but a lower risk of not being able to borrow when short-term funds are needed.

Figure 17.5 illustrates fluctuations and trends over time of net working capital at several firms. Some firms had strategies to reduce net working capital; we see the largest declines in net working capital in Dell (from almost 40 percent of total assets to almost 0 percent) and Sears (subsequent to its merger with Kmart). Both firms sought to reduce inventories and receivables to free up precious cash that was locked into current assets. Other tech firms, such as Apple, Google, and Microsoft, are flush with cash relative to total assets, thus increasing current assets and their net working capital figures.

Some firms use an aggressive financing approach, such as AT&T, as seen in its negative net working capital figures. Other firms following a maturity-matching approach as net working capital, relative to total assets, fluctuate close to or around zero percent. Such firms include a utility, Consolidated Edison, and retail businesses such as McDonald's and Wal-Mart.

EXAMPLES OF FINANCING STRATEGY PROBLEMS

Not all firms in financial difficulty get there because of poor financing decisions, but there are some cases where poor financial decisions or being overly aggressive have led to difficulties for firms.

---

3. We discussed security holders' rates of return in Chapters 6, 7, and 8 and the cost of financing a firm with long-term debt and equity in Chapter 15.

FIGURE 17.5

Net Working Capital Divided by Total Assets

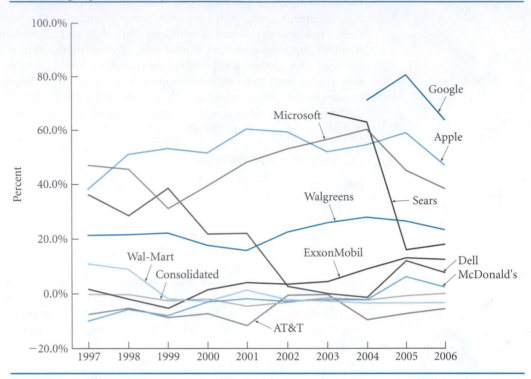

Financial Strategy Problems and Solutions

Following the high-growth 1990s, the U.S. economy cooled during 2000–2001. Some firms began to have trouble meeting sales and earnings targets. A credit crunch occurred as some formerly top-quality firms had difficulty arranging new short-term financing. Their aggressive financing strategies, with their reliance on large amounts of short-term financing and constant rollover of short-term debt, put several firms into a bind. Wary lenders demanded higher interest rates for their short-term loans. Companies such as AT&T, Lucent, and DaimlerChrysler had sharp increases in commercial paper rates.[4] As the economy weakened and corporate balance sheets deteriorated, some firms, including Xerox, Lucent, DaimlerChrysler, and Goodyear, were not able to roll over their commercial paper. Some of these firms maintained an aggressive financing policy by tapping into bank borrowing (Xerox, Tyco) to replace the funds they could not raise in the commercial paper market; others, such as DaimlerChrysler, Sprint, and GE Capital, switched to a less aggressive stance by issuing bonds to raise long-term funds. Analysts predicted that Sprint's long-term bond issues would increase its interest expenses almost $200 million annually, while others estimate GE Capital's interest costs would rise $100 million because of the shift from short-term borrowing to long-term borrowing. These examples show the magnitude of borrowing choices on the firm's expenses and profits.[5]

Caldor Corporation, a discount retailer, was using an aggressive financing approach in the early 1990s. Because of this strategy, it filed for bankruptcy in September 1995 despite earning profits.[6] Caldor chose to finance a major expansion and remodeling project with its working capital. Caldor's working capital fell precipitously, from over $60 million in early 1994 to under

4. Commercial paper is a source of unsecured short-term financing for large corporations. We mentioned it as a marketable security for investing excess cash in Chapter 16. We discuss it as a financing source later in this chapter.

5. There was a series of articles in 2000–2002 about the short-term financing difficulties of some firms. Some of these are Gregory Zuckerman, "Cash Drought: A Dwindling Supply of Short-Term Credit Plaques Corporations," *Wall Street Journal* (March 28, 2002), pp. A1, A10; Henny Sender, "Companies Feel Consequences of Borrowing for Short Term," *Wall Street Journal* (October 12, 2001), pp. C1, C13; Paul M. Scherer, "Blue-Chip Borrowers Find Solutions to Credit Crunch," *Wall Street Journal* (May 1, 2001), pp. C1, C18; Paul M. Scherer, "Commercial-Paper Chase Grows Difficult," *Wall Street Journal* (January 25, 2001), pp. C1, C16; Paul M. Scherer and Gregory Zuckerman, "Credit Crunch Starts to Hurt Big Companies as Commercial-Paper Costs Edge Upward," *Wall Street Journal* (December 21, 2000), pp. C1, C16; John Hechinger and Joseph Pereira, "Xerox Taps $7 Billion Line of Bank Credit," *Wall Street Journal* (October 16, 2000), p. A4.

6. As reviewed in Chapter 11, this is another example showing that net income and cash flow are not the same concept.

$10 million in early 1995, when it should have been flush with cash following the Christmas selling season. Caldor's short-term creditors encouraged it to borrow long-term funds or issue stock to move to a maturity-matching or less aggressive financing plan, but Caldor refused. Alarmed at Caldor's decreasing liquidity, banks subsequently grew hesitant to lend and factors— firms that guaranteed Caldor's payments to its suppliers—grew nervous.[7] Lower-than-expected sales during the 1994 Christmas season and early 1995 hurt Caldor's cash position even more. When GE Capital Corporation refused Caldor's request for a $30 million loan, suppliers and factors delayed inventory shipments and demanded that Caldor pay its bills faster. Finally, factors told Caldor's suppliers that they would no longer guarantee payment of the money Caldor owed to them, in effect shutting off Caldor's credit and inventory shipments. This was the immediate reason for Caldor's September 1995 bankruptcy filing, but it was Caldor's choice of an aggressive financing plan, relying on short-term funds to finance growing fixed assets, that was the ultimate cause of the failure.[8]

GLOBAL DISCUSSION

Nor was an overreliance on short-term debt a problem only for U.S. firms. Germany experienced a credit crunch in 1995 and 2002. Midsize firms that employed between 20 and 500 workers, the so-called Mittelstand, were filing for bankruptcy and suffering losses in large numbers. Banks, hurt by bad loans during previous recessions, were hesitant to lend and take chances. This was quite a change from past bank and borrower relationships in Germany, when Mittelstand firms could obtain low-cost financing from banks. In the past, German banks would provide much assistance to such firms, but that formerly paternalistic relationship has turned sour. Mittelstand firms had, on the whole, become too reliant on rolling over bank debt. A poll of Mittelstand companies showed over half needing capital and over a third stating that banks were being too restrictive.[9]

CONCEPT CHECK

What is a firm's working capital? A firm's net working capital?

How does the maturity-matching approach differ from more conservative or aggressive financing strategies?

Problems Not Caused by Financing Strategy

The growth of the 1990s ended in many failed dot-coms after the new millennium began. These failures were not, for the most part, because of poor financing strategy. Reasons for the failures are many, including an overly optimistic stock market and venture capital market pouring money into firms that had little more than an idea and no forecast of a profit. Changing technology saw the previous quarter's hot product get replaced in the mind of consumers by another firm's hot product. Subsequent inventory write-downs (devaluing inventory from original value to a lower value better reflecting its marketability) resulted in firms with liabilities greater than their assets (that is, book value was negative). The inability to sell products with the previous quarter's technology caused the firms to run out of cash and go bankrupt. Many firms were relying on external financing rather than internal cash flow to pay their bills. No financing strategy—save throwing good money after bad—could have saved many of these firms. The resulting bankruptcies were a reminder of the expected risk/return trade-off: get-rich-quick schemes usually aren't.

ETHICAL ISSUES

At times, financial difficulties arise because of questionable accounting practices and possible ethical lapses. Reliance on "off-balance sheet" financing in attempts to hide debt and leverage from investors, moves to "book" revenue by moving inventory from the warehouse to stores without a sales transaction or order, or stimulating this quarter's sales via aggressive marketing and price discounting with the result of harming next quarter's prospects have hurt a number of companies in recent years, most notably Enron—since defunct in an accounting scandal—and Xerox, among others.[10]

The point of these examples is that a firm's difficulties cannot always be tied to a poor financial strategy. Sometimes foolish decisions, bad management, and poor ethics are contributing factors.

---

7. Factors are an important source of financing for many firms, especially those in the retail trade. We discuss them in more detail in this chapter.

8. Laura Bird, "Caldor Files for Bankruptcy Protection in Face of Weak Sales, Jittery Suppliers," *Wall Street Journal* (September 19, 1995), p. A3; Roger Lowenstein, "Lenders' Stampede Tramples Caldor," *Wall Street Journal* (October 26, 1995), p. C1.

9. Hugh Williamson and Tony Major, "Banks Get Tough with Mittelstand," *Financial Times* (June 19, 2002), p. 12; Matt Marshall, "Timid Lending Hits Germany's Exporters," *Wall Street Journal* (November 21, 1995), p. A12.

10. Michael Schroeder, Jerry Guidera, and Mark Maremont, "Accounting Crackdown Focuses Increasingly on Top Executives," *Wall Street Journal* (April 12, 2002), pp. A1, A2.

FACTORS AFFECTING SHORT-TERM FINANCING

Whether the firm uses an aggressive approach, a conservative approach, or maturity matching depends on an evaluation of many factors. The company's operating characteristics will affect a firm's financing strategy. Other factors having an impact include cost, flexibility, the ease of future financing, and other qualitative influences.

OPERATING CHARACTERISTICS

The nature of the demand for funds depends in part on the industry in which a business operates and on the characteristics of the business itself. It is influenced by such factors as seasonal variations in sales and the growth of the company. The need for funds also depends on fluctuations of the business cycle.

Industry and Company Factors

Some industries, such as utilities and oil refineries, have larger proportions of fixed assets to current assets and will prefer to use long-term financing. Others, such as service industries, have larger proportions of current assets to fixed assets and will prefer short-term financing. Within each industry, some firms will choose different operating structures with different levels of operating leverage.

The composition of the asset structure or current assets versus fixed assets of an industry and of a firm within that industry constitute a significant factor in determining the relative proportions of long-term and short-term financing. An industry that needs large amounts of fixed capital can do more long-term financing than one that has a relatively small investment in fixed assets.

While manufacturing companies often require substantial investments in fixed assets for manufacturing purposes, they also have significant investments in inventories and receivables. Manufacturers generally have a more equal balance between current and fixed assets than electric utility and telephone companies do and so will use relatively more short-term financing. The same is true for large retail stores, which often lease their quarters and hold substantial assets in the form of inventories and receivables. They are characterized by relatively high current assets to fixed assets ratios and so will have a greater tendency than utilities to use short-term debt.

The size and age of a company and stage in its financial life cycle may also influence management's short-term/long-term financing mix decisions. A new company's only source of funds may be the owner and possibly his or her friends. Some long-term funds may be raised by mortgaging real estate and buying equipment on installment, and some current borrowing may be possible to meet seasonal needs. As a business grows, it has more access to short-term capital from finance companies and banks. Further along, its growth and good record of profitability may enable a business to arrange longer-term financing with banks or other financial agencies such as insurance companies. At this stage in its financial development, it may also expand its group of owners by issuing stock to people other than the owner and a few friends.

The growth prospects of a company also have an effect on financing decisions. If a company is growing faster than it can generate funds from internal sources, it must give careful consideration to a plan for long-term financing. Even if it can finance its needs in the current situation from short-term sources, it may not be wise to do so. Sound financial planning calls for raising long-term funds at appropriate times.

Some examples of ratios of current liabilities to total assets are presented in Figure 17.6. Google has a low amount of short-term financing as it is flush with cash from recent stock offerings. Con Ed, a regulated utility, has an asset base that is mainly fixed so it uses relatively little short-term financing. McDonald's, which relies on long-term facility leases or franchisee funds for financing its stores, also has a relatively low amount of current liabilities. Dell has a relatively high amount of short-term financing in Figure 17.6; it is well-known for its focus on liquidity with its just-in-time inventory and production environment. It has very little long-term debt financing as it relies mainly on short-term financing for its large amount of current assets.

Seasonal Variation

Our previous discussion of Figure 17.3 pointed out that seasonal variations in sales affect the demand for current assets. Inventories are built up to meet seasonal needs, and receivables rise as sales increase. The peak of receivables will come after the peak in sales, the intervening time

FIGURE 17.6

Current Liabilities Divided by Total Assets

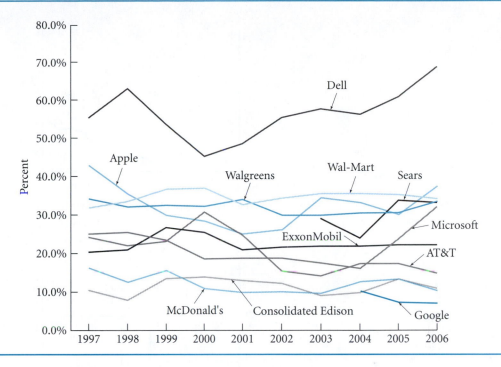

depending on the credit terms and payment practices of customers. Accounts payable will also increase as inventories are purchased. The difference between the increase in current assets and accounts payable should be financed by short-term borrowing because the need for funds will disappear as inventories are sold and accounts receivable are collected. When a need for additional funds is financed by a short-term loan, such a loan is said to be self-liquidating since funds are made available to repay it as inventories and receivables are reduced.

Sales Trend

A firm's sales trend affects the financing mix. As sales grow, fixed assets and current assets also must grow to support the sales growth, as depicted in Figure 17.3. This need for funds is ongoing unless the upward trend of sales is reversed.

If asset growth is initially financed by short-term borrowing, the outstanding borrowings will continue to rise as sales rise. The amount of debt may rise year by year as the growth trend continues upward. After a while the current ratio will drop to such a level that no financing institution will provide additional funds. The only alternative then is long-term financing. Long-term financing often rises to reduce excess levels of short-term financing.

As we learn later in this chapter, short-term financing can be increased over time in relatively small increments, if needed, by applying for loans and negotiating with borrowers, as seen in Panel A of Figure 17.7. Long-term external financing, however, is what might be termed "lumpy." Because of the time and cost of floating a bond or stock issue or negotiating a long-term loan or private placement, long-term securities are usually issued only in large quantities, as seen in Panel B of Figure 17.7.

Cyclical Variations

The need for current funds increases when there is an upswing in the business cycle or the sales cycle of an industry. Since the cycle is not regular in timing or degree, it is hard to predict exactly how much, or for how long, added funds will be needed. The need should be estimated for a year ahead in the budget and checked quarterly. When the sales volume of business decreases, the need for funds to finance accounts receivable and inventory will decrease as well. It is possible, however, that for a time during the downturn the need for financing will increase temporarily. This will occur if the cash conversion cycle lengthens as receivables are collected more slowly and inventories move more slowly and drop in value.

FIGURE 17.7

Patterns of Short-term and Long-term Financing Needs Over Time for a Growing Firm

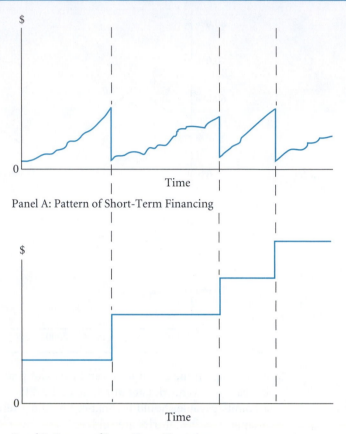

Panel A: Pattern of Short-Term Financing

Panel B: Pattern of Long-Term Financing

If cyclical needs for funds are met by current borrowing, the loan may not be self-liquidating in a year. There are hazards in financing these needs on a short-term basis. The lending institution may demand payment of all or part of the loan as business turns down. Funds may be needed more than ever at this stage of the cycle, and the need may last until receivables can be collected and inventory can be reduced. Firms in cyclical industries should use a more conservative approach that makes use of long-term financing. Major U.S automobile firms, in a highly cyclical business, have been preparing for the next recession. Ford Motor Company, for example, went through $10 billion in cash during the 1990–1991 recession and $8.5 billion during 1999–2001. At the beginning of 2006 Ford and its car financing subsidiary had over $39 billion in cash and short-term marketable securities as a cushion. It wasn't alone: General Motors had over $50 billion and DaimlerChrysler had $7.1 billion in cash and marketable securities.

OTHER INFLUENCES IN SHORT-TERM FINANCING

There are other advantages to using short-term borrowing rather than other forms of financing. Short-term borrowing offers more flexibility than long-term financing, since a business can borrow only those sums needed currently and pay them off if the need for financing diminishes. Long-term financing cannot be retired so easily, and it may include a prepayment penalty, as is the case with the call premium for callable bonds. If an enterprise finances its growing current asset requirements entirely through long-term financing during a period of general business expansion, it may be burdened with excess funds and financing costs during a subsequent period of general business contraction. Using short-term financing along with long-term financing creates a financial flexibility that is not possible with long-term financing alone.

Short-term financing has advantages that result from continuing relationships with a bank or other financial institution. The firm that depends almost entirely on long-term financing for its needs will not enjoy the close relationship with its bank that it might otherwise. A record of frequent borrowing and prompt repayment to a bank is an extremely important factor in sound financial management. A bank will make every effort to accommodate regular business customers who do this. The enterprise that has not established this type of working relationship with its bank will scarcely be in a position to seek special loans when it has emergency needs. The credit experience of a business with short-term financing may be the only basis on which its potential long-term lenders will be able to judge it. Hence, the business that intends to seek long-term loans may wish to establish a good credit reputation based on its short-term financing.

Offsetting these advantages of short-term financing is the need for frequent renewals. Even though short-term credit is usually easy to obtain, time and effort must be spent at frequent intervals because of the short duration of these loans. When sales revenues decline, for example, a great deal of negotiation may be required to receive needed credit.

Frequent maturities also create an added element of risk. The bank or finance company can call the loan whenever it is due. The bank may not want to roll over a loan. Borrowing costs also may rise if short-term interest rates increase. A company in a temporary slump due to the business cycle or some internal problem could possibly work out its problems in time with adequate financing. If the company had acquired funds on a long-term basis, it might have a better chance of resolving its problems. On the other hand, if it relies heavily on short-term financing, its loans may be reduced or not renewed, which may make it nearly impossible to recover and might even lead to liquidation.

Now that we have an understanding of short-term/long-term financing strategies and factors that affect the relative use of short-term financing, we turn our attention toward various sources of short-term financing. Short-term financing sources include bank loans, trade credit or accounts payable, and commercial paper, among others. Financial managers should recall the five C's discussed in Chapter 16's section on accounts receivable management: the ability to obtain short-term financing is made easier for firms with acknowledged character (ethics), the capacity to pay bills, a strong capital base, collateral to act as security for loans, and favorable conditions in the economy and the firm's industry.

CONCEPT CHECK

List the major influences on a firm's short-term financing mix decision.

What other influences can affect a firm's level of short-term financing?

PROVIDERS OF SHORT-TERM FINANCING

Businesses can attempt to obtain short-term financing from a number of different providers and methods. Some are financial institutions, such as banks, that lend to firms for both working capital and long-term purposes (such as equipment loans). Other providers of financing include the firm's suppliers (trade credit), other corporations (commercial finance companies), the financial markets (commercial paper) and, when a small business is deemed "too risky" for a bank loan, they may be able to obtain financing by way of a government loan guarantee through the U.S. Small Business Administration. We discuss each of these in turn.

PERSONAL FINANCIAL PLANNING
The Role of Money Market Mutual Funds

Money market mutual funds (MMMFs) are a link between an individual's savings and investment needs and a firm's need for short-term financing. MMMFs invest in money market securities— securities that mature, or come due, in less than one year. In reality, the typical MMMF invests in securities that mature much sooner than that. The average maturity of the securities held by some MMMFs is one week or less.

Money market securities exist because of the short-term financing needs of governments, banks, and businesses. The MMMFs pool the savings of many investors. The funds use the savings to invest in T-bills, short-term state and local government debt, negotiable certificates of deposit (CDs), and commercial paper. The typical denominations ($25,000 or higher) of these short-term financing sources are usually beyond the reach of the small investor. The advent of the MMMF in the early 1970s allows the small investor to tap into this market and earn returns higher than those paid on short-term bank CDs or checking accounts. In turn, the MMMF provides another source of liquidity to the short-term financing markets. By pooling the savings of small investors, borrowers of short-term funds have another outlet for obtaining short-term financing. This extra supply of loanable funds provided by MMMFs helps to keep short-term financing rates a bit lower than would be the case without them.

COMMERCIAL BANK LENDING

prime rate
interest rate the bank charges its most creditworthy customers

Although many banks require a pledge of specific assets, the unsecured loan still remains the primary type of loan arrangement. The stated rate on such loans is based on the bank's **prime rate** or the interest rate a bank charges its most creditworthy customers. Interest rates on loans typically are stated in terms of the prime rate plus a risk differential, such as prime + 2 percent. Loan papers will call this prime plus 2 or simply P + 2. Higher-risk borrowers will have higher differentials to compensate the bank for lending to riskier customers.

Bank Lines of Credit

line of credit
loan limit the bank establishes for each of its business customers

A business and a bank often have an agreement regarding the amount of credit that the business will have at its disposal. The loan limit that the bank establishes for each of its business customers is called a **line of credit**. The cost for a line of credit is the interest rate for the period during which money is actually borrowed.

Under a line of credit, the business does not wait until money is needed to negotiate the loan. Rather, it files the necessary financial statements and other evidences of financial condition with the bank prior to the need for credit. The banker is interested in how well the business has fared in the past and its probable future because the line of credit generally is extended for a year at a time. The banker may require that other debts of the business be subordinated to, or come after, the claim of the bank. Banks also usually require their business customers to "clean up" their lines of credit for a specified period of time each year—that is, to have no outstanding borrowing against the credit line, usually for a minimum of two weeks. This ensures that the credit line is being used for short-term financing purposes rather than for long-term needs.

Continued access to a line of credit may be subject to the approval of the bank if there are major changes in the operation of a business. A major shift or change in management personnel or in the manufacture or sale of particular products can greatly influence the future success of a company. Hence, the bank, having contributed substantially to the financial resources of the business, is necessarily interested in these activities. The bank may also seek information on the business through organized credit bureaus, through contact with other businesses having dealings with the firm, and through other banks.

In the event that the business needs more money than was anticipated at the time the line of credit was set up, it may request the bank to increase the limit on its line of credit. It must be prepared, however, to offer very sound evidence of the need for additional funds and the ability of the business to repay the increased loan from business operations. A request for an increased line of credit frequently occurs when a business is growing and needs more capital to make its growth possible. Banks, following the principle of maturity matching discussed previously, generally insist that expansion be financed with long-term funds, but they may assist growth by temporarily providing a part of the increased needs. The business that is unable to obtain additional unsecured credit from its bank may seek a loan secured with collateral from the bank or other lenders. These other forms of borrowing are discussed later in this chapter.

Bank mergers have affected the ability of firms to obtain credit lines. Table 17.1 lists twenty large banks that were in existence, in one form or another, from 1990 to 2005; by 2007 they had merged into only three banks, but that doesn't mean the larger banks are eager participants in meeting the line of credit needs of larger firms; the existence of fewer banks has meant tighter credit and higher fees.[11] A survey of corporate financial officers found that 78 percent believed the mergers reduced the number of loans, and 72 percent had fears of monopolistic pricing by merged banks. Fortunately, as the field of banking changes to one of financial services, other entities, such as commercial finance companies, insurance companies, and even some mutual funds are starting to lend to firms and to take the place of the traditional banking relationship.

compensating balance
requirement that 10 to 20 percent of a loan be kept on deposit at the bank

Although the practice is diminishing, some banks require that a **compensating balance** of 10 to 20 percent of unsecured loans outstanding be kept on deposit by the business. The most frequently cited justification for this requirement is that, because banks cannot lend without deposits, bank borrowers should be required to be depositors. However, compensating balances are also a means of increasing the effective cost of borrowing by increasing the amount on which interest is computed.

---

11. Jathon Sapsford and Paul Sherer, "Fewer Banks Means Costlier Credit Lines," *Wall Street Journal* (March 14, 2001), pp. C1, C16.

TABLE 17.1
Merging Banks

BANKS IN EXISTENCE SOMETIME DURING 1990–2005	SURVIVING BANKS IN 2007 AFTER MERGERS
J.P. Morgan	J.P. Morgan Chase
Manufacturers Hanover Trust	
Chemical Bank	
Chase Manhattan Bank	
Banc One	
First Chicago	
Bank of America	Bank of America
Continental Bank	
Security Pacific	
Nations Bank	
Barnett	
Bank Boston	
Bay Bank	
Fleet	
Shawmut	
Fleet Boston	
Wachovia	Wachovia
First Union	
Signet	
CoreStates	

Computing Interest Rates

Chapter 5, "The Time Value of Money," illustrated how to use time value of money concepts to calculate interest rates. The same concepts can be used to calculate the true cost of borrowing funds from a bank. If, for example, Global Manufacturing can borrow $10,000 for six months at 8 percent APR, the six-month interest cost will be 8 percent/2 × $10,000, or $400. Global will repay the $10,000 principal and $400 in interest after six months. As we learned in Chapter 5, the true or effective interest rate on this loan is:

$$EAR = (1 + APR/m)^m - 1 \qquad (17.1)$$

or

$$(1 + 0.08/2)2 - 1 = 0.0816 \text{ or } 8.16 \text{ percent}$$

discounted loan

borrower receives the principal less the interest at the time the loan is made; the principal is repaid at maturity

At times banks will discount a loan. A ***discounted loan*** is one in which the borrower receives the principal less the interest at the time the loan is made. At maturity, the principal is repaid. Discounting has the effect of reducing the available funds received by the borrower, while raising the effective interest rate. If Global's loan is discounted, Global will receive $9,600 ($10,000 less $400) and will repay $10,000, in essence paying $400 interest on the $9,600 funds received. This is a periodic rate of $400/$9,600, or 4.17 percent.[12] The effective annual rate is $(1 + 0.0417)2 - 1$, or 8.51 percent, an increase of 0.35 percentage point over the undiscounted loan.

When a loan is discounted, a firm has to borrow more money than the amount it really needs. To counteract the effect of discounting, to acquire $10,000 in usable funds it will have to borrow $10,000/(1 − 0.04) or $10,416.67. When a loan of $10,416.67 is discounted at a six-month rate of 4 percent, the net proceeds to Global will be $10,000 (that is, $10,416.67 − [0.04][10,416.67] = $10,000). In general, to receive the desired usable funds, the loan request must equal:

$$\text{Loan request} = \text{Desired usable funds}/(1 - \text{discount}). \qquad (17.2)$$

---

12. This periodic rate can also be computed using our Chapter 5 concepts. We know that $FV = PV (1 + r)^n$. Since FV equals $10,000 (the amount to be repaid), PV equals $9,600 (the usable funds received after discounting), and n is 1 for our six-month time frame, we have $10,000 = $9,600 $(1 + r)^1$. Solving for r, we see the periodic interest rate is 4.17 percent.

revolving credit agreement
legal obligation of the bank to provide up to the agreed upon borrowing limit

CONCEPT CHECK

How does a bank line of credit differ from a revolving credit agreement?

What does it mean to "clean up" a line of credit?

What is a discounted loan?

What happens to the borrower's effective interest rate when the loan is discounted?

A loan with a compensating balance is similar to a discounted loan as far as its effect on the effective interest rate and usable funds is concerned. Compensating balances are equivalent to discounting when the firm currently has no money on deposit at the bank. The firm's loan request should be large enough so that after funds are placed in the compensating balance it will have the usable funds it desires. For compensating balance loans, Equation 17.2 becomes:

$$\text{Loan request} = \frac{\text{Desired usable funds}}{(1 - \text{compensating balance requirement})} \tag{17.3}$$

which is identical to Equation 17.2, except the discount percent is replaced by the compensating balance percentage.

Revolving Credit Agreements

The officers of a business may feel rather certain that an agreed-upon line of credit will provide the necessary capital requirements for the coming year, but the bank is not obligated to continue to offer the credit line if the firm's financial condition worsens. Line of credit agreements usually allow the bank to reduce or withdraw its extension of credit to the firm.

The well-established business with an excellent credit rating may be able to obtain a ***revolving credit agreement***, which is a commitment in the form of a standby agreement for a guaranteed line of credit. Unlike a line of credit, a revolving credit agreement is a legal obligation of the bank to provide funds up to the agreed-upon borrowing limit during the time the agreement is in effect. In addition to paying interest on borrowed funds for the period of the loan, the business must pay a commission or fee to the bank based on the unused portion of the credit line, or the money it has available for it to borrow when it wants to during the agreement period. This fee is usually between 0.25 and 0.50 percent of the unused amount of the line.[13]

To compute the effective cost of a revolving credit agreement (revolver), the joint effect of interest on borrowed funds and the commitment fee on the unborrowed portion of the agreement must be considered. Suppose Global has a one-year $1 million revolving credit agreement with a local bank. The annual interest rate on the agreement is 9 percent with a commitment fee of 0.40 percent on the unborrowed portion. Global expects to have average outstanding borrowings against the revolver of $300,000. Over the year, the interest cost on the average amount borrowed is $0.09 \times \$300,000$ or $27,000. The commitment fee on the average unborrowed portion is $0.0040 \times \$700,000$, or $2,800. With total interest and fees of $29,800 ($27,000 + $2,800) on average borrowings of $300,000, the expected annual cost of the revolver is $29,800/$300,000, or 9.93 percent.

Small Business Administration

The Small Business Administration (SBA) was established by the federal government to provide financial assistance to small firms that are unable to obtain loans through private channels on reasonable terms. Created in 1953, the SBA provides a wide variety of services in addition to loan guarantees through its more than a hundred field offices.

The reason businesses use SBA loan guarantees is explained by the stated objectives of the SBA: to enable deserving small businesses to obtain financial assistance not otherwise available through private channels on reasonable terms. When the SBA was established, it was recognized that the economic development of the nation depended in large part on the freedom of new business ventures to enter into active operation. Yet the increased concentration of investable funds with large institutional investors, such as life insurance companies, investment companies, and others, made it increasingly difficult for new and small business ventures to attract investment capital. The lack of a track record made loans hard to obtain from traditional bank sources.

It is important to note that the Small Business Administration does not make loans, rather it guarantees them. Under their 7(a) loan program the SBA will guarantee up to 85 percent of the loan amount for loans of $150,000 or less. Loans larger than $150,000 up to $2 million can

---

13. Banks are a major participant in the commercial paper market (discussed later in this chapter) as they frequently support this market by offering paper issuers a line of credit or an arrangement similar to the revolving credit agreement (described in the preceding text) to act as a secondary source of funds for repaying its commercial paper loans.

INTERNET ACTIVITY

Learn about financing opportunities for small businesses through the Small Business Administration at http://www.sba.gov.

CONCEPT CHECK

How can the Small Business Administration help a firm obtain short-term financing?

obtain a guarantee of up to 75 percent. The loan guarantee means a bank can lend a sum to a small business owner by only having a small portion of the funds at risk. In case of default, the SBA will repay the loan. For example, a bank lending $100,000 under the SBA loan guarantee program has 85 percent of the loan guaranteed by the SBA. This means only 15 percent, or $15,000, of their funds is at risk. In case the borrower cannot repay the loan, the SBA will reimburse the bank for up to $85,000 in case of default.

If a firm is able to obtain financing elsewhere, its loan application to the SBA is rejected. An applicant for a loan must prove that funds needed are not available from any bank, that no other private lending sources are available, that issuing securities is not practicable, that financing cannot be arranged by disposing of business assets, and that the personal credit of the owners cannot be used. These loans may not be used for paying existing creditors or for speculative purposes.

In addition to its business-lending activities, the SBA is responsible for several related financial activities. These include loans to development companies, disaster loans, lease guarantees, surety bond support, minority enterprise programs, procurement assistance, and support for investment companies that service small businesses.

SBA working capital loans are limited to seven years, while regular business loans have a maximum maturity of twenty-five years. It also sets a maximum allowable rate that banks can charge on guaranteed loans. These rates are adjusted periodically by the SBA to reflect changes in market conditions.

TRADE CREDIT FROM SUPPLIERS

The most important single form of short-term business financing is the credit extended by one business organization to another. Accounts receivable, together with longer-term notes receivable taken by manufacturers, wholesalers, jobbers, and other businesses that sell products or services to businesses, are known as trade credit.

The establishment of trade credit is the least formal of all forms of financing. It involves only an order for goods or services by one business and the delivery of goods or performance of service by the selling business. The purchasing business receives an invoice stating the terms of the transaction and the time period within which payment is to be made. The purchaser adds the liability to accounts payable. The seller adds the claim to accounts receivable. In some situations, the seller may insist on written evidence of liability on the part of the purchaser. Such written evidence is usually in the form of a note that is payable by the purchaser and is considered as a note receivable by the seller. Before a business organization delivers goods or performs a service for another business, it must determine the ability and willingness of the purchaser to pay for the order.[14] The responsibility of such credit analysis in most businesses belongs to the credit manager.

SMALL BUSINESS PRACTICE
Bank Financing for Small Businesses

Getting a small business bank loan today is much harder than it was in the 1980s. Bankers are making greater demands on entrepreneurial or venture firms. More comprehensive financial statements must be provided and more collateral (such as equipment or working capital in the form of inventories or receivables) pledged. Banks lend at the prime rate, which is their best rate to larger businesses. In contrast, small businesses are asked to pay two or more points above prime. For example, if the prime rate is 8 percent, small businesses will have to pay interest rates of 10 percent or more to obtain bank loans.

In her book *Financing Your Business* (Prentice Hall, 1997), Iris Lorenz-Fife lists the five most common reasons given by bankers when they decide not to make loans to small businesses. The first

reason is the "owner's equity is too low relative to the size of the loan that is requested." The second reason relates to the "value of the collateral being offered is too low or unreliable." A third reason is that the "firm is a one-person business with no adequate managerial backup." A fourth reason centers on the belief that the business "will need more time to repay the loan than the bank's usual terms." The fifth reason for rejecting a loan application from a small business is that the banker believes that the small business owner/manager "has inadequate managerial experience or ability."

If a small business loan application you make is rejected by a bank, you should ask the banker why it was rejected. You also should ask what changes in the application would be necessary to be successful in obtaining a bank loan.

14. We discussed the process of credit evaluation in Chapter 16.

Terms for Trade Credit

trade discounts

provided to purchasers as an incentive for early or prompt payment of accounts

Sales may be made on terms such as cash, E.O.M. (end of month), M.O.M. (middle of month), or R.O.G. (receipt of goods). Terms such as 2/10, net 30 may be offered, which means the purchaser may deduct 2 percent from the purchase price if payment is made within ten days of shipment; if not paid within ten days, the net amount is due within thirty days. Such **trade discounts** to purchasers for early payment are common and are designed to provide incentive for prompt payment of bills. Occasionally, sellers offer only net terms such as net 30 or net 60.

A cash sale, contrary to its implication, usually involves credit. This is because the purchaser is often permitted a certain number of days within which to make payment. For example, a sale of merchandise in which the purchaser is permitted up to ten days to pay may be considered a cash transaction, but credit is outstanding to the purchaser for that time. Even for the firm that purchases products entirely on a cash basis, the volume of accounts payable outstanding on its books at any one time may be large.

Cost of Trade Credit

When trade credit terms do not provide a discount for early payment of obligations, there is no cost to the buyer for such financing. Even when discounts are available, it may seem that there is no cost for trade credit since failing to take the early payment discount simply requires the purchaser to pay the net price. There is a cost involved, however, when a discount is not taken. For example, with terms of 2/10, net 30, the cost is the loss of the 2 percent discount that could have been taken if payment were made within the ten-day period.

To compare the cost of trade credit and bank credit, the cost of the trade credit must be placed on an annual interest rate basis. For example, if the terms of sale are 2/10, net 30, the cost of trade credit is the loss of the 2 percent discount that the purchaser fails to take if she or he extends the payment period from ten days up to thirty days. The lost 2 percent is the cost of trade credit for those twenty days. If we also consider that it is the discounted price (invoice price minus the percentage discount) that is being financed, the approximate effective cost (EC) is:

$$EC = \frac{\% \text{ discount}}{100\% - \% \text{ discount}} \times \frac{365 \text{ days}}{\text{Credit period} - \text{discount days}} \quad (17.4)$$

For our 2/10, net 30 example:

$$EC = \frac{2\%}{100\% - 2\%} \times \frac{365}{30 - 10} = 2.04\% \times 18.25 = 37.2\%$$

This shows that the cost of trade credit typically is far in excess of bank rates. Thus it is usually worthwhile to borrow funds to take advantage of cash discounts on trade credit. Failure to take advantage of the trade discount is the same as borrowing from the vendor at the effective cost.[15]

The cost of trade credit in most lines of business activity is high when discounts are missed. However, it should not be assumed that high cost necessarily makes trade credit an undesirable source of short-term financing. It can be, in fact, the most important form of financing for small and growing businesses that are unable to qualify for short-term credit through customary financial channels.

---

15. Astute readers will note that these popular formulas do not take period-by-period compounding into account. The true effective cost can be determined as follows:

$$\text{Effective cost} = \left(1 + \frac{\% \text{ discount}}{100\% - \% \text{ discount}}\right)^{365/(\text{Credit period} - \text{discount days})} - 1$$

In the text example, we have:

$$\text{True effective cost} = \left(1 + \frac{2\%}{100\% - 2\%}\right)^{365/(30-10)} - 1$$

$$= (1.0204)^{365/20} - 1$$

$$= 1.446 - 1 = 0.446 \text{ or } 44.6 \text{ percent}$$

The firm in a weak financial condition will find trade credit more readily available than bank credit. The bank stands to gain only the interest on the loan if repayment is made, but it will lose the entire sum loaned if the borrower's obligation is not met. The manufacturer or merchant, on the other hand, has a profit margin on the goods sold. If the purchaser fails to meet the obligation, the seller loses at most the cost of the goods delivered to the purchaser.

COMMERCIAL FINANCE COMPANIES

The first commercial finance company in the United States was chartered about 100 years ago. Since that time, the number of these institutions has increased to more than five hundred. Some of these organizations are small, offering limited financial services to their customers, while others have vast resources and engage in broadly diversified programs of business lending.

A **commercial finance company** is an organization without a bank charter that advances funds to businesses by (1) discounting accounts receivable, (2) making loans secured by chattel mortgages on machinery or liens on inventory, or (3) financing deferred-payment sales of commercial and industrial equipment. These companies also are known as commercial credit companies, commercial receivables companies, and discount companies.

Commercial finance companies, such as CIT Group, Celtic Capital, and GE Capital, offer many of the same services as commercial banks for financing accounts receivable and inventory. Lending funds based upon the amount of a firm's accounts receivable balances was, in fact, originated by commercial finance companies and only later was adopted by commercial banks. Both consumer and business financing can be obtained from firms such as General Electric Capital Corporation and Ford Motor Credit Company.

Commercial finance companies grew to their present number because they were completely free to experiment with new and highly specialized types of credit arrangements. Also, state laws concerning lending on the basis of accounts receivable were generally more favorable to these nonbanking organizations. A third influence is that they were able to charge rates high enough to make a profitable return on high-risk loans. Frequently these rates were far above rates bankers were permitted to charge.

In addition to financing accounts receivable and inventories, commercial finance companies provide a vast amount of credit for businesses by financing commercial vehicles, industrial and farm equipment, and other types of business credit. The Commercial Finance Association estimates the total volume of business credit outstanding by the commercial finance companies to be more than $420 billion.[16]

The equity position of commercial finance companies is considerably greater than that of banks. However, these organizations do not operate on equity capital alone. Additional long-term capital is acquired by selling debenture, or unsecured, bonds. In addition, commercial banks lend a large volume of money at wholesale rates to commercial finance companies, which in turn lend it to business borrowers at retail rates. Nonbank financial intermediaries, as well as commercial and industrial firms, often find it advantageous to invest their temporary surplus funds in the commercial paper of commercial finance companies. These sources of short-term funds permit the commercial finance companies to meet their peak loan demands without having too much long-term debt, only part of which would be used during slack lending periods.

When viewing the high interest rates (sometimes as high as 15 to 20 percent) for commercial finance company loans, the question may arise why a borrower would under any circumstances use these companies. As a matter of fact, a business that has ample current assets and is in a highly liquid position may be well advised to rely on other sources of short-term financing. When business is most brisk and growth possibilities most favorable, the need for additional short-term funds becomes unusually pressing, just as it is when customers are slow in paying their bills and the company needs cash.

A business will typically first request an increase in its bank line of credit. Failing this, an additional loan from a bank may be secured by pledging either inventory or receivables as collateral. However, not all banks actively engage in this type of financial arrangement. Thus it may be necessary to deal with a commercial finance company. Commercial finance companies are able

16. R. R. Carmichael & Co., Inc., and Commercial Finance Association, *Annual Asset-Based Lending and Factoring Surveys, 2005,* http://www.cfa.com/documents/Annual_ABL_Factoring_Survey_2005.pdf (accessed March 13, 2007).

CONCEPT CHECK

What is trade credit?

What is the cost of trade credit?

Is it usually more or less expensive than bank financing?

commercial finance company
organization without a bank charter that advances funds to businesses

INTERNET ACTIVITY

The Commercial Finance Association is a trade association for commercial finance companies. Learn more about the industry at http://www.cfa.com.

CONCEPT CHECK

What is a commercial finance company?

How does a commercial finance company raise funds to lend to borrowers?

commercial paper
short-term promissory note sold by corporations with high-quality credit; notes backed solely by the credit quality of the issuer

INTERNET ACTIVITY

Visit Sungard's trading system Web site at http://mm.sungard.net. For a variety of financial market information, see the Bloomberg Web site at www.bloomberg.com.

to operate through a system of branches on a regional or national basis, unhampered by restrictions on bank branch operations. Therefore, they can acquire the volume of business necessary to cover overhead and provide the needed diversification of risks for high-risk financing. Several bank holding companies have purchased or established commercial finance companies to take advantage of their special operating characteristics.

COMMERCIAL PAPER

A final source of short-term financing is not a specific type of lender but is the financial markets itself. Large U.S. corporations with high-quality credit can issue or sell **commercial paper**, which is a short-term promissory note. This means the notes are backed solely by the credit quality of the issuer; there is no security or collateral behind them. Commercial paper may be sold directly by the issuer to financial institutions or other investors. Alternatively, it can be sold to commercial paper houses or dealers who purchase the promissory notes to resell them to individuals or businesses. A fee based on the amount of notes purchased, charged to the issuer of the notes, provides the basic income of commercial paper dealers. With about $150 billion outstanding in early 2007, trading in this short maturity form of debt surpasses $1 trillion annually.

A firm that wishes to obtain funds from a commercial paper house must have an unquestioned reputation for sound operation. First, the commercial paper house makes a thorough investigation of the firm's financial position. If it appears that the notes of the firm can be sold with little difficulty, an agreement is made for the outright sale of a block of the firm's promissory notes to the commercial paper house, which will resell these notes as quickly as possible to banks, managers of pension funds, business corporations that have surplus funds, or other investors. The notes are usually prepared in denominations of $100,000 or more with maturities ranging from a few days to 270 days.[17] The size of the notes and the maturities, however, can be adjusted to suit individual investor requirements.

Commercial paper is sold on a discount basis. Dealers will pay the borrower the face amount of the notes minus the interest charge and a fee that is usually between 0.02 and 0.05 percent. The interest charge is determined by the general level of prevailing rates in the money market and the strength of the borrowing company. When these notes are resold to banks and other lenders, only the prevailing interest charge is deducted from the face value of the notes. Hence, the commercial paper dealer receives the fee as compensation for the negotiation and intermediation.

Commercial paper is no longer sold only through dealers or brokers. Investors can now buy commercial paper online through an electronic trading system. The first firm to offer its paper online was Ford Motor Company on a commercial paper trading system designed by CS First Boston. Since then, others have developed online commercial paper systems to facilitate the direct issue of paper to investors. In recent years the most successful of them has been SunGard's Transaction Network. Online issuance of paper allows issuers to cut in half the fees usually collected by dealers.

Commercial paper is issued by large, well-known, and financially stable firms; only they have the ability to raise large sums of short-term financing quickly and with a bank's backing.[18] Many of the borrowers of commercial paper are financial firms such as commercial finance companies; they seek to finance their own lending and leasing operations by raising short-term funds through commercial paper. They will borrow at the commercial paper rate and then lend the funds to others at higher interest rates.

Suppose Global Manufacturing wants to issue $100,000 of commercial paper that will mature in nine months (270 days). The placement fee is 0.10 percent, and the interest charge will be 7.5 percent over the nine-month period. To compute Global's effective financing cost, we must determine the net proceeds or usable funds that Global will obtain from the sale, as well as the total interest charges they will pay. The net proceeds will be the $100,000 raised minus the interest less the placement fee:

---

17. Commercial paper has a maximum maturity of 270 days, as SEC regulations require that securities with maturities exceeding 270 days must go through the costly and time-consuming SEC registration process.

18. Banks are a major player in the commercial paper market, as they frequently offer issuers a line of credit equal to their amount of paper outstanding. Up until 1999, it was a requirement for S&P to award its top A-1 rating to a firm issuing paper. S&P now considers all sources of liquidity that can be used to redeem the paper.

$$\text{Net proceeds} = \$100,000 - [(0.075)(\$100,000)] - [(0.0010)(\$100,000)]$$
$$= \$100,000 - \$7,500 - \$100$$
$$= \$92,400$$

The interest charge is $0.075 \times \$100,000$, or \$7,500, and the placement fee is \$100 for total expenses of \$7,600. The nine-month financing cost for the commercial paper issue is:

$$\text{9-month cost} = \$7,600/\$92,400 = 0.0823, \text{ or } 8.23 \text{ percent}$$

The annualized cost of the commercial paper issue will be:

$$(1 + 0.0823)^{12/9} - 1 = 0.1111 \text{ or } 11.11 \text{ percent}$$

The most important reason a firm has for issuing commercial paper is that the cost of borrowing is generally less than regular bank rates. The reason for the lower rates is that only the largest, most financially stable firms can issue commercial paper. Also, unlike banks, which typically service a geographic region, commercial paper is sold by dealers to investors worldwide, so international short-term rates help determine commercial paper rates rather than bank loan committees. Also, the need for compensating bank balances that increase interest costs on short-term bank loans is avoided. Loan restrictions on the amount that can be borrowed from a single bank also may favor the issuance of commercial paper by large corporations.

Like bonds, commercial paper is rated. The rating is important to the issuer, as the higher the rating, the lower the interest expense. Industrial firms and other nonbank lenders often purchase commercial paper as a more profitable alternative to Treasury bills for investing excess cash.

Commercial paper provides a yield slightly above that of short-term government securities as we saw in Figure 16.6 in Chapter 16. Although historically commercial banks were the main purchasers of commercial paper, it is now actively held by industrial corporations, money market mutual funds, and other lenders.

Many top-rated U.S. commercial paper issuers can also issue paper overseas. The European commercial paper (Euro CP) market offers advantages to commercial paper issuers, just as the Eurodollar bond market offers advantages over the U.S. bond market. There is no SEC regulation of the Euro CP market, so commercial paper maturities are generally a little longer and interest costs lower. In addition, Euro CP is available only to the "cream" of the commercial paper issuers, so no ratings are needed. Investors already know who the safest issuers are, so not having to pay for a rating also makes the Euro CP market attractive to those firms that are able to use it.

CONCEPT CHECK

What is commercial paper?

How is commercial paper sold?

What advantages does a firm have when issuing commercial paper instead of getting a bank loan?

ADDITIONAL VARIETIES OF SHORT-TERM FINANCING

We've reviewed several types of short-term financing in our discussion of financing providers. For example, in our prior discussion of banks we discussed lines of credit, revolving credit agreements, and SBA loan guarantees. Suppliers offer trade credit. The financial markets offer the ability to sell commercial paper. In this section we discuss other important varieties of short-term financing. For the most part, these financing arrangements are available both from banks and commercial finance companies and are forms of secured financing. *Secured lending (asset-based lending)* means that there is some collateral or security backing the loan that can be claimed or sold by the lender if the borrower defaults. We have seen this type of lending before in Chapter 7's discussion of mortgage bonds. In this section we examine the use of asset-based lending for short-term financing purposes.

ACCOUNTS RECEIVABLE FINANCING

The business that does not qualify for an unsecured bank loan or that has emergency needs for funds in excess of its line of credit may decide to use its accounts receivable as a way to raise needed funds. Two methods exist for using accounts receivable as a form of asset-based lending. First, the firm can borrow against its accounts receivable balances. This is called *pledging* accounts receivable. Second, it can sell its accounts receivable to a firm called a *factor*; thus, selling accounts receivable balances is called *factoring*.

There are many similarities between these two methods of using accounts receivable to raise funds, but there also are a number of differences. We'll discuss the general process of each before reviewing the differences between them.

secured lending (asset-based lending)
collateral or security backing the loan that can be claimed or sold by the lender if the borrower defaults

pledging (pledge)
obtain a short-term loan by using accounts receivable as collateral

factor
engages in accounts receivable financing by purchasing accounts and assuming all credit risks

Pledging Accounts Receivable

Rather than wait until its customers pay on each of their accounts, a firm can pledge its accounts and get a loan. By so doing, the firm obtains funds sooner, albeit at a cost. The word *accounts* in accounts receivable is plural. When a firm pledges its accounts receivable, each customer's account is reviewed to see if it is sufficiently creditworthy to be security or collateral for a loan. The lender—usually a bank or finance company—gives close attention to the borrower's collection experience on its receivables and to certain characteristics of its accounts receivable.

The bank may spot-check the receivables of the firm and may in some cases analyze each account to determine how quickly the firm's customers make payments. It is also important for the bank to know something about these customers; it will probably check on their credit ratings from a source such as Dun & Bradstreet. Customers' ability to pay their debts will strongly influence how well the business applying for the loan will be able to collect payment.

In addition, the bank studies the type and quality of goods that are sold. If the merchandise is inferior, there may be objections from the customers and hence slower payment of bills or sales returns. Accounts receivable are of little value as security for a loan if large quantities of merchandise are returned and the amount of accounts receivable is reduced accordingly.

Generally, a loan based on accounts receivable will be no more than 80 percent of the gross receivables. This amount should be reduced by any discounts allowed to customers for quick payment and by the normal percentage of merchandise returns. If there is reason to believe that many of the loan applicant's customers are not suitable risks, or if adequate credit ratings are not available, the bank will lend a lower percentage of the face value of the receivables. Additionally, if a customer is a large proportion of the firm's credit sales, the percentage lent against that account may be less than usual; this protects the bank in case a large customer of the firm experiences financial difficulties which may, in turn, create subsequent cash flow problems for the supplying firm.

Pledging accounts receivable is not a simple process. The firm's accounts receivable are reviewed by the bank to determine their level and if they are acceptable to form the basis for a loan. At the time the loan is made, individual accounts on the ledger of the business are designated clearly as having been pledged for the bank loan. Only those accounts suitable for collateral purposes for the bank are designated. When these accounts are paid in full or become unsatisfactory, they are replaced by other accounts.

Pledging accounts receivable involves sending invoices and funds (either electronically or paper) back and forth between the firm, its customers, and the bank offering the loan. For example, the bank receives copies of all shipping invoices to show that the goods have been shipped and an account receivable is valid. Thus not only is invoice material transferred from firm to customer but also from firm to bank. Similarly, there are several transfers of funds. First the bank lends funds to the firm. Second, the firm's customers make payments on the pledged receivables. Third, the firm sends such payments to the bank to repay the loan.

It is usually more expensive to pledge receivables than to borrow funds from a bank. Under a pledged receivables arrangement, the firm pays interest on the loan (namely the funds advanced to it) and a separate fee to cover the extra work needed for such a loan. The bank must periodically check or audit the books of the business to see that it is, in fact, living up to the terms of the agreement and sending customer payments to it in a timely basis. As customers pay their bill on the pledged account that has been assigned for the loan, the proceeds must be turned over to the bank. The bank also reserves the right to make a direct audit of the business's books from time to time and to have an outside accounting firm examine the books periodically.

ETHICAL ISSUES

Factoring Accounts Receivable

Pledging involves borrowing against receivables balances; factoring involves selling the accounts. A financing firm called a *factor* purchases the accounts receivable outright and assumes all credit risks. Under **maturity factoring**, the firm selling its accounts receivable is paid on the normal collection date or net due date of the account. Under **advance factoring**, the factor pays the firm for its receivables before the account due date.

Under a factoring arrangement, customers whose accounts are sold are notified that their bills are payable to the factor. The task of collecting on the accounts is thus shifted from the seller of the accounts to the factor. Some factors include GE Capital, Platinum Funding, and units of several large banks.

maturity factoring
firm selling its receivables is paid on the normal collection date or net due date of the account

advance factoring
factor pays the firm for its receivables before the account due date

INTERNET ACTIVITY

Learn about factors and other asset-based lenders by visiting Web sites such as http://www. platinumfundingcorp.com, http://www.gecapital.com, http://www.gecfo.com, http://www.tfc.textron.com, http://www.citicapital.com, and http://www.celticcapital .com.

Factoring can be done *with recourse* or *without recourse*. With recourse, the factor can return an unpaid account to the firm and any funds advanced for that account must be returned to the factor. Without recourse, the accounts are sold to the factor and any bad or slow-paying accounts are the factor's responsibility.

Rather than just occasionally selling accounts to the factor, many times the factor becomes a partner with the firm. A typical arrangement has the factor become the firm's credit department. That is, all requests to sell goods on credit to new and existing customers are routed to the factor for approval, thus saving the firm time and expense in hiring, training, staffing, and running its own credit department. Members of the factor's credit department not only must be extremely prompt and accurate in their credit analyses but also, because they work closely with the firm's clients, must retain the goodwill of the companies that use its services.

Should the factor reject a credit request from a new customer of the firm—or reject a request to increase an existing credit limit on an existing customer of the firm—the firm can always choose to extend the credit itself. In such cases, the firm will keep those accounts on its books and have to service the accounts—send bills, collect payments, and deal with any slow or non-payers.

To use a factor, a contract is drawn establishing the duties and obligations of the seller and the factor. The contract provides that the accepted accounts be assigned to the factor for payment and that sales invoices to these customers, together with the original shipping documents, be delivered daily to the factor along with information on all credits, allowances, and returns of merchandise.

The contract includes the conditions under which accounts may be sold to the factor, such as type of firm, geographic area of the customer, and acceptable credit ratings. Another important part of the contract is the collection procedures to be followed in case a customer is slow in paying its bill. As we saw in Chapter 16, collecting accounts receivable can be a costly process, especially when a customer is alienated by aggressive collection efforts. A firm will want to know what collection process the factor follows as future sales may be lost if the factor is too aggressive.

The charge for factoring has two components. First, interest is charged on the money advanced. Second, a factoring commission or service charge is figured as a percentage of the face amount of the receivables. This charge typically ranges from 1.5 percent to 3 percent of the face amount of the accounts financed. Factors will typically lend 80 percent of the remainder, although they may reduce the amount of the loan anywhere from 5 to 15 percent of the total amount of receivables factored to make adjustments, such as for merchandise that is returned to the seller. This portion of the receivables is returned to the seller if it is not needed for adjustment purposes.

For example, suppose a firm is owed $70,000 by a customer that rarely pays its bills any sooner than sixty days after the invoice. Assuming the customer meets the factor's credit standards, the firm will receive 80 percent of the $70,000 or $56,000 within a day or two of accepting the account. If the interest rate for a sixty-day account is 2 percent and the factoring fee is 3 percent, the cost of the factoring arrangement will be $3,500 (5 percent of $70,000). Assuming the customer pays its bill in full on day sixty, the firm receives an additional $10,500, which is the amount of the invoice ($70,000) less the advance ($56,000) less the combined factoring and interest costs ($3,500). Thus, the firm collects $66,500 of the original $70,000 invoice; $56,000 was received after a one- or two-day delay, and the remainder was received around day sixty.

Although a factor's services may be used by a firm that is unable to secure financing through customary channels, financially strong companies also may at times use these services to good advantage. In fact, factors are of greatest benefit to companies that enjoy very strong sales and growth. We have noted that during such periods companies experience extreme shortages of working capital. The sale of receivables without recourse (that is, sellers do not have to repay any funds received from the factor in the case of a bad debt) has the effect of substituting cash for accounts receivable. This may make even greater growth and profitability possible in the long run.

Some firms factor their receivables for other reasons. First, the cost of doing business through credit sales is definite and can be determined in advance because the factor assumes all risks of collection. This is, in effect, a form of credit insurance. Second, factoring eliminates expenses, including bookkeeping costs, the maintenance of a credit department, and the expenses of collecting delinquent accounts. A further advantage, but of a less tangible nature, is that factoring

TABLE 17.2

Comparison of Pledging and Factoring Accounts Receivable

PLEDGING ACCOUNTS RECEIVABLE	FACTORING ACCOUNTS RECEIVABLE
It is a loan against accounts receivable.	It is a sale of accounts receivable.
Accounts receivable balances remain on the balance sheet.	Sold accounts receivable balances are removed from the balance sheet.
Customer payment is made to firm, which then submits the payment to the bank.	Customer pays the factor.
Firm makes each credit decision.	Factor makes the credit decision; firm can always choose to extend credit on its own.
Charges:	Charges:
• Interest rate on loan	• Interest rate on funds advanced
• Audit fees for periodic review of accounts, payments	• Service charge
Additional cost: paper and funds flow between firm and bank.	

GLOBAL DISCUSSION

frees the management of a business from concern with financial matters and permits it to concentrate on production and distribution. Factoring has become increasingly important in supporting export sales. The firm that is unfamiliar with the problems of financing international shipments of goods is relieved of such details by factoring foreign receivables.

Although factoring services are regarded highly by some businesses, others object to their use. The two reasons cited most frequently are the cost and the implication of financial weakness. The cost of factoring is unquestionably higher than the cost of borrowing from a bank on the basis of an unsecured loan. However, it is difficult to conclude that the net cost is higher. The elimination of overhead costs that would otherwise be necessary, plus the reality that management need not concern itself with financial matters, may completely offset the additional cost involved in factoring.

Few industries are affected by factors as much as retailing. Factors guarantee payment to suppliers of many large retail firms. With such guarantees, suppliers ship goods to the retailers, confident that they will get paid. Should factors refuse to guarantee payments to suppliers because the factors believe a retailer to be on shaky financial ground, a retailing firm can find itself with no merchandise to sell. Thus, predictions about poor finances can become a self-fulfilling prophecy. Once one factor hesitates to stand behind a retailer's credit, they all turn their backs on the retailer since no one factor wants to be left alone supporting a financially troubled firm. Factors act as an early warning signal of a retailer's real or imagined financial deterioration. In 1995 Bradlees, a discount retailer, filed for Chapter 11 bankruptcy protection after factors refused to guarantee Bradlees' receivables to its suppliers. A few months later Caldor, another discount retailer, filed for bankruptcy protection for the same reason: the factors would not support it. When factors refuse to accept a retailer's credit, the retailer's suppliers face a decision: whether to continue shipping and taking the risk of nonpayment by the financially troubled retailer or to stop shipping and possibly lose a client. With the bankruptcy filings in recent years of such retail stores as Federated Department Stores, Allied Stores, Macy's, Jamesway, Bradlees, and Caldor, it appears that the suppliers are choosing to listen to the factors.[19]

There are many similarities between pledging and factoring. To help differentiate them, Table 17.2 summarizes some of their differences.

INVENTORY LOANS

A business may use its inventory as collateral for a loan in much the same manner that it may borrow on its receivables. The bank evaluates the physical condition of the firm's inventory and the inventory's general composition. Staple items that are in constant demand serve well as

CONCEPT CHECK

What are two types of accounts receivable financing?

What is meant by pledging receivables, and how does it differ from factoring?

What are the advantages of using a factor? What are the disadvantages?

---

19. Joseph Pereira, "Bradlees Seeks Bankruptcy Protection, but Denies It Is Facing Liquidity Crisis," *Wall Street Journal* (June 26, 1995), p. A10; Susan Pulliam and Laura Bird, "Concern Rises About Retailer Caldor's Ability to Deal with Cutthroat Rivalry; Stock Sinks," *Wall Street Journal* (August 24, 1995), p. C2; Laura Bird, "Caldor Files for Bankruptcy Protection in Face of Weak Sales, Jittery Suppliers," *Wall Street Journal* (September 19, 1995), p. A3; Roger Lowenstein, "Lenders' Stampede Tramples Caldor," *Wall Street Journal* (October 26, 1995), p. C1.

collateral for a loan. Style and fashion items such as designer clothes are not as acceptable as collateral except for brief periods. Firms that use inventory as collateral usually do so because they are not in a position to obtain further funds on an unsecured basis.

blanket inventory lien
claim against a customer's inventory when the individual items are indistinguishable

The bank may protect itself when lending to a business by having a **blanket inventory lien**, or a claim against inventory when individual items are indistinguishable, as may be the case with grain or clothing items. For such loans, a borrower may receive only 60 to 80 percent of the inventory's value in a loan. A manufacturer's work-in-process inventory may receive only 20 to 30 percent of its value.

trust receipt
lien against specific identifiable items in inventory

In other cases, when goods can be clearly identified, a **trust receipt** may be used. Money is borrowed against specific items in inventory. This method of financing, sometimes called *floor plan financing*, is used by car dealerships and appliance stores, where inventory items financed by trust receipts can be identified by serial number. Under a trust receipt arrangement, the bank retains ownership of the goods until they are actually sold in the regular course of business. Audits are simply a matter of checking serial numbers of inventory items to determine if items held against a trust receipt have been sold.

warehouse receipt
inventory is placed in a bonded warehouse for safekeeping; items are removed as they are paid for

In some cases when inventory is used as collateral, the bank may insist that the inventory be placed in a bonded and licensed warehouse. The **warehouse receipt** issued by the warehouse is then turned over to the bank, which holds it until the loan is repaid.

field warehouse
an enterprise establishes a warehouse on the grounds of the borrowing business establishment

It is frequently inconvenient for a business to deliver large bulky items of inventory to a warehouse for storage. This problem is solved by using a **field warehouse**. A field warehousing enterprise has the power to establish a field warehouse on the grounds of the borrowing business establishment. Field warehouses differ from the typical public warehouse in that (1) they serve a single customer: that customer on whose property the field warehouse is established and (2) they exist only until the loan is repaid.

In setting up a field warehouse, the warehouse operator usually must first obtain a lease on that portion of the property to be used for warehousing purposes. Then he or she must establish fences, barriers, walks, and other postings to indicate clear possession of the property. This is done to avoid accidental or deliberate removal of stored items during the general course of business operations. A guard may be posted to check on the safety of the warehoused goods, or a room may be sealed and the seal inspected periodically to make sure the company is honoring its agreement.

There also must be a complete statement of the commodities or items that are to be warehoused, and agreements must be made about the maintenance of the property, proper fire precautions, insurance, and other necessary physical requirements. Under certain circumstances, the warehouse operator is authorized to release a certain quantity of goods by the day, week, or month to make possible a rotation of merchandise. Under this arrangement, physical inventories must be taken from time to time.

Field warehouses are in operation throughout the United States but are concentrated in the Central and Pacific Coast regions. Canned goods, miscellaneous groceries, lumber, timber, and building supplies fill about two-fifths of all field warehouses in this country. Those banks that make loans involving commodities will generally accept field warehouse receipts as collateral.

INTERNET ACTIVITY

Have you visited http://www.ebay.com to look for items of interest? Do a search for items that may comprise excess inventory. Another business-oriented site is http://www.salvagesale.com.

Inventory loans are somewhat more expensive than unsecured loans to business borrowers. The higher cost is due in part to the cost of warehousing operations and also because the borrower's credit rating may be low. Bank interest rates for warehouse loans ordinarily are somewhat higher than for unsecured loans.[20] In addition, a warehouse fee of 1 to 2 percent of the loan, depending on size and other factors, must be paid.

Technology can assist the valuing of inventory, especially if the inventory is equipment.[21] Digital writing and recording devices, such as digital cameras, allow items to be photographed and the information saved electronically for later recall. Business-to-business auction sites and even eBay auction prices have been used to estimate an item's value.[22]

---

20. Inventory loans, like receivable loans, are also made by commercial finance companies. Their interest rates usually are higher than those charged by banks.

21. Firms can also obtain loans against the firm's equipment used in its operations, as well as what might be manufactured or sold from inventory.

22. Hilary Rosenberg, "Mining the Balance Sheet," *CFO* (May 2001), pp. 103–108; Robert S. MacDonald, "Technology Tools Used in the Equipment Appraisal Process," *The Secured Lender* (August 2001), p. 8.

DAVE LOCKARD
Corporate Manager
Fath Management

BS, Accounting
University of Notre Dame
Certified Public Accountant

"I wear lots of hats."

Q: *Describe the firm you work for.*

A: Fath Management is a privately owned real estate management company. We own and operate about forty properties, almost all apartment buildings or complexes, in four states. In all we have about 7,000 residential units.

Q: *What is your role there?*

A: I wear lots of hats. I set the operating budgets for our properties, approve significant expenditures, oversee hiring and firing, negotiate contracts for services like waste removal, manage our insurance needs, set company policies and salary guidelines, manage our banking relationships, and evaluate properties that we may want to purchase, among other things.

Q: *You "manage banking relationships." What does that involve?*

A: Most of our properties are purchased via bank loans. Because interest rates are relatively low right now, we are continually looking for opportunities to refinance our loans at lower rates. That's basically a cost-justification issue—can we save enough in interest expense to compensate for the refinancing fees we would face? Every time there's a fall in interest rates it opens up the possibility of refinancing more of our loans. And then there are new loans when we buy new properties, of course.

Q: *Describe the acquisition process.*

A: We are not acquiring as many new properties now as we did several years ago, but we are always open to that possibility. I've developed a computer spreadsheet model that we use to assess the financial potential of a property. We use this model to identify the properties that fit best with our strategy and have the potential to generate the rate of return we need. Then we take a closer look at those properties, their condition, the neighborhoods. If we decide to purchase a property, we go to a local or regional bank and negotiate a loan.

Q: *What information do you provide the bank to secure the financing?*

A: We would provide information about the specific property—the projected cash flow, our plans for renovation or improvement, and so on—as well as information about Fath's overall financial position, our operating results, and credit history. There's another side to our interaction with banks, too. Banks compete for customers just like any other business. In many cases banks will come to us offering special deals on certain types of loans, which may encourage us to take a closer look at an acquisition we might not have pursued otherwise.

Q: *What skills do you use most in your job?*

A: The ability to understand and resolve problems is essential in this job. A lot of issues come up that you could never foresee, and you need to be able to determine the right course of action and implement it right away. You have to be able to consider the impact of your actions so that you don't create new problems when you solve an existing one. These problems make the job difficult, but interesting too. I like the variety of issues that I get involved in.

LOANS SECURED BY STOCKS AND BONDS

Stocks and bonds often are used as collateral for short-term loans. These securities are welcomed as collateral primarily because of their marketability and their value. If the securities are highly marketable and if their value is high enough to cover the amount of the loan requested even if the stock's price goes down somewhat, a banker will not hesitate to extend a loan. Securities listed on one of the national exchanges are preferred because frequent price quotations are available. Banks usually will loan from 60 to 70 percent of the market value of listed stocks and from 70 to 80 percent of the market value of high-grade bonds.

Only assignable stocks and bonds are eligible for this type of collateral financing, with the exception of nonassignable U.S. savings bonds. When assignable securities are placed with a bank, a stock or bond power is executed that authorizes the bank to sell or otherwise dispose of the securities should it become necessary to do so to protect the loan.

OTHER FORMS OF SECURITY FOR BANK LOANS

Security for short-term bank loans also may include such things as the cash surrender value of life insurance policies, guarantee of a loan by a party other than the borrower, notes, and acceptances.

Life Insurance Loans

Small businesses frequently find it possible to obtain needed short-term bank loans by pledging the cash surrender value, or the amount they will receive on cancellation, of the owner's life insurance policies. The policies must be assignable, and many insurance companies insist that their own assignment forms be used for such purposes. Because of the safety afforded the bank by the cash surrender values, these loans usually carry a lower interest rate than loans on other types of business collateral. Another reason for the favorable rates is that the borrower could borrow directly from the insurance company. Even so, bank interest rates are many times higher than those of insurance companies to their policyholders. As a result, there has been an increase in the number of these loans made by insurance companies.

Co-Maker Loans

Many small businesses find it necessary to provide the bank with a guarantor in the form of a cosigner to their notes. It is expected that the cosigner has a credit rating at least as satisfactory as, and usually far better than, the firm requesting the loan.

Acceptances

acceptance
a receivable from the sale of merchandise on the basis of a draft or bill of exchange drawn against the buyer or the buyer's bank

Another type of receivable instrument that arises out of the sale of merchandise and that may be sold to a bank is the acceptance. An ***acceptance*** is a receivable from the sale of merchandise on the basis of a draft or bill of exchange drawn against the buyer or the buyer's bank. The accepted draft or bill of exchange is returned to the seller of the merchandise who may hold it until the date payment is due. During this period, the business may discount such acceptances with its bank. Again, the seller is contingently liable for these discounted acceptances. The use of the banker's acceptance is discussed in detail in Chapter 18 in connection with an international shipment of goods.

THE COST OF SHORT-TERM FINANCING

For most asset-based and unsecured loans, a simple method can be used to combine the interest expenses and fees to determine the true interest cost of a short-term loan. Fortunately, it is a process we already discussed in this chapter when we examined commercial paper. Here we break it down into steps and then present an example.

First, determine the amount to be borrowed. Discounted loans or bank loans with compensating balances will need to use Equations 17.2 and 17.3 to determine the amount.

Second, determine the interest expenses on the borrowed funds. This is the interest rate multiplied by the amount borrowed.

Third, determine the fees and other expenses associated with using the financing source. We know, for example, that factors charge a service fee, inventory loans may carry warehouse charges, and pledged loans usually carry extra fees because of the extra analysis done by the lender.

APPLYING FINANCE TO . . .

INSTITUTIONS AND MARKETS

We've seen in previous chapters how the financial markets determine financing rates. Interest rates facing borrowers depend on the risk-free rate and a risk premium. Financial institutions have developed many ways to meet the short-term financing needs of firms, including instruments offering different maturities, security (collateral) requirements, and control—that is, who actually "supervises" the collateral—arrangements.

INVESTMENTS

Just as a capital market investor reviews the creditworthiness of a bond issuer and the share price appreciation potential of a company, similar care must be taken when analyzing a firm seeking a short-term loan or other financing arrangement. The primary concern will be the firm's ability to generate cash to repay the short-term loan. Cash generation, not sales or accounting profits, will be paramount.

FINANCIAL MANAGEMENT

Managers must balance the opportunity cost of excess cash with the costs of paying short-term financing rates and the dangers of a credit crunch when short-term financing dries up. A firm's treasurer wants to maintain liquidity, which includes the firm's access to short-term financing sources, at all times.

Fourth, estimate the net proceeds. This may be the same as the amount borrowed, but in the case of discounted loans (such as commercial paper) the net proceeds will be less than the amount borrowed.

Fifth, to estimate the financing cost, divide the sum of the interest expenses and fees (steps 2 and 3) by the net proceeds (step 4). Annualize this rate, if necessary.

Here's an example. Fluoridated Manufacturing (FM) is considering short-term financing choices. A factor is willing to advance FM 80 percent of its receivables and charge it a 2 percent fee to compensate it for analyzing the receivables and determining which it will purchase. FM estimates it will pay a 12 percent annual percentage rate (APR) in order to receive cash an average of forty-five days earlier. The current receivables balance is $10,000.

Let's do the analysis step-by-step. This process should help determine the financing cost of virtually any lending arrangement, whether by a bank, commercial finance company, factor, or other source of short-term finance:

1. Determine the amount to be received. With receivables of $10,000 and an advance rate of 80 percent, FM will receive $10,000 × 0.80 = $8,000.
2. Determine the interest expense. With a 12 percent APR the daily interest charge is 0.12/365. Factoring allows FM to receive its funds an average of forty-five days sooner, so the interest expense is $8,000 × (0.12/365) × 45 = $118.36.
3. Determine the fees and other expenses. The factor's fee is 2 percent for basing a loan on a receivables balance of $10,000. The fees are 0.02 × $10,000 = $200.
4. Estimate the net proceeds. There is no discounting, so in this case the net proceeds will be $8,000. We assume FM will pay the fees out of pocket. The net proceeds will be smaller if the $200 in fees is deducted by the factor from the loan amount.
5. The financing cost is $118.36 + $200 = $318.36 with net proceeds of $8,000. The percentage cost is $318.36/$8,000 = 0.0398 or 3.98 percent for forty-five days of financing. The annualized rate is $(1 + 0.0398)^{365/45} - 1 = 0.3724$ or 37.24 percent.

SUMMARY

Working capital, it has been said, is the grease that keeps the wheels turning in a company. Inventories are needed to meet customer demands for the firm's products. When they are sold, accounts receivable are created that will one day be converted into cash. This cash is used to pay suppliers, workers, creditors, taxes, and shareholder dividends. A firm without working capital is a firm unlikely to remain in business.

There are two classes of working capital: permanent, or the minimum necessary for smooth company operations, and tempo-

rary, which occurs because of seasonal or cyclical fluctuations in sales demand. A company financing strategy that uses long-term sources to finance its working capital is a conservative strategy that reduces profits but increases liquidity. An aggressive strategy that uses more short-term financing has less liquidity but may increase company profits. Several influences affect managers' decisions on how the firm should be financed, including the characteristics of the firm's industry, its asset base, seasonality, sales cycles, and sales trends.

Firms have many possible sources of short-term financing, from bank loans (including lines of credit and revolving credit), to commercial paper, to trade credit. Care should be taken by the treasurer to evaluate the cost of each financing source by calculating its effective annual cost, by incorporating all interest charges and fees into the analysis, and by comparing the principal of the loan with the actual usable funds received. Asset-backed financing, such as pledging, factoring receivables, or using inventory as collateral, are usually higher-cost financing sources, primarily because smaller, less creditworthy firms rely on them for financing.

KEY TERMS

acceptance

advance factoring

blanket inventory lien

commercial finance company

commercial paper

compensating balance

discounted loan

factor

field warehouse

line of credit

maturity factoring

maturity-matching approach

net working capital

pledging (pledge)

prime rate

revolving credit agreement

secured lending (asset-based lending)

trade discounts

trust receipt

warehouse receipt

working capital

DISCUSSION QUESTIONS

1. What is meant by *net working capital?* Briefly describe the financing implications when net working capital is positive.

2. What is meant by *permanent* current assets? How do *temporary* current assets differ from permanent current assets?

3. Explain the strategies businesses can use to finance their assets with short-term and long-term funds.

4. What influences affect the nature of the demand for short-term versus long-term funds?

5. Explain how a conservative approach to financing a firm's assets is a low-risk/low-expected-return strategy whereas an aggressive approach to financing is a high-risk/high-expected-return strategy.

6. Prepare a list of advantages and disadvantages of short-term bank borrowing over other short-term financing sources.

7. What is meant by an unsecured loan? Are these loans an important form of bank lending?

8. Explain what a bank line of credit is.

9. Explain how discounting and compensating balances affect the effective cost of bank financing.

10. Describe the revolving credit agreement, and compare it with the bank line of credit.

11. When might a business seek accounts receivable financing?

12. What safeguards may a bank establish to protect itself when it lends on the basis of a customer's receivables pledged as collateral for a loan?

13. When a business firm uses its inventory as collateral for a bank loan, how is the problem of storing and guarding the inventory accomplished for the bank?

14. What is meant by trade credit? Briefly describe some of the possible terms for trade credit.

15. What are the primary reasons for using trade credit for short-term financing?

16. Under what circumstances would a business secure its financing through a commercial finance company?

17. Describe how a factor differs from a commercial finance company in terms of accounts receivable financing.

18. Why would a business use the services of a factor?

19. How does the Small Business Administration provide financing to businesses?

20. What is commercial paper, and how important is it as a source of financing?

21. Is commercial paper a reliable source of financing? Why or why not?

22. How is changing technology changing the methods of raising short-term funds?

PROBLEMS

1. A supplier is offering your firm a cash discount of 2 percent if purchases are paid for within ten days; otherwise the bill is due at the end of sixty days. Would you recommend borrowing from a bank at an 18 percent annual interest rate to take advantage of the cash discount offer? Explain your answer.

2. Assume that you have been offered cash discounts on merchandise that can be purchased from either of two suppliers. Supplier A offers trade credit terms of 3/20, net 70, while supplier B offers 4/15, net 80. What is the approximate effective cost of missing the cash discounts from each supplier? If you could not take advantage of either cash discount offer, which supplier would you select?

3. Obtain a current issue of the Federal Reserve Bulletin, or review a copy from the Fed's Web site (http://www.federalreserve.gov) or the Federal Reserve Bank of St. Louis Web site (http://www.stlouisfed.org), and determine the changes in the prime rate that have occurred since the end of 1998. Comment on any trends in the data.

4. Compute the effective cost of not taking the cash discount under the following trade credit terms:

   a. 2/10, net 40

   b. 2/10, net 50

   c. 3/10, net 50

   d. 2/20, net 40

5. What conclusions can you make about credit terms from reviewing your answers to Problem 4?

6. Your firm needs to raise funds for inventory expansion.

   a. What is the effective annual rate on a loan of $150,000 if it is discounted at a 12 percent stated annual rate and it matures in five months?

   b. How much must you borrow to obtain usable funds of $150,000?

   c. What is the effective annual rate if you borrow the funds computed in (b)?

7. Bank A offers loans with a 10 percent stated annual rate and a 10 percent compensating balance. You wish to obtain $250,000 in a six-month loan.

   a. How much must you borrow to obtain $250,000 in usable funds? Assume you currently do not have any funds on deposit at the bank. What is the effective annual rate on a six month loan?

   b. How much must you borrow to obtain $250,000 in usable funds if you currently have $10,000 on deposit at the bank? What is the effective annual rate on a six-month loan?

   c. How much must you borrow to obtain $250,000 in usable funds if you currently have $30,000 on deposit at the bank? What is the effective annual rate on a six-month loan?

8. Compute the effective annual rates of the following:

   a. $1 million maturing in 90 days with a stated annual rate of 6 percent. Fees are 0.02 percent of the principal.

   b. $15 million maturing in 60 days with a stated annual rate of 7.6 percent. Fees are 0.05 percent of the principal.

   c. $500,000 maturing in 180 days with a stated annual rate of 8.25 percent. Fees are 0.03 percent of the principal.

   d. $50 million maturing in 210 days with a stated annual rate of 6.5 percent. Fees are 0.10 percent of the principal.

9. Construct a spreadsheet that computes the effective annual rates on the commercial paper offerings. Inputs to the spreadsheet should include the dollar amount of paper to be issued, the number of days the paper is outstanding, the stated annual rate, and fees. All paper is sold on a discount basis. Use it to find the effective annual rates in Problem 8.

10. Wonder Dog Leash Company is examining its accounts receivable patterns. Wonder's customers are offered terms of 1/10, net 30. Of its receivables, $150,000 are current, $75,000 are one month overdue, $30,000 are two months overdue, and $20,000 are over two months overdue.

    a. What proportion of Wonder's customers pay their bills on time?

    b. What is the effective cost of Wonder's terms of trade credit?

    c. What might happen to Wonder's receivables balance if it changed its terms to 1/15, net 30? To 2/10, net 30?

11. Wonder Dog Leash Company is seeking to raise cash and is in negotiation with Big Bucks Finance Company to pledge its receivables. BB is willing to loan funds against 75 percent of current (that is, not overdue) receivables at a 15 percent annual percentage rate (see the aging of receivables in Problem 10). To pay for its evaluation of Wonder's receivables, BB charges a 2.5 percent fee on the total balance of current receivables.

    a. If the average term of a loan is thirty days, what is the effective interest rate if Wonder pledges its receivables?

    b. What is the effective rate if Wonder negotiates a loan of forty-five days with no other changes in the loan's terms?

12. Michael's Computers is evaluating proposals from two different factors who will provide receivables financing. Big Fee Factoring will finance the receivables at an APR of 8 percent, discounted and charges a fee of 4 percent. High Rate Factoring offers an APR of 14 percent (nondiscounted) with fees of 2 percent. The average term of either loan is expected to be thirty-five days. With an average receivables balance of $250,000, which proposal should Michael's accept?

13. Michael's Computers' local bank offers the firm a twelve-month revolving credit agreement of $500,000. The APR of the revolver is 12 percent with a commitment fee of 0.5 percent on the unused portion. Over the course of a year Michael's chief financial officer believes they will have an average balance of $280,000 on the revolving credit agreement, with a low of $50,000 and a high of $450,000. What is the annual effective cost of this proposed agreement?

14. Banc Two wants to attract Michael's Computers, Inc., to become a customer. The company's sales force contacts Michael's and offers its line of credit financing. The credit line will be for $500,000 with a one month "clean-up" period. The APR on borrowed funds is 11 percent. Banc Two will offer the line of credit if Michael's opens an account and maintains an average balance of $100,000 over the next twelve months. As in Problem 13, ignoring compensating balances, Michael's CFO believes its financing needs will average $280,000 monthly over the next year with a low monthly need of $50,000 and a high need forecast of $450,000.

    a. Will the line of credit satisfy Michael's needs for short-term funds?

    b. How much money will Michael's draw down from the credit line during a low-use month?

    c. How much will Michael's need to borrow in a month before it maximizes its use of the line of credit?

    d. What is the average cost to Michael's of using the credit line for a year?

15. Montcalm Enterprises is seeking bids on short-term loans with area banks. It expects its average outstanding borrowings to equal $320,000. Which of the following terms offers Montcalm the lowest effective rate?

Town Bank: revolving credit agreement for $500,000 with a 15 percent APR, 0.5 percent commitment fee on the unused portion.

Village Bank: revolving credit agreement for $400,000 with a 12 percent APR, 1.0 percent commitment fee on the unused portion, and a 10 percent compensating balance requirement based on the size of the bank's commitment.

16. Beckheart is seeking financing for its inventory. Safe-proof Warehouses offers space in its facility for Beckheart's inventory. It offers loans with a 15 percent APR equal to 60 percent of the inventory. Monthly fees for the use of the warehouse are $500 plus 0.5 percent of the inventory's value. If Beckheart has saleable inventory of $2 million:

    a. How much money can the firm borrow?

    b. What is the interest cost of the loan in dollars over a year?

    c. What is the total amount of fees to be paid in a year?

    d. What is the effective annual rate of using Safe-proof to finance Beckheart's inventory?

17. CDRW is evaluating an inventory financing arrangement with DVD Banks. CDRW estimates an average monthly inventory balance of $800,000. DVD Bank is offering a 12 percent APR loan on 75 percent of the value of the inventory. DVD's inventory storage and evaluation fees will be 1 percent a month on the total value of the inventory. What is the annual effective rate of the inventory loan?

18. Which of the following offer the lowest effective rate for Wolf Howl jackets? Assume Wolf Howl will need to borrow $800,000 for 180 days.

    a. 14 percent APR bank loan

    b. 13 percent APR, discounted bank loan

    c. 12.5 percent APR with fees of 1 percent for receivables financing

    d. $2 million revolving credit agreement with an APR of 12 percent, a commitment fee of 0.5 percent on the unused balance, and a 10 percent compensating balance requirement

19. **Challenge Problem** Visit a firm's Web site and obtain historical quarterly balance sheet information from it or from its SEC EDGAR filings (http://www.walmart.com and http://www.walgreens.com may be two good sites to use). Use a spreadsheet to record quarterly balance sheet data for several years. Over time, compute and graph the firm's financing mix (for example, by computing the ratio of current liabilities to total assets) and asset mix (by computing the ratio of current assets to total assets). What happens to the firm's financing mix and asset mix over time? Do the financing and asset mix ratios move together over time? Are any seasonal effects in the firm's working capital position and financing evident? What conclusions can you draw about the firm's use of short-term financing?

20. **Challenge Problem** Use the information in the following table for this problem. Comfin Company has estimates on its level of current and total assets for the next two years:

    a. Estimate the levels of permanent and temporary current assets for Comfin over these months. Find the average amount for fixed assets, permanent current assets, and temporary current assets in year 200X and year 200X + 1.

    b. What average amounts of short-term and long-term financing should Comfin have during each year if it wants to follow a maturity-matching financing strategy over time?

    c. What average amounts of short-term and long-term financing should Comfin have during each year if it wants to follow an aggressive financing strategy over time?

    d. Suppose Comfin's cost of short-term funds is 8 percent and its cost of long-term funds is 15 percent. Use your answers in (b) and (c) to compute the cost of each strategy.

    e. What are the pro and con arguments toward each strategy in terms of profitability, risk, and company liquidity?

YEAR 200X	JAN	FEB	MAR	APR	MAY	JUNE	JULY	AUG	SEPT	OCT	NOV	DEC
Total Assets	$500,000	$475,000	$460,000	$470,000	$475,000	$485,000	$495,000	$555,000	$600,000	$650,000	$700,000	$750,000
Current Assets	$250,000	$220,000	$199,900	$204,698	$204,392	$208,980	$213,459	$262,829	$307,085	$351,227	$395,251	$439,156

YEAR 200X + 1	JAN	FEB	MAR	APR	MAY	JUNE	JULY	AUG	SEPT	OCT	NOV	DEC
Total Assets	$600,000	$570,000	$552,000	$564,000	$570,000	$582,000	$594,000	$660,000	$720,000	$780,000	$840,000	$900,000
Current Assets	$350,000	$350,000	$352,100	$359,302	$365,608	$373,020	$380,541	$397,171	$412,915	$428,773	$444,749	$460,844

• CHAPTER 18 •

International Finance and Trade

Chapter Learning Objectives

AFTER STUDYING THIS CHAPTER, YOU SHOULD BE ABLE TO:

- Explain how the international monetary system evolved and how it operates today.
- Describe the efforts undertaken to achieve economic unification of Europe.
- Describe how currency or foreign exchange markets are organized and operate.
- Explain how currency exchange rates are quoted.
- Describe the factors that affect currency exchange rates.
- Describe how the world banking systems facilitate financing of sales by exporters and purchases by importers.
- Identify recent developments in the U.S. balance of payments.

Where We Have Been...   *Our Part 1, "Financial Markets," discussed the purpose, evolution, and working of the financial system. The types of financial intermediaries, the savings-investment process, and types of financial assets were covered. Interest rates and the time value of money were also discussed. In Part 2, "Investments," we discussed how risk and return influence investor decisions and security prices, how securities are priced, and how securities markets work. Part 3, "Financial Management," has reviewed financial statements and financial decisions, covered how businesses make their long-term financing decisions, determine their cost of financial capital, decide on the management of working capital, and make asset investment decisions.*

Where We Are Going...   *In this last chapter we cover international aspects of financial management. Thus, we will have gone full circle—from financial markets, to investments, and finally to the coverage of financial management both domestically and internationally. This means that you will soon be at the beginning of what we hope is a successful business career—possibly one in finance.*

How This Chapter Applies to Me...   *You live in a global environment. You likely have already purchased products grown or manufactured in foreign countries and sold in the United States. For example, you may purchase fresh fruit during the winter that was grown in and shipped from South America. Or, you may have purchased a Swiss-made watch from a retail store in the United States. You may also have had to convert U.S. dollars into a foreign currency such as euros for a direct product purchase from a manufacturer in Germany. You may have traveled internationally and needed to exchange your dollars for that country's currency. You may even live and work outside the United States in the future. Thus, a basic understanding of international trade and factors that affect currency exchange rates will be useful knowledge to have.*

It is important to have an "*open view*" of other countries from the perspective of what they do and why they do it. Maria Mitchell, a U.S. astronomer, probably summed it up best when she stated:

> I have never been in any country where they did not do something better than we do it, think some thoughts better than we think, catch some inspiration from heights above their own.

Interactions among countries are quite complex. Philosophical, cultural, economic, and religious differences exist. These differences jointly establish the basis for international relations and help us understand the practice of internationalism by specific countries. Differences in philosophies, cultures, economic models, and religion also often provide the basis for establishing a nation's foreign policy. At the same time, virtually everyone would agree that it is in the best interests of worldwide economic growth and productivity for countries to work together in facilitating international trade and the flow of financial capital. While this chapter focuses on the economics of international trade and finance, we recognize the importance of being willing to try to understand the basis for differences among countries in terms of philosophies, cultures, economic models, and religions.

GLOBAL DISCUSSION

international monetary system
institutions and mechanisms to foster international trade, manage the flow of financial capital, and determine currency exchange rates

GLOBAL OR INTERNATIONAL MONETARY SYSTEM

In Part 1 we covered the role of the U.S. financial system, the monetary system, and monetary policy. When viewed in a global context, responsibilities become more complex. The global or ***international monetary system*** is a system of institutions and mechanisms to foster world trade, manage the flow of financial capital, and determine currency exchange rates. We first begin with a brief discussion of the historical development of international trade and finance. Then we turn our attention to how the international monetary system has changed or evolved over the past couple of centuries.

DEVELOPMENT OF INTERNATIONAL FINANCE

International finance probably began about 5,000 years ago when Babylonian cities rose to importance as centers of trading between the Mediterranean Sea and civilizations in the East. Gold was used for transactions and as a store of value probably beginning around 3000 B.C., when the pharaohs ruled Egypt. Centers of international finance shifted to the Greek city of Athens around 500 B.C. and to the Roman Empire and Rome around 100 B.C.[1] It appears that whenever international trade developed, financial institutions came into existence and international bankers followed.

CONCEPT CHECK

When did international finance begin?

What is meant by being on a gold standard?

Instruments and documents similar to those in use today were designed to control movement of cargo, insure against losses, satisfy government requirements, and transfer funds. Financial centers shifted to the northern European cities during the 1500s, and in more recent years to London, New York, and Tokyo. Today, international trade takes place and international claims are settled around the clock. It is no longer necessary to have a physical center, such as a city, in which to carry out international financial operations.

HOW THE INTERNATIONAL MONETARY SYSTEM EVOLVED

Before World War I

Prior to the start of World War I in 1914, the international monetary system operated mostly under a ***gold standard*** whereby the currencies of major countries were convertible into gold at fixed exchange rates. For example, an ounce of gold might be worth twenty U.S. dollars, or $1 would be worth one-twentieth (or .05) of an ounce of gold. At the same time an ounce of gold might be worth five French francs (FF), or FF1 would be worth one-fifth (or .20) of an ounce of gold. Since $20 could be converted into 1 ounce of gold that could then be used to purchase five FF or twenty U.S. dollars, the exchange rate between the dollar and franc would be 20 to 5, or 4 to 1. Alternatively, .20 ÷ .05 equals 4 to 1.

gold standard
currencies of countries are convertible into gold at fixed exchange rates

Recall from Chapter 1 that the American colonies relied primarily on the Spanish dollar to conduct business transactions prior to the 1800s. In 1792 the first U.S. monetary act was enacted and provided for a *bimetallic standard* based on both gold and silver. A standard based solely on gold was not adopted until 1879. In those days, coins were *full-bodied money* in that their metal content was worth the same as their face values. Paper money then was *representative full-bodied money* because the paper money was backed by an amount of precious metal equal to the money's face value.

---

1. For a more detailed look at the early development of international finance, see Robert D. Fraser, *International Banking and Finance,* 6th ed., Washington, DC: R & H Publishers, 1984, ch. 2.

INTERNET ACTIVITY

Go to the International Monetary Fund Web site, http://www.imf.org, and find information about "special drawing rights" and how they are used as reserve assets.

During the 1800s most other developed countries also had their own currencies tied to gold, silver, or both. By the end of the 1800s most countries had adopted just the gold standard. However, coinciding with the start of World War I, most countries went off the gold standard. For example, the Federal Reserve Act of 1913 provided for the issuance of Federal Reserve Notes, called *fiat money* because they were not backed by either gold or silver. Recall from Chapter 1 that the government decreed the notes to be "legal tender" for purposes of making payments and discharging public and private debts. Fiat money has value that is based solely on confidence in the U.S. government's being able to achieve economic growth and maintain price stability. Most foreign governments also moved to monetary systems based on fiat money.

A major criticism of the gold standard was that as the volume of world trade increased over the years, the supply of "new" gold would fail to keep pace. Thus, without some form of supplementary international money, the result would be international deflation. A second criticism of the gold standard was a lack of an international organization to monitor and report whether countries were deviating from the standard when it was in their own best interests.

World War I Through World War II: 1915–1944

During the interwar period from 1915 through 1944, which encompassed most of World War 1, the period in between, and World War II, an attempt was made to go back onto the gold standard. Many nations returned to the gold standard during the 1920s only to go off it again in the early 1930s because of financial crises associated with the Great Depression. A series of bank failures and continued outflow of gold caused the United States to abandon the gold standard in 1933.

Bretton Woods Fixed Exchange Rate System: 1945–1972

In mid-1944, authorities from all major nations met in Bretton Woods, New Hampshire, to formulate a post–World War II international monetary system. The ***International Monetary Fund (IMF)*** was created to promote world trade through monitoring and maintaining fixed exchange rates and by making loans to countries facing balance of trade and payment problems. The International Bank for Reconstruction and Development, or ***World Bank*** also was created to help economic growth in developing countries.

The most significant development of the conference was the exchange rate agreement commonly called the ***Bretton Woods system***, in which individual currencies would be tied to gold through the U.S. dollar via fixed or pegged exchange rates. One ounce of gold was set equal to $35. Each participating country's currency was then set at a "par" or fixed value in relation to the U.S. dollar. For example, one French franc might be one-seventh of a U.S. dollar or $.1429. Thus, a franc would "indirectly" be worth $5 in gold (i.e., $35 ÷ 7). In essence, one franc could be exchanged for $.1429, which could be exchanged for $5 in gold (.1429 × $35).

Countries adopting the Bretton Woods system could hold their reserves either in gold or U.S. dollars because the dollar was the only currency on the gold standard. This eliminated one of the criticisms associated with all currencies being on a gold standard system: that world economic growth was restricted to the rate of increase in new gold production since gold was the only monetary reserve. Since the Bretton Woods System allowed for the holding of both gold and U.S. dollars as foreign exchange reserves, this new monetary system allowed for less restrictive world economic growth. The negative side of the Bretton Woods system was that the U.S. government had to produce balance-of-payments deficits so that foreign exchange reserves would grow.

Unfortunately, by the 1960s the value of the U.S. gold stock was less than the amount of foreign holdings of dollars. This, of course, caused concern about the viability of the Bretton Woods system. To help keep the system operating, in 1970 the IMF created a new reserve asset called ***special drawing rights (SDRs)***, a basket or portfolio of currencies that could be used to make international payments. At first the SDR comprised a weighted average of sixteen currencies. At the beginning of the 1980s the SDR basket was reduced to include only five major currencies. The current SDR basket includes the U.S. dollar (45 percent weight), euro (29 percent weight), Japanese yen (15 percent weight), and British pound (11 percent weight).

Attempts were made to save the Bretton Woods system in 1971 when representatives of major central banks met at the Smithsonian Institution in Washington, D.C., and raised the price of gold to $38 per ounce. In early 1973 the price of gold was further increased to $42 per ounce. However, the end of fixed exchange rates was at hand.

International Monetary Fund (IMF)
created to promote world trade through monitoring and maintaining fixed exchange rates and by making loans to countries with payment problems

World Bank
International Bank for Reconstruction and Development created to help economic growth in developing countries

Bretton Woods system
international monetary system in which the U.S. dollar was valued in gold and other exchange rates were pegged to the dollar

special drawing rights (SDRs)
reserve asset created by the IMF and consisting of a basket of currencies that could be used to make international payments

CONCEPT CHECK

What was the Bretton Woods System of exchange rates?

What exchange rate system is in use today?

flexible exchange rates
a system in which currency exchange rates are determined by supply and demand

GLOBAL DISCUSSION

European Union (EU)
organization established to promote trade and economic development among European countries

European Monetary Union (EMU)
organization of European countries that agreed to have a common overall monetary policy and the euro as common currency

euro
official currency of the countries in the European Monetary Union

CONCEPT CHECK

What is the European Union?

What is the European Monetary Union?

What is a euro?

Flexible Exchange Rate System: 1973–Present

Beginning in March 1973 major currencies were allowed to "float" against one another. By the mid-1970s gold was abandoned as a reserve asset and a system of **flexible exchange rates**, in which currency exchange rates are determined by supply and demand, was accepted by IMF members. A primary objection to flexible exchange rates is the possibility of wide swings in response to changes in supply and demand, with a resulting uncertainty in world trade. Evidence indicates that exchange rates indeed have been much more volatile since the collapse of the Bretton Woods system compared to when the system was in place.

Today, many countries allow their currencies to float against others, including Australia, Japan, Canada, the United States, and the United Kingdom. The European Monetary Union also allows the euro to float freely. In contrast, India, China, and Russia employ semifloating or managed floating systems involving active government intervention. China, for example, pegs its currency to the dollar, with adjustments being related to monetary targets. Thus, the current exchange rate system is a composite of flexible or floating exchange rates, managed floating exchange rates, and pegged exchange rates.

EUROPEAN UNIFICATION

EUROPEAN UNION

Efforts to unify the countries of Europe have resulted in a common currency for twelve of the countries and major changes in the international monetary system. The **European Union (EU)** was established to promote trade and economic development among European countries. Economic integration was to be achieved by eliminating barriers that previously restricted the flow of labor, goods, and financial capital among countries. The European Union's history can be traced back to a treaty that established the *European Economic Community (EEC)* in 1957. The EEC became the *European Community (EC)* in 1978, and the EC became the EU in 1994.

In late 1991, members of the European Community met in Maastricht, Netherlands, to prepare, sign, and later ratify the *Maastricht Treaty*, which provided for economic convergence, the fixing of member country exchange rates, and the introduction of the euro as the common currency at the beginning of 1999. By 1995 the fifteen EU members were Austria, Belgium, Denmark, Finland, France, Germany, Greece, Ireland, Italy, Luxembourg, Netherlands, Portugal, Spain, Sweden, and the United Kingdom. In May 2004, the European Union grew to a total of twenty-five members with the addition of Cyprus, Czech Republic, Estonia, Hungary, Latvia, Lithuania, Malta, Poland, Slovakia, and Slovenia. At the beginning of 2007, Bulgaria and Romania were added to the European Union, resulting in a union of twenty-seven independent states.

EUROPEAN MONETARY UNION

The **European Monetary Union (EMU)** began as a twelve-member subset of the original fifteen members. By ratifying the Maastricht Treaty, the EMU agreed to have overall monetary policy set by the *European Central Bank (ECB)* and adopted the euro as its common currency. Of the original fifteen EU members, Denmark, Sweden, and the United Kingdom chose not to join the EMU. Slovenia was added to the EMU in 2004 when it was allowed to adopt the euro as its currency. None of the other eleven "new" members of the EU that joined in 2004 or 2007 currently qualify for EMU status because they do not comply with the standards for budget deficits and government debt relative to gross domestic product.

THE EURO

On January 1, 1999, the official currency of the European Monetary Union members became the **euro**, a paper currency consisting of seven denominations from 5 to 500. Coins were designed and minted separately. At the beginning of 2002, individual EMU countries' currencies began being phased out; only the euro coin and currency were legal tender by July 2002.

Designing the euro paper currency was a difficult task. It could not include images (e.g., the Eiffel Tower) that could be associated with a single country. Likewise, portraits of individuals

SMALL BUSINESS PRACTICE
Finding Foreign Customers

To conduct business in a foreign country, a domestic firm must either export to that country or produce goods or offer services in that country. Exporting may take place indirectly or directly. Indirect exporting by U.S. companies involves U.S.-based exporters. These exporters may sell for manufacturers, buy for overseas customers, buy and sell for their own account, and/or buy on behalf of middle-persons or wholesalers.

Exporters that sell for manufacturers usually are manufacturers' export agents or export management companies. A manufacturer's export agent usually represents several noncompeting domestic manufacturers. An export management company acts as an export department for a number of noncompeting domestic firms. Exporters that purchase for overseas customers are called export commission agents since they are paid a commission by foreign purchasers to buy on their behalf.

Small businesses usually find it necessary to use indirect exporting. Direct exporting uses manufacturers' agents, distributors, and retailers located in the countries where they are conducting business. Only large domestic firms are able to engage in direct exporting.

Various forms of government assistance are available to help businesses in their exporting efforts. Many states have government "trade export" departments that assist firms in their export activities. At the federal level, the Export-Import Bank of the United States was founded in 1934 to aid domestic businesses in finding foreign customers and markets for their products. Export credit insurance also is available to help exporters. The Foreign Credit Insurance Association (FCIA) provides credit insurance policies to U.S. exporters to protect against nonpayment by foreign customers.

In some instances, "countertrading" is used to foster sales to foreign customers. Under such an arrangement, a U.S. exporter sells its goods to a foreign producer in exchange for goods produced by that foreign company. Simple kinds of countertrading take the form of a barter arrangement between a domestic firm and a foreign firm.

GLOBAL DISCUSSION

(e.g., royalty, military leaders) could not be used. Ultimately, the euro was designed to include "gates" and "windows" for the front of the bills "to symbolize the future"; "bridges" were chosen for the back of the bills. The paper currency uses multicolored ink, watermarks, and three-dimensional holographic images to thwart counterfeiting efforts.

CURRENCY EXCHANGE MARKETS AND RATES

CURRENCY EXCHANGE MARKETS

currency exchange markets
electronic markets where banks and institutional traders buy and sell currencies on behalf of businesses, other clients, and themselves

We ordinarily think of a market as a specific place or institution, but this is not always so. *Currency exchange markets*, also called *foreign exchange markets*, are electronic markets where banks and institutional traders buy and sell various currencies on behalf of businesses, other clients, and themselves. The major financial centers of the world are connected electronically so that when an individual or firm engaged in a foreign transaction deals with a local bank, that individual or firm is, in effect, dealing with the exchange markets of the world. Transactions throughout the world may be completed in only a few minutes by virtue of the effective communications network serving the various financial institutions, including central banks of every nation.

foreign exchange markets
same as currency exchange markets

EXCHANGE RATE QUOTATIONS

currency exchange rate
value of one currency relative to another currency

A *currency exchange rate* indicates the value of one currency relative to another currency. Table 18.1 shows the currency exchange rates for a variety of foreign currencies relative to the U.S. dollar on March 19, 2007. Currency exchange rates are stated in two basic ways. The *direct quotation method* indicates the value of one unit of a foreign currency in terms of a home country's currency. For illustration purposes, let's focus on the U.S. dollar as the domestic or home country's currency relative to the Economic Monetary Union's euro. Notice in Table 18.1 that the "U.S. dollar equivalent" of one euro was $1.3310; stated differently, it took $1.3310 to buy one euro. The *indirect quotation method* indicates the number of units of a foreign currency needed to purchase one unit of the home country's currency. By again turning to Table 18.1, we see that it takes .7509 euros to purchase one U.S. dollar.

direct quotation method
indicates the amount of a home country's currency needed to purchase one unit of a foreign currency

indirect quotation method
indicates the number of units of a foreign currency needed to purchase one unit of the home country's currency

Table 18.1 also shows the value of other major currencies in U.S. dollar terms on March 19, 2007. An Australia dollar was worth $.7937, a United Kingdom (British) pound had a value $1.9402, a Swiss franc equaled $.8289, and a Japanese yen was worth $.008588. The corresponding indirect quotations in units relative to one U.S. dollar were Australia dollar = 1.2590, United Kingdom pound = .5151, Swiss franc = 1.2070, and Japanese yen = 116.38. It should be apparent

CONCEPT CHECK

What are currency exchange markets?

INTERNET ACTIVITY

Go to the European Central Bank Web site, http://www. ecb.int, and find information about the history of the euro.

TABLE 18.1
Selected Foreign Exchange Rates, March 19, 2007

COUNTRY	CURRENCY	U.S. DOLLAR EQUIVALENT (DIRECT METHOD)	CURRENCY PER U.S. DOLLAR (INDIRECT METHOD)
Australia	Dollar	0.7937	1.2590
Canada	Dollar	0.6492	1.1770
China	Yuan	0.1293	7.7362
Denmark	Krone	0.1788	5.5941
Hong Kong	Dollar	0.1280	7.8116
India	Rupee	0.02274	43.975
Japan	Yen	0.008588	116.3800
Mexico	Peso	0.0898	11.1371
Russia	Ruble	.03841	26.035
Singapore	Dollar	0.6555	1.5255
South Africa	Rand	0.1344	7.4405
Sweden	Krona	0.1436	6.9650
Switzerland	Franc	0.8289	1.2070
United Kingdom	Pound	1.9402	0.5151
European Monetary Union	Euro	1.3310	0.7509

Sources: http://www.Reuters.com, http://www.money.cnn.com, and other sources.

that it is easy to find the other quotation if we know either the direct quotation or the indirect quotation. For example, the indirect quotation can be calculated as follows:

$$\text{Indirect Quotation} \atop \text{(foreign currency units)} = \frac{1}{\text{Direct Quotation} \atop \text{(home currency value)}} \qquad (18.1)$$

INTERNET ACTIVITY

Go to the CNNMoney Web site, http://money.cnn.com. Access "markets" and then "currencies" and find current currency exchange rates for the U.S. dollar relative to the Australian dollar, British pound, and Canadian dollar. Find either the direct or indirect exchange rate and calculate the other one.

For illustration purposes, let's use the euro versus U.S. dollar relationships previously noted. A euro was worth $1.3310 and represents a direct quotation where the United States is the home country. To find the indirect quotation, we would calculate:

$$\text{Indirect Quotation} = \frac{1}{\$1.3310} = .7509 \text{ euros}$$

Of course, if we knew that the indirect quotation for the euro relative to the dollar was .7509 euros per U.S. dollar, we could divide that value into 1 to get the direct quotation value: 1 ÷ .7509 = 1.3310 or $1.3310.

It is worth noting that electronic and newspaper exchange rate quotes are for large unit transfers within the currency exchange markets. Consequently, individuals buying foreign currencies would not get exactly the same ratio. The currency exchange prices for an individual always favor the seller, who makes a margin of profit.

The balance in the foreign account of a U.S. bank is subject to constant drain as the bank sells foreign currency claims to individuals who import goods or obtain services from other countries. These banks may reestablish a given deposit level in their correspondent banks either through selling dollar claims in the foreign countries concerned or by buying claims from another dealer in the foreign exchange.

FACTORS THAT AFFECT CURRENCY EXCHANGE RATES

CONCEPT CHECK

What is the difference between the direct and indirect quotation methods for stating currency exchange rates?

Each currency exchange rate shown in Table 18.1 is said to be a ***spot exchange rate***, or the current rate being quoted for delivery of the currency "on the spot." Actually, it is common practice to have up to two days for delivery after the trade date. It is also possible to enter into a contract for the purchase or sale of a currency when delivery will take place at a future date. In this case, the negotiated exchange rate is referred to as a ***forward exchange rate***.

Supply and Demand Relationships

The supply and demand relationship involving two currencies is said to be in "balance" or equilibrium at the current or spot exchange rate. Demand for a foreign currency derives from the demand

spot exchange rate
rate being quoted for current delivery of the currency

forward exchange rate
rate for the purchase or sale of a currency where delivery will take place at a future date

FIGURE 18.1
Exchange Rate Determination in the Currency Exchange Market

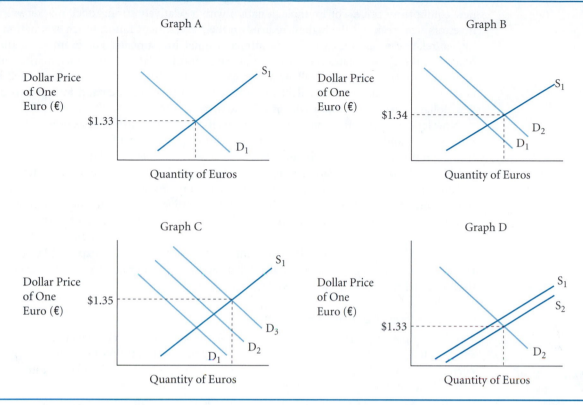

CONCEPT CHECK

What factors determine currency exchange rates?

for the goods, services, and financial assets of a country (or group of countries, such as the EMU). For example, U.S. consumers and investors demand a variety of EMU member goods, services, and financial assets, most of which must be paid for in euros. The supply of euros comes from EMU member demand for U.S. goods, services, and financial assets. A change in the relative demand for euros versus U.S. dollars will cause the spot exchange rate to change. Currency exchange rates also depend on relative inflation rates, relative interest rates, and political and economic risks.

Figure 18.1 illustrates how exchange rates are determined in a currency exchange market. Graph A depicts a supply and demand relationship between the U.S. dollar and the European Monetary Union euro (€). The market, in our example, is in balance when one euro is worth $1.33. This price reflects the market-clearing price that equates the demand (D_1) for euros relative to the supply (S_1) of euros.

Now, assume Americans increase their demand for products and services from EMU member countries such as Germany and France. These products and services would be priced in euros. Americans will need to exchange their dollars for euros to pay for their purchases. The consequence is an increase or shift in demand for euros from D_1 to D_2, as depicted in Graph B of Figure 18.1. The supply of euros reflects demand by EMU member countries for U.S. products and services, and as long as there is no change, S_1 will remain unchanged. As a consequence of this scenario, the increased demand for euros results in a new higher equilibrium price of $1.34.

A further increased demand for the goods and services from EMU member countries could cause the dollar price or value of one pound to increase even more. Graph C in Figure 18.1 depicts such an increase as a shift from D_2 to D_3. Again, with no change in the supply of euros, the new market-clearing price of a pound might be $1.35. Of course, as the euro's dollar value increases, the prices of EMU member products also increase. At some point, as EMU member products become more costly, U.S. demand for these foreign goods will decline. Graph D depicts this cutback in U.S. demand for euros as a shift downward from D_3 in Graph C to D_2. In a similar fashion, the higher dollar value of the euro in Graph C makes U.S. goods and services less costly to EMU members, and thus the supply of euros might increase or shift from S_1 to S_2. The net result could be a new equilibrium exchange rate in which the dollar price of a euro is $1.33.

A change in the demand for one country's financial assets relative to another country's financial assets also will cause the currency exchange rate between the two countries to change to a new equilibrium price. For example, a nation with a relatively strong stock market will attract investors who seek out the highest returns on their investment funds, much as a nation with a higher relative economic growth rate attracts capital investments. For example, if the stock market in the United States is expected to perform poorly relative to the stock markets in EMU member countries, investors will switch or move their debt investments denominated in U.S. dollars into euro-denominated debt investments. This increased demand for euros relative to U.S. dollars will cause the euro's dollar value to increase.

Now let's turn our attention to what happens if changes occur in relative nominal (observed) interest rates and inflation rates between two countries. Recall that for government debt securities, the nominal interest rate is composed of a "real rate" plus an inflation expectation.[2] Thus, the higher (lower) the inflation rate, the higher (lower) will be the nominal interest rate. A nation with a relatively lower inflation rate will have a relatively stronger currency. For example, if inflation becomes lower in the United States relative to EMU member countries, EMU member products of comparable quality will become increasingly more expensive. Americans will find it less expensive to buy American products, and so will EMU members. The result will be fewer EMU member imports into the United States and greater U.S. exports to EMU member countries, causing an appreciation of the dollar relative to the euro. For example, the euro might decline in value from $1.33 to, say, $1.31.

Inflation, Interest Rates, and Other Factors

purchasing power parity (PPP)

currency of a country with relatively higher inflation rate will depreciate relative to the currency of a country with a relatively lower inflation rate

Purchasing power parity (PPP) states that a country with a relatively higher expected inflation rate will have its currency depreciate relative to a country (or group of countries using a single currency) with a relatively lower inflation rate. For example, if the U.S. inflation rate is expected to be 6 percent next year and the EMU member inflation rate is expected to be 3 percent, then we would expect the U.S. dollar to depreciate and the euro to appreciate over the next year. Let's assume that the United States is the home country (hc), the EMU members represent the foreign country (fc), and the expected inflation rate is designated as InfR. In general equation form, we can say that the current or spot rate (SR_0) is equal to the future or forward rate in one year (FR_1) times the expected relative inflation rates, as follows:

$$FR_1 = SR_0 \times \frac{1 + InfR_{hc}}{1 + InfR_{fc}} \tag{18.2}$$

For our example, let's assume that the spot rate for a euro is $1.33. We estimate the forward rate as follows:

$$FR_1 = \$1.33 \times \frac{1.06}{1.03}$$

and

$$FR_1 = \$1.33 \times 1.0291 = \$1.369$$

Thus, based on relative expected inflation rates, we expect the euro to appreciate from $1.33 to $1.369 over the next year.

interest rate parity (IRP)

currency of a country with a relatively higher interest rate will depreciate relative to the currency of a country with a relatively lower interest rate

Interest rate parity (IRP) states that a country with a relatively higher nominal interest rate will have its currency depreciate relative to a country with a relatively lower nominal interest rate. For example, let's assume that the interest rate (IntR) on a one-year U.S. government debt security is 9 percent, while the interest rate on a comparable one-year EMU government debt security is 6 percent. We can use an equation similar to the one for PPP to calculate the forward rate based on IRP:

$$FR_1 = SR_0 \times \frac{1 + IntR_{hc}}{1 + IntR_{fc}} \tag{18.3}$$

---

2. We covered the factors that determine interest rates in detail in Chapter 4.

For consistency, let's assume that the spot rate for a euro is $1.33. We estimate the forward rate as follows:

$$FR_1 = \$1.33 \times \frac{1.09}{1.06}$$

and,

$$FR_1 = \$1.33 \times 1.0283 = \$1.368$$

Thus, based on relative one-year government interest rates, we expect the euro to appreciate from $1.33 to $1.368 over the next year.[3]

Political risk is the risk associated with the possibility that a national government might confiscate or expropriate assets held by foreigners. A nation with relatively lower political risk will generally have a relatively stronger currency. *Economic risk* is the risk associated with the possibility of slow or negative economic growth, as well as variability in economic growth. A nation that has a relatively higher economic growth rate, along with growth stability, will generally have a stronger currency. Furthermore, a nation with a relatively stronger economic growth rate will attract more capital inflows relative to a nation growing more slowly. For example, a stronger U.S. economy relative to the British economy will cause investors in both countries to switch from pound investments to dollar investments.

political risk

actions by a sovereign nation to interrupt or change the value of cash flows accruing to foreign investors

economic risk

risk associated with possible slow or negative economic growth, as well as with the likelihood of variability

CURRENCY EXCHANGE RATE APPRECIATION AND DEPRECIATION

The change (appreciation or depreciation) of a foreign currency (FC) relative to a domestic or home currency is typically expressed on a percentage basis:

$$\% \text{ FC Change} = \frac{\text{FC's New Value} - \text{FC's Old Value}}{\text{FC's Old Value}} \tag{18.4}$$

Let's use an example where the demand for EMU member financial assets increases relative to the demand for U.S. financial assets, causing the U.S. dollar value of the euro to increase from $1.33 to $1.36. The associated percent euro change would be:

$$\% \text{ Euro Change} = \frac{\$1.36 - \$1.33}{\$1.33} = \frac{\$0.03}{\$1.33} = 2.26\%$$

In other words, the euro would have appreciated by 2.26 percent relative to the dollar.

Previously we discussed the possibility that the value of an EMU euro might drop from $1.33 to $1.30 if the inflation rate in the United States is lower than the inflation rate for the EMU member countries. The percent change in the euro would be calculated as:

$$\% \text{ Euro Change} = \frac{\$1.30 - \$1.33}{\$1.33} = \frac{-\$0.03}{\$1.33} = -2.26\%$$

Thus, the euro has depreciated by 2.26 percent relative to the U.S. dollar because of the new and relatively higher EMU member inflation rate.

The amount of U.S. dollar ($US) appreciation or depreciation also can be easily calculated, since the value of one currency is simply the inverse of the other currency. For example, when the dollar price of a euro is $1.33, one $US is worth €.752 (i.e., 1 ÷ $1.33). Similarly, when the dollar price of a euro rises to $1.36, one $US is worth 1 ÷ $1.36, or €0.735. When the dollar value of the euro increases, one dollar can be exchanged for fewer euros, and vice versa.

An appreciation (or depreciation) of a home or domestic currency (DC) relative to a foreign currency can be expressed on a percentage basis as follows:

$$\% \text{ DC Change} = \frac{1/\text{FC's New Value} - 1/\text{FC's Old Value}}{1/\text{FC's Old Value}} \tag{18.5}$$

---

3. Notice that the PPP and IRP provide slightly different estimates of the one-year forward rate. This is due to the fact that the ratios of 1.06/1.03 and 1.09/1.06 are slightly different.

INTERNET ACTIVITY

Go to the CNNMoney Web site, http://money.cnn.com. Access "markets" and then "currencies" and find current currency exchange rates for the U.S. dollar relative to the Japanese yen, European Monetary Union euro, and the Swiss franc. Find either the direct or indirect exchange rate and calculate the other one.

arbitrage
buying commodities, securities, or bills of exchange in one market and immediately selling them in another to make a profit from price differences in the two markets

Using the preceding data for the relative interest rate example involving the American dollar and the EMU euro, we have:

$$\% \ \$US \ Change = \frac{1/\$1.36 - 1/\$1.33}{1/\$1.33} = \frac{€ \ 0.735 - € \ 0.752}{€ \ 0.752}$$

$$= \frac{-0.0017}{0.752} = -2.26\%$$

Thus, the U.S. dollar in this example depreciated by 2.26 percent relative to the euro, which is the mirror opposite of the 2.26 percent appreciation of the euro relative to the $US. The two examples produced the same percentage change (one positive and the other negative) because the base from which the calculations were made was the same.

ARBITRAGE

Arbitrage is the simultaneous, or nearly simultaneous, purchasing of commodities, securities, or bills of exchange in one market and selling them in another where the price is higher. In international exchange, variations in quotations among countries at any time are quickly brought into alignment through the arbitrage activities of international financiers. For example, if the exchange rate was reported in New York at €1 = $1.34 and in Brussels, Belgium, at €1 = $1.33, alert international *arbitrageurs* simultaneously would sell claims to euros in New York at the rate of $1.34 and would have Brussels correspondents sell claims on U.S. dollars in Brussels at the rate of $1.33 for each euro. Such arbitrage would be profitable only when dealing in large sums. Under these circumstances, if an arbitrageur sold a claim on €100 million in New York, $131 million would be received. The corresponding sale of claims on American dollars in Brussels would be at the rate of €100 million for $133 million. Hence, a profit of $1 million would be realized on the transaction. A quotation differential of as little as one-sixteenth of one cent may be sufficient to encourage arbitrage activities.

The ultimate effect of large-scale arbitrage activities on exchange rates is the elimination of the variation between the two markets. The sale of large amounts of claims to American dollars in Brussels would drive up the price for euros, and in New York the sale of claims to euros would force the exchange rate down.

EXCHANGE RATE DEVELOPMENTS FOR THE U.S. DOLLAR

The dollar continues to be an important currency for international commercial and financial transactions. Because of this, both the United States and the rest of the world benefit from a strong and stable U.S. dollar. Its strength and stability depend directly on the ability of the United States to pursue noninflationary economic policies. In the late 1960s and the 1970s, the United States failed to meet this objective. Continuing high inflation led to a dollar crisis in 1978, which threatened the stability of international financial markets.

Figure 18.2 shows the strength of the dollar relative to an index of major currencies that trade widely outside the U.S. for the years 1980 through 2006. As inflation was brought under control in the early 1980s and economic growth accelerated after the 1981–1982 recession, the dollar rose against other major currencies until it reached record highs in 1985. As discussed, relatively higher economic growth and relatively lower inflation rates lead to a relatively stronger currency. These economic developments, coupled with a favorable political climate, caused the value of the dollar to rise sharply.

However, the renewed strength of the dollar contributed to a worsening of the trade imbalance because import prices were effectively reduced while exported U.S. goods became less cost competitive. Beginning in 1985, U.S. economic growth slowed relative to economic growth in other developed countries. Also, the belief that the U.S. government wanted the dollar to decline on a relative basis so as to reduce the trade deficit contributed to a decline in the desirability of holding dollars. This resulted in a major shift toward holding more foreign assets and fewer U.S. assets. As a consequence, the dollar's value declined by 1987 to levels below those in place when flexible exchange rates were reestablished in 1973. Since 1987 the value of the dollar in international exchange has continued to fluctuate, but within a fairly narrow range compared to the 1980–1987 period. However, since 2002 and through 2006, the U.S. dollar value declined steeply relative to an index of major currencies.

FIGURE 18.2
U.S. Dollar Value Relative to an Index of Major Currencies

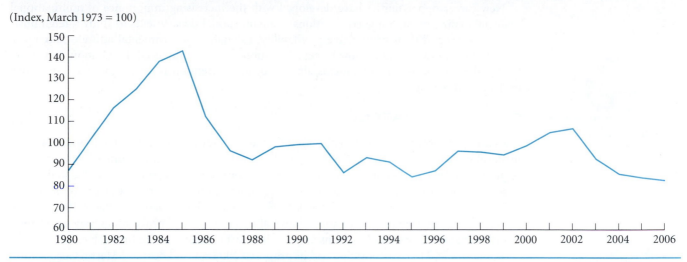

(Index, March 1973 = 100)

Source: *Federal Reserve Bulletin* and *Statistical Supplements,* (various issues).

CONCEPT CHECK

What actions can firms that have foreign sales take to reduce foreign exchange risk?

A stronger dollar leads to concern about the deficit in the U.S. trade balance, but at the same time it offers hope of lower inflation. A stronger dollar results in more imports of foreign merchandise since it requires fewer dollars for purchase. Just as a U.S. tourist abroad finds it cheaper to travel when the dollar is strong, importers find prices lower when their dollars increase in relative strength. When the dollar weakens, inflation may follow, countered by a reduced balance of trade deficit.

CONDUCTING BUSINESS INTERNATIONALLY

MANAGING FOREIGN EXCHANGE RISK

Firms that have foreign sales must be concerned with the stability of the governments and changing values of currency in the countries in which they do business. They must also pay attention to commodity price changes and other uncertainties related to monetary systems.

Large firms usually have special departments that handle international transactions. These firms may engage in foreign exchange speculation as opportunities arise, but risk reduction is their primary goal. Among the possible actions of skilled foreign exchange specialists are hedging, adjusting accounts receivable and payable procedures, cash management, and borrowing and lending activities. Existing or anticipated variations in the value of foreign currencies guide all these actions. For example, a seller with a claim for payment within ninety days may anticipate a possible decline in the currency value of his customer's country. The seller can hedge by entering into a futures contract for the delivery of that currency at the existing exchange rate on the day of the contract.[4] By so doing, a loss in the collection process is offset by a gain in the delivery process ninety days hence. The fee for the futures contract becomes a cost of the transaction.

Large multinational companies enjoy special opportunities for risk reduction and speculation since they can move cash balances from one country to another as monetary conditions warrant. For example, if a decline in the value of a particular currency is expected, cash in the branch in that country may be moved back to the United States; or a firm may borrow funds in a foreign market and move them immediately to the United States (or to another country) with the expectation of repaying the loan at a reduced exchange rate. This is speculation rather than a risk-reduction activity. An expected decline in a currency may lead to an attempt to accelerate collection of accounts receivable, with funds transferred quickly to another country. Payments on accounts payable may be delayed in the expectation of a decline in exchange rates. If, on the

---

4. We discussed futures contracts in the Learning Extension at the end of Chapter 9.

other hand, a foreign currency is expected to increase in relative value, the preceding actions would be reversed.

New career opportunities have developed with the increasing importance of multinational financial management. Some corporations maintain special departments to study foreign business activities and their prospective profitability; to analyze governmental attitudes, tax rates, and duties; and to determine how foreign operations are to be financed. In addition, to protect bank balances and other investments almost constant attention must be given to day-to-day exchange rate changes.

ETHICAL ISSUES

ETHICAL CONSIDERATIONS

The concept of acceptable ethical behavior differs across cultures and countries. In some primarily developing countries it seems to be acceptable practice for government officials and others to request "side" payments and even bribes as a means for foreign companies being able to do business in these countries. This is morally wrong. In addition, the *Foreign Corrupt Practices Act (FCPA)* prohibits U.S. firms from bribing foreign officials. For violators of the FCPA, the U.S. Justice Department may impose monetary penalties and criminal proceedings may be brought against violators. Government actions may result in lost reputations and firm values.

For example, Titan Corporation had its proposed 2004 sale to Lockheed Martin Corporation implode because it could not promptly resolve a bribery investigation brought by the Justice Department.[5] Another example was the 2004 indictment of two former HealthSouth Corporation executives for conspiracy in a bribery scheme involving a Saudi Arabian hospital. An attempt was made to conceal the bribery by setting up a bogus consulting contract for the director general of the Saudi foundation that owned the hospital. The former HealthSouth executives were indicted after a Justice Department investigation alleged that they had violated the *U.S. Travel Act* by using interstate commerce when making the bribes and the FCPA by falsely reflecting the bogus bribe payments as legitimate consulting expenses on HealthSouth's financial statements.[6]

When conducting business activities in certain foreign countries, business executives also are sometimes faced with extortion demands by organized criminals. Most of us would agree that extortion payments are morally wrong. Paying organized criminals is not different from paying corrupt government officials.

GLOBAL DISCUSSION

FINANCING INTERNATIONAL TRADE

One of the substantial financial burdens of any industrial firm is the process of manufacture itself. When a U.S. manufacturer exports goods to distant places such as India or Australia, funds are tied up not only for the period of manufacture but also for a lengthy period of transportation. To reduce costs, manufacturers may require the foreign importer to pay for the goods as soon as they are on the way to their destination. In this way, a substantial financial burden is transferred to the importer.

FINANCING BY THE EXPORTER

If the exporter has confidence in foreign customers and is in a financial position to sell to them on an open-book account, then sales arrangements should operate very much as in domestic trade, subject, of course, to the complex nature of any international transaction.

Sight and Time Drafts

draft (bill of exchange)
an unconditional order for the payment of money from one person to another

As an alternative to shipping merchandise on open-account financing, the exporter may use a collection draft. A *draft (bill of exchange)* is an unconditional written order, signed by the party drawing it, requiring the party to whom it is addressed to pay a certain sum of money to order or to bearer. A draft may require immediate payment by the importer upon its presentation—on

5. Jonathan Karp, "As Titan Mutates to Meet Needs of Pentagon, Risks Become Clear," *Wall Street Journal* (June 28, 2004), p. A1.

6. "Ex-HealthSouth Execs Indicted," http://money.cnn.com/2004/07/01/news/international/healthsouth.reut/index.htm, (accessed July 7, 2004).

FIGURE 18.3
Sight Draft or Bill of Exchange

$ 2,500.00	New Orleans, Louisiana, August 15, 20–

At sight -

_____ PAY TO THE

ORDER OF   Mervin J. Mansfield

Two thousand five hundred no/100 - - - - - - _____ DOLLARS

VALUE RECEIVED AND CHARGE TO ACCOUNT OF

TO   Brazilian Import Company   NEW ORLEANS EXPORT COMPANY

No.   11678 Rio de Janeiro, Brazil   _Theresa M. Jones_

---

sight draft
draft requiring immediate payment

time draft
draft that is payable at a specified future date

documentary draft
draft that is accompanied by an order bill of lading and other documents

order bill of lading
document given by a transportation company that lists goods to be transported and terms of the shipping agreement

clean draft
a draft that is not accompanied by any special documents

CONCEPT CHECK

What is meant by a draft or bill of exchange?

What is an order bill of lading?

demand—or it may require only acceptance on the part of the importer, providing for payment at a specified future time. An instrument requiring immediate payment is classified as a **sight draft**; one requiring payment later is a **time draft**. A draft may require remittance, or payment, in the currency of the country of the exporter or of the importer, depending on the transaction's terms. An example of a sight draft form is shown in Figure 18.3.

Drafts may be either documentary or clean. A **documentary draft** is accompanied by an order bill of lading along with other papers such as insurance receipts, certificates of sanitation, and consular invoices. The **order bill of lading** (see Figure 18.4) represents the written acceptance of goods for shipment by a transportation company and the terms under which the goods are to be transported to their destination. In addition, the order bill of lading carries title to the merchandise being shipped, and only its holder may claim the merchandise from the transportation company. The documentary sight draft is generally referred to as a D/P draft (documentary payments draft), and the documentary time draft is referred to as a D/A draft (documentary acceptance draft).

A **clean draft** is one that is not accompanied by any special documents and is generally used when the exporter has confidence in the importer's ability to meet the draft when presented. Once the merchandise is shipped to the importer, it is delivered by the transportation company, regardless of any actions by the importer in terms of the draft.

Bank Assistance in the Collection of Drafts

An importer will generally try to avoid paying for a purchase before the goods are actually shipped because several days or perhaps weeks may elapse before the goods arrive. But the exporter is often unwilling to send the draft and documents directly to the importer. Therefore, the exporter usually works through a commercial bank.

A New York exporter dealing with an importer in Portugal with whom there has been little experience may ship goods on the basis of a documentary draft that has been deposited for collection with the local bank. That bank, following the specific instructions regarding the manner of collection, forwards the draft and the accompanying documents to its correspondent bank in Lisbon. The correspondent bank holds the documents until payment is made in the case of a sight draft or until acceptance is obtained if a time draft is used. When collection is made on a sight draft, it is remitted to the exporter.

Financing Through the Exporter's Bank

It is important to recognize that throughout the preceding transaction the banking system only provided a service to the exporter and in no way financed the transaction itself. The exporter's bank, however, may offer financing assistance by allowing the exporter to borrow against the security of a documentary draft. Such loans have the financial strength of both the exporter and the importer to support them, since documents for taking possession of the merchandise are released only after the importer has accepted the draft.

FIGURE 18.4
Order Bill of Lading

UNITED STATES LINES CO.
(SPACES IMMEDIATELY BELOW FOR SHIPPERS MEMORANDA– NOT PART OF BILL OF LADING)

FORWARDING AGENT – REFERENCES	EXPORT DEC. No.
John Doe Shipping Co., #E6776 F.M.B. #9786	X67-90687

DELIVERING CARRIER TO STEAMER:	CAR NUMBER – REFERENCE
Penn Central Company	876528

BILL OF LADING
(SHORT FORM)

(NOT NEGOTIABLE UNLESS CONSIGNED "TO ORDER")

SHIP American Banker	FLAG	PIER	PORT OF LOADING
PORT OF DISCHARGE FROM SHIP Liverpool AM.		61 N.R.	NEW YORK
(Where goods are to be delivered to consignee or On-carrier)		THROUGH BILL OF LADING	
If goods to be transhipped beyond Port of Discharge, show destination Here ⟶ To			

SHIPPER _____ Midwest Printing Company

CONSIGNED TO: ORDER OF _____ M.T. Wilson & Co.

ADDRESS ARRIVAL NOTICE TO _____ Same at 15 Dock St., Liverpool, E.C. 3

PARTICULARS FURNISHED BY SHIPPER OF GOODS

MARKS AND NUMBERS	NO. OF PKGS.	DESCRIPTION OF PACKAGES AND GOODS	MEASUREMENT	GROSS WEIGHT IN POUNDS
M. T. W. & Co. Liverpool	56	Books		10,145
		SPECIMEN		

FREIGHT PAYABLE IN   NEW YORK

(10,145) @_____ PER 2240 LBS....$ _____	(TERMS OF THIS BILL OF LADING CONTINUED FROM REVERSE SIDE HEREOF)
_____ @ _____ PER 100 LBS......$ _____	IN WITNESS WHEREOF, THE MASTER OR AGENT OF SAID VESSEL HAS SIGNED.......**3**
_____ FT. @ _____ PER 40 CU. FT....$ _____	BILLS OF LADING, ALL OF THE SAME TENOR AND DATE, ONE OF WHICH BEING ACCOMPLISHED, THE OTHERS TO STAND VOID.
545 FT. @ $1.05 PER CU. FT........$ 572 25	

UNITED STATES LINES COMPANY

BY _____ *J.H.*
FOR THE MASTER

ISSUED AT NEW YORK, N.Y.

B/L No.

M-105

January	12	20--
MO.	DAY	YEAR

The amount that the exporter can borrow is less than the face amount of the draft and depends mainly on the credit standing of both the exporter and the importer. When the exporter is financially strong enough to offer suitable protection to the bank, a substantial percentage of the draft may be advanced, even though the importer may not be known to the exporter's bank. In other cases, the advance may be based on the importer's financial strength.

The character of the goods shipped also has an important bearing on the amount lent, since the goods offer collateral security for the advance. Goods that are not breakable or perishable are better as collateral; goods for which there is a ready market are preferable to those with a very limited market.

FIGURE 18.5

Banker's Acceptance

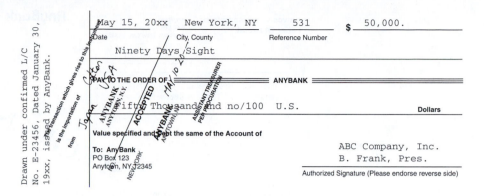

FINANCING BY THE IMPORTER

Like the exporter, the importer may also arrange payment for goods without access to bank credit. When an order is placed, payment in full may be made or a partial payment offered. The partial payment gives some protection to both the exporter and the importer. It protects the exporter against rejection of the goods for no reason, and it gives the importer some bargaining power in the event the merchandise is damaged in shipment or does not meet specifications. When the importer is required to make full payment with an order but wants some protection in the transaction, payment is sent to a bank in the exporter's country. The bank is instructed not to release payment until certain documents are presented to the bank to prove shipment of the goods according to the terms of the transaction. The bank, of course, charges a fee for this service.

Financing Through the Importer's Bank

In foreign trade, because of language barriers and the difficulty in obtaining credit information about companies in foreign countries, the use of the banker's acceptance is common. The *banker's acceptance* is a draft drawn on and accepted by a bank rather than the importing firm. An example of a banker's acceptance is shown in Figure 18.5. The importer must, of course, make arrangements with the bank in advance. The exporter, too, must know before shipment is made whether or not the bank in question has agreed to accept the draft. This arrangement is facilitated by the use of a **commercial letter of credit**, a bank's written statement to an individual or firm guaranteeing acceptance and payment of a draft up to a specified sum if the draft is presented according to the terms of the letter (see Figure 18.6).

commercial letter of credit

statement by a bank guaranteeing acceptance and payment of a draft up to a stated amount

Importer Bank Financing—An Example

The issue of a commercial letter of credit and its use in international finance are shown in this example. The owner of a small exclusive shop in Chicago wishes to import expensive perfumes from Paris. Although the shop is well known locally, its financial reputation is not known widely enough to permit it to purchase from foreign exporters on the basis of an open-book account or drafts drawn on the firm. Under these circumstances the firm would substitute the bank's credit for its own through the use of a letter of credit. Upon application by the firm, the bank issues the letter if it is entirely satisfied that its customer is in satisfactory financial condition.

The letter of credit is addressed to the French exporter of perfumes. The exporter, upon receipt of the commercial letter of credit, would not be concerned about making the shipment. Although the exporter may not have heard of the Chicago firm, the bank issuing the commercial letter of credit may be known to the exporter or to his bank. (International bank directories provide bank credit information.) The French exporter then ships the perfumes and at the same time draws a draft in the appropriate amount on the bank that issued the letter of credit. The draft and the other papers required by the commercial letter of credit are presented to the exporter's bank. The bank sends the draft and the accompanying documents to its New York correspondent, who

FIGURE 18.6

Irrevocable Commercial Letter of Credit

Irrevocable Commercial Letter Of Credit	AnyBank P.O. Box 123 Anytown, New York 12345	**AnyBank**	Cable Address: AnyBank	Letter Of Credit Division

May 2, 20-- $50,000.

Drafts drawn hereunder must be marked
"Drawn under AnyBank Anytown
L/C Ref. E-23456   *and indicate the date hereof

SPECIMEN

ABC Company, Inc.

B. Frank, President

Gentlemen:

We hereby authorize you to draw on AnyBank, Anytown

by order of   J. R. Doe & Company, New York, N.Y.

and for account of   J. R. Doe & Company

up to an aggregate amount of   Fifty Thousand Dollars U.S. Currency

available by your drafts at 90 days sight, for full invoice value, in duplicate
accompanied by   Commercial Invoice in triplicate . . .
             Consular Invoice in duplicate . . .
             Full set of onboard Bills of Lading to order of AnyBank,
Anytown, marked Notify J. R. Doe & Company, New York, N.Y., and bearing
a separate onboard endorsement signed by the Master and also marked
freight collect at port of destination . . . .

Relating to shipment of Cotton.

. . . Any charges for negotiation of the draft(s) are for your account.
. . . Marine and war risk insurance covered by buyers.

Drafts must be drawn and negotiated not later than   October 2, 20--

The amounts thereof must be endorsed on this Letter Of Credit.
We hereby agree with the drawers, endorsers, and bonafide holders of all drafts drawn under and in compliance
with the terms of this credit, that such drafts will be duly honored upon presentation to the drawee.
This letter of credit is subject to the Uniform Customs and Practice for Documentary Credits (1974 Revision) International Chamber Of Commerce Publication No. 290.

Yours very truly,

D. E. Price

D. E. Price
Vice President
Authorized Signature

---

forwards them to the importer's bank in Chicago. The importer's bank thoroughly inspects the papers that accompany the draft to make sure that all provisions of the letter of credit have been met. If the bank is satisfied, the draft is accepted and the appropriate bank officials sign it. The accepted draft, now a banker's acceptance, may be held until maturity by the accepting bank or returned to the exporter on request. If the acceptance is returned to the exporter, it may be held until maturity and sent to the accepting bank for settlement or it may be sold to other investors. An active market for banker's acceptances exists in the world's money centers.

After having accepted the draft, the Chicago bank notifies its customer that it has the shipping documents and that arrangements should be made to take them over. As the shop sells the perfume, it builds up its bank account with daily deposits until it is sufficient to retire the acceptance. The bank can then meet its obligation on the acceptance without having advanced its other funds at any time.

In releasing shipping documents to a customer, some banks prefer to establish an agency arrangement between the firm and the bank whereby the bank retains title to the merchandise. The instrument that provides for this is called a ***trust receipt***. Should the business fail, the bank would not be in the position of an ordinary creditor trying to establish its claim on the business

trust receipt

an instrument through which a bank retains title to goods until they are paid for

assets. Rather, it could repossess, or take back, the goods and place them with another agent for sale since title had never been transferred to the customer. As the merchandise is sold under a trust receipt arrangement, generally the business must deposit the proceeds with the bank until the total amount of the acceptance is reached.

In summary, the banker's acceptance and the commercial letter of credit involve four principal parties: the importer, the importer's bank, the exporter, and the exporter's bank. Each benefits to a substantial degree through this arrangement. The importer benefits by securing adequate credit. The importer's bank benefits because it receives a fee for issuing the commercial letter of credit and for the other services provided in connection with it. The exporter benefits by being assured that payment will be made for the shipment of merchandise. Thus, a sale is made that might otherwise have been rejected because of lack of guaranteed payment. Finally, the exporter's bank benefits if it discounts the acceptance, since it receives a high-grade credit instrument with a definite, short-term maturity. Acceptances held by commercial banks provide a low, but certain, yield, and banks can liquidate them quickly if funds are needed for other purposes.

CONCEPT CHECK

What is meant by a commercial letter of credit?

What is a trust receipt?

BANKER'S ACCEPTANCES

banker's acceptance
a promise of future payment issued by a firm and guaranteed by a bank

The Board of Governors of the Federal Reserve System authorizes member banks to accept drafts that arise in the course of certain types of international transactions. These include the import and export of goods, the shipment of goods between foreign countries, and the storage of highly marketable staple goods in any foreign country. A **banker's acceptance** is a promise of future payment issued by a firm and guaranteed by a bank. The maturity of a banker's acceptance arising out of international transactions may not exceed six months. This authority to engage in banker's acceptance financing is intended to encourage banks to participate in financing international trade and to strengthen the U.S. dollar abroad.

Banker's acceptances are used to finance international transactions on a wide variety of items, including coffee, wool, rubber, cocoa, metals and ores, crude oil, jute, and automobiles. Because of the growth of international trade in general and the increasing competition in foreign markets, banker's acceptances have become increasingly important. Exporters have had to offer more liberal terms on their sales to compete effectively. The banker's acceptance permits them to do so without undue risk.

The cost of financing an international transaction with the banker's acceptance involves not only the interest cost involved in the exporter's discounting the acceptance but also the commission charge of the importer's accepting bank. Foreign central banks and commercial banks regard banker's acceptances as attractive short-term funds commitments. In recent years, foreign banks have held more than half of all dollar-denominated banker's acceptances, with most of the remainder held by domestic banks. Nonfinancial corporations have played only a small role as investors in acceptances. Relatively few firms deal in banker's acceptances. These dealers arrange nearly simultaneous exchanges of purchases and sales.

CONCEPT CHECK

What are banker's acceptances and how are they used?

OTHER AIDS TO INTERNATIONAL TRADE

The Export-Import Bank

Export-Import Bank
bank established to aid in financing and facilitating trade between the United States and other countries

The **Export-Import Bank** was authorized in 1934 and became an independent agency of the government in 1945. The bank's purpose is to help finance and facilitate exports and imports between the United States and other countries. It is the only U.S. agency engaged solely in financing foreign trade.

The Export-Import Bank is a government-owned corporation with capital of $1 billion in nonvoting stock paid in by the U.S. Treasury. It may borrow from the Treasury on a revolving basis and sell short-term discount promissory notes. It pays interest on these loans and dividends on the capital stock. In performing its function, the bank makes long-term loans to private enterprises and governments abroad to finance the purchase of U.S. equipment, goods, and services. The Export-Import Bank also aids substantially in the economic development of foreign countries by giving emergency credits to assist them in maintaining their level of U.S. imports during temporary balance-of-payments difficulties. In addition, the bank finances or guarantees the payment of medium-term commercial export credit extended by exporters and, in partnership with private insurance companies, offers short- and medium-term credit insurance. It lends and guarantees only where repayment is reasonably assured and avoids competition with sources of private capital.

CONCEPT CHECK

What is the Export-Import Bank, and what does it do?

Traveler's Letter of Credit

A firm's buyer who is traveling abroad may not know in advance from which individuals or firms purchases will be made—for example, an art buyer touring several countries. The buyer could carry U.S. currency, but this involves possible physical loss of the money and sometimes a substantial discount for its conversion into the local currency. A traveler's letter of credit is a convenient and safer method for travelers who need large amounts of foreign currency.

The **traveler's letter of credit** is issued by a bank in one country and addressed to a list of foreign banks. These banks are usually correspondents of the issuing bank and have agreed to purchase sight drafts presented to them by persons with appropriate letters of credit. When a bank issues a letter of credit, it sends a copy of the signature of the person to whom the letter is issued to each of its foreign correspondent banks. When someone presents a draft for payment in foreign currency to one of these correspondent banks, his or her signature is compared with the signature the bank already has. The bank may also ask the individual for supplementary identification.

As with a commercial letter of credit, a maximum total draft amount is stated in a traveler's letter of credit. So that an individual with such a letter does not exceed authorized withdrawals, each bank to which the letter is presented enters on it the amount of the draft it has honored.

CONCEPT CHECK

What is a traveler's letter of credit and how is it used internationally?

Traveler's Checks

Traveler's checks, which are offered by banks and other financial intermediaries in the United States, are generally issued in denominations of $10, $20, $50, and $100. These checks, generally purchased by an individual before leaving for a foreign country, promise to pay on demand the even amounts indicated on the faces of the checks. Each check must be signed by the purchaser twice, once when it is bought and again in the presence of a representative of the business, hotel, or financial institution where it is presented for payment. This allows the person cashing a traveler's check to determine whether the signature is authentic.

The use of traveler's checks is widespread and offers several advantages to the traveler, including protection in the event of loss and almost certain acceptance when they are presented for payment. Traveler's checks are usually sold for their face amount plus a charge of 1 percent. They can now be purchased in the United States in major foreign currency denominations—for example, British pounds. This eliminates a traveler's exposure to varying exchange rates and the extra amount that is often charged (in the form of a less favorable exchange rate than the official rate) when U.S. dollar checks are cashed in a foreign country.

CONCEPT CHECK

What are the advantages associated with the use of traveler's checks?

GLOBAL DISCUSSION

BALANCE IN INTERNATIONAL TRANSACTIONS GOAL

Just as monetary policy plays an important role in the nation's stability, growth, interest rates, and price levels, it also helps keep international financial relationships in balance. Since the dollar is widely held as a medium of international exchange, U.S. monetary policy has especially significant effects on the world economy. No nation is a world unto itself, nor can a nation pursue whatever policies it desires without regard to other nations. Policy makers of all economies must recognize the interdependence of their actions in attempting to maintain a balance in international transactions that is sometimes referred to as *international financial equilibrium*.

Briefly, the nations of the world attempt to achieve international financial equilibrium by maintaining a balance in their exchange of goods and services. In general, international trade benefits all countries involved. Consumers benefit by getting lower-cost goods, since the goods come from the country where they are produced most efficiently. Producers benefit by expanding their markets. Well over one-tenth of the U.S. national income comes from selling goods to foreigners, and a like amount of our needs are met through imports. However, individuals and firms make the decisions to import and export, and problems arise if they are out of balance over time.

NATURE OF THE PROBLEM

Exports are sales to foreigners; they are a source of income to domestic producers. Imports divert spending to foreign producers and therefore represent a loss of potential income to domestic producers. When the two are in balance, there is no net effect on total income in the economy. However, an increase in exports over imports tends to expand the economy just as an increase in investment or government spending does. An excess of imports tends to contract the economy.

As in the domestic economy, goods and services are not exchanged directly in international trade; payment flows through monetary or financial transactions. Methods of making payments and financing international trade were discussed previously. Other short- and long-term lending and investment are conducted across national boundaries on a large scale. In addition, government grants for both military and civilian purposes and private gifts and grants are sources of international financial flows. These flows can have an important impact on domestic economies and may affect monetary policy.

Since producers, consumers, and investors in different countries use different currencies, the international financial system requires a mechanism for establishing the relative values, or exchange rates, among currencies, and for handling their actual exchange. Under the system of *flexible exchange rates* that began in 1973, rates are determined in the actual process of exchange, by supply and demand in the foreign exchange market. This system reduces the impact of international financial transactions on domestic money supplies. Still, changes in exchange rates do affect imports and exports and can thus affect domestic production, incomes, and prices. International financial markets strongly influence domestic interest rates and vice versa, so that domestic monetary policy still involves international considerations.

In short, domestic economies are linked to one another in a worldwide economic and financial system. The United States has played a leading role in the development and growth of that system. Before we take a closer look at that role, we should examine the accounting system used to keep track of international financial transactions.

BALANCE-OF-PAYMENTS ACCOUNTS

The U.S. **balance of payments** involves all of its international transactions, including foreign investment, private and government grants, U.S. military spending overseas, and many other items besides the buying and selling of goods and services. The most important element of the balance of payments is the **balance of trade**, which is the net balance of exports and imports of goods and services. A more narrow view considers only the import and export of goods and is termed the **merchandise trade balance**. The merchandise trade balance was consistently favorable between the 1950s and the beginning of the 1970s. However, imports of goods have exceeded exports since the latter part of the 1970s.

The following are exports, imports, and balance on goods amounts in billions of dollars for selected years at the beginning of each decade beginning with 1980 and for 2005:

YEAR	EXPORTS	IMPORTS	BALANCE ON GOODS
1980	$224.3	−$249.8	−$25.5
1990	387.4	−498.4	−111.0
2000	772.0	−1,224.4	−452.4
2005	894.6	−1,677.4	−782.8

Source: *Economic Report of the President*, February 2007, p. 348.

As recorded in the preceding table, exports have increased nearly four times from $224.3 billion in 1980 to $894.6 billion in 2005. However, over the same period imports have increased well over six times from $249.8 billion in 1980 to $1,677.4 billion in 2005. Over this same period, the balance on goods grew from −$25.5 billion to −$782.8 billion in 2005.

Factors that impact international trade balances include the exchange value of the U.S. dollar relative to other currencies, relative inflation rates, and economic growth. A relatively stronger U.S. economy means that more will be spent on imports, while the weaker foreign economy means that less will be spent on U.S. exports. A relatively weaker real exchange rate, where the nominal exchange rate is adjusted for inflation differences, makes for a weaker U.S. dollar, which lowers the dollar cost of U.S. goods relative to foreign goods.

INTERNET ACTIVITY

Go to the CNNMoney Web site, http://money.cnn.com. Access "markets" and then "currencies" and find current currency exchange rates for the European Monetary Union euro relative to the United Kingdom (British) pound, Japanese yen, and Swiss Franc. Find both direct and indirect currency exchange quotations.

balance of payments
summary of all economic transactions between one country and the rest of the world

balance of trade
net value of a country's exports of goods and services compared to its imports

merchandise trade balance
net difference between a country's import and export of goods

VALERIE R. COLVILLE
Vice President, Project Finance
Group, Fluor Corporation

BA, Geology, Williams College
MSc, Petroleum Geology, University
of Wisconsin
Executive MBA, University of Michigan

*"We hedge our exchange
rate positions and manage
our cross-currency positions
on a daily basis."*

Q: *Describe Fluor and its international operations.*

A: Fluor Corporation is one of the largest publicly traded engineering and construction companies in the world. With over 50,000 employees worldwide, we provide engineering, construction, procurement, and operations and maintenance services to clients in sixteen industry sectors, including energy, chemicals, mining, manufacturing, power/utilities, telecommunications, transportation, operations, and maintenance services. About 50 percent of our revenues come from international projects, and we have offices in seventy countries globally. This local presence helps us understand the business environment in which we operate.

Q: *What are your current position and responsibilities?*

A: As Vice President, Project Finance, I am one of only five women in Fluor's 200-person worldwide senior management group. I arrange debt and equity financing from the global financial markets for each of our business units for the following regions: in Europe, Africa, the former Soviet Union, the Middle East, and Latin America. Most of our deals are between $200 million and $2 billion. We also provide financial advisory services. I am responsible for the entire process, from creating the appropriate financial structure to closing the transaction.

Q: *Do you use any special financing techniques for international projects?*

A: For projects in emerging markets we often access nontraditional lending institutions such as export credit agencies and multilaterals such as the World Bank. We raise capital from a variety of internationally based financial institutions, using the best financing structure and product for each transaction, whether it's tax-exempt financing for toll roads in the United States, private finance initiative communications projects in the United Kingdom, or export credit agency financing in Indonesia.

Q: *How do exchange rate movements affect your business?*

A: Since approximately 40 to 50 percent of all project costs are for labor and local construction services, we hedge our exchange rate positions and manage our cross-currency positions on a daily basis. We also try to have as much of our contracts paid in U.S. dollars as possible. For each contract we analyze foreign exchange risk and look for ways to reduce our exposure. We consider the credit quality of our clients and their ability to convert their local currency into U.S. dollars to pay us for locally incurred costs. This is particularly important on very large emerging market transactions.

Q: *What skills are important to your position?*

A: Project finance specialists must be well-rounded bankers. I use finance skills, including corporate finance, mergers/acquisitions, accounting, and financial modeling. Also critical are general business skills like strategic planning, marketing, and computer literacy, and many "life skills": strong written and verbal communication, leadership, mentoring, and team management and building. Project finance also requires knowledge of global markets (commodities) and geopolitics. We need to understand complex financing techniques, tax treatment, and accounting standards. Project finance also requires a significant amount of legal knowledge, plus conflict resolution and negotiation skills. Success in international markets calls for a keen understanding of—and respect for—cultural diversity. Perhaps the greatest skill of all is patience coupled with a true team orientation: it is impossible to complete a project financing without collaborating with other specialists.

TABLE 18.2
U.S. Balance of Payments in 2005 ($ Billions)

	INCOME (+)	PAYMENTS (−)	NET
Current Account			
Goods and services			
Exports	$1,275.3		
Imports		$1,992.0	
Balance on goods and services			−$716.7
Income, net			11.3
Unilateral current transfers, net			−86.1
Balance on current account			−$791.5
Capital Account			
Changes in U.S. government assets			
other than official reserve assets	5.5		
Changes in U.S. private assets abroad		446.4	
Changes in foreign official assets in U.S.	199.5		
Changes in foreign private assets in U.S.	1,012.8		
Changes in U.S. official reserve assets	14.1		
Capital account transactions, net		4.4	
Balance on capital account			$781.1
Statistical discrepancy			10.4
Adjusted balance on capital account			$791.5

Source: Statistical Supplement to the Federal Reserve Bulletin (February 2007), p. 44.

We can better understand the U.S. balance of payments by examining the current account and capital account balances information shown in Table 18.2. An annual balance of trade (goods and services) deficit of $716.7 billion occurred in 2005 and reflects the net of merchandise trade, service transactions, and military transactions. We find the current account balance by adjusting the goods and services balance for net income flows that come primarily from investments and also from unilateral, or one-way, transfers. These transfers include remittances, pensions, private gifts and grants, and U.S. government grants (excluding military). Thus, the ***current account balance*** shows the flow of income into and out of the United States during a specified period. For 2005, the current account balance showed a deficit of $791.5 billion.

The ***capital account balance*** includes all foreign private and government investment in the United States netted against U.S. investments in foreign countries. Deficits or surpluses in the current account must be offset by changes in the capital account. That is, changes in the current account and the capital account must be equal except for statistical discrepancies caused by measurement errors and the inability to keep track of all international transactions. According to Table 18.2, the balance on the capital account was a surplus of $781.1 billion. Since this amount was less than the current account deficit of $791.5 billion, the difference reflects a statistical discrepancy of $10.4 billion for 2005.

The first item in the capital account section, changes in U.S. government assets other than official reserve assets, represents an income of $5.5 billion and includes government ownership of assets in foreign countries, gold, and the reserve position in the International Monetary Fund. The second item, changes in U.S. private assets abroad, reflects private investments abroad and represents an outflow of capital, which was $446.4 billion in 2005.

The third and fourth items reflect foreign ownership changes, both government and private, in investments in the United States. Among those changes are increases in bank deposits, purchases of government and corporate securities, loans, and direct investment in land and buildings. Both of these items give rise to inflows of capital with $199.5 billion coming from an increase in foreign official assets and $1,012.8 billion from foreign private assets in 2005. The fifth item reflects an increase in U.S. official reserve assets of $14.1 billion in 2005. Capital account transactions (net) reflected payments of $4.4 billion in 2005 for debt forgiveness and the disposition of certain assets.

From an international monetary management point of view, U.S. government ownership of foreign assets is of special interest. Under the current system of flexible exchange rates, a country's

current account balance
the flow of income into and out of the United States during a specified period

capital account balance
foreign government and private investment in the United States netted against similar U.S. investment in foreign countries

CONCEPT CHECK

What is meant by the U.S. balance of payments?

What are the differences between the current account balance and the capital account balance?

central bank does not have to redeem its currency. However, it may try to control its exchange rate by entering the foreign exchange market to buy or sell that currency, thus adding to demand or supply. Intervention by central banks in the flexible exchange rate system is called a *managed float*.

Under a pure flexible system in which central banks do not enter the foreign exchange market at all, there would be no change in the official government ownership of foreign assets. Note, however, that the rest of the accounts would still balance. Any surplus or deficit in current accounts would be balanced by the capital accounts. For example, a trade deficit might be balanced partly by an increase in foreign assets in the United States, including deposits in U.S. banks.

APPLYING FINANCE TO . . .

INSTITUTIONS AND MARKETS

Commercial banks play an important role in financing international trade. Banks provide commercial letters of credit that guarantee acceptance and payment of drafts. Banker's acceptances—promises of future payment issued by a firm and guaranteed by a bank—also are important financial instruments that facilitate international trade. Banks throughout the world also are important participants in the electronic currency exchange markets. Traveler's letters of credit and traveler's checks are provided by financial institutions to help travelers purchase products and cover living expenses while in foreign countries.

INVESTMENTS

Individuals and businesses interested in investing in securities issued by foreign corporations may need to use the currency exchange markets to convert U.S. dollars into the currencies of the countries where those corporations are located. Individuals traveling internationally also will need to convert their U.S. dollars into the local currencies through the aid of financial institutions. Investors may also speculate on the relative future movements of currencies through the use of spot and forward markets.

FINANCIAL MANAGEMENT

Financial managers use currency exchange markets to hedge against currency exchange risk associated with possible changes in the exchange rates between currencies. Financial managers may hedge in the forward markets or seek the aid of banks to sell unneeded currencies or to purchase currencies needed to conduct business operations. Financial managers also rely on banks and other financial institutions to aid them in their international transactions both as importers and as exporters.

SUMMARY

In this chapter we discussed the development of international finance and the international monetary system as it evolved from a gold standard system to a system of flexible exchange rates. We also covered the developments toward European economic unification through the creation of the European Union (EU) and the European Monetary Union (EMU). The EU is currently composed of twenty-seven country members, while the EMU consists of the thirteen countries that have adopted the euro as their common currency and the European Central Bank as their central monetary policy-making authority. The banking system, along with the arbitrage activities of international financiers, support and facilitate international transactions and activities. Management of foreign exchange is particularly important to multinational corporate financial managers as they attempt to protect their international claims against currency fluctuations.

Foreign exchange markets are electronic communication systems that connect major financial centers throughout the world.

Exchange rates are determined by supply and demand relationships, relative interest rate levels, relative rates of inflation, political risk, and economic risk. Alternatives to effect settlement of purchase and sale claims were explored, along with the instruments available to exporters and importers for financing their international activities.

Nations of the world try to maintain a balance in their exchange of goods and services, as well as in their payments balances. When international financial equilibrium does not exist, exchange rates usually adjust to reflect these imbalances. Furthermore, when the current account shows a surplus or deficit in the flow of income into and out of the United States, changes in the capital account must offset the current account imbalance. This is accomplished by a change in the relationship between foreign private and government investment in the United States relative to U.S. investment in foreign countries.

KEY TERMS

arbitrage

balance of payments

balance of trade

banker's acceptances

Bretton Woods system

capital account balance

clean draft

commercial letter of credit

currency exchange markets

currency exchange rate

current account balance

direct quotation method

documentary draft	forward exchange rate	purchasing power parity (PPP)
draft (bill of exchange)	gold standard	sight draft
economic risk	indirect quotation method	special drawing rights (SDRs)
euro	interest rate parity (IRP)	spot exchange rate
European Monetary Union (EMU)	International Monetary Fund (IMF)	time draft
European Union (EU)	international monetary system	traveler's letter of credit
Export-Import Bank	merchandise trade balance	trust receipt
flexible exchange rates	order bill of lading	World Bank
foreign exchange markets	political risk	

DISCUSSION QUESTIONS

1. What is the purpose of an international monetary system?

2. What is meant by the statement that the international monetary system has operated mostly under a "gold standard"? What are the major criticisms associated with being on a gold standard?

3. Describe the Bretton Woods system for setting currency exchange rates. What is meant by "special drawing rights," and how are they used to foster world trade?

4. What is meant by an international monetary system based on "flexible exchange rates"?

5. Describe the international monetary system currently in use.

6. What is the European Union (EU)? How did it develop? Who are the current members of the EU?

7. What is the European Monetary Union (EMU)? How does it differ from the EU? Who are the current members of the EMU?

8. What is the euro? Identify some of its distinguishing characteristics.

9. What are currency or foreign exchange markets?

10. Explain the role of supply and demand in establishing exchange rates between countries.

11. Describe the activities and economic role of the arbitrageur in international finance.

12. What is meant by the statement that foreign exchange quotations may be given in terms of sight drafts, cable orders, and time drafts?

13. Describe the various ways by which an exporter may finance an international shipment of goods. How may commercial banks assist the exporter in collecting drafts?

14. How do importers protect themselves against improper delivery of goods when they are required to make payment as they place an order?

15. Describe the process by which an importing firm may substitute the credit of its bank for its own credit in financing international transactions.

16. How may a bank protect itself after having issued a commercial letter of credit on behalf of a customer?

17. Describe the costs involved in connection with financing exports through banker's acceptances.

18. Describe the ultimate sources of funds for export financing with banker's acceptances. How are acceptances acquired for investment by these sources?

19. Explain the role played in international trade by the Export-Import Bank. Do you consider this bank to be in competition with private lending institutions?

20. Commercial letters of credit, traveler's letters of credit, and traveler's checks all play an important role in international finance. Distinguish among these three types of instruments.

21. Briefly indicate the problems facing the United States in its attempt to maintain international financial equilibrium.

22. The U.S. international balance of payments position is measured in terms of the current account balance. Describe the current account balance and indicate its major components.

23. Discuss the meaning of the capital account balance and identify its major components.

EXERCISES

1. You are the owner of a business that has offices and production facilities in several foreign countries. Your product is sold in all these countries, and you maintain bank accounts in the cities in which you have offices. At present you have short-term notes outstanding at most of the banks with which you maintain deposits. This borrowing is to support seasonal production activity. One of the countries in which you have offices is now strongly rumored to be on the point of a devaluation, or lowering, of its currency relative to that of the rest of the world. What actions might this rumor cause you to take?

2. Explain the concept of "balance" as it relates to a nation's balance of payments.

3. As an exporter of relatively expensive electronic equipment, you have a substantial investment in the merchandise that you ship.

Your foreign importers are typically small- or medium-size firms without a long history of operations. Although your terms of sales require payment upon receipt of the merchandise, you are concerned about the possible problem of nonpayment and the need to reclaim merchandise that you have shipped. How might the banking system assist and protect you in this situation?

4. As an importer of merchandise you depend on the sale of the merchandise for funds to make payment. Although customary terms of sale are ninety days for this type of merchandise, you are not well-known to foreign suppliers because of your recent entry into business. Furthermore, your suppliers require almost immediate payment to meet their own expenses of operations. How might the banking systems of the exporter and importer accommodate your situation?

5. As a speculator in the financial markets, you notice that for the last few minutes Swiss francs are being quoted in New York at a price of $0.5849 and in Frankfurt at $0.5851.

    a. Assuming that you have access to international trading facilities, what action might you take?

    b. What would be the effect of your actions and those of other speculators on these exchange rates?

6. You manage the cash for a large multinational industrial enterprise. As a result of credit sales on ninety-day payment terms you have a large claim against a customer in Mexico City. You have heard rumors of the possible devaluation of the Mexican peso. What actions, if any, can you take to protect your firm against the consequences of a prospective devaluation?

7. Assume, as the loan officer of a commercial bank, that one of your customers has asked for a commercial letter of credit to enable his firm to import a supply of well-known French wines. This customer has a long record of commercial success, yet has large outstanding debts to other creditors. In what way might you accommodate the customer and at the same time protect your bank?

8. For the entire year the nation's balance of trade with other nations has been in a substantial deficit position, yet, as always, the overall balance of payments will be in "balance." Describe the various factors that accomplish this overall balance, in spite of the deficit in the balance of trade.

9. Assume you are the international vice president of a small U.S.-based manufacturing corporation. You are trying to expand your business in several developing countries. You are also aware that some business practices are considered to be "acceptable" in these countries but not necessarily in the United States. How would you react to the following situations?

    a. You met yesterday with a government official from one of the countries in which you would like to make sales. He said that he could speed up the process for acquiring the necessary licenses for conducting business in his country if you would pay him for his time and effort. What would you do?

    b. You are trying to make a major sale of your firm's products to the government of a foreign country. You have identified the key decision maker. You are considering offering the official a monetary payment if she would recommend buying your firm's products. What would you do?

    c. Your firm has a local office in a developing country where you are trying to increase business opportunities. Representatives from a local crime syndicate have approached you and have offered to provide "local security" in exchange for a monthly payment to them. What would you do?

PROBLEMS

1. At the beginning of July 2004, the U.S. dollar equivalent of a euro was $1.2167. In mid-March 2007, the U.S. dollar equivalent of a euro was $1.3310. Using the indirect quotation method, determine the currency per U.S. dollar for each of these dates.

2. At the beginning of July 2004, the U.S. dollar equivalent of a euro was $1.2167. In mid-March 2007, the U.S. dollar equivalent of a euro was $1.3310. Determine the percentage change of the euro between these two dates.

3. Assume that last year a euro was trading at a direct method quotation of $.8767. Also assume that recently the indirect method quotation was .8219 euros per U.S. dollar.

    a. Calculate the euro "currency per U.S. dollar" last year.

    b. Calculate the "U.S. dollar equivalent" of a euro this year.

    c. Determine the percentage change (appreciation or depreciation) of the U.S. dollar value of one euro between last year and this year.

    d. Determine the percentage change (appreciation or depreciation) of the euro currency per U.S. dollar between last year and this year.

4. Assume that last year the Australian dollar was trading at $.5527, the Mexican peso at $.1102, and the United Kingdom (British) pound was worth $1.4233. By this year the U.S. dollar value of an Australian dollar was $.7056, the Mexican peso was $.0867, and the British pound was $1.8203. Calculate the percentage appreciation or depreciation of each of these three currencies between last year and this year.

5. Assume that the Danish krone (DK) has a current dollar ($US) value of $0.18.

    a. Determine the number of DK that can be purchased with one $US.

    b. Calculate the percentage change (appreciation or depreciation) in the Danish krone if it falls to $0.16.

    c. Calculate the percentage change (appreciation or depreciation) in the U.S. dollar if the DK falls to $0.16.

6. Assume the U.S. dollar ($US) value of the Australian dollar is $0.73 while the U.S. dollar value of the Hong Kong dollar is $0.13.

    a. Determine the number of Australian dollars that can be purchased with one $US.

    b. Determine the number of Hong Kong dollars that can be purchased with one $US.

    c. In $US terms, determine how many Hong Kong dollars can be purchased with one Australian dollar.

7. Assume one U.S. dollar ($US) can currently purchase 1.316 Swiss francs. However, it has been predicted that one $US soon will be exchangeable for 1.450 Swiss francs.

    a. Calculate the percentage change in the $US if the exchange rate change occurs.

    b. Determine the dollar value of one Swiss franc at both of the above exchange rates.

    c. Calculate the percentage change in the dollar value of one Swiss franc based on the preceding exchange rates.

8. Assume inflation is expected to be 3 percent in the United States next year compared with 6 percent in Australia. If the U.S. dollar value of an Australian dollar is currently $0.500, what is the expected exchange rate one year from now based on purchasing power parity?

9. Assume inflation is expected to be 8 percent in New Zealand next year compared with 4 percent in France. If the New Zealand dollar value of a euro is $0.400, what is the expected exchange rate one year from now based on purchasing power parity?

10. Assume the interest rate on a one-year U.S. government debt security is currently 9.5 percent compared with a 7.5 percent on a foreign country's comparable maturity debt security. If the U.S. dollar value of the foreign country's currency is $1.50, what is the expected exchange rate one year from now based on interest rate parity?

11. Assume the interest rate in Australia on one-year government debt securities is 10 percent and the interest rate on Japanese one-year debt is 5 percent. Assume the current Australian dollar value of the Japanese yen is $0.0200. Using interest rate parity, estimate the expected value of the Japanese yen in terms of Australian dollars one year from now.

12. **Challenge Problem** Following are currency exchange "crossrates" between pairs of major currencies. Currency crossrates include both direct and indirect methods for expressing relative exchange rates.

	U.S. DOLLAR	U.K. POUND	SWISS FRANC	JAPANESE YEN	EUROPEAN EURO
European Monetary Union	1.1406	?	0.6783	0.0087	————
Japan	130.66	185.98	77.705	————	114.60
Switzerland	1.6817	2.3936	————	0.0129	?
United Kingdom	?	————	0.4178	?	0.6162
United States	————	1.4231	?	0.0077	0.8767

a. Fill in the missing exchange rates in the crossrates table.

b. If the inflation rate is expected to be 3 percent in the European Monetary Union and 4 percent in the United States next year, estimate the forward rate of one euro in U.S. dollars one year from now.

c. If the one-year government interest rate is 6 percent in Japan and 4 percent in the United Kingdom, estimate the amount of yen that will be needed to purchase one British pound one year from now.

d. Based solely on purchasing power parity, calculate the expected one-year inflation rate in the United States if the Swiss inflation rate is expected to be 3.5 percent next year and the one-year forward rate of a Swiss franc is $.6100.

e. Assume the U.S. dollar is expected to depreciate by 15 percent relative to the euro at the end of one year from now and the interest rate on one-year government securities in the European Monetary Union is 5.5 percent. What would be the current U.S. one-year government security interest rate based solely on the use of interest rate parity to forecast forward currency exchange rates?

• APPENDIX •

TABLE 1

Future Value of $1 (FVIF)

TABLE 2

Present Value of $1 (PVIF)

TABLE 3

Future Value of a $1 Ordinary Annuity (FVIFA)

TABLE 4

Present Value of a $1 Ordinary Annuity (PVIFA)

TABLE I
Future Value of $1 (FVIF)

YEAR	1%	2%	3%	4%	5%	6%	7%	8%	9%
1	1.010	1.020	1.030	1.040	1.050	1.060	1.070	1.080	1.090
2	1.020	1.040	1.061	1.082	1.102	1.124	1.145	1.166	1.188
3	1.030	1.061	1.093	1.125	1.158	1.191	1.225	1.260	1.295
4	1.041	1.082	1.126	1.170	1.216	1.262	1.311	1.360	1.412
5	1.051	1.104	1.159	1.217	1.276	1.338	1.403	1.469	1.539
6	1.062	1.126	1.194	1.265	1.340	1.419	1.501	1.587	1.677
7	1.072	1.149	1.230	1.316	1.407	1.504	1.606	1.714	1.828
8	1.083	1.172	1.267	1.369	1.477	1.594	1.718	1.851	1.993
9	1.094	1.195	1.305	1.423	1.551	1.689	1.838	1.999	2.172
10	1.105	1.219	1.344	1.480	1.629	1.791	1.967	2.159	2.367
11	1.116	1.243	1.384	1.539	1.710	1.898	2.105	2.332	2.580
12	1.127	1.268	1.426	1.601	1.796	2.012	2.252	2.518	2.813
13	1.138	1.294	1.469	1.665	1.886	2.113	2.410	2.720	3.066
14	1.149	1.319	1.513	1.732	1.980	2.261	2.579	2.937	3.342
15	1.161	1.346	1.558	1.801	2.079	2.397	2.759	3.172	3.642
16	1.173	1.373	1.605	1.873	2.183	2.540	2.952	3.426	3.970
17	1.184	1.400	1.653	1.948	2.292	2.693	3.159	3.700	4.328
18	1.196	1.428	1.702	2.026	2.407	2.854	3.380	3.996	4.717
19	1.208	1.457	1.754	2.107	2.527	3.026	3.617	4.316	5.142
20	1.220	1.486	1.806	2.191	2.653	3.207	3.870	4.661	5.604
25	1.282	1.641	2.094	2.666	3.386	4.292	5.427	6.848	8.623
30	1.348	1.811	2.427	3.243	4.322	5.743	7.612	10.063	13.268

(Continues)

Note: The basic equation for finding the future value interest factor (FVIF) is:

$$FVIF_{r,n} = (1 + r)^n$$

where r is the interest rate and n is the number of periods in years.

TABLE I
Future Value of $1 *(Continued)*

10%	12%	14%	15%	16%	18%	20%	25%	30%
1.100	1.120	1.140	1.150	1.160	1.180	1.200	1.250	1.300
1.210	1.254	1.300	1.322	1.346	1.392	1.440	1.563	1.690
1.331	1.405	1.482	1.521	1.561	1.643	1.728	1.953	2.197
1.464	1.574	1.689	1.749	1.811	1.939	2.074	2.441	2.856
1.611	1.762	1.925	2.011	2.100	2.288	2.488	3.052	3.713
1.772	1.974	2.195	2.313	2.436	2.700	2.986	3.815	4.827
1.949	2.211	2.502	2.660	2.826	3.185	3.583	4.768	6.276
2.144	2.476	2.853	3.059	3.278	3.759	4.300	5.960	8.157
2.358	2.773	3.252	3.518	3.803	4.435	5.160	7.451	10.604
2.594	3.106	3.707	4.046	4.411	5.234	6.192	9.313	13.786
2.853	3.479	4.226	4.652	5.117	6.176	7.430	11.642	17.922
3.138	3.896	4.818	5.350	5.936	7.288	8.916	14.552	23.298
3.452	4.363	5.492	6.153	6.886	8.599	10.699	18.190	30.288
3.797	4.887	6.261	7.076	7.988	10.147	12.839	22.737	39.374
4.177	5.474	7.138	8.137	9.266	11.974	15.407	28.422	51.186
4.595	6.130	8.137	9.358	10.748	14.129	18.488	35.527	66.542
5.054	6.866	9.276	10.761	12.468	16.672	22.186	44.409	86.504
5.560	7.690	10.575	12.375	14.463	19.673	26.623	55.511	112.460
6.116	8.613	12.056	14.232	16.777	23.214	31.948	69.389	146.190
6.728	9.646	13.743	16.367	19.461	27.393	38.338	86.736	190.050
10.835	17.000	26.462	32.919	40.874	62.669	95.396	264.700	705.640
17.449	29.960	50.950	66.212	85.850	143.371	237.376	807.790	2,620.000

TABLE 2
Present Value of $1 (PVIF)

YEAR	1%	2%	3%	4%	5%	6%	7%	8%	9%	10%
1	0.990	0.980	0.971	0.962	0.952	0.943	0.935	0.926	0.917	0.909
2	0.980	0.961	0.943	0.925	0.907	0.890	0.873	0.857	0.842	0.826
3	0.971	0.942	0.915	0.889	0.864	0.840	0.816	0.794	0.772	0.751
4	0.961	0.924	0.888	0.855	0.823	0.792	0.763	0.735	0.708	0.683
5	0.951	0.906	0.863	0.822	0.784	0.747	0.713	0.681	0.650	0.621
6	0.942	0.888	0.837	0.790	0.746	0.705	0.666	0.630	0.596	0.564
7	0.933	0.871	0.813	0.760	0.711	0.665	0.623	0.583	0.547	0.513
8	0.923	0.853	0.789	0.731	0.677	0.627	0.582	0.540	0.502	0.467
9	0.914	0.837	0.766	0.703	0.645	0.592	0.544	0.500	0.460	0.424
10	0.905	0.820	0.744	0.676	0.614	0.558	0.508	0.463	0.422	0.386
11	0.896	0.804	0.722	0.650	0.585	0.527	0.475	0.429	0.388	0.350
12	0.887	0.788	0.701	0.625	0.557	0.497	0.444	0.397	0.356	0.319
13	0.879	0.773	0.681	0.601	0.530	0.469	0.415	0.368	0.326	0.290
14	0.870	0.758	0.661	0.577	0.505	0.442	0.388	0.340	0.299	0.263
15	0.861	0.743	0.642	0.555	0.481	0.417	0.362	0.315	0.275	0.239
16	0.853	0.728	0.623	0.534	0.458	0.394	0.339	0.292	0.252	0.218
17	0.844	0.714	0.605	0.513	0.436	0.391	0.317	0.270	0.231	0.198
18	0.836	0.700	0.587	0.494	0.416	0.350	0.296	0.250	0.212	0.180
19	0.828	0.686	0.570	0.475	0.396	0.331	0.276	0.232	0.194	0.164
20	0.820	0.673	0.554	0.456	0.377	0.312	0.258	0.215	0.178	0.149
25	0.780	0.610	0.478	0.375	0.295	0.233	0.184	0.146	0.116	0.092
30	0.742	0.552	0.412	0.308	0.231	0.174	0.131	0.099	0.075	0.057

(Continues)

Note: The basic equation for finding the present value interest factor (PVIF) is:

$$PVIF_{r,n} = \frac{1}{(1+r)^n}$$

where r is the interest or discount rate and n is the number of periods in years.

TABLE 2
Present Value of $1 (PVIF) *(Continued)*

12%	14%	15%	16%	18%	20%	25%	30%
0.893	0.877	0.870	0.862	0.847	0.833	0.800	0.769
0.797	0.769	0.756	0.743	0.718	0.694	0.640	0.592
0.712	0.675	0.658	0.641	0.609	0.579	0.512	0.455
0.636	0.592	0.572	0.552	0.516	0.482	0.410	0.350
0.567	0.519	0.497	0.476	0.437	0.402	0.328	0.269
0.507	0.456	0.432	0.410	0.370	0.335	0.262	0.207
0.452	0.400	0.376	0.354	0.314	0.279	0.210	0.159
0.404	0.351	0.327	0.305	0.266	0.233	0.168	0.123
0.361	0.308	0.284	0.263	0.225	0.194	0.134	0.094
0.322	0.270	0.247	0.227	0.191	0.162	0.107	0.073
0.287	0.237	0.215	0.195	0.162	0.135	0.086	0.056
0.257	0.208	0.187	0.168	0.137	0.112	0.069	0.043
0.229	0.182	0.163	0.145	0.116	0.093	0.055	0.033
0.205	0.160	0.141	0.125	0.099	0.078	0.044	0.025
0.183	0.140	0.123	0.108	0.084	0.065	0.035	0.020
0.163	0.123	0.107	0.093	0.071	0.054	0.028	0.015
0.146	0.108	0.093	0.080	0.060	0.045	0.023	0.012
0.130	0.095	0.081	0.069	0.051	0.038	0.018	0.009
0.116	0.083	0.070	0.060	0.043	0.031	0.014	0.007
0.104	0.073	0.061	0.051	0.037	0.026	0.012	0.005
0.059	0.038	0.030	0.024	0.016	0.010	0.004	0.001
0.033	0.020	0.015	0.012	0.007	0.004	0.001	0.000

TABLE 3

Future Value of a $1 Ordinary Annuity (FVIFA)

YEAR	1%	2%	3%	4%	5%	6%	7%	8%
1	1.000	1.000	1.000	1.000	1.000	1.000	1.000	1.000
2	2.010	2.020	2.030	2.040	2.050	2.060	2.070	2.080
3	3.030	3.060	3.091	3.122	3.152	3.184	3.215	3.246
4	4.060	4.122	4.184	4.246	4.310	4.375	4.440	4.506
5	5.101	5.204	5.309	5.416	5.526	5.637	5.751	5.867
6	6.152	6.308	6.468	6.633	6.802	6.975	7.153	7.336
7	7.214	7.434	7.662	7.898	8.142	8.394	8.654	8.923
8	8.286	8.583	8.892	9.214	9.549	9.897	10.260	10.637
9	9.369	9.755	10.159	10.583	11.027	11.491	11.978	12.488
10	10.462	10.950	11.464	12.006	12.578	13.181	13.816	14.487
11	11.567	12.169	12.808	13.486	14.207	14.972	15.784	16.645
12	12.683	13.412	14.192	15.026	15.917	16.870	17.888	18.977
13	13.809	14.680	15.618	16.627	17.713	18.882	20.141	21.495
14	14.947	15.974	17.086	18.292	19.599	21.015	22.550	24.215
15	16.097	17.293	18.599	20.024	21.579	23.276	25.129	27.152
16	17.258	18.639	20.157	21.825	23.657	25.673	27.888	30.324
17	18.430	20.012	21.762	23.698	25.840	28.213	30.840	33.750
18	19.615	21.412	23.414	25.645	28.132	30.906	33.999	37.450
19	20.811	22.841	25.117	27.671	30.539	33.760	37.379	41.466
20	22.019	24.297	26.870	29.778	33.066	36.786	40.995	45.762
25	28.243	32.030	36.459	41.646	47.727	54.865	63.249	73.106
30	34.785	40.568	47.575	56.805	66.439	79.058	94.461	113.283

(Continues)

Note: The basic equation for finding the future value interest factor of an ordinary annuity (FVIFA) is:

$$FVIFA_{r,n} = \sum_{t=1}^{n} (1+r)^{n-t} = \frac{(1+r)^n - 1}{r}$$

where r is the interest rate and n is the number of periods in years.

Future Value of a $1 Annuity Due (FVIFAD)

The future value interest factor of an annuity due (FVIFAD) may be found by using the following formula to convert FVIFA values found in Table 3:

$$FVIFAD_{r,n} = FVIFA_{r,n}(1+r)$$

where r is the interest rate and n is the number of periods in years.

TABLE 3

Future Value of a $1 Ordinary Annuity (FVIFA) *(Continued)*

9%	10%	12%	14%	16%	18%	20%	25%	30%
1.000	1.000	1.000	1.000	1.000	1.000	1.000	1.000	1.000
2.090	2.100	2.120	2.140	2.160	2.180	2.200	2.250	2.300
3.278	3.310	3.374	3.440	3.506	3.572	3.640	3.813	3.990
4.573	4.641	4.779	4.921	5.066	5.215	5.368	5.766	6.187
5.985	6.105	6.353	6.610	6.877	7.154	7.442	8.207	9.043
7.523	7.716	8.115	8.536	8.977	9.442	9.930	11.259	12.756
9.200	9.487	10.089	10.730	11.414	12.142	12.916	15.073	17.583
11.028	11.436	12.300	13.233	14.240	15.327	16.499	19.842	23.858
13.021	13.579	14.776	16.085	17.518	19.086	20.799	25.802	32.015
15.193	15.937	17.549	19.337	21.321	23.521	25.959	33.253	42.619
17.560	18.531	20.655	23.044	25.733	28.755	32.150	42.566	56.405
20.141	21.384	24.133	27.271	30.850	34.931	39.580	54.208	74.327
22.953	24.523	28.029	32.089	36.786	42.219	48.497	68.760	97.625
26.019	27.975	32.393	37.581	43.672	50.818	59.196	86.949	127.910
29.361	31.772	37.280	43.842	51.660	60.965	72.035	109.690	167.290
33.003	35.950	42.753	50.980	60.925	72.939	87.442	138.110	218.470
36.974	40.545	48.884	59.118	71.673	87.068	105.931	173.640	285.010
41.301	45.599	55.750	68.394	84.141	103.740	128.117	218.050	371.520
46.018	51.159	63.440	78.969	98.603	123.414	154.740	273.560	483.970
51.160	57.275	72.052	91.025	115.380	146.628	186.688	342.950	630.170
84.701	98.347	133.334	181.871	249.214	342.603	471.981	1,054.800	2,348.800
136.308	164.494	241.333	356.787	530.312	790.948	1,181.882	3,227.200	8,730.000

TABLE 4
Present Value of a $1 Ordinary Annuity (PVIFA)

YEAR	1%	2%	3%	4%	5%	6%	7%	8%	9%	10%
1	0.990	0.980	0.971	0.962	0.952	0.943	0.935	0.926	0.917	0.909
2	1.970	1.942	1.913	1.886	1.859	1.833	1.808	1.783	1.759	1.736
3	2.941	2.884	2.829	2.775	2.723	2.673	2.624	2.577	2.531	2.487
4	3.902	3.808	3.717	3.630	3.546	3.465	3.387	3.312	3.240	3.170
5	4.853	4.713	4.580	4.452	4.329	4.212	4.100	3.993	3.890	3.791
6	5.795	5.601	5.417	5.242	5.076	4.917	4.767	4.623	4.486	4.355
7	6.728	6.472	6.230	6.002	5.786	5.582	5.389	5.206	5.033	4.868
8	7.652	7.325	7.020	6.733	6.463	6.210	5.971	5.747	5.535	5.335
9	8.566	8.162	7.786	7.435	7.108	6.802	6.515	6.247	5.995	5.759
10	9.471	8.983	8.530	8.111	7.722	7.360	7.024	6.710	6.418	6.145
11	10.368	9.787	9.253	8.760	8.306	7.887	7.499	7.139	6.805	6.495
12	11.255	10.575	9.954	9.385	8.863	8.384	7.943	7.536	7.161	6.814
13	12.134	11.348	10.635	9.986	9.394	8.853	8.358	7.904	7.487	7.103
14	13.004	12.106	11.296	10.563	9.899	9.295	8.745	8.244	7.786	7.367
15	13.865	12.849	11.938	11.118	10.380	9.712	9.108	8.559	8.061	7.606
16	14.718	13.578	12.561	11.652	10.838	10.106	9.447	8.851	8.313	7.824
17	15.562	14.292	13.166	12.166	11.274	10.477	9.763	9.122	8.544	8.022
18	16.398	14.992	13.754	12.659	11.690	10.828	10.059	9.372	8.756	8.201
19	17.226	15.678	14.324	13.134	12.085	11.158	10.336	9.604	8.950	8.365
20	18.046	16.351	14.877	13.590	12.462	11.470	10.594	9.818	9.129	8.514
25	22.023	19.523	17.413	15.622	14.094	12.783	11.654	10.675	9.823	9.077
30	25.808	22.397	19.600	17.292	15.372	13.765	12.409	11.258	10.274	9.427

(Continues)

Note: The basic equation for finding the present value interest factor of an ordinary annuity (PVIFA) is:

$$\text{PVIFA}_{r,n} = \sum_{t=1}^{n} \frac{1}{(1+r)^t} = \frac{1 - \dfrac{1}{(1+r)^n}}{r}$$

where r is the interest or discount rate and n is the number of periods in years.

Present Value of a $1 Annuity Due (PVIFAD)
The present value interest factor of an annuity due (PVIFAD) may be found by using the following formula to convert PVIFA values found in Table 4:

$$\text{PVIFAD}_{r,n} = \text{PVIFA}_{r,n}(1+r)$$

where r is the interest or discount rate and n is the number of periods in years.

Constant Dividend = $P = \frac{D}{r}$

- Constant Growth $P_0 = \frac{D_1}{r-g}$ $D_1 = D_0(1+g)$
- NPV = PV (of all cash flows) - COST >0 accept <0 reject
- IRR $NPV_A = 5,000 \times PVIFA_{IRR, 5} - 20,000 = 0$
  - $PVIFA_{IRR, 5} = 4$ IRR > Discount Rate Accept
  - IRR = 8%   IRR < Discount Rate Reject
- PI = $\frac{PV (\text{of all cash flows})}{COST}$ >1 Accept <1 Reject

- Payback Period - How long to recover Cost?
- Stand Alone Principle - Project must be viewed separately from rest of firm
- Relevant Cash Flows
  - ① Incremental After Tax CFs - CFs w/ project vs. CFs w/o project
  - ② Cannibalization or Enhancement
  - ③ Opportunity Costs - Cost of passing up next best alternative
- Irrelevant Cash Flows
  - ① Sunk Costs - project related expense not dependent on taking project
  - ② Financing Costs
- Depreciation is tax shield - Depreciation expense x tax rate (t)
- Project Stages & CF Estimation
  - ① Initial Outlay - Purchases, transportation, construction, Opp. costs, replace., NWC Δ
  - ② CFs during projects operating life
  - ③ Salvage Value & NWC Recovery @ Project Termination
    - After tax proceeds = Selling price - t (Selling Price - BV)
- Initial Investment = New Asset Cost - After tax proceeds + Δ in NWC
- 1st yr Rev & Exp $70,000 & $30,000. Exist Asset $40,000 & $20,000. Exist Asset $18,000 in depr., New Asset $50,000. 40% tax rate

Rev	70,000		40,000
-EXP	-30,000		-20,000
	40,000		20,000
-Dep	-50,000		-18,000
EBT	-10,000		2,000
-Tax	4,000		-800
NI	-6,000		1200
+Dep	50,000		18,000
OCF	$44,000		19,200

Incremental CF = 24,800

TABLE 4

Present Value of a $1 Ordinary Annuity (PVIFA) *(Continued)*

12%	14%	16%	18%	20%	25%	30%
0.893	0.877	0.862	0.847	0.833	0.800	0.769
1.690	1.647	1.605	1.566	1.528	1.440	1.361
2.402	2.322	2.246	2.174	2.106	1.952	1.816
3.037	2.914	2.798	2.690	2.589	2.362	2.166
3.605	3.433	3.274	3.127	2.991	2.689	2.436
4.111	3.889	3.685	3.498	3.326	2.951	2.643
4.564	4.288	4.039	3.812	3.605	3.161	2.802
4.968	4.639	4.344	4.078	3.837	3.329	2.925
5.328	4.946	4.607	4.303	4.031	3.463	3.019
5.650	5.216	4.833	4.494	4.193	3.571	3.092
5.938	5.453	5.029	4.656	4.327	3.656	3.147
6.194	5.660	5.197	4.793	4.439	3.725	3.190
6.424	5.842	5.342	4.910	4.533	3.780	3.223
6.628	6.002	5.468	5.008	4.611	3.824	3.249
6.811	6.142	5.575	5.092	4.675	3.859	3.268
6.974	6.265	5.668	5.162	4.730	3.887	3.283
7.120	5.373	5.749	4.222	4.775	3.910	3.295
7.250	6.467	5.818	5.273	4.812	3.928	3.304
7.366	6.550	5.877	5.316	4.843	3.942	3.311
7.469	6.623	5.929	5.353	4.870	3.954	3.316
7.843	6.873	6.097	5.467	4.948	3.985	3.329
8.055	7.003	6.177	5.517	4.979	3.995	3.332

• GLOSSARY •

A

acceptance receivable from the sale of merchandise on the basis of a draft or bill of exchange drawn against the buyer or the buyer's bank

accommodative function Fed efforts to meet credit needs of individuals and institutions, clearing checks, and supporting depository institutions

administrative inflation the tendency of prices, aided by union-corporation contracts, to rise during economic expansion and to resist declines during recessions

advance factoring factor pays the firm for its receivables before the account due date

aftermarket period during which members of the syndicate may not sell the securities for less than the initial offering price

agency costs tangible and intangible expenses borne by shareholders because of the actual or potential self-serving actions of managers

agents hired by the principals to run the firm

American depository receipt (ADR) receipt that represents foreign shares to U.S. investors

amortized loan a loan repaid in equal payments over a specified time

annual percentage rate (APR) determined by multiplying the interest rate charged per period by the number of periods in a year

annual report contains descriptive information and numerical records on the operating and financial performance of a firm during the past year

annualize a return state the return as the annual return that would result in the observed percentage return

annuity a series of equal payments that occur over a number of time periods

annuity due exists when the equal payments occur at the beginning of each time period

arbitrage (1) buying commodities, securities, or bills of exchange in one market and immediately selling them in another to make a profit from price differences in the two markets; (2) operation that takes place if there is a mispricing between two different markets for the same asset that leads to a risk-free profit

ask price price for which the owner is willing to sell the security

asset management ratios indicate the extent to which assets are used to support sales

assets financial and physical items owned by a business

at-the-money an option's exercise price equals the current market price of the underlying asset

automatic stabilizers continuing federal programs that stabilize economic activity

automatic transfer service (ATS) accounts provide for direct deposits to, and payments from, checkable deposit accounts

average tax rate determined by dividing the taxes paid by the taxable income

B

balance of payments a summary of all economic transactions between one country and the rest of the world

balance of trade the net value of a country's exports of goods and services compared to its imports

balance sheet statement of a company's financial position as of a particular date

bank holding company company that holds voting power in two or more banks through stock ownership

bank liquidity   reflects ability to meet depositor withdrawals and to pay off other liabilities when due

bank reserves   vault cash and deposits held at Federal Reserve Banks

bank solvency   reflects ability to keep the value of a bank's assets greater than its liabilities

banker's acceptances   a promise of future payment issued by a firm and guaranteed by a bank

banking system   includes commercial banks, savings and loans, savings banks, and credit unions that operate in the U.S. financial system

bankruptcy costs   explicit and implicit costs associated with financial distress

barter   exchange of goods or services without using money

base case   firm's after-tax cash flows without the project

bearer bonds   have coupons that are literally "clipped" and presented, like a check, to the bank for payment; the bond issuer does not know who is receiving the interest payments

benefit/cost ratio (profitability index [PI])   ratio between the present values of the cash flows and the project's cost

best-effort agreement   agreement by the investment banker to sell securities to the issuing corporation; assumes no risk for the possible failure of the flotation

beta   measure of an asset's systematic risk

bid price   price that the buyer is willing to pay for the security

bimetallic standard   standard based on two metals, usually silver and gold

blanket inventory   lien claim against a customer's inventory when the individual items are indistinguishable

blue-sky laws   protect the investor from fraudulent security offerings

bond rating   assesses both the collateral underlying the bonds as well as the ability of the issuer to make timely payments of interest and principal

branch banks   bank offices under a single bank charter

breakeven analysis   used to estimate how many units of product must be sold for the firm to break even or have a zero profit

broker   one who assists in the trading process by buying or selling securities in the market for an investor

budgetary deficit   occurs when expenditures are greater than revenues

budgets   financial plans indicating expected revenues, spending, and investment needs

business finance   study of financial planning, asset management, and fund-raising by businesses and financial institutions

business risk   measured by variability in EBIT over time

buying on margin   investor borrows money and invests it along with his own funds in securities

bylaws   rules established to govern the corporation; they deal with how the firm will be managed and the rights of the stockholder

C

call deferment period   specified period after the issue during which the bonds cannot be called

call option   contract for the purchase of a security within a specified time and at a specified price

call price   price paid to the investor for redemption prior to maturity, typically par value plus a call premium of one year's interest

call risk   risk of having a bond called away and reinvesting the proceeds at a lower interest rate

callable bonds   can be redeemed prior to maturity by the issuing firm

callable preferred stock   gives the corporation the right to retire the preferred stock at its option

cannibalization   situation in which a project robs cash flow from the firm's existing lines of business

capacity   ability to pay bills

capital   adequacy of owners' equity relative to existing liabilities

capital account balance   foreign government and private investment in the United States netted against similar U.S. investment in foreign countries

Capital Asset Pricing Model (CAPM)   states that expected return on an asset depends on its level of systematic risk

capital budgeting   process of identifying, evaluating, and implementing a firm's investment opportunities

capital consumption allowances   estimates of the "using up," or depreciation of, plant and equipment assets for business purposes

capital formation   (1) process of constructing residential and nonresidential structures, manufacturing producers' durable equipment, and increasing business inventories; (2) the creation of productive facilities such as buildings, tools, and equipment

capital gains   gains or losses on capital assets held for more than one year

capital markets   markets for longer-term debt securities and corporate stocks

capital structure   firm's mix of debt and equity

cash budget   tool the treasurer uses to forecast future cash flows and estimate future short-term borrowing needs

cash conversion cycle time between a firm paying its suppliers for inventory and collecting cash from customers on a sale of the finished product

central bank a federal government agency that facilitates operation of the financial system and regulates money supply growth

central limit order book limit "book" in which the specialist keeps unexecuted limit orders

certificates of deposit (CDs) time deposits with a stated maturity

character ethical quality upon which one can base a judgment about a customer's willingness to pay bills

charter provides the corporate name, indicates the intended business activities, provides names and addresses of directors, and indicates how a firm will be capitalized with stock

chartists (technicians) study graphs of past price movements, volume, etc., to try to predict future prices

chief financial officer (CFO) responsible for the controller and the treasury functions of a firm

clean draft a draft that is not accompanied by any special documents

closed-end mortgage bond does not permit future bond issues to be secured by any of the assets pledged as security to it

coefficient of variation (CV) measures the risk per unit of return

collateral assets that are available to provide security for the potential credit

collateralized bonds pledge securities to protect the bondholders against loss in case of default

combined leverage effect on earnings produced by the operating and financial leverage

commercial bank accepts deposits, makes loans, and issues check-writing accounts

commercial finance company organization without a bank charter that advances funds to businesses

commercial letter of credit statement by a bank guaranteeing acceptance and payment of a draft up to a stated amount

commercial paper (1) short-term promissory note sold by high-credit-quality corporations; notes are backed solely by the credit quality of the issuer; (2) short-term unsecured promissory notes

commission (house) brokers act as agents to execute customers' orders for securities purchases and sales

common stock represents ownership shares in a corporation

common-size financial statement expresses balance sheet dollar figures as a percent of total assets and income statement numbers as a percent of total revenue to facilitate comparisons between different-size firms

compensating balance requirement that 10 to 20 percent of a loan be kept on deposit at the bank

compound interest interest earned on interest in addition to interest earned on the principal or investment

compounding an arithmetic process whereby an initial value increases at a compound interest rate over time to reach a future value

conditions current economic climate and state of the business cycle

Consumer Credit Protection Act of 1968 act requiring clear explanation of consumer credit costs and prohibiting overly high-priced credit transactions

contractual savings savings accumulated on a regular schedule by prior agreement

contractual savings organizations collect premiums and contributions from participants and provide insurance against major financial losses and retirement benefits

contribution margin contribution of each unit sold that goes toward paying fixed costs

controller manages accounting, cost analysis, and tax planning

conversion ratio number of shares into which a convertible bond can be converted

conversion value stock price times the conversion ratio

convertible bond can be changed or converted, at the investor's option, into a specified number of shares of the issuer's common stock

convertible preferred stock has special provision that makes it possible to convert it to common stock of the corporation, generally at the stockholder's option

corporate equity capital financial capital supplied by the owners of a corporation

corporation legal entity created under state law with unending life that offers limited financial liability to its owners

correlation statistical concept that relates movements in one set of returns to movements in another set over time

cost of capital (1) project's required rate of return; (2) minimum acceptable rate of return to a firm on a project

cost-push inflation occurs when prices are raised to cover rising production costs, such as wages

cost-volume-profit analysis used by managers for financial planning to estimate the firm's operating profits at different levels of unit sales

coupon payments interest payments paid to the bondholders

covenants impose additional restrictions or duties on the firm

credit bureaus source of credit information about business firms and individuals

credit cards provide predetermined credit limits to consumers when the cards are issued

credit money money worth more than what it is made of

credit risk (default risk) the chance of nonpayment or delayed payment of interest or principal

credit union a cooperative nonprofit organization that exists primarily to provide member depositors with consumer credit

cross-sectional analysis different firms are compared at the same point in time

crowding out lack of funds for private borrowing caused by the sale of government obligations to cover large federal deficits

cumulative preferred stock requires that before dividends on common stock are paid, preferred dividends must be paid not only for the current period but also for all previous periods in which preferred dividends were missed

currency exchange rate value of one currency relative to another

currency exchange markets electronic markets where banks and institutional traders buy and sell various currencies on behalf of businesses and other clients

current account balance the flow of income into and out of the United Sates during a specified time period

current assets cash and all other assets that are expected to be converted into cash within one year

D

dealer satisfies the investor's trades by buying and selling securities from its own inventory

dealer system depends on a small group of dealers in government securities with an effective marketing network throughout the United States

debenture bonds unsecured obligations that depend on the general credit strength of the corporation for their security

debit cards provide for immediate direct transfer of deposit amounts

debt management various Treasury decisions connected with refunding debt issues

default risk risk that a borrower will not pay interest and/or principal on a loan when due

default risk premium compensation for the possibility of the borrower's failure to pay interest and/or principal when due

defensive activities Fed activities that offset unexpected monetary developments and contribute to the smooth everyday functioning of the economy

deficit financing how a government finances its needs when spending is greater than revenues

deficit reserves the amount that required reserves are greater than total reserves

degree of combined leverage (DCL) percentage change in earnings per share that results from a 1 percent change in sales volume

degree of financial leverage (DFL) measure the sensitivity of eps to changes in EBIT

degree of operating leverage (DOL) measures the sensitivity of operating income to changes in the level of output

demand-pull inflation occurs during economic expansions when demand for goods and services is greater than supply

depository institutions commercial banks, savings and loan associations, saving banks, and credit unions

depreciation devaluing a physical asset over the period of its expected life

depreciation tax shield (1) tax reduction due to depreciation of fixed assets; equals the amount of the depreciation expense multiplied by the firm's tax rate; (2) tax reduction due to noncash depreciation expense, equals the depreciation expense multiplied by the tax rate

derivative deposit deposit of funds that were borrowed from the reserves of primary deposits

derivative security value determined by the value of another investment vehicle

derivatives markets facilitate purchase and sale of derivative securities, which are financial contracts that derive their values from underlying securities

development stage requires estimating relevant cash inflows and outflows

deviations computed as a periodic return minus the average return

direct financing involves use of securities that represent specific contracts between the savers and borrowers themselves

direct quotation method indicates the amount of a home country's currency necessary to purchase one unit of a foreign currency

dirty float intervention by central banks to control exchange rates in the foreign exchange market's flexible exchange system

discount bond bond that is selling below par value

discount rate interest rate that a bank must pay to borrow from its regional Federal Reserve Bank

discounted loan borrower receives the principal less the interest at the time the loan is made; the principal is repaid at maturity

discounting   an arithmetic process whereby a future value decreases at a compound interest rate over time to reach a present value

disintermediation   periods of significant decrease in funds moving through depository institutions to the credit markets

dissave   to liquidate savings for consumption uses

diversification   occurs when we invest in several different assets rather than just a single one

dividend payout ratio   the proportion of each dollar of earnings that is paid to shareholders as a dividend; equals one minus the retention rate

documentary draft   draft that is accompanied by an order bill of lading and other documents

draft (bill of exchange)   an unconditional order for the payment of money from one person to another

dual banking system   allows commercial banks to obtain charters either from the federal government or a state government

Du Pont analysis   technique of breaking down return on total assets and return on equity into their component parts

due diligence   detailed study of a corporation

Dutch auction   an offering process in which investors bid on prices and number of securities they wish to purchase; the securities are sold at the highest price that allows all the offered securities to be sold

dynamic actions   Fed actions that stimulate or repress the level of prices or economic activity

E

EBIT/eps analysis   allows managers to see how different capital structures affect the earnings and risk levels of their firms

economic risk   risk associated with possible slow or negative economic growth, as well as with the likelihood of variability

effective annual rate (EAR)   measures the true interest rate when compounding occurs more frequently than once a year

efficient market   market in which prices adjust quickly after the arrival of new information and the price change reflects the economic value of the information, on average

electronic data interchange   the use of communications and computer systems to convey ordering, invoice, and payment information between suppliers and customers

electronic funds transfer systems (EFTS)   electronic method of receiving and disbursing funds

eligible paper   short-term promissory notes eligible for discounting with Federal Reserve Banks

enhancement   increase in the cash flows of the firm's other products that occur because of a new project

entrepreneurial finance   study of how growth-driven, performance-focused, early-stage firms raise financial capital and manage operations and assets

equipment trust   certificate gives the bondholder a claim to specific "rolling stock" (movable assets) such as railroad cars or airplanes

equity capital   equity funds or stock investments made by the owners of a firm

equity   funds supplied by the owners that represent their residual claim on the firm

euro   common currency that has replaced the individual currencies of twelve member countries of the European Union

Eurobond   bond denominated in U.S. dollars that is sold to investors in a country outside the United States

Eurocurrencies   all non-U.S. currencies held by banks outside their country of origin

Eurodollar bonds   dollar-denominated bonds sold outside the United States

Eurodollars   U.S. dollars placed in foreign banks

ex-ante   expected or forecasted

excess reserves   the amount that total reserves are greater than required reserves

exchange rate   value of one currency in terms of another

exchange rate risk   fluctuating exchange rates lead to varying levels of U.S. dollar-denominated cash flows

exercise price (strike price)   price at which an underlying asset can be traded

expectations theory   states that shape of the yield curve indicates investor expectations about future inflation rates

Export-Import Bank   bank established to aid in financing and facilitating trade between the United States and other countries

extendable notes   have their coupons reset every two or three years to reflect the current interest rate environment and any changes in the firm's creditworthiness; the investor can accept the new coupon rate or put the bonds back to the firm

F

face value   principal amount or par value that the issuer is obligated to repay at maturity

factor   engages in accounts-receivable financing for business; purchases accounts outright and assumes all credit risks

Fed Board of Governors   seven-member board of the Federal Reserve that sets monetary policy

federal funds   temporary excess reserves loaned by banks to other banks

Federal Reserve float temporary increase in bank reserves from checks credited to one bank's reserves and not yet debited to another's

Federal Reserve System (Fed) U.S. central bank that sets monetary policy and regulates banking system

federal statutory debt limits limits on the federal debt set by Congress

fiat money legal tender proclaimed to be money by law

field warehouse enterprise establishes a warehouse on the grounds of the borrowing business establishment

finance study of how individuals, institutions, and businesses acquire, spend, and manage financial resources

finance companies provide loans directly to consumers and businesses or aid individuals in obtaining financing of durable goods and homes

finance firms provide loans directly to consumers and businesses and help borrowers obtain mortgage loans on real property

financial assets (1) claims against the income or assets of individuals, businesses, and governments; (2) claims against the income or assets of others; (3) claims in the form of obligations or liabilities issued by individuals, businesses, financial intermediaries, and governments

financial disintermediation reduction in the flow of savings through depository institutions and into the credit markets

financial environment financial system, institutions, markets, and individuals that make the economy operate efficiently

financial institutions intermediaries that help the financial system operate efficiently and transfer funds from savers and investors to individuals, businesses, and governments that seek to spend or invest the funds

financial intermediaries firms that bring about the flow of funds from savers to borrowers

financial intermediation interaction of intermediaries, markets, instruments, policy makers, and regulations to aid the flow from savings to investments

financial leverage ratios indicate the extent to which borrowed funds are used to finance assets, as well as the ability of a firm to meet its debt payment obligations

financial management involves financial planning, asset management, and fund raising decisions to enhance the value of businesses

financial markets locations or electronic forums that facilitate the flow of funds among investors, businesses, and governments

financial system interaction of intermediaries, markets, instruments, policy makers, and regulations to aid the flow from savings to investments

fiscal agent role of the Fed in collecting taxes, issuing checks, and other activities for the Treasury

fiscal policy government influence on economic activity through taxation and expenditure plans

flexible exchange rates a system in which international exchange rates are determined by supply and demand

float the delay in the payment system between when funds are sent by a payer and credited to the payee's bank account and deducted from the payer's bank account

floor brokers independent brokers who handle the commission brokers' overflow

flotation initial sale of newly issued debt or equity securities

flotation costs (1) comprised of direct costs, the spread, and underpricing; (2) costs of issuing stock; includes accounting, legal, and printing costs of offering shares to the public, as well as the commission earned by the investment bankers who market the new securities to investors

follow-up a stage in the capital budgeting process during which managers track, review, or audit a project's results

foreign bond bond issued by a corporation or government that is denominated in the currency of a foreign country where it is sold

foreign exchange markets electronic network that connects the major financial centers of the world

forward exchange rate rate for the purchase or sale of a currency where delivery will take place at a future date

fourth market large institutional investors arrange the purchase and sale of securities among themselves without the benefit of broker or dealer

fractional reserve system reserves held with the Fed that are equal to a certain percentage of bank deposits

full-bodied money coins that contain the same value in metal as their face value representative

future value value of a savings amount or investment at a specified time in the future

futures contract obligates the owner to purchase the underlying asset at a specified price on a specified day

G

generally accepted accounting principles (GAAP) set of guidelines as to the form and manner in which accounting information should be presented

Glass-Steagall Act provided for separation of commercial banking and investment banking activities in the United States

global bonds generally denominated in U.S. dollars and marketed globally

global depository receipt (GDR) listed on the London Stock Exchange; facilitates trading in foreign shares

Gordon Model (constant dividend growth model) a means of estimating common stock prices by assuming constant divided growth over time

government purchases (GP) expenditures for goods and services by federal, state, and local governments

Gramm-Leach-Bliley Act of 1999 repealed the separation of commercial banking and investment banking activities provided for in the Glass-Steagall Act

greenbacks money issued by the U.S. government to help finance the Civil War

gross domestic product (GDP) measures the output of goods and services in an economy

gross private domestic investment (GPDI) investment in residential and nonresidential structures, producers' durable equipment, and business inventories

H

hedge reduce risk

I

identification stage finding potential capital investment opportunities and identifying whether a project involves a replacement decision and/or revenue expansion

implementation stage executing accepted projects

income statement reports the revenues generated and expenses incurred by the firm over an accounting period

incremental cash flows represent the difference between the firm's after-tax cash flows with the project and the firm's after-tax cash flows without the project

independent projects projects not in direct competition with one another

indirect financing financing created by an intermediary that involves separate instruments with lenders and borrowers

indirect quotation method indicates the amount of a foreign currency necessary to purchase one unit of the home country's currency

individual net worth sum of an individual's money, real assets, and financial assets less the individual's debt obligations

industry comparative analysis compares a firm's ratios against average ratios for other companies in the industry

inflation (1) a rise in prices not offset by increases in quality; (2) occurs when an increase in the price of goods or services is not offset by an increase in quality

inflation premium average inflation rate expected over the life of the security

initial margin (1) initial equity percentage; (2) required deposit of funds for those who are purchasers and sellers of futures, usually 3–6% of the contract

initial public offering (IPO) initial sale of equity to the public

insurance companies provide financial protection to individuals and businesses for life, property, liability, and health uncertainties

interest rate price that equates the demand for and supply of loanable funds

interest rate parity (IRP) currency of a country with a relatively higher interest rate will depreciate relative to the currency of a country with a relatively lower interest rate

interest rate risk (1) fluctuating interest rates lead to varying asset prices—in the context of bonds, rising (falling) interest rates result in falling (rising) bond prices; (2) possible price fluctuations in fixed-rate debt instruments associated with changes in market interest rates

intermediation the accumulation and lending of savings by depository institutions

internal growth rate a measure of how quickly a firm can grow without needing additional outside financing

internal rate of return (IRR) method return that causes the net present value to be zero

international banking exists when banks operate in more than one country

International Monetary Fund (IMF) provides means for United Nations countries to borrow money

in-the-money option has a positive intrinsic value; for a call (put) option, the underlying asset price exceeds (is below) the stroke price

investment bank helps businesses sell their securities to raise financial capital

investment bankers (underwriters) assist corporations by raising money through the marketing of corporate securities to the securities markets

investment banking firms sell or market new securities issued by businesses to individual and institutional investors

investment companies sell shares in their firms to individuals and others and invest the pooled proceeds in corporate and government securities

investments involves sale or marketing of securities, the analysis of securities, and the management of investment risk through portfolio diversification

L

legal tender money backed only by government credit

liabilities creditors' claims on a firm

limit order maximum buying price (limit buy) or the minimum selling price (limit sell) specified by the investor

limited branch banking allows additional banking offices within a geographically defined distance of a bank's main office

limited liability company (LLC) organizational form whose owners have limited liability; the firm can have an unlimited number of shareholders; income is taxed only once as personal income of the shareholders

limited partners face limited liability; their personal assets cannot be touched to settle the firm's debt

limited partnership has at least one general partner who has unlimited liability; the liability of the limited partners is limited to their investment

line of credit loan limit the bank establishes for each of its business customers

liquidity how easily an asset can be exchanged for money

liquidity preference theory states that investors are willing to accept lower interest rates on short-term debt securities, which provide greater liquidity and less interest rate risk

liquidity premium compensation for securities that cannot easily be converted to cash without major price discounts

liquidity ratios indicate the ability of the firm to meet short-term obligations as they come due

liquidity risk likelihood that a bank will be unable to meet depositor withdrawal demands and other liabilities when due

loan amortization schedule a schedule of the breakdown of each payment between interest and principal, as well as the remaining balance after each payment

loanable funds theory states that interest rates are a function of the supply of and demand for loanable funds

lockbox payments are sent to a P.O. box and processed by a bank to reduce collection float

M

M1 money supply consists of currency, traveler's checks, demand deposits, and other checkable deposits

M2 money supply M1 plus highly liquid financial assets including savings accounts, small time deposits, and retail money market mutual funds

M3 money supply M2 plus large time deposits and institutional money market mutual funds

macro finance study of how financial intermediaries, financial markets, and policy makers interact and operate within financial systems

maintenance margin minimum margin to which an investment may fall before a margin call will be placed

margin minimum percentage of the purchase price that must represent the investor's equity or unborrowed funds

margin call investor faces the option of either closing the position or investing additional cash to increase the position's equity or margin

marginal tax rate paid on the last dollar of income

market maker one who facilitates market transactions by selling (buying) when other investors wish to buy (sell)

market order open order of an immediate purchase or sale at the best possible price

market portfolio portfolio that contains all risky assets

market segmentation theory states that interest rates may differ because securities of different maturities are not perfect substitutes for each other

market stabilization intervention of the syndicate to repurchase securities in order to maintain their price at the offer price

market timing hypothesis firms try to time the market by selling common stock when their stock price is high and repurchasing shares when their stock price is low

market value added (MVA) measures the value created by the firm's managers

market value ratios indicates the value of a firm in the market place relative to financial statement values

marketable government securities securities that may be bought and sold through the usual market channels

maturity factoring firm selling its accounts receivable is paid on the normal collection date or net due date of the account

maturity matching approach financing strategy that attempts to match the maturities of assets with the maturities of the liabilities with which they are financed

maturity risk premium compensation expected by investors due to interest rate risk on debt instruments with longer maturities

medium of exchange the basic function of money store of purchasing power when money is held as a liquid asset

merchandise trade balance the net difference between a country's import and export of goods

mission statement statement of a firm's reason for being; sometimes called a vision statement

MOGS Mission, Objectives, Goals, and Strategies

monetary base banking system reserves plus currency held by the public

monetary policy formulated by the Fed to regulate money supply growth

monetizing the deficit Fed buys government securities, which increases the money supply, to help finance the deficit

money anything that is generally accepted as payment

money market mutual funds (MMMFs) issue shares to customers and invest the proceeds in highly liquid, very short maturity, interest-bearing debt instruments

money markets markets where debt instruments of one year or less are traded

money multiplier the ratio formed by 1 divided by the reserve ratio, which indicates maximum expansion possible in the money supply

mortgage banking firms originate mortgage loans on homes and other real property by bringing together borrowers and institutional investors

mortgage bonds backed or secured by specifically pledged property of a firm (real estate, buildings, and other assets classified as real property)

mortgage markets where mortgage loans, backed by real property in the form of buildings and houses, are originated and sometimes traded

multibank holding company (MBHC) permits a firm to own and control two or more banks

municipal bond long-term debt security issued by a state or local government

mutual fund open-end investment company that can issue an unlimited number of its shares to its investors and use the pooled proceeds to purchase corporate and government securities

mutually exclusive projects selecting one project precludes others from being undertaken

N

negative correlation two time series tend to move in opposite directions

negotiable certificates of deposit debt instruments of $100,000 or more issued by banks that can be traded in the money markets

net exports (NE) exports of goods and services minus imports

net present value (NPV) present value of a project's cash flows minus its cost

net working capital dollar amount of a firm's current assets minus current liabilities

nominal interest rate interest rate that is observed in the marketplace

nonbank financial conglomerates large corporations that offer various financial services

noncumulative preferred stock makes no provision for the accumulation of past missed dividends

nonmarketable government securities issues that cannot be transferred between persons or institutions but must be redeemed with the U.S. government

NPV profile the graphical relationship between a project's NPV and cost of capital

O

odd lot sale or purchase of less than 100 shares

off-budget outlays funding for some government agencies that is not included in the federal budget

offer price price at which the security is sold to the investors

one bank holding companies (OBHCs) permits a firm to own and control only one bank

open-end mortgage bond allows the same assets to be used as security in future issues

open-market operations buying and selling of securities by the Federal Reserve to alter the supply of money

operating cycle time between receiving raw materials and collecting cash from receivables

opportunity cost cost of passing up the next best alternative

optimum debt/equity mix proportionate use of debt and equity that minimizes the firm's cost of capital

option financial contract that gives the owner the option or choice of buying or selling a particular good at a specified price on or before a specified expiration date

option premium price paid for the option itself

option writer seller of option contracts

order bill of lading document given by a transportation company that lists goods to be transported and terms of the shipping agreement

ordinary annuity exists when the equal payments occur at the end of each time period (also referred to as a deferred annuity)

out-of-the-money option has a zero intrinsic value; for a call (put) option, the underlying asset price is below (exceeds) the strike price

P

par value stated value of a stock on the balance sheet; accounting and legal concept bearing no relationship to a firm's stock price or book value

partnership form of business organization in which two or more people own a business operated for profit

payback period method determines the time in years it will take to recover, or pay back, the initial investment in fixed assets

pecking order hypothesis a theory that explains that managers prefer to use additions to retained earnings to finance the firm, then debt, and as a final resort new equity

pension funds receive contributions from employees and/or their employers and invest the proceeds on behalf of the employees for use during their retirement years

personal consumption expenditures (PCE) expenditures by individuals for durable goods, nondurable goods, and services

personal finance study of how individuals prepare for financial emergencies, protect against premature death and property losses, and accumulate wealth

pledge obtain a short-term loan by using accounts receivable as collateral

poison pills provisions in a corporate charter that make a corporate takeover more unattractive

political risk actions by a sovereign nation to interrupt or change the value of cash flows accruing to foreign investors

portfolio any combination of financial assets or investments

positive correlation two time series tend to move in conjunction with each other

precautionary motives holding funds to meet unexpected demands

preauthorized checks regular, (typically) monthly deductions by a vendor from a customer's checking account

preemptive rights rights of existing shareholders to purchase any newly issued shares

preferred stock equity security that has preference, or a senior claim, to the firm's earnings and assets over common stock

premium bond bond that is selling in excess of its par value

present value value of an investment or savings amount today or at the present time

primary deposit deposit that adds new reserves to a bank

primary market original issue market in which securities are initially sold

primary reserves vault cash and deposits held at other depository institutions and at Federal Reserve Banks

primary securities market involved in creating and issuing new securities, mortgages, and other claims to wealth

prime rate (1) interest rate on short-term unsecured loans to highest-quality business customers; (2) interest rate the bank charges its most creditworthy customers

principal-agent problem conflict of interest between the principals and agents

principals owners of the firm

private placement sale of securities to a small group of private investors

profitability index (PI) (benefit/cost ratio) ratio between the present values of the cash flows and the project's cost

profitability ratios indicate the firm's ability to generate returns on its sales, assets, and equity

program trading technique for trading stocks as a group rather than individually, defined as a minimum of at least fifteen different stocks with a minimum value of $1 million

progressive tax rate based on the concept that the higher the income the larger the percentage of income that should be paid in taxes

proprietorship business venture that is owned by a single individual who personally receives all profits and assumes all responsibility for the debts and losses of the business

prospectus highly regulated document that details the issuer's operations and finances and must be provided to each buyer of a newly issued security

public offering sale of securities to the investing public

purchasing power parity (PPP) currency of a country with relatively higher inflation rate will depreciate relative to the currency of a country with a relatively lower inflation rate

put option contract for the sale of securities within a specified time period and at a specified price

putable bonds (retractable bonds) allow the investor to force the issuer to redeem the bonds prior to maturity

R

random walk prices appear to fluctuate randomly over time, driven by the random arrival of new information

ratio analysis financial technique that involves dividing various financial statement numbers into one another

real assets (1) include ownership of land, buildings, machinery, inventory, commodities, and precious metals

real rate of interest interest rate on a risk-free debt instrument when no inflation is expected

registered bonds the issuer knows the names of the bondholders and the interest payments are sent directly to the bondholder

registered traders buy and sell stocks for their own account

Regulation Z enacts Truth in Lending section of the Consumer Credit Protection Act with intent to make consumers able to compare costs of alternate forms of credit

reinvestment rate risk (rollover risk) fluctuating interest rates cause coupon or interest payments to be reinvested at different interest rates over time

representative full-bodied money paper money fully backed by a precious metal

repurchase agreements short-term loans using Treasury bills as collateral

required reserve ratio percentage of deposits that must be held as reserves

required reserves the minimum amount of total reserves that a depository institution must hold

retention rate the proportion of each dollar of earnings that is kept by the firm

retractable bonds (putable bonds) allow the investor to force the issuer to redeem the bonds prior to maturity

revolving credit agreement legal obligation of the bank to provide up to the agreed-upon borrowing limit

risk-adjusted discount rate (RADR) adjusts the required rate of return at which the analyst discounts a project's cash flows; projects with higher (or lower) risk levels require higher (or lower) discount rates

risk-free rate of interest interest rate on a debt instrument with no default, maturity, or liquidity risks (Treasury securities are the closest example)

rollover risk (reinvestment rate risk) fluctuating interest rates cause coupon or interest payments to be reinvested at different interest rates over time

round lot sale or purchase of 100 shares

Rule of 72 used to approximate the time required for an investment to double in value

S

savings income that is not consumed but held in the form of cash and other financial assets

savings and loan association accepts individual savings and lends pooled savings to individual, primarily in the form of mortgage loans, and businesses

savings bank accepts the savings of individual and lends pooled savings to individuals primarily in the form of mortgage loans

savings deficit occurs when investment in real assets exceeds current income

savings-investment process involves the direct or indirect transfer of individual savings to business firms in exchange for their securities

savings surplus occurs when current income exceeds investment in real assets

secondary market market in which securities are traded among investors

secondary reserves short-term securities held by banks that can be quickly converted into cash at little cost

secondary securities market market for transferring existing securities between investors

secured loan loan backed by collateral

securities firms accept and invest individual savings and also facilitate the sale and transfer of securities between investors

securities markets physical locations or electronic forums where debt and equity securities are sold and traded

selection stage applying appropriate capital budgeting techniques to help make a final accept or reject decision

semi-strong-form efficient market market in which all public information, both current and past, is reflected in asset prices

settlement price determined by a special committee that determines the approximate closing price

shelf registration allows firms to register security issues (both debt and equity) with the SEC, and have them available to sell for two years

short sale sale of securities that the seller does not own

sight draft draft requiring immediate payment

simple interest interest earned only on the principal of the initial investment

sinking fund requirement that the firm retire specific portions of the bond issue over time

sinking fund payments periodic bond principal repayments to a trustee

Special Drawing Rights (SDRs) international reserve assets created by the International Monetary Fund that can be drawn upon by member nations

specialists assigned dealers who have the responsibility of making a market in an assigned security

speculative inflation caused by the expectation that prices will continue to rise, resulting in increased buying to avoid even higher future prices

speculative motives holding funds to take advantage of unusual cash discounts for needed materials

spot exchange rate rate being quoted for current delivery of the currency

spot market cash market for trading stocks, bonds, or other assets

spread difference between the offer price and the price paid by the investment bank

stand-alone principle analysis focuses on the project's own cash flows, uncontaminated by cash flows from the firm's other activities

standard deviation square root of the variance

standard of value a function of money that occurs when prices and debts are stated in terms of the monetary unit

statement of cash flows provides a summary of the cash inflows (sources) and cash outflows (uses) during a specified accounting period

statewide branch banking allows banks to operate offices throughout a state

static trade-off hypothesis a theory that states that firms attempt to balance the benefits of debt versus its disadvantages to determine an optimal capital structure

stock certificate certificate showing an ownership claim of a specific company

stock options allow managers to purchase a stated number of the firm's shares at a specified price

stop-loss order order to sell stock at the market price when the price of the stock falls to a specified level

store of purchasing power when money is held as a liquid asset

store of value money held for some period of time before it is spent

street name (1) allows stock to be held in the name of the brokerage house; (2) an investor's securities are kept in the name of the brokerage house to facilitate record keeping, settlement, safety against loss or theft, and so on

strong-form efficient market market in which prices reflect all public and private knowledge, including past and current information

subchapter S corporation has fewer than thirty-five shareholders, none of which is another corporation; its income is taxed only once, as personal income of the shareholders

subordinated debenture claims of these bonds are subordinate or junior to the claims of the debenture holders

sunk cost project-related expense not dependent on whether or not the project is undertaken

sustainable growth rate the estimate of how quickly a firm may grow by maintaining a constant mix of debt and equity

syndicate group of several investment banking firms that participate in underwriting and distributing a security issue

systematic risk (market risk) risk that cannot be eliminated through diversification

T

tax policy setting the level and structure of taxes to affect the economy

technician (chartists) study graphs of past price movements, volume, etc., to try to predict future prices

term structure relationship between interest rates or yields and the time to maturity for debt instruments of comparable quality

third market market for large blocks of listed stocks that operates outside the confines of the organized exchanges

thrift institutions savings and loans, savings banks, and credit unions

time draft draft that is payable at a specified future date

time value of money the mathematics of finance whereby interest is earned over time by saving or investing money

token coins coins containing metal of less value than their stated value

tombstones announcements of securities offerings

total reserves deposits held in Federal Reserve Banks and cash in depository institutions

trade credit credit extended on purchases to a firm's customers

trade discounts provided to purchasers as an incentive for early or prompt payment of accounts

transactions motive demand for cash needed to conduct day-to-day operations

transfer payments government payments for which no current services are given in return

traveler's letter of credit issued by a bank to banks in other countries authorizing them to cash checks or purchase drafts presented by the bearer

treasurer oversees the traditional functions of financial analysis

Treasury bills federal obligations that bear the shortest original maturities

Treasury bonds federal obligations of any maturity but usually over five years

Treasury notes federal obligations issued for maturities of one to ten years

trend or time series analysis used to evaluate a firm's performance over time

trust indenture contract that lists the various provisions and covenants of the loan arrangement

trust receipt (1) an instrument through which a bank retains title to goods until they are paid for; (2) lien against specific identifiable items in inventory

trustee individual or organization that represents the bondholders to ensure the indenture's provisions are respected by the bond issuer

U

underpricing represents the difference between the aftermarket stock price and the offering price

underwriting agreement contract in which the investment banker agrees to buy securities at a predetermined price and then resell them to the investors

undistributed profits proportion of after-tax profits retained by corporations

unit banking exists when a bank can have only one full-service office

universal bank can engage in both commercial banking and investment banking activities

unsecured loan loan that is a general claim against the borrower's assets

unsystematic risk risk that can be diversified away

V

variance derived by summing the squared deviations and dividing by $n - 1$

velocity of money the rate of circulation of the money supply

voluntary savings financial assets set aside for future use

W

warehouse receipt inventory is placed in a bonded warehouse for safekeeping; items are removed as they are paid for

weak-form efficient market market in which prices reflect all past information

weighted average cost of capital (WACC) represents the minimum required rate of return on a capital budgeting project; it is found by multiplying the marginal cost of each capital structure component by its appropriate weight, and summing the terms

working capital   assets needed to carry out the normal operations of the business

World Bank   provides loans to developing countries

Y

Yankee bonds   dollar-denominated bonds issued in the United States by a foreign issuer

yield curve   graphic presentation of the term structure of interest rates at a given point in time

yield to maturity (YTM)   return on a bond if it is held to maturity

Z

zero balance account   an arrangement between a bank and firm to transfer sufficient funds to a disbursement account to cover the day's checks presented to the bank for payment

• INDEX •

Note: Page numbers followed by an f indicate figures; those followed by t indicate tables.